Timeline of Criminological Theories (continued)

Andenaes
General Preventive Effects of Punishment (1966)

Martinson
What Works (1974)

Cohen & Felson
Routine Activities (1979)

Clarke
Situational Crime Prevention (1992)

Packer
The Limits of Criminal Sanction (1968)

Newman
Defensible Space (1973)

J. Q. Wilson
Thinking About Crime (1975)

Katz
Seductions of Crime (1988)

Montagu
Man and Aggression (1968)

Jeffery
Crime Prevention (1971)

E. O. Wilson
Sociobiology (1975)

Mednick & Volavka
Biology and Crime (1980)

Rowe
The Limits of Family Influence (1995)

Harris
The Nurture Assumption (1998)

...don
...s of Delinquent Youth (1949)

Dalton
The Premenstrual Syndrome (1971)

Ellis
Evolutionary Sociobiology (1989)

...lander
...analytic ...ch to ...ncy (1947)

Eysenck
Crime and Personality (1964)

Bandura
Aggression (1973)

Hirschi & Hindelang
Intelligence and Delinquency (1977)

Henggeler
Delinquency in Adolescence (1989)

Moffitt
Neuropsychology of Crime (1992)

Wilson & Daly
Evolutionary Psychology (1997)

Murray & Herrnstein
The Bell Curve (1994)

Vold
Theoretical Criminology (1958)

Chambliss & Seidman
Law, Order and Power (1971)

Lea & Young
Left Realism (1984)

Hagan
Structural Criminology (1989)

Braithwaite
Crime, Shame, and Reintegration (1989)

Zehr & Mika
Fundamental Concepts of Restorative Justice (1998)

Dahrendorf
Class and Class Conflict in Industrial Society (1959)

Taylor, Walton, & Young
The New Criminology (1973)

Daly & Chesney-Lind
Feminist Theory (1988)

Quinney & Pepinsky
Criminology as Peacemaking (1991)

Barak & Henry
An Integrative-Constitutive Theory of Crime (1999)

Cloward & Ohlin
Delinquency and Opportunity (1960)

Kornhauser
Social Sources of Delinquency (1978)

Wilson
The Truly Disadvantaged (1987)

Agnew
General Strain Theory (1992)

Courtwright
Violent Land (1996)

Anderson
Code of the Street (1999)

Lewis
The Culture of Poverty (1966)

Blau & Blau
The Cost of Inequality (1982)

Messner & Rosenfeld
Crime and the American Dream (1994)

LaFree
Losing Legitimacy (1998)

...rt
...y (1951)

Hirschi
Causes of Delinquency (1969)

Schur
Labeling Deviant Behavior (1972)

Akers
Deviant Behavior (1977)

Kaplan
General Theory of Deviance (1992)

Akers
Social Learning and Social Structure (1998)

Becker
Outsiders (1963)

Heimer & Matsueda
Differential Social Control (1994)

...ck & Glueck
...ng Juvenile Delinquency
(...)

West & Farrington
Delinquent Way of Life (1977)

Thornberry
Interactional Theory (1987)

Sampson & Laub
Crime in the Making (1993)

Loeber
Pathways to Delinquency (1998)

Weis
Social Development Theory (1981)

Moffitt
Adolescence-Limited and Life-Course Persistent Antisocial Behavior (1995)

Hathaway & Monachesi
Analyzing and Predicting Juvenile Delinquency with the MMPI (1953)

Wolfgang, Figlio, & Sellin
Delinquency in Birth Cohorts (1972)

Wilson & Herrnstein
Crime and Human Nature (1985)

Tittle
Control Balance: Toward a General Theory of Deviance (1995)

Eysenck
Crime and Personality (1964)

Gottfredson & Hirschi
General Theory of Crime (1990)

| 1969 | 1975 | 1980 | 1991 | 1995 | 1997 | 1998 |

Timeline

Lott
More Guns, Less Crime (2000)
(2002)

Felson
Crime and Everyday Life

Steffensmeier & Ulmer
Confessions of a Dying Thief: Understanding Criminal Careers and Illegal Enterprise **(2005)**

Simon
Governing Through Crime (2010)

Petrossian & Clarke
"The CRAVED Theft Model" (2014)

Levitt
Understanding Why Crime Fell in the 1990s **(2004)**

Ellis & Hoskin
"Criminality and the 2D:4D Ratio: Test the Prenatal Androgen Hypothesis" (2

Schoenthaler
Intelligence, Academic Performance, and Brain Function (2000)

Friedman
"Violence and Mental Illness" (2006)

Beaver
Biosocial Criminology (2009)

Wright & Cullen
"The Future of Biosocial Criminology" (2012)

Barnes & Jacobs
"Genetic Risk for Violent Behavior" (2013)

Bushman & Anderson
Media Violence (2001)

Dorn, Volavka & Johnson *"Mental Disorder and Violence" (2012)*

Sullivan & Tifft
Restorative Justice (2001)

Western
Punishment and Inequality in America (2010)

Hagan and Wymond-Richmond
Darfur and the Crime of Genocide **(2009)**

Chesney-Lind & Morash
"Transformative Feminist Criminology" (201

Sampson & Raudenbush
Disorder in Urban Neighborhoods— Does It Lead to Crime? **(2001)**

LeBlanc
Random Family: Love, Drugs, Trouble, and Coming of Age in the Bronx **(2003)**

Wilson & Taub *There Goes the Neighborhood: Racial, Ethnic, and Class Tensions in Four Chicago Neighborhoods and Their Meaning for America (2006)*

Wilson
More Than Just Race (2009

Topalli *"When Being Good Is Bad: An Expansion of Neutralization Theory" (2005)*

Conger
"Family Functioning and Crime" (201

Maruna
Making Good: How Ex-convicts Reform and Rebuild Their Lives (2001)

Conger
Long-term Consequences of Economic Hardship on Romantic Relationships (2015)

Laub & Sampson
Shared Beginnings, Divergent Lives **(2003)**

Agnew
Why Do Criminals Offend? **(2005)**

Larson & Sweeten
"Breaking Up Is Hard to Do" (2012)

Bersani & Doherty
"When the Ties That Bind Unwind" (2013)

Colvin
Crime and Coercion (2000)

Farrington
"Developmental and Life-Course Criminology" (2003)

Zimmerman, Botchkovar, Antonaccio, & Hughes *"Low Self-Control in 'Bad' Neighborhoods" (2015)*

Piquero, Farrington, Nagin, & Moffitt
Trajectories of Offending **(2010)**

Boutwell, Barnes, Deaton, & Beaver *"On the Evolutionary Origins of Life-course Persistent Offending" (2013)*

| 2000 | 2001 | 2002 | 2003 | 2004 | 2005 | 2010 | 2016 |

7 EDITION

CRIMINOLOGY

THE CORE

Larry J. Siegel

University of Massachusetts, Lowell

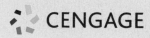 CENGAGE

Australia • Brazil • Mexico • Singapore • United Kingdom • United States

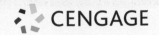

Criminology: The Core, **Seventh Edition**
Larry J. Siegel

Senior Product Director: Marta Lee-Perriard

Product Team Manager: Carolyn Henderson Meier

Senior Content Developer: Shelley Murphy

Product Assistant: Megan Nauer

Senior Marketing Manager: Mark Linton

Senior Content Project Manager: Christy Frame

Photo Development Editor: Kim Adams Fox

Photo Researcher: Ragav Seshadri, Lumina Datamatics

Text Researcher: Abdulrahman Fasihuddeen, Lumina Datamatics

Production Service: Linda Jupiter Productions

Copy Editor: Lunaea Weatherstone

Proofreaders: Mary Kanable and Susan Gall

Indexer: Do Mi Stauber

Compositor: MPS Limited

Senior Art Director: Helen Bruno

Text Designer: Diane Beasley

Cover Designer: Irene Morris Design

Cover Image: Mary DeLave

For product information and technology assistance, contact us at **Cengage Customer & Sales Support, 1-800-354-9706.**

For permission to use material from this text or product, submit all requests online at **www.cengage.com/permissions.** Further permissions questions can be e-mailed to **permissionrequest@cengage.com.**

Library of Congress Control Number: 2017945193

Student Edition:
ISBN: 978-1-337-55771-9

Loose-leaf Edition:
ISBN: 978-1-337-61664-5

Cengage
20 Channel Center Street
Boston, MA 02210
USA

Cengage is a leading provider of customized learning solutions with employees residing in nearly 40 different countries and sales in more than 125 countries around the world. Find your local representative at **www.cengage.com.**

Cengage products are represented in Canada by Nelson Education, Ltd.

To learn more about Cengage platforms and services, visit **www.cengage.com.** To register or access your online learning solution or purchase materials for your course, visit **www.cengagebrain.com.**

Printed in Mexico
Quad / Graphics México.

Print Number: 03   Print Year: 2018

This book is dedicated to

my children, **Eric, Julie, Rachel, and Andrew;**

my grandchildren, **Jack, Brooke, and Kayla Jean;**

my sons-in-law, **Jason Macy and Patrick Stephens;**

and my wife, partner, and best friend, **Therese J. Libby.**

L. J. S.

ABOUT THE AUTHOR

Therese J. Libby and Larry J. Siegel

LARRY J. SIEGEL was born in the Bronx. While living on Jerome Avenue and attending City College of New York in the 1960s, he was swept up in the social and political currents of the time. He became intrigued with the influence contemporary culture had on individual behavior: Did people shape society, or did society shape people? He applied his interest in social forces and human behavior to the study of crime and justice. Graduating from college in 1968, he was accepted into the first class of the newly opened program in criminal justice at the State University of New York at Albany, where he earned both his MA and PhD degrees. Dr. Siegel began his teaching career at Northeastern University, where he was a faculty member for nine years. He also held teaching positions at the University of Nebraska–Omaha and Saint Anselm College in New Hampshire before being appointed a full professor in the School of Criminology and Justice Studies at the University of Massachusetts, Lowell. Dr. Siegel retired from full-time classroom teaching in 2015 and now teaches exclusively online. He has written extensively in the area of crime and justice, including books on juvenile law, delinquency, criminology, criminal justice, corrections, and criminal procedure. He is a court-certified expert on police conduct and has testified in numerous legal cases. The father of four and grandfather of three, Larry Siegel and his wife, Terry, now reside in Naples, Florida, with their two dogs, Watson and Cody.

Brief Contents

Contents

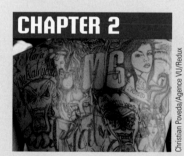

PART 2
Theories of Crime Causation

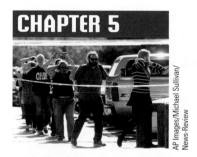

CHAPTER 5

AP Images/Michael Sullivan/
News-Review

Trait Theory 132

CHAPTER 6

AP Images/Steven Senne

Social Structure Theory 170

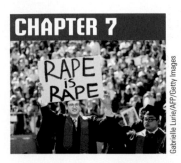

Hartford Courant/Tribune News Service/Getty Images; AP Images/ Connecticut Department of Correction

CHAPTER 9

Developmental Theories: Life Course, Propensity, and Trajectory 284

PART 3
Crime Typologies

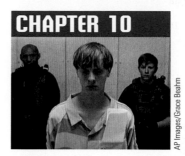

AP Images/Grace Beahm

CHAPTER 10

Violent Crime 318

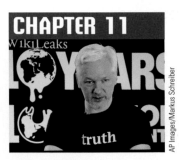

CHAPTER 11
Political Crime and Terrorism 366

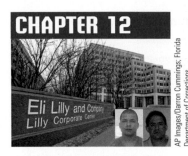

CHAPTER 12
Economic Crimes: Blue-Collar, White-Collar, and Green-Collar 404

CHAPTER 13

John Lamb/Shellys/DigitalVision/
Getty Images

Public Order Crimes 444

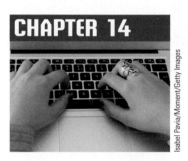

CHAPTER 14

Isabel Pavia/Moment/Getty Images

Crimes of the New Millennium: Cybercrime and Transnational Organized Crime 488

Preface

In 2017, the operator of the world's largest child pornography website was sentenced to serve 30 years in prison. The case began in August 2014, when Steven Chase created the Playpen, a website using the Tor Project hidden service protocol, which allows for an open network on the Internet where users can communicate anonymously. Tor software conceals its users' identities and their online activity from surveillance and traffic analysis by separating identification and routing. It encrypts and then randomly bounces communications through a network of relays run by volunteers around the globe.

Steven Chase

Chase served as lead administrator of Playpen, through which he and more than 150,000 other members viewed tens of thousands of postings of young victims, sorted by age, sex, and the type of sexual activity involved. In addition to Tor, website members employed other advanced technological means to thwart identification, including elaborate file encryption.

Chase chose the name of the website, selected and made payments to the website hosting company, regularly updated the site with new features and security fixes, promoted several site members to administrator and moderator status to assist with the administration of the criminal enterprise, and spent hundreds of hours logged in, personally authoring hundreds of postings. He was arrested following a court-authorized search of his home that revealed he was in possession of thousands of images depicting the sexual abuse of children as young as infants and toddlers.

Following Chase's arrest, federal agents pierced through the anonymity provided by the Tor network and obtained IP addresses and other information to identify other site users. As a result of the investigation, at least 350 US-based individuals have been arrested, 25 producers of child pornography have been prosecuted, 51 alleged hands-on abusers have been prosecuted, and 55 American children who were subjected to sexual abuse have been successfully identified or rescued. The ongoing international investigation has led to least 520 arrests, and the successful identification and rescue of at least 186 children who were subjected to sexual abuse.

The Playpen case demonstrates the complex nature of crime today. Contemporary criminals, whether they be pornographers, gang members, or terrorists, are adept at using the Internet to carry out their criminal enterprise schemes. While some crimes are local, others are global in their reach. It is not surprising that many Americans are concerned about crime and worried about becoming victims of crime themselves. We alter our behavior to limit the risk of victimization and question whether legal punishment alone can control criminal offenders. We watch movies and TV shows about law firms and their clients, fugitives, and stone-cold killers. We are shocked when the news media offers graphic accounts of school shootings, police brutality, and sexual assaults. We are swayed when politicians claim that crime is on the upswing and that we must arm ourselves to protect loved ones. Is anywhere safe? Twenty years ago, no states had laws that allowed guns on university campuses. Today, 10 states have signed such laws, while 20 others are considering college carry laws.

I, too, have had a lifelong interest in crime, law, and justice. Why do people behave the way they do? What causes someone like Steven Chase to operate a global kiddie porn site? Was his behavior the result of a diseased mind and personality? And what should be done with people who commit such horrendous crimes? Is 30 years in prison too severe a sentence for someone who distributes child pornography, or too lenient? Can draconian punishments convince others that "crime does not pay"?

Goals of This Book

For more than 40 years, I have channeled my fascination with issues related to crime and justice into a career as a student and teacher of criminology. My goal in writing this text is to help students share the same enthusiasm for criminology that has sustained me during my teaching career. What could be more important or fascinating than a field of study that deals with such wide-ranging topics as the motivation for mass murder, the effects of violent media on young people, drug abuse, and organized crime? Criminology is a dynamic field, changing constantly with the release of major research studies, Supreme Court rulings, and governmental policy. Its dynamism and diversity make it an important and engrossing area of study.

One reason why the study of criminology is so important is that debates continue over the nature and extent of crime and the causes and prevention of criminality. Some view criminals as society's victims who are forced to violate the law because of poverty and lack of opportunity. Others view antisocial behavior, such as the Playpen website, as a product of mental and physical abnormalities, present at birth or soon after, that are stable over the life course. Still another view is that crime is a function of the rational choice of greedy, selfish people who can be deterred from engaging in criminal behavior only by the threat of harsh punishments. It all comes down to this: Why do people do the things they do? How can we explain the intricacies and diversity of human behavior?

Because interest in crime and justice is so great and so timely, this text is designed to review these ongoing issues and cover the field of criminology in an organized and comprehensive manner. It is meant as a broad overview of the field, an introduction to whet the reader's appetite and encourage further and more in-depth exploration. I try to present how the academic study of criminology intersects with real-world issues. For example, diversity is a key issue in criminology and a topic that has important real-world consequences. Therefore, the text attempts to integrate issues of racial, ethnic, gender, and cultural diversity throughout. The book covers the killing of Michael Brown in Ferguson, Missouri, and racial differences in economic and social factors related to crime.

My primary goals in writing this text were as follows:

1. To separate the facts from the fiction about crime and criminality
2. To provide students with comprehensive and wide-ranging knowledge of criminology and show its diversity and intellectual content
3. To be as thorough and up-to-date as possible
4. To be objective and unbiased
5. To describe current theories, crime types, and methods of social control, and to analyze their strengths and weaknesses
6. To show how criminological thought has influenced social policy

Features

FACT OR FICTION? A main goal of this edition is to expose some of the myths that cloud people's thinking about crime and criminals. The media often paints a distorted picture of the crime problem in America and focuses only on the most sensational cases. Is the crime rate really out of control? Are unemployed people inclined to commit crime? Are immigrants more crime prone than the native-born, as some politicians suggest? Are married people less crime prone than singles? Distinguishing what is true from what is merely legend is one of the greatest challenges for instructors in criminology courses. Therefore, a goal of this text is disabuse students of incorrect notions, perceptions, and biases. Each chapter opens with a set of statements high-lighting common perceptions about crime that are related to the material discussed in the chapter. In the text, these statements are revisited so the student will become skilled at distinguishing the myths from the reality of crime and criminality.

CONCEPT SUMMARY There are ongoing debates about the nature and extent of crime and the causes and prevention of criminality. I try to present the various view-points on each topic and then draw a conclusion based on the weight of the existing evidence. Students become familiar with this kind of analysis by examining Concept Summary boxes that compare different viewpoints, reviewing both their main points and their strengths.

THINKING LIKE A CRIMINOLOGIST It is important for students to think critically about law and justice and to develop a critical perspective toward the social insti-tutions and legal institutions entrusted with crime control. Throughout the book, students are asked to critique research highlighted in boxed material and to think "outside the box," as it were. To aid in this task, each chapter ends with a brief section called Thinking Like a Criminologist, which presents a scenario that can be analyzed with the help of material found in the chapter and a suggested writing assignment to expand knowledge on the issue.

POLICIES AND ISSUES IN CRIMINOLOGY Throughout the book, every attempt is made to access the most current research and scholarship available. Most people who use the book have told me that this is one of its strongest features. I have attempted to present current research in a balanced fashion, even though this approach can be frustrating to students. It is comforting to reach an unequivocal conclusion about an important topic, but sometimes that simply is not possible. In an effort to be objec-tive and fair, I have presented each side of important criminological debates in full. Throughout the text, boxed features titled Policies and Issues in Criminology review critically important research topics. In Chapter 13, for example, this feature covers the current opioid epidemic that is sweeping the United States and analyzes its cause and effects.

PROFILES IN CRIME These features are designed to present to students actual crimes that help illustrate the position or views within the chapter. In Chapter 12, a Profiles in Crime feature entitled "Fertility Fraud" looks at the case of Allison Layton, who owned a company called Miracles Egg Donation. Layton earned a prison sentence for cheating vulnerable would-be parents out of tens of thousands of dollars for phony egg donation and surrogacy services.

CONNECTIONS are short inserts that help link the material to other areas covered in the book. A Connections insert in Chapter 14 points out how cyberspace is being used to facilitate public order crimes (covered in Chapter 13) by being a conduit to illegally distribute prescription drugs, advertise prostitution, and disseminate pornography.

CHAPTER OUTLINES provide a roadmap to coverage and serve as a useful review tool.

LEARNING OBJECTIVES spell out what students should learn in each chapter and are reinforced via a direct link to the end-of-chapter summary as well as all of the text's ancillary materials.

A RUNNING GLOSSARY in the margins ensures that students understand words and concepts as they are introduced.

In sum, the text has been carefully structured to cover relevant material in a comprehensive, balanced, and objective fashion. Every attempt has been made to make the presentation of material interesting and contemporary. No single political or theoretical position dominates the text; instead, the many diverse views that are contained within criminology and characterize its interdisciplinary nature are presented. While the text includes analysis of the most important scholarly works and scientific research reports, it also includes a great deal of topical information on recent cases and events, such as the story of Owen Labrie and the St. Paul's School rape case and Dylann Roof and the Charleston massacre.

Topic Areas

Criminology: The Core is a thorough introduction to this fascinating field and is intended for students in introductory courses in criminology. It is divided into three main sections or topic areas.

PART 1 provides a framework for studying criminology. The first chapter defines the field and discusses its most basic concepts: the definition of crime, the component areas of criminology, the history of criminology, the concept of criminal law, and the ethical issues that arise in this field. Chapter 2 covers criminological research methods, as well as the nature, extent, and patterns of crime. Chapter 3 is devoted to the concept of victimization, including the nature of victims, theories of victimization, and programs designed to help crime victims.

PART 2 contains six chapters that cover criminological theory: Why do people behave the way they do? Why do they commit crimes? These views focus on choice (Chapter 4), biological and psychological traits (Chapter 5), social structure and culture (Chapter 6), social process and socialization (Chapter 7), social conflict (Chapter 8), and human development (Chapter 9).

PART 3 is devoted to the major forms of criminal behavior. The chapters in this section cover violent crime (Chapter 10), political crime and terrorism (Chapter 11), blue-collar, white-collar, and green-collar crimes (Chapter 12), public order crimes, including sex offenses and substance abuse (Chapter 13), and cybercrime and transnational organized crime (Chapter 14).

What's New in This Edition: Chapter-by-Chapter Changes

Chapter 1

Chapter 1 now begins with a vignette on the 2015 terror attack in San Bernardino, California, that killed 14 people and wounded 22 others. There is discussion of *Glossip v. Gross*, a case that illustrates how the Supreme Court relies on social science research to reach decisions. There is also a review of research aimed at determining whether people who view pornography are also more likely to commit violence against women. A Profiles in Crime feature entitled "A Shooting in Ferguson" reviews the case of Michael Brown, an African American youth killed in what proved to be a highly controversial confrontation with a police officer. There is new information on drug legalization: a number of states have now legalized recreational use of marijuana, while others have legalized it for medical purposes. A Policies and Issues in Criminology feature, "Hate Crime in Georgia," considers whether the punishment was appropriate to the crime.

Chapter 2

Chapter 2's opening vignette looks at a recent crime committed by members of MS-13, a violent international criminal organization based in El Salvador and Honduras. The data on crime and victimization have been updated. There is new information in the Policies and Issues features on international crime trends and factors that shape criminal activity.

Chapter 3

Chapter 3 begins with the discussion of the infamous St. Paul's School rape case in which a young student was sexually assaulted by a classmate as part of a ritual in which senior boys attempt to seduce freshman girls. There is a new discussion on the different methods that have been developed to measure the cost of victimization to American society. A new section looks at the stress abuse victims encounter in childhood that endures into adulthood. There is recent data from the National Center for Educational Statistics on victimization among students. Research is covered that shows that racial stereotypes affect criminal decision making. Research showing that people with particular and distinct mental and physical traits are more likely to suffer victimization is discussed.

Chapter 4

Chapter 4 begins with a vignette on an Ohio man, Michael Wymer, whose case aptly illustrates the concept of rational choice in criminal decision making. There is a new section on criminal competence, which may be an important element in structuring criminality. Research is covered that shows that criminals choose targets in familiar places, where they know their way around and won't get lost or trapped. Research now shows that neighborhoods with medical marijuana dispensaries have a high risk of armed robbery and resulting murders. A new section called "Getting Away" discusses escape mechanisms employed during criminal acts. A new Profiles in Crime feature looks at how auto thieves plan their crimes. There is an updated section on the installation of closed-circuit television (CCTV) surveillance cameras and improved street lighting. Another new section looks at criminal compulsion. A Policies and Issues in Criminology feature looks at racial disparity in state prisons. There are new sections on courts, sentencing, corrections, and rational choice theory.

Chapter 5

Chapter 5 begins with a vignette on Chris Harper Mercer, a troubled young man who opened fire at Umpqua Community College in Oregon, killing nine people and wounding seven others before being killed after exchanging gunfire with responding police officers. There is new data on adolescent boys with antisocial substance disorder (ASD) who repeatedly engage in risky antisocial behavior. Research is covered that shows that antisocial children have lower resting heart rates than the general population. Meta-analysis of existing research finds that lack of attachment predicts involvement in a broad spectrum of criminal activity. A new Policies and Issues in Criminology feature entitled "Criminal Susceptibility" argues that the link between personality traits and crime flows through an individual's resistance or susceptibility to crime-promoting experiences. A new Profiles in Crime feature covers Adam Lanza and the Sandy Hook Elementary School massacre.

Chapter 6

Chapter 6 begins with a vignette on the tragic case of Aaron Hernandez, the pro-football star who could not shake the street values that shaped his early life. New material on economic structure and American society reviews such issues as stratification, class economic disparity, white privilege, and racial conflict. A new Policies and Issues in Criminology feature entitled "*Labor's Love Lost*" reviews the book by Andrew Cherlin that provides an explanation of the toll income and educational inequality take on society. Research is presented on how destructive commercial institutions can destabilize a neighborhood and increase the rate of violent crimes.

Chapter 7

Chapter 7's opening vignette looks at the case of Stanford University student athlete Brock Turner, who was convicted of sexually assaulting an unconscious woman behind a dumpster and received a six-month jail sentence for his crime. New research shows that youth who are suspended or expelled from school are the ones most likely to have problems over the life course. A Profiles in Crime feature entitled "The Affluenza Case" looks at what happened to Ethan Couch, a 16-year-old Texas boy, who killed four people while driving drunk. A new Policies and Issues in Criminology feature, "White-Collar Neutralization," reviews research that shows that white-collar criminals use neutralization techniques before engaging in business crimes. There is a new section covering Per-Olof H. Wikstrom's Situational Action Theory (SAT), which maintains that when people are socialized to have a strong sense of morality, if confronted or exposed to criminal opportunity, their sense of ethics and principles will guide their behavior. There is also a new section on the long-term effects of labeling.

Chapter 8

Chapter 8 opens with a vignette on the political conflict that dominated the 2016 presidential election. There is new coverage of income including research sponsored by the Pew Foundation that shows that the wealth gap between America's high-income group and everyone else has now reached record high levels. There is a new section on justice system inequality that discusses how critical thinkers believe that racial and ethnic minorities are now the target of racist police officers and unfair prosecutorial practices. A Policies and Issues in Criminology box asks the provocative question "Are Wrongful Convictions a State Crime?" There is discussion on how critical feminists show that sexual and other victimization of girls is a function of male socialization because so many young males learn to be aggressive and to exploit women.

Chapter 9

Chapter 9's opening vignette covers the horrific murders of Jennifer, Michaela, and Hayley Petit during a home invasion in Cheshire, Connecticut. A new Policies and Issues in Criminology feature entitled "Human Agency, Personal Assessment, Crime, and Desistance" looks at the research of Robert Agnew and Steven Messner, which shows that human agency plays a major role in shaping personal assessments and behaviors. A new section entitled "Personality and Offending Trajectories" shows that the reason why some offenders start early, others late, and some not at all may be linked to psychological problems and disturbance.

Chapter 10

Chapter 10 opens with an update on the Dylann Roof case; he was sentenced to death after being convicted in federal court on 33 hate crime charges. Randol Contreras's influential book *Stickup Kids: Race, Drugs, Violence, and the American Dream* is covered. A Policies and Issues in Criminology feature entitled "American Culture and Homicide" covers the work of social historian Randolph Roth, who charts changes in the homicide rate in the United States from colonial times to the present. There is a section that looks at date and acquaintance rape on college campuses; data from a national survey of sexual assault on campus are presented. A new section, "Sex in Authority Relations," reviews the legislation making it a crime for people in power to have sexual relations with those they control or supervise. A Policies and Issues in Criminology feature looks at mass shooters: Why do some live and some die? A new section, "Targeting Criminals," reviews how some robbers target fellow criminals—for example, drug dealers—because they are inviting targets.

Chapter 11

Chapter 11 updates the case of Julian Assange and WikiLeaks, and how the 2016 presidential election was influenced by the release of emails hacked from Clinton campaign computers. A Profiles in Crime feature covers the Edward Snowden case. Voting fraud is now covered in some detail. A Policies and Issues in Criminology feature on the history and activities of the Islamic State has been updated. We also review the US Freedom Act, which replaced the Patriot Act.

Chapter 12

Chapter 12 reviews the activities of the Cuban Mob, a gang of commercial thieves who made off with $60 million worth of pharmaceuticals. Data are updated on shoplifting and retail theft: in a given year, total retail losses are approximately $44 billion. There is new information on the increase in highly organized professionals involved in auto theft. A Profiles in Crime feature entitled "Fertility Fraud" looks at the crimes of Allison Layton, who cheated would-be parents at her fertility clinic. There is coverage of recent Foreign Corrupt Practices Act (FCPA) cases, illegal logging, and importation of wildlife that has brought some species, such as the northern white rhinoceros and the western black rhinoceros, to near extinction.

Chapter 13

Chapter 13 begins with a vignette on Larry Nassar, a central figure in USA gymnastics, and how his downfall began when young female athletes accused him of sexual assault and federal investigators found child pornography on his computer. The most challenged or banned library books are set out. There is new material on the history of prostitution, including how in 1908 officials in Salt Lake City, Utah, hired Dora Topham, the leading madam of Ogden, to operate a legal red-light district called the stockade. The Policies and Issues in Criminology feature "Sex Work in Contemporary Society" is updated to include survival sex among LGBTQ youth. Another Policies and Issues feature, "The International Sex Trade," is updated with the latest report by the UN on human trafficking. There is a new Policies and Issues in Criminology feature on the opioid epidemic that is sweeping the country. There is new material on the link between drugs and crime; research projects find that they are highly correlated.

Chapter 14

Chapter 14 begins with the case of Kassandra Cruz, a Miami woman sent to prison for cyberstalking and extortion. New data are presented on how the crime rate in England and Wales doubled in 2015 when cybercrime began to be included. New data are presented that show that a conservative estimate of the annual cost to the global economy from cybercrime is now more than $400 billion and losses may be as high as $575 billion. A new section entitled "Internet Extortion/Ransomware" discusses how computers around the world are attacked by hackers. There is a new Policies and Issues in Criminology box on revenge porn and efforts to penalize people who post non-consensual sexually explicit photos online. Data are presented on cyberbullying that show on average about 28 percent of kids experience this form of harassment. A Policies and Issues in Criminology feature discusses how the Islamic State uses the Internet to recruit and raise funds.

Supplements

An extensive package of supplemental aids is available for instructor and student use with this edition of *Criminology: The Core*. Supplements are available to qualified adopters. Please consult your local sales representative for details.

For the Instructor

ONLINE INSTRUCTOR'S MANUAL The manual includes learning objectives, key terms, a detailed chapter outline, student activities, and media tools. The learning objectives are correlated with the discussion topics, student activities, and media tools. The manual is available for download on the password-protected website and can also be obtained by e-mailing your local Cengage Learning representative.

ONLINE TEST BANK Each chapter of the test bank contains questions in multiple-choice, true/false, completion, and essay formats, with a full answer key. The test bank is coded to the learning objectives that appear in the main text, references to the section in the main text where the answers can be found, and Bloom's taxonomy. Finally, each question in the test bank has been carefully reviewed by experienced criminal justice instructors for quality, accuracy, and content coverage. The Test Bank is available for download on the password-protected website and can also be obtained by e-mailing your local Cengage Learning representative.

CENGAGE LEARNING TESTING, POWERED BY COGNERO This assessment software is a flexible, online system that allows you to import, edit, and manipulate test bank content from the *Criminology: The Core* test bank or elsewhere, including your own favorite test questions; create multiple test versions in an instant; and deliver tests from your LMS, your classroom, or wherever you want.

ONLINE POWERPOINT® LECTURES Helping you make your lectures more engaging while effectively reaching your visually oriented students, these handy Microsoft PowerPoint slides outline the chapters of the main text in a classroom-ready presentation. The PowerPoint slides are updated to reflect the content and organization of the new edition of the text and feature some additional examples and real-world cases for application and discussion. Available for download on the password-protected instructor companion website, the presentations can also be obtained by e-mailing your local Cengage Learning representative.

For the Student

MINDTAP FOR CRIMINOLOGY With MindTap™ Criminal Justice for *Criminology: The Core*, you have the tools you need to better manage your limited time, with the ability to complete assignments whenever and wherever you are ready to learn. Course material that is specially customized for you by your instructor in a proven, easy-to-use interface keeps you engaged and active in the course. MindTap helps you achieve better grades today by cultivating a true understanding of course concepts, and with a mobile app to keep you on track. With a wide array of course-specific tools and apps—from note taking to flashcards—you can feel confident that MindTap is a worthwhile and valuable investment in your education.

You will stay engaged with MindTap's video cases and career scenarios and remain motivated by information that shows where you stand at all times—both individually and compared to the highest performers in class. MindTap eliminates the guesswork, focusing on what's most important with a learning path designed specifically by your instructor and for your criminology course. Master the most important information with built-in study tools such as visual chapter summaries and integrated learning objectives that will help you stay organized and use your time efficiently.

Acknowledgments

The preparation of this book would not have been possible without the aid of my colleagues who helped by reviewing the previous editions and gave me important suggestions for improvement.

My partners at Cengage Learning have done their typically outstanding job of aiding me in the preparation of this text and putting up with my yearly angst. Carolyn Henderson Meier, my wonderful product team manager, is always an inspiration; Shelley Murphy is both my content developer and dear friend. Kim Adams Fox did an outstanding job on photo research. Both Mary Kanable and Susan Gall are excellent proofreaders and I'm grateful for their thoughtful and smart comments. Linda Jupiter, the book's production editor, is another confidant and friend. I really appreciate the help of Lunaea Weatherstone, who in addition to being a great copy editor is also my oracle and personal life coach. The sensational Christy Frame is an extraordinary senior content project manager, and senior marketing manager Mark Linton is equally fantastic.

CRIMINOLOGY
THE CORE

Crime and Criminology

SIERRA CLAYBORN

TIN NGUYEN

Syed Rizwan Farook

Tashfeen Malik

1

Chapter Outline

FACT OR FICTION?

▶ Sex offender registration lists help deter potential offenders and reduce the incidence of child molestation.

▶ It's a crime to ignore a drowning person's cries for help.

▶ The definitions of long-established common-law crimes such as rape, robbery, and murder never change.

On December 2, 2015, Syed Rizwan Farook and Tashfeen Malik, residents of Redlands, California, attacked a holiday party being held for employees at the San Bernardino County Department of Public Health. Armed with semi-automatic weapons, they killed 14 people; 22 others were seriously injured. Farook, who worked for the health department, was an American-born citizen of Pakistani decent, while Malik, his wife, was Pakistani-born and a lawful permanent resident; they had a 6-month-old daughter. After the shooting, the couple fled the scene in a rented SUV and were killed in a shootout with pursuing police.

Farook and Malik are considered homegrown violent extremists, inspired by but not directed by a foreign group; they were not part of any known terrorist cell. Farook visited Pakistan in 2014 and returned with Malik, who traveled on a Pakistani passport with a fiancée visa. They also visited Saudi Arabia, but their radicalization is believed to have been via the Internet. After they returned from abroad, the couple began to stockpile weapons, thousands of rounds of ammunition, and bomb-making equipment in their home.[1]

The San Bernardino attack was all too reminiscent of other terrorist incidents on American soil:

- On April 15, 2013, Dzhokhar and Tamerlan Tsarnaev set off bombs at the Boston Marathon finish line, killing three people, and maiming and injuring at least 264. The Tsarnaev brothers, though born abroad and of Chechen descent, had prospered in the United States; Dzhokhar was attending a state university. Nonetheless, the brothers clung to radical Islamic views and blamed the US government for conducting a war against Islam in Iraq and Afghanistan.[2] ▶

- On November 28, 2016, Somali refugee Abdul Razak Ali Artan deliberately drove his car into pedestrians at Ohio State University. Getting out of the car, he then attacked others with a butcher knife before being shot and killed by the first responding OSU police officer. Thirteen people were injured in the attack. Investigators believe that Artan was inspired by terrorist propaganda from the Islamic State (IS) and radical Muslim cleric Anwar al-Awlaki.[3] ■

These and other high-profile terrorist incidents have spurred an ongoing national debate over the proper response to terrorism. In 2017, President Trump issued an executive order that prohibited residents from seven predominantly Muslim countries from visiting the US to work or study. Another executive order focused on immigrants who "pose a risk to public safety" and thereby made millions of undocumented people a priority for deportation.[4] The ban provoked even greater debate. Supporters believed Tump's order enhanced national security. Critics countered that the ban was unconstitutional; federal judges sided with the latter and blocked its implementation.

Widely publicized criminal acts, including terror attacks, have stimulated interest in **criminology**, an academic discipline that uses the scientific method to study the nature, extent, cause, and control of criminal behavior. This involves using valid and reliable procedures for the systematic collection, testing, and analysis of empirical evidence relevant to the problem under study.

What motivates people like Farook and Malik to turn on coworkers and people they knew in the name of Jihad? Or was that their real motive? Was their crime a matter of rational choice and decision making or the outcome of delusional thinking and mental illness?

Unlike political figures and media commentators, whose opinions about crime may be colored by personal experiences, biases, and election concerns, criminologists remain objective as they study crime and its consequences.[5] The field itself is far reaching, and subject matter ranges from street level drug dealing to international organized crime, from lone wolf terrorism to control of kiddie porn. It is an interdisciplinary field: while many criminologists have attended academic programs that award degrees in criminology or criminal justice, many criminologists have a background in other academic disciplines, including sociology, psychology, and legal studies.

In this chapter, we review the components of this diverse field of study, how this field developed, and how criminologists view crime and justice. We begin by examining the focus and concerns of this intriguing academic discipline.

criminology
The scientific study of the nature, extent, cause, and control of criminal behavior.

What Criminologists Do: The Elements of Criminology

L01 Explain the various elements of criminology.

Several subareas exist within the broader arena of criminology. Some criminologists specialize in one area while ignoring others, and some are generalists whose research interests are wide ranging. What then are the most important subareas in the field?

Criminal Statistics/Crime Measurement

The subarea of criminal statistics/crime measurement involves creating methodologies that are able to accurately measure activities, trends, and patterns in crime and then using these tools to calculate amounts and developments in criminal activity: How much crime occurs annually? Who commits it? When and where does it occur? Which crimes are the most serious?

Criminologists interested in computing criminal statistics focus on creating **valid** and **reliable measures** of criminal behavior:

- Criminologists help formulate techniques for collecting and analyzing official measures of criminal activities, such as crimes reported to the police.
- To measure unreported criminal activity criminologists develop survey instruments designed to have victims report loss and injury that may not have been reported to the police.
- Criminologists design methods that make it possible to investigate the cause of crime. They may create a self-administered survey with questions measuring an adolescent's delinquent behaviors as well as social characteristics, education and occupation of parents, friendship patterns, and school activities. These survey items can later be correlated in order to determine the associations among a variety of social factors and criminal activities, such as whether school failure is related to drug abuse.

valid measure
A measure that actually measures what it purports to measure; a measure that is factual.

reliable measure
A measure that produces consistent results from one measurement to another.

Sociology of Law/Law and Society/Sociolegal Studies

Variously called sociology of law, law and society, or sociolegal studies, this subarea of criminology is concerned with the social, political, and intellectual influences of law and legal activity; the sociology of legal institutions and legal processes; and consequences of law on society. According to the American Sociological Association, the sociology of law involves linking the study of law with such core sociological issues as social change and stability, order and disorder, the nation-state and capitalism. Research on sociolegal issues involves methodologically sophisticated empirical investigations as the central means of studying the dynamics of law in society.[6]

Criminologists who study the impact of law on society focus their attention on the role that social forces play in shaping criminal law and the role of criminal law in shaping society. They might investigate the history of legal thought in an effort to understand how criminal acts (such as theft, rape, and murder) evolved into their present form. They may also play an active role in suggesting legal changes that benefit society.

Criminologists who are interested in sociolegal scholarship evaluate the impact that new laws have on society. Take sex offender registration laws, which require convicted sex offenders to register with local law enforcement agencies whenever they move into a community. These provisions are often called Megan's Laws, in memory of 7-year-old Megan Kanka. Megan was killed in 1994 by sex offender Jesse Timmendequas, who had moved unannounced into her New Jersey neighborhood. When criminologists conducted an in-depth study of the effectiveness of the New Jersey registration law they found that, although it was maintained at great cost to the state, the system did not produce effective results: Sex offense rates in New Jersey were in steep decline before the system was installed, and the rate of decline actually slowed down after 1995 when the law took effect; in some states arrests for sex offenses increased after the law took effect. Megan's Law did not reduce the number of rearrests for sex offenses, nor did it have any demonstrable effect on the time between when sex offenders were released from prison and the time they were rearrested for any new offense, such as a drug offense, theft, or another sex offense.[7] Such sociolegal scholarship helps policy makers determine the effectiveness of legal change.

FACT OR FICTION?

Sex offender registration lists help deter potential offenders and reduce the incidence of child molestation.

FICTION Research indicates that registration has little effect on either offenders or rates of child molesting.

Monica Almeida/New York Times/Redux

Criminologists interested in the sociology of law conduct research on the effects of legal change on society. Take for example the Supreme Court's ruling in *Miller v. Alabama*, barring mandatory life sentences for juveniles convicted of murder. Criminologists may be called upon to test public opinion on whether young offenders have the potential for rehabilitation. They may also try to explore whether adolescent brains have developed sufficiently to fully understand the consequences of their behavior.

Criminological research is also used extensively by the Supreme Court in shaping their decision making and creating legal precedence.[8] Take what happened in these two important cases:

- In *Miller v. Alabama*, the Supreme Court relied on social research that conclusively showed that juveniles are not fully capable of anticipating the consequences of their actions. This finding led the justices to conclude that it would be inappropriate and unconstitutional for juveniles to receive mandatory life sentences without the possibility of parole. If juveniles have a different mental capacity than adults, it seemed illogical that they should receive the same punishment; this would amount to cruel and unusual punishment.[9]

- In *Glossip v. Gross*, Justices Breyer and Ginsburg relied on social science research by sociolegal scholar Samuel Gross and his colleagues showing that there is a significant likelihood of a wrongful conviction in death penalty cases. Why is this so? Because capital cases typically involve horrendous murders, and they generate intense community pressure on police, prosecutors, and jurors to secure a conviction. This pressure creates a greater likelihood of convicting the wrong person.[10] Here a legal opinion was informed by social science research.

Developing Theories of Crime Causation

Criminologists also explore the causes of crime. How do the mechanisms of past experience influence an individual's propensity to offend? Is past behavior the best predictor of future behavior? Are the seeds of a criminal career planted early in life or do life events upend a person's normal life course?

Some criminologists focus on the individual and look for an association between decision making, psychological and biological traits, and antisocial behaviors. Those who have a psychological orientation view crime as a function of personality, development, social learning, or cognition. Others investigate the biological correlates of antisocial behavior and study the biochemical, genetic, and neurological linkages to crime.

Those with a sociological orientation look at the social forces producing criminal behavior, including neighborhood conditions, poverty, socialization, and group interaction. Their belief is that people are a "product of their environment" and anyone living in substandard conditions could be at risk to crime. Kids are deeply affected by what goes on in their family, school, and neighborhood, and these are the keys to understanding the development of antisocial behavior.

On November 13, 2015, 130 people were killed and another 350 injured in a series of terror attacks across Paris, including at the Stade de France (the French national stadium), at cafés and restaurants, and at the Bataclan Theater, where a concert was taking place. The attacks began when bombs were set off outside the Stade de France during a soccer match between France and Germany. Hundreds of people ran from the stadium in panic. The Islamic State (IS) claimed responsibility for the attacks, which involved groups of jihadists who simultaneously attacked numerous sites in the city. Soon after, French President François Hollande closed the nation's borders and declared a state of emergency. The Paris attacks prompted massive retaliation on IS installations by France, the United States, and Russia. Criminologists conduct research on discovering what prompts people to join terror groups and what can be done to dissuade them from joining.

AP Images/Christophe Ena

Pinning down "one true cause" of crime remains a difficult problem because most people, even those living in the poorest disorganized neighborhood, or who suffered abuse and neglect as children, do not become criminals. If they did, there would be a lot more crimes committed each year than now occur. Since most of us are law abiding, despite enduring many social and psychological problems, it's tough to pinpoint the conditions that inevitably lead to a criminal way of life. Criminologists are still unsure why, given similar conditions, some people choose criminal solutions to their problems, whereas others conform to accepted social rules of behavior.

Explaining Criminal Behavior

Another subarea of criminology involves research on specific criminal types and patterns: violent crime, theft crime, public order crime, organized crime, and so on. Numerous attempts have been made to describe and understand particular crime types. Marvin Wolfgang's 1958 study *Patterns in Criminal Homicide* is a landmark analysis of the nature of homicide and the relationship between victim and offender. Wolfgang discovered that in many instances victims caused or precipitated the violent confrontation that led to their death, spawning the term **victim-precipitated homicide**.[11] Edwin Sutherland's pioneering analysis of business-related offenses also helped coin a new phrase, **white-collar crime**, to describe economic crime activities of the affluent.[12]

Criminologists are constantly broadening the scope of their inquiry because new crimes and crime patterns are constantly emerging. Whereas 50 years ago they might have focused their attention on rape, murder, and burglary, they now may be looking at stalking, environmental crimes, cybercrime, terrorism, and hate crimes. Take for instance Internet porn, something that began being widely used in the 1990s and has been more frequently viewed ever since, especially by the younger generation.[13] Today 46 percent of men and 16 percent of women between the ages of 18 and 39 intentionally view pornography in a given week.[14] At the same time, there has been public outrage over sexual assaults on college campuses; several studies indicate that a substantial proportion of female students—between 18 and 20 percent—experience rape or some other form of sexual assault during their college years.[15] Is there a link between these two phenomena? To answer this question, criminologists are conducting research aimed at determining whether people who view pornography are also more likely to commit violence against women. So far the evidence finds a connection: watching Internet porn and sexual violence may actually be related.[16]

Penology: Punishment, Sanctions, and Corrections

The study of **penology** involves efforts to control crime through the correction of criminal offenders. Some criminologists advocate a therapeutic approach to crime prevention that relies on the application of **rehabilitation** services; they direct their efforts at identifying effective treatment strategies for individuals convicted of law violations, such as relying on community sentencing rather than prison. Others argue that crime can be prevented only through the application of formal social control, through such measures as **mandatory sentences** for serious crimes and even the use of **capital punishment** as a deterrent to murder.

Criminologists interested in penology direct their research efforts at evaluating the effectiveness of crime control programs and searching for effective treatments that can significantly lower **recidivism** rates. An evaluation of the Risk-Need-Responsivity (RNR) program, which classifies people on probation and orders the placement of some in anger management and cognitive behavioral therapy programs, has been found to cut the recidivism of high-risk offenders by as much as 20 percent.[17]

Not all penological measures work as expected. One might assume that inmates placed in the most punitive high-security prisons will "learn their lesson" and not

victim-precipitated homicide
Refers to those killings in which the victim is a direct, positive precipitator of the incident.

white-collar crime
Illegal acts that capitalize on a person's status in the marketplace. White-collar crimes may include theft, embezzlement, fraud, market manipulation, restraint of trade, and false advertising.

penology
Subarea of criminology that focuses on the correction and control of criminal offenders.

rehabilitation
Treatment of criminal offenders that is aimed at preventing future criminal behavior.

mandatory sentences
A statutory requirement that a certain penalty shall be carried out in all cases of conviction for a specified offense or series of offenses.

capital punishment
The execution of criminal offenders; the death penalty.

recidivism
Relapse into criminal behavior after apprehension, conviction, and correction for a previous crime.

Concept Summary 1.1   Criminology in Action

The following subareas constitute the discipline of criminology.

Criminal statistics	*Gathering valid crime data.* Devising new research methods; measuring crime patterns and trends.
Sociology of law/law and society/sociolegal studies	*Determining the origin of law.* Measuring the forces that can change laws and society.
Theory construction	*Predicting individual behavior.* Understanding the cause of crime rates and trends.
Criminal behavior systems	*Determining the nature and cause of specific crime patterns.* Studying violence, theft, organized crime, white-collar crime, and public order crimes.
Penology: punishment, sanctions, and corrections	*Studying the correction and control of criminal behavior.* Using the scientific method to assess the effectiveness of criminal sanctions designed to control crime through the application of criminal punishments.
Victimology	*Studying the nature and cause of victimization.* Aiding crime victims; understanding the nature and extent of victimization; developing theories of victimization risk.

dare to repeat their criminal offense. However, research shows that being sent to a high-security prison exposes inmates to the most violent peers who have a higher propensity for crime. This exposure may actually increase criminal behavior, reinforce antisocial attitudes, and ultimately increase recidivism—a finding that supports the need for careful penological research.[18]

victimology
The study of the victim's role in criminal events.

Victimology

Criminologists recognize that the victim plays a critical role in the criminal process and that the victim's behavior is often a key determinant of crime.[19] **Victimology** includes the following areas of interest:

* Using victim surveys to measure the nature and extent of criminal behavior and to calculate the actual costs of crime to victims
* Calculating probabilities of victimization risk
* Studying victim culpability in the precipitation of crime
* Designing services for crime victims, such as counseling and compensation programs

Criminologists who study victimization have uncovered some startling results. For one thing, criminals have been found to be at greater risk of victimization than noncriminals.[20] This finding indicates that rather than being passive targets who are "in the wrong place at the wrong time," victims may themselves be engaging in a high-risk behavior, such as crime, that increases their victimization risk and renders them vulnerable to crime.

The various elements of criminology in action are summarized in Concept Summary 1.1.

A Brief History of Criminology

How did this field of study develop? What are the origins of criminology? The scientific study of crime and criminality is a relatively recent development. During the Middle Ages (1200–1600), people who violated social norms or religious practices were believed to be witches or possessed by demons.[21] The use of cruel torture to extract confessions was common. Those convicted of violent or theft crimes

CHECKPOINTS

▶ Criminologists engage in a variety of professional tasks.

▶ Those who work in criminal statistics create accurate measures of crime trends and patterns.

▶ Some criminologists study the origins and sociology of law.

▶ Theorists interested in criminal development seek insight into the causes of crime.

▶ Some criminologists try to understand and describe patterns and trends in particular criminal behaviors, such as serial murder or rape.

▶ Penologists evaluate the criminal justice system.

▶ Victimologists try to understand why some people become crime victims.

suffered extremely harsh penalties, including whipping, branding, maiming, and execution.

Classical Criminology

By the mid-eighteenth century, social philosophers began to argue for a more rational approach to punishment. Reformers stressed that the relationship between crime and punishment should be balanced and fair. This more moderate view of criminal sanctions can be traced to the writings of an Italian scholar, Cesare Beccaria (1738–1794), who was one of the first scholars to develop a systematic understanding of why people commit crime.

Beccaria believed that in choosing their behavior people act in their own self-interest: they want to achieve pleasure and avoid pain. People will commit crime when the potential pleasure and reward they believe they can achieve from illegal acts outweigh the threat of future punishment. To deter crime, punishment must be sufficient—no more, no less—to counterbalance the lure of criminal gain. If it were too lenient, people would risk committing crimes; too severe a punishment would be unfair and encourage crimes. If rape were punished by death, rapists might be encouraged to kill their victims to prevent identification; after all, they would have nothing to lose if both rape and murder were punished equally. Beccaria's famous theorem was that in order for punishment to be effective it must be public, prompt, necessary, the least possible in the given circumstances, proportionate, and dictated by law.[22]

The writings of Beccaria and his followers form the core of what today is referred to as **classical criminology**. As originally conceived in the eighteenth century, classical criminology theory had several basic elements:

- People have free will to choose criminal or lawful solutions to meet their needs or settle their problems.
- Crime is attractive when it promises great benefits with little effort.
- Crime may be controlled by the fear of punishment.
- Punishment that is (or is perceived to be) severe, certain, and swift will deter criminal behavior.

This classical perspective influenced judicial philosophy, and sentences were geared to be proportionate to the seriousness of the crime. Executions were still widely used but gradually came to be employed for only the most serious crimes. The catchphrase was "Let the punishment fit the crime."

Positivist Criminology

During the nineteenth century, a new vision of the world challenged the validity of classical theory and presented an innovative way of looking at the causes of crime. The scientific method was beginning to take hold in Europe and North America.

Auguste Comte (1798–1857), considered the founder of sociology, argued that societies pass through stages that can be grouped on the basis of how people try to understand the world in which they live. People in primitive societies believe that inanimate objects have life (for example, the sun is a god); in later social stages, people embrace a rational, scientific view of the world. Comte called this the positive stage, and those who followed his writings became known as positivists.

Positivism has a number of elements:

- Use of the **scientific method** to conduct research. The scientific method is objective, universal, and culture-free.
- Predicting and explaining social phenomena in a logical manner. This means identifying necessary and sufficient conditions under which a phenomenon may or may not occur. Both human behavior and natural phenomena operate according to laws that can be measured and observed.
- All beliefs or statements must be proved through empirical investigation guided by the scientific method. Such concepts as "God" and "the soul" cannot be

classical criminology
Theoretical perspective suggesting that people choose to commit crime and that crime can be controlled if potential criminals fear punishment.

positivism
The branch of social science that uses the scientific method of the natural sciences and suggests that human behavior is a product of social, biological, psychological, or economic forces that can be empirically measured.

scientific method
The use of verifiable principles and procedures for the systematic acquisition of knowledge. Typically involves formulating a problem, creating hypotheses, and collecting data, through observation and experiment, to verify the hypotheses.

Positivists use the scientific method to explain criminal behavior. Some look at social factors while others focus on physical and biological traits. Here, Dr. Michael Nicholas, a clinical psychologist from Paducah, Kentucky, displays a small red and white cube and a model of a human brain as he testifies in the Kevin Wayne Dunlap murder trial. Nicholas was using the props to show the approximate size of an abnormality detected in Dunlap's brain on MRI and PET scans. Nicholas was a defense witness testifying as to how the abnormality may have affected Dunlap, who confessed to the killing of three children and the assault of their mother in October 2008. Dunlap stabbed and killed a 5-year-old boy and his 14- and 17-year-old sisters in their home. He then raped and attempted to murder their mother by stabbing her. When he thought that the mother was dead, he set fire to the home and left. Despite evidence that Dunlap's abnormal brain structure may have controlled his behavior, he was convicted of murder and sentenced to death.

AP Images/Paducah Sun, John Wright

measured empirically and therefore are not the subject of scientific inquiry; they remain a matter of faith.

- Science must be value-free and should not be influenced by the observer/scientist's biases or political point of view.

EARLY CRIMINOLOGICAL POSITIVISM The earliest "scientific" studies examining human behavior now seem quaint and primitive. Physiognomists, such as J. K. Lavater (1741–1801), studied the facial features of criminals and found that the shape of the ears, nose, and eyes and the distances between them were associated with antisocial behavior. Phrenologists, such as Franz Joseph Gall (1758–1828) and Johann K. Spurzheim (1776–1832), studied the shape of the skull and bumps on the head and concluded that these physical attributes were linked to criminal behavior.[23]

By the early nineteenth century, abnormality in the human mind was being linked to criminal behavior patterns. Philippe Pinel, one of the founders of French psychiatry, coined the phrase *manie sans delire* to denote what eventually was referred to as a psychopathic personality.

In Italy, Cesare Lombroso (1835–1909), known as the "father of criminology," began to study the cadavers of executed criminals in an effort to determine scientifically how criminals differed from noncriminals. Lombroso was soon convinced that serious and violent offenders had inherited criminal traits. These "born criminals" suffered from "atavistic anomalies"; physically, they were throwbacks to more primitive times when people were savages and were believed to have the enormous jaws and strong canine teeth common to carnivores that devour raw flesh. Lombroso's version of criminal anthropology was brought to the United States via articles and textbooks that adopted his ideas.[24] By the beginning of the twentieth century, American authors were discussing "the science of penology" and "the science of criminology."[25]

Sociological Criminology

At the same time that biological views were dominating criminology, another group of positivists were developing the field of sociology to study scientifically the major social changes taking place in nineteenth-century society. The foundations of **sociological criminology** can be traced to the work of Émile Durkheim (1858–1917).[26]

According to Durkheim's vision of social positivism, crime is normal because it is virtually impossible to imagine a society in which criminal behavior is totally absent.[27] Durkheim believed that crime is inevitable because people are so different

sociological criminology
Approach to criminology, based on the work of Émile Durkheim, that focuses on the relationship between social factors and crime.

CONNECTIONS

Many of us have grown up with movies showing criminals as "homicidal maniacs." Some may laugh, but *Split, No Country for Old Men, Disturbia, American Psycho, Hannibal*, and similar films are usually box office hits. See Chapter 5 for more on psychosis as a cause of crime.

from one another and use such a wide variety of methods and types of behavior to meet their needs. Even if "real" crimes were eliminated, human weaknesses and petty vices would be elevated to the status of crimes. Durkheim suggested that crime can be useful—and occasionally even healthful—for society in that it paves the way for social change. To illustrate this concept, Durkheim offered the example of the Greek philosopher Socrates, who was considered a criminal and was put to death for corrupting the morals of youth simply because he expressed ideas that were different from what people believed at that time.

In *The Division of Labor in Society*, Durkheim wrote about the consequences of the shift from a small, rural society, which he labeled "mechanical," to the more modern "organic" society with a large urban population, division of labor, and personal isolation.[28] From the resulting structural changes flowed **anomie**, or norm and role confusion. An anomic society is in chaos, experiencing moral uncertainty and an accompanying loss of traditional values. People who suffer anomie may become confused and rebellious. Is it possible that the loss of privacy created by widespread social media, a technology that can cause a private moment to go "viral," has helped create a sense of anomie in our own culture?

THE CHICAGO SCHOOL The primacy of sociological positivism was secured by research begun in the early twentieth century by Robert Ezra Park (1864–1944), Ernest W. Burgess (1886–1966), Louis Wirth (1897–1952), and their colleagues in the Sociology Department at the University of Chicago. The scholars who taught at this program created what is still referred to as the **Chicago School** in honor of their unique style of doing research.

These urban sociologists examined how neighborhood conditions, such as poverty levels, influenced crime rates. They found that social forces operating in urban areas created a crime-promoting environment; some neighborhoods were "natural areas" for crime.[29] In urban neighborhoods with high levels of poverty, the fabric of critical social institutions, such as the school and the family, came undone. Their traditional ability to control behavior was undermined, and the outcome was a high crime rate.

SOCIALIZATION VIEWS During the 1930s and 1940s, another group of sociologists began conducting research that linked criminal behavior to the quality of an individual's **socialization**—the relationship they have to important social processes, such as education, family life, and peer relations. They found that children who grew up in homes wracked by conflict, attended inadequate schools, or associated with deviant peers became exposed to forces that engendered crime. One position, championed by the preeminent American criminologist Edwin Sutherland, was that people learn criminal attitudes from older, more experienced law violators.

Conflict Criminology

In his *Communist Manifesto* and other writings, Karl Marx (1818–1883) described the oppressive labor conditions prevalent during the rise of industrial capitalism. Marx was convinced that the character of every civilization is determined by its mode of production—the way its people develop and produce material goods. The most important relationship in industrial culture is between the owners of the means of production (the capitalist bourgeoisie) and the people who perform the labor (the proletariat). The economic system controls all facets of human life; consequently, people's lives revolve around the means of production. The exploitation of the working class, Marx believed, would eventually lead to class conflict and the end of the capitalist system.[30]

These writings laid the foundation for **conflict theory**, the view that human behavior is shaped by interpersonal conflict and that crime is a product of human conflict. However, it was not until the social and political upheaval of the 1960s—fueled by the Vietnam War, the development of an antiestablishment counterculture movement, the civil rights movement, and the women's movement—that criminologists began to analyze the social conditions in the United States that promoted

anomie
A lack of norms or clear social standards. Because of rapidly shifting moral values, the individual has few guides to what is socially acceptable.

Chicago School
Group of urban sociologists who studied the relationship between environmental conditions and crime.

socialization
Process of human development and enculturation. Socialization is influenced by key social processes and institutions.

conflict theory
The view that human behavior is shaped by interpersonal conflict and that those who maintain social power will use it to further their own ends.

CONNECTIONS

Did your mother ever warn you about staying away from "bad neighborhoods" in the city? If she did, how valid were her concerns? To find out, go to Chapter 6 for a discussion of the structural conditions that cause crime.

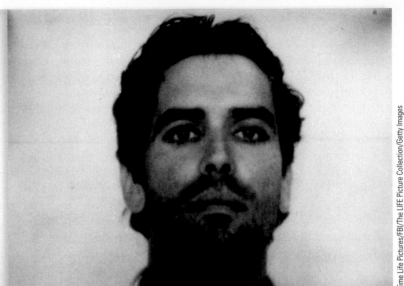

In 1980, Glen Stewart Godwin, along with his partner, Frank Soto, robbed a drug dealer and stabbed him 26 times with a butcher knife, then blew up the body to hide the evidence. Godwin was sentenced to 26 years to life in prison, but in 1987, he made a daring escape by digging a tunnel. Godwin fled to Mexico, where he got involved in the drug trade. Sent to a Mexican prison, he killed a member of a drug cartel and escaped once again. He is currently on the loose somewhere in Latin America and assumed to be dealing drugs. Developmental criminologists would view Godwin's criminal career as a product of sociological, psychological, and economic factors. His initiation into a criminal career is a developmental process, influenced by both internal and external situations, conditions, and circumstances.

critical criminology
The view that crime is a product of the capitalist system.

rational choice theory
The view that crime is a function of a decision-making process in which the would-be offender weighs the potential costs and benefits of an illegal act.

trait theory
The view that criminality is a product of abnormal biological or psychological traits.

social structure theory
The view that disadvantaged economic class position is a primary cause of crime.

class conflict and crime. What emerged from this intellectual ferment was a **critical criminology** that indicted the economic system as producing the conditions that support a high crime rate. Critical criminologists have played a significant role in the field ever since.

Developmental Criminology

In the 1940s and 1950s, Sheldon and Eleanor Glueck, a husband-and-wife team of criminologists and researchers at Harvard Law School, conducted numerous studies of delinquent and criminal behavior that profoundly influenced criminological theory. Their work integrated sociological, psychological, and economic elements into a complex developmental view of crime causation. Their most important research efforts followed the careers of known delinquents to determine what factors predicted persistent offending; they also made extensive use of interviews and records in their elaborate comparisons of delinquents and nondelinquents.[31]

The Gluecks' vision integrated biological, social, and psychological elements. It suggested that the initiation and continuity of a criminal career was a developmental process influenced by both internal and external situations, conditions, and circumstances.

Contemporary Criminology

These various schools of criminology, developed over 200 years, have been constantly evolving.

- Classical theory has evolved into modern **rational choice theory**, which argues that criminals are rational decision makers: before choosing to commit crime, criminals evaluate the benefits and costs of the contemplated criminal act; their choice is structured by the fear of punishment.
- Lombrosian biological positivism has evolved into contemporary biosocial and psychological **trait theory** views. Criminologists who consider themselves trait theorists no longer believe that a single trait or inherited characteristic can explain crime, but that biological and psychological traits interact with environmental factors to influence criminality. Contemporary trait theories suggest that there is a causal link between criminal behavior and such individual level factors as diet, hormonal makeup, personality, and intelligence.
- The original Chicago School sociological vision has transformed into a **social structure theory**, which maintains that a person's place in the social structure

Concept Summary 1.2   Criminological Perspectives

The major perspectives of criminology focus on individual factors (biological, psychological, and choice theories), social factors (structural and process theories), political and economic factors (conflict theory), and multiple factors (developmental theory).

Classical/choice perspective	*Situational forces.* Crime is a function of free will and personal choice. Punishment is a deterrent to crime.
Biological/psychological perspective	*Internal forces.* Crime is a function of chemical, neurological, genetic, personality, intelligence, or mental traits.
Structural perspective	*Ecological forces.* Crime rates are a function of neighborhood conditions, cultural forces, values, and norms.
Process perspective	*Socialization forces.* Crime is a function of upbringing, learning, and control. Peers, parents, and teachers influence behavior.
Conflict perspective	*Economic and political forces.* Crime is a function of competition for limited resources and power. Class conflict produces crime.
Developmental perspective	*Multiple forces.* Biological, social-psychological, economic, and political forces may combine to produce crime.

CHECKPOINTS

▶ Criminology has a long and rich history.

▶ The first criminologists believed that crime was a matter of free will. This outlook is referred to as classical criminology.

▶ In the nineteenth century, positivist criminologists began to use the scientific method to study crime. They were convinced that the cause of crime could be found in the individual offender.

▶ During the early twentieth century, sociological criminology was developed to explain the effect of the social environment on individual behavior.

▶ Critical criminologists attempted to explain how economic forces create crime.

▶ Developmental criminologists trace criminal careers over the life course.

▶ Contemporary criminology carries on and refines these traditions.

controls their behavior; people are a product of their environment. Those at the bottom of the social hierarchy, who find it impossible to achieve monetary and social success through conventional means, experience anomie, strain, failure, and frustration. Social pressures, and the personal turmoil they produce, lead people down a path to crime.

- The focus of **social process theory** is on socialization. Theorists who hold this view believe that children learn to commit crime by interacting with, and modeling their behavior after, others whom they admire. Some criminal offenders are people whose life experiences have shattered their social bonds to society.
- Many criminologists still view social and political conflict as the root cause of crime. These **critical criminologists** believe that crime is related to the inherently unfair economic structure of the United States and other advanced capitalist countries.
- The Gluecks' pioneering research has influenced a new generation of developmental theorists. Their focus today is identifying the personal traits and social conditions that lead to the creation and maintenance of criminal careers over the life course.

Each of the major perspectives is summarized in Concept Summary 1.2.

Deviant or Criminal? How Criminologists Define Crime

Criminologists devote themselves to measuring, understanding, and controlling crime and deviance. How are these behaviors defined, and how do we distinguish between them?

Criminologists view **deviant behavior** as any action that departs from the social norms of society.[32] Deviance thus includes a broad spectrum of behaviors, ranging from the most socially harmful, such as rape and murder, to the relatively inoffensive, such as joining a religious cult or cross-dressing. A deviant act becomes a **crime** when

social process theory
The view that criminality is a function of people's interactions with various organizations, institutions, and processes in society.

critical criminologists
Critical criminologists examine how those who hold political and economic power shape the law to uphold their self-interests.

deviant behavior
Actions that depart from the social norm. Some are considered criminal, others merely harmless aberrations.

crime
An act, deemed socially harmful or dangerous, that is specifically defined, prohibited, and punished under the criminal law.

LO2 Differentiate between crime and deviance.

What is considered deviant behavior today can be socially acceptable tomorrow. This poster is for the 1936 film *Reefer Madness*, a movie depicting the dangers of smoking marijuana. Eighty years later, pot smoking is routine behavior and legal in several states.

it is deemed socially harmful or dangerous; it then will be specifically defined, prohibited, and punished under the criminal law.

Crime and deviance are often confused because not all crimes are deviant and not all deviant acts are illegal or criminal. For example, recreational drug use such as smoking marijuana may be a crime, but is it deviant? A significant percentage of the population has used recreational drugs (including some well-known politicians—even presidents!). If an illegal act, such as smoking pot or downloading copyrighted material, becomes a norm, should society reevaluate its criminal status and let it become merely an unusual or deviant act?

To argue that all crimes are behaviors that depart from the norms of society is probably erroneous. The shifting definition of deviant behavior is closely associated with our concepts of crime. Where should society draw the line between behavior that is considered merely deviant and unusual and behavior that is considered dangerous and criminal? Many deviant acts are not criminal, even though they may be shocking or depraved. A passerby who observes a person drowning is not legally required to jump in and render aid. Although the general public would probably condemn the person's behavior as callous, immoral, and deviant, no legal action could be taken because citizens are not required by law to effect rescues. In sum, many criminal acts, but not all, fall within the concept of deviance. Similarly, some deviant acts, but not all, are considered crimes.

Becoming Deviant

To understand the nature and purpose of criminal law, criminologists study both the process by which deviant acts are criminalized (become crimes) and, conversely, how criminal acts are **decriminalized** (that is, the penalties attached to them are reduced) and/or legalized.

In some instances, individuals, institutions, or government agencies mount a campaign aimed at convincing both the public and lawmakers that what was considered merely deviant behavior is actually dangerous and must be outlawed. During the 1930s, Harry Anslinger, then head of the Federal Bureau of Narcotics, used magazine articles, public appearances, and public testimony to sway public opinion about the dangers of marijuana, which up until that time had been legal to use and possess.[33] In testimony before the House Ways and Means Committee considering passage of the Marijuana Tax Act of 1938, Anslinger stated,

> In Florida a 21-year-old boy under the influence of this drug killed his parents and his brothers and sisters. The evidence showed that he had smoked marihuana. In Chicago recently two boys murdered a policeman while under the influence of marihuana. Not long ago we found a 15-year-old boy going insane because, the doctor told the enforcement officers, he thought the boy was smoking marihuana cigarettes. They traced the sale to some man who had been growing marihuana and selling it to these boys all under 15 years of age, on a playground there.[34]

As a result of Anslinger's efforts, a deviant behavior, marijuana use, became a criminal behavior, and previously law-abiding citizens were defined as criminal offenders. Today some national organizations, such as the Drug Policy Alliance, are committed to repealing draconian drug laws and undoing Anslinger's "moral crusade." They call for an end to the "war against drugs," which they believe has become overzealous in its effort to punish drug traffickers. In fact, they maintain, many of the problems the drug war purports to resolve are actually caused by the drug war itself. So-called "drug-related" crime is a direct result of drug prohibition's distortion of immutable laws of supply and demand. Public health problems such as HIV and

FACT OR FICTION?

It's a crime to ignore a drowning person's cries for help.

FICTION Citizens are not required to risk their lives to save another unless they are bound to by occupation or status (e.g., a lifeguard).

decriminalized
Having criminal penalties reduced rather than eliminated.

hepatitis C are all exacerbated by zero-tolerance laws that restrict access to clean needles. The drug war is not the promoter of family values that some would have us believe. Children of inmates are at risk of educational failure, joblessness, addiction, and delinquency. Drug abuse is bad, but the drug war is worse.[35] Their efforts have borne some fruit: a number of states, including Colorado and Washington, have decriminalized the possession and sale of marijuana.

In sum, criminologists are concerned with the concept of deviance and its relationship to criminality. The shifting definition of deviant behavior is closely associated with our concept of crime.

The Concept of Crime

Professional criminologists usually align themselves with one of several schools of thought, or perspectives. Each of these perspectives maintains its own view of what constitutes criminal behavior and what causes people to engage in criminality. A criminologist's choice of orientation or perspective depends, in part, on his or her definition of crime. The three most common concepts of crime used by criminologists are the consensus view, the conflict view, and the interactionist view.

CONSENSUS VIEW OF CRIME According to the **consensus view**, crimes are behaviors that all elements of society consider repugnant. The rich and powerful as well as the poor and indigent are believed to agree on which behaviors are so repugnant that they should be outlawed and criminalized. Therefore, the **criminal law**—the written code that defines crimes and their punishments—reflects the values, beliefs, and opinions of society's mainstream. The term *consensus* implies general agreement among a majority of citizens on what behaviors should be prohibited by criminal law and hence be viewed as crimes.[36]

This approach to crime implies that it is a function of the beliefs, morality, and rules inherent in Western civilization. Ideally, the laws apply equally to all members of society, and their effects are not restricted to any single element of society.

CONFLICT VIEW OF CRIME Although most practicing criminologists accept the consensus model of crime, others take a more political orientation toward its content. The **conflict view** depicts society as a collection of diverse groups—such as owners, workers, professionals, and students—who are in constant and continuing conflict. Groups able to assert their political power use the law and the criminal justice system to advance their economic and social position. Criminal laws, therefore, are viewed as created to protect the haves from the have-nots. Conflict criminologists often contrast the harsh penalties inflicted on the poor for their "street crimes" (burglary, robbery, and larceny) with the minor penalties the wealthy receive for their white-collar crimes (securities violations and other illegal business practices). Whereas the poor go to prison for minor law violations, the wealthy are given lenient sentences for even serious breaches of law. The Profiles in Crime feature illustrates the conflict view of crime.

INTERACTIONIST VIEW OF CRIME According to the **interactionist view**, there is no objective reality. People, institutions, and events are viewed subjectively and labeled either good or evil according to the interpretation of the evaluator. The content of the criminal law and consequently the definition of crime are subjective and can change at any moment. The recreational use of marijuana is now legal in some jurisdictions and illegal in others. It could easily be the other way around in those same jurisdictions, depending on the voting public's views, perceptions, and beliefs.

Whether a particular act fits the definition of a crime is also a function of interaction and perception. If a death occurs in the wake of an argument, a jury may be asked to decide whether the act was murder, self-defense, or merely an accidental fatality. Each person on the jury may have his or her own interpretation of what took place. Whether the act is labeled a crime and the actor a criminal depends on the

L03 Analyze the three different views of the definition of crime.

consensus view
The belief that the majority of citizens in a society share common values and agree on what behaviors should be defined as criminal.

criminal law
The written code that defines crimes and their punishments.

conflict view
The belief that criminal behavior is defined by those in power in such a way as to protect and advance their own self-interest.

interactionist view
The belief that those with social power are able to impose their values on society as a whole, and these values then define criminal behavior.

PROFILES IN CRIME

A SHOOTING IN FERGUSON

On August 9, 2014, in Ferguson, Missouri, a suburb of St. Louis, Michael Brown, an 18-year-old unarmed African American youth, was fatally shot by Darren Wilson, a white police officer. According to most accounts, shortly before the shooting Brown and a friend, Dorian Johnson, had stolen some cigars from a local convenience store. Officer Wilson, who at the time was not aware of the theft, encountered the two young men as they were walking down the middle of the street. From his police car, Wilson ordered them to move to the sidewalk. According to Wilson, when the two refused to obey the order, a scuffle broke out during which Michael Brown punched Wilson through the window of the police car. The fight went on until Wilson fired his gun, and Brown and Johnson fled down the street. Wilson pursued Brown, eventually firing a total of 12 rounds at him from a distance ranging from 10 to 30 feet. In all Michael Brown was hit eight times, the last shot causing his death.

A grand jury called to review the evidence in the case failed to find sufficient cause to indict Darren Wilson for the death of Michael Brown, prompting nationwide protests condemning racial bias in the justice system.

Many questioned the grand jury's refusal to indict Officer Wilson, not being able to understand how the shooting of an unarmed suspect was not a crime. Legally, the grand jury's decision rested on what happened during the pursuit of Michael Brown. Did Brown, as some witnesses asserted, have his hands raised in surrender as he moved toward Officer Wilson? Or was Michael Brown madly charging at the officer in an attempt to attack him further, as Wilson claimed? If the latter, then the officer's behavior might be excused since he acted in self-defense if he actually felt threatened; if the former, Wilson's actions amounted to felony murder. Members of the jury obviously believed Wilson's story when they failed to indict.

Wilson could have been indicted, tried, and convicted for his act and be considered a callous, violent criminal. Instead, the jury decided not to indict, meaning that Wilson is not a criminal in the eyes of the law. The fact that a jury of his peers failed to indict Wilson reinforces the fact that what is a crime and who is considered a criminal are not objective facts but open to interpretation.

The death of Michael Brown certainly raised issues about the role race plays in the construction and creation of crime and criminality. Would Michael Brown have been stopped by a police officer if he was a Caucasian college student? The law should and must be color and gender blind. Did this incident occur because of racial profiling? Many people believed that the incident showed that racism still exists in the justice system.

The "Ferguson effect" refers to the belief that increased investigation of police activities following the shooting of Michael Brown has led to an increased crime rate in major US cities. Following the shooting, murder rates increased by almost 10 percent. Do you agree that police are more cautious since the Brown case? If so, has this more cautious mindset influenced the nation's violence rate? ■

Robert Cohen/Pool/epa/Corbis Wire/Corbis

Sources: Neil Gross, "Is There a 'Ferguson Effect'?" *New York Times*, September 30, 2016, https://www.nytimes.com/2016/10/02/opinion/sunday/is-there-a-ferguson-effect.html; "What Happened in Ferguson?" *New York Times*, August 10, 2015, https://www.nytimes.com/interactive/2014/08/13/us/ferguson-missouri-town-under-siege-after-police-shooting.html. (URLs accessed April 2017.)

Concept Summary 1.3   The Definition of Crime

The definition of crime affects how criminologists view the cause and control of illegal behavior and shapes their research orientation.

Consensus view	• The law defines crime. • Agreement exists on outlawed behavior. • Laws apply to all citizens equally.
Conflict view	• The law is a tool of the ruling class. • Crime is a politically defined concept. • "Real crimes" such as racism, sexism, and classism are not outlawed. • The law is used to control the underclass.
Interactionist view	• Moral entrepreneurs define crime. • Acts become crimes because society defines them that way. • Criminal labels are life-transforming events.

juror's interpretation of events. Interactionists see criminal law as conforming to the beliefs of "moral crusaders," or moral entrepreneurs, who use their influence to shape the legal process as they see fit.[37] Laws against pornography, prostitution, and drugs are believed to be motivated more by moral crusades than by capitalist sensibilities. Consequently, interactionists are concerned with shifting moral and legal standards.

A Definition of Crime

Because of their diverse perspectives, criminologists have taken a variety of approaches in explaining crime's causes and suggesting methods for its control (see Concept Summary 1.3). Considering these differences, we can take elements from each school of thought to formulate an integrated definition of crime.

Crime is a violation of societal rules of behavior as interpreted and expressed by the criminal law, which reflects public opinion, traditional values, and the viewpoint of people currently holding social and political power. Individuals who violate these rules are subject to sanctions by state authority, social stigma, and loss of status.

This definition combines the consensus view that the criminal law defines crimes, the conflict perspective's emphasis on political power and control, and the interactionist concept of stigma. Thus crime as defined here is a political, social, and economic function of modern life.

Criminology and the Criminal Law

No matter which definition of crime we embrace, criminal behavior is tied to the criminal law. It is therefore important for all criminologists to have some understanding of the development of criminal law, its objectives, its elements, and how it evolved over time.

The concept of criminal law has been recognized for more than 3,000 years. Hammurabi (1792–1750 BCE), the king of Babylon, created the most famous set of written laws of the ancient world, known today as the **Code of Hammurabi**. Preserved on basalt rock columns, the code established a system of crime and punishment based on physical retaliation (*lex talionis* or "an eye for an eye").

More familiar is the **Mosaic Code** of the Israelites (1200 BCE), including the Ten Commandments. The Mosaic Code is not only the foundation of Judeo-Christian moral teachings but also a basis for the US legal system. Prohibitions against murder, theft, perjury, and adultery preceded, by several thousand years, the same laws found in the modern United States.

LO4 Articulate the different purposes of the criminal law.

Code of Hammurabi
The first written criminal code, developed in Babylonia about 1750 BCE.

Mosaic Code
The laws of the ancient Israelites, found in the Old Testament of the Judeo-Christian Bible.

Common Law

precedent
A rule derived from previous judicial decisions and applied to future cases; the basis of common law.

common law
Early English law, developed by judges, which became the standardized law of the land in England and eventually formed the basis of the criminal law in the United States.

statutory crimes
Crimes defined by legislative bodies in response to changing social conditions, public opinion, and custom.

felony
A serious offense that carries a penalty of imprisonment, usually for one year or more, and may entail loss of political rights.

misdemeanor
A minor crime usually punished by a short jail term and/or a fine.

The present system of law can be traced back to the reign of Henry II (1154–1189), when royal judges began to publish their decisions in local cases and their legal reasoning became **precedent**, to be applied in similar cases around the land—hence the term **common law**. Crimes such as murder, burglary, arson, and rape are common-law crimes whose elements were initially defined by judges. They are referred to as *mala in se*, or inherently evil and depraved. When the situation required, the English Parliament enacted legislation to supplement the common law shaped by judges. Crimes defined by Parliament, which reflected existing social conditions, were referred to as *mala prohibitum*, or **statutory crimes**.

Before the American Revolution, the colonies, then under British rule, were subject to the common law. After the colonies acquired their independence, state legislatures standardized common-law crimes such as murder, burglary, arson, and rape by putting them into statutory form in criminal codes. As in England, whenever common law proved inadequate to deal with changing social and moral issues, the states and Congress supplemented it with legislative statutes, creating new elements in the various state and federal legal codes.

Contemporary Criminal Law

Criminal laws are now divided into felonies and misdemeanors. The distinction is based on seriousness: a **felony** is a serious offense, a **misdemeanor** a minor or petty crime. Crimes such as murder, rape, and burglary are felonies; they are punished with long prison sentences or even death. Crimes such as unarmed assault and battery, petty larceny, and disturbing the peace are misdemeanors; they are punished with a fine or a period of incarceration in a county jail.

Regardless of their classification, acts prohibited by the criminal law constitute behaviors considered unacceptable and impermissible by those in power. People who engage in these acts are eligible for severe sanctions. By outlawing these behaviors, the government expects to achieve a number of social goals:

- *Enforces social control.* Those who hold political power rely on criminal law to formally prohibit behaviors believed to threaten societal well-being or to challenge their authority.
- *Discourages revenge.* By punishing people who infringe on the rights, property, and freedom of others, the law shifts the burden of revenge from the individual to the state. Although the application of state retaliation may offend the sensibilities of some people, as Oliver Wendell Holmes stated, it prevents "the greater evil of private retribution."[38]
- *Expresses public opinion.* Criminal law reflects constantly changing public opinion on such controversial acts as using recreational drugs, selling obscene material, or performing abortions. Criminal law is used to codify these changes.
- *Teaches moral values.* By observing how the law is applied, people, especially children, learn to distinguish between appropriate and prohibited behavior. Application of the criminal law provides a moral lesson.
- *Deters criminal behavior.* Criminal law has a social control function. Because it applies criminal punishments such as fines, prison sentences and even death, it is designed to control, restrain, and direct human behavior and prevent crimes before they occur.
- *Applies "just desert."* Those who violate criminal law are subject to criminal sanctions because they have maltreated others and harmed society. It is only fair then that they should be punished for their misdeeds; offenders *deserve* their punishments.
- *Creates equity.* Criminals benefit from their misdeeds. People who violate security laws can make huge profits from their illegal transactions. Through fines, forfeiture, and other economic sanctions, the criminal law redistributes illegal gains back to society, thereby negating the criminal's unfair advantage.

- *Maintains the social order*. The legal system is designed to support and maintain the boundaries of the social system they serve. Our economic and social system is also supported and sustained by criminal law.

The Evolution of Criminal Law

The criminal law is constantly evolving in an effort to reflect social and economic conditions. Sometimes legal changes are prompted by highly publicized cases that generate fear and concern. A number of cases of celebrity stalking, including Robert John Bardo's fatal shooting of actress Rebecca Schaeffer on July 18, 1989, prompted more than 25 states to enact stalking statutes. Such laws prohibit "the willful, malicious, and repeated following and harassing of another person."[39] California's sexual predator law, which took effect on January 1, 1996, allows people convicted of sexually violent crimes against two or more victims to be committed to a mental institution after their prison terms have been served.[40]

The criminal law may also change because of shifts in culture and social conventions and thus may reflect a newfound tolerance for behavior condemned only a few years before or, conversely, condemnation of behavior that was heretofore considered normative and legal. Take these examples:

- *Rape law*. In several states, including California and Maryland, the law has evolved so that it is now considered rape if a woman consents to sex, the sex act begins, she changes her mind during the act and tells her partner to stop, and he refuses and continues. Before this legal change, such a circumstance was not considered rape but merely aggressive yet consensual sex.[41]
- *Adult same-sex relations*. Another example of how changing morals may be reflected in the law can be found in the case of *Lawrence v. Texas*, where the Supreme Court declared that state laws criminalizing sexual relations between consenting adults, heretofore classified as sodomy, were unconstitutional because they violated the due process rights of citizens because of their sexual orientation.[42] Because consensual sex between same-sex adults was now legal, the *Lawrence* decision paved the way for the eventual legalization of same-sex marriage by the Supreme Court in 2015.[43]
- *Drug legalization*. A number of states have now legalized recreational use of marijuana, while others have legalized it for medical purposes. In Colorado, an adult 21 years of age or older can now legally possess one ounce of marijuana. In addition to buds (flowers), many types of concentrated and edible forms of marijuana can be legally purchased and consumed as long as it is not in an open and public place (if caught in public, a fine will be issued). Nonresidents are allowed to purchase no more than a quarter-ounce (seven grams) in a single transaction, a restriction designed to prevent visitors from going from one retail store to another and stockpiling marijuana for export.[44] Colorado is not alone: at this writing, 25 states and Washington, DC, have legalized marijuana use in some form, most for medical purposes; recreational marijuana use is fully legal in eight states.

Criminology and Criminal Justice

Not only is the study of criminology bound up in the criminal law, it is also closely linked to the workings of the criminal justice system. Although the terms *criminology* and *criminal justice* may seem similar, and people often confuse the two or lump them together, there are major differences between these fields of study. Criminology explains the etiology (origin), extent, and nature of crime in society, whereas **criminal justice** refers to the study of the agencies of social control—police, courts, and corrections. While criminologists are mainly concerned with identifying the suspected cause of *crime*, criminal justice scholars spend their time identifying effective methods of *crime control*.

A. C. Cooper Ltd., by permission of The Inner Temple, London

Common law was created by English judges during the Middle Ages. It unified local legal practices into a national system of laws and punishments. Common law serves as the basis for the American legal system.

FACT OR FICTION?

The definitions of long-established common-law crimes such as rape, robbery, and murder never change.

FICTION Even well-established criminal laws defining murder and rape are not set in stone and may change to reflect current norms and values.

L05 Outline the criminal justice process.

criminal justice
System made up of the agencies of social control, such as police departments, courts, and correctional institutions that handle criminal offenders.

Since both fields are crime-related, they do overlap. Some criminologists devote their research to justice and social control and are concerned with how the agencies of justice operate, how they influence crime and criminals, and how justice policies shape crime rates and trends. Conversely, criminal justice experts often want to design effective programs of crime prevention or rehabilitation and to do so must develop an understanding of the nature of crime and its causation. It is common, therefore, for criminal justice programs to feature courses on criminology and for criminology courses to evaluate the agencies of justice. What is the criminal justice system, how big is it, and how does it operate?

The Criminal Justice System

criminal justice system
The agencies of government—police, courts, and corrections—that are responsible for apprehending, adjudicating, sanctioning, and treating criminal offenders.

The **criminal justice system** consists of the agencies of government charged with enforcing law, adjudicating crime, and correcting criminal conduct. It is essentially an instrument of social control: Society considers some behaviors so dangerous and destructive that it either strictly controls their occurrence or outlaws them outright. The agencies of justice are designed to prevent social harm by apprehending, trying, convicting, and punishing those who have already violated the law, as well as deterring those who may be contemplating future wrongdoing. Society maintains other types of informal social control, such as parental and school discipline, but these are designed to deal with moral, not legal, misbehavior. Only the criminal justice system maintains the power to control crime and punish those who violate the law.

The contemporary criminal justice system can be divided into three main components:

- Police and law enforcement, which consists of federal, state, and municipal agencies charged with such tasks as maintaining the peace, rendering emergency assistance, investigating crimes, and apprehending suspects
- The court system, which houses the prosecution and the judiciary, and is responsible for charging criminal suspects, carrying out trials, and sentencing those convicted of crime
- The correctional system, which incapacitates convicted offenders and attempts to aid in their treatment and rehabilitation

Because of its varied and complex mission, the contemporary criminal justice system in the United States is monumental in size. It now costs federal, state, and local governments more than $200 billion per year to administer civil and criminal justice, up more than 300 percent since 1982. There are now almost 18,000 US law enforcement agencies employing more than 1 million people; of these, more than 800,000 are full-time sworn law enforcement officers, and the remainder are part-time officers and civilian employees. There are nearly 17,000 courts, more than 8,000 prosecutorial agencies, about 6,000 correctional institutions, and more than 3,500 probation and parole departments.

The system is massive because it must process, treat, and care for millions of people. Although the crime rate has declined substantially, almost 11 million people are still being arrested each year, including about 2 million for serious felony offenses.[45] In addition, about 1.5 million juveniles are handled by the juvenile courts. Today, state and federal courts convict almost 1 million adults a year on felony charges.

Considering the massive proportions of this system, it does not seem surprising that 6.7 million people are under some form of correctional supervision, including more than 2.1 million men and women behind bars in the nation's jails and prisons and more than 4.5 million adult men and women being supervised in the community while on probation or parole.[46] While these numbers are vast, they actually represent a decline from the peak reached in 2007–2008 when the correctional system served more than 7 million people. A declining crime rate coupled with changes in the law may have finally brought an end to the nation's costly imprisonment boom (see Figure 1.1).

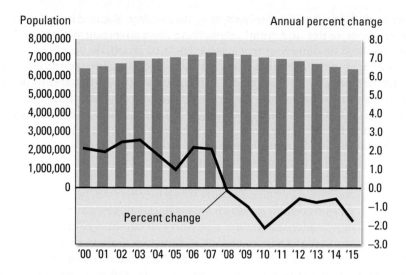

Population   Annual percent change

Percent change

'00 '01 '02 '03 '04 '05 '06 '07 '08 '09 '10 '11 '12 '13 '14 '15

FIGURE 1.1

Total Population under the Supervision of US Adult Correctional Systems and Annual Percent Change

Source: Danielle Kaeble and Lauren E. Glaze, *Correctional Populations in the United States, 2015* (Washington, DC: Bureau of Justice Statistics, 2016), https://www.bjs.gov/content/pub/pdf/cpus15.pdf.

The Process of Justice

In addition to viewing the criminal justice system as a collection of agencies, it is possible to see it as a series of decision points through which offenders flow. This process begins with initial contact with police and ends with the offender reentering society. At any point in the process, a decision may be made to drop further proceedings and allow the accused back into society without further penalty.[47] The justice process is transformative: at first a person is a suspect, then a convicted criminal, and finally an ex-offender. He is transformed from the accused to a thief, rapist, or killer. Stigma and labeling make reform efforts difficult to achieve.

Although each jurisdiction is somewhat different, a comprehensive view of the processing of a felony offender would probably contain the following decision points:

1. *Initial contact.* The initial contact an offender has with the justice system occurs when police officers observe a criminal act during patrol of city streets, parks, or highways. They may also find out about a crime through a citizen or victim complaint. Similarly, an informer may alert them about criminal activity in return for financial or other consideration. Sometimes political officials, such as the mayor or city council, ask police to look into ongoing criminal activity, such as gambling, and during their subsequent investigations police officers encounter an illegal *act.*

2. *Investigation.* An investigation may take a few minutes, as when patrol officers see a burglary in progress and apprehend the burglar at the scene of the crime. Other investigations may take years to complete and involve numerous investigators. When federal agents tracked and captured Theodore Kaczynski (known as the Unabomber) in 1996, his arrest completed an investigation that had lasted more than a decade.

3. *Arrest.* An **arrest** is legal when all of the following conditions exist: (a) the officer believes there is sufficient evidence (**probable cause**) that a crime is being or has been committed and that the suspect committed the crime; (b) the officer deprives the individual of freedom; and (c) the suspect believes that he or she is in the custody of a police officer and cannot voluntarily leave. The police officer is not required to use the word "arrest" or any similar word to initiate an arrest, nor does the officer first have to bring the suspect to the police station. For all practical purposes, a person who has been deprived of liberty is under arrest. Arrests can be made at the scene of a crime or after a warrant is issued by a magistrate.

4. *Custody.* After arrest, the suspect remains in police custody. The person may be taken to the police station to be fingerprinted and photographed and to have personal information recorded—a procedure popularly referred to as **booking**. Witnesses may be brought in to view the suspect in a lineup, and further evidence

arrest
The taking into police custody of an individual suspected of a crime.

probable cause
A set of facts, information, circumstances, or conditions that would lead a reasonable person to believe that an offense was committed and that the accused committed that offense. It is the level of proof needed to make a legal arrest.

booking
Fingerprinting, photographing, and recording personal information of a suspect in police custody.

interrogation
The questioning of a suspect in police custody.

nolle prosequi
A declaration that expresses the prosecutor's decision to drop a case from further prosecution.

indictment
A written accusation returned by a grand jury charging an individual with a specified crime, based on the prosecutor's demonstration of probable cause.

grand jury
A group of citizens chosen to hear testimony in secret and to issue formal criminal accusations (indictments).

information
A filing before an impartial lower-court judge who decides whether the case should go forward (this filing is an alternative to the use of a grand jury).

preliminary hearing
Alternative to a grand jury, in which an impartial lower-court judge decides whether there is probable cause sufficient for a trial.

arraignment
The step in the criminal justice process in which the accused is brought before the trial judge, formal charges are read, defendants are informed of their rights, a plea is entered, bail is considered, and a trial date is set.

bail
A money bond intended to ensure that the accused will return for trial.

recognizance
Pledge by the accused to return for trial, which may be accepted in lieu of bail.

plea bargain
Agreement between prosecution and defense in which the accused pleads guilty in return for a reduction of charges, a more lenient sentence, or some other consideration.

hung jury
A jury that is unable to agree on a decision, thus leaving the case unresolved and open for a possible retrial.

may be gathered on the case. Suspects may be interrogated by police officers to get their side of the story, they may be asked to sign a confession of guilt, or they may be asked to identify others involved in the crime. The law allows suspects to have their lawyer present whenever police conduct an in-custody **interrogation**.

5. *Complaint/charging.* After police turn the evidence in a case over to the prosecutor, the prosecution weighs the evidence to determine whether there are sufficient facts to support the accusation. If, in its discretion, the prosecutor's office believes there is insufficient evidence to move the case forward, it issues a **nolle prosequi** declaration, which signifies its decision to drop the case from further prosecution. If there is sufficient evidence, the case will be brought forth to a grand jury or preliminary hearing.

6. *Preliminary hearing/grand jury.* Because it is a tremendous personal and financial burden to stand trial for a serious felony crime, such as murder or rape, the US Constitution provides that before a person can be charged, the state must first prove to an impartial decision-making authority that there exists probable cause that the accused committed the crime and that there is sufficient evidence to try the person as charged. In about half the states and in the federal system, the decision is made via an **indictment** issued by a **grand jury**, which considers the case in a closed hearing during which only the prosecutor is permitted to present evidence. If sufficient facts are presented, the grand jury will issue a *true bill of indictment*; insufficient evidence will result in a *no bill*. In the remaining states, a criminal **information** is filed before an impartial lower-court judge, who decides whether the case should go forward and be heard in a felony court. At this **preliminary hearing** (sometimes called a probable cause hearing), the defendant is permitted to appear and dispute the prosecutor's charges. In both procedures, if the prosecution's evidence is found to be factual and sufficient, the suspect will be summoned to stand trial for his or her crime. (In misdemeanor cases, the term typically used in charging is *criminal complaint*, an allegation made to a court in writing by either a victim or a police officer.)

7. *Arraignment.* At an **arraignment** the accused is brought before the court that will actually try the case. At this hearing, the formal charges are read, and defendants are informed of their constitutional rights (such as the right to legal counsel). Bail is considered, and a trial date is set.

8. *Bail or detention.* **Bail** is a money bond, the amount of which is set by judicial authority; it is intended to ensure the presence of suspects at trial, while allowing them their freedom until that time. Suspects who do not show up for trial forfeit their bail. Suspects who cannot afford bail or are considered too dangerous or too great a flight risk may be required to remain in detention until trial. Many jurisdictions now allow defendants awaiting trial to be released on their own **recognizance**, without bail, if they are stable members of the community.

9. *Plea bargaining.* After arraignment, it is common for the prosecutor to meet with the defendant and his or her attorney to discuss a possible **plea bargain**. If a bargain can be struck, the accused pleads guilty as charged, thus ending the criminal trial process. In return for the plea, the prosecutor may reduce charges, request a lenient sentence, or grant the defendant some other consideration.

10. *Adjudication/trial process.* If a plea bargain cannot be arranged, a criminal trial takes place. This involves a full-scale inquiry into the facts of the case before a judge, a jury, or both. The defendant can be found guilty or not guilty, or the jury can fail to reach a decision (**hung jury**), thereby leaving the case unresolved and open for a possible retrial.

11. *Disposition/sentencing.* If found guilty by trial or plea, a defendant is sentenced by the presiding judge. Disposition usually involves a fine, a term of community supervision (probation), a period of incarceration in a penal institution, or some combination of these penalties. About two-thirds of all defendants convicted of felonies receive incarceration sentences. Of course, this means that many people convicted of serious criminal offenses, including murder and rape, are granted a community sentence—that is, probation. The Policies and Issues in Criminology

Policies and Issues in Criminology

HATE CRIME IN GEORGIA

On July 25, 2015, Kayla Rae Norton and Jose Ismael Torres drove a pickup truck around Paulding and Douglas counties in Georgia as part of a "Respect the Flag" rally; the truck sported a number of large Confederate flags. They joined about a dozen other people in a convoy of trucks waving Confederate flags. Norton and Torres stopped their truck in front of a birthday party being held for an 8-year-old African American child, featuring a bouncy castle and a snow-cone machine. The pair hurled racial slurs in the family's direction, and then pointed a shotgun at the party guests, threatening to kill them. The couple also yelled threats at African American drivers and approached one vehicle with a gun. Law enforcement officials were later able to locate numerous posts and messages indicating that members of the group were white supremacists who discussed attending KKK rallies, joining Skinheads Nation, and making numerous derogatory remarks about African Americans as a whole.

The facts of the case were not in dispute, and after conviction in 2017, Torres was sentenced to 20 years, 13 of which must be served in prison, for aggravated assault, street gang terrorism, and terroristic threats. Norton received 15 years, with six to be served behind bars, for terroristic threats and street gang terrorism.

"Many people tried to make the case about simply flying the Confederate Battle Flag," Douglas County District Attorney Brian Fortner said in a statement. "This case was about a group of people riding around our community, drinking alcohol, harassing and intimidating our citizens because of the color of their skin." Judge McClain told the couple before handing down their sentences, "If you drive around town with a Confederate flag, yelling the 'N' word, you know how it's going to be interpreted." In all, 15 people were indicted for their part in the "Respect the Flag" rally.

Critical Thinking

1. While there is no question that this behavior is despicable and outrageous, is a sentence of 13 years in prison proportional for a crime in which no one was physically injured or killed, even though it was a hate crime aimed at young children? What would you consider a fair sentence?

2. By comparison, a 17-year-old in Illinois pleaded guilty to the charge of felony hate crime after severely beating a Sikh man and calling him a terrorist. His sentence: two years' probation, a fine, and 200 hours of community service. Does this seem like a reasonable sentence to you?

3. The "Respect the Flag" incident occurred about a month after the Charleston church massacre where Dylann Roof killed nine black worshipers at Emanuel African Methodist Episcopal Church. Could this incident have influenced the judge's sentence, and if so, should it have?

4. Should a crime motivated by hate be punished more severely than one provoked by greed, anger, or lust?

Jose Torres and Kayla Rae Norton weep during sentencing.

AP Images/Henry P. Taylor/Atlanta Journal-Constitution

Sources: Associated Press, "Jose Ismael Torres, Kayla Rae Norton Sentenced for Threats at Black Child's Birthday Party," *Huffington Post*, February 28, 2017, http://www.huffingtonpost.ca/2017/02/28/jose-ismael-torres-kayla-rae-norton_n_15063698.html; Mayra Cuevas and Ralph Ellis, "Georgia Couple Gets Prison for Racist Threats at Child's Birthday Party," CNN, March 1, 2017, http://www.cnn.com/2017/02/27/us/georgia-couple-confederate-flags-threats/.

LO6 Summarize the ethical issues in criminology.

appeal
Taking a criminal case to a higher court on the grounds that the defendant was found guilty because of legal error or violation of his or her constitutional rights.

feature focuses on the sentencing process and raises some issues on how sentences are handed down.

12. *Appeal.* After conviction, if the defendant believes he or she was not treated fairly by the justice system, the individual may **appeal** the conviction. An appellate court reviews trial procedures to determine whether an error was made. Such issues as whether evidence was used properly, whether the judge conducted the trial in an approved fashion, whether the jury was representative, and whether the attorneys in the case acted appropriately may be the basis for an appeal. In most instances, if the appellate court rules in favor of the defendant, she or he is granted a new trial.

13. *Correctional treatment.* Offenders who are found guilty and are formally sentenced come under the jurisdiction of correctional authorities. They may serve a term of community supervision under control of the county probation department, they may spend time in a community correctional center, or they may be incarcerated in a large penal institution.

14. *Release.* At the end of the correctional sentence, the offender is released into the community. Most incarcerated offenders are granted parole before the expiration of the maximum term given them by the court, and therefore they finish their prison sentences in the community under supervision of the parole department.

15. *Postrelease/aftercare.* After termination of correctional treatment, the offender must successfully return to the community and be supervised by corrections department staff members, typically parole officers. Successful completion of the postrelease period marks the end of the criminal justice process.

Ethical Issues in Criminology

A critical issue facing criminology students involves recognizing the field's political and social consequences. All too often criminologists forget the social responsibility they bear as experts in the area of crime and justice. When government agencies request their views on issues, their pronouncements and opinions may become the basis for sweeping changes in social policy.

The lives of millions of people can be influenced by criminological research data. Debates over gun control, capital punishment, and mandatory sentences are ongoing and contentious. Some criminologists have argued successfully for social service, treatment, and rehabilitation programs to reduce the crime rate; others consider these a waste of time, suggesting instead that a massive prison construction program coupled with tough criminal sentences can bring the crime rate down. By accepting their roles as experts on law-violating behavior, criminologists place themselves in a position of power. The potential consequences of their actions are enormous. Therefore, they must be both aware of the ethics of their profession and prepared to defend their work in the light of public scrutiny. Major ethical issues include what to study, whom to study, and how to conduct those studies.

- *What to study.* Criminologists must be concerned about the topics they study. Their research must not be directed by the sources of funding on which research projects rely. The objectivity of research may be questioned if studies are funded by organizations that have a vested interest in the outcome of the research. A study on the effectiveness of the defensive use of handguns to stop crime may be tainted if the funding for the project comes from a gun manufacturer whose sales could be affected by the research findings. It has been shown over the past decades that criminological research has been influenced by government funding linked to the topics the government wants research on and those it wishes to avoid. Recently, funding by political agencies has increased the likelihood that criminologists will address drug issues, while spending less time on topics such as incapacitation and white-collar crime.[48] Should the nature and extent of scientific research be shaped by the hand of government, or should research remain independent of outside interference?

- *Whom to study.* Another ethical issue in criminology concerns selection of research subjects. Too often, criminologists focus their attention on the poor and minorities, while ignoring middle-class white-collar crime, organized crime, and government crime. For example, a few social scientists have suggested that criminals have lower intelligence quotients than the average citizen and that because the average IQ score is lower among some minority groups, their crime rates are high.[49] This was the conclusion reached in *The Bell Curve*, a popular but highly controversial book written by Richard Herrnstein and Charles Murray.[50] Although such research is often methodologically unsound, it brings to light the tendency of criminologists to focus on one element of the community while ignoring others.

- *How to study.* A third area of concern involves the methods used in conducting research. One issue is whether subjects are fully informed about the purpose of research. When European American and African American youngsters are asked to participate in a survey of their behavior or to take an IQ test, are they told in advance that the data they provide may later be used to demonstrate racial differences in their self-reported crime rates? Criminologists must also be careful to keep records and information confidential in order to maintain the privacy of research participants. But ethical questions still linger: Should a criminologist who is told in confidence by a research subject about a future crime report her knowledge to the police? How far should a criminologist go to protect her sources of information? Should stated intentions to commit offenses be disclosed?[51]

In studies that involve experimentation and treatment, care must be taken to protect those subjects who have been chosen for experimental and control groups. For example, is it ethical to provide a special program for one group while depriving others of the same opportunity just so the groups can later be compared? Conversely, criminologists must be careful to protect subjects from experiments that may actually cause harm. Criminologists must take extreme care to ensure that research subjects are selected in a random and unbiased manner.[52]

Of course, it is critical that criminological research do no harm to subjects, but this may not be enough: criminological research can, and should, be empowering and directly useful to research participants. To be truly ethical, criminological research must have social value to research participants rather than simply doing no harm.[53]

Thinking Like a Criminologist

Testing Violent Brains

You have been experimenting with various techniques in order to identify a surefire method for predicting violent behavior in delinquents. Your procedure involves brain scans, DNA testing, and blood analysis. Used with samples of incarcerated adolescents, your procedure has been able to distinguish with 75 percent accuracy between youths with a history of violence and those who are exclusively property offenders. Your research indicates that if all youths were tested with your techniques, potentially violence-prone career criminals could be easily identified for special treatment. For example, children in the local school system could be tested, and those identified as violence prone could be carefully monitored by teachers. Those at risk for future violence could be put into special programs as a precaution.

Some of your colleagues argue that this type of testing is unconstitutional because it violates the subjects' Fifth Amendment right against self-incrimination. There is also the problem of error: some children may be falsely labeled as violence prone.

Writing Assignment

Write an essay addressing the issue of predicting antisocial behavior. Address such issues as the following: Is it fair or ethical to label people as potentially criminal and violent, even though they have not yet exhibited any antisocial behavior? Do the risks of such a procedure outweigh its benefits?

SUMMARY

LO1   **Explain the various elements of criminology.**
The various subareas included within the scholarly discipline of criminology, taken as a whole, define the field of study. The subarea of criminal statistics/crime measurement involves calculating the amount of, and trends in, criminal activity. Sociology of law/law and society/sociolegal studies is a subarea of criminology concerned with the role that social forces play in shaping criminal law and the role of criminal law in shaping society. Criminologists also explore the causes of crime. Another subarea of criminology involves research on specific criminal types and patterns: violent crime, theft crime, public order crime, organized crime, and so on. The study of penology, correction, and sentencing involves the treatment of known criminal offenders. Criminologists recognize that the victim plays a critical role in the criminal process and that the victim's behavior is often a key determinant of crime.

LO2   **Differentiate between crime and deviance.**
Criminologists devote themselves to measuring, understanding, and controlling crime and deviance. Deviance includes a broad spectrum of behaviors that differ from the norm, ranging from the most socially harmful to the relatively inoffensive. Criminologists are often concerned with the concept of deviance and its relationship to criminality.

LO3   **Analyze the three different views of the definition of crime.**
According to the consensus view, crimes are behaviors that all elements of society consider repugnant. It is the belief that the majority of citizens in a society share common values and agree on what behaviors should be defined as criminal. The conflict view depicts criminal behavior as being defined by those in power to protect and advance their own self-interest. According to the interactionist view, those with social power are able to impose their values on society as a whole, and these values then define criminal behavior.

LO4   **Articulate the different purposes of the criminal law.**
The criminal law serves several important purposes. It represents public opinion and moral values. It enforces social controls. It deters criminal behavior and wrongdoing. It punishes transgressors. It creates equity. And it abrogates the need for private retribution.

LO5   **Outline the criminal justice process.**
The criminal justice process involves 15 stages, beginning with initial contact and ending with postrelease aftercare. At each stage of the process, the offender can either be released or moved on to a higher level. At the end, they are transformed from a suspect to a convicted criminal who bears a label such as rapist or thief.

LO6   **Summarize the ethical issues in criminology.**
Ethical issues arise when information-gathering methods appear biased or exclusionary. These issues may cause serious consequences because research findings can significantly affect individuals and groups. Criminologists must be concerned about the topics they study. Another ethical issue in criminology revolves around the selection of research subjects. A third area of concern involves the methods used in conducting research.

Key Terms

criminology 4
valid measure 5
reliable measure 5
victim-precipitated
    homicide 7
white-collar crime 7
penology 7
rehabilitation 7
mandatory sentences 7
capital punishment 7
recidivism 7
victimology 8
classical criminology 9
positivism 9
scientific method 9

sociological
    criminology 10
anomie 11
Chicago School 11
socialization 11
conflict theory 11
critical criminology 12
rational choice theory 12
trait theory 12
social structure
    theory 12
social process theory 13
critical criminologists 13
deviant behavior 13
crime 13

decriminalized 14
consensus view 15
criminal law 15
conflict view 15
interactionist view 15
Code of Hammurabi 17
Mosaic Code 17
precedent 18
common law 18
statutory crimes 18
felony 18
misdemeanor 18
criminal justice 19
criminal justice
    system 20

arrest 21
probable cause 21
booking 21
interrogation 22
nolle prosequi 22
indictment 22
grand jury 22
information 22
preliminary hearing 22
arraignment 22
bail 22
recognizance 22
plea bargain 22
hung jury 22
appeal 24

Critical Thinking Questions

1. What are the specific aims and purposes of the criminal law? To what extent does the criminal law control behavior? Do you believe that the law is too restrictive? Not restrictive enough?

2. If you ran the world, which acts that are now legal would you make criminal? Which criminal acts would you legalize? What would be the probable consequences of your actions?

3. Beccaria argued that the threat of punishment controls crime. Are there other forms of social control aside from the threat of legal punishment? What else controls your own behavior?

4. Would it be ethical for a criminologist to observe a teenage gang by hanging with them, drinking, and watching as they steal cars? Should the criminologist report that behavior to the police?

Notes

All URLs accessed in 2017.

1. Saeed Ahmed, "Who Were Syed Rizwan Farook and Tashfeen Malik?" CNN, December 4, 2015, http://www.cnn.com/2015/12/03/us/syed-farook-tashfeen-malik-mass-shooting-profile/.

2. BBC News, "Profile: Who Is Boston bomber Dzhokhar Tsarnaev?" April 8, 2015, http://www.bbc.com/news/world-us-canada-31734557.

3. Pete Williams, Tom Winter, Andrew Blankstein, and Tracy Connor, "Suspect Identified in Ohio State Attack as Abdul Razak Ali Artan," NBC News November 28, 2016, http://www.nbcnews.com/news/us-news/suspect-dead-after-ohio-state-university-car-knife-attack-n689076.

4. Emily Bazelon, "Department of Justification: Stephen Bannon and Jeff Sessions, the new attorney general, have long shared a vision for remaking America. Now the nation's top law-enforcement agency can serve as a tool for enacting it." *New York Times Magazine*, February 28, 2017, https://www.nytimes.com/2017/02/28/magazine/jeff-sessions-stephen-bannon-justice-department.html.

5. John Hagan and Alberto Palloni, "Sociological Criminology and the Mythology of Hispanic Immigration and Crime," *Social Problems* 46 (1999): 617–632.

6. The Sociology of Law Section of the American Sociological Association, http://www.departments

.bucknell.edu/soc_anthro/soclaw/textfiles/Purpose
_soclaw.txt.

7. Kristen Zgoba and Karen Bachar, "Sex Offender
    Registration and Notification: Limited Effects in
    New Jersey," National Institute of Justice, April
    2009, http://www.ncjrs.gov/pdffiles1/nij/225402.pdf;
    Jill S. Levenson and Kristen M. Zgoba, "Community
    Protection Policies and Repeat Sexual Offenses in
    Florida," *International Journal of Offender Therapy*
    and *Comparative Criminology*, first published online
    March 10, 2015; Jill S. Levenson, "An Evidence-
    Based Perspective on Sexual Offender Registration
    and Residential Restrictions," in Amy Phenix
    and Harry M. Hoberman, eds., *Sexual Offending:
    Predisposing Antecedents, Assessments and Management*
    (New York: Springer Verlag, 2015), pp. 861–870.

8. Christina Mancini and Daniel P. Mears, "U.S.
    Supreme Court Decisions and Sex Offender
    Legislation: Evidence of Evidence-Based Policy?"
    Journal of Criminal Law and Criminology 103 (2013):
    1115–1156.

9. Ibid.; see also, "Brief for the American Psychological
    Association et al. as Amici Curiae in Support of
    Petitioners," at 3–4, *Miller v. Alabama*, 132 S. Ct. 2455
    (2012) (Nos. 10-9646 and 10-9647).

10. Samuel Gross, Kristen Jacoby, Daniel Matheson,
    Nicholas Montgomery, and Sujata Patil, "Exonerations
    in the United States 1989 Through 2003," *Journal of
    Criminal Law and Criminology* 95 (2005): 531–533.

11. Marvin Wolfgang, *Patterns in Criminal Homicide*
    (Philadelphia: University of Pennsylvania Press, 1958).

12. Edwin Sutherland, *White-Collar Crime: The Uncut
    Version* (New Haven, CT: Yale University Press, 1983).

13. Joseph Price, Rich Patterson, Mark Regnerus, and
    Jacob Walley, "How Much More XXX Is Generation
    X Consuming? Evidence of Changing Attitudes and
    Behaviors Related to Pornography Since 1973,"
    Journal of Sex Research 53 (2016): 12–20.

14. Mark Regnerus, David Gordon, and Joseph Price,
    "Documenting Pornography Use in America: A
    Comparative Analysis of Methodological Approaches,"
    Journal of Sex Research 53 (2016): 873–881.

15. National Institute of Justice, "Sexual Assault on
    Campus," June 3, 2016, https://www.nij.gov
    /topics/crime/rape-sexual-violence/campus/pages
    /measuring.aspx.

16. Walter S. DeKeseredy and Marilyn Corsianos, *Violence
    Against Women in Pornography* (London: Routledge,
    2015); Megan Lim, Elise Carrotte, and Margaret
    Hellard, "The Impact of Pornography on Gender-
    Based Violence, Sexual Health and Well-Being: What
    Do We Know?" *Journal of Epidemiology and Community
    Health*, published online May 28, 2015.

17. Joan Petersilia, "Beyond the Prison Bubble," *NIJ
    Journal* 268 (2011), http://www.nij.gov/nij/journals
    /268/prison-bubble.htm.

18. M. Keith Chen and Jesse Shapiro, "Do Harsher
    Prison Conditions Reduce Recidivism? A
    Discontinuity-Based Approach," *American Law and
    Economics Review* 9 (2007): 1–29.

19. Hans von Hentig, *The Criminal and His Victim*
    (New Haven, CT: Yale University Press, 1948);
    Stephen Schafer, *The Victim and His Criminal*
    (New York: Random House, 1968).

20. Linda Teplin, Gary McClelland, Karen Abram, and
    Darinka Mileusnic, "Early Violent Death Among
    Delinquent Youth: A Prospective Longitudinal
    Study," *Pediatrics* 115 (2005): 1586–1593.

21. Eugene Weber, *A Modern History of Europe* (New York:
    W. W. Norton, 1971), p. 398.

22. Wolfgang, *Patterns in Criminal Homicide*.

23. Nicole Rafter, "The Murderous Dutch Fiddler:
    Criminology, History, and the Problem of
    Phrenology," *Theoretical Criminology* 9 (2005): 65–97.

24. Nicole Hahn Rafter, "Criminal Anthropology in the
    United States," *Criminology* 30 (1992): 525–547.

25. Ibid., p. 535.

26. See, generally, Robert Nisbet, *The Sociology of Emile
    Durkheim* (New York: Oxford University Press, 1974).

27. Emile Durkheim, *Rules of the Sociological Method*,
    reprint ed., trans. W. D. Halls (New York: Free
    Press, 1982).

28. Emile Durkheim, *The Division of Labor in Society*,
    reprint ed. (New York: Free Press, 1997).

29. Robert Park and Ernest Burgess, *The City* (Chicago:
    University of Chicago Press, 1925).

30. Karl Marx and Friedrich Engels, *Capital: A Critique of
    Political Economy*, trans. E. Aveling (Chicago: Charles
    Kern, 1906); Karl Marx, *Selected Writings in Sociology
    and Social Philosophy*, trans. P. B. Bottomore (New
    York: McGraw-Hill, 1956). For a general discussion
    of Marxist thought, see Michael Lynch and W. Byron
    Groves, *A Primer in Radical Criminology* (New York:
    Harrow and Heston, 1986), pp. 6–26.

31. Sheldon Glueck and Eleanor Glueck, *Unraveling
    Juvenile Delinquency* (Cambridge, MA: Harvard
    University Press, 1950).

32. Charles McCaghy, *Deviant Behavior* (New York:
    Macmillan, 1976), pp. 2–3.

33. Edward Brecher, *Licit and Illicit Drugs* (Boston: Little,
    Brown, 1972), pp. 413–416.

34. Hearings on H.R. 6385, April 27, 28, 29, 30, and
    May 4, 1937, http://www.druglibrary.org/schaffer/
    hemp/taxact/anslng1.htm.

35. See, generally, the Drug Policy Alliance, http://www
.drugpolicy.org.

36. Edwin Sutherland and Donald Cressey, *Criminology*,
8th ed. (Philadelphia: J. B. Lippincott, 1960), p. 8.

37. Ibid.

38. Oliver Wendell Holmes, *The Common Law*, ed. Mark
De Wolf (Boston: Little, Brown, 1881), p. 36.

39. National Institute of Justice, *Project to Develop a Model
Anti-Stalking Statute* (Washington, DC: National
Institute of Justice, 1994).

40. Associated Press, "Judge Upholds State's Sexual
Predator Law," *Bakersfield Californian*, October 2, 1996.

41. Matthew Lyon, "No Means No? Withdrawal of
Consent During Intercourse and the Continuing
Evolution of the Definition of Rape," *Journal of
Criminal Law and Criminology* 95 (2004): 277–314.

42. *Lawrence et al. v. Texas*, No. 02-102, June 26, 2003.

43. *Obergefell v. Hodges*, No. 14-556, June 26, 2015.

44. Colorado Pot Guide, Marijuana Laws in Colorado,
2016, https://www.coloradopotguide.com
/marijuana-laws-in-colorado/.

45. Federal Bureau of Investigation, "Persons Arrested,"
Crime in the United States, 2015, https://ucr.fbi.gov
/crime-in-the-u.s/2015/crime-in-the-u.s.-2015
/persons-arrested/persons-arrested.

46. Danielle Kaeble and Lauren E. Glaze, "Correctional
Populations in the United States, 2015," Bureau of
Justice Statistics, https://www.bjs.gov/content/pub
/pdf/cpus15.pdf.

47. Herbert L. Packer, *The Limits of the Criminal Sanction*
(Stanford, CA: Stanford University Press, 1968), p. 159.

48. Joachim Savelsberg, Ryan King, and Lara Cleveland,
"Politicized Scholarship? Science on Crime and the
State," *Social Problems* 49 (2002): 327–349.

49. See, for example, Michael Hindelang and Travis Hirschi,
"Intelligence and Delinquency: A Revisionist Review,"
American Sociological Review 42 (1977): 471–486.

50. Richard Herrnstein and Charles Murray, *The Bell
Curve* (New York: Free Press, 1994).

51. Dermot Feenan, "Legal Issues in Acquiring
Information About Illegal Behaviour Through
Criminological Research," *British Journal of
Criminology* 42 (2002): 762–781.

52. Victor Boruch, Timothy Victor, and Joe Cecil,
"Resolving Ethical and Legal Problems in Randomized
Experiments," *Crime and Delinquency* 46 (2000):
330–353.

53. Ida Dupont, "Beyond Doing No Harm: A Call for
Participatory Action Research with Marginalized
Populations in Criminological Research," *Critical
Criminology* 16 (2008): 197–207.

The Nature and Extent of Crime

Learning Objectives

LO1   Discuss the various forms of crime data.

LO2   Analyze recent trends in the crime rate.

LO3   List the factors that influence crime rates.

LO4   Identify the gender and racial patterns in crime.

LO5   Clarify what is meant by the term *aging-out process*.

LO6   Define the concept of chronic offending and know its causes.

2

Chapter Outline

FACT OR FICTION?

▶ Crime is out of control and is more dangerous now in the United States than at any time in history.

▶ Immigrants who are in the United States illegally commit a lot of crime, a fact that justifies limiting immigration and closing down the borders.

L a Mara Salvatrucha, also known as MS-13, is a violent international criminal organization, based in El Salvador and Honduras but with thousands of members across the United States. With numerous branches, or cliques, MS-13 is the largest and most violent street gang on Long Island. In 2016, Arnolvin Umanzor Velasquez (aka "Momia" and "Lito"), a member of the Brentwood Locos Salvatruchas (BLS) clique, pleaded guilty to his involvement in the December 18, 2011, execution-style murders of two brothers, Ricardo and Enston Ceron.[1] Why did it take so long to prosecute Momia? After committing the murders, Velasquez fled to El Salvador and then returned to a small Georgia town, Flowery Branch, where on May 19, 2015, he was arrested and transferred to the Eastern District of New York where the murders had taken place.

What motivated the murders? It turns out that members of the BLS clique agreed that Enston Ceron must be killed because he was not attending meetings or "putting in work" for the gang, and the gang members worried that he might cooperate with law enforcement authorities if he were arrested. They determined to murder Ricardo Ceron, who belonged to another MS-13 clique, fearing he would retaliate when he learned that BLS killed his brother. On December 18, 2011, Velasquez and Sergio Cerna ("Taz"), armed with .22 caliber and 9mm semi-automatic handguns, asked Enston and Ricardo for a ride home from a party. When the car stopped in a quiet Long Island neighborhood, Velasquez and Cerna executed the brothers. When another vehicle approached the murder scene, Cerna fired multiple shots at the driver, striking him once in the chest; the driver survived the shooting.

At the sentencing hearing, while acknowledging the role Velasquez played in the double homicide, his attorney asked the judge to consider that his client was only 18 at the time of the crime and during the ▶

intervening years had turned his life around: he was married, had children, and worked as a landscaper and at McDonald's to support his family. The judge was not persuaded and sentenced Velasquez to forty years in prison. ■

News stories such as the Ceron murders strike fear in the general public and convince people that crime is out of control. Are Americans justified in their fear of violent crime? Should they barricade themselves behind armed guards? Are crime rates actually rising or falling? Is there more crime today than ever before? Where do most crimes occur and who commits criminal acts? To answer these and similar questions, criminologists have devised elaborate methods of crime data collection and analysis. Without accurate data on the nature and extent of crime, it would not be possible to formulate theories that explain the onset of crime or to devise social policies that facilitate its control or elimination. Accurate data collection is also critical in assessing the nature and extent of crime, tracking changes in the crime rate, and measuring the individual and social factors that may influence criminality.

In this chapter, we review how data are collected on criminal offenders and offenses and what this information tells us about crime patterns and trends. We also examine the concept of criminal careers and discover what available crime data can tell us about the onset, continuation, and termination of criminality. We begin with a discussion of the most important sources of crime data that criminologists use to measure the nature and extent of crime.

Primary Sources of Crime Data

The primary sources of crime data are surveys and official records. Criminologists use these techniques to measure the nature and extent of criminal behavior and the personality, attitudes, and background of criminal offenders. Understanding how such data are collected provides insight into how professional criminologists approach various problems and questions in their field.

Official Records: The Uniform Crime Report

In order to understand more about the nature and extent of crime, criminologists use the records of government agencies such as police departments, prisons, and courts. The Federal Bureau of Investigation collects the most important crime record data from local law enforcement agencies and publishes it yearly in their **Uniform Crime Report (UCR)**. The UCR includes crimes reported to local law enforcement departments and the number of arrests made by police agencies.[2] The FBI receives and compiles records from about 17,000 police departments serving a majority of the US population. The FBI tallies and annually publishes the number of reported offenses by city, county, standard metropolitan statistical area, and geographical divisions of the United States for the most serious crimes. These **Part I crimes** are **murder and nonnegligent manslaughter, forcible rape, robbery, aggravated assault, burglary, larceny, motor vehicle theft**, and **arson**.

In addition to recording crimes reported to the police, the UCR also collects data on the number and characteristics (age, race, and gender) of individuals who have been arrested for committing a crime. Included in the arrest data are both people who have committed Part I crimes and people who have been arrested for all other crimes, known collectively as **Part II crimes**. This latter group includes such criminal acts as sex crimes, drug trafficking, and vandalism.

COMPILING THE UNIFORM CRIME REPORT The methods used to compile the UCR are quite complex. Each month, law enforcement agencies report the number of Part I crimes reported by victims, by officers who discovered the infractions, or by other sources.

Uniform Crime Report (UCR)
Large database, compiled by the FBI, of crimes reported and arrests made each year throughout the United States.

Part I crimes
The eight most serious offenses included in the UCR: murder and nonnegligent manslaughter, forcible rape, robbery, aggravated assault, burglary, larceny, motor vehicle theft, and arson.

murder and nonnegligent manslaughter
The willful (nonnegligent) killing of one human being by another.

forcible rape
Under common law, the carnal knowledge of a female forcibly and against her will. In 2012, a new broader definition of rape was implemented: "The penetration, no matter how slight, of the vagina or anus with any body part or object, or oral penetration by a sex organ of another person, without the consent of the victim."

L01 Discuss the various forms of crime data.

robbery
The taking or attempting to take anything of value from the care, custody, or control of a person or persons by force or threat of force or violence and/or by putting the victim in fear.

aggravated assault
An unlawful attack by one person upon another, accompanied by the use of a weapon, for the purpose of inflicting severe or aggravated bodily injury.

burglary
The unlawful entry of a structure to commit a felony or a theft.

larceny
The unlawful taking, carrying, leading, or riding away of property from the possession or constructive possession of another.

motor vehicle theft
The theft of a motor vehicle.

Whenever criminal complaints are found through investigation to be unfounded or false, they are eliminated from the actual count. However, the number of actual offenses known is reported to the FBI whether or not anyone is arrested for the crime, the stolen property is recovered, or prosecution ensues.

The UCR uses three methods to express crime data. First, the number of crimes reported to the police and arrests made are expressed as raw figures. Second, year over year percentage changes in the number of crimes are computed. Finally, the crime rate per 100,000 people is calculated. The equation used:

$$\frac{\text{Number of Repeated Crimes}}{\text{Total US Population}} \times 100{,}000$$
$$= \text{Rate per } 100{,}000$$

CLEARANCE RATES In addition, each month law enforcement agencies also report how many crimes are **cleared**. Crimes are cleared in two ways: (1) when at least one person is arrested, charged, and turned over to the court for prosecution; or (2) by exceptional means, when some element beyond police control precludes the physical arrest of an offender (i.e., the offender leaves the country).

Traditionally, about half of all violent crime and 20 percent of property crimes are cleared by arrest each year. Not surprisingly, as Figure 2.1 shows, the most serious crimes such as murder and rape are cleared at much higher rates than less serious property crimes such as larceny. What factors account for this clearance rate differential?

- The media gives more attention to serious violent crimes, and as a result local and state police departments are more likely to devote time and spend more resources in their investigations.
- There is more likely to be a prior association between victims of violent/serious crimes and their attackers, a fact that aids police investigations.
- Even if they did not know one another beforehand, violent crime victims and offenders interact so that identification is facilitated.
- Serious violent crimes often produce physical evidence—blood, body fluids, fingerprints—that can be used to identify suspects.

VALIDITY OF THE UCR Despite criminologists' continued reliance on the UCR, its accuracy has been suspect. The three main areas of concern are reporting practices, law enforcement practices, and methodological problems.

Fewer than half of all violent crimes and only one-third of property crimes are reported to the police.[3] The reasons for not reporting vary:

- *Confidence in law enforcement.* Some victims do not trust the police or have confidence in their ability to solve crimes. Cities in which people believe the police can help them are more likely to report crime.[4]
- *Insurance.* Victims without property insurance believe it is useless to report theft.
- *Reprisal.* Some victims fail to report because they fear reprisals from an offender's friends or family or, in the case of family violence, from their spouse, boyfriend, or girlfriend.[5]
- *Not important enough.* The more serious the crime and the greater the loss, the more likely citizens will report crime to police.[6] Some victims believe that the incident was "a private matter," that "nothing could be done," or that the

Charleston Police Department/HAN/EPA/Redux

Charleston Police Department
180 Lockwood Blvd., Charleston, SC 29403
June 18, 2015
Need To Identify

On June 17, 2015 at approximately 8:00PM, the below pictured white male suspect entered the Emanuel AME church located at 110 Calhoun Street and began shooting church members. The suspect was seen leaving the church in the below pictured black four door sedan.

Law Enforcement needs help to identify this individual as part of the ongoing homicide investigation. The suspect is considered armed and dangerous. Anyone with information regarding the suspect's identity or whereabouts is asked to call 1-800-CALLFBI (1-800-225-5324).

Suspect is described as a younger white male. He stands approximately 5'09" in height and has a slender build.

Official crime data are made up of crimes reported to police. Acts are included even if the crime is never solved or a suspect identified. This is the "wanted" poster released by the Charleston (South Carolina) Police Department when they were searching for the perpetrator of the shooting at the Emanuel African Methodist Episcopal Church on June 18, 2015. At the time the gunman, who we now know is Dylann Roof, was still at large. This horrific crime would have been reported to the FBI and become part of the Uniform Crime Report data regardless of whether the shooter had ever been identified.

arson
The willful or malicious burning of a dwelling house, public building, motor vehicle, aircraft, personal property of another, or the like.

Part II crimes
All other crimes, aside from the eight Part I crimes, included in the UCR arrest data. Part II crimes include drug offenses, sex crimes, and vandalism, among others.

cleared crimes
Crimes are cleared in two ways: when at least one person is arrested, charged, and turned over to the court for prosecution; or by exceptional means, when some element beyond police control precludes the physical arrest of an offender (for example, the offender leaves the country).

FIGURE 2.1
Crimes Cleared by Police

Source: FBI, *Uniform Crime Reports, 2015.*

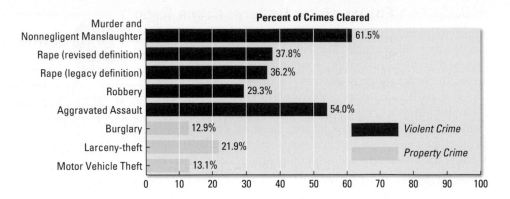

victimization was "not important enough." If they are injured, especially if a weapon was involved, they are more likely to consider the incident serious and report it to the police. If the crime was completed, and the criminal got away with their wallet, purse, car, or package, reporting is more likely to occur.

- *Dirty hands.* People who are themselves involved in criminal activities and have "dirty hands" are less likely to report crime than those whose "hands are clean." The dirty hands may not be related to criminal activity: people who cheat on their spouse, drink excessively, or have other skeletons in the closet are less likely to call the police than their less deviant peers.

- *Social support.* Nonreporters receive little social support from family, friends, and government institutions. Crimes involving strangers are more likely to be reported than those involving friends and relatives. One exception to this rule: if the crime was committed by an ex-husband or ex-wife, the police are more likely to be called than if it was committed by a stranger.[7] Crimes involving multiple offenders are also more likely to come to the attention of police than those with a single perpetrator.[8]

The way police departments record and report criminal activity also affects the validity of UCR statistics. Some departments may define crimes loosely—reporting a trespass as a burglary or an assault on a woman as an attempted rape—whereas others pay strict attention to FBI guidelines. Some make systematic errors in UCR reporting—for example, counting an arrest only after a formal booking procedure, even though the UCR requires arrests to be counted if the suspect is released without a formal charge. These reporting practices may help explain interjurisdictional differences in crime. Differences in the way crimes are defined may also influence reporting practices. Because many jurisdictions have broadened their classification of rape to include all forms of sexual assault, the FBI followed suit, in 2012 changing the definition used in the UCR to "The penetration, no matter how slight, of the vagina or anus with any body part or object, or oral penetration by a sex organ of another person, without the consent of the victim."

Some critics take issue with the way the FBI records data and counts crimes. According to the "Hierarchy Rule," in a multiple-offense incident, only the most serious crime is counted. Thus, if an armed bank robber commits a robbery, assaults a patron as he flees, steals a car to get away, and damages property during a police chase, only the robbery is reported because it is the most serious offense.

Although these issues are troubling, the UCR continues to be one of the most widely used sources of criminal statistics. Because data for the UCR are collected in a careful and systematic way, it is considered a highly reliable indicator of crime patterns and trends. That is, even if reporting problems impede a precise count of total crimes committed in a single year, measurement of year-to-year percentage change should be accurate because measurement problems are stable over time. If the UCR reports that the murder rate increased about 10 percent between 2015 and 2016, that assessment is probably accurate because the reporting and counting problems that influenced data collection in 2015 had the same effect in 2016.

NIBRS: The Future of the Uniform Crime Report

Clearly there must be a more reliable source for crime statistics than the UCR as it stands today. Beginning in 1982, a five-year redesign effort was undertaken to provide more comprehensive and detailed crime statistics. The effort resulted in the **National Incident-Based Reporting System (NIBRS)**, a program that collects data on each reported crime incident. Instead of submitting statements of the kinds of crime that individual citizens report to the police and summary statements of resulting arrests, NIBRS requires local police agencies to provide at least a brief account of each incident and arrest, including the incident, victim, and offender information.

Under NIBRS, law enforcement authorities provide information to the FBI on each criminal incident involving 49 specific offenses, including the eight Part I crimes, that occur in their jurisdiction; arrest information on 46 offenses plus 11 lesser offenses is also provided in NIBRS. In addition to common-law crimes such as rape and murder, NIBRS reporting provides information on most of the criminal justice issues facing law enforcement today—terrorism, white-collar crime, assaults on law enforcement officers, offenses in which weapons were involved, drug/narcotic offenses, hate crimes, domestic and familial abuse including elder abuse, juvenile crime, gang-related crime, parental abduction, organized crime, and pornography, as well as arrest data related to driving under the influence. In addition, NIBRS reporting captures whether the offender was suspected of using drugs/narcotics or alcohol during or shortly before the incident and whether the offender used computer equipment to perpetrate the crime; this makes it possible to develop a national database on the nature of crime, victims, and criminals.

Today, 6,520 law enforcement agencies, representing coverage of more than 93 million US inhabitants, submit NIBRS data. While not yet nationally representative, this coverage represents 35 percent of all law enforcement agencies that participate in the UCR program.[9]

Survey Research

Another important method of collecting crime data is through surveys in which people are asked about their attitudes, beliefs, values, and characteristics, as well as their experiences with crime and victimization. Surveys typically involve **sampling**, the process of selecting for study a limited number of subjects who are representative of an entire group that has similar characteristics, called the **population**. To understand the social forces that produce crime, a criminologist might interview a sample of 3,000 prison inmates drawn from the population of more than 2 million inmates in the United States; in this case, the sample represents the entire population of US inmates. It is assumed that the characteristics of people or events in a carefully selected sample will be similar to those of the population at large. If the sampling is done correctly, the responses of the 3,000 inmates should represent those of the entire population of inmates.

The National Crime Victimization Survey (NCVS)

Because many victims do not report their experiences to the police, the UCR cannot measure all the annual criminal activity. To address the nonreporting issue, the federal government sponsors the **National Crime Victimization Survey (NCVS)**, a comprehensive, nationwide survey of victimization in the United States conducted annually by the US Census Bureau for the Bureau of Justice Statistics (BJS).

In the most recent survey (2015), 95,760 households and 163,880 persons age 12 or older were interviewed for the NCVS. Each household was interviewed twice during the year. The response rate was 82 percent for households and 86 percent for eligible persons. The NCVS collects information on crimes suffered by individuals and households, whether or not those crimes were reported to law enforcement. It estimates the proportion of each crime type reported to law enforcement, and it summarizes the reasons that victims give for reporting or not reporting.

Since its inception the NCVS has undergone a number of changes to improve reliability and validity. The most important improvements include asking victims

---

National Incident-Based Reporting System (NIBRS) Program that requires local police agencies to provide a brief account of each incident and arrest involving 49 specific offenses, including incident, victim, and offender information.

sampling Selecting a limited number of people for study as representative of a larger group.

population All people who share a particular characteristic, such as all high school students or all police officers.

National Crime Victimization Survey (NCVS) The ongoing victimization study conducted jointly by the Justice Department and the US Census Bureau that surveys victims about their experiences with law violation.

A passerby writes a message related to sexual assault during an event on UCLA's campus to pay respect to students who have experienced sexual violence. While campus sexual assault is a significant problem, many victims fail to report the crime to police or other authorities, so the true extent of this vicious crime remains unknown.

directly about rape and sexual assault experiences and using computer-assisted interviewing techniques (which replaced paper and pencil recording).

Through this massive and complex survey, the NCVS provides information about victims (age, sex, race, ethnicity, marital status, income, and educational level), offenders (sex, race, approximate age, and victim–offender relationship), and crimes (time and place of occurrence, use of weapons, nature of injury, and economic consequences). Questions also cover the experiences of victims with the criminal justice system, self-protective measures used by victims, and possible substance abuse by offenders.

The greatest advantage of the NCVS over official data sources such as the UCR is that it can estimate the total amount of annual crimes, not just those that are reported to police. As a result, the NCVS provides a more nearly complete picture of the nation's crime problem. Recently, the Bureau of Justice statistics surveyed trends in reporting practices and calculated the percentage of serious violent crime—rape or sexual assault, robbery, or aggravated assault—that was not reported to police declined from 50 to 40 percent, a finding that indicates that people are more willing to report crime today than in the past. The great majority of motor vehicle theft victimizations are reported, presumably because most cars are insured for theft and car theft victims must make claims to be reimbursed by insurance companies.. However, many crimes still remain significantly unreported: only 35 percent of property crime and 47 percent of violent crimes are reported to law enforcement agencies.

VALIDITY OF THE NCVS Although its utility and importance are unquestioned, the NCVS may also suffer from some methodological problems. As a result, its findings must be interpreted with caution. Among the potential problems are the following:

• Overreporting due to victims' misinterpretation of events. A lost wallet may be reported as stolen, or an open door may be viewed as a burglary attempt.
• Underreporting due to the embarrassment of reporting crime to interviewers, fear of getting in trouble, or simply forgetting an incident.
• Inability to record the personal criminal activity of those interviewed, such as drug use or gambling; murder is also not included, for obvious reasons.
• Sampling errors, which produce a group of respondents who do not represent the nation as a whole.
• Inadequate question format that invalidates responses. Some groups, such as adolescents, may be particularly susceptible to error because of question format.

While these issues are critical, there is no substitute available that provides national information on crime and victimization with extensive detail on victims and the social context of the criminal event.

Self-Report Surveys

self-report survey
A research approach that requires subjects to reveal their own participation in delinquent or criminal acts.

Another tool commonly used by criminologists to measure crime is the **self-report survey** that asks people to describe, in detail, their recent and lifetime participation in criminal activity. Self-reports are given in groups, and the respondents are promised anonymity in order to ensure the validity and honesty of their responses. Most self-report studies have focused on juvenile delinquency and youth crime.[10] However, self-reports can also be used to examine the offense histories of prison inmates, drug users, and other segments of the criminal population.[11]

Most self-report surveys also contain questions related to the subjects' background and history: family makeup, upbringing, income, school performance, and personal beliefs. Using this information, criminologists can search for links between personal history and characteristics and criminal behaviors. For example, they can explore whether people who report being abused as children are also more likely to use drugs as adults or whether failure in school leads to delinquency.[12]

VALIDITY OF SELF-REPORTS Critics of self-report studies frequently suggest that expecting people to candidly admit illegal acts is unreasonable. This is especially true of those with official records—the very people who may be engaging in the most criminality. At the same time, some people may exaggerate their criminal acts, forget some of them, or be confused about what is being asked. Some surveys contain an overabundance of trivial offenses, such as shoplifting small items or using false identification to obtain alcohol, often lumped together with serious crimes to form a total crime index. Consequently, comparisons between groups can be highly misleading.

The "missing cases" phenomenon is also a concern. Even if 90 percent of a school population voluntarily participates in a self-report study, researchers can never be sure whether the few who refuse to participate or are absent that day constitute a significant portion of the school's population of persistent high-rate offenders. Research indicates that offenders with the most extensive prior criminality are also the most likely "to be poor historians of their own crime commission rates."[13] It is also unlikely that the most serious chronic offenders in the teenage population are willing to cooperate with criminologists administering self-report tests.[14] Institutionalized youths, who are not generally represented in the self-report surveys, not only are more delinquent than the general youth population but also are considerably more misbehaving than the most delinquent youths identified in the typical self-report survey.[15] Consequently, self-reports may measure only nonserious, occasional delinquents, while ignoring hard-core chronic offenders who may be institutionalized and unavailable for self-reports.

There is also concern that the way self-reports are administered may change their outcomes. One study in which researchers actually paid one group of subjects to be "honest and thoughtful" and compared them with those who were merely paid to participate found important differences between the two groups. Those who were paid to tell the truth reported a greater willingness to offend and lower estimates of perceived risk for drinking and driving and cheating on exams.[16] An outcome that suggests that the way a survey is administered and who is the administrator may shape responses. Can we really be sure unpaid participants are actually telling the truth?

To address these criticisms, various techniques have been used to verify self-report data. The "known group" method compares people known to be offenders with those who are not, to see whether the former report more crime, which they should. Research shows that when people are asked whether they have ever been arrested or sent to court, their responses accurately reflect their true-life experiences.[17] In addition, responses to self-reports are consistent over time: people who either exaggerate or understate their criminal activities in youth also do so as adults.[18]

MONITORING THE FUTURE One way to improve the reliability of self-reports is to use them in a consistent fashion with different groups of subjects over time. That makes it possible to measure trends in self-reported crime and drug abuse to see whether changes have occurred. One important source of longitudinal self-report data is the Monitoring the Future (MTF) study that researchers at the University of Michigan Institute for Social Research (ISR) have been conducting annually since 1978. This national survey, which typically involves more than 50,000 high school students, is one of the most important sources of self-report data on drug abuse.[19] A subsample of respondents is also asked about their self-reported delinquency.

Table 2.1 contains data from the most recent MTF survey. A surprising number of teenagers report involvement in serious criminal behavior. About 8 percent reported

CONNECTIONS

Criminologists suspect that a few high-rate offenders are responsible for a disproportionate share of all serious crime. Results would be badly skewed if even a few of these chronic offenders were absent or refused to participate in schoolwide self-report surveys. For more on chronic offenders, see "Chronic Offenders/ Criminal Careers," later in this chapter.

TABLE 2.1	Monitoring the Future Survey of Criminal Activity of High School Seniors	
Type of Delinquency	Committed at Least Once	Committed More than Once
Set fire on purpose	1%	2%
Damaged school property	4%	4%
Damaged work property	1%	2%
Auto theft	2%	2%
Auto part theft	2%	2%
Break and enter	8%	12%
Theft, less than $50	12%	9%
Theft, more than $50	3%	4%
Shoplift	10%	12%
Gang or group fight	7%	7%
Hurt someone badly enough to require medical care	6%	5%
Used force or a weapon to steal	1%	2%
Hit teacher or supervisor	1%	2%
Participated in serious fight	6%	5%

Source: Data provided by *Monitoring the Future, 2015* (Ann Arbor, MI: Institute for Social Research, 2017).

hurting someone badly enough that the victim needed medical care (4 percent said they did it more than once); about 20 percent reported stealing something worth less than $50, and another 7 percent stole something worth more than $50; 23 percent reported shoplifting one or more times; 7 percent damaged school property, 4 percent more than once.

If the MTF data are accurate, the crime problem is much greater than official statistics would lead us to believe. There are approximately 40 million youths between the ages of 10 and 18. Extrapolating from the MTF findings, this group accounts for more than 100 percent of all the theft offenses reported in the UCR. About 3 percent of high school students said they had used force to steal (which is the legal definition of a robbery). Two-thirds of them said they committed this crime more than once in a year. At this rate, high school students alone commit more than 1.6 million robberies per year. In comparison, the UCR now tallies about 330,000 robberies for all age groups yearly. The MTF finds that self-reported participation in theft, violence, and damage-related crimes have been quite stable over the past few years.

Concept Summary 2.1 reviews the primary data collection methods used by criminologists today.

Evaluating Crime Data

Each source of crime data has strengths and weaknesses. The FBI survey contains data on the number and characteristics of people arrested, information that the other data sources lack. For the most serious crimes, such as drug trafficking, arrest data can provide a meaningful measure of the level of criminal activity in a particular neighborhood environment, which other data sources cannot provide. It is also the source of information on particular crimes, such as murder, that cannot be measured by survey data.[20] The UCR remains the standard unit of analysis on which most criminological research is based. However, this survey omits the many crimes that victims choose not to report to police, and it is subject to the reporting caprices of individual police departments.

The NCVS includes unreported crime and important information on the personal characteristics of victims. However, the data consist of estimates made from relatively

Concept Summary 2.1   Data Collection Methods

Uniform Crime Report	• Data are collected from records from police departments across the nation, crimes reported to police, and arrests. • Strengths of the UCR are that it measures homicides and arrests and is a consistent national sample. • Weaknesses of the UCR are that it omits crimes not reported to police, omits most drug usage, and contains reporting errors.
National Incident-Based Reporting System	• NIBRS data are collected on every incident and arrest in 49 specified offenses. Facts about these crimes, including offense, victim, offender, property, and arrestee data, are gathered and reported. • Strength of NIBRS is that it provides much more detailed information than the UCR. • Weakness is that currently not all law enforcement agencies are engaged in the program.
National Crime Victimization Survey	• Data are collected from a large national survey. • Strengths of the NCVS are that it includes crimes not reported to the police, uses careful sampling techniques, and is a yearly survey. • Weaknesses of the NCVS are that it relies on victims' memory and honesty and that it omits substance abuse.
Self-report surveys	• Data are collected from local surveys. • Strengths of self-report surveys are that they include nonreported crimes, substance abuse, and offenders' personal information. • Weaknesses of self-report surveys are that they rely on the honesty of offenders and omit offenders who refuse or are unable, as a consequence of incarceration, to participate (and who therefore may be the most delinquent and/or criminal).

limited samples of the total US population, so even narrow fluctuations in the rates of some crimes can have a major impact on findings. It also relies on personal recollections that may be inaccurate. The NCVS does not include data on important crime patterns, including murder and drug abuse.

Self-report surveys can provide information on the personal characteristics of offenders (such as their attitudes, values, beliefs, and psychological profiles) that is unavailable from any other source. Yet, at their core, self-reports rely on the honesty of criminal offenders and drug abusers, a population not generally known for accuracy and integrity.

Although their numerical tallies of crimes are certainly not in synch, the findings on crime patterns, rates, and trends are similar. Each have their strengths and weaknesses. For example, the NCVS may have greater utility at measuring crime in rural areas where police reporting may be less accurate.[21] They all generally agree about the personal characteristics of serious criminals (such as age and gender) and where and when crime occurs (such as urban areas, nighttime, and summer months). The problems inherent in each source are consistent over time. Even if the data sources are incapable of providing a precise and valid count of crime at any given time, they are reliable indicators of changes and fluctuations in yearly crime rates.

In addition to these primary sources of crime data, criminologists use other data in their studies. These are discussed in Exhibit 2.1.

Crime Trends

Crime is not new to this century. Studies have indicated that a gradual increase in the crime rate, especially in violent crime, occurred from 1830 to 1860. Following the Civil War, this rate increased significantly for about 15 years. Then, from 1880 up to the time of World War I, with the possible exception of the years immediately preceding and following the war, the number of reported crimes decreased. After a period of readjustment, the crime rate steadily declined until the Depression (about 1930),

LO2 Analyze recent trends in the crime rate.

Exhibit 2.1   Alternative Crime Measures

In addition to the primary sources of crime data—UCR, NCVS, and self-report surveys—criminologists use several other methods to acquire data. Although this list is not exhaustive, the methods described here are routinely used in criminological research and data collection.

Cohort Research Data

Collecting cohort data involves observing over time a group of people who share certain characteristics. Researchers might select all girls born in Boston in 1990 and then follow their behavior patterns for 20 years. The research data might include their school experiences, arrests, and hospitalizations, along with information about their family life (marriages, divorces, parental relations). If the cohort is carefully drawn, it may be possible to accumulate a complex array of data that can be used to determine which life experiences are associated with criminal careers.

Experimental Data

Sometimes criminologists conduct controlled experiments to collect data on the cause of crime. To conduct experimental research, criminologists manipulate, or intervene in, the lives of their subjects to see the outcome or the effect of the intervention. True experiments usually have three elements: (1) random selection of subjects, (2) a control or comparison group, and (3) an experimental condition.

Observational and Interview Research

Sometimes criminologists focus their research on relatively few subjects, interviewing them in depth or observing them as they go about their activities. This research often results in the kind of in-depth data that large-scale surveys do not yield.

Meta-analysis and Systematic Review

Meta-analysis involves gathering data from a number of previous studies. Compatible information and data are extracted and pooled together. When analyzed, the grouped data from several different studies provide a more powerful and valid indicator of relationships than the results provided by a single study. A systematic review involves collecting the findings from previously conducted scientific studies that address a particular problem, appraising and synthesizing the evidence, and using the collective evidence to address a particular scientific question.

Data Mining

Data mining uses multiple advanced computational methods, including artificial intelligence, to analyze large data sets that usually involve one or more data sources. The goal is to identify significant and recognizable patterns, trends, and relationships that are not easily detected through traditional analytical techniques.

Crime Mapping

Criminologists use crime mapping to create graphical representations of the spatial geography of crime. Computerized crime maps enable criminologists to analyze and correlate a wide array of data to create immediate, detailed visuals of crime patterns.

---

when another crime wave was recorded. As measured by the UCR, crime rates increased gradually following the 1930s until the 1960s, when the growth rate became much greater. The homicide rate, which had actually declined from the 1930s to the 1960s, also began a sharp increase that continued through the 1980s. During the following decade, there were sharp increases in rates of robbery, motor vehicle theft, and overall homicide and a disturbing increase in youth firearm homicide rates.[22]

Contemporary Trends

After a decade of increases, crime rates peaked in 1991, when the UCR recorded almost 15 million crimes in a single year. Since then the number of crimes has been in decline; about 9.2 million total crimes were reported in 2015, a drop of about 6 million since the 1991 peak, despite a boost of more than 50 million people in the general population.

There has been a significant drop in UCR violent crimes—murder, rape, robbery, and assault—a trend that began in 1991. About 1.2 million violent crimes are now being reported to the police each year, a rate of 372 per 100,000 Americans. There are

800,000 fewer violent crimes being reported today than in 1991, when almost 2 million incidents occurred yearly, a violence rate of 758 per 100,000. This means that the violence rate has dropped almost 50 percent from its peak, because the number of violent crimes is far lower and the general population continues to increase. While this trend has been welcome, there was an uptick in violent crime in 2015 and continued into 2016. Especially concerning was a more than 10 percent increase in reported murders, especially in the nation's largest cities.

The property crimes reported in the UCR include larceny, motor vehicle theft, and arson. Property crime rates have also declined in recent years, dropping more than 10 percent during the past decade. At its peak in 1991, about 13 million property crimes were reported, a rate of almost 5,000 per 100,000 citizens. Currently, about 8 million property crimes are reported annually to police, a rate of about 2,500 per 100,000 population. Property crimes remain a serious national problem, and losses totaling an estimated $14 billion now result from property crimes each year.

How has the rest of the world fared while the United States has undergone a significant crime drop? To find out, read the Policies and Issues in Criminology feature on international crime trends.

Police departments are now using high-level data analysis tools prepared by crime analysts to identify crime trends and patterns and use their resources in a more effective manner. Here, a Command Operation Briefings to Revitalize Atlanta (COBRA) meeting is taking place at the Atlanta Police Department on January 15, 2015. The meetings are an opportunity for the Crime Analysis Unit to provide commanders with updates on citywide crime trends and evaluate responses.

Trends in Victimization

According to the latest NCVS survey, US residents aged 12 or older experienced about 20 million violent and property victimizations.[23] Like the UCR data, NCVS data show that criminal victimizations have declined significantly during the past 30 years (see Figure 2.2). In 1973, an estimated 44 million victimizations were recorded, far higher than today; since 1993, the rate of violent victimization has declined about 80 percent. Especially striking has been the decline in the rate of serious violent crime against youth ages 12 to 17, which has declined more than 70 percent since 1994, falling from 62 victimizations per 1,000 youth to fewer than 15 victimizations per 1,000.[24]

LO3 List the factors that influence crime rates.

FACT OR FICTION?

Crime is out of control and is more dangerous now in the United States than at any time in history.

FICTION Crime rates are lower now than they were 20 years ago. The violent crime rate, including murder, has been in decline. Crime rates were much higher in the nineteenth century.

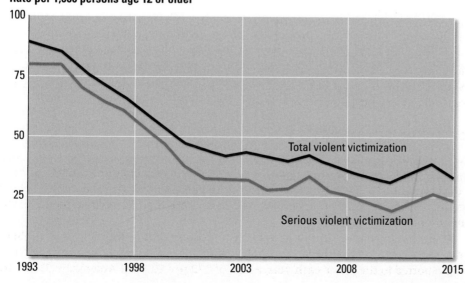

Rate per 1,000 persons age 12 or older

FIGURE 2.2
Violent and Property Victimization

Source: Jennifer Truman and Rachel Morgan, *Criminal Victimization, 2015* (Washington, DC: Bureau of Justice Statistics, 2016).

Policies and Issues in Criminology

INTERNATIONAL CRIME TRENDS

Making international comparisons is often difficult because the legal definitions of crime vary from country to country. There are also differences in the way crime is measured. In the United States, crime may be measured by counting criminal acts reported to the police or by using victim surveys, whereas in many European countries, the number of cases solved by the police is used as the measure of crime. Despite these problems, valid comparisons can still be made about crime across different countries using a number of reliable data sources.

There has been a marked decline in overall US crime rates, which are now below those of other industrial nations, including England and Wales, Denmark, and Finland.

Countries with the highest crime and victimization rate are Ireland, England and Wales, New Zealand, and Iceland. Lowest overall victimization rates are found in Spain, Japan, Hungary, and Portugal. Just as in the United States, there has been a distinct downward trend in the level of crime and victimization during the past decade. Also similarly, some cities have much higher crime rates than others. The cities in developed countries with the lowest victimization rates are Hong Kong, Lisbon, Budapest, Athens, and Madrid; highest victimization rates are found in London and Tallinn, Estonia. Similar to the US, most of the countries show a distinct downward trend in the level of victimization since 1995. The drops are most pronounced in property crimes such as vehicle-related crimes (bicycle theft, thefts from cars, and joyriding) and burglary. One reason is that people around the world are taking precautions to prevent crime. Improved security may well have been one of the main forces behind the universal drop in crimes such as joyriding and household burglary.

Homicide

The global average homicide rate is about 6 per 100,000 population, but southern Africa and Central America have rates over four times higher than that (above 24 victims per 100,000 population), making them the subregions with the highest homicide rates on record, followed by South America, central Africa, and the Caribbean (between 16 and 23 homicides per 100,000 population). Subregions with very low homicide rates include eastern Asia, southern Europe, and western Europe. Homicide levels in some countries, such as Brazil, are now stabilizing, and those in South Africa, Russia, and central Asia are actually decreasing.

Rape and Sexual Assault

Southern Africa, Oceania, and North America have the highest recorded rape rates, Asia the lowest. Violence against women is related to economic hardship and the social status of women. Rates are high in poor nations in which women are oppressed. Where women are more emancipated, the rates of violence against women are lower.

For many women, sexual violence starts in childhood and adolescence and may occur in the home, school, and community. Studies conducted in a wide variety of nations ranging from Cameroon to New Zealand found high rates of reported forced sexual initiation. In some nations, as many as half of adolescent women and 20 percent of adolescent men report sexual coercion at the hands of family members, teachers, boyfriends, or strangers.

Sexual violence has significant health consequences, including suicide, stress, mental illnesses, unwanted pregnancies, sexually transmitted diseases, HIV/AIDS, self-inflicted injuries, and (in the case of child sexual abuse) adoption of high-risk behaviors such as multiple sexual partners and drug use.

Human Trafficking

Trafficking in persons affects virtually every country in every region of the world. Most trafficking is intraregional, meaning that the origin and the destination of the trafficked victim are within the same region. However, in the rich countries of the Middle East, western Europe, and North America, trafficking victims may be imported from East and South Asia and sub-Saharan Africa. Richer countries attract victims from a variety of origins, including from other continents, whereas less affluent countries are mainly affected by domestic or subregional trafficking.

The most common form of human trafficking is sexual exploitation. The victims of sexual exploitation are predominantly women and girls. The second most common form of human trafficking is forced labor, although this may be a misrepresentation because forced labor is less frequently detected and reported than trafficking for sexual exploitation. Trafficking for exploitation that is neither sexual nor forced labor is also increasing, including trafficking of children for armed combat, petty crime, and forced begging.

Worldwide, almost 20 percent of all trafficking victims are children. However, in some parts of Africa and Asia, children are the majority (up to 100 percent in parts of West Africa). Although trafficking seems to imply people moving across continents, most exploitation takes place close to home. Data show intraregional and domestic trafficking are the major forms of trafficking in persons.

Child Abuse

According to the World Health Organization, more than 50,000 children are murdered worldwide each year. Approximately 20 percent of women and 5 to 10 percent of men report being sexually abused as children, while 25 to 50 percent of all children report being physically abused. The lifelong consequences of child maltreatment include impaired physical and mental health, poorer school performance, and job and relationship difficulties. Ultimately, child maltreatment can contribute to slowing a country's economic and social development.

Drug Crimes

Drug use continues to exact a significant toll around the world on both human lives and economic productivity. More than 180,000 drug-related deaths now occur each year; a mortality rate of 40 deaths per million among the population aged 15 to 64. Globally, it is estimated that between 160 million and 325 million people used marijuana, opium, cocaine, or amphetamine at least once in the previous year. About 40 million people can be considered drug dependent.

Today there is an annual flow of up to 450 tons of heroin into the global heroin market. Of that total, opium from Myanmar and the Lao People's Democratic

Republic yields some 50 tons, while the rest, some 380 tons of heroin and morphine, is produced in Afghanistan. While approximately 5 tons are consumed and seized in Afghanistan, the remaining bulk of 375 tons is trafficked worldwide. The most common route is through Iran via Pakistan, Turkey, Greece, and Bulgaria, then across southeastern Europe to the western European market, with an annual market value of some $20 billion. The northern route runs mainly through Tajikistan and Kyrgyzstan (or Uzbekistan or Turkmenistan) to Kazakhstan and the Russian Federation. The size of that market is estimated to total $13 billion per year. There are about 17 million opiate users in the world, and another 17 million who use cocaine.

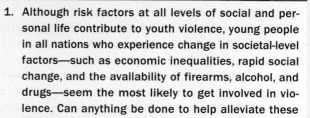

Critical Thinking

1. Although risk factors at all levels of social and personal life contribute to youth violence, young people in all nations who experience change in societal-level factors—such as economic inequalities, rapid social change, and the availability of firearms, alcohol, and drugs—seem the most likely to get involved in violence. Can anything be done to help alleviate these social problems?

2. The United States is notorious for employing much tougher penal measures than European nations. Do you believe that our tougher measures would work abroad and should be adopted there as well? Is there a downside to putting lots of people in prison?

Sources: United Nations Office on Drugs and Crime, *Drug Trafficking, 2016*, https://www.unodc.org/unodc/en/drug-trafficking/; UN Office on Drugs and Crime, *Global Report on Trafficking in Persons, 2014*, http://www.unodc.org/documents/data-and-analysis/glotip/GLOTIP_2014_full_report.pdf; United Nations, *Global Studies on Homicide, 2013*, http://www.unodc.org/gsh/; Stefan Harrendorf, Markku Heiskanen, and Steven Malby, eds., *International Statistics on Crime and Justice*, European Institute for Crime Prevention and Control, affiliated with the United Nations, http://www.heuni.fi/en/index/publications/heunireports/reportseries64.internationalstatisticsoncrimeandjustice.html; UN World Health Organization, *Child Maltreatment, 2016*, http://www.who.int/violence_injury_prevention/violence/child/en/. (URLs accessed April 2017.)

44

Policies and Issues in Criminology

EXPLAINING TRENDS IN CRIME RATES

Criminologists consider the explanation of crime trends one of their most important goals. Yet when they are asked, "Why have crime rates declined?" or "Why are rates increasing?" they tend to fumble around, mumble, and become lost in thought, because articulating a single explanation for crime rate change has proved elusive. And despite the fact that policy makers and politicians like simple solutions to complex problems, such as getting kids to watch less violence on TV, many different factors contribute to the ebb and flow of crime rates. The interplay of these social, economic, and demographic changes determines the crime rate. Let's look at a few of the most important influences.

Age Structure

As a general rule, the crime rate follows the proportion of teens in the population: more kids, more crime! Crime rates skyrocketed in the 1960s when the baby boomers became teens and the 13 to 19 population grew rapidly. Crime rate drops since 1993 can be explained in part by an aging society: the elderly commit relatively few crimes. However, the age–crime relationship may be mitigated by social factors: areas where youth are alienated and disengaged have higher crime rates than communities whose youth population are involved with prosocial institutions such as school or church. So while young people are more likely to get in trouble with the law than their elders, not all do and those who don't are the ones who have successful involvement with supportive social institutions.

Economy/Jobs

Although it seems logical that high unemployment should increase crime rates and that a good economy should reduce criminal activity, especially theft-related crimes, there is actually little evidence linking crime rates and the economy. The official crime rates have declined during some periods of high unemployment and a poor economy (such as 2000–2011), while increasing in others (the Depression era). They have also increased during periods of relative economic prosperity (the 1960s). Some crime experts believe that a poor economy actually helps lower crime rates because unemployed parents are at home to supervise children and guard their possessions. Since there is less to spend, a poor economy reduces the number of valuables worth stealing. And it is unlikely that law-abiding, middle-aged workers will suddenly turn to a life of crime if they are laid off during an economic downturn. Of course, a poor economy hurts some people more than

others, and if there is a long period of economic downturn, crime rates may eventually be impacted.

Abortion

There is evidence that the recent drop in the crime rate is linked to the availability of legalized abortion. In 1973, *Roe v. Wade* legalized abortion nationwide, and the drop in the crime rate began approximately 18 years later, in 1991. According to John Donohue and Steven Levitt's widely cited research, crime rates began to decline when the first groups of potential offenders affected by the abortion decision began reaching the peak age of criminal activity. According to the Donohue and Levitt theory, it is possible that the link between crime rates and abortion is the result of two mechanisms: (1) selective abortion on the part of women most at risk to have children who would engage in criminal activity as they matured. Because these children were unwanted to begin with they would not have gotten the care and concern afforded wanted children; (2) because fewer women were bringing pregnancies to term, more services would be available for those that were not terminated.

Recently, Gary Shoesmith found that the association between abortion and crime only applies to teen mothers and not older women. The odds of a child from an unwanted pregnancy becoming a criminal decline rapidly as the mother's age and education increase. Because the teen birth rate is in sharp decline, so too is the crime rate. The abortion–crime association is still being debated. And due to its controversial nature it will most likely be a research topic for quite some time.

Gun Availability

As the number of guns in the population increases, so too do violent crime rates. As the number of gun-toting people increases, so does the seriousness of violent crime, because a fight between gun-toting people can easily turn into murder. Tighter gun control laws would reduce murder rates.

Gang Membership

According to government sources, there are now about 850,000 gang members in the United States. Criminal gangs commit as much as 80 percent of the crime in many communities, including armed robbery, assault, auto theft, drug trafficking, extortion, fraud, home invasions, identity theft, murder, and weapons trafficking. Gang members are far more likely to possess guns than those not affiliated with gangs; criminal activity increases when kids join gangs. If gangs continue to grow, so too may crime rates.

Drug Use

The presence of drug users in the population impacts on crime rates. Drug users routinely commit property crimes to feed their habits; recreational drug users frequently commit crimes to buy marijuana and methamphetamines. Substance abusers also commit violent crimes.

As drug use increases, crime rates increase. The surge in violent crime in the 1980s has been tied directly to the crack cocaine epidemic that swept the nation's largest cities. When crack use declined in urban areas after 1991, so too did crime rates. A sudden increase in drug use may be a harbinger of future increases in the crime rate, especially if guns are easily obtained and the economy is weak. There is substantial evidence of a significant uptick in both opioid usage and drug-related deaths. Whether this increase in serious drug usage is a harbinger of rising crime rates remains to be seen.

Media

The jury is still out, but some experts believe that violent media can influence the direction of crime rates. As the availability of media with a violent theme skyrocketed with the introduction of home video players, DVDs, cable TV, and computer and video games, teen violence rates increased as well. However, crime rates have been in decline though the media thrives on providing violent programming.

Medical Technology

Some crime experts believe that the presence and quality of health care can have a significant impact on murder rates. The big breakthrough occurred in the 1970s, when technology that was developed to treat injured soldiers in Vietnam was applied to trauma care in the nation's hospitals. Ever since then, fluctuations in the murder rate have been linked to the level and availability of emergency medical services.

Aggressive Law Enforcement

Reductions in crime rates may be attributed to adding large numbers of police officers and using them in aggressive police practices that target "quality of life" crimes, such as panhandling, graffiti, petty drug dealing, and loitering. By showing that even the smallest infractions will be dealt with seriously, aggressive police departments may be able to discourage potential criminals from committing more serious crimes. Cities that encourage aggressive, focused police work may be able to lower homicide rates in the area. Not all experts believe that aggressive policing can work, and others caution against the collateral damage to community relations produced by hardline police tactics that require patrol officers to stop, search, and question community residents on a routine basis.

Incarceration

It is also possible that tough laws imposing lengthy prison terms on drug dealers and repeat offenders can affect crime rates. The fear of punishment may inhibit some would-be criminals, and placing a significant number of potentially high-rate offenders behind bars seems to help lower crime rates. As the nation's prison population has expanded, the crime rate has fallen. Even though putting people in prison may have a short-term positive effect on crime rates, in the long run, increasing punishments may backfire. The recidivism rate of paroled inmates is quite high, and about two-thirds of those released from state custody will eventually return to prison.

Cultural Change

In contemporary society, cultural change, such as increases in the number of single-parent families, in high school dropout rates, in racial conflict, and in teen pregnancies, can affect crime rates.

Internet

The number of cybercrimes is expanding yearly. It is possible that official crime rates will drop even further as former thieves and burglars turn to Internet fraud schemes that are not counted in the official statistics. Prostitution arrests have been in sharp decline as Internet hookup sites are now being used to arrange "dates," a method safer from police interference than streetwalking.

Critical Thinking

1. What current cultural changes might affect crime rates? Can political movements and trends also influence crime trends?

2. Gang membership is linked to crime rates. Would effective crime control involve convincing perspective gang bangers that crime does not pay and offering them alternative methods for economic gain, such as job training and vocational education?

Sources: Richard B. Felson and Jeremy Staff, "Committing Economic Crime for Drug Money," *Crime and Delinquency*, first published June 26, 2015; Gary L. Shoesmith, "Crime, Teenage Abortion, and Unwantedness," *Crime and Delinquency*, first published November 18, 2015; Patricia L. McCall, Kenneth Land, Cindy Brooks Dollar, and Karen F. Parker, "The Age Structure–Crime Rate Relationship: Solving a Long-Standing Puzzle," *Journal of Quantitative Criminology* 29 (2013): 167–190; John J. Donohue and Steven D. Levitt, "The Impact of Legalized Abortion on Crime," *Quarterly Journal of Economics* 116 (2001): 379–420.

On August 16, 2016, people suspected of human trafficking arrive at Soekarno-Hatta Airport in Tangerang, Indonesia. The suspects were caught smuggling 16 people from the seaport in North Sumatra province to Malaysia. Indonesia is a major source country for women, children, and men who are subjected to sex trafficking and forced labor. An estimated 6 million Indonesian laborers (70 percent of whom are female) work abroad. It is feared that many who have migrated to the Middle East and Asia are now being subjected to exploitation.

While there have been year-to-year fluctuations, there is little question that the NCVS data support the findings of the UCR: the US has experienced a significant crime drop for more than two decades. The Policies and Issues in Criminology feature on the previous pages discusses factors that cause crime rates to rise and fall.

What the Future Holds

It is risky to speculate about the future of crime trends because current conditions can change rapidly. While crime rates declined for more than 20 years, they spiked in 2015 when the murder rate jumped 10 percent. Preliminary 2016 data indicate that the rate increase has continued. It's too early to tell whether this spike in homicide is a temporary blip or a harbinger of consistent increase. Nonetheless, the recent uptick in the murder rate has police officials worried. Murders seem to be trending upward in Chicago, Baltimore, Milwaukee, and other major cities. While some blame easy access to guns as the culprit, others point to what has become known as the "Ferguson Effect." Some police officers may be reluctant to take aggressive action in the aftermath of the protests that followed the shooting of Michael Brown by a police officer in Ferguson, Missouri. However, it's unlikely that the Brown shooting alone could have influenced the crime rate: murders were ticking up in many large cities before the shooting occurred on August 9, 2014.[25]

It's also possible that crime rates may rise in the future because of limited economic opportunities. Globalization and the outsourcing of manufacturing jobs may cause the current generation of teens to have difficulty finding high-paying jobs. Income inequality remains a significant social problem. Today nearly 3 million workers are still being paid minimum wage or less.[26] As high-paid job opportunities disappear, young men and women may seek alternative sources of income and prestige. Gang membership may increase and those involved in gangs may remain in them longer.

There is also evidence of increasing drug usage, especially opioids such as heroin, morphine, and oxycodone. According to the Centers for Disease Control and Prevention (CDC), opioids were involved in 33,091 deaths in 2015, and opioid overdoses have quadrupled since 1999.[27] Increasing drug use and abuse may soon have a dramatic influence on the crime rate.

There is, of course, no telling what changes are in store that may influence crime rates. Technological developments such as e-commerce on the Internet have created new classes of crime that are not recorded by any of the traditional methods of crime measurement. It's possible that some crimes such as fraud, larceny, prostitution, obscenity, vandalism, stalking, and harassment have increased over the Internet while falling under the radar of official crime data. The number of people arrested for prostitution has declined almost 20 percent during the past decade. It's possible that

CHECKPOINTS

▶ The FBI's Uniform Crime Report is an annual tally of crime reported to local police departments. It is the nation's official crime database.

▶ The National Crime Victimization Survey (NCVS) samples more than 75,000 people annually to estimate the total number of criminal incidents, including those not reported to police.

▶ Self-report surveys ask respondents about their own criminal activity. They are useful in measuring crimes rarely reported to police, such as drug use.

▶ Crime rates peaked in the early 1990s and have been in sharp decline ever since. The murder rate has undergone a particularly steep decline.

▶ A number of factors are believed to influence the crime rate, including the economy, drug use, gun availability, and crime control policies that include adding police and putting more criminals in prison.

Policies and Issues in Criminology

ARE IMMIGRANTS CRIME PRONE?

O n June 16, 2015, as he kicked off his presidential campaign, Donald Trump made this now-famous statement about immigrants and crime: "When Mexico sends its people, they're not sending their best. They're not sending you. They're sending people that have lots of problems, and they're bringing those problems with us. They're bringing drugs. They're bringing crime. They're rapists. And some, I assume, are good people." Not surprisingly, in his first week in office, President Trump issued an executive order directing the Department of Homeland Security to deport most illegal immigrants who come in contact with law enforcement. His order was presumably based on his perception that illegal immigrants are a significant source of crime in the United States. How true is this assumption?

President Trump's fears about illegal immigrants are newsworthy because there are an estimated 11 million unauthorized immigrants in the United States, accounting for 3.5 percent of the nation's population. The number of unauthorized immigrants peaked in 2007 at 12.2 million and has actually been in decline since then.

How accurate are Trump's views? Criminologists who study the relationship conclude that that immigration has a suppressor effect on crime: immigrants are less crime prone than the general population. As the number of immigrants in the population increases, per capita crime rates decline. Places that are the destination of immigrants have had the greatest crime rate drop. During the past two decades, cities with the largest increases in immigration have experienced the largest decreases in crime rates, especially homicides and robberies. The effect seems greatest in communities with high preexisting murder rates: when immigrants arrive, homicide rates in these communities experience a significant decline.

Another indicator of the weak association between immigration and crime can be found in the incarceration rate. A recent study by the Cato Institute found that in 2014 there were an estimated 2,007,502 US-born natives, 122,939 illegal immigrants, and 63,994 legal immigrants incarcerated in correctional facilities. The incarceration rate was 1.53 percent for natives, 0.85 percent for illegal immigrants, and 0.47 percent for legal immigrants. Illegal immigrants are 44 percent less likely to be incarcerated than natives, while legal immigrants are 69 percent less likely to be incarcerated than natives. If native-born Americans were incarcerated at the same rate as illegal immigrants, about 893,000 fewer natives would be incarcerated; if native-born Americans had the same incarceration rate as legal immigrants, about 1.4 million fewer natives would be incarcerated.

It is possible that immigrants are reluctant to report crime to police, thereby undermining the accuracy of crime rate data. It is also possible that this immigrant effect may be short-lived; by the second generation, children of immigrants have begun to catch up and their crime rates begin to resemble those of the native-born population. But in the present, the fact remains that immigrants have a crime suppressing effect and are underrepresented in the prison population.

Critical Thinking

1. Why do you suppose illegal immigrants have lower crime rates than the native born?

2. Should the fact that illegal immigrants have low crime rates influence the nation's immigration policy? Or are the two issues unrelated?

Sources: *Newsday*, "Donald Trump Speech, Debates and Campaign Quotes," http://www.newsday.com/news/nation/donald-trump-speech-debates-and-campaign-quotes-1.11206532; "Executive Order: Enhancing Public Safety in the Interior of the United States," Executive Order of the President, January 25, 2017, https://www.whitehouse.gov/the-press-office/2017/01/25/presidential-executive-order-enhancing-public-safety-interior-united; Michelangelo Landgrave and Alex Nowrasteh, "Criminal Immigrants: Their Numbers, Demographics, and Countries of Origin," Cato Institute, March 15, 2017, https://www.cato.org/publications/immigration-reform-bulletin/criminal-immigrants-their-numbers-demographics-countries; Vincent Ferraro, "Immigration and Crime in the New Destinations, 2000–2007: A Test of the Disorganizing Effect of Migration," *Journal of Quantitative Criminology* 32 (2016): 23–45; Graham Ousey and Charis Kubrin, "Immigration and the Changing Nature of Homicide in US Cities, 1980–2010," *Journal of Quantitative Criminology* 30 (2014): 453–483; Carmen Gutierrez and David S. Kirk, "Silence Speaks: The Relationship Between Immigration and the Underreporting of Crime," *Crime and Delinquency*, first published September 23, 2015; Bianca Bersani, "A Game of Catch-Up? The Offending Experience of Second-Generation Immigrants," *Crime and Delinquency* 60 (2014): 60–84.

(a) there are simply fewer prostitutes, (b) police are less likely to arrest prostitutes than they were a decade ago, or (c) prostitution is booming, but because it's being conducted via the Internet, prostitutes are now better equipped to avoid detection.

One contemporary issue that may influence crime rates and trends is the presence of legal and illegal immigrants in the US population. While some citizens fear the presence of immigrants, others welcome the cultural and intellectual diversity they bring to the nation. The Policy and Issues in Criminology box feature on the previous page looks at the association between immigration and crime.

Crime Patterns

LO4 Identify the gender and racial patterns in crime.

Criminologists look for stable crime-rate patterns to gain insight into the nature of crime. The cause of crime may be better understood by examining the rate. If criminal statistics consistently show that crime rates are higher in poor neighborhoods in large urban areas, the cause of crime may be related to poverty and neighborhood decline. If, in contrast, crime rates are spread evenly across society, and rates are equal in poor and affluent neighborhoods, this would provide little evidence that crime has an economic basis. Instead, crime might be linked to socialization, personality, intelligence, or some other trait unrelated to class position or income. In this section, we examine traits and patterns that may influence the crime rate.

Place, Time, Season, Climate

There are distinct temporal and ecological patterns in the crime rate.[28] Metropolitan areas are more crime prone than suburban or rural areas. But even in large cities not all areas and neighborhoods have similar crime rates. Most reported crimes occur in confined geographical areas; there are stable block-by-block and neighborhood-by-neighborhood differences in the crime rate. These concentrated areas may contain ecological features such as housing projects that experience a disproportionate share of crime incidents. Crime-prone neighborhoods making up less than 10 percent of a city's area may experience more than 50 percent of the city's crime.[29]

There are also seasonal patterns. Crime rates are highest during the warm summer months of July and August. During the summer, teenagers, who usually have the highest crime levels, are out of school and have greater opportunity to commit crime. People spend more time outdoors during warm weather, making themselves easier targets. Homes are left vacant more often during the summer, making them more vulnerable to property crimes. Two exceptions to this trend are murders and robberies, which occur frequently in December and January (although rates are also high during the summer). One reason: robberies are more likely to take place when it gets dark, something that occurs earlier in these winter months (in the United States and Europe, at least).[30]

Crime rates also may be higher on the first day of the month than at any other time. Government welfare and Social Security checks arrive at this time, and with them come increases in such activities as breaking into mailboxes and accosting recipients on the streets. Also, people may have more disposable income at this time, and the availability of extra money may relate to behaviors associated with crime such as drinking, partying, gambling, and so on.[31]

AP Images/M. Spencer Green

Chicago has been the location of a great deal of gun violence. Here, Ge Ge Gatewood (right) reacts after hearing gunshots. A murder suspect had fired shots at officers surrounding a South Side home where he was barricaded. Gateway's two teenage children were in the home next door and fled to the basement when they heard the shots. Co-worker Alton Kelly (left) comforts Gatewood at the scene.

Some crimes are more likely to take place at night while others are more common during daytime; others are time resistant and take place at any hour of the day. Take robbery, for instance. Robbers target corner stores and fast-food restaurants at any time since these establishments may do business around the clock. In contrast, robbers who target check-cashing stores strike later in the day, after people have gotten paid and need cash. Robberies in public parks occur at times when people engage in recreational activities. ATMs are always open, but robbers seem to prefer daytime, when people feel comfortable walking away with cash; people taking money from ATMs may be more cautious at night.[32]

While large urban areas have by far the highest violence rates, there are some exceptions to this pattern. Low-population resort areas with large transient or seasonal populations typically have higher crime rates than the norm; this phenomenon has been observed in the United States and abroad.[33] Typically, the western and southern states have had consistently higher crime rates than the Midwest and Northeast. This pattern has convinced some criminologists that regional cultural values influence crime rates; others believe that regional differences can be explained by economic differences.

A great deal of crime, especially juvenile delinquency, occurs in groups, a phenomenon known as co-offending. On June 2, 2015, vandals inside Chesapeake High School in Pasadena, Maryland, caused thousands of dollars in property damage. Would a lone offender vandalize a school or is this a group experience produced and supported by peer pressure?

Co-Offending and Crime

It is generally accepted that crime tends to be a group activity and that adolescents, in particular, are overwhelmingly likely to commit crime in groups. Peer support encourages offending in adolescence.[34] Rather than being shunned by their peers, antisocial adolescents enjoy increased social status if they engage in risk-taking behaviors.[35] Of course, not all offenders enjoy being part of a group or gang; many are lone wolves who spurn peer involvement.[36] But crime, especially among the young, appears to be a group activity.

Because co-offending requires lawbreakers to collaborate on a risky endeavor, it is more likely to occur in communities that contain a supply of appropriate criminal associates who can keep their mouth shut and never cooperate with police. Co-offending is more prevalent in neighborhoods that are less disadvantaged, more stable, and contain more people who can be trusted. Ironically, this means that efforts to improve neighborhood stability and cohesiveness may also help produce an environment that encourages group offending.[37]

Does it pay to offend in groups or are you better off as a lone wolf? Recent research by Marie Skubak Tillyer and Rob Tillyer analyzed NIBRS data to determine whether co-offending in robberies actually works. Their findings are somewhat surprising: co-offending results in significantly less property value stolen per offender, while increasing the likelihood of an incident resulting in an arrest. One reason for the greater apprehension risk: the more robbers, the more likely the victim will recognize someone they know. Why do robbers commit crime in groups if co-offending produces lower gain and greater pain? Some mistakenly believe in "safety in numbers," while others have the erroneous belief that working in a group produces opportunities for more frequent offending, thus leading to higher overall profits.[38]

Gender and Crime

Male crime rates are much higher than those of females. The most recent Uniform Crime Report arrest statistics indicate that males account for about 80 percent of all arrests for serious violent crimes and more than 60 percent of the arrests for serious

While women still commit less crime per capita than men, the gap is closing. Here, Katlyn Marin appears via video arraignment on January 5, 2015, in the District Courtroom in Nashua, New Hampshire. Marin was charged with second-degree murder in the beating death of her 3-year-old daughter.

AP Images/The Telegraph, Don Himsel

property crimes. Murder arrests are 8 males to 1 female. Even though gender differences in the crime rate have persisted over time, there seems little question that females are now involved in many serious criminal activities and that there are more similarities than differences between male and female offenders.[39] UCR arrest data show that over the past decade, while male arrest rates have declined by 25 percent, female arrest rates have been more stable, declining by 11 percent. Female arrest rates have actually increased for serious property crimes during the past decade, while male rates have undergone a decline during this same time frame. Nonetheless, as measured by the arrest data, gender differences in the serious crime rate still persist. How can these persistent differences be explained?

TRAIT DIFFERENCES Early criminologists pointed to emotional, physical, and psychological differences between males and females to explain the differences in crime rates. They maintained that because females were weaker and more passive, they were less likely to commit crimes.

Although these early writings are no longer taken seriously, some criminologists still consider trait differences a key determinant of crime rate differences. They link antisocial behavior to hormonal influences by arguing that male sex hormones (androgens) account for the more aggressive male behavior; thus, gender-related hormonal differences can explain the gender gap in the crime rate.[40]

SOCIALIZATION DIFFERENCES Although there are few gender-based differences in aggression during the first few years of life, girls are socialized to be less aggressive than boys and are supervised more closely by parents. Males are taught to be more aggressive and assertive and are less likely to form attachments to others. They may seek approval by knocking down or running through peers on the playing field, while females literally cheer them on.[41] Male perceptions of power, their relative freedom, and their ability to hang with their friends help explain the gender differences in crime and delinquency.

COGNITIVE DIFFERENCES Psychologists note significant cognitive differences between boys and girls that may affect their antisocial behaviors. Girls have been found to be superior to boys in verbal ability, whereas boys test higher in visual-spatial performance. Girls acquire language faster, learning to speak earlier and with better pronunciation. Their superior verbal skills may enable girls to talk rather than fight. When faced with conflict, women might be more likely to attempt to negotiate, rather than responding passively or resisting physically, especially when they perceive increased threat of harm or death.[42]

liberal feminist theory
A view of crime that suggests that the social and economic role of women in society controls their crime rates.

SOCIAL/POLITICAL DIFFERENCES In the 1970s, **liberal feminist theory** focused attention on the social and economic role of women in society and its relationship to female crime rates.[43] This view suggested that the traditionally lower crime rate for women could be explained by their "second-class" economic and social position. It was assumed that as women's social roles changed and their lifestyles became more like men's, their crime rates would converge.

Recent trends seem to support the feminist view of crime rate differences. Although male arrest rates are still considerably higher than female rates, the gap is narrowing because male rates are declining at a much faster pace than female rates; it is possible that they may eventually converge. Of course, arrest trends may reflect changing attitudes by police who may be abandoning their traditional deference toward women, resulting in higher female arrest rates.[44] But whatever the reason, the gender gap in crime is narrowing.

Race and Crime

There is no more complex and controversial issue than that of race and crime. That is because UCR arrest data indicate that minority group members are involved in a disproportionate share of criminal activity. African Americans make up about 13 percent of the general population, yet they account for more than 40 percent of arrests for Part I violent crimes and about 25 percent of serious property crime arrests. They also are responsible for a disproportionate number of Part II arrests (except for alcohol-related arrests, which involve primarily white offenders).

Self-report studies using large samples show that about 30 percent of black males have experienced at least one arrest by age 18 (versus about 22 percent for white males), and by age 23 almost half of all black males have been arrested (versus about 38 percent for white males).[45]

While data collected by the Monitoring the Future study generally show similarity in offending patterns between African American and European American youths for most crimes, there are some significant differences in reports for serious offenses such as stealing more than $50 and robbery, where African American youth admit more participation, a finding that is reflective of the UCR arrest data. How can these differences be explained?

INSTITUTIONAL BIAS Racial differences in the arrest rate may be an artifact of institutional bias found in the justice system and not actual differences in criminal activity: police are more likely to stop, search, and arrest racial minorities than they are members of the white majority. Institutional bias creates a vicious cycle: because they are targeted more frequently, young black men are more likely to possess a criminal record; having a criminal record is associated with repeat stops and searches.[46]

The fact that police unfairly target African Americans is so widely accepted that the term **racial profiling** has been used to describe the practice of stopping and searching African Americans without probable cause or reasonable suspicion. Does such racial profiling truly exist? Numerous studies find that minority citizens are more likely to be stopped and searched than a member of the white majority, especially if they seem "out of place" (i.e., driving in a white neighborhood).[47] Minority suspects are more likely to be arrested than white suspects when stopped by police for the same behaviors.[48] Take for instance drug arrests. When Ojmarrh Mitchell and Michael Caudy looked at racial differences in the arrest of low-level drug offenders, they found that African Americans were 247 percent more likely than whites to have experienced a drug distribution arrest by age 29; Hispanics were 60 percent more likely than whites. Mitchell and Caudy reasoned that the differences are an outcome of implicit police bias. Police officers focus their attention on patrolling inner-city areas where drug offending may be readily apparent and where residents are predominately African American. These factors reinforce prevailing stereotypes linking African Americans to drug offending and in turn bolster the belief that such areas need greater drug control efforts, leading to even more arrests.[49]

Racial profiling may be more common in communities where there are relatively few racial minorities (i.e., "white neighborhoods"). In racially segregated neighborhoods and communities, police may be suspicious of people based on their race if it is inconsistent with the neighborhood racial composition.[50]

Racial profiling creates a cycle of hostility: young black men see their experience with police as unfair or degrading; they approach future encounters with preexisting hostility; police take this as a sign that young black men pose a special danger; they respond with harsh treatment; a never-ending cycle of mutual mistrust is created.[51]

Race-based differences are not confined to the arrest process. A significant body of research shows that bias can be found across the entire justice process.[52]

CONNECTIONS

Critical criminologists view gender inequality as stemming from the unequal power of men and women in a capitalist society and the exploitation of females by fathers and husbands. This perspective is considered more fully in Chapter 8.

racial profiling
Police-initiated action directed at a suspect or group of suspects based solely on race.

Critics of the New York City Police Department (NYPD) stop-and-frisk policy celebrate after City Council members voted to establish an inspector general for the NYPD. A federal judge ruled that the NYPD had violated the civil rights of minorities, including hundreds of thousands of black and Hispanic men. It remains to be seen whether future police practices will be closely monitored by the US Justice Department under the Trump administration.

When compared to whites, black and Hispanic defendants are more likely to be detained, to be incarcerated. If sent to prison, African American defendants receive longer sentences.[53] Race-based differences occur in sentencing for minor crimes (misdemeanors) as well as more serious felony offenses.[54]

RACIAL THREAT HYPOTHESIS According to the **racial threat hypothesis**, as the percentage of African Americans in the population increases, so does the amount of social control imposed on black citizens at every stage of the justice system, from arrest to final release.[55] The source of racial threat begins when white residents overestimate the proportion of minorities living in their neighborhood, a circumstance that leads to false perceptions of disorder.[56] When fear grips a neighborhood, police are more likely to aggressively patrol minority areas; suspect, search, and arrest minority group members; and make arrests for minor infractions, helping to raise the minority crime rate. As perceptions of racial threat increase, so too does the demand for greater law enforcement protection; the greater the perception of racial threat, the larger the community's police department.[57] The result is a stepped-up effort to control and punish minority citizens, which segregates minorities from the economic mainstream and reinforces the physical and social isolation of the minority community.

racial threat hypothesis
As the size of the black population increases, the perceived threat to the white population increases, resulting in a greater amount of social control imposed on African Americans.

STRUCTURAL RACISM Another assumed source of racial differences in the crime rate is the racial discrimination that has pervaded American society for hundreds of years and has resulted in economic and social disparity. Racial and ethnic minorities face a greater degree of social isolation and economic deprivation than the white majority.[58] Race-based differences in the social context that predict future crime first appear in adolescence.[59] Many black youths are forced to attend essentially segregated schools that are underfunded and run-down, a condition that elevates the likelihood of their being incarcerated in adulthood.[60] Even if they remain in school they face much harsher discipline than other students.[61] Being suspended increases the likelihood that African American youth will experience criminal involvement and incarceration as adults.[62] Family dissolution may be tied to low employment rates among African American males, which places a strain on marriages.[63] When families are weakened or disrupted, social control over their children is compromised.

In sum, racial differences in the crime rate have been linked to institutional and structural differences in society. If racial and ethnic disparity in the application of justice and the distribution of social and economic resources were to end, crime rate differences between the races would evaporate.

Use of Firearms

Firearms play a dominant role in criminal activity. According to the NCVS, firearms are typically involved in more than 280,000 nonfatal victimizations each year. According to the UCR, about 70 percent of all murders involve firearms; most of these weapons are handguns. Criminals of all races and ethnic backgrounds are equally likely to use guns in violent attacks.[64]

Because of these findings, there is an ongoing debate over gun control. Some criminologists staunchly favor gun control. In a classic work, Franklin Zimring and Gordon Hawkins believe that the proliferation of handguns and the high rate of lethal

FACT OR FICTION?

Immigrants who are in the United States illegally commit a lot of crime, a fact that justifies limiting immigration and closing down the borders.

FICTION Immigrants, whether they are in this country legally or illegally, have very low crime rates. Immigration helps reduce crime rates.

violence they cause is the single most significant factor separating the crime problem in the United States from that in the rest of the developed world.[65]

In contrast, some criminologists, particularly Gary Kleck, believe that personal gun use can actually be a deterrent to crime and that guns "almost certainly" save lives. While guns are involved in murders, suicides, and accidents, Kleck believes the benefit of guns as a crime prevention device should not be overlooked and that at least 18 national surveys have consistently confirmed that defensive gun usage by potential victims is very common, probably more common than criminal uses of guns.[66]

Though Kleck's research is widely cited, a recent study by David Hemenway and Sara Solnick on defensive gun use found that firearms are rarely used by victims to prevent crimes, and when they are used have relatively little effect on the risk of victim injury. Self-defense with any weapon is associated with a reduced risk of property loss.[67] Needless to say, this remains a very controversial issue.

While gun control remains a heated national debate, evidence out of Chicago illustrates the difficulty of keeping guns out of the hands of criminals. Research by Philip Cook and his associates found that while the vast majority of the city's homicides are committed with guns, most guns used in crime are quite old, with a median age of over 10 years and have gone through a series of transactions before being acquired by the current owner. It is very rare for guns used in crime to be purchased new from a gun dealer in a documented sale; new guns were used less than 2 percent of the time. Most of these older guns came from out of state; 60 percent of the new guns were likewise imported. Cook concludes that licensed dealers may play only a very small direct role in arming gang members, and other intermediaries such as straw purchasers, brokers, and traffickers who remain outside the law are far more important.[68]

Social Class and Crime

Crime is often considered a lower-class phenomenon: people living in inner-city, high-poverty areas are generally more likely to join gangs, sell drugs, and commit crimes than those residing in wealthy suburban areas. Neighborhoods experiencing income inequality, lack of informal social controls, and **resource deprivation** have crime rates significantly higher than those that can provide economic opportunities for their residents.[69] When these conditions exist, youth gangs flourish, resulting in high rates of the most serious violent crimes, including homicide and assault.[70]

It makes logical sense that crime is a lower-class phenomenon. After all, indigent people at the lowest rungs of the social structure, who are unable to obtain desired goods and services through conventional means, have the greatest incentive to commit crime. Their motivation comes from a lack of real opportunity in lower-class communities. As manufacturing moves overseas, less educated, untrained young males are frozen out of the legitimate job market and instead turn to gain through participation in illegal markets: selling drugs is generally more profitable than washing cars or working in a fast-food restaurant. However, when the economy turns around, drug dealers do not suddenly quit the trade and get a job with GE or IBM. As criminologist Shawn Bushway points out, lack of entry into legitimate labor markets creates incentives for teens to participate in illegal activities.[71]

Some of them commit **instrumental crimes**, illegal acts whose goal is to provide desired goods and services that cannot be obtained through legitimate economic means. People living in poverty are also believed to engage in disproportionate amounts of **expressive crimes**, such as rape and assault, as a result of their frustration with what they believe to be an unfair and unjust society. Boiling with anger over social issues such as **income inequality**, they express their rage with irrational crimes that bring them no economic gain.[72] In contrast, when middle- and upper-class people commit crime, it's typically nonviolent, business-related, white-collar crimes that do not threaten the public or produce fear and anxiety.

Not all criminologists accept the class–crime association at face value. An alternative explanation is that the relationship between crime and social class is a

CONNECTIONS

Using guns to fight back against victimization is discussed in more detail in Chapter 3. Would you carry a concealed weapon if research showed that armed people are less likely to become crime victims?

resource deprivation
The consequence of a lack of income and other resources, which cumulatively leads to poverty.

instrumental crimes
Offenses designed to improve the financial or social position of the criminal.

expressive crimes
Offenses committed not for profit or gain but to vent rage, anger, or frustration.

income inequality
The unequal distribution of household or individual income across the various participants in an economy.

function of law enforcement practices, not actual criminal behavior patterns. Police may devote more resources to poor areas, and consequently apprehension and arrest rates may be higher in these communities, giving a false picture of the true class–crime association. Prosecutors may be more likely to file charges against the poor, while handling cases involving the middle class informally, a practice which accounts for the overrepresentation of the lower class in the prison population.[73] And people in the middle and upper classes may commit white-collar crimes that are rarely detected or enforced.

Unemployment and Crime

It stands to reason that crime rates should correlate with unemployment rates, peaking during tough economic times when people are out of work and money is tight. Unemployed people may feel frustrated and discouraged, leading not only to an increase in property crimes but to angry aggression and violence. Research has linked unemployment rates to higher crime rates, especially when the government does not provide sufficient economic support such as welfare and unemployment benefits.[74]

L05 Clarify what is meant by the term *aging-out process*.

While this association seems logical, there is a great deal of conflicting research, some of which shows that the two factors are only weakly related: crime rates sometimes rise during periods of high employment and fall during periods when people are out of work.

How can the weak association be explained? One reason is that during times of full employment more people are being hired, including young people with after-school jobs, who then go unsupervised by parents. Rather than bank their wages to pay for future college tuition, some spend it on activities such as drinking and drug usage.[75] In contrast, when unemployment rates are high, jobless parents are at home to supervise teenagers, thus reducing their opportunity to commit crimes. When people are unemployed, they have less money on hand and purchase fewer things worth stealing; they are also home to guard their meager possessions. They may even sell their valuables to raise cash to pay off debts, reducing suitable targets for burglars and thieves.

Age and Crime

There is general agreement that age is inversely related to criminality. Criminologists Travis Hirschi and Michael Gottfredson state that "Age is everywhere correlated with crime. Its effects on crime do not depend on other demographic correlates of crime."[76]

Regardless of economic status, marital status, race, sex, and other factors, younger people commit crime more often than older people, and this relationship has been stable across time.[77] Official statistics tell us that young people are arrested at a rate disproportionate to their numbers in the population; victim surveys generate similar findings for crimes in which assailant age can be determined. As a general rule, the peak age for property crime is believed to be 16, and for violence, 18. The 10-to-24 age group makes up about 20 percent of the population but commits 34 percent of serious violent crimes and 35 percent of all property crimes. In contrast, the elderly are particularly resistant to the temptations of crime. Elderly males 65 and over are predominantly arrested for alcohol-related matters (such as public drunkenness and drunk driving) and elderly females for larceny (such as shoplifting). There are a few crime patterns in which adults offend at a higher rate than juveniles; for example, adults use cocaine and heroin considerably more than adolescents.[78] But for the most part, the statement "crime declines with age" has repeatedly been shown to be accurate.

AP Images/Michael Wilson

Most illegal acts are committed by teens who eventually age out of crime and become responsible adults. Here, Kayla Hassall, 15, tries to contain her emotions as she sits with her parents in court prior to a plea hearing in Bartow, Florida. Kayla was one of five teenagers accused of beating 17-year-old Victoria Lindsay. The attack was recorded on video and seen around the world via the Internet and TV. Kayla received one year of juvenile probation for her crime.

AGING OUT OF CRIME Criminologists agree that people commit less crime as they age.[79] Crime peaks in adolescence and then declines rapidly thereafter. In modern industrial societies, adolescents are given most of the privileges of adults but less supervision and fewer responsibilities. This can result in a reduced ability to cope in a legitimate manner and increased incentive to solve problems in a criminal manner.[80] Young people tend to discount the future.[81] They are impatient and are unwilling or unable to delay gratification. As they mature, troubled youths are able to develop a long-term life view and resist the need for immediate gratification.[82]

Aging out of crime may also be a function of the natural history of the human life cycle.[83] Deviance in adolescence is fueled by the need for money and sex and is reinforced by close relationships with peers who defy conventional morality. At the same time, teenagers are becoming independent from parents and other adults who enforce conventional standards of morality and behavior. They have a new sense of energy and strength and are involved with peers who are similarly vigorous and frustrated. Adults, on the other hand, develop the ability to delay gratification and forgo the immediate gains that law violations bring. They also start wanting to take responsibility for their behavior and to adhere to conventional mores, such as establishing long-term relationships and starting a family.[84] Some criminologists believe that the key to desistance and aging out is linked to human biology. Levels of hormones and brain chemicals ebb and flow over the life course. During adolescence, dopamine increases while serotonin is reduced; in adulthood, dopamine levels recede while serotonin levels become elevated. It is possible that these biological changes influence behavioral choices.[85]

While the age–crime association is a key element of criminology, the association may soon have to be rethought. Though teens are still very active in crime, according to the most recent UCR data the number of people arrested under age 18 dropped 55 percent since 2006. In contrast, arrests for people over age 18 dropped only 17 percent. If these trends continue, the rates will eventually converge, calling into question the age–crime association.

Chronic Offenders/Criminal Careers

Crime data show that most offenders commit a single criminal act and, upon arrest, discontinue their antisocial activity. Others commit a few less serious crimes. A small group of criminal offenders, however, account for a majority of all criminal offenses. These persistent offenders are referred to as **career criminals** or **chronic offenders**. The concept of the chronic, or career, offender is most closely associated with the research efforts of Marvin Wolfgang, Robert Figlio, and Thorsten Sellin.[86] In their landmark 1972 study *Delinquency in a Birth Cohort*, they used official records to follow the criminal careers of 9,945 boys born in Philadelphia in 1945 from the time of their birth until they reached 18 years of age in 1963. Official police records were used to identify delinquents. About one-third of the boys (3,475) had some police contact. The remaining two-thirds (6,470) had none. Each delinquent was given a seriousness weight score for every delinquent act.[87] The weighting of delinquent acts enabled the researchers to differentiate between a simple assault requiring no medical attention for the victim and serious battery in which the victim needed hospitalization. The best-known discovery of Wolfgang and his associates was that of the so-called chronic offender. The cohort data indicated that 54 percent (1,862) of the sample's delinquent youths were repeat offenders, whereas the remaining 46 percent (1,613) were one-time offenders. The repeaters could be further categorized as nonchronic recidivists and chronic recidivists. The former consisted of 1,235 youths who had been arrested more than once but fewer than five times and who made up 35.6 percent of all delinquents. The latter were a group of 627 boys arrested five times or more, who accounted for 18 percent of the delinquents and 6 percent of the total sample of 9,945.

CHECKPOINTS

▶ Gauging future trends is difficult. Some experts forecast an increase in crime, whereas others foresee a continued and ongoing decline in the crime rate.

▶ There are stable and enduring patterns in the crime rate.

▶ Males have a higher crime rate than females, but the gap is narrowing.

▶ Some criminologists suggest that institutional racism, such as police profiling, accounts for the racial differences in the crime rate.

▶ Others believe that African American crime rates are a function of living in a racially biased society, a phenomenon referred to as structural racism.

▶ Crime is more common during the summer and in urban areas.

▶ Crime rates are highest in areas with high rates of poverty.

▶ Young people have the highest crime rates; people commit less crime as they mature.

L06 Define the concept of chronic offending and know its causes.

aging out
Phrase used to express the fact that people commit less crime as they mature.

chronic offenders (career criminals)
The small group of persistent offenders who account for a majority of all criminal offenses.

The chronic offenders (known today as "the chronic 6 percent") were involved in the most dramatic amounts of delinquent behavior. They were responsible for 5,305 offenses, or 52 percent of all the offenses committed by the cohort. Even more striking was the involvement of chronic offenders in serious criminal acts. The chronic 6 percent committed 71 percent of the homicides, 73 percent of the rapes, 82 percent of the robberies, and 69 percent of the aggravated assaults.

Wolfgang and his associates found that arrests and court experience did little to deter the chronic offender. In fact, punishment was inversely related to chronic offending: the more stringent the sanction chronic offenders received, the more likely they were to engage in repeated criminal behavior.

In a second cohort study, Wolfgang and his associates selected a new, larger birth cohort, born in Philadelphia in 1958, which contained both male and female subjects.[88] Analysis revealed a similar pattern of chronic offending in both studies even though the study groups were born 13 years apart. The researchers were now able to look at gender differences in chronic offending, finding that chronic female delinquency was relatively rare—only 1 percent of the females in the 1958 survey were chronic offenders.

Wolfgang's pioneering effort to identify the chronic career offender has been replicated by a number of other researchers in a variety of locations in the United States.[89] The chronic offender has also been found abroad.[90]

What Causes Chronicity?

Criminologists believe that chronic offenders tend to be at-risk youth who are exposed to a variety of personal and social problems and who begin their law breaking at a very early age—a phenomenon referred to as **early onset**.[91] Research studies have also linked chronicity to relatively low intellectual development and to parental involvement in drugs.[92]

Implications of the Chronic Offender Concept

The findings of the cohort studies and the discovery of the chronic offender revitalized criminological theory. If relatively few offenders become chronic criminals, perhaps chronic offenders possess some individual trait that is responsible for their behavior. Most people exposed to troublesome social conditions, such as poverty, do not become chronic offenders, so it is unlikely that social conditions alone can cause chronic offending. Traditional theories of criminal behavior have failed to distinguish between chronic and occasional offenders. They concentrate more on explaining why people begin to commit crime and pay scant attention to why people stop offending. The discovery of the chronic offender 40 years ago forced criminologists to consider such issues as persistence and desistance in their explanations of crime; more recent theories account not only for the onset of criminality but also for its termination.

The chronic offender has become a central focus of crime control policy. Apprehension and punishment seem to have little effect on the offending behavior of chronic offenders, and most repeat their criminal acts after their release from corrections.[93] Because chronic offenders rarely learn from their mistakes, sentencing policies designed to incapacitate chronic offenders for long periods without hope of probation or parole have been established. Incapacitation rather than rehabilitation is the goal. Among the policies spurred by the chronic offender concept are mandatory sentences for violent or drug-related crimes; **three-strikes policies**, which require people convicted of a third felony offense to serve a mandatory life sentence; and truth-in-sentencing policies, which require that convicted felons spend a significant portion of their sentence behind bars. It remains to be seen whether such policies can reduce crime rates or are merely get-tough measures designed to placate conservative voters.

early onset
The view that repeat offenders begin their criminal careers at a very young age.

three-strikes policies
Laws that require offenders to serve life in prison after they are convicted of a third felony.

Thinking Like a Criminologist

Rough Justice The planning director for the State Department of Juvenile Justice has asked for your advice on how to reduce the threat of chronic offenders. Some of the more conservative members of her staff seem to believe that these kids need a strict dose of rough justice if they are to be turned away from a life of crime. They believe juvenile delinquents who are punished harshly are less likely to recidivate than youths who receive lesser punishments, such as community corrections or probation. In addition, they believe that hard-core, violent offenders deserve to be punished; excessive concern for offenders, and not enough concern for their acts, ignores the rights of victims and of society in general.

The planning director is unsure whether such an approach can reduce the threat of chronic offending. She is concerned that a strategy stressing punishment will have relatively little impact on chronic offenders and, if anything, may cause escalation in their serious criminal behaviors. She has asked you for your professional advice.

Writing Assignment

Write an essay explaining both sides of the issue, comparing the potential effects of stigma and labeling with the need for control and security. Explain how you would handle chronic offenders, and tie your answer to the aging-out process.

SUMMARY

LO1 Discuss the various forms of crime data.
The Federal Bureau of Investigation collects data from local law enforcement agencies and publishes that information yearly in its Uniform Crime Report (UCR). The National Incident-Based Reporting System (NIBRS) is a program that collects data on each reported crime incident. The National Crime Victimization Survey (NCVS) is a nationwide survey of victimization in the United States. Self-report surveys ask people to describe, in detail, their recent and lifetime participation in criminal activity.

LO2 Analyze recent trends in the crime rate.
Crime rates peaked in 1991, when police recorded almost 15 million crimes. Since then the number of crimes tallied by the FBI has been in a steep decline. In addition, NCVS data show that criminal victimizations have declined significantly during the past 40 years: in 1973, an estimated 44 million victimizations were recorded, compared to fewer than 20 million today, a drop of more than 50 percent.

LO3 List the factors that influence crime rates.
The age composition of the population, the number of immigrants, the availability of legalized abortion, the number of guns, drug use, availability of emergency medical services, numbers of police officers, the state of the economy, cultural change, and criminal opportunities all influence crime rates.

LO4 Identify the gender and racial patterns in crime.
Male crime rates are much higher than those of females. Gender differences in the crime rate have persisted over time, but there is little question that females are now involved in more crime than ever before and that there are more similarities than differences between male and female offenders. Official crime data indicate that minority group members are involved in a disproportionate share of criminal activity. Racial and ethnic differentials in crime rates may be tied to economic and social disparity and institutional racism.

LO5 Clarify what is meant by the term *aging-out process*.
Regardless of economic status, marital status, race, sex, and other factors, younger people commit crime more often than older people, and this relationship has been stable across time. Most criminologists agree that people commit less crime as they age.

LO6   Define the concept of chronic offending and know its causes.

The concept of the chronic, or career, offender is most closely associated with the research efforts of Marvin Wolfgang, Robert Figlio, and Thorsten Sellin. Chronic offenders are involved in significant amounts of delinquent behavior and tend later to become adult criminals. Unlike most offenders, they do not age out of crime. The cause of chronic offending has been linked to a variety of personal and social problems, and those who begin their lawbreaking at an early age are the most at risk to repeat offending. Chronic offenders often have problems in the home and at school, relatively low intellectual development, and parental drug involvement.

Key Terms

Uniform Crime Report
   (UCR) 32
Part I crimes 32
murder and nonnegligent
   manslaughter 32
forcible rape 32
robbery 32
aggravated
   assault 32
burglary 32

larceny 32
motor vehicle theft 32
arson 32
Part II crimes 32
cleared crimes 33
National Incident-Based
   Reporting System
   (NIBRS) 35
sampling 35
population 35

National Crime
   Victimization Survey
   (NCVS) 35
self-report survey 36
liberal feminist
   theory 50
racial profiling 51
racial threat
   hypothesis 52
resource deprivation 53

instrumental
   crimes 53
expressive crimes 53
income inequality 53
aging out 55
chronic offenders
   (career criminals) 55
early onset 56
three-strikes
   policies 56

Critical Thinking Questions

1. Would you answer honestly if a national crime survey asked you about your criminal behavior, including drinking and drug use? If not, why not? If you would not answer honestly, do you question the accuracy of self-report surveys?

2. How would you explain gender differences in the crime rate? Why do you think males are more violent than females?

3. Assuming that males are more violent than females, does that mean crime has a biological rather than a social basis (because males and females share a similar environment)?

4. The UCR reports that crime rates are higher in large cities than in small towns. What does that tell us about the effects of TV, films, and music on teenage behavior?

5. What social and environmental factors do you believe influence the crime rate?

6. Do you think a national emergency would increase or decrease crime rates?

Notes

All URLs accessed in 2017.

1. Department of Justice, US Attorney's Office, Eastern District of New York, "MS-13 Gang Member Pleads Guilty to Double-Murder," March 11, 2016, https://www.justice.gov/usao-edny/pr/ms-13-gang-member-pleads-guilty-double-murder.

2. Data in this chapter are from Federal Bureau of Investigation, *Crime in the United States, 2015*, https://ucr.fbi.gov/crime-in-the-u.s/2015/crime-in-the-u.s.-2015. Includes preliminary 2016 data.

3. Jennifer Truman and Rachel Morgan, *Criminal Victimization, 2015* (Washington, DC: Bureau of Justice Statistics, 2016), https://www.bjs.gov/content/pub/pdf/cv15.pdf.

4. Min Xie, "Area Differences and Time Trends in Crime Reporting: Comparing New York with Other Metropolitan Areas," *Justice Quarterly* 31 (2014): 43–73.

5. Richard Felson, Steven Messner, Anthony Hoskin, and Glenn Deane, "Reasons for Reporting and Not Reporting Domestic Violence to the Police," *Criminology* 40 (2002): 617–648.

6. Bradford W. Reyns and Ryan Randa, "Victim Reporting Behaviors Following Identity Theft Victimization: Results from the National Crime Victimization Survey," *Crime and Delinquency*, first published online December 18, 2015.

7. Andrew Karmen, *Crime Victims: An Introduction to Victimology* (Belmont, CA: Cengage, 2012).

8. Heather Zaykowski, "Reconceptualizing Victimization and Victimization Responses," *Crime and Delinquency* 61 (2015): 271–296.

9. "FBI Releases 2014 Crime Statistics from the National Incident-Based Reporting System," December 14, 2015, https://www.fbi.gov/about-us /cjis/ucr/nibrs/2014/resource-pages/summary-of -nibrs-2014_final.pdf.

10. A pioneering effort in self-report research is A. L. Porterfield, *Youth in Trouble* (Fort Worth, TX: Leo Potishman Foundation, 1946).

11. See John Paul Wright and Francis Cullen, "Juvenile Involvement in Occupational Delinquency," *Criminology* 38 (2000): 863–896.

12. Christiane Brems, Mark Johnson, David Neal, and Melinda Freemon, "Childhood Abuse History and Substance Use Among Men and Women Receiving Detoxification Services," *American Journal of Drug and Alcohol Abuse* 30 (2004): 799–821.

13. Leonore Simon, "Validity and Reliability of Violent Juveniles: A Comparison of Juvenile Self-Reports with Adult Self-Reports Incarcerated in Adult Prisons," paper presented at the annual meeting of the American Society of Criminology, Boston, November 1995, p. 26.

14. Stephen Cernkovich, Peggy Giordano, and Meredith Pugh, "Chronic Offenders: The Missing Cases in Self-Report Delinquency Research," *Journal of Criminal Law and Criminology* 76 (1985): 705–732.

15. Terence Thornberry, Beth Bjerregaard, and William Miles, "The Consequences of Respondent Attrition in Panel Studies: A Simulation Based on the Rochester Youth Development Study," *Journal of Quantitative Criminology* 9 (1993): 127–158.

16. Thomas A. Loughran, Ray Paternoster, and Kyle J. Thomas, "Incentivizing Responses to Self-report Questions in Perceptual Deterrence Studies: An Investigation of the Validity of Deterrence Theory Using Bayesian Truth Serum," *Journal of Quantitative Criminology* 30 (2014): 677–707.

17. Alex Piquero, Carol Schubert, and Robert Brame, "Comparing Official and Self-Report Records of Offending Across Gender and Race/Ethnicity in a Longitudinal Study of Serious Youthful Offenders," *Journal of Research in Crime and Delinquency* 51 (2014): 526–556.

18. Amanda Emmert, Arna Carlock, Alan Lizotte, and Marvin Krohn, "Predicting Adult Under- and Over-Reporting of Self-Reported Arrests from Discrepancies in Adolescent Self-Reports of Arrests: A Research Note," *Crime and Delinquency*, first published online March 12, 2015.

19. Richard Miech, Lloyd Johnston, Patrick O'Malley, Jerald Bachman, and John Schulenberg, *Monitoring the Future* (Ann Arbor, MI: Institute for Social Research, 2015), http://www.monitoringthefuture.org.

20. Sami Ansari and Ne He, "Convergence Revisited: A Multi-Definition, Multi-Method Analysis of the UCR and the NCVS Crime Series (1973–2008)," *Justice Quarterly* 32 (2015): 1–31.

21. Mark Berg and Janet L. Lauritsen, "Telling a Similar Story Twice? NCVS/UCR Convergence in Serious Violent Crime in Rural, Suburban, and Urban Places (1973–2010)," *Journal of Quantitative Criminology* 32 (2016): 61–87.

22. Clarence Schrag, *Crime and Justice: American Style* (Washington, DC: US Government Printing Office, 1971), p. 17.

23. Data in this section are from Truman and Morgan, *Criminal Victimization, 2015.*

24. Nicole White, Ph.D., and Janet L. Lauritsen, *Violent Crime Against Youth from 1994 to 2010* (Washington, DC: Bureau of Justice Statistics, 2012), http://bjs.ojp .usdoj.gov/content/pub/pdf/vcay9410.pdf.

25. Monica Davey and Mitch Smith, "Murder Rates Rising Sharply in Many U.S. Cities," *New York Times*, August 31, 2015, http://www.nytimes.com/2015 /09/01/us/murder-rates-rising-sharply-in-many-us -cities.html.

26. Bureau of Labor Statistics, "Characteristics of Minimum Wage Workers, 2015," https://www.bls .gov/opub/reports/minimum-wage/2015/home.htm.

27. Centers for Disease Control and Prevention, "Drug Overdose Death Data," https://www.cdc.gov /drugoverdose/data/statedeaths.html.

28. Timothy Hart and Terance Miethe, "Configural Behavior Settings of Crime Event Locations: Toward an Alternative Conceptualization of Criminogenic Microenvironments," *Journal of Research in Crime and Delinquency* 52 (2015): 373–402.

29. David Weisburd, "The Law of Crime Concentration and the Criminology of Place," *Criminology* 53 (2015): 133–157.

30. Lisa Tompson and Kate Bowers, "A Stab in the Dark? A Research Note on Temporal Patterns of Street Robbery," *Journal of Research in Crime and Delinquency* 50 (2013): 616–631.

31. Ellen Cohn, "The Effect of Weather and Temporal Variations on Calls for Police Service," *American Journal of Police* 15 (1996): 23–43.

32. Cory Haberman and Jerry Ratcliffe, "Testing for Temporally Differentiated Relationships Among Potentially Criminogenic Places and Census Block Street Robbery Counts," *Criminology* 53 (2015): 457–483.

33. Daniel Montolio and Simón Planells-Struse, "Does Tourism Boost Criminal Activity? Evidence from a Top Touristic Country," *Crime and Delinquency*, first published online October 28, 2013.

34. Franklin Zimring and Hannah Laqueur, "Kids, Groups, and Crime: In Defense of Conventional Wisdom," *Journal of Research in Crime and Delinquency* 52 (2015): 403–413.

35. Derek Kreager, "When It's Good to Be 'Bad': Violence and Adolescent Peer Acceptance," *Criminology* 45 (2007): 893–923.

36. Lisa Stolzenberg and Stewart D'Alessio, "Co-offending and the Age-Crime Curve," *Journal of Research in Crime and Delinquency* 45 (2008): 65–86.

37. David R. Schaefer, Nancy Rodriguez, and Scott H. Decker, "The Role of Neighborhood Context in Youth Co-offending," *Criminology* 52 (2014): 117–139.

38. Marie Skubak Tillyer and Rob Tillyer, "Maybe I Should Do This Alone: A Comparison of Solo and Co-offending Robbery Outcomes," *Justice Quarterly* 32 (2015): 1064–1088.

39. Paul Tracy, Kimberly Kempf-Leonard, and Stephanie Abramoske-James, "Gender Differences in Delinquency and Juvenile Justice Processing: Evidence from National Data," *Crime and Delinquency* 55 (2009): 171–215.

40. Alan Booth and D. Wayne Osgood, "The Influence of Testosterone on Deviance in Adulthood: Assessing and Explaining the Relationship," *Criminology* 31 (1993): 93–118.

41. Jean Bottcher, "Social Practices of Gender: How Gender Relates to Delinquency in the Everyday Lives of High-Risk Youths," *Criminology* 39 (2001): 893–932.

42. Debra Kaysen, Miranda Morris, Shireen Rizvi, and Patricia Resick, "Peritraumatic Responses and Their Relationship to Perceptions of Threat in Female Crime Victims," *Violence Against Women* 11 (2005): 1515–1535.

43. Freda Adler, *Sisters in Crime* (New York: McGraw-Hill, 1975); Rita James Simon, *The Contemporary Woman and Crime* (Washington, DC: US Government Printing Office, 1975).

44. Darrell Steffensmeier, Jennifer Schwartz, Hua Zhong, and Jeff Ackerman, "An Assessment of Recent Trends in Girls' Violence Using Diverse Longitudinal Sources: Is the Gender Gap Closing?" *Criminology* 43 (2005): 355–406.

45. Robert Brame, Shawn Bushway, Ray Paternoster, and Michael G. Turner, "Demographic Patterns of Cumulative Arrest Prevalence by Ages 18 and 23," *Crime and Delinquency* 60 (2014): 471–486.

46. Rob Tillyer, "Opening the Black Box of Officer Decision-Making: An Examination of Race, Criminal History, and Discretionary Searches," *Justice Quarterly* 31 (2014): 961–986.

47. Leo Carroll and M. Lilliana Gonzalez, "Out of Place: Racial Stereotypes and the Ecology of Frisks and Searches Following Traffic Stops," *Journal of Research in Crime and Delinquency* 51 (2014): 559–584.

48. Tammy Rinehart Kochel, David Wilson, and Stephen Mastrofski, "Effect of Suspect Race on Officers' Arrest Decisions," *Criminology* 49 (2011): 473–512.

49. Ojmarrh Mitchell and Michael S. Caudy, "Race Differences in Drug Offending and Drug Distribution Arrests," *Crime and Delinquency* 63 (2017): 91–112.

50. Kenneth Novak and Mitchell Chamlin, "Racial Threat, Suspicion, and Police Behavior: The Impact of Race and Place in Traffic Enforcement," *Crime and Delinquency* 58 (2012): 275–300.

51. Richard Rosenfeld, Jeff Rojek, and Scott Decker, "Age Matters: Race Differences in Police Searches of Young and Older Male Drivers," *Journal of Research in Crime and Delinquency* 49 (2011): 31–55.

52. Karen Parker, Brian Stults, and Stephen Rice, "Racial Threat, Concentrated Disadvantage and Social Control: Considering the Macro-Level Sources of Variation in Arrests," *Criminology* 43 (2005): 1111–1134; Lisa Stolzenberg, J. Stewart D'Alessio, and David Eitle, "A Multilevel Test of Racial Threat Theory," *Criminology* 42 (2004): 673–698.

53. Besiki Kutateladze, Nancy Andiloro, Brian Johnson, and Cassia Spohn, "Cumulative Disadvantage: Examining Racial and Ethnic Disparity in Prosecution and Sentencing," *Criminology* 52 (2014): 514–551.

54. William Hauser and Jennifer H. Peck, "The Intersection of Crime Seriousness, Discretion, and Race: A Test of the Liberation Hypothesis," *Justice Quarterly*, published online January 2016: 166–192.

55. Andres F. Rengifo and Don Stemen, "The Unintended Effects of Penal Reform: African American Presence, Incarceration, and the Abolition of Discretionary Parole in the United States," *Crime and Delinquency*, first published May 25, 2012; David Eitle and Susanne Monahan, "Revisiting the Racial Threat Thesis: The Role of Police Organizational Characteristics in Predicting Race-Specific Drug Arrest Rates," *Justice Quarterly* 26 (2009): 528–561.

56. Rebecca Wickes, John R. Hipp, Renee Zahnow, and Lorraine Mazerolle, "'Seeing' Minorities and Perceptions of Disorder: Explicating the Mediating

and Moderating Mechanisms of Social Cohesion," *Criminology* 51 (2013): 519–560.

57. David Jacobs, "Minority Threat and Police Strength from 1980 to 2000: A Fixed-Effects Analysis of Nonlinear and Interactive Effects in Large U.S. Cities," *Criminology* 52 (2014): 140–142.

58. Karen Parker and Patricia McCall, "Structural Conditions and Racial Homicide Patterns: A Look at the Multiple Disadvantages in Urban Areas," *Criminology* 37 (1999): 447–469.

59. Rebecca L. Fix, Spencer T. Fix, Christine M. Wienke Totura, and Barry R. Burkhart, "Disproportionate Minority Contact Among Juveniles Adjudicated for Sexual, Violent, and General Offending: The Importance of Home, School, and Community Contexts," *Crime and Delinquency* 63 (2017): 189–209.

60. Gary LaFree and Richard Arum, "The Impact of Racially Inclusive Schooling on Adult Incarceration Rates Among U.S. Cohorts of African Americans and Whites Since 1930," *Criminology* 44 (2006): 73–103; Michael Rocques and Raymond Paternoster, "Understanding the Antecedents of the 'School-to-Jail' Link: The Relationship Between Race and School Discipline," *Journal of Criminal Law and Criminology* 101 (2011): 633–665.

61. US Department of Education, "New Data from U.S. Department of Education Highlights Educational Inequities Around Teacher Experience, Discipline and High School Rigor," March 6, 2012, http://www.ed.gov/news/press-releases/new-data-us-department-education-highlights-educational-inequities-around-teacher-experience-discipline-and-high-school-rigor.

62. Kerrin C. Wolf and Aaron Kupchik, "School Suspensions and Adverse Experiences in Adulthood," *Justice Quarterly* 34 (2017): 407–430.

63. Bureau of Labor Statistics, "Unemployment Rates for African Americans by State in 2015," March 04, 2016, https://www.bls.gov/opub/ted/2016/unemployment-rates-for-african-americans-by-state-in-2015.htm; Kate H. Choi and Marta Tienda, "Marriage-Market Constraints and Mate-Selection Behavior: Racial, Ethnic, and Gender Differences in Intermarriage," *Journal of Marriage and Family* 79 (2017): 301–317.

64. Amie Nielsen, Ramiro Martinez, and Richard Rosenfeld, "Firearm Use, Injury, and Lethality in Assaultive Violence: An Examination of Ethnic Differences," *Homicide Studies* 9 (2005): 83–108.

65. See, generally, Franklin Zimring and Gordon Hawkins, *Crime Is Not the Problem: Lethal Violence in America* (New York: Oxford University Press, 1997).

66. Gary Kleck, "Defensive Gun Use Is Not a Myth," *Politico*, February 17, 2015, http://www.politico.com/magazine/story/2015/02/defensive-gun-ownership-gary-kleck-response-115082.html; see also the classic article, Gary Kleck and Marc Gertz, "Armed Resistance to Crime: The Prevalence and Nature of Self-Defense with a Gun," *Journal of Criminal Law and Criminology* 86 (1995): 219–249.

67. David Hemenway and Sara Solnick, "The Epidemiology of Self-Defense Gun Use: Evidence from the National Crime Victimization Surveys 2007–2011," *Preventive Medicine* 79 (2015): 22–27.

68. Philip J. Cook, Richard J. Harris, Jens Ludwig, and Harold A. Pollack "Some Sources of Crime Guns in Chicago: Dirty Dealers, Straw Purchasers, and Traffickers," *Journal of Criminal Law and Criminology* 104 (2015): 717–760.

69. John R. Hipp and Adam Boessen, "Egohoods as Waves Washing Across the City: A New Measure of 'Neighborhoods,'" *Criminology* 51 (2013): 287–327; Ramiro Martinez, Jacob Stowell, and Jeffrey Cancino, "A Tale of Two Border Cities: Community Context, Ethnicity, and Homicide," *Social Science Quarterly* 89 (2008): 1–16.

70. Robert J. Sampson, "Disparity and Diversity in the Contemporary City: Social (Dis)order Revisited," *British Journal of Sociology* 60 (2009): 1–31.

71. Shawn Bushway, "Economy and Crime," *The Criminologist* 35 (2010): 1–5.

72. Aki Roberts and Dale Willits, "Income Inequality and Homicide in the United States: Consistency Across Different Income Inequality Measures and Disaggregated Homicide Types," *Homicide Studies* 19 (2015): 28–57.

73. Nancy Rodriguez, "Concentrated Disadvantage and the Incarceration of Youth: Examining How Context Affects Juvenile Justice," *Journal of Research in Crime and Delinquency*, first published December 13, 2011.

74. Mikko Aaltonen, John M. Macdonald, Pekka Martikainen, and Janne Kivivuor, "Examining the Generality of the Unemployment–Crime Association," *Criminology* 51 (2013): 561–594.

75. R. Ramchand, M. Elliott, S. Mrug, J. Grunbaum, M. Windle, A. Chandra, M. Peskin, S. Cooper, and M. Schuster, "Substance Use and Delinquency Among Fifth Graders Who Have Jobs," *American Journal of Preventive Medicine* 36 (2007): 297–303; Jeremy Staff and Christopher Uggen, "The Fruits of Good Work: Early Work Experiences and Adolescent Deviance," *Journal of Research in Crime and Delinquency* 40 (2003): 263–290.

76. Travis Hirschi and Michael Gottfredson, "Age and the Explanation of Crime," *American Journal of Sociology* 89 (1983): 552–584, at 581.

77. Darrell Steffensmeier and Cathy Streifel, "Age, Gender, and Crime Across Three Historical Periods: 1935, 1960 and 1985," *Social Forces* 69 (1991): 869–894.

78. Wanda Leal and Carrie Mier, "What's Age Got to Do With It? Comparing Juveniles and Adults on Drugs and Crime," *Crime and Delinquency* 64 (2017): 334–352.

79. Hirschi and Gottfredson, "Age and the Explanation of Crime."

80. Robert Agnew, "An Integrated Theory of the Adolescent Peak in Offending," *Youth and Society* 34 (2003): 263–302.

81. Laurence Steinberg, Sandra Graham, Lia O'Brien, Jennifer Woolard, Elizabeth Cauffman, and Marie Banich, "Age Differences in Future Orientation and Delay Discounting," *Child Development* 80 (2009): 28–44.

82. Michael Rocque, "The Lost Concept: The (Re)emerging Link Between Maturation and Desistance from Crime," *Criminology and Criminal Justice* 15 (2015): 340–360.

83. James Q. Wilson and Richard Herrnstein, *Crime and Human Nature* (New York: Simon & Schuster, 1985), pp. 126–147.

84. Ibid., p. 219.

85. Kevin Beaver, John Paul Wright, Matt DeLisi, and Michael Vaughn, "Desistance from Delinquency: The Marriage Effect Revisited and Extended," *Social Science Research* 37 (2008): 736–752.

86. Marvin Wolfgang, Robert Figlio, and Thorsten Sellin, *Delinquency in a Birth Cohort* (Chicago: University of Chicago Press, 1972).

87. See Thorsten Sellin and Marvin Wolfgang, *The Measurement of Delinquency* (New York: Wiley, 1964), p. 120.

88. Paul Tracy, Marvin Wolfgang, and Robert Figlio, *Delinquency Careers in Two Birth Cohorts* (New York: Plenum Press, 1990); Marvin Wolfgang, "Delinquency in Two Birth Cohorts," in *Perspective Studies of Crime and Delinquency*, ed. Katherine Teilmann Van Dusen and Sarnoff Mednick (Boston: Kluwer-Nijhoff, 1983), pp. 7–17. The following sections rely heavily on these sources.

89. Lyle Shannon, *Criminal Career Opportunity* (New York: Human Sciences Press, 1988).

90. D. J. West and David P. Farrington, *The Delinquent Way of Life* (London: Heinemann, 1977).

91. Michael Schumacher and Gwen Kurz, *The 8% Solution: Preventing Serious Repeat Juvenile Crime* (Thousand Oaks, CA: Sage, 1999).

92. Peter Jones, Philip Harris, James Fader, and Lori Grubstein, "Identifying Chronic Juvenile Offenders," *Justice Quarterly* 18 (2001): 478–507.

93. Michael Ezell and Amy D'Unger, "Offense Specialization Among Serious Youthful Offenders: A Longitudinal Analysis of a California Youth Authority Sample," (Durham, NC: Duke University, 1998, unpublished report).

Victims and Victimization

3

Chapter Outline

FACT OR FICTION?

▶ Men are more likely to be victimized by strangers, women by someone they know.

▶ Most crime victims are people who are simply in the wrong place at the wrong time.

I n 2015, in a case that made national news, 19-year-old Owen Labrie (in orange jumpsuit) was tried for the rape of a fellow student at the exclusive St. Paul's School in Concord, New Hampshire. Labrie, who was 18 at the time the attack took place, used email to convince the 15-year-old freshman to meet him as part of the "senior salute" ritual in which graduating seniors seduce younger students. She claimed that she had intended merely to kiss or make out with Labrie but then as things got out of hand said no to his sexual advances and resisted him as best she could. In the end her resistance was futile and he forced himself on her and engaged in three unwanted sex acts.

Labrie, a popular scholarship student and athlete who was accepted at Harvard, testified that the young woman consented to his advances and that sexual intercourse had not actually taken place. They had exchanged pleasant emails after the assault, evidence of her consent.

The jury found Labrie not guilty of the most serious charge of forcible rape but convicted him of several lesser charges, including endangering the welfare of a child, and using a computer to "seduce, solicit, lure, or entice a child" in order to commit a sexual assault. He was also found guilty of three counts of misdemeanor sexual assault. Why was he found not guilty of the most serious charge even though the jury believed he did have sex with the young woman, who was still a minor? The reason is that under New Hampshire law, an individual can be found guilty of aggravated felonious sexual assault only if the victim clearly indicates that she doesn't "freely consent," or before she has "an adequate chance to flee and/or resist." The jury apparently concluded that Labrie did have sex with the girl, but there was no real proof that she resisted. Also, under New Hampshire law, if a person has penetrative ▶

consensual sex with a minor between the ages 13 and 16 but is within four years of that age, they are guilty of *misdemeanor* sexual assault. If the age difference is more than four years, they are guilty of *felony* sexual assault. Since Labrie was 18 and the young woman 15, he could only be convicted of a misdemeanor.[1] ■

CONNECTIONS

Sexual assault on campus will be revisited in Chapter 10 when the crime of rape is discussed in some detail. What punishment would you recommend for someone like Owen Labrie? Is a 20-year sentence too harsh? Is a one-year sentence too lenient?

Why do some people become targets of predatory criminals? Is it because of their lifestyle and environment? Could the victim here have done more to protect herself or is it unfair to expect women to always be on their guard, especially when their attackers were trusted friends and schoolmates? In this case, the young woman testified under oath that she did not consent to sex, but it seems like the jury did not fully believe her story. Did they unfairly blame the victim because they believed she should have known the consequences for her risky behavior, i.e., having a clandestine meeting with a teenage boy? Labrie, now 21, is requesting a new trial, claiming he had inadequate counsel. He must adhere to a strict curfew requiring him to be at home between 5 P.M. and 8 A.M. In a sense his appeal suggests that he believes that he was also a victim: of an unfair justice system!

The Victim's Role

LO1 Analyze the victim's role in the crime process.

For many years, crime victims were viewed by criminologists as merely the passive targets of a criminal's anger, greed, or frustration; they were considered to have been "in the wrong place at the wrong time." More than 50 years ago, a number of criminologists, including Hans Von Hentig and Stephen Schafer, conducted pioneering studies that found that, contrary to popular belief, the victim's own behavior is important in the crime process.[2] Victims influence criminal behavior by playing an active role in a criminal incident—for example, by provoking the assault that ended in their death. Victims were also found to sometimes play an indirect role in a criminal incident, such as when they travel through a dangerous, high-crime neighborhood at night without companionship or protection.

The discovery that victims play an important role in the crime process has prompted the scientific study of victims, or **victimology**. Criminologists who focus their attention on crime victims refer to themselves as **victimologists**.

In this chapter, we examine victims and their relationship to the criminal process. First, using available victim data, we analyze the nature and extent of victimization. We then discuss the relationship between victims and criminal offenders. In this context, we look at various theories of victimization that attempt to explain the victim's role in the crime problem. Finally, we examine how society has responded to the needs of victims and consider what special problems they still face.

victimology
The study of the victim's role in criminal events.

victimologists
Criminologists who focus on the victims of crime.

The Costs of Victimization

Criminal victimization exacts a heavy toll on all whom it touches, both the general society and its direct target, individual victims. The cost of victimization takes many forms, ranging from financial loss—property losses, productivity losses, and medical bills—to personal losses—stress, fear, emotional trauma, pain. We examine the social and individual costs of victimization in the following sections.

Societal-Level Costs

Victimization brings with it a bevy of costs to society, including economic losses. When the costs of goods taken during property crimes is added to productivity losses caused by injury, pain, and emotional trauma, the cost of victimization is estimated to be in the hundreds of billions of dollars.

A number of different methods have been developed to measure the cost of victimization to American society and how that cost influences the average American. Mark Cohen pioneered these efforts by focusing on the total costs of a criminal act rather than the out-of-pocket expenses incurred by victims. Cohen used complex mathematical models to estimate the additional cost of such intangibles as pain, suffering, and fear caused by crime and what a jury might award in personal injury case for similar injuries. Cohen's analysis determined that the typical career criminal causes $1.3 to $1.5 million in economic costs; a heavy drug user, $370,000 to $970,000; and a high-school dropout, $243,000 to $388,000. Eliminating duplication between crimes committed by individuals (for example, those who are both heavy drug users and career criminals) results in an overall estimate of lifetime cost for each chronic offender at between $1.7 to $2.3 million. This means that a treatment program for youth that costs thousands of dollars annually will pay for itself if it can "save" five or six youthful offenders each year.

In the aftermath of Cohen's influential research, a number of different measures have been created to gauge the cost of victimization. Kathryn McCollister and her associates determined that cost of victimization includes justice system, health care, and other costs. The crimes they could put a figure on included:

The problems faced by rape survivors are not confined to the civilian population. The Veterans Administration finds that one in four women in the military have experienced sexual harassment or assault. The problem is growing because female veterans represent the military's fastest-growing population: an estimated 2.2 million, or 10 percent, of the country's veterans are women. Army veteran Kate Weber, shown here, a survivor of military sexual trauma (MST), now spends most of her time doing MST advocacy with other victims.

- Murder: $8,982,907 (range = $4,144,677 to $11,350,687)
- Rape/sexual assault: $240,776 (range = $80,403 to $369,739)
- Robbery: $42,310 (range = $18,591 to $280,237)
- Household burglary: $6,462 (range = $1,974 to $30,197)
- Stolen property: $7,974 (range = $151 to $22,739)

According to McCollister, the cost to society of an average murder is almost $9 million. Considering that about 16,000 murders now occur each year, this crime alone costs the nation about $190 billion in losses each year.[3]

But even these huge costs may be only the tip of the iceberg. Michael Tonry reminds us that such efforts ignore the social costs of punishment that are levied on offenders and their families.[4] Imprisoning a convicted criminal places an economic burden on his family who thereafter may need government assistance and welfare. And, because there is a significant correlation between parental incarceration and children's delinquency, incarcerating parents may actually create more victimization than it saves; parental absence due to incarceration has a greater effect on kids than parental separation due to illness, death, or divorce.[5] While these factors may add to the true cost of victimization, they negate or neutralize the economic benefits accrued from incarcerating criminals

Individual-Level Costs

Some of the direct, tangible costs suffered by individual victims of crime include the cost of damaged and lost property, pain and suffering, costs of medical care, lost wages, reduced quality of life imposed by debilitating injuries and/or fear of being victimized again, and the cost of psychological counseling. Lynn Langton and Jennifer Truman found that more than two-thirds (68 percent) of serious violent-crime victims

LO2 Discuss the greatest problems faced by crime victims.

experienced socio-emotional problems including stress, anxiety, and fatigue, leading to emotional distress, increased relationship problems, and disruptions at school or work.[6]

Some victims are physically disabled, including those who suffer paralyzing spinal cord injuries and need long-term medical care. The long-term effects of the crime may have devastating financial consequences. One recent interview study assessed the economic impact of sexual assaults using data from 27 in-depth, qualitative interviews with rape survivors. Rebecca Loya found that trauma can disrupt survivors' employment in several ways, including forcing victims to take time off and diminishing their job performance once they return.[7]

There are also hidden costs. Take for instance the decline in value of a home that has been the scene of a crime. The impact of a high-profile murder on real estate can be particularly devastating. The Brentwood, California, home where Nicole Brown Simpson (wife of O. J. Simpson) and her friend Ron Goldman were murdered in 1994 hit the market the following year with a $795,000 price tag; it sat for more than two years before selling for $595,000.[8] A high-profile crime can affect the value of all homes in the neighborhood.

POSTTRAUMATIC STRESS Victims may suffer stress and anxiety long after the incident is over and the justice process has run its course. Langton and Truman found that most violent crime victims with socio-emotional problems suffered from symptoms such as feeling anxious, depressed, or angry, or having trouble sleeping, for at least a month or more after the incident. Many victims suffer from long-term **posttraumatic stress disorder (PTSD)**—the symptoms of which include depression, anxiety, and self-destructive behavior—especially when the victim does not receive adequate support from family and friends.[9] Rape victims are particularly susceptible to PTSD, and its effects are felt whether the victim acknowledges the attack or remains in denial about what happened. In other words, there is no escaping the long-term effects of sexual assault, even if the victim refuses to acknowledge having been raped.[10]

Children who are victimized by parents or other adults, who have either witnessed or experienced child abuse or have been the victim of traumatic sexual experiences, also have been found to suffer a long list of negative psychological deficits. These include but are not limited to acute stress disorders, depression, eating disorders, nightmares, anxiety, suicidal ideation, and other psychological problems.[11] Many run away to escape their environment, which puts them at risk for juvenile arrest and involvement with the justice system.[12]

The stress accrued in childhood follows victims over the life course. Young victims are at greater risk of being abused as adults than those who escaped childhood victimization.[13] They may also suffer a wide range of personal deficits as they mature. Research shows that children repeatedly victimized before the age of 12 are the ones most susceptible to a number of physical and mental health issues, smoking, and homelessness.[14]

RELATIONSHIP STRESS The stress encountered in childhood endures into adulthood, especially for those who are the victim of intimate partner violence (IPV). People who were abused as youth are more likely to become involved in abusive relationships as they mature. Early victimization has what is referred to as a "transformative effect," making childhood victims extremely vulnerable to IPV when they form co-residential romantic unions.[15]

Numerous research efforts show that people who suffer IPV experience an extremely high prevalence of psychological problems, including but not limited to depression, generalized anxiety disorder (GAD), panic disorder, substance use disorders, borderline personality disorder, antisocial personality disorder, posttraumatic stress disorder, anxiety disorder, and **obsessive-compulsive disorder** (an extreme preoccupation with certain thoughts and compulsive performance of certain behaviors).[16] One reason may be that abusive partners are as likely to mistreat their victims

posttraumatic stress disorder (PTSD)
Psychological reaction to a highly stressful event; symptoms may include depression, anxiety, flashbacks, and recurring nightmares.

obsessive-compulsive disorder
An extreme preoccupation with certain thoughts and compulsive performance of certain behaviors.

psychologically with threats and intimidation as they are to use physical force; psychological abuse can lead to depression and other long-term disabilities.[17]

VICTIM FEAR People who live in crime-ridden neighborhoods develop an overwhelming sense of fear.[18] Those who have actually experienced crime are the most fearful, dreading the possibility that they may be victimized again.[19] Fear can become generalized: people who have been assaulted may develop fears that their house will be burglarized.[20]

There are gender differences in the fear of crime, and women are more fearful than men, especially those living in crime-ridden communities.[21] In a moving book called *Aftermath: Violence and the Remaking of a Self*, rape victim Susan Brison recounts the difficult time she had recovering from her ordeal. The trauma of rape disrupted her memory, cut off events that happened before the rape from those that occurred afterward, and undermined her ability to conceive of a happy or productive future. Although sympathizers encouraged her to forget the past, she found that confronting it can have healing power.[22]

Those who experience victimization directly are the most likely to be fearful and change their behaviors; some choose to move out of their neighborhood to a safer area.[23] But even those who have escaped attack themselves may develop fears and become timid after hearing about another's victimization.[24] Not only are people likely to move out of their neighborhood if they become crime victims, but they are also likely to relocate if a friend or neighbor has suffered a break-in or burglary.[25] Their fear is exacerbated by lurid news accounts of crime and violence.[26] News stories about serial killers on a rampage or mass killers shooting people in a movie theater can cause a chill felt throughout the city. Fear of these violent crimes prompts people to protect themselves and their family by implementing some sort of protective measure, such as carrying mace or pepper spray or installing a security device in their home.[27] Some may go overboard, carry weapons for protection, and react aggressively to provocations, no matter how slight; this group is the one most likely to engage in violence themselves.[28]

VICTIM BLAME The suffering endured by crime victims does not end when their attacker leaves the scene of the crime. They may suffer innuendos or insinuations from friends and family members who suggest that they are to blame for what happened or that the crime was somehow their fault.

Being blamed for what others perceive to be a result of risky behavior is especially painful for rape victims who may be made to feel they were somehow responsible for the attack because they used poor judgment or took risks.[29] Rape survivors are often the target of negative reactions from people who are supposed to give them support, including family friends and professionals. Some rape victims report that police seem suspicious of their involvement and question them about whether they may have helped precipitate the crime; the treatment they received from legal, medical, and mental health services was so destructive that they couldn't help feeling "re-raped."[30] In some instances these negative reactions cause survivors to blame themselves for the attack and even question whether the incident was really rape.[31]

Victims are especially prone to stress, blame, and fear if it turns out they may have made a false identification and the person they thought responsible for their attack was actually not guilty of the crime. The effect of exoneration on victims is discussed in the Policies and Issues in Criminology feature.

Legal Costs of Victimization

People who are crime victims may be more likely to commit crime themselves. The process may begin early in life, because being abused or neglected as a child increases the odds of being arrested, both as a juvenile and as an adult.[32] People who were physically or sexually abused, especially young males, are much more likely

L03 Clarify the term *cycle of violence*.

Policies and Issues in Criminology

THE IMPACT OF WRONGFUL CONVICTIONS ON CRIME VICTIMS

When a wrongfully convicted individual is exonerated, the original crime victim may experience feelings of guilt, fear, helplessness, devastation, and depression. To find out more about the effect a wrongful conviction has on victims, researchers from ICF International conducted in-depth studies in six states to identify the shared experiences of victims in 11 cases of wrongful conviction for crimes ranging from rape and homicide to burglary and sex offenses.

How Wrongful Convictions May Affect Victims

The researchers found that a number of factors contributed to the wrongful convictions, including eyewitness misidentification, invalidated or improper forensic evidence and analysis, false testimony by informants, false confessions, and ineffective legal counsel. Regardless of cause, wrongful convictions have a significant impact on the original crime victims. As one victim told researchers, "For [several] years, I had been quite comfortable with my role as the victim. When the exoneration happened, that exoneree became the victim, and I, the rape victim, became the offender. The roles switch, and it's a role you don't know what to do with."

More than half of the victims in the study described the impact of the wrongful conviction as being comparable to—or worse than—that of their original victimization. Many said they were in shock when they first heard about the exoneration. The majority of the victims also reported intense feelings of guilt. This was especially true for the two-thirds of victims in the study who provided eyewitness identification. One victim recounted, "It was harder going through the re-victimization than it was through the rape. . . . Now you have the same feelings of that pain. You have the same scariness. You have the same fear. You have the same panic, but now you have this flood of guilt on top of it."

As with many cases of wrongful conviction, most received media attention, generating notoriety for both the wrongfully convicted individuals and the crime victims. Some of the victims felt that the media insinuated that they had intentionally misidentified the wrongfully convicted individuals. Many found the anger directed toward them in blogs and comments that followed news articles particularly painful. One victim stated, "This is the thing— your name's not out there, but you are out there. This is your case. This is something that happened to your body. This is what happened to your mind, to your life. . . . I didn't give anybody permission to put this out in the newspaper."

The crime victims reported being afraid of the wrongfully convicted individual following the exoneration. One victim said, "My initial thought was [the wrongfully convicted individual] is going to kill me. [They] will hurt me, and if [they] can't get to me, [they] will get to my children. So I was hyper alert. The children could not leave my side. I went to school and told the teachers, 'They are to stay with you every second.' That went on for almost two years." The crime victims also reported being afraid of the actual offenders.

Improving Support for Victims

When asked for recommendations, victims and stakeholders spoke of the need to improve notification, information, and services for the original crime victims in cases of wrongful conviction. In all of the case studies, those interviewed agreed that the criminal justice system should provide initial notification. Victims and other stakeholders recommended that, when appropriate and possible, officials involved in the original case should notify the crime victim. When this is not possible, many stakeholders suggested having a victim service provider present. Others stressed that law enforcement or prosecutors should be present, especially in cases that may involve additional litigation.

Victims and stakeholders stressed that the crime victims are often unfamiliar with the criminal justice system and need information explaining the exoneration process. Several victims in the study who provided eyewitness identification said that learning how misidentifications may occur helped them process their reactions and understand the wrongful conviction. Some officials, however, pointed out that providing such information might not be appropriate or legally advisable for law enforcement. Victims also said that information on how memories are formed helped them understand why they continued to envision the wrongfully convicted individual when they thought about the crime. Interviewees also highlighted the importance of counseling services in helping crime victims come to terms with the wrongful conviction. Victims recommended that counseling services be provided by someone with formal training and experience working with victims of trauma.

Critical Thinking

Can anything be done to ease the pain of victims who wrongfully identify an innocent person? Should the state provide counseling services at taxpayer cost?

Source: Seri Irazola, Erin Williamson, Julie Stricker, and Emily Niedzwiecki, "Addressing the Impact of Wrongful Convictions on Crime Victims," *NIJ Journal* 274 (2014): 35–38.

to smoke, drink, and take drugs than nonabused youth. Incarcerated offenders report significant amounts of posttraumatic stress disorder as a result of prior victimization, which may in part explain their violent and criminal behaviors.[33] Some may run away, increasing their risk of becoming a crime victim.[34] Others may seek revenge against the people who harmed them, and sometimes these feelings are generalized to others who exhibit the same characteristics as their attackers.[35] The abuse–crime phenomenon is referred to as the **cycle of violence**.[36]

As adults, there is evidence that crime victims themselves are more likely than nonvictims to commit crimes.[37] Fearing revictimization, they may take drastic measures and arm themselves for self-protection.[38] Such measures may amplify victimization risk.

The factors that link crime and victimization are set out more fully in Exhibit 3.1.

cycle of violence
Victims of crime, especially victims of childhood abuse, are more likely to commit crimes themselves.

Exhibit 3.1 The Link Between Victimization and Crime

Given the evidence pointing to a link between victimization and crime, how can the association be explained?

- *Victimization causes social problems.* People who are crime victims experience long-term negative consequences, including problems with unemployment and developing personal relationships, factors related to criminality. Some young victims may run away from home, taking to the streets and increasing their risk of becoming a crime victim again.
- *Victimization causes stress and anger.* Victimization may produce anger, stress, and strain. Known offenders report significant amounts of posttraumatic stress disorder as a result of prior victimization, which may in part explain their violent and criminal behaviors. Victims, especially those who lack self-control, may try to cope with this stress by self-medicating, drinking, or taking drugs, a form of behavior highly correlated with future criminality.
- *Victimization prompts revenge.* Victims may seek revenge against the people who harmed them or whom they believe are at fault for their problems. In some cases, these feelings become generalized to others who share the same characteristics of their attackers (e.g., men, Hispanics). As a result, their reactions become displaced, and they may lash out at people who are not their attackers. They may take drastic measures, fearing revictimization, and arm themselves for self-protection. In some cultures, retaliation is an expected and accepted response to victimization.
- *Crime and victimization have a common cause.* Social and personal factors predictive of crime also produce victimization—substance abuse, experiencing violence, psychological deficits. When Marie Skubak Tillyer and Emily Wright studied the victims and perpetrators of intimate partner violence they found a great deal of overlap. Perpetrators and victim-perpetrators were more likely to live with a non-spouse partner, feel isolated, display negative temperaments, and report substance use problems.
- *Spurious and/or nonlinear relationship.* While some victims engage in antisocial behaviors, others do not. Victims and criminals are actually two separate groups linked together because both have the same lifestyle and live in the same neighborhoods, making it seem they are one and the same. The personal traits that produce violent criminals may not be the same traits that produce victims. It is also possible that while there is some overlap, the association between victimization and crime fluctuates over time. Younger victims are more likely to respond with antisocial activities after an attack, while older victims refrain from violent confrontations.

Sources: Christopher Schreck, Eric Stewart, and D. Wayne Osgood, "A Reappraisal of the Overlap of Violent Offenders and Victims," *Criminology* 46 (2008): 872–906; Christopher Schreck, Mark Berg, Graham Ousey, Eric Stewart, and J. Mitchell Miller, "Does the Nature of the Victimization–Offending Association Fluctuate Over the Life Course? An Examination of Adolescence and Early Adulthood," *Crime and Delinquency*, first published online December 18, 2015; Marie Skubak Tillyer and Emily M. Wright, "Intimate Partner Violence and the Victim–Offender Overlap," *Journal of Research in Crime and Delinquency* 51 (2014): 29–55; Jillian J. Turanovic and Travis C. Pratt, "The Consequences of Maladaptive Coping: Integrating General Strain and Self-Control Theories to Specify a Causal Pathway Between Victimization and Offending," *Journal of Quantitative Criminology* 29 (2013): 321–345; Ulrich Orth, Leo Montada, and Andreas Maercker, "Feelings of Revenge, Retaliation Motive, and Posttraumatic Stress Reactions in Crime Victims," *Journal of Interpersonal Violence* 21 (2006): 229–243; Chris Melde, Finn-Aage Esbensen, and Terrance Taylor, "'May Piece Be with You': A Typological Examination of the Fear and Victimization Hypothesis of Adolescent Weapon Carrying," *Justice Quarterly* 26 (2009): 348–376.

The Nature of Victimization

How many crime victims are there in the United States, and what are the trends and patterns in victimization? The National Crime Victimization Survey (NCVS) indicates that about 20 million theft and violence victimizations occur each year.[39] And while this number has declined considerably during the past 20 years (see Chapter 2), it still means that more than 10 percent of all the households in America experience theft sometime during the year and about 20 in every 1,000 citizens are raped, robbed, or assaulted. As we have seen, these data are especially disturbing considering that becoming a victim of these violent acts can not only be immediately devastating but also have considerable long-term consequences and costs, ranging from damaged property to mental anguish.[40]

Patterns in the victimization survey findings tell us that victimization is stable and repetitive; victimization is not random but is a function of personal and ecological factors. The stability of these patterns allows judgments to be made about the nature of victimization; policies can then be created in an effort to reduce the victimization rate. Who are victims? Where does victimization take place? What is the relationship between victims and criminals? The following sections discuss some of the most important victimization patterns and trends.

The Social Ecology of Victimization

LO4 Assess the ecology of victimization risk.

Victim surveys show that violent crimes are slightly more likely to take place in an open, public area (such as a street, a park, or a field) or at a commercial establishment such as a tavern, and in daytime or early evening hours than in a private home during the morning or late evening hours.

The more serious violent crimes, such as rape and aggravated assault, typically take place after 6 P.M. Approximately two-thirds of rapes and sexual assaults occur at night—6 P.M. to 6 A.M. Less serious forms of violence, such as unarmed robberies and personal larcenies such as purse snatching, are more likely to occur during the daytime.

There are also seasonal variations in victimization. Household property crimes, such as burglaries, have higher rates in the summer and lower rates during other seasons of the year. Motor vehicle thefts do not exhibit the same seasonal patterns. Serious violent victimization rates—which include rape and sexual assault, robbery, and aggravated assault—are significantly higher during the summer than during the winter, spring, and fall. When all violent crimes are counted, including simple assault, rates of violence are highest in the fall.[41] One reason: many simple assaults occur in school, and victimization rate patterns correspond to the start of the school year.

NEIGHBORHOOD CHARACTERISTICS Community factors also affect the chances of victimization. Those living in the central city experience significantly higher rates of theft and violence than suburbanites; people living in rural areas have a victimization rate less than half that of city dwellers. The risk of murder for both men and women is significantly higher in disorganized inner-city areas where gangs flourish and drug trafficking is commonplace.

Not only does living in a disorganized neighborhood increase victimization risk, but so does the socioeconomic characteristics of surrounding areas. People who live in and next to poverty areas are more likely to suffer victimization; surrounding poverty matters beyond the effect of residential poverty. Victimization risk declines as people move farther away from extreme poverty to improved extended (residential and surrounding) neighborhoods.[42]

Even if people are not personally victimized, city dwellers, especially those living in areas with large disadvantaged populations, are more likely to observe or be exposed to violence than those living in more advantaged neighborhoods. And observing violence can contribute to stress, fear, and flight.[43]

CONNECTIONS

As we saw in Chapter 2, the NCVS is currently the leading source of information on the nature and extent of victimization. It uses a sophisticated sampling methodology to collect data; statistical techniques are then applied to estimate victimization rates, trends, and patterns for the entire US population.

CRIME IN SCHOOLS Schools, unfortunately, are the scene of a great deal of victimization because they are populated by one of the most dangerous segments of society, teenage males. The latest data available from the National Center for Educational Statistics found that among students ages 12 to 18, there were about 850,000 nonfatal victimizations at school, which included 363,700 theft victimizations and 486,400 violent victimizations.[44] During the last school year, 53 student, staff, and nonstudent school-associated violent deaths occurred, including 41 homicides, 11 suicides, and 1 legal intervention death.

One reason for the extent of school crime is that adult supervision is minimal before, during, and after school activities. School hallways and locker rooms are typically left unattended. Kids who participate in school sports may leave their valuables in locker rooms; others congregate in unguarded places, making them attractive targets for predators who come on school grounds.[45] So ironically, while for most people and most crimes summer is the most dangerous season, for adolescents victimization actually peaks in the fall when the school year begins and declines in the summer after the school year ends.[46]

The Victim's Household

The NCVS tells us that, within the United States, homes located in urban areas in the South and West are the ones most vulnerable to crime, especially those occupied by African American families. In contrast, European American homes in rural areas in the Northeast and Midwest are the least likely to become the target of crimes such as burglary and larceny. People who own their homes are less vulnerable than renters.

Population movement and changes may account for recent decreases in crime victimization. US residents have become extremely mobile, moving from urban areas to suburban and rural areas. In addition, family size has been reduced; more people than ever before are living in single-person homes, and more people than ever are not marrying. The proportion of people over 18 who are currently married is about 50 percent, down from 72 percent in 1960. Over a quarter of all households are now single person, up from 13 percent in 1960. The fact that smaller households in less populated areas have a lower victimization risk is a possible explanation for the decline in household victimization rates during the past 25 years.[47]

Victim Characteristics

Social and demographic characteristics also distinguish victims and nonvictims. The most important of these factors are gender, age, social status, and race.

L05 Categorize the most dominant victim characteristics.

GENDER Gender affects victimization risk. Except for the crimes of rape and sexual assault, males are somewhat more likely than females to be the victims of violent crime. Men are almost twice as likely as women to experience robbery. Women, however, are 10 times more likely than men to be victims of rape or sexual assault. Although males are more likely to be victimized than females, the gender difference in victimization has narrowed considerably during the past decade and is now approaching equality.[48]

Another significant gender difference is that women are much more likely to be victimized by someone they know or with whom they live. Of those offenders victimizing females, about two-thirds were described as someone the victim knew or was related to. In contrast, less than half of male victims were attacked by a friend, relative, or acquaintance.[49]

There are also gender differences in the aftermath of victimization. When men are the aggressors, injuries are more severe and victims are more likely to suffer injury. Female aggressors tend to engage in verbal rather than physical abuse.[50]

AGE Although violent crime rates declined in recent years for most age groups, victim data reveal that young people face a much greater victimization risk than older persons. Teens and young adults experience the highest rates of violent crime, but even

FACT OR FICTION?

Men are more likely to be victimized by strangers, women by someone they know.

FACT Women are much more likely than men to be victimized by someone they know or someone with whom they live.

CONNECTIONS

The association between age and victimization is undoubtedly tied to lifestyle: adolescents often stay out late at night, go to public places, and hang out with other young people who have a high risk of criminal involvement. Go back to Chapter 2 and review the association between age and crime.

the youngest kids are not immune; younger children are just as likely to be hit with an object that could cause injury, to be victimized on multiple occasions, and suffer similar injuries as their older siblings.[51]

Although the elderly are less likely to become crime victims than the young, they are most often the victims of a narrow band of criminal activities from which the young are more immune. Frauds and scams, purse snatching, pocket picking, stealing checks from the mail, and crimes committed in long-term care settings claim more older than younger victims. The elderly are especially vulnerable to fraud because they have insurance, pension plans, proceeds from the sale of homes, and money from Social Security and savings that make them attractive financial targets. Because many elderly live by themselves and are lonely, they remain more susceptible to telephone and mail fraud. Unfortunately, once victimized, the elderly have more limited opportunities either to recover their lost money or to earn enough to replace what they have lost.[52] In addition, the elderly are also subject to physical and sexual abuse, most often from family members. This topic is explored in the accompanying Policies and Issues in Criminology feature.

Policies and Issues in Criminology

ELDER VICTIMS

Elder abuse and neglect are serious yet understudied problems in the United States. One reason is that the elderly, over age 65, have far lower rates of victimization than persons ages 12 to 64. Each year, the elderly account for approximately 5 percent of violence and 2 percent of serious violent victimizations. However, many of these incidents occur at the hands of family members.

Because elder abuse was historically viewed as a social rather than a criminal problem, most states did not establish adult protective services units to address elderly victims until the mid-1980s. Elder abuse is frequently perpetrated by a spouse, relative, or acquaintance, which increases the likelihood that crimes are underreported. Low household income, unemployment or retirement, poor health, prior traumatic events, and low levels of social support can indicate both a higher likelihood that older people may experience mistreatment and that the crime will be underreported.

Ron Acierno and his colleagues surveyed more than 5,000 people 60 or older via telephone. Interviewers asked participants about their experiences in the previous year, as well as their lifetime overall. Though almost 2 percent of the respondents reported physical mistreatment, only 31 percent of those respondents had reported the problem to police. One reason is that strangers accounted for only 3 percent of these assaults as compared to family members, who were the perpetrators in 76 percent of the cases. Of those surveyed, slightly less than 1 percent reported being sexually abused in the previous year. About 16 percent of those people reported the assault to the police. Family members were responsible for about half of the assaults.

Other types of abuse include financial exploitation (5 percent), neglect (5 percent), and emotional mistreatment (5 percent). Overall, 11 percent of those surveyed reported some form of mistreatment in the previous year; 1.2 percent reported two forms of mistreatment, and 0.2 percent reported three forms.

Adding to this undercount of older victims is the rising number of elderly living in long-term care facilities who are the target of physical abuse. There is much that is unknown about the abuse and criminal victimization of adults living in residential care facilities, but what is known is troubling. Available data suggest that adults are victimized at an alarming rate, and often have much more difficulty participating in the criminal justice system and receiving the help they need.

While widespread already, elder abuse will continue to be an important issue because of shifts in the US population. Currently there are about 40 million people in the United States over age 65 and the Bureau of the Census predicts that by 2030 that population will reach 70 million people; the elderly will then make up more than 20 percent of the population (up from 12 percent in 1990).

The elderly are at particular risk for Internet fraud. Here, Ruth Wilson sits with her father while she displays some of the scam mail he has received in various attempts to defraud the elderly man. A Jamaica–US task force launched to stop a network of aggressive gangs who run fake lottery scams has failed to stop the con artists, who are now stealing an estimated $1 billion a year, largely from elderly Americans.

AP Images/Elaine Thompson

What Causes Elder Abuse?

There are a number of possible causes of elder abuse. The most important are set out below:

- *The caregiver stress view* asserts that maltreatment occurs when family members caring for an impaired older adult are unable to adequately manage their caregiving responsibilities. The elderly victim is typically described as highly dependent on the caregiver, who becomes overwhelmed, frustrated, and abusive because of the continuous caretaking demands posed by the elderly person.
- *The social learning view* holds that elder abuse results from the abusive individual learning to use violence (perhaps from their elderly parent or relative) to either resolve conflicts or obtain a desired outcome.
- *The social exchange view* holds that people who abuse the elderly perceive themselves as not receiving their fair share from their relationship with the elderly person or other family members, and their resort to violence is an effort to restore or obtain what they feel they deserve.
- *The background-situational view* asserts that long-term discord results from a combination of factors, such as a history of family violence and/or a lack of relationship satisfaction, which primes a person's acceptance of violence as a conflict resolution strategy.
- *The power and control view* highlights an abusive individual's use of an ongoing pattern of coercive tactics to gain and maintain power and control during the course of a relationship with another person.

A husband who abuses his elderly wife probably abused her when she was young.

- *The ecological view* explains elder abuse by including the impact of individual, relationship, community, and societal influences.
- *The biopsychosocial view* holds that elder maltreatment can be attributed to the characteristics of both the elderly person and the abusive individual and the influence of their environment.

Critical Thinking

1. Can you think of anything that could be done to help identify elderly victims?
2. What could be done to aid in the prosecution of their attackers? Do we need elder protective services similar to child protective services?

Sources: Rachel E. Morgan and Britney J. Mason, "Crimes Against the Elderly, 2003–2013," Bureau of Justice Statistics, 2014, http://www.bjs.gov/content/pub/pdf/cae0313.pdf; Ron Acierno, Melba Hernandez-Tejada, Wendy Muzzy, and Kenneth Steve, *National Elder Mistreatment Study*, National Institute of Justice, 2009, http://www.ncjrs.gov/pdffiles1/nij/grants/226456.pdf; Office of Justice Programs, *OJP Fact Sheet, Elder Abuse and Mistreatment, 2011*, http://ojp.gov/newsroom/factsheets/ojpfs_elderabuse.html; Philip Bulman, "Elder Abuse Emerges from the Shadows of Public Consciousness," *NIJ Journal* 26 (2010), http://www.nij.gov/journals/265/pages/elder-abuse.aspx; Shelley Jackson and Thomas Hafemeister, *Understanding Elder Abuse*, National Institute of Justice, 2013, http://www.ncjrs.gov/pdffiles1/nij/241731.pdf; data from the National Center on Elder Abuse, 2014, https://ncea.acl.gov/. (URLs accessed in 2017.)

SOCIAL STATUS The poorest Americans are the most likely to be victims of violent and property crime. This association occurs across all gender, age, and racial groups. The homeless, who are among the poorest individuals in America, suffer very high rates of assault.[53] Similarly, gang boys who are both lower class and live a high-risk lifestyle are more likely to become crime victims than the non–gang affiliated.[54]

In contrast, the wealthy are more likely to be targets of personal theft crimes such as pocket picking and purse snatching. Perhaps the affluent, who sport more expensive attire and drive better cars, attract the attention of thieves.

RACE AND ETHNICITY African Americans are significantly more likely than European Americans to be victims of violent crime. The black homicide victimization rate is more than six times the homicide victimization rate for whites. This means the homicide rate among black victims in the United States is 16 per 100,000; for whites, the national homicide rate is about 2.50 per 100,000. Nearly 85 percent of black homicide victims are shot and killed with guns.[55]

Why do these discrepancies exist? Because of income inequality, racial and minority group members are often forced to live in lower-income communities, a status that places them in the most at-risk population group. Another reason may be that offenders are more likely to attack minority group victims with weapons. Criminologist Mark Berg speculates that racial stereotypes affect criminal decision making and shape offenders' decisions about how to incapacitate a potential target. Criminals believe African American men are tough and not willing to back down or surrender their valuables without a fight. When African Americans are targeted, the use of a weapon increases their chances of injury.[56]

MARITAL STATUS Johnny Brickman Wall, a Salt Lake City pediatrician was recently convicted for killing his ex-wife, Uta von Schwedler, amid a bitter custody dispute. Wall was sentenced to 15-to-life in prison for attacking the 49-year-old woman with a knife, dosing her with the anti-anxiety drug Xanax, and drowning her in her bathtub.[57] The Wall case is certainly not unusual, considering that divorce claims about half of all first marriages and domestic violence is a significant social problem. Considering this turmoil, one might expect that married people have a greater chance of violent victimization than single people. But the data show quite the opposite effect: never-married males and females are victimized more often than married people. Widows and widowers have the lowest victimization risk. This association between marital status and victimization is probably influenced by age, gender, and lifestyle:

- Many young people, who have the highest victim risk, are actually too young to have been married.
- Young, single people also go out in public more often and sometimes interact with high-risk peers, increasing their exposure to victimization.
- Widows and widowers suffer much lower victimization rates because they are generally older, interact with older people, and are more likely to stay home at night and to avoid public places.

Victimization may also influence the decision to marry: violent crime victims are the ones most likely to marry at an early age.[58] Why victimization spurs marriage is hard to determine. It is possible that those scarred by street violence seek stable relationships to provide a sense of security and tranquility. Unfortunately, getting married at an early age is associated with divorce, so while early victimization may cause people to seek the stability of marriage their decision may not bring long-term marital bliss.

PHYSICAL AND MENTAL TRAITS A number of research efforts have found that people who have particular personality traits are more likely to become victims.

These traits include impulsivity, risk taking, lack of self-control, and low tolerance for frustration. It is possible that impulsive risk takers are more likely to get involved in dangerous situations than people who routinely take precautions.[59]

Not only do criminals seek out people with personality deficits, but those with physical disabilities are also more at risk. The rate of violent victimization for persons with disabilities (36 per 1,000) is more than twice the rate for persons without disabilities (14 per 1,000) (adjusting for age since persons with disabilities—hearing, vision, cognitive, ambulatory, self-care, or independent living limitations—are generally older). Each year persons with disabilities experience more than 1 million violent victimizations. Rates of serious violent victimization—rape, sexual assault, robbery, or aggravated assault—are more than three times higher for persons with disabilities (14 per 1,000) than the age-adjusted rate for persons without disabilities (4 per 1,000). When surveyed, many people with disabilities believed they were purposely targeted because of their physical status.[60]

REPEAT VICTIMIZATION Does prior victimization enhance or reduce the chances of future victimization? Individuals who have been crime victims have a significantly higher chance of future victimization than people who have remained nonvictims.[61]

The chances of repeat victimization may relate to lifestyle. When Marie Skubak Tillyer and her associates studied repeat sexual assault victimization among a high school sample they found that repeat victimization was normative, and that impulsive kids who hang out with antisocial peers and are involved in unsupervised social activities are the ones most at risk for repeat victimization.[62]

Repeat victimization also applies to locations: households that have experienced victimization in the past are the ones most likely to experience it again in the future.[63] People who specialize in one type of crime, such as burglary, are more likely to choose the same target over and over again, especially if it is nearby and convenient. Why travel when you can burglarize a building close to home, especially if you got away with it the first time?[64]

What factors predict chronic victimization? Most repeat victimizations occur soon after the previous crime, suggesting that repeat victims share some personal characteristic that makes them a magnet for predators.[65] Children who are shy, physically weak, or socially isolated may share a set of characteristics making them prone to being repeatedly bullied in the schoolyard.[66] David Finkelhor and Nancy Asigian have found that three specific types of characteristics increase the potential for victimization:

- *Target vulnerability*. The victims' physical weakness or psychological distress renders them incapable of resisting or deterring crime and makes them easy targets.
- *Target gratifiability*. Some victims have a quality, possession, skill, or attribute that an offender wants to obtain, use, have access to, or manipulate. Having attractive possessions, such as expensive trainers or a new iPhone, may make one vulnerable to predatory crime.
- *Target antagonism*. Some characteristics increase risk because they arouse anger, jealousy, or destructive impulses in potential offenders. Gay men risk attacks by homophobes; being argumentative and alcoholic may provoke barroom assaults.[67]

Of course, not all victims are repeaters. Some take defensive measures to lessen their chance of future victimizations. Some may change their lifestyle, take fewer risks, and cut back on associating with dangerous people; once burned, twice shy.[68] Repeat victimization may occur when the victim does not take defensive action. If an abusive husband finds that his battered wife will not call the police, he repeatedly victimizes her. If a hate crime is committed and the police do not respond to reported offenses, the perpetrators learn they have little to fear from the law.[69]

A great many victims knew or were acquainted with their attacker. Here, Chicago police remove a body from a home where 57-year-old Darnell Hudson Donerson, the mother of Oscar winner Jennifer Hudson, was found shot to death on the living room floor. Hudson's brother was also found dead in a bedroom of the home. In 2012, William Balfour, the former husband of Hudson's sister Julia, was convicted of the murders.

Victims and Their Criminals

The victim data also tell us something about the relationship between victims and criminals. Males are more likely to be violently victimized by a stranger, and females are more likely to be victimized by a friend, an acquaintance, or an intimate.

Victims report that most crimes were committed by a single offender over age 20. Crime tends to be intraracial: African American offenders victimize blacks, and European Americans victimize whites.

Although many violent crimes are committed by strangers, a surprising number are committed by relatives or acquaintances. When Yale sociologist Andrew Papachristos studied 191 murder incidents that took place between 2005 and 2010 in two low-income Chicago neighborhoods, he found that while some killings were random, more often than not the victims knew their killers or at least someone linked to the offender. Papachristos found that 70 percent of the killings occurred within a social network of just 1,600 people out of a total neighborhood population of 80,000. His data showed that the risk of people in the network being murdered was approximately 30 in 1,000, compared to less than 1 in 1,000 for the others in the study neighborhoods. His conclusion was that murder victims are part of a relatively small network of people involved in some form of interpersonal conflict and who live in close proximity to one another.[70]

▶ Males are more often the victims of crime than females; women are more likely than men to be attacked by a relative.

▶ The indigent are much more likely than the affluent to be victims of violent crime; the wealthy are more likely to be targets of personal theft.

▶ Younger, single people are more often targets than older, married people.

▶ Crime victimization tends to be intraracial.

▶ Some people and places are targets and venues of repeat victimization.

L06 Compare and contrast the most important theories of victimization.

Theories of Victimization

For many years, criminological theory focused on the actions of the criminal offender; the role of the victim was virtually ignored. More than 60 years ago, scholars began to realize that the victim was not simply a passive target in crime but someone whose behavior can influence his or her own fate, who "shapes and molds the criminal."[71] These early works helped focus attention on the role of the victim in the crime problem and led to further research efforts that have sharpened the image of the crime victim. Today a number of different theories attempt to explain the causes of victimization.

Victim Precipitation Theory

According to **victim precipitation theory**, some people actually initiate the confrontation that eventually leads to their injury or death. Victim precipitation can be either active or passive.

Active precipitation occurs when victims act provocatively, use threats or fighting words, or even attack first.[72] In 1971, Menachem Amir suggested that female rape victims often contribute to their attack by dressing provocatively or pursuing a relationship with the rapist.[73] Although Amir's findings are considered highly controversial, and there has been a great deal of change in the way rape victims are treated and the laws have been written, rape myths still exist (for example, that women make false reports of rape when they later regret consensual sexual activity). It is still not unusual for courts to exonerate defendants in rape cases unless there is overwhelming proof that the victim did not consent to sexual intimacy.[74]

In contrast, **passive precipitation** occurs when the victim was the first to act in the sequence of interactions that lead up to the criminal event; the victim encouraged the commission of the crime. Victim precipitation is a component in several different types of crime, most notably homicide, assault, rape, and robbery.[75] Passive precipitation may also be triggered when the victim exhibits some personal characteristic that unknowingly either threatens or encourages the attacker, such as their race or ethnicity. Gender

Brent Stirton/Getty Images News/Getty Images

Victim precipitation theory suggests that criminal violence may be encouraged by the active or passive behavior of its target. Consider the famous case of victimization known as the Jena 6 incident. It began when Justin Barker, 18, shown here, was beaten on December 4, 2006, by six black students at Jena High School in Jena, Louisiana. There had been an undercurrent of racial tension in the town, which had led to outbreaks of violence between white and black students. The tension escalated when a black student attempted to sit under a tree where white students congregated. The next day, three nooses were found hanging from the branches of this tree. After the incident, six black students attacked Barker, who was not involved in the incident in any way. At trial, where five of the defendants received probation and were asked to pay restitution, their lawyer read a statement apologizing to the Barker family and to the town. This statement also addressed the rumors that the attack had been provoked by Barker using a racial epithet: "To be clear, not one of us heard Justin use any slur or say anything that justified Mychal Bell attacking Justin, nor did any of us see Justin do anything that would cause Mychal to react." The Barker case is a good example of passive victim precipitation: Justin was victimized because of ongoing racial tension and hostility that were simply not his doing.

may play a role in the decision-making process: criminals may target female victims because they perceive them to be easier, less threatening targets.[76] Thus, it is possible that a fearful or anxious demeanor may make a woman more vulnerable to attack.

Lifestyle Theories

People may become crime victims because their risky lifestyle increases their exposure to criminal offenders.[77] Victimization risk is increased by such behaviors as associating with young men, going out in public places late at night, and living in an urban area. Conversely, one's chances of victimization can be reduced by staying home at night, moving to a rural area, staying out of public places, earning more money, and getting married. The basis of such **lifestyle theories** is that crime is not a random occurrence; rather, it is a function of the victim's lifestyle.

HIGH-RISK LIFESTYLES People who have high-risk lifestyles—drinking, taking drugs, going out at night, being away from home, living on the streets—have a much greater chance of victimization.[78] One reason is that offenders have similar lifestyles, and being in close proximity to dangerous people increases chances of victimization.[79]

Teenage males have an extremely high victimization risk because their lifestyle places them at risk both at school and once they leave the school grounds.[80] They spend a great deal of time hanging out with their friends and pursuing recreational fun.[81] Their friends may give them a false ID so they can drink in the neighborhood bar. They may hang out in taverns at night, which places them at risk because many fights and assaults occur in places that serve liquor. Research conducted in a variety of nations shows boys who have an active nightlife (any time after 6 P.M.), who frequent public places, and who consume alcohol significantly increase their victimization risk.[82]

Exposure to violence and associating with violent peers enmeshes young men in a violent lifestyle that increases their own risk of violent offending. One way for young males to avoid victimization is to limit their male friends and hang out with girls! The greater the number of girls in their peer group, the lower their chances of victimization.[83]

victim precipitation theory
The view that victims may initiate, either actively or passively, the confrontation that leads to their victimization.

active precipitation
Aggressive or provocative behavior of victims that results in their victimization.

passive precipitation
Personal or social characteristics of victims that make them attractive targets for criminals; such victims may unknowingly either threaten or encourage their attackers.

lifestyle theories
Views on how people become crime victims because of lifestyles that increase their exposure to criminal offenders.

Being a gang member is a classic example of having a "high-risk lifestyle." Frank Reyos sits with his defense team during his sentencing in Salt Lake City. Prosecutors said Reyos killed 16-year-old Kenyatta Winston with a single bullet to the back of the head as retribution after Winston abandoned him during a gunfight with gang members the day before. Reyos was found guilty of first-degree murder and sentenced to life in prison without parole.

AP Images/Salt Lake Tribune, Al Hartmann

FACT OR FICTION?

Most crime victims are people who are simply in the wrong place at the wrong time.

FICTION Criminologists believe that victims often engage in behaviors that increase the likelihood of their being targeted for crime. Victims are more likely to engage in risky behavior than nonvictims.

CONNECTIONS

Chapter 10 will discuss the nature and extent of intimate partner violence in greater detail. The NCVS data show that this is far more traumatic than an attack by a stranger. Why do you suppose this is true?

Those who have a history of engaging in serious delinquency, getting involved in gangs, carrying guns, and selling drugs have an increased chance of being shot and killed. Kids who have done time and have a history of family violence are the ones most at risk for becoming homicide victims.[84] Lifestyle risks continue into young adulthood. As adults, those who commit crimes increase their chances of becoming the victims of homicide.[85]

The association between victimization and criminal lifestyle is probably one of risk rather than of propensity: people who are involved simply get close to violent, dangerous people and are therefore exposed to victimization themselves.

COLLEGE LIFESTYLE On January 25, 2016, Florida State University agreed to pay $950,000 to settle a lawsuit filed by a former student, Erica Kinsman, who in 2012 accused former FSU quarterback Jameis Winston of rape. Although the university did not admit to liability in the matter, they did agree to conduct five years of sexual assault awareness programs and to publish annual reports on those programs. Winston himself was never criminally charged in the case, in part because the police investigation was not thorough enough to allow the DA to press charges. The victim received $250,000, her lawyers the rest; Winston is now the quarterback for the Tampa Bay Buccaneers.[86]

Some college students maintain a lifestyle—partying, taking recreational drugs—that makes them vulnerable to victimization. But even those who don't engage in risky activity become crime victims: research shows that the incidence of intimate partner violence is extremely high among college students.[87]

Of particular importance is the disturbing number of sexual assaults that now occur on college campuses. Most victims were acquainted with their attacker.[88] Most student rape and sexual assault victimizations (51 percent) occurred while the victim was pursuing leisure activities away from home. Only about 20 percent of the student victims reported the crime to police. Why did the college victims fail to report a rape or sexual assault victimization to police? Many felt the victimization was not important enough to report: about a quarter of the students who did not report to police believed the incident was a personal matter; one in five stated a fear of reprisal.

It is a sad fact of modern life that victimization can occur anywhere, even while socializing on a college campus with acquaintances and fellow students. Can taking precautions help? Research by Lee Michael Johnson and his colleagues show that for some students precautionary drinking behavior (e.g., limiting alcohol intake, eating before or during drinking, and having friends close by) reduced the odds of victimization, especially for men who frequently drink. Conversely, for both men and women using drugs, having multiple sex partners, and binge drinking increased the chances of becoming a victim.[89]

CRIMINAL LIFESTYLE One element of lifestyle that may place some people at risk for victimization is an ongoing involvement in a criminal career. People who get involved in a criminal lifestyle, join a gang, deal drugs, and so on, are much more likely to be victimized than noncriminals.[90] Recent research conducted by Andrew Papachristos and his associates found gun violence clustered in social networks that groups contained gang members; associating with gang boys elevated the likelihood of being the target of gun violence.[91]

Another reason why the criminal lifestyle promotes victimization is that some criminals make tempting targets. There are groups of criminal offenders who specialize in preying upon other miscreants, such as drug dealers. After all, they have a ready supply of cash and are unlikely to call the cops. One way for dealers and other criminals to avoid victimization: use highly aggressive tactics and be prepared to do violence.[92]

While becoming a criminal may increase chances of victimization, it is also possible that becoming victims themselves may convince some criminals that crime does not pay and they might be better off going straight. Scott Jacques and Richard Wright found that for at least one set of criminal offenders—drug dealers—becoming a crime victim sets the stage for their breaking away from crime. According to these investigators, serious victimizations that drug dealers define as being caused by their own lawbreaking increase the probability of their transitioning out of crime. Terminating their drug dealing is an adaptation that enables them to gain control over their lives and to reduce the probability of future victimization.[93]

On December 2, 2014, Florida State University quarterback Jameis Winston (right) and his attorney David Cornwell arrive for his student conduct code hearing, where he was found not liable of sexual misconduct. In 2016, FSU settled a lawsuit with his accuser, former student Erica Kinsman, who said the school failed to respond when she accused Winston of rape.

Deviant Place Theory

According to **deviant place theory**, the greater their exposure to dangerous places, the more likely people are to become victims of crime and violence.[94] Some communities encourage both crime and victimization. If criminals and victims are one and the same, it's because of where they live and not who they are. Victims are vulnerable because they reside in socially disorganized, high-crime areas where they have the greatest risk of coming into contact with criminal offenders.[95] Neighborhood crime levels may be more significant than individual characteristics or lifestyle for determining the chances of victimization.[96]

So-called deviant places are poor, densely populated, highly transient neighborhoods in which commercial and residential properties exist side by side.[97] The commercial establishments provide criminals with easy targets for theft crimes, such as shoplifting and larceny. Successful people stay out of these stigmatized areas. They are home to "demoralized people" who are easy targets for crime: the homeless, the addicted, the mentally ill, and the elderly poor.[98]

HONOR CODES Deviant places also may house informal "honor codes" that promote victimization. According to the code, people who become crime victims are honor bound to retaliate against their attacker. Failure to do so may damage their reputation and make them vulnerable to future attacks. Honor codes are often bound up in gang cultures, so if violence occurs against one member, there is a significant likelihood that retaliation of some sort will occur.[99] This call to honor helps promote a climate where crime leads to victimization and vice versa.

deviant place theory
The view that victimization is primarily a function of where people live.

In "less deviant" neighborhoods without a street honor culture, there is more of an emphasis on nonviolent methods of conflict resolution, a condition that minimizes the possibility of retaliation. In these communities, victims are less likely to strike back, more likely to repress their anger, and more likely to call the police to satisfy their need for justice. Victims within these settings may find it *unnecessary* to engage in a counterattack against their adversaries because it will have little bearing on their street rep and on their likelihood of future victimization.[100]

Routine Activities Theory

routine activities theory
The view that victimization results from the interaction of three everyday factors: the availability of suitable targets, the absence of capable guardians, and the presence of motivated offenders.

suitable targets
Objects of crime (persons or property) that are attractive and readily available.

capable guardians
Effective deterrents to crime, such as police or watchful neighbors.

motivated offenders
People willing and able to commit crimes.

A series of papers by Lawrence Cohen and Marcus Felson first articulated **routine activities theory**.[101] Cohen and Felson assume that both the motivation to commit crime and the supply of offenders are constant.[102] Every society will always have some people willing to break the law for revenge, greed, or some other motive. Therefore, the volume and distribution of predatory crime (violent crimes against a person and crimes in which an offender attempts to steal an object directly) are closely related to the interaction of three variables that reflect the routine activities of the typical American lifestyle:

- The availability of **suitable targets**, such as homes containing goods that are easily sold.
- The absence of **capable guardians**, such as police, homeowners, neighbors, friends, and relatives.
- The presence of **motivated offenders**, such as a large number of teenagers.

These components increase the likelihood that a predatory crime will take place and increases the likelihood of victimization. Targets are more likely to be victimized if they are poorly guarded and exposed to a large group of motivated offenders, such as teenage boys.[103] Increasing the number of motivated offenders and placing them in close proximity to valuable goods will increase property victimizations. Even after-school programs, which are designed to reduce criminal activity, may produce higher crime rates because they lump together motivated offenders, such as teenage boys, with vulnerable victims, such as teenage boys.[104] Figure 3.1 illustrates the interacting components of routine activities theory.

Lack of capable guardians
- Police officers
- Homeowners
- Security systems

Motivated offenders
- Teenage boys
- People with antisocial personalities
- Addict population

CRIME

Suitable targets
- Costly jewelry
- Expensive cars
- Easily transportable goods

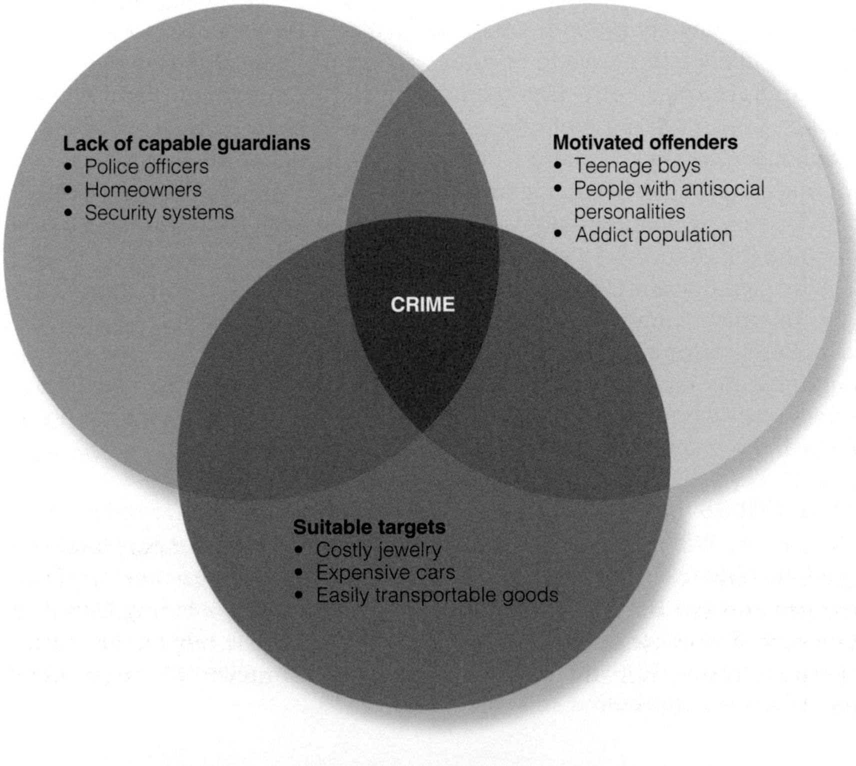

FIGURE 3.1
Routine Activities Theory

CRIME AND EVERYDAY LIFE Routine activities theory helps explain why US citizens suffer such high rates of victimization. According to Felson, crime began to increase in the United States as the country changed from a nation of small villages and towns to one of large urban environments. Because metropolitan areas provide a critical population mass, predatory criminals are better able to hide and evade apprehension. After committing crime, criminals can blend into the crowd, disperse their loot, and make a quick escape using the public transportation system.[105]

As the population became more urban, the middle class, fearing criminal victimization, fled to the suburbs. Rather than being safe from crime, the suburbs produced a unique set of routine activities that promotes victimization risk. Both parents are likely to commute to work, leaving teens unsupervised. Affluent kids own or drive cars, date, and socialize with peers in unsupervised settings—all behaviors that are related to both crime and victimization.[106] The downtown shopping district was replaced by the suburban shopping mall. Here strangers converge in large numbers, and youths hang out. The interior is filled with people, so drug deals can be concealed in the pedestrian flow. Stores have attractively displayed goods, encouraging shoplifting and employee pilferage. Substantial numbers of cars are parked in areas that make larceny and car theft virtually undetectable. Cars that carry away stolen merchandise have an undistinguished appearance: who notices people placing items in a car in a shopping mall parking lot? Also, shoppers can be attacked in parking lots as they walk in isolation to and from their cars. As car ownership increases, teens have greater access to transportation outside parental control. Thus, even though victimization rates in urban areas are still higher, the routine activities in the suburbs may also produce the risk of victimization.

AP Images/Julio Cortez

On December 15, 2013, attorney Dustin Friedland, of Hoboken, was fatally shot in the parking garage of The Mall at Short Hills, New Jersey, as he and his wife returned to their Range Rover. Basim Henry (shown here being escorted by police after an arraignment hearing) and four other suspects—Hanif Thompson, Karif Ford, and Kevin Roberts—were charged with felony murder, carjacking, and conspiracy. All four pleaded not guilty. On March 31, 2017, Henry was found guilty on all charges. His co-conspirators await their own trials.

RESEARCH SUPPORT Research supports many facets of routine activities theory. There is evidence that the convergence of targets, guardians, and motivated offenders can predict area crime rates for crimes such as robbery.[107] Cohen and Felson themselves found that crime rates increased between 1960 and 1980 because the number of adult caretakers at home during the day (guardians) decreased as a result of increased female participation in the workforce. While mothers are at work and children in day care, homes are left unguarded. Similarly, with the growth of suburbia and the decline of the traditional neighborhood, the number of such familiar guardians as family, neighbors, and friends diminished.[108] Steven Messner and his associates found that as adult unemployment rates *increase*, juvenile homicide arrest rates *decrease*. One reason for this phenomenon: it is possible that juvenile arrests decreased because unemployed adults were at home to supervise their children and make sure they did not get into trouble or join gangs.[109] The availability and cost of easily transportable goods have also been shown to influence victimization rates: as the cost of goods such as smartphones and iPads declines, so too will burglary rates.[110]

ROUTINE ACTIVITIES AND LIFESTYLE Routine activities theory and the lifestyle approach have a number of similarities. They both assume that a person's living arrangements can affect victim risk and that people who live in unguarded areas are at the mercy of motivated offenders. These two theories both rely on four basic concepts: (1) proximity to criminals, (2) time of exposure to criminals, (3) target attractiveness, and (4) guardianship.[111]

Concept Summary 3.1   Victimization Theories

Victimization Theory	Major Premise
Victim precipitation	Victims provoke criminals.
Lifestyle	Victims put themselves in danger by engaging in high-risk activities, such as going out late at night, living in a high-crime area, and associating with high-risk peers.
Deviant place	Victimization risk is related to neighborhood crime rates.
Routine activities	A pool of motivated offenders exists, and these offenders will take advantage of unguarded, suitable targets.

CHECKPOINTS

▶ Victim precipitation theory suggests that crime victims may trigger attacks by acting provocatively.

▶ Some experts link victimization to high-risk lifestyles.

▶ Some people live in places that are magnets for criminals.

▶ The routine activities approach suggests that the risk of victimization may be an interaction among suitable targets, effective guardians, and motivated criminals. Victims who have insufficient protection present motivated criminals with attractive targets.

These theories also share five predictions: people increase their victimization risk if they (1) live in high-crime areas, (2) go out late at night, (3) carry valuables such as an expensive watch, (4) engage in risky behavior such as drinking alcohol, and (5) are without friends or family to watch or help them.[112] Young women who drink to excess in bars and fraternity houses may elevate their risk of date rape, because (1) they are easy targets, and (2) their attackers can rationalize raping them because they are intoxicated. ("She's loose and immoral, so I didn't think she'd care.") Intoxication is sometimes seen as making the victim culpable for the crime.[113] Conversely, people can reduce their chances of repeat victimization if they change their lifestyle and adopt crime-suppressing routines such as getting married, having children, or moving to a small town.[114]

The various theories of victimization are summarized in Concept Summary 3.1.

Caring for the Victim

Helping the victim cope is the responsibility of all of society. Law enforcement agencies, courts, and correctional and human service systems have come to realize that due process and human rights exist not only for the criminal defendant but also for the victim of criminal behavior.

Because of public concern over violent personal crime, President Ronald Reagan created a Task Force on Victims of Crime in 1982.[115] This group suggested that a balance be achieved between recognizing the victim's rights and providing the defendant with due process. Recommendations included providing witnesses and victims with protection from intimidation, requiring restitution in criminal cases, developing guidelines for fair treatment of crime victims and witnesses, and expanding programs of victim compensation.[116]

As a result, Congress passed the Omnibus Victim and Witness Protection Act, requiring the use of victim impact statements at sentencing in federal criminal cases, greater protection for witnesses, more stringent bail laws, and the use of restitution in criminal cases. In 1984, the Comprehensive Crime Control Act and the Victims of Crime Act authorized federal funding for state victim compensation and assistance projects.[117] Another important milestone was the Crime Victims' Rights Act of 2004 that extended crime victims the right to participate in the justice system and be informed and consulted on tactics and decisions being employed by the Justice Department "and other departments and agencies of the United States engaged in the detection, investigation, or prosecution of crime." The courts were required under the act to "ensure that the crime victim is afforded the rights given by the law."[118] The most important elements of the CVRA are set out in Exhibit 3.2.

With these acts, the federal government recognized the plight of the victim and made victim assistance an even greater concern of the public and the justice system.

Exhibit 3.2 — The Rights Established Under the Crime Victims' Rights Act of 2004

The Crime Victims' Rights Act of 2004, 18 U.S.C. § 3771, provides that officers and employees of the Department of Justice shall make their best efforts to see that crime victims are notified of, and accorded, the following rights:

- The right to be reasonably protected from the accused
- The right to reasonable, accurate, and timely notice of any public court proceeding, or any parole proceeding, involving the crime or of any release or escape of the accused
- The right not to be excluded from any such public court proceeding, unless the court, after receiving clear and convincing evidence, determines that testimony by the victim would be materially altered if the victim heard other testimony at that proceeding
- The right to be reasonably heard at any public proceeding in the district court involving release, plea, sentencing, or any parole proceeding
- The reasonable right to confer with the attorney for the government in the case
- The right to full and timely restitution as provided by law
- The right to proceedings free from unreasonable delay
- The right to be treated with fairness and with respect for the victim's dignity and privacy

Source: The Justice for All Act of 2004, 18 U.S.C. § 3771, http://www.ojp.usdoj.gov/ovc/publications/factshts/justforall/fs000311.pdf (accessed April 2017).

Victim Service Programs

Thousands of **victim–witness assistance programs** have been developed throughout the United States. These programs are organized on a variety of government levels and serve a variety of clients.

VICTIM COMPENSATION A primary goal of victim advocates has been to lobby for legislation creating crime **victim compensation programs**.[119] As a result of such legislation, the victim ordinarily receives compensation from the state to pay for damages associated with the crime. Rarely are two compensation schemes alike, however, and many state programs suffer from a lack of both adequate funding and proper organization within the criminal justice system. Compensation may be provided for medical bills, loss of wages, loss of future earnings, and counseling. In the case of death, the victim's survivors may receive burial expenses and aid for loss of support.[120] Awards typically range from $100 to $15,000. Occasionally, programs provide emergency assistance to indigent victims until compensation is available. Emergency assistance may come in the form of food vouchers or replacement of prescription medicines.

In 1984, the federal government created the Victims of Crime Act (VOCA), which grants money to state compensation boards derived from fines and penalties imposed on federal offenders. The money is distributed each year to the states to fund both their crime victim compensation programs and their victim assistance programs, such as rape crisis centers and domestic violence shelters. Victims of child abuse and victims of domestic violence receive most of the funds. VOCA money goes to support victims' medical expenses, gives them economic support for lost wages, helps to compensate for the death of loved ones, and provides mental health counseling.[121] To give some idea of how much funding is available, the Consolidated Appropriations Act of 2016, increased the cap on the Crime Victims Fund from $2.361 billion in 2015 to $3.042 billion in 2016. Included in this amount was a transfer of $379 million to the Office on Violence Against Women and $10 million to the Office of the Inspector General for "oversight and auditing purposes." Of the $2.65 billion remaining for programs authorized under the VOCA statute, about $2.26 billion was made available for state VOCA victim assistance grants.[122]

VICTIM ADVOCATES Some programs assign counselors to victims to serve as advocates, help them understand the operations of the justice system, and guide them

victim–witness assistance programs
Government programs that help crime victims and witnesses; may include compensation, court services, and/or crisis intervention.

victim compensation programs
Financial aid awarded to crime victims to repay them for their loss and injuries; may cover medical bills, loss of wages, loss of future earnings, and/or counseling.

through the process. Victims of sexual assault may be assigned the assistance of a rape victim advocate to stand by their side as they negotiate the legal and medical systems that must process their case. Research shows that rape survivors who had the assistance of an advocate were significantly more likely to have police reports taken, were less likely to be treated negatively by police officers, and reported less distress from their medical contact experiences.[123] Police departments are now instituting training designed to prepare officers to work more effectively with victim advocates.[124]

Court advocates prepare victims and witnesses by explaining court procedures: how to be a witness, how bail works, and what to do if the defendant makes a threat. Lack of such knowledge can cause confusion and fear, making some victims reluctant to testify in court proceedings. Many victim programs also provide transportation to and from court, as well as counselors who remain in the courtroom during hearings to explain procedures and provide support. Court escorts are particularly important for elderly and disabled victims, victims of child abuse and assault, and victims who have been intimidated by friends or relatives of the defendant.

In some instances, victim aid is provided to surviving family members. In New Hampshire, all homicides, excluding negligent homicides, are prosecuted out of the Homicide Bureau of the Attorney General's Office, enabling a centralized victim services unit to be involved from the onset of the investigation. The office has victim/witness advocates who are on call 24 hours a day. When a homicide occurs, an advocate responds to the scene and is responsible for notifying the victim's family of the death of their loved one and for providing immediate crisis intervention and support to both family members and witnesses to the crime. From arranging for the cleanup of the homicide scene to informing the family on the results of the autopsy and assisting them with funeral arrangements, the advocate provides each family with extensive support and services at this difficult and extremely painful time.[125]

Don Hatfield reads a victim impact statement and addresses Todd Winkler who, on December 8, 2014, was sentenced to 26 years to life in El Dorado County Superior Court in Placerville, California. At right is prosecutor Lisette Suder. Winkler murdered Hatfield's daughter, Rachel Winkler, in their home during a painful marital breakup. Hatfield condemned Winkler for the "vile act" that will force the couple's three young children to have to ask, "Why did Daddy kill Mommy?"

AP Images/Sacramento Bee, Renee C. Byer

Exhibit 3.3 describes programs designed to help women who are victims of intimate partner violence.

VICTIM IMPACT STATEMENTS Every state jurisdiction allows victims to make an impact statement before the sentencing judge. Victim impact information is part of the Federal Crime Act of 1994, in which Congress gave federal victims of violent crime or sexual assault the right to speak at sentencing. Through the Child Protection Act of 1990, child victims of federal crimes are allowed to submit victim impact statements that are "commensurate with their age and cognitive development," which can include drawings, models, etc.[126] This gives the victim an opportunity to tell of his or her experiences and describe the ordeal; in the case of a murder trial, the surviving family can recount the effect the crime has had on their lives and well-being.[127]

Those who favor the use of impact statements argue that because the victim is harmed by the crime, she or he has a right to influence the outcome of the case. After all, the public prosecutor is allowed to make sentencing recommendations because the public has been harmed by the crime. Logically, the harm suffered by the victim legitimizes her or his right to make sentencing recommendations.[128]

The effect of victim impact statements on sentencing has been the topic of some debate. Some research finds that victim statements result in a higher rate of incarceration.[129] There is also evidence that impact statements

Exhibit 3.3　Advocacy for the Victims of Intimate Partner Violence

Intimate partner violence involves the abuse of a woman by a male or female partner with whom she currently is, or formerly was, in an intimate relationship. Advocacy interventions for women who have experienced intimate partner violence aim to empower women and link them to helpful services in the community. The goals of advocacy interventions include helping abused women to access necessary services, reducing or preventing incidents of abuse, and improving women's physical and psychological health.

Advocacy interventions are targeted at abused women who are still with their partners or who have left the abusive relationship. Although the interventions target women, services and support for any children involved in the abusive relationship may also be provided. They may be primary, secondary, or tertiary. Primary interventions focus on preventing the onset of abuse. Secondary interventions focus on preventing further abuse, and tertiary interventions focus on dealing with the consequences of abuse once the abuse has ceased.

The core activities of advocacy interventions varies from program to program and can include:

- Providing legal, housing, and financial advice
- Facilitating access to and use of community resources such as shelters, emergency housing, and psychological interventions
- Providing safety planning advice

In addition, advocates may also provide ongoing support and informal counseling. The amount of time that advocacy is provided for abused women will vary, depending upon the specific needs of each woman. Short-term, or crisis, advocacy usually involves the advocate working with the woman for a short period of time (though she may be referred for additional services with a specialized agency). The duration of short-term advocacy interventions can range from 1 hour to about 12 hours, whereas long-term advocacy interventions, such as counseling services, can last as long as 12 months, if necessary. Advocacy interventions can take place within health care settings such as hospitals but may also take place in other settings, such as shelters.

Advocacy interventions are based on the concept of empowerment. This includes talking with the abused woman about potential solutions (rather than being prescriptive and telling her what to do); helping her achieve goals she has set (rather than setting the goals for her); and helping her understand and make sense of the situation and how she responds. Advocates who work with abused women to identify their needs and connect them to resources in the community can include trained paraprofessionals, therapists, counselors, and social workers.

While evaluations of these programs are preliminary, they suggest that women who received advocacy interventions experienced significantly less physical abuse, compared with women in the control groups—a positive trend that substantiates the utility of advocacy.

Source: National Institute of Justice, "Advocacy Interventions for Women Who Experience Intimate Partner Violence," https://www.crimesolutions.gov/PracticeDetails.aspx?ID=55 (accessed April 2017).

are significant in deciding between community and incarceration sentences.[130] Yet, not all research efforts support the value of such statements.[131]

PUBLIC EDUCATION More than half of all victim programs include public education to help familiarize the general public with their services and with other agencies that help crime victims. In some instances, these are primary prevention programs, which teach methods of dealing with conflict without resorting to violence. School-based programs present information on spousal and dating abuse, followed by discussions of how to reduce violent incidents.[132]

CRISIS INTERVENTION Most victim programs refer victims to specific services to help them recover from their ordeal. Clients are commonly referred to the local network of public and private social service agencies that provide emergency and long-term assistance with transportation, medical care, shelter, food, and clothing. In addition, more than half of all victim programs provide **crisis intervention** for victims who feel isolated, vulnerable, and in need of immediate services. Some programs counsel at their offices; others visit victims in their homes, at the crime scene, or in the hospital. The Good Samaritan program in Mobile County, Alabama, unites

crisis intervention
Emergency counseling for crime victims.

law enforcement with faith-based and community organizations to train and mobilize volunteers who can help crime victims. Good Samaritan volunteers provide services such as:

- Making repairs to a home after a break-in
- Conducting home safety inspections to prevent revictimization
- Accompanying victims to court
- Supplying "victim care kits" or other support[133]

VICTIM–OFFENDER RECONCILIATION PROGRAMS Mediators facilitate face-to-face encounters between victims and their attackers in **victim–offender reconciliation programs (VORPs)**. The aim is to engage in direct negotiations that lead to restitution agreements and, possibly, reconciliation between the parties involved.[134] Originally designed to handle routine misdemeanors such as petty theft and vandalism, such programs now commonly hammer out restitution agreements in more serious incidents, such as residential burglary and even attempted murder.

VICTIM NOTIFICATION There have been a number of efforts to notify victims (or potential victims) of offenders' locations. Every state has sex offender registration to keep potential victims aware of the location of convicted sex offenders in their community. In addition, most states have adopted the VINE (Victim Information and Notification Everyday) service through which victims of crime can use the telephone or Internet to search for information regarding their offender's custody status and register to receive telephone and email notification when their offender's status changes. The federal system has its own program, the Department of Justice's Victim Notification System (VNS). This is a cooperative effort among the Federal Bureau of Investigation, the US Postal Inspection Service, the US Attorney's Offices, the Federal Bureau of Prisons, and the Criminal Division. This computer-based system provides federal crime victims with information on scheduled court events, as well as the outcome of those court events. It also provides victims with information on the offender's custody status and release.[135]

LEGAL PROTECTION FOR VICTIMS Another way that victims have been served is the more rigorous enforcement of laws designed specially to protect certain classes of victims. For many years victim advocates complained that states did not offer adequate protection for victims of domestic violence, sometimes treating these crimes as a "private matter." Due to the impact of victim advocacy, state courts are now more likely to issue orders of protection, which require accused abusers to immediately stop stalking or harassing a victim and to stay away from the victim's home.

Typically, there are two types of these protective orders. The first, an *ex parte* order, is a temporary measure quickly issued by the court that grants immediate relief while an investigation can be conducted. For example, Massachusetts General Laws (M.G.L.) Chapter 209A Section 1 defines the conditions under which a restraining order may be issued:

> The occurrence of one or more of the following acts between family or household members:
>
> **1.** attempting to cause or causing physical harm;
> **2.** placing another in fear of imminent serious physical harm;
> **3.** causing another to engage involuntarily in sexual relations by force, threat or duress

Note that the order may be issued when the complaining party is put in fear—no actual abuse needs to have occurred. The accused abuser does not have to be present at the hearing.

When the court issues an *ex parte* order, it sets up another hearing with notice to the defendant; this is usually called a "return" day. If evidence is presented before the court that authenticates the original complaint, a full order may be issued. This is in effect for a longer period than the *ex parte* order and may become permanent.

---

victim–offender reconciliation programs (VORPs)
Mediated face-to-face encounters between victims and their attackers, designed to produce restitution agreements and, if possible, reconciliation.

CONNECTIONS

Chapter 1 has a feature on the effectiveness of offender registration systems. As you may recall, they do not seem to work as intended. Considering their ineffectiveness, would you advocate their elimination in order to save the taxpayers money?

Have these legal changes helped protect domestic violence victims? While it is always difficult to show a direct causal relationship between legal change and criminal behavior, there has in fact been a significant decline in domestic violence cases during the past decade.[136] While providing legal redress may be responsible in part for the significant decade-long decline in domestic violence cases, it is also likely that victim advocacy programs and the availability of such services as emergency shelters and transitional housing also play a role. While these trends are encouraging, about 1 million people are still victims of intimate partner attacks each year.

Victims' Rights

Because of the influence of victims' rights advocates, every state now has a set of legal rights for crime victims in its code of laws, often called a Victims' Bill of Rights.[137] These generally include the right

- To be notified of proceedings and the status of the defendant
- To be present at criminal justice proceedings
- To make a statement at sentencing and to receive restitution from a convicted offender
- To be consulted before a case is dismissed or a plea agreement entered
- To a speedy trial
- To keep the victim's contact information confidential

A controversial element of the victims' rights movement is the development of offender registration laws that require law enforcement agencies to post the name, and sometimes the address, of known sex offenders. Every state has adopted sex offender laws, and the federal government runs a National Sex Offender Public Registry with links to every state.[138] However, there is little evidence that registration laws are effective.

Victim Advocates

Ensuring victims' rights may involve an eclectic mix of advocacy groups—some independent, others government-sponsored, and some self-help. Advocates can be especially helpful when victims need to interact with the agencies of justice. Advocates can lobby police departments to keep investigations open and can request the return of recovered stolen property. They can demand that prosecutors and judges provide protection from harassment and reprisals by making "no contact" a condition of bail (research shows that victims who hire lawyers have a better chance of getting these orders enforced).[139] They can help victims make statements during sentencing hearings and during probation and parole revocation procedures. Victim advocates can also interact with news media, making sure that reporting is accurate and that victims' privacy is not violated. Victim advocates can be part of an independent agency similar to a legal aid society. Top-notch victim advocates sometimes open private offices, similar to attorneys, private investigators, or jury consultants.

Self-Protection

Not all actual or potential victims are content with relying on victim services to provide after-the-fact comfort. Concerns about community safety have prompted some people to become their own "police force," taking an active role in community protection through creation of citizen watch and crime control groups.[140] The more crime in an area, the greater the amount of fear and the more likely residents will be to engage in self-protective measures.[141]

Another method of self-protection involves target hardening, or making one's home and business crime-proof through locks, bars, alarms, and other devices.[142] Some commonly used crime prevention techniques include a fence or barricade at the entrance; a doorkeeper, guard, or receptionist in an apartment building; an intercom or phone to gain access to the building; surveillance cameras; window bars;

Does fighting back help? Jennifer Hilchey-Reyell believes so. She is shown here carrying a .22 rifle at her mother's house near Dannemora, New York. Hilchey-Reyell has been keeping a gun close at hand since the escape of two prisoners from the maximum-security Clinton Correctional Facility near her home. David Sweat, one of the two convicted killers, was captured after being shot during a firefight with law enforcement officers; the other escapee, Richard Matt, was killed in a shootout.

warning signs; and dogs chosen for their ability to guard the house. The use of these measures is inversely proportional to perception of neighborhood safety: people who fear crime are more likely to use crime prevention techniques. Although the true relationship is still unclear, there is mounting evidence that people who protect their homes are less likely to be victimized by property crimes.[143]

FIGHTING BACK Some people take self-protection to its ultimate end by fighting back when attacked. How successful are victims when they resist? The research is decidedly mixed. Some find that victims who fight back frustrate their attackers and prevent the crime from being completed; others find that forcefully resisting increases both the chance of the crime being completed and the likelihood of personal injury.[144]

What about the use of firearms for self-protection? Each year, millions of victims use guns for defensive purposes (a number that is not surprising considering that about one-third of US households contain guns).[145] Gary Kleck has estimated that armed victims kill more attackers than police and the risk of collateral injury is relatively rare. In one study, conducted with colleague Jongyeon Tark, Kleck reviewed more than 27,000 contact-crime incidents and found that self-protection significantly reduced the likelihood of loss and injury and that the most forceful tactics, including resistance with a gun, appear to have the strongest effects in reducing the risk of injury. Importantly, the Kleck research indicated that resistance did not contribute to injury in any meaningful way. Kleck's conclusion: it is better to fight than flee.[146]

Thinking Like a Criminologist

Spare the Rod, Eliminate the Needle

The director of your state's Department of Human Services has asked you to evaluate a self-report survey of adolescents aged 12 to 18. She has provided you with the following information on physical abuse.

Adolescents experiencing abuse or violence are at high risk of immediate and lasting negative effects on their health and well-being. Of the middle school students surveyed, an alarming 1 in 5 (21 percent) said they had been physically abused. Of the older students, aged 15 to 18, 29 percent said they had been physically abused. Younger students, ages 10 and 11, also reported significant rates of abuse: 17 percent responded "yes" when asked whether they had been physically abused. Although girls were far less likely to report abuse than boys, 12 percent said they had been physically abused. Most abuse occurs at home, it occurs more than once, and the abuser is usually a family member. More than half of those physically abused had tried alcohol and drugs, and 60 percent had admitted to committing a violent act. Nonabused children were significantly less likely to abuse substances, and only 30 percent indicated that they had committed a violent act.

Writing Assignment

Write an essay describing why being abused as a child leads to substance abuse and violence as an adult. In your essay, interpret these findings from environmental, socialization, psychological, and biological points of view, and provide evidence supporting each perspective.

SUMMARY

LO1 **Analyze the victim's role in the crime process.**

Victims may influence criminal behavior by playing an active role in a criminal incident. Rather than being merely at the wrong place at the wrong time, a victim's lifestyle and activities may increase their risk of being crime targets. In some instances, victims may actually trigger or precipitate an aggressive act. The discovery that victims play an important role in the crime process has prompted the scientific study of victims, or victimology. Criminologists who focus their attention on crime victims refer to themselves as victimologists.

LO2 **Discuss the greatest problems faced by crime victims.**

The costs of victimization can include such things as damaged property, pain and suffering to victims, and the involvement of the police and other agencies of the justice system. The pain and suffering inflicted on an individual can result in the need for long-term medical care and counseling, the loss of wages from not being able to go to work, and reduced quality of life from debilitating injuries and/or fear of being victimized again.

LO3 **Clarify the term *cycle of violence*.**

People who were abused as children may be more likely to commit crimes themselves. Adult victims may seek revenge against their attackers. The abuse–crime phenomenon is referred to as the cycle of violence.

LO4 **Assess the ecology of victimization risk.**

Violent crimes are slightly more likely to take place in an open, public area, such as a street, a park, or a field. The more serious violent crimes, such as rape and aggravated assault, typically take place after 6 P.M. Those living in the central city have significantly higher rates of theft and violence than suburbanites; people living in rural areas have a victimization rate almost half that of city dwellers. Schools are the site of a great deal of victimization because they are populated by one of the most dangerous segments of society, teenage males.

LO5 **Categorize the most dominant victim characteristics.**

Except for the crimes of rape and sexual assault, males are more likely than females to be the victims of violent crime. Victim data reveal that young people face a much greater victimization risk than older persons. The poorest Americans are the most likely to be victims of violent and property crime. This association occurs across all gender, age, and racial groups. African Americans are about twice as likely as European Americans to be victims of violent crime. Never-married males and females are victimized more often than married people.

LO6 **Compare and contrast the most important theories of victimization.**

According to victim precipitation theory, some people may actually initiate the confrontation that eventually leads to their injury or death. Victim precipitation can be either active or passive. Some criminologists believe that people may become crime victims because their lifestyle increases their exposure to criminal offenders. People who have high-risk lifestyles—drinking, taking drugs, getting involved in crime—have a much greater chance of victimization. According to deviant place theory, the greater their exposure to dangerous places, the more likely people are to become victims of crime and violence. So-called deviant places are poor, densely populated, highly transient neighborhoods in which commercial and residential properties exist side by side. Routine activities theory links victimization to the availability of suitable targets, the absence of capable guardians, and the presence of motivated offenders.

Key Terms

victimology 66

victimologists 66

posttraumatic stress
    disorder (PTSD) 68

obsessive-compulsive
    disorder 68

cycle of violence 71

victim precipitation
    theory 78

active precipitation 78

passive precipitation 78

lifestyle theories 79

deviant place
    theory 81

routine activities
    theory 82

suitable targets 82

capable guardians 82

motivated offenders 82

victim–witness assistance
    programs 85

victim compensation
    programs 85

crisis intervention 87

victim–offender
    reconciliation
    programs
    (VORPs) 88

Critical Thinking Questions

1. Considering what you have learned in this chapter about crime victimization, what measures can you take to better protect yourself from crime?

2. Do you agree with the assessment that a school is one of the most dangerous locations in the community? Did you find your high school to be a dangerous environment?

3. Do people bear some of the responsibility for their victimization if they maintain a lifestyle that contributes to the chances of becoming a crime victim? That is, should we ever "blame the victim"?

4. Have you ever observed someone habitually "precipitating" crime? If so, did you do anything to improve the situation?

5. What would you advise freshman women to do to lower their risk of being sexually assaulted?

Notes

All URLs accessed in 2017.

1. Jess Bidgood, "Owen Labrie of St. Paul's School Not Guilty of Main Rape Charge," *New York Times*, August 28, 2015, http://www.nytimes.com /2015/08/29/us/st-pauls-school-rape-trial-owen -labrie.html; Andy Rosen and Peter Schworm, "Labrie Acquitted of Felony Rape in St. Paul's School Trial," *Boston Globe*, August 28, 2015.

2. Hans Von Hentig, *The Criminal and His Victim: Studies in the Sociobiology of Crime* (New Haven, CT: Yale University Press, 1948); Stephen Schafer, *The Victim and His Criminal* (New York: Random House, 1968).

3. Kathryn McCollister, Michael T. French, and Hai Fang, "The Cost of Crime to Society: New Crime-Specific Estimates for Policy and Program Evaluation," *Drug and Alcohol Dependence* 108 (2010): 98–109.

4. Michael Tonry, "The Fog Around Cost-of-Crime Studies May Finally Be Clearing, Prisoners and Their Kids Suffer Too," *Criminology and Public Policy* 14 (2015): 653–671.

5. Joseph Murray and David Farrington, "Parental Imprisonment: Effects on Boys' Antisocial Behaviour and Delinquency Through the Life-Course," *Journal of Child Psychology and Psychiatry* 46 (2005): 1269–1278.

6. Lynn Langton and Jennifer Truman, *Socio-Emotional Impact of Violent Crime*, Bureau of Justice Statistics, 2014, http://www.bjs.gov/content/pub/pdf/sivc.pdf.

7. Rebecca Loya, "Rape as an Economic Crime: The Impact of Sexual Violence on Survivors' Employment and Economic Well-being," *Journal of Interpersonal Violence* 30 (2015): 2793–2813.

8. Sheree Curry "Fate of a Murder House," AOL Real Estate, February 11, 2010, http://realestate.aol.com /blog/2010/02/11/fate-of-a-murder-house/.

9. Angela Scarpa, Sara Chiara Haden, and Jimmy Hurley, "Community Violence Victimization and Symptoms of Posttraumatic Stress Disorder: The Moderating Effects of Coping and Social Support," *Journal of Interpersonal Violence* 21 (2006): 446–469.

10. Heather Littleton and Craig Henderson, "If She Is Not a Victim, Does That Mean She Was Not Traumatized? Evaluation of Predictors of PTSD Symptomatology Among College Rape Victims," *Violence Against Women* 15 (2009): 148–167.

11. Noora Llonen, Minna Piispa, Kirsi Peltonen, and Mikko Oranen, "Exposure to Parental Violence and Outcomes of Child Psychosocial Adjustment," *Violence and Victims* 28 (2013): 3–15; N. N. Sarkar and Rina Sarkar, "Sexual Assault on Woman: Its Impact on Her Life and Living in Society," *Sexual and Relationship Therapy* 20 (2005): 407.

12. Jeanne Kaufman and Cathy Spatz Widom, "Childhood Victimization, Running Away, and Delinquency," *Journal of Research in Crime and Delinquency* 36 (1999): 347–370.

13. David Finkelhor, *Childhood Victimization: Violence, Crime, and Abuse in the Lives of Young People* (London: Oxford University Press, 2008).

14. Leana Bouffard and Maria Koeppel, "Understanding the Potential Long-Term Physical and Mental Health Consequences of Early Experiences of Victimization," *Justice Quarterly* 31 (2014): 568–587.

15. Danielle Kuhl, David Warner, and Tara Warner, "Intimate Partner Violence Risk Among Victims of Youth Violence: Are Early Unions Bad, Beneficial, or Benign?" *Criminology* 53 (2015): 427–456.

16. Gregory Stuart, Todd M. Moore, Kristina Coop Gordon, Susan Ramsey, and Christopher Kahler, "Psychopathology in Women Arrested for Domestic Violence," *Journal of Interpersonal Violence* 21 (2006): 376–389; Caron Zlotnick, Dawn Johnson, and Robert Kohn, "Intimate Partner Violence and Long-Term Psychosocial Functioning in a National Sample of American Women," *Journal of Interpersonal Violence* 21 (2006): 262–275.

17. K. Daniel O'Leary, "Psychological Abuse: A Variable Deserving Critical Attention in Domestic Violence," *Violence and Victims* 14 (1999): 1–21.

18. Jihong Solomon Zhao, Brian Lawton, and Dennis Longmire, "An Examination of the Micro-Level Crime–Fear of Crime Link," *Crime and Delinquency* 61 (2015): 19–44.

19. Ron Acierno, Alyssa Rheingold, Heidi Resnick, and Dean Kilpatrick, "Predictors of Fear of Crime in Older Adults," *Journal of Anxiety Disorders* 18 (2004): 385–396.

20. Ibid.

21. Karen A. Snedker, "Neighborhood Conditions and Fear of Crime: A Reconsideration of Sex Differences," *Crime and Delinquency* 61 (2015): 45–70.

22. Susan Brison, *Aftermath: Violence and the Remaking of a Self* (Princeton, NJ: Princeton University Press, 2001).

23. Min Xie and David McDowall, "Impact of Victimization on Residential Mobility: Explaining Racial and Ethnic Patterns Using the National Crime Victimization Survey," *Criminology* 52 (2014): 553–587.

24. Fawn T. Ngo and Raymond Paternoster, "Toward an Understanding of the Emotional and Behavioral Reactions to Stalking: A Partial Test of General Strain Theory," *Crime and Delinquency*, first published online November 7, 2013.

25. Min Xie and David McDowall, "Escaping Crime: The Effects of Direct and Indirect Victimization on Moving," *Criminology* 46 (2008): 809–840.

26. Mirka Smolej and Janne Kivivuori, "The Relation Between Crime News and Fear of Violence," *Journal of Scandinavian Studies in Criminology and Crime Prevention* 7 (2006): 211–227.

27. Matthew Lee and Erica DeHart, "The Influence of a Serial Killer on Changes in Fear of Crime and the Use of Protective Measures: A Survey-Based Case Study of Baton Rouge," *Deviant Behavior* 28 (2007): 1–28.

28. Tyler Frederick, Bill McCarthy, and John Hagan, "Perceived Danger and Offending: Exploring the Links Between Violent Victimization and Street Crime," *Violence and Victims* 28 (2013): 16–35.

29. Amy Rose Grubb and Julie Harrower, "Understanding Attribution of Blame in Cases of Rape: An Analysis of Participant Gender, Type of Rape and Perceived Similarity to the Victim," *Journal of Sexual Aggression* 15 (2009): 63–81.

30. Rebecca Campbell and Sheela Raja, "Secondary Victimization of Rape Victims: Insights from Mental Health Professionals Who Treat Survivors of Violence," *Violence and Victims* 14 (1999): 261–274.

31. Courtney Ahrens, "Being Silenced: The Impact of Negative Social Reactions on the Disclosure of Rape," *American Journal of Community Psychology* 38 (2006): 263–274.

32. Timothy Ireland and Cathy Spatz Widom, *Childhood Victimization and Risk for Alcohol and Drug Arrests* (Washington, DC: National Institute of Justice, 1995).

33. Brigette Erwin, Elana Newman, Robert McCracken, Carlo Morrissey, and Danny Kaloupek, "PTSD, Malevolent Environment, and Criminality Among Criminally Involved Male Adolescents," *Criminal Justice and Behavior* 27 (2000): 196–215.

34. Min Jung Kim, Emiko Tajima, Todd Herrenkohl, and Bu Huang, "Early Child Maltreatment, Runaway Youths, and Risk of Delinquency and Victimization in Adolescence: A Mediational Model," *Social Work Research* 33 (2009): 19–28.

35. Ulrich Orth, Leo Montada, and Andreas Maercker, "Feelings of Revenge, Retaliation Motive, and Posttraumatic Stress Reactions in Crime Victims," *Journal of Interpersonal Violence* 21 (2006): 229–243.

36. Cathy Spatz Widom, *The Cycle of Violence* (Washington, DC: National Institute of Justice, 1992), p. 1.

37. Amy Reckdenwald, Christina Mancini, and Eric Beauregard, "The Cycle of Violence: Examining

the Impact of Maltreatment Early in Life on Adult Offending," *Violence and Victims* 28 (2013): 466–482; Marie Skubak Tillyer and Emily M. Wright, "Intimate Partner Violence and the Victim-Offender Overlap," *Journal of Research in Crime and Delinquency*, first published online April 29, 2013.

38. Chris Melde, Finn-Aage Esbensen, and Terrance Taylor, "'May Piece Be with You': A Typological Examination of the Fear and Victimization Hypothesis of Adolescent Weapon Carrying," *Justice Quarterly* 26 (2009): 348–376.

39. Jennifer L. Truman and Rachel E. Morgan, *Criminal Victimization*, 2015 (Washington, DC: Bureau of Justice Statistics, 2016), https://www.bjs.gov /content/pub/pdf/cv15.pdf.

40. Arthur Lurigio, "Are All Victims Alike? The Adverse, Generalized, and Differential Impact of Crime," *Crime and Delinquency* 33 (1987): 452–467.

41. Janet Lauritsen and Nicole White, "Seasonal Patterns in Criminal Victimization Trends," Bureau of Justice Statistics, 2014, http://www.bjs.gov /content/pub/pdf/spcvt.pdf.

42. Corina Graif and Stephen Matthews, "The Long Arm of Poverty: Extended and Relational Geographies of Child Victimization and Neighborhood Violence Exposures," *Justice Quarterly*, published online January 25, 2017.

43. Chris Gibson, Zara Morris, and Kevin Beaver, "Secondary Exposure to Violence During Childhood and Adolescence: Does Neighborhood Context Matter?" *Justice Quarterly* 26 (2009): 30–57.

44. Anlan Zhang, Lauren Musu-Gillette, and Barbara Oudekerk, *Indicators of School Crime and Safety: 2015*, National Center for Education Statistics, US Department of Education, and Bureau of Justice Statistics, Office of Justice Programs, US Department of Justice, 2016, https://www.bjs.gov/content/pub /pdf/iscs15.pdf.

45. Pamela Wilcox, Marie Skubak Tillyer, and Bonnie S. Fisher, "Gendered Opportunity? School-Based Adolescent Victimization," *Journal of Research in Crime and Delinquency* 46 (2009): 245–269.

46. Kristin Carbone-Lopez and Janet Lauritsen, "Seasonal Variation in Violent Victimization: Opportunity and the Annual Rhythm of the School Calendar," *Journal of Quantitative Criminology* 29 (2013): 399–422.

47. US Census Bureau, *America's Families and Living Arrangements: 2016*, https://www.census.gov/hhes /families/data/cps2016.html.

48. Nicole White and Janet L. Lauritsen, *Violent Crime Against Youth from 1994 to 2010*, Bureau of Justice Statistics, 2012, http://bjs.ojp.usdoj.gov/content /pub/pdf/vcay9410.pdf.

49. Victoria Titterington, "A Retrospective Investigation of Gender Inequality and Female Homicide Victimization," *Sociological Spectrum* 26 (2006): 205–231.

50. Sherry Hamby, David Finkelhor, and Heather Turner, "Perpetrator and Victim Gender Patterns for 21 Forms of Youth Victimization in the National Survey of Children's Exposure to Violence," *Violence and Victims* 28 (2013): 915–939.

51. David Finkelhor, Heather Turner, and Richard Ormrod, "Kid's Stuff: The Nature and Impact of Peer and Sibling Violence on Younger and Older Children," *Child Abuse and Neglect* 30 (2006): 1401–1421.

52. Lamar Jordan, "Law Enforcement and the Elderly: A Concern for the 21st Century," *FBI Law Enforcement Bulletin* 71 (2002): 20–24.

53. Tracy Dietz and James Wright, "Age and Gender Differences and Predictors of Victimization of the Older Homeless," *Journal of Elder Abuse and Neglect* 17 (2005): 37–59.

54. David C. Pyrooz, Richard K. Moule, Jr., and Scott H. Decker, "The Contribution of Gang Membership to the Victim–Offender Overlap," *Journal of Research in Crime and Delinquency* 51 (2014): 315–348.

55. Violence Policy Center, "Black Homicide Victimization in the United States," March 2017, http://www.vpc.org/studies/blackhomicide17.pdf.

56. Mark T. Berg, "Accounting for Racial Disparities in the Nature of Violent Victimization," *Journal of Quantitative Criminology* 30 (2014): 629–650.

57. CBS News, Crimesider, "Utah Pediatrician Sentenced in Ex-wife's Death,' July 8, 2015, http://www.cbsnews.com/news/utah-pediatrician -sentenced-in-ex-wifes-death/.

58. Danielle Kuhl, David Warner, and Andrew Wilczak, "Adolescent Violent Victimization and Precocious Union Formation," *Criminology* 50 (2012): 1089–1127.

59. M. Kunst and J. Van Wilsem, "Trait Impulsivity and Change in Mental Health Problems After Violent Crime Victimization: A Prospective Analysis of the Dutch Longitudinal Internet Studies for the Social Sciences Database," *Journal of Interpersonal Violence* 28 (2013): 1642–1656.

60. Bureau of Justice Statistics, "Crime Against Persons with Disabilities, 2009–2013," May 2015, http:// www.bjs.gov/content/pub/pdf/capd0913st_sum.pdf.

61. Daniel Birks, Michael Townsley, and Anna Stewart, "Emergent Regularities of Interpersonal Victimization: An Agent-Based Investigation," *Journal of Research in Crime and Delinquency* 51 (2014): 119–140.

62. Marie Skubak Tillyer, Brooke Miller Gialopsos, and Pamela Wilcox, "The Short-Term Repeat Sexual

Victimization of Adolescents in School," *Crime and Delinquency*, first published online September 9, 2013.

63. Denise Osborn, Dan Ellingworth, Tim Hope, and Alan Trickett, "Are Repeatedly Victimized Households Different?" *Journal of Quantitative Criminology* 12 (1996): 223–245.

64. Marre Lammers, Barbara Menting, Stijn Ruiter, and Wim Bernasco, "Biting Once, Twice: The Influence of Prior on Subsequent Crime Location Choice," *Criminology* 53 (2015): 309–329.

65. Graham Farrell, "Predicting and Preventing Revictimization," in *Crime and Justice: An Annual Review of Research*, ed. Michael Tonry and David Farrington, vol. 20 (Chicago: University of Chicago Press, 1995), pp. 61–126.

66. Ibid., p. 61.

67. David Finkelhor and Nancy Asigian, "Risk Factors for Youth Victimization: Beyond a Lifestyles/Routine Activities Theory Approach," *Violence and Victimization* 11 (1996): 3–19.

68. Graham C. Ousey, Pamela Wilcox, and Bonnie S. Fisher, "Something Old, Something New: Revisiting Competing Hypotheses of the Victimization–Offending Relationship Among Adolescents," *Journal of Quantitative Criminology*, published online July 2010.

69. Graham Farrell, Coretta Phillips, and Ken Pease, "Like Taking Candy: Why Does Repeat Victimization Occur?" *British Journal of Criminology* 35 (1995): 384–399.

70. Andrew Papachristos, "The Coming of a Networked Criminology?" *Advances in Criminological Theory* 17 (2011): 101–140.

71. Von Hentig, *The Criminal and His Victim*, p. 384.

72. Marvin Wolfgang, *Patterns of Criminal Homicide* (Philadelphia: University of Pennsylvania Press, 1958).

73. Menachem Amir, *Patterns in Forcible Rape* (Chicago: University of Chicago Press, 1971).

74. Rose Corrigan, *Up Against a Wall: Rape Reform and the Failure of Success* (New York: New York University Press, 2013); Sokratis Dinos, Nina Burrowes, Karen Hammond, and Christina Cunliffe, "A Systematic Review of Juries' Assessment of Rape Victims: Do Rape Myths Impact on Juror Decision-Making?" *International Journal of Law, Crime and Justice* 43 (2015): 36–49.

75. Molly Smith and Leana Bouffard, "Victim Precipitation," in *The Encyclopedia of Criminology and Criminal Justice*, ed. Jay S. Albanese (London: Blackwell, 2014).

76. Wilcox, Tillyer, and Fisher, "Gendered Opportunity? School-Based Adolescent Victimization."

77. Jillian Turanovic, Michael Reisig, and Travis Pratt, "Risky Lifestyles, Low Self-control, and Violent Victimization Across Gendered Pathways to Crime," *Journal of Quantitative Criminology* 31 (2015): 183–206.

78. Margit Averdijk and Wim Bernasco, "Testing the Situational Explanation of Victimization Among Adolescents," *Journal of Research in Crime and Delinquency*, first published September 24, 2014; Lening Zhang, John W. Welte, and William F. Wieczorek, "Deviant Lifestyle and Crime Victimization," *Journal of Criminal Justice* 29 (2001): 133–143.

79. Joel Miller, "Individual Offending, Routine Activities, and Activity Settings: Revisiting the Routine Activity Theory of General Deviance," *Journal of Research in Crime and Delinquency*, first published online April 2, 2012.

80. See, generally, Gary Gottfredson and Denise Gottfredson, *Victimization in Schools* (New York: Plenum Press, 1985).

81. Gary Jensen and David Brownfield, "Gender, Lifestyles, and Victimization: Beyond Routine Activity Theory," *Violence and Victims* 1 (1986): 85–99.

82. Richard B. Felson, Jukka Savolainen, Mark T. Berg, and Noora Ellonen, "Does Spending Time in Public Settings Contribute to the Adolescent Risk of Violent Victimization?" *Journal of Quantitative Criminology*, first published online July 11, 2012.

83. Dana Haynie and Alex Piquero, "Pubertal Development and Physical Victimization in Adolescence," *Journal of Research in Crime and Delinquency* 43 (2006): 3–35.

84. Michael Ezell and Emily Tanner-Smith, "Examining the Role of Lifestyle and Criminal History Variables on the Risk of Homicide Victimization," *Homicide Studies* 13 (2009): 144–173; Rolf Loeber, Mary DeLamatre, George Tita, Jacqueline Cohen, Magda Stouthamer-Loeber, and David Farrington, "Gun Injury and Mortality: The Delinquent Backgrounds of Juvenile Offenders," *Violence and Victim* 14 (1999): 339–351.

85. Adam Dobrin, "The Risk of Offending on Homicide Victimization: A Case Control Study," *Journal of Research in Crime and Delinquency* 38 (2001): 154–173.

86. Marc Tracy, "Florida State Settles Suit Over Jameis Winston Rape Inquiry," *New York Times*, January 25, 2016, https://www.nytimes.com/2016/01/26/sports/football/florida-state-to-pay-jameis-winstons-accuser-950000-in-settlement.html.

87. Tara Richards, Elizabeth Tomsich, Angela Gover, and Wesley Jennings, "The Cycle of Violence Revisited: Distinguishing Intimate Partner Violence Offenders Only, Victims Only, and Victim-Offenders," *Violence and Victims* 31 (2016): 573–590.

88. Sofi Sinozich and Lynn Langton, "Rape and Sexual Assault Among College-Age Females, 1995–2013," Bureau of Justice Statistics, 2014, http://www.bjs.gov/content/pub/pdf/rsavcaf9513.pdf.

89. Lee Michael Johnson, Leah Daigle, and Sarah Napper, "Precautionary Behavior and Violent Victimization: Do Safer Drinking Strategies Reduce Risk?" *Victims and Offenders* 12 (2017): 381–400.

90. Rolf Loeber, Larry Kalb, and David Huizinga, *Juvenile Delinquency and Serious Injury Victimization* (Washington, DC: Office of Juvenile Justice and Delinquency Prevention, 2001).

91. Andrew Papachristos, Anthony Braga, Eric Piza, and Leigh Grossman, "The Company You Keep? The Spillover Effects of Gang Membership on Individual Gunshot Victimization in a Co-offending Network," *Criminology* 53 (2015): 624–650.

92. Mark Berg and Rolf Loeber, "Violent Conduct and Victimization Risk in the Urban Illicit Drug Economy: A Prospective Examination," *Justice Quarterly* 32 (2015): 32–55.

93. Scott Jacques and Richard Wright, "The Victimization–Termination Link," *Criminology* 46 (2008): 47–91.

94. Maryse Richards, Reed Larson, and Bobbi-Viegas Miller, "Risky and Protective Contexts and Exposure to Violence in Urban African American Young Adolescents," *Journal of Clinical Child and Adolescent Psychology* 33 (2004): 138–148.

95. James Garofalo, "Reassessing the Lifestyle Model of Criminal Victimization," in *Positive Criminology*, ed. Michael Gottfredson and Travis Hirschi (Newbury Park, CA: Sage, 1987), pp. 23–42.

96. Terance Miethe and David McDowall, "Contextual Effects in Models of Criminal Victimization," *Social Forces* 71 (1993): 741–759.

97. Rodney Stark, "Deviant Places: A Theory of the Ecology of Crime," *Criminology* 25 (1987): 893–911.

98. Ibid., p. 902.

99. William Wells, Ling Wu, and Xinyue Ye, "Patterns of Near-Repeat Gun Assaults in Houston," *Journal of Research in Crime and Delinquency*, first published online May 12, 2011.

100. Mark Berg, Eric Stewart, Christopher Schreck, and Ronald Simons, "The Victim–Offender Overlap in Context: Examining the Role of Neighborhood Street Culture," *Criminology* 50 (2012): 359–390.

101. Lawrence Cohen and Marcus Felson, "Social Change and Crime Rate Trends: A Routine Activities Approach," *American Sociological Review* 44 (1979): 588–608.

102. For a review, see James LeBeau and Thomas Castellano, "The Routine Activities Approach: An Inventory and Critique," unpublished paper, Center for the Studies of Crime, Delinquency, and Corrections, Southern Illinois University, Carbondale, 1987.

103. Teresa LaGrange, "The Impact of Neighborhoods, Schools, and Malls on the Spatial Distribution of Property Damage," *Journal of Research in Crime and Delinquency* 36 (1999): 393–422.

104. Denise Gottfredson and David Soulé, "The Timing of Property Crime, Violent Crime, and Substance Use Among Juveniles," *Journal of Research in Crime and Delinquency* 42 (2005): 110–120.

105. Marcus Felson, *Crime and Everyday Life: Insights and Implications for Society*, 3rd ed. (Thousand Oaks, CA: Sage, 2002).

106. Amy Anderson and Lorine Hughes, "Exposure to Situations Conducive to Delinquent Behavior: The Effects of Time Use, Income, and Transportation," *Journal of Research in Crime and Delinquency* 46 (2009): 5–34.

107. John R. Hipp, "General Theory of Spatial Crime Patterns," *Criminology* 54 (2016): 653–679.

108. Lawrence Cohen, Marcus Felson, and Kenneth Land, "Property Crime Rates in the United States: A Macrodynamic Analysis, 1947–1977, with Ex-ante Forecasts for the Mid-1980s," *American Journal of Sociology* 86 (1980): 90–118.

109. Steven Messner, Lawrence Raffalovich, and Richard McMillan, "Economic Deprivation and Changes in Homicide Arrest Rates for White and Black Youths, 1967–1998: A National Time Series Analysis," *Criminology* 39 (2001): 591–614.

110. Melanie Wellsmith and Amy Burrell, "The Influence of Purchase Price and Ownership Levels on Theft Targets: The Example of Domestic Burglary," *British Journal of Criminology* 45 (2005): 741–764.

111. Terance Miethe and Robert Meier, *Crime and Its Social Context: Toward an Integrated Theory of Offenders, Victims, and Situations* (Albany: State University of New York Press, 1994).

112. Richard Felson, "Routine Activities and Involvement in Violence as Actor, Witness, or Target," *Violence and Victimization* 12 (1997): 209–223.

113. Georgina Hammock and Deborah Richardson, "Perceptions of Rape: The Influence of Closeness of Relationship, Intoxication, and Sex of Participant," *Violence and Victimization* 12 (1997): 237–247.

114. Karin Wittebrood and Paul Nieuwbeerta, "Criminal Victimization During One's Life Course: The Effects of Previous Victimization and Patterns of Routine Activities," *Journal of Research in Crime and Delinquency* 37 (2000): 112–113.

115. US Department of Justice, *Report of the President's Task Force on Victims of Crime* (Washington, DC: US Government Printing Office, 1983).

116. Ibid., pp. 2–10; "Review on Victims: Witnesses of Crime," *Massachusetts Lawyers Weekly*, April 25, 1983, p. 26.

117. Robert Davis, *Crime Victims: Learning How to Help Them* (Washington, DC: National Institute of Justice, 1987).

118. Crime Victims' Rights Act, 18 U.S.C. § 3771 (2004).

119. Randall Schmidt, "Crime Victim Compensation Legislation: A Comparative Study," *Victimology* 5 (1980): 428–437.

120. Ibid.

121. National Association of Crime Victim Compensation Boards, http://www.nacvcb.org.

122. National Association of VOCA Assistance Administrators, http://www.navaa.org/.

123. Rebecca Campbell, "Rape Survivors' Experiences with the Legal and Medical Systems: Do Rape Victim Advocates Make a Difference?" *Violence Against Women* 12 (2006): 30–45.

124. Karen Rich and Patrick Seffrin, "Police Officers' Collaboration with Rape Victim Advocates: Barriers and Facilitators," *Violence and Victims* 28 (2013): 681–696.

125. New Hampshire Department of Justice, Office of Victim/Witness Assistance, http://doj.nh.gov /criminal/victim-assistance/.

126. Information provided by the National Center for Victims of Crime, http://www.victimsofcrime.org.

127. *Payne v. Tennessee*, 111 S.Ct. 2597, 115 L.Ed.2d 720 (1991).

128. Douglas E. Beloof, "Constitutional Implications of Crime Victims as Participants," *Cornell Law Review* 88 (2003): 282–305.

129. Stacy Hoskins Haynes, "The Effects of Victim-Related Contextual Factors on the Criminal Justice System," *Crime and Delinquency* 57 (2011): 298–328.

130. Edna Erez and Pamela Tontodonato, "The Effect of Victim Participation in Sentencing on Sentence Outcome," *Criminology* 28 (1990): 451–474.

131. Robert Davis and Barbara Smith, "The Effects of Victim Impact Statements on Sentencing Decisions: A Test in an Urban Setting," *Justice Quarterly* 11 (1994): 453–469.

132. Pater Jaffe, Marlies Sudermann, Deborah Reitzel, and Steve Killip, "An Evaluation of a Secondary School Primary Prevention Program on Violence in Intimate Relationships," *Violence and Victims* 7 (1992): 129–145.

133. Good Samaritans Program, http://www.ojp.usdoj .gov/ovc/publications/infores/Good_Samaritans /welcome.html.

134. Andrew Karmen, "Victim–Offender Reconciliation Programs: Pro and Con," *Perspectives of the American Probation and Parole Association* 20 (1996): 11–14.

135. US Department of Justice, Victim Notification System (VNS), https://www.justice.gov/criminal-vns.

136. Shannan M. Catalano, *Intimate Partner Violence, 1993–2010* (Washington, DC: Bureau of Justice Statistics, 2012), http://bjs.ojp.usdoj.gov/content /pub/pdf/ipv9310.pdf.

137. National Center for Victims of Crime, http://www .victimsofcrime.org.

138. Dru Sjodin National Sex Offender Public Website, http://www.nsopw.gov.

139. Alesha Durfee, "Victim Narratives, Legal Representation, and Domestic Violence Civil Protection Orders," *Feminist Criminology* 4 (2009): 7–31.

140. Sara Flaherty and Austin Flaherty, *Victims and Victims' Risk* (New York: Chelsea House, 1998).

141. Pamela Wilcox Rountree and Kenneth Land, "Burglary Victimization, Perceptions of Crime Risk, and Routine Activities: A Multilevel Analysis Across Seattle Neighborhoods and Census Tracts," *Journal of Research in Crime and Delinquency* 33 (1996): 1147–1180.

142. Ronald Clarke, "Situational Crime Prevention: Its Theoretical Basis and Practical Scope," in *Annual Review of Criminal Justice Research*, ed. Michael Tonry and Norval Morris (Chicago: University of Chicago Press, 1983).

143. See, generally, Dennis P. Rosenbaum, Arthur J. Lurigio, and Robert C. Davis, *The Prevention of Crime: Social and Situational Strategies* (Belmont, CA: Wadsworth, 1998).

144. Ráchael Powers, "Consequences of Using Self-Protective Behaviors in Nonsexual Assaults: The Differential Risk of Completion and Injury by Victim Sex," *Violence and Victims* 30 (2015): 846–869.

145. Gary Kleck, "Defensive Gun Use Is Not a Myth," *Politico*, February 17, 2015, http://www.politico .com/magazine/story/2015/02/defensive-gun -ownership-gary-kleck-response-115082.html; Gary Kleck, *Targeting Guns: Firearms and Their Control* (Hawthorne, NY: Aldine de Gruyter, 1997); Gary Kleck and Marc Gertz, "Armed Resistance to Crime: The Prevalence and Nature of Self-Defense with a Gun," *Journal of Criminal Law and Criminology* 86 (1995): 150–187; Gary Kleck, *Point Blank: Guns and Violence in America* (Hawthorne, NY: Aldine de Gruyter, 1991).

146. Jongyeon Tark and Gary Kleck, "Resisting Rape: The Effects of Victim Self-Protection on Rape Completion and Injury," *Violence Against Women* 20 (2014): 270–292; Jongyeon Tark and Gary Kleck, "Resisting Crime: The Effects of Victim Action on the Outcomes of Crimes," *Criminology* 42 (2004): 861–909.

Rational Choice Theory

Learning Objectives

LO1 Describe the development of rational choice theory.

LO2 Explore the concepts of rational choice.

LO3 Interpret the evidence showing that crime is rational.

LO4 Discuss the elements of situational crime prevention.

LO5 Analyze the elements of general deterrence.

LO6 Discuss the basic concepts of specific deterrence.

4

Chapter Outline

FACT OR FICTION?

▶ Neighborhood watch programs are a waste of time.

▶ Living in a gated community decreases the risk of burglary.

I n 2015, a Toledo, Ohio, man named Michael Wymer was sentenced to 27 years in prison after being convicted of charges relating to setting up a criminal enterprise designed to steal trucks, disassemble them in his chop shop, and sell them as scrap metal. Nine of his 13 co-conspirators— including his son, two brothers, and two nephews— were also convicted.

Wymer's scheme was quite complex. He and his fellow conspirators traveled outside of the Toledo area—including trips to·Michigan and Indiana—to steal trucks so they could avoid detection by one single jurisdiction. They would "shop" for semi-trucks and trailers at truck stops and other locations that were fairly close to interstate highways. If they were traveling in Wymer's own semi-truck (minus a trailer), they would back the truck up to the trailer they wanted and tow it away. If traveling by car, one or two of the thieves would break into an empty semi-truck with an attached trailer, manipulate the ignition to get it started, and drive the entire vehicle onto the closest interstate highway.

The Wymer team preferred items that could be chopped into scrap metal, so they stole things like motorcycles, all-terrain vehicles, copper wire, spools of metal, even actual loads of scrap metal. How did they know what the trucks were hauling? By breaking into the trailers and taking a look.

Once back in Toledo with the stolen property, Wymer would take the truck to one of his two chop shop locations, where he had everything he needed—from heavy moving equipment and floor jacks to blowtorches and chain saws. He would remove and sell parts from the truck and then "chop" the rest of the truck, the trailer, and the trailer's contents into scrap metal within a couple of hours. He would then load the material into one of his trucks and transport it to various businesses ▶

and/or recycling companies interested in buying scrap metal. Wymer used security cameras to keep an eye on his chop shops, and video footage from these cameras was used to convict him. All the evidence needed was on film! ■

The Wymer case clearly illustrates that the decision to commit crimes involves rational actions and planned decision making, designed to maximize profits and avoid detection. Rather than being unthinking and spontaneous, most crimes involve thought and planning designed to maximize personal gain and avoid capture and punishment.[1] Some criminologists go as far as suggesting that the source of all criminal violations—even those involving drug abuse, vandalism, and violence—are a function of rational decision making. The decision to violate the law is made only after the potential offender carefully weighs the potential benefits and consequences of the planned action and decides that the benefits of crime are greater than its consequences. Criminals may be motivated by a variety of human traits and emotions: greed, revenge, need, anger, lust, jealousy, thrill seeking, or vanity. Regardless of the motive, criminal offenders are people who make the decision to put their own needs ahead of the rest of us, even though there may be serious consequences for their actions. Why? Because after reviewing all available information they believe that the rewards of crime outweigh its risks. This view of crime causation is referred to here as **rational choice theory (choice theory)**.

In this chapter, we review the philosophical underpinnings of rational choice theory—the view that criminals rationally choose crime. We then turn to theories of crime prevention and control that flow from the concept of choice: situational crime prevention, general deterrence theory, specific deterrence theory, and incapacitation. Finally, we take a brief look at how choice theory has influenced criminal justice policy.

rational choice theory (choice theory)
The view that crime is a function of a decision-making process in which the potential offender weighs the potential costs and benefits of an illegal act.

L01 Describe the development of rational choice theory.

Development of Rational Choice Theory

Rational choice theory has its roots in the classical criminology developed by the Italian social thinker Cesare Beccaria, whose utilitarian approach powerfully influenced the criminal justice system and was widely accepted throughout Europe and the United States (see Chapter 1). Although the classical approach was influential for more than 100 years, by the end of the nineteenth century its popularity among criminologists declined, being replaced by positivist views that focused on social and personal factors rather than personal choice and decision making. The prevailing view was that crime was not a matter of choice but the by-product of destructive personal and social conditions and influences. Rather than controlling their behavior, people were at the mercy of their upbringing and environment.

Beginning in the late 1960s, criminologists once again began to embrace classical ideas, producing books and monographs expounding on the theme that criminals are rational actors who plan their crimes, who can be controlled by the fear of punishment, and who deserve to be penalized for their misdeeds. In the 1960s, Nobel Prize–winning economist Gary Becker applied his views on rational behavior and human capital (that is, human competence and the consequences of investments in human competence) to criminal activity. Becker argued that except for a few mentally ill people, criminals behave in a predictable or rational way when deciding to commit crime. Engaging in a cost-benefit analysis of crime, they weigh what they expect to gain against the risks they must undergo and the costs they may incur, such as going to prison.[2] Instead of regarding criminal activity as irrational behavior, Becker viewed criminality as rational behavior that might be controlled by increasing the costs of crime and reducing the potential for gain.

In *Thinking About Crime*, political scientist James Q. Wilson observed that people who are likely to commit crime are unafraid of breaking the law because they value the excitement and thrills of crime, have a low stake in conformity, and are willing to take greater chances than the average person. If they could be convinced that their actions would bring severe punishment, only the totally irrational would be willing to engage in crime.[3]

From these roots has evolved a more contemporary version of classical theory based on intelligent thought processes and criminal decision making; today this is referred to as the rational choice approach to crime causation.[4]

Concepts of Rational Choice

According to contemporary rational choice theory, law-violating behavior is the product of careful thought and planning. It assumes that people are self-interested and will be willing to violate the law after considering both personal factors (such as money, revenge, thrills, and entertainment) and situational factors (such as target availability, security measures, and police presence). Anyone is a potential criminal if they calculate that the profits are great and the risks are small. Below, some of the decisions made by potential criminals are set out and discussed.

Evaluating the Risks of Crime

Before deciding to commit a crime, the reasoning criminal evaluates the risk of apprehension, the seriousness of expected punishment, the potential value or benefit of the criminal enterprise, her ability to succeed, and the need for criminal gain. People who believe that the risks of crime outweigh the rewards may decide to "go straight."[5] Those who find the risks acceptable are more willing to take a gamble on crime.

Burglars seem to choose targets on the basis of their value, novelty, and resale potential. A piece of electronic gear that has not yet saturated the market and still retains high value, such as a new generation iPhone, may be a prime target.[6] The decision to commit crime is enhanced by the promise of easy gain with low risk.

In contrast, the decision to forgo crime is reached when the potential criminal believes that the risks outweigh the rewards:

- They stand a good chance of getting caught and being punished.
- They fear the consequences of punishment.
- They risk losing the respect of their peers, damaged reputations, and feelings of guilt or shame.[7]
- The risk of apprehension outweighs the profit and/or pleasure of crime.

Risk evaluations may cover a wide range of topics: What's the chance of getting caught? How difficult will it be to commit the crime? Is the profit worth the effort? How familiar am I with the target?[8]

People who decide to get involved in crime compare the chances of arrest (based on their past experiences) with the subjective psychic rewards of crime (including the excitement and social status it brings and perceived opportunities for easy gains).[9] If the rewards are great, the perceived risk small, and the excitement high, the likelihood of their committing additional crimes increases.[10]

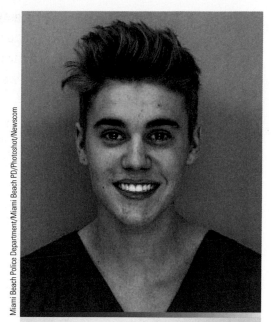

Miami Beach Police Department/Miami Beach PD/Photoshot/Newscom

Some people choose crime and deviance because it provides excitement and thrills. That might be the motive for celebrity crimes such as when, on January 2, 2014, pop singer Justin Bieber was arrested after drag racing in his yellow Lamborghini while under the influence of alcohol, marijuana, and prescription drugs and failing to cooperate when pulled over. Bieber's arrest came a week after his home in Los Angeles was searched by police following allegations he had thrown eggs at his neighbor's house. Prosecutors dropped the drunken driving charge in an agreement that required Bieber to get 12 hours of anger management counseling, attend a program that teaches about the impact on victims of drunken driving, and donate $50,000 to the Our Kids program.

LO2 Explore the concepts of rational choice.

Offense-Specific/Offender-Specific

offense-specific
The view that an offender reacts selectively to the characteristics of a particular criminal act.

offender-specific
The view that offenders evaluate their skills, motives, needs, and fears before deciding to commit the criminal act.

Rational choice theorists view crime as both **offense-specific** and **offender-specific**.[11] Crime is said to be offense-specific because offenders react selectively to the immediate characteristics of a specific criminal act. Take, for instance, the decision to commit a burglary. Potential offenders might consider:

- Their evaluation of the target yield
- The probability of security devices
- Police patrol effectiveness
- Likelihood of apprehension
- Ease of selling stolen merchandise
- Presence of occupants
- Neighbors who might notice a break-in
- Presence of guard dogs
- Escape routes
- Entry points and exits

OFFENDER-SPECIFIC Crime is also said to be offender-specific because criminals are not simply robots or automatons who engage in unthinking and unplanned acts of antisocial behavior. Before deciding to commit crime, individuals must decide whether they have the personal needs, skills, and prerequisites to commit a successful criminal act. These assessments might include evaluation of:

- Necessary skills to commit the crime
- Immediate need for money or other valuables
- Availability of legitimate financial alternatives to crime
- Available resources to commit the crime
- Fear of expected apprehension and punishment
- Availability of alternative criminal acts, such as selling drugs
- Physical ability, including health, strength, and dexterity

Note the distinction made here between "crime" and "criminality."[12] A crime is an event; criminality is a personal trait. Criminals do not commit crime all the time; conversely, even the most honest citizens may, on occasion, violate the law. Some high-risk people lacking opportunity may never commit crime. Given enough

According to rational choice theory, crime can be viewed as offender- and offense-specific. On June 10, 2015, New York Governor Andrew Cuomo and Vermont Governor Peter Shumlin appear during a news conference in front of the Clinton Correctional Facility in Dannemora, New York, after two convicted killers, David Sweat (photo on left) and Richard Matt (right), made a daring escape. The men had convinced prison employee Joyce Mitchell, who worked as an instructor in the facility's tailoring shop, to help them break out. She was convicted and sentenced to seven years in prison for helping them escape; Matt was killed in the attempt. Why would a married prison employee choose to help criminals escape, thereby putting herself in jeopardy of becoming a felon herself?

AP Images/Seth Wenig

provocation or opportunity, a low-risk, law-abiding person may commit crime. What are the factors that (a) structure criminality and (b) structure crime?

Structuring Criminality

Because crime is offender-specific, a number of personal factors and conditions must be evaluated before someone decides to choose criminality.

PEERS AND GUARDIANSHIP Though young people are believed to be more crime prone than adults, effective monitoring by parents reduces the likelihood kids will commit crime; in contrast, unsupervised activities increase the risk.[13] Kids are more likely to choose crime when they are out at night without adult supervision, partying and drinking with their buddies.[14]

Gender differences in crime may be explained by levels of guardianship and peer influence. Because adolescent girls are more likely to experience parental supervision than their brothers, they are more likely to socialize at home or at a friend's home with parents present. Adolescent boys are given more freedom to socialize away from home as they wish, thereby increasing the opportunity to engage in antisocial behaviors.[15] When girls do go out, they tend to gather in places like shopping malls, where there are security guards and cameras that monitor behavior and limit criminal choice.

NEED FOR EXCITEMENT AND THRILLS People may engage in illegal behavior because they love the excitement and the buzz that crime can provide. For some, crimes such as vandalism and shoplifting are alluring simply because they are stimulating and allow people to get what sociologist Jack Katz calls "sneaky thrills"; profit is not the primary motive.[16] The need for excitement may counter fear of apprehension: the riskier the act, the more attractive it becomes.[17]

ECONOMIC NEED/OPPORTUNITY Clearly, one important decision that people make before they embark on a life of crime is whether they need the money! The need to commit economic crimes diminishes when people are able to obtain needed funds in a legitimate fashion, either through jobs or government assistance. Other potential offenders simply may have money problems: they are in debt; their creditors are hounding them; they have nowhere else to turn.[18]

Crime may be an attractive alternative when people have little faith in the economy or believe there is little hope of advancement in the legitimate economy.[19] While these desperate people may realize that the average take from crime is not that much, it's a lot quicker and more efficient to steal a car than to get a job and save enough money to buy one from a dealer. Drug users may turn to crime to support their lifestyle and their habit, especially when entry into the legitimate job market closes.[20]

The FBI reports that the average take from a burglary is now a little more than $2,300 per crime; robberies average about $1,200 and bank robberies $3,800.[21] Despite the risk, earning $2,000 from a burglary that takes an hour is alluring to someone whose alternative is making minimum wage in a fast-food restaurant.

Adding to the allure of crime is the fact that many potential criminals may be misled about the potential of financial reward of crime. They may know people who brag about the "big scores" of $50,000 or more they have made: if their friend or brother-in-law can do well, they assume they will succeed also.[22]

There is also the potential for future riches no matter the current risks. When Steven Levitt and Sudhir Alladi Venkatesh interviewed drug gang members, they found that despite enormous risks to health, life, and freedom, average gang members earned just about minimum wage.[23] Why, then, did they continue to take risks? They believed there was a strong potential for future riches if they stayed in the drug business and earned a "management" position (gang leaders earned a lot more than street-level dealers). Like the college grad entering the executive training program

CONNECTIONS

Rational choice theory dovetails with routine activities theory, which was discussed in Chapter 3. Though not identical, these approaches both claim that crime rates are a product of criminal opportunity. They suggest that increasing the number of guardians, decreasing the suitability of targets, or reducing the offender population should lower crime rates. Conversely, increased opportunity and reduced guardianship should increase crime rates.

at a Fortune 500 company, gang kids are willing to take risks and work hard today for the promise of a high-paid position tomorrow.[24] Of course, neither the corporate trainee nor the gang boy stands much chance of getting to the top rung of the organization; there are a lot more openings at the bottom of the pyramid than there are at the top.

COMPETENCE AND EXPERIENCE Personal experience and expertise may be an important element in structuring criminality.[25] One reason is that the risk of detection, arrest, and punishment diminishes as burglars, robbers, and auto thieves become more competent at their craft. Compared to unskilled beginners, experienced criminals profit more per each crime they commit. They therefore can perpetrate fewer crimes, leaving them less exposed to detection and arrest.[26]

While criminals may learn when to commit crimes, they also become aware of when to quit. No matter how successful, a criminal's physical strength and emotional toughness eventually begin to wane, and some get the message that it may be time to turn from a risky criminal way of life to a lower-paying, safer conventional lifestyle.[27]

Structuring Crime

According to the rational choice approach, the decision to commit crime, regardless of its substance, is structured by (a) where it occurs and (b) the characteristics of the target.

CHOOSING THE PLACE OF CRIME Criminals seem to carefully choose where they will commit their crime. Crack cocaine street dealers evaluate the desirability of their sales area before setting up shop.[28] Dealers consider the middle of a long block the best choice because they can see everything in both directions; police raids can be spotted before they occur.[29] Another tactic is to entice new buyers into spaces between apartment buildings or into back lots. Although the dealers may lose the tactical edge of being on a public street, they gain a measure of protection because their colleagues can watch over the operation and come to the rescue if the buyer tries to "pull something."[30]

Criminals choose targets in familiar places, where they know their way around and won't get lost or trapped. One interesting study by Barbara Menting and her colleagues discovered that offenders not only commit crimes near their home or former home but also are more likely to target the residential areas of family members—parents, siblings, and their own children. As visitors, criminals are familiar with their families' neighborhoods, and this familiarity increases the risk of the area becoming a target.[31]

CHOOSING TARGETS Evidence of rational choice may also be found in the way criminals locate their targets. Market forces can shape decision making. Targets that decline in value due to oversupply or obsolescence are avoided; materials such as metal parts and wire may become coveted when undersupply causes their value to skyrocket.[32]

Robbers may seek targets with a great deal of cash on hand; why bother with a place that only takes credit cards? Research by Christopher Contreras found that neighborhoods with medical marijuana dispensaries have a high risk of armed robbery and resulting murders when things go awry. High crime rates, Contreras concludes, may be tied to dispensaries' lack of banking access and regulation, necessarily making them a cash economy and possibly inviting a criminal element to the areas hosting these facilities.[33]

Auto thieves are known to be very selective in their choice of targets, often making their selection based on cash value and ease of sale. German cars are selected for stripping because they usually have high-quality audio equipment that has good value on the secondhand market.[34]

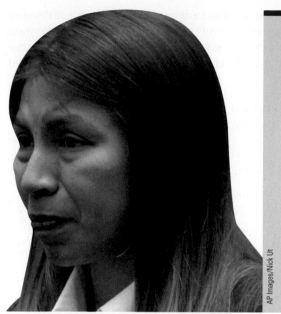

Criminals show rationality when they carefully plan and structure their illegal acts. One case that shows this type of rationality involved a criminal group called the Bling Ring, of which Diana Tamayo, shown in court, was a member. In 2012, she pleaded no contest to a burglary charge for stealing items from the home of actress Lindsay Lohan and was sentenced to three years of probation. Tamayo was one of six people charged in thefts of more than $3 million in clothes, jewelry, and art from the homes of celebrities such as Lohan, Paris Hilton, Orlando Bloom, and Megan Fox. The Bling Ring targeted victims who were considered fashion icons. If the members liked a celebrity's style, they became determined to steal the celebrity's clothes. They found their targets by using Google maps and information from a website showing where famous people live. They planned their crimes to coincide with the celebrities' schedules, such as appearances at events, through social media such as Facebook and Twitter.

AP Images/Nick Ut

Burglars also seem particularly rational when choosing targets. Interviews with active burglars indicate that they check to make sure no one is home before they enter a residence. Some call ahead; others ring the doorbell, preparing to claim they had the wrong address if someone answers. Some find out which families include star athletes, because those that do are sure to be at the weekend football game, leaving their houses unguarded.[35] Others read bridal announcements in the local newspaper, hoping to locate empty homes with expensive gifts left unguarded while the occupants are at the wedding.

Burglars seek unlocked doors and avoid the ones with deadbolts; houses with dogs are usually considered off-limits.[36] Being sensitive to the activities of their victims, burglars make note of the fact that homemakers often develop predictable behavior patterns.[37] Burglars also seem to prefer "working" between 9 A.M. and 11 A.M. and in mid-afternoon, when parents are either working or dropping off or picking up children at school. Some report monitoring car and pedestrian traffic; others avoid selecting targets on heavily traveled streets.[38] It does not seem surprising that well-organized communities that restrict traffic and limit neighborhood entrance and exit routes have experienced significant declines in property crime.[39]

GETTING AWAY Because they fear apprehension, professional criminals lay out an escape route before they commit crime. Having an effective exit strategy is just as important as planning the initial crime. Bruce Jacobs and Mark Cherbonneau found that savvy auto thieves rely on what they refer to as "normalcy illusions," a patchwork of tactics designed to prevent authorities from becoming wise to the fact that the thieves are driving a stolen vehicle. One instant precaution is affixing a fresh license plate to the stolen vehicle as quickly as possible after it is taken. Some thieves go to a local junkyard and take plates off abandoned cars.[40] Another ploy: find an innocent-looking driver to shield them from police attention. A number of male offenders interviewed by Jacobs and Cherbonneau asked females to drive the stolen vehicles because police do not generally suspect women of being auto thieves.

Just in case they are caught, car thieves plan flight strategies in advance. They are ready for high-speed chases triggered by being asked to pull over. Some knew that police were forbidden to pursue speeding cars, making high-speed getaways

L03 Interpret the evidence showing that crime is rational.

Philip Seymour Hoffman poses on the red carpet during a screening for the movie *The Master* at the Venice Film Festival in Italy. Hoffman died on February 2, 2014, of a drug overdose. Can his drug-use behavior ever be considered rational?

that much more effective. Some waited until the officer exited the patrol car and approached their vehicle before taking off, giving them a head start. Some stashed cars around the city and, during a pursuit, would simply drive to one of these vehicles or "stash spots," ditch the vehicle being pursued, and escape in the stashed vehicle.

In sum, rational choice involves both shaping and structuring criminality and crime. Personality, age, status, risk, and opportunity seem to influence the decision to become a criminal; place, target, and techniques help to structure crime.[41]

Is Crime Truly Rational?

It is relatively easy to show that some crimes are the product of rational, objective thought, especially when they involve an ongoing criminal conspiracy centered on economic gain (such as the chop shop scheme discussed in the opening vignette). When prominent bankers and financial analysts such as Bernie Madoff are indicted for criminal fraud, their elaborate schemes not only show signs of rationality but also exhibit brilliant, though flawed, financial expertise.[42] But what about street crimes? Do these also show elements of rational choice? Burglars, for example, like to target residences close to where they live so they know the territory and have access to escape routes. Because they have access to cars and vans, adult burglars are willing to travel farther than juveniles.[43]

Street robbers are likely to choose victims who are vulnerable, have low coercive power, and do not pose any threat.[44] They size up their prey and get ready to use violence if the target appears to be streetwise. During the robbery, offenders are more likely to use physical force against a victim who resists; compliant victims are treated with greater restraint. Robbers therefore take a rational approach to sizing up and dealing with their victims.[45] The Profiles in Crime feature focuses on the rational planning of auto thieves.

Is Drug Use Rational?

Did Oscar-winning actor Philip Seymour Hoffman make an objective, rational choice to overdose on heroin? Did Prince choose to overdose on the opioid fentanyl? Did rising young star Heath Ledger make a rational choice when he abused prescription drugs to the point that it killed him? And what about British singer Amy Winehouse—did she choose to drink herself to death? Or the King of Pop, Michael Jackson, who died of acute propofol and benzodiazepine intoxication? Is it possible that these and other drug users, a group not usually associated with clear thinking, make rational choices?

Research does in fact show that at its onset, drug use is controlled by rational decision making. Users report that they begin taking drugs when they believe the benefits of substance abuse outweigh its costs. That is, they believe drugs will provide a fun, exciting, thrilling experience. They choose what they consider safe sites to buy and sell drugs.[46] Their entry into substance abuse is facilitated by their perception that valued friends and family members endorse and encourage drug use and that these individuals abuse substances themselves.[47]

Drug dealers approach their profession in a businesslike fashion. Traffickers and dealers face many of the same problems as legitimate retailers.[48] If they are too successful in one location, rivals will be attracted to the area, and stiff competition may drive down prices and undermine profits. The dealer can fight back against competitors by discounting the price of drugs or increasing quality, as long as this doesn't reduce profit margins.[49] If these "business tactics" are not working, dealers can always turn to violence. They may start drug wars on their rivals' turf and then convince customers to stay away from such a dangerous area; in retaliation, rivals may cut prices to lure customers back.

Max Ross/Reuters/Corbis

PROFILES IN CRIME

PLANNING TO STEAL

Bruce Jacobs and Michael Cherbonneau recently studied the decision-making process of auto thieves, who as a group are especially concerned about the reaction of their victim targets. Their data were drawn from in-depth interviews with 35 active offenders recruited from the streets of a large midwestern US city.

Jacobs and Cherbonneau found that two factors figured prominently in the offenders' decision making: the area around the target and the target itself. They found that auto thieves could be deterred by the threat of confrontation and the self-defense measures taken by the car owners. While the wheels of justice may be slow, victim responses are immediate—and potent. Making a mistake in planning an auto theft can result in severe consequences.

Offenders "intuit" potential scenarios and plan accordingly. They must calculate whether the car owner is absent and the likelihood of his/her return, and what force the victim has at his/her disposal. These tasks require time, know-how, patience, and coolness under pressure. Thieves must figure out a way to make their behavior seem normal to observers, hide their intentions from prying eyes, and neutralize the desire of car owners to take action to protect their property.

In auto theft, such measures involve the maximization of stealth and speed during the theft. Stealth keeps victims unaware of the fact that a theft is occurring, while speed minimizes the duration of exposure within the actual offense.

To meet these requirements, auto thieves avoid situations that would bring contact with victims or people who could potentially notify victims. The mere prospect of being noticed gives auto thieves serious pause about targeting a vehicle with anyone around. One tactic is to carefully scope out an area on foot or with a drive-by to make sure there are no bystanders lurking about. If an offender sees a driver exit a vehicle, he might wait to gauge whether a return is likely. Some use an "occupancy probe," knocking on the car owner's door to see if they are home; others wait until the early morning hours when most people are asleep.

Not all offenders can count on such strategies. Some use lookouts, co-offenders who provide a critical "heads-up" if the owner or a related party is watching, approaching, or in danger of intervening. Lookouts allow thieves to make quick decisions without a lot of preparation. One thief named Will told Jacobs and Cherbonneau how he targeted a vehicle driven to a nightclub. After watching the owner go inside, Will had a co-offender follow the man into the club and keep an eye on his movements. If "he was going [to] walk off and leave," Will explained, "[My partner] was going [to] call... on the cell phone... I didn't want to be breaking somebody's car down and here he all of a sudden decides to go."

Female thieves may hook up with a car owner to catch them off guard. One told how she knocked out her target with sleeping pills and morphine (which she slipped into his drink during a date), and then took his car once he fell unconscious. "I knew that he wasn't gonna come out for a minute," she recalled. Although there is some risk of post-offense retaliation, most thieves were unconcerned, believing they could talk their way out of involvement if they were somehow tracked down.

Another concern was alarms. It didn't matter how stealthy they were if a car alarm started blaring. One method was to break a window to gain access and get away quickly. Others looked for cars with open windows or ones that already had a broken window. The faster one broke into the vehicle, the faster the offense would be over, and the quicker one could escape. Some would purposely jostle the vehicles and then wait to see whether the owner came out if an alarm went off. If the owner did appear, thieves would simply slink down the street as if uninvolved. Others felt the easiest way was to target vehicles left running in gas stations or convenience store parking lots. Although these open spaces afforded little concealment, speed of access and escape trumped the deterrent power of victim proximity: by the time the owner realized what happened, the crime would be over.

Despite all their precautions, auto thieves were afraid of run-ins with car owners. They were auto thieves, after all, not violent criminals. Some reported fear of getting shot by an irate owner. Although sneaky property crimes such as auto theft were unlikely to land offenders in the crosshairs of an angry victim, the mere prospect encouraged offenders to apply confrontation avoidance measures at the front end of the offense. By reducing the certainty of detection, the offenders sought to short-circuit consequences that they anticipated would be both swift and severe. ■

Source: Bruce Jacobs and Michael Cherbonneau, "Managing Victim Confrontation: Auto Theft and Informal Sanction Threats," *Justice Quarterly* (2016): 21–44.

Can violence be rational? Cop killer Christopher Jordan Dorner killed three LAPD officers and was the subject of an intense 2013 manhunt that resulted in his death. Dorner was a former Los Angeles police officer who believed he was unfairly dismissed from the force; the shootings were revenge for his dismissal. Would you consider killing people for revenge against an institution an example of rational behavior?

LAPD/Getty Images News/Getty Images

Street-level drug dealers also display rationality when they employ defensive measures to limit exposure to police. Some have stash spots so they do not have illegal substances on their person in case of arrest. Some employ partners for protection. Drug offenders are particularly attractive victims for robbery, since they are typically stationary in public places, have ready cash, and generally will not report crimes to the police; partners help them avoid victimization.[50]

Online drug marketers also use rational means to escape detection. Some use fake online identities while others use drop-shipping techniques (moving goods directly from the manufacturer to the buyer) so they can sell illegal drugs without the necessity of having possession.[51]

Is Violence Rational?

Is it possible that violent acts are the product of reasoned decision making? Evidence confirms that violent criminals, even serial killers, select suitable targets by picking people who are vulnerable and lack adequate defenses.[52] Street robbers use a considerable amount of rational thought before choosing a robbery, which may involve violence, over a burglary, which involves stealth and cunning.[53] Robbers generally choose targets close to their homes or in areas to which they routinely travel. Familiarity with the area gives them ready knowledge of escape routes; this is referred to as their "awareness space."[54] Robbers may be wary of people who are watching the community for signs of trouble; robbery levels are relatively low in neighborhoods where residents keep a watchful eye out for trouble and are quick to take notice of a stranger in their midst.[55]

Robbers report that they avoid freestanding buildings because these can more easily be surrounded by police; others select targets that are known to do a primarily cash business, such as bars, convenience stores, and gas stations. Robbers also tend to shy away from victims who are perceived to be armed and potentially dangerous.[56]

In some instances, however, targets are chosen in order to send a message rather than to generate capital. Bruce Jacobs and Richard Wright conducted in-depth interviews with street robbers who target drug dealers and found that their crimes are a response to one of three types of provocations:

- *Market-related* robberies emerge from disputes involving partners in trade, rivals, or generalized predators.
- *Status-based* violations involve encounters in which the robber's essential character or values have been challenged.
- *Personalistic* violations flow from incidents in which the robber's autonomy or sense of values has been jeopardized.

Robbery in this instance is an instrument used to settle scores, display dominance, and stifle potential rivals. And as Jacobs and Wright conclude, retaliation certainly is rational in the sense that actors who lack legitimate access to the law and who prize respect above everything else will often choose to resolve their grievances through a rough and ready brand of self-help.[57]

Is Hate Crime Rational?

Can hate crimes possibly be rational? Hard to believe, but when Ryan King and Gretchen Sutto examined the characteristics of an outbreak of hate crimes they found that three factors seem to trigger these events: an incident that leaves one group with a grievance against another, a definable target group held responsible for the deed, and publicity sufficient to make the event known to a broad public. All these are signs of rationality.[58] Hate crimes, then, are not merely the product of a disturbed mind, but rather a calculated response to a concrete event whose impact is often fanned and inflamed by the media.

Is Sex Crime Rational?

Are men who solicit sex workers (**johns**) rational decision makers? Recent research by Thomas Holt and his colleagues found that not only did johns make careful and rational decisions when engaging prostitutes, they shared their knowledge and expertise in Internet chat rooms and web forums. Topics ranged from what kind of car to drive and how to avoid police stops to how to spot undercover policewomen posing as street workers, with some johns suggesting that policewomen look more attractive and healthier than the average sex worker. In addition to avoiding law enforcement, johns shared information on how to protect themselves from becoming crime victims, such as finding spots for their sexual encounters that minimized the likelihood of detection or violence. After hearing horror stories like "I was robbed by a pimp," they learned to avoid motels recommended by prostitutes, as the risk of robbery or assault was too high. Homes were off limits because johns feared having their property taken; the preferred rendezvous points were alleyways, empty parking lots, and trusted hourly motels.[59] Here we can see that johns are rational decision makers who learn to take precautions before engaging in an outlawed public order crime.

Analyzing Rational Choice Theory

In sum, according to the rational choice approach, crime is not a random event but the product of calculation and planning, designed to provide the would-be criminal with an overall benefit, whether it be monetary profit or an emotional thrill. To accept this rational choice view, you must believe that criminals are decision makers who spend time calculating profit and risk. They are selfish, self-absorbed individuals who care nothing about others. If they believe they can get away with

On June 12, 2016, 49 people were killed and at least 53 injured during a Latin music event at a gay nightclub in Orlando, Florida. Here, mourners in Berlin hold photographs of the victims during a vigil in front of the United States embassy. The shooting was the worst terror attack in the US since 9/11. The American-born gunman had pledged allegiance to ISIL, though officials have yet to find credible evidence of any direct connection with foreign extremists. The incident added fuel to the ongoing debate about gun control in this country.

johns
Men who solicit sex workers.

Are sex offenses rational? Here, Heather Keith shows her tattoo that says King Koby, the street name of her pimp, Vincent George Jr., as she testifies in a Manhattan court. George and his father, Vincent George Sr., were each sentenced to three to nine years in prison for their crimes. During the trial Keith and others testified for the defense, saying they considered themselves to be one big family. They claimed they were treated to nice cars, vacations in Florida, and affection from their pimps. Keith testified she had been a drug-addicted 19-year-old stripper from upstate New York when King Koby moved her to Allentown, Pennsylvania, and helped her beat a cocaine habit. "I would say that I make my own choices," said the 26-year-old Keith.

illegal and/or immoral behavior, they will try. What holds them back: fear of apprehension and punishment.

Research shows this image of the calculating criminal can be found across all forms of illegal activities. Even those who would seem to be spontaneous in their actions—adolescents with a history of serious criminal offending, drug offenders, violent offenders—act after considering the anticipated rewards and costs of offending. If they believe they can increase rewards by taking precautions or working with co-offenders, they will chance criminal activities. As the expectations of benefits change, so does criminal involvement. Criminal propensity is neither static nor invariable but subject to the perceived availability of benefits and the absence of penalties.

Not everyone accepts this version of events. Criminologist Robert Agnew argues that the average person is just as likely to give consideration to others as they are to satisfy their own self-interests. Most people feel distress at the suffering of others and are inclined to pitch in and help in an emergency, even if it means taking a risk or inconveniencing themselves. Agnew suggests that though many individuals are self-interested, most of us are also socially concerned, a state of mind that provides a natural restraint against crime. Social concern and self-interest can exist side by side.

If Agnew's view is accurate, then the image of the calculating criminal who weighs costs and benefits without caring for other people is inaccurate. Rational choice theorists would disagree, of course, putting more stock into convincing would-be criminals that crime does not pay, rather than hoping such people will empathize with their victims. Given that conclusion, rational choice advocates have formulated a number of potential strategies for controlling crime. Among the most important of these are situational crime prevention strategies, general deterrence strategies, specific deterrence strategies, and incapacitation strategies, all of which are discussed in detail in the following sections.

Situational Crime Prevention

L04 Discuss the elements of situational crime prevention.

Desperate people may contemplate crime, but only the truly irrational would attack a well-defended, inaccessible target and risk strict punishment. Law violators of all stripes seek out targets that are attractive yet vulnerable.[60] Criminals are ready and willing to pounce if (a) there are valuable items, (such as cash), that (b) can be taken easily because victims do not take adequate precautions (they go alone to a ATM at night) without anyone around to guard or protect them (the bank is closed, the guards are gone).[61]

It follows that crime prevention can be achieved by convincing would-be criminals that a particular target is not worth the effort; "it's too hard a nut to crack." This approach is referred to as **situational crime prevention**; because crime is rational and criminals calculating, effective crime prevention strategies must be aimed at reducing immediate and particular criminal opportunities, making it more difficult to engage in successful criminal enterprise. Strategies such as target hardening and improving surveillance are designed to convince would-be criminals that, even if they believe crime pays, it does not pay to commit it here and it pays more to go elsewhere.[62] Criminal acts can be prevented if (a) potential targets are carefully guarded, (b) the means to commit crime are controlled, and (c) potential offenders are carefully monitored. Desperate people may contemplate crime, but only the truly irrational will attack a well-defended, inaccessible target and risk strict punishment.

One way of preventing crime, then, is to reduce the opportunities people have to commit particular crimes. This approach was popularized in the United States in the early 1970s by Oscar Newman, who coined the term **defensible space**. The idea is that crime can be prevented or displaced through the use of residential designs that reduce criminal opportunity, such as well-lit housing projects that maximize surveillance.[63]

situational crime prevention
A method of crime prevention that seeks to eliminate or reduce particular crimes in specific settings.

defensible space
The principle that crime can be prevented or displaced by modifying the physical environment to reduce the opportunity that individuals have to commit crime.

Exhibit 4.1   The CRAVED Model

The CRAVED model of theft suggests that the appropriation of property is most likely to occur when the target is:

- *Concealable.* Merchandise that is easily hidden is more vulnerable to shoplifters than bulkier items. Things that are difficult to identify after being stolen are desirable. While it might be possible to identify a diamond ring, commodities such as copper tubing are easily concealable.
- *Removable.* Mobile items such as cars or bikes are desirable. A laptop makes a more appealing target than a desktop. Jewelry, cash, drugs, and the like are easy to carry and quite valuable on resale. Refrigerators may cost more, but you would need three people and a truck to remove them from a home.
- *Available.* Desirable objects that are widely available and easy to find are at high risk for theft. Cars actually become at greater risk as they get older, because similar models need parts and car thieves can bring them to chop shops to be stripped.

Older cars are also owned by people living in disorganized neighborhoods with motivated offenders and limited security.

- *Valuable.* Thieves will generally choose more expensive, in-demand goods that are easily sold. Some may want to keep valuable goods for themselves and target goods that will confer status, such as a Rolex.
- *Enjoyable.* Hot products tend to be enjoyable things to own or consume, such as the newest electronic gadget or flashy bling.
- *Disposable.* Thieves tend to target items that are easy to sell. Cartons of cigarettes can be resold at a discount to a convenience store. While more valuable, it's tougher to sell a Picasso print.

Sources: Gohar Petrossian and Ronald Clarke, "Explaining and Controlling Illegal Commercial Fishing, An Application of the CRAVED Theft Model," *British Journal of Criminology* 54 (2014): 73–90; Stephen Pires and Ronald Clarke, "Are Parrots CRAVED? An Analysis of Parrot Poaching in Mexico," *Journal of Research in Crime and Delinquency* 49 (2012): 122–146.

Another approach, suggested by Ron Clarke, is the CRAVED model, which identifies the factors that make theft-related crimes attractive to potential thieves so that steps can be taken to thwart their criminal ambitions. The CRAVED model is set out in Exhibit 4.1.

Recently, Clarke along with colleague Brian Smith tested the CRAVED model in a rather unique way. They hypothesized that over-the-counter drugs, sold in supermarkets and other stores, can produce a "high" similar to illegal drugs. According to the CRAVED model, these items should be shoplifted at higher rates than other products because they are readily available, enjoyable to use, easily removed, and so on. Using data from more than 200 supermarkets, Smith and Clarke found that products with an appeal to drug users were in fact stolen at significantly higher theft rates than products that were not drug related.[64]

Crime Prevention Strategies

Situational crime prevention strategies involve developing tactics to reduce or eliminate a specific crime problem (such as shoplifting in an urban mall or street-level drug dealing). These efforts may be divided into the six strategies described in the following paragraphs.[65]

INCREASE THE EFFORT NEEDED TO COMMIT CRIME Tactics to increase effort include target-hardening techniques such as putting unbreakable glass on storefronts, locking gates, and fencing yards. Does it work? Removing signs from store windows to increase interior visibility, installing brighter lights, and instituting a pay-first policy have helped reduce thefts from gas stations and convenience stores.[66] Research by Lynn Addington and Callie Marie Rennison shows that living in a gated community reduces the risk of being targeted by burglars.[67]

INCREASE THE RISK OF COMMITTING CRIME If the risk of getting caught can be increased, rational offenders are less likely to commit crime. Marcus Felson argues that the risk of crime may be increased by improving the effectiveness of

CONNECTIONS

Shoplifting and retail theft will be discussed further in Chapter 12. While there have been ongoing efforts to prevent shoplifting, it is still a multibillion-dollar-a-year crime. It has proven difficult to deter professionals who know how to counter security measures. Do you have any new ideas?

FACT OR FICTION?

Living in a gated community decreases the risk of burglary.

FACT Research does show that the gates really help reduce the risk of burglary. Locked gates may increase the effort needed to commit crime, convincing burglars to seek out easier targets elsewhere.

crime discouragers
People who serve as guardians of property or people.

crime discouragers: people who serve as guardians of property or people and who can help control would-be criminals.[68] Discouragers can be grouped into three categories: "guardians," who monitor potential targets (such as police and store security guards), "handlers," who monitor potential offenders (such as parole officers and parents), and "managers," who monitor places (such as homeowners and garage attendants). If the discouragers do their jobs correctly, the potential criminal will be convinced that the risk of crime outweighs any potential gains.[69] Even if discouragers cannot prevent crime, their presence may convince offenders to limit the severity of offending since they know a guardian will intervene if they injure victims.[70]

Some crime discouragers are mechanical rather than human. One prominent approach is the installation of closed-circuit television (CCTV) surveillance cameras and improved street lighting, techniques that are currently being used around the world. CCTV can deter would-be criminals who fear detection and apprehension while aiding police in the detection and apprehension of suspects, aid in the prosecution of alleged offenders, and aid in the detection and prevention of terrorist activities.[71]

Nowhere is the popularity of CCTV more apparent than in Great Britain, where more than 4 million CCTV cameras, or 1 for every 14 citizens, are in operation. Some cities in the United States have large numbers of security cameras: New York City has more than 4,000 cameras in Manhattan alone; Chicago's linked public and private security cameras number around 10,000.[72] Research in a variety of locations shows that CCTV interventions have a moderate crime-reducing effect; they are more effective in reducing crimes such as assault, robbery, and burglary while having less effect on other crimes. Location, time of day, and neighborhood crime rates may influence effectiveness; as location crime rates increase, effectiveness decreases.[73]

REDUCE THE REWARDS OF CRIME Target reduction strategies are designed to reduce the value of crime to the potential criminal. Jewelry stores display expensive rings with fake diamonds (cubic zirconia), while keeping the real stones under lock and key. Retail establishments put small but valuable items in tamper-proof hard plastic cases that emit electronic signals to trigger alarms if they are taken from the store; they can only be opened by store employees. Bike owners can put an indelible identification mark on their bicycle such as a serial number; thieves are less likely to steal a bicycle that can be positively identified.

INDUCE GUILT: INCREASE SHAME Crime may be reduced or prevented if we can communicate to people the wrongfulness of their behavior and how harmful it is to society. We may tell them to "say no to drugs" or that "users are losers." By making people aware of the shamefulness of their actions, we hope to prevent their criminal activities, even if the chances that they will be detected and punished are slight.

Sometimes punishment is designed to make people ashamed and embarrass them so that they will not repeat their criminal acts. In one incident a judge in Hudson, Kansas, ordered a man who admitted molesting an 11-year-old boy to post signs reading "A Sex Offender Lives Here" on all four sides of his home and to display the warning "Sex Offender in This Car" in bold yellow lettering on both sides of his automobile.[74]

Inducing guilt or shame might include such techniques as setting strict rules to embarrass offenders. Publishing "john lists" in the newspaper punishes those arrested for soliciting prostitutes. Facilitating compliance by providing trash bins might shame chronic litterers into using them. In a classic study, Ronald Clarke found that the introduction of caller ID systems created significant reductions in the number of obscene phone calls, presumably because of the shame presented by the threat of exposure.[75]

REDUCE PROVOCATION Some crimes are the result of extreme provocation—for example, road rage. It might be possible to reduce provocation by creating programs that reduce conflict. As Philip Cook and Jens Ludwig point out, alcohol is a significant factor in various kinds of crime, including rape and assaults. One way to reduce this

sort of crime is to raise the price of beer, wine, and hard liquor. They suggest that raising the tax by 55 cents would reduce beer consumption by around 6 percent. And
there would be significant fringe benefits, including fewer auto accidents and more
money for state treasuries.[76] Another approach: mandating an early closing time in
local bars and pubs might limit assaults that result from late-night drinking and conflicts at closing time.

REMOVE EXCUSES Crime may be reduced by making it difficult for people to excuse
their criminal behavior by saying things like "I didn't know that was illegal" or "I had
no choice." Municipalities have set up roadside displays that electronically flash a car's
speed as it passes, eliminating the driver's excuse that she did not know how fast she
was going when stopped by police. Trash containers, brightly displayed, can eliminate
the claim that "I just didn't know where to throw my trash." Reducing or eliminating
excuses in this way also makes it physically easy for people to comply with laws and
regulations, thereby reducing the likelihood that they will choose crime.

Evaluating Situational Crime Prevention

Situational crime prevention efforts bring with them certain hidden costs and benefits
that can either undermine their success or increase their effectiveness. What are these
costs and benefits, and what do they tell us about the effectiveness and efficiency of
situational crime prevention?

HIDDEN BENEFITS When efforts to prevent one crime unintentionally prevent another, it is known as **diffusion**.[77] Video cameras set up in a mall to reduce shoplifting can also reduce property damage, because would-be vandals fear they are being
caught on camera. Police surveillance set up to reduce drug trafficking may unintentionally reduce the incidence of prostitution and other public order crimes by scaring
off would-be clients.[78] Intensive police patrols designed to target specifically high-
crime areas (hot spots) reduce crime in neighboring areas as well.[79]

    Discouragement occurs when crime control efforts targeting a particular locale
help reduce crime in surrounding areas and populations. Programs designed to control drug dealing in a particular area of the city have been found to decrease drug
sales not only in targeted areas but also in adjacent areas. The message that drug
dealing would not be tolerated in a particular neighborhood had a spillover effect,
decreasing the total number of people involved in drug activity, even though they did
not operate in the targeted areas.[80]

HIDDEN COSTS Situational crime prevention efforts may also contain hidden costs
that may limit their effectiveness.

- **Displacement** occurs when crime control efforts in one location simply move, or
  redirect, offenders to less heavily guarded alternative targets.[81] Beefed-up police
  patrols may appear to reduce crime but in reality merely shift it to a more vulnerable neighborhood.[82]
- **Extinction** occurs when crime reduction programs produce a short-term positive
  effect, but benefits dissipate as criminals adjust to new conditions; for example,
  burglars learn to dismantle alarms or avoid patrols. A Philadelphia police program that made use of foot patrols to lower violent crime rates found that while
  the program worked at first, the effects began to quickly fade. It is possible that at
  first publicity about the program scared would-be criminals, but as time went on
  their fear dissipated and they soon resumed illegal activities.[83]
- **Replacement** occurs when criminals try new offenses to replace those neutralized by crime prevention efforts. Foiled by burglar and car alarms, motivated offenders may turn to armed robbery, a riskier and more violent crime.

Before the effectiveness of situational crime prevention can be accepted, these
hidden costs and benefits must be weighed and balanced.

---

diffusion
An effect that occurs when
efforts to prevent one crime
unintentionally prevent another.

discouragement
An effect that occurs when crime
control efforts targeting a particular
locale help reduce crime in
surrounding areas and populations.

displacement
An effect that occurs when crime
control efforts simply move, or
redirect, offenders to less heavily
guarded alternative targets.

extinction
An effect that occurs when crime
reduction programs produce a
short-term positive effect, but
benefits dissipate as criminals
adjust to new conditions.

replacement
An effect that occurs when criminals
try new offenses they had previously
avoided because situational crime
prevention programs neutralized
their crime of choice.

General Deterrence

L05 Analyze the elements of general deterrence.

According to the rational choice view, because human beings are self-interested, rational, and reasoning, they will violate the law if they do not fear the consequences of their crimes. After all, crime left unchecked can bring profit and pleasure. It stands to reason, then, that crime can be controlled by increasing the real or perceived threat of criminal punishment; this is the concept of **general deterrence**. Based on Beccaria's famous equation, the greater the severity, certainty, and speed of legal sanctions, the less inclined people will be to commit crime and, consequently, the lower the crime rate. General deterrence would be achieved if (a) the police are effective in detecting crime and apprehending criminals, (b) judges and juries were sure to convict the guilty, who would then (c) endure harsh criminal punishments.[84]

Perception and Deterrence

According to deterrence theory, not only does the actual chance of punishment but so, too, does the *perception that punishment will almost certainly be forthcoming* if they dare commit crimes.[85] A central theme of deterrence theory is that people who believe or imagine that they will be punished for crimes in the future will avoid doing those crimes in the present.[86] Even the most committed offenders (e.g., gang members, terrorists) will forgo criminal activities if they fear legal punishments.[87] Conversely, the likelihood of being arrested or imprisoned will have little effect on crime rates if criminals believe that they have only a small chance of suffering apprehension and punishment.[88] Because criminals are rational decision makers, if they can be convinced that crime will lead to punishment, then they will be deterred.

While logical, the association between perception and deterrence is not a simple one nor does it appear to be linear—that is, the greater the perception of punishment, the less people are willing to commit crime. Perception of punishment appears to change and evolve over time, shaped by a potential offender's experience and personality. There also may be different classes and types of offenders, some being more *deterrable* than others. The most significant deterrent effects can be achieved on minor petty criminals, whereas more serious offenders such as murderers are harder to discourage.[89] High-rate serious offenders may perceive less risk and more reward from crime, while others who commit less serious crime less frequently may view illegal acts as less rewarding; they tend to overestimate the risk of apprehension and punishment.[90] More experienced offenders who may have gotten away with crime in the past are less likely to fear punishment in the future.

Marginal and Restrictive Deterrence

In some instances deterrence strategies can lead to less than perfect results. Rather than entirely eliminating crime, they may reduce its frequency, duration, and severity. **Marginal deterrence** refers to the relative effectiveness of punishments. Let's say when police are called to the scene of a domestic violence disturbance they choose to arrest some offenders and let others go with a warning. If getting arrested reduces the chance of repeat offending when compared to a warning, arrest is said to produce a higher marginal deterrent effect. Arresting someone for domestic violence may not eliminate future offending completely, but it provides a better outcome than merely warning the abuser.

Restrictive deterrence (sometimes called **partial deterrence**) refers to situations in which the threat of punishment can reduce but not eliminate the frequency, severity, and duration of a crime. Restrictive deterrence would be achieved if creating a steep fine for going 20 miles per hour or more over the posted speed limit resulted in the average motorist exceeding the speed limit by only 10 miles per hour. People still speed, but not by as much.

Criminologist Bruce Jacobs suggests that restrictive deterrence contains four separate but interrelated concepts:

- The offender reduces the number of crimes she or he commits over a particular period of time.

general deterrence
A crime control policy that depends on the fear of criminal penalties convincing the potential law violator that the pains associated with crime outweigh its benefits.

marginal deterrence
Occurs when a relatively more severe penalty will produce *some* reduction in crime.

restrictive (partial) deterrence
Refers to situations in which the threat of punishment can reduce but not eliminate crime.

- The offender commits crimes of lesser seriousness than the contemplated act, believing that punishment won't be as severe for a more minor infraction.
- The offender engages in situational measures to enhance the probability that the contemplated offense will be undertaken without risk of detection.
- The offender recognizes a risky situational context, which causes him or her to commit the same crime at a different place or time.[91]

Punishment and Deterrence

According to general deterrence theory, if the certainty, severity, and celerity or speed of arrest, conviction, and sanctioning increase, crime rates should decline. Crime will persist, however, if people believe they will get away with crime and even if they are caught, they will have a good chance of escaping punishment.[92] If people believe that their criminal transgressions will almost certainly result in punishment, then only the truly irrational will commit crime.[93] The sections below examine each of these associations in some detail.

CERTAINTY OF PUNISHMENT A number of research efforts do show a direct relationship between crime rates and the certainty of punishment. And although the issue is far from settled, people who believe that they will get caught if they commit crime are the ones most likely to be deterred from committing criminal acts.[94]

Certainty increases when local police officers are active, aggressive crime fighters, convincing would-be criminals that the risk of apprehension outweighs any benefits they can gain from crime.[95] There is a positive association between the likelihood of getting arrested and crime rate levels: the higher the arrest rate, the lower the subsequent crime rate.[96]

Proactive, aggressive law enforcement seems more effective than routine patrol. Would-be criminals are deterred when police concentrate their forces and focus on so-called "hot spots" of crime, convincing them that these areas are now unsafe and off limits to criminal activity.[97] Improving response time and increasing the number of patrol cars that respond per crime may increase police efficiency and deter people from committing crime.[98]

There is still debate whether increasing the size of the local police force can actually reduce crime rates. When Steven Durlauf and Daniel Nagin carefully reviewed the existing scientific literature, they found that jurisdictions that increased the visibility of the police, hired more officers, and used patrol officers in ways that increased the perceived risk of apprehension did enjoy deterrent effects and lower crime rates.[99]

SEVERITY OF PUNISHMENT According to deterrence theory, people who believe they will be punished severely for a crime will forgo committing criminal acts.[100] Nonetheless, there is little consensus that strict punishments alone can reduce criminal activities, and most criminologists believe that the certainty of punishment, rather than its severity, is the key to deterring criminal behaviors.[101]

One reason for this skepticism is the alleged failure of the death penalty to deter murder. Because this topic is so important, it is discussed in the accompanying Policies and Issues in Criminology feature.

AP Images/Michael Graczyk

Texas death row inmate Lester Bower is shown during a 2015 interview from a visiting cage at the Texas Department of Criminal Justice Polunsky Unit. Bower was executed on June 3, 2015, for the fatal shootings of four men at an airplane hangar in 1983. At 67, Bower was the oldest inmate executed in Texas since the state resumed carrying out the death penalty in 1982. Does Bower's execution help deter crime?

Policies and Issues in Criminology

DOES THE DEATH PENALTY DISCOURAGE MURDER?

According to deterrence theory, the death penalty—the ultimate deterrent—should deter criminals from committing murder—the ultimate crime. A majority of Americans, even convicted criminals who are currently behind bars, approve of the death penalty. But is the public's approval warranted? Does the death penalty actually discourage murder?

Empirical research on the association between capital punishment and murder can be divided into three types: immediate impact studies, comparative research, and time-series analysis.

- *Immediate impact.* If capital punishment is a deterrent, the reasoning goes, then its impact should be greatest after a well-publicized execution. However, most research has failed to find evidence that an execution produces an immediate decline in the murder rate; even highly publicized executions had little impact on the murder rate.
- *Comparative research.* It is also possible to compare murder rates in jurisdictions that have abolished the death penalty with the rates in jurisdictions that routinely employ the death penalty. Studies using this approach have found little difference between the murder rates of adjacent states, regardless of their use of the death penalty; capital punishment did not appear to affect the reported rate of homicide.
- *Time-series studies.* If capital punishment is a deterrent, then periods that have an upswing in executions should also experience a downturn in violent crime and murder. Most research efforts have failed to show such a relationship. Economic conditions, population density, and incarceration rates have a much greater impact on the murder rate than does the death penalty.

Rethinking the Deterrent Effect of Capital Punishment

Some recent studies have concluded that executing criminals may, in fact, bring the murder rate down.

These newer studies, using sophisticated data analysis, have been able to uncover a more significant association—when a state routinely uses executions, the deterrent effect becomes significant.

These recent pro–death penalty studies are not without their detractors. Jeffrey Fagan, a highly regarded criminologist, finds fault with the methodology now being used, arguing that "this work fails the tests of rigorous replication and robustness analysis that are the hallmarks of good science." Fagan and his colleagues compared homicide rates in two Asian cities with vastly different execution risks. Singapore had at one time a surge in execution rate that made it the highest in the world, before significantly reducing the number of executions. Hong Kong, by contrast, has had no executions all. Nonetheless, homicide levels and trends are remarkably similar in these two cities, with neither the surge in Singapore executions nor the more recent steep drop producing any differential impact. By comparing two closely matched places with huge contrasts in actual execution but no differences in homicide trends, Fagan disputes the relative effectiveness of capital punishment as a crime deterrent.

Similarly, John Donohue and Justin Wolfers examined recent statistical studies that claimed to show a deterrent effect from the death penalty and found that they "are simply not credible." In fact, they reach an opposite conclusion: applying the death penalty actually *increases* the number of murders.

Rethinking the Death Penalty

The death penalty debate continues. Advocates argue that even if marginally effective, capital punishment ensures that convicted criminals never again get the opportunity to kill again: about 9 percent of all inmates on death row have had prior convictions for homicide. They note that the murder rate has been in dramatic decline since capital punishment has been reinstated, and the general public approves of its use as a deterrent to murder. Further, as Meredith Martin Rountree's research shows, more than 10 percent of inmates who have been executed hastened their executions by

SWIFTNESS OF PUNISHMENT The third leg of Beccaria's equation involves the celerity, or speed, of punishment: the more rapidly punishment is applied and the more closely it is linked to the crime, the more likely it is to serve as a deterrent.[102] The deterrent effect of the law may be neutralized if there is a significant lag between apprehension and punishment. In the American justice system, court delays brought

abandoning their appeals, many because they believed their execution was actually fair and justified. If so many death row inmates approve of the death penalty, how can its abolition be justified? Writing in the *Stanford Law Review*, Cass Sunstein and Adrian Vermeule conclude that "a government that settles upon a package of crime control policies that does *not* include capital punishment might well seem, at least prima facie, to be both violating the rights and reducing the welfare of its citizens—just as would a state that failed to enact simple environmental measures promising to save a great many lives."

Far from being persuaded, abolitionists note that capital punishment has significant drawbacks. Since 1976, more than 100 people have been wrongfully convicted and sentenced to death in the United States only to be exonerated when new scientific evidence has proven their innocence; the possibility that an innocent person can be executed is real and frightening. In addition, as legal scholar David Baldus and his associates have found, racial bias may influence death penalty decisions in both civilian and military courts. People are more likely to be sentenced to death when a victim is white or in cases involving black criminals and white victims—a race-based outcome that tarnishes the validity of capital punishment.

Critical Thinking

1. Even if it is effective, the death penalty is not without serious problems. When Geoffrey Rapp studied the effect of the death penalty on the safety of police officers, he found that the introduction of capital punishment actually created an extremely dangerous environment for law enforcement officers. Because the death penalty does not have a deterrent effect, criminals are more likely to kill police officers when the death penalty is in place. Tragically, the death penalty may lull officers into a false sense of security, causing them to let down their guard—killing fewer criminals but getting killed more often themselves. Given Rapp's findings, should we still maintain the death penalty?

2. Is it possible that the insignificant effects of the death penalty on murder rates is a function in the legal delays that prolong the sentence from being carried out, leaving killers on death row for many years, even decades, before they are executed? Would you recommend that the process be accelerated and executions carried out soon after guilt is established? Or is there a real purpose to delaying executions so that people on death row can exercise every avenue of appeal, making sure an innocent person is not wrongfully executed?

Sources: Jeffrey A. Fagan, "Capital Punishment: Deterrent Effects and Capital Costs," Columbia University School of Law, http://facade1.law.columbia.edu/law_school/communications/reports/summer06/capitalpunish; Franklin Zimring, Jeffrey Fagan, and David Johnson, "Executions, Deterrence and Homicide: A Tale of Two Cities," http://papers.ssrn.com/sol3/papers.cfm?abstract_id=1436993; Meredith Martin Rountree, "'I'll Make Them Shoot Me': Accounts of Death Row Prisoners Advocating for Execution," *Law and Society Review* 46 (2012): 589–622; David Baldus, Catherine Grosso, George Woodworth, and Richard Newell, "Racial Discrimination in the Administration of the Death Penalty: The Experience of the United States Armed Forces (1984–2005)," *Journal of Criminal Law and Criminology* 101 (2011): 1227–1335; Cass R. Sunstein and Adrian Vermeule, "Is Capital Punishment Morally Required? Acts, Omissions, and Lifetime Tradeoffs," *Stanford Law Review* 58 (2006): 703–750, at 749; Tomislav Kovandzic, Lynne Vieraitis, and Denise Paquette Boots, "Does the Death Penalty Save Lives? New Evidence from State Panel Data, 1977 to 2006," *Criminology and Public Policy* 8 (2009): 803–843; Jeffrey Fagan, "Death and Deterrence Redux: Science, Law and Causal Reasoning on Capital Punishment," *Ohio State Journal of Criminal Law* 4 (2006): 255–320; Joanna Shepherd, "Deterrence versus Brutalization: Capital Punishment's Differing Impacts Among States," *Michigan Law Review* 104 (2005): 203–253; John Donohue and Justin Wolfers, "Uses and Abuses of Empirical Evidence in the Death Penalty Debate," *Stanford Law Review* 58 (2005): 791–845; Geoffrey Rapp, "The Economics of Shootouts: Does the Passage of Capital Punishment Laws Protect or Endanger Police Officers?" *Albany Law Review* 65 (2002): 1051–1084.

by numerous evidentiary hearings and requests for additional trial preparation time are common trial tactics. As a result, the criminal process can be delayed to a point where the connection between crime and punishment is broken. Take for instance how the death penalty is employed. Typically, more than 10 years elapse between the time a criminal is convicted and sentenced to death for murder and that person's execution. Delay in application of the death penalty may mitigate or neutralize the potential deterrent effect of capital punishment.

Evaluating General Deterrence

Some experts believe that the purpose of the law and justice system is to create a "threat system."[103] The threat of legal punishment should, on the face of it, deter law-breakers through fear. Nonetheless, crime rates and deterrent measures are much less closely related than choice theorists might expect. Despite efforts to punish criminals and make them fear crime, there is little evidence that the fear of apprehension and punishment alone can reduce crime rates. How can this discrepancy be explained?

RATIONALITY Deterrence theory assumes a rational offender who weighs the costs and benefits of a criminal act before deciding on a course of action. Criminals may be desperate people who choose crime because they believe there is no reasonable alternative. Some may suffer from personality disorders that impair their judgment and render them incapable of making truly rational decisions. Psychologists believe that chronic offenders suffer from an emotional state that renders them both incapable of fearing punishment and less likely to appreciate the consequences of crime.[104] Research on repeat sex offenders finds that they suffer from an elevated emotional state that negates the deterrent effect of the law.[105] There is also evidence that drinking alcohol impedes a person's ability to reasonably assess the costs and benefits of crime.[106] If the benefits of crime are exaggerated, the law's deterrent effect may be deflated.

COMPULSION Many offenders act compulsively and are therefore unlikely to be deterred by the future threat of punishment. Take for instance sex offenders whose behavior is difficult to control. As you may recall, the evidence showing that sex offender lists can control crime has been spotty. Research shows that registration lists have little effectiveness as a crime control mechanism.[107]

We know that a relatively small group of chronic offenders commits a significant percentage of all serious crimes. Some psychologists believe this select group suffers from an innate or inherited emotional state that renders them both incapable of fearing punishment and less likely to appreciate the consequences of crime.[108] Their compulsive behavior and heightened emotional state negate the deterrent effect of the law.[109]

SYSTEM EFFECTIVENESS As Beccaria's famous equation tells us, the threat of punishment involves not only its severity but also its certainty and speed. The American legal system is not very effective. About half of all crimes are reported to police, and police make arrests in only about 20 percent of reported crimes. Even when offenders are detected, police officers may choose to warn rather than arrest.[110] The odds of receiving a prison term are less than 20 per 1,000 crimes committed. As a result, some offenders believe they will not be severely punished for their acts, and they consequently have little regard for the law's deterrent power. Even those accused of murder are often convicted of lesser offenses and spend relatively short amounts of time behind bars.[111] In making their "rational choice," offenders may be aware that the deterrent effect of the law is minimal.

CRIMINALS DISCOUNT PUNISHMENTS Would-be criminals are not well informed about the actual risks of sanctions. They may know somebody who made a big score and that shapes their perceptions: according to their thinking, crime may actually pay.[112] Criminals who have already been punished may believe that the likelihood of getting caught twice for the same type of crime is remote: "Lightning never strikes twice in the same spot," they may reason; no one is that unlucky.[113]

SOME OFFENDERS—AND SOME CRIMES—ARE MORE "DETERRABLE" THAN OTHERS Not every crime can be discouraged nor is every criminal deterrable.[114] Some people may be suffering from personality disorders and mental infirmity that make them immune to the deterrent power of the law.[115] Others live in economically depressed neighborhoods, where the threat of formal sanctions is irrelevant because people living in these areas have little to lose if arrested; their opportunities are few, and they have little attachment to social institutions such as school and family. Even if they truly fear the consequences of the law, they must commit crime to survive in a hostile environment.

It also appears that it is easier to deter offenders from some crimes than from others.[116] The most significant deterrent effects appear to be achieved in minor crimes and offenses, such as recreational drug use, whereas more serious crimes such as homicide are harder to discourage.[117]

Specific Deterrence

The theory of **specific deterrence** (also called special or particular deterrence) holds that criminal sanctions should be so powerful that known criminals will never repeat their criminal acts. According to this view, the drunk driver whose sentence is a substantial fine and a week in the county jail should be convinced that the price to be paid for drinking and driving is too great to consider future violations. Similarly, burglars who spend five years in a tough, maximum-security prison should find their enthusiasm for theft dampened.[118] In principle, punishment works when a connection can be established between the planned action and memories of its consequence; if these recollections are adequately intense, the action is unlikely to occur again.[119] The theory supposes that people can "learn from their mistakes" and that those who are caught and punished will perceive greater risk than those who have escaped detection.[120] As the perceived benefits of crime decline, so too should **recidivism**.[121]

The evidence on specific deterrence is decidedly mixed: the association between experiencing punishment and desistance from crime is not always perfect. For example, while some initial research found that domestic violence offenders who received severe punishments were less likely to offend, follow-up studies failed to replicate a significant specific deterrent effect.[122] Many offenders recidivate, even after suffering a prison sentence; the effect of incarceration on rearrest sometimes appears to be minimal.[123]

Toughen Punishment?

It's possible that a specific deterrent can be achieved if the severity of punishment is increased and type of punishment is amplified. Research by Benjamin Meade and his associates found that inmates serving long sentences (five years or more) are less likely to recidivate once released than those serving shorter sentences.[124] However, other research finds that former inmates who report that their incarceration conditions were particularly severe do not report any less criminal activity upon release than those who had a better prison experience; the severity of punishment did not have the desired effect.[125]

WHY IS THE EVIDENCE MIXED? How is it possible that even the harshest treatment fails to produce the desired specific deterrent effect on future crime?

- Punishment may breed defiance rather than deterrence. People who are harshly treated may want to show that they cannot be broken by the system.
- The stigma of harsh treatment labels people and helps lock offenders into a criminal career instead of convincing them to avoid one. Teens who get arrested are more likely to join gangs. Instead of deterring crime, an arrest may intensify and or/amplify criminal motivations.[126] Experiencing the harshest punishments, such as a stay in a supermax prison, may cause severe psychological problems because these prisons isolate convicts, offer little sensory stimulation, and provide minimal opportunities for interaction with other people.[127]
- The effect of punishment is negligible in neighborhoods where almost everyone has a criminal record.[128]

Thus, although the concept of specific deterrence should work on paper, the reality can be far different.

L06 Discuss the basic concepts of specific deterrence.

specific deterrence
The view that criminal sanctions should be so powerful that offenders will never repeat their criminal acts.

recidivism
Repetition of criminal behavior.

Incapacitation

Even if severe punishments cannot effectively turn criminals away from crime, it stands to reason that if more criminals are sent to prison, the crime rate should go down. Because most people age out of crime, the duration of a criminal career is limited. Placing offenders behind bars during their prime crime years should reduce their lifetime opportunity to commit crime. The shorter the span of opportunity, the fewer offenses they can commit during their lives; hence, crime is reduced. This theory, which is known as the **incapacitation effect**, seems logical, but does it work?

> **incapacitation effect**
> The idea that keeping offenders in confinement will eliminate the risk of their committing further offenses.

Today, more than one in every hundred US adults is behind bars (about 2.3 million people).[129] Advocates of incapacitation suggest that this growth in the prison/jail population is directly responsible for the decade-long decline in the crime rate. Putting dangerous felons under lock and key for longer periods of time significantly reduces the opportunity they have to commit crime, so the crime rate declines as well.

Although it is difficult to measure precisely, there is at least some evidence that crime rates and incarceration rates are related.[130] Economist Steven Levitt, author of the widely read book *Freakonomics*, concludes that each person put behind bars results in a decrease of 15 serious crimes per year.[131] He argues that the social benefits associated with crime reduction equal or exceed the social and financial costs of incarceration.[132]

Even though Levitt's argument is persuasive, not all criminologists buy into the incapacitation effect:

- There is little evidence that incapacitating criminals will deter them from future criminality, and there *is* reason to believe they may be more inclined to commit even more crimes upon release. There is a significant correlation between incarceration and recidivism.[133]
- Former inmates often suffer postrelease personal and financial problems that cause them to commit more crimes than they might have had they not been sentenced to prison. The crimes that are "saved" while they serve time are more than made up for by the extra ones they commit because they are now ex-cons.[134]
- By its nature, the prison experience exposes young, first-time offenders to higher-risk, more experienced inmates who can influence their lifestyle and help shape their attitudes; prisons are "schools for crime."
- Imprisoning established offenders may open new opportunities for competitors. Incarcerating gang members or organized crime figures may open illegal markets to new groups that are even hungrier and more aggressive than the gangs they replaced.

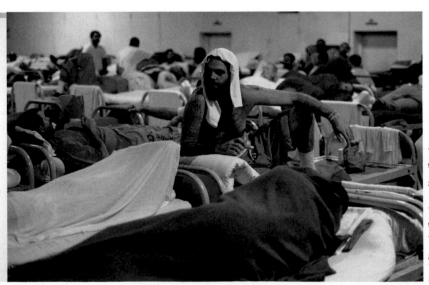

Using an incapacitation strategy to control crime may work, but it also brings unpleasant side effects such as prison overcrowding. Here, an inmate at Chino State Prison in California, which houses 5,500 inmates, relaxes on a bunk bed in a gymnasium that was modified to house 213 prisoners. In 2009, the US Supreme Court ordered the state to release 40,000 prisoners in order to cope with overcrowding so severe that it violated their human rights.

- The effect of costly incarceration sentences may not justify the modest reduction in the crime rate they produce. Incarceration reduces crime, but only up to a point. Once the incarceration rate hits a certain level (at the state level the tipping point appears to be around 325 inmates per 100,000 population), crime rates actually increase. It is possible that somewhere along the line mass incarceration destabilizes society, producing higher crime rates.[135]

- Most criminal offenses are committed by teens and very young adult offenders who are unlikely to be sent to prison for a single felony conviction. Older criminals are already past the age when they are likely to commit crime. As a result, a strict incarceration policy may keep people in prison beyond the time when they cease being a threat to society, while a new cohort of high-risk adolescents is on the street.[136] A strict incarceration policy would result in a growing number of elderly inmates whose maintenance costs are much higher than those of younger inmates.

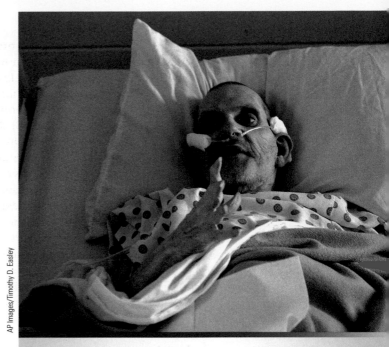

AP Images/Timothy D. Easley

Patrick O'Hara, a patient in the medical unit, speaks with staff members of the Kentucky State Reformatory in LaGrange. It costs Kentucky $3.3 million a year to care for 50 elderly inmates who can't take care of themselves, a burden the state is preparing to shift to the federal government. Do you agree that there is no real purpose in keeping inmates like O'Hara behind bars?

It is also possible that any incarceration–crime rate relationship is not linear or predictable. There are times when a surge in incarceration coincided with a significant decline in crime rates (1991–2000); however, during other time periods, crime rate increases coincided with increasing incarceration rates (1984–1991).[137] Such findings weaken the argument that the key to lower crime rates is locking people up for long periods of time.

In sum, there is little clear-cut evidence that nation's decades long "incarceration binge" has produced the expected results, and it may have done much more harm than good. The Policies and Issues in Criminology feature looks at the racial effects of mass incarceration. Concept Summary 4.1 summarizes the main features of choice theories.

Concept Summary 4.1   Choice Theories

Theory	Major Premise	Strengths	Research Focus
Rational choice	Law-violating behavior occurs after offenders weigh information on their personal needs and the situational factors involved in the difficulty and risk of committing a crime.	Explains why high-risk people do not constantly engage in crime. Relates theory to crime control policy. It is not limited by class or other social variables.	Offense patterns—where, when, and how crime takes place.
General deterrence	People will commit crime if they perceive that the benefits outweigh the risks. Crime is a function of the severity, certainty, and speed of punishment.	Shows the relationship between crime and punishment. Suggests a real solution to crime.	Perception of punishment, effect of legal sanctions, probability of punishment, and crime rates.
Specific deterrence	If punishment is severe enough, criminals will not repeat their illegal acts.	Provides a strategy to reduce crime.	Recidivism, repeat offending, punishment type, and crime.
Incapacitation	Keeping known criminals out of circulation will reduce crime rates.	Recognizes the role that opportunity plays in criminal behavior. Provides a solution to chronic offending.	Prison population and crime rates, sentence length, and crime.

Policies and Issues
in Criminology

RACIAL DISPARITY IN STATE PRISONS

One major drawback of a strict incarceration policy to reduce or prevent crime is racial disparity. Young, poor, black men are incarcerated at a far higher rate than their representation in the population. And though imprisonment rates for white, black, and Hispanic adults are now at their lowest level for any time during the past decade, racial differences have been maintained. The latest data available show that the rate of imprisonment per 100,000 population for black adults is now 1,745. Hispanics are incarcerated at the rate of 820 per 100,000 and whites 312 per 100,000 in 2015 (see Figure A).

There are significant state-based racial differences in the incarceration rate:

- African Americans are incarcerated in state prisons at a rate that is 5.1 times the imprisonment of whites. In five states (Iowa, Minnesota, New Jersey, Vermont, and Wisconsin), the disparity is more than 10 to 1.
- In twelve states, more than half of the prison population is black: Alabama, Delaware, Georgia, Illinois, Louisiana, Maryland, Michigan, Mississippi, New Jersey, North Carolina, South Carolina, and Virginia. Maryland, whose prison population is 72 percent African American, tops the nation.
- In eleven states, at least 1 in 20 adult black males is in prison.

In sum, disparities vary broadly across the states, but even in Hawaii—the state with the lowest black/white disparity—African Americans are imprisoned more than two times the rate of whites.

There are a number of suspected reasons for this race-based incarceration differential. Structural racism and bias may account for at least part. However, the most likely culprit is a series of policies that were enacted to expand the use of imprisonment for drug offenses and also to increase penalties and the amount of time served behind bars. Harsh drug laws are clearly an important factor in the persistent racial and ethnic disparities observed in state prisons, especially when combined with differential law enforcement practices. African Americans are nearly four times as likely as whites to be arrested for drug offenses and 2.5 times as likely to be arrested for drug possession. Racial differences in arrest for drug offenses are vexing because the evidence shows that whites and blacks use drugs at roughly the same rate. For example, from 1995 to 2005, African Americans comprised approximately 13 percent of drug users but 36 percent of drug arrests and 46 percent of those convicted for drug offenses.

Critical Thinking

1. What can be done to reduce racial disparity in the prison system? Would legalizing drugs be an answer?
2. Why do you suppose some states have greater racial disparity in sentencing than others?

Sources: Ashley Nellis, *The Color of Justice: Racial and Ethnic Disparity in State Prisons*, The Sentencing Project, June 14, 2016; E. Ann Carson and Elizabeth Anderson, *Prisoners in 2015* (Washington, DC: Bureau of Justice Statistics, 2016).

FIGURE A
Imprisonment Rate of Persons under the Jurisdiction of State or Federal Correction Authorities
Source: E. Ann Carson and Elizabeth Anderson, *Prisoners in 2015*, Bureau of Justice Statistics, 2016, p. 10, https://www.bjs.gov/content/pub/pdf/p15.pdf (accessed April 2017).

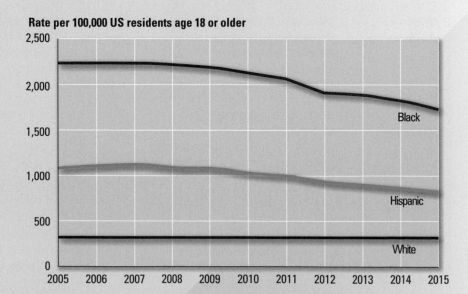

Criminal Justice and Rational Choice Theory

From the origins of classical theory to the development of modern rational choice views, the belief that criminals choose to commit crime has influenced the relationships among law, punishment, and crime. Although research on the core principles of choice theory and deterrence theories produces mixed results, these models have had an important impact on criminal justice system crime prevention strategies.

Police and Rational Choice Theory

While adding cops seems a logical way of deterring crime, this assumption has been questioned ever since the classic Kansas City patrol study found that crime rates were unaffected by merely increasing (or decreasing) the number of police on patrol. Nonetheless, some recent evidence indicates that adding to police patrol forces does in fact help reduce crime rates and that police are a more effective deterrent than toughening sentences or putting people in prison.[138] The Kansas City study was conducted in the 1970s, so it is possible that newer technologies, such as computers in police cars, have made patrol more effective.

The deterrent effect of police may depend on crime control tactics. Focused crime-fighting initiatives, targeting specific crimes such as murder or robbery, are more effective than routine patrol. Some police departments have instituted **crackdowns**, sudden changes in police activity designed to increase the communicated threat or actual certainty of punishment. Another aggressive patrol approach, instituted in New York City, was the highly controversial stop, question, and frisk (SQF) policy in which officers stopped people they considered suspicious, armed, or dangerous, and patted them down (i.e., frisked the outer clothing), without any real evidence or probable cause. Legal challenges were filed because the SQFs were far more frequent in minority communities and because blacks and Hispanics were disproportionately stopped under the policy. A federal court ordered changes to SQF and the number of police stops under the program has been dramatically reduced. Recent research by Richard Rosenfeld and Robert Fornango shows that though legally troubled, the SQF policy did have a deterrent effect on crime in the New York City neighborhoods where it was employed.[139]

Another recent approach known as "pulling levers policing" or **focused deterrence** is about activating or pulling every deterrent "lever" available to reduce the targeted problem. If it is juvenile gang violence, responses may include shutting down drug markets, serving warrants, enforcing probation restrictions, and making disorder arrests. A major component to this approach is communicating direct and explicit messages to offenders about the responses they can expect if this behavior is not stopped. Careful evaluations using sophisticated matching group comparisons finds that the program was an effective deterrent to gang crime.[140]

Courts, Sentencing, and Rational Choice Theory

The fact that punishment may deter criminals from committing crime has shaped sentencing policy. A number of states have adopted draconian sentencing policies that require mandatory prison terms for specific crimes such as drug trafficking or the use of a firearm while committing crime. Another deterrence strategy is the "three strikes and you're out" laws, which require the state courts to hand down mandatory periods of incarceration of up to life in prison to persons who have been convicted of a serious criminal offense on three or more separate occasions. While a policy of placing people convicted of a third felony behind bars for life is politically compelling, many criminologists believe these laws are ineffective and will create a growing population of expensive to maintain elderly inmates who committed relatively minor crimes.[141]

CHECKPOINTS

▶ Situational crime prevention efforts are designed to reduce or redirect crime by making it more difficult to profit from illegal acts.

▶ General deterrence models are based on the fear of punishment that is severe, swift, and certain.

▶ Specific deterrence aims at reducing crime through the application of severe punishments. Once offenders experience these punishments, they will be unwilling to repeat their criminal activities.

▶ Incapacitation strategies are designed to reduce crime by taking known criminals out of circulation, which denies them the opportunity to commit further offenses. The effectiveness of incapacitation strategies is hotly debated.

crackdowns
The concentration of police resources on particular problem areas, such as street-level drug dealing, to eradicate or displace criminal activity.

focused deterrence
The view that police can deter crime by using every strategy possible and also by directly interacting with offenders and communicating clear consequences if they engage in criminal activity.

Corrections and Rational Choice Theory

There are a number of choice theory–based correctional policies designed to convince convicted criminals that crime does not pay and they would be better off pursuing more legitimate alternatives. Some states are now employing high-security supermax prisons that apply a bare minimum of treatment and impose lockdown 23 hours a day.

Take for instance the federal facility (ADX) in Florence, Colorado. This prison has the most sophisticated security measures in the United States, including hundreds of video cameras and electronically controlled gates. Inside the cells, all furniture is immovable; the bed, the desk, and TV stand are made of cement. All potential weapons, including toilet seats, toilet handles, and soap dishes, have been removed. The cement walls are 5,000-pound quality, and steel bars are placed so they crisscross every eight inches inside the institution. Cells are angled so that prisoners can see neither each other nor the outside scenery. This cuts down on communication and denies inmates a sense of location, to prevent escapes. The newer prisons have totally automated the traditional tasks of correction officers such as opening cell doors and surveillance. Inmates are escorted by a minimum of three officers for their five hours of private recreation per week.

Certainly, such a harsh regimen should discourage future criminality. However, studies that compare supermax prisoners with inmates from more traditional prisons on a one-to-one basis show that upon release supermax prisoners had significantly higher felony recidivism rates than controls from less restrictive prisons. Those released directly into the community from a supermax prison commit new offenses sooner than supermax prisoners who were first sent to traditional institutions three months or more before their release.[142] Creating tougher prisons, then, may not produce the desired deterrent effect.

Thinking Like a Criminologist

Just Punishment   The governor has asked you, a death penalty expert, to give your advice on abolishing the death penalty in the state. He has recently read an article by philosopher Bradley Wilson that sets out the argument against the death penalty using this train of thought:

1. Capital punishment is not morally required in any case.
2. Mercy is a morally valuable trait; all things being equal, actions that demonstrate mercy have more moral worth than those that do not. Thus, a moral viewpoint that incorporates mercy is preferable to one that does not.
3. Not executing those who have committed capital crimes demonstrates mercy.
4. Just punishment of capital crimes is compatible with showing mercy.
5. Thus, not executing those who have committed capital crimes is morally preferable to executing them.[143]

Writing Assignment

Write a critical essay commenting on this reasoning. Address the issue of whether executing people is an effective crime control policy—or might it have hidden costs that undermine its effectiveness? Address the moral issue for abolition.

SUMMARY

LO1   Describe the development of rational choice theory.

Rational choice theory has its roots in the classical school of criminology developed by the eighteenth-century Italian social thinker Cesare Beccaria. In the 1960s, Nobel Prize–winning economist Gary Becker applied his views on rational behavior and human capital to criminal activity. James Q. Wilson observed that people who are likely to commit crime are unafraid of breaking the law because they value the excitement and thrills of crime, have a low stake in conformity, and are willing to take greater chances than the average person.

LO2   Explore the concepts of rational choice.

Law-violating behavior is the product of careful thought and planning. People who commit crime believe that the rewards of crime outweigh the risks. If they think they are likely to get arrested and punished, people will not risk engaging in criminal activities. Before choosing to commit a crime, reasoning criminals carefully select targets, and their behavior is systematic and selective. Rational choice theorists view crime as both offense-specific and offender-specific.

LO3   Interpret the evidence showing that crime is rational.

There is a great deal of anecdotal evidence showing that crime is rational. Even drug use is controlled by rational decision making. Users report that they began taking drugs when they believed the benefits of substance abuse outweighed its costs. Drug dealers approach their profession in a businesslike fashion. Violent criminals who are seemingly irrational, even serial killers, select suitable targets by picking people who are vulnerable and lack adequate defenses. Even johns make careful and rational decisions when engaging prostitutes and then share their knowledge and expertise in Internet chat rooms and web forums.

LO4   Discuss the elements of situational crime prevention.

Situational crime prevention involves developing tactics to reduce or eliminate a specific crime problem. Such tactics include increased efforts to discourage crime, such as putting unbreakable glass on storefronts, locking gates, and fencing yards. Another approach is to increase the risks of crime through better security efforts. Reducing the rewards of crime is designed to lessen the value of crime to the potential criminal. Crime may be reduced or prevented if we can communicate to people the wrongfulness of their behavior and how harmful it is to society. Crime may be reduced by making it difficult for people to excuse their criminal behavior by saying things like "I didn't know that was illegal" or "I had no choice."

LO5   Analyze the elements of general deterrence.

Crime can be controlled by increasing the real or perceived threat of criminal punishment. According to deterrence theory, criminality is affected not only by the actual chance of punishment but also by the *perception* that one is likely to be punished. A central theme of deterrence theory is that people who believe they will be punished for crimes will avoid committing those crimes. According to general deterrence theory, if the certainty of arrest, conviction, and sanctioning increases, crime rates should decline. The threat of severe punishment should also bring the crime rate down. The more rapidly punishment is applied and the more closely it is linked to the crime, the more likely it will serve as a deterrent. The factors of severity, certainty, and speed of punishment may also influence one another.

LO6   Discuss the basic concepts of specific deterrence.

The theory of specific deterrence holds that criminal sanctions should be so powerful that convicted criminals will never repeat their criminal acts.

However, research on specific deterrence does not provide any clear-cut evidence that punishing criminals is an effective means of stopping them from committing future crimes. Punishment may bring defiance rather than deterrence. People who are harshly treated may want to show that they cannot be broken by the system. The stigma of harsh treatment labels people and helps lock offenders into a criminal career instead of convincing them to avoid one.

Key Terms

rational choice theory (choice theory) 100
offense-specific 102
offender-specific 102
johns 109
situational crime prevention 110

defensible space 110
crime discouragers 112
diffusion 113
discouragement 113
displacement 113
extinction 113
replacement 113

general deterrence 114
marginal deterrence 114
restrictive (partial) deterrence 114
specific deterrence 119
recidivism 119

incapacitation effect 120
crackdowns 123
focused deterrence 123

Critical Thinking Questions

1. Are criminals rational decision makers, or are most of them motivated by uncontrollable psychological and emotional drives or social forces such as poverty and despair?

2. Would you want to live in a society where crime rates were quite low because they were controlled by extremely harsh punishments, such as flogging for vandalism?

3. Which would you be more afraid of if you were caught by the police while shoplifting: receiving criminal punishment or having to face the contempt of your friends or relatives?

4. Is it possible to create a method of capital punishment that would actually deter people from committing murder? Would televising executions work? What might be some of the negative consequences of such a policy?

Notes

All URLs accessed in 2017.

1. United States Attorney's Office, Northern District of Ohio, "Toledo man Sentenced to 27 Years in Prison for Operating Chop Shop, Eight Others Also Sent to Prison," http://www.justice.gov/usao-ndoh/pr /toledo-man-sentenced-27-years-prison-operating -chop-shop-0; FBI, "Multi-State Chop Shop Operation Disrupted: Criminal Enterprise Leader Among Those Convicted," June 23, 2015, https:// www.fbi.gov/news/stories/2015/june/multi-state -chop-shop-operation-disrupted/multi-state-chop -shop-operation-disrupted.

2. Gary Becker, "Crime and Punishment: An Economic Approach," *Journal of Political Economy* 76 (1968): 169–217.

3. James Q. Wilson, *Thinking About Crime*, rev. ed. (New York: Vintage Books, 1983), p. 260.

4. See, generally, Derek Cornish and Ronald Clarke, eds., *The Reasoning Criminal: Rational Choice Perspectives on Offending* (New York: Springer Verlag, 1986); Philip Cook, "The Demand and Supply of Criminal Opportunities," in *Crime and Justice*, Vol. 7, ed. Michael Tonry and Norval Morris (Chicago: University of Chicago Press, 1986), pp. 1–28; Ronald Clarke and Derek Cornish, "Modeling Offenders' Decisions: A Framework for Research and Policy," in *Crime and Justice*, Vol. 6, ed. Michael Tonry and Norval Morris (Chicago: University of Chicago Press, 1985), pp. 147–187; Morgan Reynolds, *Crime by Choice: An Economic Analysis* (Dallas: Fisher Institute, 1985).

5. Hung-en Sung and Linda Richter, "Rational Choice and Environmental Deterrence in the Retention of Mandated Drug Abuse Treatment Clients," *International Journal of Offender Therapy and Comparative Criminology* 51 (2007): 686–702.

6. Melanie Wellsmith and Amy Burrell, "The Influence of Purchase Price and Ownership Levels on Theft Targets: The Example of Domestic Burglary," *British Journal of Criminology* 45 (2005): 741–764.

7. Jeffrey Bouffard, "Predicting Differences in the Perceived Relevance of Crime's Costs and Benefits in a Test of Rational Choice Theory," *International Journal of Offender Therapy and Comparative Criminology* 51 (2007): 461–485.

8. Carlo Morselli and Marie-Noële Royer, "Criminal Mobility and Criminal Achievement," *Journal of Research in Crime and Delinquency* 45 (2008): 4–21.

9. Bouffard, "Predicting Differences."

10. Ross Matsueda, Derek Kreager, and David Huizinga, "Deterring Delinquents: A Rational Choice Model of Theft and Violence," *American Sociological Review* 71 (2006): 95–122.

11. Derek Cornish and Ronald Clarke, "Understanding Crime Displacement: An Application of Rational Choice Theory," *Criminology* 25 (1987): 933–947.

12. Michael Gottfredson and Travis Hirschi, *A General Theory of Crime* (Stanford, CA: Stanford University Press, 1990).

13. D. Wayne Osgood and Amy Anderson, "Unstructured Socializing and Rates of Delinquency," *Criminology* 42 (2004): 519–550.

14. Wim Bernasco, Stijn Ruiter, Gerben Bruinsma, Lieven Pauwels, and Frank Weerman, "Situational Causes of Offending: A Fixed-Effects Analysis of Space–Time Budget Data," *Criminology* 51 (2013): 895–926.

15. Megan Bears Augustyn and Jean Marie McGloin, "The Risk of Informal Socializing with Peers: Considering Gender Differences Across Predatory Delinquency and Substance Use," *Justice Quarterly* 30 (2013): 117–143.

16. Jack Katz, *The Seductions of Crime* (New York: Basic Books, 1988).

17. Holly Nguyen and Jean Marie McGloin, "Does Economic Adversity Breed Criminal Cooperation? Considering the Motivation Behind Group Crime," *Criminology* 51 (2013): 833–870.

18. Mikko Aaltonen, Atte Oksanen, and Janne Kivivuori, "Debt Problems and Crime," *Criminology* 54 (2016): 307–331.

19. Ting Zhang, "Addressing Unobserved Heterogeneity in the Relationship Between Crime and Consumer Confidence," *Journal of Quantitative Criminology* 32 (2016): 47–59.

20. Melissa Thompson and Christopher Uggen, "Dealers, Thieves, and the Common Determinants of Drug and Nondrug Illegal Earnings," *Criminology* 59 (2012): 1057–1087; Uggen and Thompson, "The Socioeconomic Determinants of Ill-Gotten Gains: Within-Person Changes in Drug Use and Illegal Earnings," *American Journal of Sociology* 109 (2003): 146–185.

21. FBI, *Crime in the United States, 2015*, https://ucr.fbi .gov/crime-in-the-u.s/2015/crime-in-the-u.s.-2015 /offenses-known-to-law-enforcement/robbery.

22. Pierre Tremblay and Carlo Morselli, "Patterns in Criminal Achievement: Wilson and Abrahamse Revisited," *Criminology* 38 (2000): 633–660.

23. Steven Levitt and Sudhir Alladi Venkatesh, "An Economic Analysis of a Drug-Selling Gang's Finances," NBER Working Papers 6592 (Cambridge, MA: National Bureau of Economic Research, 1998).

24. Bill McCarthy, "New Economics of Sociological Criminology," *Annual Review of Sociology* (2002): 417–442.

25. Ronald Akers, "Rational Choice, Deterrence and Social Learning Theory in Criminology: The Path Not Taken," *Journal of Criminal Law and Criminology* 81 (1990): 653–676.

26. Frédéric Ouellet and Martin Bouchard, "Only a Matter of Time? The Role of Criminal Competence in Avoiding Arrest," *Justice Quarterly*, published online August 17, 2016.

27. Neal Shover, *Aging Criminals* (Beverly Hills, CA: Sage, 1985).

28. Bruce Jacobs, "Crack Dealers' Apprehension Avoidance Techniques: A Case of Restrictive Deterrence," *Justice Quarterly* 13 (1996): 359–381.

29. Ibid., p. 367.

30. Ibid., p. 372.

31. Barbara Menting, Marre Lammers, Stijn Ruiter, and Wim Bernasco, "Family Matters: Effects of Family Members' Residential Areas on Crime Location Choice," *Criminology* 54 (2016): 413–433.

32. Aiden Sidebottom, Matt Ashby, and Shane D. Johnson, "Copper Cable Theft: Revisiting the Price–Theft Hypothesis," *Journal of Research in Crime and Delinquency* 51 (2014): 684–700.

33. Christopher Contreras, "A Block-Level Analysis of Medical Marijuana Dispensaries and Crime in the City of Los Angeles," *Justice Quarterly*, published online December 25, 2016.

34. Jessica Rust, "Regarding: Luxury Vehicle Thefts in the United States," National Insurance Crime Bureau, July 26, 2013, https://www.nicb.org/newsroom /news-releases/luxury-vehicle-thefts-in-the-us.

35. Paul Cromwell, James Olson, and D'Aunn Wester Avary, *Breaking and Entering: An Ethnographic Analysis of Burglary* (Newbury Park, CA: Sage, 1989), p. 24.

36. Ibid., pp. 30–32.

37. George Rengert and John Wasilchick, *Space, Time, and Crime: Ethnographic Insights into Residential Burglary* (Washington, DC: National Institute of Justice, 1989); see also Rengert and Wasilchick, *Suburban Burglar: A Tale of 2 Suburbs* (Springfield, IL: Charles C Thomas, 2000).

38. Matthew Robinson, "Lifestyles, Routine Activities, and Residential Burglary Victimization," *Journal of Criminal Justice* 22 (1999): 27–52.

39. Patrick Donnelly and Charles Kimble, "Community Organizing, Environmental Change, and Neighborhood Crime," *Crime and Delinquency* 43 (1997): 493–511.

40. Bruce Jacobs and Michael Cherbonneau, "Auto Theft and Restrictive Deterrence," *Justice Quarterly* 31 (2014): 344–367.

41. Ronald Clarke and Marcus Felson, "Introduction: Criminology, Routine Activity and Rational Choice," in *Routine Activity and Rational Choice* (New Brunswick, NJ: Transaction, 1993), pp. 1–14.

42. Associated Press, "Thrift Hearings Resume Today in Senate," *Boston Globe*, January 2, 1991, p. 10.

43. Michael Townsley, Daniel Birks, Wim Bernasco, Stijn Ruiter, Shane D. Johnson, and Gentry White, "Burglar Target Selection: A Cross-national Comparison," *Journal of Research in Crime and Delinquency* 52 (2015): 3–31.

44. Richard Felson and Steven Messner, "To Kill or Not to Kill? Lethal Outcomes in Injurious Attacks," *Criminology* 34 (1996): 519–545, at 541.

45. Marie Rosenkrantz Lindegaard, Wim Bernasco, and Scott Jacques, "Consequences of Expected and Observed Victim Resistance for Offender Violence During Robbery Events," *Journal of Research in Crime and Delinquency* 52 (2015): 32–61.

46. Gordon Knowles, "Deception, Detection, and Evasion: A Trade Craft Analysis of Honolulu, Hawaii's Street Crack Cocaine Traffickers," *Journal of Criminal Justice* 27 (1999): 443–455.

47. John Petraitis, Brian Flay, and Todd Miller, "Reviewing Theories of Adolescent Substance Use: Organizing Pieces in the Puzzle," *Psychological Bulletin* 117 (1995): 67–86.

48. Levitt and Venkatesh, "An Economic Analysis of a Drug-Selling Gang's Finances."

49. George Rengert, *The Geography of Illegal Drugs* (Boulder, CO: Westview Press, 1996).

50. Eric Piza and Victoria Sytsma, "Exploring the Defensive Actions of Drug Sellers in Open-Air Markets," *Journal of Research in Crime and Delinquency* 53 (2016): 36–65.

51. Judith Aldridge and Rebecca Askew, "Delivery Dilemmas: How Drug Cryptomarket Users Identify and Seek to Reduce Their Risk of Detection by Law Enforcement," *International Journal of Drug Policy* 41 (2017): 101–109.

52. Felson and Messner, "To Kill or Not to Kill? Lethal Outcomes in Injurious Attacks."

53. Richard Wright and Scott Decker, *Armed Robbers in Action: Stickups and Street Culture* (Boston: Northeastern University Press, 1997).

54. William Smith, Sharon Glave Frazee, and Elizabeth Davison, "Furthering the Integration of Routine Activity and Social Disorganization Theories: Small Units of Analysis and the Study of Street Robbery as a Diffusion Process," *Criminology* 38 (2000): 489–521.

55. Paul Bellair, "Informal Surveillance and Street Crime: A Complex Relationship," *Criminology* 38 (2000): 137–167.

56. Gary Kleck and Don Kates, *Armed: New Perspectives on Guns* (Amherst, NY: Prometheus Books, 2001).

57. Bruce A. Jacobs and Richard Wright, "Moralistic Street Robbery," *Crime and Delinquency* 54 (2008): 511–531.

58. Ryan King and Gretchen Sutto, "High Times for Hate Crimes: Explaining the Temporal Clustering of Hate-Motivated Offending," *Criminology* 51 (2013): 871–894.

59. Thomas Holt, Kristie Blevins, and Joseph Kuhns, "Examining Diffusion and Arrest Avoidance Practices Among Johns," *Crime and Delinquency* 60 (2014): 261–283.

60. Jeff Gruenewald, Kayla Allison-Gruenewald, and Brent R. Klein, "Assessing the Attractiveness and Vulnerability of Eco-Terrorism Targets: A Situational Crime Prevention Approach," *Studies in Conflict and Terrorism* 38 (2015): 433–455.

61. Mathew Ashby and Adam Thorpe, "Self-Guardianship at Automated Teller Machines," *Crime Prevention and Community Safety* 19 (2017): 1–16.

62. Patricia Brantingham, Paul Brantingham, and Wendy Taylor, "Situational Crime Prevention as a Key Component in Embedded Crime Prevention," *Canadian Journal of Criminology and Criminal Justice* 47 (2005): 271–292.

63. Ronald Clarke, *Situational Crime Prevention: Successful Case Studies* (Albany, NY: Harrow and Heston, 1992).

64. Brian Smith and Ronald Clarke, "Shoplifting of Everyday Products that Serve Illicit Drug Uses," *Journal of Research in Crime and Delinquency*, first published online September 11, 2014.

65. Derek Cornish and Ronald Clarke, "Opportunities, Precipitators and Criminal Decisions: A Reply to Wortley's Critique of Situational Crime Prevention," *Crime Prevention Studies* 16 (2003): 41–96; Ronald Clarke and Ross Homel, "A Revised Classification of Situational Prevention Techniques," in *Crime Prevention at a Crossroads,* ed. Steven P. Lab (Cincinnati: Anderson Publishing, 1997).

66. Nancy LaVigne, "Gasoline Drive-Offs: Designing a Less Convenient Environment," in *Crime Prevention Studies*, Vol. 2, ed. Ronald Clarke (Monsey, NY: Criminal Justice Press, 1994), pp. 91–114.

67. Lynn A. Addington and Callie Marie Rennison, "Keeping the Barbarians Outside the Gate? Comparing Burglary Victimization in Gated and Non-gated Communities," *Justice Quarterly* 32 (2015): 168–192.

68. Marcus Felson, "Those Who Discourage Crime," in *Crime and Place, Crime Prevention Studies*, Vol. 4, ed. John Eck and David Weisburd (New York: Criminal Justice Press, 1995), pp. 53–66.

69. John Eck, "Drug Markets and Drug Places," in *Problem-Oriented Policing: Crime-Specific Problems, Critical Issues and Making POP Work*, Vol. II, ed. Corina Solé Brito and Tracy Allan (Washington, DC: Police Executive Research Forum, 1999), p. 29.

70. Marie Tillyer, Holly Miller, and Rob Tillyer, "The Environmental and Situational Correlates of Victim Injury in Nonfatal Violent Incidents," *Criminal Justice and Behavior* 38 (2010): 433–452.

71. Brandon Welsh, David Farrington, and Sema Taheri, "Effectiveness and Social Costs of Public Area Surveillance for Crime Prevention," *Annual Review of Law and Social Science* 11 (2015): 111–130.

72. Keith Proctor, "The Great Surveillance Boom," *Fortune*, April 26, 2013, http://fortune.com/2013/04/26/the-great-surveillance-boom/.

73. Hyungjin Lim and Pamela Wilcox, "Crime-Reduction Effects of Open-street CCTV: Conditionality Considerations," *Justice Quarterly*, published online June 20, 2016; Welsh, Farrington, and Taheri, "Effectiveness and Social Costs of Public Area Surveillance for Crime Prevention"; Brandon C. Welsh and David P. Farrington, *Making Public Places Safer: Surveillance and Crime Prevention* (New York: Oxford University Press, 2008).

74. "Pervert's Tough Sign-tence," *The Sun*, March 26, 2008.

75. Ronald Clarke, "Deterring Obscene Phone Callers: The New Jersey Experience," in *Situational Crime Prevention*, ed. Ronald Clarke (Albany, NY: Harrow and Heston, 1992), pp. 124–132.

76. Philip Cook and Jens Ludwig, "The Economist's Guide to Crime Busting," *NIJ Journal* 270 (2012), http://nij.gov/nij/journals/270/economists-guide.htm.

77. Ronald Clarke and David Weisburd, "Diffusion of Crime Control Benefits: Observations of the Reverse of Displacement," in *Crime Prevention Studies*, Vol. 2, ed. Ronald Clarke (New York: Criminal Justice Press, 1994).

78. David Weisburd and Lorraine Green, "Policing Drug Hot Spots: The Jersey City Drug Market Analysis Experiment," *Justice Quarterly* 12 (1995): 711–734.

79. Anthony A. Braga, Andrew V. Papachristos, and David M. Hureau, "The Effects of Hot Spots Policing on Crime: An Updated Systematic Review and Meta-Analysis," *Justice Quarterly*, first published online May 16, 2012.

80. Lorraine Green, "Cleaning Up Drug Hot Spots in Oakland, California: The Displacement and Diffusion Effects," *Justice Quarterly* 12 (1995): 737–754.

81. Robert Barr and Ken Pease, "Crime Placement, Displacement, and Deflection," in *Crime and Justice, A Review of Research*, Vol. 12, ed. Michael Tonry and Norval Morris (Chicago: University of Chicago Press, 1990), pp. 277–319.

82. Clarke, *Situational Crime Prevention*, p. 27.

83. Evan Sorg, Cory Haberman, Jerry Ratcliffe, and Elizabeth Groff, "Foot Patrol in Violent Crime Hot Spots: The Longitudinal Impact of Deterrence and Posttreatment Effects of Displacement," *Criminology* 51 (2013): 65–101.

84. Peter Henning, "Deterrence Relevant in Sentencing White-Collar Defendants?" *Wayne Law Review* 61 (2015): 25–57.

85. Robert Apel, Greg Pogarsky, and Leigh Bates, "The Sanctions–Perceptions Link in a Model of School-Based Deterrence," *Journal of Quantitative Criminology* 25 (2009): 201–226.

86. Daniel Nagin and Greg Pogarsky, "Integrating Celerity, Impulsivity, and Extralegal Sanction Threats into a Model of General Deterrence: Theory and Evidence," *Criminology* 39 (2001): 865–892.

87. Jennifer Varriale Carson, "Counterterrorism and Radical Eco-Groups: A Context for Exploring the Series Hazard Model," *Journal of Quantitative Criminology*, first published online October 2013; Cheryl L. Maxson, Kristy N. Matsuda, and Karen Hennigan, "Deterrability Among Gang and Nongang Juvenile Offenders: Are Gang Members More (or Less) Deterrable than Other Juvenile Offenders?" *Crime and Delinquency* 57 (2011): 516–543.

88. Robert Bursik, Harold Grasmick, and Mitchell Chamlin, "The Effect of Longitudinal Arrest Patterns on the Development of Robbery Trends at the Neighborhood Level," *Criminology* 28 (1990): 431–450; Theodore Chiricos and Gordon Waldo, "Punishment and Crime: An Examination of Some Empirical Evidence," *Social Problems* 18 (1970): 200–217.

89. Dieter Dolling, Horst Entorf, Dieter Hermann, and Thomas Rupp, "Deterrence Effective? Results of a Meta-Analysis of Punishment," *European Journal on Criminal Policy and Research* 15 (2009): 201–224.

90. Thomas Loughran, Alex Piquero, Jeffrey Fagan, and Edward Mulvey, "Differential Deterrence: Studying Heterogeneity and Changes in Perceptual

Deterrence Among Serious Youthful Offenders," *Crime and Delinquency* 58 (2012): 3–27.

91. Bruce Jacobs, "Deterrence and Deterrability," *Criminology* 48 (2010): 417–441.

92. R. Steven Daniels, Lorin Baumhover, William Formby, and Carolyn Clark-Daniels, "Police Discretion and Elder Mistreatment: A Nested Model of Observation, Reporting, and Satisfaction," *Journal of Criminal Justice* 27 (1999): 209–225.

93. Nagin and Pogarsky, "Integrating Celerity, Impulsivity, and Extralegal Sanction Threats."

94. Daniel Nagin, "Criminal Deterrence Theory at the Outset of the Twenty-First Century," in *Crime and Justice: An Annual Review of Research*, Vol. 23, ed. Michael Tonry (Chicago: University of Chicago Press, 1998), pp. 51–92; for an opposing view, see Bursik, Grasmick, and Chamlin, "The Effect of Longitudinal Arrest Patterns on the Development of Robbery Trends at the Neighborhood Level."

95. Michael White, James Fyfe, Suzanne Campbell, and John Goldkamp, "The Police Role in Preventing Homicide: Considering the Impact of Problem-Oriented Policing on the Prevalence of Murder," *Journal of Research in Crime and Delinquency* 40 (2003): 194–226.

96. Hope Corman and Naci Mocan, "Alcohol Consumption, Deterrence and Crime in New York City," *Journal of Labor Research* 36 (2015): 103–128.

97. Braga, Papachristos, and Hureau, "The Effects of Hot Spots Policing on Crime."

98. Richard Timothy Coupe and Laurence Blake, "The Effects of Patrol Workloads and Response Strength on Arrests at Burglary Emergencies," *Journal of Criminal Justice* 33 (2005): 239–255.

99. Steven Durlauf and Daniel Nagin, "Imprisonment and Crime: Can Both Be Reduced?" *Criminology and Public Policy* 10 (2011): 13–54.

100. Antonio Tavares, Silvia Mendes, and Claudia Costa, "The Impact of Deterrence Policies on Reckless Driving: The Case of Portugal," *European Journal on Criminal Policy and Research* 14 (2008): 417–429; Greg Pogarsky, "Identifying 'Deterrable' Offenders: Implications for Research on Deterrence," *Justice Quarterly* 19 (2002): 431–453.

101. Ed Stevens and Brian Payne, "Applying Deterrence Theory in the Context of Corporate Wrongdoing: Limitations on Punitive Damages," *Journal of Criminal Justice* 27 (1999): 195–209; Jeffrey Roth, *Firearms and Violence* (Washington, DC: National Institute of Justice, 1994); Thomas Marvell and Carlisle Moody, "The Impact of Enhanced Prison Terms for Felonies Committed with Guns," *Criminology* 33 (1995): 247–281; Gary Green, "General Deterrence and Television Cable Crime: A Field Experiment in Social Crime," *Criminology* 23 (1986): 629–645.

102. Richard D. Clark, "Celerity and Specific Deterrence: A Look at the Evidence," *Canadian Journal of Criminology* 30 (1988): 109–122.

103. Ernest Van Den Haag, "The Criminal Law as a Threat System," *Journal of Criminal Law and Criminology* 73 (1982): 709–785.

104. David Lykken, "Psychopathy, Sociopathy, and Crime," *Society* 34 (1996): 30–38.

105. George Lowenstein, Daniel Nagin, and Raymond Paternoster, "The Effect of Sexual Arousal on Expectations of Sexual Forcefulness," *Journal of Research in Crime and Delinquency* 34 (1997): 443–473.

106. Lyn Exum, "The Application and Robustness of the Rational Choice Perspective in the Study of Intoxicated and Angry Intentions to Aggress," *Criminology* 40 (2002): 933–967.

107. Cynthia Najdowski, Hayley Cleary, and Margaret Stevenson, "Adolescent Sex Offender Registration Policy: Perspectives on General Deterrence Potential from Criminology and Developmental Psychology," *Psychology, Public Policy, and Law* 22 (2016): 114–125.

108. David Lykken, "Psychopathy, Sociopathy, and Crime," *Society* 34 (1996): 30–38.

109. George Lowenstein, Daniel Nagin, and Raymond Paternoster, "The Effect of Sexual Arousal on Expectations of Sexual Forcefulness," *Journal of Research in Crime and Delinquency* 34 (1997): 443–473.

110. David Klinger, "Policing Spousal Assault," *Journal of Research in Crime and Delinquency* 32 (1995): 308–324.

111. James Williams and Daniel Rodeheaver, "Processing of Criminal Homicide Cases in a Large Southern City," *Sociology and Social Research* 75 (1991): 80–88.

112. Raymond Paternoster, "How Much Do We Really Know About Criminal Deterrence?" *Journal of Criminal Law and Criminology* 100 (2010): 765–823.

113. Greg Pogarsky and Alex R. Piquero, "Can Punishment Encourage Offending? Investigating the 'Resetting' Effect," *Journal of Research in Crime and Delinquency* 40 (2003): 92–117.

114. Pogarsky, "Identifying 'Deterrable' Offenders: Implications for Deterrence Research."

115. Nagin and Pogarsky, "Integrating Celerity, Impulsivity, and Extralegal Sanction Threats."

116. Michael Tonry, "Learning from the Limitations of Deterrence Research," *Crime and Justice: A Review of Research* 37 (2008): 279–311.

117. Owen Gallupe and Stephen Baron, "Morality, Self-Control, Deterrence, and Drug Use: Street Youths and Situational Action Theory," *Crime and Delinquency* 60 (2014): 284–305.

118. James Q. Wilson, *Thinking About Crime* (New York: Basic Books, 1975).

119. James Q. Wilson and Richard Herrnstein, *Crime and Human Nature* (New York: Simon & Schuster, 1985), p. 494.

120. Shamena Anwar and Thomas Loughran, "Testing a Bayesian Learning Theory of Deterrence Among Serious Juvenile Offenders," *Criminology* 49 (2011): 667–698.

121. Ibid.; Rudy Haapanen, Lee Britton, and Tim Croisdale, "Persistent Criminality and Career Length," *Crime and Delinquency* 53 (2007): 133–155.

122. Frank Sloan, Alyssa Platt, Lindsey Chepke, and Claire Blevins, "Deterring Domestic Violence: Do Criminal Sanctions Reduce Repeat Offenses?" *Journal of Risk and Uncertainty* 46 (2013): 51–80.

123. Daniel Nagin and G. Matthew Snodgrass, "The Effect of Incarceration on Re-offending: Evidence from a Natural Experiment in Pennsylvania," *Journal of Quantitative Criminology* 29 (2013): 601–642.

124. Benjamin Meade, Benjamin Steiner, Matthew Makarios, and Lawrence Travis, "Estimating a Dose–Response Relationship Between Time Served in Prison and Recidivism," *Journal of Research in Crime and Delinquency* 50 (2013): 525–550.

125. Ellen Raaijmakers, Thomas Loughran, Jan de Keijser, Paul Nieuwbeerta, and Anja Dirkzwager, "Exploring the Relationship Between Subjectively Experienced Severity of Imprisonment and Recidivism: A Neglected Element in Testing Deterrence Theory," *Journal of Research in Crime and Delinquency* 54 (2017): 3–28.

126. Stephanie A. Wiley, Dena C. Carson, and Finn-Aage Esbensen, "Arrest and the Amplification of Deviance: Does Gang Membership Moderate the Relationship?" *Justice Quarterly*, published online September 5, 2016.

127. Bruce Arrigo and Jennifer Bullock, "The Psychological Effects of Solitary Confinement on Prisoners in Supermax Units: Reviewing What We Know and Recommending What Should Change," *International Journal of Offender Therapy and Comparative Criminology* 52 (2008): 622–640.

128. Jeffrey Fagan and Tracey Meares, "Deterrence and Social Control: The Paradox of Punishment in Minority Communities," *Ohio State Journal of Criminal Law* 6 (2008): 173–229.

129. Bureau of Justice Statistics, "U.S. Correctional Population Declined by Less than 1 Percent for the Second Consecutive Year," December 19, 2014, http://www.bjs.gov/content/pub/press/cpus13pr.cfm; see also Pew Charitable Trust, *One in 100: Behind Bars in America 2008* (Washington, DC: Pew Charitable Trusts, 2008), http://www.pewtrusts.org/en/research-and-analysis/reports/2008/02/28/one-in-100-behind-bars-in-america-2008.

130. William Spelman, "Specifying the Relationship Between Crime and Prisons," *Journal of Quantitative Criminology* 24 (2008): 149–178.

131. Steven D. Levitt and Stephen J. Dubner, *Freakonomics: A Rogue Economist Explores the Hidden Side of Everything* (New York: William Morrow, 2006).

132. Steven Levitt, "Why Do Increased Arrest Rates Appear to Reduce Crime: Deterrence, Incapacitation, or Measurement Error?" *Economic Inquiry* 36 (1998): 353–372; see also Thomas Marvell and Carlisle Moody, "The Impact of Prison Growth on Homicide," *Homicide Studies* 1 (1997): 205–233.

133. Ojmarrh Mitchell, Joshua C. Cochran, Daniel P. Mears, and William D. Bales, "Examining Prison Effects on Recidivism: A Regression Discontinuity Approach," published online August 18, 2016.

134. Michael Ostermann and Joel Caplan, "How Much Do the Crimes Committed by Released Inmates Cost?" *Crime and Delinquency*, first published November 5, 2013.

135. James Byrne and Karin Tusinski Miofsky, "From Preentry to Reentry: An Examination of the Effectiveness of Institutional and Community-Based Sanctions," *Victims and Offenders* 4 (2009): 348–356.

136. Jose Canela-Cacho, Alfred Blumstein, and Jacqueline Cohen, "Relationship Between the Offending Frequency of Imprisoned and Free Offenders," *Criminology* 35 (1997): 133–171.

137. Cook and Ludwig, "The Economist's Guide to Crime Busting."

138. Daniel Nagin, "Deterrence in the Twenty-First Century: A Review of the Evidence," in *Crime and Justice: An Annual Review of Research*, ed. Michael Tonry (Chicago: University of Chicago Press, 2013).

139. Richard Rosenfeld and Robert Fornango, "The Relationship Between Crime and Stop, Question, and Frisk Rates in New York City Neighborhoods," *Justice Quarterly*, published online January 9, 2017.

140. Anthony Braga, David Hureau, and Andrew Papachristos, "Deterring Gang-Involved Gun Violence: Measuring the Impact of Boston's Operation Ceasefire on Street Gang Behavior," *Journal of Quantitative Criminology* 30 (2014): 113–139.

141. Marc Mauer, testimony before the U.S. Congress, House Judiciary Committee, on "Three Strikes and You're Out," March 1, 1994.

142. David Lovell, L. Clark Johnson, and Kevin Cain, "Recidivism of Supermax Prisoners in Washington State," *Crime and Delinquency* 53 (2007): 633–656.

143. Bradley Wilson, "Justice with Mercy: An Argument Against Capital Punishment," *International Journal of Applied Philosophy* 26 (2012): 119–135.

Trait Theory

Learning Objectives

LO1 Outline the development of trait theory.

LO2 Differentiate between the biochemical conditions that produce crime.

LO3 Describe the link between genetics and crime, according to trait theory.

LO4 List the elements of the psychodynamic perspective.

LO5 Correlate behavior theory with criminal activities.

LO6 Analyze the controversy surrounding the link between intelligence and crime.

AP Images/Michael Sullivan/News-Review

5

Chapter Outline

FACT OR FICTION?

▶ You are what you eat! "Eating healthy" can reduce antisocial behaviors.

▶ The acorn does not fall far from the tree; that is, the children of deviant parents are more likely than other kids to be antisocial themselves.

A neighbor said that 26-year-old Chris Harper Mercer would "sit by himself in the dark in the balcony with this little light." Mercer was the man who opened fire at Umpqua Community College on October 1, 2015, killing nine people and wounding seven others; some people, like those shown here in the photo, were able to escape unharmed. Mercer was killed after exchanging gunfire with responding officers. He left behind a long, rambling letter that told of being depressed and angry; it turns out that Mercer was an angry person who had a low opinion of himself and obsessed about his place in the world, which he apparently did not think was very good. He had an online blog that referenced other multiple shooting incidents. In one post he discussed Vester Flanagan, the man who on August 26, 2015, killed reporter Allison Parker and photojournalist Adam Ward while they were reporting live on camera in Moneta, Virginia. About this horrific case, Mercer wrote, "I have noticed that so many people like [Flanagan] are alone and unknown, yet when they spill a little blood, the whole world knows who they are. A man who was known by no one, is now known by everyone. His face splashed across every screen, his name across the lips of every person on the planet, all in the course of one day. Seems like the more people you kill, the more you're in the limelight."[1] ■

Senseless tragedies such as these help convince some criminologists that the root cause of crime may be linked to mental or physical abnormality. How could a young man such as Chris Harper Mercer engage in mass murder unless he were suffering from some form of mental instability or collapse? And yet, while in the aftermath of the killings there seemed to be ample evidence that he was under severe psychological stress, no one was able to foresee or predict his violent actions.

These events remind us that, at least in some instances, it is hard to conclude that crime is a matter of rational choice—rather than being rational, crime is anything but. Take for instance Jared Lee Loughner, a deeply disturbed person who on January 8, 2011, opened fire in a supermarket parking lot in Tucson, Arizona, in an attempt to kill Congresswoman Gabrielle Giffords. Before the shooting stopped, six bystanders had been killed. As a college student Loughner had numerous run-ins with campus security and bizarre outbursts in class. Pima Community College school officials sent a letter to his parents stating that if he wished to return to the school, he would have to "obtain a mental health clearance indicating, in the opinion of a mental health professional, his presence at the college does not present a danger to himself or others." Rather than get help, Loughner decided to drop out; he was later diagnosed with schizophrenia.

Why would people like Mercer and Loughner, who had at one time attended college, gone out on dates, and had friendships, engage in mass murder unless they were suffering from some form of mental instability or collapse? People who knew them claimed they seemed to have gone through a significant personality change just before the murders took place. Hardly a case for concluding that all criminals are rational and calculating, as choice theory maintains.

The image of a disturbed, mentally ill offender seems plausible because generations of Americans have grown up watching films and TV shows that portray violent criminals as mentally deranged and physically abnormal. Beginning with Alfred Hitchcock's film *Psycho*, producers have made millions depicting the ghoulish acts of people who at first seem normal and even friendly but turn out to be demented and dangerous. As children they are possessed (*Paranormal Activity*, *The Omen*), maybe because they play with demonic dolls (*Chucky*, *Annabelle*). As they grow older, they turn into deranged female (*Obsession*) and male (*Fear*) teens who have lunatic high school friends (*Scream*), who evolve into even crazier college classmates (*Scream II*) and then grow up to become deranged young adults (*Scream III*). Some of these psychos do not act alone but are part of extended demented families (*Texas Chainsaw Massacre*, *The Hills Have Eyes*) with loony fathers (*The Stepfather*), mothers (*Mama*, *Friday the 13th, Part 1*), and grandparents (*The Visit*). Some have multiple personalities (*Split*) while others are totally delusional (*Shutter Island*). No one is safe when doctors, psychologists, and psychiatrists turn out to be demonic murderers themselves (*The Human Centipede*, *Silence of the Lambs*, *Hannibal*, *Red Dragon*). And even after they are dead, they can turn into zombies (*28 Days Later*, *Zombieland*, *World War Z*). Is it any wonder that we respond to a particularly horrible crime by saying of the perpetrator, "That guy must be crazy" or "She is a monster"?

This chapter reviews the theories that suggest that criminality is an outgrowth of abnormal human traits. These **trait theories** can be subdivided into two major categories: those that stress biological makeup and those that stress psychological functioning. Although these views often overlap (that is, brain function may have a biological basis), each branch has its unique characteristics and will be discussed separately.

trait theories
View criminality as a product of abnormal biological or psychological traits.

Development of Trait Theory

L01 Outline the development of trait theory.

As you may recall (Chapter 1), the view that criminals have physical or mental traits that make them different and abnormal is not restricted to movie plots but began with the Italian physician and criminologist Cesare Lombroso and his contemporaries, who conducted the first "scientific" studies of crime. Today their efforts are regarded as historical curiosities, not scientific fact, mainly because the research methodology used was slipshod and invalid, not employing control groups and the scientific method. What they assumed was a biological cause could just as easily have resulted from environment or upbringing.

As criticism of biological explanations mounted, the view that human traits were responsible for antisocial behaviors fell out of favor and were abandoned in the early twentieth century.[2] Then, spurred by the publication of Edmund O. Wilson's *Sociobiology: The New Synthesis* in 1975, explanations of crime based on human traits received renewed interest from criminologists.[3]

Sociobiology stresses the following principles:

- Behavioral traits are shaped by both inherited traits and the environment.
- Biological and genetic conditions affect how social behaviors are learned and perceived.
- Behavior is determined by the need to ensure survival of offspring and replenishment of the gene pool.
- Biology, environment, and learning are mutually interdependent factors.

Simply put, sociobiology assumes that while social behavior is genetically transmitted, it adapts to and is shaped by existing environmental conditions. This view revived interest in finding a biological or psychological basis for crime and delinquency. It prompted some criminologists to conclude that personal traits must be what separates the deviant members of society from the nondeviant. Possessing these traits may help explain why, when faced with the same life situation, one person commits crime whereas another obeys the law. Living in a disadvantaged neighborhood will not cause a well-adjusted person to commit crime, and living in an affluent area will not stop a maladapted person from offending.[4] All people may be aware of and even fear the sanctioning power of the law, but their behavior is controlled by traits that are present at birth or developed soon afterwards. Possession of these traits does not guarantee that their bearer will commit crime, but given equivalent environmental conditions those who possess the suspect traits will be more likely to employ deviant or outlawed behaviors to attain their life goals and desires.

Contemporary Trait Theory

For years many criminologists ignored any linkage made between traits and crime. To suggest so would mean that personal differences and not social factors such as poverty and racism were responsible for antisocial behavior. Today that view is softening, and trait theory has entered the criminological mainstream. As criminologists John Paul Wright and Francis Cullen put it:

> . . . the ideological dam preventing the development of biosocial perspectives is weakening and has sprung some leaks. The reality that humans are biological creatures who vary in biological traits is becoming too obvious to ignore.[5]

As a result of this newfound acceptance, more criminologists are conducting research on the individual traits related to crime and their findings are being published in mainstream journals.

Unlike their forebears, these contemporary trait theorists do not suggest that a single biological or psychological attribute adequately explains all criminality. Rather, each offender is considered physically and mentally unique, so there must be different explanations for each person's behavior. Some may have inherited criminal tendencies; others may be suffering from neurological problems; still others may have blood chemistry disorders that heighten their antisocial activity. What often appears as an effect of environment and socialization may actually be linked to genetically determined physical and/or mental traits. Personal traits and biological conditions, not parenting or social environment, best explain behavioral choices.[6]

sociobiology
The view that human behavior is motivated by inborn biological urges to survive and preserve the species.

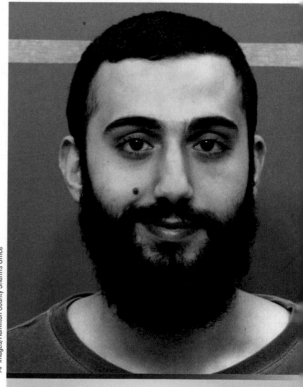

AP Images/Hamilton County Sheriffs Office

Muhammad Youssef Abdulazeez killed five servicemen at two Chattanooga military facilities before taking his own life. Was he a terrorist or someone suffering from a mental disease or defect? People who knew him said he was a quiet kid but well liked. One told the press, "He was friendly, funny, kind. I never would have thought it would be him." She added that his whole family seemed normal: "They were your average Chattanooga family." On the other hand, Abdulazeez sent the *Times Free Press* photos of what appears to be his high school senior picture and senior quote in the school's yearbook. "My name causes national security alerts," the quote reads. "What does yours do?"

Individual Vulnerability vs. Differential Susceptibility

Trait theorists today recognize that crime-producing interactions involve both personal traits (such as defective intelligence, impulsive personality, and abnormal brain chemistry) and environmental factors (such as family life, educational attainment, socioeconomic status, and neighborhood conditions). People living in a disadvantaged community may be especially at risk to crime, but that risk is significantly increased if they also bear a genetic makeup that makes them vulnerable to the crime-producing influences in their environment.[7]

There are actually two views on how this interaction unfolds. The **individual vulnerability model** supposes a direct link between traits and crime: some people develop physical or mental conditions at birth, or soon thereafter, that affect their social functioning no matter where they live or how they are raised.[8]

In contrast, the **differential susceptibility model** suggests that there is an indirect association between traits and crime: some people possess physical or mental traits that make them vulnerable to adverse environmental influences. While a positive environment provides benefits, those people whose genetic makeup makes them predisposed to violence manifest more aggression when their surroundings become troubled. Someone like this may benefit from a supportive, therapeutic environment, but a more adverse one may trigger a violent response.

Biological Trait Theories

One branch of contemporary trait theory focuses on the biological conditions that control human behavior (see Figure 5.1). Criminologists who work in this area typically refer to themselves as biocriminologists, biosocial criminologists, or biologically oriented criminologists; the terms are used here interchangeably.

The following sections examine some important subareas within biological criminology. First we review the biochemical factors that are believed to affect how proper behavior patterns are learned. Then we consider the relationship between brain

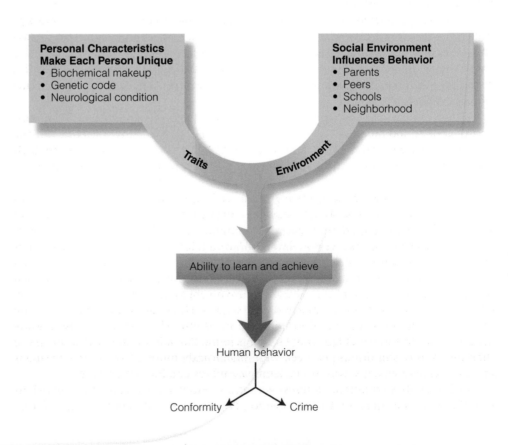

FIGURE 5.1
Biosocial Perspectives on Criminality

function and crime. Next we analyze current ideas about the association between genetic factors and crime. Finally, we evaluate evolutionary views of crime causation.

Biochemical Conditions and Crime

In 1978, the biology of crime began to receive national attention when Dan White, the confessed killer of San Francisco Mayor George Moscone and city councilman Harvey Milk, claimed that his behavior was precipitated by an addiction to sugar-laden junk foods.[9] White's successful "Twinkie defense" prompted a California jury to find him guilty of the lesser offense of diminished-capacity manslaughter rather than first-degree murder. (In 1985, White committed suicide after serving his prison sentence; 24 years later he was played by Josh Brolin in the film *Milk*, for which Sean Penn won an Oscar for his portrayal of Harvey Milk.)

Today, trait theorists believe that biochemical conditions, including both those that are genetically predetermined and those that are acquired through diet and environment, influence antisocial behavior. In some cases, the influence of chemicals and minerals is direct. Adolescent drinking may have a direct and long-term influence on antisocial behavior.[10] The association between biochemical factors may also be indirect: chemical imbalance can lead to intellectual deficits that produce school underachievement; educational failure has been linked to antisocial behaviors.[11] Similarly, blood mercury levels of children diagnosed with attention deficit hyperactivity disorder (ADHD) are significantly higher than the levels found in the general population, indicating a clear association between an environmental pollutant and a behavior disorder linked to antisocial behavior.[12]

Some of the biochemical factors that have been linked to criminality are discussed in detail here.

DIET Biocriminologists maintain that a healthful diet can provide minimal levels of minerals and chemicals needed for normal brain functioning and growth, especially in the early years of life. An improper diet can cause chemical and mineral imbalance and can lead to cognitive and learning deficits and problems, and these factors in turn are associated with antisocial behaviors.[13]

Research conducted over the past decade shows that an oversupply or undersupply of certain chemicals and minerals (including caffeine, sodium, mercury, potassium, calcium, amino acids, and iron) can lead to depression, hyperactivity, cognitive problems, memory loss, or abnormal sexual activity.[14] Either eliminating harmful substances or introducing beneficial ones into the diet can reduce the threat of antisocial behaviors.[15]

People whose diets lack sufficient polyunsaturated fats, minerals, and vitamins, and/or contain too much saturated fat (or other elements, including sugar and a range of food and agricultural chemicals), seem to be at higher risk of developing psychological disturbances, such as schizophrenia, that are directly related to antisocial acts.[16]

SUGAR INTAKE One area of diet that has received a great deal of attention is the association between high intake of both sugar and high fructose corn syrup and antisocial/aggressive behavior. Experiments have been conducted in which children's diets were altered so that sweet drinks were replaced with fruit juices, table sugar with honey, molasses substituted for sugar in cooking, and so on; results indicate that aggression levels are associated with sugar intake.[17] A British study of the long-term effects of childhood diet on adult violence found that kids aged 10 who engaged in excessive consumption of confectionary (food items that are rich in sugar such as candy and soda) were the ones most likely to be convicted for violence in adulthood.[18] More recently, a study conducted in Boston with high school students found that adolescents who drank more than five cans of soft drinks per week were significantly more likely to carry weapons and to engage in violence with peers, family members and intimate partners.[19]

Although these results are impressive, some questions remain about the actual interaction between sugar intake and violence, and not all research projects have found

L02 Differentiate between the biochemical conditions that produce crime.

a significant sugar–violence effect. One recent study by Nathan DeWall and his associates found that some sugar intake may actually help *reduce* aggression.[20]

HYPOGLYCEMIA When blood glucose (sugar) falls below levels necessary for normal and efficient brain functioning, a condition called **hypoglycemia** occurs. Symptoms of hypoglycemia include irritability, anxiety, depression, crying spells, headaches, and confusion. Research studies have linked hypoglycemia to outbursts of antisocial behavior and violence.[21] High levels of reactive hypoglycemia have been found in groups of habitually violent and impulsive offenders.[22]

HORMONAL INFLUENCES A number of biosocial theorists are now evaluating the association between criminal activities ranging from fraud to violent behavior episodes and hormone levels.[23] Biosocial research has found that abnormal levels of male sex hormones (**androgens**) can produce aggressive behavior.[24] Other androgen-related male traits include sensation seeking, impulsivity, dominance, and reduced verbal skills; all of these traits are related to antisocial behavior.[25] A growing body of evidence suggests that hormonal changes are also related to mood and behavior. Adolescents experience more intense mood swings, anxiety, and restlessness than their elders, explaining in part the high violence rates found among teenage males.[26]

AP Images/Daytona Beach News-Journal, David Tucker

On March 17, 2014, Ebony Wilkerson enters the courtroom with attorney Craig Dyer for a bail hearing at the Justice Center in Daytona Beach, Florida. Wilkerson was charged with attempted murder for driving her three children into the ocean. At the time of the incident, Wilkerson's blood showed a glucose level of 44. A normal reading would be between 70 and 80; her heart was racing at 146 beats per minute. Could her action have been caused by hypoglycemia that affected her thought process?

hypoglycemia
A condition that occurs when glucose (sugar) in the blood falls below levels necessary for normal and efficient brain functioning.

androgens
Male sex hormones.

testosterone
The principal male hormone.

premenstrual syndrome (PMS)
Condition, postulated by some theorists, wherein several days before and during menstruation excessive amounts of female sex hormones stimulate antisocial, aggressive behavior.

FACT OR FICTION?

You are what you eat! "Eating healthy" can reduce antisocial behaviors.

FACT Biocriminologists link antisocial behavior to diet and chemical intake. You may in fact be what you eat.

Testosterone, the most abundant androgen, which controls secondary sex characteristics such as facial hair and voice timbre, has been linked to criminality and violence.[27] Research conducted on both human and animal subjects has found that prenatal exposure to unnaturally high levels of testosterone permanently alters behavior. Girls who were unintentionally exposed to elevated amounts of testosterone during their fetal development display a marked, long-term tendency toward aggression.[28]

Conversely, boys who were prenatally exposed to steroids that decrease testosterone levels display decreased aggressiveness.[29] Gender differences in the crime rate, therefore, may be explained by the relative difference in testosterone and other androgens between the two sexes. Females may be biologically protected from deviant behavior in the same way that they enjoy immunity from some diseases that strike males.[30] Hormone levels also help explain the aging-out process: levels of testosterone decline during the life cycle, and so do violence rates.[31] They have also been linked to specific crime patterns such as intimate partner violence. [32]

PREMENSTRUAL SYNDROME The suspicion has long existed that the onset of the menstrual cycle triggers excessive amounts of the female sex hormones, which stimulate antisocial, aggressive behavior. This condition is commonly referred to as **premenstrual syndrome (PMS)**.[33] The link between PMS and delinquency was first popularized more than 40 years ago by Katharina Dalton, whose studies of English women indicated that females are more likely to commit suicide and to be aggressive and otherwise antisocial just before or during menstruation.[34]

Diana Fishbein, a noted expert on biosocial theory, also concludes that there is in fact an association between menstruation and elevated levels of female aggression. Research efforts, she argues, show that (a) a significant number of incarcerated females committed their crimes during the premenstrual phase, and (b) at least a small percentage of women appear vulnerable to cyclical hormonal changes that make them more prone to anxiety and hostility.[35]

LEAD EXPOSURE Exposure to lead has been linked to emotional and behavioral disorders.[36] This association is especially important because so many children suffer harmful levels of lead exposure. According to the Centers for Disease Control and Prevention, even low levels of lead in the blood have been shown to affect IQ, ability to pay attention, and academic achievement. And effects of lead exposure cannot be corrected. Experts now use a reference level of 5 micrograms per deciliter (of blood) to identify children with blood lead levels that are much higher than most children's levels. That means that about 2 million kids 18 and under have dangerously high lead levels according to CDC standards.[37]

Delinquents have been found to have much higher bone lead levels than children in the general population.[38] There is also evidence linking lead exposure to mental illnesses, such as schizophrenia.[39] Locales with the highest concentrations of lead also report the highest levels of homicide.[40] Long-term worldwide trends in crime levels correlate significantly with changes in environmental levels of lead.[41]

Some experts, have gone as far as linking the decrease in the use of leaded gasoline, which began to be phased out in the mid-1970s, to a drop in violent crimes in the United States and abroad. Research shows a significant fit between the rise and fall of gas lead and the rise and fall of the violent crime rate with a time lag of 23 years. As the presence of lead in the bloodstream of schoolchildren declined, so eventually did the crime rate.[42]

ENVIRONMENTAL CONTAMINANTS Research has linked prenatal exposure to PCBs (polychlorinated biphenyls) to lower IQs and attention problems, both considered risk factors for serious behavioral and learning problems.[43] Similarly, exposure to severe air pollution has been found to cause cognitive deficits and changes in the brain structure of otherwise healthy children. These destructive changes affect intelligence, influence cognitive control, and produce other neurological deficits that have been associated with school failure; educational underachievement is a condition that has long been associated with delinquency and adult criminality.[44] In addition, PCBs, polybrominated diphenyl ethers (PBDEs), polycyclic aromatic hydrocarbons (PAHs), and inorganic gases such as chlorine and nitrogen dioxide can cause severe illness or death. These environmental contaminants can be especially harmful to the brains of babies and small children because they may affect their developing nervous systems; they can be exposed to harmful chemicals even before they are born.[45]

Neurophysiological Conditions and Crime

Some researchers focus their attention on **neurophysiology**, the study of brain activity. Using brain-scanning techniques such as magnetic resonance imaging (MRI), positron emission tomography (PET), brain electrical activity mapping (BEAM), and the superconducting quantum interference device (SQUID), they assess areas of the brain that are directly linked to antisocial behavior.[46]

neurophysiology
The study of brain activity.

Studies carried out in the United States and elsewhere have shown that both violent criminals and substance abusers have impairment in the prefrontal lobes, thalamus, medial temporal lobe, and superior parietal and left angular gyrus areas of the brain.[47] Adolescent boys with antisocial substance disorder (ASD) repeatedly engage in risky antisocial and drug-using behaviors. Research has linked this behavior with misfiring in particular areas of the brain and suppressed neural activity.[48]

Such damage may be associated with a reduction in executive functioning (EF), a condition that refers to impairment of the cognitive processes that facilitate the planning and regulation of goal-oriented behavior (such as abstract reasoning, problem solving, and motor skills). Impairments in EF have been implicated in a range of developmental disorders, including attention deficit hyperactivity disorder (ADHD), conduct disorder (CD), autism, and Tourette syndrome. EF impairments also have been implicated in a range of neuropsychiatric and medical disorders, including schizophrenia, major depression, alcoholism, structural brain disease, diabetes mellitus, and normal aging.[49]

Neurological impairment may also lead to the development of personality traits linked to antisocial behaviors. There is now evidence that low self-control may in fact be regulated and controlled by the prefrontal cortex of the brain.[50] Under this scenario, neurological impairment reduces impulse management and self-control, a condition that often results in antisocial behaviors.

There is a suspected link between brain dysfunction and **conduct disorder (CD)**, which is considered a precursor of long-term chronic offending. Children with CD lie, steal, bully other children, get into fights frequently, and break schools' and parents' rules; many are callous and lack empathy and/or guilt.[51]

Links between CD and violent extremism have also been found. It's possible that similar psychological deficits are responsible for one youth joining a violent street gang and another an extremist group may be quite similar.[52]

conduct disorder (CD)
A pattern of repetitive behavior in which the rights of others or social norms are violated.

attention deficit hyperactivity disorder (ADHD)
A developmentally inappropriate lack of attention, along with impulsivity and hyperactivity.

BRAIN STRUCTURE Research psychiatrist Guido Frank finds that aggressive teen behavior may be linked to the amygdala, an area of the brain that processes information regarding threats and fear, and to a lessening of activity in the frontal lobe, a brain region linked to decision making and impulse control. Frank investigated why some teenagers are more prone than others to "reactive" aggression—that is, unpremeditated aggression in response to a trigger (for instance, an accidental bump from a passerby). He found that reactively aggressive adolescents—most commonly boys—frequently misinterpret their surroundings, feel threatened, and act inappropriately aggressive. They tend to strike back when being teased, blame others when getting into a fight, and overreact to accidents. Their behavior is emotionally "hot," defensive, and impulsive; teens with this behavior are at high risk for lifelong social, career, or legal problems.

Frank's research helps explain what goes on in the brains of some teenage boys who respond with inappropriate anger and aggression to perceived threats. It is possible that such behavior is associated with brain functioning and not environment, socialization, personality, or other social and psychological functions.[53]

ATTENTION DEFICIT HYPERACTIVITY DISORDER Many parents have noticed that their children do not pay attention to them—they run around and do things in their own way. Sometimes this inattention is a function of age; in other instances it is a symptom of **attention deficit hyperactivity disorder (ADHD)**, in which a child shows a developmentally inappropriate lack of attention, along with impulsivity and hyperactivity. Some of the various symptoms of ADHD include easy distraction, acting without thinking, and inability to sit still. About 3 percent of American children, most often boys, are believed to suffer from this disorder, and it is the most common reason why children are referred to mental health clinics. The condition has been associated with poor school performance, retention for another year in the same grade, placement in classes for those with special needs, bullying, stubbornness, and lack of response to discipline.[54]

Although the origin of ADHD is still unknown, suspected causes include neurological damage, prenatal stress, and even reactions to food additives and chemical allergies; some research suggests a genetic link.[55] There are also links to family turmoil: mothers of children with ADHD are more likely to be divorced or separated, and they are much more likely than others to move to new locales.[56] It may be possible that emotional turmoil either produces symptoms of ADHD or, if they already exist, causes them to intensify.

Many children with ADHD also suffer from conduct disorder (CD) and continually engage in aggressive and antisocial behavior in early childhood.[57] Children diagnosed with ADHD are more likely to be suspended from school and to engage in criminal behavior as adults.[58] A series of research studies now links ADHD to the onset and sustenance of a criminal career.[59] Children with ADHD are more likely than non-ADHD youths to use illicit drugs, alcohol, and cigarettes, be physically aggressive, and engage in sex offenses in adolescence. In addition to adolescent misbehavior, hyperactive or ADHD children are at greater risk for antisocial activity and drug use/abuse that persists into adulthood. They are more likely to be arrested, to be charged with a felony, and to have multiple arrests.[60]

There are two views on the association between ADHD and aggressive behavior. One view is that the association is direct and that hyperactivity leads to aggressive antisocial behaviors.[61] Others view the association as being more indirect: hyperactivity results in poor school achievement; school failure leads to substance abuse and depression, conditions that have long been associated with the onset of antisocial behaviors.[62]

BRAIN CHEMISTRY Chemical compounds called **neurotransmitters** influence or activate brain functions. Those studied in relation to aggression and other antisocial behaviors include dopamine, norepinephrine, serotonin, monoamine oxidase (MAO), and gamma-aminobutyric acid (GABA).[63] Evidence exists that abnormal levels of these chemicals are associated with aggression.[64]

Research efforts have linked low levels of MAO to high levels of violence and property crime, as well as defiance of punishment, impulsivity, hyperactivity, poor academic performance, sensation seeking and risk taking, and recreational drug use.[65] Abnormal MAO levels may explain both individual and group differences in the crime rate. Females naturally have higher MAO levels than males, which may contribute to gender differences in the crime rate.[66] The effect of MAO on crime persists throughout the life span: delinquent youth with low levels of MAO have been found to have a greater likelihood of engaging in physical aggression later in adulthood than those with normal or higher levels.[67]

What is the link between brain chemistry and crime? One view is that prenatal exposure of the brain to high levels of androgens can result in a brain structure that is less sensitive to environmental inputs and more prone to criminal behavior choices.[68] Affected individuals seek more intense and varied stimulation and are willing to tolerate more adverse consequences than individuals not so affected.[69] Because this link has been found, it is not uncommon for violence-prone people to be treated with antipsychotic drugs such as Haldol, Stelazine, Prolixin, and Risperdal. These drugs, which help control levels of neurotransmitters (such as serotonin or dopamine), are sometimes referred to as chemical restraints or chemical straitjackets.

AROUSAL THEORY According to **arousal theory**, for a variety of genetic and environmental reasons, people's brains function differently in response to environmental stimuli. All of us seek to maintain a preferred or optimal level of arousal: too much stimulation leaves us anxious and stressed, whereas too little makes us feel bored and weary. However, people vary in the way their brains process sensory input. Some nearly always feel comfortable with little stimulation, whereas others require a high degree of environmental input to feel comfortable. The latter group of "sensation seekers" looks for stimulating activities, which may include aggressive, violent behavior patterns.[70]

Although the factors that determine a person's level of arousal are not fully understood, suspected sources include brain chemistry (such as serotonin levels) and brain structure. Some people's brains have many more nerve cells, with receptor sites for neurotransmitters. Another view is that people with low heart rates are more likely to commit crime because they seek stimulation to increase their arousal to normal levels. Adrian Raine has found that antisocial children have lower resting heart rates than the general population.[71] In one recent study, Raine and his associates found that low heart rate may produce a need for stimulation that is associated with aggressive behavior patterns. It is also associated with impulsivity, which in turn is associated with lack of self-control, and involvement in delinquent and criminal behaviors.[72]

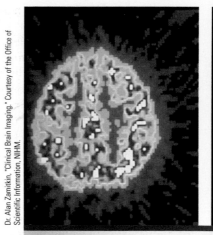
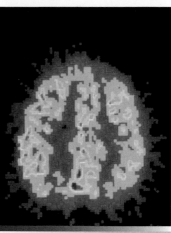

Dr. Alan Zametkin, "Clinical Brain Imaging." Courtesy of the Office of Scientific Information, NIHM.

This scan compares a normal brain (left) and the brain of an individual with ADHD (right). Areas of orange and white demonstrate a higher rate of metabolism, whereas areas of blue and green represent an abnormally low metabolic rate. Why is ADHD so prevalent in the United States today? Some experts believe that our immigrant forebears, risk takers who impulsively left their homelands for life in a new world, may have brought with them a genetic predisposition to ADHD.

neurotransmitters
Chemical compounds that influence or activate brain functions.

arousal theory
The view that people seek to maintain a preferred level of arousal but vary in how they process sensory input. A need for high levels of environmental stimulation may lead to aggressive, violent behavior patterns.

CONNECTIONS

Gottfredson and Hirschi's self-control theory of delinquency that proposes that low self-control constitutes the most important causal factor in explaining antisocial behavior will be discussed in Chapter 9.

LO3 Describe the link between genetics and crime, according to trait theory.

Genetics and Crime

Another biosocial theme is that the human traits associated with criminality have a genetic basis.[73] Over the course of human history, the most aggressive violent people have gained reproductive advantages that ensure survival of their genetics and have created a population of aggressive young males. The genes that produce aggression are still present in the population and those that inherit them are responsible for violent crimes.[74]

The genes–crime association may be direct: (1) antisocial behavior is inherited, (2) the genetic makeup of parents is passed on to children, and (3) genetic abnormality is directly linked to a variety of antisocial behaviors.[75]

It is also possible that the association is indirect: genes are related to some personality or physical trait linked to antisocial behavior.[76] Genetic makeup may shape friendship patterns and orient people toward deviant peer associations, which cause them to become crime prone.[77] Adolescent attachment to parents may be controlled by their genetic makeup; attachment that is weak and attenuated has been linked to criminality.[78]

Whether it be direct or indirect, the genes–crime relationship has been explored by a number of different methods, described below:

PARENTAL DEVIANCE If criminal tendencies are inherited, children of criminal parents should be more likely to become law violators than the offspring of conventional parents. A number of studies have found that growing up in a family with criminal or otherwise troubled parents has a powerful influence on criminal behavior.[79] The Cambridge Youth Survey, a longitudinal cohort study conducted in England, indicates that a significant number of delinquent youths have criminal fathers.[80] David Farrington found that one type of parental deviance—schoolyard aggression, or bullying—may be both inter- and intragenerational. Bullies have children who bully others, and these second-generation bullies grow up to father children who are also bullies, in a never-ending cycle.[81]

ADOPTION STUDIES Several studies indicate that some relationship exists between biological parents' behavior and the behavior of their children, even when they have been adopted at birth and had no contact.[82] Studies of adopted youths have found that the biological father's criminality strongly predicted the child's criminal behavior even if the adopting parent was noncriminal.[83] When the biological father and the adoptive father were both criminal, the probability that the youth would engage in criminal behavior greatly increased.

TWIN BEHAVIOR If, in fact, inherited traits cause criminal behavior, we might expect that twins would be quite similar in their antisocial activities. And as predicted, research efforts confirm a significant correspondence of twin behavior in activities ranging from frequency of sexual activity to crime.[84] However, because twins are usually brought up in the same household and exposed to the same social conditions, determining whether their similar behavior is a result of similar biological, sociological, or psychological conditions is difficult. To control for environmental factors, criminologists have compared identical, **monozygotic (MZ) twins** with fraternal, **dizygotic (DZ) twins**.[85] MZ twins are genetically identical, whereas DZ twins

FACT OR FICTION?

The acorn does not fall far from the tree; that is, the children of deviant parents are more likely than other kids to be antisocial themselves.

FACT Research shows that there is a significant association between parental and child deviance levels, although investigators are still not sure whether it is a matter of environment or genetics.

monozygotic (MZ) twins
Identical twins.

dizygotic (DZ) twins
Fraternal (nonidentical) twins.

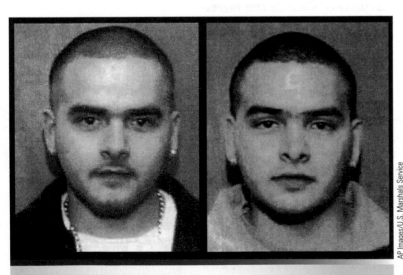

Research using twin subjects indicates that there might be a genetic basis for crime. On January 27, 2015, Pedro Flores (left) and his twin brother, Margarito Flores, were sentenced to 14 years in prison each for running a nearly $2 billion North American drug ring. Their sentence was reduced for agreeing with prosecutors to testify against Joaquin "El Chapo" Guzman and other Mexican cartel leaders.

AP Images/U.S. Marshals Service

have only half their genes in common. Studies of MZ twins reared apart, who have never met, show that their behavior is nearly identical.

Studies conducted on twin behavior have detected a significant relationship between the criminal activities of MZ twins and a much lower association between those of DZ twins; these genetic effects can be seen in children as young as 3 years old.[86] MZ twins are closer than DZ twins in such crime-relevant measures as level of aggression and verbal skills.[87]

IS CRIME INHERITED? Those who support a gene–crime relationship maintain that antisocial behavior is roughly 50 percent heritable; some calculate that the influence of genes on deviant behaviors may be as high as 85 percent. Genetic influences appear strongest for chronic offenders whose behavior is persistent, severe, and involves callous unemotional symptoms, such as a lack of remorse; these conditions have been linked to crime and antisocial behavior.[88]

The theoretical association between crime and genes is by no means certain. There has been and continues to be serious debate over the heritability of human behavior. Some critics, such as Callie Burt and Ronald Simons, believe the social environment plays a more critical role in shaping behavior than genes and heredity, especially during the critical periods of childhood and adolescence. The environment, they argue, shapes biological processes and enables people to function and survive in existing social conditions; human biological makeup helps people respond to the everyday situations and events they face in their social world. As environmental conditions change, so do the brain and nervous system. Adverse, dangerous, and negative environments sculpt or change an individual's brain functioning, causing them to respond to environmental events with aggression, violence, and coercion.[89] However, when Burt and Simons called for an end to gene-based research they were challenged by groups of criminologists who found fault with their assumptions and who believe that a great deal of human behavior is shaped by inherited rather than learned traits.[90] Needless to say, the debate over the heritability of criminal tendencies remains an open issue among criminologists.

Evolutionary Views of Crime

Some criminologists believe that the human traits that produce violence and aggression have been advanced by the long process of human evolution.[91] According to this evolutionary view, the competition for scarce resources has influenced and shaped the human species.[92] Over the course of human existence, people whose personal characteristics enabled them to accumulate more than others were the most likely to breed successfully, have more offspring, and (genetically speaking) dominate the species. People have been shaped to engage in actions that promote their well-being and ensure the survival and reproduction of their genetic line. Males who are impulsive risk takers may be able to father more children because they are reckless in their social relationships and have sexual encounters with numerous partners. If, according to evolutionary theories, such behavior patterns are inherited, impulsive behavior becomes intergenerational, passed down from parents to children. It is therefore not surprising that human history has been marked by war, violence, and aggression.

THE EVOLUTION OF GENDER AND CRIME Evolutionary concepts that have been linked to gender differences in violence rates are based loosely on mammalian mating patterns. To ensure survival of the gene pool (and the species), it is beneficial for a male of any species to mate with as many suitable females as possible because each can bear his offspring. Those males that maximize an aggressive mating effort strategy also possess traits such as a strong sexual drive, a reduced ability to form strong emotional bonds, a lack of conscience, and aggressive and violent tendencies. Not surprisingly, those individuals who possess the traits associated with a high-mating-effort strategy (i.e., sexual promiscuity) are also more likely to engage in antisocial conduct.[93] They are also likely to produce offspring who are also prone to criminal behaviors.

CHECKPOINTS

▶ Brain chemistry and hormonal differences are related to aggression and violence.

▶ The male hormone testosterone is linked to criminality.

▶ Neurological impairments have been linked to crime.

▶ Genetic theory holds that violence-producing traits are passed from generation to generation.

▶ According to evolutionary theory, instinctual drives control behavior. The urge to procreate influences male violence.

Concept Summary 5.1   Biosocial Theories of Crime

Biochemical	• The major premise of the theory is that crime, especially violence, is a function of diet, vitamin intake, hormonal imbalance, or food allergies. • The strengths of the theory are that it explains irrational violence and shows how the environment interacts with personal traits to influence behavior. • The research focuses of the theory are diet, hormones, enzymes, environmental contaminants, and lead intake.
Neurological	• The major premise of the theory is that criminals and delinquents often suffer brain impairment. Attention deficit hyperactivity disorder and minimal brain dysfunction are related to antisocial behavior. • The strengths of the theory are that it explains irrational violence and shows how the environment interacts with personal traits to influence behavior. • The research focuses of the theory are CD, ADHD, learning disabilities, brain injuries, and brain chemistry.
Genetic	• The major premise of the theory is that criminal traits and predispositions are inherited. The criminality of parents can predict the delinquency of children. • The strengths of the theory include the fact that it explains why only a small percentage of youths in high-crime areas become chronic offenders. • The research focuses of the theory are twin behavior, sibling behavior, and parent–child similarities.
Evolutionary	• The major premise of the theory is that as the human race evolved, traits and characteristics became ingrained. Some of these traits make people aggressive and predisposed to commit crime. • The strengths of the theory include its explanation of high violence rates and aggregate gender differences in the crime rate. • The research focuses of the theory are gender differences and understanding human aggression.

Therefore, over the long history of the human species, aggressive males have had the greatest impact on the gene pool. The descendants of these aggressive males now account for the disproportionate amount of male aggression and violence.[94] In contrast, because of the long period of gestation, females require a secure home and a single, stable, nurturing partner to ensure their survival.

Crime rate differences between the genders, then, may be less a matter of socialization than of inherent differences in mating patterns that have developed over time.[95] The various biosocial views of crime are set out in Concept Summary 5.1.

Psychological Trait View

The second branch of trait theory focuses on the psychological aspects of crime, including the associations among intelligence, personality, learning, and criminal behavior. This view has a long history, and psychologists, psychiatrists, and other mental health professionals have long played an active role in formulating criminological theory.

Among nineteenth-century pioneers in this area were Charles Goring (1870–1919) and Gabriel Tarde (1843–1904). Goring studied 3,000 English convicts and found little difference in the physical characteristics of criminals and noncriminals. However, he uncovered a significant relationship between crime and a condition he referred to as "defective intelligence," which involved such traits as feeblemindedness, epilepsy, insanity, and defective social instinct.[96] Tarde was the forerunner of modern learning theorists, who hold that people learn from one another through imitation.[97]

In their quest to understand and treat all varieties of abnormal mental conditions, psychologists have encountered clients whose behavior falls within the categories that society has labeled criminal, deviant, violent, and antisocial. A number of different psychological views have various implications for the causation of criminal behavior. The most important of these theoretical perspectives and their association with criminal conduct are discussed in the following sections.

psychodynamic (psychoanalytic) psychology Theory, originated by Freud, that the human personality is controlled by unconscious mental processes that develop early in childhood and involve the interaction of id, ego, and superego.

id The primitive part of people's mental makeup, present at birth, that represents unconscious biological drives for food, sex, and other life-sustaining necessities. The id seeks instant gratification without concern for the rights of others.

The Psychodynamic Perspective

Psychodynamic (or **psychoanalytic**) **psychology** was originated by Viennese psychiatrist Sigmund Freud (1856–1939) and has remained a prominent segment of psychological theory ever since.[98] Freud believed that we all carry with us the residue of the most significant emotional attachments of our childhood, which then guides our future interpersonal relationships.

According to psychodynamic theory, the human personality has a three-part structure. The **id** is the primitive part of people's mental makeup, is present at birth, and represents unconscious biological drives for food, sex, and other life-sustaining necessities. The id seeks instant gratification without concern for the rights of others. The ego develops early in life, when a child begins to learn that his or her wishes cannot be instantly gratified. The **ego** is the part of the personality that compensates for the demands of the id by helping the individual keep his or her actions within the boundaries of social convention. The **superego** develops as a result of incorporating within the personality the moral standards and values of parents, community, and significant others. It is the moral aspect of people's personalities; it judges their own behavior.

The psychodynamic model of the criminal offender depicts an aggressive, frustrated person dominated by events that occurred early in childhood. Because they had unhappy experiences in childhood or had families that could not provide proper love and care, criminals suffer from weak or damaged egos that make them unable to cope with conventional society. Weak egos are associated with immaturity, poor social skills, and excessive dependence on others. People with weak egos may be easily led into crime by antisocial peers and drug abuse. Some have underdeveloped superegos and consequently lack internalized representations of those behaviors that are punished in conventional society. They commit crimes because they have difficulty understanding the consequences of their actions.[99]

In sum, the psychodynamic tradition links crime to a manifestation of feelings of oppression and the inability to develop the proper psychological defenses and rationales to keep these feelings under control. Criminality enables troubled people to survive by producing positive psychic results: it helps them to feel free and independent, and it offers them the possibility of excitement and the chance to use their skills and imagination.

ATTACHMENT THEORY According to psychologist John Bowlby's **attachment theory**, the ability to form an emotional bond to another person has important psychological implications that follow people across the life span.[100] Attachments are formed soon after birth, when infants bond with their mothers. Babies will become frantic, crying and clinging, to prevent separation or to reestablish contact with a missing parent. Attachment figures, especially the mother, must provide support and care, and without attachment an infant would be helpless and could not survive.

Failure to develop proper attachment may cause people to fall prey to a number of psychological disorders, some of which resemble attention deficit hyperactivity disorder (ADHD). Such individuals may be impulsive and have difficulty concentrating—and consequently experience difficulty in school. As adults, they often have difficulty initiating and sustaining relationships with others and find it difficult to sustain romantic relationships.

Meta-analysis of existing research finds that lack of attachment predicts involvement in a broad spectrum of criminal activity.[101] Criminologists have linked people who have detachment problems with a variety of antisocial behaviors, including sexual assault and child abuse.[102] It has been suggested that boys disproportionately experience disrupted attachment and that these disruptions are causally related to disproportionate rates of male offending.[103]

The Behavioral Perspective: Social Learning Theory

Behavior theory maintains that human actions are developed through learning experiences. The major premise of behavior theory is that people alter their

L04 List the elements of the psychodynamic perspective.

ego
The part of the personality developed in early childhood that helps control the id and keep people's actions within the boundaries of social convention.

superego
The part of the personality representing the conscience, formed in early life by internalization of the standards of parents and other models of behavior.

attachment theory
Bowlby's theory that being able to form an emotional bond to another person is an important aspect of mental health throughout the life span.

behavior theory
The view that all human behavior is learned through a process of social reinforcement (rewards and punishment).

CONNECTIONS

Chapter 1 discussed how some of the early founders of psychiatry tried to understand the criminal mind. Early theories suggested that mental illness and insanity were inherited and that deviants were inherently mentally damaged by their inferior genetic makeup.

L05 Correlate behavior theory with criminal activities.

social learning theory
The view that human behavior is modeled through observation of human social interactions, either directly from observing those who are close and from intimate contact, or indirectly through the media. Interactions that are rewarded are copied, while those that are punished are avoided.

behavior in accordance with the response it elicits from others. In other words, behavior is supported by rewards and extinguished by negative reactions or punishments. The behaviorist views crimes—especially violent acts—as learned responses to life situations, which do not necessarily represent abnormality or moral immaturity.

The branch of behavior theory most relevant to criminology is **social learning theory**.[104] Social learning theorists argue that people are not born with the ability to act violently; rather, they learn to be aggressive through their life experiences.

Policies and Issues in Criminology

VIOLENT MEDIA/VIOLENT BEHAVIOR?

Does the media influence behavior? Does broadcast violence cause aggressive behavior in viewers? This has become a hot topic because of the persistent theme of violence in video games, television, and films. Critics have called for drastic measures, ranging from banning TV violence to limiting access to video games.

If there is in fact a media–violence link, the problem is indeed alarming. Systematic viewing of TV begins at 2.5 years of age and continues at a high level during the preschool and early school years. Children 6 and under spend an average of two hours a day using screen media (TV and computer games)—about the same amount of time they spend playing outside and significantly more time than they spend reading or being read to (about 39 minutes per day). Marketing research indicates that adolescents ages 11 to 14 view violent horror movies at a higher rate than any other age group. Children this age use older peers and siblings and apathetic parents to gain access to R-rated films. In all, the average child views 8,000 TV murders before finishing elementary school.

Not all experts believe that media violence is a direct *cause* of violent behavior (if it were, there would be millions of daily incidents in which viewers imitated the aggression they watched on games, on TV, or in movies), but many do agree that media violence *contributes* to aggression. Developmental psychologists have concluded that viewing media violence is related to both short- and long-term increases in aggressive attitudes, values, and behaviors; the effects of media violence are both real and strong.

One source of influence is violent video games. In 2015, a research team sponsored by the American Psychological Association investigated the effects of violent video games on the onset of aggressive behavior. Team members conducted a review of the research literature published between 2005 and 2013 that involved analysis of more than 170 research reports. They found clear evidence that playing violent video games increases aggressive behavior, aggressive cognitions, and aggressive

affect, and decreases prosocial behavior, empathy, and sensitivity to aggression. No single risk factor consistently leads a person to act aggressively or violently, the report states. It is the accumulation of risk factors that tends to lead to aggressive or violent behavior. The research reviewed here demonstrates that playing violent video games is one such risk factor.

There is also evidence that kids who watch violent media are more likely to persist in aggressive behavior as adults. Kids who watch more than an hour of violent media each day show an increase in assaults, fights, robberies, and other acts of aggression later in life and into adulthood. One reason may be that violent media viewing in childhood creates changes in personality and cognition that produce long-term behavioral changes.

There are several explanations for the effects of games, television, and film violence on behavior:

- Media violence can provide aggressive "scripts" that children store in memory. Repeated exposure to these scripts can increase their retention and lead to changes in attitudes.
- Children learn from what they observe. In the same way that they learn cognitive and social skills from their parents and friends, children learn to be violent from violent media.
- Media violence increases the arousal levels of viewers and makes them more prone to act aggressively. Studies measuring the galvanic skin response of subjects—a physical indication of arousal based on the amount of electricity conducted across the palm of the hand—show that viewing violent media led to increased arousal levels in young children.
- Watching media violence promotes such negative attitudes as suspiciousness and the expectation that the viewer will become involved in violence. Those who watch violent media frequently come to view aggression and violence as common and socially acceptable behavior.
- Media violence enables aggressive youths to justify their behavior. It is possible that, instead of causing violence, media violence helps violent youths rationalize their behavior as a socially acceptable and common activity.

These experiences include personally observing others acting aggressively to achieve some goal or watching people being rewarded for violent acts on television or in movies (see the Policies and Issues in Criminology feature entitled "Violent Media/Violent Behavior?"). People learn to act aggressively when, as children, they model their behavior after the violent acts of adults. Later in life, these violent behavior patterns persist in social relationships.[105] The boy who sees his father repeatedly strike his mother with impunity is likely to become a battering parent and husband.

- Media violence may disinhibit aggressive behavior, which is normally controlled by other learning processes. Disinhibition takes place when adults are viewed as being rewarded for violence and when violence is seen as socially acceptable. This contradicts previous learning experiences in which violent behavior was viewed as wrong.

Debating the Link Between Media Violence and Violent Behavior

Even though this research is quite persuasive, not all criminologists are convinced that watching violent incidents on TV and in the movies or playing violent video games predisposes young people to violent behavior. Even the APA report linking video games to aggressive attitudes did not find sufficient evidence to extend the link to actual criminal violence or delinquency.

There is little evidence that areas that experience the highest levels of violent media viewing also have rates of violent crime that are above the norm. Millions of children watch violence every day but do not become violent criminals. If violent media did, indeed, cause interpersonal violence, then there should be few ecological and regional patterns in the crime rate, but in fact there are many. To put it another way, how can regional differences in the violence rate be explained, considering the fact that people all across the nation watch the same TV shows and films? Nor can the link between media violence and violent behavior explain recent crime trends. Despite a rampant increase in violent TV shows, films, and video games, the violence rate among teens has been in significant decline.

One possibility is that media violence may affect one subset of the population but have relatively little effect on other groups. Sociologist George Comstock has identified the attributes that make some people especially prone to the effects of media violence:

- Predisposition to aggressive or antisocial behavior
- Rigid or indifferent parenting
- Unsatisfactory social relationships
- Low psychological well-being

- Having been diagnosed as suffering from DBD—disruptive behavior disorder

Thus, if the impact of media on behavior is not in fact universal, it may have the greatest effect on those who are the most socially and psychologically vulnerable.

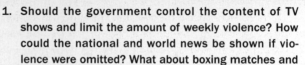

Critical Thinking

1. Should the government control the content of TV shows and limit the amount of weekly violence? How could the national and world news be shown if violence were omitted? What about boxing matches and hockey games?

2. How can we explain the fact that millions of kids watch violent TV shows and remain nonviolent? If there is a link between violence in the media and violent behavior, how can we explain the fact that violence rates were higher before media was invented?

Sources: Sarah Coyne, "Effects of Viewing Relational Aggression on Television on Aggressive Behavior in Adolescents: A Three-Year Longitudinal Study," *Developmental Psychology* 52 (2016): 284–295; Sarah Coyne, Mark Callister, Laura Stockdale, Holly Coutts, and Kevin Collier, "Just How Graphic Are Graphic Novels? An Examination of Aggression Portrayals in Manga and Associations with Aggressive Behavior in Adolescents," *Violence and Victims* 30 (2015): 208–224; Mark Appelbaum, Sandra Calvert, Kenneth Dodge, Sandra Graham, Gordon N. Hall, Sherry Hamby, and Larry Hedges, "The American Psychological Association Task Force on Violent Media: Technical Report on the Review of Violent Video Game Literature," http://www.apa .org/news/press/releases/2015/08/technical-violent-games.pdf (accessed April 2017); Sukkyung You, Euikyung Kim, and Unkyung No, "Impact of Violent Video Games on the Social Behaviors of Adolescents: The Mediating Role of Emotional Competence," *School Psychology International* 36 (2015): 94–111; George Comstock, "A Sociological Perspective on Television Violence and Aggression," *American Behavioral Scientist* 51 (2008): 1184–1211; John Murray, "Media Violence: The Effects Are Both Real and Strong," *American Behavioral Scientist* 51 (2008): 1212–1230; Craig Anderson and Brad J. Bushman, "The Effects of Media Violence on Society," *Science* 295 (2002): 2377–2379; Brad Bushman and Craig Anderson, "Media Violence and the American Public," *American Psychologist* 56 (2001): 477–489.

Although social learning theorists agree that mental or physical traits may predispose a person toward violence, they believe a person's violent tendencies are activated by factors in the environment. The specific form of aggressive behavior, the frequency with which it is expressed, the situations in which it is displayed, and the specific targets selected for attack are largely determined by social learning. However, people are also self-aware and engage in purposeful learning. Their interpretations of behavior outcomes and situations influence the way they learn from experiences. One adolescent who spends a weekend in jail for drunk driving may find it the most awful experience of her life—an ordeal that convinces her never to drink and drive again. Another person, however, may find it an exciting experience about which he can brag to his friends.

behavior modeling
The process of learning behavior (notably, aggression) by observing others. Aggressive models may be parents, criminals in the neighborhood, or characters on television or in movies.

SOCIAL LEARNING AND VIOLENCE Social learning theorists view violence as something learned through a process called **behavior modeling**. In modern society, aggressive acts are usually modeled after three principal sources:

*   *Family interactions.* Studies of family life show that aggressive children have parents who use aggressive tactics when dealing with others. The children of wife batterers are more likely to use aggressive tactics themselves than children in the general population, especially if the victims (their mothers) suffer psychological distress from the abuse.[106]
*   *Environmental experiences.* People who reside in areas where violence occurs daily are more likely to act violently than those who dwell in low-crime areas whose norms stress conventional behavior.
*   *Mass media.* Films, video games, and television shows commonly depict violence graphically. Violence is often portrayed as acceptable, especially for heroes who never have to face legal consequences for their actions.[107] As the Policies and Issues in Criminology feature suggests, viewing violence is believed to influence behavior in a number of ways.

Social learning theorists have tried to determine what triggers violent acts. One position is that a direct, pain-producing, physical assault will usually set off a violent response. Yet the relationship between painful attacks and aggressive responses has been found to be inconsistent. Whether people counterattack depends, in part, on their fighting skill and their perception of the strength of their attackers. Verbal taunts and insults have also been linked to aggressive responses. People who are predisposed to aggression by their learning experiences are likely to view insults from others as a challenge to their social status and to react violently.

In sum, social learning theorists suggest that the following factors may contribute to violent or aggressive behavior:

*   *An event that heightens arousal.* For example, a person may frustrate or provoke another through physical assault or verbal abuse.
*   *Aggressive skills.* Learned aggressive responses picked up from observing others, either personally or through the media.
*   *Expected outcomes.* The belief that aggression will somehow be rewarded. Rewards can come in the form of reducing tension or anger, gaining some financial reward, building self-esteem, or receiving praise from others.

Everett Collection

Social learning theory holds that kids who watch violent media, including TV, films, and video games are more likely to become violent themselves. This still is from *Batman: The Killing Joke.* Would an adolescent actually become more violence prone if they watch Batman (voice: Kevin Conroy) fight the Joker (voice: Mark Hamill) than if they viewed *Mulan, Moana,* or *Finding Dory*?

- *Consistency of behavior with values*. The belief, gained from observing others, that aggression is justified and appropriate, given the circumstances of the current situation.

Cognitive Theory

One area of psychology that has received increasing recognition in recent years is **cognitive theory**. Psychologists with a cognitive perspective focus on mental processes—how people perceive and mentally represent the world around them and solve problems. The pioneers of this school were Wilhelm Wundt (1832–1920), Edward Titchener (1867–1927), and William James (1842–1920). Today the cognitive area includes several subdisciplines. The moral development branch is concerned with how people morally represent and reason about the world. Humanistic psychology stresses self-awareness and getting in touch with feelings. **Information-processing theory** focuses on how people process, store, encode, retrieve, and manipulate information to make decisions and solve problems.

Cognitive theorists explain antisocial behavior in terms of mental perception and how people use information to understand their environment. When people make decisions, they engage in a sequence of cognitive thought processes. First, they encode information so that it can be interpreted; next, they search for a proper response and decide on the most appropriate action; and finally, they act on their decision.[108]

According to this cognitive approach, people who use information properly, who are better conditioned to make reasoned judgments, and who can make quick and reasoned decisions when facing emotion-laden events are best able to avoid antisocial behavior choices. In contrast, crime-prone people may have cognitive deficits and use information incorrectly when they make decisions. They view crime as an appropriate means to satisfy their immediate personal needs, which take precedence over more distant social needs such as obedience to the law.[109] They are not deterred by the threat of legal punishments because when they try to calculate the costs and consequences of an action—that is, when they are deciding whether to commit a crime—they make mistakes because they are imperfect processors of information. As a result of their faulty calculations, they pursue behaviors that they perceive as beneficial and satisfying but that turn out to be harmful and detrimental.[110]

Law violators may be sensation seekers who are constantly looking for novel experiences, whereas others lack deliberation and rarely think through problems.[111] Others maintain inappropriate attitudes and beliefs; they are thrill-seeking, manipulative, callous, deceptive, and hold rule-breaking attitudes. Some may give up easily, whereas others act without thinking when they get upset.[112]

People with inadequate cognitive processing perceive the world as stacked against them; they believe they have little control over the negative events in their life. They find it difficult to understand or sympathize with other people's feelings and emotions, which leads them to blame their victims for their problems. Thus, the sexual offender believes his target either led him on or secretly wanted the forcible sex to occur: "She was asking for it."

MENTAL SCRIPTS One reason for this faulty reasoning is that people may be relying on mental scripts learned in childhood that tell them how to interpret events, what to expect, how they should react, and what should be the outcome of the interaction.[113] Some may have learned improper scripts because as children they had early, prolonged exposure to violence (such as child abuse), which increased their sensitivity to slights and maltreatment.[114] Violence becomes a stable behavior because the scripts that emphasize aggressive responses are repeatedly rehearsed as the child matures. These errors in cognition and information processing have been used to explain the behavior of pedophiles. They may perceive children as being able

cognitive theory
Psychological perspective that focuses on the mental processes by which people perceive and represent the world around them and solve problems.

information-processing theory
Theory that focuses on how people process, store, encode, retrieve, and manipulate information to make decisions and solve problems.

## Concept Summary 5.2	Psychological Theories

Theory	Major Premise	Strengths	Research Focus
Psychodynamic	The development of the unconscious personality early in childhood influences behavior for the rest of a person's life. Criminals have weak egos and damaged personalities.	Explains the onset of crime and why crime and drug abuse cut across class lines.	Mental illness and crime.
Behavioral	People commit crime when they model their behavior after others they see being rewarded for the same acts. Behavior is reinforced by rewards and extinguished by punishment.	Explains the role of significant others in the crime process. Shows how media can influence crime and violence.	Media and violence; effects of child abuse.
Cognitive	Individual reasoning processes influence behavior. Reasoning is influenced by the way people perceive their environment.	Shows why criminal behavior patterns change over time as people mature and develop their reasoning powers. May explain the aging-out process.	Perception; environmental influences.

to and wanting to engage in sexual activity with adults and also as not harmed by such sexual contact.[115]

The various psychological theories of crime are set out in Concept Summary 5.2.

Personality and Crime

personality
The reasonably stable patterns of behavior, including thoughts and emotions, that distinguish one person from another.

Personality can be defined as the reasonably stable patterns of behavior, including thoughts and emotions, that distinguish one person from another.[116] One's personality reflects a characteristic way of adapting to life's demands and problems. The way we behave is a function of how our personality enables us to interpret life events and make appropriate behavioral choices. Can the cause of crime be linked to personality?

Several research efforts have attempted to identify criminal personality traits. Surveys show that traits such as impulsivity, hostility, narcissism, hedonism, and aggression are highly correlated with criminal and antisocial behaviors.[117]

Personal feelings and emotions have been found to help shape behavior. Take for instance feelings of regret. People who are remorseful and feel bad about their prior bad acts are less likely to recidivate than those who are neither contrite nor apologetic.[118]

Personality defects have been linked not only to aggressive antisocial behaviors such as assault and rape but also to white-collar and business crimes.[119] Hans Eysenck's PEN model contains three elements: psychoticism (P), extraversion (E), and neuroticism (N). He associates two personality traits, extroversion and introversion, with antisocial behavior:

- Extroverts are energetic, enthusiastic, action-oriented, chatty, glib, and self-confident.
- Introverts tend to be quiet, low-key, deliberate, and detached from others.

People who fall at the far ends of either trait, either extremely extroverted or extremely introverted, are at risk for antisocial behaviors. Extroverts who are also unstable, a condition that Eysenck calls neuroticism, are anxious, tense, and emotionally volatile.[120] They may act self-destructively by abusing drugs and repeating their criminal activity over and over.[121] The Policies and Issues in Criminology box sets forth one new vision on the link between personality and crime.

Policies and Issues in Criminology

CRIMINAL SUSCEPTIBILITY

Robert Agnew suggests that the link between personality traits and crime flows through an individual's resistance or susceptibility to crime-promoting experiences. Some people have a personality that helps them resist the lures of crime, while others are more susceptible. Those who have personalities that make them susceptible to crime are inclined to model their own behavior after the criminal behavior of others. They are inclined to accept the antisocial beliefs and attitudes they encounter as accurate and valid, they are willing to conform their behavior to the antisocial behaviors of their peers, and they are more easily influenced by others than the average person. Some susceptibles are more inclined to conform than others, and this inclination to conform controls antisocial behaviors. Furthermore, susceptible individuals are more likely to experience some crimes and their consequences as pleasurable: crime provides them with thrills and excitement, a sense of power or control, and feelings of self-worth. Susceptibles obtain much pleasure from the money and property they obtain and the status accorded to them by others. In contrast, those whose personalities are high in resistance are less likely to have these reactions.

Susceptibles also are more easily upset by stressful situations. When they experience social pressures, they view them as very bad, unjust, and uncontrollable through legal channels but controllable through crime. The strong negative emotional reactions to stresses and strain lead them to feel an inclination to respond to them in an aggressive or rebellious manner. Resistors are in better control of their reactions, less likely to overreact, and less likely to try to resolve stressful situations with aggression.

The research suggests that four factors may play key roles in determining the individual's level of resistance and susceptibility to criminogenic events and conditions. Susceptible individuals:

- Tend to react to the environment in a negative manner. Their personality is shaped by such traits as difficult temperament; neuroticism, especially the hostility or anger facet; negative emotionality; hostile orientation; perceptual negativity; hostile attribution of intent; poor emotional regulation; sensitivity to punishment; sensitivity to injustice directed at oneself, and the belief that one is unjustly treated; and pessimism (low optimism).
- Place emphasis on pleasure and sensation seeking. Those high in pleasure and sensation seeking place a premium on the quick acquisition of money, material possessions, power over and autonomy from others, prestige, thrills and excitement, and physical pleasure. And they place a low emphasis on the hard work and sacrifice that are ordinarily required to achieve most such goals.
- Are low in conventional efficacy and perceived social support but high in criminal efficacy and support. Those low in conventional efficacy and perceived social support believe that they cannot legally address the challenges and opportunities they confront in the major life domains, including family, school, work, peer group, and community. In particular, they believe that they do not have the ability, motivation, and resources to cope legally with strains and achieve conventional success.
- Are more sensitive than others to environmental influences, both criminal and prosocial. Those who are environmentally sensitive are more susceptible to crime in criminogenic environments while being more resistant to crime in conventional environments.

Critical Thinking

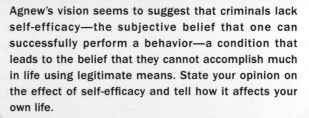

Agnew's vision seems to suggest that criminals lack self-efficacy—the subjective belief that one can successfully perform a behavior—a condition that leads to the belief that they cannot accomplish much in life using legitimate means. State your opinion on the effect of self-efficacy and tell how it affects your own life.

Sources: Robert Agnew, "A Theory of Crime Resistance and Susceptibility," *Criminology* 54 (2016): 181–211; Dominique Laferrière and Carlo Morselli, "Criminal Achievement and Self-Efficacy," *Journal of Research in Crime and Delinquency* 52 (2015): 856–889.

Psychopathic/Antisocial Personality

Some people lack affect, cannot empathize with others, and are short-sighted and hedonistic. These traits make them prone to problems ranging from psychopathology to drug abuse, sexual promiscuity, and violence.[122] As a group, people who share these traits are believed to have a character defect referred to as sociopathic, psychopathic,

antisocial personality
Combination of traits, such as hyperactivity, impulsivity, hedonism, and inability to empathize with others, that make a person prone to deviant behavior and violence; also referred to as sociopathic or psychopathic personality.

or **antisocial personality**. Although these terms are often used interchangeably, some psychologists distinguish between sociopaths and psychopaths by suggesting that the former are a product of a destructive home environment, whereas the latter are a product of a defect or aberration within themselves.[123] Today antisocial personality is the more accepted term.

From an early age, people suffering from antisocial behavior disorder experience home lives that are filled with frustration, bitterness, and quarreling. Antisocial youths exhibit low levels of guilt and anxiety and persistently violate the rights of others. Their intelligence may alter their criminal career development and render it quite different from other criminals; high intelligence appears to enhance their destructive potential, while intelligence may mediate the criminality of most other offenders.[124] As a result of this instability and frustration, antisocial individuals develop personalities that are unreliable, unstable, demanding, and egocentric.

There are different types of psychopaths/sociopaths who fall along a continuum of critical behavior and personality traits, such as instability, inhibition, and attachment.[125] Most but not all are risk-takers and sensation seekers who are constantly involved in a wide variety of antisocial behaviors. There are also differences in the need for stimulation: Some may become almost addicted to thrill seeking, resulting in repeated and dangerous risky behaviors. Others can be described as grandiose, egocentric, manipulative, forceful, and cold-hearted, with shallow emotions and the inability to feel remorse, empathy with others, or anxiety over their misdeeds. When they commit antisocial acts, they are less likely to feel shame or empathize with their victims. Considering these personality traits, it is not surprising that research studies show that antisocials tend to continue their criminal careers long after other offenders burn out or age out of crime.

After reviewing available data, forensic psychologist James Blair and his colleagues conclude that approximately 15 to 25 percent of US prison inmates meet diagnostic criteria for psychopathy. Once they are released, former inmates who suffer from psychopathy are three times more likely to reoffend within a year of release than other prisoners, and four times more likely to reoffend violently.[126] The Profiles in Crime feature looks at the life of a notorious psychopathic killer.

THE CAUSE OF ANTISOCIAL PERSONALITY DISORDER There is still disagreement on the cause of antisocial personality disorder. Some explanations reflect sociopathy and focus on family experiences. According to this view, a sociopathic personality may be formed by experiencing an unstable parent, parental rejection, lack of love during childhood, and inconsistent discipline. Children who lack the opportunity to form an attachment to a mother figure in the first three years of life, who suffer sudden separation from the mother figure, or who see changes in the mother figure are most likely to develop psychopathic personalities. According to this view, the path runs from antisocial parenting to sociopathy to criminality.[127]

A second view is that antisocial personality is passed down genetically and inherited.[128] Supporting evidence shows that psychopaths may suffer from lower than normal levels of arousal.[129] Research studies show that psychopaths have lower skin conductance levels and fewer spontaneous responses than normal subjects. There may be a link between psychopathy and autonomic nervous system (ANS) dysfunction. The ANS mediates physiological activities associated with emotions and is manifested in such measurements as heartbeat rate, blood pressure, respiration, muscle tension, capillary size, and electrical activity of the skin (called galvanic skin resistance). Psychopaths may be less capable of regulating their activities than other people. While some people may become anxious and afraid when facing the prospect of committing a criminal act, psychopaths in the same circumstances feel no such fear. James Ogloff and Stephen Wong conclude that their reduced anxiety levels result in behaviors that are more impulsive and inappropriate and in deviant behavior, apprehension, and incarceration.

Another view is that psychopathy is related to abnormal brain structures. Consequently, psychopaths may need greater than average stimulation to bring them up

PROFILES IN CRIME

THE ICEMAN: A TRUE SOCIOPATH

Richard Kuklinski, known as the Iceman, fits the description of sociopath better than almost anyone on record.

Kuklinski's early life was punctuated by savage abuse from his father, who beat his wife and children so badly that one son, Florian, died at his hands. Fearing for their lives, the family covered up the crime. Richard, an eighth-grade dropout, worked out his hatred of his father by killing his neighbors' pets. He soon progressed to people. His first victim, whom he killed when he was just 14, was a young boy who had bullied him at school. Kuklinski dumped his victim's body off a bridge in South Jersey after removing his teeth and chopping off his fingertips in an effort to prevent identification of the body. Kuklinski routinely made trips to New York City looking for victims to beat and kill.

At 6-foot-5, 300 pounds, Kuklinski soon became known to organized crime families in New Jersey looking for a cold-blooded enforcer. His career took off when he became one of the top enforcers for the Gambino family. He killed his victims with guns, ice picks, crossbows, and chain saws, but his favorite weapon was cyanide solution administered with a nasal-spray bottle in the victim's face. He earned his nickname by his practice of freezing corpses to disguise the time of death and confound authorities.

During his career, he killed somewhere between 100 and 200 people, but through the efforts of undercover agents, the Iceman was convicted of five murders and given consecutive life sentences. While in prison, he confessed to killing Peter Calabro, a New York City police detective, and got another 30 years tacked on to his life sentence. Never shy or remorseful, Kuklinski gave many interviews and appeared in two HBO documentaries before he died in prison in 2006 at age 70.

Kuklinski's home life was not what you would expect from a mass killer. He married his wife, Barbara, in 1961, lived a suburban, relatively affluent lifestyle, and had three kids. His wife called them "the all-American family." And while he occasionally struck his wife, the Iceman would never harm a child, including his own.

Was Kuklinski a true sociopath? The evidence is mixed. His murderous behavior seems to have been a product of his disturbed, violent childhood. He exhibited a great deal of superficial charm and had above-average intelligence, positive traits that often mask a disturbed personality that continually involves sociopaths in deviant behaviors such as violence, risk taking, substance abuse, and impulsivity.

Another indicator: Kuklinski was a chronic offender, beginning in childhood and continuing until he was caught and imprisoned as an adult. As many as 80 percent of high-end chronic offenders exhibit sociopathic behavior patterns. Though comprising about 4 percent of the total male population and less than 1 percent of the total female population, they are responsible for half of all serious felony offenses committed annually. Not all high-rate chronic offenders are sociopaths, but enough are to support a strong link between personality dysfunction and long-term criminal careers.

Despite this evidence, one factor remains puzzling: Kuklinski had a long-term marriage and was a loving father; sociopaths are believed to be incapable of forming enduring relationships with others. ■

Sources: Douglas Martin, "Richard Kuklinski, 70, a Killer of Many People and Many Ways, Dies," *New York Times*, March 9, 2006, http://www.nytimes.com/2006/03/09/nyregion/09kuklinski.html (accessed April 2017); Philip Carlo, *The Ice Man: Confessions of a Mafia Contract Killer* (New York: Macmillan, 2009).

Everett Collection

to comfortable levels (similar to arousal theory, discussed earlier). This may be linked to an impairment of the amygdala, that part of the brain that plays a crucial role in processing emotions. As James Blair and his colleagues suggest, amygdala dysfunction gives rise to impairments in aversive conditioning, instrumental learning, and the processing of fearful and sad expressions.[130]

Intelligence and Criminality

LO6 Analyze the controversy surrounding the link between intelligence and crime.

nature theory
The view that intelligence is largely determined genetically and that low intelligence is linked to criminal behavior.

nurture theory
The view that intelligence is not inherited but is largely a product of environment. Low IQ scores do not cause crime but may result from the same environmental factors.

mood disorder
A condition in which the prevailing emotional mood is distorted or inappropriate to the circumstances.

oppositional defiant disorder (ODD)
A pattern of negativistic, hostile, and defiant behavior, during which a child often loses her or his temper, often argues with adults, and often actively defies or refuses to comply with adults' requests or rules.

Early criminologists maintained that many delinquents and criminals have below-average intelligence and that low IQ causes their criminality. However, there was disagreement over the development of intellectual ability. Some believed that law violators had inherently substandard intelligence and thus were naturally inclined to commit crimes. These proponents of **nature theory** argued that intelligence is largely determined genetically, that ancestry determines IQ, and that low intelligence, as demonstrated by low IQ, is linked to criminal behavior. In contrast, proponents of **nurture theory** argued that environmental stimulation from parents, relatives, social contacts, schools, peer groups, and innumerable others accounts for a child's IQ level and that low IQs may result from an environment that also encourages delinquent and criminal behavior. Thus, if low IQ scores are recorded among criminals, these scores may reflect the criminals' cultural background, not their inherited mental ability.[131] These ideas led to the "nature versus nurture" controversy that continues to rage today.

The IQ–crime link controversy was reignited nearly 40 years ago, when the influential criminologists Travis Hirschi and Michael Hindelang suggested a link existed between intelligence and crime. Youths with low IQs, they found, do poorly in school, and school failure and academic incompetence are highly related to delinquency and later to adult criminality.[132] Their findings were supported by James Q. Wilson and Richard Herrnstein in their influential albeit controversial book *Crime and Human Nature*, which also concluded that low intelligence leads to poor school performance, which enhances the chances of criminality.[133] In another widely read and equally controversial book, *The Bell Curve*, Herrnstein with Charles Murray claimed that adolescents with low IQs are more likely to commit crime, get caught, and be sent to prison. Conversely, at-risk kids with higher IQs seem to be protected from becoming criminals by their superior ability to succeed in school and in social relationships.[134]

On an individual level, there is evidence linking low IQ scores with violent crimes, including murder.[135] There is also evidence of a macro-level connection;

In 2012, Pedro Hernandez (shown here in Manhattan criminal court in New York) confessed to killing a long-missing New York City boy, Etan Patz. When the case went to trial in 2015, the prosecution had little evidence to back up his confession, since Patz's body has never been found. Hernandez's defense claimed his confessions were the false imaginings of a man who has an IQ in the lowest 2 percent of the population, and doctors testified that he had trouble telling reality from illusion. "Pedro Hernandez is the only witness against himself," defense lawyer Harvey Fishbein said during his closing argument. "The stories he told over the years . . . are the only evidence. Yet he is inconsistent and unreliable." During 18 days of deliberations, the jury emerged three times with a deadlock before the judge declared a mistrial. Since 11 members voted to convict, the prosecution retried the case; Hernandez was convicted and sentenced to 25 years in prison.

AP Images/Louis Lanzano

national state and county data have found that IQ and crime rates are associated.[136] A number of research projects have found evidence that residents living in geographic areas—nations, states, and counties—whose residents have higher than average IQs experience lower crime rates than those whose citizens have lower than average IQ scores.[137] In sum, some criminologists maintain that intelligence can function as a protective factor for offending.[138]

The IQ–criminality debate is unlikely to be settled soon. Measurement is beset by many methodological problems and charges that IQ tests are biased against members of racial minority groups. Even if it can be shown that known offenders have lower IQs than the general population, it is difficult to reconcile the effect of intelligence with some important correlates of crime: Why do crime rates vary by time of year and even weather patterns? Why does aging out occur? IQs do not rise with age or fall with temperature and season, so why should these factors affect crime rates?

Mental Disorders and Crime

Psychologists and psychiatrists have long debated the origin of mental disorders and mental illness, linking it to a variety of sources such as genetic predisposition, traumatic family and upbringing, brain trauma, and substance abuse. Cognitive theories link learning to development of mental disorders. Children growing up in an abusive home may be "rewarded" by not getting beaten if they learn to be quiet, introverted, and withdrawn, a condition that often leads to clinical depression in adulthood.[139]

Regardless of its source, criminologists have connected antisocial behavior to mental instability and turmoil. Offenders may suffer from a wide variety of mood and/or behavior disorders rendering them histrionic, depressed, antisocial, or narcissistic.[140]

Some have been diagnosed with some form of **mood disorder** characterized by disturbance in expressed emotions. Children with **oppositional defiant disorder (ODD)**, for example, experience an ongoing pattern of uncooperative, defiant, and hostile behavior toward authority figures that seriously interferes with day-to-day functioning. Symptoms of ODD may include frequent loss of temper, constant arguing with adults, defying adults or refusing adult requests or rules, deliberately annoying others, blaming others for mistakes or misbehavior, being angry and resentful, being spiteful or vindictive, swearing or using obscene language, or having a low opinion of oneself.[141] ODD has been linked to a great many social problems, including delinquency and bullying.[142]

Adolescent boys with antisocial substance disorder (ASD) repeatedly engage in risky antisocial and drug-using behaviors. Research has linked this disorder with misfiring in particular areas of the brain and suppressed neural activity.[143] Children who are diagnosed with conduct disorder (CD) have great difficulty following rules and behaving in a socially acceptable way.[144] They are often viewed by other children, adults, and social agencies as severely antisocial. Research shows that they are frequently involved in such activities as bullying, fighting, committing sexual assaults, and behaving cruelly toward animals.[145]

Crime and Mental Illness

The most serious forms of mental illness are psychotic disorders, such as **schizophrenia** and **bipolar disorder** (manic-depression), which affect the mind and alter a person's ability to understand reality, think clearly, respond emotionally, communicate effectively, and behave appropriately. People with psychotic disorders may hear nonexistent voices,

schizophrenia
A severe disorder marked by hearing nonexistent voices, seeing hallucinations, and exhibiting inappropriate responses.

bipolar disorder
An emotional disturbance in which moods alternate between periods of wild elation and deep depression.

AP Images/Keith Srakocic

Laurel Schlemmer is escorted by Allegheny County sheriffs to court for the verdict in her murder trial, March 16, 2017, in Pittsburgh. Schlemmer, charged with drowning her two youngest sons in the bathtub because she wanted to be a better mother to their remaining older brother, was found guilty of third-degree murder. Judge Jeffrey Manning found that Schlemmer's mental capacity was diminished by mental illness so that she could not form the specific intent to kill required of the first-degree murder conviction prosecutors sought for the 2014 killings.

hallucinate, and make inappropriate behavioral responses. Others exhibit illogical and incoherent thought processes and a lack of insight into their own behavior. They may see themselves as agents of the devil, avenging angels, or the recipients of messages from animals and plants.

There is evidence that law violators, especially those involved in violent crime, suffer from a disproportionate amount of severe mental health problems. Recently, Richard Dorn and his associates, using a longitudinal sample of about 35,000 subjects, examined the association between mental disorder and violence. They found that when compared to the mentally sound, people suffering mental illness were significantly more likely to engage in violent episodes, especially if they abused drugs and alcohol.[146] The diagnosed mentally ill also appear in arrest and court statistics at a rate disproportionate to their presence in the population and if sentenced to prison are more likely to recidivate upon release.[147]

Mental illness dogs offenders across the life course. Delinquent adolescents have higher rates of clinical mental disorders than adolescents in the general population.[148] As adult criminals, people who have been arrested for multiple crimes are more likely to suffer from a psychiatric disorder, particularly a psychotic disorder, than non-chronic offenders.[149] Even if apprehended, the mentally ill are much more likely to experience repeated incarcerations if they continue to suffer from major psychiatric disorders (such as depressive disorder, bipolar disorder, schizophrenia, and non-schizophrenic psychotic disorders).[150] In sum, there is a body of research showing that people who suffer from severe mental illness and distress seem to be more antisocial than members of the general population and that punishment may do little to reduce their criminal offending.[151]

IS THE LINK VALID? Although these findings are persuasive, the association between crime and mental illness must be interpreted with some caution. Only a small minority of seriously mentally ill people commit violent crimes. But people with serious mental illness are significantly more likely to commit violent crimes than are people who are not seriously mentally ill. However, closer examination shows that serious mental illness is a crime risk mainly when that illness is accompanied by other risk factors, such as alcoholism or unemployment. So helping seriously mentally ill people improve their lives—such as by holding a steady job—will also have large crime-reducing effects. Helping people with untreated serious mental illness is particularly relevant to reducing homicides and even more so for reducing mass attacks against strangers.

It is possible that the link between mental illness and crime is spurious and that, in fact, both mental illness and criminal behavior are caused by some other, independent factor:

- People who suffer from prior social problems (for example, child abuse) may be more likely to commit criminal acts, use drugs and alcohol to cope, and to suffer mental illness.[152]
- Mentally ill people may also be more likely than the mentally sound to lack financial resources. They are thus forced to reside in deteriorated high-crime neighborhoods, a social factor that may increase criminal behavior.[153] Living in a stress-filled urban environment may produce symptoms of both mental illness and crime.[154]
- The police may be more likely to arrest the mentally ill, which fosters the impression that they are crime prone.[155]
- People with severe mental illness are more at risk to violent victimization than the mentally healthy. Violent victimization has been linked to increased crime rates.[156]
- Those suffering from mental illness may self-medicate by using illegal substances, a practice linked to criminal behavior.[157]

The Profiles in Crime feature looks at one of the most notorious crimes committed by a mentally ill young man.

CHECKPOINTS

▶ According to psychodynamic theory, unconscious motivations developed early in childhood propel some people into destructive or illegal behavior.

▶ Behaviorists view aggression as a learned behavior.

▶ Learning may be either direct and experiential or observational, such as watching TV and movies.

▶ Cognitive theory stresses knowing and perception. Some people have a warped view of the world.

▶ Some evidence suggests that people with abnormal or antisocial personalities are more likely than others to commit crime.

▶ Although some criminologists find a link between intelligence and crime, others dispute any link between IQ level and law-violating behaviors.

▶ Mental illness has been linked to crime, but the association is still actively debated.

PROFILES IN CRIME

ADAM LANZA AND THE NEWTOWN MASSACRE

On December 14, 2012, Adam Lanza shot his mother at her home in Newtown, Connecticut, and then took her car to the nearby Sandy Hook Elementary School, where he shot and killed 20 first-graders, aged 6 and 7, and six adult teachers and school employees. After firing 50 to 100 shots at the children and staff, Lanza fatally shot himself in the head as first responders began arriving on scene.

What could have driven this seemingly intelligent and articulate young man to commit one of the worst crimes in American history? Adam Peter Lanza was born in Exeter, New Hampshire, on April 22, 1992. His parents, Peter and Nancy Lanza, were both wealthy and successful. He had an older brother, Ryan Lanza, six years his senior. Then in 2008, when Adam was 16 years old, his parents divorced. Soon after, his classmates began to describe his behavior as "fidgety" and "deeply troubled"; he may have suffered from Asperger's syndrome. Adam began to lose his connection to reality and developed severe mental illness. By 2010, his illness had become so severe he broke off relations with almost everyone in his life and secluded himself in his bedroom, where he spent hours playing violent video games and obsessing over mass murderers. The fact that his mother was a gun enthusiast did not help matters. Lanza's home was filled with weapons and ammunition to which he had easy access. Lanza also had a number of books and articles on other mass killings.

Adam joined the Columbine mass murder website, *Shocked Beyond Belief*, using the screen name "Smiggles," and began to express his paranoia and his belief that society was trying to manipulate him into following an immoral value system that led to both mental and physical sickness. On December 7, 2011, he posted a note showing his disdain for society and his interest in mass murder:

When civilization exists in a form where all forms of alienation (among many other things) are rampant ... new children will end up "not well" in all sorts of ways. You don't even have to touch a topic as cryptic as mass murder to see an indication of this: you can look at a single symptom as egregious as the proliferation of antidepressants.

In Adam's worldview, children were indoctrinated from a very young age to become part of a sick society. They were manipulated to live unhealthy lives and doomed to live in a joyless world where they would be used and abused. By killing them, he'd be doing them a favor, saving them from the hell he was enduring. Lanza's father said in his first public comments about the massacre that what his son did couldn't "get any more evil" and that he wished Adam had never been born. ■

Source: Matthew Lysiak, "Why Adam Lanza Did It," *Newsweek*, January 17, 2014, http://www.newsweek.com/why-adam-lanza-did-it-226565 (accessed April 2017).

Evaluation of Trait Theory

Trait theories have raised some challenging questions. Critics find some of these theories racist and faulty in other ways as well. If there are biological and/or psychological explanations for street crimes such as assault, murder, or rape (the argument goes), and if, as official crime statistics suggest, the poor and minority-group members commit a disproportionate number of such acts, then by implication, trait theory is suggestive of the fact that members of these groups are different, flawed, or inferior.

Trait-based explanations for the geographic, social, and temporal patterns in the crime rate are also problematic. Is it possible that more people are genetically predisposed to crime in the South and the West than in New England and the Midwest? Or that people in large cities are psychologically impaired compared to people in small towns and villages? Furthermore, trait theory seems to divide

primary prevention programs
Programs, such as substance abuse clinics and mental health associations, that seek to treat personal problems before they manifest themselves as crime.

secondary prevention programs
Programs that provide treatment, such as psychological counseling, to youths and adults after they have violated the law.

people into criminals and noncriminals on the basis of their makeup, ignoring self-reports that indicate that almost everyone has engaged in some type of illegal activity.

Trait theorists counter that their views should not be confused with the early deterministic views of Lombroso and his contemporaries, which suggest that people are born either criminals or noncriminals, and nothing can alter their life course. Contemporary trait theories instead maintain that some people carry the potential to be violent or antisocial, and antisocial behavior occurs when these preexisting tendencies are triggered by environmental conditions.[158]

Social Policy and Trait Theory

For quite some time, biological and psychological views of criminality have influenced crime control and prevention policy. The result has been **primary prevention programs** that seek to treat personal problems before they manifest themselves as crime. To this end, thousands of family therapy organizations, substance abuse clinics, and mental health associations operate throughout the United States. Teachers, employers, courts, welfare agencies, and others make referrals to these facilities.

These services are based on the premise that if a person's problems can be treated before they become overwhelming, some future crimes will be prevented. **Secondary prevention programs** provide treatment such as psychological counseling to youths and adults *after* they have violated the law. Attendance at such programs may be a requirement of a probation order, part of a diversionary sentence, or aftercare at the end of a prison sentence.

Biologically oriented therapy is also being used in the criminal justice system. Programs have altered diets, changed lighting, compensated for learning disabilities, treated allergies, and so on.[159] More controversial has been the use of mood-altering chemicals, such as lithium, pemoline, imipramine, phenytoin, and benzodiazepines, to control behavior. Another practice that has elicited concern is the use of psychosurgery (brain surgery) to control antisocial behavior. Surgical procedures have been used to alter the brain structure of convicted sex offenders in an effort to eliminate or control their sex drives.

The numerous psychologically based treatments that are available range from individual counseling to behavior modification. Treatment based on how people process information takes into account that people are more likely to respond aggressively to provocation if their thoughts intensify the insult or otherwise stir feelings of anger. Cognitive therapists attempt to teach explosive people to control aggressive impulses by viewing social provocations as problems demanding a solution rather than retaliation. Programs are aimed at teaching problem-solving skills such as self-disclosure, role playing, listening, following instructions, joining in, and using self-control.

One popular approach to treat emotional issues linked to criminality—cognitive behavioral therapy—is discussed in detail in the Policies and Issues in Criminology feature.

AP Images/Capital Times, Mike DeVries

Treatment programs based on trait theory can take many forms. Here, Wensdae Rauls and Linda Miles participate in a meditation class held in the gym at the Dane County Jail in Madison, Wisconsin. The stress management and relaxation class, which incorporates basic yoga poses, is offered to female inmates at the jail.

Policy and Issues in Criminology

COGNITIVE BEHAVIORAL THERAPY

Few mental health interventions have attracted more attention across the criminal justice system than cognitive behavioral therapy (CBT). First widely used in the latter half of the twentieth century, when large numbers of people with mental illness were deinstitutionalized and treated in community settings, CBT has since found its way into nearly every aspect of the justice system, often supplementing or displacing other programs and interventions. Practitioners today use CBT to reduce recidivism among adults and juveniles; help victims deal with the aftermath of crimes; and address substance abuse, depression, violence, and other problematic behavior.

So what is CBT? And more importantly, does it work? CBT is a class of therapeutic interventions based on a common theory about the connection between our thoughts, attitudes, and beliefs—cognitions—and our behavior. The therapy assumes that most people can become conscious of their own thoughts and behaviors and then make positive changes to them. A person's thoughts are often the result of experience, and behavior is often influenced and prompted by these thoughts. The way we think about situations shapes our choices, behavior, and actions. Flawed or maladaptive thoughts, attitudes, and beliefs lead to inappropriate and even destructive behavior. Characteristics of distorted thinking may include:

- Immature or developmentally arrested thoughts
- Poor problem solving and decision making
- An inability to consider the effects of one's behavior
- An egocentric viewpoint with a negative view or lack of trust in other people

- A hampered ability to reason and accept blame for wrongdoing
- A mistaken belief of entitlement, including an inability to delay gratification, confusing wants and needs, and ignoring the rights of other people
- A tendency to act on impulse, including a lack of self-control and empathy
- An inability to manage feelings of anger
- The use of force and violence as a means to achieve goals

It follows that changing those thoughts, attitudes, and beliefs can lead to more appropriate, prosocial behavior. That is the therapeutic promise of CBT.

CBT focuses on providing, through individual or group therapy, the means to correct flawed cognitive-behavior processes. Evaluations of these programs show that they are effective at deterring crime, assisting victims, and preventing recidivism.

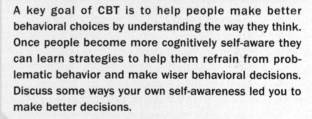

Critical Thinking

A key goal of CBT is to help people make better behavioral choices by understanding the way they think. Once people become more cognitively self-aware they can learn strategies to help them refrain from problematic behavior and make wiser behavioral decisions. Discuss some ways your own self-awareness led you to make better decisions.

Sources: "Does Cognitive Behavioral Therapy Work in Criminal Justice? A New Analysis from CrimeSolutions.gov," *NIJ Journal* 277 (2016), https://www.nij.gov/journals/277/Pages/crimesolutions -cbt.aspx; Patrick Clark, "Preventing Future Crime with Cognitive Behavioral Therapy," *NIJ Journal* 265 (2010), https://www.nij.gov /journals/265/pages/therapy.aspx (URLs accessed April 2017).

Thinking Like a Criminologist

Girl Interrupted Fourteen-year-old Daphne is a product of Boston's best private schools; she lives with her wealthy family on Beacon Hill. Her father is an executive at a local financial services conglomerate and makes close to $1 million per year. Daphne, however, has a hidden, darker side. She is always in trouble at school, and teachers report that she is impulsive and has poor self-control. At times she can be kind and warm, but on other occasions she is obnoxious, unpredictable, insecure, and hungry for attention. She is overly self-conscious about her body and has a drinking problem. Daphne attends AA meetings and is on the waiting list at High Cliff Village, a residential substance abuse treatment program. Her parents seem intimidated by her and confused by her complexities; her father even filed a harassment complaint against her once, saying she had slapped him.

Despite repeated promises to get her life together, Daphne likes to hang out most nights in the Public Gardens and drink with neighborhood kids. On more than one occasion she went to the park with her friend and confidant Chris, a quiet boy who had his own set of personal problems. His parents had separated, and subsequently he began to suffer severe anxiety attacks. He stayed home from school and was diagnosed with depression for which he took two drugs—Zoloft, an antidepressant, and Lorazepam, a sedative.

One night, Daphne and Chris met up with Michael, a 44-year-old man with a long history of alcohol problems. After a night of drinking, a fight broke out and Michael was stabbed, his throat cut, and his body dumped in the pond. Daphne was quickly arrested when soon after the attack she placed a 911 call to police, telling them that a friend had "jumped in the lake and didn't come out." Police searched the area and found Michael's slashed and stabbed body in the water; he had been disemboweled by Chris and Daphne in an attempt to sink the body.

At a waiver hearing, Daphne admits that she participated in the killing but cannot articulate what caused her to get involved. She had been drinking and remembers little of the events. She says that she was flirting with Michael and that Chris stabbed him in a jealous rage. She speaks in a flat, hollow voice and shows little remorse for her actions. It was a spur-of-the-moment thing, she claims, and after all it was Chris, not she herself, who had the knife. Later Chris testifies, claiming that Daphne instigated the fight and egged him on, taunting him that he was too scared to kill someone. Chris says that when she was drunk, Daphne often talked of killing an adult because she hated older people, especially her parents.

Daphne's parents claim that although she has been a burden with her mood swings and volatile behavior, she is still a child and can be helped with proper treatment. They are willing to supplement any state intervention with privately funded psychiatrists. Given that this is her first real offense and because of her age (14), her parents believe that home confinement with intense treatment is the best course.

The district attorney, however, wants Daphne treated as an adult and waived to adult court where, if she is found guilty, she can receive a 25-year sentence for second-degree murder; there is little question of her legal culpability.

Writing Assignment

Take the role of a defense lawyer in the juvenile court. Write a brief to the juvenile court judge that could be used at the waiver hearing. Use your essay to persuade the judge to keep Daphne in the juvenile court, where she could be treated rather than punished. How would you convince the court that Daphne's crime was a function of some abnormal trait or condition that is amenable to treatment? Be sure to refute the notion that she is a calculating criminal who understood the seriousness of her actions. If you want to read about the actual case, search online for "Daphne Abdela," or go to this website: http://topics.nytimes.com/top/reference/timestopics/people/a/daphne _abdela/. But do that after you write your essay—no cheating.

SUMMARY

LO1 Outline the development of trait theory.

The view that criminals have physical or mental traits that make them different originated with the Italian physician and criminologist Cesare Lombroso. In the early 1970s, spurred by the publication of *Sociobiology: The New Synthesis*, by Edmund O. Wilson, biological explanations of crime once again emerged. Trait theorists today recognize crime-producing interactions that involve both personal traits and environmental factors. If only a few offenders become persistent repeaters, what sets them apart from the rest of the criminal population may be some crime-producing trait.

LO2 Differentiate between the biochemical conditions that produce crime.

Biochemical conditions influence antisocial behavior. Biocriminologists maintain that an improper diet can cause chemical and mineral imbalance and lead to cognitive and learning deficits and problems, and these factors in turn are associated with antisocial behaviors. Abnormal levels of male sex hormones (androgens) can incline individuals to aggressive behavior. Exposure to lead has been linked to emotional and behavioral disorders.

LO3 Describe the link between genetics and crime, according to trait theory.
Another biosocial theme is that the human traits associated with criminality have a genetic basis. According to this view, (1) antisocial behavior is inherited, (2) the genetic makeup of parents is passed on to children, and (3) genetic abnormality is linked to a variety of antisocial behaviors.

LO4 List the elements of the psychodynamic perspective.
The id is the primitive part of people's mental makeup. The ego is shaped by learning and experience, and the superego reflects the morals and values of parents and significant others. Criminals are id-driven people who suffer from weak or damaged egos. Crime is a manifestation of feelings of oppression and the inability to develop the proper psychological defenses and rationales to keep these feelings under control.

LO5 Correlate behavior theory with criminal activities.
People are not born with the tendency to act violently; rather, they learn to be aggressive through their life experiences. These experiences include personally observing others acting aggressively to achieve some goal or observing people being rewarded for violent acts.

LO6 Analyze the controversy surrounding the link between intelligence and crime.
Proponents of nature theory argue that intelligence is largely determined genetically, that ancestry determines IQ, and that low intelligence is linked to criminal behavior. Proponents of nurture theory argue that intelligence is not inherited and that low-IQ parents do not necessarily produce low-IQ children. The debate about any link between IQ and criminality is unlikely to be settled soon. Measurement is beset by many methodological problems.

Key Terms

trait theories 134
sociobiology 135
individual vulnerability model 136
differential susceptibility model 136
hypoglycemia 138
androgens 138
testosterone 138
premenstrual syndrome (PMS) 138
neurophysiology 139
conduct disorder (CD) 140
attention deficit hyperactivity disorder (ADHD) 140
neurotransmitters 141
arousal theory 141
monozygotic (MZ) twins 142
dizygotic (DZ) twins 142
psychodynamic (psychoanalytic) psychology 145
id 145
ego 145
superego 145
attachment theory 145
behavior theory 145
social learning theory 146
behavior modeling 148
cognitive theory 149
information-processing theory 149
personality 150
antisocial personality 152
nature theory 154
nurture theory 154
mood disorder 155
oppositional defiant disorder (ODD) 155
schizophrenia 155
bipolar disorder 155
primary prevention programs 158
secondary prevention programs 158

Critical Thinking Questions

1. If research could show that the tendency to commit crime is inherited, what should be done with the young children of violence-prone criminals? Would it be fair to monitor their behavior from an early age?
2. Considering the evidence on the association between media and crime, would you recommend that young children be forbidden to view films with violent content?

3. Knowing what you do about trends and patterns in the crime rate and where and when crime takes place, how would you counteract the assertion that people who commit crime are physically or mentally abnormal?

4. Aside from becoming a criminal, what other career paths are open to psychopaths?

5. Should sugar be banned from school lunches?

6. Can gender differences in the crime rate be explained by evolutionary factors? Do you agree that male aggression is linked to mating patterns developed millions of years ago?

Notes

All URLs accessed in 2017.

1. Jack Healy and Ian Lovett, "Oregon Killer Described as Man of Few Words, Except on Topic of Guns," *New York Times*, Oct. 2, 2015, http://www.nytimes.com/2015/10/03/us/chris-harper-mercer-umpqua-community-college-shooting.html; CBS News, "What We Know About Oregon Shooter Chris Harper Mercer," http://www.cbsnews.com/news/umpqua-community-college-shooting-chris-harper-mercer/.

2. Lee Ellis, "A Discipline in Peril: Sociology's Future Hinges on Curing Biophobia," *American Sociologist* 27 (1996): 21–41.

3. Edmund O. Wilson, *Sociobiology: The New Synthesis* (Cambridge, MA: Harvard University Press, 1975).

4. Per-Olof Wikstrom and Rolf Loeber, "Do Disadvantaged Neighborhoods Cause Well-Adjusted Children to Become Adolescent Delinquents?" *Criminology* 38 (2000): 1109–1142.

5. John Paul Wright and Francis T. Cullen, "The Future of Biosocial Criminology: Beyond Scholars' Professional Ideology," *Journal of Contemporary Criminal Justice* 28 (2012): 237–253, at 244.

6. Bernard Rimland, *Dyslogic Syndrome: Why Today's Children Are "Hyper," Attention Disordered, Learning Disabled, Depressed, Aggressive, Defiant, or Violent—and What We Can Do About It* (London: Jessica Kingsley Publishers, 2008).

7. J. C. Barnes and Bruce Jacobs, "Genetic Risk for Violent Behavior and Environmental Exposure to Disadvantage and Violent Crime: The Case for Gene-Environment Interaction," *Journal of Interpersonal Violence* 28 (2013): 92–120.

8. Rimland, *Dyslogic Syndrome*.

9. John Cloud, "Harvey Milk: People Told Him No Openly Gay Man Could Win Political Office. Fortunately, He Ignored Them," *Time*, June 14, 1999, http://www.time.com/time/time100/heroes/profile/milk01.html.

10. F. T. Crews, A. Mdzinarishvili, D. Kim, J. He, and K. Nixon, "Neurogenesis in Adolescent Brain Is Potently Inhibited by Ethanol," *Neuroscience* 137 (2006): 437–445.

11. G. B. Ramirez, O. Pagulayan, H. Akagi, A. Francisco Rivera, L. V. Lee, A. Berroya, M. C. Vince Cruz, and D. Casintahan, "Tagum Study II: Follow-Up Study at Two Years of Age After Prenatal Exposure to Mercury," *Pediatrics* 111 (2003): 289–295.

12. D. K. L. Cheuk and Virginia Wong, "Attention Deficit Hyperactivity Disorder and Blood Mercury Level: A Case-Control Study in Chinese Children," *Neuropediatrics* 37 (2006): 234–240.

13. Ramirez et al., "Tagum Study II."

14. L. Kristjansson, I. D. Sigfusdottir, S. S. Frost, and J. E. James, "Adolescent Caffeine Consumption and Self-Reported Violence and Conduct Disorder," *Journal of Youth and Adolescence* 43 (2013): 1053–1062; Eric Konofal, Samuele Cortese, Michel Lecendreux, Isabelle Arnulf, and Marie Christine Mouren, "Effectiveness of Iron Supplementation in a Young Child with Attention-Deficit/Hyperactivity Disorder," *Pediatrics* 116 (2005): 732–734.

15. Alexandra Richardson and Paul Montgomery, "The Oxford-Durham Study: A Randomized Controlled Trial of Dietary Supplementation with Fatty Acids in Children with Developmental Coordination Disorder," *Pediatrics* 115 (2005): 1360–1366.

16. Crystal Haskell, Andrew Scholey, Philippa Jackson, Jade Elliott, Margaret Defeyter, Joanna Greer, Bernadette Robertson, Tom Buchanan, Brian Tiplady, and David Kennedy, "Cognitive and Mood Effects in Healthy Children During 12 Weeks' Supplementation with Multi-Vitamin/Minerals," *British Journal of Nutrition* 100 (2008): 1086–1096.

17. Stephen Schoenthaler and Walter Doraz, "Types of Offenses Which Can Be Reduced in an Institutional Setting Using Nutritional Intervention," *International Journal of Biosocial Research* 4 (1983): 74–84.

18. Simon Moore, Lisa Carter, and Stephanie Van Goozen, "Confectionary Consumption in Childhood and Adult Violence," *British Journal of Psychiatry* 195 (2009): 366–367.

19. Sara J. Solnick, and David Hemenway, "The Twinkie Defense," *Injury Prevention* 18 (2012): 259–263.

20. Nathan DeWall, Timothy Deckman, Matthew Gailliot, and Brad Bushman, "Sweetened Blood Cools Hot Tempers: Physiological Self-Control and Aggression," *Aggressive Behavior* 37 (2011): 73–80.

21. Diana Fishbein, "Neuropsychological Function, Drug Abuse, and Violence: A Conceptual Framework," *Criminal Justice and Behavior* 27 (2000): 139–159.

22. Matti Virkkunen, "Reactive Hypoglycemic Tendency Among Habitually Violent Offenders," *Nutrition Reviews Supplement* 44 (1986): 94–103.

23. Jooa Julia Lee, Francesca Gino, Ellie Shuo Jin, Leslie Rice, and Robert Josephs, "Hormones and Ethics: Understanding the Biological Basis of Unethical Conduct," *Journal of Experimental Psychology* 144 (2015): 891–897; Cave Sinai, Tatja Hirvikoski, Anna-Lena Nordström, Peter Nordström, Åsa Nilsonne, Alexander Wilczek, Marie Åsberg, and Jussi Jokinen, "Thyroid Hormones and Adult Interpersonal Violence Among Women with Borderline Personality Disorder," *Psychiatry Research* 227 (2015): 253–257.

24. Stephanie H. M. van Goozen, Walter Matthys, Peggy Cohen-Kettenis, Jos Thijssen, and Herman van Engeland, "Adrenal Androgens and Aggression in Conduct Disorder Prepubertal Boys and Normal Controls," *Biological Psychiatry* 43 (1998): 156–158.

25. Paul Bernhardt, "Influences of Serotonin and Testosterone in Aggression and Dominance: Convergence with Social Psychology," *Current Directions in Psychological Science* 6 (1997): 44–48.

26. Christy Miller Buchanan, Jacquelynne Eccles, and Jill Becker, "Are Adolescents the Victims of Raging Hormones? Evidence for Activational Effects of Hormones on Moods and Behavior at Adolescence," *Psychological Bulletin* 111 (1992): 62–107.

27. Angel Romero-Martínez, Marisol Lila, Patricia Sariñana-González, Esperanza González-Bono, and Luis Moya-Albiol, "High Testosterone Levels and Sensitivity to Acute Stress in Perpetrators of Domestic Violence with Low Cognitive Flexibility and Impairments in Their Emotional Decoding Process: A Preliminary Study," *Aggressive Behavior* 39 (2013): 355–369.

28. Celina Cohen-Bendahan, Jan Buitelaar, Stephanie van Goozen, Jacob Orlebeke, and Peggy Cohen-Kettenis, "Is There an Effect of Prenatal Testosterone on Aggression and Other Behavioral Traits? A Study Comparing Same-Sex and Opposite-Sex Twin Girls," *Hormones and Behavior* 47 (2005): 230–237.

29. Albert Reiss and Jeffrey Roth, eds., *Understanding and Preventing Violence* (Washington, DC: National Academy Press, 1993), p. 118.

30. Anthony Walsh, "Genetic and Cytogenetic Intersex Anomalies: Can They Help Us to Understand Gender Differences in Deviant Behavior?" *International Journal of Offender Therapy and Comparative Criminology* 39 (1995): 151–166.

31. Walter Gove, "The Effect of Age and Gender on Deviant Behavior: A Biopsychosocial Perspective," in *Gender and the Life Course*, ed. A. S. Rossi (New York: Aldine, 1985), pp. 115–144.

32. A. Romero-Martínez, M. Lila, and L. Moya-Albiol, "The Testosterone/Cortisol Ratio Moderates the Proneness to Anger Expression in Antisocial and Borderline Intimate Partner Violence Perpetrators," *Journal of Forensic Psychiatry and Psychology* 27 (2016): 135–144.

33. For a review of this concept, see Anne E. Figert, "The Three Faces of PMS: The Professional, Gendered, and Scientific Structuring of a Psychiatric Disorder," *Social Problems* 42 (1995): 56–72.

34. Katharina Dalton, *The Premenstrual Syndrome* (Springfield, IL: Charles C Thomas, 1971).

35. Diana Fishbein, "Selected Studies on the Biology of Antisocial Behavior," in *New Perspectives in Criminology*, ed. John Conklin (Needham Heights, MA: Allyn & Bacon, 1996), pp. 26–38.

36. David C. Bellinger, "Lead," *Pediatrics* 113 (2004): 1016–1022.

37. Centers for Disease Control and Prevention, "Lead: What Do Parents Need to Know to Protect Their Children?" http://www.cdc.gov/nceh/lead/ACCLPP/blood_lead_levels.htm.

38. Jeff Evans, "Asymptomatic, High Lead Levels Tied to Delinquency," *Pediatric News* 37 (2003): 13.

39. Mark Opler, Alan Brown, Joseph Graziano, Manisha Desai, Wei Zheng, Catherine Schaefer, Pamela Factor-Litvak, and Ezra S. Susser, "Prenatal Lead Exposure, [Delta]-Aminolevulinic Acid, and Schizophrenia," *Environmental Health Perspectives* 112 (2004): 548–553.

40. Paul Stretesky and Michael Lynch, "The Relationship Between Lead Exposure and Homicide," *Archives of Pediatric Adolescent Medicine* 155 (2001): 579–582.

41. Rick Nevin, "Understanding International Crime Trends: The Legacy of Preschool Lead Exposure," *Environmental Research* 104 (2007): 315–336.

42. Ibid.

43. Paul Stewart, Edward Lonky, Jacqueline Reihman, James Pagano, Brooks Gump, and Thomas Darvill, "The Relationship Between Prenatal PCB Exposure and Intelligence (IQ) in 9-Year-Old Children," *Environmental Health Perspectives* 116 (2008): 1416–1422.

44. Lilian Calderón-Garcidueñas et al., "Air Pollution, Cognitive Deficits and Brain Abnormalities: A Pilot Study with Children and Dogs," *Brain and Cognition* 68 (2008): 117–127.

45. Centers for Disease Control and Prevention, "Developmental Disabilities: Exposure and Risk," http://ephtracking.cdc.gov/showDevelopmental DisabilitiesExposureRisk.action.

46. Nathaniel Pallone and James Hennessy, "Brain Dysfunction and Criminal Violence," *Society* 35 (1998): 21–27.

47. Kristy Lane, Maria St. Pierre, Margo Lauterbach, and Vassilis Koliatsos, "Patient Profiles of Criminal Behavior in the Context of Traumatic Brain Injury," *Journal of Forensic Sciences* 62 (2017): 545–548.

48. Thomas Crowley, Manish S. Dalwani, Susan K. Mikulich-Gilbertson, Yiping P. Du, Carl W. Lejuez, Kristen M. Raymond, and Marie T. Banich, "Risky Decisions and Their Consequences: Neural Processing by Boys with Antisocial Substance Disorder," *PLoS One* 5 (2010), http://www.ncbi.nlm .nih.gov/pmc/articles/PMC2943904/.

49. James Ogilvie, Anna Stewart, Raymond Chan, and David Shum, "Neuropsychological Measures of Executive Function and Antisocial Behavior: A Meta-Analysis," *Criminology* 49 (2011): 1063–1107.

50. Kevin Beaver, John Paul Wright, and Matt DeLisi, "Self-Control as an Executive Function: Reformulating Gottfredson and Hirschi's Parental Socialization Thesis," *Criminal Justice and Behavior* 34 (2007): 1345–1361.

51. Alice Jones, Kristin Laurens, Catherine Herba, Gareth Barker, and Essi Viding, "Amygdala Hypoactivity to Fearful Faces in Boys with Conduct Problems and Callous-Unemotional Traits," *American Journal of Psychiatry* 166 (2009): 95–102.

52. Peter Simi, Karyn Sporer, and Bryan Bubolz, "Narratives of Childhood Adversity and Adolescent Misconduct as Precursors to Violent Extremism," *Journal of Research in Crime and Delinquency* 53 (2016): 536–563.

53. Society for Neuroscience, "Studies Identify Brain Areas and Chemicals Involved in Aggression; May Speed Development of Better Treatment," http://www .sfn.org/Press-Room/News-Release-Archives/2007 /studies-identify-brain.

54. Stephen Faraone et al., "Intellectual Performance and School Failure in Children with Attention Deficit Hyperactivity Disorder and in Their Siblings," *Journal of Abnormal Psychology* 102 (1993): 616–623.

55. Leonore M. J. Simon, "Does Criminal Offender Treatment Work?" *Applied and Preventive Psychology* 7 (1998): 137–159.

56. Ibid.

57. Molina Pelham Jr., "Childhood Predictors of Adolescent Substance Use in a Longitudinal Study of Children with ADHD," *Journal of Abnormal Psychology* 112 (2003): 497–507; Peter Muris and Cor Meesters, "The Validity of Attention Deficit Hyperactivity and Hyperkinetic Disorder Symptom Domains in Nonclinical Dutch Children," *Journal of Clinical Child and Adolescent Psychology* 32 (2003): 460–466.

58. Elizabeth Hart et al., "Criterion Validity of Informants in the Diagnosis of Disruptive Behavior Disorders in Children: A Preliminary Study," *Journal of Consulting and Clinical Psychology* 62 (1994): 410–414.

59. Michael Kofler, Ross Larsen, Dustin Sarver, and Patrick Tolan, "Developmental Trajectories of Aggression, Prosocial Behavior, and Social-Cognitive Problem Solving in Emerging Adolescents with Clinically Elevated Attention-Deficit/Hyperactivity Disorder Symptoms," *Journal of Abnormal Psychology* 124 (2015): 1027–1042.

60. W. R. Lindsay, D. Carson, A. J. Holland, J. L. Taylor, G. O'Brien, and J. R. Wheeler, "The Impact of Known Criminogenic Factors on Offenders with Intellectual Disability: Previous Findings and New Results on ADHD," *Journal of Applied Research in Intellectual Disabilities* 26 (2013): 71–80.

61. Joseph Biederman, Michael Monuteaux, Eric Mick, Thomas Spencer, Timothy Wilens, Julie Silva, Lindsey Snyder, and Stephen Faraone, "Young Adult Outcome of Attention Deficit Hyperactivity Disorder: A Controlled 10-Year Follow-Up Study," *Psychological Medicine* 36 (2006): 167–179.

62. Jukka Savolainen, Alex Mason, Jonathan Bolen, Mary Chmelka, Tuula Hurtig, Hann Ebeling, Tanja Nordström, and Anja Taanila, "The Path from Childhood Behavioural Disorders to Felony Offending: Investigating the Role of Adolescent Drinking, Peer Marginalisation and School Failure," *Criminal Behaviour and Mental Health* 25 (2015): 375–388; Ivy Defoe, David Farrington, and Rolf Loeber, "Disentangling the Relationship Between Delinquency and Hyperactivity, Low Achievement, Depression, and Low Socioeconomic Status: Analysis of Repeated Longitudinal Data," *Journal of Criminal Justice* 41 (2013): 100–107.

63. Ronald Simons, Man Kit Lei, Steven Beach, Gene Brody, Robert Philibert, and Frederick Gibbons, "Social Environmental Variation, Plasticity Genes, and Aggression: Evidence for the Differential Susceptibility Hypothesis," *American Sociological Review* 76 (2011): 833–912.

64. Susan Young, Andrew Smolen, Robin Corley, Kenneth Krauter, John DeFries, Thomas Crowley, and John Hewitt, "Dopamine Transporter

Polymorphism Associated with Externalizing Behavior Problems in Children," *American Journal of Medical Genetics* 114 (2002): 144–149.

65. M. Skondras, M. Markianos, A. Botsis, E. Bistolaki, and G. Christodoulou, "Platelet Monoamine Oxidase Activity and Psychometric Correlates in Male Violent Offenders Imprisoned for Homicide or Other Violent Acts," *European Archives of Psychiatry and Clinical Neuroscience* 254 (2004): 380–386.

66. Lee Ellis, "Monoamine Oxidase and Criminality: Identifying an Apparent Biological Marker for Antisocial Behavior," *Journal of Research in Crime and Delinquency* 28 (1991): 227–251.

67. Rose McDermott, Chris Dawes, Elizabeth Prom-Wormley, Lindon Eaves, and Peter Hatemi, "MAOA and Aggression: A Gene–Environment Interaction in Two Populations," *Journal of Conflict Resolution* 57 (2013): 1043–1064.

68. Lee Ellis and Anthony Hoskin, "Criminality and the 2D:4D Ratio: Testing the Prenatal Androgen Hypothesis," *International Journal of Offender Therapy and Comparative Criminology* 59 (2015): 295–312.

69. Lee Ellis, "Left and Mixed-Handedness and Criminality: Explanations for a Probable Relationship," in *Left-Handedness: Behavioral Implications and Anomalies,* ed. S. Coren (Amsterdam: Elsevier, 1990), pp. 485–507.

70. Lee Ellis, "Arousal Theory and the Religiosity–Criminality Relationship," in *Contemporary Criminological Theory*, ed. Peter Cordella and Larry Siegel (Boston: Northeastern University, 1996), pp. 65–84.

71. Jill Portnoy, Adrian Raine, Frances Chen, Dustin Pardini, Rolf Loeber, and J. Richard Jennings, "Heart Rate and Antisocial Behavior: The Mediating Role of Impulsive Sensation Seeking," *Criminology* 52 (2014): 292–311.

72. Olivia Choy, Adrian Raine, Jill Portnoy, Anna Rudo-Hutt, Yu Gao, and Liana Soyfer, "The Mediating Role of Heart Rate on the Social Adversity-Antisocial Behavior Relationship: A Social Neurocriminology Perspective," *Journal of Research in Crime and Delinquency* 52 (2015): 303–341.

73. Thomas Frisell, Yudi Pawitan, Niklas Långström, and Paul Lichtenstein, "Heritability, Assortative Mating and Gender Differences in Violent Crime: Results from a Total Population Sample Using Twin, Adoption, and Sibling Models," *Behavior Genetics* 42 (2012): 3–18.

74. Kevin Beaver, Joseph Nedelec, Joseph Schwartz, and Eric Connolly, "Evolutionary Behavioral Genetics of Violent Crime" in Todd Shackelford and Ranald D. Hansen, eds., "The Evolution of Violence," special issue of *Evolutionary Psychology* (2014): 117–135.

75. Ronald L. Simons, Man Kit Lei, Eric A. Stewart, Steven R. H. Beach, Gene H. Brody, Robert A. Philibert, and Frederick X. Gibbons, "Social Adversity, Genetic Variation, Street Code, and Aggression: A Genetically Informed Model of Violent Behavior," *Youth Violence and Juvenile Justice* 10 (2012): 3–24; Anita Thapar, Kate Langley, Tom Fowler, Frances Rice, Darko Turic, Naureen Whittinger, John Aggleton, Marianne Van den Bree, Michael Owen, and Michael O'Donovan, "Catechol O-methyltransferase Gene Variant and Birth Weight Predict Early-Onset Antisocial Behavior in Children with Attention-Deficit/Hyperactivity Disorder," *Archives of General Psychiatry* 62 (2005): 1275–1278.

76. Kevin Beaver, John Paul Wright, and Matt DeLisi, "Delinquent Peer Group Formation: Evidence of a Gene X Environment Correlation," *Journal of Genetic Psychology* 169 (2008): 227–244.

77. Kevin Beaver, Chris Gibson, Michael Turner, Matt DeLisi, Michael Vaughn, and Ashleigh Holand, "Stability of Delinquent Peer Associations: A Biosocial Test of Warr's Sticky-Friends Hypothesis," *Crime and Delinquency* 57 (2011): 907–927.

78. Kevin M. Beaver, "The Effects of Genetics, the Environment, and Low Self-Control on Perceived Maternal and Paternal Socialization: Results from a Longitudinal Sample of Twins," *Journal of Quantitative Criminology* 27 (2011): 85–105.

79. K. Dean, P. B. Mortensen, H. Stevens, R. M. Murray, E. Walsh, and E. Agerbo, "Criminal Conviction Among Offspring with Parental History of Mental Disorder," *Psychological Medicine* 42 (2012): 571–581.

80. D. J. West and D. P. Farrington, "Who Becomes Delinquent?" in *The Delinquent Way of Life*, ed. D. J. West and D. P. Farrington (London: Heinemann, 1977), pp. 1–28; D. J. West, *Delinquency: Its Roots, Careers, and Prospects* (Cambridge, MA: Harvard University Press, 1982).

81. David Farrington, "Understanding and Preventing Bullying," in *Crime and Justice*, Vol. 17, ed. Michael Tonry (Chicago: University of Chicago Press, 1993), pp. 381–457.

82. R. J. Cadoret, C. Cain, and R. R. Crowe, "Evidence for a Gene–Environment Interaction in the Development of Adolescent Antisocial Behavior," *Behavior Genetics* 13 (1983): 301–310.

83. Barry Hutchings and Sarnoff A. Mednick, "Criminality in Adoptees and Their Adoptive and Biological Parents: A Pilot Study," in *Biological Bases in Criminal Behavior*, ed. S. A. Mednick and K. O. Christiansen (New York: Gardner Press, 1977).

84. Michael Lyons, Karestan Koenen, Francisco Buchting, Joanne Meyer, Lindon Eaves, Rosemary Toomey, Seth Eisen, et al., "A Twin Study of Sexual Behavior in Men," *Archives of Sexual Behavior* 33 (2004): 129–136.

85. Sarnoff Mednick and Jan Volavka, "Biology and Crime," in *Crime and Justice*, ed. Norval Morris and Michael Tonry (Chicago: University of Chicago Press, 1980), pp. 85–159, at p. 94.

86. Edwin J. C. G. van den Oord, Frank Verhulst, and Dorret Boomsma, "A Genetic Study of Maternal and Paternal Ratings of Problem Behaviors in 3-Year-Old Twins," *Journal of Abnormal Psychology* 105 (1996): 349–357.

87. Ginette Dionne, Richard Tremblay, Michel Boivin, David Laplante, and Daniel Perusse, "Physical Aggression and Expressive Vocabulary in 19-Month-Old Twins," *Developmental Psychology* 39 (2003): 261–273.

88. Alex Piquero, "No Remorse, No Repent: Linking Lack of Remorse to Criminal Offending in a Sample of Serious Adolescent Offenders," *Justice Quarterly* 34 (2017): 350–376.

89. Callie Burt and Ronald Simons, "Pulling Back the Curtain on Heritability Studies: Biosocial Criminology in the Postgenomic Era," *Criminology* 52 (2014): 223–262.

90. J. C. Barnes, John Paul Wright, Brian B. Boutwell, Joseph A. Schwartz, Eric J. Connolly, Joseph L. Nedelec, and Kevin M. Beaver, "Demonstrating the Validity of Twin Research in Criminology," *Criminology* 52 (2014): 588–626.

91. Lawrence Cohen and Richard Machalek, "A General Theory of Expropriative Crime: An Evolutionary Ecological Approach," *American Journal of Sociology* 94 (1988): 465–501.

92. For a general review, see Martin Daly and Margo Wilson, "Crime and Conflict: Homicide in Evolutionary Psychological Theory," in *Crime and Justice: An Annual Edition*, ed. Michael Tonry (Chicago: University of Chicago Press, 1997), pp. 51–100.

93. Joseph Nedelec and Kevin Beaver, "The Association Between Sexual Behavior and Antisocial Behavior: Insights from an Evolutionary Informed Analysis," *Journal of Contemporary Criminal Justice* 28 (2012): 329–345.

94. Ibid.

95. David Rowe, Alexander Vazsonyi, and Aurelio Jose Figuerdo, "Mating-Effort in Adolescence: A Conditional Alternative Strategy," *Personal Individual Differences* 23 (1997): 105–115.

96. Edwin Driver, "Charles Buckman Goring," in *Pioneers in Criminology*, ed. Hermann Mannheim (Montclair, NJ: Patterson Smith, 1970), p. 440.

97. Gabriel Tarde, *Penal Philosophy*, trans. R. Howell (Boston: Little, Brown, 1912).

98. See, generally, Donn Byrne and Kathryn Kelly, *An Introduction to Personality* (Englewood Cliffs, NJ: Prentice Hall, 1981).

99. See, generally, D. A. Andrews and James Bonta, *The Psychology of Criminal Conduct* (Cincinnati: Anderson, 1994), pp. 72–75.

100. John Bowlby, *Maternal Care and Mental Health*, World Health Organization Monograph, WHO Monographs Series No. 2 (Geneva: World Health Organization, 1951).

101. Claire Ogilvie, Emily Newman, Lynda Todd, and David Peck, "Attachment and Violent Offending: A Meta-analysis," *Aggression and Violent Behavior* 19 (2014): 322–339.

102. Eric Wood and Shelley Riggs, "Predictors of Child Molestation: Adult Attachment, Cognitive Distortions, and Empathy," *Journal of Interpersonal Violence* 23 (2008): 259–275.

103. Helmut Hirtenlehner and Brenda Sims Blackwell, "Can Differences in Attachment to Parents and Level of Self-Control Explain the Gender Gap in Juvenile Delinquency? Testing a Gendered Attachment—Self-Control Theory," *Journal of Current Issues in Crime, Law and Law Enforcement* 8 (2015): 406–424; Karen L. Hayslett-McCall and Thomas J. Bernard, "Attachment, Masculinity, and Self-Control: A Theory of Male Crime Rates," *Theoretical Criminology* 6 (2002): 5–33.

104. This discussion is based on three works by Albert Bandura: *Aggression: A Social Learning Analysis* (Englewood Cliffs, NJ: Prentice Hall, 1973); *Social Learning Theory* (Englewood Cliffs, NJ: Prentice Hall, 1977); and "The Social Learning Perspective: Mechanisms of Aggression," in *Psychology of Crime and Criminal Justice*, ed. Hans Toch (New York: Holt, Rinehart & Winston, 1979), pp. 198–236.

105. Glenn Walters, "Forging a Link Between Conduct Disorder and Adolescent/Adult Offending via Externalizing Behavior and Reading Performance," *Youth Violence and Juvenile Justice* 14 (2016): 61–75.

106. Amy Street, Lynda King, Daniel King, and David Riges, "The Associations Among Male-Perpetrated Partner Violence, Wives' Psychological Distress and Children's Behavior Problems: A Structural Equation Modeling Analysis," *Journal of Comparative Family Studies* 34 (2003): 23–46.

107. David Phillips, "The Impact of Mass Media Violence on U.S. Homicides," *American Sociological Review* 48 (1983): 560–568.

108. Kenneth Dodge, "A Social Information Processing Model of Social Competence in Children," in *Minnesota Symposium in Child Psychology*, Vol. 18,

ed. M. Perlmutter (Hillsdale, NJ: Erlbaum, 1986), pp. 77–125.

109. Tony Ward and Claire Stewart, "The Relationship Between Human Needs and Criminogenic Needs," *Psychology, Crime and Law* 9 (2003): 219–225.

110. David Ward, Mark Stafford, and Louis Gray, "Rational Choice, Deterrence, and Theoretical Integration," *Journal of Applied Social Psychology* 36 (2006): 571–585.

111. Glenn Walters and Matt DeLisi, "Antisocial Cognition and Crime Continuity: Cognitive Mediation of the Past Crime–Future Crime Relationship," *Journal of Criminal Justice* 41 (2013): 135–140.

112. Donald Lynam and Joshua Miller, "Personality Pathways to Impulsive Behavior and Their Relations to Deviance: Results from Three Samples," *Journal of Quantitative Criminology* 20 (2004): 319–341.

113. L. Huesman and L. Eron, "Individual Differences and the Trait of Aggression," *European Journal of Personality* 3 (1989): 95–106.

114. Rolf Loeber and Dale Hay, "Key Issues in the Development of Aggression and Violence from Childhood to Early Adulthood," *Annual Review of Psychology* 48 (1997): 371–410.

115. Vincent Marziano, Tony Ward, Anthony Beech, and Philippa Pattison, "Identification of Five Fundamental Implicit Theories Underlying Cognitive Distortions in Child Abusers: A Preliminary Study," *Psychology, Crime and Law* 12 (2006): 97–105.

116. See, generally, Walter Mischel, *Introduction to Personality*, 4th ed. (New York: Holt, Rinehart & Winston, 1986).

117. Edelyn Verona and Joyce Carbonell, "Female Violence and Personality," *Criminal Justice and Behavior* 27 (2000): 176–195.

118. Piquero, "No Remorse, No Repent."

119. Gerhard Blickle, Alexander Schlegel, Pantaleon Fassbender, and Uwe Klein, "Some Personality Correlates of Business White-Collar Crime," *Applied Psychology: An International Review* 55 (2006): 220–233.

120. Hans Eysenck and M. W. Eysenck, *Personality and Individual Differences* (New York: Plenum, 1985).

121. Catrien Bijleveld and Jan Hendriks, "Juvenile Sex Offenders: Differences Between Group and Solo Offenders," *Psychology, Crime and Law* 9 (2003): 237–246.

122. Laurie Frost, Terrie Moffitt, and Rob McGee, "Neuropsychological Correlates of Psychopathology in an Unselected Cohort of Young Adolescents," *Journal of Abnormal Psychology* 98 (1989): 307–313.

123. David Lykken, "Psychopathy, Sociopathy, and Crime," *Society* 34 (1996): 30–38.

124. Ashley Hampton, Deborah Drabick, and Laurence Steinberg, "Does IQ Moderate the Relation Between Psychopathy and Juvenile Offending?" *Law and Human Behavior* 38 (2014): 23–33.

125. Baris Yildirim and Jan Derksen, "Clarifying the Heterogeneity in Psychopathic Samples: Towards a New Continuum of Primary and Secondary Psychopathy," *Aggression and Violent Behavior* 24 (2015): 9–41.

126. James Blair, Derek Mitchell, and Karina Blair, *The Psychopath: Emotion and the Brain* (New York: Blackwell Publishing, 2005).

127. Sonja Krstic, Raymond A. Knight, and Carrie A. Robertson, "Developmental Antecedents of the Facets of Psychopathy: The Role of Multiple Abuse Experiences," *Journal of Personality Disorders*, printed online 2015.

128. Kevin Beaver, Meghan Rowland, Joseph Schwartz, and Joseph Nedelec, "The Genetic Origins of Psychopathic Traits in Adult Males and Females: Results from an Adoption-Based Study," *Journal of Criminal Justice* 39 (2011): 426–432.

129. Rolf Holmqvist, "Psychopathy and Affect Consciousness in Young Criminal Offenders," *Journal of Interpersonal Violence* 23 (2008): 209–224.

130. James Blair, Derek Mitchell, and Karina Blair, *The Psychopath: Emotion and the Brain* (New York: Blackwell Publishing, 2005).

131. Joseph Lee Rogers, H. Harrington Cleveland, Edwin van den Oord, and David Rowe, "Resolving the Debate over Birth Order, Family Size and Intelligence," *American Psychologist* 55 (2000): 599–612.

132. Travis Hirschi and Michael Hindelang, "Intelligence and Delinquency: A Revisionist Review," *American Sociological Review* 42 (1977): 471–586.

133. James Q. Wilson and Richard Herrnstein, *Crime and Human Nature* (New York: Simon & Schuster, 1985), p. 148.

134. Richard Herrnstein and Charles Murray, *The Bell Curve: Intelligence and Class Structure in American Life* (New York: Free Press, 1994).

135. Matt DeLisi, Alex Piquero, and Stephanie Cardwell, "The Unpredictability of Murder," *Youth Violence and Juvenile Justice* 14 (2016): 26–42.

136. Kevin M. Beaver, Joseph A. Schwartz, Joseph L. Nedelec, Eric J. Connolly, Brian B. Boutwell, and J. C. Barnes, "Intelligence Is Associated with Criminal Justice Processing: Arrest Through Incarceration," *Intelligence* 41 (2013): 277–288.

137. Kevin Beaver and John Paul Wright, "The Association Between County-Level IQ and

County-Level Crime Rates," *Intelligence* 39 (2011): 22–26; Jared Bartels, Joseph Ryan, Lynn Urban, and Laura Glass, "Correlations Between Estimates of State IQ and FBI Crime Statistics," *Personality and Individual Differences* 48 (2010): 579–583; Philippe Rushton and Donald Templer, "National Differences in Intelligence, Crime, Income, and Skin Color," *Intelligence* 37 (2009): 341–346.

138. Maria Ttofi, David Farrington, Alex Piquero, Friedrich Lösel, Matthew DeLisi, and Joseph Murray, "Intelligence as a Protective Factor Against Offending: A Meta-analytic Review of Prospective Longitudinal Studies," *Journal of Criminal Justice* 45 (2016): 4–18.

139. Aaron Beck, Neil Rector, Neal Stolar, and Paul Grant, *Schizophrenia: Cognitive Theory, Research, and Therapy* (New York, Guilford Press, 2008).

140. Paige Crosby Ouimette, "Psychopathology and Sexual Aggression in Nonincarcerated Men," *Violence and Victimization* 12 (1997): 389–397.

141. Ellen Kjelsberg, "Gender and Disorder-Specific Criminal Career Profiles in Former Adolescent Psychiatric In-Patients," *Journal of Youth and Adolescence* 33 (2004): 261–270.

142. Paula Fite, Spencer Evans, John Cooley, and Sonia Rubens, "Further Evaluation of Associations Between Attention-Deficit/Hyperactivity and Oppositional Defiant Disorder Symptoms and Bullying-Victimization in Adolescence," *Child Psychiatry and Human Development* 45 (2014): 32–41.

143. Crowley et al., "Risky Decisions and Their Consequences."

144. Barbara Maughan, Richard Rowe, Julie Messer, Robert Goodman, and Howard Meltzer, "Conduct Disorder and Oppositional Defiant Disorder in a National Sample: Developmental Epidemiology," *Journal of Child Psychology and Psychiatry and Allied Disciplines* 45 (2004): 609–621.

145. Cyril Boonmann et al., "Mental Disorders in Juveniles Who Sexually Offended: A Meta-analysis," *Aggression and Violent Behavior* 24 (2015): 241–249.

146. Richard Dorn, Jan Volavka, and Norman Johnson, "Mental Disorder and Violence: Is There a Relationship Beyond Substance Use?" *Social Psychiatry and Psychiatric Epidemiology* 47 (2012): 487–503.

147. Michael Ostermann and Jason Matejkowski, "Estimating the Impact of Mental Illness on Costs of Crimes," *Criminal Justice and Behavior* 41 (2014): 20–40.

148. Robert Vermeiren, "Psychopathology and Delinquency in Adolescents: A Descriptive and Developmental Perspective," *Clinical Psychology Review* 23 (2003): 277–318.

149. David Vinkers, Edwin de Beurs, and Marko Barendregt, "Psychiatric Disorders and Repeat Offending," *American Journal of Psychiatry* 166 (2009): 489.

150. Jacques Baillargeon, Ingrid Binswanger, Joseph Penn, Brie Williams, and Owen Murray, "Psychiatric Disorders and Repeat Incarcerations: The Revolving Prison Door," *American Journal of Psychiatry* 166 (2009): 103–109.

151. John Monahan, *Mental Illness and Violent Crime* (Washington, DC: National Institute of Justice, 1996).

152. Thomas O'Hare, Ce Shen, and Margaret Sherrer, "High-Risk Behaviors and Drinking-to-Cope as Mediators of Lifetime Abuse and PTSD Symptoms in Clients with Severe Mental Illness," *Journal of Traumatic Stress* 23 (2010): 255–263; Eric Silver, "Mental Disorder and Violent Victimization: The Mediating Role of Involvement in Conflicted Social Relationships," *Criminology* 40 (2002): 191–212.

153. Eric Silver, "Extending Social Disorganization Theory: A Multilevel Approach to the Study of Violence Among Persons with Mental Illness," *Criminology* 38 (2000): 1043–1074.

154. B. Lögdberg, L-L. Nilsson, M. T. Levander, and S. Levander, "Schizophrenia, Neighbourhood, and Crime," *Acta Psychiatrica Scandinavica* 110 (2004): 92–97; Stacy DeCoster and Karen Heimer, "The Relationship Between Law Violation and Depression: An Interactionist Analysis," *Criminology* 39 (2001): 799–837.

155. Courtenay Sellers, Christopher Sullivan, Bonita Veysey, and Jon Shane, "Responding to Persons with Mental Illnesses: Police Perspectives on Specialized and Traditional Practices," *Behavioral Sciences and the Law* 23 (2005): 647–657.

156. Tamsin B. R. Short, Stuart Thomas, Stefan Luebbers, Paul Mullen, and James Ogloff, "A Case-Linkage Study of Crime Victimisation in Schizophrenia-Spectrum Disorders over a Period of Deinstitutionalization," *BMC Psychiatry* 13 (2013): 1–9.

157. David Kopel and Clayton Cramer, "Reforming Mental Health Law to Protect Public Safety and Help the Severely Mentally Ill," *Howard Law Journal* 58 (2015): 715–778.

158. Beaver, Wright, and DeLisi, "Delinquent Peer Group Formation."

159. Susan Pease and Craig T. Love, "Optimal Methods and Issues in Nutrition Research in the Correctional Setting," *Nutrition Reviews Supplement* 44 (1986): 122–131.

Social Structure Theory

Learning Objectives

LO1 Explain the association between social structure and crime.

LO2 Identify the elements of social disorganization theory.

LO3 Analyze the views of Shaw and McKay.

LO4 Differentiate between the various elements of ecological theory.

LO5 Discuss the concept of strain.

LO6 List and compare the elements of cultural deviance theory.

Aaron Hernandez in court.

AP Images/Steven Senne

6

Chapter Outline

FACT OR FICTION?

▶ Very few children today live in poverty, because the government has made ending child poverty a top priority.

▶ Political, social, and economic programs such as affirmative action have erased the economic gulf between whites and minorities.

▶ Crime rates go down in a healthy economy and rise along with unemployment.

I n 2012, Aaron Hernandez signed a $40 million contract with the New England Patriots. Only 22 years old, Hernandez had grown up poor, working menial jobs in Bristol, Connecticut. He hung with a tough crowd in a bad neighborhood; he had gang tats. He was saved by his incredible athletic ability. Hernandez set scoring records in high school football and was recruited to the University of Florida where he became a collegiate All-American. He entered the NFL as its youngest player.

But despite his success, Hernandez could not shake his early life and often hung out with his old friends from the hood. While in college, he got into a fight with a bouncer at a bar. He was questioned by the police about a shooting that injured two men; he was supposedly with his Connecticut crew. Hernandez was suspended as a sophomore for an undisclosed violation of team rules and by his junior year he acknowledged testing positive for marijuana.

On June 26, 2013, in an incident that made national headlines, Hernandez was arrested on suspicion of the murder of Odin Lloyd, a 27-year-old semiprofessional football player, who was dating the sister of Hernandez's fiancée, Shayanna Jenkins. It seems that the two men had begun socializing together and sharing secrets. Hernandez became angry at Lloyd when he suspected he was talking to people about a prior incident: the shooting of two men with whom Hernandez had a disagreement at a Boston club. Although no murder weapon was found, and no witness to the shooting of Lloyd came forward, prosecutors had overwhelming physical evidence and were able to get a jury to convict Hernandez; he received a life sentence without hope of parole. Hernandez was also charged with the earlier double murder.[1]

On April 19, 2017, Hernandez was found dead in his cell at the Souza-Baranowski Correctional ▶

Center, in Shirley, Massachusetts. He had hanged himself by a bed sheet that he attached to a window. Ironically, just five days before, he had been found not guilty in the double murder case. Things seemed to be going his way, and he was appealing his conviction in the Lloyd case.

In the aftermath of his suicide, friends and fellow athletes lamented the tragic life and death of this gifted but troubled young man. Many argued that he could not shake off his roots and brought his gang associations with him first to college and then to professional football. ■

To criminologists it comes as no surprise that someone who grew up in a poor, deteriorated urban neighborhood, who was immersed in street culture and values, will get involved in violent behavior—even someone like Aaron Hernandez, who seemed to have escaped poverty.[2] Many kids in these areas grow up hopeless and alienated, believing that they have little chance of being part of the American Dream.[3] Many, like Hernandez, become involved in gang culture. There are now an estimated 30,700 gangs and 850,000 gang members in the United States; the numbers of gangs and gang members are increasing. There are more than 2,300 gang-related homicides each year, more than 15 percent of all the murders that occur in the US.[4] And even when opportunity presents itself, the lure of the gangster lifestyle is hard to shake.

Noting the universal associations between poverty, neighborhood conditions, and criminal behavior, social structure theorists suggest that antisocial behavior is a direct result of destructive social forces on human behavior.[5] According to this view, it is *social forces*—not individual traits—that cause crime. Inner-city residents are indigent and desperate, not abnormal, calculating, or evil. Raised in deteriorated parts of town, they lack the social support and economic resources available to more affluent members of society. Dealing drugs or joining a gang holds the promise of economic rewards and status enhancements that the conventional world simply cannot provide.

Economic Structure and American Society

People in the United States live in a **stratified society**; social strata are created by the unequal distribution of wealth, power, and prestige. **Social classes** are segments of the population whose members have a relatively similar portion of desirable things and who share attitudes, values, norms, and an identifiable lifestyle.

In US society, it is common to identify people as belonging to the upper, middle, or lower socioeconomic class, although a broad range of economic variations exist within each group. The upper-upper class is reserved for a small number of exceptionally well-to-do families who control enormous financial and social resources; income inequality has become a national social and political concern. The top 1 percent of households have an annual income of about $400,000 and/or about $1.5 million in liquid assets. The top 1/10th of the 1 percent have an income of almost $2 million a year; the top 1/100th of the top 1 percent have an annual income of at least $10 million. The 16,000 wealthiest families in the United States have more than $6 trillion in total assets.[6]

Living in Poverty

While the wealthy live lives of affluence, there are now about 46 million Americans living in poverty, defined as a family of four earning about $24,000 per year, who have scant, if any, resources and suffer socially and economically as a result.[7]

stratified society
Grouping according to social strata or levels. American society is considered stratified on the basis of economic class and wealth.

social classes
Segments of the population whose members are at a relatively similar economic level and who share attitudes, values, norms, and an identifiable lifestyle.

FACT OR FICTION?

Very few children today live in poverty, because the government has made ending child poverty a top priority.

FICTION Despite residing in the richest country in the world, more than 20 percent of all American children live in poverty.

Poverty is not always an urban problem. Here, a Montgomery County sheriff's deputy walks away from an old school bus where two children were found living on their own in Spendora, Texas. Their parents, Mark and Sherrie Shorten, were in prison when the children, then 11 and 5, were found living alone. The Shortens had left the children in the care of an aunt, but she became overwhelmed and left them to fend for themselves.

Those living below the poverty line are often forced to live in inadequate housing, have poor health care, and suffer from disrupted family lives, underemployment, and despair. They are more prone to depression, less likely to have achievement motivation, and are unable to put off immediate gratification for future gain; kids living in poverty areas may drop out before graduation because the rewards for educational achievement are in the distant future.

Clearly the wealth gap creates two Americas, one that can afford the finest luxuries the world can offer and the other just scraping by, often with government assistance to supplement meager earnings.

Child Poverty

More than 20 percent of all youth—about 15 million—live in families with incomes below the poverty line. Another 22 percent escape poverty but live in families considered "poor."[8] Many kids living in poverty have working parents, but low wages and unstable employment leave their families struggling to make ends meet.[9] Being a child in a low-income or poor family does not happen by chance and is a function of parental education and employment, race/ethnicity, and other factors associated with economic insecurity.

Economic disadvantage and poverty can be especially devastating to younger children.[10] Children who grow up in low-income homes are less likely to achieve in school and less likely to complete their schooling than children with more affluent parents.[11] Poor kids are also more likely to suffer from health problems and to receive inadequate health care. Not only are they poor, but the number of homeless children in the US has surged in recent years to an all-time high, amounting to one child in every 30. The National Center on Family Homelessness calculates that nearly 2.5 million American children were homeless at some point in the past year.[12]

Minority Group Poverty

The burdens of underclass life are often felt most acutely by minority group members. Many Americans are able to take full advantage of the educational and vocational opportunities in

Income inequality and poverty have become major social issues in the United States. While the top 1 percent can live comfortable lives, those living below the poverty line suffer inadequate health care, housing, and education. Poverty hits the African American community the hardest. These men in Detroit are queuing up at a local soup kitchen to receive free food to ward off their hunger. Considering the assumed linkage between poverty and crime, how can a recently declining crime rate be explained?

American society, however, the door to these advantages is often closed to racial and ethnic minorities.[13]

The African American household median income is about $35,000 compared to $54,000 for non-Hispanic white households and almost $75,000 for Asian homes. About 28 percent of African Americans are living at the poverty level, compared to 11 percent of non-Hispanic whites. The unemployment rate for blacks is twice that for non-Hispanic whites (about 10 percent versus about 5 percent), a finding consistent for both men and women.[14] There are also race-based differences in high school completion; white and Asian rates are higher.[15]

These economic and social disparities haunt members of the minority underclass and their children despite efforts to erase race-based inequality.[16] Though most minority group members value education and other middle-class norms, their desperate life circumstances, such as high unemployment and nontraditional family structures, prevent them from developing the skills and habits that lead first to educational success and later to success in the workplace; these deficits have been linked to crime and drug abuse.[17]

Race-based social and economic disparity can take a terrific toll. Whereas many urban European Americans use their economic, social, and political advantages—**white privilege**—to live in sheltered, gated communities patrolled by security guards and police, most minorities do not have access to similar protections and opportunities.[18] In contrast, a significant proportion of minority group members are relegated to living in segregated inner-city areas, where they are hit hard by race-based disparity such as income inequality and institutional racism.[19] As Ruth Peterson and Lauren Krivo point out in their groundbreaking book *Divergent Social Worlds*, among urban dwellers, more than two-thirds of all whites, half of all African Americans, and one-third of Latinos live in segregated local neighborhoods. While fewer than 10 percent of white neighborhoods can be considered poverty stricken, 75 percent of black and Latino communities can be classified as impoverished.[20]

There is also the perception in the minority community that the justice system is biased and racist. Minority citizens often believe that the police are overzealous in their duties when dealing with minorities, stopping them for no reason, searching them, and arresting them when they would treat Caucasians informally—a practice that has spurred the creation of the **Black Lives Matter (BLM)** movement. And if they do commit crime, minority youth are more likely to be officially processed to the juvenile court than Caucasian youths, helping them develop an official record at an early age, an outcome that may increase their chances of incarceration as adults.[21] In the United States today, about 1 in 30 men between the ages of 20 and 34 is behind bars; for black males in that age group, the figure is 1 in 9. One in 100 black women in their mid- to late-30s are incarcerated compared to 1 in 355 European American women.[22] In some neighborhoods, a significant portion—up to half—of all minority males are under criminal justice system control.[23]

white privilege
The assumed societal privileges that benefit Caucasians and provide them with opportunities not available to non-white people under the same social, political, or economic circumstances.

Black Lives Matter (BLM)
A movement whose aim is to reduce institutional violence and perceived systemic racism toward black people.

culture of poverty
A separate lower-class culture, characterized by apathy, cynicism, helplessness, and mistrust of social institutions such as schools, government agencies, and the police, that is passed from one generation to the next.

AP Images/Ted S. Warren

African Americans earn considerably less than other racial groups, preventing them from partaking in the American Dream. The Black Lives Matter (BLM) movement has developed in response to racial inequality. BLM is an activist movement, originating in the African American community, that campaigns against violence and perceived systemic racism toward black people. Here, on October 19, 2016, Janett Du Bois (right), a special education teacher at Garfield High School in Seattle, speaks at a rally to promote racial equity in schools.

Problems of the Lower Class

In 1966, sociologist Oscar Lewis argued that the crushing lifestyle of lower-class areas produces a **culture of poverty** that is passed from one generation to the next.[24] Apathy, cynicism, helplessness, and mistrust of social institutions such as schools, government agencies, and the police, mark the culture of poverty. This mistrust prevents the inner-city poor from taking advantage of the meager opportunities available to them. Lewis's work was the first of a number of studies that described the plight of at-risk children and adults. In 1970, Swedish economist Gunnar Myrdal described a worldwide **underclass** that was cut off from society, its members lacking the education and skills needed to function successfully in modern society.[25]

Lower-class areas are scenes of inadequate housing and health care, disrupted family lives, underemployment, and despair. Members of the lower class also suffer in other ways. They are more prone to depression, less likely to have achievement motivation, and less likely to put off immediate gratification for the sake of future gain or security. Members of the lower classes may be less willing to stay in school because the rewards for educational achievement are in the distant future.

THE TRULY DISADVANTAGED In his classic work *The Truly Disadvantaged*, William Julius Wilson, one of the nation's most prominent sociologists, described the plight of the lowest levels of the underclass, which he labels the truly disadvantaged.[26] These socially isolated people live in areas in which the basic institutions of society—family, school, housing—have long since declined. Their weakening triggers similar breakdowns in the strengths of inner-city areas, including the loss of community cohesion and the ability of people living in the area to control the flow of drugs and criminal activity. In more affluent areas, neighbors might complain to parents that their children were acting out. In distressed areas, this element of informal social control may be absent because parents are under stress or all too often absent. These effects magnify the isolation of the underclass from mainstream society and promote a ghetto culture and behavior.

Because the truly disadvantaged rarely come into contact with the actual source of their oppression, they direct their anger and aggression at those with whom they are in close and intimate contact, such as neighbors, businesspeople, and landlords. Members of this group, plagued by under- or unemployment, begin to lose self-confidence, a feeling supported by the plight of kin and friendship groups who also experience extreme economic marginality. Self-doubt is a neighborhood norm, overwhelming those forced to live in areas of concentrated poverty. More recently (2016), Wilson argued that when income segregation is coupled with racial segregation, low-income African Americans cluster in neighborhoods where they often become innocent victims of crime, an event that frequently goes unnoticed or unreported in the media. Recognizing the close association between crime, victimization, and joblessness, Wilson calls for a policy that enhances the employment prospects of jobless youth, who are disproportionally involved in criminal offenses, especially those stigmatized by prison records.[27]

The Policies and Issues in Criminology feature *"Labor's Love Lost"* shows how social and economic factors impact on human lives.

Social Structure and Crime

According to **social structure theory**, the root cause of crime can be traced directly to the socioeconomic disadvantages that have become embedded in American society. The social problems found in lower-class areas have been described as an "epidemic" that spreads through a community, destroying the inner workings that enable neighborhoods to survive; they become "hollowed out."[28] As neighborhood quality decreases, the probability that residents will develop problems sharply increases. Because they lack ties to the mainstream culture, some lower-class people are driven to desperate measures, such as crime and substance abuse, to cope with their economic plight.[29] Crime and violence may also take the form of a "slow epidemic," with a course consisting of stages: onset, peak, and decline. Violence and crime have been found to spread and then contract in a pattern similar to a contagious disease.[30]

Because lower-class kids are exposed to a continual stream of violence, they are more likely to engage in violent acts themselves.[31] Their involvement with conventional social institutions, such as schools and after-school programs, is either absent

---

CONNECTIONS

Concern about the ecological distribution of crime, the effect of social change, and the interactive nature of crime itself has made sociology the foundation of modern criminology. This chapter reviews sociological theories that emphasize the relationship between social status and criminal behavior. In Chapter 7, the focus shifts to theories that emphasize socialization and its influence on crime and deviance; Chapter 8 covers theories based on the concept of social conflict.

L01 Explain the association between social structure and crime.

---

underclass
The lowest social stratum in any country, whose members lack the education and skills needed to function successfully in modern society.

social structure theory
The view that disadvantaged economic class position is a primary cause of crime.

Policies and Issues in Criminology

LABOR'S LOVE LOST

In his book *Labor's Love Lost*, Andrew Cherlin provides an explanation of the toll income and educational inequality takes on society. Cherlin points out that 50 years ago high school graduates were able to enter the workforce and have plentiful opportunities in industrial occupations that at that time sustained the middle-class ideal of a male-breadwinner family. Such jobs have all but vanished due to automation and globalization, and in their place are low-paid jobs with few fringe benefits. Ever-growing numbers of young adults now face insecure economic prospects. Consequently, less-educated young adults, both men and women, are increasingly forgoing marriage and are having children within unstable cohabiting relationships. This has created a large marriage gap between the marginally educated and more affluent, college-educated peers, exacerbating the income gap in American society. These social and economic shifts have contributed to the collapse of this once-stable lower-middle social class.

Cherlin points out that the marriage gap today seems similar to what occurred during the late nineteenth century, when society was divided between families of great wealth and the working poor. Sadly, the prosperity of working-class families in the mid-twentieth century, when both income inequality and the marriage gap were low, was unique in the history of the American family. The changing economy, the end of high-paid factory jobs, and their replacement with low-paid service jobs have had such a significant impact that traditional working-class family patterns have largely disappeared.

The primary problem of the end of the working-class family is not that the traditional male-breadwinner family has declined, but that it has not been replaced with any other stable model. As a result of the breakdown, there have been serious consequences for children of low-income families, many of whom underperform in school, thereby reducing their future employment prospects and perpetuating an intergenerational cycle of economic disadvantage. American children experience the highest rates of family turnover in the developed world. Large numbers live with single parents or with parents in cohabitating unions of short duration and high breakup rates. As a result, American children experience parents, parents' partners, and stepparents moving in and out of their households far more than in other developed countries. The percentage of children who aren't living with two biological parents has increased sharply among the moderately educated. It is now common for high school educated women to have at least one child outside of marriage. Cherlin finds that these problems are more pronounced in the African American community, where men did not fully share in the wage gains of the post-war period. As a result, marriage rates among African Americans did not rise as high as whites during the 1950s and 1960s, and now they have fallen further.

Can This Cycle Be Broken?

Cherlin argues that rather than stress college as the answer for all, vocational opportunities for working-class children must be enhanced through programs stressing apprenticeships and internships as paths to steady employment for high school graduates. Wage subsidies and other income enhancements may also help break the cycle.

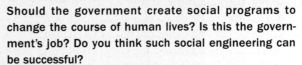

Critical Thinking

Should the government create social programs to change the course of human lives? Is this the government's job? Do you think such social engineering can be successful?

Source: Andrew Cherlin, *Labor's Love Lost* (New York: Russell Sage Foundation, 2014).

or blocked, which puts them at risk for recruitment into gangs.[32] When informal and formal avenues of social control have become frayed, kids are given a free hand to mix with deviant peers.[33] The impact of poverty is felt most often during the teen years and diminishes over time, helping to explain why crime involvement drops in adulthood.[34]

Aggravating this dynamic is the constant media bombardment linking material possessions to self-worth. Because they are unable to obtain desired goods and services through conventional means, members of the lower class may turn to illegal solutions to their economic plight. They may deal drugs for profit, steal cars and sell them to "chop shops," or commit armed robberies for desperately needed funds. They may become so depressed that they use alcohol and drugs as a form of self-tranquilization, and because of their poverty, they may acquire the drugs and alcohol through illegal channels.

Because of income inequality, minority group members are the citizens most likely to be hit hard economically and forced to live in the most deteriorated neighborhoods in the city. Interracial differences in the crime rate could be significantly reduced by improving levels of education, lowering levels of poverty, ending racial segregation in housing and neighborhood makeup, and reducing the extent of male unemployment among minority populations.[35]

Social Structure Theories

At their core, social structure theories have a basic theme: a person is the product of his or her environment. These theories view the cause of crime through the lens of poverty, income inequality, hopelessness, and despair. Social and economic forces operating in deteriorated lower-class areas push many of their residents into criminal behavior patterns. It seems logical that if crime rates are higher in lower-class urban centers than in middle-class suburbs, social forces must influence or control behavior.

The social structure perspective encompasses three independent yet overlapping branches:

- According to **social disorganization theory**, crime flourishes in a disorganized area in which institutions of social control, such as the family, commercial establishments, and schools, have broken down and can no longer perform their expected or stated functions. There are high unemployment and school dropout rates, deteriorated housing, low income levels, and large numbers of single-parent households. Young people living in these areas experience conflict and despair, are more likely to join gangs, and as a result, cannot avoid the lure of antisocial behaviors.
- **Strain theory** holds that crime occurs when members of the lower class experience anger and frustration over their inability to achieve success. Because they fail to achieve success through conventional means, lower-class people feel **strain**, pushing some to find alternative means of achieving their life goals. Striving for success may involve engaging in criminal activities.
- **Cultural deviance theory** combines elements of both strain and social disorganization: in disorganized neighborhoods, the presence of strain locks people into an independent **subculture** with unique values and beliefs. Criminal behavior is an expression of conformity to lower-class subcultural values and traditions that often are at odds with conventional society.

Although these views differ in critical aspects, each approach has at its core the view that socially isolated people, living in disorganized neighborhoods, are likely to experience crime-producing social forces.

Social Disorganization Theory

Social disorganization theory links crime rates to neighborhood ecological characteristics. Crime rates are highest in transient, mixed-use (where residential and commercial property exist side by side), and changing neighborhoods in which the fabric of social life has become frayed. When these failing communities are numerous, contiguous, or in close proximity the criminogenic effect may multiply. Youths living in one disorganized area who visit friends and family in adjoining communities discover that these areas are equally dangerous and deteriorated. They may begin to feel

social disorganization theory
Branch of social structure theory that focuses on the breakdown in inner-city neighborhoods of institutions such as the family, school, and employment.

strain theory
Branch of social structure theory that sees crime as a function of the conflict between people's goals and the means available to obtain them.

strain
The anger, frustration, and resentment experienced by people who believe they cannot achieve their goals through legitimate means.

cultural deviance theory
Branch of social structure theory that sees strain and social disorganization together resulting in a unique lower-class culture that conflicts with conventional social norms.

subculture
A set of values, beliefs, and traditions unique to a particular social class or group within a larger society.

L02 Identify the elements of social disorganization theory.

Disorganized neighborhoods lack the ability to apply social control. Institutions of social control are weak and attenuated. In the absence of formal (police) and informal (families, neighbors) social control mechanisms, gangs and law-violating youth groups are free to rule the streets. Under such conditions, crime flourishes and people seek to relocate if they have sufficient financial resources.

Kirsten Luce/New York Times/Redux

FACT OR FICTION?

Political, social, and economic programs such as affirmative action have erased the economic gulf between whites and minorities.

FICTION Despite governmental efforts and programs, the income differential between European Americans and minority group members persists.

helpless and hopeless. "Why bother trying to move out," they reason, "when every place I go to is equally bad?" Feelings of hopelessness increase the lure of gangs and law-violating groups.[36]

These localities are unable to provide essential services, such as education, health care, and proper housing, and as a result, they experience significant levels of unemployment, single-parent families, and families on welfare.

The few residents in crime-ridden neighborhoods that can leave do so at the earliest opportunity. Those planning to leave take little interest in community matters, so the common sources of control—the family, school, business community, and social service agencies—are weak and disorganized. Personal relationships are strained because neighbors are constantly moving. Continuous resident turnover weakens communications and blocks attempts at solving neighborhood problems or establishing common goals.[37]

Because social institutions are frayed or absent, law-violating youth groups and gangs form and are free to recruit neighborhood youth. Both boys and girls who feel detached and alienated from their social world are at risk to become gang members.[38]

Not surprisingly, then, there are now more than 30,000 law-violating gangs in the United States, containing about 850,000 members.[39] This represents a 15 percent increase from 2006 and is the highest annual estimate since 1996.

The Work of Shaw and McKay

LO3 Analyze the views of Shaw and McKay.

Social disorganization theory was popularized by the work of two Chicago sociologists, Clifford R. Shaw and Henry McKay, who linked life in transitional slum areas to the inclination to commit crime. Shaw and McKay began their pioneering work on Chicago crime during the early 1920s, while working as researchers for a state-supported social service agency.[40]

Shaw and McKay explained crime and delinquency within the context of the changing urban environment and ecological development of the city. They saw that Chicago had developed into distinct neighborhoods (natural areas), some affluent and others wracked by extreme poverty. These poverty-ridden **transitional neighborhoods** suffered high rates of population turnover and were incapable of inducing residents to remain and defend the neighborhoods against criminal groups.

transitional neighborhoods
Areas undergoing shifts in population and structure, usually from middle-class residential to lower-class mixed-use.

In transitional areas, successive changes in population composition, disintegration of traditional cultures, diffusion of divergent cultural standards, and gradual industrialization dissolve neighborhood culture and organization. The continuity of conventional neighborhood traditions and institutions is broken, leaving people feeling displaced and without a strong or definitive set of values.

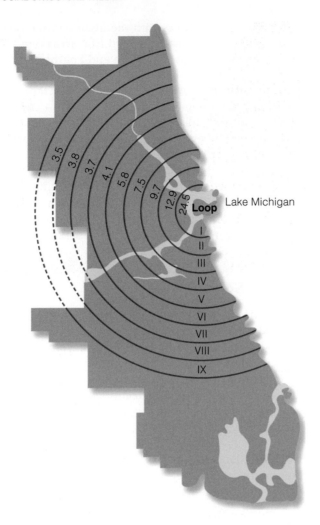

FIGURE 6.1
Shaw and McKay's Concentric Zones Map of Chicago

Note: Arabic numbers represent the rate of male delinquency. Numbers indicate the crime rate in various zones; the crime rates decline in zones farthest from inner-city Chicago.

Source: Clifford R. Shaw et al., *Delinquency Areas*. Reprinted with permission. Copyright 1929 by the University of Chicago. All rights reserved.

CONCENTRIC ZONES Shaw and McKay identified the areas in Chicago that had excessive crime rates. They noted that distinct ecological areas had developed in the city, forming a series of nine concentric circles, or zones, and that there were stable and significant interzone differences in crime rates (see Figure 6.1). The areas beset by the most crime appeared to be the transitional inner-city zones, where large numbers of the city's poorest citizens had settled.[41] The zones farthest from the city's center had correspondingly lower crime rates.

Analysis of these data indicated a surprisingly stable pattern of criminal activity in the nine ecological zones over a period of 65 years. Shaw and McKay concluded that multiple cultures and diverse values, both conventional and deviant, coexist in the transitional neighborhoods. People growing up in the street culture often find residents who have adopted a deviant lifestyle (gamblers, pimps, drug dealers) are the most financially successful people in the neighborhood. Forced to choose between conventional and deviant lifestyles, many slum kids opt for the latter. They join other like-minded youths and form law-violating gangs and cliques. The development of teenage law-violating groups is an essential element of misbehavior in slum areas. The values that slum youths adopt often conflict with existing middle-class norms, which demand strict obedience to the legal code. Consequently, a value conflict further separates the delinquent youth and his or her peer group from conventional society; the result is a more solid embrace of deviant goals and behavior. To further justify their choice of goals, these youths seek support for their choice by recruiting new members and passing on the delinquent tradition.

Shaw and McKay's statistical analysis confirmed that even though crime rates changed, the highest rates were always in Zones I and II (the central city and a

CHECKPOINTS

▶ Because crime rates are higher in lower-class areas, many criminologists believe that the causes of crime are rooted in socioeconomic factors.

▶ Despite economic headway, there are still more than 30 million indigent Americans. Minority groups are more likely than the white majority to be poor.

▶ Some criminologists believe that destructive social forces in poverty-stricken areas are responsible for high crime rates.

▶ The strain and frustration inflicted by poverty are a suspected cause of crime.

▶ Indigents may become involved in a deviant subculture that sustains and supports criminality.

transitional area, respectively). The areas with the highest crime rates retained high rates even when their ethnic composition changed (the areas that Shaw and McKay examined shifted from German and Irish to Italian and Polish).[42]

THE LEGACY OF SHAW AND MCKAY The social disorganization concepts articulated by Shaw and McKay have remained prominent within criminology for more than 75 years. Although cultural and social conditions have changed over time, and today we live in a much more heterogeneous, mobile society, the most important of Shaw and McKay's findings—crime rates correspond to neighborhood structure—still holds up.[43]

Their research supported the fact that crime is a constant fixture in areas of poverty, regardless of residents' racial or ethnic identity. Because the basis of their theory was that neighborhood disintegration is the primary cause of criminal behavior, Shaw and McKay paved the way for many of the community action and development programs that have been developed in the last half-century.

The Social Ecology School

Contemporary social disorganization theory seeks to identify the ecological conditions—poverty, disorganization, instability, incivility, economy—that produce high crime rates and while so doing formulate strategies to bring these community-level crime rates down.[44] Referred to as the **social ecology school**, what has been developed is a purer form of structural theory that emphasizes the association of community deterioration and economic decline with criminality but places less emphasis on value conflict. The following sections discuss some of the more recent social-ecological research.

COMMUNITY DISORDER Contemporary social ecologists believe that crime rates are associated with community deterioration: disorder, poverty, alienation, disassociation, and fear of crime.[45] Even in rural areas, which normally have low crime rates, increased levels of crime and violence are associated with indicators of social disorganization such as residential instability (a large number of people moving in and out), family disruption, and changing ethnic composition.[46]

In larger cities, neighborhoods with a high percentage of deserted houses and apartments experience high crime rates; abandoned buildings serve as a "magnet for crime."[47] One reason is that criminals target neighborhoods that are near and similar to where they live themselves, especially if they are highly disadvantaged or disorganized. They look for characteristics such as residential instability and disadvantage, because these neighborhoods are the ones with lower social control and a correspondingly lower risk of detection.[48]

COMMUNITY FEAR In neighborhoods where people help each other, residents are less likely to fear crime or to be afraid of becoming a crime victim.[49] In disorganized neighborhoods that suffer social and physical incivilities, residents experience unruly youths, trash and litter, graffiti, abandoned storefronts, burned-out buildings, littered lots, strangers, drunks, vagabonds, loiterers, prostitutes, noise, congestion, angry words, dirt, and stench. Having parks and playgrounds where teens hang out and loiter may contribute to fear.[50]

And as fear increases, quality of life deteriorates.[51]

Fear is often based on experience: people living in areas with especially high crime rates are the ones most

CONNECTIONS

If social disorganization causes crime, why are most low-income people law abiding? To explain this anomaly, some sociologists have devised theoretical models suggesting that individual socialization experiences mediate environmental influences. These theories will be discussed in Chapter 7.

L04 Differentiate between the various elements of ecological theory.

social ecology school
An interdisciplinary approach to the study of interdependent social and environmental problems that cause crime.

Reuters/Jim Young

On July 3, 2015, people gather for a candlelight vigil against gun violence in the Englewood neighborhood of Chicago. Extra police patrols were not enough to prevent 9 deaths and about 50 injuries from gun violence in Chicago over the Fourth of July weekend, when homicides increase almost every year. Chicago is currently experiencing an upswing in violence, with poverty, street gangs, and a pervasive gun culture all contributing to the problem.

likely to experience fear.[52] People who live in public housing projects, who come into daily contact with civil disorder, are not surprisingly the ones most likely to see their community as disorderly and dangerous.[53] Residents who have already been victimized or know someone who has are more fearful of the future than those who have escaped crime.[54] People become afraid when they are approached by someone in the neighborhood selling drugs. They may fear that their children will also be approached and will be seduced into the drug life.[55] The presence of such incivilities, especially when accompanied by relatively high crime rates, convinces residents that their neighborhood is dangerous; becoming a crime victim seems inevitable.[56]

Fear can be contagious. People tell others when they have been victimized, thus spreading the word that the neighborhood is getting dangerous and that the chance of future victimization is high.[57] As a result, people dread leaving their homes at night and withdraw from community life.

SIEGE MENTALITY People who live in neighborhoods that experience high levels of crime and civil disorder become suspicious and mistrusting.[58] Minority group members may experience greater levels of fear than whites, perhaps because they may have fewer resources to address ongoing social problems.[59] They develop a sense of powerlessness, which increases levels of mistrust. Some residents become so suspicious of authority that they develop a "siege mentality," in which the outside world is considered an enemy bent on their destruction.

Siege mentality often results in an expanding mistrust of social institutions, including law enforcement, business, government, and schools. Government officials seem arrogant and haughty. The police are believed to ignore crime in minority communities and, when they do take action, they use excessive force against young black men.[60] When a seemingly unjust shooting occurs, such as the case when on August 9, 2014, Michael Brown was killed in Ferguson, Missouri, people in the community lose respect for the police: they are forced to protest that "Black Lives Matter."[61]

The Michael Brown case is not unique: research does show that police are more likely to use higher levels of force when suspects are encountered in disadvantaged neighborhoods, regardless of the suspects' behaviors or reactions.[62] When police ignore crime in poor areas, or, conversely, when they are violent and corrupt, anger flares, and people take to the streets and react in violent ways.

COMMUNITY CHANGE Change, not stability, is the hallmark of inner-city areas. A neighborhood's residents, wealth, density, and purpose are constantly evolving. Even disorganized neighborhoods acquire new identifying features. Some may become multiracial and others racially homogeneous. Some areas become stable and family-oriented, whereas in others, mobile, never-married people predominate.[63] Urban areas undergoing rapid structural changes in racial and economic composition also seem to experience the greatest change in crime rates.[64] In contrast, stable neighborhoods, even those with a high rate of poverty, experience relatively low crime rates and have the strength to restrict substance abuse and criminal activity.[65]

As areas decline, residents flee to safer, more stable localities. Those who can move to more affluent neighborhoods find that their lifestyles and life chances improve immediately and continue to

AP Images/David Goldman

Living in segregated neighborhoods may cause minority group members to develop a sense of powerlessness that in turn creates a "siege mentality" characterized by mistrust of social institutions, including law enforcement, business, government, and schools. Local police are believed to ignore crime in minority communities and, when they do take action, they use excessive force against young black men. When an arrest or use of force seems unjust, such as when Michael Brown was killed in Ferguson, Missouri, people take to the streets in angry protests, as seen here.

do so over their life span.[66] Those who cannot leave because they cannot afford to live in more affluent communities face an increased risk of victimization. Because of racial differences in economic well-being, those who remain are all too often minority citizens.[67] Whites may feel threatened as the percentage of minorities in the population increases and there is more competition for jobs and political power.[68] As racial prejudice increases, the call for "law and order" aimed at controlling the minority population grows louder.[69] Some of course adapt and create new friendship networks which may cross ethnic and racial lines. While multicultural networks should be a good thing, they often exist in neighborhoods that have limited forces of social control.[70]

Those who cannot move find themselves surrounded by a constant influx of new residents. In response to this turnover, a culture may develop that dictates to neighborhood youths' standards of dress, language, and behavior that are in opposition to those of conventional society. All these factors are likely to produce increased crime rates.

As communities change, neighborhood deterioration precedes increasing rates of crime and delinquency.[71] Neighborhoods most at risk for increased crime contain large numbers of single-parent families and unrelated people living together, have changed from owner-occupied to renter-occupied units, and have lost semiskilled and unskilled jobs (hence the growing number of discouraged workers who are no longer seeking employment).[72] These ecological disruptions strain existing social control mechanisms and undermine their ability to control crime and delinquency.

POVERTY CONCENTRATION One aspect of community change may be the concentration of poverty in deteriorated urban neighborhoods.[73] Working- and middle-class families flee inner-city areas where poverty is pervasive, resulting in a poverty **concentration effect** in which the most disadvantaged population is consolidated in the most disorganized urban neighborhoods. Poverty concentration has been associated with income and wealth disparities, nonexistent employment opportunities, inferior housing patterns, and unequal access to health care.[74] Urban areas marked by concentrated poverty become isolated and insulated from the social mainstream and more prone to criminal activity, violence, and homicide.[75] Young men growing up in neighborhood characterized by poverty concentration are the most likely to engage in risk taking and delinquency, especially those who perceive few opportunities for legitimate success.[76]

How does neighborhood poverty concentration produce high crime rates? White families are more likely to leave an area when they perceive that the surrounding neighborhoods have become predominantly minority.[77] As the working and middle classes move out to the suburbs, they take with them their financial and institutional resources and support.[78] The people left behind have an even tougher time coping with urban decay and conflict and controlling youth gangs and groups; after all, the most successful people in the community have left for "greener pastures." Businesses are disinclined to locate in poverty-stricken areas; banks become reluctant to lend money for new housing or businesses.[79] Unemployment rates skyrocket, destabilizing households, and unstable families are likely to produce children who use violence and aggression to deal with limited opportunity. Large groups or cohorts of people of the same age are forced to compete for relatively scarce resources.[80]

Limited employment opportunities reduce the stabilizing influence of parents and other adults, who might once have counteracted the allure of youth gangs. In a classic study, sociologist Elijah Anderson's analysis of Philadelphia neighborhood life found that "old heads" (respected neighborhood residents), who at one time played an important role in socializing youths, were displaced by younger street hustlers and drug dealers. Although the old heads may complain that these newcomers have not earned or worked for their fortunes in the old-fashioned way, they nevertheless envy these young people whose grills and luxury cars advertise their wealth

concentration effect
As working-class and middle-class families flee inner-city poverty-ridden areas, the most disadvantaged population is consolidated in urban ghettos.

amid poverty.[81] So the old heads admire the fruits of crime, even as they disdain the violent manner in which they are acquired.

Collective Efficacy

Cohesive communities with high levels of social control and social integration, where people know one another and develop interpersonal ties, develop **collective efficacy**: a sense of mutual trust, a willingness to intervene in the supervision of children, and the maintenance of public order.[82] Cohesion among neighborhood residents, combined with shared expectations for informal social control of public space, promotes collective efficacy.[83] Residents in these areas enjoy a better life because the fruits of cohesiveness can be better education, health care, and housing opportunities.[84]

In contrast, in socially disorganized neighborhoods, where the population is transient, and interpersonal relationships remain superficial and nonsupportive, efforts at social control are weak and attenuated.[85] In these unstable neighborhoods, residents find that the social support they need to live a conventional life is absent or lacking. The resulting lack of social cohesion produces an atmosphere where antisocial behavior becomes normative.[86] As the number of people who have a stake in the community (i.e., they are homeowners) increases, crime rates drop.[87] These more cohesive neighborhoods report less disorder than less-unified communities.[88]

In Richmond, California, Tommie Woods, 19 (left), and Lonnie Holmes, 21 (right), discuss their involvement in a program of the Office of Neighborhood Safety (ONS). In order to curb firearm assaults and retaliations in Richmond, the city's ONS works to use their positive influences, including money, to engage potentially active firearms users.

People living in economically disadvantaged areas are significantly more likely to perceive their immediate surroundings in more negative terms (with higher levels of incivilities) than those living in areas that maintain collective efficacy.[89] When community social control efforts are blunted, crime rates increase, further weakening neighborhood cohesiveness.[90] This suggests that there are spillover effects that extend beyond the geographic boundaries of a single neighborhood. As assessments of disorder, crime rates, and neighborhood conditions worsen, they can impact perceptions of collective efficacy. So rather than being set in stone, collective efficacy is an elastic concept, influenced by fluctuations in perceived social disorder.[91]

There are three forms of collective efficacy—informal social control, institutional social control, and public social control—and all three contribute to community stability.

collective efficacy
Social control exerted by cohesive communities and based on mutual trust, including intervention in the supervision of children and maintenance of public order.

INFORMAL SOCIAL CONTROL Some elements of collective efficacy operate on the primary, or private, level and involve peers, families, and relatives. These sources exert informal control by either awarding or withholding approval, respect, and admiration. Informal control mechanisms include direct criticism, ridicule, ostracism, desertion, and physical punishment.[92]

The most important wielder of informal social control is the family, which may keep at-risk kids in check through such mechanisms as effective parenting, withholding privileges, or ridiculing lazy or disrespectful behavior. The informal social control provided by the family takes on greater importance in neighborhoods with few social ties among adults and limited collective efficacy. In these areas, parents cannot call upon neighborhood resources to take up the burden of controlling children; family members face the burden of providing adequate supervision.[93] In neighborhoods with high levels of collective efficacy, parents are better able to function and effectively supervise their children. Confident and authoritative parents who live in areas that have developed collective efficacy are able to effectively deter their children from affiliating with deviant peers and getting involved in delinquent behavior.[94] However, in areas with low levels of collective efficacy, many parents cannot cope with the strain of living in a deteriorated neighborhood. Some become abusive, increasing the likelihood that children will suffer from neglect and emotional, physical, or sexual abuse. Others engage in domestic violence and/or substance abuse. These outcomes are a precursor of high levels of youth crime and delinquency.[95]

Crime rates and the chances of victimization are lower in communities where residents trust one another and are ready to lend help and assistance when needed.[96] In some neighborhoods, even high-risk areas, people are willing to participate in anticrime programs.[97] Neighbors may get involved in informal social control through surveillance practices—for example, by keeping an "eye out" for intruders when their neighbors go out of town. Informal surveillance has been found to reduce the levels of some crimes such as street robberies; however, if robbery rates remain high, surveillance may be terminated because people become fearful for their safety.[98]

INSTITUTIONAL SOCIAL CONTROL   Social institutions such as schools and churches cannot work effectively in a climate of alienation and mistrust. Unsupervised peer groups and gangs, which flourish in disorganized areas, disrupt the influence of those neighborhood control agents that do exist.[99] Children who reside in these neighborhoods find that involvement with conventional social institutions, such as schools and afternoon programs, is blocked; they are instead at risk for recruitment into gangs and law-violating groups.[100] As crime flourishes, neighborhood fear increases, which in turn decreases a community's cohesion and thwarts the ability of its institutions to exert social control over its residents.[101]

To combat these influences, communities that have collective efficacy attempt to use their local institutions to control crime. Sources of institutional social control include businesses, stores, schools, churches, and social service and volunteer organizations. When these institutions are effective, rates for some crimes (such as burglary) decline.[102] Some institutions, such as neighborhood youth organizations and recreation centers for teens, have been found to lower crime rates because they exert a positive effect on both the individual level (for example, they improve participants' self-control) and institutional level (for example, they encourage informal social control).[103] Others, such as taverns and bars, tend to destabilize a neighborhood and increase the rate of violent crimes such as rape and robbery.[104] Adding coffee shops and cafés may help; their presence seems to increase social action and may help neutralize the effect of taverns and bars.[105]

PUBLIC SOCIAL CONTROL   Stable neighborhoods are also able to arrange for external sources of social control. If they can draw on outside help and secure external resources—a process referred to as public social control—they are better able to reduce the effects of disorganization and maintain lower levels of crime and victimization.[106]

One primary source of public social control is the police. Neighborhoods that are sufficiently organized to demand and get additional police resources are likely to have lower crime rates than neighborhoods that lack such political clout.[107] An effective police presence, cracking down on hot spots and strictly enforcing the law at a neighborhood level,

Public social control promotes a sense of collective efficacy. On June 3, 2015, teens attend a meeting in East New York, a neighborhood that in recent years has been plagued by gun violence. Organized by the city Department of Probation and the Mayor's Office of Criminal Justice, the "One Message Many Voices: Anti-Gun Violence Town Hall" meeting featured a number of speakers and an inspirational dance performance. Following news of a more than 20 percent increase in murders and a 9 percent increase in shootings in the first half of 2015, the NYPD started its Summer All Out program a month early. This anticrime program trains and puts 330 administrative officers on the streets to help deter shootings and gun crimes.

Spencer Platt/Getty Images News/Getty Images

sends a message that the area will not tolerate deviant behavior.[108] Because they can respond vigorously to crime, police prevent criminal groups from gaining a toehold in the neighborhood.[109] Criminals and drug dealers avoid such areas and relocate to easier and more appealing "targets."[110]

In disorganized areas, the absence of political power brokers limits access to external funding and protection. Without money from the outside, the neighborhood lacks the ability to "get back on its feet."[111] In these areas there are fewer police, and those that do patrol the area are less motivated and their resources are stretched thinner.[112]

THE EFFECTS OF COLLECTIVE EFFICACY In areas where collective efficacy remains high, children are less likely to become involved with deviant peers and engage in problem behaviors.[113] In these more stable areas, kids are better able to avoid violent confrontations and to feel safe in their own neighborhood, a concept referred to as **street efficacy**.[114]

In contrast, people who live in neighborhoods with concentrated disadvantage and low collective efficacy begin to lose confidence in their ability to avoid violence. They perceive that the community cannot provide the level of social control needed to neutralize or make up for what they lack in personal self-control.[115]

The lack of community controls may convince them to take matters into their own hands—for example, joining a gang or carrying a weapon for self-protection. In these disorganized areas, interpersonal relationships remain superficial and non-supportive. People who are forced to live in these areas either because of limited finances or legal restrictions, such as sex offenders, may find that the social support they need to live a conventional life is absent or lacking.[116] And even when an attempt is made in these areas to revitalize a disorganized neighborhood by creating institutional support programs such as community centers and better schools, the effort may be neutralized by the ongoing drain of deep-rooted economic and social deprivation.[117]

In sum, the more crime, the lower the levels of community cohesion.[118] The more interconnected and organized the community, the lower the crime rate.[119]

Concept Summary 6.1 lists some of the basic concepts and theories of the social disorganization view.

street efficacy
A concept in which more cohesive communities with high levels of social control and social integration foster the ability for kids to use their wits to avoid violent confrontations and to feel safe in their own neighborhood. Adolescents with high levels of street efficacy are less likely to resort to violence themselves or to associate with delinquent peers.

Concept Summary 6.1 Social Disorganization Theories

Theory	Major Premise	Strengths	Research Focus
Shaw and McKay's concentric zones theory	Crime is a product of transitional neighborhoods that manifest social disorganization and value conflict.	Identifies why crime rates are highest in slum areas. Points out the factors that produce crime. Suggests programs to help reduce crime.	Poverty; disorganization.
Social ecology theory	The conflicts and problems of urban social life and communities (including fear, unemployment, deterioration, and siege mentality) influence crime rates.	Accounts for urban crime rates and trends.	Social control; fear; collective efficacy; unemployment.

Strain Theories

L05 Discuss the concept of strain.

Inhabitants of a disorganized inner-city area feel isolated, frustrated, ostracized from the economic mainstream, hopeless, and eventually angry. How do these feelings affect criminal activities?

Strain theorists view crime as a direct result of frustration and anger among the lower socioeconomic classes. Although most people share similar values and goals, the ability to achieve personal goals is stratified by socioeconomic class. Strain is limited in affluent areas because educational and vocational opportunities are available. In disorganized areas, strain proliferates because legitimate avenues for success are all but closed. To relieve strain, indigent people may achieve their goals through deviant methods, such as theft or drug trafficking, or they may reject socially accepted goals and substitute more deviant goals, such as being tough and aggressive.

Theory of Anomie

Sociologist Robert Merton applied the sociological concepts first identified by Durkheim to criminology in his theory of anomie.[120] He found that two elements of culture interact to produce potentially anomic conditions: culturally defined goals and socially approved means for obtaining them. US society stresses the goals of acquiring wealth, success, and power. Socially permissible means include hard work, education, and thrift.

Merton argues that, in the United States, legitimate means to acquire wealth are stratified across class and status lines. Those with little formal education and few economic resources soon find that they are denied the ability to legally acquire wealth—the preeminent success symbol. When socially mandated goals are uniform throughout society and access to legitimate means is bound by class and status, the resulting strain produces anomie among those who are locked out of the legitimate opportunity structure. Consequently, they may develop criminal or delinquent solutions to the problem of attaining goals.

SOCIAL ADAPTATIONS Merton argues that each person has his or her own concept of society's goals and his or her own degree of access to the means to attain them. Some people have inadequate means of attaining success; others, who have the means, reject societal goals. The result is a variety of social adaptations:

According to strain theories, the lack of opportunity produces strain. People attempt to overcome strain by retreating, committing crime, becoming a revolutionary, joining a cult, or trying to lead a conventional lifestyle. Here, lawyer David Lee Windecher shows some of his tattoos in Judge Asha Jackson's courtroom. He was appearing as part of a program in her court for nonviolent, first-time offenders under the age of 25 called "Project Pinnacle." Windecher, the son of Argentine immigrants, grew up in a tough, poor neighborhood in Miami where he became a gang member and drug dealer as a young teenager. He was arrested 13 times and jailed for eight months before he turned 19. Around that time, several things happened that changed the trajectory of his life. He found religion, he met a girl from the other side of the tracks who urged him to make something better of himself, he noticed that his younger siblings were starting to follow his bad example, and his best friend and gang running mate got sentenced to hard time in prison. David enrolled in a local college, still selling a little weed to support himself, and began to wean himself from his gang days. He set his sights on becoming a lawyer and moved to Atlanta to attend John Marshall Law School. It was a long, hard struggle, but he finally graduated and passed the bar exams in Georgia and then Florida, despite his lengthy criminal record. Now a criminal defense attorney in Atlanta, he has written a book about overcoming his checkered past, titled *The American Dream: HisStory in the Making*.

AP Images/Bob Andres/Atlanta Journal-Constitution

- *Conformity*. When individuals embrace conventional social goals and also have the means to attain them, they can choose to conform. They remain law abiding.
- *Innovation*. When individuals accept the goals of society but are unable or unwilling to attain them through legitimate means, the resulting conflict forces them to adopt innovative solutions to their dilemma: they steal, sell drugs, or extort money. Of the five adaptations, innovation is most closely associated with criminal behavior.
- *Ritualism*. Ritualists gain pleasure from practicing traditional ceremonies, regardless of whether they have a real purpose or goal. The strict customs in religious orders, feudal societies, clubs, and college fraternities encourage and appeal to ritualists.

- *Retreatism*. Retreatists reject both the goals and the means of society. They attempt to escape their lack of success by withdrawing, either mentally or physically, through taking drugs or becoming drifters.
- *Rebellion*. Some individuals substitute an alternative set of goals and means for conventional ones. Revolutionaries who wish to promote radical change in the existing social structure and who call for alternative lifestyles, goals, and beliefs are engaging in rebellion. Rebellion may be a reaction against a corrupt, hated government or an effort to create alternative opportunities and lifestyles within the existing system.

EVALUATION OF ANOMIE THEORY According to **anomie theory**, social inequality leads to perceptions of anomie. To resolve the goals–means conflict and relieve their sense of strain, some people innovate by stealing or extorting money; others retreat into drugs and alcohol; some rebel by joining revolutionary groups; and still others get involved in ritualistic behavior by joining a religious cult.

Merton's view of anomie has been one of the most enduring and influential sociological theories of criminality and has been successfully tested by numerous studies conducted in the United States and abroad.[121] By linking deviant behavior to the success goals that control social behavior, anomie theory attempts to pinpoint the cause of the conflict that engenders personal frustration and consequent criminality. By acknowledging that society unfairly distributes the legitimate means to achieving success, anomie theory helps explain the existence of high-crime areas and the apparent predominance of delinquent and criminal behavior in the lower class. By suggesting that social conditions, not individual personalities, produce crime, Merton greatly influenced the directions taken to reduce and control criminality during the latter half of the twentieth century.

Even so, anomie theory leaves a number of questions unanswered.[122] Merton does not explain why people choose to commit certain types of crime. For example, why does one anomic person become a mugger whereas another deals drugs? Anomie may explain differences in crime rates, but it cannot explain why most young criminals desist from crime as adults. Does this mean that perceptions of anomie dwindle with age? Is anomie short-lived?

Institutional Anomie Theory

Steven Messner and Richard Rosenfeld's **institutional anomie theory (IAT)** is an updating of Merton's work.[123] For them, the **American Dream** refers to both a goal and a process. As a goal, the American Dream involves accumulating material goods and wealth via open individual competition. As a process, it involves both being socialized to pursue material success and believing that prosperity is achievable in American culture. Anomic conditions arise because the desire to succeed at any cost drives people apart, weakens the collective sense of community, fosters ambition, and restricts the desire to achieve anything other than material wealth. Achieving respect is not sufficient.

Why does anomie pervade American culture? According to Messner and Rosenfeld, it is because institutions that might otherwise control the exaggerated emphasis on financial success, such as religious or charitable institutions, have been rendered powerless or obsolete. These social institutions have been undermined in three ways:

- Noneconomic functions and roles have been devalued. Performance in other institutional settings—the family, school, or community—is assigned a lower priority than the goal of financial success.
- When conflicts emerge, noneconomic roles become subordinate to and must accommodate economic roles. The schedules, routines, and demands of the workplace take priority over those of the home, the school, the community, and other aspects of social life. People think nothing of leaving their neighborhood,

anomie theory
The view that anomie results when socially defined goals (such as wealth and power) are universally mandated but access to legitimate means (such as education and job opportunities) is stratified by class and status.

institutional anomie theory (IAT)
The view that anomie pervades US culture because the drive for material wealth dominates and undermines social and community values.

American Dream
The goal of accumulating material goods and wealth through individual competition; the process of being socialized to pursue material success and to believe it is achievable.

city, or state for a better job, disrupting family relationships and undermining informal social control.

- Economic language, standards, and norms penetrate noneconomic realms. Economic terms become part of the common vernacular: People want to get to the "bottom line." Spouses view themselves as "partners" who "manage" the household. Retired people say they want to "downsize" their household. We "outsource" home repairs instead of doing them ourselves. Corporate leaders run for public office promising to "run the country like a business."

According to Messner and Rosenfeld, the relatively high American crime rates can be explained by the interrelationship of culture and institutions. At the cultural level, the dominance of the American Dream mythology ensures that many people will develop desires for material goods that cannot be satisfied by legitimate means. Anomie becomes a norm, and extralegal means become a strategy for attaining material wealth. At the institutional level, the dominance of economic concerns weakens the informal social control exerted by family, church, and school. These institutions have lost their ability to regulate behavior and have instead become a conduit for promoting material success. Schools are evaluated not in terms of their effectively imparting knowledge but in terms of their ability to train students to get high-paying jobs. Social conditions reinforce each other: culture determines institutions, and institutional change influences culture.[124] Crime rates may rise in a healthy economy because national prosperity heightens the attractiveness of monetary rewards, encouraging people to gain financial success by any means necessary, including illegal means. In this culture of competition, self-interest prevails and generates amorality, acceptance of inequality, and disdain for the less fortunate.[125]

A number of research efforts have found support for the principles set out in the IAT. On a macro level, research shows that there is an association between national homicide rates and cultural stress on individual achievement and the fetishism of money.[126] On an individual or micro level, commitment to economic success is positively related to criminality. The more people say that making money is what's important to them, the more likely they are to get involved in crime.[127] And while there is general support for the IAT, a number of issues remain, such as developing an understanding of gender differences in the crime rate.[128] Assuming that women desire money, success, and the American Dream as much as men, why is their crime rate lower?

Relative Deprivation Theory

There is ample evidence that neighborhood-level income inequality is a significant predictor of neighborhood crime rates.[129] Sharp divisions between the rich and the poor create an atmosphere of envy and mistrust. Criminal motivation is fueled both by perceived humiliation and by the perceived right to humiliate a victim in return.[130] Psychologists warn that under these circumstances young males will begin to fear and envy "winners" who are doing very well at their expense. If they fail to use risky aggressive tactics, they are surely going to lose out in social competition and have little chance of future success.[131] These generalized feelings of **relative deprivation** are precursors to high crime rates.[132]

relative deprivation
Envy, mistrust, and aggression resulting from perceptions of economic and social inequality.

The concept of relative deprivation was proposed by sociologists Judith Blau and Peter Blau, who combined concepts from anomie theory with those derived from social disorganization models.[133] According to the Blaus, lower-class people may feel both deprived and embittered when they compare their life circumstances to those of the more affluent. People who feel deprived because of their race or economic class eventually develop a sense of injustice and discontent. The less fortunate begin to distrust the society that has nurtured social inequality and reduced their chances of progressing by legitimate means. The constant frustration that results from these feelings of inadequacy produces pent-up aggression and hostility, eventually leading to violence and crime. The effect of inequality may be greatest when the impoverished believe that they are becoming less able to compete in a society whose balance of economic and social power is shifting further toward the already affluent. Under these conditions, the relatively poor are increasingly likely to choose illegitimate life-enhancing activities.[134] Research studies using national data sets do show a strong positive association between income inequality and violent crime, a finding that supports the relative deprivation concept.[135]

Relative deprivation is felt most acutely by African American youths because they consistently suffer racial discrimination and economic deprivation that inflict on them a lower status than that of other urban residents.[136] Wage inequality may motivate young African American males to enter the drug trade, an enterprise that increases the likelihood that they will become involved in violent crimes.[137]

In sum, according to the relative deprivation concept, people who perceive themselves as economically deprived relative to people they know, as well as to society in general, may begin to form negative self-feelings and hostility, which motivate them to engage in deviant and criminal behaviors.[138]

General Strain Theory (GST)

Sociologist Robert Agnew's **general strain theory (GST)** helps identify the micro-level, or individual-level, influences of strain. Whereas Merton and Messner and Rosenfeld try to explain social class differences in the crime rate, Agnew tries to explain why individuals who feel stress and strain are likely to commit crimes. Agnew also offers a more general explanation of criminal activity among all elements of society, rather than restricting his views to crime among the lower socioeconomic classes.[139]

general strain theory (GST)
The view that multiple sources of strain interact with an individual's emotional traits and responses to produce criminality.

negative affective states
Anger, frustration, and adverse emotions produced by a variety of sources of strain.

MULTIPLE SOURCES OF STRAIN Agnew suggests that criminality is the direct result of **negative affective states**—the anger and frustration that emerge in the wake of destructive social relationships. He finds that negative affective states are produced by a variety of sources of strain. These are described below and summarized in Figure 6.2.

- *Failure to achieve positively valued goals.* This cause of strain, similar to what Merton speaks of in his theory of anomie, is a result of the disjunction between aspirations and expectations. This type of strain occurs when someone aspires to wealth and fame but, lacking financial and educational resources, assumes that such goals are impossible to achieve; he or she then turns to crime and drug dealing.
- *Disjunction of expectations and achievements.* Strain can also be produced by a disjunction between expectations and achievements. When people compare themselves

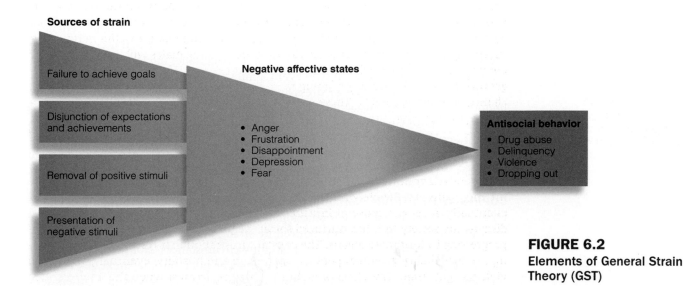

FIGURE 6.2
Elements of General Strain Theory (GST)

to peers who seem to be doing a lot better financially or socially (making more money, for example, or getting better grades), even those doing relatively well feel strain. When a high school senior is accepted at a good college but not at a prestigious school, like some of her friends, she will feel strain. Perhaps she is not being treated fairly because the playing field is tilted against her: "Other kids have connections," she may say. Perceptions of inequity may result in many adverse reactions, ranging from running away from its source to lowering others' benefits through physical attacks or property vandalism.

- *Removal of positively valued stimuli.* Strain may occur because of the actual or antici-pated loss of positively valued stimuli.[140] The loss of a girlfriend or boyfriend can produce strain, as can the death of a loved one, or moving to a new neighbor-hood or school, or the divorce or separation of parents. The loss of positive stim-uli may lead to delinquency as the adolescent tries to prevent the loss, retrieve what has been lost, obtain substitutes, or seek revenge against those responsible for the loss. Recent research by Matthew Larson and Gary Sweeten shows that both males and females increase their involvement in antisocial activities after they suffer a romantic breakup.[141]
- *Presentation of negative stimuli.* Strain may also be caused by negative or noxious stimuli, such as child abuse or neglect, crime victimization, physical punishment, family or peer conflict, school failure, or stressful life events ranging from verbal threats to air pollution.[142] The onset of delinquency has been linked to mal-treatment through the rage and anger it generates. Children who are abused at home may take out their rage on younger children at school or become involved in violent delinquency.[143] Nor is the effect of negative stimuli a one-shot deal: victims who continually interact with the source of negative stimuli (the school-yard bully, the abusive parent, the demanding boss) may find that the cumulative effects of strain are overwhelming. Negative affective states experienced in child-hood can follow a person to the grave.[144]

Although these sources of strain are independent of one another, they may over-lap. If a teacher insults a student, it may be viewed as an unfair application of neg-ative stimuli that interferes with a student's academic aspirations. The greater the intensity and frequency of strain experiences, the greater their impact and the more likely they are to cause delinquency.

CONSEQUENCES OF STRAIN According to Agnew, each type of strain increases the likelihood of experiencing negative emotions such as disappointment, depression, fear, and (most important) anger. Anger increases perceptions of injury and of being wronged. It produces a desire for revenge, energizes individuals to take action, and lowers inhibitions. Violence and aggression seem justified if you have been wronged and are righteously angry. Because it produces these emotions, chronic, repetitive strain can be considered a predisposing factor for delinquency when it creates a hos-tile, suspicious, aggressive attitude. Individual strain episodes may trigger delinquency, such as when a particularly stressful event ignites a violent reaction.

Kids who report feelings of stress and anger are more likely to interact with de-linquent peers and to engage in criminal behaviors.[145] They may join deviant groups and gangs whose law-violating activities produce even more strain and pressure to commit even more crime. For example, the angry youngster who gets involved with substance-abusing peers may feel forced to go on unwanted shoplifting sprees to pay for drugs.[146]

COPING WITH STRAIN Not all people who experience strain eventually resort to criminality. Some marshal their emotional, mental, and behavioral resources to cope with the anger and frustration produced by strain. Some defenses are cognitive; in-dividuals may be able to rationalize frustrating circumstances. Not getting the career they desire is "just not that important"; they may be poor, but the "next guy is worse off"; and if things didn't work out, then they "got what they deserved." Others seek behavioral solutions: they run away from adverse conditions or seek revenge against those who caused the strain. Others will try to regain emotional equilibrium with techniques ranging from physical exercise to drug abuse. Some may change their daily routine in order to avoid the negative influences that are causing emotional duress.[147] Some people, especially those who are overly sensitive or emotional and who have an explosive temperament, low tolerance for adversity, and poor problem-solving skills, are less likely to cope well with strain.[148] As their perception of strain increases, so does their involvement in antisocial behaviors.[149]

Although these traits, which are linked to aggressive, antisocial behavior, seem to be stable over the life cycle, they may peak during adolescence.[150] This is a period of social stress caused by weakening parental supervision and the development of relationships with a diverse peer group. Many adolescents going through the trauma of family breakup and frequent changes in family structure feel a great deal of strain. They may react by becoming involved in precocious sexuality or by turning to substance abuse to mask the strain.[151]

As children mature, their expectations increase. Some are unable to meet academic and social demands. Adolescents are very concerned about their standing with peers. Teenagers who are deficient in these areas may find they are social outcasts, another source of strain. In adulthood, crime rates may drop because these sources of strain are reduced. New sources of self-esteem emerge, and adults seem more likely to align their goals with reality.

EVALUATING GST Agnew's model has been shown to predict crime and deviance within a number of different cultures and nations.[152] It also adds to the body of literature describing how social and life history events influence patterns of offending. As levels of strain increase, so does involvement in antisocial activities; as strain levels decrease, so do individual crime rates.[153]

There is also empirical support for GST:[154]

- Early indicators of strain—family breakup, poor nurturing, running away, and substance use—are associated with long-term social problems, including sexual exploitation.[155]
- As predicted by GST, kids who report feelings of stress and anger are more likely to interact with delinquent peers and to engage in criminal behaviors.[156]
- Minority group members are forced to live in difficult and unique social conditions that produce strain, and they may cope with strain and negative emotions through crime.[157]
- People who perceive strain because their success goals are blocked are more likely to engage in criminal activities.[158]
- The interactions predicted by GST have cross-cultural validity.[159]

RACE AND DISCRIMINATION While GST has become a cornerstone of criminological theory, there are still issues that need to be fully explored. Take for instance the effect of racism and racial discrimination on strain. Minority youth are exposed to racist attitudes at school and in public places. Some of these incidents are overt and intentionally hostile, while others are a product of microaggressions—typically defined as routine slights, snubs, or insults that communicate derogatory or negative meanings based solely upon race, ethnicity, or sexual orientation. Research by Stacy De Coster and Maxine Thompson shows a clear link between perceptions of racial hostility strain and aggressive responses.[160] Their research shows that African American middle-schoolers constantly grapple with racial microaggressions. They are called names, disrespected, and treated as intellectually inferior and dangerous on account of their race. Perceptions of racial hostility are not only linked to strain but also exacerbate the influence of general stresses on offending. These findings indicate that the association between race, strain, and antisocial behaviors needs to be more fully explored.

Concept Summary 6.2 reviews major concepts and theories of the strain perspective.

CHECKPOINTS

▶ Strain theories hold that economic deprivation causes frustration, which leads to crime.

▶ According to Merton's anomie theory, many people who desire material goods and other forms of economic success lack the means to achieve their goals. Some may turn to crime.

▶ Messner and Rosenfeld's institutional anomie theory argues that the goal of success at all costs has invaded every aspect of American life.

▶ Agnew's general theory of strain suggests that there is more than one source of anomie.

Concept Summary 6.2 Strain Theories

Theory	Major Premise	Strengths	Research Focus
Anomie theory	People who adopt the goals of society but lack the means to attain them seek alternatives, such as crime.	Points out how competition for success creates conflict and crime. Suggests that social conditions, and not personality, can account for crime. Explains high lower-class crime rates.	Frustration; anomie; effects of failure to achieve goals.
Institutional anomie theory	Material goods pervade all aspects of American life.	Explains why crime rates are so high in American culture.	Frustration; effects of materialism.
Relative deprivation theory	Crime occurs when the wealthy and the poor live close to one another.	Explains high crime rates in deteriorated inner-city areas located near more affluent neighborhoods.	Relative deprivation.
General strain theory	Strain has a variety of sources. Strain causes crime in the absence of adequate coping mechanisms.	Identifies the complexities of strain in modern society. Expands on anomie theory. Shows the influence of social events on behavior over the life course. Explains middle-class crimes.	Strain; inequality; negative affective states; influence of negative and positive stimuli.

Cultural Deviance Theory

L06 List and compare the elements of cultural deviance theory.

The third branch of social structure theory combines the effects of social disorganization and strain to explain how people living in deteriorated neighborhoods react to social isolation and economic deprivation. Because their lifestyle is draining, frustrating, and dispiriting, members of the lower socioeconomic class create an independent subculture with its own set of rules and values. Whereas middle-class culture stresses hard work, delayed gratification, formal education, and being cautious, the lower-class subculture stresses excitement, toughness, taking risks, fearlessness, immediate gratification, and street smarts.

The subculture of the lower socioeconomic class is an attractive alternative because the urban poor find it impossible to meet the behavioral demands of middle-class society. However, subcultural norms often clash with conventional values. Urban dwellers must violate the law in order to obey the rules of the deviant culture with which they are in immediate contact.

Focal Concerns

More than 50 years ago, sociologist Walter Miller identified the unique conduct norms that help define lower-class culture.[161] Miller referred to these norms as

Exhibit 6.1   Focal Concerns

- *Trouble*. In lower-class communities, people are evaluated by their actual or potential involvement in making trouble. Getting into trouble includes such behaviors as fighting, drinking, and sexual misconduct. Dealing with trouble can confer prestige—for example, when a man establishes a reputation for being able to handle himself well in a fight. Not being able to handle trouble, and having to pay the consequences, can make a person look foolish and incompetent.
- *Toughness*. Lower-class males want local recognition of their physical and spiritual toughness. They refuse to be sentimental or soft and instead value physical strength, fighting ability, and athletic skill. Those who cannot meet these standards risk getting a reputation for being weak, inept, and effeminate.
- *Smartness*. Members of the lower-class culture want to maintain an image of being streetwise and savvy, using their street smarts, and having the ability to outfox and out-con the opponent. Although formal education is not admired, knowing essential survival techniques (such as gambling, conning, and outsmarting the law) is a requirement.
- *Excitement*. Members of the lower class search for fun and excitement to enliven an otherwise drab existence. The search for excitement may lead to gambling, fighting, getting drunk, and sexual adventures. In between, the lower-class citizen may simply "hang out" and "be cool."
- *Fate*. Lower-class citizens believe their lives are in the hands of strong spiritual forces that guide their destinies. Getting lucky, finding good fortune, and hitting the jackpot are the daily dreams of most slum dwellers.
- *Autonomy*. Being independent of authority figures, such as the police, teachers, and parents, is required; losing control is an unacceptable weakness, incompatible with toughness.

Source: Walter Miller, "Lower-Class Culture as a Generating Milieu of Gang Delinquency," *Journal of Social Issues* 14 (1958): 5–19.

focal concerns, values that have evolved specifically to fit conditions in lower-class environments. The major lower-class focal concerns are set out in Exhibit 6.1.[162]

According to Miller, clinging to lower-class focal concerns promotes illegal or violent behavior. Toughness may mean displaying fighting prowess; street smarts may lead to drug deals; excitement may result in drinking, gambling, or drug abuse. In lower-class culture, violence helps young men acquire social power, while insulating them from becoming victims. Violence is also seen as a means to acquire the trappings of wealth (such as nice clothes, flashy cars, and access to clubs), control or humiliate another person, defy authority, settle drug-related disputes, attain retribution, satisfy the need for thrills or risk taking, and respond to challenges to one's manhood.[163] These subcultural values are handed down from one generation to the next in a process called **cultural transmission**.

To some criminologists, the influence of lower-class focal concerns and culture seems as relevant today as when it was first identified by Miller more than half a century ago. One of the most important statements of this culture is Elijah Anderson's "code of the streets," which is discussed in the accompanying Policies and Issues in Criminology feature.

GANG CULTURE The cultural deviance model assumes that kids will be drawn to the culture of the gang. Adolescents who feel alienated from the normative culture can find a home in the gang. In a disorganized area, gangs are a stable community feature rather than a force of disruption. Gang membership has appeal to adolescents who are alienated from their families as well as the mainstream of society. It is not surprising that kids who have had problems with the law and suffer juvenile justice processing are more likely to join gangs than nonstigmatized kids.[164]

focal concerns
Values, such as toughness and street smarts, that have evolved specifically to fit conditions in lower-class environments.

cultural transmission
Process whereby values, beliefs, and traditions are handed down from one generation to the next.

Policies and Issues in Criminology

THE CODE OF THE STREETS

A widely cited view of the interrelationship of culture and behavior is Elijah Anderson's concept of the "code of the streets." He sees that life circumstances are tough for the "ghetto poor"—lack of jobs that pay a living wage, stigma of race, fallout from rampant drug use and drug trafficking, and alienation and lack of hope for the future. Living in such an environment places young people at special risk of crime and deviant behavior.

There are two cultural forces running through the neighborhood that shape their reactions. Decent values are taught by families committed to middle-class values and representing mainstream goals and standards of behavior. Though they may be better off financially than some of their street-oriented neighbors, they are generally "working poor." They value hard work and self-reliance and are willing to sacrifice for their families; they harbor hopes for a better future for their children. Most go to church and take a strong interest in education. Some see their difficult situation as a test from God and derive great support from their faith and from the church community.

In opposition, street values are born in the despair of inner-city life and are in opposition to those of mainstream society. The street culture has developed what Anderson calls a code of the streets, a set of informal rules setting down both proper attitudes and ways to respond if challenged. If the rules are violated, there are penalties and sometimes violent retribution.

At the heart of the code is the issue of respect—loosely defined as being "treated right." The code demands that disrespect be punished or hard-won respect will be lost. With the right amount of respect, a person can avoid being bothered in public. If he is bothered, not only may he be in physical danger, but he has been disgraced or "dissed" (disrespected). Some forms of dissing, such as maintaining eye contact for too long, may seem pretty mild. But to street kids who live by the code, these actions become serious indications of the other person's intentions and a warning of imminent physical confrontation.

These two orientations—decent and street—socially organize the community. Their coexistence means that kids who are brought up in decent homes must be able to successfully navigate the demands of the street culture. Even in decent families, parents recognize that the code must be obeyed or at the very least negotiated; it cannot simply be ignored.

The Respect Game

Young men in poor inner-city neighborhoods build their self-image on the foundation of respect. Having "juice" (as respect is sometimes called on the street) means that they can take care of themselves even if it means resorting to violence. For street youth, losing respect on the street can be damaging and dangerous. Once they have demonstrated that they can be insulted, beaten up, or stolen from, they become an easy target. Kids from decent families may be able to keep their self-respect by getting good grades or a scholarship. Street kids do not have that luxury. With nothing to fall back on, they cannot walk away from an insult. They must retaliate with violence.

One method of preventing attacks is to go on the offensive. Aggressive, violence-prone people are not seen as easy prey. Robbers do not get robbed, and street fighters are not the favorite targets of bullies. A youth who communicates an image of not being afraid to die

Joining a gang is a type of turning point that changes the direction of people's lives. Gang membership portends a substantial change in emotions, attitudes, and social controls conducive to criminality.[165] The more embedded a boy becomes in the gang and its processes, the less likely he is to leave. When David Pyrooz and his research team interviewed gang members, they found that most of the less-involved gang boys leave within six months of their first gang contact, while more involved kids stay at least two more years.[166] Similarly, Pyrooz found that gang membership can have a significant effect on critical life domains: youth who join gangs are 30 percent less likely to graduate from high school and 58 percent less likely to earn a four-year degree than a matched sample of non-gang peers. The effects of gang membership on educational attainment begin within one year of joining; gang membership's influence is both quick and long lasting.[167]

and not being afraid to kill has given himself a sense of power on the street.

Testing the Theory Does the Code Exist?

Anderson's work has been well received by the criminological community. A number of researchers have found that the "code of the streets" does in fact exist and that Anderson's observations are in fact valid. Jeffery Fagan found that the street code's rules for getting and maintaining respect through aggressive behavior forced many "decent" youths to situationally adopt a tough demeanor and perhaps behave violently in order to survive an otherwise hostile and possibly dangerous environment. Similarly, Eric Stewart and Ronald Simons found that adolescents living in urban neighborhoods are often forced to accept the street code even if it violates their own personal values and attitudes. Failure to do so threatens their life and well-being. In another recent study Kristy Matsuda and her associates found that kids who join a gang also increase their street code–related attitudes and emotions. Those whose loyalty to the code of the streets is the greatest also experience the greatest frequency of violent offending.

Gender and social differences have also been found to exist. Males seem more likely to accept the code than females, though many girls embrace the principles as a personal code. Boys who report experiencing racial discrimination maintain stronger street code beliefs that last into adulthood. Adolescents with strong family ties are more likely to embrace decent values while those whose family is less influential are more likely to hold street code beliefs. Stephen Baron observed that kids who follow and apply the street code are more likely to engage in violence if they are angry and self-centered. Not surprisingly, being homeless and suffering abuse intensifies the effect of the street code. All these research efforts in some form support Anderson's view of the association between the code of the street and antisocial behaviors.

In sum, the weight of the evidence supports the validity of Anderson's groundbreaking research.

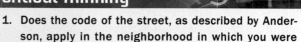

Critical Thinking

1. Does the code of the street, as described by Anderson, apply in the neighborhood in which you were raised? Is it universal?

2. Is there a form of "respect game" being played out on college campuses? If so, what is the substitute for violence?

Sources: Elijah Anderson, *Code of the Street: Decency, Violence, and the Moral Life of the Inner City* (New York: Norton, 2000); Stephen W. Baron, "It's More than the Code: Exploring the Factors that Moderate the Street Code's Relationship with Violence," *Justice Quarterly* 34 (2017): 491–516; Elijah Anderson, "Violence and the Inner-City Street Code," in *Violence and Children in the Inner City*, ed. Joan McCord (New York: Cambridge University Press, 1998), pp. 1–30; Elijah Anderson, "The Code of the Streets," *Atlantic Monthly* 273 (May 1994): 80–94; Richard Moule Jr., Callie Burt, Eric Stewart, and Ronald Simons, "Developmental Trajectories of Individuals' Code of the Street Beliefs Through Emerging Adulthood," *Journal of Research in Crime and Delinquency* 52 (2015): 342–372; Jeffrey Nowacki, " Sugar, Spice, and Street Codes: The Influences of Gender and Family Attachment on Street Code Adoption," *Deviant Behavior* 33 (2012): 831–844; Eric Stewart and Ronald Simons, "Race, Code of the Street, and Violent Delinquency: A Multilevel Investigation of Neighborhood Street Culture and Individual Norms of Violence," *Criminology* 482 (2010): 569–606; Eric Stewart and Ronald Simons, "Structure and Culture in African American Adolescent Violence: A Partial Test of the 'Code of the Street' Thesis," *Justice Quarterly* 23 (2006): 1–33; Jeffrey Fagan, "Adolescent Violence: A View from the Street," *NIJ Research Preview* (Washington, DC: National Institute of Justice, 1998).

Theory of Delinquent Subculture

Albert Cohen first articulated the theory of **delinquent subculture** in his classic 1955 book *Delinquent Boys*.[168] Cohen's central argument was that delinquent behavior of lower-class youths is actually a protest against the norms and values of middle-class US culture. Because social conditions prevent them from achieving success legitimately, lower-class youths experience a form of culture conflict that Cohen labels **status frustration**.[169] As a result, many of them join gangs and engage in behavior that is "non-utilitarian, malicious, and negativistic."[170]

Cohen viewed the delinquent gang as a separate subculture possessing a value system directly opposed to that of the larger society. He described the subculture as one that "takes its norms from the larger culture, but turns them upside down. The

delinquent subculture
A value system adopted by lower-class youths that is directly opposed to that of the larger society.

status frustration
A form of culture conflict experienced by lower-class youths because social conditions prevent them from achieving success as defined by the larger society.

Community programs have been aimed at improving neighborhood climate in order to counteract negative subcultural forces. Here, children get off a bus in front of the headquarters for the DC Promise Neighborhood Initiative (DCPNI), which provides afterschool programs in the Kenilworth-Parkside neighborhood of Washington. Backed by a multiyear $28 million Education Department grant, DCPNI vows to tackle generational poverty with a fresh approach: if a parent's level of education improves, so do a child's prospects. In Kenilworth-Parkside, helping the children get a good education is a primary focus, but it's the adults they must first engage.

AP Images/Charles Dharapak

delinquent's conduct is right by the standards of his subculture precisely because it is wrong by the norms of the larger culture."[171]

According to Cohen, the development of the delinquent subculture is a consequence of socialization practices in lower-class environments. Here children lack the basic skills necessary to achieve social and economic success, including a proper education, which renders them incapable of developing the skills they need to succeed in society. Lower-class parents are incapable of teaching children the necessary techniques for entering the dominant middle-class culture. The consequences of this deprivation include developmental handicaps, poor speech and communication skills, and inability to delay gratification.

MIDDLE-CLASS MEASURING RODS One significant handicap that lower-class children face is the inability to positively impress authority figures, such as teachers, employers, or supervisors. In US society, these positions tend to be held by members of the middle class, who have difficulty relating to the lower-class youngster. Cohen calls the standards set by these authority figures **middle-class measuring rods**.

The conflict and frustration that lower-class youths experience when they fail to meet these standards is a primary cause of delinquency. They may find themselves prejudged by others and not measuring up in the final analysis. Negative evaluations become part of a permanent "file" that follows an individual for the rest of his or her life. When the individual wants to improve, evidence of prior failures is used to discourage advancement.

FORMATION OF DEVIANT SUBCULTURES Cohen believes that lower-class boys rejected by middle-class decision makers usually join one of three existing subcultures: the corner boy, the college boy, or the delinquent boy.

The "corner boy" role is the most common response to middle-class rejection. The corner boy is not a chronic delinquent but may be a truant who engages in petty or status offenses, such as precocious sex and recreational drug abuse. His main loyalty is to his peer group, on which he depends for support, motivation, and interest. His values, therefore, are those of the group with which he is in close contact. The corner boy, well aware of his failure to achieve the standards of the American Dream, retreats into the comforting world of his lower-class peers and eventually becomes a

middle-class measuring rods
The standards by which authority figures, such as teachers and employers, evaluate lower-class youngsters and often prejudge them negatively.

stable member of his neighborhood, holding a menial job, marrying, and remaining in the community.

The "college boy" embraces the cultural and social values of the middle class. Rather than scorning middle-class measuring rods, he actively strives to succeed by those standards. Cohen views this type of youth as one who is embarking on an almost hopeless path because he is ill-equipped academically, socially, and linguistically to achieve the rewards of middle-class life.

The "delinquent boy" adopts a set of norms and principles that directly oppose middle-class values. He engages in short-run hedonism, living for today and letting "tomorrow take care of itself."[172] Delinquent boys strive for group autonomy. They resist efforts by family, school, or other sources of authority to control their behavior. Frustrated by their inability to succeed, these boys resort to a process to which Cohen attaches the psychoanalytic term **reaction formation**. This process includes overly intense responses that seem disproportionate to the stimuli that trigger them. For the delinquent boy, this takes the form of irrational, malicious, and unaccountable hostility to the enemy, which in this case is "the norms of respectable middle-class society."[173]

Cohen's approach skillfully integrates strain and social disorganization theories and has become an enduring element of criminological literature.

Theory of Differential Opportunity

In their classic 1960 work *Delinquency and Opportunity*, Richard Cloward and Lloyd Ohlin combined strain and social disorganization principles to portray a gang-sustaining criminal subculture.[174] The centerpiece of Cloward and Ohlin's theory is **differential opportunity**. According to this concept, people in all strata of society share the same success goals; however, those in the lower socioeconomic class have limited means of achieving them. People who perceive themselves as failures within conventional society will seek alternative or innovative ways to succeed. People who conclude that there is little hope for legitimate advancement may join like-minded peers to form a gang, which can provide them with emotional support. The youth who is considered a failure at school and is qualified for only a menial job at the minimum wage can earn thousands of dollars, plus the respect of his or her peers, by joining a gang and taking part in drug deals or armed robberies.

Cloward and Ohlin recognize that the opportunity for success in both conventional and criminal careers is limited. In stable areas, adolescents may be recruited by professional criminals, drug traffickers, or organized crime groups. Unstable areas, however, cannot support flourishing criminal opportunities. In these socially disorganized neighborhoods, adult role models are absent, and young criminals have few opportunities to join established gangs or learn the fine points of professional crime. Their most important finding, then, is that all opportunities for success, both illegal and conventional, are closed for the most disadvantaged youths. Because of differential opportunity, young people are likely to join one of three types of gangs:

- *Criminal gangs.* These gangs exist in stable neighborhoods where close connections among adolescent, young adult, and adult offenders create an environment for successful criminal enterprise.[175] Youths are recruited into established criminal gangs that provide training for a successful criminal career. Gang membership is a learning experience in which the knowledge and skills needed for success in crime are acquired. During this apprenticeship, older, more experienced members of the criminal subculture hold youthful trainees on tight reins, limiting activities that might jeopardize the gang's profits (for example, engaging in nonfunctional, irrational violence).
- *Conflict gangs.* These gangs develop in communities unable to provide either legitimate or illegitimate opportunities.[176] They attract tough adolescents who fight

reaction formation
Irrational hostility evidenced by young delinquents, who adopt norms directly opposed to middle-class goals and standards that seem impossible to achieve.

differential opportunity
The view that lower-class youths, whose legitimate opportunities are limited, join gangs and pursue criminal careers as alternative means to achieve universal success goals.

Concept Summary 6.3   Cultural Deviance Theories

Theory	Major Premise	Strengths	Research Focus
Miller's focal concern theory	Citizens who obey the street rules of lower-class life (focal concerns) find themselves in conflict with the dominant culture.	Identifies the core values of lower-class culture and shows their association to crime.	Cultural norms; focal concerns.
Cohen's theory of delinquent subculture	Status frustration of lower-class boys, created by their failure to achieve middle-class success, causes them to join gangs.	Shows how the conditions of lower-class life produce crime. Explains violence and destructive acts. Identifies conflict of lower class with middle class.	Gangs; culture conflict; middle-class measuring rods; reaction formation.
Cloward and Ohlin's theory of opportunity	Blockage of conventional opportunities causes lower-class youths to join criminal, conflict, or retreatist gangs.	Shows that even illegal opportunities are structured in society. Indicates why people become involved in a particular type of criminal activity. Presents a way of preventing crime.	Gangs; cultural norms; culture conflict; effects of blocked opportunity.

CHECKPOINTS

▶ Cultural deviance theory shows how subcultures develop with norms in opposition to the general society.

▶ Walter Miller describes the focal concerns that shape this subculture.

▶ Albert Cohen analyzes the lifestyle of delinquent boys, revealing how they obey an independent social code with its own values.

▶ Cohen shows how members of the lower class fail when they are judged by "middle-class measuring rods."

▶ Richard Cloward and Lloyd Ohlin find that deviant subcultures form when people believe that their legitimate opportunities are blocked or impaired.

▶ Crime prevention efforts have been aimed at increasing the conventional options for success open to members of the lower class.

with weapons to win respect from rivals and engage in unpredictable and destructive assaults on people and property. Conflict gang members must be ready to fight to protect their own and their gang's integrity and honor. By doing so, they acquire a "rep," which gains them admiration from their peers and consequently helps them buttress their self-image.

- *Retreatist gangs.* Retreatists are double failures, unable to gain success through legitimate means and unwilling to do so through illegal ones. Members of the retreatist subculture constantly search for ways of getting high—alcohol, pot, heroin, unusual sexual experiences, music. To feed their habits, retreatists develop a "hustle"—pimping, conning, selling drugs, or committing petty crimes. Personal status in the retreatist subculture is derived from peer approval.

Cloward and Ohlin's theory integrates cultural deviance and social disorganization variables and recognizes different modes of criminal adaptation. The fact that criminal cultures can be supportive, rational, and profitable seems to reflect the actual world of the delinquent more realistically than Cohen's original view of purely negativistic, destructive delinquent youths who reject all social values. Concept Summary 6.3 reviews the major concepts of cultural deviance theory.

Social Structure Theory and Public Policy

Social structure theory has significantly influenced public policy. If the cause of criminality is viewed as a schism between lower-class individuals and conventional goals, norms, and rules, it seems logical that alternatives to criminal behavior can be provided by giving inner-city youth opportunities to share in the rewards of conventional society.

One approach is to give indigent people direct financial aid through public assistance or welfare. Although welfare has been curtailed under the Federal Welfare Reform Act of 1996, research shows that crime rates decrease when families receive supplemental income through public assistance payments.[177]

Efforts have also been made to reduce crime by improving the community structure in inner-city high-crime areas. Crime prevention efforts based on social structure precepts can be traced back to the Chicago Area Project supervised by Clifford Shaw. This program attempted to organize existing community structures to develop social stability in otherwise disorganized slums. The project sponsored recreation programs for neighborhood children, including summer camping. It campaigned for community improvements in education, sanitation, traffic safety, resource conservation, and law enforcement. Project members also worked with police and court agencies to supervise and treat gang youth and adult offenders.

Social structure concepts, especially Cloward and Ohlin's views, were a critical ingredient in the Kennedy and Johnson administrations' War on Poverty, begun in the early 1960s. War on Poverty programs—Head Start, Neighborhood Legal Services, and the Community Action Program—have continued to help people. Another similar program, called Weed and Seed, involved a two-pronged approach: law enforcement agencies and prosecutors cooperated in "weeding out" violent criminals and drug abusers, and public agencies and community-based private organizations collaborated to "seed" much-needed human services, including prevention, intervention, treatment, and neighborhood restoration programs. Unfortunately, government funding for this program ended in 2012.[178]

Broken Windows

Social structural views can be seen in so-called broken windows policing, more commonly called community policing, which is based on the belief that police administrators would be well advised to deploy their forces where they can encourage public confidence, strengthen feelings of safety, and elicit cooperation from citizens. Community preservation, public safety, and order maintenance—not crime fighting—are the primary focus of patrol. Put another way, just as physicians and dentists practice preventive medicine and dentistry, police should help maintain an intact community structure rather than simply fighting crime.

Community-oriented policing (COP) also emphasizes sharing power with local groups and individuals. A key element of the community-oriented policing philosophy is that citizens must actively participate with police to fight crime. Such participation is essential because the community climate is influenced by the informal social control created by a concerned citizenry coupled with effective policing.[179] Participation might involve providing information in area-wide crime investigations or helping police reach out to troubled youths.

To achieve the goals of COP, some police agencies have tried to decentralize. According to this view, problem solving is best done at the neighborhood level where issues originate, not at a far-off central headquarters.[180] Because each neighborhood has its own particular needs, police decision making must be flexible and adaptive. Neighborhoods undergoing change in racial composition may experience high levels of racially motivated violence and require special police initiatives to reduce tensions.[181]

Does it work? New York City's emphasis on broken windows policing was credited with producing significant declines in that city's crime rate. In one of the most rigorous tests of broken windows theory in researchers identified 34 crime-ridden areas in Lowell, Massachusetts, half of which received broken windows policing; the other half regular patrol. Results revealed substantial reductions in crime, disorder, and calls for service in the treatment areas, but not in the control areas.[182]

Some recent community-oriented programs based on social structure concepts are set out in Exhibit 6.2.

Exhibit 6.2   Community-Based Crime Prevention Programs

- Communities That Care (CTC) is a national program that emphasizes the reduction of risk factors and the enhancement of protective factors against crime and delinquency. One example of the CTC approach is Project COPE, which serves the Lynn, Massachusetts, area. Established in 2004, COPE works collaboratively with multiple local agencies, including Girls Incorporated of Lynn, the city's health department, police department, public schools, and other agencies whose goals include reducing risk factors for youth and promoting healthy family and neighborhood development. The coalition includes a large and active youth subcommittee. Originally focused on substance abuse prevention in youth, the coalition expanded its initiatives to include the prevention of fatal and nonfatal opiate overdoses, teen suicide, teen pregnancy, bullying and violence, and obesity. Project COPE cares for individuals of all ages. As an advocate for individuals needing specialized services, COPE assumes the responsibility for leadership in developing new and creative programs and addressing the needs of the many populations it serves. In 2014, COPE merged with Bridgewell, a larger service organization that provides residential services, day habilitation, behavioral health services, employment training, transitional homeless services, affordable housing, and substance abuse and addiction services.

- In Tulsa, Oklahoma, the Educare I/Kendall-Whittier School is part of the Educare Learning Network, a national early childhood education program that operates about 18 schools across the nation in cities such as Denver, Omaha, and Chicago. The program seeks to disrupt the cycle of poverty in communities by eliminating the academic achievement gap among low-income children. Four core features compose the Educare model: data

utilization, embedded professional development, high-quality teaching practices, and intensive family engagement. The goal is to develop a culture for high-quality early childhood education and family support services, while connecting with community-based programs that help children and families access additional resources, such as health and mental health services. The program maintains small class sizes, high staff–child ratios, and continuity of care—whereby children remain with the same teacher for their first three years at the school. Evaluations show that the program helps reduce community-level violence rates.

- In Seattle, the Neighborhood Matching Fund (NMF), program was created in 1988 to provide matching dollars for neighborhood improvement, organizing, or projects that are developed and implemented by community members. The program requires the service providers to match their award from the city with contributions from the community (volunteer time, donated materials, donated professional services or cash). Since 1988, the Fund has awarded more than $49 million to more than 5,000 projects throughout Seattle and generated an additional $72 million of community match. Evaluations of the programs show that it can reduce neighborhood-level crime rates, especially in the city's poorest areas.

Sources: Project COPE, http://www.bridgewell.org/projectcope/; Arelys Madero-Hernandez, Rustu Deryol, M. Murat Ozer, and Robin S. Engel, "Examining the Impact of Early Childhood School Investments on Neighborhood Crime," *Justice Quarterly*, published online September 9, 2016; Seattle Department of Neighborhoods, http://www.seattle.gov/neighborhoods /programs-and-services; David Ramey and Emily Shrider, "New Parochialism, Sources of Community Investment, and the Control of Street Crime," *Criminology and Public Policy* 13 (2014): 193–216.

Thinking Like a Criminologist

Mean Streets   You have accepted a position in Washington as an assistant to the undersecretary of urban affairs. The undersecretary informs you that he wants to initiate a demonstration project in a major city to show that government can reduce poverty, crime, and drug abuse.

The area he has chosen is a large inner-city neighborhood in a midwestern city of more than 3 million people. It suffers from disorganized community structure, poverty, and hopelessness. Predatory delinquent gangs run free, terrorizing local merchants and citizens. The school system has failed to provide opportunities and educational experiences sufficient to dampen enthusiasm for gang recruitment. Stores, homes, and public buildings are deteriorated and decayed. Commercial enterprise has fled the area, and civil servants are reluctant to enter the neighborhood. There is an uneasy truce among the varied ethnic and racial groups that populate the area. Residents feel that little can be done to bring the neighborhood back to life. Merchants are afraid to open stores, and there is little outside development from major retailers or manufacturers. People who want to start their own businesses find that banks will not lend them money.

One of the biggest problems has been the large housing projects built in the 1960s. These are now overcrowded and deteriorated. Police are actually afraid to enter the buildings unless they arrive with a SWAT team. Each building is controlled by a gang whose members demand tribute from the residents.

Writing Assignment

Write a proposal outlining a redevelopment program to revitalize the area and eventually bring down the crime rate. In your essay, describe how the public or private sector can help with this overwhelming problem. Discuss how private industry can help in the struggle. What programs would you recommend to break the cycle of urban poverty?

SUMMARY

L01 **Explain the association between social structure and crime.**
According to social structure theory, the root cause of crime is the socioeconomic disadvantages that have become embedded in American society. People in the lower class are driven to desperate measures, such as crime and substance abuse, to cope with their economic plight. Aggravating this dynamic is the constant media bombardment linking material possessions to self-worth.

L02 **Identify the elements of social disorganization theory.**
This theory focuses on the urban conditions that affect crime rates. Crime occurs in disorganized areas where institutions of social control, such as the family, commercial establishments, and schools, have broken down and can no longer perform their expected or stated functions. Indicators of social disorganization include high unemployment and school dropout rates, deteriorated housing, low income levels, and large numbers of single-parent households. Residents in these areas experience conflict and despair, and as a result, antisocial behavior flourishes.

L03 **Analyze the views of Shaw and McKay.**
Shaw and McKay explained crime and delinquency within the context of the changing urban environment and ecological development of the city. Poverty-ridden transitional neighborhoods suffer high rates of population turnover and often cannot induce residents to remain and defend the neighborhoods against criminal groups. The values that slum youths adopt often conflict with existing middle-class norms, which demand strict obedience to the legal code. Consequently, a value conflict further separates the delinquent youth and his or her peer group from conventional society; the result is a more solid embrace of deviant goals and behavior.

L04 **Differentiate between the various elements of ecological theory.**
Crime rates and the need for police services are associated with community deterioration: disorder, poverty, alienation, disassociation, and fear of crime. In larger cities, neighborhoods with a high percentage of deserted houses and apartments experience high crime rates. As fear increases, quality of life deteriorates. People who live in neighborhoods that experience high levels of crime and civil disorder become suspicious, distrust authorities, and may develop a "siege mentality." As areas decline, residents flee to safer, more stable localities.

LO5 **Discuss the concept of strain.**
Strain theorists argue that although people in all economic strata share similar social and economic goals, the ability to obtain these goals is class dependent. Most people in the United States desire wealth, material possessions, power, prestige, and other life comforts. Members of the lower class are unable to obtain these symbols of success through conventional means. Consequently, they feel anger, frustration, and resentment, referred to collectively as strain. To resolve the goals–means conflict and relieve their sense of strain, some people innovate by stealing or extorting money; others retreat into drugs and alcohol; some rebel by joining revolutionary groups; and still others get involved in ritualistic behavior by joining a religious cult.

LO6 **List and compare the elements of cultural deviance theory.**
Cultural deviance theory combines elements of both strain theory and social disorganization theory. A unique lower-class culture has developed in disorganized neighborhoods. These independent subcultures maintain unique values and beliefs that conflict with conventional social norms. Criminal behavior is an expression of conformity to lower-class subcultural values and traditions, not a rebellion from conventional society. Subcultural values are handed down from one generation to the next in a process called cultural transmission.

Key Terms

stratified society 172
social classes 172
white privilege 174
Black Lives Matter
    (BLM) 174
culture of poverty 174
underclass 175
social structure
    theory 175
social disorganization
    theory 177

strain theory 177
strain 177
cultural deviance
    theory 177
subculture 177
transitional
    neighborhood 178
social ecology
    school 180
concentration effect 182
collective efficacy 183

street efficacy 185
anomie theory 187
institutional
    anomie theory
    (IAT) 187
American Dream 187
relative deprivation 188
general strain theory
    (GST) 189
negative affective
    states 189

focal concerns 193
cultural transmission 193
delinquent
    subculture 195
status frustration 195
middle-class measuring
    rods 196
reaction formation 197
differential
    opportunity 197

Critical Thinking Questions

1. Is there a "transitional" area in your town or city? Does the crime rate remain constant there, regardless of who moves in or out?

2. Is it possible that a distinct lower-class culture exists? Do you know anyone who has the focal concerns Miller talks about? Were there focal concerns in your high school or college experience?

3. Have you ever perceived anomie in your own life? How did you cope with these feelings

4. How would Merton explain Aaron Hernandez's violent behavior? How would Agnew?

5. Could "relative deprivation" produce crime among college-educated white-collar workers?

Notes

All URLs accessed in 2017.

1. Ron Borges and Paul Solotaroff, "Aaron Hernandez: Inside Dark, Tragic Life of Former Patriots Star," *Rolling Stone*, August 28, 2013, http://www.rollingstone.com/feature/the-gangster-in-the-huddle.

2. Cleve R. Wootson Jr., "Aaron Hernandez was a man who couldn't leave 'gang member' life behind, Shannon Sharpe says," *Washington Post*, April 19, 2017, https://www.washingtonpost.com/news/early-lead/wp/2017/04/19/aaron-hernandez-was-a-man-who-couldnt-leave-gang-member-life-behind-shannon-sharpe-says/.

3. Steven Messner and Richard Rosenfeld, *Crime and the American Dream* (Belmont, CA: Wadsworth, 1994), p. 11.

4. Arlen Egley Jr., James Howell, and Meena Harris, *Highlights of the 2012 National Youth Gang Survey*, Office of Juvenile Justice and Delinquency Prevention, 2014, http://www.ojjdp.gov/pubs/248025.pdf.

5. Sara Thompson and Rosemary Gartner, "The Spatial Distribution and Social Context of Homicide in Toronto's Neighborhoods," *Journal of Research in Crime and Delinquency* 51 (2014): 88–118.

6. Drew DeSilver, "High-income Americans pay most income taxes, but enough to be 'fair'?" March 24, 2015, http://www.pewresearch.org/fact-tank/2015/03/24/high-income-americans-pay-most-income-taxes-but-enough-to-be-fair/; Phil DeMuth, "Are You Rich Enough? The Terrible Tragedy of Income Inequality Among the 1%," *Forbes Magazine*, November 25, 2013, http://www.forbes.com/sites/phildemuth/2013/11/25/are-you-rich-enough-the-terrible-tragedy-of-income-inequality-among-the-1/.

7. US Census Bureau, "Poverty," https://www.census.gov/library/publications/2016/demo/p60-256.html.

8. National Center for Children in Poverty (NCCP), *Child Poverty, 2015*, http://www.nccp.org/publications/pub_1100.html.

9. Ibid.

10. Jeanne Brooks-Gunn and Greg J. Duncan, "The Effects of Poverty on Children," *Future of Children* 7 (1997): 34–39.

11. Greg Duncan, W. Jean Yeung, Jeanne Brooks-Gunn, and Judith Smith, "How Much Does Childhood Poverty Affect the Life Chances of Children?" *American Sociological Review* 63 (1998): 406–423.

12. National Center on Family Homelessness, "America's Youngest Outcasts," http://new.homelesschildrenamerica.org/mediadocs/275.pdf.

13. Maria Velez, Lauren Krivo, and Ruth Peterson, "Structural Inequality and Homicide: An Assessment of the Black-White Gap in Killings," *Criminology* 41 (2003): 645–672.

14. US Department of Health and Human Services, "Profile: Black/African Americans," http://minorityhealth.hhs.gov/omh/browse.aspx?lvl=3&lvlid=61.

15. National Center for Education Statistics, *The Condition of Education 2014* (NCES 2014-083), Status Dropout Rates, http://nces.ed.gov/fastfacts/display.asp?id=16.

16. Deirdre Bloome, "Racial Inequality Trends and the Intergenerational Persistence of Income and Family Structure," *American Sociological Review* 79 (2014): 1196–1225.

17. James Ainsworth-Darnell and Douglas Downey, "Assessing the Oppositional Culture Explanation for Racial/Ethnic Differences in School Performances," *American Sociological Review* 63 (1998): 536–553.

18. Bruce Jacobs and Lynn Addington, "Gating and Residential Robbery," *Prevention and Community Safety* 18 (2016): 19–37; Lynn Addington and Callie Marie Rennison, "Keeping the Barbarians Outside the Gate? Comparing Burglary Victimization in Gated and Non-Gated Communities," *Justice Quarterly* 32 (2015): 168–192; Maria Velez, Lauren Krivo, and Ruth Peterson, "Structural Inequality and Homicide: An Assessment of the Black-White Gap in Killings," *Criminology* 41 (2003): 645–672.

19. Karen Parker and Matthew Pruitt, "Poverty, Poverty Concentration, and Homicide," *Social Science Quarterly* 81 (2000): 555–582.

20. Ruth Peterson and Lauren Krivo, *Divergent Social Worlds: Neighborhood Crime and the Racial-Spatial Divide*, reprint ed. (New York: Russell Sage, 2012).

21. Michael Leiber and Joseph Johnson, "Being Young and Black: What Are Their Effects on Juvenile Justice Decision Making?" *Crime and Delinquency* 54 (2008): 560–581.

22. Pew Foundation, *One in 100: Behind Bars in America 2008*, http://www.pewtrusts.org/en/research-and-analysis/reports/2008/02/28/one-in-100-behind-bars-in-america-2008.

23. John Hagan, Carla Shedd, and Monique Payne, "Race, Ethnicity, and Youth Perceptions of Criminal Injustice," *American Sociological Review* 70 (2005): 381–407.

24. Oscar Lewis, "The Culture of Poverty," *Scientific American* 215 (1966): 19–25.

25. Gunnar Myrdal, *The Challenge of World Poverty* (New York: Vintage Books, 1970).

26. William Julius Wilson, *The Truly Disadvantaged* (Chicago: University of Chicago Press, 1987); see also Wilson, *More than Just Race: Being Black and Poor in the Inner City* (New York: Norton, 2009); William Julius Wilson and Richard Taub, *There Goes the Neighborhood: Racial, Ethnic, and Class Tensions in Four Chicago Neighborhoods and Their Meaning for America* (New York: Knopf, 2006); William Julius Wilson, *When Work Disappears: The World of the Urban Poor* (New York: Alfred Knopf, 1996); *The Bridge over the Racial Divide: Rising Inequality and Coalition Politics* (Wildavsky Forum Series, 2) (Berkeley: University of California Press, 1999).

27. William Julius Wilson, "Black Youths, Joblessness, and the Other Side of 'Black Lives Matter,'" *Ethnic and Racial Studies* 39 (2016): 1450–1457.

28. Jonathan Crane, "The Epidemic Theory of Ghettos and Neighborhood Effects on Dropping Out and Teenage Childbearing," *American Journal of Sociology* 96 (1991): 1226–1259; see also Rodrick Wallace, "Expanding Coupled Shock Fronts of Urban Decay and Criminal Behavior: How U.S. Cities Are Becoming 'Hollowed Out,'" *Journal of Quantitative Criminology* 7 (1991): 333–355.

29. Barbara Warner, "The Role of Attenuated Culture in Social Disorganization Theory," *Criminology* 41 (2003): 73–97.

30. April Zeoli, Jesenia Pizarro, Sue Grady, and Christopher Melde, "Homicide as Infectious Disease: Using Public Health Methods to Investigate the Diffusion of Homicide," *Justice Quarterly* 31 (2014): 609–632; Jeffrey Fagan and Garth Davies, "The Natural History of Neighborhood Violence," *Journal of Contemporary Criminal Justice* 20 (2004): 127–147.

31. Justin Patchin, Beth Huebner, John McCluskey, Sean Varano, and Timothy Bynum, "Exposure to Community Violence and Childhood Delinquency," *Crime and Delinquency* 52 (2006): 307–332.

32. For a classic look, see Frederick Thrasher, *The Gang* (Chicago: University of Chicago Press, 1927).

33. Dana Haynie, Eric Silver, and Brent Teasdale, "Neighborhood Characteristics, Peer Networks, and Adolescent Violence," *Journal of Quantitative Criminology* 22 (2006): 147–169.

34. Richard Stansfield, Kirk Williams, and Karen Parker, "Economic Disadvantage and Homicide: Estimating Temporal Trends in Adolescence and Adulthood," *Homicide Studies* 21 (2017): 59–81.

35. John Hipp, "Spreading the Wealth: The Effect of the Distribution of Income and Race/Ethnicity Across Households and Neighborhoods on City Crime Trajectories," *Criminology* 49 (2011): 631–665; Julie A. Phillips, "White, Black, and Latino Homicide Rates: Why the Difference?" *Social Problems* 49 (2002): 349–374.

36. Matt Vogel and Scott J. South, "Spatial Dimensions of the Effect of Neighborhood Disadvantage on Delinquency," *Criminology* 54 (2016): 434–458.

37. See Ruth Kornhauser, *Social Sources of Delinquency* (Chicago: University of Chicago Press, 1978), p. 75.

38. Kerryn E. Bell, "Gender and Gangs: A Quantitative Comparison," *Crime and Delinquency* 55 (2009): 363–387.

39. National Gang Center (NGC), "Measuring the Extent of Gang Problems," National Youth Gang Survey Analysis, http://www.nationalgangcenter.gov/Survey-Analysis/Measuring-the-Extent-of-Gang-Problems#estimatednumbergangs.

40. Clifford R. Shaw and Henry D. McKay, *Juvenile Delinquency and Urban Areas*, rev. ed. (Chicago: University of Chicago Press, 1972).

41. Ibid., p. 52.

42. Ibid., p. 171.

43. Claire Valier, "Foreigners, Crime and Changing Mobilities," *British Journal of Criminology* 43 (2003): 1–21.

44. For a general review, see James Byrne and Robert Sampson, eds., *The Social Ecology of Crime* (New York: Springer Verlag, 1985).

45. See, generally, Robert Bursik, "Social Disorganization and Theories of Crime and Delinquency: Problems and Prospects," *Criminology* 26 (1988): 521–539.

46. D. Wayne Osgood and Jeff Chambers, "Social Disorganization Outside the Metropolis: An Analysis of Rural Youth Violence," *Criminology* 38 (2000): 81–117.

47. William Spelman, "Abandoned Buildings: Magnets for Crime?" *Journal of Criminal Justice* 21 (1993): 481–493.

48. Alyssa Chamberlain and Lyndsay Boggess, "Relative Difference and Burglary Location," *Journal of Research in Crime and Delinquency* 53 (2016): 872–906.

49. Marc Swatt, Sean Varano, Craig Uchida, and Shellie Solomon, "Fear of Crime, Incivilities, and Collective Efficacy in Four Miami Neighborhoods," *Journal of Criminal Justice* 41 (2013): 1–11; Matthew Lee and Terri Earnest, "Perceived Community Cohesion and Perceived Risk of Victimization: A Cross-National Analysis," *Justice Quarterly* 20 (2003): 131–158.

50. Pamela Wilcox, Neil Quisenberry, and Shayne Jones, "The Built Environment and Community Crime Risk Interpretation," *Journal of Research in Crime and Delinquency* 40 (2003): 322–345.

51. Yili Xu, Mora Fiedler, and Karl Flaming, "Discovering the Impact of Community Policing: The Broken Windows Thesis, Collective Efficacy, and Citizens' Judgment," *Journal of Research in Crime and Delinquency* 42 (2005): 147–186.

52. Michael Hanslmaier, "Crime, Fear and Subjective Well-Being: How Victimization and Street Crime Affect Fear and Life Satisfaction," *European Journal of Criminology* 10 (2013): 515–533.

53. Wendy Kilewer, "The Role of Neighborhood Collective Efficacy and Fear of Crime in Socialization of Coping with Violence in Low-Income Communities," *Journal of Community Psychology* 41 (2013): 920–930; Danielle Wallace, "A Test of the Routine Activities and Neighborhood Attachment Explanations for Bias in Disorder Perceptions," *Crime and Delinquency*, first published online December 7, 2011.

54. Michele Roccato, Silvia Russo, and Alessio Vieno, "Perceived Community Disorder Moderates the Relation Between Victimization and Fear of Crime," *Journal of Community Psychology* 39 (2011): 884–888.

55. C. L. Storr, C. Y. Chen, and J. C. Anthony, "'Unequal Opportunity': Neighborhood Disadvantage and the Chance to Buy Illegal Drugs," *Journal of Epidemiology and Community Health* 58 (2004): 231–238.

56. Pamela Wilcox Rountree and Kenneth Land, "Burglary Victimization, Perceptions of Crime Risk, and Routine Activities: A Multilevel Analysis Across Seattle Neighborhoods and Census Tracts," *Journal of Research in Crime and Delinquency* 33 (1996): 147–180.

57. Ted Chiricos, Ranee McEntire, and Marc Gertz, "Social Problems, Perceived Racial and Ethnic Composition of Neighborhood and Perceived Risk of Crime," *Social Problems* 48 (2001): 322–341; Wesley Skogan, "Fear of Crime and Neighborhood Change," in *Communities and Crime*, ed. Albert Reiss and Michael Tonry (Chicago: University of Chicago Press, 1986), pp. 191–232.

58. Catherine E. Ross, John Mirowsky, and Shana Pribesh, "Powerlessness and the Amplification of Threat: Neighborhood Disadvantage, Disorder, and Mistrust," *American Sociological Review* 66 (2001): 568–580.

59. Jodi Lane and James Meeker, "Social Disorganization Perceptions, Fear of Gang Crime, and Behavioral Precautions Among Whites, Latinos, and Vietnamese," *Journal of Criminal Justice* 32 (2004): 49–62.

60. John Hagan, Carla Shedd, and Monique Payne, "Race, Ethnicity, and Youth Perceptions of Criminal Injustice," *American Sociological Review* 70 (2005): 381–407.

61. Jane Sprott and Anthony Doob, "The Effect of Urban Neighborhood Disorder on Evaluations of the Police and Courts," *Crime and Delinquency* 55 (2009): 339–362.

62. Bradley Smith, "Structural and Organizational Predictors of Homicide by Police," *Policing: An International Journal of Police Strategies and Management* 27 (2004): 539–557; William Terrill and Michael Reisig, "Neighborhood Context and Police Use of Force," *Journal of Research in Crime and Delinquency* 40 (2003): 291–321.

63. Finn-Aage Esbensen and David Huizinga, "Community Structure and Drug Use: From a Social Disorganization Perspective," *Justice Quarterly* 7 (1990): 691–709.

64. Karen Parker, Brian Stults, and Stephen Rice, "Racial Threat, Concentrated Disadvantage, and Social Control: Considering the Macro-Level Sources of Variation in Arrests," *Criminology* 43 (2005): 1111–1134.

65. Bridget Freisthler, Elizabeth Lascala, Paul Gruenewald, and Andrew Treno, "An Examination of Drug Activity: Effects of Neighborhood Social Organization on the Development of Drug Distribution Systems," *Substance Use and Misuse* 40 (2005): 671–686.

66. Micere Keels, Greg Duncan, Stefanie Deluca, Ruby Mendenhall, and James Rosenbaum, "Fifteen Years Later: Can Residential Mobility Programs Provide a Long-Term Escape from Neighborhood Segregation, Crime, and Poverty?" *Demography* 42 (2005): 51–72.

67. Allen Liska and Paul Bellair, "Violent-Crime Rates and Racial Composition: Convergence over Time," *American Journal of Sociology* 101 (1995): 578–610.

68. Patricia McCall and Karen Parker, "A Dynamic Model of Racial Competition, Racial Inequality, and Interracial Violence," *Sociological Inquiry* 75 (2005): 273–294.

69. Steven Barkan and Steven Cohn, "Why Whites Favor Spending More Money to Fight Crime: The Role of Racial Prejudice," *Social Problems* 52 (2005): 300–314.

70. Barbara Warner, Kristin Swartz, and Shila René Hawk, "Racially Homophilous Social Ties and Informal Social Control," *Criminology* 53 (2015): 204–230.

71. Leo Scheurman and Solomon Kobrin, "Community Careers in Crime," in *Communities and Crime*, ed. Reiss and Tonry, pp. 67–100.

72. Ibid.

73. Paul Stretesky, Amie Schuck, and Michael Hogan, "Space Matters: An Analysis of Poverty, Poverty Clustering, and Violent Crime," *Justice Quarterly* 21 (2004): 817–841.

74. Gregory Squires and Charis Kubrin, "Privileged Places: Race, Uneven Development and the Geography of Opportunity in Urban America," *Urban Studies* 42 (2005): 47–68; Matthew Lee, Michael Maume, and Graham Ousey, "Social Isolation and Lethal Violence Across the Metro /Nonmetro Divide: The Effects of Socioeconomic Disadvantage and Poverty Concentration on Homicide," *Rural Sociology* 68 (2003): 107–131.

75. Lee, Maume, and Ousey, "Social Isolation and Lethal Violence Across the Metro/Nonmetro Divide"; Charis E. Kubrin, "Structural Covariates of Homicide Rates: Does Type of Homicide Matter?" *Journal of Research in Crime and Delinquency* 40 (2003): 139–170; Darrell Steffensmeier and Dana Haynie, "Gender, Structural Disadvantage, and Urban Crime: Do Macrosocial Variables Also Explain Female Offending Rates?" *Criminology* 38 (2000): 403–438.

76. Corina Graif, "Delinquency and Gender Moderation in the Moving to Opportunity Intervention: The Role of Extended Neighborhoods," *Criminology* 53 (2015): 366–398.

77. Kyle Crowder and Scott South, "Spatial Dynamics of White Flight: The Effects of Local and Extralocal Racial Conditions on Neighborhood Out-Migration," *American Sociological Review* 73 (2008): 792–812.

78. Paul Jargowsky and Yoonhwan Park, "Cause or Consequence? Suburbanization and Crime in U.S. Metropolitan Areas," *Crime and Delinquency* 55 (2009): 28–50.

79. Jeffrey Morenoff, Robert Sampson, and Stephen Raudenbush, "Neighborhood Inequality, Collective Efficacy, and the Spatial Dynamics of Urban Violence," *Criminology* 39 (2001): 517–560.

80. Scott Menard and Delbert Elliott, "Self-Reported Offending, Maturational Reform, and the Easterlin Hypothesis," *Journal of Quantitative Criminology* 6 (1990): 237–268.

81. Elijah Anderson, *Streetwise: Race, Class and Change in an Urban Community* (Chicago: University of Chicago Press, 1990), pp. 243–244.

82. Jeffrey Michael Cancino, "The Utility of Social Capital and Collective Efficacy: Social Control Policy in Nonmetropolitan Settings," *Criminal Justice Policy Review* 16 (2005): 287–318; Chris Gibson, Jihong Zhao, Nicholas Lovrich, and Michael Gaffney, "Social Integration, Individual Perceptions of Collective Efficacy, and Fear of Crime in Three Cities," *Justice Quarterly* 19 (2002): 537–564; Felton Earls, *Linking Community Factors and Individual Development* (Washington, DC: National Institute of Justice, 1998).

83. Robert J. Sampson and Stephen W. Raudenbush, *Disorder in Urban Neighborhoods: Does It Lead to Crime?* (Washington, DC: National Institute of Justice, 2001).

84. Andrea Altschuler, Carol Somkin, and Nancy Adler, "Local Services and Amenities, Neighborhood Social Capital, and Health," *Social Science and Medicine* 59 (2004): 1219–1230.

85. Kelly Socia and Janet Stamatel, "Neighborhood Characteristics and the Social Control of Registered Sex Offenders," *Crime and Delinquency* 58 (2012): 565–587.

86. Andrea Cantora and Lauren Restivo, "Understanding Drivers of Crime in East Baltimore: Resident Perceptions of Why Crime Persists," *American Journal of Criminal Justice* 41 (2016): 686–709; Todd Armstrong, Charles Katz, and Stephen M. Schnebly, "The Relationship Between Citizen Perceptions of Collective Efficacy and Neighborhood Violent Crime," *Crime and Delinquency* 61 (2015): 121–142.

87. M. R. Lindblad, K. R. Manturuk, and R. G. Quercia, "Sense of Community and Informal Social Control Among Lower Income Households: The Role of Homeownership and Collective Efficacy in Reducing Subjective Neighborhood Crime and Disorder," *American Journal of Community Psychology* 51 (2013): 123–139.

88. Rebecca Wickes, John Hipp, Renee Zahnow, and Lorraine Mazerolle, "'Seeing' Minorities and Perceptions of Disorder: Explicating the Mediating and Moderating Mechanisms of Social Cohesion," *Criminology* 51 (2013): 519–560.

89. Michael Reisig and Jeffrey Michael Cancino, "Incivilities in Nonmetropolitan Communities: The Effects of Structural Constraints, Social Conditions, and Crime," *Journal of Criminal Justice* 32 (2004): 15–29.

90. Robert Sampson, Jeffrey Morenoff, and Felton Earls, "Beyond Social Capital: Spatial Dynamics of Collective Efficacy for Children," *American Sociological Review* 64 (1999): 633–660.

91. John Hipp, "Collective Efficacy: How Is It Conceptualized, How Is It Measured, and Does It Really Matter for Understanding Perceived Neighborhood Crime and Disorder?" *Journal of Criminal Justice* 46 (2016): 32–44.

92. Donald Black, "Social Control as a Dependent Variable," in *Toward a General Theory of Social Control*, ed. D. Black (Orlando, FL: Academic Press, 1990).

93. Jennifer Beyers, John Bates, Gregory Pettit, and Kenneth Dodge, "Neighborhood Structure, Parenting Processes, and the Development of Youths' Externalizing Behaviors: A Multilevel Analysis," *American Journal of Community Psychology* 31 (2003): 35–53.

94. Ronald Simons, Leslie Gordon Simons, Callie Harbin Burt, Gene Brody, and Carolyn Cutrona, "Collective Efficacy, Authoritative Parenting and Delinquency: A Longitudinal Test of a Model Integrating Community and Family-Level Processes," *Criminology* 43 (2005): 989–1029.

95. Michael Baglivio, Kevin Wolff, Nathan Epps, and Randy Nelson, "Predicting Adverse Childhood Experiences: The Importance of Neighborhood

Context in Youth Trauma Among Delinquent Youth," *Crime and Delinquency* 63 (2017): 166–188.

96. Justin Medina, "Neighborhood Firearm Victimization Rates and Social Capital Over Time," *Violence and Victims* 30 (2015): 81–96.

97. April Pattavina, James Byrne, and Luis Garcia, "An Examination of Citizen Involvement in Crime Prevention in High-Risk versus Low- to Moderate-Risk Neighborhoods," *Crime and Delinquency* 52 (2006): 203–231.

98. Paul Bellair, "Informal Surveillance and Street Crime: A Complex Relationship," *Criminology* 38 (2000): 137–170.

99. Wesley G. Skogan, *Disorder and Decline: Crime and the Spiral of Decay in American Neighborhoods* (New York: Free Press, 1990), pp. 15–35.

100. Robert Sampson and W. Byron Groves, "Community Structure and Crime: Testing Social Disorganization Theory," *American Journal of Sociology* 94 (1989): 774–802; Denise Gottfredson, Richard McNeill, and Gary Gottfredson, "Social Area Influences on Delinquency: A Multilevel Analysis," *Journal of Research in Crime and Delinquency* 28 (1991): 197–206.

101. Fred Markowitz, Paul Bellair, Allen Liska, and Jianhong Liu, "Extending Social Disorganization Theory: Modeling the Relationships Between Cohesion, Disorder, and Fear," *Criminology* 39 (2001): 293–320.

102. George Capowich, "The Conditioning Effects of Neighborhood Ecology on Burglary Victimization," *Criminal Justice and Behavior* 30 (2003): 39–62.

103. Gregory Zimmerman, Brandon Welsh, and Chad Posick, "Investigating the Role of Neighborhood Youth Organizations in Preventing Adolescent Violent Offending: Evidence from Chicago," *Journal of Quantitative Criminology* 31 (2015): 565–593.

104. Ruth Peterson, Lauren Krivo, and Mark Harris, "Disadvantage and Neighborhood Violent Crime: Do Local Institutions Matter?" *Journal of Research in Crime and Delinquency* 37 (2000): 31–63.

105. James Wo, "Community Context of Crime," *Crime and Delinquency* 62 (2016): 1286–1312.

106. Lee Ann Slocum, Andres Rengifo, Tiffany Choi, and Christopher Herrmann, "The Elusive Relationship Between Community Organizations and Crime: An Assessment Across Disadvantaged Areas of the South Bronx," *Criminology* 51 (2013): 167–216; Maria Velez, "The Role of Public Social Control in Urban Neighborhoods: A Multi-Level Analysis of Victimization Risk," *Criminology* 39 (2001): 837–864.

107. Tammy Rinehart Kochel, "Robustness of Collective Efficacy on Crime in a Developing Nation: Association with Crime Reduction Compared to Police Services," *Journal of Crime and Justice* 36 (2013): 334–352.

108. David Weisburd, Michael Davis, and Charlotte Gill, "Increasing Collective Efficacy and Social Capital at Crime Hot Spots: New Crime Control Tools for Police," *Policing: A Journal of Policy and Practice* 9 (2015): 265–274.

109. David Klinger, "Negotiating Order in Patrol Work: An Ecological Theory of Police Response to Deviance," *Criminology* 35 (1997): 277–306.

110. Rodney Stark, "Deviant Places: A Theory of the Ecology of Crime," *Criminology* 25 (1987): 893–911.

111. Robert Bursik and Harold Grasmick, "Economic Deprivation and Neighborhood Crime Rates, 1960–1980," *Law and Society Review* 27 (1993): 263–278.

112. Robert Kane, "Compromised Police Legitimacy as a Predictor of Violent Crime in Structurally Disadvantaged Communities," *Criminology* 43 (2005): 469–498.

113. Suzanna Fay-Ramirez, "The Comparative Context of Collective Efficacy: Understanding Neighbourhood Disorganisation and Willingness to Intervene in Seattle and Brisbane," *Australian and New Zealand Journal of Criminology* 48 (2015): 513–542; Keri Burchfield and Eric Silver, "Collective Efficacy and Crime in Los Angeles Neighborhoods: Implications for the Latino Paradox," *Sociological Inquiry* 83 (2013): 154–176.

114. Patrick Sharkey, "Navigating Dangerous Streets: The Sources and Consequences of Street Efficacy," *American Sociological Review* 71 (2006): 826–846.

115. Per-Olof H. Wikström and Kyle Treiber, "The Role of Self-Control in Crime Causation," *European Journal of Criminology* 4 (2007): 237–264.

116. Socia and Stamatel, "Neighborhood Characteristics and the Social Control of Registered Sex Offenders."

117. Peterson, Krivo, and Harris, "Disadvantage and Neighborhood Violent Crime: Do Local Institutions Matter?"

118. John R. Hipp and Wouter Steenbeek, "Types of Crime and Types of Mechanisms: What Are the Consequences for Neighborhoods Over Time?" *Crime and Delinquency*, 62 (2016): 1203–1234.

119. Ibid.

120. Robert Merton, *Social Theory and Social Structure*, enlarged ed. (New York: Free Press, 1968).

121. Lonnie Schaible and Irshad Altheimer, "Social Structure, Anomie, and National Levels of Homicide," *International Journal of Offender Therapy and Comparative Criminology* 60 (2016): 936–963.

122. Albert Cohen, "The Sociology of the Deviant Act: Anomie Theory and Beyond," *American Sociological Review* 30 (1965): 5–14.

123. Messner and Rosenfeld, *Crime and the American Dream.*

124. Jon Gunnar Bernburg, "Anomie, Social Change and Crime: A Theoretical Examination of Institutional-Anomie Theory," *British Journal of Criminology* 42 (2002): 729–743.

125. John Hagan, Gerd Hefler, Gabriele Classen, Klaus Boehnke, and Hans Merkens, "Subterranean Sources of Subcultural Delinquency Beyond the American Dream," *Criminology* 36 (1998): 309–340.

126. Lorine Hughes, Lonnie Schaible, and Benjamin Gibbs, "Economic Dominance, the 'American Dream,' and Homicide: A Cross-National Test of Institutional Anomie Theory," *Sociological Inquiry* 85 (2015): 100–128.

127. Brian Stults and Christi Falco, "Unbalanced Institutional Commitments and Delinquent Behavior: An Individual-Level Assessment of Institutional Anomie Theory," *Youth Violence and Juvenile Justice* 12 (2014): 77–100.

128. Steven Messner and Samantha Applin, "Her American Dream: Bringing Gender into Institutional-Anomie Theory," *Feminist Criminology* 10 (2015): 36–59.

129. Morenoff, Sampson, and Raudenbush, "Neighborhood Inequality, Collective Efficacy, and the Spatial Dynamics of Urban Violence."

130. John Braithwaite, "Poverty, Power, White-Collar Crime and the Paradoxes of Criminological Theory," *Australian and New Zealand Journal of Criminology* 24 (1991): 40–58.

131. Margo Wilson and Martin Daly, "Life Expectancy, Economic Inequality, Homicide, and Reproductive Timing in Chicago Neighbourhoods," *British Journal of Medicine* 314 (1997): 1271–1274.

132. Judith Blau and Peter Blau, "The Cost of Inequality: Metropolitan Structure and Violent Crime," *American Sociological Review* 147 (1982): 114–129.

133. Ibid.

134. Tomislav Kovandzic, Lynne Vieraitis, and Mark Yeisley, "The Structural Covariates of Urban Homicide: Reassessing the Impact of Income Inequality and Poverty in the Post-Reagan Era," *Criminology* 36 (1998): 569–600.

135. Aki Roberts and Dale Willits, "Income Inequality and Homicide in the United States: Consistency Across Different Income Inequality Measures and Disaggregated Homicide Types," *Homicide Studies* 19 (2015): 28–57.

136. Scott South and Steven Messner, "Structural Determinants of Intergroup Association," *American Journal of Sociology* 91 (1986): 1409–1430; Steven Messner and Scott South, "Economic Deprivation, Opportunity Structure, and Robbery Victimization," *Social Forces* 64 (1986): 975–991.

137. Richard Fowles and Mary Merva, "Wage Inequality and Criminal Activity: An Extreme Bounds Analysis for the United States 1975–1990," *Criminology* 34 (1996): 163–182.

138. Beverly Stiles, Xiaoru Liu, and Howard Kaplan, "Relative Deprivation and Deviant Adaptations: The Mediating Effects of Negative Self Feelings," *Journal of Research in Crime and Delinquency* 37 (2000): 64–90.

139. Robert Agnew, "Foundation for a General Strain Theory of Crime and Delinquency," *Criminology* 30 (1992): 47–87.

140. Ibid., p. 57.

141. Matthew Larson and Gary Sweeten, "Breaking Up Is Hard to Do: Romantic Dissolution, Offending, and Substance Use During the Transition to Adulthood," *Criminology* 50 (2012): 605–636.

142. Stephen Watts and Thomas McNulty, "Childhood Abuse and Criminal Behavior: Testing a General Strain Theory Model," *Journal of Interpersonal Violence* 28 (2013): 3023–3040.

143. Timothy Brezina, "Adolescent Maltreatment and Delinquency: The Question of Intervening Processes," *Journal of Research in Crime and Delinquency* 35 (1998): 71–99.

144. Susan Sharp, Mitchell Peck, and Jennifer Hartsfield, "Childhood Adversity and Substance Use of Women Prisoners: A General Strain Theory Approach," *Journal of Criminal Justice* 40 (2012): 202–211.

145. Paul Mazerolle, Velmer Burton, Francis Cullen, T. David Evans, and Gary Payne, "Strain, Anger, and Delinquent Adaptations Specifying General Strain Theory," *Journal of Criminal Justice* 28 (2000): 89–101; Paul Mazerolle and Alex Piquero, "Violent Responses to Strain: An Examination of Conditioning Influences," *Violence and Victimization* 12 (1997): 323–345.

146. George E. Capowich, Paul Mazerolle, and Alex Piquero, "General Strain Theory, Situational Anger, and Social Networks: An Assessment of Conditioning Influences," *Journal of Criminal Justice* 29 (2001): 445–461.

147. Fawn Ngo and Raymond Paternoster, "Toward an Understanding of the Emotional and Behavioral Reactions to Stalking: A Partial Test of General Strain Theory," *Crime and Delinquency*, first published online November 7, 2013.

148. Robert Agnew, Timothy Brezina, John Paul Wright, and Francis T. Cullen, "Strain, Personality Traits, and Delinquency: Extending General Strain Theory," *Criminology* 40 (2002): 43–71.

149. Robert Agnew, "When Criminal Coping Is Likely: An Extension of General Strain Theory," *Deviant Behavior* 34 (2013): 653–670; Lee Ann Slocum, Sally Simpson, and Douglas Smith, "Strained Lives

and Crime: Examining Intra-Individual Variation in Strain and Offending in a Sample of Incarcerated Women," *Criminology* 43 (2005): 1067–1110.

150. Robert Agnew, "Stability and Change in Crime over the Life Course: A Strain Theory Explanation," in *Advances in Criminological Theory: Vol. 7, Developmental Theories of Crime and Delinquency*, ed. Terence Thornberry (New Brunswick, NJ: Transaction Books, 1995), pp. 113–137.

151. Lawrence Wu, "Effects of Family Instability, Income, and Income Instability on the Risk of Premarital Birth," *American Sociological Review* 61 (1996): 386–406.

152. Ekaterina Botchkovar and Lisa Broidy, "Accumulated Strain, Negative Emotions, and Crime: A Test of General Strain Theory in Russia," *Crime and Delinquency* 59 (2013): 837–860.

153. Jacob Bucher, Michelle Manasse, and Jeffrey Milton, "Soliciting Strain: Examining Both Sides of Street Prostitution Through General Strain Theory," *Journal of Crime and Justice* 38 (2015): 435–453.

154. Robert Agnew and Helene Raskin White, "An Empirical Test of General Strain Theory," *Criminology* 30 (1992): 475–499.

155. Joan Reid and Alex Piquero, "Applying General Strain Theory to Youth Commercial Sexual Exploitation," *Crime and Delinquency* 62 (2016): 341–367; John Hoffman and Alan Miller, "A Latent Variable Analysis of General Strain Theory," *Journal of Quantitative Criminology* 13 (1997): 111–113.

156. Mazerolle, Burton, Cullen, Evans, and Payne, "Strain, Anger, and Delinquent Adaptations: Specifying General Strain Theory."

157. Joanne Kaufman, Cesar Rebellon, Sherod Thaxton, and Robert Agnew, "A General Strain Theory of Racial Differences in Criminal Offending," *Australian and New Zealand Journal of Criminology* 41 (2008): 421–437.

158. Stephen Cernkovich, Peggy Giordano, and Jennifer Rudolph, "Race, Crime and the American Dream," *Journal of Research in Crime and Delinquency* 37 (2000): 131–170.

159. Byongook Moon, Merry Morash, Cynthia Perez McCluskey, and Hye-Won Hwang, "A Comprehensive Test of General Strain Theory: Key Strains, Situational- and Trait-Based Negative Emotions, Conditioning Factors, and Delinquency," *Journal of Research in Crime and Delinquency* 46 (2009): 182–212.

160. Stacy De Coster and Maxine Thompson, "Race and General Strain Theory: Microaggressions as Mundane Extreme Environmental Stresses," *Justice Quarterly*, published online September 26, 2016.

161. Walter Miller, "Lower-Class Culture as a Generating Milieu of Gang Delinquency," *Journal of Social Issues* 14 (1958): 5–19.

162. Ibid., pp. 14–17.

163. Jeffrey Fagan, *Adolescent Violence: A View from the Street*, NIJ Research Preview (Washington, DC: National Institute of Justice, 1998).

164. Jon Gunnar Bernburg, Marvin Krohn, and Craig Rivera, "Official Labeling, Criminal Embeddedness, and Subsequent Delinquency: A Longitudinal Test of Labeling Theory," *Journal of Research in Crime and Delinquency* 43 (2006): 67–88.

165. Chris Melde and Finn-Aage Esbensen, "Gang Membership as a Turning Point in the Life Course," *Criminology* 49 (2011): 513–552.

166. David C. Pyrooz, Gary Sweeten, and Alex R. Piquero, "Continuity and Change in Gang Membership and Gang Embeddedness," *Journal of Research in Crime and Delinquency*, published online February 7, 2012.

167. David C. Pyrooz, "From Colors and Guns to Caps and Gowns? The Effects of Gang Membership on Educational Attainment," *Journal of Research in Crime and Delinquency* 51 (2014): 56–87.

168. Albert Cohen, *Delinquent Boys* (New York: Free Press, 1955).

169. Ibid., p. 25.

170. Ibid., p. 28.

171. Ibid.

172. Ibid., p. 30.

173. Ibid., p. 133.

174. Richard Cloward and Lloyd Ohlin, *Delinquency and Opportunity* (New York: Free Press, 1960).

175. Ibid., p. 171.

176. Ibid., p. 73.

177. James DeFronzo, "Welfare and Burglary," *Crime and Delinquency* 42 (1996): 223–230.

178. Weed and Seed FAQ, https://ojp.gov/ccdo/faqs.html.

179. Brian Renauer, "Reducing Fear of Crime," *Police Quarterly* 10 (2007): 41–62

180. Susan Sadd and Randolph Grinc, *Implementation Challenges in Community Policing* (Washington, DC: National Institute of Justice, 1996).

181. Donald Green, Dara Strolovitch, and Janelle Wong, "Defended Neighborhoods: Integration and Racially Motivated Crime," *American Journal of Sociology* 104 (1998): 372–403.

182. Anthony A. Braga and Brenda J. Bond, "Policing Crime and Disorder Hot Spots: A Randomized Controlled Trial," *Criminology* 46 (2008): 577–606.

Social Process Theory

Learning Objectives

LO1 Explain the concepts of social process and socialization.

LO2 Discuss the effect of family relationships on crime.

LO3 Describe how the educational setting influences crime.

LO4 Summarize the link between peers and delinquency.

LO5 Contrast social learning, social control, and social reaction (labeling) theories.

LO6 Link social process theory to crime prevention efforts.

Brock Turner

Gabrielle Lurie/AFP/Getty Images

7

Chapter Outline

FACT OR FICTION?

▶ Gang members reduce their criminal activity if they receive effective parental monitoring.

▶ "Idle hands are the devil's workshop" is not merely an old saying. Getting involved in sports and other activities helps prevent crime and delinquency.

On January 18, 2015, Stanford University student athlete Brock Turner was arrested for sexually assaulting an unconscious woman behind a dumpster.[1] He was apprehended during the act by two Swedish exchange students who quickly called the police. On March 30, 2016, Turner was found guilty of three felonies: assault with intent to rape an intoxicated woman, sexually penetrating an intoxicated person with a foreign object, and sexually penetrating an unconscious person with a foreign object.

It is what happened after guilt was established that made national headlines. The judge in the case, Aaron Persky, heard from all parties at the sentencing hearing. The victim read in court a poignant statement setting out the pain she had endured: "You don't know me, but you've been inside me, and that's why we're here today," she said. "Your damage was concrete; stripped of titles, degrees, enrollment. My damage was internal, unseen, I carry it with me. You took away my worth, my privacy, my energy, my time, my safety, my intimacy, my confidence, my own voice, until today." Turner said the woman had consented to his sexual advances and blamed "the party culture and risk-taking behavior" of college for his actions. Turner's father pleaded with the judge for leniency, saying that his son should not be punished for what amounted to "20 minutes of action."

The prosecutor asked for a six-year sentence, telling the court, "He purposefully took her to an isolated area, away from all of the party goers, to an area that was dimly lit, and assaulted her on the ground behind a dumpster. He deliberately took advantage of the fact that she was so intoxicated that she could not form a sentence, let alone keep her eyes open or stand. This behavior is not typical assaultive behavior that you find on campus, but it is more akin to a predator who is searching for prey." The shock came when the judge ▶

sentenced Turner to six months in county jail. In his opinion, Judge Persky said, he believed Turner's side of the story, that the victim consented to sex, something that the jury had rejected. The judge took into account the fact that Turner was remorseful, was not previously convicted of any crimes, was young, was not armed during the crime, that he would comply with the terms of probation, and he would not be a danger to others if not imprisoned. He said the role alcohol played in the assault is "not an excuse" but "is a factor that, when trying to assess moral culpability in this situation, is mitigating." He said a prison sentence would have "a severe impact" and "adverse collateral consequences" on Turner.

Turner's sentence was reduced to three months due to "automatically applied 'credits'" for good behavior prior to sentencing. He was also in protective custody during his entire time behind bars. As for Judge Persky, he has been reassigned to the civil division of the California court system.

The case raises a number of critical issues. First, the Turner case shows that crime is a highly subjective concept. An act is considered a crime only when a judge or jury label it as such. In this case, if the jury believed that the victim had actually consented to sex and later fell unconscious, as Turner claimed, then no crime would have occurred and he would have been found not guilty. However, here the jury did not believe Turner, rejected this claim, and found him guilty as charged; the act was indeed a rape because the jury labeled it as such. In contrast, the judge was willing to believe Turner's story and as a result neutralized the jury's decision by granting him a very lenient sentence.

The outcome may also have hinged on Brock Turner's personal characteristics. He was not a gang member or an ex-offender but an attractive Stanford student who during the trial was labeled "promising" and a "successful athlete." Would he have been treated differently if he was poor, African American, and/or a high school dropout? Are labels and stigma subjectively applied? What does his being labeled a "successful athlete" have to do with his raping a vulnerable woman?

As part of his sentence, Turner, who later moved to his family's home in the suburbs of Dayton, Ohio, was required to register as a sex offender for life. His picture, conviction information, and address are publicly available on Ohio's sex offender registry. Additionally, anyone living within 1,250 feet of Turner's address will be notified with a postcard of his sex offender status, and he will not be allowed to live within 1,000 feet of schools or playgrounds. Despite Turner's lenient sentence, his conviction and status as a convicted sex offender will label him as violent, dangerous, and abnormal for the rest of his life. His status will bar him from certain occupations, and he will be looked on with disdain by those who know of his criminal status. ■

The Turner case illustrates that both the concept of crime and criminality are shaped by social forces and institutions. People are not born criminals but rather engage in antisocial behaviors as a result of their involvement with significant social groups, such as family, peers, and neighbors, and critical social institutions such as schools and law enforcement agencies. As people are **socialized** over the life course, relationships can be either positive and supportive or dysfunctional and destructive. Depending on the interaction, some people may learn to be a criminal and then consider themselves as such. Others may feel that social institutions have let them down and not given them guidance or control. Others may run afoul of social institutions, as Brock Turner did, and be labeled a deviant or outcast. This view of crime is referred to as **social process theory**.

The social process approach has several independent branches: **social learning theory**, **social control theory**, and **social reaction (labeling) theory**, discussed in detail later in this chapter.

Social learning theories assume that people are born good and learn to be bad; social control theory assumes that people are born bad and must be controlled in order to be good; and social reaction theory assumes that whether good or bad, people are shaped, directed, and influenced by the evaluations of others.

All three forms of social process theories share some basic concepts:

- Socialization is the key to understanding criminal behavior choices.
- Socialization occurs through contact with significant others.
- Anyone can turn to antisocial behavior if their socialization is damaging and/or destructive; crime is not solely a lower-class phenomenon.
- Because criminal behavior is a function of socialization, it can be reversed and criminals turned around by proper resocialization and prosocial interactions.

Institutions of Socialization

Social process theorists have long studied the critical elements of socialization to determine how they contribute to a burgeoning criminal career. Their view relies on the fact that interaction with key social institutions helps control human behavior. Prominent among these elements are the individual's family, peer group, school, and church.

Family Relations

Family relationships are considered a major determinant of behavior.[2] Parenting factors, such as the ability to communicate and to provide proper discipline, may play a critical role in determining whether people misbehave as children and even later as adults. The family–crime relationship is significant across racial, ethnic, and gender lines, and this is one of the most replicated findings in the criminological literature.[3]

Even gang boys will be better able to reduce their criminal activity if they receive parental monitoring; being left alone to engage in unstructured and unsupervised socializing, partying, and drinking with peers significantly increased the likelihood of delinquent and criminal involvement.[4]

FAMILY STRESS While the family can help neutralize the lure of the streets, living in a disadvantaged neighborhood places terrific strain on family functioning, especially in single-parent families that experience social isolation from relatives, friends, and neighbors. Children who are raised within such distressed families are at risk for delinquency.[5] Ongoing studies by sociologist Rand Conger and his associates find economic stress appears to have a harmful effect on parents and children.[6] According to his Family Stress Model of economic hardship, such factors as low income and income loss increase parents' sadness, pessimism about the future, anger, despair, and withdrawal from other family members. Economic stress has this impact on parents'

socialized
The process of acquiring social norms, values, behavior, and skills through interaction with significant others such as parents, peers, and teachers.

social process theory
The view that criminality is a function of people's interactions with various organizations, institutions, and processes in society.

social learning theory
The view that people learn the techniques and attitudes of crime from close relationships with criminal peers: crime is a learned behavior.

social control theory
The view that everyone has the potential to become a criminal, but most people are controlled by their bonds to society. Crime occurs when the forces that bind people to society are weakened or broken.

social reaction (labeling) theory
The view that people become criminals when significant members of society label them as such and they accept those labels as a personal identity.

L01 Explain the concepts of social process and socialization.

L02 Discuss the effect of family relationships on crime.

FACT OR FICTION?

Gang members reduce their criminal activity if they receive effective parental monitoring.

FACT Research shows that proper parenting can reduce delinquent activity even among committed gang members.

Bonnie Jo Mount/Washington Post/Getty Images

According to social process theories, socialization at home, in school, and in the community is the key element in determining adolescent behavior. A strong, positive relationship with significant others insulates youth from delinquency promoting forces in the environment. Here, Reginald Wilson II, age 9, learns a math trick from his father, Reginald Wilson, at their home in Rockville, Maryland. Parental attachment and guidance are important elements of socialization.

social-emotional functioning through the daily pressures it creates for them, such as being unable to pay bills or acquire basic necessities such as adequate food, housing, clothing, and medical care. Disrupted parenting, in turn, increases children's risk of suffering developmental problems, such as depressed mood, substance abuse, and engaging in delinquent behaviors. These economic stress processes also decrease children's ability to function in a competent manner in school and with peers.

Adolescents who do not receive affection from their often hostile parents during childhood are more likely to use illicit drugs and to be more aggressive as they mature.[7] In contrast, those growing up in a home where parents are supportive and effectively control their children in a noncoercive way are more likely to refrain from delinquency; this phenomenon is referred to as **parental efficacy**.[8] Delinquency is reduced when parents provide the type of structure that integrates children into families, while giving them the ability to assert their individuality and regulate their own behavior.[9] Children who have warm and affectionate ties to their parents report greater levels of self-esteem beginning in adolescence and extending into their adulthood; high self-esteem is inversely related to criminal behavior.[10]

parental efficacy
The ability of parents to be supportive of their children and effectively control them in noncoercive ways.

THE EFFECTS OF DIVORCE The relationship between family structure and crime is critical when the high rates of divorce and single parents are considered. Today more than 30 percent of children live in single-family homes.[11] Family disruption or change can have a long-lasting impact on children. Research conducted in both the United States and abroad shows that children raised in homes with one or both parents absent may be prone to antisocial behavior.[12] It is not surprising that the number of single-parent households in the population is significantly related to arrest rates.[13]

FAMILY DEVIANCE A number of studies have found that parental deviance has a powerful influence on children's future behavior. When parents drink, take drugs, and commit crimes, the effects can be both devastating and long term. The effect is intergenerational: the children of deviant parents produce delinquent children themselves.[14] One reason is self-control: parents who lack self-control produce children with the same or similar personalities.[15] If they get arrested and wind up in prison, the effects of parental misbehavior are enhanced.[16] Children of incarcerated parents are more likely to act out and engage in expressive crimes of violence.[17] In the long term, children of incarcerated parents have more physical health problems (migraines, asthma, high cholesterol), school problems (absenteeism, dropping out), and adult life problems (lower incomes, homelessness, feelings of powerlessness).[18]

VIOLENCE AND ABUSE Children who grow up in homes where parents use overly strict discipline become prone to antisocial behavior.[19] A recent meta-analysis of 33 studies reviewing the association between violence and physical and sexual abuse showed clear-cut evidence that the two factors are closely linked.[20]

The more often a child is physically disciplined and the harsher the discipline, the more likely he or she will engage in antisocial behaviors.[21] The effects of abuse appear to be long term: exposure to abuse in early life provides a foundation for violent and antisocial behavior in late adolescence and adulthood.[22] Kids who were abused are less likely to graduate from high school, hold a job, and be happily married; they are more likely to encounter juvenile and adult arrests.[23] They are also more likely to grow up to be abusers themselves.[24]

Abused kids also suffer more from other social problems, such as depression, suicide attempts, and self-injurious behaviors.[25] Mental health and delinquency experts have found that abused kids experience mental and social problems across their life span, problems ranging from substance abuse to damaged personality.[26] Children who experienced indirect types of family violence, such as exposure to the physical abuse of a sibling, are even more likely to externalize antisocial behaviors.[27]

The effects of family dysfunction are felt well beyond childhood.[28] Children whose parents are harsh, angry, and irritable are likely to behave in the same way toward their own children, putting their own offspring at risk.[29] Thus, the seeds of adult dysfunction are planted early in childhood.

Educational Experience

The educational process and adolescent achievement in school have been linked to criminality. Children who do poorly in school, fail at their coursework, do not have a strong bond to the educational experience, lack educational motivation, and feel alienated are the most likely to engage in criminal acts.[30] Children who fail in school commit more serious and violent offenses and persist in their offending into adulthood.[31]

Schools contribute to criminality when they label problem youths and set them apart from conventional society. One way in which schools perpetuate this stigmatization is the "track system," which identifies some students as college bound and others as special needs.[32]

All too often educational problems lead students to leave school early and become dropouts. Even though national dropout rates are in decline, more than 10 percent of Americans ages 16 to 24 have left school permanently without a diploma; of these, more than 1 million withdrew before completing 10th grade. Most kids who drop out show danger signs as early as the 4th grade and serious problems begin to manifest in their first year of high school.[33]

Why do kids drop out? Reasons include a lack of interest in the educational curriculum, a development that leads to course failure and low grade point average.[34] Some kids are pushed out of school because they lack attention, have poor attendance records, and are labeled troublemakers.

RACE AND EDUCATIONAL PROBLEMS African American children are much more likely than their European American peers to suffer problems at school.[35] As a result, minority students are more likely to disengage from school at a younger age than Caucasian students.[36] One reason may be their being the focus of school disciplinary practices. According to the US Department of Education, minority students, especially boys, face

L03 Describe how the educational setting influences crime.

> ### CONNECTIONS
>
> Chapter 2's analysis of the relationship between socioeconomic class and crime showed why this relationship is still a hotly debated topic. Although serious criminals may be found disproportionately in lower-class areas, self-report studies show that criminality cuts across class lines. Middle-class use and abuse of recreational drugs, discussed in Chapter 13, suggests that law violators are not necessarily economically motivated.

While racial inequality continues to plague America, there are many success stories that tell us that anyone can achieve the American Dream. On February 26, 2016, young supporters peek into the huddle as Eisenhower High School boys' basketball team chaplain Rev. Courtney Carson says a prayer before a game in Decatur, Illinois. Carson, expelled from Eisenhower as a student 18 years ago, says he is thankful to the head coach and the school for allowing him to be the team's chaplain. Carson was a drug dealer/gangster at the age of 17 who got involved in a fight in Decatur that became a national news story. Since then, he has experienced a transformation and now lives the life of a minister and mentor heavily involved in helping his community.

AP Images/Jim Bowling/Herald & Review

Bullying has become a major national issue. Others have fought back. Isabella "Belle" Hankey, 18, shown walking with her mother, filed a $2 million lawsuit against the Concord-Carlisle school system in Massachusetts for repeated bullying by other students, including death threats. The case was dismissed on technical grounds, though the judge found school administrators' responses to the obvious bullying and harassment "ineffective and unreasonable."

John Tlumacki/Boston Globe/Getty Images

much harsher discipline in public schools than other students. One in five African American boys and more than one in ten African American girls received an out-of-school suspension, and were three and a half times more likely to be suspended or expelled than white students. Many of the nation's largest districts had very different disciplinary rates for students of different races. In Los Angeles, for example, black students made up 9 percent of those enrolled, but 26 percent of those suspended; in Chicago, they made up 45 percent of the students, but 76 percent of the suspensions.[37] Research shows that youth who are suspended or expelled from school are the ones most likely to have problems over the life course; being suspended increases the likelihood that students will experience criminal victimization, criminal involvement, and incarceration as adults.[38]

GETTING BULLIED Students are also subject to violence and intimidation on school grounds. National data indicate that in a single year about 22 percent of all public schools report that bullying occurred among students on a daily or weekly basis.[39] Seven percent of students ages 12 to 18 report being cyberbullied, and about 3 percent report being subject to harassing text messages; girls are twice as likely to be subject to cyberbullying as boys. It may come as no surprise that a majority of lesbian, gay, bisexual, transgender, and queer young people experience harassment each year in an educational setting. Most LGBTQ students have experienced harassment and discrimination. National surveys have found that more than 8 in 10 (85 percent) experience verbal harassment and nearly two-thirds (66 percent) experience LGBTQ-related discrimination at school. Due to feeling unsafe or uncomfortable, nearly a third (32 percent) of LGBTQ students missed at least one day of school in the last month, and over a third avoid bathrooms (39 percent) and locker rooms (38 percent).[40]

Peer Relations

L04 Summarize the link between peers and delinquency.

Criminologists have long recognized that peer group relations have a powerful effect on human conduct and can dramatically influence decision making and behavior choices.[41] The more antisocial the peer group, the more likely its members will engage in delinquency.[42] Even virtual exposure to antisocial peers they meet online can trigger antisocial behaviors.[43]

Peer effects follow people over the life course, through adolescence into adulthood. Prolonged attachment and exposure to deviant friends eventually shapes the content and character of illegal involvement: those who have violent friends eventually become violent themselves; those whose friends abuse substances will eventually specialize in substance abuse.[44] This relationship continues into college: having a roommate who is a binge drinker is highly correlated with personal binge drinking.[45]

Friendship helps reduce antisocial behaviors: kids who have lots of friends and a variety of peer group networks tend to be less delinquent than their less popular mates.[46] However, some of the most popular kids get to hang out with their friends without parental supervision.[47] If their peer group includes kids who take risks, drink, and take drugs, the lack of parental supervision gives them the opportunity to get into trouble.[48] In contrast, conventional friendship networks help to moderate antisocial behavior.[49] Having prosocial friends who are committed to conventional success may help shield people from crime-producing inducements in their environment.[50]

Even kids who are not usually at risk to crime (young girls, immigrants, college students) may find themselves outside the law if their peers engage in or support antisocial activities.[51] Conversely, children born into high-risk families—such as those with single teen mothers—can avoid delinquency if their friends refrain from drug use and criminality.[52]

In disorganized neighborhoods, deviant peers may help kids become independent and socially accepted.[53] Joining a gang or deviant group may help members increase their social standing and popularity within their age cohort. By ninth grade, kids who belong to a group that engages in underage drinking gain social capital. Participation in the "party" subculture has some short-term costs (e.g., lower grades, detachment from school), but in the long term provides gains in the form of social capital and popularity.[54]

Not all kids join law-violating groups out of choice. Some find it tough to make friends and therefore choose antisocial peers out of necessity rather than desire.[55] Being a social outcast causes them to choose friends who are dangerous and get them into further trouble.[56] Because group involvement helps them neutralize their fear of punishment, loyalty to deviant peers can help sustain or amplify antisocial behavior and reinforce criminal careers.[57] Antisocial friends tend to be, as criminologist Mark Warr puts it, "sticky": once acquired, they are not easily lost; peer influence therefore may continue through the life span.[58]

While the association between having antisocial peers and engaging in antisocial behavior seems solid, the causal direction of these associations is still open to debate. A number of possible scenarios have been suggested, including:

- Impressionable adolescents are led astray by antisocial peers.
- Troubled youth seek out like-minded peers; "birds of a feather flock together."
- Criminal tendencies are reinforced and expanded by like-minded peers.
- Members of friendship groups created in disorganized neighborhoods are all exposed to destructive, crime-producing social forces. What appears to be a peer effect on crime is in reality an ecological one.[59]

Recent research by Evelien Hoeben and Frank Weerman sheds light on the direction of the peer–crime relationship. They found at least three reasons for the significant relationship between peer relations and antisocial behaviors:

- Adolescents are often exposed to delinquent peers in situations of unstructured socializing.
- Exposure to delinquent peers increases the temptation kids have to engage in delinquency.
- Exposure to delinquent peers increases tolerance for substance use.

In sum, when young people are exposed to delinquent peers without adult monitoring, their temptation to commit crime escalates as their fear of using drugs abates. The combination of perceived temptations, reduced inhibitions, and lack of guardianship is a recipe for disaster.[60]

Religion and Belief

Logic would dictate that people who hold high moral values and beliefs, who have learned to distinguish right from wrong, and who regularly attend religious services should also eschew crime and other antisocial behaviors. Religion binds people together and forces them to confront the consequences of their behavior. Having high moral beliefs may enhance the deterrent effect of punishment by convincing even motivated offenders not to risk apprehension and punishment. Committing crimes would violate the principles of all organized religions.[61]

Recent research findings suggest that attending religious services does in fact have a significant negative impact on crime.[62] Kids living in disorganized, high-crime areas who attend religious services are better able to resist illegal drug use than nonreligious youths.[63] Interestingly, participation seems to be a more significant inhibitor of crime than merely having religious beliefs and values. That is, actually attending religious services has a more dramatic effect on behavior than merely holding religious beliefs.[64] Figure 7.1 summarizes the various views of how socialization influences behavioral choices.

CONNECTIONS

One aspect of the peer effect on crime and delinquency is the development of gangs. Chapter 6 showed how law-violating peer groups exist in all levels of the social strata, from rural counties to metropolitan areas. The number of gangs and gang members has been increasing in recent years.

FIGURE 7.1
The Complex Web of Social
Processes that Controls
Human Behavior

Social learning theory
Criminal behavior is
learned through human
interaction.

Social control theory
Human behavior is
controlled through
close associations with
institutions and individuals.

**SOCIAL
PROCESS
APPROACH**

**Social reaction theory
(labeling theory)**
People given negative labels by
authority figures accept those
labels as a personal identity,
setting up a self-fulfilling
prophecy.

Social Learning Theories

L05 Contrast social learning, social control, and social reaction (labeling) theories.

Social learning theorists believe that crime is a product of learning the norms, values, and behaviors associated with criminal activity. Social learning can involve the actual techniques of crime (how to steal a car, sell drugs, or engage in identity theft) as well as the psychological aspects of criminality (how to deal with the guilt or shame associated with illegal activities).

Learning negative attitudes and beliefs can start early in life. Some kids become jaundiced, pessimistic, and cynical early in their adolescence. They learn to trust no one, take a dim view of their future, and figure out that the only way to get ahead in life is to break social rules. Their life experience teaches them a contemptuous view of accepted social rules. Learning to disparage conventional norms increases the probability of their engaging in criminal behavior. Criminologists Ronald Simons and Callie Burt find that persistent exposure to antagonistic social circumstances and lack of exposure to positive conditions increase the chances of someone developing social schemas involving a hostile view of relationships. Embracing these schemas fosters situational definitions that lead to actions that are aggressive, opportunistic, and criminal. According to Simons and Burt, learning to distrust the world and the people in it, to embrace a here-and-now orientation, and to discount prohibitions against deviance is what drives people into a criminal way of life.[65]

This section briefly reviews three of the most prominent forms of social learning theory: differential association theory, differential reinforcement theory, and neutralization theory.

Differential Association Theory

differential association theory
The view that people commit crime when their social learning leads them to perceive more definitions favoring crime than favoring conventional behavior.

One of the most prominent social learning theories is Edwin H. Sutherland's **differential association theory**. Often considered the preeminent US criminologist, Sutherland first put forth his theory in 1939 in *Principles of Criminology*.[66] The final version of the theory appeared in 1947. When Sutherland died in 1950, his long-time associate Donald Cressey continued his work until his own death in 1987.

Sutherland believed crime was a function of a learning process that could affect any individual in any culture. Acquiring a behavior is a socialization process, not a political or legal process. Skills and motives conducive to crime are learned as a result of contact with procrime values, attitudes, and definitions and other patterns of criminal behavior.

PRINCIPLES OF DIFFERENTIAL ASSOCIATION Sutherland and Cressey explain the basic principles of differential association as follows:[67]

- *Criminal behavior is learned.* This statement differentiates Sutherland's theory from prior attempts to classify criminal behavior as an inherent characteristic of criminals. Sutherland implies that criminality is learned in the same manner as any other learned behavior, such as writing, painting, or reading.

- *Criminal behavior is learned as a by-product of interacting with others.* An individual does not start violating the law simply by living in a criminogenic environment or by manifesting personal characteristics associated with criminality, such as low IQ or family problems. People actively learn as they are socialized and interact with other individuals who serve as teachers and guides to crime. Some kids may meet and associate with criminal "mentors" who teach them how to be successful criminals and to reap the greatest benefits from their criminal activities.[68] Criminality cannot occur without the aid of others.

- *Learning criminal behavior occurs within intimate personal groups.* People's contacts with their most intimate social companions—family, friends, and peers—have the greatest influence on their development of deviant behavior and an antisocial attitude. Relationships with these influential individuals color and control the way individuals interpret everyday events.

- *Learning criminal behavior involves assimilating the techniques of committing crime, including motives, drives, rationalizations, and attitudes.* Novice criminals learn from their associates the proper way to pick a lock, shoplift, and obtain and use narcotics. They must learn the proper terminology for their acts and acquire approved reactions to law violations. Criminals must learn how to react properly to their illegal acts, such as when to defend them, when to rationalize them, and when to show remorse.

- *The specific direction of motives and drives is learned from perceptions of various aspects of the legal code as favorable or unfavorable.* Because the reaction to social rules and laws is not uniform across society, people constantly meet others who hold different views on the utility of obeying the legal code. Some people admire others who may openly disdain or flout the law or ignore its substance. People experience what Sutherland calls **culture conflict** when they are exposed to opposing attitudes toward right and wrong or moral and immoral. The conflict of social attitudes and cultural norms is the basis for the concept of differential association.

- *A person becomes a criminal when he or she perceives more favorable than unfavorable consequences to violating the law.* According to Sutherland's theory, individuals become law violators when they are in contact with persons, groups, or events that produce an excess of definitions favorable toward criminality and are isolated from counteracting forces. A definition favorable toward criminality occurs, for example, when a person hears friends talking about the virtues of getting high on drugs. A definition unfavorable toward crime occurs when friends or parents demonstrate their disapproval of crime.

- *Differential associations may vary in frequency, duration, priority, and intensity.* Whether a person learns to obey the law or to disregard it is influenced by the quality of that person's social interactions. Those of lasting duration have greater influence than those that are brief. Similarly, frequent contacts have greater effect than rare, haphazard contacts. "Priority" means the age of children when they first encounter definitions of criminality. Contacts made early in life probably have more

Fred R. Conrad/New York Times/Redux Pictures

Do kids learn delinquent attitudes and values from their parents? According to differential association, they do, and that may be why Bernard Peters and his son Scott have shared a cell for the last 18 years at the Elmira Correctional Facility in New York. In the summer of 1995, they embarked on a brief but violent string of robberies that netted them $2,900 in cash. Among their victims was Mary Halloran, 61, the manager of a Salvation Army thrift shop. The Peterses shot and robbed Halloran in the parking lot of the store as she carried a bag filled with $726 to her car.

culture conflict
Result of exposure to opposing norms, attitudes, and definitions of right and wrong, moral and immoral.

influence than those developed later. Finally, "intensity" is generally interpreted to mean the importance and prestige attached to the individuals or groups from whom the definitions are learned. The influence of a father, mother, or trusted friend far outweighs that of more socially distant figures.

- *The process of learning criminal behavior by association with criminal and anticriminal patterns involves all of the mechanisms that are involved in any other learning process.* Learning criminal behavior patterns is similar to learning nearly all other patterns and is not a matter of mere imitation.

- *Although criminal behavior expresses general needs and values, it is not excused by those general needs and values, because noncriminal behavior expresses the same needs and values.* This principle suggests that the motives for criminal behavior cannot logically be the same as those for conventional behavior. Sutherland rules out such motives as desire to accumulate money or social status, personal frustration, and low self-concept as causes of crime because they are just as likely to produce noncriminal behavior, such as getting a better education or working harder on a job. Only the learning of deviant norms through contact with an excess of definitions favorable toward criminality produces illegal behavior.

In sum, differential association theory holds that people learn criminal attitudes and behavior during their adolescence from close, trusted friends or relatives. A criminal career develops if learned antisocial values and behaviors are not matched or exceeded by the conventional attitudes and behaviors the individual learns. Criminal behavior, then, is learned in a process that is similar to learning any other human behavior.

TESTING DIFFERENTIAL ASSOCIATION THEORY Studies testing differential association theory have found it predicts a variety of criminal behavior patterns, ranging from schoolyard bullying to domestic violence.[69]

Learning from parents is related to criminal behaviors in children: Adolescents who receive more effective parenting, who grow up in homes where conventional behavior is the norm, are less likely to have delinquent attitudes, associate with delinquent peers, or engage in delinquent behaviors.[70]

We know that crime is intergenerational; a number of studies have found that parental deviance has a powerful influence on delinquent behavior.[71] Kids whose parents are deviant and criminal are more likely to become criminals themselves and eventually to produce criminal children.[72] In sum, the more that kids are involved with criminal parents, the more likely they are to commit crime, suggesting a pattern of learning rather than inheritance.[73]

The effect of peer influence also supports differential association. Learning from deviant friends is highly supportive of delinquency, regardless of race and/or class.[74] Deviant peer groups help support and sustain criminal involvement. Youths who believe their legitimate aspirations are blocked by negative social forces such as school failure and limited economic opportunities turn to deviant peers as a mechanism of social mobility. In such circumstances, gangs provide an effective and efficient social organization in which to sell drugs and engage in delinquent behavior.[75]

People who engage in antisocial activities also perceive and believe that their best friends and close associates engage in antisocial activities as well.[76] Kids who are "followers" will soon learn to copy the behaviors of more popular "leaders," even if it means engaging in illegal behaviors.[77] Deviant peers interfere with the natural process of aging out of crime by providing the support that keeps kids in criminal careers.[78] Romantic partners who engage in antisocial activities may influence their partner's behavior, which suggests that partners learn from one another.[79] Adolescents with deviant romantic partners are more delinquent than those youths with more prosocial partners, regardless of friends' and parents' behavior.[80]

ANALYSIS OF DIFFERENTIAL ASSOCIATION THEORY Differential association theory is important because it does not specify that criminals come from a disorganized area or are members of the lower class. Outwardly law-abiding, middle-class parents can encourage delinquent behavior by their own drinking, drug use, or family violence. The influence of differential associations is not dependent on social class; deviant learning experiences can affect youths in all classes.[81]

There are, however, a number of valid criticisms of Sutherland's work. It fails to account for the origin of criminal definitions. How did the first "teacher" learn criminal attitudes and definitions in order to pass them on? Another criticism of differential association theory is that it assumes criminal and delinquent acts to be rational and systematic. This ignores spontaneous, wanton acts of violence and damage that appear to have little utility or purpose, such as the isolated psychopathic killing that is virtually unsolvable because of the killer's anonymity and lack of delinquent associations.

Some critics suggest that the reasoning behind the theory is circular: How can we know when a person has experienced an excess of definitions favorable toward criminality? When he or she commits a crime! Why do people commit crime? When they are exposed to an excess of criminal definitions!

The Profiles in Crime feature looks at a well-known case involving the concepts of differential association theory.

PROFILES IN CRIME

THE AFFLUENZA CASE

On June 15, 2013, Ethan Couch, a 16-year-old Texas boy, killed four people while driving drunk. It seems that Couch and seven friends had been drinking for hours before the crash. At around 11:45 P.M., the intoxicated teens were in a Ford F350 pickup going 70 mph (30 over the speed limit) when Couch swerved off the road and into a stalled SUV on the roadside, throwing the owner and three good Samaritans who were trying to help her get the car going 60 yards in the air. They were killed on impact; kids driving with Couch were severely injured. Couch was three times over the legal alcohol limit when he slammed into the victims.

What was unusual about the case was that Couch was sentenced to a decade of probation even though prosecutors had sought a maximum sentence of 20 years in prison. One reason for the light sentence was that during his trial, a defense psychologist testified that Couch suffered from "affluenza"—in other words, on the night of the crash he did not understand the consequences of his actions because his parents had taught him that wealth buys privilege and he could do anything he wanted without consequences.

After trial, Couch was sent to a state rehabilitation facility which required the family to only pay $1,100 per month, leaving taxpayers to pay the remaining bill for his therapy. The facility offers a 90-day treatment program that included horseback riding, mixed martial arts, massage, cookery classes, a swimming pool, and basketball.

But that was not the end of the saga of Ethan Couch. On December 2, 2015, a video was found showing Couch at a party where alcohol was being served, a clear violation of his probation agreement. The next day Ethan was contacted by his probation officer and told to report for a drug test. Instead of complying, his mother, Tonya, withdrew $30,000 from her bank account and the two fled to Mexico. A directive to apprehend Couch for a probation violation was issued, and the two were taken into custody in the Mexican resort city of Puerto Vallarta. Tonya Couch was deported and jailed on a charge of hindering the apprehension of a felon. In February 2016, the case was transferred to the adult court system where Ethan Couch was placed on probation until 2024 and required to serve four consecutive terms of 180 days (a total of two years) in jail, as punishment regarding his original drunk driving case from 2013 in light of his recent trip to Mexico.

The Couch case illustrates the belief that the way we are brought up or socialized can have long-term influence over behavior. If we are to believe the defense, Couch learned that his wealth shielded him from responsibility for his actions, freeing him to engage in deviant and criminal behaviors. And the state reinforced these values by granting him a lenient sentence and subsidizing his rehabilitation costs. Who could blame him if he walked away believing that his parents were correct, that he was privileged? ■

Sources: Hunter Stuart, "Ethan Couch, 'Affluenza' Teen, Facing 5 Lawsuits," *Huffington Post*, December 12, 2013, http://www.huffingtonpost.com/2013/12/18/ethan-couch-affluenza-lawsuits-car-crash-texas_n_4461585.html; Ramit Plushnick-Masti, "'Affluenza' Isn't a Recognized Diagnosis, Experts Say After 'Brat' Spared from Jail in Drunk Driving Case," *National Post*, December 12, 2013, http://news.nationalpost.com/2013/12/12/affluenza-defence-used-to-protect-teen-driver-who-killed-four-was-never-meant-to-be-used-in-court-expert-says/; *USA Today*, "'Affluenza' Teen Ethan Couch Transferred to Adult Jail," http://www.usatoday.com/story/news/nation-now/2016/02/06/affluenza-teen-ethan-couch-jail-time-adult/79920884/. (URLs accessed May 2017.)

Differential Reinforcement Theory

First proposed by Ronald Akers in collaboration with Robert Burgess in 1966, differential reinforcement theory is a version of the social learning view that employs both differential association concepts and elements of psychological learning theory.[82]

According to Akers, the same process is involved in learning both deviant and conventional behavior. People learn to be neither "all deviant" nor "all conforming," but rather strike a balance between the two opposing poles of behavior. This balance is usually stable, but it can undergo revision over time.

A number of learning processes shape behavior. Direct conditioning, also called **differential reinforcement**, occurs when behavior is reinforced by being either rewarded or punished while interacting with others. **Negative reinforcement** occurs when the rate of a behavior increases because an aversive event or stimulus is removed or prevented from happening. If a person discovers that drinking heavily results in a severe and painful hangover, he or she can switch to coffee and soft drinks in order to avoid the pains associated with binge drinking; the negative stimulus is removed. Positive reinforcement occurs when a pleasurable result is linked to a particular behavior: studying hard results in getting an A on a test, encouraging a student to continue to study in order to receive more As.

According to Akers, people learn to evaluate their own behavior through their interactions with significant others and groups in their lives. These groups control sources and patterns of reinforcement, define behavior as right or wrong, and provide behaviors that can be modeled through observational learning. The more individuals learn to define their behavior as good or at least as justified, rather than as undesirable, the more likely they are to engage in that behavior. Adolescents who join a peer group whose members value drugs and alcohol, encourage their use, and provide opportunities to observe people abusing substances will be encouraged, through this social learning experience, to use drugs themselves.[83]

Akers's theory suggests that the principal influence on behavior comes from "those groups that control individuals' major sources of reinforcement and punishment and expose them to behavioral models and normative definitions." The important groups are the ones with which a person is in differential association—peer and friendship groups, schools, churches, and similar institutions. Within the context of these critical groups, according to Akers, "deviant behavior can be expected to the extent that it has been differentially reinforced over alternative behavior . . . and is defined as desirable or justified." Once people are indoctrinated into crime, their behavior can be reinforced by being exposed to deviant behavior models—associating with deviant peers—without being subject to negative reinforcements for their antisocial acts. The deviant behavior, originally executed by imitating someone else's behavior, is sustained by social support. Kids who engage in computer crime and computer hacking may find their behavior reinforced by peers who are playing the same game.[84] Similarly, adolescents whose deviant behavior (recreational drug use) is reinforced by significant others (parents and/or peers) are more likely to accelerate their rates of deviance than those who do not receive reinforcements.[85]

Neutralization Theory

Neutralization theory is identified with the writings of Gresham Sykes and his associate David Matza.[86] These criminologists also view the process of becoming a criminal as a learning experience. They theorize that law violators must learn and master techniques that enable them to neutralize conventional values and attitudes, which enables them to drift back and forth between illegitimate and conventional behavior.

Neutralization theory points out that even the most committed criminals and delinquents are not involved in criminality all the time; they also attend schools, family functions, and religious services. Thus, their behavior falls along a continuum between total freedom and total restraint. This process of **drift**, or movement from one extreme to another, produces behavior that is sometimes unconventional or deviant and at other times constrained and sober.[87] Learning **neutralization techniques** equips

---

differential reinforcement
Behavior is reinforced by being either rewarded or punished while interacting with others; also called direct conditioning.

negative reinforcement
Using either negative stimuli (punishment) or loss of reward (negative punishment) to curtail unwanted behaviors.

neutralization theory
The view that law violators learn to neutralize conventional values and attitudes, enabling them to drift back and forth between criminal and conventional behavior.

drift
Movement in and out of delinquency, shifting between conventional and deviant values.

neutralization techniques
Methods of rationalizing deviant behavior, such as denying responsibility or blaming the victim.

a person to temporarily drift away from conventional behavior and become involved in antisocial behaviors, including crime and drug abuse.[88]

NEUTRALIZATION TECHNIQUES Sykes and Matza suggest that people develop a distinct set of justifications for their law-violating behavior. Several observations form the basis of their theoretical model:[89]

- *Criminals sometimes voice guilt over their illegal acts.* If they truly embraced criminal or antisocial values, criminals would probably not exhibit remorse for their acts, apart from regret at being apprehended.
- *Offenders frequently respect and admire honest, law-abiding persons.* Those admired may include entertainers, sports figures, priests and other members of the clergy, parents, teachers, and neighbors.
- *Criminals define whom they can victimize.* Members of similar ethnic groups, churches, or neighborhoods are often off-limits. This practice implies that criminals are aware of the wrongfulness of their acts.
- *Criminals are not immune to the demands of conformity.* Most criminals participate in the same social functions as law-abiding people, such as school, church, and family activities. Few engage in illegal activity all the time.

Sykes and Matza conclude that criminals must first neutralize accepted social values before they are free to commit crimes; they do so by learning a set of techniques that allow them to counteract the moral dilemmas posed by illegal behavior.[90] Through their research, Sykes and Matza have identified the following techniques of neutralization:

- *Denial of responsibility.* Young offenders sometimes claim that their unlawful acts are not their fault—that such acts result from forces beyond their control or are accidents.
- *Denial of injury.* By denying the injury their acts cause, criminals neutralize illegal behavior. For example, stealing is viewed as borrowing; vandalism is considered mischief that has gotten out of hand. Offenders may find that their parents and friends support their denial of injury. In fact, parents and friends may claim that the behavior was merely a prank, which helps affirm the offender's perception that crime can be socially acceptable.
- *Denial of the victim.* Criminals sometimes neutralize wrongdoing by maintaining that the crime victim "had it coming." Vandalism may be directed against a disliked teacher or neighbor, or a gang may engage in gay bashing.
- *Condemnation of the condemners.* An offender views the world as a corrupt place with a dog-eat-dog code. Because police and judges are on the take, teachers show favoritism, and parents take out their frustrations on their children, offenders claim it is ironic and unfair for these authorities to condemn criminal misconduct. By shifting the blame to others, criminals repress their awareness that their own acts are wrong.
- *Appeal to higher loyalties.* Novice criminals often argue that they are caught in the dilemma of being loyal to their peer group while attempting to abide by the rules of society. The needs of the group take precedence because group demands are immediate and localized.

In sum, neutralization theory states that people neutralize conventional norms and values by using excuses that enable them to drift into crime (see Figure 7.2).

TESTING NEUTRALIZATION THEORY Attempts have been made to verify neutralization theory empirically, but the results have been inconclusive.[91] One area of research has been directed at determining whether law violators really need to neutralize moral constraints. The thinking behind this research is that if criminals hold values in opposition to accepted social norms, there is really no need to neutralize. So far, the evidence is mixed. Some studies show that law violators approve of criminal behavior such as theft and violence, whereas other studies yield evidence that even though

FIGURE 7.2
Techniques of Neutralization

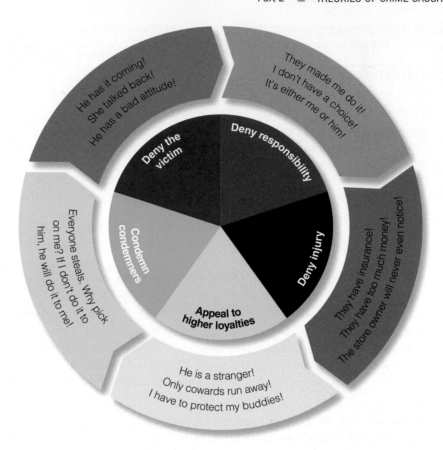

they may be active participants themselves, criminals voice disapproval of illegal behavior.[92] Some studies indicate that law violators approve of social values such as honesty and fairness; other studies support the opposite conclusion.[93]

Although the existing research findings are ambiguous, the weight of the evidence suggests that most adolescents generally disapprove of deviant behaviors such as violence, and that neutralizations do in fact enable youths to engage in socially disapproved behavior.[94] And, as Matza predicted, people seem to drift into and out of antisocial behavior, rather than being committed solely to a criminal way of life.[95] As the Policies and Issues in Criminology feature suggests, even white-collar offenders seem to use neutralization techniques.

DO CRIMINALS REALLY NEUTRALIZE? Not all criminologists accept Matza's vision. Volkan Topalli conducted in-depth interviews with active criminals in St. Louis, Missouri, and found that street criminals living in disorganized, gang-ridden neighborhoods "disrespect authority, lionize honor and violence, and place individual needs above those of all others." Rather than having to neutralize conventional values in order to engage in deviant ones, these offenders do not experience guilt that requires neutralizations; they are "guilt free." There is no need for them to "drift" into criminality, Topalli finds, because their allegiance to nonconventional values and their lack of guilt perpetually leave them in a state of openness to crime. Rather than being embarrassed, they take great pride in their criminal activities and abilities. In fact, rather than neutralizing conventional values, these street kids embrace criminal values: they are expected to be bad and have to explain good behavior! Street criminals are expected to seek vengeance if they themselves are the target of theft or violence. If they don't, their self-image is damaged and they look weak and ineffective. If they decide against vengeance, they must neutralize their decision by convincing themselves that they are being merciful out of respect for their enemies' friends and family.[96]

Policies and Issues in Criminology

WHITE-COLLAR NEUTRALIZATION

Do white-collar criminals use neutralization techniques before engaging in business crimes? To find out, Paul M. Klenowski interviewed 40 inmates in federal custody who had been convicted of white-collar crimes.

Klenowski found that, like common-law criminals, white-collar offenders routinely used neutralizations before committing law violations. The most commonly used technique for all offenders was the appeal to higher loyalties. Those using this technique believed they committed their crimes for the betterment of others, namely family and friends. One inmate, incarcerated for his wrongdoings in the investment industry, told Klenowski:

> My parents never really supported me. So, I guess when I was committing my acts, I believed that maybe I was doing some of this for my family. I wanted to have the time and the financial security to be around my family to make sure I would be there for my children, so I guess family also subconsciously played into why I did what I did.

The denial-of-injury technique was the second most frequently offered account by participants. Some explained that "nobody is getting hurt," "it's only money," or "I am only borrowing it." One respondent incarcerated for bribery said, "I wasn't stealing from anybody. I didn't take that money. It wasn't for me." Some claimed that they did not intend to cause any real harm and if given more time they would have paid their victims back in full.

It was not uncommon for the offenders to redirect the focus of their own actions toward those whom they felt unfairly condemned or judged their actions. Those who used this technique typically pointed out hypocrisy within the government that allowed them to carry out their illicit activities. Some said the laws are too strict and almost force people to be criminals if they are going to make any money. "Why," one asked, "should we follow regulations that the government itself does not follow?"

Another common white-collar neutralization technique was to put blame for crime onto the victims: victims were deserving of victimization. The offenders were actually the "real" victim and the person they were stealing from "had it coming" for the way they had treated others. Greedy corporations and banks should not be considered victims because of their prior actions of preying on individuals. Some felt it was okay to cheat on their taxes because the government did things they disagreed with, such as legalize abortion. Why give tax money to an organization that will only spend it on disagreeable activities?

Many participants claimed they should not be held responsible for the commission of their crimes because their actions were the result of social conditions or bad advice from others whom they trusted. They blamed the business culture or their colleagues for their decision to engage in their trust-violating behavior.

Those using the defense of necessity claimed to be in a desperate situation—their crimes were born out of need, not greed. They had no choice. One told how she was desperate for money—her husband was ill and had filed bankruptcy—and she only committed crime so her family could stay in their home.

Offenders using the defense-of-necessity technique often coupled it with the fulfilling of the caregiver role (i.e., the appeal to higher loyalties). They claimed that the necessity of their crimes was heightened because of their desire to protect or shield their family from harm.

Some of the neutralizations seemed unique to white-collar crime. Offenders claimed that what they did was common business practice, and their crimes were justifiable because others in their respective industries were committing the same types of behaviors with impunity. They had to commit crime to keep up with the competition. Others simply felt that they worked so hard they were entitled to a greater share of profit than they were actually getting. One engaged in theft because the boss denied her a raise to which she felt entitled; she compensated herself through larceny. When participants were asked what had allowed them to psychologically cross that moral and legal boundary to commit their individual acts, all of those using this technique indicated that their legitimate efforts were not meeting their financial expectations. Thus, they were entitled to the extra benefits they obtained.

Where did they learn to use these techniques? Most of the research sample said that they learned both the knowledge of how to and the language necessary to pacify the feelings of guilt prior to the commission of their crimes from coworkers or colleagues. Thus, neutralizations can be learned through interaction with others, especially coworkers and colleagues in the field.

Critical Thinking

Do you believe that people learn and assimilate neutralization techniques prior to committing crime, or are they actually rationalizations formulated after the act to explain away their illegal acts? In other words, are neutralizations a cause or an effect of crime?

Source: Paul Klenowski, "'Learning the Good with the Bad: Are Occupational White-Collar Offenders Taught How to Neutralize Their Crimes?" *Criminal Justice Review* 37 (2012): 461–477.

Evaluating Learning Theories

Learning theories contribute significantly to our understanding of the onset of criminal behavior. Nonetheless, the general learning model has been criticized. One complaint is that learning theorists fail to account for the origin of criminal definitions. How did the first criminal learn the necessary techniques and definitions? Who came up with the original neutralization technique?

Learning theories imply that people systematically learn techniques that enable them to be active, successful criminals. However, as Topalli's research indicates, street criminals may be proud of their felonious exploits and have little need to neutralize their guilt. Learning theory also fails to adequately explain spontaneous, wanton acts of violence, damage, and other expressive crimes that appear to have little utility or purpose. Although principles of differential association can easily explain shoplifting, is it possible that a random shooting is caused by excessive deviant definitions? It is estimated that about 70 percent of all arrestees were under the influence of drugs and alcohol when they committed their crimes. Do "crackheads" pause to neutralize their moral inhibitions before mugging a victim? Do drug-involved kids stop to consider what they have learned about moral values? Little evidence exists that people learn the techniques that enable them to become criminals before they actually commit criminal acts. It is equally plausible that people who are already deviant seek others with similar lifestyles to learn from. Early onset of deviant behavior is now considered a key determinant of criminal careers. It is difficult to see how very young children have had the opportunity to learn criminal behavior and attitudes within a peer group setting.

Despite these criticisms, learning theories have an important place in the study of delinquent and criminal behavior. They help explain the role that peers, family, and education play in shaping criminal and conventional behaviors. If crime were a matter of personal traits alone, these elements of socialization would not play such an important part in determining human behavior. And unlike social structure theories, learning theories are not limited to explaining a single facet of antisocial activity; they explain criminality across all class structures. Even corporate executives may be exposed to procrime definitions and learn to neutralize moral constraints. Learning theories can thus be applied to a wide variety of criminal activity.

Social Control Theory

Social control theorists maintain that all people have the potential to violate the law and that modern society presents many opportunities for illegal activity. Criminal activities, such as drug abuse and car theft, are often exciting pastimes that hold the promise of immediate reward and gratification.

Considering the attractions of crime, social control theorists question why people obey the rules of society. They argue that people obey the law because behavior and passions are controlled by internal and external forces. Some individuals have **self-control**—a strong moral sense that renders them incapable of hurting others and violating social norms.

Other people have been socialized to have a **commitment to conformity**. They have developed a real, present, and logical reason to obey the rules of society, and they instinctively avoid behavior that will jeopardize their reputation and achievements.[97] The stronger people's commitment to conventional institutions, individuals, and processes, the less likely they are to commit crime. If that commitment is absent, there is little to lose, and people are free to violate the law.[98]

Hirschi's Social Control Theory

The version of control theory articulated by Travis Hirschi in his influential 1969 book *Causes of Delinquency* is today the dominant version of control theory.[99] Hirschi links the onset of criminality to weakening of the ties that bind people to society. He assumes that all individuals are potential law violators, but most are kept under control

self-control
A strong moral sense that renders a person incapable of hurting others or violating social norms.

commitment to conformity
Obedience to the rules of society and the avoidance of nonconforming behavior that may jeopardize an individual's reputation and achievement.

According to Hirschi's version of social control theory, having a strong bond to society helps neutralize the lure of delinquency. Here, Normandy High School senior Eboni Boykin talks with her mother, Lekista Flurry, about her day at school before heading to her job at Johnny Rockets in St. Louis. Boykin spent a lot of time in homeless shelters, and her family moved so often she could barely keep track of the schools she's attended. But that didn't stop the teenager from pursuing her dream of attending an Ivy League school. Despite a childhood with enough hardship to last several lifetimes, Boykin's hard work and perseverance paid off, and she was given a full scholarship to attend Columbia University in New York.

because they fear that illegal behavior will damage their relationships with friends, family, neighbors, teachers, and employers. Without these social bonds, or ties, a person is free to commit criminal acts. Across all ethnic, religious, racial, and social groups, people whose bond to society is weak may fall prey to criminogenic behavior patterns. People who care little for others are the ones most likely to prey upon them.

Hirschi argues that the social bond a person maintains with society is divided into four main elements: attachment, belief, commitment, and involvement (see Figure 7.3).

- Attachment consists of a person's sensitivity to and interest in others.[100] Hirschi views parents, peers, and schools as the important social institutions with which a person should maintain ties. Of these, attachment to parents is the most important.
- Commitment involves the time, energy, and effort expended in conventional actions such as getting an education and saving money for the future. If people build a strong commitment to conventional society, they will be less likely to

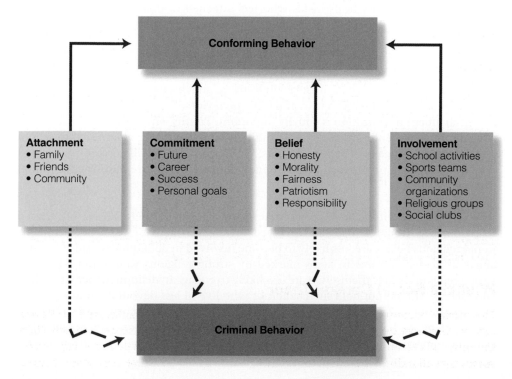

FIGURE 7.3
Elements of the Social Bond

engage in acts that jeopardize their hard-won position. Conversely, the lack of commitment to conventional values may foreshadow a condition in which risk-taking behavior, such as crime, becomes a reasonable behavior alternative.

- People who live in the same social setting often share common moral beliefs; they may adhere to such values as sharing, sensitivity to the rights of others, and admiration for the legal code. If these beliefs are absent or weakened, individuals are more likely to participate in antisocial or illegal acts.
- Involvement in conventional activities such as sports, clubs, and school leaves little time for illegal behavior. Hirschi believes that involvement in school, recreation, and family insulates people from the lure of criminal behavior. Idleness, on the other hand, enhances that lure.

Hirschi further suggests that the interrelationship among the elements of the social bond controls subsequent behavior. People who feel kinship and sensitivity to parents and friends should be more likely to adopt and work toward legitimate goals. A person who rejects such social relationships is more likely to lack commitment to conventional goals. Similarly, people who are highly committed to conventional acts and beliefs are more likely to be involved in conventional activities.

Testing Social Control Theory: Supportive Research

One of Hirschi's most significant contributions to criminology was his attempt to test the principal hypotheses of social control theory. He administered a detailed self-report survey to a sample of more than 4,000 junior and senior high school students in Contra Costa County, California.[101] In a detailed analysis of the data, Hirschi found considerable evidence to support the control theory model society.

Even when the statistical significance of Hirschi's findings was less than he expected, the direction of his research data was notably consistent. Only rarely did his findings contradict the theory's most critical assumptions. Hirschi's version of social control theory has been corroborated by numerous research studies showing that delinquent youths often feel detached from society.[102] What are some of the most important findings?

ATTACHMENT Kids who are attached to their families, friends, and school are less likely to get involved in a deviant peer group and consequently are less likely to engage in criminal activities.[103] Kids who feel attached to their parents, especially if they are authoritative and respected, are the ones less likely to engage in antisocial behaviors.[104] In contrast, unattached kids are more likely to get involved in a deviant peer group and consequently prone to engage in criminal activities.[105] Attachment is significant regardless of gender or family structure.[106] Even if a family is shattered by divorce or separation, a child must retain a strong attachment to one or both parents in order to avoid involvement with antisocial behaviors.[107]

Attachment to education is equally important. Youths who are detached from the educational experience are at risk of criminality; those who are committed to school are less likely to engage in delinquent acts.[108] Detachment and alienation from school may be even more predictive of delinquency than school failure and/or educational underachievement.[109]

BELIEF Research efforts have shown that holding positive beliefs is inversely related to criminality. Children who are involved in religious activities and hold conventional religious beliefs are less likely to become involved in delinquency and substance abuse.[110] Teens who live in areas marked by strong religious values and who hold strong religious beliefs themselves are less likely to engage in delinquent activities than adolescents who do not hold such beliefs or who live in less devout communities.[111]

According to Per-Olof H. Wikstrom's Situational Action Theory (SAT), if people are socialized to have a strong sense of morality, when confronted or exposed to criminal opportunity, their sense of ethics and principles will guide their behavior.

FACT OR FICTION?

"Idle hands are the devil's workshop" is not merely an old saying. Getting involved in sports and other activities helps prevent crime and delinquency.

FACT Old sayings are sometimes accurate. Kids who are involved in conventional leisure activities, such as supervised social activities and noncompetitive sports, are less likely to engage in delinquency.

This **moral filtering** process means that there are internal boundaries that guide and shape the way people make choices. People with a strong moral sense cannot imagine crime as a viable or acceptable behavioral alternative even when facing an immediate situation in which a less moral person might turn to illegal actions.[112] And if they do commit crime, they may be filled with remorse and regret, emotions that may prevent them from repeating their criminal activities.[113]

moral filtering
The process of making socially and morally responsible decisions.

COMMITMENT As predicted by Hirschi, kids who are committed to school and educational achievement are less likely to become involved in delinquent behaviors than those who lack such commitment.[114] The association may be reciprocal: kids who drink and engage in deviant behavior are more likely to fail in school; kids who fail in school are more likely to later drink and engage in deviant behavior.[115]

INVOLVEMENT Research shows that youths who are involved in conventional leisure activities, such as supervised social activities and noncompetitive sports, are less likely to engage in delinquency than those who are involved in unconventional leisure activities and unsupervised, peer-oriented social pursuits.[116] Although there are gender differences in involvement, members of both sexes are less likely to commit crime if they are engaged in conventional activities.[117]

Critiquing Social Control Theory

Few theoretical models in criminology have garnered as much attention as Hirschi's social control theory. And although there is a great deal of supportive research, a number of questions have been raised about the validity of his work.

THE INFLUENCE OF FRIENDSHIP One significant concern is Hirschi's contention that delinquents are detached loners whose bond to friends has been broken. A number of researchers have argued that delinquents seem not to be "lone wolves" whose only personal relationships are exploitive; rather, their friendship patterns seem quite close to those of conventional youths.[118] Some types of offenders, such as drug abusers, have been found to maintain even more intimate relations with their peers than nonabusers do.[119] Hirschi would counter that what appears to be a close friendship is really a relationship of convenience and that "birds of a feather flock together" only when it suits their criminal activities. His view is supported by a number of research studies that question the influence of peers and suggest that deviant youth do not accurately perceive their friends' behavior and that their perceptions of peer deviance influence their own behavior.[120] It comes as no surprise, then, that most juvenile offenses are committed by individuals acting alone and that group offending, when it does occur, is incidental and of little importance to explaining the onset of delinquency. Committed delinquents, as Hirschi suggests, may truly be "lone wolves."[121]

FAILURE TO ACHIEVE Hirschi argues that commitment to career and economic advancement reduces criminal involvement. But he does not deal with the issue of failure: what about kids who are committed to the future but fail in school and perceive few avenues for advancement? Some research indicates that people who are committed to success but fail to achieve it may be crime prone.[122]

DEVIANT INVOLVEMENT Adolescents who report high levels of involvement, which Hirschi suggests should reduce delinquency, actually engage in high levels of criminal behavior. Typically, these are teenagers who are involved in activities outside the home without parental supervision.[123] Teens who spend a lot of time hanging out with their friends, unsupervised by parents and/or other authority figures, and who own cars that give them the mobility to get into even more trouble, are the ones most likely to get involved in antisocial acts such as drinking and taking drugs.[124] This is especially true of dating relationships: teens who date, especially if they have multiple partners, are the ones who are likely to get into trouble and engage in delinquent acts.[125] It is possible that although involvement is important, it depends on the behavior in which a person is involved!

DEVIANT PEERS AND PARENTS Perhaps the most controversial of Hirschi's conclusions is that any form of social attachment is beneficial, even attachment to deviant peers and parents. Despite Hirschi's claims, there is evidence that rather than deterring youths from delinquency, attachment to deviant peers and parents may support and nurture antisocial behavior.[126] A number of research efforts have found that youths attached to drug-abusing parents are more likely to use drugs themselves.[127] Attachment to deviant family members, peers, and associates may help motivate youths to commit crime and facilitate their antisocial acts.[128]

MISTAKEN CAUSAL ORDER Hirschi's theory proposes that a weakened bond leads to delinquency, but there is evidence that the chain of events may flow in the opposite direction: youngsters who break the law find that their bonds to parents, schools, and society are weakened.[129] *Increases* in adolescent behavior problems, such as substance abuse, may result in *decreases* in parental control and support. Attachment to parents may actually weaken *after* kids get involved in delinquency and not vice versa.[130]

While antisocial behavior may fray parents' nerves, even the most distraught may not totally abandon their delinquent kids. Sonja Siennick found that young adult offenders receive more parental financial assistance than do their nonoffending peers (and siblings). Parents are not adverse to helping troubled teens even after they have engaged in criminal activity.[131]

These criticisms are important, but Hirschi's views still constitute one of the preeminent theories in criminology.[132] It has been successfully tested using samples of teens in the United States and abroad.[133] Many criminologists consider social control theory the primary way of understanding the onset of youthful misbehavior.

Social Reaction (Labeling) Theory

The third type of social process theory, social reaction theory, also called labeling theory (the two terms are used interchangeably), explains criminal careers in terms of stigma-producing encounters. Social reaction theory has a number of key points:

- *Behaviors that are considered criminal are highly subjective.* Even such crimes as murder, rape, and assault are bad or evil only because people label them as such. The difference between a forcible rape and a consensual sexual encounter often rests on whom the members of a jury believe and how they interpret the events that took place. The difference between an excusable act and a criminal one is often subject to change and modification. Acts such as performing an abortion, using marijuana, possessing a handgun, and gambling have been legal at some times and places and illegal at others.

- *Crime is defined by those in power.* The content and shape of criminal law are defined by the values of those who rule and are not an objective standard of moral conduct. Howard Becker refers to people who create rules as **moral entrepreneurs**. An example of a moral entrepreneur is someone who campaigns against violence in the media and wants laws passed to restrict the content of television shows.

- *Not only acts are labeled but also people.* Labels define not just an act but also the actor. Valued labels, such as "smart," "honest," and "hardworking," suggest overall competence. Sometimes labels are highly symbolic, such as being named "most likely to succeed" or class valedictorian. People who hold these titles are automatically assumed to be leaders who are well on their way to success. Without meeting them, we know that they are hardworking, industrious, and bright. These positive labels can improve self-image and social standing. Research shows that people who are labeled with one positive trait, such as being physically attractive, are assumed to have other positive traits, such as being

moral entrepreneurs
Individuals who create moral rules that reflect the values of those in power rather than any objective, universal standards of right and wrong.

intelligent and competent.[134] In contrast, people who run afoul of the law or other authorities, such as school officials, are given negative labels, including "troublemaker," "mentally ill," and "stupid," that **stigmatize** them and reduce their self-image. Negative labels also define the whole person. People labeled "insane" are also assumed to be dangerous, dishonest, unstable, violent, strange, and otherwise unsound.

- *Both positive and negative labels involve subjective interpretation of behavior.* A "troublemaker" is merely someone whom people label as "troublesome."

These symbolic messages and their interpretation also determine how people view themselves—that is, develop a self-image. More than 100 years ago, Charles Horton Cooley presented his idea of the "looking-glass self": an individual's view of self is formed by interpreting how others in society view him or her; people shape their self-concepts based on their understanding of how they are perceived by others.[135] If we believe others see us as smart, attractive, and appealing, this appraisal will form the basis of our own self-image. If we believe, through thought or action, that people view us as unappealing, foolish, and dangerous, these negative traits will shape our selves.

In a famous statement, Howard Becker sums up the importance of the audience's reaction:

> Social groups create deviance by making rules whose infractions constitute deviance, and by applying those rules to particular people and labeling them as outsiders. From this point of view, deviance is not a quality of the act a person commits, but rather a consequence of the application by others of rules and sanctions to an "offender." The deviant is one to whom the label has successfully been applied; deviant behavior is behavior that people so label.[136]

Even if some acts are labeled as bad or evil, those who participate in them can be spared a negative label. It is possible to take another person's life but not be considered a murderer, because the killing was considered self-defense or even an accident. Acts have negative consequences only when they are labeled by others as being wrong or evil.

Consequences of Labeling

Although a label may be a function of rumor, innuendo, or unfounded suspicion, its adverse impact can be immense. If a devalued status is conferred by a significant other—a teacher, police officer, parent, or valued peer—the negative label may permanently harm the target. The degree to which a person is perceived as a social deviant may affect his or her treatment at home, at work, at school, and in other social situations. Children may find that their parents consider them a bad influence on younger brothers and sisters. School officials may limit them to classes reserved for people with behavioral problems. Likewise, when adults are labeled as "criminal," "ex-con," or "drug addict," they may find their eligibility for employment severely restricted. If the label is bestowed as the result of conviction for a criminal offense, the labeled person may also be subjected to official sanctions ranging from a mild reprimand to incarceration. The simultaneous effects of labels and sanctions reinforce feelings of isolation and detachment.

Public denunciation plays an important part in the labeling process. Condemnation is often carried out in "ceremonies" in which the individual's identity is officially

AP Images/Jeff Chiu

Once labeled deviant, a person's identity becomes damaged. Here, Kenneth Barillas is interviewed under a sign he attached to his home, which is near the residence of sex offender Donald Robinson, in East Palo Alto, California. After being locked away for 25 years for sex crimes, Robinson, now 57 years old, moved to a little block of unassuming homes. The timing was particularly bad. The day before, Philip Garrido's arrest for kidnapping 11-year-old Jaycee Lee Dugard and keeping her for 18 years made headlines around the world. The spotlight was on sex offenders. And Robinson, who had spent 12 years after his release from prison in a state mental hospital for recidivist sex offenders, remained under state-sponsored treatment as an outpatient. His release caused a significant neighborhood reaction despite assurances he was no longer a danger to the community.

stigmatize
To apply negative labeling with enduring effects on a person's self-image and social interactions.

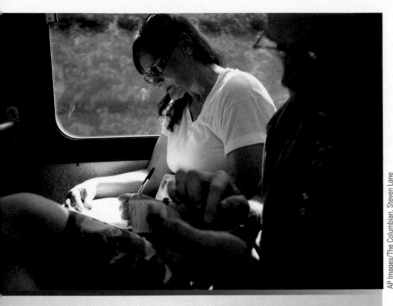

One problem faced by those bearing a criminal label is that it sends a negative message to potential employers. Here, Debra Lepak, who is serving the last 6 months of a 17-month prison sentence, fills out a job application. When the economy is bad and unemployment high, it becomes difficult for those with the ex-con label to find jobs, especially when experienced workers without criminal records are applying for jobs they traditionally wouldn't pursue in a better economy.

transformed. One example of such a reidentification ceremony is a competency hearing in which a person is declared "mentally ill"; another is a public trial in which a person is found to be a "rapist" or "child molester." During the process, a permanent record is produced, such as an arrest or conviction record, so that the denounced person is ritually separated from a place in the legitimate order and set outside the world occupied by citizens of good standing. Harold Garfinkle has called transactions that produce irreversible, permanent labels **successful degradation ceremonies**.[137]

SELF-LABELING According to labeling theory, depending on the visibility of the label and the manner and severity with which it is applied, negatively labeled individuals will become increasingly committed to a deviant career. Labeled persons may find themselves turning for support and companionship to others who have been similarly stigmatized.

Isolated from conventional society, labeled people may identify themselves as members of an outcast group and become locked into deviance. Kids who view themselves as delinquents after being labeled as such are giving an inner voice to their perceptions of how parents, teachers, peers, and neighbors view them. When they believe that others view them as antisocial or as troublemakers, they take on attitudes and roles that reflect this assumption; they expect to become suspects and then to be rejected.[138]

JOINING DEVIANT CLIQUES People labeled as deviant may join with similarly outcast peers who facilitate their behavior. Eventually, antisocial behavior becomes habitual and automatic.[139] The desire to join deviant cliques and groups may stem from self-rejecting attitudes ("At times, I think I am no good at all") that eventually weaken commitment to conventional values and behaviors. In turn, stigmatized individuals may acquire motives to deviate from social norms because they now share a common bond with similarly labeled social outcasts.[140]

RETROSPECTIVE READING Beyond any immediate results, labels tend to redefine the whole person. The label "ex-con" may evoke in people's imaginations a whole series of behavior descriptions—tough, mean, dangerous, aggressive, dishonest, sneaky—that may or may not apply to a particular person who has been in prison. People react to the label and its connotations instead of reacting to the actual behavior of the person who bears it. The labeled person's past is reviewed and reevaluated to fit his or her current status—a process known as **retrospective reading**. Boyhood friends of an assassin or serial killer, interviewed by the media, may report that the suspect was withdrawn, suspicious, and negativistic as a youth; they were always suspicious but never thought to report their concerns to the authorities. According to this retrospective reading, we can now understand what prompted his current behavior; therefore, the label must be accurate.[141]

Labels, then, become the basis of personal identity. As the negative feedback of law enforcement agencies, parents, friends, teachers, and other figures amplifies the force of the original label, stigmatized offenders may begin to reevaluate their own identities (see Figure 7.4). If they are not really evil or bad, they may ask themselves, "Why is everyone making such a fuss?" This process has been referred to as the "dramatization of evil."[142]

successful degradation ceremony
A course of action or ritual in which someone's identity is publicly redefined and destroyed and he or she is thereafter viewed as socially unacceptable.

retrospective reading
The reassessment of a person's past to fit a current generalized label.

Primary and Secondary Deviance

One of the better-known views of the labeling process is Edwin Lemert's concept of primary deviance and secondary deviance.[143] According to Lemert, **primary deviance** involves norm violations or crimes that have little influence on the actor and can be quickly forgotten. A college student successfully steals a textbook at the campus bookstore, gets an A in the course, graduates, is admitted to law school, and later becomes a famous judge. Because his shoplifting goes unnoticed, it is a relatively unimportant event that has little bearing on his future life.

In contrast, **secondary deviance** occurs when a deviant event comes to the attention of significant others or social control agents, who apply a negative label. The newly labeled offender then reorganizes his or her behavior and personality around the consequences of the deviant act. The shoplifting student is caught by a security guard and expelled from college. With his law school dreams dashed and his future cloudy, his options are limited; people say he lacks character, and he begins to share their opinion. He eventually becomes a drug dealer and winds up in prison (see Figure 7.5).

Secondary deviance involves resocialization into a deviant role. The labeled person is transformed into one who, according to Lemert, "employs his behavior or a role based upon it as a means of defense, attack, or adjustment to the overt and covert problems created by the consequent social reaction to him."[144] Secondary deviance produces a **deviance amplification** effect: offenders feel isolated from the mainstream of society and become locked within their deviant role. They may seek others similarly labeled to form deviant groups. Ever more firmly enmeshed in their deviant role, they are trapped in an escalating cycle of deviance, apprehension, more powerful labels, and identity transformation. Lemert's concept of secondary deviance expresses the core of social reaction theory: deviance is a process in which one's identity is transformed. Efforts to control offenders, whether by treatment or punishment, simply help to lock them in their deviant role.

Criminal Careers

Because the process of becoming stigmatized is essentially interactive, labeling theorists blame the establishment of criminal careers on the social agencies originally designed for crime control, such as police, courts, and correctional agencies. These institutions, labeling theorists claim, are inflicting the very stigma that harms the people they are trying to treat or correct. As a result, they actually help to maintain and amplify criminal behavior.

Because crime and deviance are defined by the social audience's reaction to people and their behavior and by the subsequent effects of that reaction, these institutions form the audience that helps define behavior as evil or wrong, locking people into deviant identities.

FIGURE 7.4
The Labeling Process

Initial criminal act
People commit crimes for a number of reasons.

Detection by the justice system
Arrest is influenced by racial, economic, and power relations.

Decision to label
Some are labeled "official" criminals by police and court authorities.

Creation of a new identity
Those labeled are known as troublemakers, criminals, and so on, and are shunned by conventional society.

Acceptance of labels
Labeled people begin to see themselves as outsiders (secondary deviance, self-labeling).

Deviance amplification
Stigmatized offenders are now locked into criminal careers.

primary deviance
A norm violation or crime that has little or no long-term influence on the violator.

secondary deviance
A norm violation or crime that comes to the attention of significant others or social control agents, who apply a negative label that has long-term consequences for the violator's self-identity and social interactions.

deviance amplification
Process whereby secondary deviance pushes offenders out of mainstream society and locks them into an escalating cycle of deviance, apprehension, labeling, and criminal self-identity.

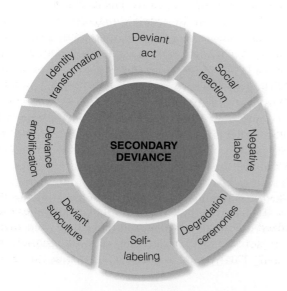

FIGURE 7.5
**Secondary Deviance:
The Labeling Process**

Racial profiling involves the use of race or ethnicity as grounds for suspecting someone of having committed an offense. According to the American Civil Liberties Union (ACLU), racial profiling is patently illegal, violating the Fourteenth Amendment's promise of equal protection under the law to all and the Fourth Amendment's guarantee of freedom from unreasonable searches and seizures. Racial profiling alienates communities from law enforcement, hinders community policing efforts, and causes law enforcement to lose credibility and trust among the people they are sworn to protect and serve.

Differential Enforcement

An important principle of social reaction theory is that the law is differentially applied, benefiting those who hold economic and social power and penalizing the powerless. From the police officer's decision on whom to arrest to the prosecutor's decisions on whom to charge and for how many and what kind of charges, to the court's decision on release or bail, to the grand jury's decision on indictment, to the judge's decision on the length of the sentence, discretion works to the detriment of minorities, including African Americans, Hispanics, Asian Americans, and Native Americans.[145]

The term **racial profiling** has been used to signify that police suspicion is often directed at minority group males.[146] Minorities and the poor are more likely to be prosecuted for criminal offenses and to receive harsher punishments when convicted. Judges may sympathize with white defendants and help them avoid criminal labels, especially if they seem to come from "good families," whereas minority defendants are not afforded that luxury.[147]

There is evidence that from the police officer's decision on whom to arrest, to the prosecutor's decision on whom to charge and how many and what kinds of charges to bring, to the court's decision on whom to release or free on bail or personal recognizance, to the grand jury's decision on indictment, to the judge's decision on sentence length—at every step, discretion works to the detriment of minorities.[148] The fact that labels are unfairly applied has focused attention on such practices as racial profiling. Minority suspects stopped by police are significantly more likely to be arrested than are white suspects.[149]

Race is not the only factor that influences the decision to apply labels. When Chongmin Na studied the effects of dropping out of high school he found that while dropping out did not influence the likelihood of future offending it did in fact escalate the chances a person would be arrested. The conclusion: having an identity damaged by one social institution may intensify the likelihood of future labeling.[150]

racial profiling
The use of racial and ethnic characteristics by police in their determining whether a person is likely to commit a crime or engage in deviant and/or antisocial activities.

Long-Term Effects of Labeling

Empirical evidence shows that negative labels may cause significant long-term damage to both how a person views themselves—self-image—and how they are viewed by others.[151] These effects may be both long-term and cumulative. As they mature, kids who perceive that they have been negatively labeled by significant others, such as peers and teachers, are also more likely to self-report delinquent behavior and to adopt a deviant self-concept.[152] They are likely to make deviant friends and join gangs, associations that escalate their involvement in criminal activities.[153]

Negative labels can plague people over the life course. Children who get involved with the police in adolescence suffer long-term effects of this negative labeling experience well into their 30s. Early police intervention is indirectly related to adult social problems such as substance abuse, unemployment, and welfare receipt.[154] Rather than deter future crime, gaining an arrest record actually produces higher levels of antisocial behaviors.[155] Arrest may amplify a person's "cumulative disadvantage" and trigger exclusionary processes that limit conventional opportunities. In addition to these significant and often overlapping challenges, an extra set of punishments, or "collateral consequences," may be imposed on individuals as a direct result of their criminal convictions. These legal restrictions create barriers to jobs, housing, benefits, and voting.

CONNECTIONS
The Brock Turner case discussed in the opening vignette touched upon this subject. Would he have been treated as deferentially if he were a poor minority group member? Was his lenient sentence the result of "white privilege"?

RESTRICTING OPPORTUNITY One of the damaging long-term effects of deviant labels is the restrictions they place on future economic opportunities. Nearly one-third of American adults have been arrested by age 23.[156] This record will keep many people from obtaining employment, even if they have paid their dues, are qualified for the job, and are unlikely to reoffend. The impact of having a criminal record is most often felt among African Americans, who may already experience racial discrimination in the labor market and are more likely than whites to have a criminal record. Research shows that a criminal record reduces the likelihood of a job callback or offer by approximately 50 percent. This criminal record "penalty" is substantially greater for African Americans than for white applicants. Latinos suffer similar penalties in the employment market. And, regardless of the legal restrictions, when asked, the majority of employers indicate they would "probably" or "definitely" not be willing to hire an applicant with a criminal record.

The National Employment Law Project (NELP) has found frequent use of blanket "no-hire" policies among major corporations. Employers do not want to hire individuals who might commit future crimes and who may be a risk to their employees' and customers' safety. The assumption, of course, is that a prior record signals higher odds that the individual will commit more crimes in the future. NELP argues that removing conviction inquiries from job applications will ease hiring barriers and create a fair chance for those with criminal records to compete for jobs. Known as "ban the box," this change allows employers to judge applicants on their qualifications first, without the stigma of a record. NELP believes that employers should make individualized assessments instead of blanket exclusions and consider the age of the offense and its relevance to the job.[157]

Is Labeling Theory Valid?

Labeling theory has been the subject of much debate among criminologists. Those who criticize it point to its inability to specify the conditions that must exist before an act or individual is labeled deviant—that is, why some people are labeled and others remain "secret deviants." There are also questions about whether stigma produces crime. Labeling often comes after, rather than before, chronic offending. Getting labeled by the justice system and having an enduring criminal record may have little effect on people who have been burdened with social and emotional problems since birth.[158]

While these criticisms are telling, there has been significant research showing that, as the theory predicts, people who suffer official labels are prone to a delinquent and criminal way of life. Recent research by Emily Restivo and Mark Lanier found that official labeling may lead to an increased delinquent self-identity, decreased prosocial expectations, and an increased association with delinquent peers, which then lead to an increased likelihood of engaging in subsequent delinquency. Restivo and Lanier conclude that the labeling process creates a new damaged identity for the individual that places them in the company of other damaged people. The result is they are expected to fail and their association with delinquent peers helps make sure that happens.[159]

Criminologists Raymond Paternoster and Leeann Iovanni have identified features of the labeling perspective that are important contributions to the study of criminality:[160]

- The labeling perspective identifies the role played by social control agents in crime causation. Criminal behavior cannot be fully understood if the agencies and individuals empowered to control and treat it are neglected.
- Labeling theory recognizes that criminality is not a disease or pathological behavior. It focuses attention on the social interactions and reactions that shape individuals and their behavior.
- Labeling theory distinguishes between criminal acts (primary deviance) and criminal careers (secondary deviance) and shows that these concepts must be interpreted and treated differently.

Labeling theory also contributes to understanding crime by focusing on interaction as well as the situation surrounding the crime. Rather than viewing the criminal as a robot-like creature whose actions are predetermined, it recognizes that

CHECKPOINTS

▶ According to labeling theory, stigma helps lock people into deviant careers.

▶ Labels amplify deviant behavior rather than deterring people from future criminality.

▶ Primary deviants view themselves as good people who have done a bad thing; secondary deviants accept a negative label as an identity.

▶ Labels are bestowed in a biased way. The poor and members of minority groups are more likely than others to receive negative labels.

crime often results from complex interactions and processes. The decision to commit crime involves actions of a variety of people, including peers, victim, police, and other key characters. Labels may foster crime by dictating the actions of all parties involved in these criminal interactions. Actions deemed innocent when performed by one person are considered provocative when performed by someone who has been labeled deviant. Similarly, labeled people may become quick to judge, take offense, or misinterpret others' behavior because of past experience.

Social Process Theory and Public Policy

LO6 Link social process theory to crime prevention efforts.

Social process theories have had a major influence on public policy since the 1950s. Learning theories have greatly influenced the way criminal offenders are treated. The effect of these theories has been felt mainly by young offenders, who are viewed as being more salvageable than hardened criminals. Advocates of the social learning approach argue that if people become criminal by learning definitions and attitudes favoring criminality, they can unlearn these attitudes by being exposed to definitions favoring conventional behavior.

This philosophy has been applied in numerous treatment facilities modeled in part on two pioneering efforts: the Highfields Project in New Jersey and the Silverlake Program in Los Angeles. These residential treatment programs, geared toward young male offenders, used group interaction sessions to attack criminal behavior orientations while promoting conventional modes of behavior. It is common today for residential and nonresidential programs to offer similar treatment, teaching children and adolescents to refuse drugs, to forgo delinquent behavior, and to stay in school. It is even common for celebrities to return to their old neighborhoods to urge young people to stay in school or stay off drugs. If learning did not affect behavior, such exercises would be futile.

Control theories have also influenced criminal justice and other social policies. Programs have been developed to increase people's commitment to conventional lines of action. Some focus on trying to create and strengthen bonds early in life before the onset of criminality. The educational system has hosted numerous programs designed to improve students' basic skills and create an atmosphere in which youths will develop a bond to their schools.

Control theory's focus on the family has played a key role in programs designed to strengthen the bond between parent and child. Other programs attempt to repair bonds that have been frayed or broken. Examples of this approach are the career, work furlough, and educational opportunity programs being developed in the nation's prisons. These programs are designed to help inmates maintain a stake in society so they will be less willing to resort to criminal activity after their release.

It is common for community programs to be based on social process principles. Here, on July 8, 2015, Robert Griffin III (aka RGIII) helps kick off the JetBlue airline summer reading initiative Soar with Reading. RGIII helped launch the pilot program that put three customized, one-of-a-kind book vending machines at locations in Washington, DC, to provide free books to kids in the area. The program is designed to help kids and families who have little or no ability to purchase age-appropriate books. Since 2011, JetBlue's Soar with Reading has donated over $1,250,000 worth of books to kids and communities in need. Can such a reading program help socialize kids and insulate them from crime?

AP Images for JetBlue's Soar with Reading Program/John Spaulding

Although labeling theorists caution that too much intervention can be harmful, programs aimed at reconfiguring an offender's self-image may help him or her develop a revamped identity and desist from crime. With proper treatment, labeled offenders can cast off their damaged identities and develop new ones. As a result, they develop an improved self-concept that reflects the positive reinforcement they receive while in treatment.[161]

The influence of labeling theory can also be seen in diversion and restitution programs. **Diversion programs** remove both juvenile and adult offenders from the normal channels of the criminal justice process by placing them in rehabilitation programs. A college student whose drunken driving hurts a pedestrian may, before trial, be placed for six months in an alcohol treatment program. If he successfully completes the program, charges against him will be dismissed; thus he avoids the stigma of a criminal label. Such programs are common throughout the United States. They frequently offer counseling, medical advice, and vocational, educational, and family services.

Another popular label-avoiding program is **restitution**. Rather than face the stigma of a formal trial, an offender is asked either to pay back the victim of the crime for any loss incurred or to do some useful work in the community in lieu of receiving a court-ordered sentence.

Despite their good intentions, stigma-reducing programs have not met with great success. Critics charge that they substitute one kind of stigma for another—for instance, attending a mental health program in lieu of undergoing a criminal trial. In addition, diversion and restitution programs usually screen out violent and repeat offenders. Finally, there is little hard evidence that these alternative programs improve recidivism rates.

Concept Summary 7.1 outlines the major concepts of social process theories.

diversion programs
Programs of rehabilitation that remove offenders from the normal channels of the criminal justice process, thus enabling them to avoid the stigma of a criminal label.

restitution
Permitting an offender to repay the victim or do useful work in the community rather than facing the stigma of a formal trial and a court-ordered sentence.

Concept Summary 7.1   Social Process Theories

Theory	Major Premise	Strengths	Research Focus
Social Learning Theories			
Differential association theory	People learn to commit crime from exposure to antisocial definitions.	Explains onset of criminality. Explains the presence of crime in all elements of social structure. Explains why some people in high-crime areas refrain from criminality. Can apply to adults and juveniles.	Measures definitions toward crime; influence of deviant peers and parents.
Neutralization theory	Youths learn ways of neutralizing moral restraints and periodically drift in and out of criminal behavior patterns.	Explains why many delinquents do not become adult criminals. Explains why youthful law violators can participate in conventional behavior.	Whether people who use neutralizations commit more crimes; beliefs, values, and crime.
Social Control Theory			
Hirschi's control theory	A person's bond to society prevents him or her from violating social rules. If the bond weakens, the person is free to commit crime.	Explains the onset of crime. Can apply to both middle- and lower-class crime. Explains its theoretical constructs adequately so they can be measured. Has been empirically tested.	The association among commitment, attachment, involvement, belief, and crime.
Social Reaction Theory			
Labeling theory	People enter into law-violating careers when they are labeled and organize their personalities around the labels.	Explains society's role in creating deviance. Explains why some juvenile offenders do not become adult criminals. Develops concepts of criminal careers.	Measures the association between self-concept and crime; differential application of labels; the effect of stigma.

Thinking Like a Criminologist

Bound for Trouble The principal of the local high school, a big fan of control theory (she used to be in your class), asks for your opinion on a new policy she intends to propose to the school board. She wants to increase students' bond to education and the school experience by creating three tracks of students: one college bound, another average, and the third for kids who need remedial help. The college-bound students would take advanced math and science, the average track would be reserved for those who plan to forgo college, and the remedial track would offer less-challenging course work and be designed to get the students through high school. She argues that the college-bound students will be recognized for their achievements and rewarded for their efforts, a process that will solidify their bond to the educational experience, all the while insulating them from more disruptive teens.

The principal wants you to comment on her plan. You know that the practice of placing students in tracking programs with preset courses has given way to having students engage in self-tracking: the ability to choose classes that match educational comfort levels. Many schools have totally eliminated nonacademic lower tracks, allowing administrators and school boards to claim that all students are now in college preparatory programs. Nonetheless, some administrators still believe in tracking and covertly maintain the system by steering students to classes that are structured according to the student's innate ability. As a result, students taking AP English and math get a much different educational experience than those in the basic and remedial sections.

Writing Assignment

Write a memo outlining the pros and cons of the three-track plan. What is the major downside of placing kids in tracks? Will it help create or weaken bonds to education? Is it ethical to label kids educationally deficient at a young age? Might that create a self-fulfilling prophecy and encourage them to drop out?

SUMMARY

LO1 Explain the concepts of social process and socialization.
Social process theories view criminality as a function of people's interaction with various organizations, institutions, and processes in society. People in all walks of life have the potential to become criminals if they maintain destructive social relationships. Improper socialization is a key component of crime.

LO2 Discuss the effect of family relationships on crime.
Family dysfunction can lead children to have long-term social problems. Interactions between parents and children provide opportunities for children to acquire or inhibit antisocial behavior patterns. Good parenting, known as parental efficacy, lowers the risk of delinquency for children living in high-crime areas. Parents who closely supervise their children and have close ties with them help reduce the likelihood of adolescent delinquent behavior. Kids who suffer abuse are likely to be deeply affected and externalize problem behavior.

LO3 Describe how the educational setting influences crime.
School failure is linked to delinquency. Kids who are alienated or do poorly in school are more likely to drop out, a decision that can later influence criminality. Minority kids are often the target of school discipline and are more likely to suffer alienation and drop out. School violence and conflict are also problems.

LO4 Summarize the link between peers and delinquency.
Delinquent peers sustain individual offending patterns. Delinquent friends may help kids neutralize the fear of punishment. Both popular kids and loners can have problems.

L05 Contrast social learning, social control, and social reaction (labeling) theories.

Social learning theory suggests that criminal behavior is learned. The most significant model, known as differential association theory, was formulated by Edwin Sutherland. It holds that criminality is a result of a person's perceiving an excess of definitions in favor of crime. Gresham Sykes and David Matza formulated the theory of neutralization, which stresses that youths learn mental techniques that enable them to overcome societal values and hence break the law. In contrast, social control theory maintains that all people have the potential to become criminals, but their bonds to conventional society prevent them from violating the law. Travis Hirschi's social control theory describes the social bond as containing elements of attachment, belief, commitment, and involvement. Weakened bonds allow youths to behave antisocially. Social reaction or labeling theory holds that criminality is promoted by becoming negatively labeled by significant others. Such labels as "criminal," "ex-con," and "junkie" isolate people from society and lock them into lives of crime. Edwin Lemert suggests that people who accept labels are involved in secondary deviance, while primary deviants are able to maintain an undamaged identity.

L06 LInk social process theory to crime prevention efforts.

Social process theories have greatly influenced social policy. They have been applied in treatment orientations as well as community action policies. Some programs teach kids conventional attitudes and behaviors. Others are designed to improve the social bond. Those based on social reaction theory attempt to shield people from criminal labels by diverting them from the system in order to avoid stigma.

Key Terms

socialized 213
social process theory 213
social learning theory 213
social control theory 213
social reaction (labeling)
    theory 213
parental efficacy 214
differential association
    theory 218

culture conflict 219
differential
    reinforcement 222
negative
    reinforcement 222
neutralization theory 222
drift 222
neutralization
    techniques 222

self-control 226
commitment to
    conformity 226
moral filtering 229
moral entrepreneur 230
stigmatize 231
successful degradation
    ceremony 232
retrospective reading 232

primary deviance 233
secondary
    deviance 233
deviance
    amplification 233
racial profiling 234
diversion programs 237
restitution 237

Critical Thinking Questions

1. If criminal behavior is learned, who taught the first criminal?

2. Have you ever been exposed to procrime definitions? How did you handle them? Did they affect your behavior?

3. Which element of Hirschi's theory is supported by the school failure–delinquency link?

4. Have you ever been given a negative label, and, if so, did it cause you social harm? How did you lose the label, or did it become a permanent marker that still troubles you today?

5. If negative labels are damaging, do positive ones help insulate people from crime-producing forces in their environment? Has a positive label ever changed your life?

6. How would a social process theorist explain the fact that many children begin offending at an early age and then desist from crime as they mature? Take for instance differential association and other learning theories. If you learn criminal definitions, how do you "unlearn" them as you mature?

Notes

All URLs accessed May 2017.

1. Veronica Rocha and Richard Winton, "Stanford Rape Sentence Unusually Light, Legal Experts Say," *Los Angeles Times*, June 7, 2016, http://www .latimes.com/local/lanow/la-me-ln-judge-stanford -rape-20160607-snap-story.html; Emanuella Grinberg, "Brock Turner to Leave Jail After Serving 3 Months for Sexual Assault," CNN, September 2, 2016, http://www.cnn.com/2016/09/02/us/brock -turner-release-jail/.

2. Sheldon Glueck and Eleanor Glueck, *Unraveling Juvenile Delinquency* (Cambridge, MA: Harvard University Press, 1950); Ashley Weeks, "Predicting Juvenile Delinquency," *American Sociological Review* 8 (1943): 40–46.

3. Alexander Vazsonyi and Lloyd Pickering, "The Importance of Family and School Domains in Adolescent Deviance: African American and Caucasian Youth," *Journal of Youth and Adolescence* 32 (2003): 115–129; Denise Kandel, "The Parental and Peer Contexts of Adolescent Deviance: An Algebra of Interpersonal Influences," *Journal of Drug Issues* 26 (1996): 289–315; Ann Goetting, "The Parenting– Crime Connection," *Journal of Primary Prevention* 14 (1994): 167–184.

4. Lorine Hughes and James Short, "Partying, Cruising, and Hanging in the Streets: Gangs, Routine Activities, and Delinquency and Violence in Chicago, 1959–1962," *Journal of Quantitative Criminology* 30 (2014): 415–451.

5. Roslyn Caldwell, Jenna Silverman, Noelle Lefforge, and Clayton Silver, "Adjudicated Mexican-American Adolescents: The Effects of Familial Emotional Support on Self-Esteem, Emotional Well-Being, and Delinquency," *American Journal of Family Therapy* 32 (2004): 55–69.

6. Rand Conger, "Evaluation of the Interactionist Model of Socioeconomic Status and Problem Behavior: A Developmental Cascade Across Generations," Center for Poverty Research at UC Davis, http://poverty.ucdavis.edu/research-paper /evaluation-interactionist-model-socioeconomic -status-and-problem-behavior; Rand Conger and Katherine Conger, "Understanding the Processes Through Which Economic Hardship Influences Families and Children," in *Handbook of Families and Poverty*, ed. D. Russell Crane and Tim B. Heaton (Thousand Oaks, CA: Sage Publications, 2008), pp. 64–81.

7. Glen A. Ishoy, "Exploring Morality as a Mediator of the Association Between Parenting Practices and Violent and Property Offending Among a Sample of Juvenile Delinquents," *Crime and Delinquency* 63 (2017): 113–136.

8. John Paul Wright and Francis Cullen, "Parental Efficacy and Delinquent Behavior: Do Control and Support Matter?" *Criminology* 39 (2001): 677–706.

9. Carter Hay, "Parenting, Self-Control, and Delinquency: A Test of Self-Control Theory," *Criminology* 39 (2001): 707–736.

10. Robert Roberts and Vern Bengston, "Affective Ties to Parents in Early Adulthood and Self-Esteem Across 20 Years," *Social Psychology Quarterly* 59 (1996): 96–106.

11. Annie E. Casey Foundation, Kids Count, 2014, http://datacenter.kidscount.org/data/Tables/106 -children-in-single-parent-families.

12. Andre Sourander, Henrik Elonheimo, Solja Niemelä, Art-Matti Nuutila, Hans Helenius, Lauri Sillanmäki, Jorma Piha, Tuulk Tamminen, Kirsti Kumpulkinen, Irma Moilanen, and Frederik Almovist, "Childhood Predictors of Male Criminality: A Prospective Population-Based Follow-Up Study from Age 8 to Late Adolescence," *Journal of the American Academy of Child and Adolescent Psychiatry* 45 (2006): 578–586.

13. Jukka Savolainen, "Relative Cohort Size and Age-Specific Arrest Rates: A Conditional Interpretation of the Easterlin Effect," *Criminology* 38 (2000): 117–136.

14. Daniel Shaw, "Advancing Our Understanding of Intergenerational Continuity in Antisocial Behavior," *Journal of Abnormal Child Psychology* 31 (2003): 193–199.

15. Ryan Meldrum, George Connolly, Jamie Flexon, and Rob Guerette, "Parental Low Self-Control, Family Environments, and Juvenile Delinquency,"

International Journal of Offender Therapy and Comparative Criminology 60 (2016): 1623–1644.

16. Michael Roettger and Raymond Swisher, "Associations of Fathers' History of Incarceration with Sons' Delinquency and Arrest Among Black, White, and Hispanic Males in the United States," *Criminology* 49 (2011): 1109–1148; Marieke van de Rakt, Joseph Murray, and Paul Nieuwbeerta, "The Long-Term Effects of Paternal Imprisonment on Criminal Trajectories of Children," *Journal of Research in Crime and Delinquency* 49 (2012): 81–108.

17. Lauren Porter and Ryan King, "Absent Fathers or Absent Variables? A New Look at Paternal Incarceration and Delinquency," *Journal of Research in Crime and Delinquency* 52 (2015) 414–443.

18. Christopher Uggen and Suzy McElrath, "Parental Incarceration: What We Know and Where We Need to Go," *Journal of Criminal Law and Criminology* 104 (2014): 596–604.

19. Eric Slade and Lawrence Wissow, "Spanking in Early Childhood and Later Behavior Problems: A Prospective Study of Infants and Young Toddlers," *Pediatrics* 113 (2004): 1321–1330; Ronald Simons, Chyi-In Wu, Kuei-Hsiu Lin, Leslie Gordon, and Rand Conger, "A Cross-Cultural Examination of the Link Between Corporal Punishment and Adolescent Antisocial Behavior," *Criminology* 38 (2000): 47–79.

20. Teresa Braga, Leonel Cunha Gonçalves, Miguel Basto-Pereira, and Ângela Maia, "Unraveling the Link Between Maltreatment and Juvenile Antisocial Behavior: A Meta-Analysis of Prospective Longitudinal Studies," *Aggression and Violent Behavior* 33 (2017): 37–50.

21. Jennifer Lansford, Laura Wager, John Bates, Gregory Pettit, and Kenneth Dodge, "Forms of Spanking and Children's Externalizing Behaviors," *Family Relations* 6 (2012): 224–236.

22. Sara Culhane and Heather Taussig, "The Structure of Problem Behavior in a Sample of Maltreated Youths," *Social Work Research* 33 (2009): 70–78.

23. Maureen A. Allwood and Cathy Spatz Widom, "Child Abuse and Neglect, Developmental Role Attainment, and Adult Arrests," *Journal of Research in Crime and Delinquency* 50 (2013): 551–578.

24. Egbert Zavala, "Testing the Link Between Child Maltreatment and Family Violence Among Police Officers," *Crime and Delinquency*, first published online November 22, 2010.

25. Kristi Holsinger and Alexander Holsinger, "Differential Pathways to Violence and Self-Injurious Behavior: African American and White Girls in the Juvenile Justice System," *Journal of Research in Crime and Delinquency* 42 (2005): 211–242; Carolyn Smith and Terence Thornberry, "The Relationship Between Childhood Maltreatment and Adolescent Involvement in Delinquency," *Criminology* 33 (1995): 451–479.

26. Fred Rogosch and Dante Cicchetti, "Child Maltreatment and Emergent Personality Organization: Perspectives from the Five-Factor Model," *Journal of Abnormal Child Psychology* 32 (2004): 123–145.

27. Lynette M. Renner, "Single Types of Family Violence Victimization and Externalizing Behaviors Among Children and Adolescents," *Journal of Family Violence* 27 (2012): 177–186.

28. Todd Herrenkohl, Rick Kosterman, David Hawkins, and Alex Mason, "Effects of Growth in Family Conflict in Adolescence on Adult Depressive Symptoms: Mediating and Moderating Effects of Stress and School Bonding," *Journal of Adolescent Health* 44 (2009): 146–152.

29. Rand Conger, Center for Poverty Research, University of California, Davis, http://poverty.ucdavis.edu/profile/rand-conger.

30. Daniel Seddig, "Crime-Inhibiting, Interactional and Co-Developmental Patterns of School Bonds and the Acceptance of Legal Norms," *Crime and Delinquency*, first published online April 1, 2015.

31. Eugene Maguin and Rolf Loeber, "Academic Performance and Delinquency," in *Crime and Justice: A Review of Research*, Vol. 20, ed. Michael Tonry (Chicago: University of Chicago Press, 1996), pp. 145–264.

32. Jeannie Oakes, *Keeping Track, How Schools Structure Inequality* (New Haven, CT: Yale University Press, 1985).

33. Jessica B. Heppen and Susan Bowles Therriault, "Developing Early Warning Systems to Identify Potential High School Dropouts," National High School Center, http://www.earlywarningsystems.org/wp-content/uploads/2008/07/IssueBrief_EarlyWarningSystemsGuide.pdf.

34. Kimberly Henry, Kelly Knight, and Terence Thornberry, "School Disengagement as a Predictor of Dropout, Delinquency, and Problem Substance Use During Adolescence and Early Adulthood," *Journal of Youth and Adolescence* 41 (2012): 156–166.

35. Allison Ann Payne and Kelly Welch, "Modeling the Effects of Racial Threat on Punitive and Restorative School Discipline Practices," *Criminology* 48 (2010): 1019–1062.

36. Michael Rocques and Raymond Paternoster, "Understanding the Antecedents of the 'School-to-Jail' Link: The Relationship Between Race and School Discipline," *Journal of Criminal Law and Criminology* 101 (2011): 633–665.

37. Department of Education, "New Data from U.S. Department of Education Highlights Educational Inequities Around Teacher Experience, Discipline and High School Rigor," March 6, 2012, http://www.ed.gov/news/press-releases/new-data-us-department-education-highlights-educational-inequities-around-teacher-experience-discipline-and-high-school-rigor.

38. Kerrin C. Wolf and Aaron Kupchik, "School Suspensions and Adverse Experiences in Adulthood," *Justice Quarterly* 34 (2017): 407–430.

39. Anlan Zhang, Lauren Musu-Gillette, and Barbara A. Oudekerk, *Indicators of School Crime and Safety: 2015*, National Center for Educational Statistics, https://nces.ed.gov/pubs2016/2016079.pdf.

40. Joseph G. Kosciw, Emily A. Greytak, Noreen M. Giga, Christian Villenas, and David J. Danischewski, *The 2015 National School Climate Survey: The Experiences of Lesbian, Gay, Bisexual, Transgender, and Queer Youth in Our Nation's Schools* (New York: GLSEN, 2016).

41. Jean Marie McGloin and Wendy Povitsky Stickle, "Influence or Convenience? Disentangling Peer Influence and Co-offending for Chronic Offenders," *Journal of Research in Crime and Delinquency* 48 (2011): 419–447.

42. Callie H. Burt and Carter Rees, "Behavioral Heterogeneity in Adolescent Friendship Networks," *Justice Quarterly*, first published online January 3, 2014.

43. Brooke Miller and Robert G. Morris, "Virtual Peer Effects in Social Learning Theory," *Crime and Delinquency* 62 (2016): 1543–1569.

44. Kyle Thomas, "Delinquent Peer Influence on Offending Versatility: Can Peers Promote Specialized Delinquency?" *Criminology* 5 (2015): 280–308.

45. Guang Guo, Yi Li, Hongyu Wang, Tianji Cai, and Greg J. Duncan, "Peer Influence, Genetic Propensity, and Binge Drinking: A Natural Experiment and a Replication," *American Journal of Sociology* 121 (2015): 914–954.

46. Caterina Gouvis Roman, Meagan Cahill, Pamela Lachman, Samantha Lowry, Carlena Orosco, and Christopher McCarty, with Megan Denver and Juan Pedroza, *Social Networks, Delinquency, and Gang Membership: Using a Neighborhood Framework to Examine the Influence of Network Composition and Structure in a Latino Community* (Washington, DC: Urban Institute, 2012), http://www.urban.org/research/publication/social-networks-delinquency-and-gang-membership.

47. Jean Marie McGloin, "Delinquency Balance and Time Use: A Research Note," *Journal of Research in Crime and Delinquency* 49 (2012): 109–121.

48. Wesley Younts, "Status, Endorsement and the Legitimacy of Deviance," *Social Forces* 87 (2008): 561–590; Amy Anderson and Lorine Hughes, "Exposure to Situations Conducive to Delinquent Behavior: The Effects of Time Use, Income, and Transportation," *Journal of Research in Crime and Delinquency* 46 (2009): 5–34.

49. Sara Battin, Karl Hill, Robert Abbott, Richard Catalano, and J. David Hawkins, "The Contribution of Gang Membership to Delinquency Beyond Delinquent Friends," *Criminology* 36 (1998): 93–116.

50. John Paul Wright and Francis Cullen, "Employment, Peers, and Life-Course Transitions," *Justice Quarterly* 21 (2004): 183–205.

51. Stephanie Dipietro and Jean Marie McGloin, "Differential Susceptibility? Immigrant Youth and Peer Influence," *Criminology* 50 (2012): 711–742; Raymond Paternoster, Jean Marie McGloin, Holly Nguyen, and Kyle Thomas, "The Causal Impact of Exposure to Deviant Peers: An Experimental Investigation," *Journal of Research in Crime and Delinquency*, first published online July 20, 2012.

52. J. C. Barnes and Robert Morris, "Young Mothers, Delinquent Children: Assessing Mediating Factors Among American Youth," *Youth Violence and Juvenile Justice* 10 (2012): 172–189.

53. Gregory Zimmerman and Bob Edward Vásquez, "Decomposing the Peer Effect on Adolescent Substance Use: Mediation, Nonlinearity, and Differential Nonlinearity," *Criminology* 49 (2011): 1235–1272.

54. Frank Weerman, "Delinquent Peers in Context: A Longitudinal Network Analysis of Selection and Influence Effects," *Criminology* 49 (2011): 253–286.

55. Paul Friday, Xin Ren, Elmar Weitekamp, Hans-Jürgen Kerner, and Terrance Taylor, "A Chinese Birth Cohort: Theoretical Implications," *Journal of Research in Crime and Delinquency* 42 (2005): 123–146.

56. Daneen Deptula and Robert Cohen, "Aggressive, Rejected, and Delinquent Children and Adolescents: A Comparison of Their Friendships," *Aggression and Violent Behavior* 9 (2004): 75–104; Stephen W. Baron, "Self-Control, Social Consequences, and Criminal Behavior: Street Youth and the General Theory of Crime," *Journal of Research in Crime and Delinquency* 40 (2003): 403–425.

57. Shelley Keith Matthews and Robert Agnew, "Extending Deterrence Theory: Do Delinquent Peers Condition the Relationship Between Perceptions of Getting Caught and Offending?" *Journal of Research in Crime and Delinquency* 45 (2008): 91–118; Sylvie Mrug, Betsy Hoza, and William Bukowski, "Choosing or Being Chosen by

Aggressive-Disruptive Peers: Do They Contribute to Children's Externalizing and Internalizing Problems?" *Journal of Abnormal Child Psychology* 32 (2004): 53–66.

58. Mark Warr, "Age, Peers, and Delinquency," *Criminology* 31 (1993): 17–40; David Fergusson, L. John Horwood, and Daniel Nagin, "Offending Trajectories in a New Zealand Birth Cohort," *Criminology* 38 (2000): 525–551.

59. Jacob Young, Cesar Rebellon, J. C. Barnes, and Frank Weerman, "Unpacking the Black Box of Peer Similarity in Deviance: Understanding the Mechanisms Linking Personal Behavior, Peer Behavior, and Perceptions," *Criminology* 52 (2014): 60–86.

60. Evelien M. Hoeben and Frank M. Weerman, "Why Is Involvement in Unstructured Socializing Related to Adolescent Delinquency?" *Criminology* 54 (2016): 242–281.

61. Alex R. Piquero, Jeffrey A. Bouffard, Nicole Leeper Piquero, and Jessica M. Craig, "Does Morality Condition the Deterrent Effect of Perceived Certainty Among Incarcerated Felons?" *Crime and Delinquency*, first published online October 20, 2013.

62. Colin Baier and Bradley Wright, "'If You Love Me, Keep My Commandments': A Meta-Analysis of the Effect of Religion on Crime," *Journal of Research in Crime and Delinquency* 38 (2001): 3–21; Byron Johnson, Sung Joon Jang, David Larson, and Spencer De Li, "Does Adolescent Religious Commitment Matter? A Reexamination of the Effects of Religiosity on Delinquency," *Journal of Research in Crime and Delinquency* 38 (2001): 22–44.

63. Sung Joon Jang and Byron Johnson, "Neighborhood Disorder, Individual Religiosity, and Adolescent Use of Illicit Drugs: A Test of Multilevel Hypothesis," *Criminology* 39 (2001): 109–144.

64. T. David Evans, Francis Cullen, R. Gregory Dunaway, and Velmer Burton Jr., "Religion and Crime Reexamined: The Impact of Religion, Secular Controls, and Social Ecology on Adult Criminality," *Criminology* 33 (1995): 195–224.

65. Ronald L. Simons and Callie Harbin Burt, "Learning to Be Bad: Adverse Social Conditions, Social Schemas, and Crime," *Criminology* 49 (2011): 553–598.

66. Edwin H. Sutherland, *Principles of Criminology* (Philadelphia: Lippincott, 1939).

67. See Edwin Sutherland and Donald Cressey, *Criminology*, 8th ed. (Philadelphia: Lippincott, 1970), pp. 77–79.

68. Carlo Morselli, Pierre Tremblay, and Bill McCarthy, "Mentors and Criminal Achievement," *Criminology* 44 (2006): 17–43.

69. Byongook Moon, Hye-Won Hwang, and John McCluskey, "Causes of School Bullying: Empirical Test of a General Theory of Crime, Differential Association Theory, and General Strain Theory," *Crime and Delinquency* 57 (2011): 849–877; John Cochran, Christine Sellers, Valerie Wiesbrock, and Wilson Palacios, "Repetitive Partner Victimization: An Exploratory Application of Social Learning," *Deviant Behavior* 32 (2011): 790–817.

70. Heleen Janssen, Veroni Eichelsheim, Maja Deković, and Gerben Bruinsma, "How Is Parenting Related to Adolescent Delinquency? A Between- and Within-Person Analysis of the Mediating Role of Self-Control, Delinquent Attitudes, Peer Delinquency, and Time Spent in Criminogenic Settings," *European Journal of Criminology* 13 (2016): 169–194.

71. For an early review, see Barbara Wooton, *Social Science and Social Pathology* (London: Allen and Unwin, 1959).

72. Joseph Murray, Rolf Loeber, and Dustin Pardini, "Parental Involvement in the Criminal Justice System and the Development of Youth Theft, Marijuana Use, Depression, and Poor Academic Performance," *Criminology* 50 (2012): 255–312; Michael Roettger and Raymond Swisher, "Associations of Fathers' History of Incarceration with Sons' Delinquency and Arrest Among Black, White, and Hispanic Males in the United States," *Criminology* 49 (2011): 1109–1148; Marieke van de Rakt, Joseph Murray, and Paul Nieuwbeerta, "The Long-Term Effects of Paternal Imprisonment on Criminal Trajectories of Children," *Journal of Research in Crime and Delinquency* 49 (2012): 81–108; Daniel Shaw, "Advancing Our Understanding of Intergenerational Continuity in Antisocial Behavior," *Journal of Abnormal Child Psychology* 31 (2003): 193–199.

73. Terence P. Thornberry, "The Apple Doesn't Fall Far from the Tree (or Does It?): Intergenerational Patterns of Antisocial Behavior—The American Society of Criminology 2008 Sutherland Address," *Criminology* 47 (2009): 297–325; Terence Thornberry, Adrienne Freeman-Gallant, Alan Lizotte, Marvin Krohn, and Carolyn Smith, "Linked Lives: The Intergenerational Transmission of Antisocial Behavior," *Journal of Abnormal Child Psychology* 31 (2003): 171–184.

74. Wesley Church II, Tracy Wharton, and Julie Taylor, "An Examination of Differential Association and Social Control Theory: Family Systems and Delinquency," *Youth Violence and Juvenile Justice* 7 (2009): 3–15.

75. Julia Dickson-Gomez, Maria Pacella, Michelle Renee Broaddus, Katherine Quinn, Carol Galletly, and Justin Rivas, "Convention Versus Deviance: Moral

Agency in Adolescent Gang Members' Decision Making," *Substance Use and Misuse* 52 (2017): 562–573.

76. Ryan Meldrum and Jamie Flexon, "Is Peer Delinquency in the Eye of the Beholder? Assessing Alternative Operationalizations of Perceptual Peer Delinquency," *Criminal Justice and Behavior: An International Journal* 42 (2015): 938–951.

77. Brett Laursen, Christopher Hafen, Margaret Kerr, and Hakin Stattin, "Friend Influence over Adolescent Problem Behaviors as a Function of Relative Peer Acceptance: To Be Liked Is to Be Emulated," *Journal of Abnormal Psychology* 121 (2012): 88–94; Joel Hektner, Gerald August, and George Realmuto, "Effects of Pairing Aggressive and Nonaggressive Children in Strategic Peer Affiliation," *Journal of Abnormal Child Psychology* 31 (2003): 399–412.

78. Warr, "Age, Peers, and Delinquency."

79. Dana Haynie, Peggy Giordano, Wendy Manning, and Monica Longmore, "Adolescent Romantic Relationships and Delinquency Involvement," *Criminology* 43 (2005): 177–210.

80. Robert Lonardo, Peggy Giordano, Monica Longmore, and Wendy Manning, "Parents, Friends, and Romantic Partners: Enmeshment in Deviant Networks and Adolescent Delinquency Involvement," *Journal of Youth and Adolescence* 38 (2009): 367–383.

81. Craig Reinerman and Jeffrey Fagan, "Social Organization and Differential Association: A Research Note from a Longitudinal Study of Violent Juvenile Offenders," *Crime and Delinquency* 34 (1988): 307–327.

82. Ronald Akers, *Deviant Behavior: A Social Learning Approach*, 2nd ed. (Belmont, CA: Wadsworth, 1977).

83. Ronald Akers, Marvin Krohn, Lonn Lanza-Kaduce, and Marcia Radosevich, "Social Learning and Deviant Behavior: A Specific Test of a General Theory," *American Sociological Review* 44 (1979): 638.

84. Robert G. Morris and Ashley G. Blackburn, "Cracking the Code: An Empirical Exploration of Social Learning Theory and Computer Crime," *Journal of Crime and Justice* 32 (2009): 1–34.

85. Jonathan Brauer, "Testing Social Learning Theory Using Reinforcement's Residue: A Multilevel Analysis of Self-Reported Theft and Marijuana Use in the National Youth Survey," *Criminology* 47 (2009): 929–970.

86. Gresham Sykes and David Matza, "Techniques of Neutralization: A Theory of Delinquency," *American Sociological Review* 22 (1957): 664–670; David Matza, *Delinquency and Drift* (New York: John Wiley, 1964).

87. Matza, *Delinquency and Drift*, p. 51.

88. Sykes and Matza, "Techniques of Neutralization"; see also David Matza, "Subterranean Traditions of Youths," *Annals of the American Academy of Political and Social Science* 378 (1961): 116.

89. Sykes and Matza, "Techniques of Neutralization."

90. Ibid.

91. Ian Shields and George Whitehall, "Neutralization and Delinquency Among Teenagers," *Criminal Justice and Behavior* 21 (1994): 223–235; Robert A. Ball, "An Empirical Exploration of Neutralization Theory," *Criminologica* 4 (1966): 22–32. See also M. William Minor, "The Neutralization of Criminal Offense," *Criminology* 18 (1980): 103–120; Robert Gordon, James Short, Desmond Cartwright, and Fred Strodtbeck, "Values and Gang Delinquency: A Study of Street Corner Groups," *American Journal of Sociology* 69 (1963): 109–128.

92. Michael Hindelang, "The Commitment of Delinquents to Their Misdeeds: Do Delinquents Drift?" *Social Problems* 17 (1970): 500–509; Robert Regoli and Eric Poole, "The Commitment of Delinquents to Their Misdeeds: A Reexamination," *Journal of Criminal Justice* 6 (1978): 261–269.

93. Larry Siegel, Spencer Rathus, and Carol Ruppert, "Values and Delinquent Youth: An Empirical Reexamination of Theories of Delinquency," *British Journal of Criminology* 13 (1973): 237–244.

94. Robert Agnew, "The Techniques of Neutralization and Violence," *Criminology* 32 (1994): 555–580.

95. Jeffrey Fagan, *Adolescent Violence: A View from the Street*, NIJ Research Preview (Washington, DC: National Institute of Justice, 1998).

96. Volkan Topalli, "When Being Good Is Bad: An Expansion of Neutralization Theory," *Criminology* 43 (2005): 797–836.

97. Scott Briar and Irving Piliavin, "Delinquency: Situational Inducements and Commitment to Conformity," *Social Problems* 13 (1965–1966): 35–45.

98. Lawrence Sherman and Douglas Smith, with Janell Schmidt and Dennis Rogan, "Crime, Punishment, and Stake in Conformity: Legal and Informal Control of Domestic Violence," *American Sociological Review* 57 (1992): 680–690.

99. Travis Hirschi, *Causes of Delinquency* (Berkeley: University of California Press, 1969).

100. Ibid., p. 231.

101. Ibid., pp. 66–74.

102. Michael Wiatroski, David Griswold, and Mary K. Roberts, "Social Control Theory and Delinquency," *American Sociological Review* 46 (1981): 525–541.

103. Abigail A. Fagan, M. Lee Van Horn, J. David Hawkins, and Thomas Jaki, "Differential Effects of Parental Controls on Adolescent Substance Use: For

Whom Is the Family Most Important?" *Journal of Quantitative Criminology* 29 (2013): 347–368.

104. Rick Trinkner, Ellen S. Cohn, Cesar J. Rebellon, and Karen Van Gundy, "Don't Trust Anyone over 30: Parental Legitimacy as a Mediator Between Parenting Style and Changes in Delinquent Behavior over Time," *Journal of Adolescence* 35 (2012): 119–132.

105. Jennifer Kerpelman and Sondra Smith-Adcock, "Female Adolescents' Delinquent Activity: The Intersection of Bonds to Parents and Reputation Enhancement," *Youth and Society* 37 (2005): 176–200.

106. Tiffiney Barfield-Cottledge, "The Triangulation Effects of Family Structure and Attachment on Adolescent Substance Use," *Crime and Delinquency* 61 (2015): 297–320; Sonia Cota-Robles and Wendy Gamble, "Parent–Adolescent Processes and Reduced Risk for Delinquency: The Effect of Gender for Mexican American Adolescents," *Youth and Society* 37 (2006): 375–392.

107. Barfield-Cottledge, "The Triangulation Effects of Family Structure and Attachment on Adolescent Substance Use."

108. Allison Ann Payne, "A Multilevel Analysis of the Relationships Among Communal School Organization, Student Bonding, and Delinquency," *Journal of Research in Crime and Delinquency* 45 (2008): 429–455.

109. Norman White and Rolf Loeber, "Bullying and Special Education as Predictors of Serious Delinquency," *Journal of Research in Crime and Delinquency* 45 (2008): 380–397.

110. P. Elizabeth Kelly, Joshua Polanin, Sung Joon Jang, and Byron Johnson, "Religion, Delinquency, and Drug Use: A Meta-Analysis," *Criminal Justice Review* 40 (2015): 505–523.

111. Mark Regnerus and Glen Elder, "Religion and Vulnerability Among Low-Risk Adolescents," *Social Science Research* 32 (2003): 633–658; Mark Regnerus, "Moral Communities and Adolescent Delinquency: Religious Contexts and Community Social Control," *Sociological Quarterly* 44 (2003): 523–554.

112. Per-Olof H. Wikstrom, Dietrich Oberwittler, Kyle Treiber, and Beth Hardie, *Breaking Rules: The Social and Situational Dynamics of Young People's Urban Crime* (Oxford, UK: Oxford University Press, 2012).

113. Alex Piquero, "'No Remorse, No Repent': Linking Lack of Remorse to Criminal Offending in a Sample of Serious Adolescent Offenders," *Justice Quarterly* 34 (2017): 350–376.

114. Eugene Maguin and Rolf Loeber, "Academic Performance and Delinquency," *Justice Review* 28 (2003): 254–277.

115. Robert Crosnoe, "The Connection Between Academic Failure and Adolescent Drinking in Secondary School," *Sociology of Education* 79 (2006): 44–60.

116. Jonathan Zaff, Kristin Moore, Angela Romano Papillo, and Stephanie Williams, "Implications of Extracurricular Activity Participation During Adolescence on Positive Outcomes," *Journal of Adolescent Research* 18 (2003): 599–631; Robert Agnew and David Peterson, "Leisure and Delinquency," *Social Problems* 36 (1989): 332–348.

117. Jeb Booth, Amy Farrell, and Sean Varano, "Social Control, Serious Delinquency, and Risky Behavior: A Gendered Analysis," *Crime and Delinquency* 54 (2008): 423–456.

118. Peggy Giordano, Stephen Cernkovich, and M. D. Pugh, "Friendships and Delinquency," *American Journal of Sociology* 91 (1986): 1170–1202.

119. Denise Kandel and Mark Davies, "Friendship Networks, Intimacy, and Illicit Drug Use in Young Adulthood: A Comparison of Two Competing Theories," *Criminology* 29 (1991): 441–467.

120. Young, Rebellon, Barnes, and Weerman, "Unpacking the Black Box of Peer Similarity in Deviance."

121. Lisa Stolzenberg and Stewart D'Alessio, "Co-offending and the Age–Crime Curve," *Journal of Research in Crime and Delinquency* 45 (2008): 65–86.

122. Stephen Cernkovich, Peggy Giordano, and Jennifer Rudolph, "Race, Crime and the American Dream," *Journal of Research in Crime and Delinquency* 37 (2000): 131–170.

123. Velmer Burton, Francis Cullen, T. David Evans, R. Gregory Dunaway, Sesha Kethineni, and Gary Payne, "The Impact of Parental Controls on Delinquency," *Journal of Criminal Justice* 23 (1995): 111–126.

124. Amy Anderson and Lorine Hughes, "Exposure to Situations Conducive to Delinquent Behavior: The Effects of Time Use, Income, and Transportation," *Journal of Research in Crime and Delinquency* 46 (2009): 5–34.

125. Patrick Seffrin, Peggy Giordano, Wendy Manning, and Monica Longmore, "The Influence of Dating Relationships on Friendship Networks, Identity Development, and Delinquency," *Justice Quarterly* 26 (2009): 238–267.

126. Michael Hindelang, "Causes of Delinquency: A Partial Replication and Extension," *Social Problems* 21 (1973): 471–487.

127. Gary Jensen and David Brownfield, "Parents and Drugs," *Criminology* 21 (1983): 543–554. See also M. Wiatrowski, D. Griswold, and M. Roberts,

"Social Control Theory and Delinquency," *American Sociological Review* 46 (1981): 525–541.

128. Leslie Samuelson, Timothy Hartnagel, and Harvey Krahn, "Crime and Social Control Among High School Dropouts," *Journal of Crime and Justice* 18 (1990): 129–161.

129. David Huh, Jennifer Tristan, Emily Wade, and Eric Stice, "Does Problem Behavior Elicit Poor Parenting? A Prospective Study of Adolescent Girls," *Journal of Adolescent Research* 21 (2006): 185–204.

130. Martha Gault-Sherman, "It's a Two-Way Street: The Bidirectional Relationship Between Parenting and Delinquency," *Journal of Youth and Adolescence* 41 (2012): 121–145.

131. Sonja Siennick, "Tough Love? Crime and Parental Assistance in Young Adulthood," *Criminology* 49 (2011): 163–196.

132. Wiatrowski, Griswold, and Roberts, "Social Control Theory and Delinquency."

133. Bryce Elling Peterson, Daiwon Lee, Alana Henninger, and Michelle Cubellis, "Social Bonds, Juvenile Delinquency, and Korean Adolescents," *Crime and Delinquency* 62 (2016): 1337–1363; Özden Özbay and Yusuf Ziya Özcan, "A Test of Hirschi's Social Bonding Theory," *International Journal of Offender Therapy and Comparative Criminology* 50 (2006): 711–726.

134. Linda Jackson, John Hunter, and Carole Hodge, "Physical Attractiveness and Intellectual Competence: A Meta-Analytic Review," *Social Psychology Quarterly* 58 (1995): 108–122.

135. Charles Horton Cooley, *Human Nature and the Social Order* (New York: Scribner's, 1902).

136. Howard Becker, *Outsiders: Studies in the Sociology of Deviance* (New York: Macmillan, 1963), p. 9.

137. Harold Garfinkle, "Conditions of Successful Degradation Ceremonies," *American Journal of Sociology* 61 (1956): 420–424.

138. Stacy DeCoster and Karen Heimer, "The Relationship Between Law Violation and Depression: An Interactionist Analysis," *Criminology* 39 (2001): 799–837.

139. Karen Heimer and Ross Matsueda, "Role-Taking, Role-Commitment and Delinquency: A Theory of Differential Social Control," *American Sociological Review* 59 (1994): 365–390.

140. See, for example, Howard Kaplan and Hiroshi Fukurai, "Negative Social Sanctions, Self-Rejection, and Drug Use," *Youth and Society* 23 (1992): 275–298; Howard Kaplan and Robert Johnson, "Negative Social Sanctions and Juvenile Delinquency: Effects of Labeling in a Model of Deviant Behavior," *Social Science Quarterly* 72 (1991): 98–122; Howard Kaplan, Robert Johnson, and Carol Bailey, "Deviant

Peers and Deviant Behavior: Further Elaboration of a Model," *Social Psychology Quarterly* 30 (1987): 277–284.

141. John Lofland, *Deviance and Identity* (Englewood Cliffs, NJ: Prentice Hall, 1969).

142. Frank Tannenbaum, *Crime and the Community* (New York: Columbia University Press, 1938), pp. 19–20.

143. Edwin Lemert, *Social Pathology* (New York: McGraw-Hill, 1951).

144. Ibid., p. 75.

145. Bruce Western, *Punishment and Inequality in America* (New York: Russell Sage Foundation, 2006); Sara Steen, Rodney Engen, and Randy Gainey, "Images of Danger and Culpability: Racial Stereotyping, Case Processing, and Criminal Sentencing," *Criminology* 43 (2005): 435–468; Stephanie Bontrager, William Bales, and Ted Chiricos, "Race, Ethnicity, Threat and the Labeling of Convicted Felons," *Criminology* 43 (2005): 589–622.

146. Ojmarrh Mitchell and Michael S. Caudy, "Examining Racial Disparities in Drug Arrests," *Justice Quarterly* 32 (2015): 288–313.

147. Christina DeJong and Kenneth Jackson, "Putting Race into Context: Race, Juvenile Justice Processing, and Urbanization," *Justice Quarterly* 15 (1998): 487–504.

148. Carl Pope and William Feyerherm, "Minority Status and Juvenile Justice Processing," *Criminal Justice Abstracts* 22 (1990): 327–336. See also Carl Pope, "Race and Crime Revisited," *Crime and Delinquency* 25 (1979): 347–357; National Minority Council on Criminal Justice, *The Inequality of Justice* (Washington, DC: National Minority Advisory Council on Criminal Justice, 1981), p. 200.

149. Tammy Rinehart Kochel, David Wilson, and Stephen Mastrofski, "Effect of Suspect Race on Officers' Arrest Decisions," *Criminology* 49 (2011): 473–512.

150. Chongmin Na, "The Consequences of School Dropout Among Serious Adolescent Offenders: More Offending? More Arrest? Both?" *Journal of Research in Crime and Delinquency* 54 (2017): 78–110.

151. Howard Kaplan and Robert Johnson, "Negative Social Sanctions and Juvenile Delinquency: Effects of Labeling in a Model of Deviant Behavior," *Social Science Quarterly* 72 (1991): 98–122.

152. Mike Adams, Craig Robertson, Phyllis Gray-Ray, and Melvin Ray, "Labeling and Delinquency," *Adolescence* 38 (2003): 171–186.

153. Jón Gunnar Bernburg, Marvin Krohn, and Craig Rivera, "Official Labeling, Criminal Embeddedness, and Subsequent Delinquency: A Longitudinal Test of Labeling Theory," *Journal of Research in Crime and Delinquency* 43 (2006): 67–88.

154. Robert Morris and Alex Piquero, "For Whom Do Sanctions Deter and Label?" *Justice Quarterly* 30 (2013): 837–868; Giza Lopes, Marvin Krohn, Alan Lizotte, Nicole Schmidt, Bob Edward Vásquez, and Jón Gunnar Bernburg, "Labeling and Cumulative Disadvantage: The Impact of Formal Police Intervention on Life Chances and Crime During Emerging Adulthood," *Crime and Delinquency* 58 (2012): 456–488.

155. Stephanie Ann Wiley, Lee Ann Slocum, and Finn-Aage Esbensen, "The Unintended Consequences of Being Stopped or Arrested: An Exploration of the Labeling Mechanisms Through Which Police Contact Leads to Subsequent Delinquency," *Criminology* 51 (2013): 927–966.

156. This section depends heavily on Amy Solomon, "In Search of a Job: Criminal Records as Barriers to Employment," *NIJ Journal* 270 (2012), https://www.ncjrs.gov/pdffiles1/nij/238488.pdf.

157. National Employment Law Project, "'Ban the Box' Is a Fair Chance for Workers with Records," February 2017, http://www.nelp.org/content/uploads/Ban-the-Box-Fair-Chance-Fact-Sheet.pdf.

158. Megan Kurlychek, Robert Brame, and Shawn Bushway, "Enduring Risk? Old Criminal Records and Predictions of Future Criminal Involvement," *Crime and Delinquency* 53 (2007): 64–83.

159. Emily Restivo and Mark M. Lanier, "Measuring the Contextual Effects and Mitigating Factors of Labeling Theory," *Justice Quarterly* 32 (2015): 116–141.

160. Raymond Paternoster and Leeann Iovanni, "The Labeling Perspective and Delinquency: An Elaboration of the Theory and an Assessment of the Evidence," *Justice Quarterly* 6 (1989): 358–394.

161. Shadd Maruna, Thomas Lebel, Nick Mitchell, and Michelle Maples, "Pygmalion in the Reintegration Process: Desistance from Crime Through the Looking Glass," *Psychology, Crime and Law* 10 (2004): 271–281.

Social Conflict, Critical Criminology, and Restorative Justice

Learning Objectives

LO1 List the core ideas of critical criminology.

LO2 Link globalization to crime and criminality.

LO3 Define the concept of state-organized crime.

LO4 Explain the goals and findings of critical research.

LO5 Articulate the basic ideas of critical feminism.

LO6 Discuss how restorative justice is related to peacemaking criminology.

8

Chapter Outline

FACT OR FICTION?

▶ It is illegal for the police to monitor people in public places with cameras and secretly record their activities.

▶ The CIA has sent terror suspects to foreign prisons where they can be subjected to harsh interrogation tactics.

When billionaire candidate Donald Trump was campaigning for president in 2016, he claimed that America was losing ground and was being brought to heel by outsiders who were undermining the nation. He focused his attention on religious and ethnic minorities, namely calling for a ban on Muslims entering the United States and a wall to be built along the Mexican border to keep out illegal immigrants. He said, "We are not talking about isolation, we're talking about security. We're not talking about religion, we're talking about security. Our country is out of control." "Tens of thousands of people" were entering America with "cell phones with ISIS flags on them." He said he would triple the number of federal agents to enforce immigration laws, end birthright citizenship, and deport more than 11 million illegal immigrants if elected president. "They have to go," Trump said. "What they're doing, they're having a baby. And then all of a sudden, nobody knows . . . the baby's here." Trump said he would get Mexico to construct a wall along the border. If Mexico refuses, a Trump administration would penalize the US ally with measures such as increasing fees on border crossings and visas, imposing tariffs and cutting foreign aid.[1] His critics claimed that his campaign base consisted of disaffected voters who felt abandoned by the government—racists, xenophobes, and others whom his rival Hillary Clinton referred to as a "basket of deplorables."[2]

True to his word, soon after he took office Trump issued an executive order barring people from seven majority-Muslim countries—Iran, Iraq, Syria, Yemen, Somalia, Sudan, and Libya—from entering the United States for 90 days. It also halted refugee resettlement for 120 days and banned Syrian refugees indefinitely; the ban was struck down by a federal court judge. Protests against his policies erupted around the country. ◼

The political conflict that dominated the 2016 election and its aftermath is nothing new or unusual. We live in a world rife with political, social, and economic conflict in nearly every corner of the globe. Conflict comes in many forms, occurs at many levels of society, and involves a whole slew of adversaries: workers and bosses, the United States and its overseas enemies, religious zealots and apostates, citizens and police. It occurs within cities, in neighborhoods, and even within the family.

Conflict can be destructive when it leads to war, violence, and death. It can be functional when it results in positive social change, though sometimes it's hard to distinguish between the two. Take for instance the uprisings referred to as the Arab Spring, which occurred in the Middle East between 2010 and 2014 and brought political and social change to Egypt, Libya, Tunisia, and Syria. While many observers applauded this upheaval, the aftermath left a fractured region. Syria became embroiled in a seemingly never-ending civil war that killed hundreds of thousands of people and displaced millions, causing a major refugee crisis in Europe.[3] The Egyptian military took control of the nation with an iron hand. The Islamic State (IS) was able to take over a huge swath of Syria and Iraq.

Conflict promotes crime by creating a social atmosphere in which the law is a mechanism for controlling dissatisfied, have-not members of society while the wealthy maintain their power. This is why crimes that are the province of the wealthy, such as illegal corporate activities, are sanctioned much more leniently than those, such as burglary, that are considered lower-class activities.

Criminologists who view crime as a function of social conflict are most commonly referred to as **critical criminologists** and their field of study as critical criminology. As their title hints, critical criminologists view themselves as social critics who dig beneath the surface of society to uncover its inequities. They reject the notion that law is designed to maintain a tranquil, fair society and that criminals are malevolent people who wish to trample the rights of others. They believe that the law is an instrument of power, wielded by those who control society in order to maintain their wealth, social position, and class advantage.

Critical criminologists consider acts of racism, sexism, imperialism, unsafe working conditions, inadequate child care, substandard housing, pollution of the environment, and war-making used as a tool of foreign policy to be the "true crimes." The crimes of the helpless—burglary, robbery, and assault—are more often expressions of rage over unjust economic conditions more than actual crimes. Some groups in society, particularly the working class and ethnic minorities, are seen as the most likely to suffer oppressive social relations based on class conflict and racism and hence to be more prone to criminal behavior.

Contemporary critical criminologists try to explain crime within economic and social contexts and to express the connection between social class, crime, and social control. They are concerned with issues such as these:

- The role government plays in creating a criminogenic environment
- The relationship between personal or group power and the shaping of criminal law
- The prevalence of bias in justice system operations
- The relationship between a capitalist, free enterprise economy and crime rates

Critical criminologists reject strictly legal definitions of crime, viewing racism, ageism, sexism, and classism as causing greater social harm than burglary, robbery, and rape.

This chapter briefly reviews the development of critical criminology. It covers its principal ideas, and then looks at policies that have been embraced by critical thinkers that focus on peace and restoration rather than punishment and exclusion. Figure 8.1 illustrates the various independent branches of critical theory.

critical criminologists
Criminologists who believe that the cause of crime can be linked to economic, social, and political disparity.

Origins of Critical Criminology

LO1 List the core ideas of critical criminology.

The roots of critical criminology can be traced to the political-economic vision created by philosopher Karl Marx, who believed that modern capitalism had turned workers into a dehumanized mass who lived an existence that was at the mercy of

FIGURE 8.1
The Branches of Critical Criminology

their employers. Young children were being sent to work in mines and factories from dawn to dusk. Workers were being beaten down by a system that demanded obedience and cooperation and offered little in return. These oppressive conditions led Marx to conclude that the character of every civilization is determined by its mode of production—the way its people develop and produce material goods.

Marx's vision of economic inequality, and the resulting social conflict it produced, had a profound influence on twentieth-century thought. Willem Bonger, Ralf Dahrendorf, and George Vold employed a Marxist perspective to identify the crime-producing social and economic forces in capitalist society. Dutch scholar Bonger proclaimed in his 1916 work *Criminality and Economic Conditions* that in every society that is divided into a ruling class and an inferior class, penal law serves the will of the ruling class. Even though criminal laws may appear to protect members of both classes, hardly any act is punished that does not injure the interests of the dominant ruling class. Crimes, then, are considered to be antisocial acts because they are harmful to

CONNECTIONS

As you may recall
from Chapter 1, the
philosophical and
economic analysis of
Karl Marx forms the
historical roots of the
conflict perspective of
criminology.

those who have the power at their command to control society. Under capitalism, the legal system discriminates against the poor by defending the actions of the wealthy. Because the proletariat are deprived of the materials that are monopolized by the bourgeoisie, they are more likely to violate the law.

However, it was the social ferment of the 1960s that gave birth to critical criminology and placed it within the criminological mainstream. In 1968, a group of British sociologists formed the National Deviancy Conference (NDC). With about 300 members, this organization sponsored several national symposiums and dialogues. Members came from all walks of life, but at its core was a group of academics who were critical of the positivist criminology being taught in British and American universities. More specifically, they rejected the conservative stance of criminologists and their close association with the government that funded many of their research projects. The NDC called attention to ways in which social control might actually cause deviance rather than just being a response to antisocial behavior. Many conference members became concerned about the political nature of social control.

In 1973, critical theory was given a powerful academic boost when British scholars Ian Taylor, Paul Walton, and Jock Young published *The New Criminology*. This brilliant, thorough, and well-constructed critique of existing concepts in criminology called for the development of new methods of criminological analysis and critique. *The New Criminology* became the standard resource for scholars critical of both the field of criminology and the existing legal process. Since its publication, critical criminologists have established a tradition of focusing on the field itself and questioning the role criminology plays in supporting the status quo and collaborating in the oppression of the poor and powerless.

Critical Criminology in the United States

In the United States, scholars were also influenced, during the late 1960s and early 1970s, by the widespread unrest and social change that shook the world. The war in Vietnam, prison struggles, and the civil rights and feminist movements produced a climate in which criticism of the ruling class seemed a natural by-product. Mainstream, positivist criminology was criticized as being overtly conservative, pro-government, and antihuman. Critical criminologists scoffed when their fellow scholars used statistical analysis of computerized data to describe criminal and delinquent behavior. Several influential scholars embraced the idea that the social conflict produced by the unequal distribution of power and wealth was the root cause of crime. William Chambliss and Robert Seidman wrote the well-respected treatise *Law, Order, and Power*, which documented how the justice system protects the rich and powerful. Chambliss and Seidman's work showed how control of the political and economic system affects the way criminal justice is administered and demonstrated that the definitions of crime used in contemporary society favor those who control the justice system.

In *The Social Reality of Crime*, sociologist Richard Quinney also proclaimed that in contemporary society, criminal law represents the interests of those who hold power in society. Where there is conflict between social groups—the wealthy and the poor—those who hold power will create laws that benefit themselves and keep rivals in check. Criminals are not simply social misfits but people who have come up short in the struggle for success and are seeking alternative means of achieving wealth, status, or even survival.

In his numerous works, including *Disobedience and Democracy*, historian and social commentator Howard Zinn forcibly argued that the American criminal justice system was far from just. He lambasted unjust laws and a judicial tyranny that created cruel punishments that treated convicted criminals as less than human. The application of due process, Zinn argued, was counterbalanced by the unchecked discretion and arbitrary judgments of those given state-sanctioned authority over the lives of others.

And of course, greedy white-collar criminals who engage in million-dollar frauds are treated far more leniently than indigent and desperate common-law criminals who commit burglaries and larcenies, even if the social harm they cause is significantly greater.

Contemporary Critical Criminology

Today, critical criminologists devote their attention to a number of important themes and concepts. One is to show how, in our postindustrial, capitalist society, the economic system invariably produces haves and have-nots, shapes social life, and controls behavior. Economic competitiveness increases interpersonal conflict and eventually destabilizes both social institutions and social groups.

Another concern is the widening gap between rich and poor, referred to as *income inequality*. While spending is being cut on social programs for the indigent, corporations are now more powerful than ever and corporate execs more highly paid. According to the prestigious Pew Foundation, the wealth gap between America's high-income group and everyone else has now reached record high levels. Economic predictions show a clear pattern of increasing wealth for the upper-income families and no wealth growth for the middle- and lower-income families. And while the rich are getting richer, conservatives renew their calls for dismantling welfare and health programs, resisting any increase in the minimum wage, increasing tax cuts that favor the wealthy, ending affirmative action, and reducing environmental control and regulation. The result is a growing income inequality that has created both public outrage and political movements such as Occupy Wall Street and Black Lives Matter.

JUSTICE SYSTEM INEQUALITY Trends in the criminal justice system are equally disturbing to critical thinkers. By controlling the justice system, the elites can preserve political-economic, racial, and ethnic domination. Domination is demonstrated in the racism and sexism that still pervade the American justice system and is manifested in a wide variety of justice system practices, ranging from the racial profiling of minorities to discriminatory sentencing practices.

The rapid buildup of the prison system is also seen as the result of draconian criminal laws that threaten civil rights and liberties—the death penalty, three-strikes laws, and especially the decades long "war on drugs" that has resulted in hundreds of thousands of people being incarcerated, most of whom are poor and powerless minority group members. Critical thinkers criticize the use of mass incarceration as a crime control device, fearing that it has racial overtones. In her provocative book *The New Jim Crow: Mass Incarceration in the Age of Colorblindness* (2010), legal scholar Michelle Alexander notes that the number of people in prison has skyrocketed in the past 30 years; there are now more African Americans behind bars than there were slaves at the time of the Civil War. This system of mass incarceration now works as a "tightly networked system of laws, policies, customs, and institutions that operate collectively to ensure the subordinate status of a group defined largely by race." In a sense, the Jim Crow laws, which worked to segregate minorities and prevented them from voting, have been replaced by the war on drugs, which has placed millions behind bars and restricted their civil rights upon release. And when they are released, existing laws prevent convicted felons from gaining employment, education, or housing, obtaining loans, and voting.

How Critical Criminologists Define Crime

According to critical theorists, crime is a political concept designed to protect the power and position of the upper classes at the expense of the poor. Some, but not all, would include in a list of "real" crimes such acts as violations of human rights due to racism, sexism, and imperialism and other violations of human dignity and physical

CHECKPOINTS

▶ Critical criminologists view themselves as social critics who dig beneath the surface of society to uncover its inequities.

▶ They consider acts of racism, sexism, imperialism, and unsafe working conditions to be the "true crimes."

▶ Contemporary critical criminologists try to explain crime within economic and social contexts and to express the connections among social class, crime, and social control.

▶ One of the roots of criminological theory is the political-economic vision created by philosopher Karl Marx.

▶ Even though criminal laws may appear to protect members of both classes, the crimes committed by the dominant ruling class receive more lenient treatment.

▶ Racial and ethnic discrimination causes social conflict and unrest.

needs and necessities. Take for instance what Alette Smeulers and Roelof Haveman call supranational crimes: war crimes, crimes against humanity, genocide, and other human rights violations. Smeulers and Haveman believe that these types of crimes should merit more attention by criminologists, and therefore they call for a separate specialization, **supranational criminology**.[4]

The nature of a society controls the direction of its criminality; criminals are not social misfits but products of the society and its economic system.[5] Criminals are not a group of outsiders who can be controlled by increased law enforcement. Criminality, instead, is a function of social and economic organization. To control crime and reduce criminality, societies must remove the social conditions that promote crime.[6]

In our advanced technological society, those with economic and political power control the definition of crime and the manner in which the criminal justice system enforces the law.[7] Consequently, the only crimes available to the poor are the severely sanctioned "street crimes": rape, murder, theft, and mugging. Members of the middle class cheat on their taxes and engage in petty corporate crime (employee theft), acts that generate social disapproval but are rarely punished severely. The wealthy routinely are involved in corporate acts that should be described as crimes but escape sanctions. Regulatory laws control illegal business activities, but these are rarely enforced, and violations are lightly punished. One reason is that an essential feature of capitalism is the need to expand business and create new markets. This goal often conflicts with laws designed to protect the environment and creates clashes with those who seek their enforcement. In our postindustrial society, the need for expansion usually triumphs. For example, corporate spokespeople and their political allies will brand environmentalists as "tree huggers" who stand in the way of jobs and prosperity.[8]

The rich are insulated from street crimes because they live in areas far removed from crime. Those in power use the fear of crime as a tool to maintain their control over society. The poor are controlled through incarceration, and the middle class is diverted from caring about the crimes of the powerful by their fear of the crimes of the powerless.[9] Ironically, they may have more to lose from the economic crimes committed by the rich than from the street crimes of the poor. Stock market swindles and scams cost the public billions of dollars but are typically settled with fines and probationary sentences.

Because private ownership of property is the true measure of success in American society (as opposed to, say, being a worthy person), the state becomes an ally of the wealthy in protecting their property interests. As a result, theft-related crimes are often punished more severely than are acts of violence because although the former may be interclass, the latter are typically intraclass.

How Critical Criminologists View the Cause of Crime

Critical thinkers believe that the key crime-producing element of modern corporate capitalism is the effort to create **surplus value**—the profits produced by the laboring classes that are accrued by business owners. Once accumulated, surplus value can be either reinvested or used to enrich the owners. To increase the rate of surplus value, workers can be made to toil harder for less pay, be made more efficient, or be replaced by machines or technology. Therefore, economic growth does not benefit all elements of the population, and in the long run it may produce the same effect as a depression or recession.

As the rate of surplus value increases, more people are displaced from productive relationships and the size of the marginal population swells. As corporations downsize to increase profits, high-paying labor and managerial jobs are lost to computer-driven machinery. Displaced workers are forced into service jobs at minimum wage. Many become temporary employees without benefits or a secure position.

supranational criminology
The study of war crimes, crimes against humanity, and the supranational penal system in which such crimes are prosecuted and tried.

surplus value
The Marxist view that the laboring classes produce wealth that far exceeds their wages and goes to the capitalist class as profits.

As more people are thrust outside the economic mainstream, a condition referred to as **marginalization**, a larger portion of the population is forced to live in areas conducive to crime. Once people are marginalized, commitment to the system declines creating another crime-producing force: a weakened bond to society.

The government may be quick to respond during periods of economic decline because those in power assume that poverty breeds crime and social disorder. When unemployment is increasing, public officials assume the worst and devote greater attention to the criminal justice system, perhaps building new prisons to prepare for the coming "crime wave."[10] Empirical research confirms that economic downturns are indeed linked to both crime rate increases and government activities such as passing anticrime legislation.[11] As the level of surplus value increases, so too do police expenditures, most likely because of the perceived or real need for the state to control those on the economic margin.[12]

Scott Olson/Getty Images News/Getty Images

According to critical theory, income inequality occurs when the wealthy classes have the power to control the law, creating conflict and social unrest. On April 14, 2016, in Chicago, demonstrators demanding an increase in the minimum wage protest in front of a McDonald's restaurant. The demonstration was one of about 300 that took place nationwide that day.

Failing Social Institutions

Critical thinkers often focus on contemporary social institutions to show how they operate as instruments of class and racial oppression. Critical scholars find that class bias and racial oppression exist from the cradle to the grave. There are significant race-based achievement differences in education, ranging from scores on standardized tests to dropout and high school completion rates. There are high schools, mostly in poverty-stricken inner-city neighborhoods, where the high school completion rate is 40 percent or less; these are referred to as **dropout factories**. There about 1,000 of these failing schools in the United States. Although they represent only a small fraction of all public high schools in America, they account for about half of all high school dropouts each year.[13] While the number of dropout factories has plummeted along with the dropout rate, the fact that almost a million American children attend failing educational institutions is troubling.

One reason for these persistent problems may be linked to differences in discipline meted out in poor and wealthy districts. Research shows that African American children receive more disciplinary infractions than children from other racial categories, despite the fact that their behavior is quite similar. Having a higher percentage of black students in a school translates into a greater use of disciplinary tactics, a factor that may explain why minority students fare less well and are more likely to disengage from school at a younger age than whites.[14] Critical thinkers might suggest that these class- and race-based burdens make crime inevitable.

Globalization

Globalization, which usually refers to the process of creating transnational markets and political and legal systems, has shifted the focus of critical inquiry to a world perspective. Globalization began when large companies decided to establish themselves in foreign markets by adapting their products or services to the local culture. The process took off with the fall of the Soviet Union, which opened new European markets. The development of China into a super industrial power encouraged foreign investors to take advantage of China's huge supply of workers. Capitalists hailed China's entry into the World Trade Organization in 2001 as a significant economic event.

Despite China's emergence as a world power, critical thinkers point out that the economic boom has significant costs. While wages in China have increased

marginalization
Displacement of workers, pushing them outside the economic and social mainstream.

dropout factories
High schools in which the completion rate is consistently 40 percent or less.

globalization
The process of creating transnational markets, politics, and legal systems in an effort to form and sustain a global economy.

L02 Link globalization to crime and criminality.

steadily over the last decade, hundreds of millions of Chinese workers are still struggling to make a living wage. The cost of living in Chinese cities increases all the time, and the gap between the rich and the poor is constantly growing. The average monthly wage increased from 1,120 yuan in 2010 to 2,190 yuan ($327) in 2016. The minimum wage for most major cities and provincial capitals also doubled, to around 1,600 yuan ($239) per month. In smaller cities and poorer provinces, the monthly minimum wage is about 1,000 yuan, or less than $150. In addition, many thousands of Chinese workers are killed at work each year and millions more disabled.[15]

As the Internet and communication revolution unfolded, companies were able to establish instant communications with their far-flung corporate empires, a technological breakthrough that further aided trade and foreign investments. A series of transnational corporate mergers and takeovers (such as when Ford bought Swedish car maker Volvo in 1999 and then in 2010 sold Volvo to the Chinese car company Geely) produced ever-larger transnational corporations. In some instances, the mergers were designed to avoid paying taxes in the United States. In 2015, Pfizer and the Irish pharmaceutical company Allergan announced a $160 billion merger that created the world's largest drug maker. Though the company is still called Pfizer, with headquarters in New York City, the deal was structured so that Allergan is technically the buyer. The reason is that corporate taxes in Ireland are significantly lower than those in the United States. As a result, tax proceeds from this giant company will go to Ireland even though most of its business is in the United States; Pfizer is subject to a tax rate of more than 25 percent, while Allergan enjoys a 4.8 percent tax rate.[16]

THE DOWNSIDE OF GLOBALIZATION Some experts believe globalization can improve the standard of living in third-world nations by providing jobs and training, but critical theorists question the altruism of multinational corporations. Their motives are exploiting natural resources, avoiding regulation, and taking advantage of desperate workers. When these giant corporations set up a factory in a developing nation, it is not to help the local population but to get around environmental laws and take advantage of needy workers who may be forced to labor in substandard conditions. In some instances, transnational companies take advantage of national unrest and calamity in order to engage in profiteering.[17] While millions have died in African civil unrest, mining operations go on unabated. Conflict diamonds are those sold in order to fund armed conflict and civil war, and profits are in the billions. Conflict diamonds mined in Côte d'Ivoire and Liberia are also being smuggled into neighboring countries and exported as part of the legitimate diamond trade.[18]

Globalization has replaced imperialism and colonization as a new form of economic domination and oppression and now presents, according to critical thinkers, a threat to the world economy:

- Growing global dominance and the reach of the free-market capitalist system, which disproportionately benefits wealthy and powerful organizations and individuals
- Increasing vulnerability of indigenous people with a traditional way of life to the forces of globalized capitalism
- Growing influence and impact of international financial institutions (such as the World Bank) and the related relative decline of power of local or state-based institutions
- Nondemocratic operation of international financial institutions[19]

state-organized crime
Acts defined by law as criminal and committed by state officials, either elected or appointed, in pursuit of their jobs as government representatives.

Globalization may have a profound influence on class relations. Workers in the United States are being replaced in high-paying manufacturing jobs not by machines but by foreign workers. Instant communication via the Internet and global communications, a development that Marx could not have foreseen, has sped the effect immeasurably. Globalization will have a profound effect both on the economy and eventually on crime rates.

Globalization has its downsides. One is environmental threats that occur when capitalists fight to cut costs and increase profits. In efforts to curb pollution, China has become a global leader in establishing renewable energy sources such as wind and solar power. To reduce emissions of carbon dioxide, authorities are pushing to shut down privately owned steel, coal, and other high-polluting factories scattered across rural areas. But in many cases, factory owners merely pay informal "fines" to local inspectors and then reopen. Here, a Chinese laborer loads coal into a furnace as smoke and steam rise from an unauthorized steel factory in Inner Mongolia, China.

Kevin Frayer/Getty Images News/Getty Images

GLOBALIZATION AND CRIME Globalization may be responsible for unrest in financial systems and in so doing has created a fertile ground for contemporary enterprise crimes. By expanding the reach of both criminal and noncriminal organizations, globalization also increases the vulnerability of indigenous people with a traditional way of life.[20] With money and power to spare, criminal enterprise groups can recruit new members, bribe government officials, and even fund private armies. International organized crime has globalized its activities for the same reasons legitimate multinational corporations have expanded around the world: new markets bring new sources of profits.

Technological advances such as efficient and widespread commercial airline traffic, improvements in telecommunications (ranging from the Internet to global cell phone connectivity), and the growth of international trade have all aided the growth in illicit transnational activities. These changes have facilitated the cross-border movement of goods and people, conditions exploited by criminals who now use Internet chat rooms to plan their activities. On a cultural level, globalization brings with it an ideology of free markets and free trade. The cultural shift means less intervention and regulation, conditions exploited by crime groups to cross un-patrolled borders and to expand their activities to new regions of the world. Transnational crime groups freely exploit this new freedom to travel to regions where they cannot be extradited, base their operations in countries with ineffective or corrupt law enforcement, and launder their money in countries with bank secrecy or few effective controls. Globalization has allowed both individual offenders and criminal gangs to gain tremendous operational benefits while reducing risks of apprehension and punishment.

State-Organized Crime

While mainstream criminologists focus on the crimes of the poor and powerless, critical criminologists focus their attention on the law violations of the powerful. One area of concern is referred to as **state-organized crime**—acts defined by law as criminal and committed by state officials, elected or appointed, in pursuit of their jobs as government representatives. Their actions, or in some cases failure to act, amount to a violation of the criminal law they are bound by oath or duty to uphold.

Among the most controversial claims made by critical criminologists are those linking the United States to state-organized crime and violence. Those who study state-organized crime argue that these antisocial behaviors arise from efforts to either maintain governmental power or to uphold the race, class, and gender advantages of those who support the government. In industrial society, the state will do every-thing to protect the property rights of the wealthy while opposing the real interests of

LO3 Define the concept of state-organized crime.

State-organized crimes are criminal acts committed by state officials, both elected and appointed, in pursuit of their jobs as government officials. Here, Hamilton Township Mayor John Bencivengo (center), 58, walks from federal court with his attorney Jerome A. Ballarotto (right), in Trenton, New Jersey, after surrendering to the FBI to face an extortion charge. Federal prosecutors charged Bencivengo with taking $12,400 in bribes in exchange for using his influence over a health insurance contact with the township's school district. Bencivengo served 18 months in federal prison.

the poor. They might even go to war to support the capitalist classes who need the wealth and resources of other nations. The desire for natural resources such as rubber, oil, and metals was one of the primary reasons for Japan's invasion of China and other Eastern nations that sparked their entry into World War II. Fifty years later, the US was accused by many media commentators and political pundits of invading Iraq in order to secure its oil for American use.[21]

Why do states and their representatives get caught up in illegal enterprises such as money laundering and human trafficking. There may be a variety of reasons ranging from gaining revenue to controlling more territory.[22] The categories of state-organized crime are set out in some detail below.[23]

ILLEGAL DOMESTIC SURVEILLANCE In 2013, a leak of documents stolen from the National Security Agency (NSA) by contract employee Edward Snowden set off an international firestorm. Among other things, Snowden's documents revealed that the NSA had programs that gave it access to a vast quantity of emails, chat logs, and other data directly from Internet companies, including Google, Facebook, and Apple. Snowden revealed that the NSA was collecting millions of email and instant messaging contact lists, searching email content, and tracking and mapping the location of cell phones. The NSA was shown to be secretly tapping into Yahoo and Google data centers to collect information from "hundreds of millions" of account holders worldwide by monitoring undersea cables.[24]

Before fleeing to Russia, Edward Snowden's illegal copying and dissemination of NSA documents showed that the US government was engaging in a wide range of domestic and foreign surveillance activities. Among other things, without a warrant the agency was collecting and analyzing the content of communications of foreigners talking to persons inside the United States. They were able to collect data and information off of fiber optic cables used by the communication industry. Was this a crime? The government was quick to point out that the programs were designed to combat terrorism and protect US citizens. While the NSA programs disturbed many people in the United States and abroad, their actions would be considered criminal only if government agents listen in on telephone conversations or intercept emails without proper approval in order to stifle dissent and monitor political opponents.

The dangers of illegal surveillance by government agencies have become magnified because technology now allows snoopers wide latitude to intercept messages and to enter computers through the Internet without being detected. In addition, closed-circuit TV cameras are now routinely used by metropolitan police agencies. Britain employs an estimated 6 million CCTV cameras, one for every 11 citizens. Many cities in the United States, including Washington, New York, Chicago, and Los Angeles, have installed significant numbers of police-operated cameras trained on public spaces. Globally, there are now almost 250 million security cameras in operation.[25] This surveillance capability worries civil libertarians as well as critical criminologists.[26]

HUMAN RIGHTS VIOLATIONS Some governments, such as Iran, routinely deny their citizens basic civil rights, holding them without trial and using "disappearances" and summary executions to rid themselves of political dissidents. The Chinese government has been criticized for taking a heavy hand with the Muslim Uighur minority. The Beijing government claims that its crackdown is necessary to fight separatism and terrorism, but its tactic is to impose discriminatory policies against Uighurs, including prohibitions on wearing beards and veils, restrictions on fasting, and overt discrimination with respect to religious education. Protests against these human rights violations have been repressed. Lawyers and activists have been detained, held in secret, and not allowed to communicate with their families. Families, lawyers, and supporters who inquired about the cases or sought the detainees' release also became targets of state repression.[27]

The United Arab Emirates (UAE) is another government that has been accused of serious human rights problems.[28] The government detains, and in some cases forcibly disappears, individuals who criticize the authorities, and its security forces have used torture against detainees. Most troubling have been allegations that imported foreign workers are used as slave labor. The workers obtain the visas needed to work in the UAE by paying hefty fees to "labor-supply agencies"; many workers sell their homes or land or borrow money at high rates of interest to pay the agencies' fees. Upon arrival in the UAE, the indebted workers—many of whom are illiterate—are required to sign contracts with the construction companies on much worse terms than they had been promised back home, ensuring that their debts can never be paid off. In the worst cases, they are subjected to what may be considered forced labor or virtual slavery. Female domestic workers are excluded from regulations that apply to workers in other sectors.

Another state-organized crime involves the operation of the correctional systems in nations that are notorious for depriving detainees of basic necessities and routinely using hard labor and torture to punish political dissidents. The CIA has made use of these brutal regimes to soften up terror suspects for interrogation and sent suspected terror suspects to secret prisons abroad, without trial or indictment. There they can be subject to harsh interrogation tactics forbidden in the United States.[29]

Is it possible that such human rights violations occur in the United States? Some critical criminologists would agree, especially those concerned with the operations of the justice system. The following Policies and Issues in Criminology feature looks at one of these possible violations and asks the provocative question: are wrongful convictions a state crime?

On September 14, 2016, in New York City, Edward Snowden speaks via video link at a news conference for the launch of a campaign asking President Barack Obama for a pardon. The campaign included representatives from the American Civil Liberties Union, Human Rights Watch, and Amnesty International. ACLU attorney Ben Wizner hoped to have the whistleblower pardoned from charges filed against him under the Espionage Act. Before leaving office, Obama denied the request.

Can terror groups commit state-organized crime? Malala Yousafzai, a 16-year-old girl from Pakistan, was shot in the head by the Taliban in Afghanistan for advocating education for girls. She survived and became an international activist for women's and children's rights; in 2014, she received the Nobel Peace Prize for her work. Can terror groups such as the Taliban and ISIL be considered "states"?

Policies and Issues
in Criminology

ARE WRONGFUL CONVICTIONS
A STATE CRIME?

Before 1990, most lawyers and judges thought that wrongful convictions were extremely rare. The use of DNA profiling to exonerate factually innocent wrongfully convicted prisoners made it clear that wrongful convictions regularly occur. In 2016, the National Registry of Exonerations listed about 1,800 exonerations of innocent prisoners since 1989. Although this is a tiny percentage of all felony convictions, experts believe that about 10,000 wrongful felony convictions occur every year, or about 1 percent of all convictions.

In 1992, Barry Scheck (who gained notoriety by serving on O. J. Simpson's defense team) and Peter Neufeld, two attorneys, formed the Innocence Project in response to their familiarity with both DNA testing and the prospect of wrongful convictions. In collaboration with the Cardozo Law School in New York, the Innocence Project's mission is to exonerate wrongfully convicted persons through DNA testing.

The Innocence Project receives in excess of 200 letters each month from convicted individuals who claim their innocence. Yet the organization has only a handful of attorneys and can take on around 160 cases at a time. To date, more than 240 innocent persons have been freed through DNA testing in the United States. The Innocence Project provided direct representation or critical assistance in most of these cases.

The reasons uncovered for miscarriages of justice have included mistaken eyewitness identification, faulty forensic science, false confessions, police investigation "tunnel vision," perjury by jailhouse snitches and others, police and prosecutorial misconduct, and ineffective assistance of counsel. Jon Gould and John Firman found that the accused's age matters the most: younger defendants are the ones most likely to be falsely convicted. Why is that? First, younger defendants are not as sophisticated as more mature and experienced defendants and were unable to be as helpful to their attorneys in preparing a defense as their older more mature peers. Second, younger defendants are less likely to be employed and thus don't have the kind of corroborating evidence enjoyed by older defendants: They clock into work at a particular time, and there is corroborating evidence that proves they could not have been at the crime scene because "Look, here—I was at work," hence, less false convictions.

A second important factor is having any prior criminal record. Being known to the police or having your photo in a mug shot book means that you are more likely—even if you are innocent—to be erroneously identified and thereafter wrongly convicted.

Does this amount to state crime? A number of criminologists think so. Greg Stratton finds that most false convictions are a function of errors of omission or commission or purposeful obstruction by investigators. Saundra Westervelt and Kimberly Cook found that police, prosecutors, and judges have engaged in activities that fall short of criminal behavior but nonetheless result in convictions of innocent people, including carelessness, sloppiness, shortcutting, cynicism, routine processing, stereotyping, tunnel vision, and/or the presumption of guilt. Westervelt and Cook charge that police create inducements to falsely confess, feed information to witnesses, conduct misleading lineups and photo arrays, lose and contaminate evidence, ignore conflicting evidence or alternative leads due to tunnel vision, and mishandle informants. Prosecutors fail to provide complete files to the defense, lose evidence, mishandle witnesses, use inflammatory and misleading evidence at trial, and intentionally exempt people of color from juries. Westervelt and Cook find that many aspects of false convictions coincide with the concept of state crime: victims are powerless; victimizers generally fail to recognize and understand the nature, extent, and harmfulness of institutional policies; victimizers have a sense of entitlement; illegal state policies and practices are manifestations of the attempt to achieve organizational, bureaucratic, or institutional goals.

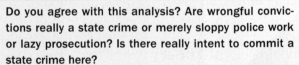

Critical Thinking

Do you agree with this analysis? Are wrongful convictions really a state crime or merely sloppy police work or lazy prosecution? Is there really intent to commit a state crime here?

Sources: Jon Gould and John Firman, "Wrongful Convictions: The Latest Scientific Research and Implications for Law Enforcement," presentation at a National Institute of Justice seminar, March 25, 2013, http://www.jrsa.org/pubs/enews/jrsa-enews-may28-2013 .pdf (accessed April 2017); Greg Stratton, "Wrongfully Convicting the Innocent: A State Crime?" *Critical Criminology* 23 (2015): 21–37; Saundra D. Westervelt and Kimberly J. Cook, "Framing Innocents: The Wrongly Convicted as Victims of State Harm," *Crime Law and Social Change* 53 (2010): 259–275.

STATE-CORPORATE CRIME This type of state-organized crime is committed by individuals who abuse their state authority or who fail to exercise it when working with people and organizations in the private sector. For example, a state environmental agency may fail to enforce laws, resulting in the pollution of public waterways or airways. This oversight can cause significant damage. When Michael Lynch and Kimberly Barrett examined deaths and diseases associated with pollution from coal-fired power plants (CFPPs) they found that the small particle pollution these plants produce cause more deaths in the US each year than homicide.[30] These disasters are not caused by corporations ignoring or violating regulations designed to protect citizens. They are a function of collusion between the state and corporate interests in which states guarantee business operations latitude in conducting operations, such as polluting the environment, in order to further the expansion of the capitalist system and the accumulation of profits. Here the crime is not someone violating state-created rules, but rather the state creating rules that are ultimately harmful and destructive to the average citizen worker while enriching corporate coffers.[31]

State-corporate crime is particularly alarming, considering that regulatory law aimed at controlling private corporations is being scaled back while globalization has made corporations worldwide entities both in production and in advancing the consumption of their products.

STATE VIOLENCE Sometimes nations engage in violence to maintain their power over dissident groups. Army or police officers form death squads—armed vigilante groups that kill suspected political opponents or other undesirables. These groups commit assassinations and kidnappings using extremely violent methods to intimidate the population and deter political activity against the government.

While the use of death squads is common in third-world countries, police violence and use of deadly force are not uncommon in Western industrialized nations. In some nations, almost all political detainees are subjected to torture, including electric shocks, burnings, and severe beating with boots, sticks, plastic bottles filled with water or sand, and heavy rubber-coated cables. Other detainees are subject to psychological pressure, such as threats or imitation of sexual abuse or execution, as well as threats to harm their relatives. The Profiles in Crime feature discusses state-organized crime involving state violence.

Instrumental vs. Structural Theory

Not all critical thinkers share a similar view of society and its control by the means of production. **Instrumental theorists** view criminal law and the criminal justice system solely as instruments for controlling the poor, have-not members of society. They view the state as the tool of capitalists. In contrast, **structural theorists** believe that the law is not the exclusive domain of the rich; rather, it is used to maintain the long-term interests of the capitalist system and to control members of any class who threaten its existence.

Instrumental Theory

According to the instrumental view, the law and justice system serve the powerful and rich and enable them to impose their morality and standards of behavior on the entire society. Those who wield economic power are able to extend their self-serving definition of illegal or criminal behavior to encompass those who might threaten the status quo or interfere with their quest for ever-increasing profits.[32] The concentration of economic assets in the nation's largest industrial firms translates into the political power needed to control tax laws to limit the firms' tax liabilities.[33] Some have the economic clout to hire top attorneys to defend them against antitrust actions, making them almost immune to regulation.

The poor, according to this branch of critical theory, may or may not commit more crimes than the rich, but they certainly are arrested and punished more often. Under the capitalist system, the poor are driven to crime because a natural frustration exists

instrumental theorists
Hold the view that criminal law and the criminal justice system are capitalist instruments for controlling the lower class.

structural theorists
Hold the view that criminal law and the criminal justice system are means of defending and preserving the capitalist system.

PROFILES IN CRIME

RUSSIAN STATE-ORGANIZED CRIME

Russia has not hesitated to send troops to neighboring countries that threaten its hegemony, a practice that amounts to state-organized crime. Its two wars against breakaway province Chechnya went on from the mid-1990s until 2009, when with massive firepower they crushed the separatist rebel groups; hundreds of thousands died during the conflict. Enraged by terrorist attacks by Chechen fighters who attacked targets in the homeland, the Russians created death squads made up of elite Russian special forces commandos who would stop at nothing to find, torture, and kill enemy combatants. Intelligence was often extracted by breaking limbs with a hammer, administering electric shocks, and forcing men to perform sexual acts on one another. The bodies were either buried in unmarked pits or pulverized. The scenes would occasionally be filmed and circulated among enemy combatants as a form of psychological warfare.

In February and March 2014, the independent nation of Ukraine was in turmoil after days and nights of clashes between antigovernment protesters and police that ended with a vote in parliament to oust President Viktor Yanukovych, a close ally and supporter of Russia and its president, Vladimir Putin. The cause of the rioting was the government's rejection of an accord with the European Union in favor of stronger ties with Russia. With a population of 45 million people, a majority of Ukrainians sought ties with the West, something that was considered unacceptable to the Russian president. On February 20, 2014, the streets become a battlefield. At least 77 people were killed and hundreds wounded in clashes between protesters and police, including many shot by uniformed snipers. Russia then sent in troops on the pretext that it was necessary to protect Russian citizens. Most were sent to Ukraine's autonomous republic of Crimea where Russia's Black Sea fleet

is based at Sevastopol. Pro-Russian forces gradually took control of the Crimean peninsula. Soon the Crimean parliament and the city council of Sevastopol adopted a resolution to show their intention of joining the Russian Federation. A vote was held and 96 percent of those who voted in Crimea supported joining Russia. On March 17, 2014, the Crimean parliament officially declared its independence from Ukraine and requested to join the Russian Federation; a day later, President Putin declared Crimea a part of Russia. ■

Sources: Andrew Osborn, "Russia Uses Death Squads and Torture in Chechnya, Says Amnesty," *The Independent*, June 24, 2004, http://www.independent.co.uk/news/world/europe/russia-uses-death-squads-and-torture-in-chechnya-says-amnesty-733296.html; BBC News, "Ukraine Crisis: What's Going On in Crimea," August 12, 2016, http://www.bbc.com/news/world-europe-25182823; Human Rights Watch, "Chechnya: Research Shows Widespread and Systematic Use of Torture," http://hrw.org/english/docs/2006/11/13/russia14557_txt.htm. (URLs accessed April 2017.)

in a society in which affluence is well publicized but unattainable. When class conflict becomes unbearable, frustration can spill out in riots and urban unrest. Because of class conflict, a deep-rooted hostility is generated among members of the lower class toward a social order they are not allowed to shape and whose benefits are unobtainable.[34]

Instrumental theorists consider it essential to **demystify** law and justice—that is, to unmask its true purpose. Criminological theories that focus on family structure,

demystify
To unmask the true purpose of law, justice, or other social institutions.

intelligence, peer relations, and school performance keep the lower classes servile by showing why they are more criminal, less intelligent, and more prone to school failure and family problems than the middle class. Demystification involves identifying the destructive intent of capitalist inspired and funded criminology. Instrumental theory's goal for criminology is to show how capitalist law preserves ruling-class power.[35]

Structural Theory

Structural theorists disagree with the view that the relationship between law and capitalism is unidirectional, always working for the rich and against the poor.[36] If law and justice were purely instruments of the wealthy, why would laws controlling corporate crimes, such as price-fixing, false advertising, and illegal restraint of trade, have been created and enforced?

To a structuralist, the law is designed to keep the system operating efficiently, and anyone, worker or owner, who rocks the boat is targeted for sanction. For example, antitrust legislation is designed to prevent any single capitalist from dominating the system. If the free enterprise system is to function, no single person can become too powerful at the expense of the economic system as a whole. Structuralists would regard the efforts of the US government to break up Microsoft as an example of a conservative government using its clout to keep the system on an even keel. The long prison sentences given to corporate executives who engage in insider trading are a warning to capitalists that they must play by the rules.

Ting Shen/Xinhua/Eyevine/Redux

According to instrumental theory, criminal law and the criminal justice system are capitalist instruments for controlling the lower classes. Here, protesters clash with police during a demonstration that followed the police killing of Laquan McDonald in downtown Chicago. Are the police a tool being used by capitalists to control the lower classes or civil servants attempting to enforce the law?

L04 Explain the goals and findings of critical research.

Research on Critical Criminology

Among the most important research carried out by critical criminologists are studies aimed at determining whether the criminal justice system operates as an instrument of class oppression or as a fair, even-handed social control agency.

Critical researchers have found disturbing evidence that at every stage of justice, criminal members of powerless, disenfranchised groups are treated less favorably than the wealthy and powerful.[37] Those convicted of crime tend to receive stricter sentences if their personal characteristics (single, young, urban, male) show them to be members of the "dangerous classes."[38] Research has found that jurisdictions with significant levels of economic disparity are also the most likely to have large numbers of people killed by police officers. Police may act more forcefully in areas where class conflict creates the perception that extreme forms of social control are needed to maintain order.[39]

Race and Justice

Critical research also shows that racial bias is present in the justice system, beginning with police contact and continuing through arrest, prosecution, and sentencing. As the numbers of racial and ethnic minorities in the population increase, so too do calls for harsher punishments. As you may recall (Chapter 2), the *racial threat hypothesis* states that as the number of minority group members in the community increases, law enforcement agents become more punitive.[40] There are cries for more "law and order" even when crime rates are declining. As a result, charges of racial profiling

CONNECTIONS

The enforcement of laws against illegal business activities such as price fixing, restraint of trade, environmental crimes, and false advertising is discussed in Chapter 12. Although some people are sent to prison for these white-collar offenses, many offenders are still punished with a fine or economic sanction. Should white-collar criminals be sent to prison or merely pay large fines? After all, they are not too dangerous.

have become common. Police are more likely to use racial profiling to stop black motorists as they travel further into the boundaries of predominantly white neighborhoods: black motorists driving in an all-white neighborhood send up a red flag because they are "out of place."[41] All too often these unwarranted stops lead to equally unfair arrests.[42] Police brutality complaints are highest in minority neighborhoods, especially those that experience relative deprivation (African American residents earn significantly less money than the European American majority).[43]

African American defendants are more likely to be prosecuted under habitual offender statutes if they commit crimes where there is a greater likelihood of a white victim—for example, larceny and burglary—than if they commit violent crimes that are largely intraracial; where there is a perceived "racial threat," punishment is enhanced.[44] After conviction, criminal courts also are more likely to dole out harsh punishments to members of powerless, disenfranchised groups.[45] Unemployed racial minorities may be perceived as "social dynamite" who present a real threat to society and must be controlled and incapacitated.[46] States with a substantial minority population have a much higher imprisonment rate than those with predominantly white populations.[47] Critical analysis also shows that despite legal controls the use of the death penalty seems to be skewed against racial minorities.[48]

Taken in sum, critical criminologists claim that these and other studies underpin the foundations of their view: social institutions are designed to favor the rich and powerful and to oppress those who lack economic power and social standing.

Alternative Views of Critical Theory

Critical criminologists are exploring avenues of inquiry that fall outside the traditional models of conflict and critical theories. The following sections discuss in detail some of these alternative views of the conflict approach to crime.

Left Realism

Some critical scholars are now addressing the need for the left wing to respond to the increasing power of right-wing conservatives. They are troubled by the emergence of a strict "law and order" philosophy, which has as its centerpiece a policy of punishing juveniles severely in adult court. At the same time, they find the focus of most left-wing scholarship—the abuse of power by the ruling elite—too narrow. It is wrong, they argue, to ignore inner-city gang crime and violence, which often target indigent people.[49] The approach of **left realism** is most often connected to the writings of British scholars John Lea and Jock Young. In their well-respected 1984 work *What Is to Be Done About Law and Order?* they reject the utopian views of idealists who portray street criminals as revolutionaries.[50] They take the more "realistic" approach that street criminals prey on the poor and disenfranchised, thus making the poor doubly abused, first by the capitalist system and then by members of their own class.

Lea and Young's view of crime causation borrows from conventional sociological theory and closely resembles the relative deprivation approach, which posits that experiencing poverty in the midst of plenty creates discontent and breeds crime. As they put it, "The equation is simple: relative deprivation equals discontent; discontent plus lack of political solution equals crime."[51]

In *Crime in Context: A Critical Criminology of Market Societies,* Ian Taylor recognizes that anyone who expects an instant socialist revolution to take place is simply engaging in wishful thinking.[52] He uses data from both Europe and North America to show that the world is currently in the midst of multiple crises that are shaping all human interaction, including criminality. These crises include lack of job creation, social inequality, social fear, political incompetence and failure, gender conflict, and family and parenting issues. These crises have led to a society in which the government seems incapable of creating positive social change: people have become more fearful and isolated from one another, and some are excluded from the mainstream because of racism and

left realism
An approach that views crime as a function of relative deprivation under capitalism and that favors pragmatic, community-based crime prevention and control.

discrimination; manufacturing jobs have been exported overseas to nations that pay extremely low wages; and fiscal constraints inhibit the possibility of reform. These problems often fall squarely on the shoulders of young black men, who suffer from exclusion and poverty and who now feel the economic burden created by the erosion of manufacturing jobs due to the globalization of the economy. In response, they engage in a form of hypermasculinity, which helps increase their crime rates.[53]

Can the concepts suggested by left realists help explain terrorism? This is the subject of the Policies and Issues in Criminology feature below.

Policies and Issues in Criminology

LEFT REALISM AND TERROR

Left realists typically have focused their attention on street crime and how it affects its targets: lower-class citizens are forced to live in dangerous neighborhoods and communities. Left realist Jennifer Gibbs uses a different lens and applies the basic concepts to explain the motivation for terrorist activity.

Gibbs finds four key elements of left realism that should, if valid, underpin terrorist involvement:

- People are recruited into terrorist organizations because of relative deprivation.
- Terrorist organizations are subcultures that provide peer support.
- Victims/targets are selected based on opportunity/routine activities.
- "Get tough" policies that create a police state may backfire.

Gibbs finds evidence to support the first proposition: terrorists are drawn not from extremely poor populations but from those who realize they have fallen behind other groups. Absolute deprivation (e.g., the inability to provide basic necessities) is not the cause of terrorism; relative deprivation (e.g., being less well off than one's peers) seems to carry more weight, an association predicted by left realism. Feelings of deprivation are exacerbated by new technology. Advancements like the Internet make communication easier, and people can see how much better off others are, increasing the perception of relative deprivation.

Second, left realism theory argues that men who experience stress as a result of relative deprivation and do not have socially appropriate coping mechanisms turn to similarly situated peers who provide support; they often form subcultures. Likewise, terrorist group members seek peer support with like-minded people, forming subcultures supportive of these values or ideology. In today's postmodern world, technology has created the opportunity for virtual peer groups and subcultures. Peer support does not necessarily need to be face to face within groups but can exist in blogs and chat rooms. Those adhering to a particular ideology may find peer support in written communications such as magazines and social media.

Gibbs finds weaker support for the role of opportunity in terrorist activities because they tend to be planned rather than spontaneous events. However, there is some evidence that opportunity plays a role in choosing victims: targeting businesses and citizens is easier than targeting government entities or military installations or personnel. Other reasons may include having the "biggest bang for the buck" by targeting businesses—symbolic of capitalism—or civilians, whose deaths generate widespread attention.

The final proposition of left realism theory addressed by Gibbs is that "get tough" policies will not reduce crime. She notes that left realism focuses on individualized or community-focused responses to crime. Get-tough policies alienate people and legitimate terrorist organizations. The war on terror legitimized groups like al-Qaeda, attracting more terrorism instead of decreasing it. Also, the military response to terrorism is not a deterrent. Military "solutions," in particular, lead to retaliation, generating a cycle of violence because they tend to be reactive rather than proactive. They provide short-term solutions that fail to address the underlying causes that led to terrorism in the first place. Instead, left realism theory directs policy toward minimal official response and maximizing informal social control. With terrorism, attempting to address the underlying grievances may be helpful.

Critical Thinking

Do you agree that the way to fight terror is to address the underlying grievances? Sounds good, but is it truly possible in a world with shifting conflicts and myriad points of view? Can we ever satisfy a terrorist? And would we even if we knew how?

Source: Jennifer Gibbs, "Looking at Terrorism Through Left Realist Lenses," *Crime, Law and Social Change* 54 (2010): 171–185.

CRIME PROTECTION Left realists argue that crime victims in all classes need and deserve protection; crime control reflects community needs. They do not view police and the courts as inherently evil tools of capitalism whose tough tactics alienate the lower classes. In fact, they recognize that these institutions offer life-saving public services. The left realists wish, however, that police would reduce their use of force and increase their sensitivity to the public.[54] They want the police to be more responsive to community needs, end racial profiling, and improve efforts at self-regulation and enforcement through citizen review boards and other control mechanisms.

Preemptive deterrence is an approach in which community organization efforts eliminate or reduce crime before police involvement becomes necessary. The reasoning behind this approach is that if the number of marginalized youths (those who feel they are not part of society and have nothing to lose by committing crime) could be reduced, then delinquency rates would decline.[55]

Although implementing a socialist economy might help eliminate the crime problem, left realists recognize that something must be done to control crime under the existing capitalist system. To develop crime control policies, left realists not only welcome critical ideas but also build on the work of strain theorists, social ecologists, and other mainstream views. Community-based efforts seem to hold the greatest promise of crime control.

Left realism has been criticized by critical thinkers as legitimizing the existing power structure: by supporting existing definitions of law and justice, it suggests that the "deviant" and not the capitalist system causes society's problems. Critics question whether left realists advocate the very institutions that "currently imprison us and our patterns of thought and action."[56] In rebuttal, left realists say that it is unrealistic to speak of a socialist state lacking a police force or a system of laws and justice. They believe the criminal code does, in fact, represent public opinion.

preemptive deterrence
Efforts to prevent crime through community organization and youth involvement.

critical feminism
The study of gender from a critical perspective. It typically involves such issues as the effects of gender inequality and the unequal power of men and women in a capitalist society.

LO5 Articulate the basic ideas of critical feminism.

Critical Feminist Theory: Gendered Criminology

Critical feminist writers have attempted to explain the cause of crime, gender differences in crime rates, and the exploitation of female victims through a gendered lens. **Critical feminism** views gender inequality as stemming from the unequal power of men and women in a capitalist/post-modern society. Some of the most important issues focused on by critical feminist criminologists include the role of masculinity in creating female victimization, the exploitation of women in the workplace, and the unequal treatment of men and women in the justice system. There is also concern about the role of media in "demonizing" girls and women of color.[57]

QUEER CRIMINOLOGY As part of their interest in gender roles and crime, some critical scholars focus their attention on the treatment of the lesbian, gay, bisexual, transgender, and queer (LGBTQ) population by society in general and the justice system in particular.[58] Among the issues being studied is how damaging stereotypes and representations of people as sexual deviants developed.[59] They claim that mainstream criminologists have either ignored LGBTQ people or portrayed them in a negative light. Areas of interest include defining deviance, crimes against LGBTQ people, and gaining equality before the law.[60] There are also international studies that look at the treatment of

AP Images/Matt Rourke

Critical feminists identify ways in which women are objectified and victimized. One concern is that incidents of sexual assaults and Internet attacks on women occur regularly on college campuses. Here, on March 20, 2015, students and others demonstrate on the Penn State campus in support of women who were depicted on the Kappa Delta Rho fraternity's Facebook pages. Kappa Delta Rho fraternity members used two secret Facebook pages to post photos of nude females, some of whom appeared to be sleeping or passed out, as well as posts relating to hazing or drug deals.

LGBTQ people around the world, such as in places like Russia and Nigeria, where denial of due process, physical violence to coerce confessions, and disproportionate sentencing (including the death penalty) are routine.[61]

PATRIARCHAL SOCIETY The origin of gender differences can be traced to the development of private property and male domination of the laws of inheritance, which led to male control over property and power.[62] A patriarchal system developed in which men's work was valued and women's work was devalued. As capitalism prevailed, the division of labor by gender made women responsible for the unpaid maintenance and reproduction of the current and future labor force, which was derisively called "domestic work." Although this unpaid work done by women is crucial and profitable for capitalists, who reap its free benefits, such labor is exploitative and oppressive for women.[63] Even when women gained the right to work for pay, they were exploited as cheap labor. The dual exploitation of women within the household and in the labor market means that women produce far greater surplus value for capitalists than men.

Patriarchy, or male supremacy, has been and continues to be supported by capitalists. This system sustains female oppression at home and in the workplace.[64] Although the number of traditional patriarchal families is in steep decline, in those that still exist, a wife's economic dependence ties men more securely to wage-earning jobs, further serving the interests of capitalists by undermining potential rebellion against the system.

patriarchy
A society in which men dominate public, social, economic, and political affairs.

PATRIARCHY AND CRIME Critical feminists link criminal behavior patterns to the gender conflict created by the economic and social struggles common in postindustrial societies. In *Capitalism, Patriarchy, and Crime*, James Messerschmidt argues that capitalist society is marked by both patriarchy and class conflict. Capitalists control the labor of workers, and men control women both economically and biologically.[65] This "double marginality" explains why females in a capitalist society commit fewer crimes than males. Because they are isolated in the family, they have fewer opportunities to engage in elite deviance (white-collar and economic crimes). Although powerful females as well as males will commit white-collar crimes, the female crime rate is restricted because of the patriarchal nature of the capitalist system.[66] Women are also denied access to male-dominated street crimes.

Because capitalism renders lower-class women powerless, they are forced to commit less serious, nonviolent, self-destructive crimes, such as abusing drugs. Recent efforts of the capitalist classes to undermine the social support of the poor has hit women particularly hard. The end of welfare, concentration on welfare fraud, and cutbacks to social services have all directly and uniquely affected women.[67]

In *Masculinities and Crime*, Messerschmidt expands on these themes.[68] He suggests that in every culture males try to emulate "ideal" masculine behaviors. In Western culture, this means being authoritative, in charge, combative, and controlling. Failure to adopt these roles leaves men feeling effeminate and unmanly. Their struggle to dominate women in order to prove their manliness is called "doing gender." Crime is a vehicle for men to "do gender" because it separates them from the weak and allows them to demonstrate physical bravery. Violence directed toward women is an especially economical way to demonstrate manhood: would a weak, effeminate male ever attack a woman?

Feminist writers have supported this view by maintaining that in contemporary society men achieve masculinity at the expense of women. In the best-case scenario, men must convince others that in no way are they feminine nor do they have female qualities. They are sloppy and don't cook or do housework because these are female activities. More ominously, men may work at excluding, hurting, denigrating, exploiting, or otherwise abusing women. Even in all-male groups, men often prove their manhood by treating the weakest member of the group as "woman-like" and abusing him accordingly. Men need to defend themselves at all costs from being contaminated with femininity, and these efforts begin in children's playgroups and continue into adulthood and marriage.[69]

SEXUAL VICTIMIZATION Critical feminists also focus on the social forces that shape women's lives and experiences to explain female criminality. They attempt to show how sexual and other victimization of girls is a function of male socialization because so many young males learn to be aggressive and to exploit women. Males seek out same-sex peer groups for social support; these groups encourage members to exploit and sexually abuse women. On college campuses, peers encourage sexual violence against women who are considered "sluts." Such derogatory labels allow the males to justify their actions. Slut-shaming, the practice of embarrassing, humiliating, or attacking a woman for being sexual or acting on sexual feelings, has become common on college campuses.

This attitude has produced numerous incidents of sexual assault against young women, in which gender-centered humiliation, such as taking nude photos and videos of unsuspecting victims and posting them online, plays a major role. College fraternities have become notorious for this type of behavior, prompting closings or suspensions at major schools such as Penn State.[70] This attitude also helps explain the sexual assault culture that dominates the club scene in which men feel free to victimize women because that is just what men do. According to Philip Kavanaugh, various types of unwanted sexual contact become expected in bars, clubs, and lounges because sexually aggressive or coercive behavior is considered a normal part of gendered interactions in public places devoted to urban nightlife.[71]

POWERLESSNESS According to the critical feminist view, when female victims run away and abuse substances, they may be reacting to abuse they have suffered at home or at school.[72] Those who are on the street, who are homeless, are more likely to have experienced significant social problems, including childhood molestation, adult sexual assault, and arrests for prostitution, and to have been in treatment for substance misuse.[73]

Powerlessness increases the likelihood that women will become targets of violent acts.[74] When lower-class males are shut out of the economic opportunity structure, they try to build their self-image through acts of machismo; such acts may involve violent abuse of women. This type of reaction accounts for a significant percentage of female victims who are attacked by a spouse or intimate partner. It is not surprising to find that incarcerated female offenders report higher rates of interpersonal violence and mental health problems than incarcerated men and that there is a strong association between suffering intimate partner violence, mental health issues, and involvement with the justice system.[75]

It follows that female victimization should decline as women's place in society is elevated and they are able to obtain more power at home, in the workplace, and in government. Empirical research seems to support this view. In nations where the status of women is generally high, sexual violence rates are significantly lower than in nations where women do not enjoy similar educational and occupational opportunities.[76] Women's victimization rates decline as they are empowered socially, economically, and legally.[77]

GENDER AND THE JUSTICE SYSTEM When the exploited girl finds herself in the arms of the justice system, her problems may just be beginning. Boys who get in trouble may be considered "overzealous" youth or kids who just went too far. Girls who get in trouble are seen as a threat to acceptable images of femininity; their behavior is considered even more unusual and dangerous than male delinquency.[78]

Critical feminists such as Meda Chesney-Lind have found gender differences not only in criminality but also in the way girls and women are treated in both the juvenile and criminal justice system.[79] While it is true males are sanctioned more heavily than females, and they are overrepresented in the correctional system, it is also true that they commit more serious violent crimes.

These outcomes may be misleading. As Chesney-Lind has repeatedly found, women and girls receive more punitive treatment than men and boys, especially in cases involving sexual matters or offenses. This is not a recent phenomenon.

Throughout history females have been more likely to be punished for their immoral behavior than for their criminal activities. Chesney-Lind's now classic research first identified the fact that police are more likely to arrest female adolescents for sexual activity while ignoring similar behaviors when engaged in by males. Girls are more likely than boys to be picked up by police for status offenses such as being truant, runaways, or disobedient, and are more likely to be kept in detention for such offenses.[80]

The sexual stigmatization of girls is not a thing of the past. Critical feminists note that girls are still disadvantaged if their behavior is viewed as morally incorrect by government officials or if they are considered beyond parental control.[81] Girls may still be subject to harsh punishments if they are considered dangerously immoral or fail to measure up to stereotypes of proper female behavior.[82] Research by Tia Stevens and her associates found that over the past decades, regardless of racial/ethnic group, young girls who are involved in behavior considered inappropriate for females are more likely to be formally charged and involved in the juvenile justice system. Tolerance for misbehavior significantly decreases when girls violate gender norms.[83] Lisa Pasko's research confirms that the focus of the juvenile justice system continues to be on girls' sexual behavior. While girls are not directly arrested and adjudicated for sexual immorality, they are still told to take responsibility for their "bad choices." In the contemporary era, the correctional focus remains on the control and micromanagement of girls' bodies and sexuality.[84]

The justice system also seems biased against people who identify as lesbian, gay, bisexual, transgender, or queer (LGBTQ), who are disproportionately incarcerated. Though they make up approximately 6 percent of the youth population, it is now estimated that LGBTQ youth comprise 13 to 15 percent of youth involved in the juvenile justice system.[85]

As they mature, women may become more adept at navigating the justice system and use their street smarts and savvy to control their experience. When Corey S. Shdaimah and Chrysanthi Leon interviewed female prostitutes who were placed in justice system programs, they found that rather than acting passively the women demonstrated skills and moral reasoning that included the ability to make choices, work the systems that dominate their lives, and assert power and control. Rather than being passive, they were creative, resilient, and rational in their efforts to deal with the life circumstances in which they were placed.[86]

Power–Control Theory

John Hagan and his associates have created a critical feminist model that uses gender differences to explain the onset of criminality.[87] Hagan's view is that crime and delinquency rates are a function of two factors: class position (power) and family functions (control).[88] The link between these two variables is that, within the family, parents reproduce the power relationships they hold in the workplace; a position of dominance at work is equated with control in the household. As a result, parents' work experiences and class position influence the criminality of children.[89]

In **paternalistic families**, fathers assume the traditional role of breadwinners, while mothers tend to have menial jobs or remain at home to supervise domestic matters. Within the paternalistic home, mothers are expected to control the behavior of their daughters while granting greater freedom to sons. In such a home, the parent–daughter relationship can be viewed as a preparation for the "cult of domesticity," which makes girls' involvement in delinquency unlikely, whereas boys are freer to deviate because they are not subject to maternal control. Girls growing up in patriarchal families are socialized to fear legal sanctions more than are males; consequently, boys in these families exhibit more delinquent behavior than their sisters. The result is that boys not only engage in more antisocial behaviors but have greater access to legitimate adult behaviors, such as working at part-time jobs or possessing their own transportation. In contrast, without these legitimate behavioral outlets, girls who are unhappy or dissatisfied with their status are forced to seek out risky **role exit behaviors**, including such desperate measures as running away and contemplating suicide.

paternalistic families
Traditional family model in which fathers assume the role of breadwinners, while mothers tend to have menial jobs or remain at home to supervise domestic matters.

role exit behaviors
In order to escape from a stifling life in male-dominated families, girls may try to break away by running away and or even attempting suicide.

egalitarian families
Families in which spouses share similar positions of power at home and in the workplace.

power–control theory
The view that gender differences in crime are a function of economic power (class position, one-earner versus two-earner families) and parental control (paternalistic versus egalitarian families).

peacemaking
An approach that considers punitive crime control strategies to be counterproductive and favors the use of humanistic conflict resolution to prevent and control crime.

In **egalitarian families**—those in which the husband and wife share similar positions of power at home and in the workplace—daughters gain a kind of freedom that reflects reduced parental control. These families produce daughters whose law-violating behavior mirrors their brothers'. In an egalitarian family, girls may have greater opportunity to engage in legitimate adult status behaviors and less need to enact deviant role exits.[90]

Ironically, Hagan believes that these relationships also occur in female-headed households with absent fathers. Hagan and his associates found that when fathers and mothers hold equally valued managerial positions, the similarity between the rates of their daughters' and sons' delinquency is greatest. By implication, middle-class girls are the most likely to violate the law because they are less closely controlled than their lower-class counterparts. In homes in which both parents hold positions of power, girls are more likely to have the same expectations of career success as their brothers. Consequently, siblings of both sexes will be socialized to take risks and engage in other behavior related to delinquency.

EVALUATING POWER–CONTROL THEORY This **power–control theory** has received a great deal of attention in the criminological community because it encourages a new approach to the study of criminality, one that includes gender differences, class position, and the structure of the family. Empirical analysis of its premises has generally been supportive. Brenda Sims Blackwell's research supports a key element of power–control theory: females in paternalistic households have learned to fear legal sanctions more than have their brothers.[91]

Not all research is as supportive.[92] Some critics have questioned its core assumption that power and control variables can explain crime. More specifically, critics fail to replicate the finding that upper-class girls are more likely to deviate than their lower-class peers or that class and power interact to produce delinquency.[93] Some researchers have found few gender-based supervision and behavior differences in worker-, manager-, or owner-dominated households.[94] Research indicates that single-mother families may be different from two-parent egalitarian families, though Hagan's theory equates the two.[95] Some suggest that the theory may be more valid with white populations and gets mixed support only when used in cross-cultural settings.[96]

It is possible that the concept of family employed by Hagan may have to be reconsidered. Power–control theorists should consider the multitude of power and control relationships that are emerging in postmodern society: blended families, families where mothers hold managerial positions and fathers are blue-collar workers, same-sex parents, and so forth.[97]

Finally, power and control may interact with other personal traits, such as personality and self-control, to shape behavior.[98] Further research is needed to determine whether power–control can have an independent influence on behavior and can explain gender differences in the crime rate.

Peacemaking Criminology

LO6 Discuss how restorative justice is related to peacemaking criminology.

To members of the **peacemaking** movement, the main purpose of criminology is to promote a peaceful, just society. Rather than standing on empirical analysis of data, peacemaking draws its inspiration from religious and philosophical teachings ranging from Quakerism to Zen.[99] For example, rather than seeing socioeconomic status as a "variable" that is correlated with crime, as do mainstream criminologists, peacemakers view poverty as a source of suffering—almost a crime in and of itself. Poverty enervates people, makes them suffer, and becomes a master status that subjects them to lives filled with suffering. From a peacemaking perspective, a key avenue for preventing crime is, in the short run, diminishing the suffering poverty causes and, in the long run, embracing social policies that reduce the prevalence of economic suffering in contemporary society.[100]

Today, advocates of peacemaking try to find humanist solutions to crime and other social problems.[101] Rather than punishment and prison, they advocate such

Concept Summary 8.1 Emerging Forms of Critical Criminology

Theory	Major Premise	Strengths	Research Focus
Left realism	Crime is a function of relative deprivation; criminals prey on the poor.	Represents a compromise between conflict and traditional criminology	Deterrence; protection
Critical feminist theory	The capitalist system creates patriarchy, which oppresses women.	Explains gender bias, violence against women, and repression	Gender inequality; oppression; patriarchy
Power–control theory	Girls are controlled more closely than boys in traditional male-dominated households. There is gender equity in contemporary egalitarian homes.	Explains gender differences in the crime rate as a function of class and gender conflict	Power and control; gender differences; domesticity
Peacemaking criminology	Peace and humanism can reduce crime; conflict resolution strategies can work.	Offers a new approach to crime control through mediation	Punishment; nonviolence; mediation

policies as mediation and conflict resolution.[102] They reject the vocabulary that social problems should be met with a "war on..." approach, such as the war on drugs. Instead, peaceful and collaborative solutions can be found for social problems ranging from narcotics addiction to climate change.[103]

Concept Summary 8.1 summarizes the various emerging forms of critical criminology.

Critical Theory and Public Policy: Restorative Justice

At the core of all the varying branches of social conflict theory is the fact that conflict causes crime. If conflict and competition in society could somehow be reduced, it is possible that crime rates would fall. Some critical theorists believe this goal can be accomplished only by thoroughly reordering society so that capitalism is destroyed and a socialist state is created. Others call for a more "practical" application of conflict principles. Nowhere has this been more successful than in applying peacemaking principles in the criminal justice system.

Rather than punish law violators harshly and make them outcasts of society, peacemakers look for ways to bring them back to the community. This peacemaking movement has adopted nonviolent methods and applied them to what is known as **restorative justice**. Springing both from academia and justice system personnel, the restorative approach relies on nonpunitive strategies for crime prevention and control.[104] The next sections discuss the foundation and principles of restorative justice.

restorative justice
Using humanistic, nonpunitive strategies to right wrongs and restore social harmony.

The Concept of Restorative Justice

The term *restorative justice* is often hard to define because it encompasses a variety of programs and practices. According to a leading restorative justice scholar, Howard Zehr, restorative justice requires that society address victims' harms and needs, hold offenders accountable to put right those harms, and involve victims, offenders, and communities in the process of healing. Zehr maintains that the core value of the restoration process can be translated into respect for all, even those who are different from us, even those who seem to be our enemies. At its core, Zehr argues, restorative justice is a set of principles, a philosophy, an alternate set of guiding questions that provide an alternative framework for thinking about wrongdoing.[105] Restorative justice would reject concepts such as "punishment," "deterrence," and "incarceration" and embrace "apology," "rehabilitation," "reparation," "healing," "restoration," and "reintegration."

Restorative justice takes many forms. Here, the program coordinator, a policewoman, and volunteers on the board of the Neighborhood Restoration Justice Program in Apoka, Florida, meet for an accountability conference. This pretrial diversion program for first-time juvenile offenders is an alternative to juvenile court. At this meeting, youths were given sanctions for the crimes they committed.

shame
The feeling we get when we don't meet the standards we have set for ourselves or that significant others have set for us.

Restorative justice has grown out of a belief that the traditional justice system has done little to involve the community in the process of dealing with crime and wrongdoing. What has developed is a system of coercive punishments, administered by bureaucrats, that are inherently harmful to offenders and reduce the likelihood offenders will ever become productive members of society. This system relies on punishment, stigma, and disgrace. In his controversial book *The Executed God: The Way of the Cross in Lockdown America*, theology professor Mark Lewis Taylor discusses the similarities between this contemporary, coercive justice system and that which existed in imperial Rome when Jesus and many of his followers were executed because they were an inspiration to the poor and slave populations. They represented a threat to the ruling Roman power structure. So, too, is our modern justice system designed to keep the downtrodden in their place. Taylor suggests that there should be a movement to reduce such coercive elements of justice as police brutality and the death penalty before our "lockdown society" becomes the model used around the globe.[106]

Advocates of restorative justice argue that rather than today's lockdown mentality, what is needed is a justice policy that repairs the harm caused by crime and that includes all parties who have suffered from that harm: the victim, the community, and the offender. They have made an ongoing effort to reduce the conflict created by the criminal justice system when it hands out harsh punishments to offenders, many of whom are powerless social outcasts. Based on the principle of reducing social harm, restorative justice advocates argue that the old methods of punishment are a failure: after all, upward of two-thirds of all prison inmates recidivate soon after their release. And tragically, not all inmates are released. Some are given life sentences for relatively minor crimes under three-strikes laws, which mandate such a sentence for a third conviction; some are given sentences of life with no parole, which are in essence death sentences.[107]

Reintegrative Shaming

One of the key foundations of the restoration movement is contained in John Braithwaite's influential book *Crime, Shame, and Reintegration*.[108] Braithwaite's vision rests on the concept of **shame**: the feeling we get when we don't meet the standards we have set for ourselves or that significant others have set for us. Shame can lead people to believe that they are defective, that there is something wrong with them. Braithwaite notes that countries such as Japan in which conviction for crimes brings an inordinate amount of shame have extremely low crime rates. In Japan, criminal prosecution proceeds only when the normal process of public apology, compensation, and the victim's forgiveness breaks down.

Shame is a powerful tool of informal social control. Citizens in cultures in which crime is not shameful, such as the United States, do not internalize an abhorrence for crime because when they are punished, they view themselves as mere victims of the justice system. Their punishment comes at the hands of neutral strangers, such as police and judges, who are being paid to act. In contrast, shaming relies on the victim's participation.[109]

Braithwaite divides the concept of shame into two distinct types. The most common form of shaming typically involves stigmatization, an ongoing process of degradation in which the offender is branded as an evil person and cast out of society. Shaming can occur at a school disciplinary hearing or a criminal court trial. Bestowing stigma and degradation may have a general deterrent effect: it makes people afraid of social rejection and public humiliation.[110] As a specific deterrent, stigma is doomed to failure; people who suffer humiliation at the hands of the justice system "reject their rejectors" by joining a deviant subculture of like-minded people who collectively resist social control. Despite these dangers, there has been an ongoing effort to brand offenders and make their shame both public and permanent. For example, states have passed sex offender registry and notification laws that make public the names of those convicted of sex offenses and warn neighbors of their presence in the community.[111]

But the fear of shame can backfire or be neutralized. When shame is managed well, people acknowledge they made mistakes and suffered disappointments, and try to work out what can be done to make things right; this is referred to as shame management. However, in some cases, to avoid the pain of shaming, people engage in improper shame management, a psychological process in which they deny shame by shifting the blame of their actions to their target or to others.[112] They may blame others, get angry, and take out their frustrations on those whom they can dominate. Improper shame management of this sort has been linked to antisocial acts ranging from schoolyard bullying to tax evasion.

Massive levels of improper shame management may occur on a societal scale during periods of social upheaval. Because of this, some nations that previously have had low crime rates may experience a surge of antisocial behavior during periods of war and revolution. Rape, an act which may have been unthinkable to most men, suddenly becomes commonplace because of the emergence of narcissistic pride, feeling dominant and arrogant, and developing a sense of superiority over others, in this case your enemy. This sense of hubris fosters aggressive actions and allows combatants to rape women whom they perceive as belonging to an enemy group. Braithwaite argues that crime control can be better achieved through a policy of **reintegrative shaming**. Here disapproval is extended to the offenders' evil deeds, while at the same time they are cast as respected people who can be reaccepted by society. A critical element of reintegrative shaming occurs when the offenders begin to understand and recognize their wrongdoing and shame themselves. To be reintegrative, shaming must be brief and controlled and then followed by ceremonies of forgiveness, apology, and repentance.

reintegrative shaming
A method of correction that encourages offenders to confront their misdeeds, experience shame because of the harm they caused, and then be reincluded in society.

To prevent crime, Braithwaite charges, society must encourage reintegrative shaming. For example, the women's movement can reduce domestic violence by mounting a crusade to shame spouse abusers. Similarly, parents who use reintegrative shaming techniques in their childrearing practices may improve parent–child relationships and ultimately reduce the delinquent involvement of their children. Because informal social controls may have a greater impact than legal or formal ones, it may not be surprising that the fear of personal shame can have a greater deterrent effect than the fear of legal sanctions. It may also be applied to produce specific deterrence. Offenders can meet with victims so that the offenders can experience shame. Family members and peers can be present to help the offender reintegrate. Such efforts can humanize a system of justice that today relies on repression rather than forgiveness as the basis of specific deterrence.

The Process of Restoration

The restoration process begins by redefining crime in terms of a conflict among the offender, the victim, and affected constituencies (families, schools, workplaces, and so forth). Therefore, it is vitally important that the resolution take place within the context in which the conflict originally occurred rather than being transferred to a specialized institution that has no social connection to the community or group from which the conflict originated. In other words, most conflicts are better settled in the community than in a court.

By maintaining "ownership" or jurisdiction over the conflict, the community is able to express its shared outrage about the offense. Shared community outrage is directly communicated to the offender. The victim is also given a chance to voice his or her story, and the offender can directly communicate his or her need for social reintegration and treatment. All restoration programs involve an understanding among all the parties involved in a criminal act: the victim, the offender, and community. Although processes differ in structure and style, they generally include these elements:

- The offender is asked to recognize that he or she caused injury to personal and social relations along with a determination and acceptance of responsibility (ideally accompanied by a statement of remorse). Only then can the offender be restored as a productive member of the community.

- Restoration involves turning the justice system into a "healing" process rather than being a distributor of retribution and revenge.
- Reconciliation is a big part of the restorative approach. Most people involved in offender–victim relationships actually know one another or were related in some way before the criminal incident took place. Instead of treating one of the involved parties as a victim deserving of sympathy and the other as a criminal deserving of punishment, it is more productive to address the issues that produced conflict between these people.
- The effectiveness of justice ultimately depends on the stake a person has in the community (or a particular social group). If a person does not value his or her membership in the group, the person will be unlikely to accept responsibility, show remorse, or repair the injuries caused by his or her actions. In contrast, people who have a stake in the community and its principle institutions, such as work, home, and school, find that their involvement enhances their personal and familial well-being.[113]
- The offender must make a commitment to both material (monetary) restitution and symbolic reparation (an apology). A determination must also be made of community support and assistance for both victim and offender.

The intended result of the process is to repair injuries suffered by the victim and the community while ensuring reintegration of the offender.

RESTORATION PROGRAMS Negotiation, mediation, consensus-building, and peace-making have been part of the dispute resolution process in European and Asian communities for centuries.[114] Native American and First Nations (native Canadian) people have long used the type of community participation in the adjudication process (for example, sentencing circles, sentencing panels, elders panels) that restorative justice advocates are now embracing.[115]

In some Native American communities, people accused of breaking the law meet with community members, victims (if any), village elders, and agents of the justice system in a **sentencing circle**. Each member of the circle expresses his or her feelings about the act that was committed and raises questions or concerns. The accused can express regret about his or her actions and a desire to change the harmful behavior. People may suggest ways the offender can make things up to the community and those he or she harmed. A treatment program, such as Alcoholics Anonymous, can be suggested, if appropriate.

Restorative justice is now being embraced on many levels within our society and the justice system:

- *Community.* Communities that isolate people and have few mechanisms for interpersonal interaction encourage and sustain crime. Those that implement forms of community dialogue to identify problems and plan tactics for their elimination, guided by restorative justice practices and principles, may create a climate in which violent crime is less likely to occur.[116]
- *Schools.* Some schools have embraced restorative justice practices to deal with students who are involved in drug and alcohol abuse without having to resort to more punitive measures such as expulsion. Schools in Minnesota, Colorado, and elsewhere are now trying to involve students in "relational rehabilitation" programs that strive to improve individuals' relationships with key figures in the community who may have been harmed by their actions.[117]
- *Police.* Restorative justice has also been implemented by police when crime is first encountered. The new community policing models are an attempt to bring restorative concepts into law enforcement. Restorative justice relies on the fact that criminal justice policymakers need to listen and respond to the needs of those who are to be affected by their actions, and community policing relies on policies established with input and exchanges between officers and citizens.[118]

sentencing circle
A peacemaking technique in which offenders, victims, and other community members are brought together in an effort to formulate a sanction that addresses the needs of all.

- *Courts.* Restorative programs in the courts typically involve diverting the formal court process. These programs encourage meeting and reconciling the conflicts between offenders and victims via victim advocacy, mediation programs, and sentencing circles, in which crime victims and their families are brought together with offenders and their families in an effort to formulate a sanction that addresses the needs of each party. Victims are given a chance to voice their stories, and offenders can help compensate them financially or provide some service (for example, fixing damaged property).[119] The goal is to enable offenders to appreciate the damage they have caused, to make amends, and to be reintegrated back into society.

Restoration programs are being used in court systems around the world. One example is the justice system in Australia, which makes use of a conferencing process to divert offenders from the justice system.[120] This offers offenders the opportunity to attend a conference to discuss and resolve their offense instead of being charged and appearing in court. (Those who deny guilt are not offered conferencing.) The conference, normally lasting one to two hours, is attended by the victims and their supporters, the defendant and his or her supporters, and other concerned parties. The conference coordinator focuses the discussion on condemning the act without condemning the character of the actor. Offenders are asked to tell their side of the story, what happened, how they have felt about the crime, and what they think should be done. The victims and others are asked to describe the physical, financial, and emotional consequences of the crime. This discussion may lead the offenders, their families, and their friends to experience the shame of the act, prompting an apology to the victim. A plan of action is developed and signed by key participants. The plan may include the offender paying compensation to the victim, doing work for the victim or the community, or similar solutions. It is the responsibility of the conference participants to determine the outcomes that are most appropriate for these particular victims and these particular offenders. All eight states and territories in Australia have used the conference model at some time or another. Research indicates the conferencing approach is well received by young offenders who believe the outcomes are fair, but it remains to be seen whether it can reduce future crime rates.[121]

RECONCILIATION Restoration has also been used as a national policy to heal internal rifts. For example, after 50 years of oppressive white rule in South Africa, the race-dividing apartheid policy was abolished in the early 1990s, and in 1994 Nelson Mandela, leader of the African National Congress (ANC), was elected president.[122] Some black leaders wanted revenge for the political murders carried out during the apartheid era, but Mandela established the Truth and Reconciliation Commission. Rather than seeking vengeance for the crimes, this government agency investigated the atrocities with the mandate of granting amnesty to those individuals who confessed their roles in the violence and could prove that their actions served some political motive rather than being based on personal factors such as greed or jealousy.

Supporters of the commission believed that this approach would help heal the nation's wounds and prevent years of racial and ethnic strife. Mandela, who had been unjustly jailed for 27 years by the regime, had reason to desire vengeance. Yet he wanted to move the country forward after the truth of what happened in the past had been established. Though many South Africans, including some ANC members, believed that the commission was too lenient, Mandela's attempts at reconciliation prevailed. The commission was a model of restoration over revenge.

In sum, restoration can be or has been used at the following stages of justice:

- As a form of final warning to young offenders
- As a tool for school officials
- As a method of handling complaints to police
- As a diversion from prosecution
- As a presentencing, postconviction add-on to the sentencing process
- As a supplement to a community sentence (probation)
- As a preparation for release from long-term imprisonment[123]

The Challenge of Restorative Justice

Restorative justice holds great promise, but there are also some concerns:

- Is it a political movement or a treatment process? Restorative justice is viewed as an extremely liberal alternative, and its advocates often warn of the uneven exercise of state power. Some view it as a social movement rather than a method of rehabilitation.[124] Can it survive in a culture that is becoming increasingly conservative and focused on security rather than personal freedom?
- Restorative justice programs must be wary of the cultural and social differences that can be found throughout our heterogeneous society. What may be considered "restorative" in one subculture may be considered insulting and damaging in another.[125]
- There is still no single definition of what constitutes restorative justice.[126] Consequently, many diverse programs that call themselves restorative-oriented pursue objectives that seem remote from the restorative ideal.
- Restorative justice programs face the difficult task of balancing the needs of offenders with those of their victims. If programs focus solely on victims' needs, they may risk ignoring the offenders' needs and increase the likelihood of reoffending. Declan Roache, a lecturer in law at the London School of Economics, makes the argument that the seductive promise of restorative justice may blind admirers to the benefits of traditional methods and prevent them from understanding or appreciating some of the pitfalls of restoration. There is danger, he warns, in a process that is essentially informal, without lawyers, and with little or no oversight on the outcome. The restoration process gives participants unchecked power without the benefit of procedural safeguards.[127]
- Benefits may work only in the short term while ignoring long-term treatment needs. Sharon Levrant and her colleagues suggest that restorative justice programs that feature short-term interactions with victims fail to help offenders learn prosocial ways of behaving. Restorative justice advocates may falsely assume that relatively brief interludes of public shaming will change deeply rooted criminal predispositions.[128]

These are a few of the obstacles that restorative justice programs must overcome to be successful and productive. Yet because the method holds so much promise, criminologists are conducting numerous demonstration projects to find the most effective means of returning the ownership of justice to the people and the community.[129]

Thinking Like a Criminologist

Is It a Bribe? A student wants to discuss a personal matter. It seems that a few weeks ago she was at a party when she was sexually assaulted by a fellow student. The attack was quite traumatic, and she suffered both physical and emotional injury. The police were called and the boy charged with rape. Now that a few weeks have passed, she has been contacted by a local program that bills itself as a restorative treatment program. It seems that her attacker is now a client and wants to engage in some form of reconciliation. At an arranged meeting, he professes his regret for the attack and wishes to make amends. He and the program director have worked out a schedule in which the victim will be compensated for her pain and suffering in the amount of $5,000 in exchange for her agreeing to a recommendation to the prosecutor that the case be treated informally rather than going to trial. She doesn't know what to do: she needs the money, having missed work after the attack, but at the same time is concerned that people will think she has accepted a bribe to withdraw the charges.

Writing Assignment

Write a paper describing the advice you would give to the student in this situation. How would you suggest that she respond to the program director? Do you consider the payment a bribe or restitution for an evil deed? Can restorative justice be used in a crime such as rape?

SUMMARY

LO1 **List the core ideas of critical criminology.**
Critical criminology is based on the view that crime is a function of the conflict that exists in society. Critical theorists suggest that crime in any society is caused by economic and class conflict. Laws are created by those in power to protect their own rights and to serve their own interests. Criminal law is designed to protect the wealthy and powerful and to control the poor, have-not members of society. The poor commit crimes because of their frustration, anger, and need. The wealthy engage in illegal acts because they are used to competition and because they must do so to maintain their position in society. Crime would disappear if equality rather than discrimination was the norm.

LO2 **Link globalization to crime and criminality.**
Globalization disproportionately benefits wealthy and powerful organizations and individuals and impoverishes indigenous people. As the influence and impact of international financial institutions increase, there is a related relative decline in power of local or state-based institutions, resulting in the recent unrest in world financial systems. With money and power to spare, global criminal enterprise groups can recruit new members, bribe government officials, and even fund private armies.

LO3 **Define the concept of state-organized crime.**
State crimes involve a violation of citizen trust. They are acts defined by law as criminal and committed by state officials in pursuit of their jobs as government representatives. Some state crimes are committed by individuals who abuse their state authority, or fail to exercise it, when working with people and organizations in the private sector. State–corporate crime involves the deviant activities by which the privileged classes strive to maintain or increase their power.

LO4 **Explain the goals and findings of critical research.**
Research on critical theory focuses on how the justice system was designed and how it operates to further class interests. It sometimes employs historical analysis to show how the capitalist classes have exerted control over the police, the courts, and correctional agencies. Contemporary research exposes how race and class influence decision making in the criminal justice system.

LO5 **Articulate the basic ideas of critical feminism.**
Critical feminist writers draw attention to the influence of patriarchal society on crime. According to power–control theory, gender differences in the crime rate can be explained by the structure of the family in a capitalist society.

LO6 **Discuss how restorative justice is related to peacemaking criminology.**
Peacemaking criminology brings a call for humanism to criminology. The restorative justice model holds that reconciliation rather than retribution should be applied to prevent and control crime. Restoration programs are now being used around the United States in schools, justice agencies, and community forums. They employ mediation, sentencing circles, and other techniques.

Key Terms

Critical Thinking Questions

1. How would a conservative reply to a call for more restorative justice? How would a restorative justice advocate respond to a conservative call for more prisons?

2. Considering recent changes in American culture, how would a power–control theorist explain recent drops in the US crime rate? Can it be linked to changes in the structure of the American family?

3. Is conflict inevitable in all cultures? If not, what can be done to reduce the level of conflict in our own society?

4. If Marx were alive today, what would he think about the prosperity enjoyed by the working class in industrial societies? Might he alter his vision of the capitalist system?

5. Has religious conflict replaced class conflict as the most important issue facing modern society? Can anything be done to heal the rifts between people of different faiths?

Notes

All URLs accessed in 2017.

1. Russell Berman, Donald Trump's Call to Ban Muslim Immigrants, *Atlantic*, December 7, 2015, http://www.theatlantic.com/politics/archive/2015/12/donald-trumps-call-to-ban-muslim-immigrants/419298/.

2. Dan Merica and Sophie Tatum, "Clinton Expresses Regret for Saying 'Half' of Trump Supporters Are 'Deplorables,'" CNN News, September 12, 2016, http://www.cnn.com/2016/09/09/politics/hillary-clinton-donald-trump-basket-of-deplorables/.

3. United Nations, "Alarmed by Continuing Syria Crisis, Security Council Affirms Its Support for Special Envoy's Approach in Moving Political Solution Forward," August 17, 2015, http://www.un.org/press/en/2015/sc12008.doc.htm; Emad El-Din Shahin, "Brutality, Torture, Rape: Egypt's Crisis Will Continue Until Military Rule Is Dismantled," *The Guardian*, March 5, 2014, http://www.theguardian.com/commentisfree/2014/mar/06/brutality-torture-rape-egypt-military-rule.

4. Alette Smeulers and Roelof Haveman, eds., *Supranational Criminology: Towards a Criminology of International Crimes* (Belgium: Intersentia, 2008).

5. Ibid., p. 4.

6. Michael Lynch and W. Byron Groves, *A Primer in Radical Criminology*, 2nd ed. (Albany, NY: Harrow & Heston, 1989), p. 7.

7. Jeffery Reiman, *The Rich Get Richer and the Poor Get Prison* (New York: Wiley, 1984), pp. 43–44.

8. Rob White, "Environmental Harm and the Political Economy of Consumption," *Social Justice* 29 (2002): 82–102.

9. Barbara Sims, "Crime, Punishment, and the American Dream: Toward a Marxist Integration," *Journal of Research in Crime and Delinquency* 34 (1997): 5–24.

10. Steven Box, *Recession, Crime, and Unemployment* (London: Macmillan, 1987).

11. David Barlow, Melissa Hickman-Barlow, and W. Wesley Johnson, "The Political Economy of

Criminal Justice Policy: A Time-Series Analysis of Economic Conditions, Crime, and Federal Criminal Justice Legislation, 1948–1987," *Justice Quarterly* 13 (1996): 223–241.

12. Mahesh Nalla, Michael Lynch, and Michael Leiber, "Determinants of Police Growth in Phoenix, 1950–1988," *Justice Quarterly* 14 (1997): 144–163.

13. America's Promise Alliance, "Building a Grad Nation: Progress and Challenge in Raising High School Graduation Rates," 2017 Annual Report, http://gradnation.americaspromise.org/sites/default/files/d8/2017-05/18754_BGN_Report_v6.pdf.

14. Michael Rocques and Raymond Paternoster, "Understanding the Antecedents of the 'School-to-Jail' Link: The Relationship Between Race and School Discipline," *Journal of Criminal Law and Criminology* 101 (2011): 633–665.

15. China Labour Bulletin, "Wages and Employment, 2017," http://www.clb.org.hk/content/wages-and-employment.

16. Jim Puzzanghera and Samantha Masunaga, "Pfizer and Allergan's $160-billion Pharmaceutical Merger Puts New Twist on Tax-Avoiding Inversion," *LA Times*, November 23, 2015, http://www.latimes.com/business/la-fi-pfizer-allergan-merger-20151123-story.html.

17. Dawn L. Rothe, Jeffrey Ian Ross, Christopher W. Mullins, David Friedrichs, Raymond Michalowski, Gregg Barak, David Kauzlarich, and Ronald C. Kramer, "That Was Then, This Is Now, What About Tomorrow? Future Directions in State Crime Studies," *Critical Criminology* 17 (2009): 3–13.

18. Amnesty International, "Conflict Diamonds," http://www.amnestyusa.org/our-work/issues/business-and-human-rights/oil-gas-and-mining-industries/conflict-diamonds.

19. David Friedrichs and Jessica Friedrichs, "The World Bank and Crimes of Globalization: A Case Study," *Social Justice* 29 (2002): 13–36.

20. Ibid.

21. Greg Palast, "Secret US Plan for Iraqi Oil, BBC News," March 17, 2005, http://news.bbc.co.uk/1/hi/programmes/newsnight/4354269.stm.

22. Jonathan H. C. Kelman, "States Can Play, Too: Constructing a Typology of State Participation in Illicit Flows," *Crime, Law and Social Change* 64 (2015): 37–55.

23. Jeffrey Ian Ross, *The Dynamics of Political Crime* (Thousand Oaks, CA: Sage, 2003).

24. Charlie Savage and Mark Mazzetti, "Cryptic Overtures and a Clandestine Meeting Gave Birth to a Blockbuster Story," *New York Times*, June 10, 2013, http://www.nytimes.com/2013/06/11/us/how-edward-j-snowden-orchestrated-a-blockbuster-story.html.

25. Niall Jenkins, "245 Million Video Surveillance Cameras Installed Globally in 2014," IHS Markit, June 11, 2015, https://technology.ihs.com/532501/245-million-video-surveillance-cameras-installed-globally-in-2014.

26. American Civil Liberties Union, "What's Wrong with Public Video Surveillance? The Four Problems with Public Video Surveillance," https://www.aclu.org/other/whats-wrong-public-video-surveillance.

27. Human Rights Watch, "World Report 2017," https://www.hrw.org/world-report/2017.

28. Human Rights Watch, "United Arab Emirates," https://www.hrw.org/middle-east/n-africa/united-arab-emirates.

29. MSNBC News, "Bush Acknowledges Secret CIA Prisons," September 6, 2006, http://www.msnbc.msn.com/id/14689359/; American Civil Liberties Union, "FBI Inquiry Details Abuses Reported by Agents at Guantanamo," January 3, 2007, https://www.aclu.org/news/fbi-inquiry-details-abuses-reported-agents-guantanamo.

30. Michael Lynch and Kimberly Barrett, "Death Matters: Victimization by Particle Matter from Coal Fired Power Plants in the US, a Green Criminological View," *Critical Criminology* 23 (2015): 219–234.

31. Ignasi Bernat and David Whyte, "State-Corporate Crime and the Process of Capital Accumulation: Mapping a Global Regime of Permission from Galicia to Morecambe Bay," *Critical Criminology* 25 (2017): 71–86.

32. Gresham Sykes, "The Rise of Critical Criminology," *Journal of Criminal Law and Criminology* 65 (1974): 211–229.

33. David Jacobs, "Corporate Economic Power and the State: A Longitudinal Assessment of Two Explanations," *American Journal of Sociology* 93 (1988): 852–881.

34. Richard Quinney, "Crime Control in Capitalist Society," in *Critical Criminology*, ed. Ian Taylor, Paul Walton, and Jock Young (London: Routledge & Kegan Paul, 1975), p. 199.

35. Ibid.

36. John Hagan, *Structural Criminology* (New Brunswick, NJ: Rutgers University Press, 1989), pp. 110–119.

37. Darrell Steffensmeier and Stephen Demuth, "Ethnicity and Judges' Sentencing Decisions: Hispanic-Black-White Comparisons," *Criminology* 39 (2001): 145–178; Alan Lizotte, "Extra-Legal Factors in Chicago's Criminal Courts: Testing the Conflict Model of Criminal Justice," *Social Problems* 25 (1978): 564–580.

38. Terance Miethe and Charles Moore, "Racial Differences in Criminal Processing: The Consequences of Model Selection on Conclusions

About Differential Treatment," *Sociological Quarterly* 27 (1987): 217–237.

39. David Jacobs and David Britt, "Inequality and Police Use of Deadly Force: An Empirical Assessment of a Conflict Hypothesis," *Social Problems* 26 (1979): 403–412.

40. Graham Ousey and James Unnever, "Racial-Ethnic Threat, Out-Group Intolerance, and Support for Punishing Criminals: A Cross-National Study," *Criminology* 50 (2012): 565–603.

41. Albert Meehan and Michael Ponder, "Race and Place: The Ecology of Racial Profiling African American Motorists," *Justice Quarterly* 29 (2002): 399–431.

42. Tammy Rinehart Kochel, David Wilson, and Stephen Mastrofski, "Effect of Suspect Race on Officers' Arrest Decisions," *Criminology* 49 (2011): 473–512.

43. Malcolm Homes, "Minority Threat and Police Brutality: Determinants of Civil Rights Criminal Complaints in U.S. Municipalities," *Criminology* 38 (2000): 343–368.

44. Charles Crawford, Ted Chiricos, and Gary Kleck, "Race, Racial Threat, and Sentencing of Habitual Offenders," *Criminology* 36 (1998): 481–511.

45. Steffensmeier and Demuth, "Ethnicity and Judges' Sentencing Decisions"; Alan Lizotte, "Extra-Legal Factors in Chicago's Criminal Courts: Testing the Conflict Model of Criminal Justice," *Social Problems* 25 (1978): 564–580.

46. Tracy Nobiling, Cassia Spohn, and Miriam DeLone, "A Tale of Two Counties: Unemployment and Sentence Severity," *Justice Quarterly* 15 (1998): 459–485.

47. David Greenberg and Valerie West, "State Prison Populations and Their Growth, 1971–1991," *Criminology* 39 (2001): 615–654.

48. Michael Lenza, David Keys, and Teresa Guess, "The Prevailing Injustices in the Application of the Missouri Death Penalty (1978 to 1996)," *Social Justice* 32 (2005): 151–166.

49. Anthony Platt, "Criminology in the 1980s: Progressive Alternatives to 'Law and Order,'" *Crime and Social Justice* 21–22 (1985): 191–199.

50. John Lea and Jock Young, *What Is to Be Done About Law and Order?* (Harmondsworth, England: Penguin, 1984).

51. Ibid., p. 88.

52. Ian Taylor, *Crime in Context: A Critical Criminology of Market Societies* (Boulder, CO: Westview Press, 1999).

53. Ibid., pp. 30–31.

54. Richard Kinsey, John Lea, and Jock Young, *Losing the Fight Against Crime* (London: Blackwell, 1986).

55. Martin Schwartz and Walter DeKeseredy, *Contemporary Criminology* (Belmont, CA: Wadsworth, 1993), p. 249.

56. Martin D. Schwartz and Walter S. DeKeseredy, "Left Realist Criminology: Strengths, Weaknesses and the Feminist Critique," *Crime, Law, and Social Change* 15 (1991): 51–72.

57. Meda Chesney-Lind and Merry Morash, "Transformative Feminist Criminology: A Critical Re-thinking of a Discipline," *Critical Criminology* 21 (2013): 287–304.

58. Matthew Ball, "Queer Criminology as Activism," *Critical Criminology* 24 (2016): 473–487.

59. Jordan Blair Woods, "Queer Contestations and the Future of a Critical 'Queer' Criminology," *Critical Criminology* 22 (2014): 5–19.

60. Matthew Ball, "What's Queer About Queer Criminology?" in *Handbook of LGBT Communities, Crime, and Justice*, ed. Dana Peterson and Vanessa Panfil (New York: Springer Science + Business Media, 2014), pp. 531–555.

61. Carrie Buist and Emily Lenning, *Queer Criminology* (London: Routledge, 2016).

62. Kathleen Daly and Meda Chesney-Lind, "Feminism and Criminology," *Justice Quarterly* 5 (1988): 497–538.

63. Janet Saltzman Chafetz, "Feminist Theory and Sociology: Underutilized Contributions for Mainstream Theory," *Annual Review of Sociology* 23 (1997): 97–121.

64. Ibid.

65. James Messerschmidt, *Capitalism, Patriarchy, and Crime* (Totowa, NJ: Rowman & Littlefield, 1986); for a critique of this work, see Herman Schwendinger and Julia Schwendinger, "The World According to James Messerschmidt," *Social Justice* 15 (1988): 123–145.

66. Kathleen Daly, "Gender and Varieties of White-Collar Crime," *Criminology* 27 (1989): 769–793.

67. Gillian Balfour, "Re-imagining a Feminist Criminology," *Canadian Journal of Criminology and Criminal Justice* 48 (2006): 735–752.

68. James Messerschmidt, *Masculinities and Crime: Critique and Reconceptualization of Theory* (Lanham, MD: Rowman & Littlefield, 1993).

69. Angela P. Harris, "Gender, Violence, Race, and Criminal Justice," *Stanford Law Review* 52 (2000): 777–810.

70. Fox News, "Penn State Frat Suspended for Year Over Nude Facebook Pics," March 17, 2015, http://www.foxnews.com/us/2015/03/17/penn-state-frat-suspended-for-year-over-nude-facebook-pics/.

71. Philip Kavanaugh, "The Continuum of Sexual Violence: Women's Accounts of Victimization in Urban Nightlife," *Feminist Criminology* 8 (2013): 20–39.

72. Daly and Chesney-Lind, "Feminism and Criminology." See also Drew Humphries and Susan Caringella-MacDonald, "Murdered Mothers, Missing Wives: Reconsidering Female Victimization," *Social Justice* 17 (1990): 71–78.

73. Kia Asberg and Kimberly Renk, "Safer in Jail? A Comparison of Victimization History and Psychological Adjustment Between Previously Homeless and Non-Homeless Incarcerated Women," *Feminist Criminology* 10 (2015): 165–187.

74. Jane Roberts Chapman, "Violence Against Women as a Violation of Human Rights," *Social Justice* 17 (1990): 54–71.

75. Shannon Lynch, April Fritch, and Nicole Heath, "Looking Beneath the Surface: The Nature of Incarcerated Women's Experiences of Interpersonal Violence, Treatment Needs, and Mental Health," *Feminist Criminology* 7 (2012): 381–400.

76. Carrie Yodanis, "Gender Inequality, Violence Against Women, and Fear," *Journal of Interpersonal Violence* 19 (2004): 655–675.

77. Victoria Titterington, "A Retrospective Investigation of Gender Inequality and Female Homicide Victimization," *Sociological Spectrum* 26 (2006): 205–236.

78. Kjersti Ericsson and Nina Jon, "Gendered Social Control: 'A Virtuous Girl' and 'a Proper Boy,'" *Journal of Scandinavian Studies in Criminology and Crime Prevention* 9 (2006): 126–141.

79. Meda Chesney-Lind and Vickie Paramore, "Are Girls Getting More Violent? Exploring Juvenile Robbery Trends," *Journal of Contemporary Criminal Justice* 17 (2001): 142–166; Joanne Belknap, Kristi Holsinger, and Melissa Dunn, "Understanding Incarcerated Girls," *Prison Journal* 77 (1997): 381–404.

80. Thomas J. Gamble, Sherrie Sonnenberg, John Haltigan, and Amy Cuzzola-Kern, "Detention Screening: Prospects for Population-Management and the Examination of Disproportionality by Race, Age, and Gender," *Criminal Justice Policy Review* 13 (2002): 380–395; Kimberly Kempf-Leonard and Lisa Sample, "Disparity Based on Sex: Is Gender-Specific Treatment Warranted?" *Justice Quarterly* 17 (2000): 89–128.

81. Holly Hartwig and Jane Myers, "A Different Approach: Applying a Wellness Paradigm to Adolescent Female Delinquents and Offenders," *Journal of Mental Health Counseling* 25 (2003): 57–75; Meda Chesney-Lind and Randall Shelden, *Girls, Delinquency, and Juvenile Justice* (Belmont, CA: West/ Wadsworth, 1998).

82. Hartwig and Myers, "A Different Approach: Applying a Wellness Paradigm to Adolescent Female Delinquents and Offenders."

83. Tia Stevens, Merry Morash, and Meda Chesney-Lind, "Are Girls Getting Tougher, or Are We Tougher on Girls? Probability of Arrest and Juvenile Court Oversight in 1980 and 2000," *Justice Quarterly* 28 (2011): 719–744.

84. Lisa Pasko, "Damaged Daughters: The History of Girls' Sexuality and the Juvenile Justice System," *Journal of Criminal Law and Criminology* 100 (2010): 1099–1130.

85. Kristi Holsinger and Jessica P. Hodge, "The Experiences of Lesbian, Gay, Bisexual, and Transgender Girls in Juvenile Justice Systems," *Feminist Criminology*, first published online February 2014.

86. Corey S. Shdaimah and Chrysanthi Leon, "First and Foremost They're Survivors: Selective Manipulation, Resilience, and Assertion Among Prostitute Women," *Feminist Criminology* 1–22, first published online 2014.

87. Hagan, *Structural Criminology*.

88. John Hagan, A. R. Gillis, and John Simpson, "The Class Structure and Delinquency: Toward a Power-Control Theory of Common Delinquent Behavior," *American Journal of Sociology* 90 (1985): 1151–1178; John Hagan, John Simpson, and A. R. Gillis, "Class in the Household: A Power-Control Theory of Gender and Delinquency," *American Journal of Sociology* 92 (1987): 788–816.

89. John Hagan, Bill McCarthy, and Holly Foster, "A Gendered Theory of Delinquency and Despair in the Life Course," *Acta Sociologica* 45 (2002): 37–47.

90. Brenda Sims Blackwell, Christine Sellers, and Sheila Schlaupitz, "A Power-Control Theory of Vulnerability to Crime and Adolescent Role Exits—Revisited," *Canadian Review of Sociology and Anthropology* 39 (2002): 199–219.

91. Brenda Sims Blackwell, "Perceived Sanction Threats, Gender, and Crime: A Test and Elaboration of Power-Control Theory," *Criminology* 38 (2000): 439–488.

92. Christopher Uggen, "Class, Gender, and Arrest: An Intergenerational Analysis of Workplace Power and Control," *Criminology* 38 (2001): 835–862.

93. Gary Jensen and Kevin Thompson, "What's Class Got to Do with It? A Further Examination of Power-Control Theory," *American Journal of Sociology* 95 (1990): 1009–1023. For some critical research, see Simon Singer and Murray Levine, "Power-Control Theory, Gender and Delinquency: A Partial Replication with Additional Evidence on the Effects of Peers," *Criminology* 26 (1988): 627–648.

94. Kevin Thompson, "Gender and Adolescent Drinking Problems: The Effects of Occupational Structure," *Social Problems* 36 (1989): 30–38.

95. Kristin Mack and Michael Leiber, "Race, Gender, Single-Mother Households, and Delinquency: A Further Test of Power-Control Theory," *Youth and Society* 37 (2005): 115–144.

96. David Eitle, Fallon Niedrist, and Tamela McNulty Eitle, "Gender, Race, and Delinquent Behavior: An Extension of Power-Control Theory to American Indian Adolescents," *Deviant Behavior* 35 (2014): 1023–1042; Helmut Hirtenlehner, Brenda Sims Blackwell, Heinz Leitgoeb, and Johann Bacher, "Explaining the Gender Gap in Juvenile Shoplifting: A Power-Control Theoretical Analysis," *Deviant Behavior* 35 (2014): 41–65.

97. See, generally, Uggen, "Class, Gender, and Arrest."

98. Brenda Sims Blackwell and Alex Piquero, "On the Relationships Between Gender, Power Control, Self-Control, and Crime," *Journal of Criminal Justice* 33 (2005): 1–17.

99. Liz Walz, "One Blood," *Contemporary Justice Review* 6 (2003): 25–36.

100. John F. Wozniak, "Poverty and Peacemaking Criminology: Beyond Mainstream Criminology," *Critical Criminology* 16 (2008): 209–223.

101. Richard Quinney, "The Way of Peace: On Crime, Suffering, and Service," in *Criminology as Peacemaking*, ed. Harold Pepinsky and Richard Quinney (Bloomington: Indiana University Press, 1991), pp. 8–9.

102. For a review of Quinney's ideas, see Kevin B. Anderson, "Richard Quinney's Journey: The Marxist Dimension," *Crime and Delinquency* 48 (2002): 232–242.

103. Bill McClanahan and Avi Brisman, "Climate Change and Peacemaking Criminology: Ecophilosophy, Peace and Security in the 'War on Climate Change,'" *Critical Criminology* 23 (2015): 417–431.

104. Kathleen Daly and Russ Immarigeon, "The Past, Present and Future of Restorative Justice: Some Critical Reflections," *Contemporary Justice Review* 1 (1998): 21–45.

105. Howard Zehr, *The Little Book of Restorative Justice* (Intercourse, PA: Good Books, 2002): 1–10.

106. Mark Lewis Taylor, *The Executed God: The Way of the Cross in Lockdown America* (Minneapolis: Fortress Press, 2001).

107. Alfred Villaume, "'Life Without Parole' and 'Virtual Life Sentences': Death Sentences by Any Other Name," *Contemporary Justice Review* 8 (2005): 265–277.

108. John Braithwaite, *Crime, Shame, and Reintegration* (Melbourne, Australia: Cambridge University Press, 1989).

109. Eliza Ahmed, Nathan Harris, John Braithwaite, and Valerie Braithwaite, *Shame Management Through Reintegration* (Cambridge, England: Cambridge University Press, 2001).

110. Eliza Ahmed, "'What, Me Ashamed?' Shame Management and School Bullying," *Journal of Research in Crime and Delinquency* 41 (2004): 269–294.

111. John Braithwaite, "Rape, Shame and Pride," *Journal of Scandinavian Studies in Criminology and Crime Prevention* 7 (2006): 2–16.

112. Carter Hay, "An Exploratory Test of Braithwaite's Reintegrative Shaming Theory," *Journal of Research in Crime and Delinquency* 38 (2001): 132–153.

113. Rick Shifley, "The Organization of Work as a Factor in Social Well-Being," *Contemporary Justice Review* 6 (2003): 105–126.

114. Kay Pranis, "Peacemaking Circles: Restorative Justice in Practice Allows Victims and Offenders to Begin Repairing the Harm," *Corrections Today* 59 (1997): 74–78.

115. Carol LaPrairie, "The 'New' Justice: Some Implications for Aboriginal Communities," *Canadian Journal of Criminology* 40 (1998): 61–79.

116. Diane Schaefer, "A Disembodied Community Collaborates in a Homicide: Can Empathy Transform a Failing Justice System?" *Contemporary Justice Review* 6 (2003): 133–143.

117. David R. Karp and Beau Breslin, "Restorative Justice in School Communities," *Youth and Society* 33 (2001): 249–272.

118. Paul Jesilow and Deborah Parsons, "Community Policing as Peacemaking," *Policing and Society* 10 (2000): 163–183.

119. Gordon Bazemore and Curt Taylor Griffiths, "Conferences, Circles, Boards, and Mediations: The 'New Wave' of Community Justice Decision Making," *Federal Probation* 61 (1997): 25–37.

120. Heather Strang, "Restorative Justice Programs in Australia," http://www.criminologyresearchcouncil.gov.au/reports/strang/report.pdf.

121. Hennessey Hayes, Tara Renae McGee, Helen Punter, and Michael John Cerruto, "Agreements in Restorative Justice Conferences: Exploring the Implications of Agreements for Post-conference Offending Behaviour," *British Journal of Criminology* 54 (2014): 109–127.

122. John W. De Gruchy, *Reconciliation: Restoring Justice* (Minneapolis: Fortress, 2002).

123. Lawrence W. Sherman and Heather Strang, *Restorative Justice: The Evidence* (London: Smith Institute, 2007).

124. John Braithwaite, "Setting Standards for Restorative Justice," *British Journal of Criminology* 42 (2002): 563–577.

125. David Altschuler, "Community Justice Initiatives: Issues and Challenges in the U.S. Context," *Federal Probation* 65 (2001): 28–33.

126. Lois Presser and Patricia van Voorhis, "Values and Evaluation: Assessing Processes and Outcomes of Restorative Justice Programs," *Crime and Delinquency* 48 (2002): 162–189.

127. Declan Roche, *Accountability in Restorative Justice* (Clarendon Studies in Criminology) (London: Oxford University Press, 2004).

128. Sharon Levrant, Francis Cullen, Betsy Fulton, and John Wozniak, "Reconsidering Restorative Justice: The Corruption of Benevolence Revisited?" *Crime* and *Delinquency* 45 (1999): 3–28.

129. Edward Gumz, "American Social Work, Corrections and Restorative Justice: An Appraisal," *International Journal of Offender Therapy and Comparative Criminology* 48 (2004): 449–460.

Developmental Theories: Life Course, Propensity, and Trajectory

Steven Hayes

Joshua Komisarjevsky

Dr. William Petit

Hartford Courant/Tribune News Service/Getty Images

AP Images/Connecticut Department of Correction

9

Chapter Outline

Foundations of Developmental Theory
Three Views of Criminal Career Development
Population Heterogeneity vs. State Dependence

Life Course Theory
Age of Onset
Problem Behavior Syndrome
Continuity of Crime
Age-Graded Theory

Policies and Issues in Criminology
HUMAN AGENCY, PERSONAL ASSESSMENT, CRIME, AND DESISTANCE

Social Schematic Theory (SST)

Policies and Issues in Criminology
SHARED BEGINNINGS, DIVERGENT LIVES

Latent Trait/Propensity Theory
Crime and Human Nature
General Theory of Crime (GTC)

Trajectory Theory
Age and Offending Trajectories
Personality and Offending Trajectories
Chronic Offenders and Non-offenders
Pathways to Crime
Adolescent-Limited and Life Course Persistent Offenders

Public Policy Implications of Developmental Theory

FACT OR FICTION?

▶ Getting married helps people stay out of trouble.

▶ Criminals are impulsive risk takers.

F ew crimes are as horrific as the murder of Jennifer, Michaela, and Hayley Petit during a home invasion in the leafy suburb of Cheshire, Connecticut. The crime began on July 23, 2007, when career criminals Steven Hayes and Joshua Komisarjevsky (shown in the chapter opening photo) spotted the Petits at a grocery store and followed them home. At first, Hayes and Komisarjevsky had planned to rob the Petit house and leave the family unharmed, but things went terribly wrong. When they entered the home, they found William Petit sleeping on a couch, hit him with a baseball bat, and tied him up. They then subdued and bound Mrs. Petit and the children.

When they did not find sufficient funds in the house, Hayes left and filled two cans with gasoline at a local filling station, and then forced Mrs. Petit to go to her bank and withdraw money. While in the bank Jennifer Petit passed a note to the teller, who alerted the bank manager, who called the police. Rather than storming the house or letting the intruders know they were surrounded, the police spent time assessing the situation and setting up a vehicle perimeter around the house. While this was happening, Komisarjevsky raped 11-year-old Michaela while Hayes raped and strangled Jennifer Petit. When the pair realized that William Petit had escaped, they doused the house with gasoline, including the bedrooms where the girls lay bound and helpless. Hayes and Komisarjevsky then started a fire and fled, only to be quickly apprehended by police—but not before Hayley and Michaela had both died of smoke inhalation; the first officer to respond heard the girls screaming as the flames rose inside their rooms. The crime was so gruesome that some jurors had to be treated for PTSD.

During the trial, defense lawyers presented evidence in an effort to spare Hayes and ▶

Komisarjevsky the death penalty. Komisarjevsky was portrayed as a damaged person who was sexually abused as a child, suffered from mood disorders and head injuries, abused drugs, and cut himself with glass, knives, and razors. His evangelical Christian adoptive parents denied him proper care, relying instead on religion.

Dr. Eric Goldsmith, a psychiatrist who interviewed Hayes for about 37 hours over eight sessions, noted that Hayes had a troubled and abusive upbringing, was sexually molested by a teenage babysitter when he was 10 or 11, and had developed a sexual fetish that caused him to associate an object—a woman's old sneaker—with sexual arousal; he said Hayes sought out women who shared his fetish. Hayes claimed that he had killed 17 women in the Northeast and also committed date rapes.

Despite defense efforts, bother Hayes and Komisarjevsky were found guilty and sentenced to death. Connecticut Governor Jodi Rell issued a statement soon after the verdicts were released: "The crimes that were committed on that brutal July night were so far out of the range of normal understanding that now, more than three years later, we still find it difficult to accept that they happened in one of our communities," Komisarjevsky's family issued a statement: "From the very beginning, we have spoken out about the horror of the crime and taken the position that whatever verdict the jury reached was the right verdict. With today's jury decision, our view is the same. The crime was monstrous and beyond comprehension. There are no excuses." When Connecticut ended capital punishment in 2015, Hayes and Komisarjevsky were spared the death penalty and will serve life in prison.[1] ∎

developmental theories
The view that criminality is a dynamic process, influenced by social experiences as well as individual characteristics.

criminal career
Engaging in antisocial acts early in adolescence and continuing illegal behaviors into adulthood. A pattern of persistent offending across the life course.

LO1 Discuss the history of and influences on developmental theory.

CONNECTIONS

Chapter 2 discussed how Wolfgang found that although many offenders commit a single criminal act and thereafter desist from crime, a small group of chronic offenders engage in frequent and repeated criminal activity and continue to do so across their life span.

Developmental criminologists try to understand why some people, like Steven Hayes and Joshua Komisarjevsky begin their involvement in illegal activity as children, while others are late starters. Some offenders may engage in petty crimes; others continually increase the severity and frequency of their offending. Some may be deeply affected by criminal penalties, while others are career criminals who persist in their illegal activities over their life course despite being caught and punished many times. Efforts to understand the onset, continuity, and termination of crime and criminality have resulted in the construction of a variety of **developmental theories** that focus not so much on a single criminal act but on the creation and persistence of a **criminal career** over the life course.

Foundations of Developmental Theory

As you may recall (Chapter 1), the research efforts of Sheldon and Eleanor Glueck formed the basis of today's developmental approach. Soon after the publication of their work, the Gluecks' methodology and their integration of biological, psychological, and social factors were sharply criticized, and for many years their work was ignored in criminology texts and overlooked in the academic curriculum.

During the 1990s, the Glueck legacy was rediscovered by criminologists Robert Sampson and John Laub, who used modern statistical techniques to reanalyze the Gluecks' carefully drawn empirical measurements. Laub and Sampson's findings, published in a series of books and articles, fueled the popularity of the developmental approach.[2]

The Philadelphia cohort research by Marvin Wolfgang and his associates also sparked interest in explaining criminal career development. Wolfgang's research focused attention on criminal careers. His work prompted criminologists to ask this fundamental question: What prompts one person to engage in persistent criminal activity, while another, who on the surface suffers the same life circumstances, finds a way to steer clear of crime and travel a more conventional path?

A 1990 review paper by Rolf Loeber and Marc Le Blanc was another important contribution that spurred interest in developmental criminology. In this landmark work, Loeber and Le Blanc proposed that criminologists should devote time and effort to understanding basic questions about the evolution of criminal careers. Rather than viewing criminality as static and constant—a person simply is either a criminal or a noncriminal—they viewed criminality as a dynamic process, with a beginning, middle, and end and changes all along the way. Loeber and Le Blanc challenged criminologists to answer these questions: Why do some people begin committing antisocial acts in adulthood, while most begin offending at a very early age? Why do some stop, whereas others continue? Why do some escalate the severity of their criminality (that is, go from shoplifting to drug dealing to armed robbery), whereas others deescalate and commit less serious crimes as they mature? If some terminate their criminal activity, what (if anything) causes them to begin again? Why do some criminals specialize in certain types of crime, whereas others are generalists engaging in a variety of antisocial activities? Loeber and Le Blanc's developmental view suggests that criminologists must pay attention to how a criminal career unfolds—how it begins, why it is sustained, and how it comes to an end.[3]

From these and similar efforts, a view of crime has emerged that incorporates personal change and growth. The factors that produce crime and criminality at one point in the life cycle may not be relevant at another; as people mature, the social, physical, and environmental influences on their behavior are transformed. People may show a propensity to offend early in their lives, but the nature and frequency of their activities are often affected by forces beyond their control, which elevate and sustain their criminal activity.[4]

Three Views of Criminal Career Development

As criminologists began to explore this concept of criminal careerism, three independent yet interrelated developmental views gained traction. The first, referred to as **life course theory**, suggests that criminal behavior is a dynamic process, influenced by individual characteristics as well as social experiences and that the factors that cause antisocial behaviors change dramatically over a person's life span.

A second view, referred to here as **propensity theory**, suggests that human development is controlled by a master **latent trait** that remains stable and unchanging throughout a person's lifetime. As people travel through their life course, this propensity is always present, directing their behavior. Because this hidden trait is enduring, the ebb and flow of criminal behavior are shaped less by personal change and more by the impact of external forces such as environment and opportunity. Criminality may increase upon joining a gang, a status that provides more opportunities to steal, take drugs, and attack others. Put another way: the propensity to commit criminal acts is constant, but the opportunity to commit them is constantly fluctuating.

A third view, **trajectory theory**, suggests there are multiple trajectories or paths into a criminal career. According to this approach, there are subgroups within a population that follow distinctively different developmental routes toward and away from a criminal career. Some people may begin early in antisocial activities and demonstrate a lifetime propensity for crime, while others begin later and are influenced by life circumstances. Unlike the latent trait and life course views, trajectory theory suggests that there are different types and classes of offenders.[5]

life course theory
Theory that focuses on changes in criminality over the life course brought about by shifts in experience and life events.

propensity theory
The view that a stable unchanging feature, characteristic, property, or condition, such as defective intelligence or impulsive personality, makes some people crime prone.

latent trait
A stable feature, characteristic, property, or condition, such as defective intelligence or impulsive personality, that makes some people crime prone over the life course.

trajectory theory
The view that there are multiple independent paths to a criminal career and that there are different types and classes of offenders.

population heterogeneity
The propensity to commit crime is stable; those who have it continue to commit crime over their life course.

state dependence
The propensity to commit crime is constantly changing, affected by environmental influences and changing life events.

CHECKPOINTS

▸ Pioneering criminologists Sheldon and Eleanor Glueck tracked the onset and termination of criminal careers.

▸ Their work led to the creation of developmental theories.

▸ Developmental theories attempt to provide a global vision of a criminal career that encompasses its onset, continuation, and termination.

▸ Developmental theories come in three different varieties: life course, propensity or latent trait, and trajectory.

▸ Life course theories look at such issues as the onset of crime, escalation of offenses, continuity of crime, and desistance from crime.

▸ Latent trait theories assume that a "master trait" exists that guides human development.

▸ Trajectory theories assume there is more than one type of criminal and more than one criminal path.

▸ The concept of population heterogeneity assumes that the propensity of an individual to participate in antisocial and/or criminal behaviors is a relatively stable trait, unchanging over their life course.

▸ The concept of state dependence suggests that life events have a significant influence on future behavior.

Concept Summary 9.1 Three Developmental Theories

Life course theory	People have multiple traits: social, psychological, economic. People change over the life course. Family, job, peers influence behavior.
Propensity theory/ Latent trait theory	People do not change, criminal opportunities change; maturity brings fewer opportunities. People have a master trait: personality, intelligence, genetic makeup. Early social control and proper parenting can reduce criminal propensity.
Trajectory theory	There is more than one path to a criminal career. There are different types of offenders and offending.
Similarities	Focus on criminal careers. Criminality must be viewed as a path rather than an event. Criminal careers are enduring, begin early in adolescence, and continue into adulthood. Integration of multiple factors.
Differences	Life course: People are constantly evolving and so is their criminal behavior. Propensity: An unchanging master trait controls antisocial behavior. Trajectory: There is more than one path to crime and more than one crime-producing trait.

The main points, similarities, and differences of these positions are set out in Concept Summary 9.1.

Population Heterogeneity vs. State Dependence

Are people truly different, or are we more or less all the same but shaped by our different experiences? This question is the core issue separating the various branches of developmental theory.

The concept of **population heterogeneity** assumes that the propensity of an individual to participate in antisocial and/or criminal behaviors is a relatively stable trait, unchanging over their life course. Within a given population people differ in their behavior choices: some are hotheaded, violent, and inclined to commit crime, while others remain reasonable, unruffled, and presumably law abiding. According to this view, individual differences remain stable and are not affected by the consequences of participation in crime or any other changing life circumstances.[6] Because people affect their environment and not vice versa, the best predictor of future behavior is past behavior: people who are criminally active in their childhood should remain so in their adulthood, no matter what happens to them in the meantime. The cause of misbehavior remains the same as people traverse the life course.

In contrast, the concept of **state dependence** suggests that people change and develop as they mature; life events have a significant influence on future behavior. Life course theorists embrace this concept because it can explain continuity and desistance from crime: while positive experiences can help the troubled person adjust and conform, damaging encounters and events have the potential to increase future criminal involvement. Adolescents who are at risk for crime can avoid a criminal way of life if they encounter people who help, nurture, and support them in their adolescence and adulthood. If past antisocial behavior influences future offending, it's not because they have a similar cause, but because offending disrupts prosocial bonds and informal mechanisms of social control. Those people who have the propensity to commit crime find that life events disrupt socialization and thereafter increase the risk of prolonged antisocial behavior. Early rule breaking increases the probability of future rule breaking because it weakens inhibitions to crime and/or strengthens criminal motivation. Some adolescents who get a taste of antisocial behavior like it and want to continue down a deviant path during the teenage years and into and through their adulthood.[7]

Life Course Theory

According to the life course view, even as toddlers, people begin relationships and behaviors that will determine their entire life course. As children they must learn to conform to social rules and function effectively in society. Later as teens, they are expected to begin thinking about careers, complete their schooling, leave their parents' home, enter the workforce. In young adulthood, people find permanent relationships, eventually marry, and begin their own families.[8] These transitions are expected to take place in an orderly fashion. Disruptions in life's major transitions can be destructive and ultimately promote criminality. Those who are already at risk because of socioeconomic problems or family dysfunction are the most susceptible during these awkward transitions. The cumulative impact of these disruptions sustains criminality from childhood into adulthood.

> **LO2** List the principles of the life course approach to developmental theory.

In some cases, transitions can occur too early—an adolescent girl engages in precocious sex and becomes pregnant. In other cases, transitions may occur too late—an 18-year-old boy fails to graduate on time because of bad grades, drops out, and is unemployed. Sometimes disruption of one trajectory can harm another—becoming a teenage parent is likely to disrupt future educational and career development. These negative life experiences can become cumulative; as kids acquire more personal deficits, the chances of acquiring additional ones increase.[9]

People who get in trouble early in life, especially those who are arrested and given an official criminal label, may find it difficult to shake the criminal way of life as they mature.[10] Racial disparity in the criminal justice system helps put minority group members at a disadvantage, increasing the likelihood that they will become embedded in criminal careers.[11]

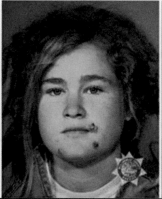

AP Images/Multnomah County Sheriff's Office/Portland Police

Life course theory suggests that while most people age out of crime, a small segment are not able to knife off from a criminal path and continue to commit crimes into adulthood. They may escalate the seriousness of their acts as they mature. In 2015, Sean Michael Angold, Lila Scott Alligood, and Morrison Haze Lampley were charged with two murders, a Canadian backpacker and a yoga instructor walking his dog. At trial, testimony by the group indicated that they had selected their victims—the first in San Francisco and the second in Marin County—almost randomly while dreaming of moving to Oregon to start a pot farm. They chose 23-year-old Audrey Carey because "she was foreign and possibly had money." Two days later, the three singled out 67-year-old Steve Carter because they wanted his station wagon for their journey north. They followed Carter as he walked his Doberman pinscher, Coco, and then attacked him. All three pleaded guilty to murder and were given long prison sentences.

While most kids age out of crime, the ability to change wilts with age as people become embedded in a criminal lifestyle. What may help a person resist a life of crime while they are still in their teens—for example, school achievement and positive family relations—may have little impact once they reach their 20s.[12]

One way of getting embedded in a criminal way of life is to join a youth gang, a choice that has both short- and long-term consequences. Those who join gangs are more likely to get involved in antisocial behavior after they leave the gang than before they joined.[13] Gang membership disrupts conventional life transitions and provides roadblocks to success long after membership has ceased.[14]

So a young man who deals with anger issues in early adolescence, who joins a gang, gets in trouble with the law, and drops out of school, is also the one who is more likely to become involved in antisocial behavior as a teen and to mature into a law-violating behavior as an adult.[15] While most adolescents age out of crime and become responsible adults, those growing up in a criminogenic environment and engaging in antisocial behavior as adolescents are the ones who are most likely to engage in antisocial behavior as adults.[16]

But even those who have been in trouble throughout their adolescence may manage to find stable work and maintain intact marriages as adults; positive life events help them desist from crime. It is the less fortunate adolescents who develop arrest records and get involved with the wrong crowd who may find themselves at risk for delinquency and later adult criminal careers.

Life course theories also recognize that as people mature, the factors that influence their behavior change.[17] As people make important life transitions—from child to adolescent, from adolescent to adult, from unwed to married—the nature of social interactions also changes.[18] At first, family relations may be most influential; it comes as no shock to life course theorists when research shows that criminality runs in families and that having criminal relatives is a significant predictor of future misbehaviors.[19] In later adolescence, school and peer relations predominate; in adulthood, vocational achievement and marital relations may be the most critical influences. Some antisocial children who are in trouble throughout their adolescence manage to find stable work and maintain intact marriages as adults. These life events help them desist from crime. In contrast, less fortunate adolescents who develop arrest records and get involved with the wrong crowd may find themselves limited to menial jobs and at risk for criminal careers.

The following sections review and discuss some prominent life course concepts.

Age of Onset

We know that most young criminals desist and do not become adult offenders.[20] But some do go on to have a long career as a chronic offender. The seeds of a criminal career are planted early in life (preschool); **early onset** of deviance strongly predicts more frequent, varied, and sustained criminality later in life.[21] What causes some kids to begin offending at an early age? Among the suspected root causes are inadequate emotional support, distant peer relationships, and psychological issues and problems.[22] Among the psychological conditions associated with early onset are attention deficit hyperactivity disorder (ADHD) and conduct disorder (CD).[23]

Poor parental discipline and monitoring also seem to be keys to the early onset of criminality, and these influences may follow kids into their adulthood. Research by Kristin Carbone-Lopez and Jody Miller shows that for girls, early entry into adult roles—precocious sexuality, motherhood, independent living, romantic relationships—is a key ingredient in the entry into a substance-abusing lifestyle as an adult.[24] The psychic scars of childhood are hard to erase.[25]

Most of these early onset delinquents begin their careers with disruptive behavior, truancy, cruelty to animals, lying, and theft.[26] They also appear to be more violent than their less precocious peers.[27] The earlier the onset, the more likely an adolescent will engage in serious criminality and for a longer period of time. Studies of the juvenile justice system show that many incarcerated youths began their offending careers

early onset
The view that kids who begin engaging in antisocial behaviors at a very early age are the ones most at risk for a criminal career.

Exhibit 9.1 Problem Behaviors

Social

Family dysfunction
Unemployment
Educational underachievement
School misconduct

Personal

Substance abuse
Suicide attempts
Early sexuality
Premature death
Poor health
Sensation seeking

Early parenthood
Accident prone
Medical problems
Mental disease
Anxiety
Eating disorders (bulimia, anorexia)

Environmental

High-crime area
Disorganized area
Racism
Exposure to poverty

very early in life and that a significant number had engaged in heavy drinking and drug abuse by age 10 or younger.[28]

Problem Behavior Syndrome

One life course view is that criminality is but one of many social and personal problems faced by people who live a risky lifestyle. Referred to collectively as **problem behavior syndrome (PBS)**, these behaviors include social, personal, and environmental dysfunction ranging from poor health to unemployment (see Exhibit 9.1).[29]

Those who exhibit PBS are prone to more difficulties than the general population. They find themselves experiencing personal dilemmas ranging from drug abuse to being accident prone, requiring more health care and hospitalization, becoming teenage parents, or having mental health problems.[30] PBS has been linked to individual-level personality problems (such as impulsiveness, rebelliousness, and low ego), family problems (such as intrafamily conflict and parental mental disorder), substance abuse, poor health, and educational failure.[31] Adolescents who get in trouble with the law are likely to exhibit a combination of externalizing behaviors, including conduct disorder, attention deficit hyperactivity disorder (ADHD), drug abuse, familial and interpersonal difficulties (such as conflict with parents), and low intelligence.[32] All varieties of antisocial behavior, including violence, theft, and drug offenses, may be part of a generalized PBS, indicating that all forms of criminal behavior have similar developmental patterns.[33]

Considering the types of problems that cluster together, it is not surprising that people who have a long and varied criminal career are more likely than others to die early and to have greater than average mortality rates.[34] Criminal conduct has been found to increase the chances of premature death due to both natural and unnatural causes, including deaths from accidents, homicide, and suicide. The more crime a person commits, the more likely he or she is to suffer premature death.[35]

In sum, problem behavior syndrome portrays crime as a type of social problem rather than as the product of other social problems.[36] People involved in crime may fall prey to other social problems, ranging from poverty to premature death.[37]

Continuity of Crime

Another aspect of life course theory is continuity of crime: the best predictor of future criminality is past criminality. Children who are repeatedly in trouble during early adolescence will generally still be antisocial in their middle teens; people who display

L03 Explain the term *problem behavior syndrome.*

problem behavior syndrome (PBS) Antisocial behaviors that cluster together, including family dysfunction, substance abuse, smoking, precocious sexuality and early pregnancy, educational underachievement, suicide attempts, sensation seeking, and unemployment, as well as criminality.

conduct problems in youth are the ones most likely to commit crime as adults.[38] As adults, people involved in the most serious crimes continue to misbehave even when they are behind bars.[39]

Life course theorists believe that the continuity of crime is state dependent: criminal activity is sustained because law violators and rule breakers seem to lack the social survival skills necessary to find work or to develop the interpersonal relationships they need to allow them to desist. As a result, antisocial behavior may be *contagious*: people at risk for criminality may infect those around them, thereby creating an ever-widening circle of peers and acquaintances who support deviant behavior.[40]

Research shows that as they emerge into adulthood, persisters are beset with additional social and personal problems (as was predicted by PBS): they report less emotional support, lower job satisfaction, distant peer relationships, and more psychiatric problems than those who desist.[41] But even if they manage to forgo criminal activity, they are still at risk for a large variety of social behavior problems.

A number of systematic life course theories have been formulated that account for such factors as early onset, the clustering of behavioral problems, and the continuance (and/or termination) of a criminal career.[42] As a group, these theories integrate *personal factors* such as personality and intelligence, *social factors* such as income and neighborhood, *socialization factors* such as marriage and military service, *cognitive factors* such as information processing and attention/perception, and *situational factors* such as criminal opportunity, effective guardianship, and apprehension risk into complex multifactor explanations of human behavior. They do not focus on the relatively simple question of why people commit crime but, rather, on more complex issues: Why do some offenders persist in criminal careers, whereas others desist from or alter their criminal activity as they mature?[43] Why do some people continually escalate their criminal involvement, whereas others slow down and turn their lives around? The most prominent life course theory is Robert Sampson and John Laub's **age-graded theory**, which is discussed next.

One of the key principles of life course theory is that the seeds of a criminal career are planted early in life and the early onset of antisocial behavior strongly predicts later and more serious criminality. The psychic scars of a crippling childhood are hard to erase. Here, attorney John Henry Browne places his hand on the shoulder of Colton Harris-Moore, after Browne concluded defense testimony that included details of Harris-Moore's troubled childhood. Harris-Moore, known as the "Barefoot Bandit," was sentenced to more than seven years in prison after pleading guilty to dozens of state charges stemming from a two-year crime spree.

Age-Graded Theory

L04 Outline the basic principles of Sampson and Laub's age-graded life course theory.

In an important 1993 work, *Crime in the Making*, Robert Sampson and John Laub find that the course of a criminal career can be affected by events that occur later in life, even after a chronic criminal career has been undertaken.[44] While in some cases a career in crime begins early in life and continues over the life course, it is wrong to believe that once this course is set nothing can impede its progress. There are **turning points** in a criminal career that can alter its course and direction, changing a lifetime ne'er-do-well into a productive citizen.

To conduct their research, Sampson and Laub reanalyzed the data originally collected by the Gluecks more than 50 years before. Using modern statistical analysis, Sampson and Laub found that discrete factors influence people at different stages of their development, and therefore the propensity to commit crimes is neither stable nor unyielding. Children who enter delinquent careers are those who have trouble at home and at school; their parents and family life are the greatest influence on their behavior. Supervision, parental styles of discipline, and parental attachment are the most important predictors of serious and persistent delinquency. Later as adolescents, peer relations become all important, and kids who maintain deviant friends are the ones most at risk of committing crime. In adulthood,

age-graded theory
A state dependence theory formulated by Sampson and Laub that assumes that the causal association between early delinquent offending and later adult deviant behavior involves the quality of relationships encountered at different times in human development.

behavior choices are influenced by elements of informal social control such as marriage, family, and work.

SOCIAL CAPITAL Social scientists have long recognized that people build **social capital**—positive relations with individuals and institutions that are life-sustaining. In the same manner that building financial capital improves the chances for personal success, building social capital supports conventional behavior and inhibits deviant behavior.[45]

In their age-graded theory, Sampson and Laub recognize the role of social capital and its ability to create turning points, allowing some at-risk people to *knife off* from a criminal career.[46] People who can make the right connections and gain advantage through family connections are the ones most likely to knife off from crime. Sampson and Laub found that criminal careers can be reversed if life conditions improve by such fortunate events as moving to a more attractive environment, doing well in school, or finding a good job and a supportive mate. Social capital is also gained by joining the military, serving overseas, and receiving veterans' benefits. Gaining social capital may help erase some of the damage caused by its absence.

In contrast, some people not only fail to accumulate social capital, but instead experience social problems that weigh down their life chances. Nor do these social problems simply go away; they linger and vex people throughout their lives. Past miscues are highly correlated with future social problems—for example, people arrested in their teens are less likely to find jobs as adults. People who acquire this **cumulative disadvantage** are more likely to commit criminal acts and become victims of crime.[47] When faced with personal crisis, they lack the social supports that can help them reject criminal solutions and maintain a conventional behavior trajectory. Not surprisingly, research shows that adolescents whose parents were convicted of crime and suffered incarceration were also more likely to engage in theft offenses. Parental incarceration erases social capital and escalates cumulative disadvantage: it reduces family income, gives kids the opportunity to gain antisocial peers, and subjects them to negative labels and stigma.[48] Kids whose fathers were incarcerated are more likely to suffer an arrest by age 25 than the offspring of conventional, law-abiding parents.[49] Adolescents lacking capital may also suffer criminal victimization. Criminologist Joan Reid found that kids who were the victims of sex traffickers had limited social capital that led to them experiencing initial exploitation during young adulthood; those trafficked internationally lost even more capital because of their citizenship status and language or cultural barriers.[50]

turning points
According to Laub and Sampson, the life events that alter the development of a criminal career.

social capital
Positive, life-sustaining relations with individuals and institutions.

cumulative disadvantage
The tendency of prior social problems to produce future ones that accumulate and undermine success.

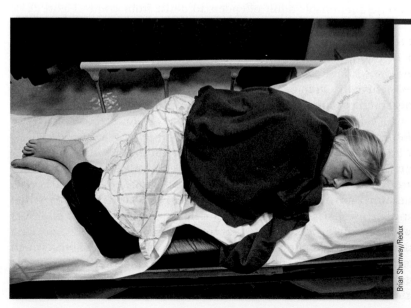

Social and personal disadvantages tend to accumulate. Here, homeless teenager Pamila sleeps in the emergency room of an Orange County hospital, waiting to find out if she is sick or pregnant again. At only 18, Pamila found herself homeless. She was living with her boyfriend Rob, 32, in a tent in a small wooded area beside a freeway off-ramp. Pamila had followed Rob west from Baltimore in an attempt to find his father. They had gotten heavily into drugs and Pamila became pregnant. The search for Rob's father, along with their relationship, failed. Rob was arrested on a warrant from the Midwest, and Pamila moved in with a mother and daughter she had befriended, who lived at a motel. She bounced around to different motel rooms, dating a new guy. Eventually, Pamila got out of Orange County, but she continues to struggle with life, a failed marriage, and pregnancy.

Brian Shumway/Redux

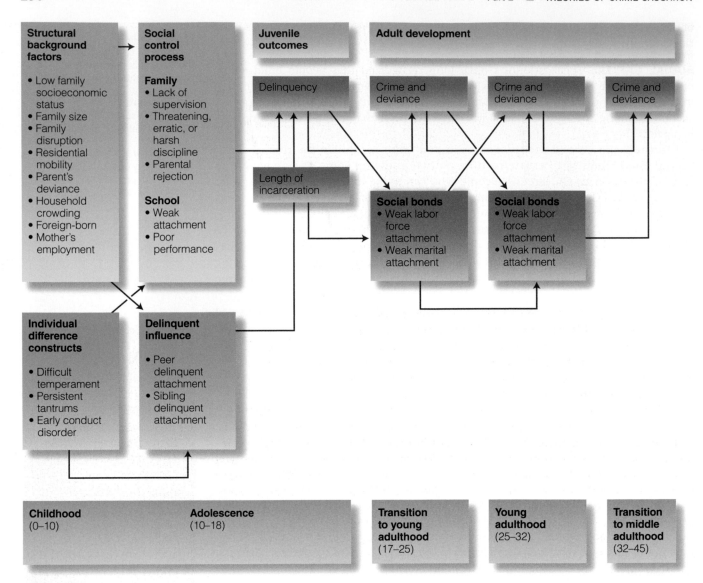

FIGURE 9.1

Sampson and Laub's Age-Graded Theory

Source: Robert Sampson and John Laub, *Crime in the Making: Pathways and Turning Points through Life* (Cambridge, MA: Harvard University Press, 1993) pp. 244–245.

TURNING POINTS   One of Sampson and Laub's most important contributions is identifying the life events that enable adult offenders to desist from crime (Figure 9.1). Because criminal careers are a dynamic process, an important life event or turning point can change the direction of a person's life course trajectory. Two critical turning points are marriage and military service. Adolescents who are at risk for crime can live conventional lives if they can find a supportive mate and serve some time in the military. The Policies and Issues in Criminology feature on page 296 discusses how life changes can affect both personal assessments and subsequent behaviors.

LOVE, MARRIAGE, AND CRIMINALITY   Age-graded theory places a lot of emphasis on the stability brought about by romantic relationships leading eventually to a good marriage. When they achieve adulthood, adolescents who had significant problems with the law are able to desist from crime if they become attached to a spouse who supports and sustains them even when the spouse knows they were in trouble when they were young. Happy marriages are life-sustaining, and marital quality improves over time (as people work less and have fewer parental responsibilities).[51] Spending time in marital and family activities also reduces exposure to deviant peers, which in turn reduces the opportunity to become involved in criminal activities.[52] People who cannot sustain secure marital relations are less likely than others to desist from crime.

FACT OR FICTION?

Getting married helps people stay out of trouble.

FACT Marriage, according to Sampson and Laub, is one of those turning points that help people get out of a criminal career.

Emotions catch up with classmates Shaneecia Tyson, Erin Van Cleve, and Zakeera Ward at their Lincoln Challenge Academy graduation in Springfield, Illinois. The academy is a rigorous 22-week military-style residential program for high school dropouts on the former Chanute Air Force Base. Such programs can help people change their life trajectories and reduce the chance of becoming enmeshed in a criminal career.

AP Images/State Journal-Register, Rich Saal

The marriage effect is supported by research on both a societal and individual level. On a societal level, communities with high marriage rates have correspondingly low crime rates.[53] On an individual level, people headed toward a life of crime can knife off from that path if they meet the right mate, fall in love, and get married. Getting married has a crime suppression effect.[54] Even unstable marriages appear to reduce conviction frequency, at least while they last.[55]

What is it about love that prevents criminality? Romantic love can help fill the emotional void that occurs between the time people break free of parental bonds and when they learn to accept adult responsibilities.[56] But only meaningful relationships seem to work: love, not sex, is the key to success. Kids who get involved in sexual activity without the promise of love actually increase their involvement in crime and criminality; only true love reduces the likelihood of offending. Loveless sexual relations produce feelings of strain, which are correlated with antisocial activity. It is possible that kids who engage in sex without love or romance are willing to partake in other risky and/or self-indulgent behaviors, including criminality and drug usage. In contrast, romantic love discourages offending by strengthening the social bond.

BREAKING UP Romantic breakups, pre- and post-marriage, are a precursor to increased criminal activity.[57] Even unstable marriages appear to reduce conviction frequency, at least while they last.[58] However, things don't always work out as planned: an estimated 40 to 50 percent of first marriages, 67 percent of second marriages, and 74 percent of third marriages end in divorce. And while a happy marriage can reduce crime, separation and divorce seem to have an opposite effect: both men and women have a greater likelihood of arrest when divorced (or legally separated) compared with when they were married.[59]

It is tough to stay married when life circumstances are chaotic, especially when people are in trouble with the law. And the roots of divorce may be traced back to adolescence: kids who get involved with police during adolescence are also the ones most likely to experience financial hardship during young adulthood, which, in turn, decreases the odds of entering into a stable marriage.[60]

Of course, not all marriages are the same. Research indicates that, as expected, people in long-term marriages increase their antisocial behavior when they divorce.[61] However, shorter marriages, those that dissolve prior to the first anniversary, have little effect on offending rates. It's possible that "bad marriages" that are doomed to quickly fail may produce so much tension and conflict that marriage does little to suppress antisocial behaviors even while the couple is still married.[62] Those who can find the right mate and stick with them for the duration are the most likely to live happier, crime-free lives.

CONNECTIONS

Discrete factors influence people at different stages of their development, so the propensity to commit crimes is neither stable nor unyielding. The likelihood of committing crime is linked to the accumulation (or absence) of social capital, social control, and human decision making. This conclusion seems to intersect with the rational choice theory discussed in Chapter 4. Is it possible that the reasons people choose to commit crime fluctuate according to their position in the life course?

Policies and Issues in Criminology

HUMAN AGENCY, PERSONAL ASSESSMENT, CRIME, AND DESISTANCE

Criminologists Robert Agnew and Steven Messner have made a convincing argument that human agency—the ability to intentionally make choices that are not fully determined by forces beyond the individual's control—plays a major role in shaping personal assessments and behaviors, including crime.

Agnew and Messner find that given the same set of prior conditions, one person may choose crime to get what they want while another person relies on more conventional and law-abiding solutions. Why do people make such choices? It's because they use agency to assess their life experiences and immediate personal situation. Crime becomes a reasonable alternative when after making this assessment they come to believe:

1. Crime pays. Offenders believe that crime is the best and maybe the only way for them to get ahead financially, and provides emotional benefits as well, such as satisfaction and excitement.
2. Conventional success, such as decent jobs and respectable status, are beyond their reach.
3. There is no guilt for crimes, because crime is considered acceptable, attractive, and desirable.
4. People come to believe that their bond to conventional society is severed beyond repair and that consequently they have little to lose by committing crime.
5. People decide to adopt identities favorable to crime, although they do not necessarily think of themselves as "criminals." They may view themselves as thieves, hustlers, gangstas, gang bangers, thugs, crazy, wild, outlaws, hardmen, badasses, real men, and/or other identities conducive to crime. Choosing a "bad identity" involves an emphasis on masculinity, as well as physical and emotional toughness.

Assessments are also made when an offender decides to desist. Agnew and Messner find that offenders begin to desist following major life changes or "turning points," such as getting married or finding a good job. These changes in life circumstances are most likely to lead to desistance when they are associated with or prompt "cognitive transformations" (or "cognitive shifts" or the adoption of "redemption scripts"). These shifts correspond with reassessing one's life circumstances: something happens, something changes, and suddenly the criminal lifestyle is no longer attractive. Familiar criminal identities, such as gangsta or playa, seem incompatible with the current lifestyle. Thereafter, the person chooses another persona—devoted husband, good father, enterprising worker—that is incompatible with crime.

Here we can see how change in life circumstances may bring about personal reassessment, cognitive change, and desistance from crime. Why then do some people choose to remain chronic offenders even if their life circumstances change? They decide not to take that step toward cognitive transformations. They find it impossible to take the initiative to reassess their lives and make a commitment to stop offending. They lack self-efficacy—confidence in the ability to succeed in tasks and to control motivation, behavior, and the social environment—a key trait of desisters.

The decision to commit crime and the decision to stop rest on the general assessment of life circumstances. Because people assess their lives differently, the concept of assessment can help explain why given the same set of circumstances one person will choose crime while another remains law abiding and conventional.

Critical Thinking

Do you agree with Agnew and Messner? Are self-assessment and cognitive change responsible for the aging-out process? Or might something else be responsible for desistance?

Source: Robert Agnew and Steven F. Messner, "General Assessments and Thresholds for Chronic Offending: An Enriched Paradigm for Explaining Crime," *Criminology* 53 (2015): 571–596.

MARITAL SUCCESS What prompts some people to engage in loving relationships, while others are doomed to fall in and out of love without finding lasting happiness? Sociologist Rand Conger and his colleagues have discovered that the seeds of marital success are planted early in childhood: kids who grow up with warm, nurturing parents are the ones most likely to have positive romantic relationships and later intact marriages. Well-nurtured kids develop into warm and supportive romantic partners who have relationships that are likely to endure.[63] It is the quality of parenting, not the observation of adult romantic relations, that socializes a young person to engage in behaviors likely to promote successful and lasting romantic unions as an adult.

Do love and other prosocial life experiences work to help kids avoid antisocial behavior over the long haul? To find out, Laub and Sampson conducted an important follow-up to their original research. They found and interviewed survivors from the original Glueck research, the oldest subject being 70 years old and the youngest 62. This study is the subject of the Policies and Issues in Criminology feature Shared Beginnings, Divergent Lives.

HOW VALID IS AGE-GRADED THEORY? There has been a great deal of effort to prove the validity of age-graded theory. Empirical research now shows that, just as Laub and Sampson predicted, people change over the life course, and the factors that predict criminal involvement change as an offender moves from adolescent misbehavior to adult criminality. Criminal careers appear to be dynamic and evolving, not static and constant. Cumulative disadvantage can indeed lock a person into a criminal way of life. Ex-offenders find that their career paths are blocked well into adulthood. If they accumulate deviant peers, criminal behavior may escalate. If they cannot find relevant work, the lure of crime may escalate: the unemployed or underemployed report higher criminal participation rates than those in the workforce.

Despite the support given to age-graded theory some important questions remain, including the theory's time order. Are people who desist from crime able to find a suitable mate, get married, and find a good job? Or are people who find an appropriate mate and a good job then able to desist from crime? In other words, does desistance result in the accumulation of social capital or does the accumulation of social capital produce desistance? Laub and Sampson believe the latter, but there is also evidence that people who desist from crime undergo a cognitive change, and only after they quit a criminal way of life are they able to acquire mates, jobs, and other benefits that support their life change.[64]

Another issue is the current relevance of the Glueck data used in the study. The data were collected at a time when there was no TV or Internet, when divorce was less common, and drug abuse relatively unknown.

Social Schematic Theory (SST)

Age-graded theory is not the only life course view. In what they call a life course learning approach, social schematic theory (SST), criminologists Callie Burt and Ronald Simons propose that social **schemas**—cognitive frameworks that help people quickly process and sort through information—are the key theoretical mechanisms that account for the development of criminal behavior patterns.

The SST relies on how people develop these cognitive shortcuts to organize and interpret information. In some instances schemas can exclude pertinent information and instead focus only on things that confirm preexisting beliefs and ideas. If a member of some group commits a notorious crime, we think "those people are all criminals," forgetting that the vast majority in any grouping are law-abiding citizens. Or if someone is hassled by a police officer, the experience can shape the way they view all police officers and cause them to alter their behavior accordingly (i.e., avoid contact with cops, refuse to cooperate, call them names, and so on). Schemas can contribute to stereotypes and make it difficult to retain new information that does not conform to our established ideas about the world.

Burt and Simons argue that seemingly unrelated family, peer, and community conditions—harsh parenting, racial discrimination, and community disadvantage—lead to crime because the lessons communicated by these events are actually similar and promote social schemas involving (a) a hostile view of people and relationships, (b) a preference for immediate rewards, and (c) a cynical view of conventional norms.[65] Because these negative schemas are interconnected they combine to form a **criminogenic knowledge structure (CKS)**. When someone with a CKS forged by negative life events encounters a stressful situation, their past experiences compel

schemas
Cognitive frameworks that help people quickly process and sort through information.

criminogenic knowledge structure (CKS)
The view that negative life events are connected and produce a hostile view of people and relationships, preference for immediate rewards, and a cynical view of conventional norms.

Policies and Issues in Criminology

SHARED BEGINNINGS, DIVERGENT LIVES

Why are some people destined to become persistent criminals as adults? To find out, John Laub and Robert Sampson located the survivors of the sample first collected by Sheldon and Eleanor Glueck. At the time of the follow-up study, the oldest was 70 years old and the youngest was 62. The study involved three sources of new data collection—criminal record checks (both local and national), death record checks (local and national), and personal interviews with a sample of 52 of the original Glueck men, stratified to ensure variability in patterns of persistence and desistance in crime.

They found that explanations of desistance from crime and also for persistent offending in crime are two sides of the same coin. Desistance is a process rather than an event, and it must be continually renewed. The processes of desistance operate simultaneously at different levels (individual, situational, and community) and across different contextual environments (especially family, work, and military service). The process of desistance is more than mere aging and more than individual predisposition.

The interviews showed that criminality and other forms of antisocial conduct in childhood are strongly related to adult criminality and drug and alcohol abuse. Former delinquents also suffer consequences in other areas of social life, such as school, work, and family life. They are far less likely to finish high school than are nondelinquents and subsequently are more likely to be unemployed, receive welfare, and experience separation or divorce as adults.

Laub and Sampson also addressed a key question posed by life course theories: Is it possible for former delinquents to turn their lives around as adults? The researchers found that most antisocial children do not remain antisocial as adults. Of men in the study cohort who survived to 50 years of age, 24 percent had no arrests for delinquent acts of violence and property (predatory criminality) after age 17 (6 percent had no arrests for total criminality); 48 percent had no arrests for predatory criminality after age 25 (19 percent for total criminality); 60 percent had no arrests for predatory criminality after age 31 (33 percent for total criminality); and 79 percent had no arrests for predatory criminality after age 40 (57 percent for total criminality). Laub and Sampson concluded that desistance from criminality is the norm and that most, if not all, serious delinquents desist from criminality.

Why Do People Desist?

Laub and Sampson's earlier research indicated that building social capital through marriage and jobs was the key component of desistance from criminality. The follow-up showed a dramatic drop in criminal activity as the men aged. Between 17 and 24 years of age, 84 percent of the subjects had committed violent crimes; in their 30s and 40s, that number dropped to 14 percent; it fell to 3 percent as the men reached their 60s and 70s. Property crimes and alcohol- and drug-related crimes showed significant decreases. Former delinquents who desisted from crime were rooted in structural routines and had strong social ties to family and community. They found that one important element for going straight is the knifing off of individuals from their immediate environment, offering the men a new script for the future. Joining the military can provide this knifing-off effect, as can marriage or changing one's residence. One former criminal (age 69) told them:

I'd say the turning point was, number one, the Army. You get into an outfit, you had a sense of belonging, you made your friends. I think I became a pretty good judge of character. In the Army, you met some good ones, you met some foul balls. Then I met the wife. I'd say probably that would be the turning point. Got married, then naturally, kids come. So now you got to get a better job, you got to make more money. And that's how I got to the Navy Yard and tried to improve myself.

them to respond with criminal and antisocial behavior. Prior negative life experiences allow them to legitimize their behavior: people abused me, so it's okay to abuse other people. CKS exists on a continuum: those at the low end possess benign views of relationships, see the wisdom of following conventional norms and the value of delaying gratification. Those at the high end of the CKS have a learned view of the world that is more harsh, unpredictable, and unforgiving, and thus are more likely to define situations as requiring or justifying crime.[66]

Former delinquents who went straight were able to put structure into their lives. Structure often led the men to disassociate from criminal peers, reducing the opportunity to get into trouble. Getting married may limit the number of nights available to "hang with the guys." As one wife of a former offender said, "It is not how many beers you have, it's who you drink with." Even multiple offenders who did time in prison were able to desist with the help of a stabilizing marriage. So love does in fact conquer all!

People who can turn their life around, who have acquired a degree of maturity by taking on family and work responsibilities, and who have forged new commitments are most likely to make a fresh start and find new direction and meaning in life. It seems that men who desisted changed their identity as well, and this, in turn, affected their outlook and sense of maturity and responsibility. The ability to change did not reflect any criminality "specialty": violent offenders followed the same path as property offenders.

Although many former delinquents desisted, others did not and continued a life of crime late into adulthood. These persisters experienced considerable residential instability, marital instability, job instability, failure in the school and the military, and relatively long periods of incarceration. Many were "social nomads," without permanent addresses, steady jobs, spouses, or children. As a consequence of chaotic and unstructured routines, the persisters had increased contact with those individuals who were similarly situated—in this case, similarly unattached and free from nurturing and informal social control. And they paid the price for their unstructured lives: they faced the risk of an early and untimely death. Thirteen percent (N = 62) of the criminal subjects as compared to 6 percent (N = 28) of the noncriminal subjects died unnatural deaths, such as by violence, cirrhosis of the liver caused by alcoholism, poor self-care, and suicide. By 65 years of age, 29 percent (N = 139) of the offenders and 21 percent (N = 95) of the non-offenders

had died from natural causes. Frequent involvement in criminality during adolescence and alcohol abuse were the strongest predictors of an early and untimely death. So, while many troubled youths are able to reform, their early excesses may haunt them across their life span.

These findings are important because they suggest that criminality and other social problems are cumulative. Consequently, early prevention efforts that reduce criminality in adolescence will probably also reduce alcohol abuse, drunk driving, drug abuse, sexual promiscuity, and family violence in adulthood. The best way to achieve these goals is through four significant life-changing events: marriage, joining the military, getting a job, and changing one's environment or neighborhood. What appears to be important about these processes is that they all involve, to varying degrees, the following items: a knifing off of the past from the present; new situations that provide both supervision and monitoring as well as new opportunities of social support and growth; and new situations that provide the opportunity for transforming identity.

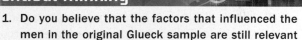

Critical Thinking

1. Do you believe that the factors that influenced the men in the original Glueck sample are still relevant for change—for example, a military career?

2. Would it be possible for men such as these to join the military today?

3. Do you believe that some sort of universal service program might be beneficial and help people turn their lives around?

Sources: John Laub and Robert Sampson, *Shared Beginnings, Divergent Lives: Delinquent Boys to Age 70* (Cambridge, MA: Harvard University Press, 2003); John Laub and Robert Sampson, "Understanding Desistance from Criminality," in *Criminality and Justice: An Annual Review of Research*, Vol. 28, ed. Michael Tonry (Chicago: University of Chicago Press, 2001), pp. 1–71.

While developed at an early age, the CKS can improve when people experience positive life events, such as having a healthy romantic relationship, or worsen when experiencing some negative life event, such as racial discrimination. Negative social schemas combined with situational events that set them off produce antisocial behavior. Actions, including crime, result from the combination of individual characteristics and situational cues. Moreover, individuals are not randomly placed in various contexts, but they actively seek out settings consistent with their aims and preferences.

Consequently, any preexisting thought patterns will be reinforced by surrounding influences in a never-ending loop.

While still being tested, early results have given strong support for the SST.[67]

Latent Trait/Propensity Theory

In a popular 1985 book, *Crime and Human Nature*, two prominent social scientists, James Q. Wilson and Richard Herrnstein, argued that personal traits, such as genetic makeup, intelligence, and body build, operate in tandem with social variables that include poverty and family function. Together these factors influence people to "choose criminality" over noncriminal behavioral alternatives.[68]

Following their lead, David Rowe, D. Wayne Osgood, and W. Alan Nicewander proposed the concept of latent traits, the idea that a number of people in the population have a personal attribute or propensity that controls their inclination to commit criminal acts.[69] This disposition, or latent trait, is either present at birth or established early in life, and it remains stable over time. Suspected latent traits include defective intelligence, impulsive personality, genetic abnormalities, the physical–chemical functioning of the brain, and environmental influences on brain function, such as drugs, chemicals, and injuries.[70] Those who carry one of these latent traits are in danger of becoming career criminals; those who lack the propensity to commit crime have a much lower risk.[71]

According to this view, the *propensity* to commit crime is stable, but the *opportunity* to commit crime fluctuates over time. People age out of crime because as they mature there are simply fewer opportunities to commit such acts and greater inducements to remain "straight." They may marry, have children, and obtain jobs. The former delinquents' newfound adult responsibilities leave them little time to hang with their friends, abuse substances, and get into scrapes with the law.

Assume, for example, that a stable latent trait such as low IQ causes some people to commit criminal acts. Teenagers have more opportunity to do so than adults, so at every level of intelligence, adolescent criminality rates will be higher. As they mature, however, teens with both high and low IQs will slowly age out of crime, not due to a change in makeup or propensity, but because adult responsibilities provide them with fewer opportunities to engage in antisocial acts.

Crime and Human Nature

Wilson and Herrnstein's *Crime and Human Nature* was a milestone in the development of propensity theory. Quite controversial at the time, they speculated that individual-level factors played a significant role in shaping behavior choices.[72]

According to Wilson and Herrnstein, all human behavior, including criminality, is determined by its perceived consequences. A criminal incident occurs when an individual chooses criminal over conventional behavior (which Wilson and Herrnstein refer to as non-crime) after weighing the potential gains and losses associated with each: "The larger the ratio of net rewards of crime to the net rewards of non-crime, the greater the tendency to commit the crime."[73]

Wilson and Herrnstein's model assumes that both biological and psychological traits influence the choice between crime and non-crime. They see a close link between a person's decision to choose crime and such biosocial factors as low intelligence, mesomorphic body type, genetic influences (parental criminality), and possessing an autonomic nervous system that responds too quickly to stimuli. Psychological traits, such as an impulsive or extroverted personality or generalized hostility, also affect the potential to commit crime.

In their focus on the association between these constitutional and psychological factors and crime, Wilson and Herrnstein seem to be suggesting the existence of an elusive latent trait that predisposes people to commit crime.[74] Their vision helped inspire other criminologists to identify the elusive latent trait that causes criminal behavior. The most prominent latent trait/propensity theory is Gottfredson and Hirschi's general theory of crime (GTC).

CONNECTIONS

Hirschi's original theory was reviewed in Chapter 7. At first he linked crime to a lack of social control due to the weakening of social bonds. In this newer version, he shifts his focus to self-control.

General Theory of Crime (GTC)

In their **general theory of crime (GTC)**, Michael Gottfredson and Travis Hirschi attribute the tendency to commit crime to a single and powerful latent trait: a person's level of **self-control**.[75]

People with limited self-control tend to be **impulsive**; they are insensitive to other people's feelings, physical (rather than mental), risk takers, shortsighted, and nonverbal.[76] They have a here-and-now orientation and refuse to work for distant goals; they lack diligence, tenacity, and persistence. People lacking self-control tend to be adventuresome, active, and self-centered. Criminality is only one aspect of their problems. As they mature, they often have unstable marriages, jobs, and friendships.[77] They are less likely to feel shame if they engage in deviant acts and are more likely to find them pleasurable.[78] They are also more likely to engage in dangerous behaviors such as drinking.

Because those with low self-control enjoy risky, exciting, or thrilling behaviors with immediate gratification, they are more likely to enjoy criminal acts, which require stealth, agility, speed, and power, than conventional acts, which demand long-term study and cognitive and verbal skills. As Gottfredson and Hirschi put it, they derive satisfaction from "money without work, sex without courtship, revenge without court delays."[79] Many of these individuals who have a propensity for committing crime also engage in other risky, impulsive behaviors such as smoking, drinking, gambling, and illicit sexuality.[80] Although these acts are not illegal, they too provide immediate, short-term gratification. Unlike other theoretical models that explain only narrow segments of criminal behavior (i.e., teenage gang formation), Gottfredson and Hirschi's self-control theory applies to all crimes and deviant acts, ranging from murder to suicide.[81]

WHAT CAUSES IMPULSIVITY/LOW SELF-CONTROL TO DEVELOP? Gottfredson and Hirschi trace the root cause of poor self-control to inadequate child-rearing practices. Parents who refuse or are unable to monitor a child's behavior, to recognize deviant behavior when it occurs, and to punish that behavior will produce children who lack self-control. Children whose social bond is weak and frayed, who are not attached to their parents, who are poorly supervised, and whose parents are criminal or deviant themselves are the most likely to develop poor self-control.[82] Even in disadvantaged communities, children whose parents provide adequate and supportive discipline are the ones most likely to develop self-control.[83]

The association between poor parents and lack of self-control may be both reciprocal and intergenerational. Kids who have low self-control may strain parental attachments and the ability of parents to control children; parents who themselves have low self-control are the ones most likely to use damaging and inappropriate supervision and punishment mechanisms. Impulsive kids grow up to become poor parents who themselves use improper discipline, producing yet another generation of impulsive kids who lack self-control.[84]

LEARNING OR BIOLOGY? There may also be a genetic/biosocial component to the development of impulsivity. Children of impulsive parents are the ones most likely to exhibit a lack of self-control.[85] Research by David Farrington and his colleagues shows that antisocial behavior runs in families and that having criminal relatives is a significant predictor of future misbehaviors.[86] While these studies are not definitive, they raise the possibility that the intergenerational transfer of impulsivity has a biological basis.

Measures of neuropsychological deficits, birth complications, and low birth weight have all been found to have significant direct or indirect effects on levels of self-control.[87] Recent research shows that children who suffer anoxia (oxygen starvation) during the birthing process are the ones most likely to lack self-control later in life, which suggests that impulsivity may have a biological basis.[88] When Kevin Beaver and his associates examined impulsive personality and self-control in twin pairs, they discovered evidence that these traits may be inherited rather than developed. That might help explain the stability of these latent traits over the life course.[89]

LO5 Explain the concept of the latent trait and the basic principles of the general theory of crime (GTC).

general theory of crime (GTC) Gottfredson and Hirschi's developmental theory that links crime to impulsivity and a lack of self-control.

self-control Refers to a person's ability to exercise restraint and control over his or her feelings, emotions, reactions, and behaviors.

impulsive Lacking in thought or deliberation in decision making. An impulsive person lacks close attention to details, has organizational problems, and is distracted and forgetful.

FACT OR FICTION?

Criminals are impulsive risk takers.

FACT According to the general theory of crime (GTC), criminals are impulsive people who lack the self-control to curb their criminal activities.

Another biological basis for impulsivity may be low resting heart rate. People with low heart rates may seek out dangerous and arousing behaviors, such as criminality, to compensate for their biological condition; they become thrill seekers who engage in dangerous behaviors simply because it gives them the jolt they need to feel good, that is, normal.[90]

THE ACT AND THE OFFENDER Not all impulsive people become criminals, nor does impulsivity mean that someone is consistently antisocial. In their general theory of crime (GTC), Gottfredson and Hirschi consider the criminal offender and the criminal act as separate concepts. On the one hand, criminal acts, such as robberies or burglaries, are illegal events or deeds that offenders engage in when they perceive them to be advantageous. Burglaries are typically committed by young males looking for cash, liquor, and entertainment; the crime provides "easy, short-term gratification."[91]

On the other hand, criminal offenders are people predisposed to commit crimes. They are not, however, robots who commit crime without restraint; their days are also filled with conventional behaviors, such as going to school, parties, concerts, and church. But given the same set of criminal opportunities, such as having a lot of free time for mischief and living in a neighborhood with unguarded homes containing valuable merchandise, crime-prone people have a much higher probability of violating the law than do noncriminals. It bears repeating: according to the GTC, the propensity to commit crimes remains stable throughout a person's life. Change in the frequency of criminal activity is purely a function of change in criminal opportunity. Exhibit 9.2 lists the elements of impulsivity, or low self-control.

TESTING THE GENERAL THEORY OF CRIME Following the publication of *A General Theory of Crime*, dozens of research efforts tested the validity, both directly and indirectly, of Gottfredson and Hirschi's theoretical views.[92] Meta-analysis of these studies indicate that the GTC is a valid theory of the onset of deviant behavior.[93] The patterns of antisocial behavior predicted by Gottfredson and Hirschi seem to be valid.[94]

There have been a variety of approaches to test the theory. Some criminologists have identified indicators of impulsiveness and self-control and then determined whether these factors correlate with measures of criminal activity. According to the GTC, as self-control declines the likelihood that someone will engage in future antisocial behaviors increases.[95] Low self-control has been linked to a variety of crime types ranging from texting while driving to serious sex offending.[96] Studies using this approach have found that teens measuring low on self-control are the ones most likely to fall in with a bad crowd, and once they do so their impulsivity makes them vulnerable to antisocial peer influence.[97] Career criminals have been shown to have significantly lower levels of self-control than non-offenders.[98]

CRITICISMS AND QUESTIONS Although the GTC seems persuasive, several questions and criticisms remain to be answered. Among the most important are the following:

- *Impulsivity is only one of many personality traits correlated with crime.* Lack of self-control may in fact be a trait associated with crime, but so are many others.[99] There is too much variety in personality traits, ranging from psychopathy to decision-making style, to say that a single element is responsible for

One criticism of the general theory of crime is that people actually do change over their lifetime. Here are early photos of Stanley "Tookie" Williams, executed cofounder of the Crips gang, as seen in a memorial service program. Sentenced to prison for the 1979 murders of four people, Williams spent several years involved with violent activities in prison, but around 1993 he changed his behavior and became an antigang activist. Williams coauthored such books as *Life in Prison*, which encouraged kids to stay out of gangs, and his memoir *Blue Rage, Black Redemption*. Williams was nominated for the Nobel Peace Prize for his efforts. Do you believe that a gang leader such as "Tookie" Williams really can change? Or did his changing life circumstances simply prevent him from committing violent criminal acts? Regardless of his change, Williams was executed in 2005.

David McNew/Getty Images News/Getty Images

Exhibit 9.2 Elements of Impulsivity: Signs that a Person Has Low Self-Control

- Insensitive
- Physical (rather than mental)
- Shortsighted
- Nonverbal
- Here-and-now orientation
- Unstable social relations
- Enjoys deviant behaviors
- Risk taker
- Refuses to work for distant goals

- Lacks diligence
- Lacks tenacity
- Adventuresome
- Self-centered
- Shameless
- Imprudent
- Lacks cognitive and verbal skills
- Enjoys danger and excitement

all crimes.[100] People who score low on scales measuring an honesty-humility personality dimension (honesty-humility refers to individuals who are willing to use others for personal gain and includes greed, immodesty, and active violations of social norms through insincerity and unfairness) are more likely than high scorers to make criminal choices.[101] Other personality traits such as low self-direction (the tendency not to act in one's long-term benefit) may be a better predictor of criminality than impulsivity or lack of self-control.[102]

- *The GTC does not explain racial and gender differences.* Although distinct gender differences in the crime rate exist, there is little evidence that males are more impulsive or lacking in self-control than females.[103] It is equally likely that gender differences in the crime rate can be explained by differences in socialization and gender role differentials. Cognitive differences may also play a role: because they acquire social cognitive skills earlier in life than males, females develop better prosocial skills and verbal dexterity; these factors may help lower their rates of offending. Gottfredson and Hirschi explain racial differences in the criminality rate as a failure of childrearing practices in the African American community.[104] In so doing, they overlook issues of institutional racism, poverty, and relative deprivation, which have been shown to have a significant impact on crime rates.[105] In sum, impulsivity alone may not be able to explain all the gender and racial variations in the crime rate.[106]

- *People change and so does their level of self-control.* The general theory of crime assumes that criminal propensity does not change; opportunities change. This is a critical issue because it assumes that critical elements of human personality are stable from childhood into adulthood. However, social scientists recognize that behavior-shaping factors that are dominant in early adolescence, such as peer groups, may fade in adulthood and be replaced by others, such as the nuclear family.[107] Personality also undergoes change and so does its impact on antisocial behavior.[108] There is evidence that impulsivity, a key element of the GTC, declines over the life course, perhaps explaining the age-graded decline in the crime rate.[109] It is not surprising that research efforts show that the stability in self-control predicted by Gottfredson and Hirschi may be an illusion.[110] As kids mature, the focus of their lives likewise changes and they may be better able to control their impulsive

David Wallace/Arizona Republic/Reuters

Jodi Arias (center) talks to defense attorneys Jennifer Willmott and Kirk Nurmi during her trial at Maricopa County Superior Court in Phoenix, Arizona, April 3, 2013. Arias was on trial for the 2008 killing of her boyfriend, Travis Alexander, whom she claimed repeatedly abused her. Was hers an impulsive response to a violent environment or a calculated act of murder? The jury did not believe her claims: on May 8, 2013, Arias was found guilty of first-degree murder. In 2015, she was sentenced to life in prison without the possibility of parole.

behavior.[111] As Callie Burt and her associates recently found, adolescence is a period of dramatic biological, behavioral, and social changes; a young person's physical and neurological makeup is undergoing remodeling and restructuring. Environmental influences operate in concert with neurobiological changes to create a period of heightened change. During this period levels of impulsivity also change, a result that is not predicted by the GTC.[112]

- *Environmental patterns are not adequately explained.* The GTC fails to address ecological patterns in the crime rate. If crime rates are higher in Los Angeles than in Boston, can it be assumed that Angelenos are more impulsive than Bostonians? There is little evidence of regional differences in impulsivity or self-control. Gottfredson and Hirschi might counter that crime rate differences may reflect criminal opportunity: one area may have more effective law enforcement, tougher criminal laws, and higher levels of guardianship. In their view, opportunity is controlled by economy and culture.

Environments may interact with personality to shape behaviors, a condition not foreseen by the GTC.[113] Some research indicates that social factors do in fact mediate the influence of self-control on crime and that such factors as community solidarity, morality, and general levels of self-control moderate the effects of individual-level low self-control.[114]

Recently, criminologist Gregory Zimmerman found that in disadvantaged neighborhoods, most people tend to possess a feeling of fatalism and adopt an "I have nothing to lose" attitude. These factors cause both non-impulsive and impulsive individuals to take advantage of criminal opportunities. In these disorganized neighborhoods, nearly everyone commits crime, so having self-control means relatively little.[115] In disadvantaged neighborhoods, then, people's behavior seems to be more closely influenced by environmental factors and conditions; individual-level factors, such as lack of self-control, remain in the background.[116] This observation contradicts the GTC.

Although questions remain, the strength of the general theory of crime lies in its scope and breadth. By integrating concepts of criminal choice, criminal opportunity, socialization, and personality, Gottfredson and Hirschi make a plausible argument that all deviant behaviors may originate from the same source. Continued efforts are needed to test the GTC and establish the validity of its core concepts. It remains one of the key developments of modern criminological theory.

Trajectory Theory

LO6 Articulate the basic principles of trajectory theory.

Trajectory theory is a third developmental approach that combines elements of propensity and life course theories. The basic premise is that there is more than one path to crime and more than one class of offender; there are different *trajectories* in a criminal career. Because people are different, no single model of criminality can hope to describe every person's journey through life. People offend at a different pace, commit different kinds of crimes, and are influenced by different external forces.[117] As external influences, both individual and social, shift and change so too do offending trajectories.[118]

Because there is little question that there is more than a single route to a criminal career, and criminal careerists travel down many paths, criminologists have sought to identify different trajectories to crime.[119] What are some of the factors that may influence criminal trajectories?

Age and Offending Trajectories

Some people begin at an early age and later become adult offenders, while others begin their violent careers in adulthood, having escaped and/or avoided crime as juveniles.[120] As they mature, people who begin offending at an early age may later segue into more age-appropriate crimes—the violent adolescent schoolyard bully matures into the abusive husband in adulthood—but they remain violent over the life course.[121] Other offenders stay out of trouble in early adolescence and do not begin to violate the law until much later in the life cycle. While some later starters reach their offending peak during adolescence, others persist at a high rate into adulthood.[122]

Personality and Offending Trajectories

The reason why some offenders start early, others late, and some not at all, may be linked to psychological problems and disturbance. Mental disease and personality disorders progress differently, affecting some people in early adolescence and others later in life.[123] Research shows that offending trajectories do in fact differ among people with mental disorders, creating different classes of offenders. There are early starters (ES) who begin to engage in antisocial behavior at a young age before the onset of the psychiatric disorder, most likely because they maintain other psychological issues such as an antisocial personality. There are also late starters (LS) who begin to engage in antisocial behavior after the onset of the psychiatric disorder. Their criminal and deviant behavior is attributed to symptoms of the disorder.[124] Another category, called first offenders (FO), are people in their late 30s with a schizophrenia disorder who suddenly commit a very serious, typically violent, offense.[125]

Chronic Offenders and Non-offenders

There is also a spectrum of offending frequency, ranging from people who have never committed a crime to those who repeatedly commit criminal offenses.

CHRONIC OFFENDING As you may recall from Chapter 2, Marvin Wolfgang first identified the concept of chronic offending when he analyzed data from the Philadelphia cohort study. Now research shows that even chronic offenders can be divided into subgroupings.[126] Alex Piquero and his associates found five classes based on their offending histories:

- Non-offenders (62 percent)
- Low-rate adolescence peak offenders (19 percent)
- Very-low-rate chronic offenders (11 percent)
- High-rate adolescence peak offenders (5 percent)
- High-rate chronic offenders (3 percent)

Following them over time until they reached their 40s, Piquero found that boys in each of these offending trajectories faced a different degree of social and personal problems, such as poor housing, a troubled romantic life, mental illness, and drug involvement. Not surprisingly, those youth classified as high-rate chronic offenders were the ones most likely to experience life failure. Piquero, along with Wesley Jennings and David Farrington, calculated that the cost to society presented by each high-rate chronic offender could be up to 10 times greater than the cost of those in the other offending categories.[127]

ABSTAINERS AND LATE BLOOMERS There is also a group of abstainers, or non-offenders. Despite the fact that most of their peers engage in a wide variety of antisocial activities, these people never break the law; their conventional behavior makes them deviant because offending is the norm! Why do some people refrain from antisocial activity of any sort? Who are these folks who never ever shoplifted, smoked pot, got drunk, or had a fight? According to social psychologist Terrie Moffitt, abstainers are social introverts as teens, whose unpopularity shields them from group pressure to commit delinquent acts.[128] Still another explanation may be biological: abstainers maintain a genetic code that insulates them from criminality-producing factors in the environment.[129] Xiaojin Chen and

Sylvia Plachy/Redux

Kids who have close parental monitoring and/or family relations are able to abstain from crime. Here, Regina Saiz, 15, a Mexican American from Goshen, California, and her grandmother share a moment in their Catholic church before her quinceañera mass. Although some girls' quinceañeras are focused around a big party, Regina's also included a strong religious component. A crown was placed on her head, signifying, as the deacon who officiated said, "the victory that she has won so far in her life" as a Christian. Regina saw the church service as "a way to show people that ever since baptism, I've been following God's path and living my life with God." Afterward, her family and all her friends, who served as a sort of homecoming court wearing fancy dresses and zoot suits, had a party at a local Elks Club.

Michele Adams found that rather than being shy loners, abstainers are just normal kids who have prosocial friends, the kind who shun deviant activities.[130] Not surprisingly, abstainers are more likely than other youth to become successful, well-adjusted adults.[131]

Pathways to Crime

Trajectory theory recognizes that criminals may travel more than a single road. Some may specialize in violence and extortion; some may be involved in theft and fraud; others may engage in a variety of criminal acts.[132] Each type of specialist may be unique: people who commit violent crimes may be different from nonviolent property and drug offenders.[133]

There are unique criminal career paths. Some start out as violent kids whose violent behavior declines with age and who eventually desist. Another group are *escalators* whose severity of violence increases over time. Escalators are more likely to live in racially mixed communities, experience racism, and have less parental involvement than people who avoid or decrease their violent behaviors.[134] Late-onset escalators begin their violent careers relatively late in their adolescence after suffering a variety of psychological and social disturbances earlier in childhood, including high levels of social anxiety.[135]

Pathways may also be created by the effect of early childhood risk factors. Kids who experience risk factors (difficult infant temperament, low cognitive ability, weak parental closeness, and disadvantaged family background) very early in their lives, by age 3, seem to travel down a variety of paths: a normative, prosocial pathway; a pathway marked by oppositional behavior and fighting; a pathway marked by impulsivity and inattention; and a few who engage in a wide range of antisocial tendencies. Children who enter on an antisocial pathway early in their lives are more likely to engage in preteen delinquency and substance use by 11 years of age.[136]

Some of the most important research on delinquent paths or trajectories has been conducted by Rolf Loeber and his associates. Using data from a longitudinal study of Pittsburgh youth, Loeber identified three distinct paths to a criminal career (Figure 9.2):[137]

- The **authority conflict pathway** begins at an early age with stubborn behavior. This leads to defiance (doing things one's own way, disobedience) and then to authority avoidance (staying out late, truancy, running away).
- The **covert pathway** begins with minor, underhanded behavior (lying, shoplifting) that leads to property damage (setting nuisance fires, damaging property). This behavior eventually escalates to more serious forms of criminality, ranging from joyriding, pocket picking, larceny, and fencing to passing bad checks, using stolen credit cards, stealing cars, dealing drugs, and breaking and entering.
- The **overt pathway** escalates to aggressive acts beginning with aggression (annoying others, bullying), leading to physical (and gang) fighting, and then to violence (attacking someone, forced theft).

The Loeber research indicates that each of these paths may lead to a sustained deviant career. Some people enter two and even three paths simultaneously: they are stubborn, lie to teachers and parents, are bullies, and commit petty thefts. Those taking more than one path are the most likely to become persistent offenders as they mature.

Although some persistent offenders may specialize in one type of behavior, others engage in varied criminal acts and antisocial behaviors as they mature. As adolescents, they cheat on tests, bully kids in the schoolyard, take drugs, commit burglary, steal a car, and then shoplift from a store. Later as adults, some specialize in a particular criminal activity such as drug trafficking, while others are involved in an assortment of deviant acts—selling drugs, committing robberies, and getting involved in break-ins—when the situation arises and the opportunities are present.[138] There may be a multitude of criminal career subgroupings (for example, prostitutes, drug dealers), each with its own distinctive career path.

Adolescent-Limited and Life Course Persistent Offenders

According to psychologist Terrie Moffitt, most young offenders follow one of two paths. **Adolescent-limited offenders** may be considered typical teenagers who get into

authority conflict pathway
The path to a criminal career that begins with early stubborn behavior and defiance of parents.

covert pathway
A path to a criminal career that begins with minor underhanded behavior and progresses to fire starting and theft.

overt pathway
Pathway to a criminal career that begins with minor aggression, leads to physical fighting, and eventually escalates to violent crime.

adolescent-limited offenders
Kids who get into minor scrapes as youth but whose misbehavior ends when they enter adulthood.

Age of Onset
Late

% Boys
Few

FIGURE 9.2
Loeber's Pathways
to Crime

Source: "Serious and Violent
Juvenile Offenders," *Juvenile
Justice Bulletin*, May 1998.

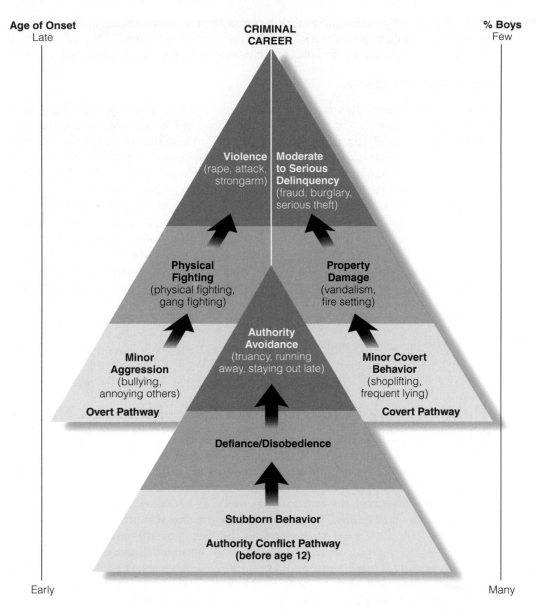

CRIMINAL
CAREER

Violence
(rape, attack,
strongarm)

**Moderate
to Serious
Delinquency**
(fraud, burglary,
serious theft)

**Physical
Fighting**
(physical fighting,
gang fighting)

**Property
Damage**
(vandalism,
fire setting)

**Authority
Avoidance**
(truancy, running
away, staying out late)

**Minor
Aggression**
(bullying,
annoying others)

**Minor Covert
Behavior**
(shoplifting,
frequent lying)

Overt Pathway

Covert Pathway

Defiance/Disobedience

Stubborn Behavior

Authority Conflict Pathway
(before age 12)

Early

Many

minor scrapes and engage in what might be considered rebellious teenage behavior with their friends.[139] As they reach their mid-teens, adolescent-limited delinquents begin to mimic the antisocial behavior of more troubled teens, only to reduce the frequency of their offending as they mature to around age 18.[140]

The second path is the one taken by a small group of **life course persisters** who begin their offending career at a very early age and continue to offend well into adulthood.[141] Moffitt finds that life course persisters combine family dysfunction with severe neurological problems that predispose them to antisocial behavior patterns. These afflictions can be the result of maternal drug abuse, poor nutrition, or exposure to toxic agents such as lead. Research using twin pairs indicates that there may be a genetic basis to life course persistence that may be linked through neurological deficiencies.[142] It is not surprising that life course persisters display social and personal dysfunctions, including lower than average verbal ability, reasoning skills, learning ability, and school achievement.

Research shows that the persistence patterns predicted by Moffitt are valid and accurate.[143] Life course persisters offend more frequently and engage in a greater variety of antisocial acts than other offenders; they also manifest significantly more mental health problems, including psychiatric pathologies, than adolescent-limited offenders.[144] Many have deviant friends who support their behavior choices.[145] Persisters are more likely to manifest traits such as low verbal ability and hyperactivity; they display a

life course persisters
Delinquents who begin their offending career at a very early age and continue to offend well into adulthood.

Life course persistent offenders begin their aggressive acts early in life and continue uninterrupted into maturity. Here, David Kalac, accused of killing his girlfriend Amber Coplin and posting grisly nude photos of her body online, is led into his arraignment hearing at Kitsap County Superior Court, in Port Orchard, Washington. Kalac was charged with first-degree murder with a special allegation of domestic violence and an aggravated circumstance of having an impact on people other than the victim. After he committed the crime, he wrote: "I killed Amanda Coplin. I strangled her with my hands, then a shoelace. I had no reason other than I was drunk and she pissed me off. Running from the cops was so fun."

AP Images/Kitsap Sun, Meegan M. Reid

negative or impulsive personality and seem particularly impaired on spatial and memory functions.[146] Individual traits rather than environment seem to have the greatest influence on life course persistence.[147]

Public Policy Implications of Developmental Theory

Policies based on the premises of developmental theory have inspired a number of initiatives. Since the aim is to set people on the right developmental track, these efforts typically feature multisystemic treatment efforts designed to provide at-risk youths with personal, social, educational, and family services. Interventions are aimed at promoting academic success, social competence, and educational enhancement during the elementary grades.[148] Many of the most successful programs are aimed at strengthening children's social-emotional competence and positive coping skills and suppressing the development of antisocial, aggressive behavior.[149]

The most promising multicomponent prevention programs are designed to improve developmental skills. They may include a school component, an after-school component, and a parent-involvement component. All of these components share the goal of increasing protective factors and decreasing risk factors in the areas of the family, the community, the school, and the individual.[150] One example is the Boys and Girls Clubs and School Collaborations' Substance Abuse Prevention Program, which includes a school component called SMART (Skills Mastery And Resistance Training), an after-school component called SMART Kids, and a parent-involvement component called SMART Parents. Each component is designed to reduce specific risk factors in the children's school, family, community, and personal environments.[151] Another effort, Guiding Good Choices (GGC, formerly known as Preparing for the Drug Free Years), is designed to aid parents on many fronts, including teaching them about the risk and protective factors for substance abuse. GGC is a multimedia substance abuse prevention program that gives parents of children in grades 4 through 8 (ages 9 to 14) the knowledge and skills needed to guide their children through early adolescence.[152]

AP Images for Boys & Girls Clubs of America/Steve Ruark

Programs based on developmental theory try to help kids knife off from a pathway to crime. Here, staff and volunteers huddle during the Triple Play Mobile Tour in Baltimore. With the support of partners Coca-Cola and the Anthem Foundation, the tour brings Boys and Girls Clubs' healthy lifestyles program to clubs around the country, providing a unique experience focused on mind, body, and soul.

Thinking Like a Criminologist

A Question of Life or Death You are a state supreme court judge. Before you is the case of Gary L. Sampson, 41, a man addicted to alcohol and cocaine, a deadbeat dad, a two-bit thief, and a bank robber with a long history of violence. On August 1, 2001, he turned himself in to the Vermont State Police after fleeing from pursuit for a string of three murders he committed in Massachusetts and New Hampshire.

Those who knew Sampson speculated that his murders were a desperate finale to a troubled life. During his early life in New England, he once bound, gagged, and beat three elderly women in a candy store. He had hijacked cars at knifepoint and was medically diagnosed as schizophrenic. In 1977, he married a 17-year-old girl he had impregnated; two months later he was arrested and charged with rape for having "unnatural intercourse with a child under 16." Although he was acquitted of that charge, his wife noticed that Sampson had developed a hair-trigger temper and had become increasingly violent; their marriage soon ended. As the years passed, Sampson had at least four failed marriages, was an absentee father to two children, and became an alcoholic and a drug user. He spent nearly half of his adult life behind bars.

Jumping bail after being arrested for theft from an antique store, he headed south to North Carolina and took on a new identity: Gary Johnson, a construction worker. He took up with Ricki Carter, a transvestite, but their relationship was anything but stable. Sampson once put a gun to Carter's head, broke his ribs, and threatened to kill his family. After his breakup with Carter, Sampson moved in with a new girlfriend, Karen Anderson, and began robbing banks. When the police closed in, Sampson fled north. Needing transportation, he pulled three carjackings and killed the drivers, one a 19-year-old college freshman who had stopped to give Sampson a hand. In December 2003, Sampson received a sentence of death from a jury that was not swayed by his claim that he was mentally unfit.

Writing Assignment

Write an opinion on whether Sampson should receive the death penalty or a sentence of life in prison. Do you believe that Sampson's crimes were a product of his impaired development, and if so, should his life be spared?

SUMMARY

L01 Discuss the history of and influences on developmental theory.
The developmental theory of criminality looks at the onset, continuity, and termination of a criminal career. The foundation of developmental theory can be traced to the pioneering work of Sheldon and Eleanor Glueck, who identified a number of personal and social factors related to persistent offending. A 1990 review paper by Rolf Loeber and Marc Le Blanc proposed that criminologists should devote time and effort to understanding basic questions about the evolution of criminal careers.

L02 List the principles of the life course approach to developmental theory.
Life course theory suggests that the development of a criminal career is a dynamic process. Behavior is influenced by individual characteristics as well as social experiences, and the factors that cause antisocial behaviors change dramatically over a person's life span. Even as toddlers, people begin relationships and behaviors that will determine their adult life course. Some individuals are incapable of maturing in a reasonable and timely fashion because of family, environmental, or personal problems. The propensity to commit crimes is neither stable nor constant; it is a developmental process. Disruptions in life's major transitions can be destructive and ultimately can promote criminality.

LO3　Explain the term *problem behavior syndrome*.

One element of life course theory is that criminality may best be understood as one of many social problems faced by people. This is referred to as problem behavior syndrome (PBS), which typically involves family dysfunction, sexual and physical abuse, substance abuse, smoking, precocious sexuality and early pregnancy, educational underachievement, suicide attempts, sensation seeking, and unemployment.

LO4　Outline the basic principles of Sampson and Laub's age-graded life course theory.

According to Sampson and Laub's age-graded theory, the course of a criminal career can be affected by events that occur across the life span. There are turning points in a criminal career that can alter its course and direction, changing a lifetime ne'er do well into a productive citizen. Acquiring social capital helps some at-risk people to knife off from a criminal career. However, people who acquire cumulative disadvantage are more likely to commit criminal acts and become victims of crime. Because criminal careers are a dynamic process, an important life event or turning point can change the direction of a person's life course trajectory.

LO5　Explain the concept of the latent trait and the basic principles of the general theory of crime (GTC).

Propensity or latent trait theory suggests that a stable feature, characteristic, property, or condition, such as defective intelligence or impulsive personality, makes some people crime prone over the life course. Suspected latent traits include defective intelligence, damaged or impulsive personality, genetic abnormalities, the physical–chemical functioning of the brain, and environmental influences on brain function such as drugs, chemicals, and injuries. In *A General Theory of Crime*, Michael Gottfredson and Travis Hirschi argue that the propensity to commit antisocial acts is tied directly to a person's level of self-control. By integrating the concepts of socialization and criminality, Gottfredson and Hirschi help explain why some people who lack self-control can escape criminality, and, conversely, why some people who have self-control might live conventional lives.

LO6　Articulate the basic principles of trajectory theory.

Trajectory theorists recognize that career criminals may travel more than a single road. Some may specialize in violence and extortion; some may be involved in theft and fraud; others may engage in a variety of criminal acts. Some offenders begin their careers early in life, whereas others are late bloomers who begin committing crime when most people desist. Some are frequent offenders, while others travel a more moderate path or are even abstainers. Experiences in young adulthood and beyond can redirect criminal trajectories or paths. In some cases people can be turned in a positive direction, while in others negative life experiences can be harmful and injurious.

Key Terms

Critical Thinking Questions

1. Do you consider yourself a holder of "social capital"? If so, what form does it take?

2. A person gets a 1600 on the SAT. Without knowing this person, what personal, family, and social characteristics would you assume he or she has? Another person becomes a serial killer. Without knowing this person, what personal, family, and social characteristics would you assume he or she has? If "bad behavior" is explained by multiple problems, is "good behavior" explained by multiple strengths?

3. Do you believe there is a latent trait that makes a person criminality prone, or is criminality a function of environment and socialization?

4. Do you agree with Loeber's multiple pathways model? Do you know people who have traveled down those paths?

5. Do you think that marriage is different than merely being in love? Having a romantic relationship may help reduce crime; if so, what happens when the couple breaks up? Does that increase the likelihood of criminal involvement?

Notes

All URLs accessed April 2017.

1. David Gardner. "'Things Got Out of Control': Chilling Confession of Connecticut Massacre 'Killer,'" *Daily Mail*, September 23, 2010; Alaine Griffin, "Judge Sentences Komisarjevsky to Death," *Hartford Courant*, January 27, 2012, http://www.courant.com/community/cheshire/cheshire-home-invasion/hc-komisarjevsky-sentenced-0128-20120127,0,1199254.story.

2. See, generally, John Laub and Robert Sampson, "The Sutherland–Glueck Debate: On the Sociology of Criminological Knowledge," *American Journal of Sociology* 96 (1991): 1402–1440; John Laub and Robert Sampson, "Unraveling Families and Criminality: A Reanalysis of the Gluecks' Data," *Criminology* 26 (1988): 355–380.

3. Rolf Loeber and Marc Le Blanc, "Toward a Developmental Criminology," in *Crime and Justice*, Vol. 12, ed. Norval Morris and Michael Tonry (Chicago: University of Chicago Press, 1990), pp. 375–473; Rolf Loeber and Marc Le Blanc, "Developmental Criminology Updated," in *Crime and Justice*, Vol. 23, ed. Michael Tonry (Chicago: University of Chicago Press, 1998), pp. 115–198.

4. Raymond Paternoster, Charles Dean, Alex Piquero, Paul Mazerolle, and Robert Brame, "Generality, Continuity, and Change in Offending," *Journal of Quantitative Criminology* 13 (1997): 231–266.

5. Alex Piquero, "Taking Stock of Developmental Trajectories of Criminal Activity Over the Life Course," in *The Long View of Crime: A Synthesis of Longitudinal Research*, ed. Akiva Liberman (New York: Springer, 2008), pp. 23–78.

6. Shawn Bushway, Robert Brame, and Raymond Paternoster, "Assessing Stability and Change in Criminal Offending: A Comparison of Random Effects, Semiparametric, and Fixed Effects Modeling Strategies," *Journal of Quantitative Criminology* 15 (1999): 23–61.

7. Sarah Bacon, Raymond Paternoster, and Robert Brame, "Understanding the Relationship Between Onset Age and Subsequent Offending During Adolescence," *Journal of Youth and Adolescence* 38 (2009): 301–311.

8. Marvin Krohn, Alan Lizotte, and Cynthia Perez, "The Interrelationship Between Substance Use and Precocious Transitions to Adult Sexuality," *Journal of Health and Social Behavior* 38 (1997): 88.

9. Peggy Giordano, Stephen Cernkovich, and Jennifer Rudolph, "Gender, Crime, and Desistance: Toward a Theory of Cognitive Transformation?" *American Journal of Sociology* 107 (2002): 990–1064.

10. Lara DePadilla, Molly Perkins, Kirk Elifson, and Claire Sterk, "Adult Criminal Involvement: A Cross-Sectional Inquiry into Correlates and Mechanisms Over the Life Course," *Criminal Justice Review* 37 (2012): 110–126.

11. Besiki Kutateladze, Nancy Andiloro, Brian Johnson, and Cassia Spohn, "Cumulative Disadvantage: Examining Racial and Ethnic Disparity in Prosecution and Sentencing," *Criminology* 52 (2014): 514–551.

12. Shawn Bushway, Marvin Krohn, Alan Lizotte, Matthew Phillips, and Nicole Schmidt, "Are Risky Youth Less Protectable as They Age? The Dynamics of Protection During Adolescence and Young Adulthood," *Justice Quarterly* 30 (2013): 84–116.

13. Chris Melde and Finn-Aage Esbensen, "The Relative Impact of Gang Status Transitions: Identifying the Mechanisms of Change in Delinquency," *Journal of Research in Crime and Delinquency* 51 (2014): 349–376.

14. David C. Pyrooz, "From Colors and Guns to Caps and Gowns? The Effects of Gang Membership on Educational Attainment," *Journal of Research in Crime and Delinquency* 51 (2014): 56–87.

15. John Hagan and Holly Foster, "S/He's a Rebel: Toward a Sequential Stress Theory of Criminality and Gendered Pathways to Disadvantage in Emerging Adulthood," *Social Forces* 82 (2003): 53–86.

16. Patrick Lussier, David Farrington, and Terrie Moffitt, "Is the Antisocial Child Father of the Abusive Man? A 40-Year Prospective Longitudinal Study on the Development Antecedents of Intimate Partner Violence," *Criminology* 47 (2009): 741–780.

17. Gerald Patterson, Barbara DeBaryshe, and Elizabeth Ramsey, "A Developmental Perspective on Antisocial Behavior," *American Psychologist* 44 (1989): 329–335.

18. Robert Sampson and John Laub, "Crime and Deviance in the Life Course," *American Review of Sociology* 18 (1992): 63–84.

19. David Farrington, Darrick Jolliffe, Rolf Loeber, Magda Stouthamer-Loeber, and Larry Kalb, "The Concentration of Offenders in Families, and Family Criminality in the Prediction of Boys' Criminality," *Journal of Adolescence* 24 (2001): 579–596.

20. Lila Kazemian, David Farrington, and Marc Le Blanc, "Can We Make Accurate Long-Term Predictions About Patterns of De-escalation in Offending Behavior?" *Journal of Youth and Adolescence* 38 (2009): 384–400.

21. Alex R. Piquero and He Len Chung, "On the Relationships Between Gender, Early Onset, and the Seriousness of Offending," *Journal of Delinquent Justice* 29 (2001): 189–206.

22. Mary Campa, Catherine Bradshaw, John Eckenrode, and David Zielinski, "Patterns of Problem Behavior in Relation to Thriving and Precocious Behavior in Late Adolescence," *Journal of Youth and Adolescence* 37 (2008): 627–640; Alex Mason, Rick Kosterman, J. David Hawkins, Todd Herrenkohl, Liliana Lengua, and Elizabeth McCauley, "Predicting Depression, Social Phobia, and Violence in Early Adulthood from Childhood Behavior Problems," *Journal of the American Academy of Child and Adolescent Psychiatry* 43 (2004): 307–315; Rolf Loeber and David Farrington, "Young Children Who Commit Crime: Epidemiology, Developmental Origins, Risk Factors, Early Interventions, and Policy Implications," *Development and Psychopathology* 12 (2000): 737–762.

23. Matt DeLisi, Tricia K. Neppl, Brenda J. Lohman, Michael G. Vaughn, and Jeffrey J. Shook, "Early Starters: Which Type of Criminal Onset Matters Most for Delinquent Careers?" *Journal of Criminal Justice* 41 (2013): 12–17.

24. Kristin Carbone-Lopez and Jody Miller, "Precocious Role Entry as a Mediating Factor in Women's Methamphetamine Use: Implications for Life-Course and Pathways Research," *Criminology* 50 (2012): 187–220.

25. David Gadd and Stephen Farrall, "Criminal Careers, Desistance and Subjectivity: Interpreting Men's Narratives of Change," *Theoretical Criminology* 8 (2004): 123–156.

26. Rolf Loeber and David Farrington, "Young Children Who Commit Criminality: Epidemiology, Developmental Origins, Risk Factors, Early Interventions, and Policy Implications," *Development and Psychopathology* 12 (2000): 737–762.

27. Mason, Kosterman, Hawkins, Herrenkohl, Lengua, and McCauley, "Predicting Depression, Social Phobia, and Violence in Early Adulthood from Childhood Behavior Problems"; Loeber and Farrington, "Young Children Who Commit Crime"; Patrick Lussier, Jean Proulx, and Marc Le Blanc, "Criminal Propensity, Deviant Sexual Interests and Criminal Activity of Sexual Aggressors Against Women," *Criminology* 43 (2005): 249–282.

28. Ronald Prinz and Suzanne Kerns, "Early Substance Use by Juvenile Offenders," *Child Psychiatry and Human Development* 33 (2003): 263–268.

29. Magda Stouthamer-Loeber and Evelyn Wei, "The Precursors of Young Fatherhood and Its Effect on Criminality of Teenage Males," *Journal of Adolescent Health* 22 (1998): 56–65; Richard Jessor, John Donovan, and Francis Costa, *Beyond Adolescence: Problem Behavior and Young Adult Development* (New York: Cambridge University Press, 1991).

30. James Marquart, Victoria Brewer, Patricia Simon, and Edward Morse, "Lifestyle Factors Among Female Prisoners with Histories of Psychiatric Treatment," *Journal of Criminal Justice* 29 (2001): 319–328; Rolf Loeber, David Farrington, Magda Stouthamer-Loeber, Terrie Moffitt, Avshalom Caspi, and Don Lynam, "Male Mental Health Problems, Psychopathy, and Personality Traits: Key Findings from the First 14 Years of the Pittsburgh Youth Study," *Clinical Child and Family Psychology Review* 4 (2002): 273–297.

31. John Stogner, Chris Gibson, and J. Mitchell Miller, "Examining the Reciprocal Nature of the Health-Violence Relationship: Results from a Nationally Representative Sample," *Justice Quarterly* 31 (2014): 473–499.

32. J. Rayner, T. Kelly, and F. Graham, "Mental Health, Personality and Cognitive Problems in Persistent Adolescent Offenders Require Long-Term Solutions:

Pilot Study," *Journal of Forensic Psychiatry and Psychology* 16 (2005): 248–262.

33. Deborah Capaldi and Gerald Patterson, "Can Violent Offenders Be Distinguished from Frequent Offenders? Prediction from Childhood to Adolescence," *Journal of Research in Crime and Criminality* 33 (1996): 206–231.

34. Alex Piquero, David Farrington, Jonathan Shepherd, and Katherine Auty, "Offending and Early Death in the Cambridge Study in Delinquent Development," *Justice Quarterly* 31 (2014): 445–472.

35. Paul Nieuwbeerta and Alex Piquero, "Mortality Rates and Causes of Death of Convicted Dutch Criminals 25 Years Later," *Journal of Research in Crime and Criminality* 45 (2008): 256–286.

36. David Fergusson, L. John Horwood, and Elizabeth Ridder, "Show Me the Child at Seven II: Childhood Intelligence and Later Outcomes in Adolescence and Young Adulthood," *Journal of Child Psychology and Psychiatry and Allied Disciplines* 46 (2005): 850–859.

37. Krysia Mossakowski, "Dissecting the Influence of Race, Ethnicity, and Socioeconomic Status on Mental Health in Young Adulthood," *Research on Aging* 30 (2008): 649–671.

38. Nicole Leeper Piquero and Terrie Moffitt, "Can Childhood Factors Predict Workplace Deviance?" *Justice Quarterly* 31 (2014): 664–693; Margit Wiesner and Michael Windle, "Young Adult Substance Use and Depression as a Consequence of Criminality Trajectories During Middle Adolescence," *Journal of Research on Adolescence* 16 (2006): 239–264.

39. Alan Drury and Matt DeLisi, "Gangkill: An Exploratory Empirical Assessment of Gang Membership, Homicide Offending, and Prison Misconduct," *Crime and Criminality* 57 (2011): 130–146.

40. Marshall Jones and Donald Jones, "The Contagious Nature of Antisocial Behavior," *Criminology* 38 (2000): 25–46.

41. W. G. Clingempeel and S. W. Henggeler, "Aggressive Juvenile Offenders Transitioning into Emerging Adulthood," *American Journal of Orthopsychiatry* 73 (2003): 310–323.

42. Robert Agnew, *Why Do Criminals Offend? A General Theory of Crime and Criminality* (Los Angeles: Roxbury Publishing, 2005); Terence Thornberry, "Toward an Interactional Theory of Criminality," *Criminology* 25 (1987): 863–891; Richard Catalano and J. David Hawkins, "The Social Development Model: A Theory of Antisocial Behavior," in *Criminality and Crime: Current Theories*, ed. J. David Hawkins (New York: Cambridge University Press, 1996), pp. 149–197.

43. Stephen Farrall and Benjamin Bowling, "Structuration, Human Development, and Desistance from Crime," *British Journal of Criminology* 39 (1999): 253–268.

44. Robert Sampson and John Laub, *Crime in the Making: Pathways and Turning Points Through Life* (Cambridge, MA: Harvard University Press, 1993).

45. Matthew Moore and Nicholas Recker, "Social Capital, Type of Crime, and Social Control," *Crime and Delinquency*, first published online November 15, 2013.

46. John Laub and Robert Sampson, *Shared Beginnings, Divergent Lives: Delinquent Boys to Age 70* (Cambridge, MA: Harvard University Press, 2003), p. 149.

47. Daniel Nagin and Raymond Paternoster, "Personal Capital and Social Control: The Deterrence Implications of a Theory of Criminal Offending," *Criminology* 32 (1994): 581–606.

48. Joseph Murray, Rolf Loeber, and Dustin Pardini, "Parental Involvement in the Criminal Justice System and the Development of Youth Theft, Marijuana Use, Depression, and Poor Academic Performance," *Criminology* 50 (2012): 255–302.

49. Michael Roettger and Raymond Swisher, "Associations of Fathers' History of Incarceration with Sons' Criminality and Arrest Among Black, White, and Hispanic Males in the United States," *Criminology* 49 (2011): 1109–1148.

50. Joan Reid, "Exploratory Review of Route-Specific, Gendered, and Age-Graded Dynamics of Exploitation: Applying Life Course Theory to Victimization in Sex Trafficking in North America," *Aggression and Violent Behavior* 17 (2012): 257–271.

51. Terri Orbuch, James House, Richard Mero, and Pamela Webster, "Marital Quality over the Life Course," *Social Psychology Quarterly* 59 (1996): 162–171; Lee Lillard and Linda Waite, "'Til Death Do Us Part': Marital Disruption and Mortality," *American Journal of Sociology* 100 (1995): 1131–1156.

52. Mark Warr, "Life-Course Transitions and Desistance from Crime," *Criminology* 36 (1998): 183–216.

53. Michael Rocque, Chad Posick, Steven Barkan, and Ray Paternoster, "Marriage and County-Level Crime Rates: A Research Note," *Journal of Research in Crime and Delinquency* 52 (2015): 130–145; Ronald Simons and Ashley Barr, "Shifting Perspectives: Cognitive Changes Mediate the Impact of Romantic Relationships on Desistance from Crime," *Justice Quarterly*, first published online July 20, 2012.

54. Sonja Siennick, Jeremy Staff, D. Wayne Osgood, John Schulenberg, Jerald Bachman, and Matthew VanEseltine, "Partnership Transitions and Antisocial Behavior in Young Adulthood: A Within-Person, Multi-Cohort Analysis," *Journal of Research in Crime and Delinquency* 51 (2014): 735–758.

55. Marieke van Schellen, Robert Apel, and Paul Nieuwbeerta, "'Because You're Mine, I Walk the

Line'? Marriage, Spousal Criminality, and Criminal Offending over the Life Course," *Journal of Quantitative Criminology*, first published online April 9, 2012.

56. Bill McCarthy and Teresa Casey, "Love, Sex, and Crime: Adolescent Romantic Relationships and Offending," *American Sociological Review* 73 (2008): 944–969.

57. Matthew Larson, Gary Sweeten, and Alex Piquero, "With or Without You? Contextualizing the Impact of Romantic Relationship Breakup on Crime Among Serious Adolescent Offenders," *Journal of Youth and Adolescence* 45 (2016): 54–72.

58. van Schellen, Apel, and Nieuwbeerta, "'Because You're Mine, I Walk the Line'? Marriage, Spousal Criminality, and Criminal Offending over the Life Course."

59. Centers for Disease Control and Prevention, "Marriage and Divorce," http://www.cdc.gov /nchs/fastats/marriage-divorce.htm; Matthew Larson and Gary Sweeten, "Breaking Up Is Hard to Do: Romantic Dissolution, Offending, and Substance Use During the Transition to Adulthood," *Criminology* 50 (2012): 605–636.

60. Nicole M. Schmidt, Giza Lopes, Marvin D. Krohn, and Alan J. Lizotte, "Getting Caught and Getting Hitched: An Assessment of the Relationship Between Police Intervention, Life Chances, and Romantic Unions," *Justice Quarterly*, first published online January 3, 2014.

61. Torkild Hovde Lyngstad and Torbjørn Skardhamar, "Changes in Criminal Offending Around the Time of Marriage," *Journal of Research in Crime and Delinquency* 50 (2013): 608–615.

62. Bianca Bersani and Elaine Eggleston Doherty, "When the Ties that Bind Unwind: Examining the Enduring and Situational Processes of Change Behind the Marriage Effect," *Criminology* 51 (2013): 399–433.

63. Rand Conger, "Long-Term Consequences of Economic Hardship on Romantic Relationships," Center for Poverty Research, University of California, Davis, http://poverty.ucdavis.edu /research-paper/long-term-consequences-economic -hardship-romantic-relationships.

64. Torbjørn Skardhamar and Jukka Savolainen, "Changes in Criminal Offending Around the Time of Job Entry: A Study of Employment and Desistance," *Criminology* 52 (2014): 263–291.

65. Ronald L. Simons and Callie Harbin Burt, "Learning to Be Bad: Adverse Social Conditions, Social Schemas, and Crime," *Criminology* 49 (2011): 553–598.

66. Callie Burt and Ronald Simons, "Interpersonal Racial Discrimination, Ethnic-Racial Socialization, and Offending: Risk and Resilience Among African American Females," *Justice Quarterly* 32 (2015): 532–579.

67. Ronald L. Simons, Callie H. Burt, Ashley B. Barr, Man-Kit Lei, and Eric A. Stewart, "Incorporating Routine Activities, Activity Spaces, and Situational Definitions into the Social Schematic Theory of Crime," *Criminology* 52 (2014): 655–687.

68. James Q. Wilson and Richard Herrnstein, *Crime and Human Nature* (New York: Simon and Schuster, 1985).

69. David Rowe, D. Wayne Osgood, and W. Alan Nicewander, "A Latent Trait Approach to Unifying Criminal Careers," *Criminology* 28 (1990): 237–270.

70. Lee Ellis, "Neurohormonal Bases of Varying Tendencies to Learn Delinquent and Criminal Behavior," in *Behavioral Approaches to Crime and Criminality*, ed. E. Morris and C. Braukmann (New York: Plenum, 1988), pp. 499–518.

71. David Rowe, Alexander Vazsonyi, and Daniel Flannery, "Sex Differences in Crime: Do Means and Within-Sex Variation Have Similar Causes?" *Journal of Research in Crime and Criminality* 32 (1995): 84–100.

72. Wilson and Herrnstein, *Crime and Human Nature*.

73. Ibid., p. 44.

74. Ibid., p. 171.

75. Michael Gottfredson and Travis Hirschi, *A General Theory of Crime* (Stanford, CA: Stanford University Press, 1990).

76. Ibid., p. 90.

77. Ibid., p. 89.

78. Alex Piquero and Stephen Tibbetts, "Specifying the Direct and Indirect Effects of Low Self-Control and Situational Factors in Offenders' Decision Making: Toward a More Complete Model of Rational Offending," *Justice Quarterly* 13 (1996): 481–508.

79. Gottfredson and Hirschi, *A General Theory of Crime*, p. 112.

80. Ibid.

81. Stacey Nofziger and Valerie Callanan, "Predicting Suicidal Tendencies Among High Risk Youth with the General Theory of Crime," *Deviant Behavior* 37 (2016): 167–183.

82. Jeffrey Bouffard and Stephen Rice, "The Influence of the Social Bond on Self-Control at the Moment of Decision: Testing Hirschi's Redefinition of Self-Control," *American Journal of Criminal Justice* 36 (2011): 138–157.

83. Chris L. Gibson, Christopher J. Sullivan, Shayne Jones, and Alex R. Piquero, "Does It Take a Village? Assessing Neighborhood Influences on Children's Self-Control," *Journal of Research in Crime and Criminality* 47 (2010): 31–62.

84. Ryan Meldrum, Jacob Young, Carter Hay, and Jamie Flexon, "Does Self-Control Influence Maternal Attachment? A Reciprocal Effects Analysis from

Early Childhood Through Middle Adolescence," *Journal of Quantitative Criminology*, first published online March 24, 2012; Stacey Nofziger, "The 'Cause' of Low Self-Control: The Influence of Maternal Self-Control," *Journal of Research in Crime and Criminality* 45 (2008): 191–224.

85. Brian Boutwell and Kevin Beaver, "The Intergenerational Transmission of Low Self-Control," *Journal of Research in Crime and Criminality* 47 (2010): 174–209.

86. Farrington, Jolliffe, Loeber, Stouthamer-Loeber, and Kalb, "The Concentration of Offenders in Families, and Family Criminality in the Prediction of Boys' Criminality."

87. Marie Ratchford and Kevin Beaver, "Neuropsychological Deficits, Low Self-Control, and Delinquent Involvement: Toward a Biosocial Explanation of Criminality," *Criminal Justice and Behavior* 36 (2009): 147–162.

88. Kevin Beaver and John Paul Wright, "Evaluating the Effects of Birth Complications on Low-Control in a Sample of Twins," *International Journal of Offender Therapy and Comparative Criminology* 49 (2005): 450–472.

89. Kevin M. Beaver, J. Eagle Shutt, Brian Boutwell, Marie Ratchford, Kathleen Roberts, and J. C. Barnes, "Genetic and Environmental Influences on Levels of Self-Control and Delinquent Peer Affiliation: Results from a Longitudinal Sample of Adolescent Twins," *Criminal Justice and Behavior* 36 (2009): 41–60.

90. Jill Portnoy, Adrian Raine, Frances R. Chen, Dustin Pardini, Rolf Loeber, and J. Richard Jennings, "Heart Rate and Antisocial Behavior: The Mediating Role of Impulsive Sensation Seeking," *Criminology* 52 (2014): 292–311.

91. Gottfredson and Hirschi, *A General Theory of Crime*, p. 27.

92. Christopher Sullivan, Jean Marie McGloin, Travis Pratt, and Alex Piquero, "Rethinking the 'Norm' of Offender Generality: Investigating Specialization in the Short-Term," *Criminology* 44 (2006): 199–233; Annemaree Carroll, Francene Hemingway, Julie Bower, Adrian Ashman, Stephen Houghton, and Kevin Durkin, "Impulsivity in Juvenile Criminality: Differences Among Early-Onset, Late-Onset, and Non-Offenders," *Journal of Youth and Adolescence* 35 (2006): 517–527. Michael Reisig, Scott Wolfe, and Travis Pratt, "Low Self-Control and the Religiosity-Crime Relationship," *Criminal Justice and Behavior* 39 (2012): 1172–1191; Michael Reisig, Scott Wolfe, and Kristy Holtfreter, "Legal Cynicism, Legitimacy, and Criminal Offending: The Non-confounding Effect of Low Self-Control," *Criminal Justice and Behavior* 38 (2011): 1170–1184; Daniel Nagin and Greg Pogarsky, "Time and Punishment: Delayed

Consequences and Criminal Behavior," *Journal of Quantitative Criminology* 20 (2004): 295–317.

93. Alexander Vazsonyi, Jakub Mikuška, and Erin Kelley, "It's Time: A Meta-Analysis on the Self-Control-Deviance Link," *Journal of Criminal Justice* 48 (2017): 48–63.

94. Sullivan, McGloin, Pratt, and Piquero, "Rethinking the 'Norm' of Offender Generality: Investigating Specialization in the Short-Term"; Carroll, Hemingway, Bower, Ashman, Houghton, and Durkin, "Impulsivity in Juvenile Criminality: Differences Among Early-Onset, Late-Onset, and Non-Offenders."

95. Reisig, Wolfe, and Pratt, "Low Self-Control and the Religiosity-Crime Relationship."

96. Olivia Katherine Ha and Eric Beauregard, "Sex Offending and Low Self-Control: An Extension and Test of the General Theory of Crime," *Journal of Criminal Justice* 47 (2016): 62–73; Philip Quisenberry, "Texting and Driving: Can It Be Explained by the General Theory of Crime?" *American Journal of Criminal Justice* 40 (2015): 303–316.

97. Kyle Thomas and Jean Marie McGloin, "A Dual-Systems Approach for Understanding Differential Susceptibility to Processes of Peer Influence," *Criminology* 51 (2013): 435–474.

98. Matt DeLisi and Michael Vaughn, "The Gottfredson-Hirschi Critiques Revisited: Reconciling Self-Control Theory, Criminal Careers, and Career Criminals," *International Journal of Offender Therapy and Comparative Criminology* 52 (2008): 520–537.

99. Jeffrey Ward, Matt Nobles, and Kathleen Fox, "Disentangling Self-Control from Its Elements: A Bifactor Analysis," *Journal of Quantitative Criminology* 31 (2015): 595–627.

100. Michael Courey and Paul-Philippe Pare, "A Closer Look at the Relationship Between Low Self-Control and Delinquency: The Effects of Identity Styles," *Crime and Delinquency*, first published online September 16, 2013.

101. Jean-Louis Van Gelder and Reinout E. De Vries, "Traits and States: Integrating Personality and Affect into a Model of Criminal Decision Making," *Criminology* 50 (2012): 637–371.

102. Richard Wiebe, "Reconciling Psychopathy and Low Self-Control," *Justice Quarterly* 20 (2003): 297–336.

103. Alan Feingold, "Gender Differences in Personality: A Meta-Analysis," *Psychological Bulletin* 116 (1994): 429–456.

104. Gottfredson and Hirschi, *A General Theory of Crime*, p. 153.

105. James Unnever, J. C. Barnes, and Francis Cullen, "The Racial Invariance Thesis Revisited," *Journal of Contemporary Criminal Justice* 32 (2016): 7–26.

106. Maria Koeppel, "How General Is the General Theory of Crime? Using Self-Control to Predict Substance Use Between Sexual Orientation Groups," *Journal of Drug Issues* 45 (2015): 80–94.

107. Scott Menard, Delbert Elliott, and Sharon Wofford, "Social Control Theories in Developmental Perspective," *Studies on Crime and Criminality Prevention* 2 (1993): 69–87.

108. Dustin Pardini, Jelena Obradovic, and Rolf Loeber, "Interpersonal Callousness, Hyperactivity/Impulsivity, Inattention, and Conduct Problems as Precursors to Criminality Persistence in Boys: A Comparison of Three Grade-Based Cohorts," *Journal of Clinical Child and Adolescent Psychology* 35 (2006): 46–59.

109. Brie Diamond, Robert G. Morris, and Alex R. Piquero, "Stability in the Underlying Constructs of Self-Control," *Crime and Delinquency* 63 (2017): 235–266.

110. Ojmarrh Mitchell and Doris Layton MacKenzie, "The Stability and Resiliency of Self-Control in a Sample of Incarcerated Offenders," *Crime and Criminality* 52 (2006): 432–449.

111. Charles R. Tittle and Harold G. Grasmick, "Delinquent Behavior and Age: A Test of Three Provocative Hypotheses," *Journal of Criminal Law and Criminology* 88 (1997): 309–342.

112. Callie Burt, Gary Sweeten, and Ronald Simons, "Self-Control Through Emerging Adulthood: Instability, Multidimensionality, and Criminological Significance," *Criminology* 52 (2014): 450–487.

113. Adrian Jones, "When in Rome: Testing the Moderating Influence of Neighborhood Composition on the Relationship Between Self-Control and Juvenile Offending," *Crime and Delinquency*, first published online July 30, 2015; Chris Gibson, "An Investigation of Neighborhood Disadvantage, Low Self-Control, and Violent Victimization Among Youth," *Youth Violence and Juvenile Justice* 10 (2012): 41–63.

114. Gregory Zimmerman, Ekaterina Botchkovar, Olena Antonaccio, and Lorine Hughes, "Low Self-Control in 'Bad' Neighborhoods: Assessing the Role of Context on the Relationship Between Self-Control and Crime," *Justice Quarterly* 32 (2015): 56–84; Burt, Sweeten, and Simons, "Self-Control Through Emerging Adulthood: Instability, Multidimensionality, and Criminological Significance."

115. Gregory Zimmerman, "Impulsivity, Offending, and the Neighborhood: Investigating the Person–Context Nexus," *Journal of Quantitative Criminology* 26 (2010): 301–332.

116. Gibson, "An Investigation of Neighborhood Disadvantage, Low Self-Control, and Violent Victimization Among Youth."

117. Alex Piquero, Robert Brame, Paul Mazerolle, and Rudy Haapanen, "Crime in Emerging Adulthood," *Criminology* 40 (2002): 137–170.

118. Ryan Schroeder and Thomas Mowen, "Parenting Style Transitions and Delinquency," *Youth and Society* 46 (2014): 228–254.

119. Wesley Jennings and Jennifer Reingle, "On the Number and Shape of Developmental/Life-Course Violence, Aggression, and Delinquency Trajectories: A State-of-the-Art Review," *Journal of Criminal Justice* 40 (2012): 472–489.

120. Stacy Tzoumakis, Patrick Lussier, Marc Le Blanc, and Garth Davies, "Onset, Offending Trajectories, and Crime Specialization in Violence," *Youth Violence and Juvenile Justice* 11 (2013): 143–164.

121. Alex Piquero, Delphine Theobald, and David Farrington, "The Overlap Between Offending Trajectories, Criminal Violence, and Intimate Partner Violence," *International Journal of Offender Therapy and Comparative Criminology* 58 (2014): 286–302.

122. Amy D'Unger, Kenneth Land, Patricia McCall, and Daniel Nagin, "How Many Latent Classes of Delinquent/Criminal Careers? Results from Mixed Poisson Regression Analyses," *American Journal of Sociology* 103 (1998): 1593–1630.

123. Selma Salihovic, Metin Özdemir, and Margaret Kerr, "Trajectories of Adolescent Psychopathic Traits," *Journal of Psychopathology and Behavioral Assessment* 36 (2014): 47–59.

124. Ibid.

125. Josanne van Dongen, Nicole Buck, and Hjalmar van Marle, "First Offenders with Psychosis: Justification of a Third Type Within the Early/Late Start Offender Typology," *Crime and Delinquency* 60 (2014): 126–142.

126. D'Unger, Land, McCall, and Nagin, "How Many Latent Classes of Delinquent/Criminal Careers? Results from Mixed Poisson Regression Analyses."

127. Alex Piquero, Wesley Jennings, and David Farrington, "The Monetary Costs of Crime to Middle Adulthood: Findings from the Cambridge Study in Delinquent Development," *Journal of Research in Crime and Delinquency* 50 (2013): 53–74.

128. Terrie Moffitt, "A Review of Research on the Taxonomy of Life-Course Persistent versus Adolescence-Limited Antisocial Behavior," in *Taking Stock: The Status of Criminological Theory*, Vol. 15, ed. F. T. Cullen, J. P. Wright, and K. R. Blevins (New Brunswick, NJ: Transaction Publications, 2006), pp. 277–311.

129. C. Barnes, Kevin Beaver, and Brian Boutwell, "Examining the Genetic Underpinnings to Moffitt's Developmental Taxonomy: A Behavioral Genetic Analysis," *Criminology* 49 (2011): 923–954.

130. Xiaojin Chen and Michele Adams, "Are Teen Criminality Abstainers Social Introverts? A Test of

Moffitt's Theory," *Journal of Research in Crime and Criminality* 47 (2010): 439–468.

131. Jennifer Gatewood Owens and Lee Ann Slocum, "Abstainers in Adolescence and Adulthood: Exploring the Correlates of Abstention Using Moffitt's Developmental Taxonomy" *Crime and Criminality*, published online February 7, 2012.

132. Margit Wiesner and Ranier Silbereisen, "Trajectories of Delinquent Behaviour in Adolescence and Their Covariates: Relations with Initial and Time-Averaged Factors," *Journal of Adolescence* 26 (2003): 753–771.

133. Donald Lynam, Alex Piquero, and Terrie Moffitt, "Specialization and the Propensity to Violence: Support from Self-Reports but Not Official Records," *Journal of Contemporary Criminal Justice* 20 (2004): 215–228.

134. Jennifer Reingle, Wesley Jennings, and Mildred Maldonado-Molina, "Risk and Protective Factors for Trajectories of Violent Criminality Among a Nationally Representative Sample of Early Adolescents," *Youth Violence and Juvenile Justice*, first published online February 16, 2012.

135. Georgia Zara and David Farrington, "Childhood and Adolescent Predictors of Late Onset Criminal Careers," *Journal of Youth and Adolescence* 38 (2009): 287–300.

136. Jeremy Staff, Corey Whichard, Sonja E. Siennick, and Jennifer Maggs, "Early Life Risks, Antisocial Tendencies, and Preteen Delinquency," *Criminology* 53 (2015): 677–701.

137. Rolf Loeber, Phen Wung, Kate Keenan, Bruce Giroux, Magda Stouthamer-Loeber, Wemoet van Kammen, and Barbara Maughan, "Developmental Pathways in Disruptive Behavior," *Development and Psychopathology* (1993): 12–48.

138. Sheila Royo Maxwell and Christopher Maxwell, "Examining the 'Criminal Careers' of Prostitutes Within the Nexus of Drug Use, Drug Selling, and Other Illicit Activities," *Criminology* 38 (2000): 787–809.

139. Alex Piquero and Timothy Brezina, "Testing Moffitt's Account of Adolescent-Limited Criminality," *Criminology* 39 (2001): 353–370.

140. Terrie Moffitt, "Adolescence-Limited and Life-Course Persistent Antisocial Behavior: A Developmental Taxonomy," *Psychological Review* 100 (1993): 674–701.

141. Terrie Moffitt, "Natural Histories of Criminality," in *Cross-National Longitudinal Research on Human Development and Criminal Behavior*, ed. Elmar Weitekamp and Hans-Jurgen Kerner (Dordrecht, Netherlands: Kluwer, 1994), pp. 3–65.

142. J. C. Barnes, Kevin Beaver, and Brian Boutwell, "Examining the Genetic Underpinnings to Moffitt's Developmental Taxonomy: A Behavioral Genetic Analysis," *Criminology* 49 (2011): 923–954.

143. Andrea Donker, Wilma Smeenk, Peter van der Laan, and Frank Verhulst, "Individual Stability of Antisocial Behavior from Childhood to Adulthood: Testing the Stability Postulate of Moffitt's Developmental Theory," *Criminology* 41 (2003): 593–609.

144. Robert Vermeiren, "Psychopathology and Criminality in Adolescents: A Descriptive and Developmental Perspective," *Clinical Psychology Review* 23 (2003): 277–318; Paul Mazerolle, Robert Brame, Ray Paternoster, Alex Piquero, and Charles Dean, "Onset Age, Persistence, and Offending Versatility: Comparisons Across Sex," *Criminology* 38 (2000): 1143–1172.

145. Margit Wiesner, Deborah Capaldi, and Hyoun Kim, "General versus Specific Predictors of Male Arrest Trajectories: A Test of the Moffitt and Patterson Theories," *Journal of Youth and Adolescence* 42 (2012): 217–228.

146. Adrian Raine, Rolf Loeber, Magda Stouthamer-Loeber, Terrie Moffitt, Avshalom Caspi, and Don Lynam, "Neurocognitive Impairments in Boys on the Life-Course Persistent Antisocial Path," *Journal of Abnormal Psychology* 114 (2005): 38–49.

147. Per-Olof Wikstrom and Rolf Loeber, "Do Disadvantaged Neighborhoods Cause Well-Adjusted Children to Become Adolescent Delinquents? A Study of Male Juvenile Serious Offending, Individual Risk and Protective Factors, and Neighborhood Context," *Criminology* 38 (2000): 1109–1142.

148. Heather Lonczk, Robert Abbott, J. David Hawkins, Rick Kosterman, and Richard Catalano, "Effects of the Seattle Social Development Project on Sexual Behavior, Pregnancy, Birth, and Sexually Transmitted Disease Outcomes by Age 21 Years," *Archive of Pediatrics and Adolescent Medicine* 156 (2002): 438–447.

149. Kathleen Bodisch Lynch, Susan Rose Geller, and Melinda G. Schmidt, "Multi-Year Evaluation of the Effectiveness of a Resilience-Based Prevention Program for Young Children," *Journal of Primary Prevention* 24 (2004): 335–353.

150. This section leans on Thomas Tatchell, Phillip Waite, Renny Tatchell, Lynne Durrant, and Dale Bond, "Substance Abuse Prevention in Sixth Grade: The Effect of a Prevention Program on Adolescents' Risk and Protective Factors," *American Journal of Health Studies* 19 (2004): 54–61.

151. Nancy Tobler and Howard Stratton, "Effectiveness of School Based Drug Prevention Programs: A Meta-Analysis of the Research," *Journal of Primary Prevention* 18 (1997): 71–128.

152. Alex Mason, Rick Kosterman, J. David Hawkins, Kevin P. Haggerty, and Richard L. Spoth, "Reducing Adolescents' Growth in Substance Use and Criminality: Randomized Trial Effects of a Parent-Training Prevention Intervention," *Prevention Science* 4 (2003): 203–212.

Violent Crime

Dylann Roof appears by video uplink at a bond hearing on June 19, 2015.

AP Images/Grace Beahm

10

Chapter Outline

FACT OR FICTION?

▶ Rape is essentially a sex crime.

▶ You can't be convicted of murder unless you personally and intentionally kill someone.

On the evening of June 17, 2015, 21-year-old Dylann Roof entered the Emanuel African Methodist Episcopal Church in downtown Charleston, South Carolina, spent an hour in Bible study with the parishioners, and then opened fire. Nine people were shot and killed, including the senior pastor, state Senator Clementa C. Pinckney; a tenth person was shot but survived. Police arrested Roof in Shelby, North Carolina, the morning after the attack.

Roof's website gave hints as to why he chose the Emanuel Church for his unprovoked slaughter. In a long, hate-filled screed, Roof claimed that the shooting of Trayvon Martin had prompted him to research what he called "black on White" crime. He wrote, "At this moment I realized that something was very wrong. How could the news be blowing up the Trayvon Martin case while hundreds of these black on White murders got ignored?" His online manifesto concluded:

> I have no choice. I am not in the position to, alone, go into the ghetto and fight. I chose Charleston because it is most historic city in my state, and at one time had the highest ratio of blacks to Whites in the country. We have no skinheads, no real KKK, no one doing anything but talking on the Internet. Well someone has to have the bravery to take it to the real world, and I guess that has to be me.

His website, called "The Last Rhodesian," contained photos of him wearing a jacket with the flags of apartheid-era South Africa and Rhodesia. Other photos showed Roof taking aim with a .45-caliber Glock pistol, posing in front of a sign that said, "Sacred burial site. Our African ancestors" as well as outside South Carolina's Museum and Library of Confederate History, and burning an American flag.[1] ▶

In 2017, Roof was sentenced to death after being convicted in federal court on 33 federal hate crime charges; in March 2017, he chose to plead guilty in South Carolina on nine counts of murder, three counts of attempted murder, and possession of a firearm during the commission of a felony to avoid a second death sentence in that state.[2]

In the aftermath of his crime, South Carolina passed legislation ordering the removal of the Confederate battle flag from the state capitol building. Protesters argued that the flag was a symbol of racism and white supremacy that shouldn't remain on the capitol grounds after the Charleston massacre. ■

expressive violence
Violence that is designed not for profit or gain but to vent rage, anger, or frustration.

instrumental violence
Violence used in a rational, controlled, and purposeful fashion; for example, an attempt to improve the financial or social position of the criminal.

LO1 Differentiate among the various causes of violent crime.

This terrible case reminds us that violence and violent acts are part of the human condition. Some violent acts, such as Roof's deadly attack, are deemed **expressive violence**, acts that vent rage, anger, frustration, or in his case hate and racial animus. Some acts are called **instrumental violence**, designed to improve the financial or social position of the criminal—for example, an armed robbery or murder for hire.

This chapter explores the concept of violence in some depth. It first reviews some of the possible causes of violent crime and the various types of interpersonal violence, such as rape, homicide, assault, and robbery. It then addresses some types of interpersonal violence, such as stalking and workplace violence, that have more recently developed in contemporary society.

Causes of Violence

What sets off a violent person such as Dylann Roof? Criminologists have a variety of views on this subject. Some believe that violence is a function of human traits and makeup. Others point to improper socialization and upbringing. Violent behavior may be culturally determined and relate to destructive social values. This section explores a number of the suspected causes of individual and group violence.

Personal Traits

While mental illness is only weakly related to violence, other psychological and personal traits may have greater impact.[3] Research has shown that a significant number of people involved in violent episodes may be suffering from mental abnormalities.[4] Young people convicted of murder have been shown to suffer signs of neurological impairment such as abnormal electroencephalograms (EEGs), multiple psychomotor impairments, and severe seizures; low intelligence as measured on standard IQ tests; psychotic close relatives; psychotic symptoms such as paranoia, illogical thinking, hallucinations; mental impairment and intellectual dysfunction; and animal cruelty.[5] Other elements of personality associated with violence include depression, impulsivity, aggression, dishonesty, pathological lying, lack of remorse, borderline personality syndrome, and psychopathology.[6] Aggressive men have been found to have a long history of torturing and killing animals.[7] Animal cruelty has been associated with a number of psychiatric disorders, including antisocial personality disorder.[8]

Is there is a connection between psychological instability and/or brain structure and violence? One recent effort to test the linkage between violence and mental process used a magnetic resonance imaging device (MRI) to assess brain function in male domestic batterers and compared the results with a matched sample of non-batterers. The brain scans indicated that men who engaged in domestic violence had distinctive brain structures that made them hypersensitive to threat stimuli in a variety of regions of the brain. Hypersensitive men are hard-wired to respond with violence to even mild provocations; they have a neurobiological predisposition that makes them prone to spousal abuse.[9]

Child Abuse and Neglect

There are also indications that children who are subject to all forms of childhood emotional and physical abuse may be more likely one day to use violence themselves; this can include emotional abuse, physical abuse, sexual abuse, emotional neglect, physical neglect, and observation of domestic violence.[10] Sociologist Murray Straus reviewed the concept of discipline in a series of surveys and found a powerful relationship between exposure to physical punishment and later aggression.[11] We now know that the more often a child is physically disciplined and the harsher the punishment, the more likely they will later engage in antisocial behaviors.[12] When kids experience physical punishment they feel angry and unjustly treated and are more willing to defy their parents and engage in antisocial behavior.[13] Abuse has long-term effects: Physical abuse leads to childhood antisocial behavior and later to adult criminality; emotional abuse is directly related to adult antisocial behavior. The more intense and longer lasting the abuse the more likely the later occurrence of adult criminality.[14]

In a series of research studies, criminologist Cathy Widom identified a **cycle of violence**, in which physical abuse by parents or caregivers is a direct cause of subsequent violent behavior among youth.[15] Kids who were abused are then likely to grow up to be abusers themselves, creating a never-ending cycle of abuse and violence. They are significantly more likely to be arrested for violent crime sometime during their life course.

The abuse–violence link can take different forms. Some violent offenders have long histories of abuse and neglect, and this condition is a direct conduit to their personal involvement in violence. Others develop posttraumatic stress disorder (PTSD) in the aftermath of their abuse; their subsequent violence can be linked to the emotional upheaval brought on by their history of personal traumas; whatever its form, the abuse–violence association is quite significant.[16]

Of course, not all abused children become violent criminals. Many do not, and many violent youths come from what appear to be model homes.[17] Widom herself finds that the majority of both abused and nonabused kids do not engage in antisocial behavior, so more research is needed to clarify this very important association.

Human Instinct

Some anthropologists trace the roots of violence back to our prehistory, when our ancestors lived in social groups and fought for dominance. The earliest humans would not hesitate to retaliate violently against aggressors, and it was common for family, tribe, or clan members to protect one another if they were attacked.[18] According to Harvard psychologist Steven Pinker, violence declined during the period of human evolution when our hunter-gatherer ancestors began to settle into agricultural civilizations, which he calls the *pacification process*.[19]

The fact that our ancient ancestors were so violent seems to suggest that violence is instinctual and part of the human condition. Sigmund Freud believed that human aggression and violence are produced by instinctual drives.[20] Freud maintained that humans possess two opposing instinctual drives that interact to control behavior: **eros**, the life instinct, which drives people toward self-fulfillment and enjoyment; and **thanatos**, the death instinct, which impels toward self-destruction. Thanatos can be expressed externally (as violence and sadism) or internally (as suicide, alcoholism, or other self-destructive habits). Because aggression is instinctual, Freud saw little hope for its treatment.

A number of biologists and anthropologists have also speculated that instinctual violence-promoting traits may be common in the human species. One view is that

cycle of violence
A hypothesis that suggests that a childhood history of physical abuse predisposes the survivor to becoming violent themselves in later years.

eros
The life instinct, which drives people toward self-fulfillment and enjoyment.

thanatos
The death instinct, which impels people toward self-destruction.

aggression and violence are the result of instincts inborn in all animals, humans among them.[21] Unlike other animals, however, humans lack the inhibition against killing members of their own species, which protects animals from self-extinction, and are capable of killing their own kind in war or as a result of interpersonal conflicts.

As the Policies and Issues in Criminology feature suggests, not all social scientists are convinced that humans have an instinct for violence.

Policies and Issues in Criminology

VIOLENCE AND HUMAN NATURE

In his important work *Violence: A Micro-sociological Theory*, sociologist Randall Collins proposes a theory that humans are inherently passive and violence is a function of social interaction. Collins argues that most humans shirk from hostile behavior and even those who talk aggressively are fearful and tense during violent encounters. Humans typically resort to violence only when they have overwhelming superiority over their opponents in terms of arms and numbers. While the thought of violence makes most people weak and scared, a supportive audience helps it become more palatable. Whether it's gang boys acting in a group or terrorists being supported by their leaders, violence is more of a group process than an individual choice.

Collins finds that the myth that humans enjoy bloodshed is perpetuated by media depictions of violence. Take for instance the barroom brawl shown in numerous films and TV shows. A fight breaks out in a bar and soon everyone joins in, joyfully punching one another and smashing up the premises. If the crowd doesn't join in, they generally will make a space for the individuals to fight, cheering and shouting encouragement. Fights are drawn out with two evenly matched opponents punching each other for long periods of combat. While normative in the movies, Collins points out that these events never actually happen in real life. When a fight does break out, most patrons typically back away to a safe distance and watch, shrinking away as far as possible. Rather than shouting encouragement, onlookers tend to withdraw vocally as well as physically. And rather than drawn-out brawls, fights are over quickly, typically with a single punch.

If violence is not normative and against human nature, what enables some people to become violent? The core of Collins's micro-sociological theory is the concept of "confrontational tension." When antagonistic interactions occur, the perspective combatants begin to feel tension and fear, emotions that will typically dampen their martial spirit; these emotions form a roadblock to violence. In order to engage in violence, people must find a pathway around this roadblock, leading them into a "tunnel of violence." There are several pathways into this tunnel, one being "forward panic." In these situations, confrontational tension builds up and is suddenly and violently released, allowing people to engage in inexplicable atrocities. "A forward panic," Collins states, "is a zone in time where the emotional impulses are overwhelming, above all because they are shared by everyone: by one's supporters and fellow attackers, and in a reciprocal way, by the passive victims."

Forward panics may occur when police confront an aggressive suspect and a beating occurs, or when sports fans riot when their team wins (or loses). Other paths open to relieve confrontational tension are to attack a weak victim or to be encouraged by an audience to do violence. These pathways can be interactive: a bully is encouraged by a crowd to beat up a weaker student. So, though most brawlers are willing to quit without a clear-cut victory as soon as a few punches are launched, a fight can get out of hand when there is a group brawl and people are encouraging violent confrontations. Prior organization, group identity, and support, Collins finds, are what enable individuals to overcome their own pervasive fear of violence and confrontation; if it were not well-organized, wide-participation group fighting would not be possible.

Critical Thinking

1. **What is your immediate reaction when violence breaks out: flee or fight? Do you agree with Collins that most of us are not violent by nature and will only resort to aggressive behavior under the most extreme circumstances?**

2. **How do we explain the behavior of people drawn to terrorist groups if violence is neither instinctual nor normative?**

Source: Randall Collins, *Violence: A Micro-sociological Theory* (Princeton, NJ: Princeton University Press, 2008).

Exposure to Violence

People who are constantly exposed to violence at home, at school, or in the environment may adopt violent methods themselves.[22] In disadvantaged neighborhoods, people of all ages are exposed to violence on a routine basis.[23] Much of the racial difference in violent crime rates can be explained by the fact that African American citizens are often forced to live in poverty areas, which increases their risk of exposure to violence.[24] Areas where people have little confidence in the police and are therefore reluctant to call for help—a condition common in minority communities—may also experience higher levels of violent behavior.[25]

Even a single exposure to firearm violence doubles the chance that a young person will later engage in violent behavior.[26] Children living in areas marked by extreme violence may in time become desensitized to the persistent neighborhood brutality and conflict they witness, eventually succumbing to violent behaviors themselves.[27] And not surprisingly, those children who are exposed to violence in the home and also live in neighborhoods with high violence rates are the ones most likely to engage in violent crime themselves.[28]

Substance Abuse

On a micro level, substance abusers have higher rates of violence than nonabusers; on a macro level, neighborhoods with high levels of drug and alcohol usage have higher than average violence rates.[29]

Substance abuse influences violence in three ways:[30]

- A **psychopharmacological relationship** may be the direct consequence of ingesting mood-altering substances. Binge drinking, for example, has been closely associated with violent crime rates.[31] Heavy drinking reduces cognitive ability, information-processing skills, and the ability to process and react to verbal and nonverbal behavior. As a result, miscommunication becomes more likely, and the capacity for rational dialogue is compromised.[32] It is not surprising that males involved in sexual assaults often claim that they were drinking and misunderstood their victim's intentions.[33] Eric Sevigny and Andrea Allen found that only those drug dealers who are users themselves routinely carry and use firearms. They speculate that personal drug use induces a mercurial or irritable temperament that increases the likelihood of gun possession and use.[34]
- Drug ingestion may also cause **economic compulsive behavior**, in which drug users resort to violence to support their habit. Studies conducted in the United States and Europe show that addicts commit hundreds of crimes each year.[35]
- A **systemic link** occurs as violence escalates when drug-dealing gangs flex their muscle to dominate territory and drive out rivals. Studies of gangs that sell drugs show that their violent activities may result in a significant proportion of all urban homicides.[36] Drug dealers/traders also are more likely to carry and use firearms in their daily activities. When Richard Felson and Luke Bonkiewicz studied the drug–violence nexus, they found relatively high levels of gun possession among traffickers who handle stashes of moderately large market value, who have central roles in the trade, and who are members of drug organizations.[37]

Firearm Availability

Although firearm availability alone does not cause violence, it may be a facilitating factor. A petty argument can escalate into a fatal encounter if one party has a handgun. The nation has also been rocked by the recent slew of well-publicized school shootings. Research indicates that a significant number of kids routinely carry guns to school; those who have been the victims of crime themselves and those who hang with peers who carry weapons are most likely to bring guns to school.[38]

The Uniform Crime Report (UCR) indicates that about 70 percent of all murders, 40 percent of all robberies, and 24 percent of all aggravated assaults involve firearms.[39] Handguns kill two-thirds of all police who die in the line of duty.[40] The presence of

psychopharmacological relationship
In such a relationship, violence is the direct consequence of ingesting mood-altering substances.

economic compulsive behavior
Violence committed by drug users to support their habit.

systemic link
A link between drugs and violence that occurs when drug dealers turn violent in their competition with rival gangs.

firearms in the home also significantly increases the risk of suicide among adolescents, regardless of how carefully the guns are secured or stored.[41]

Cultural Values

In urban areas, neighborhoods that experience violence seem to cluster together.[42] To explain this phenomenon, criminologists Marvin Wolfgang and Franco Ferracuti formulated the famous concept that some areas are characterized by an independent **subculture of violence.**[43]

The subculture's norms are separate from society's central, dominant value system. In this subculture, a potent theme of violence influences lifestyles, the socialization process, and interpersonal relationships. Even though the members of the subculture share some of the dominant culture's values, they expect that violence will be used to solve social conflicts and dilemmas.

In some cultural subgroups, then, violence has become legitimized by customs and norms. In these areas, people do not kill because they are poor, young, or live in a socially disadvantaged neighborhood but rather because they live in a culture that maintains norms conducive to violent retaliation.[44] It is considered appropriate behavior within culturally defined conflict situations in which an individual who has been offended by a negative outcome in a dispute seeks reparations through violent means ("disputatiousness").[45] That is, in some neighborhoods residents resolve interpersonal conflicts informally—without calling the police—even if it means injuring or killing their opponent; neighbors understand and support violent methods of retaliation.[46] Because police and other agencies of formal social control are viewed as weak and devalued, understaffed, and/or corrupt, people are willing to take matters into their own hands and commit what is referred to as "cultural retaliatory homicide."[47]

It is routine for teens in the subculture of violence to join gangs, another precursor of increased violent activity; violent behavior declines significantly after leaving the gang.[48] A good example of the link between subcultural values, gangs, and violence can be found in Randol Contreras's influential book *The Stickup Kids: Race, Drugs, Violence, and the American Dream.* Contreras returned to his old neighborhood in the South Bronx to do participant observation with a group of Dominican drug robbers known on the streets as "stickup kids." He observed them as they raided and tortured drug dealers in order to find the whereabouts of their heroin, cocaine, marijuana, and cash.[49] Rather than being despised for their violence, the gang was held in high esteem by the neighborhood. After all, they had plenty of flash—clothes, cars, and money. As the crack epidemic abated in New York, the stickup kids became even more violent, holding up more drug dealers to keep up their lifestyles. Instead of aging out of crime like most criminals, they continued their campaign of assault and robbery well into their adulthood.

The association between gang membership and violence has a number of roots. It can result from drug trafficking activities and turf protection, but it may also stem from personal vendettas and a perceived need for self-protection.[50] Once a gang shooting occurs, there is a significant likelihood that violent retaliation of some sort will occur.[51]

National Values

Some nations—including Colombia, Brazil, Sri Lanka, Angola, Uganda, and the Philippines—have relatively high violence rates, while others such as Japan are relatively nonviolent. There are two possible explanations for this discrepancy. One is that high-violence nations embrace value structures that support violence, while others that have a strong communitarian spirit and an emphasis on forgiveness and restorative justice have low violence rates.[52]

The other explanation is that nations with high violence rates also have negative structural factors such as a high level of poverty, income inequality, illiteracy, and alcohol consumption level, and it is the presence of these components, rather than a regional culture of violence, that produces high crime rates.[53]

In the Policies and Issues in Criminology feature, America's national values are related to its homicide rate.

---

subculture of violence
A segment of society in which violence has become legitimized by the custom and norms of that group.

rape
Under common law, the carnal knowledge of a female forcibly and against her will. Contemporary statues are gender neutral ("a person") and can include various acts of sexual penetration.

Policies and Issues in Criminology

AMERICAN CULTURE AND HOMICIDE

In *American Homicide*, social historian Randolph Roth charts changes in the homicide rate in the United States from colonial times to the present. Using a variety of data sources, including court records, newspaper accounts, vital records, and attitudes expressed in diaries and letters, he finds that murder rates are closely correlated with four distinct sociocultural factors: political instability; a loss of government legitimacy; a lack of civility among members of society caused by racial, religious, or political conflict; and a loss of confidence in those who hold power.

Roth argues that the United States has a unique culture and the level of interpersonal violence is much higher than in comparable Western nations. These differences were not always present. During the seventeenth century, murder rates were very high, but by the mid-eighteenth century they declined and the colonies were relatively non-homicidal. After the Revolutionary War, murder rates soared as the newly formed United States struggled to absorb British loyalists. While murder rates remained high in the Georgia–South Carolina backcountry, where the revolution was a genuine civil war, they held steady or fell in the Shenandoah Valley of Virginia, which enjoyed political stability under patriot control throughout the revolution, and where support for the war effort and the new federal government was stronger than anywhere else in the South.

Murder rates eventually declined, and by the early nineteenth century, rates in the North and parts of the South were extremely low. But the homicide rate rose substantially across the United States from the late 1840s through the mid-1870s due to the social conflict that grew up around the slavery issue; at the same time, homicide rates in most other Western nations held steady or fell. The end of the Civil War did not end the bitterness many Southerners felt toward the government and consequently there was a dramatic rise in homicides in the rural South.

Homicide rates rose during the Depression and Prohibition eras in the early twentieth century, but fell during the 1930s when Franklin Roosevelt was elected president and Americans had increased faith in their nation and its leadership. The establishment of government legitimacy through the New Deal, World War II, and the Cold War appeared to have reduced homicide rates through the 1950s. The crisis of government legitimacy in the 1960s and 1970s (especially among African Americans) may have contributed to soaring homicide rates.

In sum, Roth argues that American homicide rates are not related to social factors such as poverty and drug abuse, unemployment, alcohol, race, or ethnicity, but instead are controlled by the feelings that people have toward their government, the degree to which they identify with members of their own communities, and the opportunities they have to earn respect without resorting to violence. If an individual feels secure in his social standing, it's easier to get over life's disappointments. But for a person who feels alienated from the American Dream, even the smallest insult can provoke a murderous rage. To reduce homicide rates, we must learn to trust one another and the government too.

Critical Thinking

Roth says, "State breakdowns and political crises of legitimacy produce surges in nondomestic homicides; the restoration of order and legitimacy produces declines in homicides." Do you agree that homicides involving strangers are a function of the political and social world in which we live? Or is it more personal and a function of intense and immediate interpersonal conflict? How does a political crisis affect someone who robs a liquor store and shoots the owner?

Source: Randolph Roth, *American Homicide* (Cambridge, MA: Harvard University Press; Gold edition, 2012).

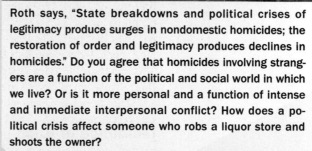

Rape

The common-law definition of **rape** (from the Latin *rapere*, "to take by force") is "the carnal knowledge of a female forcibly and against her will."[54] It is one of the most loathed, misunderstood, and frightening crimes. Under traditional common-law definitions, rape involves nonconsensual sexual intercourse inflicted on a female by a male. There are, of course, other forms of sexual assault, including

LO2 Define rape and be familiar with why men commit rape.

Rape has long been associated with war and invasion. Recent events are no exception. Here, displaced people from the minority Yazidi sect walk toward the Syrian border, fleeing violence from forces loyal to the Islamic State (IS). Yazidi women are routinely raped by IS fighters.

male-on-male and female-on-male sexual assaults (some studies estimate that up to 25 percent of males have been the target of unwanted sexual advances by women), but these are not considered here within the traditional concept of rape.[55] Recognizing these other forms of sexual assault, states have now revised their rape statutes to make them gender neutral. As you may recall (Chapter 2), the FBI has revised its definition of rape to include crimes involving other forms of sexual assault, including oral and anal penetration. Regardless of what form it takes, rape can have devastating long-term effects on the victim's emotional and physical well-being.[56]

Rape was often viewed as a sexual offense in the traditional criminological literature. It was presented as a crime that involved overwhelming lust, driving a man to force his attentions on a woman. Criminologists now consider rape a violent, coercive act of aggression, not a forceful expression of sexuality. Take for instance the use of rape in warfare, a practice that became routine during the civil war in the former Yugoslavia; human rights groups have estimated that more than 30,000 Bosnian women and young girls were sexually abused during the fighting.[57] Though shocking, the war crimes discovered in Bosnia have not deterred conquering armies from using rape as a weapon. Pro-government militias in the Darfur region of Sudan were accused of using rape and other forms of sexual violence "as a weapon of war" to humiliate African women and girls as well as the rebels fighting the Sudanese government in Khartoum.[58] More recently, the Boko Haram terror group in Nigeria has made kidnapping and sexual assaults of young women a centerpiece of its campaign to unseat the government and replace it with one based on their religious beliefs.[59] In May 2014, group members kidnapped 276 high school girls with the intent of selling them into sexual slavery, an act that prompted worldwide outrage; after lengthy negotiations, 82 of the captured girls were released on May 7, 2017.[60] Members of the Islamic State (IS) were given a free hand to rape captured Yazidi women (followers of a unique religion that blends elements of Islam, Judaism, and Christianity) after being told that rape would turn these women into Muslims.[61]

FACT OR FICTION?

Rape is essentially a sex crime.

FICTION Most criminologists consider rape an aggressive act in which sex is merely a means of inflicting violence and intimidation.

Incidence of Rape

According to the most recent UCR data, an estimated 90,000 rapes are now being reported each year in the United States, a rate of almost 40 per 100,000 inhabitants.[62] As is true of other violent crimes, the incidence of rape as reported in the UCR was in a decade-long decline, and current totals are significantly below 1992 levels, when more than 100,000 rapes were reported to police. However, there has been a significant increase in the number of reported rapes in the past two years. It is still early to tell whether this is the beginning of a long-term trend or a short-term development.

Victimization surveys indicate that rape is far more prevalent than what is recorded by the UCR. According to the National Crime Victimization Survey (NCVS), more than 430,000 people were victims of rape and sexual assault during the last survey year, a significant increase over the prior survey.[63] However, care should be taken in interpreting this change because the estimates of rape or sexual assault are based on a small number of cases reported to the survey (103 in 2015 versus 69 in 2014). Therefore, small changes and fluctuations in the rates of victimization could have resulted in the very large year-to-year change estimates.

While the overwhelming percentage of rape victims are female, hundreds of men report being sexually assaulted each year. One significant difference: while women most often are attacked by strangers, almost every male rape involves a friend or acquaintance. Male sexual victimization is most common among a small strata of men, including gay and bisexual men, veterans, inmates, and men seeking mental and physical health services.[64]

Patterns of Rape and Sexual Assault

Rape is a warm-weather crime—most incidents occur during July and August, with the lowest rates occurring during December, January, and February. Population density also influences the rape rate. Metropolitan areas today have rape rates significantly higher than rural areas; nonetheless, urban areas have experienced a much greater drop in rape reports than rural areas.

The police make arrests in somewhat less than 40 percent of all reported rape offenses. The racial and age patterns of rape arrests have been fairly consistent for some time. Of the offenders arrested, the great majority were adults; about two-thirds were Caucasian.

There is little question that rape may be significantly underreported to police and that there are significantly more rape victims than the official data suggest.[65] Some research efforts have found that less than 20 percent of all rapes are reported to police.[66] The NCVS indicates that about a third of all rapes are reported to police, a reporting rate far less than any other violent crime.[67]

Why the significant discrepancy between incidents and reporting? Many victims of rape and sexual assault fail to report the crime to the police because they are embarrassed, think it a personal matter, believe nothing can be done, or blame themselves. Some even question whether they have really been raped; research indicates that victims may not label their experience as a "real" rape when the assault involved an acquaintance or boyfriend, if they were severely impaired by alcohol or drugs, or if the act involved oral or digital sex.[68] Some victims refuse to report rape because they have histories of excessive drinking and sexual promiscuity, convincing themselves that their intemperate and/or immoderate behavior contributed to their victimization. A Bureau of Justice Statistics national survey found that about a quarter of rape victims who did not report to police believed the incident was a personal matter, and one in five stated a fear of reprisal. Others felt the incident was just not important enough.[69] But whether or not victims acknowledge that their attack is a "real" rape, the experience can have shattering psychological effects that last long after the attack itself is over.[70]

Types of Rapists

Some rapes are planned, whereas others are spontaneous; some focus on a particular victim, whereas others occur almost as an afterthought during the commission of another crime, such as a burglary. Some rapists commit a single crime, whereas others are multiple offenders; some attack alone, and others engage in group or gang rapes. Because there is no single type of rape or rapist, criminologists have attempted to define and categorize the vast variety of rape situations.

Criminologists now recognize that there are numerous motivations for rape—and, consequently, various types of rapists. One of the best-known attempts to classify the personalities of rapists was that of A. Nicholas Groth, an expert in treating sex offenders. According to Groth, every rape encounter contains at least one of three elements: anger, power, or sadism.[71] Consequently, rapists can be classified according to one of the three dimensions described in Exhibit 10.1. In treating rape offenders, Groth found that about 55 percent represented the power type, about 40 percent the anger type, and about 5 percent the sadistic type. Groth's major contribution has been his recognition that rape is generally a crime of violence, not a sexual act. In all of these circumstances, rape involves a violent criminal offense in which a predatory criminal chooses to attack a victim.[72]

Exhibit 10.1   Varieties of Forcible Rape

- *Anger rape* occurs when sexuality becomes a means of expressing and discharging pent-up anger and rage. The rapist uses far more brutality than would have been necessary if his real objective had been simply to have sex with his victim. His aim is to hurt his victim as much as possible; the sexual aspect of rape may be an afterthought. Often the anger rapist acts on the spur of the moment after an upsetting incident has caused him conflict, irritation, or aggravation. Surprisingly, anger rapes are less psychologically traumatic for the victim than might be expected. Because a woman is usually physically beaten during an anger rape, she is more likely to receive sympathy from her peers, relatives, and the justice system and consequently be immune from any suggestion that she complied with the attack.

- *Power rape* involves an attacker who does not want to harm his victim as much as he wants to possess her sexually. His goal is sexual conquest, and he uses only the amount of force necessary to achieve his objective. The power rapist wants to be in control, to be able to dominate women and have them at his mercy. Yet it is not sexual gratification that drives the power rapist; in fact, he often has a consenting relationship with his wife or girlfriend. Rape is instead a way of putting personal insecurities to rest, asserting heterosexuality, and preserving a sense of manhood. The power rapist's victim is usually a woman equal in age to or younger than the rapist. The lack of physical violence may reduce the support given the victim by family and friends. Therefore, the victim's personal guilt over her rape experience is increased—perhaps, she thinks, she could have done something to get away.

- *Sadistic rape* involves both sexuality and aggression. The sadistic rapist is bound up in ritual—he may torment his victim, bind her, or torture her. In the rapist's view, victims are usually related to a personal characteristic that he wants to harm or destroy. The rape experience is intensely exciting to the sadist; he gets satisfaction from abusing, degrading, or humiliating his captive. This type of rape is particularly traumatic for the victim. Victims of such crimes need psychiatric care long after their physical wounds have healed.

Source: A. Nicholas Groth and Jean Birnbaum, *Men Who Rape* (New York: Plenum Press, 1979).

Types of Rape

In addition to the variety of types of rapists, there are also different categories of rapes.

date rape
A rape that involves people who are in some form of courting relationship.

DATE RAPE One disturbing trend involves people who are in some form of courting relationship—this type of attack is known as **date rape**. Some date rapes occur on first dates, others after a relationship has begun developing, and still others after the couple has been involved for some time. In long-term or close relationships, the male partner may feel he has invested so much time and money in his partner that he is owed sexual relations or that sexual intimacy is an expression or acknowledgment that the involvement is progressing.[73]

Date rape was first identified as a significant social problem in the 1980s when Mary Koss conducted surveys and found that a significant number of college-age women had been sexually assaulted by a dating partner; about 27 percent of the respondents had been the victim of rape or attempted rape. However, only about a quarter of the women called what had happened to them "rape"; the majority either blamed themselves or denied they had really been raped.[74]

Koss's research helped identify a social problem that all too long had remained below the radar. Even though the problem has been identified, many victims still fail to report date rape. Some do not view their experience as a "real" rape, which, they believe, involves a strange man "jumping out of the bushes." Other victims are embarrassed and frightened. Many tell their friends about their rape while refusing to let authorities know what happened. Reporting is most common in the most serious cases, such as when a weapon is used; it is less common when drugs or alcohol is involved.[75] This leads to significant underreporting of rape, especially on college campuses, since many incidents involve the victim's voluntary involvement in drinking or substance abuse before the assault occurred.[76] Underreporting of these incidents is important because so many victims who abused substances before the rape suffer PTSD and other disorders and require help and counseling.[77]

RAPE ON CAMPUS A great deal of date and acquaintance rape is committed on college campuses. The most extensive national survey of sexual assault on college campuses was conducted by the Westat research corporation for the Association of American Universities.[78] The survey involved 150,000 students at 27 universities and found that by 2015 campus rape had reached epidemic proportions: nearly a quarter of women reported nonconsensual sexual contact by physical force, threats of physical force, or incapacitation while enrolled at a university. About 12 percent of all students experienced misconduct: while the majority were female students, about 5 percent of male students reported being sexually assaulted. Students identifying themselves as transgender or gay faced an extremely high risk of being victimized. A significant portion of the incidents involved drugs and alcohol.

While the risk of the most serious types of nonconsensual sexual contact due to physical force or incapacitation declines from freshman to senior year, the fact remains that about 1 in 10 female students say they have experienced sexual assault involving penetration by force or incapacitation sometime during their college experience. But some women, especially those in marginalized populations such as lesbian and transgendered, may even be more vulnerable than the norm. Take for instance recent research that found that within a sample of female undergraduate students who are hearing impaired more than two-thirds (69 percent) experienced at least one assault and more than half (56 percent) experienced multiple assaults.[79]

Despite its prevalence, many campus rapes go unreported. A recent survey by the Bureau of Justice Statistics found that only about 20 percent of campus rape and sexual assault victimizations are reported to police and that students were less likely to report than nonstudents.[80] One reason for underreporting may be that many campus police officers are not sensitive to rape victims and believe in "rape myths" that the victim is somehow responsible for the assault or that they made it up to conceal consensual sex.[81] Campus police are less likely to believe victims who admitted to drinking before the attack or who knew their attacker. In contrast, campus police officers who attend training on victim sensitivity, the trauma of victimization, the identification of drug-facilitated sexual assaults, and the role of alcohol and/or intoxication in sexual assault were significantly less likely to accept rape myths than those who had not received such training.[82]

Another reason for the limited reporting of campus rapes is that many students consider themselves responsible for the attack because they did not take adequate precautions or engaged in reckless behavior—for example, getting drunk at a frat house. More than 50 percent of victims say they did not report the event because they did not consider it "serious enough." A significant percentage of students say they did not report because they felt "embarrassed, ashamed, or that it would be too emotionally difficult" or they "did not think anything would be done about it." This misplaced guilt may also explain why so many college women suffer PTSD and other disorders soon after they are attacked.

Colleges and universities are notorious for trying to sweep sexual assault incidents under the rug to protect their image of a safe environment for young women. This persists despite the protections of Title IX of the Education Amendments of 1972, a federal civil rights law that prohibits discrimination on the basis of sex in any education program or activity that receives federal funding.[83] Under Title IX, discrimination on the basis of sex can include sexual harassment, rape, and sexual assault. A college or university that receives federal funds may be held legally responsible when it knows about and ignores sexual harassment or assault in its programs or activities. The school can be held responsible whether the harassment is committed by a faculty member, staff, or a student.[84] Despite this injunction, critics claim that schools either fail to prosecute miscreants or give them a slap on the wrist, such as making them send a letter of apology or perform a community service; even these mild sanctions may not be enforced.

CONNECTIONS

Chapter 3 introduced the concept of victim precipitation. The jury in the Labrie case may have concluded the victim precipitated the rape by agreeing to accompany the boy to a darkened room and removing her outer clothing. Is this an instance of blaming the victim?

In order to reduce campus rape, California became the first state to enact legislation requiring affirmative consent before a sexual encounter can take place. The law states, "Lack of protest or resistance does not mean consent, nor does silence mean consent. Affirmative consent must be ongoing throughout a sexual activity and can be revoked at any time." This bill removes the requirement that a rape victim prove she or he said "no" and instead requires that the accused prove that the alleged victim said "yes."[85] Lack of protest does not mean agreement; consent can't be given if someone is asleep or incapacitated by drugs or alcohol.

MARITAL RAPE Traditionally, a legally married husband could not be charged with raping his wife; this immunity was referred to as the **marital exemption**. However, research indicates that many women are raped each year by their husbands as part of an overall pattern of spousal abuse, and these women deserve the protection of the law. Many spousal rapes are accompanied by brutal, sadistic beatings and have little to do with normal sexual interests.[86] Not surprisingly, the marital exemption has undergone significant revision. In 1980, only three states had laws against marital rape; today every state recognizes marital rape as a crime.[87]

STATUTORY RAPE The term **statutory rape** refers to sexual relations between an underage minor female and an adult male. Although the sex is not forced or coerced, the law says that young girls are incapable of giving informed consent, so the act is legally considered nonconsensual. In most instances, state law cites an age of consent above which there can be no criminal prosecution for consensual sexual relations. Those accused of statutory rape can defend themselves by claiming the victim lied about their age or provided false documentation such as a fake driver's license. However, mistake is not an absolute defense and a defendant can still be convicted in some courts even if they were mistaken about the victim's age.

Some states have passed so-called **Romeo and Juliet laws** that decriminalize a sexual act that occurred between individuals with a few years' age difference from being considered a criminal offense. The age range allowed by a Romeo and Juliet provision is typically between two and four years. In some states, a Romeo and Juliet provision can only apply if the younger of the individuals has reached a certain age, such as 15. The state may also require the older of the individuals to be under a certain age, such as 21. Florida's Romeo and Juliet law does not legalize sexual relations between an 18-year-old and a 15-year-old; however, it does allow the offender to petition or make a motion to the court to remove the requirement to register as a sexual offender.[88]

RAPE BY DECEPTION Rape by deception occurs when the rapist uses fraud or trickery to convince the victim to engage in sex or impersonates someone with whom the victim has been intimate.[89] In one Massachusetts case, a man was convicted of rape after he allegedly impersonated his brother in order to have sex with his brother's girlfriend in the middle of the night. The conviction was later overturned because Massachusetts law does not recognize that sex by deception can be considered rape.

A few jurisdictions recognize rape by deception.[90] California passed a rape by deception law in 2013.[91] In Tennessee, the legal definition of rape includes "sexual penetration . . . accomplished by fraud"; in Idaho, sex with a woman is defined as rape when because of his "artifice, pretense or concealment," the victim believes him to be "someone other than" who he is. Despite these exceptions, rape by deception is not universally recognized in American criminal law. However, a number of legal scholars believe that sex by deception ought to be defined as rape because "a consent procured through deception is no consent at all."[92]

SEX IN AUTHORITY RELATIONS A growing number of states have passed legislation making it a crime for people in power to have sexual relations with those whom they control or supervise.[93] These "sex in authority relations" (SAR) laws criminalize such behaviors as a psychologist who pressures his patient into sex or suggests it's part of a treatment plan; a boss or supervisor who propositions his or her subordinate;

---

marital exemption
The formerly accepted tradition that a legally married husband could not be charged with raping his wife.

statutory rape
Sexual relations between an underage minor female and an adult male.

Romeo and Juliet laws
Apply to cases of statutory rape when both members engage in consensual sexual intercourse, but the age gap between the older alleged offender and the younger alleged victim is narrow, typically two to four years.

a university professor who persuades or coerces an unwilling research assistant into having sex. Criminalization of sexual contact in relationships between a person of authority and a person under his or her authority is a contemporary trend in many legal systems, including the United States, Israel, Great Britain, and Canada.

Some SAR laws do not require an element of force or physical threat; they prohibit what appears to be consensual sexual relations as long as one participant is in a position of power while the other is a subordinate; it is considered a crime even if he or she is a willing participant in the act. Other SAR laws do require coercive threats by the authority figure, such as a workplace supervisor who threatens to fire an employee if she refuses his sexual demands.

Many of these laws focus on health care providers. Texas's "sex without consent" law identifies sexual relations as nonconsensual in cases where "the actor is a mental health services provider or a health care services provider who causes the other person, who is a patient or former patient of the actor, to submit or participate by exploiting the other person's emotional dependency on the actor." Other jurisdictions specify a per se rule prohibiting sexual contact during therapy and do not require any additional elements such as fraud, coercion, or exploitation, as Texas does. The North Dakota code is illustrative of this point:

> Any person who is or who holds oneself out to be a therapist and who intentionally has sexual contact, as defined in section 12.1-20-02, with a patient or client during any treatment, consultation, interview, or examination is guilty of a class C felony. Consent by the complainant is not a defense under this section."[94]

Causes of Rape

What factors predispose some men to commit rape? Criminologists' responses to this question are almost as varied as the crime itself. However, most explanations can be grouped into a few consistent categories.

EVOLUTIONARY FACTORS According to the evolutionary psychology view, sexual violence may be instinctual, developed over the ages as a means of perpetuating the species.[95] The evolutionary view is that the sexual urge corresponds to the unconscious need to preserve the species by spreading one's genes as widely as possible. Males who were sexually aggressive had a reproductive edge over their more passive peers. These prehistoric drives remain active in some males who still have a natural sexual drive that encourages them to have intimate relations with as many women as possible. From the evolutionary perspective, it makes sense that women at the peak of their fertility would be preferential targets, and rape studies have documented that younger women are most often victimized by rapists.[96] However, in a civilized society such as ours sexual violence is subject to both social and legal disapproval and punishment so that rape as a reproductive strategy brings with it significant disadvantages.[97]

MALE SOCIALIZATION In contrast to the evolutionary biological view, some researchers argue that rape is a function of socialization. Some men have been socialized to be aggressive with women and believe that the use of violence or force is legitimate if their sexual advances are rebuffed ("Women like to play hard to get and expect to be forced to have sex"). Those who have been socialized to believe that "no means yes" are more likely to be sexually aggressive.[98] The use of sexual violence is aggravated if pro-force socialization is reinforced by peers who share similar values.[99]

Diana Russell describes the **virility mystique**—the belief that males must separate their sexual feelings from their need for love, respect, and affection. She believes men are socialized to be the aggressors and expect to be sexually active with many women; consequently, male virginity and sexual inexperience are shameful. Similarly, sexually aggressive women frighten some men and cause them to doubt their own masculinity. Sexual insecurity may lead some men to commit rape to bolster their self-image and masculine identity.[100]

virility mystique
The belief that males must separate their sexual feelings from their need for love, respect, and affection.

CONNECTIONS

The social learning view of rape will be explored further in Chapter 13 when the issue of pornography and violence is analyzed in greater detail.

narcissistic personality disorder
A pattern of traits and behaviors indicating infatuation and fixation with one's self to the exclusion of all others, along with the egotistic and ruthless pursuit of one's own gratification, dominance, and ambition.

A rape culture is not unique to the United States. India has experienced a significant rise in rapes. An incident that received worldwide attention involved Jyoti Singh, a 23-year-old medical student, who was raped and tortured by six men on a bus; she later died from the horrific injuries she sustained during the attack. When one of the rapists, Mukesh Singh, was interviewed in prison he claimed: "A decent girl won't roam around at 9 o'clock at night. A girl is far more responsible for rape than a boy. Housework and housekeeping is for girls, not roaming in discos and bars at night doing wrong things, wearing wrong clothes."[101]

PSYCHOLOGICAL ABNORMALITY Rapists often have undergone a traumatic childhood marked by sexual abuse and parental detachment. Not surprisingly, many suffer from some type of personality disorder or mental illness, and may have psychotic tendencies, including hostile, sadistic feelings toward women.[102] A high proportion of serial rapists and repeat sexual offenders exhibit psychopathic personality structures.[103] There is evidence linking rape proclivity with **narcissistic personality disorder**, a pattern of traits and behaviors that indicate infatuation and fixation with one's self to the exclusion of all others and the egotistic and ruthless pursuit of one's own gratification, dominance, and ambition.[104]

SOCIAL LEARNING According to this perspective, men learn to commit rapes in much the same way they learn any other behavior. Sexual aggression may be learned through interaction with peers who articulate attitudes supportive of sexual violence.[105] Observing or experiencing sexual violence has also been linked to sexual aggression. Groth found that 40 percent of the rapists he studied were sexually victimized as adolescents.[106] Experiencing sexual trauma has been linked with the desire to inflict sexual trauma on others.[107] Watching violent or pornographic films featuring women who are beaten, raped, or tortured has been linked to sexually aggressive behavior in men.[108]

GENDER CONFLICT VIEW According to the gender conflict view, as women make progress toward social, political, and economic equality, men fear them as a threat to their long-held dominance.[109] Men react through efforts of formal and informal controls over women. One informal method of social control is to dominate women sexually through the commission of rape. The male-dominated criminal justice system may exert less effort in handling rape cases in an effort to maintain male superiority. Research by Richard Johnson does in fact show that regions with higher levels of progress toward gender equality actually experience higher rates of rape and lower rates of rape case clearances.[110]

SEXUAL MOTIVATION Even though criminologists now consider rape a violent act without sexual motivation, there is evidence that at least some rapists have sexual feelings for their victim.[111] NCVS data reveal that rape victims tend to be young and that rapists prefer younger, presumably more attractive victims. Data show an association between the ages of rapists and those of their victims, indicating that men choose rape targets of approximately the same age as their consensual sex partners. And despite the fact that younger criminals are usually the most violent, older rapists tend to harm their victims more than younger rapists. This pattern indicates that older criminals may rape for motives of power and control, whereas younger offenders may be seeking sexual gratification. Victims may, therefore, suffer less harm from severe beatings and humiliation from younger attackers.

Rape and the Law

L03 Discuss the issues involving rape and the law.

As you may recall (Chapter 3), the jury in the St. Paul rape case may have believed that the young victim consented to a sexual encounter even though her testimony suggested the opposite; the jury doubted the veracity of her version of the events that took place. She is not alone nor is her case unique. Unlike other crime victims, women may find that they have to prove they did not engage in consensual sex and then develop remorse afterward. Research shows that people are more likely to "blame the victim" in a case of sexual assault than they are in other common-law crimes such as armed robbery. Victim blaming is exacerbated if a prior relationship existed or if the victim did not fight back because she was intoxicated—factors that have less impact in other crimes.[112]

However, police and courts are becoming more sensitive to the plight of rape victims and are now just as likely to investigate acquaintance rape as they are **aggravated rape** involving multiple offenders, weapons, and victim injuries. In some jurisdictions, the justice system takes all rape cases seriously and does not ignore those in which victim and attacker have had a prior relationship or those that did not involve serious injury.[113]

PROVING RAPE On March 13, 2006, after a performance by two strippers at a private residence, three members of Duke University's men's lacrosse team were accused of raping one of the women who had been hired to entertain the team. Media outlets had a field day with a case involving a young African American victim and her alleged attackers, who were wealthy and white. However, evidence soon emerged that the charges were false, the players falsely accused and wrongfully vilified.[114] The Duke case is not unique. In 2014, a *Rolling Stone* article claimed that a University of Virginia student identified only as "Jackie" was gang raped at a frat house. The article made headlines when it described a culture of binge-drinking and casual sex tolerated by a university administration that ignored protocol when students filed sexual assault complaints. A thorough investigation turned up no evidence of a sexual assault or any wrongdoing by the school, suggesting the entire incident was a made-up story.[115] Some criminologists claim that upward of 15 percent of all people convicted of rape were falsely accused and innocent of the charges.[116]

Stories such as these can make proving guilt in a rape case extremely challenging for prosecutors. Some judges fear that women may charge men with rape because of jealousy, withdrawn marriage proposals, revenge, or pregnancy. There is evidence that juries may consider the race of the victim and offender in their decision making; they may believe victims and convict defendants more often in interracial rapes than when both parties are the same race.[117] Although the law does not recognize it, jurors are sometimes swayed by the insinuation that the rape was victim precipitated; thus, the blame is shifted from rapist to victim. To get a conviction, prosecutors must establish that the act was forced and violent and that no question of voluntary compliance exists. They may be reluctant to prosecute cases where they have questions about the victim's moral character or if they believe the victim's demeanor and attitude will turn off the jury and undermine the chance of conviction.[118]

CONSENT It is essential to prove that the attack was forced and that the victim did not give voluntary **consent** to her attacker. In a sense, the burden of proof is on the victim to show that her character is beyond question and that she in no way encouraged, enticed, or misled the accused rapist. A common defense tactic is to introduce suspicion into the minds of the jury that the woman may have consented to the sexual act and later regretted her decision or suspicion that her dubious moral character casts doubt on the veracity of her claims. Even the appearance of impropriety can undermine a case. Proving the victim has a good character is not a requirement in any other crime.

LEGAL REFORM Because of the difficulty that rape victims have in obtaining justice, rape laws have been changing around the country. Reform efforts include changing the language

> **aggravated rape**
> Rape involving multiple offenders, weapons, and victim injuries.
>
> **consent**
> The victim of rape must prove that she in no way encouraged, enticed, or misled the accused rapist.

Brendan McDermid/Reuters; Barry Gutierrez/Reuters

Proving rape can be challenging because the prosecution must prove the victim did not consent. Actress Lili Bernard (center) and writer Sammie Mays (right), two alleged victims of Bill Cosby, speak at a press conference in New York City. More than 40 women have accused Cosby of sexual assault. While the famed comedian denies the charges, he has admitted to acquiring Quaaludes and giving them to women with whom he wanted to have sex. Cosby's first trial on sexual assault charges resulted in a hung jury.

shield laws
Laws that protect women from being questioned about their sexual history unless such questioning directly bears on the case.

murder
The unlawful killing of a human being with malice aforethought.

first-degree murder
Killing a person after premeditation and deliberation.

premeditation
Considering the criminal act beforehand, which suggests that it was motivated by more than a simple desire to engage in an act of violence.

L04 Analyze the different types of murder.

of statutes, dropping the condition of victim resistance, and changing the requirement of *use* of force to include the *threat* of force or injury.[119] **Shield laws**, which protect women from being questioned about their sexual history unless it directly bears on the case, have become universal. Although some are quite restrictive, others grant the trial judge considerable discretion to admit prior sexual conduct in evidence if it is deemed relevant for the defense. In an important case, *Michigan v. Lucas*, the Supreme Court upheld the validity of shield laws and ruled that excluding evidence of a prior sexual relationship between the parties did not violate the defendant's right to a fair trial.[120]

In addition to requiring evidence that consent was not given, the common law of rape required corroboration that the crime of rape actually took place. This involved the need for independent evidence from police officers, physicians, and witnesses that the accused was actually the person who committed the crime, that sexual penetration took place, and that force was present and consent absent. This requirement shielded rapists from prosecution in cases where the victim delayed reporting the crime or physical evidence had been compromised or lost. Corroboration is no longer required except under extraordinary circumstances, such as when the victim is too young to understand the crime, has had a previous sexual relationship with the defendant, or gives a version of events that is improbable and self-contradictory.[121]

The federal government may have given rape victims another source of redress when it passed the Violence Against Women Act in 1994. This statute allows rape victims to sue in federal court on the grounds that sexual violence violates their civil rights; so far, the provisions of this act have been upheld by appellate courts.[122] Despite these reform efforts, prosecutors may be influenced in their decision to bring charges by the circumstances of a crime.[123] Another important piece of legislation, the Campus Sexual Violence Elimination (Campus SaVE) Act, increases transparency on campus about incidents of sexual violence, guarantees victims enhanced rights, sets standards for disciplinary proceedings, and requires campus-wide prevention education programs. The act broadens this requirement to mandate fuller reporting of sexual violence to include incidents of domestic violence, dating violence, and stalking. Signed into law on March 7, 2013, it also requires schools to protect victim confidentiality when reporting criminal threats to the campus community.[124]

Murder and Homicide

The common-law definition of **murder** is "the unlawful killing of a human being with malice aforethought."[125] It is the most serious of all common-law crimes and the only one in the United States that can still be punished by death. Western society's abhorrence of murderers is illustrated by the fact that there is no statute of limitations in murder cases. Whereas state laws limit prosecution of other crimes to a fixed period (usually 7 to 10 years), accused killers can be brought to justice at any time after their crimes were committed.

- In 1991, the abused and decomposed body of 4-year-old Anjelica Castillo—known as "Baby Hope"—was found in an ice chest by the side of a New York roadway; in 2013, her killer, Conrado Juarez, was arrested in New York City, 22 years after that infamous crime took place.[126]
- In 2015, Michael R. Jones, 62, of Champaign, Illinois, was arrested and charged with two counts of murder and one count of aggravated criminal sexual assault in the 1985 death of Kristina Wesselman.[127]
- Putting an end to one of America's most notorious cases, Pedro Hernandez confessed in 2017 to luring 6-year-old Etan Patz into a basement in 1979 and killing him. Hernandez was found guilty of murder and kidnapping.[128]

To legally prove that a murder has taken place, most state jurisdictions require prosecutors to show that the accused *maliciously* intended to kill the victim. "Express or actual malice" is the state of mind assumed to exist when someone kills another person in the absence of any apparent provocation. "Implied or constructive malice" is considered to exist when a death results from negligent or unthinking behavior. In these cases, even though the perpetrator did not wish to kill the victim, the killing resulted from an inherently dangerous act and therefore is considered murder.

Degrees of Murder

There are different levels, or degrees, of homicide. **First-degree murder** occurs when a person kills another after premeditation and deliberation. **Premeditation** means that the killing was considered beforehand and suggests that it was motivated by more than a simple desire to engage in an act of violence. **Deliberation** means the killing was planned after careful thought rather than carried out on impulse: "To constitute a deliberate and premeditated killing, the slayer must weigh and consider the question of killing and the reasons for and against such a choice; having in mind the consequences, he decides to and does kill."[129] The planning implied by this definition need not be a long process; it may be an almost instantaneous decision to take another's life. Also, a killing that accompanies a felony, such as robbery or rape, usually constitutes first-degree murder (**felony murder**).

Second-degree murder requires the killer to have malice aforethought but not premeditation or deliberation. A second-degree murder occurs when a person's wanton disregard for the victim's life and his or her desire to inflict serious bodily harm on the victim result in the victim's death. Homicide without malice is called **manslaughter** and is usually punished by anywhere from 1 to 15 years in prison. **Voluntary or nonnegligent manslaughter** refers to a killing committed in the heat of passion or during a sudden quarrel that provoked violence. Although intent may be present, malice is not. **Involuntary or negligent manslaughter** refers to a killing that occurs when a person's acts are negligent and without regard for the harm they may cause others. Most involuntary manslaughter cases involve motor vehicle deaths—a drunk driver kills a pedestrian.

DELIBERATE INDIFFERENCE MURDER Murder is often considered an intentional act, but a person can also be held criminally liable for the death of another even if she or he did not intend to injure another person but exhibited *deliberate indifference* to the danger her or his actions might cause. The deliberate indifference standard is met when a person knows of and yet disregards or ignores an excessive risk to another's health or safety. One of the most famous cases illustrating deliberate indifference murder occurred on January 26, 2001, when Diane Whipple, a San Francisco woman, died after two large dogs attacked her in the hallway of her apartment building. One of the dogs' owners/keepers, Robert Noel, was found guilty of manslaughter, and his wife, Marjorie Knoller, was convicted on charges of second-degree murder, because they knew that the dogs were highly dangerous but did little or nothing to control the animals' behavior. Their deliberate indifference put their neighbor at risk, with tragic consequences. After a long series of appeals, on June 1, 2007, the California Supreme Court ruled that a dog owner who knows the animal is a potential killer and exposes other people to that danger may be guilty of murder even though he or she did not intend that particular victim to be injured or killed. In a unanimous decision, the appellate court ruled that Knoller could be convicted of murder because she acted with "conscious disregard of the danger to human life." On September 22, 2008, the court sentenced Marjorie Knoller to serve 15 years to life for the death of Diane Whipple.[130]

"BORN AND ALIVE" One issue that has received national attention is whether a murder victim can be a fetus that has not yet been delivered; this is referred to as **feticide**. Today about 38 states have some form of fetal homicide laws and more than two-thirds of the states have passed some form of legislation that criminalizes the killing of a fetus as murder even if it is not "born and alive."[131] In some states, there exists legislation creating a separate class of crime that increases criminal penalties when a person causes injury to a woman he or she knows is pregnant, and the injury results in miscarriage or stillbirth. There is still a great deal of state-to-state variation in feticide laws. Some make it a separate crime to kill a fetus or commit an act of violence against a pregnant woman. Others have a viability requirement: feticide can occur only if the unborn child could at the time potentially live outside the mother's body.[132]

---

deliberation
Planning a criminal act after careful thought, rather than carrying it out on impulse.

felony murder
A killing that accompanies a felony, such as robbery or rape.

second-degree murder
A person's wanton disregard for the victim's life and his or her desire to inflict serious bodily harm on the victim, which results in the victim's death.

manslaughter
Homicide without malice.

voluntary or nonnegligent manslaughter
A killing committed in the heat of passion or during a sudden quarrel that provoked violence.

involuntary or negligent manslaughter
A killing that occurs when a person's acts are negligent and without regard for the harm they may cause others.

feticide
Intentional or negligent killing of a human fetus.

FACT OR FICTION?

You can't be convicted of murder unless you personally and intentionally kill someone.

FICTION A person can be convicted of murder if he is aware that his behavior can cause lethal danger but does nothing to stop it from occurring, even though he did not intend the victim to be killed; this is known as deliberate indifference. Someone can also be convicted of murder if he merely participates in a felony, such as a robbery, and someone is killed by a partner or co-conspirator.

Nature and Extent of Murder

It is possible to track the trends in US murder rates from 1900 to the present with the aid of coroners' reports and UCR data. The murder rate peaked in 1933, a time of prolonged economic depression and lawlessness, and then fell until 1958. The homicide rate doubled from the mid-1960s to a peak in 1991 when almost 25,000 people were killed in a single year, a rate of about 10 per 100,000 people.

Since they reached a peak in the 1990s, the number and rate of murders declined until 2015, when there was a spike in murders. In 2015, there were 15,696 murders, at a rate of 4.9 per 100,000, representing an increase of almost 11 percent over the preceding year. Preliminary 2016 data show another 5 percent increase in the murder rate. While this new trend is disturbing, there are still about 10,000 fewer people being killed now than there were 25 years ago, even though the population has become much larger! Whether this two-year increase in the number and rate of murder is going to be a long-term trend remains to be seen.

What else do official crime statistics tell us about murder today? Murder tends to be an urban crime. More than half of all homicides occur in cities with a population of 100,000 or more; nearly one-quarter of homicides occur in cities with a population of more than 1 million. Why is homicide an urban phenomenon? Large cities experience the greatest rates of structural disadvantage—poverty, joblessness, racial heterogeneity, residential mobility, family disruption, and income inequality—that are linked to high murder rates.[133] Not surprisingly, large cities are much more commonly the site of drug-related killings and gang-related murders and are relatively less likely to be the location of family-related homicides, including murders of intimates.

Murder victims and offenders tend to be males; about 80 percent of homicide victims and nearly 90 percent of offenders are male. Murder, like rape, tends to be an intraracial crime; about 90 percent of victims are slain by members of their own race. More than half of all murder victims are African American men. Approximately one-third of murder victims and almost half of offenders are under the age of 25. In contrast, less than 10 percent of murder victims were over 60 in 2015. Some murders involve very young children, a crime referred to as **infanticide** (killing older children is called **filicide**), and others involve senior citizens, a crime referred to as **eldercide**.[134] The younger the child, the greater the risk for infanticide.

Murderers typically have a long involvement in crime; few people begin a criminal career by killing someone. Research shows that people arrested for homicide are significantly more likely to have been in trouble with the law prior to their arrest than people arrested for other crimes.[135] David Farrington and his associates found that among the risk predictors for homicide, prior criminal offenses up to age 14 was the most important; 95 percent of offenders had records of violence.[136]

A murderer's choice of weapon is related to their association with the victim. Those who knew or who had an intimate relationship with the victim are more likely to use a weapon found at the scene—a knife or blunt instrument—and attack their target in the head or face; stranger homicides are more likely to use a gun.[137]

Unlike other crimes, more than two-thirds of all murders are cleared by arrest or other means. Why are murders so solvable? Police devote more time and resources to identifying murderers; most victims and killers were acquainted; there is a significant chance of forensic evidence being left at the scene.

Murderous Relations

Most murders are expressive—that is, motivated by rage or anger—and they typically involve friends, relatives, and acquaintances. Stranger homicides typically involve commission of another crime (such as a robbery, rape, or drug deal) where the perpetrator applied too much force in completing the crime.[138]

Murderous relations are also shaped by gender: males are more likely to kill others of similar social standing in more public contexts, whereas women kill family members and intimate partners in private locations.[139] What forms do murderous relations take?

---

infanticide
Murder of a very young child.

filicide
Murder of an older child.

eldercide
Murder of a senior citizen.

INTIMATE PARTNER MURDER Many murders involve husbands and wives, boyfriends and girlfriends, and others involved in romantic relationships. Intimate partner murder is a gendered phenomenon. When women commit homicide, the most likely victim is an intimate partner; about 40 percent of all female homicide incidents involve killing a male partner. However, while less than 10 percent of all murders committed by men involve a female partner, intimate partner homicides make up 40 to 50 percent of all murders of women in the United States.[140]

Men who kill romantic partners typically have a long history of violence, while for women killing their partner may be their first violent offense.[141] This may be the reason that there is a "chivalry effect" in domestic violence murders. In death penalty states such as California, the death-sentence rate for single-victim domestic violence murders is significantly lower than the overall death-sentence rate for other kinds of killings. Not surprisingly, when women in these states are found guilty of capital murder, they are far less likely than men to be sentenced to death.[142]

Research also shows most females who kill their mates do so after suffering repeated violent attacks.[143] Women who kill or seriously assault intimate partners are often battered women unable to flee a troubled relationship.[144] Perhaps the number of males killed by their partners has declined because alternatives to abusive relationships, such as shelters for battered women, are becoming more prevalent around the United States. Regions that provide greater social support for battered women and that have passed legislation to protect abuse victims also have lower rates of female-perpetrated homicide.[145] This escape valve may help them avoid retaliation through lethal violence.

Some people kill their mates because they find themselves involved in a love triangle.[146] Interestingly, women who kill out of jealousy aim their aggression at their partners; in contrast, men are more likely to kill their rivals (their mates' suitors). Love triangles tend to become lethal when the offenders believe they have been lied to or betrayed. Lethal violence is more common when (1) the rival initiated the affair, (2) the killer knew the spouse was already in a steady relationship outside the marriage, and (3) the killer was repeatedly lied to or betrayed.[147]

AP Images/Telegraph Herald, Dave Kettering

Older people tend to be victimized by a family member. Isaiah Sweet, 18, pleaded guilty to two charges of first-degree murder for the May 2012 killings of his grandparents. Sweet told friends he hated his grandparents before shooting both in the head. He received a life sentence for the murders.

ACQUAINTANCE MURDERS Most murders occur among people who are acquainted. Although on the surface the killing might seem senseless, it is often the result of a long-simmering dispute motivated by revenge, dispute resolution, jealousy, drug deals, racial bias, or threats to identity or status.[148] A prior act of violence, motivated by profit or greed, such as when a buyer robs his dealer during a drug transaction, may generate revenge killing.

How do these murderous relations develop between two people who may have had little prior conflict? In a classic study, David Luckenbill examined murder transactions to determine whether particular patterns of behavior are common between the killer and the victim.[149] He found that many homicides follow a sequential pattern. First, the victim makes what the offender considers an offensive move. The offender typically retaliates verbally or physically. An agreement to end things violently is forged with the victim's provocative response. The battle ensues, leaving the victim dead or dying. The offender's escape is shaped by his or her relationship to the victim or by the reaction of the audience, if any.

STRANGER MURDERS About 20 percent of all murders involve strangers. Stranger homicides occur most often as felony murders during rapes, robberies, and burglaries. Others are random acts of urban violence that fuel public fear: a homeowner tells a motorist to move his car because it is blocking the driveway, an argument ensues, and the owner gets a pistol and kills the motorist. Stranger homicides can result from random gang violence: someone is killed inadvertently in a drive-by shooting. They may also stem from hate crimes (covered later in this chapter) directed at victims merely because of their race, class, gender, and so on. The killing of homeless people by adolescent groups and gangs has become all too common.[150]

SEXUALLY BASED MURDERS Some murders are sexually related. Research indicates that sexually related homicide can take a variety of forms:[151]

- Domestic disputes involving husbands and wives, boyfriends and girlfriends, same-sex couples, and even on occasion siblings. Sometimes these events are triggered by a partner's unwanted or unexpected pregnancy: homicidal injury is a leading cause of death among pregnant and postpartum women in the United States.[152]
- Love triangles involving former husbands and/or wives and jilted lovers.
- Rape and/or sodomy oriented assault in which a person intends to commit a rape or sexual assault but uses excessive force to overcome resistance, resulting in the victim's death.
- "Lust murders" that are motivated by obsessive sexual fantasies.
- Vengeance for sexual violence. In these cases someone exacts vengeance on a sexual violence perpetrator, either on his or her own behalf or on the behalf of a sexual violence victim.

Policies and Issues in Criminology

HONOR KILLINGS

Saba Qaiser, a young Pakistani woman, fell in love against her family's wishes and ran off to marry her boyfriend. Hours after the marriage, her father and uncle got her into their car and took her to a spot along a riverbank to murder her for her defiance. After beating her, Saba's uncle held her so that her father could shoot her in the head. The two men packed her bloody body into a large sack and threw it into the river to sink. Saba was unconscious but alive. The river water revived her, and she managed to crawl out of the sack and made her way to a gas station, where patrons called for help.

After the two men were arrested, Saba's father said, "She took away our honor. . . . If you put one drop of piss in a gallon of milk, the whole thing gets destroyed. That's what she has done. . . . So I said, 'No, I will kill you myself.'" Other relatives urged Saba to forgive her father and uncle and she reluctantly complied; the father and uncle were released from prison. "After this incident, everyone says I am more respected," her father later boasted. "I can proudly say that for generations to come none of my descendants will ever think of doing what Saba did." He promised not to try again to kill Saba. Her story was told in a 2015 Academy Award–winning documentary, *A Girl in the River: The Price of Forgiveness*, directed by Sharmeen Obaid-Chinoy.

Saba's story is sadly not unique: more than 1,000 people are victims of honor killings in Pakistan each year. The attacks are provoked by the belief or perception that an individual's or family's honor has been threatened because of the actual or perceived sexual misconduct of the female. In 2014, a young newlywed couple, Sajjad Ahmed, 26, and Muawia Bibi, 18, were killed by the bride's family in northeastern Pakistan because they did not approve of the marriage. The bride's father and uncles lured the couple back to the village of Satrah in the Punjab province, where the pair were tied up and decapitated. The family members turned themselves in to police, maintaining that their brutal attack was a matter of honor.

In some instances the killer was encouraged by friends and/or relatives who objected to a relationship. Mubeen Rajhu's sister, Tasleem, was only 18 when she fell in love with a Christian man. He loved her too, so much so that he was willing to, and in fact did, convert to Islam in hopes that he could marry her. However, her brother Rajhu's coworkers taunted him, saying, "Can't you do anything? What is the matter with you? You are not a man. . . . It would be better to kill your sister. It is better than letting her have this relationship."

Before he killed her, Rajhu pleaded with his sister. "I told her I would have no face to show at the mill, to show to my neighbors, so don't do it. Don't do it. But she wouldn't listen."

Honor killing and honor crime involve violence against women and girls, including such acts as beating, battering, or killing, by a family member or relative. Honor killings are most common in traditional societies

- Self-defense during sexual violence. In these incidents, sexual violence was taking place and the victim defended herself or himself resulting in the death of the perpetrator, or another person intervened to defend the sexual violence victim and this resulted in the death of the perpetrator.

Although not much is known about sexually motivated killers, Paul Greenall and Michelle Wright recently found that they tend to be generalists and that sexual homicide was part of a long history of antisocial acts that included a variety of violent crimes in addition to murder.[153] Offenders tend to suffer from neurological and personality disorders, including antisocial, borderline, and schizoid; physical abuse and parental conflict are often present.[154]

Asphyxiation is a frequent method of killing, although knives and blunt instruments are also weapons of choice. It is not uncommon for the sexual killer to use excessive violence and mutilation. Not all sexually based murders involve sex, and evidence of an actual encounter is often missing. These killers displayed behavioral problems, were poor achievers, and experienced social isolation. In adulthood, they became isolated single men who abuse substances and have criminal records.[155]

The Policies and Issues in Criminology feature discusses one type of sexually based murder: a woman killed by relatives for damaging the family's honor.

in the Middle East, Southwest Asia, India, China, and Latin America, and they are increasing rapidly in other areas such as the Palestinian territories, where the number has more than doubled in the past few years. They are also being exported to Europe and the United States. In one US incident, Yaser Abdel Said took his two teenaged daughters for a ride in his taxi cab, under the guise of taking them to get something to eat, then drove them to Irving, Texas, where he allegedly shot both girls to death. The reason: dating boys against his will.

The killings seem illogical to an outsider. Even when a woman is raped she may be accused of being the sexual aggressor who must be punished. According to criminologist Linda Williams, men consider honor killings culturally necessary because any suspicion of sexual activity or suggestion that a girl or a woman is unchaste is enough to raise questions about the family's honor. Strict control of women and girls within the home and outside the home is justified. Women are restricted in their activities in the community, religion, and politics. These institutions, in turn, support the control of females. Williams believes that honor killing is designed for maintaining male dominance. Submissiveness may be seen as a sign of sexual purity, and a woman's or girl's attempts to assert her rights is a violation of the family's honor that needs to be redressed. Rules of honor and threats against females who violate such rules reinforce the control of women and have a powerful impact on their lives. Honor killings/crimes serve to

keep women and girls from "stepping out of line." The manner in which such behaviors silence women and kill their spirit has led some to label honor killings/crimes more broadly as "femicide."

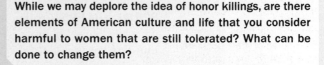

Critical Thinking

While we may deplore the idea of honor killings, are there elements of American culture and life that you consider harmful to women that are still tolerated? What can be done to change them?

Sources: Fred Barbash, "'She Wouldn't Listen': A Wrenching Story of an 'Honor Killing' in Pakistan," *Washington Post*, October 5, 2016, https://www.washingtonpost.com/news/morning-mix/wp/2016/10/05/she-wouldnt-listen-pakistani-man-explains-honor-killing-of-sister/; Nicholas Kristof, "Her Father Shot Her in the Head, as an 'Honor Killing,'" *New York Times*, January 30, 2016, http://www.nytimes.com/2016/01/31/opinion/sunday/her-father-shot-her-in-the-head-as-an-honor-killing.html; Shelby Lin Erdman, "Pakistani Newlyweds Decapitated by Bride's Family in Honor Killing," CNN, June 29, 2014, http://www.cnn.com/2014/06/28/world/asia/pakistan-honor-murders/; Anne-Marie O'Connor, "Honor Killings Rise in Palestinian Territories, Sparking Backlash," *Washington Post*, March 3, 2014, http://www.washingtonpost.com/world/middle_east/honor-killings-rise-in-palestinian-territories-sparking-backlash/2014/03/02/1392d144-940c-11e3-9e13-770265cf4962_story.html; Julia Dahl, "'Honor Killing' Under Growing Scrutiny in the U.S.," CBS News, April 5, 2012, http://www.cbsnews.com/news/honor-killing-under-growing-scrutiny-in-the-us/; Linda M. Williams, "Honor Killings," in *Encyclopedia of Interpersonal Violence*, ed. Claire M. Renzetti and Jeffrey I. Edelson (Thousand Oaks, CA: Sage Publications, 2007). (All URLs accessed April 2017.)

AP Images/Greg Lynch/Journal-News

Though schools should be a safe haven, they are actually the locale for a great deal of violence. Here, on April 5, 2016, James Austin Hancock, a teen charged with attempted murder in a school shooting near Cincinnati, sits next to his attorney for a pretrial hearing. Hancock claimed the shooting was a response to his home life—his mom wouldn't watch any of his sporting events and his dad was on his case about his grades. He also had a lot of chores and was always grounded (at least seven months out of the year). Hancock will be kept in a juvenile facility until age 21.

SCHOOL MURDERS Sadly, violence in schools has become commonplace. There have been a number of mass killings, such as the 1999 shootings at Columbine High School in Colorado that resulted in the deaths of 15 people, and the Newtown, Connecticut, massacre in 2012 in which Adam Lanza killed 20 children and 6 staff members. On average, about 25 students are killed each year at school, on the way to or returning from regular sessions at school, or while attending or traveling to or from an official school-sponsored event.[156] School massacres tend to be committed by white males, but the presence of female perpetrators is not unknown, especially when the attack is not carried out with a firearm but with a knife or some other instrument.[157] Most shooting incidents occur around the start of the school day, the lunch period, or the end of the school day.[158] In most of the shootings (55 percent), a note, threat, or other action indicating risk for violence occurred before the event. Shooters were also likely to have expressed some form of suicidal behavior and to have been bullied by their peers.[159]

Serial Killers, Mass Murderers, and Spree Killers

For years, citizens of Wichita, Kansas, lived in fear of the serial killer self-described as BTK (for Bind, Torture, Kill). During his murder spree, BTK sent taunting letters and packages to the police and the media. Suddenly, after committing gruesome killings in the 1970s, he went underground and disappeared from view. Then, after 25 years of silence, he renewed contact with a local news station. His last communication contained a computer disk, which was analyzed by the FBI and traced to 59-year-old Dennis Rader, who later confessed to 10 murders, in an effort to escape the death penalty.

serial killer
A person who kills three or more persons in three or more separate events.

SERIAL KILLERS Criminologists consider a **serial killer**, such as Rader, to be a person who kills three or more persons in three or more separate events. In between the murders, a serial killer reverts to his or her normal lifestyle. Serial killers come from all walks of life, though the majority are white males.[160] Approximately 17 percent of all serial homicides in the United States are committed by women and 20 percent by African Americans.[161]

Most serial killers are solo males, though there are also solo female and partnered offenders.[162] Female serial killers are typically white, educated, have been married, and held a caregiving role (such as mother or health care worker); about 40 percent have some form of mental illness. Why do they kill? Usually for financial gain: they tend to poison a family member or friend in order to collect an inheritance or insurance policy. They target people who have little chance of fighting back: children, elders, or the infirm.[163]

TYPES OF SERIAL KILLERS Some experts have attempted to classify serial killers on the basis of their motivations and offense patterns.[164] According to James A. Fox and Jack Levin, there are at least three different types of serial killers:[165]

- "Thrill killers" strive for either sexual sadism or dominance. They enjoy the thrill, the sexual gratification, and the dominance they achieve over the lives of their victims. Serial killers rarely use a gun because this method is too quick and would deprive them of their greatest pleasure—exulting in the victim's suffering. Extending the time it takes the victim to die increases the pleasure they experience from killing and prolongs their ability to ignore or enjoy their victims' suffering. They typically have a propensity for basking in the media limelight when apprehended for their crimes. Killing provides a way for them to feed their emotional hunger and reduce their anxiety levels.[166]

- "Mission killers" want to reform the world or have a vision that drives them to kill. Dr. Harold Frederick Shipman, Britain's most notorious serial killer, was convicted of 15 murders, though he may have killed more than 200 patients, most of them elderly, claiming his actions were motivated by compassion rather than psychosis.[167]
- "Expedience killers" are out for profit or want to protect themselves from a perceived threat.

There has been a great deal of public interest in serial killing, and a great many myths have developed about their activities and motivations. These are explored in Exhibit 10.2.

Exhibit 10.2 Myths and Realities of Serial Killers

Myth #1: All Serial Killers Are Men.

Reality: This is simply not true, but it is understandable why the public would hold this erroneous belief. As late as 1998, a highly regarded former FBI profiler said, "There are no female serial killers." The news and entertainment media also perpetuate the stereotypes that all serial offenders are male and that women do not engage in horrible acts of violence. In fact, approximately 17 percent of all serial homicides in the United States are committed by women; in contrast, only 10 percent of total murders in the US are committed by women. Therefore, relative to men, women represent a larger percentage of serial murders than all other homicide cases in the United States.

Myth #2: All Serial Killers Are Caucasian.

Reality: Contrary to popular mythology, not all serial killers are white. Serial killers span all racial and ethnic groups in the United States. The racial diversity of serial killers generally mirrors that of the overall US population. There are well-documented cases of African American, Latino, and Asian American serial killers. African Americans comprise the largest racial minority group among serial killers, representing approximately 20 percent of the total. Significantly, however, only white (and normally, male) serial killers such as Ted Bundy become popular culture icons.

Myth #3: All Serial Killers Are Isolated and Dysfunctional Loners.

Reality: Real-life serial killers are not the isolated monsters of fiction. The majority of serial killers are not reclusive, social misfits who live alone. Frequently, they do not appear to be strange or stand out from the public in any meaningful way. Many serial killers are able to hide out in plain sight for extended periods of time. Those who successfully blend in are typically employed, have families and homes, and outwardly appear to be nonthreatening, normal members of society. In fact, many are highly functioning and appear to be completely normal.

Myth #4: All Serial Murderers Travel Widely and Kill Interstate.

Reality: The roaming, homicidal maniac such as Freddy Krueger in the cult film *A Nightmare on Elm Street* is another stereotype that is rarely found in real life. Serial killers typically have a comfort zone—that is, an area that they are intimately familiar with and where they like to stalk and kill their prey. The comfort zone of a serial killer is often defined by an anchor point such as a place of residence or employment. Crime statistics reveal that serial killers are most likely to commit their first murder very close to their place of residence due to the comfort and familiarity it offers them.

Myth #5: All Serial Killers Are Either Mentally Ill or Evil Geniuses.

Reality: The images presented in the news and entertainment media suggest that serial killers either have a debilitating mental illness such as psychosis or they are brilliant but demented geniuses like Dr. Hannibal Lecter. Neither of these two stereotypes is quite accurate. In fact, very few serial killers suffer from any mental illness. Serial killers such as John Wayne Gacy and Dennis Rader may be psychopaths, but they were entirely aware of the illegality of murder while in the process of killing their victims. Their understanding of right and wrong does nothing to impede their crimes, however, because psychopaths have an overwhelming

(Continued)

Exhibit 10.2 Myth and Realities of Serial Killers (*Continued*)

desire and compulsion to kill that causes them to ignore the criminal law with impunity.

There is a popular culture stereotype that serial killers are cunning, criminal geniuses. The reality is that most serial killers who have had their IQ tested score between borderline and above average intelligence. This is very consistent with the general population. Contrary to mythology, it is not high intelligence that makes serial killers successful. Instead, it is obsession, meticulous planning, and a cold-blooded, often psychopathic personality that enables serial killers to operate over long periods of time without detection.

Myth #6: All Serial Killers Must Keep On Killing.

Reality: Another common myth is that once serial killers start killing, they cannot stop. Although this claim may seem reasonable, it is inaccurate. There are serial killers who stop murdering altogether before ever being caught.

Myth #7: All Serial Killers Want to Get Caught.

Reality: It is popularly believed that serial killers secretly want to get caught. For the vast majority of

them, however, this is simply not true. They love the act of killing. Serial killers take satisfaction in their success, particularly at the beginning of their killing careers. The skills and confidence gained through their experience make serial killers very difficult to apprehend. As they continue to operate and avoid capture, serial killers become increasingly emboldened and empowered.

Myth #8: All Serial Killer Victims Are Female.

Reality: According to the stereotypical imagery presented in Hollywood films and best-selling novels, male serial killers prey exclusively on female victims. This is not true. Just as not all serial killers are male, not all serial-killer victims are female, although females do represent the majority of victims. The presence of a sexual motive often leads a male serial killer to prey on women, but in reality about 30 percent of victims are men.

Source: Scott Bonn, *Why We Love Serial Killers: The Curious Appeal of the World's Most Savage Murderers* (New York: Skyhorse Press, 2014).

---

mass murder
The killing of four or more victims by one or a few assailants within a single event.

MASS MURDERERS In contrast to serial killings, **mass murder**, such as the mass shooting by James Holmes, who killed 12 people at a movie theater in Aurora, Colorado, on July 20, 2012, involves the killing of four or more victims by one or a few assailants within a single event; Exhibit 10.3 sets out other notable mass killing incidents.[168] The murderous incident can last but a few minutes or as long as several hours. In order to qualify as a mass murder, the incident must be carried out by one or a few offenders. Highly organized or institutionalized killings (such as war crimes and large-scale acts of political terrorism, as well as certain acts of organized crime rings), though atrocious, are not considered mass murder and are motivated by a totally different set of factors.

Fox and Levin define four types of mass murderers:

- "Revenge killers" want to get even with individuals or society at large. Their typical target is an estranged wife and "her" children or an employer and "his" employees.
- "Love killers" are motivated by a warped sense of devotion. They are often despondent people who commit suicide and take others, such as a wife and children, with them.
- "Profit killers" are usually trying to cover up a crime, eliminate witnesses, and carry out a criminal conspiracy.
- "Terrorist killers" are trying to send a message. Gang killings tell rivals to watch out; cult killers may actually leave a message behind to warn society about impending doom.

A survey by the FBI of mass shooting incidents that occurred between 2000 and 2013 found an average of 11 active shooting incidents occurred annually, including six incidents in the first seven years studied, and an average of 16 occurred in the last

Exhibit 10.3 Mass Killings

- On December 14, 2012, Adam Lanza walked into the Sandy Hook Elementary School in Newtown, Connecticut, and, methodically took the lives of 20 children and 6 adults. Before he went on his murderous rampage, he shot his own mother in the home they shared.
- On April 20, 1999, at Columbine High School in Littleton, Colorado, two heavily armed students, Eric Harris, 18, and Dylan Klebold, 17, went on a shooting spree that claimed the lives of 12 students and 1 teacher and wounded 24 others, many seriously. When police entered the school, the two boys committed suicide.
- On April 16, 2007, 23-year-old Seung-Hui Cho methodically took the lives of 32 people—27 students and 5 professors—at Virginia Tech before taking his own life. In the aftermath of the tragedy, Cho was described as a loner unable to make social connections. He had been involuntarily institutionalized in a mental health facility.
- On February 14, 2008, Steven Kazmierczak, a former student at Northern Illinois University, entered a large auditorium-style lecture hall with a shotgun and three handguns. Standing on the stage, he began shooting into the crowded classroom, killing 5 and wounding 16 others before taking his own life.
- On January 8, 2011, Jared Lee Loughner opened fire in a supermarket parking lot in Tucson, Arizona, in an attempt to kill Congresswoman Gabrielle Giffords. Before the shooting stopped, 19 people were hit, 6 of them fatally.
- On July 20, 2012, James Holmes walked into the Century movie theater in Aurora, Colorado, set off tear gas grenades, and shot into the audience; when he was done, 12 people were dead and 58 more wounded. Holmes had a history of mental illness.
- Aaron Alexis, 34, a contractor for a private information technology firm, used a shotgun and a Beretta handgun to kill 12 victims and wound 4 others before he was shot and killed by law enforcement officers at the Washington Navy Yard.
- In 2014, Elliot Rodger, 22, killed six people and injured fourteen others near the campus of University of California, Santa Barbara, before killing himself inside his vehicle.

Sources: David M. Halbfinger, "A Gunman, Recalled as Intelligent and Shy, Who Left Few Footprints in Life," *New York Times*, December 14, 2012, http://www.nytimes.com/2012/12/15/nyregion/adam-lanza-an-enigma-who-is-now-identified-as-a-mass-killer.html; Abbie Boudreau and Scott Zamost, "Girlfriend: Shooter Was Taking Cocktail of 3 Drugs," CNN, February 20, 2008, http://www.cnn.com/2008/CRIME/02/20/shooter.girlfriend/; BBC, "Profile: Aurora Cinema Shooting Suspect James Holmes," July 21, 2012, http://www.bbc.co.uk/news/world-us-canada-18937513. (All URLs accessed April 2017.)

seven years. As the data show, active shooting incidents have now become routine. About 70 percent of the incidents occurred in either a commerce/business or educational environment. Shootings occurred in 40 of 50 states and the District of Columbia. In all, active shooting incidents produced 1,043 casualties, including 486 victims killed and 557 wounded. All but two incidents involved a single shooter. In at least nine incidents, the shooter first shot and killed a family member(s) in a residence before moving to a more public location to continue shooting. In 64 incidents (40 percent), the shooters committed suicide; 54 shooters did so at the scene of the crime.[169] Adam Lankford compared mass murderers who took their own life with those who survived their attack. His research is set out in the Policies and Issues in Criminology feature, "Mass Shooters: Why Do Some Live and Why Do Some Die."

SPREE KILLERS Unlike mass murders, spree killing is not confined to a single outburst, and unlike serial killers, spree killers do not return to their normal identities in between killings. **Spree killers** engage in a rampage of violence over a period of days or weeks. The most notorious spree killing to date occurred in October 2002 in the Washington, DC, area.[170] John Lee Malvo, 17, a Jamaican citizen, and his traveling companion John Allen Muhammad, 41, an army veteran with an expert's rating in marksmanship, went on a rampage that left at least 10 people dead.

Some spree killers target a specific group or class. Joseph Paul Franklin targeted mixed-race couples (African Americans and Jews), committing more than 20 murders

spree killers
Individuals who kill multiple victims over a relatively short span of time and often follow no discernible pattern.

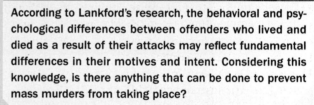

Policies and Issues in Criminology

MASS SHOOTERS: WHY DO SOME LIVE AND WHY DO SOME DIE?

Very few (4 percent) murderers and even fewer (3 percent) terrorists commit suicide after their attacks. In contrast, about 10 times as many (38 percent) mass shooters commit suicide by their own hand, while others commit "suicide by cop" (accomplished by pointing a weapon and threatening police until they are shot and killed). In all, 48 percent of mass shooters died as a result of their attacks—a consequence that suggests that mass shooters are quite different than other perpetrators of murder or terrorism. What makes the mass killer more suicidal?

To find out, Adam Lankford studied mass shooters whose attacks occurred between 1966 and 2010. He found that there are significant differences between mass shooters who died as a result of their attacks and those who remained alive. Those who died had unique behavior patterns: they armed themselves with more weapons, killed more victims, and often struck at different locations (i.e., public places, open commercial establishments) than those who survived their attacks.

What psychological factors distinguished these suicidal killers? Suicidal killers tend to engage in profound self-loathing, feeling guilty and ashamed about their perceived inadequacies and weaknesses, including their uncontrolled anger and violent tendencies. Those who commit suicide are not only consumed by hopelessness and guilt but also by a vengeful desire to punish themselves. Feeling rage and a consuming desire to punish others—resulting in the death of more victims—their self-loathing results in a desire to punish themselves,

and what better way is there to inflict pain than taking their own lives by one means or another?

Lankford found that mass killers' murderous outbursts may be propelled by powerful perceptions of personal victimization, social injustice, and general hopelessness. They may be acting in response to perceived failures in social control; they feel like they can no longer count on the system to protect them, so they take matters into their own hands. Mass murder is their violent exercise of direct control—an attempt to right past wrongs. Mass shooters who attack random victims at open commercial sites may feel hopeless about their ability to have a healthy future anywhere in society.

There are also those mass shooters who target specific individuals at the factories, offices, and warehouses where they work. Because working men have embraced a masculine ideal, they may prefer to go out in a blaze of glory, killing themselves or shooting it out with cops, rather than showing they are weak or effeminate by surrendering to law enforcement.

Critical Thinking

According to Lankford's research, the behavioral and psychological differences between offenders who lived and died as a result of their attacks may reflect fundamental differences in their motives and intent. Considering this knowledge, is there anything that can be done to prevent mass murders from taking place?

Source: Adam Lankford, "Mass Shooters in the USA, 1966–2010: Differences Between Attackers Who Live and Die," *Justice Quarterly* 32 (2015): 360–379.

in 12 states in an effort to instigate a race war. (Franklin also shot and paralyzed *Hustler* publisher Larry Flynt because he published pictures of interracial sex.)[171] Others, such as the DC snipers Malvo and Muhammad, kill randomly and do not seek a specific class of victim; their targets included the young and old, African Americans and whites, men and women.[172]

Though serial sexual murderers typically take some time to plan their next killing, there is a subset who engage in homicides in rapid-sequence fashion, with fewer than 14 days between all or some of the murders. These killers seem to be more likely to act impulsively, taking much less time to plan, and as a result may leave careless evidence at the crime scene, which makes their apprehension more likely. Research studies show that spree sexual killers have various types of personality disorders, many with antisocial traits, but not significant mental illness that would prevent them from planning crimes.[173]

Assault and Battery

Although many people mistakenly believe that the phrase "assault and battery" refers to a single act, they are actually two separate crimes. **Battery** requires offensive touching, such as slapping, hitting, or punching a victim. **Assault** requires no actual touching but involves either attempted battery or intentionally frightening the victim by word or deed. Although common law originally intended these two crimes to be misdemeanors, most jurisdictions now upgrade them to felonies either when a weapon is used or when they occur during the commission of a felony (a person is assaulted during a robbery).

Under common law, battery required bodily injury, such as broken limbs or wounds. However, under modern law, an assault and battery occurs if the victim suffers a temporarily painful blow, even if no injury results. Battery can also involve offensive touching, such as a man kissing a woman against her will or putting his hands on her body. In some legal jurisdictions, biting someone when one is infected with AIDS is considered an aggravated assault; some people with AIDS have been convicted of aggravated assault for spitting on their victims.[174]

Spree killers retain their own identity while they go on a murderous rampage over time. Here, Iztcoatl Ocampo appears at his arraignment in Santa Ana, California. Ocampo, an ex-Marine who stabbed six people to death in California, told investigators he targeted homeless people in part because they were vulnerable, and that he believes he has a "killer gene." Ocampo seemed to relish the media attention of the crime, and he stalked each victim until he got his prey.

Nature and Extent of Assault

The pattern of criminal assault is quite similar to that of homicide and rape; one could say that the only difference is that the victim survives.[175] Assaults may be common in our society simply because of common life stresses. Motorists who assault each other have become such a familiar phenomenon that the term **road rage** has been coined. There have even been frequent incidents of violent assault among frustrated airline passengers who lose control while traveling.[176]

About 765,000 assaults are now being reported to police agencies annually—about 237 per 100,000 inhabitants. Just as for other violent crimes, the number of assaults has been in decline, down more than one-third from its peak in 1993, when 1.1 million assaults were reported to the police. People arrested for assault and those identified by victims are usually young, male (about 75 percent), and white (65 percent). Assault victims tend to be male, but females also face a significant danger. Assault rates are highest in urban areas, during summer, and in southern and western regions. The weapons most commonly used in assaults are blunt instruments and hands and feet.

The NCVS indicates that about 4 million assaults take place each year; about 800,000 are considered aggravated, and 3 million are simple or weaponless assaults.

Acquaintance and Family Assaults

Violent attacks in the home are one of the most frightening types of assault. Criminologists recognize that assault among friends and intimates and within the family has become an enduring social problem in the United States and abroad. What forms do these attacks take?

CHILD ABUSE One area of intrafamily violence that has received a great deal of media attention is **child abuse**. This term describes any physical or emotional trauma

battery
Offensive touching, such as slapping, hitting, or punching a victim.

assault
Either attempted battery or intentionally frightening the victim by word or deed (actual touching is not required).

road rage
Violent assault by a motorist who loses control of his or her emotions while driving.

child abuse
Any physical or emotional trauma to a child for which no reasonable explanation, such as an accident or ordinary disciplinary practices, can be found.

AP Images/Rick Cinclair/Worcester Telegram & Gazette

Child abuse is one of the most serious forms of family assault. Here, Randall Lints is brought into court in East Brookfield, Massachusetts, for a hearing and bail review on August 19, 2015. Lints was accused of beating and starving his 7-year-old son, Jack, who weighed 38 pounds and was taken to a hospital in a coma.

neglect
Not providing a child with the care and shelter to which he or she is entitled.

child sexual abuse
The exploitation of children through rape, incest, and molestation by parents or other adults.

inflicted on a child for which no reasonable explanation, such as an accident or ordinary disciplinary practice, can be found.[177] Child abuse can result from physical beatings administered to a child by hands, feet, weapons, belts, sticks, burning, and so on. Another form of abuse results from **neglect**—not providing a child with the care and shelter to which he or she is entitled.

Estimating the actual number of child abuse cases is difficult, because many incidents are never reported to the police. The most recent Department of Health and Human Services (DHHS) survey found that US state and local child protective services (CPS) received an estimated 3.4 million referrals of children being abused or neglected each year.[178] Of these, CPS estimate that 678,000 children (9 per 1,000) were actual and confirmed victims of maltreatment. The CPS data indicate that about 60,000 children are the victims of sexual abuse each year. However, these reported cases may vastly undercount the true nature of the problem.

The most serious cases of abuse result in death, and the last available data indicate that about 1,600 children die from child maltreatment each year (rate of 2.2 per 100,000). If anything, the CPS data underestimate the true occurrence of abuse because so many cases go unreported and many victims are too young to seek help. Although child abuse is still a serious social problem, child maltreatment rates are lower today than they were a decade ago. It is difficult to pinpoint the reason for the reduction in reported abuse, but it may be the result of better treatment strategies, lower substance abuse rates, reduced reliance on physical punishment, and the availability of abortion (which reduces the number of unwanted children).

Child sexual abuse is the exploitation of children through rape, incest, and molestation by parents or other adults. The CPS data indicate that about 65,000 children are the victims of sexual abuse each year. Many of these are subjected to some form of sexual exploitation, which often begins with sexual assaults by relatives and acquaintances, such as a teacher, a coach, or a neighbor. Sexual abuse is of particular concern because children who have been abused experience a long list of symptoms, including fear, posttraumatic stress disorder, behavior problems, sexualized behavior, and poor self-esteem.[179] As they mature, abused girls are more likely than other girls to drop out of high school, become teen parents, experience image problems, and experience psychiatric problems, substance dependence, and domestic violence.[180] Women who were abused as children are also at greater risk of being abused as adults than those who escaped childhood victimization.[181]

CAUSES OF CHILD ABUSE Why do parents physically assault their children? Such maltreatment is a highly complex problem with neither a single cause nor a readily available solution. It cuts across ethnic, religious, and socioeconomic lines. Abusive parents cannot be categorized by sex, age, or educational level, and they come from all walks of life.[182]

A number of factors have been commonly linked to child abuse and neglect:

- Abusive parents may themselves have been abused, creating an intergenerational cycle of violence.
- Blended families, which include children living with an unrelated adult such as a stepparent or with another unrelated co-resident, have a higher incidence of abuse.[183]
- Parents may become abusive if they are isolated from friends, neighbors, or relatives who can help in times of crisis.[184]
- Abusive parents may be suffering from depression and other forms of psychological distress.[185]

Regardless of its cause, child abuse can have devastating long-term effects, ranging from depression to loss of self-esteem.[186] Not surprisingly, a history of childhood sexual and physical abuse is observed at a disproportionately high rate among persons with severe mental illness.[187]

PARENTAL ABUSE Parents are sometimes the target of abuse from their own children. The following facts emerge from studies of child-to-parent violence (CPV):

- The younger the child, the higher the rate of CPV.
- At all ages, more children were violent to mothers than to fathers.
- Both boys and girls hit mothers more than they hit fathers.
- At all ages, slightly more boys than girls hit parents.
- Child-to-parent violence is associated with some form of earlier violence by parents: husband-to-wife, wife-to-husband, or child abuse.[188]

SPOUSAL ABUSE Spousal abuse has occurred throughout recorded history. By the mid-nineteenth century, severe wife beating fell into disfavor, and accused wife beaters were subject to public ridicule. Nonetheless, limited chastisement of wives was still the rule. These ideas form the foundation of men's traditional physical control of women and have led to severe cases of spousal assault. Spousal abuse is still a significant problem. In their classic study of family violence, Richard Gelles and Murray Straus found that 16 percent of surveyed families had experienced husband-to-wife assaults.[189] The consequences of abuse can be significant, ranging from physical injury to psychological trauma or exposure to sexually transmitted disease.[190] Moreover, physical abuse is commonly accompanied by mental abuse and coercion that can have long-term damaging psychological effects.[191]

Dating Violence

Date rape is not the only form of violence aimed at a boyfriend or girlfriend.[192] A significant portion of all teens have been the target of dating violence, and it is estimated that one high school girl in five may suffer sexual or physical abuse from a boyfriend. Dating violence has been linked to substance abuse, unsafe sex, and eating disorders.[193]

Physical dating violence can involve a wide spectrum of activities ranging from moderate to severe: scratching, slapping, pushing, slamming or holding someone against a wall, biting, choking, burning, beating someone up, and assault with a weapon. There is also emotional and psychological abuse that includes insulting, criticizing, threatening, humiliating, or berating. An emerging form of emotional abuse is referred to as **relational aggression** in which a partner tries to damage a person's relationship with friends by spreading smears and false rumors or by revealing information or images intended to be private.

Robbery

The common-law definition of **robbery** (and the one used by the FBI) is "the taking or attempting to take anything of value from the care, custody, or control of a person or persons by force or threat of force or violence and/or by putting the victim in fear."[194] A robbery is considered a violent crime because it involves the use of force to obtain money or goods. Robbery is punished severely because the victim's life is put in jeopardy. In fact, the severity of punishment is based on the amount of force used during the crime, not on the value of the items taken.

The FBI records about 327,000 robberies a year, a rate of about 102 per 100,000 population. As with most other violent crimes, there has been a significant reduction in the robbery rate during the past decade; the robbery rate is down more than 40 percent since 1991, when about 687,000 robberies were committed. According

relational aggression
Psychological and emotional abuse that involves the spreading of smears, rumors, and private information in order to harm a partner.

robbery
Taking or attempting to take anything of value from the care, custody, or control of a person or persons by force or threat of force or violence and/or by putting the victim in fear.

L05 Explain the nature and patterns of robbery.

to the NCVS, about 578,000 robberies are committed or attempted each year, a discrepancy that illustrates that many of the most serious crimes go unreported to police agencies.

The ecological pattern for robbery is similar to that of other violent crimes, with one significant exception: northeastern states have the highest robbery rates by far. Whereas most crime rates are higher in the summer, robberies seem to peak during the winter months. One reason may be that the cold weather allows for greater disguise; another reason is that robbers may be attracted to the large amounts of cash people and merchants carry during the Christmas shopping season.[195] Robbers may also be more active in winter because days are shorter, affording them greater concealment in the dark.

Robbers in Action

Even though most robbers may be opportunistic rather than professional, robberies still demonstrate rationality and planning. Marcus Felson describes robbers as foragers, predators who search for victims, preferably close to their homes, where numerous "nutritious" victims are abundant, where the robbers know the territory so that their prey cannot easily escape, and where their victims may be less vigilant because they are on their home turf.[196] Robbers, then, select targets that are *vulnerable, accessible,* and *profitable.* Their choice of victim dictates whether violence is used. If a victim looks tough—"street credible"—the robber may choose to use violence at the outset rather than wait for the victim to resist. During the robbery itself, victims who fight back are the ones most likely to be attacked and injured. Victim passivity may work best during a robbery.[197]

Choosing Targets

In their important book *Armed Robbers in Action: Stickups and Street Culture,* Richard Wright and Scott Decker interviewed active robbers in St. Louis, Missouri, and found that robbers are rational decision makers who look for easy prey. One ideal target is the married man who is looking for illicit sexual adventures and hires a prostitute, only to be robbed by her and her pimp. The robbers know that this victim will not be inclined to call the police and bring himself to their attention.

Because they realize that the risk of detection and punishment is the same whether the victim is carrying a load of cash or is penniless, experienced robbers use discretion in selecting targets. People whose clothing, jewelry, and demeanor mark them as carrying substantial amounts of cash make suitable targets; people who look like they can fight back are avoided. Some robbers station themselves at cash machines to spot targets who are flashing stacks of money.[198]

Wright and Decker are not the only researchers who found that most robbers seek out vulnerable victims. According to research by criminologist Jody Miller, female armed robbers are likely to choose female targets, reasoning that they will be more vulnerable and offer less resistance.[199] When robbing males, women "set them up" to catch them off guard; some feign sexual interest or prostitution to gain the upper hand.[200]

AP Images/Jordan Strauss/Invision

Even the rich and famous can be the victims of robbery. Kim Kardashian was robbed at gunpoint in the Paris apartment where she was staying and lost more than $10 million worth of jewelry. Six people were eventually arrested, several of whom confessed to being involved in the heist.

Wright and Decker found that most armed robberies are motivated by a pressing need for cash. Many robbers career from one financial crisis to the next, prompted by their endless quest for stimulation and thrills. Interviewees described how they partied, gambled, drank, and abused substances until they were broke. Their partying not only provided excitement but also helped generate a street reputation as someone who can "make things happen." Robbers had a "here and now" mentality and required a constant supply of cash to fuel their appetites.

TARGETING CRIMINALS Some robbers target fellow criminals—for example, drug dealers—because they are inviting targets.[201] Although these targets may be dangerous, robbers recognize that people with "dirty hands" are unlikely to call police and get entangled with the law. When Bruce Jacobs interviewed armed robbers, he found that some specialize in targeting drug dealers because they believe that even though their work is hazardous, the rewards outweigh the risks. Drug dealers are plentiful, visible, and accessible, and they carry plenty of cash. Their merchandise is valuable, is easily transported, and can be used by the robber or sold to another. Drug dealers are not particularly popular, so they cannot rely on bystanders to come to their aid. Nor can they call the police and ask them to recover their stolen goods! Of course, drug dealers may be able to "take care of business" themselves, but surprisingly Jacobs found that many choose not to carry a pistol.[202] Drug dealers may be tough and bad, the robbers claim, but *they* are tougher and badder.

ACQUAINTANCE ROBBERY Some robbers target people they know, a phenomenon referred to as **acquaintance robbery**. This seems puzzling, because victims can easily identify their attackers and report them to the police. However, despite this threat, acquaintance robbery may be attractive for a number of reasons:[203]

- Victims may be reluctant to report these crimes because they do not want to get involved with the police.
- Some robberies are motivated by street justice. The robber has a grievance against the victim and settles the dispute by stealing the victim's property. In this instance, robbery may be considered a substitute for an assault—that is, the robber wants retribution and revenge rather than remuneration.[204]
- Because the robber knows the victim personally, the robber has inside information that there will be a "good take." Offenders may target people whom they know to be carrying a large amount of cash or who just purchased expensive jewelry.
- When a person in desperate need for immediate cash runs out of money, the individual may target people in close proximity simply because they are convenient targets.[205] Similarly, robberies of family members were more likely to have a bigger pay-off than stranger robberies, an indication that the offender was aware that the target had a large amount of cash on hand.

CARJACKING We can see this element of rationality and planning in the strategies of one type of robber: carjackers, who attack occupied vehicles for the purpose of theft. Carjacking is not a random event committed by amateurs but is carefully planned and carried out by experienced criminals. To be successful, carjackers must develop both perceptual skills (choosing the vehicle) and procedural skills (commandeering the vehicle).[206] Carjackers must learn when their efforts are having the desired effect: scaring the victim. Developing these perceptual skills lets carjackers know exactly how effective their efforts are and helps them instantly adjust the application of those skills. They must constantly process information and make split-second decisions to react properly to a rapidly changing environment—not a task for amateurs.[207]

---

acquaintance robbery
Robbery in which the victim or victims are people the robber knows.

CHECKPOINTS

▸ Forcible rape has been known throughout history and is often linked with war and violence.

▸ Types of rape include date rape, marital rape, and statutory rape; types of rapists include serial rapists and sadists.

▸ Suspected causes of rape include male socialization, hypermasculinity, and biological determinism.

▸ Murder can involve either strangers or acquaintances. Typically, stranger murder occurs during a felony; acquaintance murder involves an interaction or interpersonal transaction between people who may be related romantically, through business dealings, or in other ways.

▸ Mass murder is the killing of numerous victims in a single outburst; serial killing involves numerous victims over an extended period of time. Spree killers attack multiple victims over a short period of time.

▸ Patterns of assault are quite similar to those for homicide.

▸ Numerous cases of child abuse and spousal abuse occur each year. There are also numerous cases of parental abuse.

▸ Robbers use force to steal. Some are opportunists looking for ready cash; others are professionals who have a long-term commitment to crime. Both types pick their targets carefully, which suggests that their crimes are calculated rather than spontaneous.

Contemporary Forms of Interpersonal Violence

LO6 Discuss newly emerging forms of violence, such as stalking, hate crimes, and workplace violence.

Assault, rape, robbery, and murder are traditional forms of interpersonal violence. As more data have become available, criminologists have recognized relatively new subcategories of these types of crimes, such as serial murder and date rape. Additional new categories of interpersonal violence are also receiving attention in criminological literature; the next sections describe three of these forms of violent crime.

Hate Crimes

hate crimes (bias crimes)
Violent acts directed toward a particular person or members of a group merely because the targets share a discernible racial, ethnic, religious, or gender characteristic.

Hate crimes (bias crimes) are violent acts directed toward a particular person or members of a group merely because the targets share a discernible racial, ethnic, religious, or gender characteristic. Such crimes range from desecration of a house of worship or cemetery to racially motivated murder.

Though normally associated with racially motivated attacks, hate crimes can involve convenient, vulnerable targets who are incapable of fighting back. There have been numerous reported incidents of teenagers attacking vagrants and the homeless in an effort to rid their town or neighborhood of people they consider undesirable.[208]

Another group targeted for hate crimes are members of the LGBTQ community. The murder of Matthew Shepard, a gay college student who was kidnapped and beaten to death in Wyoming in 1998, was a grim reminder that gay bashing is all too common in America.[209] A national survey of gay, lesbian, and bisexual adults, conducted by psychologist Gregory Herek, found that approximately 20 percent of the sample reported having experienced a crime based on their sexual orientation; gay men were significantly more likely than lesbians or bisexuals to experience violence and property crimes.[210]

ROOTS OF HATE Why do people commit bias crimes? What motivates someone like Dylann Roof to kill? In a series of research studies, Jack McDevitt, Jack Levin, and Susan Bennett identify four motivations for hate crimes:[211]

- *Thrill-seeking hate crimes.* In the same way some kids like to get together to shoot hoops, hatemongers join forces to have fun by bashing minorities or destroying property. Inflicting pain on others gives them a sadistic thrill.
- *Reactive (defensive) hate crimes.* Perpetrators of these crimes rationalize their behavior as a defensive stand taken against outsiders whom they believe threaten their community or way of life. A gang of teens that attacks a new family in the neighborhood because they are the "wrong" race is committing a reactive hate crime.

Hate crimes are most often based on race, religion, or sexual orientation. Here, Jonathan Whyte and his wife, Sol, holding a friend's child, talk about finding a cross and the letters "KKK" burned into their lawn in Medford, Oregon. Chief US District Judge Ann Aiken sentenced two Medford men, Gary Moss, 37, and Devan Klausegger, 30, to federal prison for the burning incidents. The two, both white, pleaded guilty to conspiracy to deprive individuals of civil rights related to fair housing.

AP Images/Bob Pennell

- *Mission hate crimes.* Some disturbed individuals see it as their duty to rid the world of evil. Those "on a mission," such as skinheads, the Ku Klux Klan (KKK), and white supremacist groups, may seek to eliminate people who threaten their religious beliefs because they are members of a different faith or threaten "racial purity" because they are of a different race.
- *Retaliatory hate crimes.* These offenses are committed in response to a hate crime either real or perceived; whether the original incident actually occurred is irrelevant. Sometimes a rumor of an incident may cause a group of offenders to exact vengeance, even if the original information was unfounded or inaccurate; the retaliatory crimes are perpetrated before anyone has had a chance to verify the accuracy of the original rumor. Attacks based on revenge tend to have the greatest potential for fueling and refueling additional hate offenses.

The research by McDevitt and his colleagues indicates that most hate crimes can be classified as thrill-motivated (66 percent), followed by defensive (25 percent) and retaliatory hate crimes (8 percent); few if any cases had mission-oriented offenders.

NATURE AND EXTENT OF HATE CRIMES At last count, law enforcement agencies receive reports of about 6,000 hate crimes each year from about 7,000 victims (some crimes involved more than a single victim).[212] However, according to the NCVS, the official reports significantly undercount the actual incidence of hate crimes. Victims report almost 300,000 violent and property hate crimes in a single year. About half of hate crimes were motivated by ethnicity bias (the victim's ancestral, cultural, social, or national affiliation), up from 22 percent in 2004. The percentage of hate crimes motivated by religious bias nearly tripled from 10 percent in 2004 to 28 percent today, and the percentage of hate crimes motivated by gender bias more than doubled, from 12 percent to 26 percent during the same period. About 27 percent of hate crimes reported by victims could be classified as serious violent crimes—rape or sexual assault, robbery, and aggravated assault.[213]

Most such incidents are motivated by race; a lesser proportion by religion (most often anti-Semitism), sexual orientation, or ethnicity; and about 1 percent by victim disability. Vandalism and property crimes are the products of hate crimes motivated by religion. However, criminals are more likely to turn to violent acts when race, ethnicity, and sexual orientation are the motivation. Most targets of hate crimes, especially the violent variety, are young white men. Similarly, the majority of known hate crime offenders are young white men.

In crimes where victims could identify the culprits, most victims reported that they were acquainted with their attackers or that their attackers were actually friends, coworkers, neighbors, or relatives.[214] Younger victims were more likely to be victimized by persons known to them. Hate crimes can occur in many settings, but most are perpetrated in public settings.

CONTROLLING HATE CRIMES Hate crime laws actually originated after the Civil War and were designed to safeguard the rights of freed slaves.[215] Today, almost every state jurisdiction has enacted some form of legislation designed to combat hate crimes: 45 states have enacted laws against bias-motivated violence and intimidation; 27 states have statutes that specifically mandate the collection of hate crime data.[216]

Some critics argue that it is unfair to punish criminals motivated by hate any more severely than those who commit similar crimes and whose motivation is revenge, greed, or anger. There is also the danger that what appears to be a hate crime, because the target is a minority group member, may actually be motivated by some other factor such as vengeance or monetary gain. Aaron McKinney, who is serving a life sentence for killing Matthew Shepard, told ABC News correspondent Elizabeth Vargas that he was high on methamphetamine when he killed Shepard, and that his intent was robbery, not hate. His accomplice, Russell Henderson, also claims that the killing was simply a robbery gone bad: "It was not because me and Aaron had anything against gays."[217]

However, in his important book *Punishing Hate: Bias Crimes Under American Law*, Frederick Lawrence argues that criminals motivated by bias deserve to be punished more severely than those who commit identical crimes for other motives.[218] He suggests that a society dedicated to the equality of all its people must treat bias crimes differently than other crimes for several reasons:[219]

- Bias crimes are more likely to be violent and to involve serious physical injury to the victim.
- Bias crimes will have significant emotional and psychological impact on the victim; they result in a "heightened sense of vulnerability," which causes depression, anxiety, and feelings of helplessness.
- Bias crimes harm not only the victim but also the "target community."
- Bias crimes violate the shared value of equality among citizens and racial and religious harmony in a heterogeneous society.

FREE SPEECH? Should symbolic acts of hate, such as drawing a swastika or burning a cross, be banned, or are they protected by the free speech clause of the First Amendment? The US Supreme Court helped answer this question in the case of *Virginia v. Black* (2003) when it upheld a Virginia statute that makes it a felony "for any person . . . with the intent of intimidating any person or group . . , to burn . . . a cross on the property of another, a highway or other public place," and specifies that "[a]ny such burning . . . shall be prima facie evidence of an intent to intimidate a person or group." In its decision, the Court upheld Virginia's law, which criminalized cross burning. The Court ruled that cross burning was intertwined with the Ku Klux Klan and its reign of terror throughout the South. The Court has long held that statements in which the speaker communicates intent to commit an act of unlawful violence to a particular individual or group of individuals are not protected free speech and can be criminalized; the speaker need not actually intend to carry out the threat.[220]

workplace violence
Violence such as assault, rape, or murder committed at the workplace.

AP Images/Steve Helber

One of the most horrifying incidents of workplace violence occurred on August 26, 2015, when WDBJ-TV news reporter Alison Parker and photojournalist Adam Ward were fatally shot during an on-air interview. Here, investigators look at the body of cameraman Ward. The killer was Vester Lee Flanagan II, who had appeared on WDBJ as Bryce Williams before he was fired from the station. After committing the revenge murders, Flanagan shot himself during a car chase with police officers.

Workplace Violence

Workplace violence is now considered the second leading cause of occupational injury or death.[221] Who engages in workplace violence? The typical offender is a middle-aged white male who faces termination in a worsening economy. The fear of economic ruin is especially strong in agencies such as the US Postal Service, where long-term employees fear job loss because of automation and reorganization. In contrast, when younger workers kill, it is usually while committing a robbery or some other felony. A number of factors precipitate workplace violence. One suspected cause is a management style that appears cold and insensitive to workers. As corporations cut their staffs because of an economic downturn or workers are summarily replaced with cost-effective technology, long-term employees may become irate and irrational; their unexpected layoff can lead to violent reactions.

Not all workplace violence is triggered by management-induced injustice. In some incidents, coworkers have been killed because they refused romantic relationships with the assailants or reported them for sexual harassment. Others have been killed because they got a job the assailant coveted. Irate clients and customers have also killed because of poor service or perceived slights.[222] Hospital patients whose demands are not met may attack people who are there to be caregivers. In fact, health care and social services workers have the highest rate of nonfatal assault injuries. Nurses and nursing assistants are significantly more likely to experience workplace violence than any other professional group.[223]

Stalking

A complex phenomenon, **stalking** can be defined as a course of conduct that is directed at a specific person and involves repeated physical or visual proximity, nonconsensual communication, or verbal, written, or implied threats sufficient to cause fear in a reasonable person.[224] An estimated 3.3 million people are stalked each year.[225]

Stalkers use a number of strategies:

- *Surveillance*. The most common strategy is spying, watching, showing up unexpectedly in places where victims are, and waiting in places where victims are likely to appear.
- *Life invasion*. This strategy includes phone calls, emails, texts, and other uninvited contact, such as leaving gifts. It involves unwanted entry directly or through electronic means into the victim's private life—even though it can occur in public settings. This form of stalking includes property invasion, spreading rumors, and public humiliation. Invasion often expands from a target's home, phone, or computer into other spaces like work, grocery stores, and recreational activities.
- *Intimidation*. This form of stalking includes direct and indirect threats of harm, property damage, forced confrontations (other than attack), and threats to harm friends and family members.
- *Interference through sabotage or attack*. This category includes tactics that have direct consequences to victims, including financial or work sabotage, kidnapping or deliberately keeping the target from leaving or going somewhere, attacking friends and family members, and physical or sexual attack of the target. This dimension also includes tactics that are used to ruin a target's reputation, such as threatening to post (or actually posting) embarrassing pictures and spreading harmful rumors on social media.[226]

Some stalkers may be juveniles who use text messages and emails, along with direct contact, to harass their victims.[227] Women are much more likely to be stalked than men. In nearly 75 percent of stalking cases, victims know their stalker in some way; in about 30 percent of cases, the stalker is a current or former intimate partner. Former partners have leverage over their victim; they can use the information they have about their former partner's friends and family members, where they work, shop, and go for entertainment.[228]

Although stalking usually stops within one or two years, victims experience its social and psychological consequences long afterward. About one-third seek psychological treatment, and about one-fifth lose time from work; indeed, some never return to work at all. Stalking can also be lethal. More than 75 percent of women who were murdered by their current or former intimate partners were stalked by their killers before the murder.[229] The harm from stalking goes beyond the risk of physical injury to the victim and also includes social and financial harm (referred to as life sabotage) and harm to someone close to the target such as family members and new partners. Social relationships, employment, finances, day-to-day routines, and future plans are all compromised by stalkers. Stalking also poses a risk to public safety, as other persons can be collateral victims.

Even though stalking is a serious problem, research indicates that many cases are dropped by the courts despite the fact that stalkers often have extensive criminal histories and are frequently the subject of protective orders. A lenient response may be misplaced, considering that stalkers very often repeat their criminal activity within a short time after a stalking charge is lodged with police authorities.[230]

stalking
A course of conduct that is directed at a specific person and involves repeated physical or visual proximity, nonconsensual communication, or verbal, written, or implied threats sufficient to cause fear in a reasonable person.

CHECKPOINTS

▶ Hate crimes are violent acts against targets selected because of their religion, race, ethnic background, gender, or sexual orientation.

▶ Some hate criminals are thrill seekers; others are motivated by hatred of outsiders; still others believe they are on a mission. More than 6,000 people are the targets of hate crimes each year in the United States.

▶ Workplace violence has become commonplace. It is believed to be related to a number of factors, including job stress and insensitive management style.

▶ About 3.3 million people are victims of stalking each year.

Thinking Like a Criminologist

Enforcing Statutory Rape Laws
The state legislature has asked you to prepare a report on statutory rape because of the growing number of underage girls who have been impregnated by adult men. Studies reveal that many teenage pregnancies result from affairs that underage girls have with older men, with age gaps ranging from 7 to 10 years. For example, the typical relationship prosecuted in California involves a 13-year-old girl and a 22-year-old male partner. Some outraged parents adamantly support a law that will provide state grants to counties to prosecute statutory rape. These grants would allow more vigorous enforcement of the law and could result in the conviction of more than 1,500 offenders each year.

However, some critics suggest that implementing statutory rape laws to punish males who have relationships with minor girls does not solve the problems of teenage pregnancies and out-of-wedlock births. Liberals dislike the idea of using criminal law to solve social problems, because doing so does not provide for the girls and their children and focuses only on punishing offenders. In contrast, conservatives fear that such laws give the state power to prosecute people for victimless crimes, thereby increasing the government's ability to control people's private lives. Not all cases involve much older men, and critics ask whether we should criminalize the behavior of 19-year-old boys and their 15-year-old girlfriends.

Writing Assignment
Write an essay on statutory rape and how different states address sex with minors. Decide whether current laws should be changed to reflect current social behaviors.

SUMMARY

LO1   Differentiate among the various causes of violent crime.
Research has shown that a significant number of people involved in violent episodes may be suffering from severe mental abnormalities. Absent or deviant parents, inconsistent discipline, physical abuse, and lack of supervision have all been linked to persistent violent offending. A number of criminologists have speculated that instinctual violence-promoting traits may be common in the human species. Kids who are constantly exposed to violence at home, at school, or in the environment may adopt violent methods themselves. Substance abuse has been associated with violence on both the individual and social levels. Although firearm availability alone does not cause violence, it may be a facilitating factor. Furthermore, some areas contain an independent subculture of violence in which a potent theme of violence influences lifestyles, the socialization process, and interpersonal relationships. Some nations have cultures that support relatively high violence rates.

LO2   Define rape and be familiar with why men commit rape.
The common-law definition of rape is "the carnal knowledge of a female forcibly and against her will." One explanation for rape focuses on the evolutionary, biological aspects of the male sexual drive. Some researchers argue that rape is a function of socialization. Rapists may suffer from some type of personality disorder or mental illness. Men may learn to commit rapes much as they learn any other behavior. Rape arises primarily from a desire to inflict pain and humiliation, but there is evidence that at least some rapists have sexual feelings for their victim.

LO3   Discuss the issues involving rape and the law.
Proving guilt in a rape case is extremely challenging for prosecutors. It is essential to prove that the attack was forced and that the victim did not give

voluntary consent to her attacker. Shield laws that protect women from being questioned about their sexual history unless it directly bears on the case have become universal.

LO4   Analyze the different types of murder.

First-degree murder occurs when a person kills another after premeditation and deliberation. Second-degree murder is the charge when the killer had malice aforethought but not premeditation or deliberation. Voluntary or nonnegligent manslaughter is a killing committed in the heat of passion or during a sudden quarrel that provoked violence. Involuntary or negligent manslaughter is a killing that occurs when a person's acts are negligent and without regard for the harm they may cause others. Serial killers murder three or more persons in three or more separate events. Mass murder involves the killing of four or more victims by one or a few assailants within a single event. Spree killers engage in a rampage of violence over a period of days or weeks.

LO5   Explain the nature and patterns of robbery.

The common-law definition of robbery is "the taking or attempting to take anything of value from the care, custody, or control of a person or persons by force or threat of force or violence and/or by putting the victim in fear." Some robbers are opportunists looking for ready cash; others are professionals who have a long-term commitment to crime. The typical armed robber is a rational decision maker. Many robbers choose victims who themselves are involved in illegal behavior, most often drug dealers. Female armed robbers are likely to choose female targets, reasoning that women will be more vulnerable and offer less resistance.

LO6   Discuss newly emerging forms of violence, such as stalking, hate crimes, and workplace violence.

Hate crimes, or bias crimes, are violent acts directed toward a particular person or members of a particular group merely because the targets share a discernible racial, ethnic, religious, or gender characteristic. Workplace violence is now considered the second leading cause of occupational injury or death. Stalking can be defined as conduct that is directed at a specific person and involves repeated physical or visual proximity, nonconsensual communication, and/or verbal, written, or implied threats sufficient to cause fear in a reasonable person.

Key Terms

expressive violence 320
instrumental violence 320
cycle of violence 321
eros 321
thanatos 321
psychopharmacological relationship 323
economic compulsive behavior 323
systemic link 323
subculture of violence 324
rape 325
date rape 328

marital exemption 330
statutory rape 330
Romeo and Juliet laws 330
virility mystique 331
narcissistic personality disorder 332
aggravated rape 333
consent 333
shield laws 334
murder 334
first-degree murder 335
premeditation 335
deliberation 335
felony murder 335

second-degree murder 335
manslaughter 335
voluntary or nonnegligent manslaughter 335
involuntary or negligent manslaughter 335
feticide 335
infanticide 336
filicide 336
eldercide 336
serial killer 340
mass murder 342
spree killer 343

battery 345
assault 345
road rage 345
child abuse 345
neglect 346
child sexual abuse 346
relational aggression 347
robbery 347
acquaintance robbery 349
hate crimes (bias crimes) 350
workplace violence 352
stalking 353

Critical Thinking Questions

1. Should the perpetrators of different types of rape receive different legal sanctions? For example, should someone who rapes a stranger be punished more severely than someone who is convicted of marital rape or date rape? If your answer is yes, do you think someone who kills a stranger should be punished more severely than someone who kills a spouse or a friend?

2. Is there a subculture of violence in your home city or town? If so, how would you describe the environment and values of that subculture?

3. There have been significant changes in rape law involving issues such as corroboration and shield laws. What other measures would you take to protect victims of rape when they have to testify in court?

4. Should hate crimes be punished more severely than crimes motivated by greed, anger, or revenge? Why should crimes be distinguished in terms of the motivations of the perpetrator? Is hate a more heinous motivation than revenge?

Notes

All URLs accessed April 2017.

1. Ray Sanchez and Ed Payne, "Charleston Church Shooting: Who Is Dylann Roof?" CNN, June 23, 2015, http://www.cnn.com/2015/06/19/us/charleston-church-shooting-suspect/.

2. Meg Kinnard, "Dylann Roof to Plead Guilty to State Murder Charges, Avoiding Second Death Penalty Trial," *Chicago Tribune*, March 31, 2017, http://www.chicagotribune.com/news/nationworld/ct-dylann-roof-state-charges-20170331-story.html.

3. Emma Cashman and Stuart Thomas, "Does Mental Illness Impact the Incidence of Crime and Victimisation Among Young People?" *Psychiatry, Psychology and Law* 24 (2017): 33–46.

4. Rokeya Farrooque, Ronnie Stout, and Frederick Ernst, "Heterosexual Intimate Partner Homicide: Review of Ten Years of Clinical Experience," *Journal of Forensic Sciences* 50 (2005): 648–651; Miltos Livaditis, Gkaro Esagian, Christos Kakoulidis, Maria Samakouri, and Nikos Tzavaras, "Matricide by Person with Bipolar Disorder and Dependent Overcompliant Personality," *Journal of Forensic Sciences* 50 (2005): 658–661.

5. David P. Farrington, Rolf Loeber, and Mark T. Berg, "Young Men Who Kill: A Prospective Longitudinal Examination from Childhood," *Homicide Studies* 16 (2012): 99–128; Roman Gleyzer, Alan Felthous, and Charles Holzer, "Animal Cruelty and Psychiatric Disorders," *Journal of the American Academy of Psychiatry and the Law* 30 (2002): 257–265.

6. Richard Rogers, Randall Salekin, Kenneth Sewell, and Keith Cruise, "Prototypical Analysis of Antisocial Personality Disorder," *Criminal Justice and Behavior* 27 (2000): 234–255.

7. Christopher Hensley and Suzanne Tallichet, "Childhood and Adolescent Animal Cruelty Methods and Their Possible Link to Adult Violent Crimes," *Journal of Interpersonal Violence* 24 (2009): 147–158.

8. Gleyzer, Felthous, and Holzer, "Animal Cruelty and Psychiatric Disorders."

9. Tatia M. C. Lee, Siu-Ching Chan, and Adrian Raine, "Hyperresponsivity to Threat Stimuli in Domestic Violence Offenders: A Functional Magnetic Resonance Imaging Study," *Journal of Clinical Psychiatry* 70 (2009): 36–45.

10. Michael Baglivio, Kevin Wolff, Nathan Epps, and Randy Nelson, "Predicting Adverse Childhood Experiences: The Importance of Neighborhood Context in Youth Trauma Among Delinquent Youth," *Crime and Delinquency* 63 (2017): 166–188.

11. Murray Straus, "Discipline and Deviance: Physical Punishment of Children and Violence and Other Crime in Adulthood," *Social Problems* 38 (1991): 101–123.

12. Jennifer Lansford, Laura Wager, John Bates, Gregory Pettit, and Kenneth Dodge, "Forms of Spanking and Children's Externalizing Behaviors," *Family Relations* 6 (2012): 224–236.

13. Ronald Simons, Chyi-In Wu, Kuei-Hsiu Lin, Leslie Gordon, and Rand Conger, "A Cross-Cultural Examination of the Link Between Corporal Punishment and Adolescent Antisocial Behavior," *Criminology* 38 (2000): 47–79.

14. Hyunzee Jung, Todd Herrenkohl, Jungeun Lee, Bart Klika, and Martie Skinner, "Effects of Physical and Emotional Child Abuse and Its Chronicity on Crime into Adulthood," *Violence and Victims* 30 (2015): 1004–1018.

15. Cathy Widom, "The Cycle of Violence," *Science* 244 (1989): 160–166; "Understanding Child Maltreatment and Juvenile Delinquency: The Research," Welfare League of America, 2010, http://www.rfknrcjj.org /images/PDFs/Understanding_Child_Maltreatment _and_Juvenile_Delinquency_From_Research_to _Effective_Program_Practice_and_Systemic _Solutions.pdf.

16. Cathy Spatz Widom, "Varieties of Violent Behavior," *Criminology* 52 (2014): 313–344.

17. Emily M. Wright and Abigail A. Fagan, "The Cycle of Violence in Context: Exploring the Moderating Roles of Neighborhood Disadvantage and Cultural Norms," *Criminology* 51 (2013): 217–249.

18. Christopher Boehm, "Retaliatory Violence in Human Prehistory," *British Journal of Criminology* 51 (2011): 518–534.

19. Steven Pinker, *The Better Angels of Our Nature: Why Violence Has Declined* (New York: Viking, 2011).

20. Sigmund Freud, *Beyond the Pleasure Principle* (London: Inter-Psychoanalytic Press, 1922).

21. Konrad Lorenz, *On Aggression* (New York: Harcourt Brace Jovanovich, 1966).

22. Wade Myers, *Sexual Homicide by Juveniles* (London: Academic Press, 2002).

23. Gregory M. Zimmerman, "Do Age Effects on Youth Secondary Exposure to Violence Vary Across Social Context?" *Justice Quarterly* 32 (2015): 193–222.

24. Darrell Steffensmeier, Ben Feldmeyer, Casey T. Harris, and Jeffery T. Ulmer, "Reassessing Trends in Black Violent Crime, 1980–2008: Sorting Out the 'Hispanic Effect' in Uniform Crime Reports Arrests, National Crime Victimization Survey Offender Estimates, and U.S. Prisoner Counts," *Criminology* 49 (2011): 197–251.

25. Barbara Warner, "Robberies with Guns: Neighborhood Factors and the Nature of Crime," *Journal of Criminal Justice* 35 (2007): 39–50.

26. Jeffrey B. Bingenheimer, Robert T. Brennan, and Felton J. Earls, "Firearm Violence Exposure and Serious Violent Behavior," *Science* 308 (2005): 1323–1326; "Witnessing Gun Violence Significantly Increases Likelihood that a Child Will Also Commit Violent Crime; Violence May Be Viewed as Infectious Disease," *A Scribe Health News Service*, May 26, 2005.

27. Eric Stewart, Ronald Simons, and Rand Conger, "Assessing Neighborhood and Social Psychological Influences on Childhood Violence in an African-American Sample," *Criminology* 40 (2002): 801–830.

28. David Farrington, Rolf Loeber, and Magda Stouthamer-Loeber, "How Can the Relationship Between Race and Violence Be Explained?" in *Violent Crimes: Assessing Race and Ethnic Differences*, ed. D. F. Hawkins (New York: Cambridge University Press, 2003), pp. 213–237.

29. William Alex Pridemore and Tony Grubesic, "Alcohol Outlets and Community Levels of Interpersonal Violence: Spatial Density, Outlet Type, and Seriousness of Assault," *Journal of Research in Crime and Delinquency*, first published May 17, 2011; Chris Allen, "The Links Between Heroin, Crack Cocaine and Crime: Where Does Street Crime Fit In?" *British Journal of Criminology* 45 (2005): 355–372.

30. Paul Goldstein, Henry Brownstein, and Patrick Ryan, "Drug-Related Homicide in New York: 1984–1988," *Crime and Delinquency* 38 (1992): 459–476.

31. Robert Brewer and Monica Swahn, "Binge Drinking and Violence," *JAMA: Journal of the American Medical Association* 294 (2005): 16–20.

32. Tomika Stevens, Kenneth Ruggiero, Dean Kilpatrick, Heidi Resnick, and Benjamin Saunders, "Variables Differentiating Singly and Multiply Victimized Youth: Results from the National Survey of Adolescents and Implications for Secondary Prevention," *Child Maltreatment* 10 (2005): 211–223; James Collins and Pamela Messerschmidt, "Epidemiology of Alcohol-Related Violence," *Alcohol Health and Research World* 17 (1993): 93–100.

33. Antonia Abbey, Tina Zawacki, Philip Buck, Monique Clinton, and Pam McAuslan, "Sexual Assault and Alcohol Consumption: What Do We Know About Their Relationship and What Types of Research Are Still Needed?" *Aggression and Violent Behavior* 9 (2004): 271–303.

34. Eric Sevigny and Andrea Allen, "Gun Carrying Among Drug Market Participants: Evidence from Incarcerated Drug Offenders," *Journal of Quantitative Criminology* 31 (2015): 435–458.

35. Martin Grann and Seena Fazel, "Substance Misuse and Violent Crime: Swedish Population Study," *British Medical Journal* 328 (2004): 1233–1234; Susanne Rogne Gjeruldsen, Bjørn Myrvang, and Stein Opjordsmoen, "Criminality in Drug Addicts: A Follow-Up Study Over 25 Years," *European Addiction Research* 10 (2004): 49–56; Kenneth Tardiff, Peter Marzuk, Kira Lowell, Laura Portera, and Andrew Leon, "A Study of Drug Abuse and Other Causes of Homicide in New York," *Journal of Criminal Justice* 30 (2002): 317–325.

36. Paul Goldstein, Patricia Bellucci, Barry Spunt, and Thomas Miller, "Volume of Cocaine Use and Violence: A Comparison Between Men and Women," *Journal of Drug Issues* 21 (1991): 345–367.

37. Richard Felson and Luke Bonkiewicz, "Guns and Trafficking in Crack-Cocaine and Other Drug Markets," *Crime and Delinquency*, first published February 10, 2011.

38. Pamela Wilcox and Richard Clayton, "A Multilevel Analysis of School-Based Weapon Possession," *Justice Quarterly* 18 (2001): 509–542.

39. FBI, *Crime in the United States, 2015*, https://ucr.fbi.gov/crime-in-the-u.s/2015/crime-in-the-u.s.-2015.

40. FBI, *Law Enforcement Officers Killed and Assaulted, 2013*, http://www.fbi.gov/about-us/cjis/ucr/leoka/2013/officers-feloniously-killed/felonious_topic_page_-2013.

41. David Brent, Joshua Perper, Christopher Allman, Grace Moritz, Mary Wartella, and Janice Zelenak, "The Presence and Accessibility of Firearms in the Home and Adolescent Suicides," *Journal of the American Medical Association* 266 (1991): 2989–2995.

42. Robert Baller, Luc Anselin, Steven Messner, Glenn Deane, and Darnell Hawkins, "Structural Covariates of U.S. County Homicide Rates Incorporating Spatial Effects," *Criminology* 39 (2001): 561–590.

43. Marvin Wolfgang and Franco Ferracuti, *The Subculture of Violence* (London: Tavistock, 1967).

44. Andrew Papachristos, "Murder by Structure: Dominance Relations and the Social Structure of Gang Homicide," *American Journal of Sociology* 115 (2009): 74–128.

45. David Luckenbill and Daniel Doyle, "Structural Position and Violence: Developing a Cultural Explanation," *Criminology* 27 (1989): 419–436.

46. Charis Kubrin and Ronald Weitzer, "Retaliatory Homicide: Concentrated Disadvantage and Neighborhood Culture," *Social Problems* 50 (2003): 157–180.

47. Robert J. Kane, "Compromised Police Legitimacy as a Predictor of Violent Crime in Structurally Disadvantaged Communities," *Criminology* 43 (2005): 469–499.

48. Chris Melde and Finn-Aage Esbensen, "Gangs and Violence: Disentangling the Impact of Gang Membership on the Level and Nature of Offending," *Journal of Quantitative Criminology*, first published online January 24, 2012.

49. Randol Contreras, *The Stickup Kids: Race, Drugs, Violence, and the American Dream* (Berkeley: University of California Press, 2012).

50. Daniel Neller, Robert Denney, Christina Pietz, and R. Paul Thomlinson, "Testing the Trauma Model of Violence," *Journal of Family Violence* 20 (2005): 151–159; James Howell, "Youth Gang Homicides: A Literature Review," *Crime and Delinquency* 45 (1999): 208–241.

51. William Wells, Ling Wu, and Xinyue Ye, "Patterns of Near-Repeat Gun Assaults in Houston," *Journal of Research in Crime and Delinquency*, first published May 12, 2011.

52. Lonnie Schaible and Lorine Hughes, "Crime, Shame, Reintegration, and Cross-national Homicide: A Partial Test of Reintegrative Shaming Theory," *Sociological Quarterly* 52 (2011): 104–131.

53. Marc Ouimet, "A World of Homicides: The Effect of Economic Development, Income Inequality, and Excess Infant Mortality on the Homicide Rate for 165 Countries in 2010," *Homicide Studies* 16 (2012): 238–258; Don Chon, "Contributing Factors for High Homicide Rate in Latin America: A Critical Test of Neapolitan's Regional Subculture of Violence Thesis," *Journal of Family Violence* 26 (2011): 299–307.

54. William Green, *Rape* (Lexington, MA: Lexington Books, 1988), p. 5.

55. Barbara Krahé, Renate Scheinberger-Olwig, and Steffen Bieneck, "Men's Reports of Nonconsensual Sexual Interactions with Women: Prevalence and Impact," *Archives of Sexual Behavior* 32 (2003): 165–176.

56. Heidi Zinzow, Heidi Resnick, Ananda Amstadter, Jenna McCauley, Kenneth Ruggiero, and Dean Kilpatrick, "Drug- or Alcohol-Facilitated, Incapacitated, and Forcible Rape in Relationship to Mental Health Among a National Sample of Women," *Journal of Interpersonal Violence* 25 (2010): 2217–2236.

57. Marlise Simons, "Bosnian Serb Pleads Guilty to Rape Charge Before War Crimes Tribunal," *New York Times*, March 10, 1998, p. 8.

58. Joshua Kaiser and John Hagan, "Gendered Genocide: The Socially Destructive Process of Genocidal Rape, Killing, and Displacement in Darfur," *Law and Society Review* 49 (2015): 69–107.

59. Jacob Zenn and Elizabeth Pearson, "Women, Gender and the Evolving Tactics of Boko Haram," *Journal of Terrorism Research* 5 (2014), jtr.st-andrews.ac.uk/articles/10.15664/jtr.828/.

60. Stephanie Busari and Kelly McCleary, "82 Chibok Schoolgirls Released in Nigeria," CNN, May 7, 2017, http://www.cnn.com/2017/05/06/africa/chibok-girls-released/; CNN, "Boko Haram Kidnapping of Nigerian Schoolgirls, a Year Later," April 14, 2015, http://www.cnn.com/2015/04/14/africa/nigeria-kidnapping-anniversary/.

61. Atika Shubert and Bharati Naik, "ISIS Soldiers Told to Rape Women 'To Make Them Muslim,'" CNN, October 8, 2015, http://www.cnn.com/2015/10/08/middleeast/isis-rape-theology-soldiers-rape-women-to-make-them-muslim/.

62. FBI, *Crime in the United States, 2015*, https://ucr.fbi .gov/crime-in-the-u.s/2015/crime-in-the-u.s.-2015. Crime data in this chapter come from this source and from preliminary 2016 data.

63. Jennifer Truman and Rachel Morgan, *Criminal Victimization, 2015*, Bureau of Justice Statistics, 2016.

64. Samantha Lundrigan and Katrin Mueller-Johnson, "Male Stranger Rape: A Behavioral Model of Victim-Offender Interactions," *Criminal Justice and Behavior* 40 (2013): 763–783.

65. Sarah Cook, Christine Gidycz, Mary Koss, and Megan Murphy, "Emerging Issues in the Measurement of Rape Victimization," *Violence Against Women* 17 (2011): 201–218; Bonnie S. Fisher, "The Effects of Survey Question Wording on Rape Estimates: Evidence from a Quasi-Experimental Design," *Violence Against Women* 15 (2009): 133–147; Amy Buddie and Maria Testa, "Rates and Predictors of Sexual Aggression Among Students and Nonstudents," *Journal of Interpersonal Violence* 20 (2005): 713–725.

66. Dean Kilpatrick, Heidi Resnick, Kenneth Ruggiero, Lauren Conoscenti, and Jenna McCauley, "Drug-Facilitated, Incapacitated, and Forcible Rape: A National Study," US Department of Justice, 2007, http://www.ncjrs.gov/pdffiles1/nij/grants/219181.pdf.

67. Truman and Morgan, *Criminal Victimization, 2015*.

68. Carol Vanzile-Tamsen, Maria Testa, and Jennifer Livingston, "The Impact of Sexual Assault History and Relationship Context on Appraisal of and Responses to Acquaintance Sexual Assault Risk," *Journal of Interpersonal Violence* 20 (2005): 813–822.

69. Lynn Langton and Sofi Sinozich, "Rape and Sexual Assault Among College-Age Females, 1995–2013," Bureau of Justice Statistics, 2014, http://www.bjs .gov/content/pub/pdf/rsavcaf9513.pdf.

70. Heather Littleton and Craig Henderson, "If She Is Not a Victim, Does That Mean She Was Not Traumatized? Evaluation of Predictors of PTSD Symptomatology Among College Rape Victims," *Violence Against Women* 15 (2009): 148–167.

71. A. Nicholas Groth and Jean Birnbaum, *Men Who Rape* (New York: Plenum Press, 1979).

72. For another typology, see Raymond Knight, "Validation of a Typology of Rapists," in *Sex Offender Research and Treatment: State-of-the-Art in North America and Europe*, ed. W. L. Marshall and J. Frenken (Beverly Hills, CA: Sage, 1997), pp. 58–75.

73. R. Lance Shotland, "A Model of the Causes of Date Rape in Developing and Close Relationships," in *Close Relationships*, ed. C. Hendrick (Newbury Park, CA: Sage, 1989), pp. 247–270.

74. Mary Koss, "Hidden Rape: Sexual Aggression and Victimization in a National Sample of Students in Higher Education," in *Rape and Sexual Assault*,

Vol. 2, ed. Anne Wolbert Burgess (New York: Garland Publishing, 1988), p. 824.

75. Bonnie Fisher, Leah Daigle, Francis Cullen, and Michael Turner, "Reporting Sexual Victimization to the Police and Others: Results from a National-Level Study of College Women," *Criminal Justice and Behavior* 30 (2003): 6–39.

76. Steven Lawyer, Heidi Resnick, Von Bakanic, Tracy Burkett, and Dean Kilpatrick, "Forcible, Drug-Facilitated, and Incapacitated Rape and Sexual Assault Among Undergraduate Women," *Journal of American College Health* 58 (2010): 453–460.

77. Heidi M. Zinzow, Heidi S. Resnick, Jenna L. McCauley, Ananda B. Amstadter, Kenneth J. Ruggiero, and Dean G. Kilpatrick, "The Role of Rape Tactics in Risk for Posttraumatic Stress Disorder and Major Depression: Results from a National Sample of College Women," *Depression and Anxiety* 27 (2010): 708–715.

78. David Cantor, Bonnie Fisher, Susan Chibnall, Reanne Townsend, Hyunshik Lee, Carol Bruce, and Gail Thomas, *Report on the AAU Campus Climate Survey on Sexual Assault and Sexual Misconduct, 2015*, https://www.aau.edu/sites/default/files/%40%20 Files/Climate%20Survey/AAU_Campus_Climate _Survey_12_14_15.pdf.

79. Rebecca Elliott Smith and Lawrence Pick, "Sexual Assault Experienced by Deaf Female Undergraduates: Prevalence and Characteristics," Violence and Victims 30 (2015): 948–959.

80. Lynn Langton, *Rape and Sexual Assault Among College-age Females, 1995–2013*, Bureau of Justice Statistics, 2014, http://www.bjs.gov/content/pub/pdf /rsavcaf9513.pdf.

81. Molly Smith, Nicole Wilkes, and Leana Bouffard, "Rape Myth Adherence Among Campus Law Enforcement Officers," *Criminal Justice and Behavior*, first published September 4, 2015.

82. Ibid.

83. US Department of Justice, Overview of Title IX of the Education Amendments of 1972, 20 U.S.C. A§ 1681 et seq., http://www.justice.gov/crt/overview -title-ix-education-amendments-1972-20-usc-1681 -et-seq.

84. American Civil Liberties Union, "Know Your Rights: Title IX and Sexual Assault," https://www.aclu.org /know-your-rights/title-ix-and-sexual-assault.

85. California Senate Bill No. 967, Chapter 748, An Act to Add Section 67386 to the Education Code, Relating to Student Safety, 2014, https://leginfo .legislature.ca.gov/faces/billNavClient.xhtml?bill_id =201320140SB96.

86. David Finkelhor and K. Yllo, *License to Rape: Sexual Abuse of Wives* (New York: Holt, Rinehart and Winston, 1985).

87. Raquel Kennedy Bergen, with contributions from Elizabeth Barnhill, "Marital Rape: New Research and Directions," National Online Resource Center for Violence Against Women, http://www.ncdsv .org/images/VAWnet_MaritalRapeNewResearch Directions_2-2006.pdf.

88. Florida Statute s. 943.04354, F.S. (2007).

89. Jed Rubenfeld, "The Riddle of Rape-by-Deception and the Myth of Sexual Autonomy," *Yale Law Journal* 122 (2013): 1372–1443.

90. Tennessee Code Annotated § 39-i3-5O3(a)(4) (2010); Idaho Tennessee Code Annotated § 18-6101(8) (Supp. 2011).

91. Robert Lopez, "Man Gets Prison in Rape Impersonation Case that Sparked New State Law," *Los Angeles Times*, May 8, 2014, http://www.latimes .com/local/lanow/la-me-ln-man-gets-prison-rape -impersonation-case-20140508-story.html.

92. Rubenfeld, "The Riddle of Rape-by-Deception and the Myth of Sexual Autonomy."

93. Galia Schneebaum, "What Is Wrong with Sex in Authority Relations? A Study in Law and Social Theory," *Journal of Criminal Law and Criminology* 105 (2015): 345–385.

94. N.D. Cent. Code. [section]12.1-20-06.1 (2012).

95. William McKibbin, Todd Shackelford, Aaron Goetz, and Valerie Starratt, "Why Do Men Rape? An Evolutionary Psychological Perspective," *Review of General Psychology* 12 (2008): 86–97.

96. Lawrence Miller, "Rape: Sex Crime, Act of Violence, or Naturalistic Adaptation?" *Aggression and Violent Behavior* 19 (2014): 67–81.

97. Ibid.

98. Suzanne Osman, "Predicting Men's Rape Perceptions Based on the Belief that 'No' Really Means 'Yes,'" *Journal of Applied Social Psychology* 33 (2003): 683–692.

99. Martin Schwartz, Walter DeKeseredy, David Tait, and Shahid Alvi, "Male Peer Support and a Feminist Routine Activities Theory: Understanding Sexual Assault on the College Campus," *Justice Quarterly* 18 (2001): 623–650.

100. Diana Russell and Rebecca M. Bolen, *The Epidemic of Rape and Child Sexual Abuse in the United States* (Thousand Oaks, CA: Sage, 2000).

101. Lynn Elber, "Student's Horrific, Fatal Rape Inspires 'India's Daughter,'" *Associated Press*, November 13, 2015, http://federalnewsradio.com/entertainment -news/2015/11/students-horrific-fatal-rape-inspires -indias-daughter/.

102. Calvin Langton, Zuwaina Murad, and Bianca Humbert, "Childhood Sexual Abuse, Attachments in Childhood and Adulthood, and Coercive Sexual Behaviors in Community Males," *Sexual Abuse: A Journal of Research and Treatment* 29 (2017): 207–238; Paul Gebhard, John Gagnon, Wardell Pomeroy, and Cornelia Christenson, *Sex Offenders: An Analysis of Types* (New York: Harper & Row, 1965), pp. 198–205; Richard Rada, ed., *Clinical Aspects of the Rapist* (New York: Grune & Stratton, 1978), pp. 122–130.

103. Stephen Porter, David Fairweather, Jeff Drugge, Huues Herve, Angela Birt, and Douglas Boer, "Profiles of Psychopathy in Incarcerated Sexual Offenders," *Criminal Justice and Behavior* 27 (2000): 216–233.

104. Brad Bushman, Angelica Bonacci, Mirjam van Dijk, and Roy Baumeister, "Narcissism, Sexual Refusal, and Aggression: Testing a Narcissistic Reactance Model of Sexual Coercion," *Journal of Personality and Social Psychology* 84 (2003): 1027–1040.

105. Schwartz, DeKeseredy, Tait, and Alvi, "Male Peer Support and a Feminist Routine Activities Theory."

106. Groth and Birnbaum, *Men Who Rape*, p. 101.

107. See, generally, Edward Donnerstein, Daniel Linz, and Steven Penrod, *The Question of Pornography* (New York: Free Press, 1987); Diana Russell, *Sexual Exploitation* (Beverly Hills, CA: Sage, 1985), pp. 115–116.

108. Neil Malamuth and John Briere, "Sexual Violence in the Media: Indirect Effects on Aggression Against Women," *Journal of Social Issues* 42 (1986): 75–92.

109. Richard Johnson, "Rape and Gender Conflict in a Patriarchal State," *Crime and Delinquency* 60 (2014): 1110–1128.

110. Ibid.

111. Richard Felson and Marvin Krohn, "Motives for Rape," *Journal of Research in Crime and Delinquency* 27 (1990): 222–242.

112. Steffen Bieneck and Barbara Krahé, "Blaming the Victim and Exonerating the Perpetrator in Cases of Rape and Robbery: Is There a Double Standard?" *Journal of Interpersonal Violence* 26 (2011): 1785–1797.

113. Julie Horney and Cassia Spohn, "The Influence of Blame and Believability Factors on the Processing of Simple versus Aggravated Rape Cases," *Criminology* 34 (1996): 135–163.

114. "Duke Lacrosse 'Rape' Accuser Changes Story Again, Says Seligmann Didn't Touch Her," *Associated Press*, January 12, 2007, http://www .foxnews.com/story/2007/01/12/duke-lacrosse -rape-accuser-changes-story-again-says-seligmann -didnt-touch-her.html; Sal Ruibal, "Rape Allegations Cast Pall at Duke," *USA Today*, March 29, 2006, http://usatoday30.usatoday.com/sports/college /lacrosse/2006-03-29-duke-fallout_x.htm.

115. Juliet Linderman, "Victim Advocates Worry About Discredited UVa Rape Account," Associated Press, March 24, 2015, http://koin.com/ap/police-report-on-virginia-gang-rape-not-the-final-word/.

116. Katie Hail-Jares, Belén Lowrey-Kinberg, Katherine Dunn, and Jon Gould, "False Rape Allegations and Wrongful Convictions," *Sexual Assault Report* 20 (2017): 53–66.

117. Patricia Landwehr, Robert Bothwell, Matthew Jeanmard, Luis Luque, Roy Brown III, and Marie-Anne Breaux, "Racism in Rape Trials," *Journal of Social Psychology* 142 (2002): 667–670.

118. Cassia Spohn, Dawn Beichner, and Erika Davis-Frenzel, "Prosecutorial Justifications for Sexual Assault Case Rejection," *Social Problems* 48 (2001): 206–235.

119. Susan Estrich, *Real Rape* (Cambridge, MA: Harvard University Press, 1987), pp. 58–59.

120. *Michigan v. Lucas* 90-149 (1991); Andrew Z. Soshnick, "Comment: The Rape Shield Paradox: Complainant Protection Amidst Oscillating Trends of State Judicial Interpretation," *Journal of Criminal Law and Criminology* 78 (1987): 644–698.

121. Andrew Karmen, *Crime Victims* (Pacific Grove, CA: Brooks/Cole, 1990), p. 252.

122. "Court Upholds Civil Rights Portion of Violence Against Women Act," *Criminal Justice Newsletter* 28 (1997): 3.

123. Cassia Spohn and David Holleran, "Prosecuting Sexual Assault: A Comparison of Charging Decisions in Sexual Assault Cases Involving Strangers, Acquaintances, and Intimate Partners," *Justice Quarterly* 18 (2001): 651–688.

124. Campus Sexual Violence Elimination Act, http://www.cleryact.info/campus-save-act.html.

125. Donald Lunde, *Murder and Madness* (San Francisco: San Francisco Books, 1977), p. 3.

126. "'Baby Hope' Case: Cousin Confesses to Sexually Assaulting, Killing Toddler Anjelica Castillo More than Two Decades Ago," *New York Daily News*, October 13, 2013, http://www.nydailynews.com/news/crime/relative-arrested-baby-hope-case-article-1.1483690.

127. Genevieve Bookwalter, "30-Year-Old Glen Ellyn Murder Case Had Twists, Turns—and Now an Arrest," *Chicago Tribune*, September 21, 2015, http://www.chicagotribune.com/suburbs/glen-ellyn/news/ct-dupage-cold-case-kristy-wesselman-20150920-story.html.

128. Rick Rojas, "Pedro Hernandez Found Guilty of Kidnapping and Killing Etan Patz in 1979," *New York Times*, February 14, 2017, https://www.nytimes.com/2017/02/14/nyregion/etan-patz-pedro-hernandez-guilty.html.

129. Wayne LaFave and Austin Scott, *Criminal Law* (St. Paul: West, 1986; updated 1993).

130. Bob Egelko, "State's Top Court OKs Dog Maul Murder Charge, Judge Ordered to Reconsider Owner's Original Conviction," *San Francisco Chronicle*, June 1, 2007, http://www.sfgate.com/bayarea/article/SAN-FRANCISCO-State-s-top-court-OKs-dog-maul-2557910.php; Evelyn Nieves, "Woman Gets 4-Year Term in Fatal Dog Attack," *New York Times*, July 16, 2002, p. 1.

131. National Conference of State Legislatures, "Fetal Homicide State Laws," April 2012, http://www.ncsl.org/issues-research/health/fetal-homicide-state-laws.aspx.

132. Ibid.

133. Dana Haynie and David Armstrong, "Race and Gender-Disaggregated Homicide Offending Rates: Differences and Similarities by Victim-Offender Relations Across Cities," *Homicide Studies* 10 (2006): 3–32.

134. Todd Shackelford, Viviana Weekes-Shackelford, and Shanna Beasley, "An Exploratory Analysis of the Contexts and Circumstances of Filicide-Suicide in Chicago, 1965–1994," *Aggressive Behavior* 31 (2005): 399–406.

135. Philip Cook, Jens Ludwig, and Anthony Braga, "Criminal Records of Homicide Offenders," *Journal of the American Medical Association* 294 (2005): 598–601.

136. David P. Farrington, Rolf Loeber, and Mark T. Berg, "Young Men Who Kill: A Prospective Longitudinal Examination from Childhood," *Homicide Studies* 16 (2012): 99–128.

137. William Parkin, Joshua Freilich, and Steven Chermak, "Ideological Victimization: Homicides Perpetrated by Far-Right Extremists," *Homicide Studies* 19 (2015): 211–236.

138. C. Gabrielle Salfati and Paul Taylor, "Differentiating Sexual Violence: A Comparison of Sexual Homicide and Rape," *Psychology, Crime and Law* 12 (2006): 107–125.

139. Terance Miethe and Wendy Regoeczi with Kriss Drass, *Rethinking Homicide: Exploring the Structure and Process Underlying Deadly Situations* (Cambridge, England: Cambridge University Press, 2004).

140. National Institute of Justice, "How Widespread Is Intimate Partner Violence?" https://www.nij.gov/topics/crime/intimate-partner-violence/Pages/extent.aspx.

141. Carol Jordan, James Clark, Adam Pritchard, and Richard Charnigo, "Lethal and Other Serious Assaults: Disentangling Gender and Context," *Crime and Delinquency* 58 (2012): 425–455.

142. Steven Shatz and Naomi Shatz, "Chivalry Is Not Dead: Murder, Gender, and the Death Penalty,"

Berkeley Journal of Gender, Law and Justice 27 (2012): 64–112.

143. Linda Saltzman and James Mercy, "Assaults Between Intimates: The Range of Relationships Involved," in *Homicide: The Victim/Offender Connection,* ed. Anna Victoria Wilson (Cincinnati: Anderson Publishing, 1993), pp. 65–74.

144. Jordan, Clark, Pritchard, and Charnigo, "Lethal and Other Serious Assaults: Disentangling Gender and Context."

145. Angela Browne and Kirk Williams, "Exploring the Effect of Resource Availability and the Likelihood of Female-Perpetrated Homicides," *Law and Society Review* 23 (1989): 75–94.

146. Richard Felson, "Anger, Aggression, and Violence in Love Triangles," *Violence and Victimization* 12 (1997): 345–363.

147. Ibid., p. 361.

148. Scott Decker, "Deviant Homicide: A New Look at the Role of Motives and Victim–Offender Relationships," *Journal of Research in Crime and Delinquency* 33 (1996): 427–449.

149. David Luckenbill, "Criminal Homicide as a Situational Transaction," *Social Problems* 25 (1977): 176–186.

150. Jeff Gruenewald, "A Comparative Examination of Homicides Perpetrated by Far-Right Extremists," *Homicide Studies* 15 (2011): 177–203.

151. Sharon Smith, Kathleen Basile, and Debra Karch, "Sexual Homicide and Sexual Violence–Associated Homicide: Findings from the National Violent Death Reporting System," *Homicide Studies* 15 (2011): 132–153; Vernon J. Geberth, "The Classification of Sex-Related Homicides," http://www.practicalhomicide.com/Research/sexrelatedhomicides.htm.

152. Peter Lin and James Gill, "Homicides of Pregnant Women," *American Journal of Forensic Medicine and Pathology* 32 (2011): 161–163.

153. Paul Greenall and Michelle Wright, "Exploring the Criminal Histories of Stranger Sexual Killers," *Journal of Forensic Psychiatry and Psychology* 26 (2015): 242–259.

154. Paul Greenall and Michelle Wright, "Exploring the Criminal Histories of Stranger Sexual Killers," *Journal of Forensic Psychiatry and Psychology* 26 (2015): 242–259.

155. Paul Greenall and Clare Richardson, "Adult Male-on-Female Stranger Sexual Homicide: A Descriptive (Baseline) Study from Great Britain," *Homicide Studies* 19 (2015): 237–225.

156. National Center for Education Statistics, "Violent Deaths at School and Away from School," https://nces.ed.gov/programs/crimeindicators/ind_01.asp.

157. Laura Agnich, "A Comparative Analysis of Attempted and Completed School-Based Mass Murder Attacks," *American Journal of Criminal Justice* 40 (2015): 1–22.

158. Mark Anderson, Joanne Kaufman, Thomas Simon, Lisa Barrios, Len Paulozzi, George Ryan, Rodney Hammond, William Modzeleski, Thomas Feucht, Lloyd Potter, and the School-Associated Violent Deaths Study Group, "School-Associated Violent Deaths in the United States, 1994–1999," *Journal of the American Medical Association* 286 (2001): 2695–2702.

159. Bryan Vossekuil, Marisa Reddy, Robert Fein, Randy Borum, and William Modzeleski, *Safe School Initiative, An Interim Report on the Prevention of Targeted Violence in Schools* (Washington, DC: United States Secret Service, 2000).

160. Anthony Walsh, "African Americans and Serial Killing in the Media: The Myth and the Reality," *Homicide Studies* 9 (2005): 271–291.

161. Scott Bonn, *Why We Love Serial Killers: The Curious Appeal of the World's Most Savage Murderers* (New York: Skyhorse Press, 2014).

162. Elizabeth Gurian, "Reframing Serial Murder Within Empirical Research: Offending and Adjudication Patterns of Male, Female, and Partnered Serial Killers," *International Journal of Offender Therapy and Comparative Criminology* 61 (2017): 544–560.

163. Marissa Harrison, Erin Murphy, Lavinia Ho, Thomas Bowers, and Claire Flaherty, "Female Serial Killers in the United States: Means, Motives, and Makings," *Journal of Forensic Psychiatry and Psychology* 26 (2015): 383–406.

164. Christopher Ferguson, Diana White, Stacey Cherry, Marta Lorenz, and Zhara Bhimani, "Defining and Classifying Serial Murder in the Context of Perpetrator Motivation," *Journal of Criminal Justice* 31 (2003): 287–293.

165. James Alan Fox and Jack Levin, "Multiple Homicide: Patterns of Serial and Mass Murder," in *Crime and Justice: An Annual Edition*, Vol. 23, ed. Michael Tonry (Chicago: University of Chicago Press, 1998): 407–455. See also James Alan Fox and Jack Levin, *Overkill: Mass Murder and Serial Killing Exposed* (New York: Plenum, 1994); James Alan Fox and Jack Levin, "A Psycho-Social Analysis of Mass Murder," in *Serial and Mass Murder: Theory, Policy, and Research,* ed. Thomas O'Reilly-Fleming and Steven Egger (Toronto: University of Toronto Press, 1993); James Alan Fox and Jack Levin, "Serial Murder: A Survey," in *Serial and Mass Murder;* Jack Levin and James Alan Fox, *Mass Murder* (New York: Plenum Press, 1985).

166. Terry Whitman and Donald Akutagawa, "Riddles in Serial Murder: A Synthesis," *Aggression and Violent Behavior* 9 (2004): 693–703.

167. Aneez Esmail, "Physician as Serial Killer—The Shipman Case," *New England Journal of Medicine* 352 (2005): 1843–1844.

168. Fox and Levin, "Multiple Homicide: Patterns of Serial and Mass Murder"; Fox and Levin, *Overkill: Mass Murder and Serial Killing Exposed*; James Alan Fox, Jack Levin, and Kenna Quinet, *The Will to Kill: Making Sense of Senseless Murder*, 2nd ed. (Boston: Allyn & Bacon, 2004); Fox and Levin, "A Psycho-Social Analysis of Mass Murder."

169. FBI, "A Study of Active Shooter Incidents in the United States Between 2000 and 2013," https://www.fbi.gov/news/stories/2014/september/fbi-releases-study-on-active-shooter-incidents/pdfs/a-study-of-active-shooter-incidents-in-the-u.s.-between-2000-and-2013.

170. Elissa Gootman, "The Hunt for a Sniper: The Victim; 10th Victim Is Recalled as Motivator on Mission," *New York Times,* October 14, 2002, p. A15; Sarah Kershaw, "The Hunt for a Sniper: The Investigation; Endless Frustration but Little Evidence in Search for Sniper," *New York Times,* October 14, 2002, p. A1.

171. "Serial Killers, Part 4: White Supremacist Joseph Paul Franklin," https://www.fbi.gov/news/stories/serial-killers-part-4.

172. Francis X. Clines with Christopher Drew, "Prosecutors to Discuss Charges as Rifle Is Tied to Sniper Killings," *New York Times*, October 25, 2002, p. A1.

173. Louis B. Schlesinger, Stephanie Ramirez, Brittany Tusa, John P. Jarvis, and Philip Erdberg, "Rapid-Sequence Serial Sexual Homicides," *Journal of the American Academy of Psychiatry and the Law Online* 45 (2017): 72–80.

174. Associated Press, "Woman with HIV Gets 3 Years for Spitting in Face," http://www.foxnews.com/story/2008/07/22/woman-with-hiv-gets-3-years-for-spitting-in-another-woman-face.html.

175. Gabrielle Salfati and Paul Taylor, "Differentiating Sexual Violence: A Comparison of Sexual Homicide and Rape," *Psychology, Crime and Law* 12 (2006): 107–125; Keith Harries, "Homicide and Assault: A Comparative Analysis of Attributes in Dallas Neighborhoods, 1981–1985," *Professional Geographer* 41 (1989): 29–38.

176. Laurence Zuckerman, "The Air-Rage Rage: Taking a Cold Look at a Hot Topic," *New York Times*, October 4, 1998, p. A3.

177. See, generally, Ruth S. Kempe and C. Henry Kempe, *Child Abuse* (Cambridge, MA: Harvard University Press, 1978).

178. Data in this and the following sections come from the Centers for Disease Control and Prevention, "Child Abuse and Neglect Prevention," http://www.cdc.gov/violenceprevention/childmaltreatment/.

179. Eva Jonzon and Frank Lindblad, "Adult Female Victims of Child Sexual Abuse," *Journal of Interpersonal Violence* 20 (2005): 651–666.

180. Jennie Noll, Penelope Trickett, William Harris, and Frank Putnam, "The Cumulative Burden Borne by Offspring Whose Mothers Were Sexually Abused as Children: Descriptive Results from a Multigenerational Study," *Journal of Interpersonal Violence* 24 (2009): 424–449.

181. Jane Siegel and Linda Williams, "Risk Factors for Sexual Victimization of Women," *Violence Against Women* 9 (2003): 902–930.

182. Glenn Wolfner and Richard Gelles, "A Profile of Violence Toward Children: A National Study," *Child Abuse and Neglect* 17 (1993): 197–212.

183. Martin Daly and Margo Wilson, "Violence Against Stepchildren," *Current Directions in Psychological Science* 5 (1996): 77–81.

184. Ruth Inglis, *Sins of the Fathers: A Study of the Physical and Emotional Abuse of Children* (New York: St. Martin's Press, 1978), p. 53.

185. Cindy Schaeffer, Pamela Alexander, Kimberly Bethke, and Lisa Kretz, "Predictors of Child Abuse Potential Among Military Parents: Comparing Mothers and Fathers," *Journal of Family Violence* 20 (2005): 123–129.

186. April Chiung-Tao Shen, "Self-Esteem of Young Adults Experiencing Interparental Violence and Child Physical Maltreatment: Parental and Peer Relationships as Mediators," *Journal of Interpersonal Violence* 24 (2009): 770–794.

187. Christina Meade, Trace Kershaw, Nathan Hansen, and Kathleen Sikkema, "Long-Term Correlates of Childhood Abuse Among Adults with Severe Mental Illness: Adult Victimization, Substance Abuse, and HIV Sexual Risk Behavior," *AIDS and Behavior* 13 (2009): 207–216.

188. Arina Ulman and Murray Straus, "Violence by Children Against Mothers in Relation to Violence Between Parents and Corporal Punishment by Parents," *Journal of Comparative Family Studies* 34 (2003): 41–63.

189. Richard Gelles and Murray Straus, "Violence in the American Family," *Journal of Social Issues* 35 (1979): 15–39.

190. Lauren Josephs and Eileen Mazur Abel, "Investigating the Relationship Between Intimate Partner Violence and HIV Risk-Propensity in Black/African-American Women," *Journal of Family Violence* 24 (2009): 221–229.

191. Maureen Outlaw, "No One Type of Intimate Partner Abuse: Exploring Physical and Non-physical Abuse Among Intimate Partners," *Journal of Family Violence* 24 (2009): 263–272.

192. This section leans heavily on Priscilla Offenhauer and Alice Buchalter, *Teen Dating Violence: A Literature Review and Annotated Bibliography, A Report Prepared by the Federal Research Division, Library of Congress Under an Interagency Agreement with the Violence and Victimization Research Division, National Institute of Justice, April 2011,* http://www.ncjrs.gov/pdffiles1/nij /grants/235368.pdf.

193. Jay Silverman, Anita Raj, Lorelei Mucci, and Jeanne Hathaway, "Dating Violence Against Adolescent Girls and Associated Substance Abuse, Unhealthy Weight Control, Sexual Risk Behavior, Pregnancy and Suicidality," *Journal of the American Medical Association* 286 (2001): 572–579.

194. FBI, *Crime in the United States, 2000,* p. 29.

195. Peter Van Koppen and Robert Jansen, "The Time to Rob: Variations in Time of Number of Commercial Robberies," *Journal of Research in Crime and Delinquency* 36 (1999): 7–29.

196. Marcus Felson, *Crime and Nature* (Thousand Oaks, CA: Sage, 2006).

197. Marie Rosenkrantz Lindegaard, Wim Bernasco, and Scott Jacques, "Consequences of Expected and Observed Victim Resistance for Offender Violence During Robbery Events," *Journal of Research in Crime and Delinquency* 52 (2015): 32–61.

198. Richard Wright and Scott Decker, *Armed Robbers in Action: Stickups and Street Culture* (Boston: Northeastern University Press, 1997).

199. Jody Miller, "Up It Up: Gender and the Accomplishment of Street Robbery," *Criminology* 36 (1998): 37–67.

200. Ibid., pp. 54–55.

201. Elizabeth Ehrhardt Mustaine and Richard Tewksbury, "Predicting Risks of Larceny Theft Victimization: A Routine Activity Analysis Using Refined Lifestyle Measures," *Criminology* 36 (1998): 829–858.

202. Bruce A. Jacobs, *Robbing Drug Dealers: Violence beyond the Law* (Hawthorne, NY: Aldine de Gruyter, 2000).

203. Richard Felson, Eric Baumer, and Steven Messner, "Acquaintance Robbery," *Journal of Research in Crime and Delinquency* 37 (2000): 284–305.

204. Ibid., p. 287.

205. Ibid.

206. Volkan Topalli, Scott Jacques, and Richard Wright, "It Takes Skills to Take a Car: Perceptual and Procedural Expertise in Carjacking," *Aggression and Violent Behavior* (2014): 19–25.

207. Heith Copes, Andy Hochstetler, and Michael Cherbonneau, "Getting the Upper Hand: Scripts for Managing Victim Resistance in Carjackings," *Journal*

of Research in Crime and Delinquency*, published online May 3, 2011.

208. "Boy Gets 18 Years in Fatal Park Beating of Transient," *Los Angeles Times*, December 24, 1987, p. 9B.

209. James Brooke, "Gay Student Who Was Kidnapped and Beaten Dies," *New York Times*, October 13, 1998, p. A1.

210. Gregory Herek, "Hate Crimes and Stigma-Related Experiences Among Sexual Minority Adults in the United States: Prevalence Estimates from a National Probability Sample," *Journal of Interpersonal Violence* 24 (2009): 54–74.

211. Jack McDevitt, Jack Levin, and Susan Bennett, "Hate Crime Offenders: An Expanded Typology," *Journal of Social Issues* 58 (2002): 303–318; Jack Levin and Jack McDevitt, *Hate Crimes: The Rising Tide of Bigotry and Bloodshed* (New York: Plenum, 1993).

212. FBI, *Hate Crime Statistics, 2015,* https://ucr.fbi.gov /hate-crime/2015.

213. Bureau of Justice Statistics, "U.S. Residents Experienced About 293,800 Hate Crime Victimizations in 2012—Unchanged from 2004," http://www.bjs.gov/content/pub/press/hcv0412stpr .cfm.

214. Gregory Herek, Jeanine Cogan, and Roy Gillis, "Victim Experiences in Hate Crimes Based on Sexual Orientation," *Journal of Social Issues* 58 (2002): 319–340.

215. Brian Levin, "From Slavery to Hate Crime Laws: The Emergence of Race- and Status-Based Protection in American Criminal Law," *Journal of Social Issues* 58 (2002): 227–246.

216. National LGBTQ Task Force, "Hate Crime Laws in the U.S., 2013," http://www.thetaskforce.org /static_html/downloads/reports/issue_maps/hate _crimes_06_13_new.pdf.

217. Felicia Lee, "Gays Angry over TV Report on a Murder," *New York Times*, November 26, 2004, A3.

218. Frederick M. Lawrence, *Punishing Hate: Bias Crimes Under American Law* (Cambridge, MA: Harvard University Press, 1999).

219. Ibid., p. 3.

220. *Virginia v. Black et al.*, No. 01-1107, 2003.

221. Bureau of Labor Statistics, "Census of Fatal Occupational Injuries Summary, 2015," http:// www.bls.gov/news.release/cfoi.nr0.htm.

222. Robert Simon, *Bad Men Do What Good Men Dream* (Washington, DC: American Psychiatric Press, 1999).

223. Bureau of Labor Statistics, "Census of Fatal Occupational Injuries Summary, 2015."

224. Patrick Kinkade, Ronald Burns, and Angel Ilarraza Fuentes, "Criminalizing Attractions: Perceptions of Stalking and the Stalker," *Crime and Delinquency* 51 (2005): 3–25.

225. Shannan Catalano, "Stalking Victims in the United States—Revised," Bureau of Justice Statistics, 2012, https://www.bjs.gov/content/pub/pdf/svus_rev.pdf.

226. T. K. Logan and Robert Walker, "Stalking: A Multidimensional Framework for Assessment and Safety Planning," *Trauma, Violence, and Abuse* 18 (2017): 200–222.

227. Rosemary Purcell, Bridget Moller, Teresea Flower, and Paul Mullen, "Stalking Among Juveniles," *British Journal of Psychiatry* 194 (2009): 451–455.

228. *Michelle Garcia,* "Voices from the Field: Stalking," *NIJ Journal* 266 (2010), http://www.nij.gov/journals /266/stalking.htm.

229. Ibid.

230. Carol Jordan, T. K. Logan, and Robert Walker, "Stalking: An Examination of the Criminal Justice Response," *Journal of Interpersonal Violence* 18 (2003): 148–165.

Political Crime and Terrorism

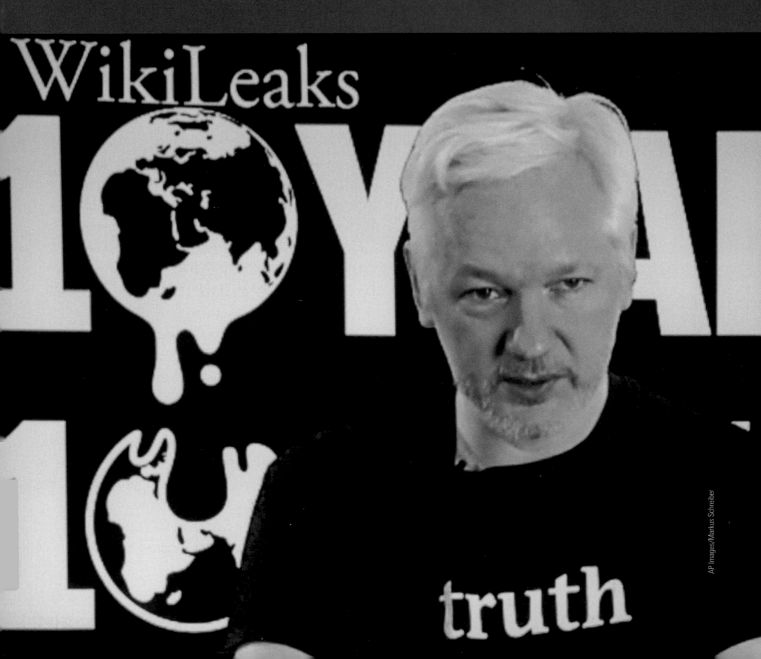

Learning Objectives

LO1 Define the term *political crime*.

LO2 Assess the cause of political crime.

LO3 Compare and contrast the terms *espionage* and *treason*.

LO4 List the components of state political crime.

LO5 Distinguish among terrorists, insurgents, guerillas, and revolutionaries.

LO6 Enumerate the various forms of terrorism.

11

Chapter Outline

FACT OR FICTION?

▶ Treason is the only crime mentioned in the United States Constitution.

▶ Terrorist attacks have been increasing every year; the world is becoming more dangerous.

Americans have become very familiar with a previously little-known website called WikiLeaks, an international organization that publishes classified and secret documents submitted by anonymous sources. Launched in 2006 and run by Julian Assange (see photo), an Australian who emigrated to Sweden, WikiLeaks has supporters around the globe. A few years ago, the site began to post videos and documents that had been illegally appropriated from US diplomatic and military computers by unknown hackers. One video showed a 2007 incident in which Iraqi civilians and journalists were killed by US forces. It also leaked more than 76,000 classified war documents from Afghanistan, including US State Department cables. In the aftermath of the leaks, Army Specialist Bradley Manning, 22, was arrested after an informant told federal authorities that he had overheard Manning bragging about giving WikiLeaks a video of a helicopter assault in Iraq, along with more than 260,000 classified US diplomatic cables taken from government computers. Both the US and foreign governments were mortified when the confidential cables hit the Net.[1] Manning was sentenced to 35 years in prison for leaking classified material.

WikiLeaks again made headlines in April 2015 when it published 30,287 documents and 173,132 emails hacked from Sony Pictures Entertainment. The material allegedly had been stolen by North Korea's intelligence service in revenge for Sony producing the comedy film *The Interview*, depicting a future overthrow of the North Korean government and the assassination of its leader, Kim Jong-un. Many of the hacked emails proved embarrassing to the studio, including ones mentioning actors' pay and others joking about President Obama and race. ▶

But WikiLeaks was not done. During the 2016 presidential election, the site published emails that had been hacked from Clinton presidential campaign computers. While the revelations were not particularly controversial, the site was accused of playing politics; Russian hackers were suspected of being behind the data breach. If the Russian connection could be proven, it meant that WikiLeaks was aiding foreign interference in US elections. In response, Assange issued a statement that read in part:

> The right to receive and impart true information is the guiding principle of WikiLeaks—an organization that has a staff and organizational mission far beyond myself. Our organization defends the public's right to be informed.
>
> This is why, irrespective of the outcome of the 2016 US Presidential election, the real victor is the US public which is better informed as a result of our work.
>
> The US public has thoroughly engaged with WikiLeaks' election related publications which number more than one hundred thousand documents. Millions of Americans have pored over the leaks and passed on their citations to each other and to us. It is an open model of journalism that gatekeepers are uncomfortable with, but which is perfectly harmonious with the First Amendment.[2]

Is Assange a hero or a criminal? Depends on one's point of view. In the meantime, wanted on a series of charges stemming from an alleged sexual assault in Sweden and threatened with extradition to the United States to face charges of espionage, Assange was granted asylum by the government of Ecuador and remained in their London embassy for years. In 2017, the fate of these two notorious people suddenly took a new twist. First, Bradley Manning (now known as Chelsea Elizabeth Manning) had her sentence commuted by President Obama just before he left office; on May 17, 2017, she walked out of prison, a free woman.[3] Then Sweden decided to drop rape charges against Assange. While he remains in the embassy, his future now looks considerably rosier. ■

Political crime can be both nonviolent, such as Chelsea Manning's violation of the espionage act, and extremely violent, such as a terrorist act designed to undermine the government. It has become an important area of criminological inquiry, and many criminologists who previously paid scant attention to the interaction between political motivation and crime have now made it the focus of intense study.

In this chapter, we will briefly discuss the concept of political crime and some of the forms it takes. We will then go into its most extreme form, terrorism, which now occupies the center stage of both world opinion and government policy. It is important for students of criminology to develop a basic understanding of terrorism's definition, history, and structure, and review the steps being taken to limit or eliminate its occurrence.

Political Crime

The term **political crime** is used to signify illegal acts that are designed to undermine an existing government and threaten its survival.[4] However, unlike other crimes, it is often difficult to decide who is the criminal and who is the victim. Take the series of uprisings that began in 2011 and are known as the "Arab Spring." Some targeted people widely viewed as dictators, such as the popular revolt in February 2011 that toppled the regime of longtime Egyptian dictator Hosni Mubarak. Similar protests broke out in Tunisia, Yemen, and Libya, where the regime of dictator Muammar Gaddafi was ousted. These revolts were not viewed as terrorist acts but popular political upheavals against hated and evil dictators. The world did not recoil when Gaddafi was apprehended and brutally killed on camera.

When an act becomes a political crime and when an actor is considered a political criminal are often extremely subjective. In highly repressive nations, any form of unsanctioned political activity, including writing a newspaper article critical of the regime, may be considered a political crime, punishable by a prison term or even death. In contrast, people whom some label as terrorists and insurrectionists are viewed by others as freedom fighters and revolutionaries. What would have happened to George Washington and Benjamin Franklin had the British won the Revolutionary War? Would they have been hanged for their political crimes or considered heroes and freedom fighters? What about Julian Assange and Chelsea Manning, the subjects of the opening vignette? Are they heroes or traitors? According to a (now closed) website maintained by supporters, Manning revealed information that showed us "the true human cost of our wars in Iraq and Afghanistan, and changed journalism forever, for revealing the video that exposed the killing of unarmed civilians and two Reuters journalists by a US Apache helicopter crew in Iraq and the release of US diplomatic cables that revealed the role that corporate interests and spying play in international diplomacy." Of course, not everyone sees it that way. Shortly after his inauguration, President Trump tweeted, "Ungrateful TRAITOR Chelsea Manning, who should never have been released from prison, is now calling President Obama a weak leader. Terrible!"[5]

Another well-known figure involved in political acts that are considered a crime by some and heroic by others is Edward Snowden, the subject of the Profiles in Crime feature.

Take for instance the ongoing civil war in Syria. In 2011, troops loyal to the ruling party cracked down hard when protests erupted against the government of Bashar al-Assad. The world watched in horror and dismay when state security forces killed hundreds of protesters and arbitrarily arrested thousands, many of whom, including children, were beaten and tortured. At first, world leaders denounced the violence: Turkish Prime Minister (now President) Recep Tayyip Erdoğan called the crackdown a "barbarity" that is "inhumane" and "cannot be digested."[6] However, as in many political conflicts, things soon became murky: Syrian government officials blamed the violence on "terrorist groups" and "armed gangs." One rebel group, the Al-Nusra Front (ANF), is associated with **al-Qaeda** and the Syrian Islamic Front, whose aim is overthrowing the Syrian government and establishing an Islamic state. The fighting soon took on sectarian overtones, and Shia and Sunni factions emerged. According to the government, the rebels were really jihadists looking to establish a base in Syria; according to the opposition, the rebels were freedom fighters looking to oust an evil dictator and establish democracy. The conflict evolved into a full-blown civil war in which more than 400,000 combatants and noncombatants have been killed, including many who died after being poisoned by chemical weapons used by government forces, such as Sarin gas.[7]

In the midst of the turmoil, the Islamic State (IS) emerged and carved out a caliphate spanning part of Syria and Iraq. In response to horrific terror acts, first the United States and then Russia began a bombing campaign against IS as the three-way civil war dragged on.

L01 Define the term *political crime*.

political crime
Illegal acts that are designed to undermine an existing government and threaten its survival. Political crimes can include both violent and nonviolent acts and range in seriousness from dissent, treason, and espionage to violent acts such as terrorism or assassination.

al-Qaeda (Arabic for "the base")
An international fundamentalist Islamist organization comprising independent and collaborative cells, whose goal is reducing Western influence upon Islamic affairs. Also spelled al-Qa'ida.

PROFILES IN CRIME

EDWARD SNOWDEN

Edward Snowden, born in North Carolina in 1983, worked for Booz Allen Hamilton, a provider of management and technology consulting services to the US government. In May 2013, Snowden began collecting top-secret documents regarding NSA domestic surveillance practices and leaking them to the press. Why did he engage in what some people consider treason? He was disturbed that the NSA was engaged in spying on millions of American citizens, a practice he considered an illegal invasion of privacy. When the documents appeared in the press, Snowden was charged with two counts of violating the Espionage Act of 1917. He was also charged with theft of government property (18 USC § 641), unauthorized communication of national defense information (18 USC § 793[d]), and willful communication of classified communications intelligence information to an unauthorized person (18 USC § 798[a][3]). He fled to Russia to avoid prosecution, where he has been given asylum and where he remains to this day.

In a series of interviews given in Hong Kong and Russia, Snowden told the press, "I'm willing to sacrifice [my former life] because I can't in good conscience allow the US government to destroy privacy, Internet freedom, and basic liberties for people around the world with this massive surveillance machine they're secretly building." He saw himself as a truth teller, informing the press that the American people have a right to know about government abuses that were being kept hidden:

> The secret continuance of these programs represents a far greater danger than their disclosure. . . . So long as there's broad support amongst a people, it can be argued there's a level of legitimacy even to the most invasive and morally wrong program, as it was an informed and willing decision. . . . However, programs that are implemented in secret, out of public oversight, lack that legitimacy, and that's a problem. It also represents a dangerous normalization of "governing in the dark," where decisions with enormous public impact occur without any public input.

Is Snowden a patriot who exposed illegal government practices or a political criminal who engaged in treasonous activity that endangered national security? He has been given awards for his actions, including Norway's Ossietzky Prize, awarded for "outstanding efforts for freedom of expression." He also received the Bjørnson Prize, awarded annually by the Bjørnstjerne Bjørnson Academy—the Norwegian Academy of Literature and Freedom of Expression—for particularly important acts of cultural expression. ■

Sources: Charlie Savage and Mark Mazzetti, "Cryptic Overtures and a Clandestine Meeting Gave Birth to a Blockbuster Story," *New York Times*, June 10, 2013, http://www.nytimes.com/2013/06/11/us/how-edward-j-snowden-orchestrated-a-blockbuster-story.html; James Risen, "Snowden Says He Took No Secret Files to Russia," *New York Times*, January 20, 2014, http://www.nytimes.com/2013/10/18/world/snowden-says-he-took-no-secret-files-to-russia.html; Gordon Hunt, "Edward Snowden: I've Applied for Asylum in 21 Countries," Silicon Republic, June 5, 2015, https://www.siliconrepublic.com/enterprise/2015/06/05/edward-snowden-ive-applied-for-asylum-in-21-countries (URLs accessed May 2017).

AP Images

The Nature of Political Crimes

Political crimes may stem from religious or ideological sources. Because their motivations shift between selfish personal needs and selfless, noble, or altruistic desires, political crimes often occupy a gray area between conventional and outlawed behavior. It is easy to condemn interpersonal violent crimes such as rape or murder because their goals are typically selfish and self-centered (e.g., revenge or profit). In contrast, political criminals may be motivated by principle, faith, or conviction. While it is true that some political crime involves profit (such as selling state secrets for money), most political criminals, including Edward Snowden, do not consider themselves antisocial but instead patriotic and altruistic. They are willing to sacrifice themselves for what they consider to be the greater good. While some concoct elaborate schemes to hide or mask their actions, others are quite brazen, hoping to provoke the government to overreact in their zeal to crack down on dissent. Because state authorities may engage in a range of retaliatory actions that result in human rights violations, even those who support the government may begin to question its activities: maybe the government is corrupt and authoritarian? On the other hand, if the government does nothing, it appears weak and corrupt and unable to protect citizens.

Even those political criminals who profit personally from their misdeeds, such as someone who spies for an enemy nation for financial payoffs, may believe that their acts are motivated by a higher calling than common theft. "My ultimate goal is to weaken or overthrow a corrupt government," they reason, "so selling secrets to the enemy is justified." Political criminals may believe that their acts are criminalized only because the group holding power fears them and wants to curtail their behavior. And while the general public has little objection to laws that control extreme behaviors such as plotting a bloody revolution, they may have questions when a law criminalizes ordinary political dissent or bans political meetings in order to control suspected political criminals.

Becoming a Political Criminal

Why does someone become a political criminal? There is no set pattern or reason; motivations vary widely. Some use political crime as a stepping stone to public office, while others use it as a method to focus their frustrations. Others hope they can gain respect from their friends and family. Although the motivations for political crime are complex and varied, there does appear to be some regularity in the way ideas are formed. Political crime expert Randy Borum finds that this pattern takes the form of a series of cognitive stages:

L02 Assess the cause of political crime.

- Stage 1: *"It's not right."* An unhappy, dissatisfied individual identifies some type of undesirable event or condition. It could be economic (e.g., poverty, unemployment, poor living conditions), social (e.g., government-imposed restrictions on individual freedoms, lack of order, or morality), or personal ("I am being cheated because of discrimination against my religious beliefs"). While the conditions may vary, those involved perceive the experience as "things are not as they should be."
- Stage 2: *"It's not fair."* The prospective political criminal concludes that the undesirable condition is a product of "injustice"—that is, it does not apply to everyone equally. A worker may believe that because of racial or religious bias someone with less skill is making more money and getting more benefits. Feeling deprived facilitates emotions of resentment and injustice.
- Stage 3: *"It's your fault."* Someone or some group must be held accountable for the extremist's displeasure. It always helps to identify a potential target. An angry employee is convinced that minorities get all the good jobs while he is underpaid and suffering financially. He is a receptive target for propaganda put out by extremist groups looking to attract recruits.
- Stage 4: *"You're evil."* When a group is cast as evil, it is dehumanized and an appropriate target for revenge and/or violence. The disaffected immigrant worker concludes that since his adopted country has let him down he is justified in joining a terrorist group or even taking matters into his own hands. Aggression becomes justifiable when aimed at bad people, particularly those who intentionally cause harm to others.[8]

election fraud
Illegal interference with the process of an election. Acts of fraud tend to involve affecting vote counts to bring about a desired election outcome, whether by increasing the vote share of the favored candidate, depressing the vote share of the rival candidates, or both. Varieties of election fraud include intimidation, disruption of polling places, distribution of misinformation such as the wrong election date, registration fraud, and vote buying.

Kelli Jo Griffin wipes away tears as she is embraced by Sister Peggy from the Holy Family Catholic Church of Fort Madison, Iowa, following her not-guilty verdict. The former drug offender, who believed her voting rights had been restored when she cast a ballot last year, was acquitted of perjury in a voter fraud case. Some states have begun to crack down on alleged voter fraud, and in some cases, such as Griffin's, prosecutions may be overzealous.

This chain of events described by Borum can be viewed in the events that led up to Dylann Roof's deadly attack on the Emanuel African Methodist Episcopal Church (discussed in Chapter 10). In his online manifesto, Roof stated:

> The event that truly awakened me was the Trayvon Martin case. I kept hearing and seeing his name, and eventually I decided to look him up. I read the Wikipedia article and right away I was unable to understand what the big deal was. It was obvious that Zimmerman was in the right. But more importantly this prompted me to type in the words "black on White crime" into Google, and I have never been the same since that day. The first website I came to was the Council of Conservative Citizens. There were pages upon pages of these brutal black on White murders. I was in disbelief. At this moment I realized that something was very wrong. How could the news be blowing up the Trayvon Martin case while hundreds of these black on White murders got ignored?[9]

Here we can see how Roof thought in terms of "it's not right, it's not fair, it's your fault, and you're evil" as justifications for what amounts to a terror attack. His beliefs made him receptive to propaganda put out by radical groups, with the result being a murderous rampage.

Types of Political Crimes

Considering this cognitive thought that produces political crime and terrorism, what are the specific crimes and what form do they take?

Election Fraud

Three city officials, including the mayor, in the small town of Cudahy, California, took part in a widespread corruption scheme that included accepting cash bribes from a marijuana dispensary, abusing drugs at City Hall, and tampering in city elections so they could continue their illegal activities. The three men opened mail-in absentee ballots: those cast in favor of the incumbent candidates were resealed and counted; ballots for challengers were discarded. Former mayor David Silva was sentenced to one year in federal prison, former councilman Osvaldo Conde received a three-year sentence, and former head of code enforcement and acting city manager Angel Perales was sentenced to five years' probation.[10]

Some political criminals want to shape elections to meet their personal needs. In some instances their goal is altruistic: the election of candidates who reflect their personal political views. In others, their actions are motivated by profit: they are paid by a candidate to rig the election. And in some cases, such as Silva, Conde, and Perales, the aim is to both get elected and profit from their political office.

Whatever the motive, **election fraud** is illegal interference with the political process. Acts of fraud tend to involve affecting vote counts to bring about a desired election outcome, whether by increasing the vote share of the favored candidate, depressing the vote share of the rival candidates, or both.

Election fraud has been a feature of political life since Roman times. In addition to discarding absentee ballots, it includes a variety of behaviors designed to give a candidate or his/her party an unfair advantage:

- *Intimidation.* Voters can be scared away from the polls through threats or intimidation. Having armed guards posted at polling places may convince people it is dangerous to vote. Lists of registered voters can be obtained and people subjected to threatening calls before the election.
- *Disruption.* Bomb threats can be called into voting places in areas that are known to heavily favor the opposing party,

AP Images/Hawk Eye, John Gaines

with the goal of suppressing the vote. There can be outright sabotage of polling places, ballots, ballot boxes, and voting machines.

- *Misinformation.* Flyers are sent out to voters registered with the opposition party containing misleading information such as the wrong election date or saying that rules have been changed about who is eligible to vote.

- *Registration fraud.* Political operatives may try to shape the outcome of an election by busing in ineligible voters from other districts. Because many jurisdictions require minimal identification and proof of citizenship, political criminals find it easy to get around residency requirements. They may provide conspirators with change-of-address forms to allow them to vote in a particular election, when in fact no actual change of address has occurred.

- *Vote buying.* Securing votes by payment or other rewards or the selling of one's vote is an age-old problem that still exists. One popular method is to buy absentee ballots from people who are in need of cash. The fraudulent voter can then be sure the vote goes his way, an outcome that cannot be guaranteed if the co-conspirator casts a secret ballot at a polling place.

Most states have created laws to control and punish vote fraud. The federal government has a number of statutes designed to control and/or restrict fraud, including 18 U.S.C. § 594, which provides:

> Whoever intimidates, threatens, coerces, or attempts to intimidate, threaten, or coerce, any other person for the purpose of interfering with the right of such other person to vote or to vote as he may choose, or of causing such other person to vote for, or not to vote for, any candidate for the office of President, Vice President, Presidential elector, Member of the Senate, Member of the House of Representatives, Delegate from the District of Columbia, or Resident Commissioner, at any election held solely or in part for the purpose of electing such candidate, shall be fined under this title or imprisoned not more than one year, or both.

Another provision that applies to voting is 18 U.S.C. § 245(b)(1)(A):

> Whoever, whether or not acting under color of law, by force or threat of force willfully injures, intimidates or interferes with, or attempts to injure, intimidate or interfere with (1) any person because he is or has been, or in order to intimidate such person or any other person or any class of persons from (A) voting or qualifying to vote, qualifying or campaigning as a candidate for elective office, or qualifying or acting as a poll watcher, or any legally authorized election official, in any primary, special, or general election.

This provision is in the Civil Rights section of Title 18, the federal criminal code, and it protects the right of all citizens to vote and campaign for office.

How common is voting fraud? According to NYU Law School's Brennan Center for Justice, while claims of voter fraud are common, actual cases in the United States are rare. There have only been a handful of substantiated cases of individual ineligible voters attempting to defraud the election system. One reason is that fraud by individual voters is an ineffective way to attempt to win an election. Each act of voter fraud in connection with a federal election risks five years in prison and a $10,000 fine, in addition to any state penalties, and yields at most one vote. When properly investigated, most accusations turn out to be a matter of mistake rather than intentional fraud—for example, a person attempting to vote under a false name can be traced back to a typo.[11]

Despite the evidence, not all groups are convinced election fraud is a rare occurrence, and many government officials consider it rampant.[12] In response, most states have passed laws requiring voter IDs in order to cut down on fraud. Today, at least 33 states have voter identification requirements: 19 states require voters to present photo identification; 14 states accept other forms of identification. Most common IDs include a driver's license, a state-issued identification card, or a military identification card.

Abuse of Office/Public Corruption

In 2015, Senator Bob Menendez became the 12th United States senator to be indicted while in office. Menendez, the top Democrat on the Senate Foreign Relations Committee, was accused of corruption, the charges alleging that he used his office to help Salomon Melgen, a Florida ophthalmologist and political donor, who was found guilty of Medicare fraud.[13] Menendez is believed to have received personal favors from Melgen, including plane tickets to vacation resorts; he has denied all charges and his case is now wending its way through the court system.

Menendez is not the only well-known politician accused of using their office for personal enrichment. Former Illinois governor Rod Blagojevich is serving a 14-year sentence in federal prison following conviction for corruption and the soliciting of bribes for political appointments, including an attempt to sell the US Senate seat formerly occupied by Barack Obama. Detroit Mayor Kwame Kilpatrick was sentenced in 2013 to a 28-year prison term for his role in a wide-ranging racketeering conspiracy. Kilpatrick extorted money from people doing business with the city, rigged bids, took bribes, and illegally appropriated funds from nonprofit civic organizations.[14]

Public corruption involves a breach of public trust and/or abuse of position by government officials and their private sector accomplices. Whether elected, appointed, or hired, they are committing a crime if while in office they demand, solicit, accept, or agree to receive anything of value in return for being manipulated in the performance of their official duties. They and their relatives and friends may be the recipients of illegal funds from businesspeople willing to bribe to gain public contracts and other government actions. The victims of public corruption are the general public, who pay for corruption through inflated costs and sometimes higher taxes.

Treason

LO3 Compare and contrast the terms *espionage* and *treason*.

treason
An act of disloyalty to one's nation or state.

Treason, is an act of disloyalty to one's nation or state. While the crime of treason is well known and the word "traitor" is a generic term, there have actually been fewer than 40 prosecutions for treason in the entire history of the United States, and most have resulted in acquittal.

Because treason is considered such a heinous crime, and to deter would-be traitors, many nations apply or have applied the death penalty to those convicted of attempting to overthrow the existing government. Treason was considered particularly loathsome under English common law, and until the nineteenth century it was punishable by being "drawn and quartered," a method of execution that involved hanging the offender, removing their intestines while still living, and finally cutting the offender into four pieces for public display.

Acts can be considered treasonous in order to stifle political dissent. In eighteenth-century England, it was considered treasonous to merely criticize the king or his behavior, and not surprisingly, the American colonists feared giving their own central government that much power. Therefore *treason is the only crime mentioned in the United States Constitution*, which defines treason as levying war against the United States or "in adhering to their Enemies, giving them Aid and Comfort," and requires the testimony of two witnesses or a confession in open court for conviction. The purpose of this was to limit the government's ability to bring charges of treason against opponents and to make it more difficult to prosecute those who are so charged.[15]

Today, the United States Criminal Code codifies treason as "whoever, owing allegiance to the United States, levies war against them or adheres to their enemies, giving them aid and comfort within the United States or elsewhere, is guilty of treason and shall suffer death, or shall be imprisoned not less than five years and fined under this title but not less than $10,000; and shall be incapable of holding any office under the United States."[16] Helping or cooperating with the enemy in a time of war would be considered treason; so too would be creating or recruiting a military force to help a foreign nation overthrow the government.

Some of the most famous cases of treason in US history include:

- In 1807, former Vice President Aaron Burr, a man best known for killing Secretary of the Treasury Alexander Hamilton in 1804 in a duel over a matter of honor, was accused of hatching a plot to separate the western states from the Union. When that plot went awry, he conspired to seize Mexico and set up a puppet government with himself as king! Arrested on charges of treason, he was acquitted when the Supreme Court, headed by Justice John Marshall, ruled that to be guilty of treason an overt act must be committed; planning is not enough.[17]
- On the evening of October 16, 1859, John Brown, a staunch abolitionist, and a group of his supporters captured prominent citizens and seized the federal armory and arsenal at Harpers Ferry, Virginia (now part of West Virginia). Brown had hopes of creating a popular slave rebellion. He was convicted of treason against the Commonwealth of Virginia and executed for attempting to organize armed resistance to slavery.[18]
- After World War II, Iva Ikuko Toguri D'Aquino, a Japanese American woman born in Los Angeles and known as Tokyo Rose, and Mildred Elizabeth Gillars, born in Portland, Maine, and known as Axis Sally, served prison terms for broadcasting for the Axis powers in an effort to demoralize American troops.[19]

Espionage

Robert Hanssen was a counterintelligence agent for the FBI assigned to detect and identify Russian spies. A former Chicago police officer, Hanssen's assignment required him to have access to sensitive top-secret information. In one of the most shocking cases in US history, Hanssen volunteered to become a paid spy for the KGB during the Cold War and over a period of 15 years received at least $1.4 million in cash and diamonds. He was arrested on February 18, 2001, after leaving a package of classified documents for his Russian handlers under a footbridge in a park outside Washington. During his years as a double agent, Hanssen not only provided more than 6,000 pages of documents to the Soviet Union but also caused the death of two US double agents whose identities were uncovered with the aid of his secret documents. The Hanssen case was the subject of the 2007 film *Breach*, which starred Chris Cooper as the corrupt agent.[20] He is currently serving multiple life sentences in a supermax prison.

Espionage (more commonly called "spying") is the practice of obtaining information about a government, organization, or society that is considered secret or confidential without the permission of the holder of the information. Espionage involves obtaining the information illegally by covertly entering the area where the information is stored, secretly photographing forbidden areas, or subverting through threat or payoff people who know the information and will divulge it through subterfuge.[21]

Espionage is typically associated with spying on potential or actual enemies, by a foreign agent who is working for his or her nation's intelligence service. With the end of the Cold War, the threat of espionage seemed reduced until 2010, when a major Russian spy group was unraveled and 10 people arrested. These were sleeper agents who had spent decades fitting seamlessly in their new environment. Neighbors were shocked to find out that "Richard Murphy" and "Cynthia Murphy" were actually spies named Vladimir Guryev and Lydia Guryev, while "Michael Zottoli" and "Patricia Mills" were in reality Mikhail Kutsik and Natalia Pereverzeva, agents of the Russian Federation. The case was settled when the Russians were exchanged for four American spies being held in Russian prisons.

Not all spies are foreign nationals. There are numerous cases of homegrown spies who are motivated by misguided altruism or belief. Others, like Robert Hanssen, were looking for profit:

- Aldrich Ames was a 31-year veteran of the Central Intelligence Agency (CIA) who spied for the Russians. In the four years he spent turning over secrets to the KGB, Ames was paid $1.88 million. He is now serving a life sentence.[22]

FACT OR FICTION?

Treason is the only crime mentioned in the United States Constitution.

FACT Treason is considered so serious that it is the only crime set out in the Constitution. Article 3, Section 3 defines treason and its punishment:

Treason against the United States, shall consist only in levying War against them, or in adhering to their Enemies, giving them Aid and Comfort. No Person shall be convicted of Treason unless on the Testimony of two Witnesses to the same overt Act, or on Confession in open Court. The Congress shall have Power to declare the Punishment of Treason, but no Attainder of Treason shall work Corruption of Blood, or Forfeiture except during the Life of the Person attainted.

The phrase "Corruption of Blood" refers to the fact that the children of people convicted of treason would not be punished or attainted as they were in England.

---

espionage
The practice of obtaining information about a government, organization, or society that is considered secret or confidential without the permission of the holder of the information. Commonly called spying.

- Harold Nicholson was the highest ranking CIA official ever convicted for spying for a foreign country. He sold American secrets to Russia for more than $1.4 million in cash and diamonds; he is currently serving a prison sentence and is scheduled for release in 2024.[23]

INDUSTRIAL ESPIONAGE In 2014, five Chinese men were indicted for stealing thousands of "sensitive, internal communications" from US companies, including Alcoa, United States Steel Corporation, and Westinghouse.[24] The concept of espionage has been extended to spying involving corporations, referred to as industrial espionage. This involves such unethical or illegal activities as bribing employees to reveal trade secrets such as computer codes or product formulas. The traditional methods of industrial espionage include recruiting agents and inserting them into the target company or breaking into an office to take equipment and information. It can also involve surveillance and spying on commercial organizations in order to determine the direction of their new product line or even what bid they intend to make on a government contract. Such knowledge can provide vast profits when it allows a competitor to save large sums on product development or to win an undeserved contract by underbidding.[25]

A report from the National Counterintelligence Center lists biotechnology, aerospace, telecommunications, computer software, transportation, advanced materials, energy research, defense, and semiconductor companies as the top targets for foreign economic espionage.[26]

The FBI has seen a sharp rise in economic espionage cases aimed at US companies, with a vast majority of the perpetrators originating from China with ties to that nation's government. Industrial spying on large corporations such as DuPont and Lockheed Martin has led to the loss of hundreds of billions of dollars. A recent survey conducted by the FBI found that more than 80 private companies have been victims of economic espionage or theft of trade secrets; about 95 percent of those attempts originated from individuals associated with the Chinese government.[27] Espionage is often carried out with "insider threats," or employees who are familiar with the inner workings of a particular technology being recruited by foreign agents in exchange for large amounts of cash.

A number of factors have combined to facilitate private-sector technology theft. Globalization, while generating major gains for the US economy, has given foreigners unprecedented access to US firms and to sensitive technologies. There has also been a proliferation of devices that have made it easy for private-sector experts to illegally retrieve, store, and transfer massive amounts of information, including trade secrets and proprietary data; such devices are increasingly common in the workplace.

In addition to private citizens conducting espionage, foreign government organizations also mount their own operations, including targeting US firms for technology that would strengthen their foreign defense capabilities. One method is to employ commercial firms in the United States in a covert effort to target and acquire US technology. They also form ventures with US firms in the hope of placing collectors in proximity to sensitive technologies or else establishing foreign research.

LEGAL CONTROLS Until 1996, there was no federal statute that explicitly penalized industrial espionage. Recognizing the increasingly important role that intellectual property plays in the well-being of the American economy, Congress enacted the Economic Espionage Act (EEA) of 1996, which criminalizes the theft of trade secrets. The EEA actually contains two separate provisions, one that specifically penalizes foreign agents for stealing American trade secrets and one directed at all forms of spying.

Convictions of foreign agents under the Economic Espionage Act have been relatively rare. One well-known case involved former Boeing engineer Dongfan "Greg" Chung, who was sentenced to 16 years in prison in 2009; it was the first trial conviction under the EEA. Chung, a native of China, was convicted of selling Boeing trade secrets related to the US space shuttle program and the Delta IV rocket technologies to China; he had more than 350,000 stolen documents hidden underneath his house.[28]

state political crime
Political crime that arises from the efforts of the state to either maintain governmental power or to uphold the race, class, and gender advantages of those who support the government. It is possible to divide state political crimes into five varieties: (1) political corruption, (2) illegal domestic surveillance, (3) human rights violations, (4) state violence such as torture, illegal imprisonment, police violence and use of deadly force, and (5) state corporate crime committed by individuals who abuse their state authority or who fail to exercise it when working with people and organizations in the private sector.

State Political Crime

While some political crimes are committed by people who oppose the state, others are perpetrated by state authorities against the people they are supposed to serve; this is referred to as **state political crime**. Critical criminologists argue that rather than being committed by disaffected people, a great deal of political crime arises from the efforts of the state to either maintain governmental power or to uphold the race, class, and gender advantages of those who support the government. In industrial society, the state will do everything to protect the property rights of the wealthy while opposing the real interests of the poor. They might even go to war to support the capitalist classes who need the wealth and resources of other nations. The desire for natural resources such as rubber, oil, and metals was one of the primary reasons for Japan's invasion of China and other Eastern nations that sparked their entry into World War II.

USING TORTURE Of all state political crimes, the use of **torture** such as using electric shocks or **waterboarding** to gain information from suspected political criminals is perhaps the most notorious.

Can the torture of a suspected terrorist determined to destroy the government and harm innocent civilians ever be permissible or is it always an example of state-sponsored political crime? While most people loathe the thought of torturing anyone, some experts argue that torture can sometimes be justified in what they call the **ticking bomb scenario**. Suppose the government found out that a captured terrorist knew the whereabouts of a dangerous explosive device that was set to go off and kill thousands of innocent people. Would it be permissible to use torture on this single suspect if it would save the population of a city?

The ticking bomb scenario has appeal. Famed social commentator and legal scholar Alan Dershowitz argues that the "vast majority" of Americans would expect law enforcement agents to use any means necessary to obtain information needed to prevent a terror attack. To protect against abuse, Dershowitz proposes the creation of a "torture warrant" that can only be issued by a judge in cases where (a) there is an absolute need to obtain immediate information in order to save lives and (b) there is probable cause that the suspect has such information and is unwilling to reveal it to law enforcement agents. The suspect would be given immunity from prosecution based on information elicited by the torture; it would only be to save lives. The warrant would limit the torture to nonlethal means, such as sterile needles being inserted beneath the nails to cause excruciating pain without endangering life.[29]

Not everyone agrees with Dershowitz.[30] Opponents of torture believe that even imminent danger does not justify state violence. There is a danger that such state-sponsored violence would become calculated and premeditated; torturers would have to be trained, ready, and in place for the ticking bomb argument to work. We couldn't be running around looking for torturers with a bomb set to go off, could we? Because torturers would be part of the government bureaucracy, there is no way to ensure that they would only use their skills in certain morally justifiable cases.[31] What happens if a superior officer tells them to torture someone, but they believe the order is unjustified? Should they follow orders or risk a court-martial for being disobedient? Furthermore, there is very little empirical evidence suggesting that torture provides any real benefits and much more that suggests it can create serious problems. It can damage civil rights and democratic institutions and cause the general public to have sympathy for the victims of torture no matter their evil intent.[32]

LO4 List the components of state political crime.

torture
An act that causes severe pain or suffering, whether physical or mental, that is intentionally inflicted on a person for such purposes as obtaining a confession, punishing them for a crime they may have committed, or intimidating or coercing them into a desired action.

waterboarding
Immobilizing a person on his or her back, with the head inclined downward, and pouring water over the face and into the breathing passages, producing an immediate gag reflex and an experience akin to drowning; the subject believes his or her death is imminent.

ticking bomb scenario
A scenario that some experts argue in which torture can perhaps be justified if the government discovers that a captured terrorist knows the whereabouts of a dangerous explosive device that is set to go off and kill thousands of innocent people.

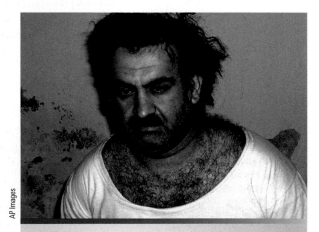

AP Images

Khalid Sheikh Mohammed, the mastermind of the 9/11 attacks, is shown here shortly after his capture. He was interrogated using waterboarding and other extreme measures. Held at Guantánamo Bay, he has asked for the death penalty so that he can become a martyr. Can the use of torture with suspected terrorists ever be appropriate or morally justified? Would someone like Mohammed ever give intelligence voluntarily?

Terrorism

On November 13, 2015, a coordinated series of terrorist attacks stunned Paris. There were suicide bombings and mass shootings at a stadium, cafés, restaurants, and the Bataclan theatre, where an American rock group was playing. In all, the attacks took the lives of 130 people and injured 368. Seven of the attackers were killed, though others were able to flee. IS (Islamic State) claimed responsibility. The attack was a follow-up to the January 2015 attacks on the offices of the satirical newspaper *Charlie Hebdo* and a Jewish supermarket in Paris, which killed 17 people and wounded 22, including civilians and police officers.[33] The Paris attacks were followed by a truck attack in Nice: on July 14, 2016, as people were celebrating Bastille Day on the Promenade des Anglais, an IS follower named Mohamed Lahouaiej-Bouhlel drove a 19-ton cargo truck into the crowds, killing 86 people and injuring 434, before being shot and killed by police.[34] Other European nations have not escaped IS wrath, including England, where patrons leaving an Ariana Grande concert were attacked by Salman Abedi, a suicide bomber who managed to kill 22 people and injure scores of others in the attack.[35]

These attacks hammer home the fact that the political crime that the general public, law enforcement agents, and criminologists are most concerned with is terrorism. What could possibly motivate people to commit such horrific acts of random violence? Scholars and experts debated the causes, but IS had begun warning Western nations a year earlier that its fighters would kill enemies of Islam wherever they could be found. The attackers were not seeking a homeland or to topple a government, they merely wanted bloody retribution for perceived wrongs. Their intent is revealed in the statement they issued after the Manchester attack in which they claimed the attack against the young concert-goers was motivated by revenge:

> With Allah's grace and support, a soldier of the Khilafah managed to place explosive devices in the midst of the gatherings of the Crusaders in the British city of Manchester, in revenge for Allah's religion, in an endeavor to terrorize the mushrikin, and in response to their transgressions against the land of the Muslims. The explosive devices were detonated in the shameless concert arena, resulting in 30 Crusaders being killed and 70 others being wounded. And what comes next will be more severe on the worshipers of the Cross and their allies, by Allah's permission. And all praises due to Allah, Lord of the creation.

Defining Terrorism

Despite its long history, it is often difficult to precisely define terrorism (from the Latin *terrere*, which means to frighten) and to separate terrorist acts from interpersonal crimes of violence. If a group robs a bank to obtain funds for its revolutionary struggles, should the act be treated as terrorism or as a common bank robbery? In this instance, defining a crime as terrorism depends on the kind of legal response the act evokes from those in power. To be considered **terrorism**, which is a political crime, an act must carry with it the intent to disrupt and change the government and must not be merely a common-law crime committed for greed or egotism.

According to the US State Department, the term *terrorism* means premeditated, politically motivated violence perpetrated against noncombatant targets by subnational groups or clandestine agents, usually intended to influence an audience. The term *international terrorism* means terrorism involving citizens or the territory of more than one country.[36] The United Nations has employed this definition created by Alex Schmid and A. Jongman:

> Terrorism is an anxiety-inspiring method of repeated violent action, employed by (semi-)clandestine individual, group or state actors, for idiosyncratic, criminal or political reasons, whereby—in contrast to assassination—the direct targets of violence are not the main targets. The immediate human victims of violence are generally chosen randomly (targets of opportunity) or selectively (representative or symbolic targets) from a target population, and serve as message generators. Threat- and violence-based communication processes between terrorist (organization),

Tamerlan Tsarnaev and Dzhokhar Tsarnaev, the two brothers who carried out the Boston Marathon bombings, are shown here on a video capture as they prepare to plant their bombs. The marathon bombing shows that the threat of domestic terror is real and that a terrorist may be the young man sitting next to you in class (Dzhokhar Tsarnaev was a student at the University of Massachusetts at Dartmouth at the time of the bombing).

(imperiled) victims, and main targets are used to manipulate the main target (audience[s]), turning it into a target of terror, a target of demands, or a target of attention, depending on whether intimidation, coercion, or propaganda is primarily sought.[37]

Terrorism usually involves a type of political crime that emphasizes violence as a mechanism to promote change. Whereas some political criminals sell secrets, spy, and the like, terrorists systematically murder and destroy or threaten such violence to terrorize individuals, groups, communities, or governments into conceding to the terrorists' political demands.[38] Because terrorists lack large armies and formidable weapons, their use of subterfuge, secrecy, and hit-and-run tactics is designed to give them a psychological advantage and the power to neutralize the physical superiority of their opponents. They can strike anywhere at any time; the government can do nothing to stop the attacks.

However, it may be erroneous to assume that all terrorists have political goals. Some may try to bring about what they consider to be social reform—for example, by attacking women wearing fur coats or sabotaging property during a labor dispute. Terrorism must also be distinguished from conventional warfare, because it requires secrecy and clandestine operations to exert social control over large populations.[39] So terrorist activities may be aimed at promoting an ideology other than political change.

LO5 Distinguish among terrorists, insurgents, guerillas, and revolutionaries.

Terrorist and Guerilla

The word *terrorist* is often used interchangeably with the word *guerilla*, but the terms are quite different. **Guerilla** comes from the Spanish term meaning "little war," which developed out of the Spanish rebellion against French troops after Napoleon's 1808 invasion of the Iberian Peninsula.[40] Terrorists have an urban focus. Operating in small bands, or cadres, of three to five members, they target the property or persons of their enemy, such as members of the ruling class.[41] However, terrorists may not have political ambitions, and their actions may be aimed at stifling or intimidating other groups who oppose their political, social, or economic views. Terrorists who kill abortion providers in order to promote their "pro-life" agenda are not aiming for regime change. Guerillas, on the other hand, are armed military bands, typically located in rural areas, that attack military, police, and government officials in an effort to destabilize the existing government. Their organizations can grow quite large and eventually take the form of a conventional military force. Some guerilla bands infiltrate urban areas (urban guerillas). For the most part, guerillas are a type of insurgent band.

terrorism
The illegal use of force against innocent people to achieve a political objective.

guerilla
The term means "little war" and developed out of the Spanish rebellion against French troops after Napoleon's 1808 invasion of the Iberian Peninsula. Today the term is often used interchangeably with the term *terrorist*.

Here, militants from the Islamic State lead away captured Iraqi soldiers. The militants boasted on Twitter that they had executed 1,700 Iraqi government soldiers. IS has beheaded and burned to death those who oppose their regime and destroyed ancient relics in their effort to create an independent and all-powerful caliphate in Syria and Iraq.

Terrorist and Insurgent

An insurgency is a political movement that may use terror tactics to achieve their goals. **Insurgents** wish to confront the existing government for control of all or a portion of its territory, or force concessions in sharing political power by competing with the opposition government for popular support.[42] What makes the insurgent unique is that they have the luxury of receiving aid from neighboring sympathizers, allowing them to base their insurgency outside the target nation, thereby protecting them from their enemies. Taliban members took shelter in Pakistan when the US military drove them out of Afghanistan. Insurgencies may attract recruits who do not actually live in the disputed area but are sympathetic to the cause. In 2014, insurgents from ISIL (the Islamic State in Iraq and the Levant) surged into Iraq from Syria, routed the Iraqi army, and occupied major cities such as Mosul. ISIL, now commonly referred to as the Islamic State (IS), is a violent Sunni extremist group that has the goal of creating a caliphate, based on a very conservative Islamic religious code, that spans Sunni-dominated sections of Iraq and Syria. IS is made up of Islamist fighters from around the world, highly trained and motivated. They were able to launch their insurgency after organizing outside of Iraq and then filtering through the porous border with Syria where they play a major role in the ongoing civil war.[43]

Insurgents tend to live isolated and stressful lives and enjoy varying levels of public support.[44] Although insurgents may engage in violence, they also may use nonviolent methods or political tactics. They may set up food distribution centers and schools in areas in which they gain control. Their good deeds provide the population with needed services while contrasting their benevolent rule with the government's incompetence and corruption.

insurgent
The typical goal of an insurgency is to confront the existing government for control of all or a portion of its territory, or force concessions in sharing political power. While terrorists may operate in small bands with a narrow focus, insurgents represent a popular movement and may also seek external support from other nations to bring pressure on the government.

Terrorist and Revolutionary

A revolution (from the Latin *revolutio*, "a revolving," and *revolvere*, "turn, roll back") is generally seen as a civil war fought between nationalists and a sovereign power that holds control of the land, or between the existing government and local groups over issues of ideology and power. Historically, the American Revolution may be considered an example of a struggle between nationalistic groups and an imperialistic overseas government. Classic examples of ideological rebellions are the French Revolution, which pitted the middle class and urban poor against the aristocracy, and the Russian Revolution of 1917, during which the Czarist government was toppled by the Bolsheviks. More recent ideological revolutions have occurred in China, Cuba, Nicaragua, and Chile, to name but a few.

While some revolutions (such as the American, French, and Russian) rely on armed force, terror activities, and violence, others can be nonviolent, depending on large urban protests and threats. Such was the case when the Shah Mohammad Reza Pahlavi was toppled in Iran in the 1979 revolution that transformed Iran into an Islamic republic under the rule of Ayatollah Ruhollah Khomeini. Similar events unfolded in Egypt in early 2011 in the effort to topple the government of Hosni Mubarak that had been in power for 30 years.

Concept Summary 11.1 describes the components of various types of radical political groups.

Concept Summary 11.1   The Various Forms of Radical Political Groups

	Terrorist	Guerilla	Insurgent	Revolutionary
Description	Groups who engage in premeditated, politically motivated violence perpetrated against noncombatant targets.	Armed groups operating in rural areas who attack the military, the police, and other government officials.	Groups who engage in armed uprising, or revolt against an established civil or political authority.	Engages in civil war against sovereign power that holds control of the land.
Examples	Al-Qaeda, Hamas	Mao's People's Liberation Army, Ho Chi Minh's Viet Cong	Iraqi insurgent groups	American Revolution, French Revolution, Russian Revolution
Goals	Personal, criminal, or political gain or change.	Replace or overthrow existing government.	Win over population by showing government's incompetence. Force government into political concessions and/or power sharing.	Gain independence or oust existing government or monarchy.
Methods	Small, clandestine cells who use systematic violence for purpose of intimidation.	Use unconventional warfare and mobile tactics. May grow large and use tactics similar to conventional military force.	May use violent (bombings and kidnappings) or nonviolent means (food distribution centers and creating schools).	Can use violent armed conflict or nonviolent methods such as Gandhi used in India.

A Brief History of Terrorism

While terrorist-like activities have been known since Roman times, the term *terrorist* first became popular during the French Revolution. Use of the word *terrorism* began in 1793 in reference to the **Reign of Terror** initiated by the revolutionary government during which agents of the Committee of Public Safety and the National Convention were referred to as terrorists. In response, royalists and opponents of the revolution employed terrorist tactics in resistance to the revolutionists. The widespread use of the guillotine is an infamous reminder of the revolutionary violence; urban mobs demanded blood, and many government officials and aristocrats were beheaded in gruesome public spectacles. From the fall of the Bastille on July 14, 1789, until July 1794, thousands suspected of counterrevolutionary activity were killed on the guillotine. Here again, the relative nature of political crime is documented: most victims of the French Reign of Terror were revolutionaries who had been denounced by rival factions, whereas thousands of the hated nobility lived in relative tranquility. The end of the terror was signaled by the death of its prime mover, Maximilien Robespierre, on July 28, 1794, as the result of a successful plot to end his rule. He was executed on the same guillotine to which he had sent almost 20,000 people.

Reign of Terror
The origin of the term *terrorism*, the French Revolution's Reign of Terror began in 1793 and was initiated by the revolutionary government during which agents of the Committee of Public Safety and the National Convention were referred to as terrorists.

In the hundred years following the French Revolution, terrorism continued to be a political tool around the world. Terrorist acts became the preferred method of political action for national groups in the early years of the twentieth century. In Eastern Europe, the Internal Macedonian Revolutionary Organization campaigned against the Turkish government, which controlled its homeland (Macedonia became part of the former Yugoslavia). Similarly, the protest of the "Union or Death" society, or Black Hand, against the Austro-Hungarian Empire's control of Serbia led to the group's assassination of Archduke Franz Ferdinand, which started World War I. Russia was the scene of left-wing revolutionary activity, which killed the tsar in 1918 and gave birth to the Marxist state.

After the war ended, the Treaty of Versailles restructured Europe and broke up the Austro-Hungarian Empire. The result was a hodgepodge of new nations controlled by majority ethnic groups. Self-determination was limited to European nations and ethnic groups and denied to others, especially the colonial possessions of the major European powers, creating bitterness and setting the stage for the long conflicts of the anticolonial period. The Irish Republican Army, established around 1916, steadily battled British forces from 1919 to 1922, culminating in the Republic of Ireland gaining independence.

Between the World Wars, right-wing terrorism existed in Germany, Spain, and Italy. One source of tension, according to author Michael Kellogg, was the virulently anti-Communist exiles (called White Russians) who fled Russia after the 1917 revolution and took up residence in Germany and other Western nations. According to Kellogg, between 1920 and 1923, Adolf Hitler was deeply influenced by the émigrés' Aufbau Vereinigung (Reconstruction Organization). Members of the Aufbau allied with the Nazis to overthrow the legitimate German government and thwart German communists from seizing power. The White Russians' deep-seated anti-Semitism may have inspired Hitler to go public with his campaign to kill European Jews, prompting both the Holocaust and the invasion of Russia, which spelled the eventual doom of Hitler and National Socialism.

During World War II, resistance to the occupying German troops was common throughout Europe. The Germans considered the resistors to be terrorists, but the rest of the world considered them heroes. Meanwhile, in Palestine, Jewish terrorist groups—the Haganah, the Irgun, and the Stern Gang, whose leaders included Menachem Begin, who later became Israel's prime minister—waged war against the British to force them to allow Jewish survivors of the Holocaust to settle in their traditional homeland. Today, of course, many of these alleged terrorists are considered freedom fighters who laid down their lives for a just cause.

After the war, Arab nationalists felt that they had been betrayed. Believing they were promised postwar independence, they were doubly disappointed—first when the French and British were given authority over their lands, and then especially when the British allowed Zionist immigration into Palestine in keeping with a promise contained in the Balfour Declaration. Hence, the creation of the PLO and Hamas.

Since the end of World War II, terrorism has accelerated its development into a major component of contemporary conflict. Primarily in use immediately after the war as a subordinate element of anticolonial insurgencies, it has expanded beyond that role. In the service of various ideologies and aspirations, terrorism sometimes supplanted other forms of conflict completely. It became a far-reaching weapon capable of effects no less global than the intercontinental bomber or missile.

Contemporary Forms of Terrorism

LO6 Enumerate the various forms of terrorism.

Today the term *terrorism* encompasses many different behaviors and goals. Some of the more common forms are briefly described here.

Political Terrorism

Political terrorism is directed at people or groups who oppose the terrorists' political ideology or whom the terrorists define as "outsiders" who must be destroyed. Political terrorists may not want to replace the existing government but to shape it so that it accepts the terrorists' views.

RIGHT-WING POLITICAL GROUPS Domestic terrorists in the United States can be found across the political spectrum. On the right, they tend to be heavily armed groups organized around such themes as white supremacy, anti-abortion, militant tax resistance, and religious revisionism. Identified groups have included, at one time or another, the Aryan Republican Army, the Aryan Nation, the Posse Comitatus, and the Ku Klux Klan. These groups want to shape US government policy over a range of matters, including ending abortion rights, extending the right to bear arms, and eliminating federal taxation. According to federal officials, they are often organized into paramilitary groups that follow a military-style rank hierarchy.[45] They tend to stockpile illegal weapons and ammunition, trying illegally to get their hands on fully automatic firearms or attempting to convert weapons to fully automatic. They also try to buy or manufacture improvised explosive devices and typically engage in wilderness, survival, or other paramilitary training. Many militia extremists view themselves as protecting the US Constitution, other US laws, or their own individual liberties. They believe that the Constitution grants citizens the power to take back the federal government by force or violence if they feel it's necessary. They oppose gun control efforts and fear the widespread disarming of Americans by the federal government. Militia extremists often subscribe to various conspiracy theories regarding government. One of their primary theories is that the United Nations—which they refer to as the New World Order, or NWO—has the right to use its military forces anywhere in the world. The extremists often train and prepare for what they foresee as an inevitable invasion of the US by United Nations forces. Many militia extremists also wrongly believe that the federal government will relocate citizens to camps controlled by the Federal Emergency Management Agency (FEMA) or force them to undergo vaccinations. Although unlikely to topple the government, these individualistic acts of terror are difficult to predict or control. On April

Political terrorists may target groups whom they consider outsiders who must be eliminated. Here, Frazier Glenn Cross, also known as Frazier Glenn Miller, is escorted by police in Overland Park, Kansas. Cross, 73, a white supremacist and former Ku Klux Klan leader, was convicted of killing three people in attacks at a Jewish community center and Jewish retirement complex near Kansas City. At his 2015 trial he called the shootings "righteous" and "honorable"; none of his three victims was Jewish. Cross is currently on death row awaiting execution.

19, 1995, in the most deadly right-wing attack, 168 people were killed in the Oklahoma City bombing, the most severe example of homegrown political terrorism in the United States so far.

Some right-wing militants target specific groups. Activists have demonstrated at abortion clinics, attacked clients, bombed offices, and killed doctors who perform abortions. On October 23, 1998, Dr. Barnett Slepian was shot by a sniper and killed in his Buffalo, New York, home; he was one of a growing number of abortion providers believed to be the victims of terrorists who ironically claim to be "pro-life." Another favorite target is law enforcement officers. Between 1990 and 2013, far-right extremists killed 50 federal, state, and local law enforcement officers in the line of duty in 33 separate incidents. More than two-thirds were killed during ideologically motivated attacks; the remaining officers were killed in non-ideological confrontations (e.g., while arresting an individual during a bank robbery). In addition, corrections officers, private security guards, and a judge have been killed during ideologically motivated attacks.[46]

LEFT-WING POLITICAL GROUPS During the turmoil of the 1960s, a number of left-wing political groups, such as the Weather Underground, emerged to challenge the existing power structure. Today, left-leaning domestic terror groups are committed to the protection of the environment. Of these groups, the Earth Liberation Front (ELF) is perhaps the best known. Founded in 1992 in Brighton, England, by members of the Earth First! environmental movement, ELF has been active since 1994 throughout the world, including the United States. Operating in secret, ELF cells have conducted a series of actions intent on damaging individuals or corporations they consider a threat to the environment. On October 19, 1998, ELF members claimed responsibility for fires that were set atop Vail Mountain, a luxurious ski resort in Colorado, claiming that the action was designed to stop the resort from expanding into animal habitats (especially that of the mountain lynx); the fires caused an estimated $12 million in damages.

Another group, the Animal Liberation Front (ALF), focuses their efforts on protecting animals from being used as food, in clothing, or as experimental subjects. Their philosophy is that animals are entitled to the moral right to possess their own lives and control their own bodies, while rejecting the view that animals are merely capital goods or property intended for the benefit of humans and can be bought, sold, or killed by humans.[47] ALF is still active—in 2015, members were responsible for "liberating" 5,740 mink from farms in Idaho, Iowa, Pennsylvania, Wisconsin, and Minnesota and also vandalizing property and destroying breeding records in an attempt to disrupt the fur breeding economy.[48]

Despite a few such incidents, left-wing terror groups have all but ceased operations.

Revolutionary Terrorism

Revolutionary terrorists use violence to frighten those in power and their supporters in order to replace the existing government with a regime that holds political or religious views that the terror group finds acceptable. Terrorist actions such as kidnapping, assassination, and bombing are designed to draw repressive responses from governments trying to defend themselves. These responses help revolutionaries to expose, through the skilled use of media coverage, the government's inhumane nature. The original reason for the government's harsh response may be lost as the effect of counterterrorist activities is felt by uninvolved people.

Jemaah Islamiyah, an Indonesian terrorist organization aligned with al-Qaeda, is believed to be intent on driving away foreign tourists and ruining the nation's economy so they can usurp the government and set up a pan-Islamic nation in Indonesia and neighboring Malaysia. Another example is Boko Haram, a fundamentalist Islamic group that has caused havoc in Nigeria, Africa's most populous country, through bombings, assassinations, and abductions. Its aim is to overthrow the government and create an Islamic state based on the concept "Anyone who is not governed by what Allah has revealed is among the transgressors." Boko Haram promotes a version of Islam that makes it *haram* (forbidden) for Muslims to take part in any political or social activity associated with Western society. This includes voting in elections, wearing shirts and trousers, and receiving a secular education. Boko Haram regards the Nigerian state as being run by nonbelievers—even when the country had a Muslim president—and it has extended its military campaign by targeting neighboring African states. It made international news in 2014 when the group abducted nearly 300 girls attending a Western school, saying it would treat them as slaves and marry them off—a reference to an ancient Islamic belief that women captured in conflict are part of the "war booty." A number of these girls have been repatriated, but the majority are still missing.[49]

Nationalist Terrorism

Nationalist terrorism promotes the interests of a minority ethnic or religious group that believes it has been persecuted under majority rule. Terrorist acts are designed to force the government to cede land so that the minority group can have its own independent nation. While revolutionary terrorists are aiming for regime change in their home country, nationalists want to create a separate country of their own.

In the Middle East, terrorist activities have been linked to the Palestinians' desire to create an independent state. At first, the Palestinian Liberation Organization (PLO), led by Yasser Arafat, directed terrorist activities against Israel. Now the group Hamas is perpetuating the conflict with Israel and is behind terrorist attacks that have sent thousands of missiles into Israeli territory, designed to elicit a sharp response from the Israeli army and air force in order to demonstrate to the world the righteousness of their cause. In 2014, three Israeli youths were kidnapped and killed by Hamas members, prompting Israeli military retaliation. Hamas amped up the tension by sending thousands of missiles into Israel, prompting increased intervention. Worldwide outrage prompted both sides to eventually back down and honor a ceasefire.

Hezbollah (from the Arabic, meaning "party of God") is a Lebanese Shi'ite Islamist organization founded in 1982 in response to the presence of Israeli forces in southern Lebanon. At inception, its goals were to both drive Israeli troops out of Lebanon and to form a Shi'ite Islamic republic in Lebanon. Taking its inspiration from Iran, Hezbollah members follow a distinct version of Shia ideology developed in Iran and have also received arms and financial support from Iran. Hezbollah is anti-West and anti-Israel and has engaged in a series of terrorist actions, including kidnappings, car bombings, and airline hijackings.[50] Recently, Hezbollah has shifted its focus and has become increasingly embroiled in the Syrian civil war, fighting for the Assad regime. Ironically, this shift has alienated some of its Lebanese constituents and prompted deadly reprisals in Beirut from partisans of the predominantly Sunni Muslim Syrian rebels. The US government and its European allies consider Hezbollah a global terrorist threat and a menace to Middle East stability.

The Middle East is not the only source of nationalistic fervor and terrorism. The Chinese government has been trying to suppress separatist groups fighting for an independent state in the northwestern province of Xinjiang. The rebels are drawn from the region's Uyghur people, most of whom practice Sufi Islam, speak a Turkic language, and wish to set up a Muslim state called Eastern Turkistan. During the past decade, the Uyghur separatists have organized demonstrations, bombings, and political assassinations. To control their rebellion, over the past decade, many prominent Uyghurs have been imprisoned after being accused of terrorism. Mass immigration of Han Chinese to Xinjiang have made Uyghurs a minority group in their own region.[51]

Retributive Terrorism

Some terrorist groups are not nationalist, political, or revolutionary organizations. Their main goal is not to set up their own homeland or topple a government (though that may be part of their plan) but rather want to punish people or governments for ideological, political, or religious reasons.[52] Al-Qaeda is the paradigm of the **retributive terrorist** organization. Rather than fighting for a homeland, its message is a call to take up a cause: there is a war of civilizations in which "Jews and Crusaders" want to destroy Islam and must therefore be defeated. Armed **jihad** is the individual obligation of every Muslim; terrorism and violence are appropriate methods for defeating even the strongest powers. The end product would be a unified Muslim world, the destruction of the West, and the end of decadent and depraved Western influence.

These themes are preached in schools and on the Internet, and disseminated in books and pamphlets. Videos are distributed in which al-Qaeda's leaders expound on political topics, going as far as calling Western leaders liars and drunkards. As a result of this media strategy, al-Qaeda's messages have penetrated deeply into Muslim communities around the world, finding a sympathetic response among many Muslims who have a sense of helplessness both in the Arab world and in the Western Muslim diaspora. Al-Qaeda offers a sense of empowerment to young men who feel lost in their adopted cultures, prompting many to travel to the Middle East to receive terror training.[53]

In Somalia, another retributive terror group, al-Shabaab, has shifting goals and priorities. They do not hesitate to attack real or imagined opponents in other nations. In 2013, they attacked the Westgate Mall in Nairobi, Kenya, resulting in hundreds of casualties and more than 60 deaths. On April 2, 2015, al-Shabaab gunmen attacked the Garissa University campus in Kenya, killing 148 students before being rooted out by security forces. In the aftermath of the attack, al-Shabaab spokespersons pledged a "long, gruesome war" in retaliation for Kenya's security forces joining with other nations of the African Union to fight al-Shabaab.[54] The group has also been linked to criminal activity. They require a share of the payment of ransoms given to Somali pirates who launch cross-ocean raids from the al-Shabaab–controlled territory; piracy would be impossible without cooperation from al-Shabaab. The group is also heavily involved in smuggling, slapping taxes on illegal charcoal exports to the Gulf, arms shipments from Yemen, and electronic goods destined for the region.[55] The most dangerous and well-known retributive group is the so-called Islamic State, discussed in the Policies and Issues in Criminology feature.

retributive terrorists
Terror groups who refrain from tying specific acts to direct demands for change. They want to instead redirect the balance between what they believe is good and evil. They see their revolution as existing on a spiritual plane; their mission is to exact retribution against sinners.

jihad
Has three meanings: (1) a true believer's internal struggle to live as a devout Muslim, (2) to build a Muslim society, (3) to defend Islam, with force if necessary, against nonbelievers.

AP Images/Rex Features

Here, on May 22, 2017, police and other emergency services are seen helping a victim near the Manchester (England) Arena after a terrorist exploded a suicide bomb following an Ariana Grande concert. Twenty-two people, including an eight-year-old girl, were killed and 59 injured. The Islamic State (IS) claimed responsibility for the attack.

Policies and Issues in Criminology

THE ISLAMIC STATE

The Islamic State of Iraq and the Levant (ISIL), also known as the Islamic State of Iraq and al-Sham (ISIS) or simply the Islamic State (IS), startled the world in the summer of 2014 when it took control of cities in Syria and Iraq defended by large contingents of enemy soldiers, who threw down their weapons and abandoned their posts. Those who actually fought were captured and killed in extremely brutal ways, through burning or decapitation. In the aftermath of its success, IS declared itself a caliphate, governed by Sharia law. Nonbelievers and opponents were killed in public executions. When Iraqi and Syrian forces tried to recapture lost territory, they only made headway under cover of US and other allies' air strikes. Despite this show of force, IS still held sway over significant territory.

Where did this deadly group come from? How did it get its start? IS origins can be traced back to 2002, when Abu Musab al-Zarqawi founded a jihadist organization called Tawhid wal-Jihad (the Party of Monotheism and Jihad) in the north of Iraq. Affiliated with al-Qaeda, Tawhid wal-Jihad focused its attention on elements of the Islamic world rather than the West. When the United States invaded Iraq, Zarqawi's organization morphed into al-Qaeda in Iraq (AQI) and began to recruit locally as a jihadist organization, while at the same time allowing al-Qaeda to gain a foothold in Iraq. The first terrorist attack attributed to this group was the assassination of American diplomat Laurence Foley in Amman, Jordan, in October 2002. Since then, it has undergone a complex evolution, including name changes, leadership changes, and shifts in allegiance to other jihadist organizations, most notably al-Qaeda. In addition, the reach of IS's violence includes attacks carried out by other groups and individuals who have pledged allegiance to IS regardless of whether or not formal ties exist.

Al-Qaeda in Iraq was involved in internal conflicts until Zarqawi was killed in an airstrike in 2006 and the group joined with other hard-core Islamist groups to create the Islamic State of Iraq (ISI), whose goal was creating an ultra-religious caliphate, governed by Islamic law, to which all Muslims owed allegiance. Abu Bakr became the ISI leader in 2010 and was believed killed in a 2017 bombing. This change in leadership, coupled with the withdrawal of US forces from Iraq and the start of the Syrian civil war, helped revive the group's prospects. ISI, now called ISIL, ISIS, and most commonly the Islamic State or IS, gained significant amounts of territory in both Syria and Iraq, including the Syrian city of Raqqa. The major Iraqi cities of Tikrit and Fallujah fell in 2014, followed by Mosul, Iraq's second-largest city. In 2015, IS began to be the target of attacks by Kurdish forces. Other Muslim nations, including Jordan and Turkey, have either heavily criticized or actually attacked IS. Russia began bombing targets in September 2015. A major effort to retake Mosul was under way in 2017, impeded by strong defenses and the threat of civilian casualties. On March 17, 2017, a US airstrike in Mosul was alleged to have killed more than 200 civilians, prompting worldwide calls for a greater effort to protect noncombatants and illustrating why it is so tough to dislodge IS fighters. When elements of

Retributive terrorists have a number of characteristics that are unique and separate them from guerrillas, revolutionaries, and other terrorists:[56]

- Violence is used as a method of influence, persuasion, or intimidation. The true target of the terrorist act extends far beyond those directly affected by the attack and is designed to lead to some desired behavior on the part of the larger target population or government.
- Victims are usually selected for their maximum propaganda value, ensuring a high degree of media coverage. The message is that the target population had better comply with their demands because the terrorists are desperate enough to "do anything."
- Unconventional military tactics are used, especially secrecy and surprise, as well as targeting civilians, including women and children. Because the goal is to inflict maximum horror, it makes sense to choose targets that contain the largest number of victims from all walks of life. The message: everyone is a target; no one is safe.

IS branched into Afghanistan in 2017, the United States bombed their network of fortified underground tunnels located in the Nangarhar province near the Pakistan border, using a GBU-43/B Massive Ordnance Air Blast bomb, or MOAB (nicknamed the "Mother of All Bombs"). The 22,000-pound bomb killed 94 IS fighters.

In addition to its terrorist activities, IS is a governing body that imposes a very strict version of Islamic law in the territory it holds. It guarantees protection in exchange for the payment of a tax and the acceptance of second-class citizenship for minorities, including Shia Muslims. IS has engaged in massacres, beheadings, burnings, and executions of foreign journalists and humanitarian aid workers who have fallen into their hands. Ironically, this brutality has helped them draw an estimated 30,000 recruits who applaud their ruthlessness and want to be part of an Islamic caliphate that will not abide any element of Western culture. Western leaders fear that some of the recruits will return to their homes after being trained in jihad, as Salman Abedi did in Manchester, England, creating tremendous danger for their home nations since they can blend in and have families and friends for support.

Reuters/Yaser Al-Khodor

Islamic State fighters carry their weapons in the Syrian town of Tel Abyad, located near the Turkish border.

Sources: Barbara Starr and Ryan Browne, "US Drops Largest Non-nuclear Bomb in Afghanistan," CNN, April 14, 2017, http://www.cnn.com/2017/04/13/politics/afghanistan-isis-moab-bomb/; Euan McKirdy, "ISIS Kills 33 Execution-Style in Syria; 22 People in Iraq Attack," CNN, April 6, 2017, http://www.cnn.com/2017/04/06/middleeast/isis-deir-ezzor-killings/; Peter Welby, "What Is ISIS?" Centre on Religion and Geopolitics, January 10, 2017, http://www.religionandgeopolitics.org/isis/what-isis; BBC News, "What Is 'Islamic State'?" December 2, 2015, http://www.bbc.com/news/world-middle-east-29052144; Tim Arango, Kareem Fahim, and Ben Hubbard, "Rebels' Fast Strike in Iraq Was Years in the Making," *New York Times*, June 14, 2014, http://www.nytimes.com/2014/06/15/world/middleeast/rebels-fast-strike-in-iraq-was-years-in-the-making.html; Andrew Silke, "Holy Warriors: Exploring the Psychological Processes of Jihadi Radicalization," *European Journal of Criminology* 5 (2008): 99–123; Farouk Chothia, "Who Are Nigeria's Boko Haram Islamists?" BBC News Africa, May 20, 2014, http://www.bbc.com/news/world-africa-13809501 (URLs accessed May 2017).

Critical Thinking

Considering the refugee crisis caused by people desperately trying to flee violence, should Western states intervene militarily every time a group such as IS or the Taliban forms in the Middle East? Are there solutions other than military intervention?

State-Sponsored Terrorism

State-sponsored terrorism occurs when a repressive government regime forces its citizens into obedience, oppresses minorities, and stifles political dissent. Death squads and the use of government troops to destroy political opposition parties are often associated with political terrorism. Much of what we know about state-sponsored terrorism comes from the efforts of human rights groups such as London-based Amnesty International, whose research shows that tens of thousands of people continue to become victims of security operations that result in disappearances and executions. Political prisoners are now being tortured in about 100 countries, people have disappeared or are being held in secret detention in about 20 countries, and government-sponsored death squads have been operating in more than 35 countries. Countries known for encouraging violent control of dissidents include Brazil, Colombia, Guatemala, Honduras, Peru, Iraq, and Sudan.

state-sponsored terrorism
Terrorism that occurs when a repressive government regime forces its citizens into obedience, oppresses minorities, and stifles political dissent.

State-sponsored terrorism became a world issue when South and Central American dictatorships in the 1970s and 1980s unleashed state violence against political dissidents through forced disappearance, political imprisonment, torture, blacklisting, and massive exile. The region-wide *state* repression in this period emerged in response to the rise of the 1960s radical movements, which demanded public reforms and programs to help the lower classes in urban areas and agricultural workers in the countryside. Local authoritarian governments, which used repression to take control of radical political groups, were given financial support by the economic elites who dominated Latin American politics and were fearful of a socialist revolution.[57]

As might be expected, governments claim that repressive measures are needed to control terror and revolutionary groups that routinely use violence. Thus the use of terror is sometimes a way of defending the nation against violence, a conundrum that supports the idea that a state is both protective and destructive.[58]

It is sometimes difficult to assess blame for state terror—is it a few rogue government agents who act on their own authority or the government itself? The issue of responsibility for improper acts hit home during the Abu Ghraib scandal in Iraq. Photos beamed around the world embarrassed the United States when they showed military personnel victimizing suspected insurgents. The US government's response was to prosecute and imprison the perpetrators. However, some critics, such as criminologist Mark Hamm, suggest that these images constitute the photographic record of a state-sponsored crime.[59] He argues that rather than being the work of a few rogue officers, the sophisticated interrogation practices at Abu Ghraib were designed and executed by the CIA and that the torturing of detainees at Abu Ghraib followed directly from decisions made by top government officials to get tough with prisoner interrogations. So while we condemn state-sponsored violence, it is not easy to identify who is truly responsible.

Lone Actor Terrorists

A lone actor or lone wolf terrorist (LWT) uses violence or the threat of violence to achieve some political or social goal, and does not receive orders, direction, support, or aid from some outside group. Thorough evaluation of this phenomenon by Mark Hamm and Ramon Spaaj found evidence that most LWTs are unemployed, single, white males with a criminal record.[60] Compared to members of terrorist groups, lone wolves are older, less educated, and more prone to mental illness. They are more likely to be unmoored from society, deprived of what they perceive as the status and benefits to which they are entitled; this encourages them to form grievances against the government they hold responsible for unemployment, discrimination, and injustices. One reason for this relatively high level of alienation is that more than half of the lone wolves embrace right-wing or anti-government ideologies. Nationalistic movements—such as American white supremacy movements—have tended to produce terrorists from the lower classes, while religious terrorists like al-Qaeda come from all classes.

Though LWTs may be in sympathy with extremist groups, they are neither guided by nor answer to some collective entity. They are often helped or encouraged by an enabler, someone who either unknowingly performs tasks that make an attack possible, or someone who indirectly encourages terrorism by example.

While lone wolves physically isolate from society, at the same time they communicate with outsiders through spoken statements, threats, letters, manifestos, and videotaped proclamations. They are prone to proclaim that an attack is imminent; broadcasting intent may occur in the weeks, days, and even hours before an attack.

Lone actors tend to be socially isolated; they are loners with few friends. Many have a military background and have recently suffered some form of serious personal disruption that triggered a violent attack, such as divorce or the death of a partner. They are grievance-fueled individuals, likely to have weapons experience, but who also suffer from depression or other mental disorders. Not all LWTs fit this profile. Some are motivated by an emotionally charged event that sets them off on a

Concept Summary 11.2 The Variety of Terror Groups

Revolutionary terrorists	Use violence to frighten those in power and their supporters in order to replace the existing government with a regime that holds acceptable political or religious views.
Political terrorists	Political terrorism is directed at people or groups who oppose the terrorists' political ideology or whom the terrorists define as "outsiders" who must be destroyed.
Eco-terrorists	Political terror groups involved in violent actions to protect the environment.
Nationalist terrorists	Groups whose actions promote the interests of a minority ethnic or religious group that has been persecuted under majority rule and/or wishes to carve out its own independent homeland.
Retributive terrorists	Groups that use violence as a method of influence, persuasion, or intimidation in order to achieve a particular aim or objective.
State-sponsored terrorism	Carried out by a repressive government regime in order to force its citizens into obedience, oppress minorities, and stifle political dissent.
Lone wolf terrorists	Individuals who carry out terror acts without involvement or participation in an organized group.

CHECKPOINTS

▶ Revolutionary terrorists use violence to frighten those in power and their supporters in order to replace the existing government with a regime that holds acceptable political or religious views.

▶ Political terrorism is directed at people or groups who oppose the terrorists' political ideology or whom the terrorists define as "outsiders" who must be destroyed.

▶ Nationalist terrorism promotes the interests of a minority ethnic or religious group that believes it has been persecuted under majority rule and wishes to carve out its own independent homeland.

▶ Retributive terrorist groups want to impose their social and religious code on others.

▶ State-sponsored terrorism occurs when a repressive government regime forces its citizens into obedience, oppresses minorities, and stifles political dissent.

▶ Lone actor terrorists do not belong to an organized group but act on their own, motivated by political, religious, or social beliefs.

destructive path: the political becomes personal. They are radicalized by feelings of moral obligation to right a perceived wrong: a man bombs abortion clinics after a family member loses a child at birth; a woman burns down a factory farm after witnessing the suffering of animals.[61]

The various forms that terror groups take are summarized in Concept Summary 11.2.

What Motivates the Terrorist?

In the aftermath of the September 11, 2001, destruction of the World Trade Center in New York City, many Americans asked themselves the same simple question: Why? What could motivate someone like Osama bin Laden to order the deaths of thousands of innocent people? How could someone who had never been to the United States or suffered personally at its hands develop such lethal hatred? Some experts believed the attacks had a political basis, claiming that bin Laden's anger was fueled by American Middle East policies. Others saw a religious motivation and claimed that bin Laden was a radical Muslim at war with the liberal religions of the West. Another view was that bin Laden's rage was fueled by deep-rooted psychological problems.

As such, there have been a number of competing visions of why terrorists engage in criminal activities such as bombings, shootings, and kidnappings to achieve a political end. Several views stand out.

Psychological View

One of the most controversial views of terrorists is that some if not all suffer from psychological deficits, and that the typical terrorist can be described as an emotionally disturbed individual who acts out his or her psychoses within the confines of violent groups. According to this view, terrorist violence is not so much a political instrument as an end in itself; it is the result of compulsion or psychopathology. Terrorists do what they do because of garden variety emotional problems, including but not limited to self-destructive urges and disturbed emotions combined with problems with authority.[62]

Other terror experts say that the majority of research on terrorists indicates that most are not psychologically abnormal.[63] Even suicide bombers, a group that should show signs of psychological abnormality, exhibit few signs of the mental problems such as depression that are typically found in people who choose to take their own life. Rather than acting disturbed and disoriented, those terrorists willing to die for their cause display a heightened sense of purpose, group allegiance, and task focus.[64]

After carefully reviewing existing evidence on the psychological state of terrorists, mental health expert Randy Borum concludes:

- Mental illness is not a critical factor in explaining terrorist behavior. Also, most terrorists are not psychopaths.
- There is no "terrorist personality," nor is there any accurate profile—psychological or otherwise—of the terrorist.
- Histories of childhood abuse and trauma and themes of perceived injustice and humiliation often are prominent in terrorist biographies, but do not really help to explain terrorism.[65]

Alienation View

Another explanation for terrorist activity is that a lack of opportunity creates a sense of alienation that motivates men and women to embrace terrorism.[66] Regions such as South Asia breed terrorists because they house an incendiary mix of strong ethnic identities and diverse religious communities, many of which are concentrated within exclusionary ghettos. Young men and women residing in these areas are motivated to join terror groups when they feel left out of the social and economic mainstream because of their religious or ethnic status.[67] According to this view, terror recruits suffer alienation from friends, family, and society.[68] Many have been raised to hate the groups who are in power and believe that they have been victimized by state authorities whom they view as oppressors.

Terrorism has also become an alternative for people whose religious beliefs alienate them from our postmodern, technological, global society in which foreign influences routinely clash with age-old traditions. They may believe that modern forms of communication, entertainment, and social interaction have brought foreign influences that are corrupting and disrespectful to their traditional way of life. Some may join terror groups whose goal is to eliminate these corrupting external influences—for example, the name of the terrorist group Boko Haram can be translated as "Western education is sin." Alienation can become so powerful that the terrorist may even believe that a suicide mission will help cleanse them of the corruption of the modern world while at the same time scaring off outsiders.

While at first glance terrorists seem alienated from modern society, when Marc Sageman studied members of extremist Islamist groups he found that most tend to be well educated; about 60 percent had some form of higher education. More than 75 percent came from upper- or middle-class backgrounds. When they joined a terror organization, the majority had professional occupations such as doctor or engineer, or semiskilled employment, such as being a civil servant; fewer than 25 percent were unemployed or working in unskilled jobs. Surprisingly, Sageman found that almost three-quarters were married and that most had children.[69] These findings suggest that terrorists are not suffering from the social problems usually associated with alienation: poverty, lack of education, and ignorance.

Family Conflict View

Terrorists report that they are products of dysfunctional families in which the father was absent or, even if present, was a distant and cold figure.[70] Because of this family estrangement, the budding terrorist may have been swayed to join a group or cult by a charismatic leader who serves as an alternative father figure. Some find it in religious schools run by strong leaders who demand strict loyalty from their followers while indoctrinating them in political causes.[71] In this sense, terror groups, similar to what happens in urban street gangs, provide a substitute family–like environment, which can nurture a heretofore emotionally underprivileged youth.

Political View

When people are left out of the political process, having their votes restricted or even losing the right to vote, they may be inclined to join terror groups.[72] Analyzing cross-national data, Laura Dugan and Gary LaFree, of the National Consortium for the Study of Terrorism and Responses to Terrorism, found that most of the risk for political violence lies in those nations that are nearly democracies, which experience three times as many terror attacks as full democracies. Ironically, the most autocratic countries, governed by dictators and without free elections, generally had the lowest average number of attacks. In contrast, **failed states**—those where governments have lost physical control of their own territory, are unable to provide reasonable public services, and cannot interact properly with other states—have extremely high rates of terrorist activity. Dugan and LaFree also found evidence that terrorist attacks against failed states were much more lethal than attacks against other nations. Their finding suggests that nations that provide access to the political process for people holding a wide range of diverse viewpoints create a culture that helps reduce the frustration that could lead to terrorist violence. Those states that cannot maintain order or provide services to its citizens are fertile grounds for terrorists. And while iron-handed dictators may keep terrorism under control in the short term, their long-term prospects are sketchy at best, as recent events in Egypt, Libya, and Syria have shown.

failed state
A nation whose government has lost control of its own territory, is unable to provide public services and protection, and lacks the ability to interact with other states as a full member of the international community.

Socialization/Friendship View

Many jihadist recruits were living in foreign countries when they got involved with terrorist organizations. Feeling homesick, they sought out people with similar backgrounds, whom they would often find at mosques.[73] If they appeared to be motivated by religious fervor, it was because they were seeking friends in a foreign land. They moved in together in order to share the rent and also to eat together under strict Muslim dietary laws. The group solidified their beliefs and created a sense of solidarity with like-minded people. If one became committed to terror, others might follow rather than let him down.

Ideological View

Another view is that terrorists hold extreme ideological beliefs that prompt their behavior. They may have developed heightened perceptions of oppressive conditions, believing they are being victimized by some group or government for their beliefs or way of life. Once they conclude that the government will not help people with their beliefs, they decide to resort to violence to encourage change.

Facilitating the use of violence is the ability to divide people into two categories based on religious, ethnic, racial, or other cultural criteria: those with common interests and beliefs who are avenged through terrorist activities ("us") and those against whom the terrorist activities are to be directed ("them"). Those associated with "us" are viewed as moral, right, good, and strong. Those associated with "them" are seen as immoral, wrong, bad, and weak.[74] Once this division is made, the terrorist can act with impunity to further their ideological beliefs because those harmed have beliefs that make them less than human.

RELIGIOUS FANATICISM Some terrorists, like the Tsarnaev brothers, are motivated by extreme religious beliefs, which often coincide with their ideological views. But how can they justify using violence if they are truly religious, since most of the world's religions eschew violence? Islamist terrorists believe that their commitment to God justifies their extreme actions. They regard the actions of people they trust as a testimony to the righteousness of their acts. They trust significant others, rely on their wisdom, experience, and testimony, and accept their expressions of faith. To the terrorist, someone like Osama bin Laden has demonstrated the strength of his faith by living in poverty and giving up a more luxurious and leisurely life in the name of God. When he calls them to jihad, they are likely to follow, even if it means killing those who deny their faith or beliefs. Perceived miracles, such as the defeat of a superpower through faith alone (e.g., the Soviet/Afghan war or the fight against the United States in Iraq), also increase confidence in the righteousness of the cause. Some have mystical experiences during prayers or dreams that demonstrate the existence of God and reinforce faith. In a videotape in the fall of 2001, Osama bin Laden said that he had banned the reporting of dreams of airplanes flying into buildings prior to September 11 for fear of revealing the plot.[75]

Explaining State-Sponsored Terrorism

How can state-sponsored terrorism be explained? After all, these violent acts are not directed at a foreign government or overseas adversaries but against natives of one's own country. In her book *Reigns of Terror*, Patricia Marchak finds that people willing to kill or maim their fellow countrymen are likely to be highly susceptible to unquestioning submission to authority. They are conformists who want to be part of the central group and who are quite willing to be part of a state regime. They are vulnerable to ideology that dehumanizes their targets and can utilize propaganda to distance themselves psychologically from those they are terrorizing.[76] So the Nazis had little trouble recruiting people to carry out horrific acts during the Holocaust because many Germans wanted to be part of the popular social/political movement and were easily indoctrinated by the Nazi propaganda that branded Jews as subhuman. Stalin was able to carry out his reign of terror in Russia because his victims were viewed as state enemies who were trying to undermine the Communist regime.

How can these tendencies be neutralized? Marchak sees little benefit to international intervention that results in after-the-fact punishment of the perpetrators, a course of action that was attempted in the former Yugoslavia after death squads had performed "ethnic cleansing" of undesirables. Instead she argues for a prevention strategy that involves international aid and economic development by industrialized nations to those in the Third World that are on the verge of becoming collapsed states, the construction of social welfare systems, and the acceptance of international legal norms and standards of human rights.[77]

Extent of the Terrorism Threat

Does the pressure being put on IS, al-Qaeda, the Taliban, and other terror groups through drone attacks and commando raids mean that the end of the global terrorism threat is at hand? Not likely. Terror cells have now dispersed around the world, helping to offset this loss in leadership. When one leader is killed, a new and even more violent one may take command.

It is difficult to enumerate terror groups and incidents because new ones emerge daily and attacks are quite frequent. The most recent data from the National Consortium for the Study of Terrorism and Responses to Terrorism (START) supports the fact that the terrorist danger has not diminished, quite the opposite in fact. Between 2002 and 2015, a single group—IS and its supporters—carried out more than 4,900 terrorist attacks. These attacks caused more than 33,000 deaths and 41,000 injuries (including perpetrator casualties), and involved more than 11,000 individuals held hostage or kidnapped. Excluding incidents where the perpetrator group was not identified, these attacks represented 13 percent of all terrorist attacks worldwide, 26 percent of all deaths, 28 percent of all injuries, and 24 percent of all kidnap victims or hostages due to terrorism during the same time period.[78]

In the United States, between 1993 and 2016, there were 109 terror plots of which more than 70 percent were foiled by law enforcement efforts. Most perpetrators were American citizens or residents (75 percent). Only three were returned foreign fighters, and none were refugees. Lone wolves were rare—only nine plots in more than 20 years were orchestrated by someone acting alone throughout the course of the plot. About 25 percent of the plots could credibly be linked to a known terrorist organization.

Private citizens and property were the most common targets, accounting for about 20 percent of all plots. Military institutions and personnel, airports and aircraft, and general government were the next most frequently targeted, followed by other transportation and business targets.[79]

Who were the most active groups? They include IS, Taliban in Afghanistan, Boko Haram in Nigeria, al-Qaeda in the Arabian Peninsula and Iraq, Tehrik-i-Taliban Pakistan, and al-Shabaab in Somalia. While many of these organizations have been active for many years, if not decades, new groups are emerging all the time. The Donetsk People's Republic and the Luhansk People's Republic, both active in Ukraine, carried out bombings, armed assaults, kidnappings, and facility/infrastructure attacks. The Donetsk People's Republic was attributed responsibility for more than 1,000 total fatalities, including the deaths of nearly 300 passengers killed by a surface-to-air missile launched at a Malaysia Airlines commercial flight.[80]

Criminal Justice Response to Terrorism

After the 9/11 attacks, agencies of the criminal justice system began to focus their attention on combating the threat of terror. Even local police agencies created anti-terror programs designed to protect their communities from the threat of attack. How should the nation best prepare itself to thwart potential attacks? The National Commission on Terrorist Attacks Upon the United States (also known as the 9/11 Commission), an independent, bipartisan commission, was created in late 2002 and given the mission of preparing an in-depth report of the events leading up to the 9/11 attacks. Part of their goal was to create a comprehensive plan to ensure that no further attacks of that magnitude take place.

To monitor the more than 500 million people who annually cross in and out of America, the commission recommended that a single agency should be created to screen border crossings. They also recommended creation of an investigative agency to monitor all aliens in the United States and to gather intelligence on the way terrorists travel across borders. The commission suggested that people who wanted passports be tagged with biometric measures to make them easily identifiable.

In response to the commission report, a **Director of National Intelligence (DNI)** was created and charged with coordinating data from the nation's primary intelligence-gathering agencies. The DNI serves as the principal intelligence adviser to the president and the statutory intelligence adviser to the National Security Council. President George W. Bush named US Ambassador to Iraq John Negroponte to be the first person to hold the post; he was confirmed on April 21, 2005. The current director is Daniel Coats, who was sworn in as the fifth DNI on March 16, 2017.

Among the agencies reporting to the DNI are the National Counterterrorism Center (NCTC), which is staffed by terrorism experts from the CIA, FBI, and the Pentagon; the Privacy and Civil Liberties Board; and the National Counterproliferation Center. The NCTC serves as the primary organization in the US government for analyzing and integrating all intelligence possessed or acquired by the government pertaining to terrorism and counterterrorism, excepting purely domestic counterterrorism information.

The 9/11 Commission report outlined what had already been done, what had not been done, and what needs to be done. Agencies of the justice system have begun to respond to the challenge.

Combating Terrorism with Law Enforcement

Ending the threat of terror is not easy. One reason is the very nature of American society. Because we live in a free and open nation, it is extremely difficult to seal

FACT OR FICTION?

Terrorist attacks have been increasing every year; the world is becoming more dangerous.

TRUE The number of terror attacks has risen sharply in the past few years.

Director of National Intelligence (DNI) Government official charged with coordinating data from the nation's primary intelligence-gathering agencies.

AP Images/Elaine Thompson

Law enforcement agencies at every level are preparing for terror attacks. During a drill, SWAT team members step over a downed "terrorist" while clearing the Washington State ferry MV *Salish*, out of Bainbridge Island, Washington. In winds that kicked up whitecaps and drenched the small boarding boats, the Coast Guard and several police agencies drilled for a potential terrorist attack on a state ferry.

the borders and prevent the entry of terrorist groups. In his book *Nuclear Terrorism*, Graham Allison, an expert on nuclear weapons and national security, describes the almost superhuman effort it would take to seal the nation's borders from nuclear attack considering the thousands of trucks, rail cars, and ships that deliver goods every day. The potential for terrorists to obtain bombs is significant: there are more than 100 nuclear research reactors now in operation around the world, and many are contained in states hostile to the United States, such as Iran and North Korea. Even if terrorists lack the knowledge to build their own bomb, they may be able to purchase an intact device on the black market. Russia alone has thousands of nuclear warheads and material for many thousands of additional weapons; all of these are vulnerable to theft. Terrorists may also be able to buy the knowledge to construct bombs. In one well-known incident, Pakistan's leading nuclear scientist, A. Q. Khan, sold comprehensive "nuclear starter kits" that included advanced centrifuge components, blueprints for nuclear warheads, and uranium samples in quantities sufficient to make a small bomb, and even provided personal consulting services to assist in nuclear development.[81]

Recognizing this problem, law enforcement agencies around the country began to realign their resources to combat future terrorist attacks. In response to 9/11, law enforcement agencies undertook a number of steps: increasing the number of personnel engaged in emergency response planning; updating response plans for chemical, biological, or radiological attacks; and reallocating internal resources or increasing departmental spending to focus on terrorism preparedness.[82] Actions continue to be taken on the federal, state, and local levels.

FEDERAL LAW ENFORCEMENT One of the most significant changes has been a realignment of the Federal Bureau of Investigation (FBI), the federal government's main law enforcement agency. Post-9/11, the FBI announced a reformulation of its priorities, making protecting the United States from terrorist attack its number one commitment. It is now charged with coordinating intelligence collection with the Border Patrol, Secret Service, and the CIA. The FBI must also work with and share intelligence with the National Counterterrorism Center (NCTC). Another initiative has been the creation of Joint Terrorism Task Forces (JTTFs), which are now located in 103 US cities. The JTTFs include more than 4,400 members nationwide, hailing from over 600 state and local agencies and 50 federal agencies (the Department of Homeland Security, the US military, Immigration and Customs Enforcement, and the Transportation Security Administration, to name a few). JTTFs enable a shared intelligence base across many agencies, among other benefits.[83]

DEPARTMENT OF HOMELAND SECURITY (DHS) Soon after the 2001 attack, President George W. Bush proposed the creation of a new cabinet-level agency called the **Department of Homeland Security (DHS)**, which is engaged in:

- Preventing terrorist attacks within the United States
- Reducing America's vulnerability to terrorism
- Minimizing the damage and recovering from attacks that do occur

Rather than start from the ground up, the DHS combined a number of existing agencies into a superagency. Among its components are:

- *Border and transportation security.* The Department of Homeland Security is responsible for securing our nation's borders and transportation systems, which

Department of Homeland Security (DHS)
An agency of the federal government charged with preventing terrorist attacks within the United States, reducing America's vulnerability to terrorism, and minimizing the damage and aiding recovery from attacks that do occur.

include 350 ports of entry. The department manages who and what enters the country, and works to prevent the entry of terrorists and the instruments of terrorism while simultaneously ensuring the speedy flow of legitimate traffic. The DHS also is in charge of securing territorial waters, including ports and waterways.

- *Emergency preparedness and response.* The department ensures the preparedness of emergency response professionals, provides the federal government's response, and aids America's recovery from terrorist attacks and natural disasters. The department is responsible for reducing the loss of life and property and protecting institutions from all types of hazards through an emergency management program of preparedness, mitigation, response, and recovery.
- *Chemical, biological, radiological, and nuclear countermeasures.* The department leads the federal government's efforts in preparing for and responding to the full range of terrorist threats involving weapons of mass destruction. To do this, the department sets national policy and establishes guidelines for state and local governments. It directs exercises and drills for federal, state, and local chemical, biological, radiological, and nuclear (CBRN) response teams and plans. The department is assigned to prevent the importation of nuclear weapons and material.
- *Information analysis and infrastructure protection.* The department analyzes information from multiple available sources, including the CIA and FBI, in order to assess the dangers facing the nation. It also analyzes law enforcement and intelligence information.[84]

The DHS has numerous and varied duties. It is responsible for port security and transportation systems and manages airport security with its Transportation Security Administration (TSA). It has its own intelligence section, and it covers every special event in the United States, including political conventions.

STATE AND COUNTY LAW ENFORCEMENT In the wake of the 9/11 attacks, a number of states have beefed up their intelligence-gathering capabilities and aimed them directly at homeland security. Arizona maintains the Arizona Counter Terrorism Information Center (ACTIC), a statewide intelligence system designed to combat terrorism.[85] It consists of two divisions. One is unclassified and draws together personnel from various public safety agencies. The other operates in a secretive manner and is made up of personnel from the FBI's Joint Terrorism Task Force. Its Fusion Center is responsible for sharing information about situations that might affect jurisdictions in the state and combs through diverse informational sources to provide early warning of incidents at the local, regional, and state levels.[86] ACTIC also has an outreach program known as the Community Liaison Program (CLP). Community partners, including religious groups, businesses, and community crime watches, provide intelligence information to ACTIC personnel as the need arises.

LOCAL LAW ENFORCEMENT Federal law enforcement agencies are not alone in responding to the threat of terrorism. And, of course, nowhere is the threat of terrorism being taken more seriously than in New York City, one of the main targets of the 9/11 attacks, which has established a Counterterrorism Bureau.[87] After the 9/11 attacks, the NYPD augmented its anti-terrorism forces from 17 to 125 and assigned them to the operational control of the Counterterrorism Bureau. Teams within the bureau have been trained to examine potential targets in the city and attempt to insulate them from possible attack. Viewed as prime targets are the city's bridges, the Empire State Building, Rockefeller Center, and the United Nations. Bureau detectives are assigned overseas to work with the police in several foreign cities, including cities in Canada and Israel. Detectives have been assigned as liaisons with the FBI and with INTERPOL, in Lyon, France. The city recruits detectives with language skills from Pashtun and Urdu to Arabic, Fujianese, and other dialects. The New York City Police Intelligence Division has been revamped, and agents are examining foreign newspapers and monitoring Internet sites. The department has set up several backup command centers in different parts of the city in case a terror attack puts headquarters out of operation. Backup senior command teams have been created so that if people at the highest levels of the department are killed, individuals will already have been tapped to step into their jobs. The Lower Manhattan Security Initiative (LMSI) is a networked surveillance project designed to detect threats and perform preoperational terrorist surveillance south of Canal Street in lower Manhattan.

The department is also drawing on the expertise of other institutions around the city. Medical specialists have been enlisted to monitor daily developments in the city's hospitals to detect any suspicious outbreaks of illness that might reflect a biological attack. And the police are conducting joint drills with the New York Fire Department to avoid the problems in communication and coordination that marked the emergency response on September 11. In January 2015, the NYPD announced it was expanding the counterterrorism unit by creating a Strategic Response Group, whose officers will receive training on counterterrorism and be equipped with heavy protective gear, including long rifles and machine guns.[88]

Combating Terrorism with the Law

The Supreme Court has been involved in terror issues ever since Congress authorized President Bush to use "all necessary and appropriate force" against those responsible for the attacks in New York and Washington, DC. Yaser Hamdi, an American citizen who had left the United States in his youth, was captured in Afghanistan and detained by military forces at Guantánamo Bay, Cuba, for supposedly aiding the Taliban. He was later moved to a military prison in Norfolk, Virginia, where he filed a writ of *habeas corpus*, arguing that, as a US citizen, he was entitled to challenge the constitutionality of his confinement in federal court. In *Hamdi v. Rumsfeld* (2004), the Supreme Court agreed with his argument, holding in a 6–3 decision that the due process clause of the Fifth Amendment requires that US citizens be given the opportunity to challenge their confinement in this way.[89] The Court also decided in *Rasul v. Bush* (2004) that the federal courts have jurisdiction to hear *habeas corpus* petitions from foreign nationals captured outside the United States.[90]

One year later, the Supreme Court heard a case involving Salim Hamdan, a Yemeni and former driver for Osama bin Laden. He was captured by Afghan warlords and turned over to US forces in 2001. He was then transferred in 2002 to Guantánamo Bay and, in 2003, was slated to be tried for various conspiracy offenses before a military tribunal. He filed a *habeas corpus* petition in the US District Court for the Western District of Washington, claiming that he could not legally be tried by a military tribunal. In a 5–3 decision, the Supreme Court agreed.[91] It held that the military commission at issue violated the Uniform Code of Military Justice and the four Geneva Conventions signed in 1949. Charges against him were subsequently dropped, but Hamdan was later deemed an "unlawful enemy combatant," tried once again before a military tribunal, and convicted. He was sentenced to five and a half years in prison, given credit for time served, and sent back to Yemen. He was not named a combatant before going into his first trial, which is partly why the first military tribunal was illegal.

Shortly after Hamdan's case was decided, Congress passed the Military Commissions Act of 2006, which stripped the federal courts of jurisdiction to hear *habeas corpus* petitions from detainees who have been designated as "enemy combatants." In a 5–4 decision, the Supreme Court held that prisoners (even foreign nationals held at Guantánamo Bay) had the right to *habeas corpus* under the US Constitution and that their arguments could be heard in the federal courts.[92] In effect, the Court held that the Military Commissions Act of 2006 was an unconstitutional suspension of the right to *habeas corpus*. In October 2009, President Obama signed into law the Military Commissions Act of 2009, which attempted to improve on—and address some of the deficiencies of—the earlier legislation. The law does not permit a US citizen to be tried by a military commission.[93]

USA PATRIOT ACT Soon after the September 11 terrorist attacks, the US government enacted several laws focused on preventing further acts of violence against the United States and creating greater flexibility in the fight to control terror activity. Most importantly, Congress passed the **USA Patriot Act (USAPA)** on October 26, 2001.

The Patriot Act expanded all four traditional tools of surveillance—wiretaps, search warrants, pen/trap orders (installing devices that record phone calls), and subpoenas. The Foreign Intelligence Surveillance Act (FISA) allowed domestic operations by intelligence agencies. The USAPA gave greater power to the FBI to check and monitor phone, Internet, and computer records without first needing to demonstrate that they were being used by a suspect or target of a court order.

> **USA Patriot Act (USAPA)**
> Legislation giving US law enforcement agencies a freer hand to investigate and apprehend suspected terrorists.

The government was given permission to serve a single wiretap, or pen/trap order, on any person regardless of whether that person or entity is named in a court order. Prior to the Patriot Act, telephone companies could be ordered to install pen/trap devices on their networks that would monitor calls coming to a surveillance target and to whom the surveillance target made calls; the USAPA extended this monitoring to the Internet. Law enforcement agencies were able to obtain the email addresses and websites visited by a target, and emails of the people with whom they communicated. It is possible to require that an Internet service provider install a device that records email and other electronic communications on its servers, looking for communications initiated or received by the target of an investigation. Under the USAPA, the government did not need to show a court that the information or communication was relevant to a criminal investigation, nor did it have to report where it served the order or what information it received.

The act also allowed enforcement agencies to monitor cable operators and obtain access to their records and systems. Before the act, a cable company had to give prior notice to the customer, even if that person was a target of an investigation. Information could be obtained on people with whom the cable subscriber communicated, the content of the person's communications, and the person's subscription records; prior notice was still required if law enforcement agencies wanted to learn what television programming a subscriber purchased.

The act also expanded the definition of "terrorism" and enabled the government to monitor more closely those people suspected of "harboring" and giving "material support" to terrorists (Sections 803, 805). It increased the authority of the US attorney general to detain and deport noncitizens with little or no judicial review. The attorney general could also certify that he had "reasonable grounds to believe" that a noncitizen endangers national security and was therefore eligible for deportation. The attorney general and secretary of state were also given the authority to designate domestic groups as terrorist organizations and deport any noncitizen who was a member.

US FREEDOM ACT When the Patriot Act ended in 2015 it was replaced by the US Freedom Act.[94] The main change was to Section 215, the section that most bothered civil libertarians. Under Section 215 of the Patriot Act, the National Security Agency routinely collected metadata from some of the biggest cellular companies—not the contents of conversations, but the phone numbers, dates, times, and duration of the calls. If someone inside the United States called a number linked to one of three terrorist organizations (including al-Qaeda), an NSA alert system would note that fact. The NSA could then ask the US Foreign Intelligence Surveillance Court for permission to search the database for a list of all the other numbers that the American phone had called, as well as all the numbers that *those* numbers had called, going back as far as five years. If this search revealed a suspicious pattern, the NSA could then turn the materials over to the FBI, which could seek a warrant to listen to conversations.

Under the new reform law, the NSA would no longer possess the database, so it would seek a FISA court order to get it from the telecom companies—and the FISA court would then include a privacy advocate who could argue against relinquishing the data. If the court sided with the NSA, what happened next would be exactly the same as before the new law passed.

Combating Terrorism with Politics

In the long run, it may simply be impossible to defeat terror groups and end terrorism using military, law enforcement, or legal solutions. Using force may play into terrorists' hands and convince them that they are freedom fighters valiantly struggling against a better armed and more ruthless foe. No matter how many terrorists are killed and/or captured, military/deterrence-based solutions may be doomed. Aggressive reprisals will cause terrorist ideology to spread and gain greater acceptance in the underdeveloped world. The resulting anger and alienation will produce more terrorists than can be killed off through violent responses. In contrast, if the terrorist ideology is countered and discredited, the appeal of terror groups such as al-Qaeda will wither and die.

One approach suggested by policy experts is to undermine support for terrorist groups by being benevolent nation-builders giving aid to the nations that house terror groups.[95] This is the approach the United States took after World War II to rebuild Germany and Japan (the Marshall Plan) all the while gaining support for its Cold War struggle against the Soviet Union. According to the Rand Corporation, a nonprofit research group, the following steps are required to defeat jihadist groups such as al-Qaeda:

- Attack the ideological underpinnings of global jihadism
- Sever ideological and other links between terrorist groups
- Strengthen the capabilities of front-line states to counter local jihadist threats

This approach may work because al-Qaeda's goal of toppling "apostate" regimes in Saudi Arabia, Egypt, and Pakistan and creating an ultraorthodox pan-Islamic government spanning the world does not sit well with large groups of Muslims. Al-Qaeda's monolithic vision has no room for other Muslim sects such as Shi'ites and Sunni moderates. Therefore, political and social appeals may help fracture local support for al-Qaeda. In addition, the United States should seek to deny sanctuaries to terrorist groups and strengthen the capabilities of foreign governments to deal with terrorist threats, but in an advisory capacity by providing intelligence.

Thinking Like a Criminologist

Torture or Not?   As a criminologist, your specialty is terrorism, so it comes as no surprise that the director of the CIA asks you to draw up a protocol setting out the rules for the use of torture with suspected terrorists. The reason for his request is that a series of new articles has exposed the agency's practice of sending suspected terrorists to friendly nations that are less squeamish about using torture. Shocking photo evidence of torture from detention facilities at the Guantánamo base in Cuba support these charges. Legal scholars have argued that these tactics violate both international treaties and domestic statutes prohibiting torture. Some maintain that the US Constitution limits the authority of an executive agency like the CIA to act against foreigners abroad and also limits physical coercion by the government under the Fifth Amendment due process and self-incrimination clauses and the Eighth Amendment prohibition against cruel and unusual punishments. Legally, it is impermissible for United States authorities to engage in indefinite detention or torture regardless of the end, the place, or the victim.

Writing Assignment

Write a memo to the CIA director outlining the protocol you recommend for the use of torture with suspected terrorists. In your document, address when torture should be used, who it should be used on, and what tortures you recommend using. Of course, if you believe the use of torture is always unethical, you could let the director know why you have reached this conclusion.

SUMMARY

LO1 Define the term *political crime*.

Political crime is used to signify illegal acts that are designed to undermine an existing government and threaten its survival. Political crimes can include both violent and nonviolent acts and range in seriousness from dissent, treason, and espionage to violent acts such as terrorism or assassination.

LO2 Assess the cause of political crime.

The political criminal and political crimes may stem from religious or ideological sources. They often occupy a gray area between conventional and outlawed behavior. While common criminals may be motivated by greed, vengeance, or jealousy, political criminals have a somewhat different agenda from common criminals. There is no set pattern or reason why someone becomes a political criminal. Some use political crime as a stepping stone to public office while others use it as a method to focus their frustrations.

LO3 Compare and contrast the terms *espionage* and *treason*.

Helping or cooperating with the enemy in a time of war would be considered treason. Espionage is the practice of obtaining information about a government, organization, or a society that is considered secret or confidential without the permission of the holder of the information. Industrial espionage involves unethical or illegal activities such as bribing employees to reveal trade secrets such as computer codes or product formulas.

LO4 List the components of state political crime.

While some political crimes are committed by people who oppose the state, others are perpetrated by state authorities against the people they are supposed to serve. There are five varieties of state political crime: political corruption, illegal domestic surveillance, human rights violations, state violence, and state-corporate crime.

LO5 Distinguish among terrorists, insurgents, guerillas, and revolutionaries.

Terrorism is generally defined as the illegal use of force against innocent people to achieve a political objective. The term *guerilla* refers to antigovernment forces located in rural areas that attack the military, the police, and government officials. The typical goal of an insurgency is to confront the existing government for control of all or a portion of its territory, or force political concessions in sharing political power. A revolution is generally seen as a civil war fought between nationalists and a sovereign power that holds control of the land, or between the existing government and local groups over issues of ideology and power.

LO6 Enumerate the various forms of terrorism.

Revolutionary terrorists use violence to frighten those in power and their supporters in order to replace the existing government with a regime that holds acceptable political or religious views. Political terrorism is directed at people or groups who oppose the terrorists' political ideology or whom the terrorists define as "outsiders" who must be destroyed. Nationalist terrorism promotes the interests of a minority ethnic or religious group that believes it has been persecuted under majority rule and wishes to carve out its own independent homeland. Retributive terrorists want to impose their social and religious code on others. State-sponsored terrorism occurs when a repressive government regime forces its citizens into obedience, oppresses minorities, and stifles political dissent. Sometimes terrorist groups become involved in common-law crimes such as drug dealing and kidnapping, even selling nuclear materials.

Key Terms

political crime 369
al-Qaeda 369
election fraud 372
treason 374
espionage 375
state political crime 377

torture 377
waterboarding 377
ticking bomb scenario 377
terrorism 378
guerilla 379
insurgent 380

Reign of Terror 381
retributive terrorists 385
jihad 385
state-sponsored
    terrorism 387
failed state 391

Director of National
    Intelligence (DNI) 393
Department of Homeland
    Security (DHS) 394
USA Patriot Act
    (USAPA) 397

Critical Thinking Questions

1. Would you be willing to give up some of your civil rights in order to aid the war on terror?

2. Should foreign terror suspects arrested abroad by US agents be given the same rights and privileges as an American citizen accused of crime?

3. What groups in America might be the breeding ground for terrorist activity in the United States?

4. In light of the 9/11 attack, should acts of terrorism be treated differently from other common-law violent crimes? Should terrorists be executed for their acts even if no one is killed during their attack?

5. Can the use of torture ever be justified? Is the "ticking bomb" scenario valid?

6. A spy gives plans for a new weapon to the enemy. They build the weapon and use it to kill American soldiers. Is the spy guilty of murder?

Notes

All URLS accessed in 2017.

1. Articles about the Manning case can be found at "Chelsea Manning," *New York Times*, https://www .nytimes.com/topic/person/bradley-manning; John F. Burns and Ravi Somaiya, "WikiLeaks Founder on the Run, Trailed by Notoriety," *New York Times*, October 23, 2010, http://www.nytimes .com/2010/10/24/world/24assange.html.

2. Julian Assange, "Assange Statement on the US Election," WikiLeaks, November 8, 2016, https:// wikileaks.org/Assange-Statement-on-the-US -Election.html.

3. Charlie Savage, "Chelsea Manning Leaves Prison, Closing an Extraordinary Leak Case," *New York Times*, May 16, 2017, https://www.nytimes.com/2017/05/16 /us/politics/chelsea-manning-leaves-prison.html.

4. Jeffrey Ian Ross, *The Dynamics of Political Crime* (Thousand Oaks, CA: Sage, 2003).

5. David Wright, "Trump Calls Chelsea Manning 'Ungrateful TRAITOR' for Obama Criticism," CNN, January 26, 2017, http://www.cnn.com/2017/01/26 /politics/trump-chelsea-manning-traitor-obama/.

6. Human Rights Watch, "UN: Reject Syria's Human Rights Council Candidacy, Country Under Investigation by Rights Body Not Fit to Join," May 6, 2011, http://www.hrw.org/en/news/2011/05/06 /un-reject-syrias-human-rights-council-candidacy.

7. Louisa Loveluck, "Deadly Nerve Agent Sarin Used in Syria Attack, Turkish Health Ministry Says," *Washington Post*, April 6, 2017, https://www .washingtonpost.com/world/turkish-autopsies -confirm-chemical-weapons-used-in-syria-attack -that-killed-scores/2017/04/06/4d660ac4-1aa7 -11e7-8003-f55b4c1cfae2_story.html; Micah Zenko, "Counting the Dead in Syria," *The Atlantic*, September 15, 2015, http://www.theatlantic.com /international/archive/2015/09/syria-civil-war -civilian-deaths/405496/.

8. Randy Borum, "Understanding the Terrorist Mind-Set," *FBI Law Enforcement Bulletin* 72 (2003): 7–10.

9. Brendan O'Connor, "Here Is What Appears to Be Dylann Roof's Racist Manifesto," *Gawker*, June 20, 2015, http://gawker.com/here-is-what-appears-to -be-dylann-roofs-racist-manifest-1712767241.

10. Olsen Ebright, Melissa Pamer, and Jason Kandel, "Election Fraud Alleged in Cudahy; 2 Accept Plea Deal," http://www.nbclosangeles.com/news/local/Cudahy-Officials-Corruption-Bribery-Ballots-Voting-162259065.html.

11. Justin Levitt, *The Truth About Voter Fraud* (New York: Brennan Center for Justice, 2007), https://www.brennancenter.org/sites/default/files/legacy/The%20Truth%20About%20Voter%20Fraud.pdf.

12. Michael Gilbert, "The Problem of Voter Fraud," *Columbia Law Review* 115 (2015): 739–775.

13. Evan Perez and Shimon Prokupecz, "Sen. Bob Menendez: 'I Am Not Going Anywhere,'" CNN, March 9, 2015, http://www.cnn.com/2015/03/06/politics/robert-menendez-criminal-corruption-charges-planned/.

14. Jason Meisner and Patrick M. O'Connell, "Blagojevich Faces 8 Years More in Prison after Judge Sticks to 14-Year Term," *Chicago Tribune*, August 9, 2016, http://www.chicagotribune.com/news/ct-rod-blagojevich-appeal-20160809-story.html; US Attorney's Office, Eastern District of Michigan, "Former Detroit Mayor Kwame Kilpatrick, Contractor Bobby Ferguson, and Bernard Kilpatrick Sentenced on Racketeering, Extortion, Bribery, Fraud, and Tax Charges," press release, October 17, 2013, www.fbi.gov/detroit/press-releases/2013/former-detroit-mayor-kwame-kilpatrick-contractor-bobby-ferguson-and-bernard-kilpatrick-sentenced-on-racketeering-extortion-bribery-fraud-and-tax-charges.

15. John Ziff and Austin Sarat, *Espionage and Treason* (New York: Chelsea House, 1999).

16. United States Criminal Code at 18 U.S.C. § 2381.

17. Douglas Linder, "The Treason Trial of Aaron Burr," http://famous-trials.com/burr.

18. "John Brown's Harpers Ferry Raid," Civil War Trust, https://www.civilwar.org/learn/collections/john-browns-harpers-ferry-raid.

19. History Net, "Tokyo Rose: They Called Her a Traitor," http://www.historynet.com/tokyo-rose-they-called-her-a-traitor.htm.

20. CNN, "Accused FBI Spy Hanssen Pleads Not Guilty," May 31, 2001, http://edition.cnn.com/2001/LAW/05/31/hanssen.arraignment.02/.

21. David Owen, *Hidden Secrets: The Complete History of Espionage and the Technology Used to Support It* (Ontario, Canada: Firefly Books, 2002).

22. FBI, "Famous Cases and Criminals: Aldrich Hazen Ames," http://www.fbi.gov/about-us/history/famous-cases/aldrich-hazen-ames/.

23. Lawrence Schiller, *Into the Mirror: The Life of Master Spy Robert P. Hanssen* (Darby, PA: Diane Publications, 2004).

24. Tim Culpan, "China's Clock-Punching Hackers Show Spying as Routine Job," *Bloomberg News*, May 27, 2014.

25. Hedieh Nasheri, *Economic Espionage and Industrial Spying* (Cambridge, England: Cambridge University Press, 2004).

26. Office of the National Counterintelligence Executive, "Annual Report to Congress on Foreign Economic Collection and Industrial Espionage, 2005," http://www.fas.org/irp/ops/ci/docs/2005.pdf.

27. Wesley Bruer. "FBI Sees Chinese Involvement Amid Sharp Rise in Economic Espionage Cases," CNN, July 24, 2015, http://www.cnn.com/2015/07/24/politics/fbi-economic-espionage/index.html.

28. US Department of Justice, "Former Boeing Engineer Convicted of Economic Espionage in Theft of Space Shuttle Secrets for China," Thursday, July 16, 2009, https://www.justice.gov/opa/pr/former-boeing-engineer-convicted-economic-espionage-theft-space-shuttle-secrets-china.

29. Alan M. Dershowitz, *Shouting Fire: Civil Liberties in a Turbulent Age* (New York: Little, Brown, 2002); Dershowitz, "Want to Torture? Get a Warrant," *San Francisco Chronicle*, January 22, 2002.

30. Human Rights Watch, "The Twisted Logic of Torture," January 2005, http://pantheon.hrw.org/legacy/wr2k5/darfurandabughraib/6.htm.

31. Jessica Wolfendale, "Training Torturers: A Critique of the 'Ticking Bomb' Argument," *Social Theory and Practice* 31 (2006): 269–287. Elizabeth Sepper, "The Ties That Bind: How the Constitution Limits the CIA's Actions in the War on Terror," *New York University Law Review* 81 (2006): 1805–1843.

32. Vittorio Bufacchi and Jean Maria Arrigo, "Torture, Terrorism and the State: A Refutation of the Ticking-Bomb Argument," *Journal of Applied Philosophy* 23 (2006): 355–373.

33. BBC News, "Paris Attacks: What Happened on the Night," http://www.bbc.com/news/world-europe-34818994.

34. Alissa Rubin, Lilia Blaise, Adam Nossiter, and Aurelien Breeden, "France Says Truck Attacker Was Tunisia Native with Record of Petty Crime," *New York Times*, July 15, 2016, https://www.nytimes.com/2016/07/16/world/europe/attack-nice-bastille-day.html.

35. "The Latest on the Manchester Bombing Investigation," *New York Times*, May 25, 2017, https://www.nytimes.com/2017/05/24/world/europe/manchester-uk-bombing-live.html.

36. US Department of State, "Patterns of Global Terrorism," http://www.state.gov/j/ct/rls/pgtrpt/.

37. Alex Schmid and Albert Jongman, *Political Terrorism: A New Guide to Actors, Authors, Concepts, Data Bases,*

Theories, and Literature (Amsterdam: North-Holland Publishing Company, 1988).

38. Paul Wilkinson, *Terrorism and the Liberal State* (New York: Wiley, 1977), p. 49.

39. Jack Gibbs, "Conceptualization of Terrorism," *American Sociological Review* 54 (1989): 329–340, at 330.

40. Robert Friedlander, *Terrorism* (Dobbs Ferry, NY: Oceana Publishers, 1979), p. 14.

41. Daniel Georges-Abeyie, "Political Crime and Terrorism," in *Crime and Deviance: A Comparative Perspective*, ed. Graeme Newman (Beverly Hills: Sage, 1980), pp. 313–333.

42. "Differences Between Terrorism and Insurgency," http://www.terrorism-research.com/insurgency/.

43. Tim Arango, Kareem Fahim and Ben Hubbard, "Rebels' Fast Strike in Iraq Was Years in the Making," *New York Times*, June 15, 2014, http://www.nytimes.com/2014/06/15/world/middleeast/rebels-fast-strike-in-iraq-was-years-in-the-making.html.

44. Andrew Silke, "Holy Warriors: Exploring the Psychological Processes of Jihadi Radicalization," *European Journal of Criminology* 5 (2008): 99–123.

45. FBI, "Domestic Terrorism, Focus on Militia Extremism," September 22, 2011, https://www.fbi.gov/news/stories/domestic-terrorism-focus-on-militia-extremism.

46. National Consortium for the Study of Terrorism and Responses to Terrorism (START), "Far-Right Violence in the United States: 1990–2013," https://www.start.umd.edu/pubs/START_ECDB_FarRightViolence_FactSheet_June2014.pdf.

47. Fiona Proffitt, "Costs of Animal Rights Terror," *Science* 304 (2004): 1731–1739.

48. "Animal Activists Face 'Domestic Terrorism' Charge in Freeing 5,740 Mink," *Guardian*, July 25, 2015, http://www.theguardian.com/us-news/2015/jul/25/animal-activists-minks-domestic-terrorism-charges.

49. Farouk Chothia, "Who Are Nigeria's Boko Haram Islamists?" BBC News Africa, May 20, 2014, http://www.bbc.com/news/world-africa-13809501.

50. Council on Foreign Relations, "Hezbollah," https://www.cfr.org/backgrounder/hezbollah.

51. BBC News, "Who Are the Uighurs?" April 30, 2014, http://www.bbc.com/news/world-asia-china-22278037.

52. Angel Rabasa, Peter Chalk, Kim Cragin, Sara A. Daly, Heather S. Gregg, Theodore W. Karasik, Kevin A. O'Brien, and William Rosenau, *Beyond al-Qaeda Part 1, The Global Jihadist Movement*, xviii, and *Part 2, The Outer Rings of the Terrorist Universe* (Santa Monica, CA: Rand Corporation, 2006).

53. Ibid.

54. Josh Levs and Holly Yan, "147 Dead, Islamist Gunmen Killed after Attack at Kenya College," CNN, April 2, 2015, http://www.cnn.com/2015/04/02/africa/kenya-university-attack/.

55. Richard Lough, "Piracy Ransom Cash Ends Up with Somali Militants," Reuters, July 6, 2011, http://www.reuters.com/article/2011/07/06/somalia-piracy-idUSLDE7650U320110706.

56. Lawrence Miller, "The Terrorist Mind: A Psychological and Political Analysis, Part I," *International Journal of Offender Therapy and Comparative Criminology* 50 (2006): 121–138.

57. Gabriela Fried, "Piecing Memories Together After State Terror and Policies of Oblivion in Uruguay: The Female Political Prisoner's Testimonial Project (1997–2004)," *Social Identities* 12 (2006): 543–562.

58. Martin Miller, "Ordinary Terrorism in Historical Perspective." *Journal for the Study of Radicalism* 2 (2008): 125–154.

59. Mark Hamm, "'High Crimes and Misdemeanors': George W. Bush and the Sins of Abu Ghraib," *Crime, Media, Culture: An International Journal* 3 (2007): 259–284.

60. Mark Hamm and Ramon Spaaj, "Lone Wolf Terrorism in America: Using Knowledge of Radicalization Pathways to Forge Prevention Strategies, Final Report to the US Department of Justice, 2015," https://www.ncjrs.gov/pdffiles1/nij/grants/248691.pdf.

61. Clark McCauley and Sophia Moskalenko, "Two Possible Profiles of Lone-Actor Terrorists," National Consortium for the Study of Terrorism and Responses to Terrorism (START), 2013, http://www.start.umd.edu/publication/two-possible-profiles-lone-actor-terrorists.

62. Andrew Silke, "Courage in Dark Places: Reflections on Terrorist Psychology," *Social Research* 71 (2004): 177–198.

63. Charles Ruby, "Are Terrorists Mentally Deranged?" *Analyses of Social Issues and Public Policy* 2 (2002): 15–26.

64. David Lester, Bijou Yang, and Mark Lindsay, "Suicide Bombers: Are Psychological Profiles Possible?" *Studies in Conflict and Terrorism* 27 (2004): 283–295.

65. Randy Borum, *Psychology of Terrorism* (Tampa: University of South Florida, 2004), http://www.ncjrs.gov/pdffiles1/nij/grants/208552.pdf.

66. Ethan Bueno de Mesquita, "The Quality of Terror," *American Journal of Political Science* 49 (2005): 515–530.

67. Saroj Kumar Rath, *Social Research Reports* 21 (2012): 23–36.

68. Jerrold Post, "When Hatred Is Bred in the Bone: Psycho-cultural Foundations of Contemporary

Terrorism," *Political Psychology* 25 (2005): 615–637.

69. Marc Sageman, *Understanding Terror Networks* (Philadelphia: University of Pennsylvania Press, 2004), Ch. 4.

70. Anthony Stahelski, "Terrorists Are Made, Not Born: Creating Terrorists Using Social Psychological Conditioning," *Journal of Homeland Security* (March 2004).

71. Sageman, *Understanding Terror Networks*.

72. Seth Schwartz, Curtis Dunkel, and Alan Waterman, "Terrorism: An Identity Theory Perspective," *Studies in Conflict and Terrorism* 32 (2009): 537–559.

73. Ibid.

74. Ibid.

75. Sageman, *Understanding Terror Networks*.

76. Patricia Marchak, *Reigns of Terror* (Montreal: McGill-Queen's University Press, 2003).

77. Ibid., pp. 153–155.

78. National Consortium for the Study of Terrorism and Responses to Terrorism (START), "Patterns of Islamic State-Related Terrorism, 2002–2015," http://www.start.umd.edu/pubs/START_IslamicStateTerrorism Patterns_BackgroundReport_Aug2016.pdf.

79. National Consortium for the Study of Terrorism and Responses to Terrorism (START), "Jihadist Plots in the United States, Jan. 1993 to Feb. 2016, Interim Findings," http://www.start.umd.edu/pubs/START _FailedFoiled_JihadistPlotsInterimFindings _Infographic_Jan2017.pdf.

80. National Consortium for the Study of Terrorism and Responses to Terrorism (START), "Overview: Terrorism in 2014," https://www.start.umd.edu /pubs/START_GTD_OverviewofTerrorism2014 _Aug2015.pdf.

81. Graham Allison, *Nuclear Terrorism: The Ultimate Preventable Catastrophe* (New York: Times Books, 2004).

82. K. Jack Riley, "How Prepared Are State and Local Law Enforcement for Terrorism?" Rand Corporation, https://www.rand.org/pubs/research_briefs/RB9093 .html.

83. FBI, "Joint Terrorism Task Forces," https://www.fbi .gov/investigate/terrorism/joint-terrorism-task-forces.

84. Homeland Security, "Information Sharing," http:// www.dhs.gov/topic/information-sharing.

85. Arizona Department of Public Safety, Arizona Fusion Center, https://www.azdps.gov/about/programs /actic. Also see http://www.azactic.gov/.

86. Arizona Department of Public Safety, "How Does the ACTIC Work?" http://www.azactic.gov/About /Operation/.

87. NYPD, Counterterrorism Bureau, http://www1.nyc .gov/site/nypd/bureaus/investigative/counterterrorism .page.

88. Pervaiz Shallwani, "New York City Police Department to Create New Counterterrorism Unit," *Wall Street Journal*, January 29, 2015, http://www .wsj.com/articles/new-york-city-police-department -to-create-new-counterterrorism-unit-1422570131.

89. *Hamdi v. Rumsfeld*, 542 U.S. 507 (2004).

90. *Rasul v. Bush*, 542 U.S. 466 (2004).

91. *Hamdan v. Rumsfeld*, 548 U.S. 557 (2006).

92. *Boumediene v. Bush*, 553 U.S. 723 (2008).

93. See Section 948c of the Military Commissions Act of 2009, http://www.mc.mil/Portals/0/MCA20Pub20 Law200920.pdf.

94. USA Freedom Act (H.R. 2048, Pub.L. 114–23).

95. Rabasa et al., *Beyond al-Qaeda Part 1*.

Economic Crimes: Blue-Collar, White-Collar, and Green-Collar

Learning Objectives

LO1 Discuss the history of theft offenses.

LO2 Differentiate between professional and amateur thieves.

LO3 Describe the various forms of shoplifting.

LO4 Summarize the various forms of white-collar crime.

LO5 Explain what is meant by the term *Ponzi scheme*.

LO6 Discuss efforts to control white-collar and green-collar crime.

Eli Lilly and Company
Lilly Corporate Center

AP Images/Darron Cummings

Amaury Villa   Amed Villa

Florida Department of Corrections

12

Chapter Outline

FACT OR FICTION?

▶ Most theft offenses are committed by trained professionals who know what they are doing and escape detection.

▶ Most white-collar and green-collar criminals get a slap on the wrist if they are convicted of crime.

In 2010, a gang of commercial thieves made off with $60 million worth of pharmaceuticals from a warehouse in Enfield, Connecticut; it was the largest theft in the state's history. The group known, as the Cuban Mob, was led by Amaury and Amed Villa, along with two other gang members, Yosmany Nunez and Alexander Marquez. These professional criminals targeted facilities that stored drugs, cigarettes, and consumer electronics such as cell phones. Cuban Mob members knew how to conduct surveillance, were proficient at recognizing and disarming alarm systems, and knew all about storing and selling stolen merchandise.

How did the Enfield crime go down? On the night of March 13, 2010, in the middle of a powerful storm that was lashing the East Coast with rain and wind, a tractor-trailer backed into a loading dock at a secluded Eli Lilly warehouse. After checking for security guards, two of the burglars jumped out of the truck and retrieved a ladder they had stashed earlier in the rear parking lot. They climbed atop the warehouse, cut a hole in the roof and, using ropes, lowered themselves into the facility. They proceeded to disable the alarm system; to security agents monitoring the system, it looked as if the storm had knocked out the power. Once in the warehouse, they loaded the truck with 40 shrink-wrapped pallets of pharmaceuticals, including thousands of boxes of popular medicines such as Cymbalta and Prozac; they left behind their burglars' tools.

As news of the theft spread in the media, an anonymous caller tipped the police that the people involved in the heist were Cubans, and one of the thieves was known as El Gato—the cat. To solve the crime, federal agents began checking hotels, car rentals, airline reservations, cell phone tower analysis, and other indicators that would identify the thieves. They checked for recent purchases ▶

of burglary tools—cutters, work gloves, and other items—and found that similar items had been recently purchased in a hardware store in Flushing Meadows, New York. A big clue came from a plastic water bottle left at the crime scene that contained DNA quickly matched to one of the culprits. The stolen merchandise was located in a Miami warehouse and placed under surveillance. In October 2011, authorities raided the storage facility and recovered the stolen drugs; the Villa brothers and their co-conspirators were arrested and charged with the crime. During the course of the investigation it was discovered that the gang had stolen $13.3 million in pharmaceuticals from the GlaxoSmithKline warehouse in Virginia in 2009; more than $8 million in cigarettes and a cargo trailer from an Illinois warehouse in 2010; approximately $7.8 million in cell phones and tablets from a Florida warehouse in 2011; and more than $1.5 million in cigarettes from a Kentucky warehouse in 2011. The gang used the same techniques for each theft—gained entry into the warehouse through the roof, disabled the alarm system, and loaded the stolen goods onto tractor-trailers. Each member of the Cuban Mob eventually received lengthy prison sentences for their $100 million burglary spree.[1] ■

economic crime
An act committed in violation of the criminal law for the purpose of monetary gain and financial benefits.

blue-collar crimes
Traditional common-law theft crimes such as larceny, burglary, and arson.

white-collar crimes
Crimes of business enterprise such as embezzlement, price fixing, and bribery.

green-collar crimes
Crimes that affect the environment.

theft
The intentional taking, keeping, or using of another's property without authorization or permission.

The crimes of the Cuban Mob, while inventive and elaborate, are certainly not unique. Each year millions of people suffer billions in losses to some form of **economic crime**. As a group, these offenses can be defined as illegal acts designed to bring financial reward, ranging in scope from simple theft involving a few dollars to burglaries, such as the ones pulled off by the Cuban Mob, that involve millions. Some involve amateurs who steal without expertise or planning, others are committed by professionals who carefully plan their crimes.

Economic crimes are here divided into three distinct categories:

- **Blue-collar crimes**—common-law theft crimes such as larceny, burglary, and arson
- **White-collar crimes**—crimes that involve business enterprise such as embezzlement, price fixing, and bribery
- **Green-collar crimes**—violations of laws designed to protect the environment

The development of these crime types and their nature and extent are discussed in some detail below.

History of Economic Crimes

LO1 Discuss the history of theft offenses.

Economic crimes have occurred throughout recorded history. Three thousand years ago, the Code of Hammurabi ordered the death penalty for such crimes as stealing from a palace or temple treasury, selling stolen goods, or making false claim to goods.[2] Theft was a problem in Roman bath houses, and slaves were assigned to watch bathers' property and clothes; of course, some slaves stole the clothes themselves and made a tidy profit.[3]

Under English common law, **theft** was defined as the taking of another person's property without their permission or consent. To be convicted of theft, the thief had to (a) deliberately deprive the owner of their lawful property (b) using stealth, trickery, or fraud and (c) with the intent of permanently keeping the item for themselves.

Taking something by accident or mistake was not considered theft if there was no intent to deprive the victim of their property (for example, someone accidentally takes the wrong jacket from the restaurant's coat rack). However, taking something by accident becomes a theft if once the mistake is discovered no effort is made to return the item to its rightful owner.

While first committed by amateur thieves and pickpockets, as cities developed and a permanent class of urban poor came into being, theft became professional.[4] By the eighteenth century, three separate groups of property criminals were active:

- *Skilled thieves* typically worked in the larger cities, such as London and Paris. This group included pickpockets, forgers, and counterfeiters, who operated freely. They congregated in "flash houses"—public meeting places, often taverns, that served as headquarters for gangs. Here deals were made, crimes were plotted, and the sale of stolen goods was negotiated.[5]
- *Smugglers* moved freely in sparsely populated areas and transported goods, such as spirits, gems, gold, and spices, without paying tax or duty.
- *Poachers* typically lived in the country and supplemented their diet and income with game that belonged to a landlord.

By the eighteenth century, professional thieves in the larger cities had banded together into gangs to protect themselves, increase the scope of their activities, and help dispose of stolen goods.

An eighteenth-century woodcut shows what happened when smugglers were discovered by authorities. One watches through the keyhole, another loads a pistol, and a third hides contraband. High customs duties meant that smuggling was common at that time.

Development of White-Collar and Green-Collar Crime

While we sometimes think of these business-related crimes as a new phenomenon, they have actually been around for hundreds of years, ever since the Industrial Revolution began. The period between 1750 and 1850 witnessed the widespread and unprecedented emergence of financial offenses—such as fraud and embezzlement—frequently perpetrated by respectable middle-class offenders as the banking and commercial systems developed.[6] In 1907, pioneering sociologist Edward Alsworth Ross recognized the phenomenon when he coined the phrase "the criminaloid" to describe the kind of person who hides behind his or her image as a pillar of the community and paragon of virtue to get personal gain through any means necessary.[7]

In the late 1930s, the distinguished criminologist Edwin Sutherland first used the phrase "white-collar crime" to describe the criminal activities of the rich and powerful. He defined white-collar crime as "a crime committed by a person of respectability and high social status in the course of his occupation."[8] As Sutherland saw it, white-collar crime involved conspiracies by members of the wealthy classes to use their position in commerce and industry for personal gain without regard to the law. Often, these actions were handled by civil courts because injured parties were more concerned with recovering their losses than with seeing the offenders punished criminally. Consequently, Sutherland believed that the great majority of white-collar criminals did not become the subject of criminological study. Yet the cost of white-collar crime is probably several times greater than all the crimes customarily regarded as the crime problem. And, in contrast to street crimes, white-collar offenses breed distrust in economic and social institutions, lower public morale, and undermine faith in business and government.[9]

Green-collar crime, a relatively new concept, can be viewed as a subdivision of white-collar crime. Green criminals are motivated by profit and are therefore not ecoterrorists or vandals. They want to make profits by logging in restricted areas, poaching protected fish and animals, or avoiding the payment of governmental fees. Each of these elements of economic crimes is discussed in the sections that follow.

LO2 Differentiate between professional and amateur thieves.

Blue-Collar Crimes and Criminals

Of the millions of common-law property- and theft-related crimes that occur each year, such as larceny, burglary, and arson, most are committed by amateur **occasional criminals** who do not define or view themselves as committed career criminals. Their crimes are in the moment, spontaneous, unplanned, and often not very lucrative. They may be teens seeking excitement rather than monetary gain or even angry people out for revenge who break into a rival's home to take valuables or do damage.[10]

Occasional property crime often occurs when an unplanned opportunity to commit crime, known as a **situational inducement**, suddenly presents itself: an unlocked car, a purse left out on a counter, an unobservant store manager. Situational inducements are short-term influences on a person's behavior that increase risk taking. When coupled with financial and social problems, such as substance abuse, they help push people into theft. But these amateur thieves lack planning and expertise; their crimes are likely to put them behind bars.[11]

Occasional criminals may deny their criminality and instead view their transgressions as out of character. They claim they were only "borrowing" the car when stopped by police; when confronted by the store security guard they contend they really were going to pay for the merchandise they had hidden under their coat. Because of their lack of commitment to a criminal lifestyle, occasional offenders may be the most likely to respond to the general deterrent effect of the law.

In contrast to these amateur offenders, **professional criminals** make a significant portion of their income from crime. Professionals do not delude themselves with the belief that their acts are impulsive, one-time efforts, nor do they use elaborate rationalizations to excuse the harmfulness of their actions. While the amateur may try to neutralize their guilt by claiming that their victim was insured, the professional's only regret is a slow market for stolen goods. Guiltless, professionals pursue their craft with vigor, attempting to learn from older, experienced criminals the techniques that will enable them to "earn" the most money with the least risk. Although they are relatively few in number, professionals engage in crimes that inflict the greater losses on society and perhaps cause the more significant social harm.

Professional theft consists of nonviolent forms of criminal behavior that are undertaken with a high degree of skill for monetary gain and that maximize financial opportunities and minimize the odds of apprehension. These include burglary, shoplifting, car theft, and other common-law crimes. Let's look at some of these blue-collar theft offense categories in some detail.

Larceny

Theft, or **larceny** (from *latrocinium*, Latin for "theft," and *latio*, "robber"), was one of the earliest common-law crimes created by English judges to define acts in which one person took for his or her own use the property of another. According to common law, larceny was defined as "the trespassory taking and carrying away of the personal property of another with intent to steal."[12]

As originally construed, larceny involved taking property that was in the possession of the rightful owner. It would have been considered larceny for someone to sneak into a farmer's field and steal a cow. Thus, the original common-law definition required a "trespass in the taking"; that is, for an act to be considered larceny, goods had to have been taken from the physical possession of the rightful owner. In creating this definition of larceny, English judges were more concerned with disturbance of the peace than with theft itself. They reasoned that if someone tried to steal property from another's possession, the act could eventually lead to a physical confrontation and—possibly—to the death of one party or the other. Consequently, the original definition of larceny did not include the misappropriation of goods by trickery or deceit.

The definition of larceny evolved with the growth of manufacturing and the development of the free enterprise system. Because commercial enterprise often requires that property be entrusted to a second party, larceny evolved to include the

FACT OR FICTION?

Most theft offenses are committed by trained professionals who know what they are doing and escape detection.

FICTION Most theft is the work of amateurs whose acts are spontaneous and unskilled.

occasional criminals
Offenders who do not define themselves by a criminal role or view themselves as committed career criminals.

situational inducement
Short-term influence on a person's behavior, such as financial problems or peer pressure, which increases risk taking.

professional criminals
Offenders who make a significant portion of their income from crime.

misappropriation of goods that had come into a person's possession through legitimate means. The commercial system would grind to a halt if people who were given merchandise to sell or transport could not be held liable for keeping the merchandise for their own use.

To get around the element of "trespass in the taking," English judges created the concept of **constructive possession**. This legal fiction applies to situations in which persons voluntarily give up temporary custody of their property but still believe that the property is legally theirs. If a person gives a jeweler her watch for repair, she still believes she owns the watch, in spite of the fact that she has handed it over to the jeweler. If the jeweler kept the watch or sold it, he would be guilty of larceny even though he did not "take" the watch; rather, it was given to him on a temporary basis. Over the years, new forms of larceny have been created, including shoplifting, purse snatching, and auto theft.

The FBI now records about 5.7 million acts of larceny annually, a rate of about 1,775 per 100,000 persons. Larceny rates declined about 20 percent in the past decade.[13] According to the National Crime Victimization Survey (NCVS), more than 11 million larceny thefts occur each year. And like the Uniform Crime Reports (UCR), the victim survey indicates that a steep decline (more than 33 percent) has occurred in the number and rate of larcenies during the past decade.[14]

Most US state criminal codes separate larceny into **petit (petty) larceny** and **grand larceny**. The former involves small amounts of money or property and is punished as a misdemeanor. Grand larceny, involving merchandise of greater value, is a felony punished by a sentence to serve time in the state prison. Each state sets its own boundary between grand larceny and petty larceny, but $100 to $500 is not unusual.

How larceny is categorized can have a significant influence on the level of punishment. Contemporary legal codes include a variety of theft offenses within the general category of larceny. The following sections cover the various forms of larceny that have been defined in law.

SHOPLIFTING **Shoplifting** is a very common form of larceny/theft involving the taking of goods from retail stores. Usually shoplifters try to snatch goods—such as jewelry, clothes, phones, and appliances—when store personnel are otherwise occupied and to hide the goods on their bodies.

The "five-finger discount" is an extremely common crime, and retailers lose billions annually to inventory shrinkage. In a given year, total retail losses are approximately $44 billion, accounting for 30 to 40 percent of all goods taken from stores illegally; the average shoplifting case involves about $50.[15] The most recent survey by the National Retail Federation found that every responding retail company said it had been a victim of shoplifting and other organized retail crimes in the past 12 months. The survey also uncovered a trend showing that shoplifters are becoming "more aggressive and brazen"; 97 percent reported an increase in the levels of aggression, and one in six felt the level of aggression was much higher than the previous year.[16] How much is at stake? A national survey of 25 large retail companies with 21,288 stores and over $700 billion in retail sales stores found that about 1,170,000 shoplifters were apprehended in a single year (2015); store security agents were able to recover about $300 million worth of goods.[17]

Retail security measures add to the already high cost of this crime, all of which is passed on to the consumer. Shoplifting may be attractive to some thieves because discount stores, such as Lowes, Walmart, and Target, have minimal sales help and depend on highly visible merchandise displays to attract purchasers, all of which makes them particularly vulnerable to shoplifters.

Most shoplifters are amateurs whose crimes are of minimal value.[18] In a classic study, Mary Owen Cameron found that the majority of shoplifters are amateur pilferers, called **snitches** in thieves' argot.[19] Snitches are "otherwise respectable people" who do not conceive of themselves as thieves but systematically steal merchandise for their own use. If they are not professionals and want to deny their culpability, why do they steal? Some are impulsive sensation seekers who are driven to shoplift by their psychological need to live on the edge.[20] Others are motivated by rational choice and

larceny
Taking for one's own use the property of another, by means other than force or threats on the victim or forcibly breaking into a person's home or workplace; simple theft.

constructive possession
A legal fiction that applies to situations in which persons voluntarily give up physical custody of their property but still retain legal ownership.

petit (petty) larceny
Theft of a small amount of money or property, punished as a misdemeanor.

grand larceny
Theft of money or property of substantial value, punished as a felony.

shoplifting
The taking of goods from retail stores.

snitch
Amateur shoplifter who does not self-identify as a thief but who systematically steals merchandise for personal use.

L03 Describe the various forms of shoplifting.

the desire to get something for nothing. Still another motivation for shoplifting seems to be psychological distress; some amateur shoplifters are looking for a release from anxiety and depression.[21] Another type of snitch needs to get quick cash to feed a drug habit. Research shows that products that serve a role in illicit drug use are actually the ones most often stolen from retail stores.[22] Both male and female drug users report that shoplifting is a form of work which helps support their habits, preferable and less dangerous than robbery for men and sex work for women.[23]

Criminologists view amateur shoplifters as people who are most likely to reform if apprehended. Cameron reasoned that because snitches are not part of a criminal subculture and do not think of themselves as criminals, they are deterred by initial contact with the law. Because getting arrested traumatizes them, they will not risk a second offense.

Cameron also found that about 10 percent of all shoplifters were professionals, who derived the majority of their income from shoplifting. Called **boosters** or **heels**, professional shoplifters steal with the intention of reselling stolen merchandise to pawnshops or fences, or sell on the Internet.

These professionals can walk into a department store, fill up a cart with expensive medicines, electronics, and other high-cost items, and use deceptive techniques to slip past security guards.[24] Hitting several stores in a day and the same store once a month, a professional thief can make between $100,000 and $200,000 a year. Some enter a store carrying a "shopping list" provided by a fence who will pay them in cash or drugs. Pros wear or carry devices and implements that help them avoid detection while shoplifting. They place a large open shopping bag obtained from another store, name prominently displayed, on the floor by their feet and casually drop in merchandise. They use a **booster box**, a device with a false bottom that can be open and shut by the operator; placed over merchandise, the bottom is opened and then closed, capturing the goods.

A professional female shoplifter will stroll into a store with a baby carriage accompanied by a friend wearing maternity clothes. Carriages are useful because no one wants to disturb a sleeping baby wrapped in blankets, which of course can also be used to hide stolen merchandise. And who would suspect a visibly pregnant woman, even though the expandable outfit is perfect for stuffing in high-priced merchandise and walking casually out the door.

Pros will later sell the merchandise in their own discount stores, at flea markets, or through online auctions. Some sell to fences who repackage—or "scrub"—the goods and pawn them off on retailers at prices that undercut legitimate distributors. Ironically, some stolen merchandise can actually make its way back onto the shelves of the chain store from which it was stolen.[25]

To encourage the arrest of shoplifters, a number of states have passed **merchant privilege laws** designed to offer retailers and their employees some protection from lawsuits stemming from improper or false arrests of suspected shoplifters. These laws require that arrests be made on reasonable grounds or probable cause, that detention be short, and that store employees or security guards conduct themselves reasonably. In addition, security systems now feature source tagging, a process by which manufacturers embed the tag in the packaging or in the product itself. Thieves have trouble removing or defeating such tags, and retailers save on the time and labor needed to attach the tags at the store.

CREDIT CARD THEFT Use of stolen credit cards and credit card numbers has become a major problem in the United States, costing consumers and merchants hundreds of billions each year.[26] Most credit card abuse is the work of amateurs who steal cards or use illegally obtained card numbers, and then use them at local stores or online. However, professional credit card rings have gotten into the act.

To curtail individual losses from credit card theft, in 1971 Congress limited a cardholder's liability to $50 per stolen card. Similarly, some states, such as California, have passed laws making it a misdemeanor to obtain property or services by means of cards that have been stolen, forged, canceled, or revoked, or whose use is unauthorized for any reason.[27]

booster (heel)
Professional shoplifter who steals with the intention of reselling stolen merchandise.

booster box
Device with a false bottom that can be open and shut by a professional shoplifter, lined with metal or some other substance to prevent security tags from setting off alarms, placed over merchandise.

merchant privilege laws
Legislation that protects retailers and their employees from lawsuits if they arrest and detain a suspected shoplifter on reasonable grounds.

AUTO THEFT Motor vehicle theft is another common larceny offense. Almost every state requires owners to insure their vehicles, and auto theft is one of the most highly reported of all major crimes (75 percent of all auto thefts are reported to police). The FBI now records 700,000 auto thefts per year, which account for a total loss of about $5 billion. Just as for other crimes, there has been a significant reduction in motor vehicle theft rates over the past decade, and the number of car thefts has declined more than 40 percent.

There are two distinct categories of auto thieves, amateur and professional. A significant number of auto thefts are carried out by amateur thieves who steal cars for a number of reasons that involve some form of temporary personal use. Among the reasons why an amateur would steal a car:

- *Joyriding*. Many car thefts are motivated by teenagers' desire to acquire the power, prestige, sexual potency, and recognition associated with an automobile. Joyriders steal cars to experience, even briefly, the benefits associated with owning an automobile.
- *Short-term transportation*. Auto theft for short-term transportation is similar to joyriding. It involves the theft of a car simply to go from one place to another. In more serious cases, the thief may drive to another city or state and then steal another car to continue the journey.
- *Long-term transportation*. Thieves who steal cars for long-term transportation intend to keep the cars for their personal use. Usually older than joyriders, these auto thieves may repaint and otherwise disguise cars to avoid detection.
- *Parts*. Some amateurs are auto strippers who steal batteries, tires, and wheel covers to reequip their own cars.
- *Commission of another crime*. A few auto thieves steal cars to use in other crimes, such as robberies and thefts. This type of auto thief desires both mobility and anonymity.

In recent years, there has been an increase in the number of highly organized professionals involved in auto theft. Some are involved in **car cloning**—reselling expensive cars after altering their identification numbers and falsifying their registration papers. How does cloning work? After stealing a luxury car from a mall or parking lot, car thieves later visit a large car dealership in another state and look for a car that's the exact make and model (and even the same color) as the stolen one. The thieves jot down the vehicle identification number (VIN) stamped on the top of the dashboard and drive off. The manufacturer-installed VIN plate on the stolen car is removed and replaced with a homemade counterfeit, similar to the original, only this one bears the VIN of the legitimate vehicle. Phony ownership and registration documents complete the cloning. At that point, the stolen vehicle can be easily registered with a motor vehicle agency in another state and sold to an unwary buyer.[28]

car cloning
Using a vehicle identification number (VIN) from a legally registered car to hide the identity of a stolen vehicle for resale.

Some cars are stolen in order to be sold to chop shops for spare parts, including blue-white, high-intensity discharge headlights, air bags, and custom rims.[29] What cars are stolen most? Rather than a brand new Porsche or Mercedes, stolen cars tend to be older, popular models that can be quickly sold to chop shops where their parts are stripped for resale. The most commonly stolen cars today include:

1. 1996 Honda Accord
2. 1998 Honda Civic
3. 2006 Ford pickup
4. 2004 Chevrolet pickup (full size)
5. 2014 Toyota Camry[30]

How much can a thief expect to get for these stolen spare parts? Among the most attractive targets are these parts:

- *Global positioning system*. It now costs approximately $950 to replace a GPS on a Mercedes. The whole unit for a Honda Odyssey can cost up to $1,200, navigation included.
- *Air conditioning*. Today, the air conditioning compressor for a Toyota Camry costs up to $1,000. One for a Ford goes between $500 and $1,000.

- *Air bags.* These life savers do well in the auto-part seller's market. Air bags go for about $200.
- *Exhaust.* The exhaust system carries emissions from the engine to the atmosphere. An overall exhaust system—including catalytic converter in some vehicles—can range up to $2,800 for luxury cars such as BMW and Mercedes.[31]

BAD CHECKS Another form of larceny involves intentionally cashing checks on a nonexistent or underfunded bank account. In general, for a person to be guilty of passing a bad check, the bank the check is drawn on must refuse payment and the check casher must fail to make the check good within 10 days after finding out the check was not honored.

Edwin Lemert conducted the best-known study of check forgers 60 years ago.[32] Lemert found that the majority of check forgers—he called them **naive check forgers**—are amateurs who do not believe their actions will hurt anyone. Most naive check forgers come from middle-class backgrounds and have little identification with a criminal subculture. They pass bad checks because of a financial crisis that demands an immediate resolution—perhaps they have lost money at the racetrack and have some pressing bills to pay.

Lemert found that a few professionals, whom he called **systematic forgers**, make a substantial living passing bad checks. Estimating the number of such forgeries committed each year or the amounts involved is difficult. Stores and banks may choose not to press charges because it is not worth it to them to make the effort to collect the money due them. It is also difficult to separate the true check forger from the neglectful shopper.

Some of the different techniques used in check fraud schemes, which may cost retail establishments upward of $1 billion per year, are set out in Exhibit 12.1.

RECEIVING AND FENCING STOLEN PROPERTY The crime of receiving stolen goods is a type of larceny/theft that involves the buying or acquiring possession of property by a person who knows (or should know) that the seller acquired it through theft or

---

naive check forgers
Amateurs who cash bad checks because of some financial crisis but have little identification with a criminal subculture.

systematic forgers
Professionals who make a living by passing bad checks.

Exhibit 12.1   Check Fraud Schemes and Techniques

- *Forged signatures.* Legitimate blank checks with an imitation of the payor's signature.
- *Forged endorsements.* The use of a stolen check, which is then endorsed and cashed or deposited by someone other than the payee.
- *Identity assumption.* Identity assumption occurs when criminals learn information about a financial institution customer, such as name, address, financial institution account number, Social Security number, home and work telephone numbers, or employer, and use the information to misrepresent themselves as the valid financial institution customer.
- *Counterfeit checks.* Counterfeit checks are presented based on fraudulent identification or are false checks drawn on valid accounts. Due to the advancement in color copying and desktop publishing capabilities, this is the fastest-growing source of fraudulent checks today.

- *Altered checks.* After a legitimate maker creates a valid check to pay a debt, a criminal then takes the good check and uses chemicals or other means to erase the amount or the name of the payee, so that new information can be entered. The new information can be added by typewriter, in handwriting, or with a laser printer or check imprinter.
- *Closed account fraud.* This is based on checks being written against closed accounts. This type of fraud generally relies upon the float time involved in interfinancial institution transactions.
- *Check kiting.* The process of depositing a check from one bank account into a second bank account without sufficient funds to cover the amount.

Sources: Check Fraud Working Group, "Check Fraud, A Guide to Avoiding Losses," Washington, DC, https://www.occ.gov/static /publications/chckfrd/chckfrd.pdf; National Check Fraud Center, http://www.ckfraud.org/ (URLs accessed May 2017).

some other illegal means. For this to constitute a crime, the receiver must know the goods were stolen at the time he receives them and must have the intent to aid the thief. Depending on the value of the property received, *receiving* stolen property is either a misdemeanor or a felony. *Fencing* is a crime that involves an ongoing effort to be a middleman or distributor of illegally received goods.

Today, the professional **fence**, who earns his or her living solely by buying and reselling stolen merchandise, seems more like the "professional criminal" described by Sutherland earlier in the chapter than almost any other kind of criminal offender. Fences use stealth rather than violence, guile and knowledge rather than force or threat, as they buy and sell stolen merchandise ranging from diamonds to wheel rims.[33] The advent of the Internet, which allows for the international sale of goods, has changed the nature of fencing from a local to global crime, and created a new breed of fence whose customers and clients can be found anywhere in the world. In the Internet age, some fences have begun to sell their merchandise online on a variety of merchandising websites. About one-third of auction and blog sites' listings for "new in box" or "new with tags" items are actually goods that were stolen through organized retail theft. E-fencers like to sell, at a discount, small items in bulk—razor blades, makeup, skincare products, baby formula, over-the-counter medications and teeth-whitening strips—as well as more expensive items—disposable cell phones, digital cameras, and electric shavers—that can bring big online profits.[34]

fence
A buyer and seller of stolen merchandise.

burglary
Entering a home by force, threat, or deception with intent to commit a crime.

Burglary

Under common law, the crime of **burglary** was defined as "the breaking and entering of a dwelling house of another in the nighttime with the intent to commit a felony within." Burglary is considered a much more serious crime than larceny/theft because it involves entering another's home, which threatens occupants. Even though the home may be unoccupied at the time of the burglary, the potential for harm to the occupants is so significant that most state jurisdictions punish burglary as a felony.

The legal definition of burglary has undergone considerable change since its common-law origins. When first created by English judges during the late Middle Ages, laws against burglary were designed to protect people whose homes might be set upon by wandering criminals. Including the phrase "breaking and entering" in the definition protected people from unwarranted intrusions; if an invited guest stole something, it would not be considered a burglary. Similarly, the requirement that the crime be committed at nighttime was added because evening was considered the time when honest people might fall prey to criminals.[35]

More recent US state laws have changed the requirements of burglary, and most have discarded the necessity of forced entry. Entry through deceit (for example, by posing as a deliveryman), through threat, or through conspiracy with others (such as guests or servants) is deemed legally equivalent to breaking and is called "constructive breaking." Many states now protect all structures, not just dwelling houses. A majority of states have also removed the nighttime element from their definitions of burglary. States commonly enact laws creating different degrees of burglary. The more serious, heavily punished crimes involve nighttime forced entry into the home; the least serious involve daytime entry into a nonresidential structure by an unarmed offender.

NATURE AND EXTENT OF BURGLARY The FBI's definition of burglary is not restricted to burglary from a person's home; it includes any unlawful entry of a structure to

Maine State Police/Handout/Reuters

Most burglars are not professionals. Christopher Knight, arrested by Maine police on suspicion of being involved in 1,000 burglaries since 1986, is pictured here on surveillance cameras at the Pine Tree Camp in Rome, Maine. Knight lived in a makeshift camp in the woods for 27 years and supported himself through burglary.

commit a theft or felony. Burglary is further categorized into three subclasses: forcible entry, unlawful entry where no force is used, and attempted forcible entry.

According to the UCR, about 1.5 million burglaries now take place each year. Like other crimes, burglaries and burglary rates have declined for the past decade: The number of burglaries decreased 28 percent during the past decade.[36]

Burglars target homes more often than nonresidential structures such as factories and stores. Most residential burglaries occur during the day, from 6:00 A.M. to 6:00 P.M., when few people are home, whereas nonresidential structures are targeted in the evening, when businesses and shops are closed. The average dollar loss per burglary offense is more than $2,300; in all, burglaries cost victims about $4 billion per year.

While the NCVS also recorded a decline in the number of annual burglaries reported by victims, it reports that about 3 million residential burglaries are either attempted or completed each year, almost double the number computed by the UCR, a discrepancy explained by the fact that only about half of all burglary victims report the crime to police.[37]

According to the NCVS, those most likely to be burglarized are relatively poor Hispanic and African American families. Owner-occupied and single-family residences had lower burglary rates than renter-occupied and multiple-family dwellings.

PROFESSIONAL BURGLARS While most burglaries may be carried out by amateurs and occasional thieves, some offenders make burglary their career and continually develop new specialized skills.[38] They develop technical competence, including finding ways to gain entry into homes and apartment houses, selecting targets with high potential payoffs, choosing items with a high resale value, opening safes properly without damaging their contents, and using the proper equipment, including cutting torches, electric saws, explosives, and metal bars.

Professional burglars seem to embody rational decision making in their choice of targets. They follow a script when they decide where to burgle. Most adapt their behavior to the community in which they reside. They avoid difficult and well-guarded targets with security gates.[39] Whether they operate alone or in groups, experienced burglars like to choose targets in neighborhoods they know so they can make their way home undetected if things go awry.[40]

Burglars learn to target areas with minimum security and lucrative targets. Once they find an easy target area they return time and again, creating a booster effect in the neighborhood burglary rate.[41] They avoid difficult and well-guarded targets with security gates.[42] Most prefer to burglarize in their own neighborhood where escape routes are well known; some are willing to travel farther to commit crimes when there are good roadways and getting around is easy.[43] And while security guards may deter some burglars, alarms and other devices designed to protect homes may actually have an opposite effect on a savvy burglar: why have an alarm unless there was something worth taking inside?[44]

Successful burglars must be able to adjust to social, technical, and legal change. In states where "stand your ground" laws have been passed, burglars seem willing to switch their targets from residential to commercial properties in order to avoid armed homeowners who are willing to shoot to protect their property.[45] Nonetheless, professional burglars also take into account the fact that social change has created a rise in dual-income families, leaving many residential properties with no one at home during the daytime.[46]

Arson

arson
The willful, malicious burning of a home, building, or vehicle.

Arson is the willful, malicious burning of a home, public building, vehicle, or commercial building. Although arson data can be sketchy since only a limited number of jurisdictions report arsons, the FBI reports that about 45,000 arsons are now recorded annually, with an average cost of about $14,000 each. Arson attacks are not unique to the United States.

CONNECTIONS

According to the rational choice approach discussed in Chapter 4, burglars make rational and calculated decisions before committing crimes. If circumstances and culture dictate their activities, their decisions must be considered a matter of choice.

There are several motives for arson. Adult arsonists may be motivated by severe emotional turmoil or a disturbed personality.[47] Research on the background characteristics of juvenile fire setters shows that their acts are often associated with antisocial behavior and psychopathology.[48] These findings support the claim that arson should be viewed as a mental health problem, not a criminal act, and should be treated with counseling and other therapeutic measures, rather than with severe punishments.[49]

Not all fires are the work of emotionally disturbed people; some are set by professionals who engage in arson for profit. People who want to collect insurance money but are afraid or unable to set the fires themselves hire professional arsonists who know how to set fires and make the cause seem accidental (such as an electrical short circuit). Another form is arson fraud, which involves a business owner burning his or her own property.

AP Images/Damian Dovarganes

Some arsons cause millions in damages. On December 8, 2014, Los Angeles firefighters battled a fire in the seven-story Da Vinci apartment complex under construction in downtown Los Angeles. Investigators later determined that arson caused the massive fire, resulting in an estimated $100 million in damages. The intense heat also melted freeway signs and cracked or shattered hundreds of windows in nearby office buildings. Fifty-six-year-old Dawud Abdulwali was arrested and later sentenced to 15 years. His motive: anger at police over the shooting of Michael Brown in Ferguson, Missouri. "Cops kill my people . . . We should go do this, we should go burn some [expletive] down."

White-Collar Crime

White-collar crime is defined as any business-related act that uses deceit, deception, or dishonesty to carry out criminal enterprise. Included within the scope of white-collar crime are such diverse acts as income tax evasion, employee theft, soliciting bribes, accepting kickbacks, and embezzlement. Nor do criminologists restrict the definition to the wealthy and powerful; members of all social classes may engage in white-collar crimes.

L04 Summarize the various forms of white-collar crime.

How much white-collar crime takes place each year? While it's difficult to calculate, the National White Collar Crime Center conducts periodic national surveys of thousands of people and taps into individual experiences with business crimes to give a picture of how widespread white-collar crime is and how many citizens are affected by these business enterprise crimes.[50] The most recent survey found that:

- About 24 percent of households and 17 percent of individuals reported experiencing at least one form of white-collar crime within the previous year.
- White-collar crimes happened at both household and individual levels, most often as a result of credit card fraud, price misrepresentation, and unnecessary repairs.
- More than half (55 percent) of the households surveyed reported a white-collar crime to a credit card company, the business or person involved, law enforcement, consumer protection agency, or their personal attorney.
- Only about 12 percent of the crimes were reported to law enforcement or some other crime control agency.
- The general public views white-collar crimes as a serious problem, considering them more damaging than traditional crimes.[51]

It is not surprising, then, that some estimate that the annual cost of white-collar crime in the United States is over $600 billion; globally it's in the trillions.[52] These losses far outstrip the expense of any other type of crime. Nor is it likely that the full extent of white-collar crime will ever be known because many victims (70 percent) are reluctant to report their crime to police, believing that nothing can be done and that getting further involved is pointless.[53]

White-collar crime today represents a wide spectrum of behaviors involving individuals acting alone and within the context of a business structure. The victims of white-collar crime can be the general public, the organization that employs the offender, or a competing organization. Here we break down white-collar crime into a number of independent yet interrelated criminal activities, ranging from an individual using a business enterprise to commit theft-related crimes to a business enterprise engaging in activities that violate laws that regulate business and commerce.[54]

Business Frauds and Swindles

Business frauds and swindles occur when someone uses his institutional or business position to trick others out of their money. One type is called contract fraud, in which a swindler lures a victim into signing a long-term agreement without informing them that the fine print on the sales contract obligates them to purchase some high-priced services they did not really want in the first place. Another ploy is to trick the victim into thinking the contract is from a legitimate vendor because it has a familiar look. A business office receives an invoice in the mail with a self-addressed envelope that without close examination looks like a legitimate bill from Verizon or AT&T. On the back, in small print, is written, "By returning this confirmation, you're signing a contract to be an advertiser in the upcoming, and all subsequent, issues of the 'People's Yellow Pages.'" If an employee returns the invoice, the business soon finds that it has agreed to a costly long-term contract to advertise in some private publication that is not widely distributed.

L05 Explain what is meant by the term *Ponzi scheme*.

PONZI SCHEMES A Ponzi scheme is a type of swindle that involves the payment of purported returns to existing investors from funds contributed by new investors. Someone sets up a mutual fund and promises a 20 percent interest guaranteed. The scheme organizers solicit new investors by promising these high returns with little or no risk. However, nothing is actually invested; the 20 percent interest is paid by returning part of the principle each year. At that rate the scheme can go on for at least five years. It can even go on longer if new investors are brought in and their capital is used to pay the original shareholders' interest payments. The swindlers take the bulk of the money and stash it away in hidden bank accounts. Ponzi schemes collapse when it becomes difficult to recruit new investors or when a large number of investors ask to cash out and find that the money has disappeared.

Why are they called "Ponzi schemes"? The term comes from one Charles Ponzi, who duped thousands of New England residents into investing in a postage stamp speculation scheme back in the 1920s. At a time when the annual interest rate for bank accounts was 5 percent, Ponzi promised investors that he could provide a 50 percent return in just 90 days. Ponzi used incoming funds to pay off earlier investors.[55]

The most famous and costly Ponzi scheme involved financier Bernard Madoff, who collected billions from celebrity clients. Rather than investing any of the money he instead deposited it in various banks. He used money given to him by new clients to pay dividends and interest owed to previous investors. He encouraged people to keep their money in the account and reinvest profit and dividends. Every month investors got a statement showing more and more paper profits. When the stock market melted down in 2007 and people wanted to cash in their stock, Madoff's house of cards fell apart: all the money was gone. Losses amounted to about $18 billion. He eventually pleaded guilty to an 11-count criminal complaint for violations sentenced to 150 years in prison, a life sentence. In the end, Madoff was regarded as the symbol of the greed run amuck that almost destroyed the nation's financial system.

The Profiles in Crime feature looks at a fraud scheme that was emotionally devastating to the victims.

PROFILES IN CRIME

FERTILITY FRAUD

Allison Layton owned a California company called Miracles Egg Donation. She claimed to be in the business of helping infertile couples have children. Would-be parents paid Miracles tens of thousands of dollars—sometimes their life savings—for egg donation and surrogacy services. But Layton's business turned out to be a fraud, and she ended up stealing her victims' hopes and dreams as well as their money.

During a three-year period, she defrauded couples, egg donors, and surrogate mothers while living a lavish lifestyle off the proceeds. Many of the victims were in a vulnerable place in their lives—working against their biological clocks and trying to afford this expensive and time-consuming procedure. The fees paid to Miracles by would-be parents—known in the surrogacy world as intended parents—were supposed to go into escrow accounts to be withdrawn for expenses related to surrogacy or egg donation. But Layton took the money and spent it on her own $60,000 wedding, a new vehicle for her husband, and high-end shopping sprees she flaunted on social media.

As a result, egg donors, surrogates, attorneys, and others often were not paid for the services they provided, and many intended parents—including some who lived overseas—failed to get the services they paid for in advance; some effectively missed the opportunity to have children.

Layton's criminal enterprise was a classic Ponzi scheme: Early on, some people got the services they paid for, but then she began shuffling funds to cover some clients' services and not others. And when it all finally collapsed, nobody was getting anything.

When confronted by clients, Layton lied about why payments had not been made and refunds not issued. She led victims to believe they might soon be paid, when, in fact, many were not. More than 40 victims lost in excess of $270,000. Clients contacted law enforcement authorities, and Layton was charged with wire fraud. In a plea agreement with federal prosecutors, she admitted to defrauding the victims, and in September 2015, a judge sentenced the 38-year-old to 18 months in prison. ■

Source: US Attorney's Office Central District of California, "Owner of San Gabriel Valley Surrogacy Agency Sentenced to Federal Prison for Ripping Off Would-Be Parents Who Paid for Egg Donations," September 28, 2015, https://www.fbi.gov/losangeles/press-releases/2015/owner-of-san-gabriel-valley-surrogacy-agency-sentenced-to-federal-prison-for-ripping-off-would-be-parents-who-paid-for-egg-donations (accessed May 2017).

TELEMARKETING SWINDLES Telemarketing swindles occur when someone calls the victim, makes a false statement, and the misrepresentation causes the victim to give money to the caller. Some victims are told that they won a prize and personal information is required to receive the prize. In another example, the scammer calls the victim, claiming to be from an antivirus software company, and convinces the victim to allow the caller to access his or her computer in order to rid it of a fictional virus. Once the scammer has the victim's personal information, he can use it to access the victim's bank accounts. Here are some typical telemarketing swindle come-ons:

- "You must act now or the offer won't be good."
- "You've won a 'free' gift, vacation, or prize." But you have to pay for "postage and handling" or other charges.
- "You must send money, give a credit card or bank account number, or have a check picked up by courier." You may hear this before you have had a chance to consider the offer carefully.
- "You don't need to check out the company with anyone."
- "You don't need any written information about their company or their references."
- "You can't afford to miss this 'high-profit, no-risk' offer."[56]

chiseling
Using illegal means to cheat an
organization, its consumers, or
both, on a regular basis.

insider trading
Illegal buying of stock in a
company on the basis of
information provided by someone
who has a fiduciary interest in
the company.

Chiseling

Another type of business swindle, **chiseling** involves an ongoing conspiracy to use one's business position to cheat institutions or individuals by providing them with faulty or bogus goods and services or by providing services that violate legal controls on business practices. Chiselers may be individuals who want to make quick profits in their own business or employees of large organizations who deceive their superiors and violate company policy to make illegal gains.

Chiseling schemes sometimes involve overbilling or charging for goods and services that the customer never received, such as for bogus auto repairs that were not required and never performed. It can also involve substituting cheap off-brand merchandise for higher priced name brands, or short weighting (intentionally tampering with the accuracy of scales used to weigh products) in supermarkets. Typically chiseling is an ongoing criminal enterprise in which rules are bent and broken.[57]

PROFESSIONAL CHISELING Some chiselers are highly educated professionals who are in a position to defraud clients. Pharmacists have been known to alter prescriptions or substitute low-cost generic drugs for more expensive name brands.[58] The most notorious case of professional chiseling involved Kansas City pharmacist Robert R. Courtney, who was charged with fraud when it was discovered that he had been selling diluted mixtures of the medications Taxol, Gemzar, Paraplatin, and Platinol, which are used to treat cancer.[59] After he pleaded guilty, Courtney told authorities that his criminal activities affected the patients of 400 doctors, involved 98,000 prescriptions, and harmed approximately 4,200 patients.[60]

FINANCIAL CHISELING A great deal of professional chiseling takes place on the commodities and stock markets, where individuals engage in deceptive schemes to defraud clients. For example, dishonest investment counselors and insurance agents may use their positions to cheat individual clients by misleading them on the quality of their investments; financial organizations cheat their clients by promoting risky investments as being iron-clad safe.

Financial chiseling schemes can involve stockbrokers, mortgage brokers, bankers, and other fiduciary agents who violate accepted commercial practices. Their schemes include *churning*, in which a stockbroker manipulates a client's account by repeated, excessive, and unnecessary buying and selling of stock, and *front running*, where a broker places personal orders ahead of a customer's large order to profit from the market effects of the trade.[61]

Financial chiselers also engage in **insider trading**, which occurs when someone uses their position of trust to profit from information unavailable to the public in order to buy and sell securities for personal profit. The law prohibiting insider trading was originally conceived to make it illegal for corporate employees with direct knowledge of market-sensitive information to use that information for their own benefit or that of their friends and relatives. It would be illegal for employees to buy stock, using their insider information, in a company that their employer was about to take over at a much higher price. In recent years, the definition of insider trading has been expanded by federal courts to include employees of financial institutions, such as law or banking firms, who have access to confidential information about corporate clients.[62] Federal laws and the rules of the Securities and Exchange Commission require that all profits from such trading be returned and provide for both fines and a prison sentence.

Exploitation

It is sad but true that some individuals exploit their position, even during times of war, in order to extort people to make an illegal profit. They use their power to take advantage of others who have an interest in how that power is used. A fire inspector who threatens a restaurant owner with a safety violation unless he is given a financial consideration is abusing his institutional position. In 2017, Arnaldo Echevarria, a former Immigration and Customs Enforcement (ICE) officer, was convicted on federal charges that he demanded $75,000 in bribes along with sex in exchange for work papers.[63]

Echevarria's crimes are considered a form of **exploitation**: a victim has a clear right to expect a service, and the offender threatens to withhold the service unless an additional payment or bribe is forthcoming. Echevarria's victims believed they would be arrested or deported unless they complied with his demands.

Exploitation can also occur in private industry. A company employee might refuse to award a contract to a supplier unless they gave him or her a "piece of the action." Purchasing agents in large companies often demand payment for awarding contracts to suppliers and distributors. Managing agents in some of New York City's most luxurious buildings have been convicted on charges that they routinely extorted millions of dollars from maintenance contractors and building suppliers before awarding them contracts that they deserved on the merits of their service.[64]

Influence Peddling

In 2014, a scam was exposed in which corrupt state employees and their accomplices were selling California driver's licenses for cash. A man who owned a driving school let his students know that—for a price—he could guarantee them a license, even if they had already failed the driving test. Those willing to pay anywhere from $500 to $2,500 to corrupt Department of Motor Vehicle (DMV) employees could get a license with no questions asked. As word got around, people actually flew in from other states just to take a California driving test. A number of DMV employees who participated in the scam went to prison for up to 18 months.[65]

Sometimes individuals holding important institutional positions sell power, influence, and information to outsiders who have an interest in manipulating the activities of the institution or buying information on what the institution may do in the future. In addition to DMV employees selling licenses to people who do not deserve them, offenses within this category include government employees taking kickbacks from contractors in return for awarding them contracts they could not have won on merit, or outsiders bribing government officials to give them special privileges they do not deserve, such as green cards, driver's licenses, and liquor licenses.[66]

While exploiters are extortionists who force victims to pay for services to which they are legally entitled, influence peddlers take bribes in exchange for granting undeserved favorable treatment. The "victim" of **influence peddling** is the organization whose integrity is compromised by one of its employees for their own interests.

INFLUENCE PEDDLING IN GOVERNMENT In 2015, Sheldon Silver, speaker of the New York state assembly and one of the state's most powerful politicians, was convicted of numerous charges of influence peddling. In one scheme, he secretly directed $500,000 in state money to Columbia University doctor Robert Taub's mesothelioma research. In return, the doctor gave Silver leads on his patients who were suffering from the deadly effects of asbestos exposure. Silver then directed those patients to the personal injury firm Weitz and Luxenberg, which paid Silver $3 million in referral fees. In the second scheme, Silver directed two major developers to use the law firm Goldberg and Iryami for litigation challenging city tax assessments. That firm secretly paid Silver $700,000 in referral fees.[67]

exploitation
Forcing victims to pay for services or contracts to which they have a clear right.

influence peddling
Using one's institutional position to grant favors and sell information to which one's co-conspirators are not entitled.

AP Images/Scranton Times-Tribune, Michael J. Mullen

Sandy Fonzo confronts former Luzerne County Judge Mark A. Ciavarella as he leaves the federal courthouse in Scranton, Pennsylvania. Fonzo's son, who was jailed when he was 17 by Ciavarella, committed suicide at the age of 23. Ciavarella is serving a 28-year sentence and fellow ex-judge Michael Conahan 17 years for taking $2.6 million from companies looking to build and fill a youth detention center for Luzerne County. The scam entangled thousands of innocent children in Pennsylvania's juvenile court system and sent many to the detention center who should never have been incarcerated.

It is unfortunately common for government workers and office holders to engage in official corruption, a circumstance that is particularly disturbing because society expects a higher standard of moral integrity from people empowered to uphold the law and judge their fellow citizens.

One of the worst and most notorious cases of influence peddling involved two judges who took bribes to put kids in detention. Pennsylvania judges Mark Ciavarella and Michael Conahan were convicted for accepting $2.6 million in payoffs to put juvenile offenders in lockups run by a privately managed youth detention corporation. Thousands of kids were put away for minor infractions so that the judges could earn millions in illegal payoffs, and the detention centers were kept filled at the expense of the state. Both judges eventually pleaded guilty and received long prison sentences.[68]

INFLUENCE PEDDLING IN BUSINESS Politicians and government officials are not the only ones accused of bribery; business has had its share of scandals. People who hold power in a business may force those wishing to work with the company to pay them some form of bribe or gratuity to gain a contract. In the building industry, a purchasing agent may demand a kickback from contractors hoping to gain a service contract. Other employees are willing to disclose confidential company information, giving competitors and suppliers a market advantage, in exchange for payments.[69]

Business-related bribery is not unique to the United States. It is common for foreign officials to solicit bribes to allow American firms to do business in their countries. Even such prestigious companies as International Business Machines Corporation (IBM) have been accused of bribery: IBM settled a case and agreed to pay some $10 million over improper gifts to government officials in South Korea and China.[70] Some important recent cases are set out in Exhibit 12.2.

In response to these revelations, Congress passed the Foreign Corrupt Practices Act (FCPA), which makes it a criminal offense to bribe foreign officials or to make other questionable overseas payments. Violations of the FCPA draw strict penalties for both the defendant company and its officers.[71] Moreover, all fines imposed on corporate officers are paid by them, not absorbed by the company. If a domestic company violates the anti-bribery provisions of the FCPA, it can be fined up to $1 million.

Exhibit 12.2   Recent Foreign Corrupt Practices Act (FCPA) Enforcement Actions

- *Biomet.* The Warsaw, Indiana–based medical device manufacturer agreed to pay more than $30 million to resolve SEC and Justice Department investigations into the company's anti-bribery violations in Brazil and Mexico.

- *Teva Pharmaceutical.* The global generic drug manufacturer agreed to pay $519 million to settle parallel civil and criminal charges that it paid bribes to foreign government officials in Russia, Ukraine, and Mexico.

- *JPMorgan.* The firm agreed to pay $264 million to the SEC, Justice Department, and Federal Reserve to settle charges that it corruptly influenced government officials and won business in the Asia-Pacific region by giving jobs and internships to their relatives and friends.

- *Anheuser-Busch InBev.* The Belgium-based global brewery agreed to pay $6 million to settle charges that it violated the FCPA by using third-party sales promoters to make improper payments to government officials in India and "chilled" a whistleblower who reported the misconduct.

- *Johnson Controls.* The Wisconsin-based global provider of HVAC systems agreed to pay more than $14 million to settle charges that its Chinese subsidiary used sham vendors to make improper payments to employees of Chinese government-owned shipyards and other officials to win business.

Source: Securities and Exchange Commission, SEC Enforcement Actions: FCPA Cases, 2017, https://www.sec.gov/spotlight/fcpa/fcpa-cases.shtml (accessed May 2017).

Company officers, employees, or stockholders who are convicted of bribery may have to serve a prison sentence of up to five years and pay a $10,000 fine.

Employee Fraud and Embezzlement

Another type of white-collar crime involves individuals' use of their positions to embezzle company funds or appropriate company property for themselves. Here the company or organization that employs the criminal, rather than an outsider, is the victim of white-collar crime.

EMPLOYEE THEFT AND PILFERAGE Each year thousands of employees are caught stealing from their employers and coworkers. National surveys show that one out of every 38 employees is now being apprehended for theft each year. Stolen funds recovered from dishonest employee apprehensions totaled over $55 million in a single year (2015).

What causes employees to pilfer from the workplace? Employee theft is most accurately explained by factors relevant to the work setting, such as job dissatisfaction and the workers' belief that they are being exploited by employers or supervisors; economic problems play a relatively small role in the decision to pilfer. So, although employers attribute employee fraud to economic conditions and declining personal values, workers themselves say they steal because of strain and conflict.

MANAGEMENT FRAUD Management-level fraud is also quite common. Such acts include converting company assets for personal benefit; fraudulently receiving increases in compensation (such as raises or bonuses); fraudulently increasing personal holdings of company stock; retaining one's present position within the company by manipulating accounts; and concealing unacceptable performance from stockholders.[72]

Management fraud has involved some of the nation's largest companies and richest people. Multibillionaire L. Dennis Kozlowski was imprisoned for taking excessive bonuses totaling $430 million, tax evasion, and stealing more than $100 million from his firm Tyco International.[73] In an even greater scandal, chief financial officer (CFO) Andrew Fastow, chief executive officer (CEO) Jeffrey Skilling, and chairman and CEO Kenneth Lay of Enron, one of the nation's largest companies, were charged with conspiracy, securities fraud, wire fraud, bank fraud, and making false statements. The three fooled the public into believing that the company was doing great and would reach its profit targets, even though they knew it was losing billions of dollars. People who had invested heavily in Enron lost their life savings when the company collapsed. Fastow was sentenced to six years in prison for his role in the accounting scandal, and Skilling was sentenced to 24 years and four months in prison. CEO Kenneth Lay died of natural causes before he could be sentenced.[74] Kenneth Lay alone received approximately $300 million from the sale of Enron stock options and restricted stock and made over $217 million in profit; he was also paid more than $19 million in salary and bonuses.

EMBEZZLEMENT Embezzlement occurs when someone who is trusted with someone else's personal property fraudulently converts it—that is, keeps it for his or her own use or for the use of others. Such acts include converting company assets for personal benefit, fraudulently receiving increases in compensation (such as raises or bonuses), fraudulently increasing personal holdings of company stock, retaining one's present position within the company by manipulating accounts, and concealing unacceptable performance from stockholders.[75]

The number of people arrested for embezzlement in the United States has increased in the past decade, indicating that (1) more employees are willing to steal from their employers, (2) more employers are willing to report instances of embezzlement, and/or (3) law enforcement officials are more willing to prosecute embezzlers. There has also been a rash of embezzlement-type crimes around the

embezzlement
A type of larceny in which someone who is trusted with someone else's personal property fraudulently converts it to his or her own use or for the use of others.

Craig Ruttle/Redux

Dozens of people were arrested on January 7, 2014, including former NYPD officers, in a Social Security fraud. Four people were the masterminds of a scheme that defrauded taxpayers of an estimated $400 million by coaching faked mental problems to get Social Security payments for as many as 1,000 ineligible people. The four architects of the scheme and 102 recipients of the benefits were indicted on grand larceny charges. More than 70 defendants pleaded guilty and were ordered to repay $14.6 million to Social Security.

world, especially in third-world countries where poverty is all too common and the economy is poor and supported by foreign aid and loans. Government officials and businesspeople through whose hands this money passes may be tempted to convert it to their own use, a scenario that is sure to increase the likelihood of embezzlement.[76]

Client Fraud

Client fraud involves cheating an organization (such as a government agency or insurance company) by filing false claims for reimbursement for services provided or, conversely, failing to pay what is owed. The victim is an organization that reimburses clients for their loss, such as an insurance company, or who should collect money for services rendered, such as the US government. An example might be an insurance policy holder who reports the loss of a diamond ring even though the ring has not been lost or stolen.

HEALTH CARE FRAUD Crooked health care providers find it lucrative to engage in fraud in obtaining patients and administering their treatment and for patients to try to scam the system for their own benefit. The FBI estimates that health care fraud now costs the nation $80 billion per year.[77] There are numerous health care–related schemes, including:

- Billing for services that were never rendered by using genuine patient information to fabricate entire claims or by adding to claims charges for procedures or services that did not take place.
- Billing for more expensive services or procedures than were actually provided or performed, commonly known as "upcoding." This practice requires "inflation" of the patient's diagnosis code to a more serious condition consistent with the false procedure code.
- Performing medically unnecessary services solely for the purpose of generating insurance payments. This scheme occurs most often in nerve-conduction and other diagnostic-testing schemes. Some Southern California clinics performed unnecessary, and sometimes harmful, surgeries on patients who had been recruited and paid to have these unnecessary surgeries performed.
- Misrepresenting noncovered treatments as medically necessary covered treatments for purposes of obtaining insurance payments. This scheme occurs in cosmetic surgery in which noncovered procedures such as nose jobs, tummy tucks, liposuction, or breast augmentations are billed to patients' insurers as deviated-septum repairs, hernia repairs, or lumpectomies.[78]

The numbers involved are enormous. A 2015 federal investigation of Medicare fraud resulted in the arrest of 240 individuals. Doctors, nurses, and other licensed professionals were arrested for their participation in Medicare fraud schemes involving approximately $712 million in false billings. The schemes included submitting claims to Medicare for treatments that were medically unnecessary and often not provided. In many of the cases, Medicare beneficiaries and other co-conspirators were allegedly paid cash kickbacks for supplying beneficiary information so providers could submit fraudulent bills to Medicare.[79]

The government has attempted to tighten control over the industry in order to restrict the opportunity for physicians to commit fraud. Health care companies providing services to federal health care programs are also regulated by federal laws that prohibit kickbacks and self-referrals. It is now a crime, punishable by up to five years in prison, to provide anything of value, money or otherwise, directly or indirectly, with the intent to induce the referral of a patient to a health care service. Liability attaches to both parties in the transaction—the entity or individual providing the kickbacks and the individual receiving payment for the referral.

Federal law also prohibits physicians and other health care providers from referring beneficiaries in federal health care programs to clinics or other facilities in which the physician or health care provider has a financial interest. It is illegal for a doctor to refer her patients to a blood-testing lab in which she has an ownership share. These practices—kickbacks and self-referrals—are prohibited under federal law because they would compromise a medical professional's independent judgment. Federal law prohibits arrangements that tend to corrupt medical judgment and tempt the prescriber to put the provider's bottom line ahead of the patient's well-being.[80]

TAX EVASION Another important aspect of client fraud is tax evasion. Here, the victim is the government that is cheated by one of its clients, the errant taxpayer to whom it extended credit by allowing the taxpayer to delay paying taxes on money he or she had already earned. Underpaying or avoiding taxes is considered client fraud because the taxpayer has received a service, such as military protection or use of national parks, and is now avoiding payment. Tax fraud is a particularly challenging area for criminological study because so many US citizens regularly underreport their income, and it is often difficult to separate honest error from deliberate tax evasion.

The basic law on tax evasion is contained in the US Internal Revenue Code, section 7201, which states that

> Any person who willfully attempts in any manner to evade or defeat any tax imposed by this title or the payment thereof shall, in addition to other penalties provided by law, be guilty of a felony and, upon conviction thereof, shall be fined not more than $100,000 or imprisoned not more than five years, or both, together with the costs of prosecution.

To prove tax fraud, the government must find that the taxpayer either underreported his or her income or did not report taxable income. No minimum dollar amount is stated before fraud exists, but the government can take legal action when there is a "substantial underpayment of tax." A second element of tax fraud is "willfulness" on the part of the tax evader. In the major case on this issue, willfulness was defined as a "voluntary, intentional violation of a known legal duty and not the careless disregard for the truth."[81] Finally, to prove tax fraud, the government must show that the taxpayer has purposely attempted to evade or defeat a tax payment. If the offender is guilty of passive neglect, the offense is a misdemeanor. "Passive neglect" means simply not paying taxes, not reporting income, or not paying taxes when due. On the other hand, "affirmative tax evasion," such as keeping double books, making false entries, destroying books or records, concealing assets, or covering up sources of income, constitutes a felony.

Corporate Crime

Yet another component of white-collar crime involves situations in which powerful institutions or their representatives willfully violate the laws that restrain these institutions from doing social harm or require them to do social good. This is also known as **corporate crime** or **organizational crime**.

Corporate crimes are socially injurious acts committed to further the business interests of people who control companies. The target of these crimes can be the general public, the environment, or even company workers. What makes these crimes unique is that the perpetrator is a legal fiction—a corporation—and not an individual. In reality, it is company employees or owners who commit corporate crimes and who ultimately benefit through career advancement or greater profits.

Some of the acts included within corporate crime are price fixing and illegal restraint of trade, false advertising, and the use of company practices that violate environmental protection statutes. The variety of crimes contained within this

corporate (organizational) crime
Powerful institutions or their representatives willfully violate the laws that restrain these institutions from doing social harm or require them to do social good.

category is great, and they cause vast damage. The following subsections examine some of the most important offenses.

ILLEGAL RESTRAINT OF TRADE A restraint of trade involves a contract or conspiracy designed to stifle competition, create a monopoly, artificially maintain prices, or otherwise interfere with free market competition.[82] The control of restraint-of-trade violations has its legal basis in the **Sherman Antitrust Act**, which subjects to criminal or civil sanctions any person "who shall make any contract or engage in any combination or conspiracy" in restraint of interstate commerce.[83] For violations of its provisions, this federal law created criminal penalties of up to three years' imprisonment and $100,000 in fines for individuals and $10 million in fines for corporations.[84] The act outlaws conspiracies between corporations that are designed to control the marketplace.

In most instances, the act lets the presiding court judge decide whether corporations have conspired to "unreasonably restrain competition." However, through the Sherman Antitrust Act, four types of market conditions considered inherently anticompetitive have been defined by federal courts as illegal per se, without regard to the facts or circumstances of the case:

- *Division of markets*. Firms divide a region into territories, and each firm agrees not to compete in the others' territories.
- *Tying arrangement*. A corporation requires customers of one of its services to use other services it offers. It would be an illegal restraint of trade if a railroad required that companies doing business with it or supplying it with materials ship all goods they produce on trains owned by the rail line.[85]
- *Group boycott*. An organization or company boycotts retail stores that do not comply with its rules or desires.
- *Price fixing*. A conspiracy to set and control the price of a necessary commodity is considered an absolute violation of the act.

PRICE FIXING A violation of the Sherman Antitrust Act occurs when two or more business competitors conspire to sell the same or similar products or services at an agreed-on price. The purpose is to maximize prices, reduce the costs of competition, and sell the product at a price higher than would be possible with normal competition.

An example of **price fixing** occurred in 2013, when nine Japan-based companies pleaded guilty and were forced to pay a total of more than $740 million in criminal fines for their roles in conspiracies to fix the prices of more than 30 different products sold to US car manufacturers, including Chrysler, Ford, and General Motors, as well as to the US subsidiaries of Honda, Mazda, Mitsubishi, Nissan, Toyota, and Subaru. Executives in the companies attended meetings and communicated by telephone in the United States and Japan to set prices, to conspire to keep bids for merchandise higher than needed, and to control the supply of auto parts sold to the car manufacturers. They took measures to keep their conduct secret by using code names and meeting in remote locations. Afterward they had further secret communications to monitor and enforce their illegal agreements.[86]

DECEPTIVE PRICING Deceptive pricing occurs when contractors provide the government or other corporations with incomplete or misleading information on how much it will actually cost to fulfill the contracts on which they are bidding, or use mischarges once the contracts are signed.[87] For example, defense contractors have been prosecuted for charging the government for costs incurred on work they are doing for private firms or for shifting the costs on fixed-price contracts to ones in which the government reimburses the contractor for all expenses ("cost-plus" contracts).

Sherman Antitrust Act
Federal law that subjects to criminal or civil sanctions any person "who shall make any contract or engage in any combination or conspiracy" in restraint of interstate commerce.

price fixing
The illegal control by agreement among producers or manufacturers of the price of a commodity to avoid price competition and deprive the consumer of reasonable prices.

Ryan Henriksen/New York Times/Redux

Does the prohibition against illegal price fixing, aimed at controlling large corporations, also apply to individuals? Sierra Poulson, shown here on October 16, 2015, in Omaha, Nebraska, has donated her eggs three times and helped start an online forum for egg donors. On their websites, next to adorable pictures of babies, some fertility clinics and egg-donor agencies refer to eggs as "priceless gifts" from caring young women who want to help people with fertility problems. There is a price tag for eggs, though, that is now the subject of a legal battle. In a federal lawsuit, a group of women are challenging industry guidelines that say it is "inappropriate" to pay a woman more than $10,000 for her eggs. The women say the $10,000 limit amounts to illegal price fixing, and point out that there is no price restriction on the sale of human sperm. Should the courts set a price limit on what a woman can charge for her eggs?

FALSE CLAIMS ADVERTISING Executives in even the largest corporations sometimes face stockholders' expectations of ever-increasing company profits that seem to demand that sales be increased at any cost. At times they respond to this challenge by making claims about their products that cannot be justified by actual performance. However, there is a fine line between clever, aggressive sales techniques and fraudulent claims. It is traditional to show a product in its best light, even if that involves resorting to fantasy. Showing a delivery service vehicle taking off into outer space or implying that taking one sip of beer will make people feel they have just jumped into a freezer are not fraudulent. But it is illegal to knowingly and purposely advertise a product as possessing qualities that the manufacturer realizes it does not have, such as the ability to cure the common cold, grow hair, or turn senior citizens into rock stars (though some rock stars are senior citizens these days).

Green-Collar Crime

In 2016, Southern Grease Company, based in Dickson, Tennessee, was ordered to pay a criminal fine of $280,000 and to forfeit an additional $113,500 for felony violations arising from its illegal disposal of waste grease. Southern Grease contracted with restaurants and other customers in Tennessee and Kentucky to collect and dispose of the customers' waste grease. Rather than haul the grease to licensed waste treatment plants, Southern Grease discharged the toxic waste into municipal sewer systems. This illegal dumping caused substantial damage by clogging pipes and interrupting the operation of pump stations. Company executives pleaded guilty to violating the Clean Water Act, conspiring to violate the Clean Water Act, and making false statements to the Environmental Protection Agency (EPA).[88]

The grease dumping case, while gross, is not unique. Green crimes involve a wide range of actions and outcomes that harm the environment and that stem from decisions about what is produced, where it is produced, and how it is produced.[89] The harm they cause is universal, affecting people in every community.[90] Global warming, overdevelopment, population growth, and other changes will continue to bring these issues front and center.[91] Environmental activists have long called attention to a variety of ecological threats that they feel should be deemed criminal.

While crimes targeting the environment have received scant attention in the criminological literature, recent events have shifted attention to what is variously called green crime, green criminology, and green-collar crime. The Gulf Coast disaster in 2010 (a topic covered in the Policies and Issues in Criminology feature on page 430) is a powerful and tragic example of how environmental destruction and green crimes may be linked to enterprise systems: the need for corporate profit may outweigh attention to safety, with subsequent catastrophic consequences.

Defining Green-Collar Crime

There is no single vision to define the concept of green-collar crimes. Four independent views exist:

- *Legalist.* According to the legalist perspective, environmental crimes are violations of existing criminal laws designed to protect people, the environment, or both. This definition would include crimes against workers such as occupational health and safety crimes, as well as laws designed to protect nature and the environment (the Clean Air Act, Clean Water Act, and so on).
- *Environmental justice.* According to the environmental justice view, limiting environmental crimes to actual violations of the criminal law is too narrow. Green crime should include all acts that have identifiable environmental damage outcomes and originated in human action but that may or may not violate existing rules and environmental regulations.[92] A great deal of environmental damage occurs in third-world nations desperate for funds and willing to give mining and oil companies a free hand to develop resources. These nations have meager

CHECKPOINTS

▶ White-collar crime has a number of different subcategories.

▶ White-collar fraud involves people using their institutional or business position to trick others out of their money.

▶ Chiseling involves regular cheating of an organization or its customers.

▶ People who engage in exploitation demand payment for services to which victims are entitled by threatening consequences if their victims refuse. The victim here is the client.

▶ Influence peddling and bribery occur when a person in authority demands payment for a service to which the payer is clearly not entitled. The victim here is the organization.

▶ Embezzlement and employee fraud occur when a person uses a position of trust to steal from an organization.

▶ Client fraud involves theft from an organization that advances credit, covers losses, or reimburses for services.

▶ Corporate, or organizational, crime involves various illegal business practices, such as price fixing, restraint of trade, and false advertising.

regulatory laws and therefore allow businesses wide latitude in environmental contamination that would be forbidden in the United States. In addition, environmental justice advocates believe that corporations themselves have attempted to co-opt or manipulate environmental laws, thereby limiting their scope and reach. Executives fear that the environmental movement will force changes in their production practices and place limits on their growth and corporate power. Some have tried to co-opt green laws by public relations and advertising campaigns that suggest they are doing everything in their power to respect the environment, thereby reducing the need for government regulation. Criminologists must take a broader view of green crimes than the law allows.

- *Biocentric.* According to the biocentric approach, environmental harm is viewed as any human activity that disrupts a biosystem, destroying plant and animal life. This more radical approach would criminalize any intentional or negligent human activity or manipulation that impacts negatively on the earth's natural resources, resulting in trauma to those resources.[93] Environmental harm, according to this view, is much greater than what is defined by law as environmental crimes. As criminologist Rob White points out, this is because some of the most ecologically destructive activities, such as clear felling of old-growth forests, are quite legal. Environmental crimes are typically oriented toward protecting humans and their property and have a limited interest in the protection of animals and plants.[94] Environmental laws protect animal and fish processing plants that treat "nature" and "wildlife" simply and mainly as resources for human exploitation. Human beings are the cause of environmental harm and need to be controlled.

- *The harms perspective.* "Green crimes include various forms of violence that directly impact ecological stability. This violence produces secondary harm affecting human and nonhuman species that inhabit these ecosystems. For example, green crimes produce numerous public health consequences for communities, and these consequences can vary in type and intensity for people in different geographical regions."[95] So say green criminologists Bruce Arrigo and Michael Lynch, whose statement is a good representation of what is known as the **harms perspective** in order to conceptualize crime and deviance.[96] Accordingly, crime is a social construct that can and should be expanded to include all serious *social harms*, activities that cause any discomfort, present or future, to individuals. Harms may include physical, financial/economic, emotional or psychological, and cultural safety harm. Using the harms perspective, it would be appropriate to sanction toxic waste dumping or air pollution severely because they cause residual harm that will last many years, poisoning the environment and producing diseases such as cancer. However, in many instances this action is punished civilly, not criminally.

harms perspective
The view that all activities that cause physical, financial/economic, emotional or psychological, and cultural harm to individuals and/or the environment should be criminalized.

Forms of Green Crime

Green crime can take many different forms, ranging from deforestation and illegal logging to violations of worker safety. A few of the most damaging forms are set out below.

WORKER SAFETY/ENVIRONMENTAL CRIMES Some corporations endanger the lives of their own workers by maintaining unsafe conditions in their plants and mines. It has been estimated that more than 20 million workers have been exposed to hazardous materials while on the job. Some industries have been hit particularly hard by complaints and allegations. The control of workers' safety in the United States has been the province of the Occupational Safety and Health Administration (OSHA), which sets industry standards for the proper use of such chemicals as benzene, arsenic, lead, and coke (from coal). Intentional violation of OSHA standards can result in criminal penalties. One of the key concerns following the 2016 presidential race was the new administration's plan to roll back Environmental Protection Agency (EPA) standards in order to encourage domestic energy production in the oil, gas, and coal industries. Critics fear that any rollback will have a devastating effect on the environment, leading to pollution of both air and groundwater.[97]

ILLEGAL LOGGING Illegal logging involves harvesting, processing, and transporting timber or wood products in violation of existing laws and treaties. It is a universal phenomenon in major timber-producing countries, especially in the third world where enforcement is lax. Logging violations include taking trees in protected areas such as national parks, going over legally prescribed logging quotas, processing logs without acquiring licenses, and exporting logs without paying export duties. By sidestepping the law, loggers can create greater profits than those generated through legal methods.

Illegal logging operations rely on corruption and could not occur without some form of cooperation from government officials responsible for protecting forests who may take bribes so that criminals can obtain logging permits, avoid detection, and export illegal timber. This results in the loss of crucial resources for developing countries, while damaging their economies, public trust, and institutional structures.[98]

The situation is serious because illegal logging can have severe environmental and social impact:

- Illegal logging destroys wildlife and damages its habitats. Illegal logging in central Africa is threatening the survival of populations of the great apes, including gorillas and chimpanzees.

- Illegal logging causes ruinous damage to the forests, including deforestation and forest degradation worldwide. The destruction of forest cover can cause flash floods and landslides that can kill thousands of people.

- By reducing forest cover, illegal logging impairs the ability of land to absorb carbon emissions. Forests are vital to mitigating climate change because they absorb carbon dioxide from the atmosphere. Deforestation accounts for an estimated 17 percent of global carbon emissions, greater than from all the world's air, road, rail, and shipping traffic combined.[99]

- Illegal logging costs billions each year in government revenue, impairing the ability of third-world nations to provide needed social services.

- Illegal logging creates unsustainable economic devastation in the poorest countries. Vietnam, for example, has lost a third of its forest cover, while in nearby Cambodia, the harvest from illegal logging is at least 10 times the size of the legal harvest. These rates of extraction are clearly unsustainable, destroying valuable sources of employment and export revenues for the future.

- The substantial revenues from illegal logging fund national and regional conflict. In Asia, terrorist and insurgent groups have been sustained primarily by the revenue from logging areas under their control.[100]

AriantoSilalahi/Barcroft Images/Barcroft Media/Getty Images

While the scale of illegal logging is difficult to estimate, according to Interpol illegal logging accounts for 50 to 90 percent of all forestry activities in key producer tropical forests, such as those of the Amazon basin, central Africa, and southeast Asia, and 15 to 30 percent of all wood traded globally. Illegal logging continues to occur in many formally protected forests, especially in tropical countries. And it's likely to continue since trade in illegally harvested timber is highly lucrative and estimated to be worth between $51 and $150 billion annually.[101]

ILLEGAL WILDLIFE EXPORTING The smuggling of wildlife across national borders is a serious matter.[102] Exporters find a lucrative trade in the demand for such illicit wildlife commodities as tiger parts, caviar, elephant ivory, rhino horn, and exotic birds and reptiles. Wildlife contraband may include live pets, hunting trophies, fashion accessories, cultural artifacts, ingredients for traditional medicines, wild meat for human consumption (or bush meat), and other products. Illegal profits can be immense.

On February 22, 2017, in Riau, Indonesia, a baby Langur monkey is secured by officers from a suspected illegal wildlife trader. Langurs are one of the world's rarest monkeys and are found in northeast Vietnam and in two Chinese provinces: Guangxi and Guizhou. The population of Langurs has been in significant decline increasing their value for illegal traders.

In some instances, endangered species are killed by poachers in one country and their hides and body parts illegally exported abroad. Tigers are the target of a highly lucrative illegal trade spanning countries and continents. These big cats are killed due to their fur being prized on the black market and the demand for their body parts for traditional medicines and other uses.[103] Elephants and rhinoceroses are also prized by poachers for their tusks and horns. The northern white rhinoceros has been shot into near extinction during the past five years; at this writing, there is only one male white rhino left. The western black rhinoceros population has fared somewhat better, though it is still critically endangered. In 1960, there were more than 70,000 black rhinos; by 1993, there were only 2,500. Today numbers are slowly increasing, thanks to conservation efforts and public awareness of their plight.[104] Since 2010, record numbers of elephants—more than 30,000 per year—have been reported poached, and record amounts of contraband ivory have been seized by authorities. Why poach? Ivory is going for around $1,000 per pound on the black market. A pair of tusks measuring 92 inches around the outside curve and weighing over 100 pounds can bring close to $100,000.[105] Rhino horns go for about $45,000. While they can be safely harvested from farmed rhinos, that has not stopped poachers from decimating the species.

There are numerous problems presented by illegal wildlife exporting. Poachers imperil endangered species and threaten them with extinction. By evading government controls, they create the potential for introducing pests and diseases into formerly unaffected areas.[106] They import nonnative species, which could harm the receiving habitats. Florida's Everglades have been overrun with nonnative species such as pythons, imported as pets and released into the wild. Illegal wildlife traders range from independent one-person operations that sell a single item to complex, multi-ton, commercial-sized consignments shipped all over the world. Adding all these sources together, the global trade in illegal wildlife is a growing phenomenon and is now estimated to be upward of $20 billion annually.[107]

There have been ongoing efforts to control illegal wildlife importation. In the United States, Congress has passed numerous laws that regulate and restrict wildlife imports and exports, including the Endangered Species Act of 1973 and the Lacey Act, which protects both plants and wildlife by creating civil and criminal penalties for a wide array of violations. The original act was directed at preserving game and wild birds and prohibiting the introduction of nonnative birds and animals into native ecosystems. The act has been amended and in 1981 was changed to include illegal trade in plants, fish, and wildlife both domestically and abroad. The maximum penalty was increased to $10,000 with possible imprisonment for one year. Additionally, the mental state required for a criminal violation was increased to "knowingly and willfully"; civil penalties were expanded to apply to negligent violations.[108]

There are also international laws restricting the wildlife trade. The United Nations Convention on International Trade in Endangered Species of Wild Fauna and Flora (CITES) serves as the primary vehicle for regulating wildlife trade. These efforts may be paying off: recent reports from China, the leading importer of ivory, indicate that illegal imports have declined sharply. One reason may be stricter enforcement policies, another the lack of product because elephant herds have been decimated. China's Forestry Administration announced a three-year ban on ivory imports in March 2016 and vowed to ban all commercial ivory trading and processing by the end of 2017.[109] Yet the trade persists: in April 2017, Malaysian authorities seized about $3 million (112 pounds) worth of rhinoceros horns flown in from Mozambique via Qatar.

ILLEGAL FISHING Unlicensed and illegal fishing practices are another billion-dollar green crime. They can take on many forms and involve highly different parties, ranging from huge factory ships operating on the high seas that catch thousands of tons of fish on each voyage, to smaller, locally operating ships that confine themselves to national waters. Illegal fishing occurs when these ships sign on to their home nation's rules but then choose to ignore their scope and boundary, or operate in a country's waters without permission or on the high seas without a flag. When catches are not reported by the fishing vessels, their illegal fishing can have a detrimental effect on species because government regulators have no idea how many are being caught. Stocks become depleted and species endangered. In addition, illegal fishing techniques, including fishermen using the wrong sized nets or fishing in prohibited areas, can damage fragile marine ecosystems, threatening coral reefs, turtles, and seabirds. Fishermen in a number of nations—stretching from Tanzania to the Philippines—are using explosives to maximize their catch. Called blast fishing or dynamite fishing, the practice can kill hundreds of fish in seconds while transforming coral reefs into rubble.[110]

In underdeveloped nations, regulators may look the other way because the need for short-term economic, social, or political gains is given more weight than long-term sustainability. As a result, species of whales, abalone, lobsters, and Patagonian toothfish (known in the United States as Chilean sea bass) have become endangered.[111] Take for instance the global demand for shark fin soup, desired for its healing and medicinal value, that has led to a catastrophic decline in shark populations; some species have been reduced by 99 percent since the 1950s due to legal and illegal fishing. In 2013, animal rights groups in Thailand launched a campaign against the sale and consumption of shark fin soup, calling on businesses to ban the dish and advising people to refrain from eating the traditional Chinese delicacy.

ILLEGAL DUMPING AND POLLUTING Some green-collar criminals want to skirt local, state, and federal restrictions on dumping dangerous substances in the environment. Rather than pay expensive processing fees, they may secretly dispose of hazardous wastes in illegal dump sites. Illegally dumped wastes can be hazardous or nonhazardous materials that are discarded in an effort to avoid disposal fees or the time and effort required for proper disposal. Materials dumped range from used motor oil to waste from construction sites.

Criminal environmental pollution is defined as the intentional or negligent discharge of a toxic or contaminating substance into the biosystem that is known to have an adverse effect on the natural environment or life. It may involve the ground release of toxic chemicals such as kepone, vinyl chloride, mercury, PCBs, and asbestos. Illegal and/or controlled air pollutants include hydrochlorofluorocarbons (HCFCs), aerosols, asbestos, carbon monoxide, chlorofluorocarbons (CFCs), criteria air pollutants, lead, mercury, methane, nitrogen oxides (NO_x), radon, refrigerants, and sulfur oxides (SO_2). Water pollution is defined as the dumping of a substance that degrades or alters the quality of the waters to an extent that is detrimental to their use by humans or by an animal or a plant that is useful to humans. This includes the disposal into rivers, lakes, and streams of:

criminal environmental pollution
A crime involving the intentional or negligent discharge into the biosystem of a toxic waste that destroys plant or animal life.

- Excess fertilizers, herbicides, and insecticides from agricultural lands and residential areas
- Oil, grease, and toxic chemicals from urban runoff and energy production
- Sediment from improperly managed construction sites, crop and forest lands, and eroding stream banks
- Salt from irrigation practices and acid drainage from abandoned mines
- Bacteria and nutrients from livestock, pet wastes, and faulty septic systems

One of the largest and fastest growing problems is the disposal of 7 million tons of obsolete high-tech electronics, called e-waste, such as televisions, desktop computers and monitors, laptops, VCRs, and so on.[112] While most e-waste in the United States is disposed of in landfills or is incinerated, the toxic material contained in electronic gear (such as lead) encourages illegal dumping in order to avoid recycling costs. Consequently, a considerable amount of e-waste is sent abroad to developing nations for recycling, often in violation of international laws restricting such commerce. All too often, the material overwhelms recycling plants and is instead dumped in local villages near people and water sources. Illegal dump sites have been documented in Nigeria, Ghana, China, the Philippines, Indonesia, Pakistan, and India, and they pose severe threats to both human health and the natural environment.

One of the most famous incidents of green crime and efforts by the government to punish offenders is covered in the Policies and Issues in Criminology feature.

Policies and Issues in Criminology

THE DEEPWATER HORIZON

On April 20, 2010, an explosion occurred on the *Deepwater Horizon* oil rig, killing 11 platform workers and injuring 17 others. The rig was built by Hyundai Heavy Industries of Korea, owned by the Transocean Drilling Corporation, and leased by BP (formerly British Petroleum) in order to drill a deep-water oil well in the Gulf of Mexico. The drilling was overseen by Halliburton.

Following the explosion, the *Deepwater Horizon* burned for 36 hours before sinking to the ocean floor 5,000 feet below, where oil was gushing from the now-uncapped well. At first, estimates of the oil spill were 5,000 barrels a day, but they quickly rose to 60,000. For more than three months, company officials frantically tried to stem the flow with a variety of failed schemes, while millions of barrels of escaping oil created a slick that covered thousands of square miles, devastating wildlife and causing one of the greatest environmental disasters in US history.

On June 1, 2010, the Obama administration announced that it had launched a criminal probe in order to "prosecute to the fullest extent of the law" any persons or companies that broke the law in the time leading up to the spill. Under federal environmental laws, a company may be charged with a misdemeanor for negligent conduct, or a felony if there is evidence that company personnel knowingly engaged in conduct risking injury. It would be a criminal act if, for example, employees of BP or its subcontractors, Transocean and Halliburton:

- Lied in the permit process of obtaining a drilling license
- Tried to cover up the severity of the spill
- Knowing of negligence in construction, chose to ignore the danger it imposed
- Engaged in or approved of unsafe, risky, or dangerous methods to remove the drill, knowing that such methods could injure those on board

To prove a felony, and potentially put BP executives in prison, the government had to show that company officials knew in advance that its actions would lead to the explosion and oil spill but chose to ignore the danger; a misdemeanor requires only mere negligence. But even a misdemeanor conviction would amp up the loss to the company, because the Federal Alternative Fines Act allows the government to request monetary fines that are twice the loss associated with an offense. This provision can also have a devastating effect on employees, because fines imposed on individuals under the act may *not* be paid by their employer.

On September 4, 2014, US District Judge Carl Barbier ruled BP was guilty of gross negligence and willful misconduct. He apportioned 67 percent of the blame for the spill to BP, 30 percent to Transocean, and 3 percent to Halliburton. Judge Barbier found that BP had acted with "conscious disregard of known risks" and that "employees took risks that led to the largest environmental disaster in US history." In the final tally, the company paid almost $54 billion in order to settle all claims: federal Clean Water Act fines, claims by states (Alabama, Florida, Louisiana, Mississippi, and Texas), and 400 local government entities. However, while a number of BP employees were indicted on criminal charges relating to their negligence in the spill and their efforts to cover up company involvement and responsibility, not one served jail time. On December 2, 2015, federal prosecutors moved—and a judge agreed—to drop manslaughter charges against two supervisors who were aboard the *Deepwater Horizon* when it exploded.

While some may argue that it is overly harsh to put company executives in prison for what is essentially an accident, civil penalties do not seem to deter companies such as BP. Before the Gulf of Mexico oil spill, BP had already paid hundreds of millions in civil penalties for similar if lesser disasters. One fine of $87 million was paid to the Occupational Safety and Health Administration—the largest fine in OSHA's history—for a Texas refinery explosion; an additional $50 million was paid to the Department of Justice for the same explosion. BP also paid $3 million to OSHA for 42 safety violations at an Ohio refinery and was fined $20 million by the Department of Justice for another spill that violated the Clean Water Act.

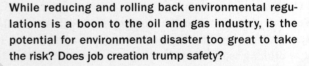

Critical Thinking

While reducing and rolling back environmental regulations is a boon to the oil and gas industry, is the potential for environmental disaster too great to take the risk? Does job creation trump safety?

Sources: "Manslaughter Charges Dropped Against Two BP Employees in Deepwater Spill," *The Guardian*, December 2, 2015, http://www.theguardian.com/environment/2015/dec/03/manslaughter-charges-dropped-bp-employees-deepwater-horizon-oil-spill; Thomas Catan and Guy Chazan, "Spill Draws Criminal Probe," *Wall Street Journal*, June 2, 2010, http://online.wsj.com/article/SB10001424052748704875604575280983140254458.html; Tyson Slocum, "BP: The Worst Safety and Environmental Record of All Oil Companies Operating in the United States," *Monthly Review*, http://mrzine.monthlyreview.org/2010/slocum060510.html; Helene Cooper and Peter Baker, "US Opens Criminal Inquiry into Oil Spill," *New York Times*, June 1, 2010, http://www.nytimes.com/2010/06/02/us/02spill.html; Alternative Fines Act, 18 U.S.C. § 3571(d); Terry Wade and Kristen Hays, "BP Reaches $18.7 Billion Settlement over Deadly 2010 Spill," Reuters, July 2, 2015, http://www.reuters.com/article/2015/07/02/us-bp-gulfmexico-settlement-idUSKCN0PC1BW20150702 (URLS accessed May 2017).

Theories of White-Collar and Green-Collar Crime

Why do people get involved in risky schemes to use their institutional positions to steal money? Why do people risk going to prison because they pollute the environment? Can the same factors that predict other types of criminal offenses also apply to crimes of criminal enterprise? After all, unlike other criminal offenses, white-collar and green-collar crimes are not committed by impoverished teenagers living in the inner city, but by otherwise respectable people, many of whom are educated and financially well off. By their very nature, business and environmental crimes require that offenders attain a position of power and trust before they can be committed. Therefore, can the theories that predict and explain common-law crime be applied to enterprise-type crime?

Rational Choice: Greed

When Kansas City pharmacist Robert Courtney was asked after his arrest why he substituted improper doses of drugs instead of what doctors had prescribed, he told investigators he cut the drugs' strength "out of greed."[113] Courtney is not alone. One view is that white-collar and green-collar criminals are greedy people who rationally choose to take shortcuts to acquire wealth, believing that the potential profits far outweigh future punishments. Most believe they will not get caught; they are far too clever to be detected by mere civil servants who work for government agencies.

Greed was rampant in the 1980s. Ivan Boesky was a famous Wall Street trader who had amassed a fortune of about $200 million by betting on corporate takeovers, a practice called *arbitrage*. In 1986, he was investigated by the Securities and Exchange Commission for insider trading. To escape serious punishment, he informed on several associates. In exchange for cooperation, Boesky received a sentence of three and a half years in prison and a $100 million fine. Released after serving two years, Boesky was barred from working in the securities business for the remainder of his life. Caught in Boesky's web was billionaire junk bond trader Michael Milken. Indicted by a federal grand jury, Milken pleaded guilty to five securities and reporting violations and was sentenced to 10 years in prison; he served 22 months. He also paid a $200 million fine and another $400 to $800 million in settlements relating primarily to civil lawsuits. Today Milken has an estimated net worth of $3.5 billion. In 2014, he pledged $50 million to George Washington University to fund the Milken Institute School of Public Health.[114]

LURE Greed unfortunately did not end in the 1980s, and the greed that begat the Wall Street crash in 2008 almost sank the world economy. Criminologists Neal Shover and Peter Grabosky introduced the concept of "lure" to help explain why some people succumb to the illegal yet alluring benefits of crime.[115] Tempted individuals possess qualities or experiences that make them more likely than peers who lack these distinctions to weigh illicit exploitation of lure.[116] Lure is something that is alluring— something that is so attractive and covetable that it can turn the heads of those who are tempted or predisposed. When a would-be green-collar criminal sees the wide expanses of uninhabited countryside, he becomes tempted to dispose of trash quickly and cheaply. When states create loopholes in the law that provide opportunities that can be manipulated easily for criminal purposes—such as tax incentives, subsidies, low-interest loans, and other forms of access to public funds—these benefits may prove too much of a lure for businessmen to resist. The lure of crime expands in the absence of capable control systems. When financial oversight was absent in the United States economic markets, the crash of 2008 became inevitable.

Rational Choice: Need

Greed is not the only motivation for white-collar and green-collar crime; need also plays an important role. Some people turn to crime to fulfill an overwhelming financial or psychological need. Executives may tamper with company books because they feel the need to keep or improve their jobs, satisfy their egos, or support their children. Even people in the upper echelons of the financial world, such as Bernie Madoff, may carry scars from an earlier needy period in their lives that can be healed only by accumulating ever-greater amounts of money. As one of Ivan Boesky's (a principal in a 1980s insider trading scandal) associates put it:

> I don't know what his devils were. Maybe he's greedy beyond the wildest imaginings of mere mortals like you and me. And maybe part of what drives the guy is an inherent insecurity that was operative here even after he had arrived. Maybe he never arrived.[117]

White-collar crime becomes a convenient vehicle for filling this need. When in need, violating business law saves time and effort to solve a financial problem, where legal alternatives seem less attractive, and future threats of detection and punishment are minimal.[118]

Rationalization/Neutralization View

Rationalizing guilt is a common trait of white-collar and green-collar criminals.[119] What they did was not so bad; what some call crime is merely a "technicality." They didn't really break the law, just bent it slightly.

In his research on fraud, Donald Cressey found that the door to solving personal financial problems through criminal means is opened by the rationalizations people develop for white-collar crime: "Some of our most respectable citizens got their start in life by using other people's money temporarily." "In the real estate business, there is nothing wrong about using deposits before the deal is closed." "All people steal when they get in a tight spot."[120] Offenders use these and other rationalizations to resolve the conflict they experience over engaging in illegal behavior.

It is especially easy for corporate offenders to neutralize wrongdoing when the target is a fellow businessperson or government regulatory agency. Because the victim is knowledgeable and sophisticated, they should have known better. *Caveat emptor*, as they say: let the buyer beware. The line between smart business practice and corporate crime is typically blurry. When the victim can be denied, it is often difficult to accept blame.

Cultural View

Business culture may also influence white-collar and green-collar crime. According to this view, some business organizations promote criminality in the same way that lower-class culture encourages the development of juvenile gangs and street crime. They may place excessive demands on employees while at the same time maintaining a business climate tolerant of employee deviance. New employees learn the attitudes and techniques needed to commit crime from their business peers. Under these circumstances, the attitudes of close coworkers and the perceived attitudes of executives have a more powerful control over decision making.[121]

Self-Control View

In their general theory of crime, Travis Hirschi and Michael Gottfredson suggest that the motives that produce white-collar and green-collar crimes—quick benefits with minimal effort—are the same as those that produce any other criminal behaviors.[122] Those who violate business or environmental laws have low self-control and are inclined to follow momentary impulses without considering the long-term costs of such behavior.[123] Hirschi and Gottfredson have collected data showing that the demographic distribution of white-collar crime is similar to other crimes. For example, gender, race, and age ratios are the same for crimes such as embezzlement and fraud as they are for street crimes such as burglary and robbery.

Controlling White-Collar and Green-Collar Crime

On the federal level, detection of these crimes is primarily in the hands of administrative departments and agencies.[124] The decision whether to pursue these activities as criminal or civil violations is usually based on the seriousness of the case and the perpetrator's intent, on any actions taken to conceal the violation, and on the individual's prior record. Any evidence of criminal activity is then sent to the Department of Justice or the FBI for investigation. Some other federal agencies, such as the Securities and Exchange Commission and the US Postal Service, have their own investigative arms. Enforcement is generally reactive (generated by complaints) rather than proactive (involving ongoing investigations or the monitoring of activities). Investigations are carried out by the various federal agencies and the FBI. If criminal prosecution is called for, the case will be handled by attorneys from the criminal, tax, antitrust, and civil rights divisions of the Justice Department. If insufficient evidence is available to warrant a criminal prosecution, the case will be handled civilly or administratively by some other federal agency. For example, the Federal Trade Commission can issue a cease and desist order in antitrust or merchandising fraud cases.

The number of state-funded technical assistance offices to help local prosecutors has increased significantly; more than 40 states offer such services. On the state and local levels, law enforcement officials have made progress in a number of areas, such as controlling consumer fraud. For example, the Environmental Crimes Strike Force in Los Angeles County is considered a model for the control of illegal dumping and pollution. Some of the more common environmental offenses investigated and prosecuted by the task force are oil spills, fraudulent certification of automobile smog tests, and illegal transportation, treatment, storage, or disposal of hazardous waste.[125]

Nonetheless, although local agencies recognize the seriousness of enterprise-type crimes, they rarely have the funds necessary for effective enforcement.[126] Local prosecutors pursue white-collar criminals more vigorously if the prosecutors are part of a team effort involving a network of law enforcement agencies.[127] National surveys of local prosecutors find that many do not consider white-collar crimes particularly serious problems. They are more willing to prosecute cases if the offense causes substantial harm and if other agencies fail to act. Relatively few prosecutors participate in interagency task forces designed to investigate white-collar criminal activity.[128]

L06 Discuss efforts to control white-collar and green-collar crime.

Environmental Laws

The United States and most sovereign nations have passed laws making it a crime to pollute or damage the environment. For example, among environmental laws in the United States are the following:

- *Clean Water Act (1972)*. Establishes and maintains goals and standards for US water quality and purity. It was amended in 1987 to increase controls on toxic pollutants, and in 1990 to more effectively address the hazard of oil spills.
- *Emergency Planning and Community Right-to-Know Act (1986)*. Requires companies to disclose information about toxic chemicals they release into the air and water and dispose of on land.
- *Endangered Species Act (1973)*. Designed to protect and recover endangered and threatened species of fish, wildlife, and plants in the United States and beyond. The law works in part by protecting species habitats.
- *Oil Pollution Act (1990)*. Enacted in the aftermath of the *Exxon Valdez* oil spill in Alaska's Prince William Sound, this law streamlines federal response to oil spills by requiring oil storage facilities and vessels to prepare spill-response plans and provide for their rapid implementation. The law also increases polluters' liability for cleanup costs and damage to natural resources.

Enforcing the Law

A typical environmental crime—such as the knowing discharge of raw sewage into one of the nation's waterways or the killing of a bald eagle—is investigated by federal authorities such as special agents of the US Fish and Wildlife Service. These agents are plainclothes criminal investigators who enforce federal wildlife laws throughout the United States. They target crimes that undermine US efforts to conserve wildlife resources, such as wildlife trafficking and habitat destruction.[129] Service special agents protect threatened and endangered species, migratory birds, marine mammals, and imperiled animals and plants around the world. Their investigations document violations of federal wildlife laws as well as such crimes as smuggling, conspiracy, money laundering, mail and wire fraud, and making false statements.

Another agency empowered to investigate environmental crimes is the EPA, which was given full law enforcement authority in 1988. The EPA has successfully prosecuted significant violations across all major environmental statutes, including data fraud cases (for instance, private laboratories submitting false environmental data to state and federal environmental

On May 21, 2015, cleanup workers gather oil-contaminated sandbags at Refugio State Beach, north of Goleta, California. This was the largest coastal oil spill in California in the past 25 years, and cost more than $90 million. Such spills and their costs to society underscore the need for enforcement agencies to ramp up their investigations of both potential and active polluters.

AP Images/Jae C. Hong

agencies); indiscriminate hazardous waste dumping that resulted in serious injuries and death; industry-wide ocean dumping by cruise ships; oil spills that caused significant damage to waterways, wetlands, and beaches; international smuggling of CFC refrigerants that damage the ozone layer and increase skin cancer risk; and illegal handling of hazardous substances such as pesticides and asbestos that exposed children, the poor, and other especially vulnerable groups to potentially serious illness.[130] Its Criminal Investigation Division (EPA CID) investigates allegations of criminal wrongdoing prohibited by various environmental statutes. Such investigations involve but are not limited to:

- The illegal disposal of hazardous waste
- The export of hazardous waste without the permission of the receiving country
- The illegal discharge of pollutants to a body of water of the United States
- The removal and disposal of regulated asbestos-containing materials in a manner inconsistent with the law and regulations
- The illegal importation of certain restricted or regulated chemicals into the United States
- Tampering with a drinking water supply
- Mail fraud
- Wire fraud
- Conspiracy and money laundering relating to environmental criminal activities

If a culprit is identified by the EPA or other agency investigators, the offender is prosecuted by the Environmental Crime Section (ECS) of the US Justice Department. The prosecutor often gets involved early in an investigation, such as when the investigator swears out a search warrant or when a grand jury's investigative power is needed. Once the necessary evidence is collected, the prosecutor presents the case to the grand jury for indictment. After indictment, the prosecutor guides the case through complex white-collar and environmental law issues and prepares it for trial. Although many cases settle through plea agreements, some do not. From October 1, 1998, through September 30, 2014, ECS prosecutors concluded criminal cases against more than 1,083 individuals and 404 corporate defendants, leading to 774 years of incarceration (903 years with incarceration, halfway house, and home detentions) and $825 million in criminal fines and restitution.[131]

In many instances, the same criminal actions may be violations of federal, state, and local laws. In order to conserve resources and improve the efficiency of environmental enforcement efforts, ECS attorneys help assemble environmental crime task forces made up of federal, state, and local personnel. These task forces have successfully identified and handled many environmental crime cases.

Deterrence vs. Compliance

The prevailing wisdom is that, unlike common-law criminals, white-collar and green-collar criminals are rarely prosecuted and, when convicted, receive relatively light sentences. There have also been charges that efforts to control white-collar and green-collar crime are biased against specific classes and races. Authorities seem to be less diligent when victims are poor or minority group members or when the crimes take place in areas populated largely by minority groups. When Michael Lynch and his associates studied whether petroleum refineries violating environmental laws in black, Latino, and low-income communities receive smaller fines than those refineries in white and affluent communities, they found that violations of the Clean Air Act, the Clean Water Act, and the Resource Conservation and Recovery Act in minority areas received much smaller fines than the same types of violations occurring in white areas ($108,563 compared to $341,590).[132]

What efforts have been made to bring violators of the public trust to justice? White-collar criminal enforcement typically involves two strategies designed to control organizational deviance: compliance and deterrence.[133]

Compliance strategies rely on the threat of economic sanctions or civil penalties to control potential violators. They attempt to create a marketplace incentive to obey the law. Under this system, the greater the violation, the larger the economic penalty. Compliance strategies also avoid stigmatizing and shaming businesspeople by focusing on the act, rather than the actor, in white-collar crime.[134] Compliance is regulated by administrative agencies set up to oversee business activity. The Securities and Exchange Commission regulates Wall Street activities, and the Food and Drug Administration regulates drugs, cosmetics, medical devices, meats, and other foods. The legislation creating these agencies usually spells out the penalties for violating regulatory standards. This approach has been used to control environmental crimes by levying heavy fines based on the quantity and dangerousness of the pollution released into the environment.[135]

In contrast, **deterrence strategies** rely on the punishment of individual offenders to deter other would-be violators. Deterrence systems are oriented toward apprehending violators and punishing them, rather than creating conditions that induce conformity to the law. Law enforcement agencies and the courts have traditionally been reluctant to throw corporate executives in jail, but a number of well-publicized cases (such as that of Bernard Madoff) indicate that the gloves are off and the government is willing to punish high-profile white-collar criminals by seeking long prison sentences. Because Madoff and other billion-dollar swindlers have deprived so many people of their life savings and caused such disruptions in the financial markets, both justice system personnel and the general public now consider white-collar crimes as more serious than common-law theft offenses and believe they should be punished accordingly.[136]

Both fines and penalties have been increasing, and long prison sentences are being routinely handed out for white-collar crimes. In fact, deterrence strategies have become so routine—and punishments so severe—that some commentators now argue that the government may actually be going overboard in its efforts to punish white-collar and green-collar criminals, especially for crimes that are the result of negligent business practices rather than intentional criminal conspiracy.[137] Is this a welcome change or an instance of governmental overkill? It depends on one's perspective.

compliance strategies
Methods of controlling white-collar crime that rely on the threat of economic sanctions or civil penalties to control potential violators, creating a marketplace incentive to obey the law.

deterrence strategies
Methods of controlling white-collar crime that rely on the punishment of individual offenders to deter other would-be violators.

FACT OR FICTION?

Most white-collar and green-collar criminals get a slap on the wrist if they are convicted of crime.

FICTION The recent trend has been to toughen sentences and send offenders to jail.

CHECKPOINTS

▶ There are numerous explanations for white-collar crime.

▶ Some offenders are motivated by greed; others offend in response to personal problems.

▶ The rationalization view is that white-collar crime enables offenders to meet their financial needs without compromising their values.

▶ Corporate culture theory suggests that some businesses actually encourage employees to cheat or cut corners.

▶ The self-control view is that white-collar criminals are like any other law violators: impulsive people who lack self-control.

▶ Compliance strategies for controlling white-collar crime rely on the threat of civil penalties for violating the law.

▶ Deterrence systems seek to control white-collar crime by threatening to punish individuals with prison sentences.

Thinking Like a Criminologist

Who Are the Real Criminals? You may recall that style guru Martha Stewart was imprisoned as a result of an investigation into an insider-trading scheme. The case caused quite a bit of controversy since Martha did not present a danger to society, and she was not convicted of insider trading but of the charge of lying to federal investigators. As trial attorney Kevin Mahoney put it:

> It is a shameful day. The federal government will imprison a woman for lying to its investigators. Not a lie that stampeded a country into an unnecessary war, that defrauded the country of millions of dollars, or endangered people's lives. The lie was no more than the denial of wrongdoing, a protestation of innocence. Shame on us for permitting our government to terrorize us.

Yet the people who were shocked when décor diva Stewart did time seem to have no problem with imprisoning a lower-class woman who is caught possessing drugs. Even though both crimes have no discernible victim, Martha's white-collar crime seemed like the more trivial offense—or was it?

Writing Assignment

Write an essay that confronts this critical issue: Is it ethical to imprison nondangerous white-collar criminals to set an example, or should they merely suffer financial penalties? What is the purpose of putting someone like Martha Stewart in prison for a trivial white-collar offense? Is she a danger to society? Is multibillion-dollar swindler Bernard Madoff? Or would it be better, to quote Billy Ray Valentine (Eddie Murphy in the classic 1983 film *Trading Places*), "You know, it occurs to me that the best way you hurt rich people is by turning them into poor people"?

SUMMARY

LO1   Discuss the history of theft offenses.
Common theft offenses include larceny, fraud, and embezzlement. These are common-law crimes, originally defined by English judges. Skilled thieves included pickpockets, forgers, and counterfeiters, who operated freely. Smugglers transported goods, such as spirits, gems, gold, and spices, without paying tax or duty. Poachers supplemented their diet and income with game that belonged to a landlord.

LO2   Differentiate between professional and amateur thieves.
Economic crimes are designed to reap financial rewards for the offender. Opportunistic amateurs commit the majority of economic crimes. Economic crime has also attracted professional criminals. Professionals earn most of their income from crime, view themselves as criminals, and possess skills that aid them in their law-breaking behavior. An example of the professional criminal is the fence who buys and sells stolen merchandise.

LO3   Describe the various forms of shoplifting.
Some shoplifters are amateurs who steal on the spur of the moment. These snitches are otherwise respectable persons who do not conceive of themselves as thieves but systematically steal merchandise for their own use. Some adolescents become shoplifters because they have been coerced by older kids. Called boosters or heels, professional shoplifters steal with the intention of reselling stolen merchandise to pawnshops or fences, usually at half the original price. Boosters know how to hit stores without being detected and have partners who can unload merchandise after it is stolen.

LO4   Summarize the various forms of white-collar crime.
White-collar fraud involves using a business enterprise as a front to swindle people. Chiseling involves professionals who cheat clients. Embezzlement and employee fraud occur when a person uses a position of trust to steal

from an organization. Client fraud involves theft from an organization that advances credit, covers losses, or reimburses for services. Corporate, or organizational, crime involves various illegal business practices such as price fixing, restraint of trade, and false advertising.

L05   Explain what is meant by the term *Ponzi scheme*.

A Ponzi scheme is an investment fraud that involves the payment of purported returns to existing investors from funds contributed by new investors. In many Ponzi schemes, the fraudsters focus on attracting new money to make promised payments to earlier-stage investors and to use for personal expenses, instead of engaging in any legitimate investment activity. The term comes from one Charles Ponzi, who duped thousands of New England residents into investing in a postage stamp speculation scheme back in the 1920s.

L06   Discuss efforts to control white-collar and green-collar crime.

The government has used various law enforcement strategies to combat white-collar and green-collar crime. Some involve deterrence, which uses punishment to frighten potential abusers. Others involve economic or compliance strategies, which create economic incentives to obey the law. Most offenders do not view themselves as criminals and therefore do not seem to be deterred by criminal statutes. Although thousands of white-collar criminals are prosecuted each year, their numbers are insignificant compared with the magnitude of the problem. Detection and enforcement are primarily in the hands of administrative departments and agencies, including the FBI, the Internal Revenue Service, the Secret Service, US Customs, the Environmental Protection Agency, and the Securities and Exchange Commission. On the state and local levels, law enforcement officials have made progress in a number of areas, such as controlling consumer fraud and environmental pollution.

Key Terms

economic crime 406
blue-collar crimes 406
white-collar crimes 406
green-collar crimes 406
theft 406
occasional criminals 408
situational
    inducement 408
professional
    criminals 408
larceny 408

constructive
    possession 409
petit (petty) larceny 409
grand larceny 409
shoplifting 409
snitch 409
booster (heel) 410
booster box 410
merchant privilege
    laws 410
car cloning 411

naive check forgers 412
systematic forgers 412
fence 413
burglary 413
arson 414
chiseling 418
insider trading 418
exploitation 419
influence peddling 419
embezzlement 421

corporate (organizational)
    crime 423
Sherman Antitrust
    Act 424
price fixing 424
harms perspective 426
criminal environmental
    pollution 429
compliance
    strategies 435
deterrence strategies 435

Critical Thinking Questions

1. Differentiate between an occasional and a professional criminal. Which one would be more likely to resort to violence?

2. What crime occurs when an antiques store owner sells a customer an "original" Tiffany lamp that she knows is a fake? Would it still be a crime if the seller were not aware that the lamp was a copy? Should antiques dealers have a duty to determine the authenticity of the products they sell?

3. What is the difference between a booster and a snitch? If caught, should they receive different punishments?

4. Should corporate crimes such as price fixing or false advertising be punished with a stiff fine or imprisonment? Is it fair to put a nonviolent businessperson in prison? Is it fair to punish a billionaire with a fine that merely requires them to write a check?

5. Which is worse: breaking into a home and stealing a television or getting involved in an insider trading scheme to make a million in the stock market? Which act should be punished most severely?

Notes

All URLs accessed in 2017.

1. Department of Justice, US Attorney's Office, District of Connecticut, Citizen of Cuba Sentenced to 7 Years in Prison for Eli Lilly Theft, Additional Multimillion Dollar Burglaries," December 16, 2016, https://www.justice.gov/usao-ct/pr/citizen-cuba-sentenced-7-years-prison-eli-lilly-theft-additional-multimillion-dollar; FBI, "Pharmaceutical Theft: $60 Million Heist Largest in Connecticut History," April 10, 2017, https://www.fbi.gov/news/stories/pharmaceutical-theft.

2. Code of Hammurabi, http://avalon.law.yale.edu/ancient/hamframe.asp.

3. Garrett Fagan, *Bathing in Public in the Roman World* (Ann Arbor: University of Michigan Press, 1999).

4. J. J. Tobias, *Crime and Police in England, 1700–1900* (London: Gill and Macmillan, 1979).

5. Ibid., p. 9.

6. John Locker and Barry Godfrey, "Ontological Boundaries and Temporal Watersheds in the Development of White-Collar Crime," *British Journal of Criminology* 46 (2006): 976–999.

7. Edward Alsworth Ross, *Sin and Society: An Analysis of Latter-Day Iniquity* (Boston: Houghton Mifflin, 1907), pp. 45–71.

8. Edwin Sutherland, *White-Collar Crime: The Uncut Version* (New Haven, CT: Yale University Press, 1983).

9. Edwin Sutherland, "White-Collar Criminality," *American Sociological Review* 5 (1940): 2–10.

10. Bryanna Hahn Fox and David Farrington, "Is the Development of Offenders Related to Crime Scene Behaviors for Burglary? Including Situational Influences in Developmental and Life-Course Theories of Crime," *International Journal of Offender Therapy and Comparative Criminology* 60 (2016): 1897–1927.

11. Joseph Kuhns, Kristie Blevins, Riane Bolin, and Josie Cambareri, "Drug Use and Abuse as Primary Motivators for Involvement in Burglary," *Journal of Drug Issues* 47 (2017): 116–131.

12. Wayne LaFave and Austin Scott, *Handbook on Criminal Law* (St. Paul, MN: West, 1972).

13. FBI, "Larceny-Theft," *Crime in the United States, 2015*, https://ucr.fbi.gov/crime-in-the-u.s/2015/crime-in-the-u.s.-2015/offenses-known-to-law-enforcement/larceny-theft.

14. Jennifer Truman and Rachel Morgan, *Criminal Victimization, 2015*, Bureau of Justice Statistics, *2016*, https://www.bjs.gov/content/pub/pdf/cv15.pdf.

15. Jack Hayes International, "Annual Retail Theft Survey, 2015," http://hayesinternational.com/news/annual-retail-theft-survey/.

16. Liz Parks, "ORC on the Rise," National Retail Federation News, December 14, 2016, https://nrf.com/news/orc-the-rise.

17. Jack Hayes International, "Annual Retail Theft Survey, 2015."

18. Darrell Steffensmeier, Casey Harris, and Noah Painter-Davis, "Gender and Arrests for Larceny, Fraud, Forgery, and Embezzlement: Conventional or Occupational Property Crime Offenders? *Journal of Criminal Justice* 43 (2015): 205–221.

19. Mary Owen Cameron, *The Booster and the Snitch* (New York: Free Press, 1964).

20. Ellen Beate Hansen and Gunnar Breivik, "Sensation Seeking as a Predictor of Positive and Negative Risk Behavior Among Adolescents," *Personality and Individual Differences* 30 (2001): 627–640.

21. Yves Lamontagne, Richard Boyer, Celine Hetu, and Celine Lacerte-Lamontagne, "Anxiety, Significant Losses, Depression, and Irrational Beliefs in First-Offense Shoplifters," *Canadian Journal of Psychiatry* 45 (2000): 64–66.

22. Brian Smith and Ronald Clarke, "Shoplifting of Everyday Products that Serve Illicit Drug Uses," *Journal of Research in Crime and Delinquency* 52 (2015): 245–269.

23. Gail Caputo and Anna King, "Shoplifting by Male and Female Drug Users: Gender, Agency, and Work," *Criminal Justice Review* 40 (2015): 47–66.

24. FBI, "Organized Retail Theft: A $30 Billion-a-Year Industry," https://www.fbi.gov/news/stories/organized-retail-theft.

25. Ibid.

26. Jennifer Conlin, "Credit Card Fraud Keeps Growing on the Net," *New York Times*, May 11, 2007, http://www.nytimes.com/2007/05/11/your-money/11iht-mcredit.1.5664687.html.

27. LaFave and Scott, *Handbook on Criminal Law*, p. 672.

28. Gerry Wagschal, Gio Benitez, and Lisa Khoury, "VIN Cloning: How Thieves Can Steal Your Car's Identity," ABC News, January 24, 2015, http://abcnews.go.com/US/vin-cloning-thieves-masking-car-thefts/story?id=28401709.

29. "Hot Cars: Parts Crooks Love Best," *BusinessWeek,* September 15, 2003, p. 104.

30. National Insurance Crime Bureau, "NICB's Hot Wheels: America's 10 Most Stolen Vehicles," August 1, 2016, http://www.multivu.com/players/English/7665254-nicb-americas-most-stolen-vehicles/.

31. All prices here were obtained on eBay, March 2016.

32. Edwin Lemert, "An Isolation and Closure Theory of Naive Check Forgery," *Journal of Criminal Law, Criminology and Police Science* 44 (1953): 297–298.

33. Carl Klockars, *The Professional Fence* (New York: Free Press, 1976); Darrell Steffensmeier, *The Fence: In the Shadow of Two Worlds* (Totowa, NJ: Rowman and Littlefield, 1986).

34. National Retail Federation, "2015 Organized Retail Crime Survey," https://nrf.com/resources/retail-library/2015-organized-retail-crime-survey.

35. William Blackstone, *Commentaries on the Laws of England* (London: Clarendon Press, 1769), p. 224.

36. FBI, "Burglary," *Crime in the United States, 2015,* https://ucr.fbi.gov/crime-in-the-u.s/2015/crime-in-the-u.s.-2015/offenses-known-to-law-enforcement/burglary.

37. Jennifer Truman and Rachel Morgan, "Criminal Victimization, 2015," Bureau of Justice Statistics, 20164, https://www.bjs.gov/content/pub/pdf/cv15.pdf.

38. Jeffrey Roth and Vanessa Trecki, "Burglary Expertise: Comparing Burglars to Other Offenders," *Deviant Behavior* 38 (2017): 188–207; Neal Shover, "Structures and Careers in Burglary," *Journal of Criminal Law, Criminology and Police Science* 63 (1972): 540–549.

39. Lynn A. Addington and Callie Marie Rennison, "Keeping the Barbarians Outside the Gate? Comparing Burglary Victimization in Gated and Non-Gated Communities," *Justice Quarterly* 32 (2015): 168–192.

40. Wim Bernasco, "Co-Offending and the Choice of Target Areas in Burglary," *Journal of Investigative Psychology and Offender Profiling* 3 (2006): 139–155.

41. Joseph Ornstein and Ross Hammond, "The Burglary Boost: A Note on Detecting Contagion Using the Knox Test," *Journal of Quantitative Criminology* 33 (2017): 65–75.

42. Addington and Rennison, "Keeping the Barbarians Outside the Gate?"

43. Christophe Vandeviver, Stijn Van Daele, and Tom Vander Beken, "What Makes Long Crime Trips Worth Undertaking? Balancing Costs and Benefits in Burglars' Journey to Crime," *British Journal of Criminology* 55 (2014): 399–420.

44. Nick Tilley, Rebecca Thompson, Graham Farrell, Louise Grove, and Andromachi Tseloni, "Do Burglar Alarms Increase Burglary Risk? A Counter-Intuitive Finding and Possible Explanations," *Crime Prevention and Community Safety* 17 (2015): 1–19.

45. Mitchell Chamlin and Andrea Krajewski, "Use of Force and Home Safety: An Impact Assessment of Oklahoma's Stand Your Ground Law," *Deviant Behavior* 37 (2016): 237–245; Ling Ren, Yan Zhang, and Jihong Solomon Zhao, "The Deterrent Effect of the Castle Doctrine Law on Burglary in Texas," *Crime and Delinquency* 61 (2015): 1127–1151.

46. Hahn Fox and Farrington, "Is the Development of Offenders Related to Crime Scene Behaviors for Burglary? Including Situational Influences in Developmental and Life-Course Theories of Crime."

47. Nancy Webb, George Sakheim, Luz Towns-Miranda, and Charles Wagner, "Collaborative Treatment of Juvenile Firestarters: Assessment and Outreach," *American Journal of Orthopsychiatry* 60 (1990): 305–310.

48. Pekka Santtila, Helina Haikkanen, Laurence Alison, and Carrie Whyte, "Juvenile Firesetters: Crime Scene Actions and Offender Characteristics," *Legal and Criminological Psychology* 8 (2003): 1–20.

49. John Taylor, Ian Thorne, Alison Robertson, and Ginny Avery, "Evaluation of a Group Intervention for Convicted Arsonists with Mild and Borderline Intellectual Disabilities," *Criminal Behaviour and Mental Health* 12 (2002): 282–294.

50. Rodney Huff, Christian Desilets, and John Kane, "2010 National Public Survey on White Collar Crime," http://www.nw3c.org/docs/publications/2010-national-public-survey-on-white-collar-crime.pdf.

51. Ibid.

52. Ibid.

53. Natalie Taylor, "Under-Reporting of Crime Against Small Business: Attitudes Towards Police and Reporting Practices," *Policing and Society* 13 (2003): 79–90.

54. This structure is based on an analysis contained in Mark Moore, "Notes Toward a National Strategy to Deal with White-Collar Crime," in *A National*

Strategy for Containing White-Collar Crime, ed. Herbert Edelhertz and Charles Rogovin (Lexington, MA: Lexington Books, 1980), pp. 32–44.

55. Securities and Exchange Commission, "Ponzi Schemes," https://www.sec.gov/fast-answers /answersponzihtm.html.

56. FBI, "Telemarketing Fraud," https://www.fbi.gov /scams-and-safety/common-fraud-schemes /telemarketing-fraud.

57. Joel Grover and Matt Goldberg, "Jiffy Lube Reacts to Hidden Camera Report," NBC LA News, October 17, 2008, http://www.nbclosangeles.com/news /Jiffy_Lube_Reacts_to_Hidden_Camera_Report .html. See also Channel 6 News, "Buried Secret: Quick Lube Chain Cheats Customers: Customers Pay Premium for Low-Priced Oil," November 1, 2007, http://www.theindychannel.com/news /buried-secret-quick-lube-chain-cheats-customers.

58. Richard Quinney, "Occupational Structure and Criminal Behavior: Prescription Violation of Retail Pharmacists," *Social Problems* 11 (1963): 179–185. See also John Braithwaite, *Corporate Crime in the Pharmaceutical Industry* (London: Routledge and Kegan Paul, 1984).

59. Pam Belluck, "Prosecutors Say Greed Drove Pharmacist to Dilute Drugs," *New York Times,* August 18, 2001, p. 3.

60. FBI press release, April 22, 2002, Kansas City Division.

61. James Armstrong et al., "Securities Fraud," *American Criminal Law Review* 33 (1995): 973–1016.

62. *Carpenter v. United States* 484 U.S. 19 (1987). See also John Boland, "The SEC Trims the First Amendment," *Wall Street Journal,* December 4, 1986, p. 28.

63. Alana Abramson, "ICE Officer Convicted of Accepting Bribes and Sex for Immigration Documents," *Time,* March 10, 2017, http://time .com/4698789/ice-officer-arnaldo-echevarria -bribes-sex-work-papers/

64. Charles V. Bagli, "Kickback Investigation Extends to Middle-Class Buildings in New York," *New York Times,* October 14, 1998, p. A19.

65. FBI, "A (Driver's) License to Steal: Corruption in a San Diego Motor Vehicle Office," February 25, 2014, http://www.fbi.gov/news/stories/2014/february /corruption-in-a-san-diego-motor-vehicle-office.

66. FBI, "Cheating in Contracts: A $30 Million Case of Corruption," July 19, 2013, https://www.fbi.gov /news/stories/30-million-dollar-case-of-corruption.

67. Victoria Bekiempis and Stephen Rex Brown, "Sheldon Silver Guilty of All 7 Corruption Charges in Twin Kickback Schemes, Faces Up to 130 Years

in Prison," *New York Daily News,* December 1, 2015, http://www.nydailynews.com/news/crime /sheldon-silver-guilty-7-corruption-charges -article-1.2450685.

68. MSNBC, "Pa. Judges Accused of Jailing Kids for Cash: Judges Allegedly Took $2.6 Million in Payoffs to Put Juveniles in Lockups," February 11, 2009, http://www.nbcnews.com/id/29142654/ns /us_news-crime_and_courts/t/pa-judges-accused -jailing-kids-cash/.

69. Henry Blodget, "Apple Manager Paul Shin Devine Busted in $1 Million Kickback Scheme," *Business Insider,* August 15, 2010, http://www.businessinsider .com/apple-manager-paul-shin-devine-busted-in-1 -million-kickback-scheme-2010-8.

70. Alina Selyukh, "U.S. Judge Approves IBM's Foreign Bribery Case Settlement with SEC," Reuters, July 25, 2013, http://www.reuters.com/article/2013/07/25 /us-ibm-sec-idUSBRE96O1FB20130725.

71. PL No. 95-213, 101-104, 91 Stat. 1494.

72. J. Sorenson, H. Grove, and T. Sorenson, "Detecting Management Fraud: The Role of the Independent Auditor," in *White-Collar Crime, Theory and Research,* eds. G. Geis and E. Stotland (Beverly Hills: Sage, 1980), pp. 221–251.

73. Jason Knott, "Ex-Tyco CEO Dennis Kozlowski Released from Prison," January 17, 2014, http:// www.cepro.com/article/ex_tyco_ceo_dennis _kozlowski_released_from_prison/.

74. Bethany McLean and Peter Elkind, *The Smartest Guys in the Room: The Amazing Rise and Scandalous Fall of Enron* (New York: Penguin, 2003); Kurt Eichenwald, "Ex-Andersen Partner Pleads Guilty in Record-Shredding," *New York Times,* April 12, 2002, p. C1; John A. Byrne, "At Enron, the Environment Was Ripe for Abuse," *BusinessWeek,* February 25, 2002, p. 12;. Peter Behr and Carrie Johnson, "Govt. Expands Charges Against Enron Execs," *Washington Post,* May 1, 2003, p. 1.

75. Sorenson, Grove, and Sorenson, "Detecting Management Fraud: The Role of the Independent Auditor."

76. To learn more about fraud in the United States and abroad, go to the StopFraud.gov website, http:// www.stopfraud.gov.

77. FBI, "Health Care Fraud," http://www.fbi.gov /about-us/investigate/white_collar/health-care -fraud.

78. National Health Care Anti-Fraud Association, "The Challenge of Health Care Fraud," 2014, http://www.nhcaa.org/resources/health-care -anti-fraud-resources/the-challenge-of-health -care-fraud.aspx.

79. FBI, "Health Care Fraud Takedown: 243 Arrested, Charged with $712 Million in False Medicare Billings," June 18, 2015, https://www.fbi.gov/news/stories/2015/june/health-care-fraud-takedown/health-care-fraud-takedown.

80. 42 USC 1320a-7b(b); 42 USC 1320a-7b(b)(3); 42 CFR 1001.952 (regulatory safe harbors); 42 USC 1395nn (codifying "Stark I" and "Stark II" statutes).

81. *United States v. Bishop*, 412 U.S. 346 (1973).

82. Kylie Cooper and Adrienne Dedjinou, "Antitrust Violations," *American Criminal Law Review* 42 (2005): 179–221.

83. 15 U.S.C. section 1 (1994).

84. 15 U.S.C. 1–7 (1976).

85. *Northern Pacific Railways v. United States*, 356 U.S. 1 (1958).

86. US Department of Justice, "Nine Automobile Parts Manufacturers and Two Executives Agree to Plead Guilty to Fixing Prices on Automobile Parts Sold to U.S. Car Manufacturers and Installed in U.S. Cars: Companies Agree to Pay Total of More than $740 Million in Criminal Fines," September 26, 2013, http://www.fbi.gov/news/pressrel/press-releases/nine-automobile-parts-manufacturers-and-two-executives-agree-to-plead-guilty-to-fixing-prices-on-automobile-parts-sold-to-u.s.-car-manufacturers-and-installed-in-u.s.-cars.

87. Tim Carrington, "Federal Probes of Contractors Rise for Year," *Wall Street Journal*, February 23, 1987, p. 50.

88. United States Attorney, Middle District of Tennessee, "Grease Hauling Company and Executives Sentenced for Clean Water Act Violations," February 19, 2016, https://www.epa.gov/sites/production/files/2016-02/documents/southern-grease-press-release.pdf.

89. Michael J. Lynch and Paul Stretesky, "Green Criminology in the United States," in *Issues in Green Criminology*, ed. Piers Beirne and Nigel South (Portland, OR: Willan, 2008), pp. 248–269, at 249.

90. Matthew Greife, Paul Stretesky, Tara O'Connor Shelley, and Mark Pogrebin, "Corporate Environmental Crime and Environmental Justice," *Criminal Justice Policy Review* 28 (2017): 327–346.

91. Michael M. O'Hear, "Sentencing the Green-Collar Offender: Punishment, Culpability, and Environmental Crime," *Journal of Criminal Law and Criminology* 95 (2004): 133–276.

92. Anh Ngoc Cao and Tanya Wyatt, "The Conceptual Compatibility Between Green Criminology and Human Security: A Proposed Interdisciplinary Framework for Examinations into Green Victimisation," *Critical Criminology* 24 (2016): 413–430.

93. F. J. W. Herbig and S. J. Joubert, "Criminological Semantics: Conservation Criminology—Vision or Vagary?" *Acta Criminologica* 19 (2006): 88–103.

94. Rob White, "Researching Transnational Environmental Harm: Toward an Eco-Global Criminology," *International Journal of Comparative and Applied Criminal Justice* 33 (2009): 229–248.

95. Bruce Arrigo and Michael Lynch, "The Human Consequences of Ecological Violence and Corporate Victimization: Public Sector Psychology and Green Criminology," *International Journal of Offender Therapy and Comparative Criminology* 59 (2015): 227–229.

96. Paddy Hillyard, Christina Pantazis, Dave Gordon, and Steve Tombs, *Beyond Criminology: Taking Harm Seriously* (London: Pluto Press, 2004).

97. Juliet Eilperin and Steven Mufson, "Trump to Roll Back Obama's Climate, Water Rules Through Executive Action," *Washington Post*, February 20, 2017, https://www.washingtonpost.com/news/energy-environment/wp/2017/02/20/trump-to-roll-back-obamas-climate-water-rules-through-executive-action/.

98. Interpol, "Project Leaf," https://www.interpol.int/Crime-areas/Environmental-crime/Projects/Project-Leaf.

99. Ibid.

100. Ibid.

101. Interpol, "Project Leaf."

102. This section leans heavily on Liana Sun Wyler and Pervaze A. Sheikh, *International Illegal Trade in Wildlife: Threats and U.S. Policy* (Washington, DC: Congressional Research Service, 2008), https://fas.org/sgp/crs/misc/RL34395.pdf.

103. Interpol, "Project Predator," http://www.interpol.int/Crime-areas/Environmental-crime/Projects/Project-Predator.

104. Interpol, "Project Wisdom," http://www.interpol.int/Crime-areas/Environmental-crime/Projects/Project-Wisdom.

105. Patterson Clark and Darryl Fears, "The Horn and Ivory Trade," *Washington Post*, August 10, 2014, https://www.washingtonpost.com/apps/g/page/national/the-horn-and-ivory-trade/1163/; World Wildlife Fund, "Black Rhino," http://wwf.panda.org/what_we_do/endangered_species/rhinoceros/african_rhinos/black_rhinoceros/.

106. White, "Researching Transnational Environmental Harm: Toward an Eco-Global Criminology."

107. For more information, go to the World Wildlife Fund, http://www.worldwildlife.org/.

108. The Lacey Act, 16 U.S.C. §§ 3371–3378.

109. International Centre for Trade and Sustainable Development, "Wildlife Trade: China Reports Drop in Smuggled Ivory, South Africa Debates Rhino Horn Law," March 23, 2017, http://www.ictsd.org/bridges-news/bridges/news/wildlife-trade-china-reports-drop-in-smuggled-ivory-south-africa-debates.

110. Jani Actman, "Watch Fishermen Bomb Their Catch Out of the Water," *National Geographic*, June 3, 2016, http://news.nationalgeographic.com/2016/06/blast-fishing-dynamite-fishing-tanzania/.

111. National Oceanic and Atmospheric Administration, "Endangered and Threatened Marine Species Under NMFS' Jurisdiction," http://www.nmfs.noaa.gov/pr/species/esa/listed.htm#fish; U. R. Sumaila, J. Alder, and H. Keith, "Global Scope and Economics of Illegal Fishing," *Marine Policy* 30 (2006): 696–703.

112. Carole Gibbs, Edmund F. McGarrell, and Mark Axelrod, "Transnational White-Collar Crime and Risk: Lessons from the Global Trade in Electronic Waste," *Criminology and Public Policy* 9 (2010): 543–560.

113. Belluck, "Prosecutors Say Greed Drove Pharmacist to Dilute Drugs," p. 3.

114. Forbes Profile, "Michael Milken," April 17, 2017, https://www.forbes.com/profile/michael-milken/.

115. See also Neal Shover and Andrew Hochstetler, *Choosing White-Collar Crime* (Cambridge, England: Cambridge University Press, 2006).

116. Neal Shover and Peter Grabosky, "White-Collar Crime and the Great Recession," *Criminology and Public Policy* 9 (2010): 429–433.

117. Quoted in Tim Metz and Michael Miller, "Boesky's Rise and Fall Illustrate a Compulsion to Profit by Getting Inside Track on Market," *Wall Street Journal*, November 17, 1986, p. 28.

118. Petter Gottschalk, "Convenience in White-Collar Crime: Introducing a Core Concept," *Deviant Behavior* 38 (2017): 605–619.

119. Mandeep Dhami, "White-Collar Prisoners' Perceptions of Audience Reaction," *Deviant Behavior* 28 (2007): 57–77.

120. Donald Cressey, *Other People's Money: A Study of the Social Psychology of Embezzlement* (Glencoe, IL: Free Press, 1973), p. 96.

121. Nicole Leeper Piquero, Stephen Tibbetts, and Michael Blankenship, "Examining the Role of Differential Association and Techniques of Neutralization in Explaining Corporate Crime," *Deviant Behavior* 26 (2005): 159–188.

122. Travis Hirschi and Michael Gottfredson, "Causes of White-Collar Crime," *Criminology* 25 (1987): 949–974.

123. Michael Gottfredson and Travis Hirschi, *A General Theory of Crime* (Stanford, CA: Stanford University Press, 1990), p. 191.

124. This section relies heavily on Daniel Skoler, "White-Collar Crime and the Criminal Justice System: Problems and Challenges," in *A National Strategy for Containing White-Collar Crime*, ed. Edelhertz and Rogovin, pp. 57–76.

125. *United States Attorneys' Bulletin, Environmental Crimes, 2011*, https://www.justice.gov/sites/default/files/usao/legacy/2011/12/16/usab5904.pdf.

126. Ronald Burns, Keith Whitworth, and Carol Thompson, "Assessing Law Enforcement Preparedness to Address Internet Fraud," *Journal of Criminal Justice* 32 (2004): 477–493.

127. Michael Benson, Francis Cullen, and William Maakestad, "Local Prosecutors and Corporate Crime," *Crime and Delinquency* 36 (1990): 356–372.

128. Ibid., pp. 369–370.

129. US Fish and Wildlife Service, "About Service Special Agents," http://www.fws.gov/le/special-agents.html.

130. Environmental Protection Agency, "Criminal Enforcement," https://www.epa.gov/enforcement/criminal-enforcement.

131. US Department of Justice, Environmental Crimes Section, http://www.justice.gov/enrd/environmental-crimes-section.

132. Michael Lynch, Paul Stretesky, and Ronald Burns, "Slippery Business," *Journal of Black Studies* 34 (2004): 421–440.

133. This section relies heavily on Albert Reiss Jr., "Selecting Strategies of Social Control over Organizational Life," in *Enforcing Regulation*, ed. Keith Hawkins and John M. Thomas (Boston: Kluwer, 1984), pp. 25–37.

134. Michael Benson, "Emotions and Adjudication: Stat Degradation Among White-Collar Criminals," *Justice Quarterly* 7 (1990): 515–528; John Braithwaite, *Crime, Shame, and Reintegration* (Sydney, Australia: Cambridge University Press, 1989).

135. John Braithwaite, "The Limits of Economism in Controlling Harmful Corporate Conduct," *Law and Society Review* 16 (1981–1982): 481–504.

136. Sean Rosenmerkel, "Wrongfulness and Harmfulness as Components of Seriousness of White-Collar Offenses," *Journal of Contemporary Criminal Justice* 17 (2001): 308–328.

137. Kris Dighe and Lana Pettus, "Environmental Justice in the Context of Environmental Crimes," *United States Attorneys' Bulletin, Environmental Crimes, 2011*, https://www.justice.gov/sites/default/files/usao/legacy/2011/12/16/usab5904.pdf.

Public Order Crimes

Learning Objectives

LO1 Interpret what is meant by the term *social harm*.

LO2 Discuss the activities of moral crusaders.

LO3 Describe the various forms of outlawed deviant sexuality.

LO4 Distinguish among the different types of prostitutes.

LO5 State the arguments for and against legalizing prostitution.

LO6 Discuss the causes of substance abuse.

John Lamb/Shellys/DigitalVision/Getty Images

Larry Nassar

AP Images/Michigan Attorney General's office

13

Chapter Outline

FACT OR FICTION?

▶ Prostitution should be legalized because it is a victimless crime and many prostitutes make a substantial amount of money.

▶ Fewer kids are drinking today than 20 years ago.

For decades, Larry Nassar was a central figure in the American gymnastics world. He was a doctor at Michigan State University's sports medicine clinic and the team physician for Team USA during four Olympic Games, treating many Olympic champions. His downfall came in 2017 when dozens of women and girls came forward to accuse him of sexual assault. Nassar's victims said they were molested numerous times by the coach during medical exams and treatment sessions. Nassar did not ask for consent, did not tell the victims what he was about to do, and did not wear gloves. In some cases a parent was present, but Nassar would position them so the parents couldn't see what was happening or used a sheet to cover up that part of a gymnast's body.

While Nassar's sexual assault case was ongoing, and Nassar has denied the allegations, he was also indicted by a federal grand jury on charges that he received and attempted to receive child pornography, and that he possessed thousands of images of kiddie porn on his computer. The charges against Nassar were the result of a joint investigation by various law enforcement agencies that was part of a Project Safe Childhood investigation. This national initiative, designed to protect children from online exploitation and abuse, is carried out by the US Attorney's Office, county prosecutor's offices, the Internet Crimes Against Children task force (ICAC), and federal, state, and local law enforcement.[1] On July 10, 2017, Nassar agreed to plead guilty to charges of obtaining and possessing child pornography. ■

public order crimes
Behaviors that are outlawed because they threaten the general well-being of society and challenge accepted moral principles.

Societies have long banned or limited behaviors believed to run contrary to social norms, customs, and values; viewing and possessing child pornography would certainly fall into this category. These behaviors are often referred to as **public order crimes** and are sometimes called victimless crimes, although as the Nassar case aptly shows, the latter term can be misleading.[2] Public order crimes can greatly harm victims and involve acts that interfere with the operations of society and the ability of people to function efficiently. Whereas common-law crimes such as rape and robbery are banned because they cause social harm to a victim, other behaviors, such as prostitution and pornography, are outlawed because they conflict with social policy, prevailing moral rules, and current public opinion. Society takes these acts so seriously that they create multi-agency law enforcement task forces to identify and apprehend public order offenders.

Statutes designed to uphold public order usually prohibit the manufacture and distribution of morally tinged goods and services such as erotic material, commercial sex, and mood-altering drugs. Prohibition of these acts can be controversial because they selectively criminalize desired goods or services. By outlawing sin and vice, they turn millions of otherwise law-abiding citizens into law violators. On the other hand, these acts may bring terrible harm and victimize people who are forced to participate without consent or free will.

Public order crimes typically create *boundaries* rather than *bright lines*: it is legal to drink at age 21, but a crime at age 20, even though 20-year-olds can fight for their country and vote in elections. Such boundaries often create confusion and ambivalence: if an act is immoral and illegal, why is it okay for some people to engage in it but not others? How can an act be considered a crime in one legal jurisdiction but perfectly legal in another?

This chapter covers these public order crimes. It first briefly discusses the relationship between law and morality. Next, it addresses public order crimes of a sexual nature: prostitution, pornography, and deviant sex acts called paraphilias. The chapter concludes by focusing on the abuse of drugs and alcohol.

Law and Morality

In 2011, rising political star Anthony Weiner was forced to resign from office after compromising photos he "tweeted" to young women were posted online. At first, Weiner denied responsibility, telling the media that his account had been hacked and/or that the pictures had possibly been altered. On June 6, 2011, Weiner admitted that he had sent sexually explicit text messages and photographs to several women, both before and after he had gotten married.[3] When Weiner tried a political comeback in 2013, his campaign for mayor of New York City came to an abrupt halt when the media found out that he had sent other women even more explicit photos of himself using the alias "Carlos Danger." Ironically, Weiner was back in the public eye during the 2016 presidential campaign when a political firestorm broke out over the use of his computer to store emails by his then-wife, Huma Abedin, one of Hillary Clinton's closest advisors. After an FBI investigation, it was determined that almost every email discovered in the laptop was a duplicate of previously produced documents or personal emails. Nonetheless, the damage had already been done.

In 2017, Weiner agreed to plead guilty to charges of transferring obscene material to a minor, a crime that carries a maximum penalty of 10 years in prison; he must also register as a sex offender and not to appeal a sentence of between 21 and 27 months in prison. In court, Weiner acknowledged his problem, saying, "These destructive impulses brought great devastation to family and friends, and destroyed my life's dream of public service. And yet I remained in denial even as the world around me fell apart."[4]

Did Weiner's behavior actually cause public harm? Some may view Weiner's behavior as odd yet essentially harmless. After all, he never had physical contact with his victims, and his texts, tweets, and emails could be deleted or discarded.

Nonetheless, his actions amounted to a felony offense under the existing criminal law. If it is a crime to expose oneself in public (indecent exposure), why not on the Internet? Weiner's behavior crossed the line between a harmless prank and a serious criminal offense.

The debate over morality has existed for all of recorded history. The line between behavior considered merely immoral and that which is considered criminal is often a fine one, but the consequences of crossing that line, as Weiner found out, can be significant. As the Bible (Genesis 18:20) tells us, despite Abraham's intervention, God destroyed the "Cities of the Plain" because "The outcry against Sodom and Gomorrah is so great and their sin so grievous."[5] What was the sin that God felt deserved such drastic punishment? According to modern Bible scholars, despite having exhibited pride, excess of food, and prosperous ease, their citizens did not aid the poor and needy.[6]

Today, acts that most of us deem highly immoral are not necessarily criminal. There are no laws banning *superbia* (hubris/pride), *avaritia* (avarice/greed), *luxuria* (extravagance or lust), *invidia* (envy), *gula* (gluttony), *ira* (wrath), and *acedia* (sloth), even though they are considered the "seven deadly sins." Nor is it a crime for a private citizen to ignore the pleas of a drowning child, even though to do so might be considered callous, coldhearted, and unfeeling.

Conversely, some acts that seem both well intentioned and moral are nonetheless considered criminal:

- It is a crime (euthanasia) to kill a loved one who is suffering from an incurable disease to spare him or her further pain; attempting to take your own life (attempted suicide) is also a crime.
- Stealing a rich person's money in order to feed a poor family is still considered larceny.
- Marrying more than one woman is considered a crime (bigamy), even though multiple marriages may conform to some groups' religious beliefs.[7]

As legal experts Wayne LaFave and Austin Scott Jr., put it, "A good motive will not normally prevent what is otherwise criminal from being a crime."[8]

Are Victimless Crimes Victimless?

To answer this question, we might first consider whether there is actually a victim in so-called **victimless crimes**. Some participants may have been coerced into their acts; if so, then they are victims. Opponents of pornography, such as Andrea Dworkin, charge that women involved in adult films, far from being highly paid stars, are "dehumanized—turned into objects and commodities."[9] Although taking drugs may be a matter of personal choice, it too has serious consequences. One study of crack cocaine–using women found that more than half had suffered a physical attack, one-third had been raped, and more than half had had to seek medical care for their injuries.[10] It has been estimated that women involved in street prostitution are 60 to 100 times more likely to be murdered than the average woman and that most of these murders result from a dispute over money rather than being sexually motivated.[11]

Some scholars argue that pornography, prostitution, and drug use erode the moral fabric of society and therefore should be prohibited and punished. They are crimes, according to the great legal scholar Morris Cohen, because "it is one of the functions of the criminal law to give expression to the collective feeling of revulsion toward certain acts, even when they are not very dangerous."[12]

According to this view, so-called victimless crimes are prohibited because one of the functions of criminal law is to express a shared sense of public morality.[13] However, basing criminal definitions on moral beliefs is often an impossible task. Who defines morality? Are we not punishing mere differences rather than social harm? As Supreme Court Justice William O. Douglas so succinctly put it, "What may be trash to me may be prized by others."[14] Would not any attempt to control or limit "objectionable" material eventually lead to the suppression of free speech and political dissent?

victimless crimes
Public order crimes that violate the moral order but have no specific victim other than society as a whole.

FACT OR FICTION?

Prostitution should be legalized because it is a victimless crime and many prostitutes make a substantial amount of money.

FICTION Although they may be glamorized in films like *Pretty Woman*, most prostitutes can be viewed as victims likely to suffer coercion, rape, and physical attacks.

Is this not a veiled form of censorship? After all, many of the great works of Western art depict nude males and females, some quite young. Are the paintings of Rubens or the sculpture of Michelangelo obscene? The nude paintings of Amedeo Modigliani were considered obscene during his time. A 1917 exhibition in Paris was closed due to public outcry over his sensuous images; in 2015 one of his nudes sold for $170 million.[15] What was once considered obscene is now a highly valued work of art.

Research indicates that people who define themselves as liberals are also the most tolerant of sexually explicit material. Demographic attributes such as age, educational attainment, and occupational status may also influence views of pornography: the young and better educated tend to be more tolerant than older, less-educated people.[16] Whose views should prevail? If a majority of the population chooses to engage in what might objectively be considered immoral or deviant behavior, would it be fair or just to prohibit or control such behavior or render it criminal? While it's difficult to measure or calculate the visits to porn sites on the Internet, according to Google's DoubleClick Ad Planner, which uses cookies to track users across the Web, dozens of adult destinations populate the top 500 websites; the largest gets 4.4 billion page views per month, three times more than CNN or ESPN. Adult entertainment websites are responsible for more than 4 percent of all site visits worldwide.[17] Interestingly, the countries with the highest share of adult websites are Iraq, Egypt, Japan, and Peru; the United States does not rank in the top ten! Should all obscenity and pornography be legalized if so many people are active users and wish to enjoy its content? Or, conversely, should adults be prohibited from viewing objectionable content in the privacy of their homes? And if a small segment of society tried to define or limit objectionable material, might it not eventually inhibit free speech and political dissent? Not so, according to social commentator Irving Kristol:

> If we start censoring pornography and obscenity, shall we not inevitably end up censoring political opinion? A lot of people seem to think this would be the case—which only shows the power of doctrinaire thinking over reality. We had censorship of pornography and obscenity for 150 years, until almost yesterday, and I am not aware that freedom of opinion in this country was in any way diminished as a consequence of this fact.[18]

Cultural clashes may ensue when behavior that is considered normative in one society is deplored by those living in another. Take for instance the practice of female genital mutilation, which has been performed on more than 100 million of the world's females; there are millions of girls who still suffer the procedure each year.[19] Custom and tradition are by far the most frequently cited reasons for mutilation, and it is often carried out in a ritual during which the young woman is initiated into adulthood. The surgery is done to ensure virginity, remove sexual sensation, and render the females suitable for marriage; a girl in these societies cannot be considered an adult unless she has undergone genital mutilation. Critics of this practice, led by American author Alice Walker (*The Color Purple*), consider the procedure mutilation and torture; others argue that this ancient custom should be left to the discretion of the indigenous people who consider it part of their culture. "Torture," counters Walker, "is not culture." Can an outsider define the morality of another culture?[20] Amnesty International and the United Nations have worked to end the practice. Because of outside pressure, the procedure is now forbidden in Senegal, Egypt, Guinea, and Togo, among other countries. However, it is growing in Western nations because immigrants continue the practice.

The Theory of Social Harm

L01 Interpret what is meant by the term *social harm*.

There is little disagreement that the purpose of criminal law is to protect society and reduce social harm. When a store is robbed or a child assaulted, it is relatively easy to see and condemn the harm done to the victim. It is, however, more difficult to identify the victims of immoral acts, such as pornography or prostitution, where the parties involved may be willing participants. Some men and women who work for high-paid adult escort services earn more in a few days than a waitress or kindergarten teacher earns in a year. Can we consider high-paid escorts who dispense sexual favors "crime victims"? People who employ sex workers may be wealthy and powerful people who freely and voluntarily spend their money for sexual services; certainly they are not victims either. If there is no victim, can there be a crime? Should acts be made illegal merely because they violate prevailing moral standards? And if so, who defines morality?

According to the theory of **social harm**, immoral acts can be distinguished from crimes on the basis of the injury they cause. Acts that cause harm or injury are outlawed and punished as crimes; acts, even those that are vulgar, offensive, and depraved, are not outlawed or punished if they harm no one.

The theory of social harm can explain most criminal acts, but not all of them. Some acts that cause enormous amounts of social harm are perfectly legal, whereas others that many people consider virtually harmless are outlawed and severely punished. It is now estimated that more than 500,000 deaths in the United States each year can be linked to the consumption of tobacco and alcohol, yet these "deadly substances" remain legal to produce and sell. Similarly, sports cars and motorcycles that can accelerate to more than 150 miles per hour are perfectly legal to sell and possess, even though more than 30,000 people die each year in car accidents. On the other hand, using marijuana is not only nonfatal but is now sold for medical purposes in more than 25 states and has been decriminalized for personal use in a number of other states including Alaska, California, Colorado, Oregon, Maine, Massachusetts, Nevada, and Washington. Yet the sale of marijuana is still banned both by the federal government and most state jurisdictions and punished with a prison sentence. According to the theory of social harm, if more people die each year from alcohol, tobacco, and automobile-related causes, whereas smoking pot is relatively safe, then marijuana should be legalized everywhere and Corvettes, scotch, and Marlboros outlawed. But they are not.

Moral Crusaders and Moral Crusades

Public order crimes often trace their origin to moral crusaders who seek to shape the law to reflect their own way of thinking; Howard Becker calls them **moral entrepreneurs**. These rule creators, argues Becker, operate with an absolute certainty that their way is right and that they are justified in employing any means to get their way: "The crusader is fervent and righteous, often self-righteous."[21] Today's moral crusaders take on such issues as prayer in school, gun ownership, same-sex marriage, abortion, and the distribution of sexually explicit books and magazines.

While some moral crusades are in fact aimed at curbing behavior that most of us find objectionable—for instance, animal cruelty or drunk driving—they can also create controversy when they are directed at behaviors engaged in by the majority of citizens. One popular focus for moral crusaders is anti-smut campaigns that target books considered too "racy" or controversial to be suitable for a public school library. According to the American Library Association, between 2000 and 2009, the *Harry Potter* series topped the yearly list of books challenged by critics who demanded their removal from school library shelves on charges they promoted Satanism and witchcraft. The most challenged books in recent years include *The Absolutely True Diary of a Part-Time Indian*, by Sherman Alexie; *Extremely Loud and Incredibly Close*, by Jonathan Safran Foer; *Persepolis*, by Marjane Satrapi; *The Kite Runner*, by Khaled Hosseini; *The Perks of Being a Wallflower*, by Stephen Chbosky; *Drama*, by Raina Telgemeier; and *A Stolen Life*, by Jaycee Dugard.[22] Are these books actually objectionable? Should librarians accede to the demands of a vocal minority or to the will of the mostly silent majority?

THE SAME-SEX MARRIAGE CRUSADE   One of the most heated moral crusades of this century has focused on marriage equality. One group of crusaders was determined to prevent the legalization of same-sex marriage; its objective was passage of an amendment to the US Constitution declaring that marriage is between one man and one woman. The Defense of Marriage Act, which was passed in 1996 and defined marriage, for the purposes of federal law, as a union of one man and one woman, was one of this group's legal achievements.[23]

---

social harm
The injury caused to others by willful wrongful conduct

moral entrepreneurs
Individuals who create moral rules, which thus reflect the values of those in power, rather than any objective, universal standards of right and wrong.

L02   Discuss the activities of moral crusaders.

CONNECTIONS
Moral entrepreneurs are likely to use the interactionist definition of crime discussed in Chapter 1: acts are illegal because they violate the moral standards of those in power and those who try to shape public opinion.

Opposing them were activists who tirelessly campaigned for the civil rights of gay men and women. One of their most important victories occurred in 2003 when the Supreme Court delivered, in *Lawrence v. Texas*, a historic decision that made it impermissible for states to criminalize oral and anal sex (and all other forms of intercourse that are not conventionally heterosexual) under statutes prohibiting sodomy, deviant sexuality, or what used to be referred to as "buggery."[24] The *Lawrence* case involved two gay men who had been arrested in 1998 for having sex in the privacy of their Houston home. In overturning their convictions, the Court said this:

> Although the laws involved here do not more than prohibit a particular sexual act, their penalties and purposes have more far-reaching consequences, touching upon the most private human conduct, sexual behavior, and in the most private of places, the home. They seek to control a personal relationship that, whether or not entitled to formal recognition in the law, is within the liberty of persons to choose without being punished as criminals. The liberty protected by the Constitution allows homosexual persons the right to choose to enter upon relationships in the confines of their homes and their own private lives and still retain their dignity as free persons.

As a result of this decision, all sodomy laws in the United States were suddenly unconstitutional and unenforceable; acts that were once a crime were legalized. The *Lawrence* decision paved the way for states to rethink their marriage laws. In 2003, Massachusetts's highest court ruled that same-sex couples are legally entitled to wed under the state constitution and that the state may not "deny the protections, benefits, and obligations conferred by civil marriage to two individuals of the same sex who wish to marry."[25] After a long, drawn-out legal process, the issue of same-sex marriage was resolved in 2015, when the US Supreme Court ruled in *Obergefell v. Hodges* that state-level bans on same-sex marriage are unconstitutional. The Court ruled that the denial of marriage licenses to same-sex couples and the refusal to recognize those marriages performed in other jurisdictions violates the due process and equal protection clauses of the Fourteenth Amendment of the US Constitution.[26]

The same-sex marriage crusade raised a number of important issues: Is it fair to prevent one group of loyal tax-paying citizens from engaging in a behavior that is allowed others? Are there objective standards of morality or should society respect people's differences? After all, opponents of same-sex marriage claim, polygamy is banned, and there are age standards for marriage in every state. If same-sex marriage is legal, what about marriage to multiple partners or with underage minors? The debate continues: The Supreme Court will hear the case of a Christian baker who refused to make a wedding cake for a gay couple.

The public order crimes discussed in this chapter are divided into two broad areas. The first relates to what conventional society considers deviant sexual practices: paraphilias, prostitution, and pornography. The second area concerns the use of substances that have been outlawed or controlled because of the harm they are alleged to cause: drugs and alcohol.

Sex-Related Offenses

On August 24, 2009, Phillip Garrido, a long-time sex offender, was placed under arrest for the kidnapping of Jaycee Lee Dugard, a California girl who had been abducted on June 10, 1991, when she was 11 years old. She had been held captive for 18 years and raped repeatedly, bearing him two children. In 2011, Garrido was sentenced to 431 years in prison; his wife received a sentence of 36 to life.

There have been similar cases that made national headlines. On June 5, 2002, Elizabeth Smart was abducted from her bedroom in Salt Lake City, Utah, and held captive until found nine months later. Elizabeth had been kidnapped by Brian David Mitchell, who was indicted for her kidnapping and sent to a mental health facility after being ruled mentally unfit to stand trial. After six years in psychiatric custody Mitchell was deemed fit to stand trial. Found guilty of rape and kidnapping, he was sentenced to life in prison in 2011. Between 2002 and 2004, Ariel Castro kidnapped Michelle

Knight, Amanda Berry, and Georgina "Gina" DeJesus and held them in his house on Seymour Avenue in Cleveland until May 6, 2013, when Berry was able to shout through a locked door and alert her neighbors. The women had been raped and beaten continually. Knight had become pregnant five times and endured miscarriages brought on by beatings and starvation. Berry had also become pregnant and had a 6-year-old daughter at the time of her rescue. Castro pleaded guilty to 937 criminal counts of rape, kidnapping, and aggravated murder and was sentenced to life in prison without the chance of parole plus 1,000 years. Castro hanged himself in his prison cell within a month of his incarceration.

Although these sex-related kidnappings are stunning in their sordidness, they are not rare. Each year thousands of children are abducted by strangers, and hundreds of thousands of women are subjected to some form of sexual exploitation, including sexual abuse, prostitution, pornography, and molestation. These sex-related offenses are discussed in detail in the sections that follow.

Paraphilias

Paraphilias, a term derived from the Greek *para*, "to the side of," and *philos*, "loving," are bizarre or abnormal sexual practices that involve recurrent sexual urges focused on (a) nonhuman objects (such as underwear, shoes, or leather), (b) humiliation or the experience of receiving or giving pain (as in sadomasochism or bondage), or (c) children or others who cannot grant consent.[27] Paraphilias have existed and been recorded for thousands of years. Buddhist texts more than 2,000 years old contain references to sexually deviant behaviors among monastic communities, including sexual activity with animals and sexual interest in corpses. Richard von Krafft-Ebing's *Psychopathia Sexualis*, published in 1887, was the first text to discuss such paraphilias as sadism, bestiality, and incest.[28]

When paraphilias such as wearing clothes normally worn by the opposite sex (transvestite fetishism) are engaged in by adults in the privacy of their homes, they remain outside the law's reach. However, when paraphilias involve unwilling or underage victims, they are considered socially harmful and subject to criminal penalties. Outlawed paraphilias include:

- *Frotteurism.* Rubbing against or touching a nonconsenting person in a crowd, elevator, or other public area.
- *Voyeurism.* Obtaining sexual pleasure from spying on a stranger while he or she disrobes or engages in sexual behavior with another.
- *Exhibitionism.* Deriving sexual pleasure from exposing the genitals to surprise or shock a stranger.
- *Sadomasochism.* Deriving pleasure from receiving pain or inflicting pain on another.
- *Pedophilia.* Attaining sexual pleasure through sexual activity with prepubescent children.

Pedophilia

On February 24, 2005, 9-year-old Jessica Lunsford was reported missing. Known sex offender John Evander Couey, 46, had kidnapped her from her home, kept her captive for three days, and then buried her alive when he believed investigators were closing in. When captured he showed investigators the shallow grave where they found Jessica's body inside two tied plastic garbage bags. Her wrists were bound, but she had

Molly Shattuck (center) ex-wife of former Constellation Energy CEO Mayo A. Shattuck, leaves the Sussex County Courthouse, June 16, 2015, in Georgetown, Delaware, after pleading guilty to raping a 15-year-old boy at a vacation rental home. Shattuck, a former Baltimore Ravens cheerleader, was sentenced to spend every other weekend in a Delaware work-release detention center for nearly two years and register as a sex offender.

AP Images/Algerina Perna/Baltimore Sun

L03 Describe the various forms of outlawed deviant sexuality.

paraphilias
Bizarre or abnormal sexual practices that may involve nonhuman objects, humiliation, or children.

managed to poke two fingers through the plastic in an attempt to free herself. In the aftermath of Jessica Lunsford's abduction, Florida passed legislation that requires increased prison sentences, electronic tracking of all convicted sex offenders on probation, and the mandatory use of state databases by all local probation officials so that known sex offenders could not avoid the scrutiny of law enforcement.[29] Couey was sentenced to death but died in prison before the sentence could be carried out. Couey suffered from pedophilia, a psychiatric disorder in which an adult or teen over age 16 is sexually attracted to prepubescent children, generally ages 11 to 13 years or younger.

Of all the commonly practiced paraphilias, pedophilia is the one that most concerns the general public. One focus of concern has been the ongoing scandals that have rocked the Catholic Church. Numerous priests have been accused of sexually molesting young children, among the most notorious being Father James Porter, convicted of molesting at least 200 children of both sexes over a 30-year period. Porter was sentenced to an 18- to 20-year prison term and died of cancer while incarcerated. Pope Francis has called the scandal a "grave problem" and declared that "one priest abusing a minor is reason enough to move the Church's whole structure." Francis told clergy that they had "suffered greatly in the not distant past by having to bear the shame of some of your brothers who harmed and scandalized the Church in the most vulnerable of her members."[30]

Men are not the only sexual predators; women are also involved. In one recent case that made national headlines, former Baltimore Ravens cheerleader Molly Shattuck was sentenced to two years of probation for engaging in a sex act with a 15-year-old boy.[31] At sentencing the prosecutor claimed, "This was not a momentary lapse in judgment. She groomed him, seduced him, supplied him with alcohol, then took advantage of him, all for her own gratification." Shattuck received a suspended 15-year prison sentence. She must report every other weekend to a probation center, register as a sex offender, and receive therapy. The Shattuck case is far from unique: one study of more than 100 adult female sex offenders found that 77 percent of the cases involved sexual abuse of their own child and in about two-thirds of the cases the women had a male co-offender.[32]

The cause of pedophilia has not been determined, but suspected factors include abnormal brain structure, social maladaptation, and neurological dysfunction. Research using brain scans shows that the central processing of sexual stimuli in pedophiles may be controlled by a disturbance in the prefrontal networks of the brain.[33] Brain trauma has also been linked to child molesting. And although injury may occur before or at birth, it is also possible that the damage caused by injury and/ or accident can produce the brain malfunctions linked to pedophilia.[34] There is also some evidence that pedophilia is heritable and that genetic factors are responsible for the development of pedophilia.[35] Other suspected connections range from cognitive distortions to exposure to pornography.[36]

Prostitution

LO4 Distinguish among the different types of prostitutes.

On July 16, 2007, Senator David Vitter of Louisiana apologized to the public after his telephone number showed up in the phone records of Pamela Martin and Associates, the prostitution ring run in the nation's capital by so-called "D.C. Madam" Deborah Jeane Palfrey. "This was a very serious sin in my past for which I am, of course, completely responsible," Vitter said remorsefully. Soon after he issued his statement, Jeanette Maier, a former madam who ran a house of prostitution in New Orleans, claimed Vitter was also a client in her brothel. She told the press: "As far as the girls coming out after seeing David, all they had was nice things to say. It wasn't all about sex. In fact, he just wanted to have somebody listen to him, you know. And I said his wife must not be listening."[37] Vitter asked voters for forgiveness, and his plea must have worked since he was reelected; he retired in 2017. Frequenting brothels and employing prostitutes is hardly the behavior expected from a married senator known for his strong advocacy of family values. While in the senate, Vitter called marriage "the most important social institution in human history." He opposed sex education and abortion and earmarked money for Christian groups who oppose the teaching of evolution.[38]

Vitter's involvement with a prostitute did not cost him political capital, most likely because he is neither alone nor unique in his choice of vices. Prostitution has existed for thousands of years. The term derives from the Latin *prostituere*, which means "to cause to stand in front of." The prostitute is viewed as publicly offering his or her body for sale.

History of Prostitution

The earliest record of prostitution appears in ancient Mesopotamia, where priests engaged in sex to promote fertility in the community. All women were required to do temple duty, and passing strangers were expected to make donations to the temple after enjoying their services.[39]

Modern commercial sex appears to have its roots in ancient Greece, where Solon established licensed brothels in 500 BCE. The earnings of Greek prostitutes helped pay for the temple of Aphrodite. Famous men openly went to prostitutes to enjoy intellectual, aesthetic, and sexual stimulation; prostitutes, however, were prohibited from marrying.[40]

Prostitution remains a worldwide industry, and young women from poor nations are often forced to sell themselves in wealthier nations in order to survive. Here, Romanian prostitutes pose in the Pussy Club brothel in Schoenefeld, Germany, one of the few Western countries where prostitution is legal. But even in Germany prostitution has suffered during the recent economic downturn. The industry has responded with an economic stimulus package: modern marketing tools, rebates, and gimmicks to boost falling demand.

Prostitution was common in early America.[41] Western towns demanded brothels pay monthly fines, fees, and taxes. In 1908, officials in Salt Lake City, Utah, hired Dora Topham, the leading madam of Ogden, to operate a legal red-light district called the stockade. Topham's district consisted of nearly 100 small brick "cribs" that were ten feet square with a door and window; girls paid one to four dollars a day for their residence. The stockade had three entrances, each guarded to keep children and undesirable guests from entering as well as to warn of the periodic police raids.[42]

As the twentieth century began, there was fear over "white slavery," whereby young girls were abducted and turned out on the street as prostitutes. Prostitution was also associated with disease, and the desire to protect young men from harm helped to end almost all experiments with legalization.[43] Some reformers attempted to paint pimps and procurers as immigrants who used their foreign ways to snare unsuspecting American girls into prostitution. These fears prompted passage of the federal Mann Act (1910), which prohibited bringing women into the country or transporting them across state lines for the purpose of prostitution. Often called the "white slave act," it carried a $5,000 fine, five years in prison, or both.[44]

Jane Addams, one of the most famous and influential social reformers of the era, was deeply concerned about the white slave trade.[45] In her 1912 book *A New Conscience and an Ancient Evil*, she described accounts of victims of white slavery during her work at Hull House, a Chicago refuge for the needy.[46] Addams believed that rural American or immigrant girls who became sex workers were victims of sexual slavery and in need of rescue and reform. Addams was a vocal opponent of legalized prostitution. Her work and writings spurred efforts to regulate prostitution in the United States through medical supervision and the licensing and zoning of brothels in districts outside residential neighborhoods.[47]

Today, **prostitution** can be defined as granting nonmarital sexual access for remuneration, under terms established by mutual agreement of the prostitutes, their clients, and their employers. Included in this process are the following elements:

- *Activity that has sexual significance for the customer.* This includes the entire range of sexual behavior, from sexual intercourse to exhibitionism, sadomasochism, oral sex, and so on.
- *Economic transaction.* Something of economic value, not necessarily money, is exchanged for the activity.

prostitution
The granting of nonmarital sexual access for remuneration.

Policies and Issues in Criminology

SEX WORK IN CONTEMPORARY SOCIETY

Meredith Dank and her colleagues at the Urban Institute recently conducted two studies of sex work in contemporary society. The first focused on adult sex work in eight US cities: Atlanta, Dallas, Denver, Kansas City, Miami, Seattle, San Diego, and Washington, DC. In the second, Dank and her colleagues conducted a three-year study of lesbian, gay, bisexual, transgender, and queer or questioning (LGBTQ) youth who engaged in survival sex in New York City.

Contemporary Prostitution

In the eight cities Dank studied, sex work runs the gamut from high-end escort services to high school "sneaker pimps." As a result, the sex trade leaves no demographic unrepresented and circuits almost every major US city. The study found that the underground sex economy's worth to these cities was between $40 million and $290 million. Almost all types of commercial sex venues—massage parlors, brothels, escort services, and street- and Internet-based prostitution—existed in some degree.

Profiting from this vast enterprise were pimps and traffickers, who took home between $5,000 and $33,000 a week. Most pimps believed that the media portrayals exaggerated their violence; some even saw the term "pimp" as derogatory. They told the research team that they rarely used physical abuse for punishment, but instead relied on frequent use of psychological coercion to maintain control over their employees. Pimps used a variety of tactics to recruit and retain employees. Some even credited their entry into pimping with a natural capacity for manipulation. Rarely, however, were pimps the sole influence for an individual's entry into the sex trade.

Not all sex workers had pimps; some solicited protection from friends and acquaintances, some of whom had exposed them to the sex trade at a young age and influenced their decision to participate.

The Internet Is Changing the Limitations of the Trade

Dank and her associates found that prostitution is decreasing on the street but thriving online. Pimps and sex workers advertise on social media and sites like Backpage.com to attract customers and new employees, and to gauge business opportunities in other cities. An increasing online presence makes it both easier for law enforcement to track activity in the underground sex economy and for an offender to promote and provide access to the trade.

The study also looked at the distribution of obscene material and found that explicit content involving younger victims is becoming increasingly available and graphic on the Internet. Online child pornography communities frequently trade content for free; offenders often consider their participation a "victimless crime."

The Underground Sex Economy Is Perceived as Low Risk

Pimps, traffickers, and child pornography offenders said that their crimes were low risk despite some fears of prosecution. Those who got caught for child pornography generally had low technological know-how, and multiple pimp offenders expressed that "no one actually gets locked up for pimping," despite their own incarcerations.

- *Emotional indifference.* The sexual exchange is simply for economic consideration. Although the participants may know one another, their interaction has nothing to do with affection for one another.[48]

Incidence of Prostitution

It is difficult to assess the number of prostitutes operating in the United States. According to the Uniform Crime Report (UCR), fewer than 50,000 prostitution arrests are now being made annually, a number that has been trending downward for some time; about 100,000 arrests were made in 1995.

How can these changes be accounted for? Changing sexual mores, brought about by the "sexual revolution," have liberalized sexuality. Men may be less likely to use prostitutes because legitimate alternatives for sexuality are more open to them.

What can be done to reduce or control the incidence of prostitution?

- Cross-train drug, sex, and weapons trade investigators to better understand circuits and overlaps
- Continue using federal and local partnerships to disrupt travel circuits and identify pimps
- Offer law enforcement trainings for both victim and offender interview techniques, including identifying signs of psychological manipulation
- Increase awareness among school officials and the general public about the realities of sex trafficking to deter victimization and entry into the trade
- Consistently enforce the laws for offenders to diminish low-risk perception
- Impose more fines for ad host websites

Survival Sex Among LGBTQ Youth

Dank's second study involved in-depth interviews with a total of 283 LGBTQ youth in New York City, including young men who have sex with men (YMSM) and young women who have sex with women (YWSW). Dank found that many are dealing with issues rooted in poverty, homophobia, transphobia, racism, child abuse, and criminalization. Many reported experiences of social and familial discrimination and rejection, familial dysfunction, familial poverty, physical abuse, sexual abuse and exploitation, and emotional and mental trauma.

Dank found that there is no single path into sex work. Some young people are recruited by an exploiter but then eventually trade independently to meet their basic needs. Other LGBTQ youth tend to have large peer networks including other youth who engage in

survival sex; many were introduced to the survival-sex economy through peer networks.

One reason LGBTQ, YMSM, and YWSW youth stay in the sex trade is because they lack access to voluntary and low-threshold services, including short- and long-term housing, affordable housing and shelter options, livable-wage employment opportunities, food security, and gender-affirming health care. They report high rates of service denial, as well as violence from breach of confidentiality, and unsafe and discriminatory treatment by staff and other recipients of these services, on the basis of their sexual orientation, gender identity, gender expression, and age. They also experience frequent arrests for various "quality-of-life" and misdemeanor crimes, creating further instability and perpetuating the need to engage in survival sex.

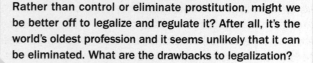

Critical Thinking

Rather than control or eliminate prostitution, might we be better off to legalize and regulate it? After all, it's the world's oldest profession and it seems unlikely that it can be eliminated. What are the drawbacks to legalization?

Sources: Meredith Dank, Jennifer Yahner, Kuniko Madden, Isela Banuelos, Lilly Yu, Andrea Ritchie, Mitchyll Mora, and Brendan Conner, "Surviving the Streets of New York: Experiences of LGBTQ Youth, YMSM, and YWSW Engaged in Survival Sex," Urban Institute, February 25, 2015, http://www.urban.org/research/publication/surviving-streets-new-york-experiences-lgbtq-youth-ymsm-and-ywsw-engaged-survival-sex/view/full_report; Meredith Dank, Bilal Khan, P. Mitchell Downey, Cybele Kotonias, Debbie Mayer, Colleen Owens, Laura Pacifici, and Lilly Yu, *Estimating the Size and Structure of the Underground Commercial Sex Economy in Eight Major US Cities* (Washington, DC: Urban Institute, 2014), http://www.urban.org/publications/413047.html (URLs accessed May 2017).

In addition, the prevalence of sexually transmitted diseases has caused many men to avoid visiting prostitutes for fear of irreversible health hazards.[49]

Of course, arrest trends must be interpreted with some caution. While it is possible that fewer people are seeking the services of prostitutes, the downward trend may also be explained by the fact that police are reluctant to make arrests in prostitution cases, or that more sophisticated prostitutes who use the Internet or other forms of technology to "make dates" are better able to avoid detection by police. In fact, e-hooking, in which prostitutes use the Internet to shield their identities and contact clients, may be responsible for a resurgence in sex for hire, especially in times of economic turmoil.[50] So despite this two-decade decline in the arrest rate, a recent survey by the Urban Institute shows that prostitution still flourishes in major cities; these findings are set out in the Policies and Issues in Criminology box, Sex Work in Contemporary Society.

Policies and Issues in Criminology

THE INTERNATIONAL SEX TRADE

In the popular 2008 film *Taken*, Bryan Mills, a former CIA agent played by Liam Neeson, must save his daughter Kim, who has been abducted while on a trip to Paris. Almost as soon as she arrives, Kim and a friend are kidnapped. As Bryan searches frantically for his beloved daughter, he uncovers an international scheme in which young women are taken, abused, forcibly addicted to drugs, and used as sex slaves. Luckily for Kim, Brian, who has a special set of skills, kills about 35 people and rescues her from her abductors. The film was so popular that two sequels were made, *Taken 2* (2012) and *Taken 3* (2014), and the *Taken* TV series was launched in 2017. Can these dreadful scenarios be based on reality?

Unfortunately, they may be all too real. Every year, hundreds of thousands of men, women, and children are lured by the promise of good jobs and then end up in the sex trade in industrialized countries. Victims are trafficked within countries, between neighboring countries, or even across different continents. Police in western and southern Europe have detected victims of 137 different citizenships. Trafficking for sexual exploitation and for forced labor are the most common, but trafficking victims can also be exploited in many other ways: begging, forced or sham marriages, benefit fraud, pornography, and organ removal for transplants.

Over the last 10 years, the profile of detected trafficking victims has changed. Although most detected victims are still women or underage girls, children (28 percent of detected victims) and men (21 percent of detected victims) now make up larger shares of the total number of victims than they did a decade ago. One reason is that about 4 in 10 victims are now being trafficked for forced labor, and out of these victims, 63 percent were men.

In the least developed countries, children often comprise large shares of the detected victims. The majority of these victims are runaway or thrown-away youths who live on the streets and become victims of prostitution. These children generally come from homes where they have been abused or from families who have abandoned them. Often, they become involved in prostitution to support themselves financially or to get the things they feel they need or want (like drugs).

While the traffickers are overwhelmingly male, women comprise a relatively large share of convicted offenders compared to most other crimes. This share is even higher among traffickers convicted in the victims' home country. Females tend to be more trusted, enabling them to snare unsuspecting victims. Many were in the sex trade themselves and were encouraged by their recruiter/trafficker to return home and recruit other women, often under the scrutiny of people working for the trafficker to make sure they don't try to escape.

Contributing Factors

Human trafficking is facilitated by social problems and disorder, such as disruptions in the global economy, war, and social unrest. Economic crisis hits young girls especially hard. Female victims are often poor and aspire to a better life. They may be forced, coerced, deceived, and psychologically manipulated into industrial or agricultural work, marriage, domestic servitude, organ donation, or sexual exploitation. Some traffickers exploit victims' frustration with low salaries in their home countries, and others take advantage of a crisis in the victim's family that requires her to make

---

PROSTITUTION ABROAD Prostitution flourishes abroad. In some nations it is legal and regulated by the government, whereas other nations punish prostitution with the death penalty. Germany, where the sex trade has been legalized, has at least 400,000 prostitutes—more than any other European nation per capita—serving 1.2 million men every day and bringing in more than $15 billion per year.[51] In contrast, many Islamic countries punish prostitution with death, a punishment that is sometimes carried out by stoning in the public square.

There is also a troubling overseas trade in prostitution in which men from wealthy countries frequent marginally regulated sex areas in needy nations such as Thailand in

money. The traffickers then promise the victim to take her abroad and find her a traditionally female service-sector job, such as waitress, salesperson, domestic worker, or au pair/babysitter.

Whereas victims often come from poorer countries, the market for labor and sex is found in wealthier countries or in countries that, though economically poor, cater to the needs of citizens from wealthy countries, of corporations, or of tourists.

Combating Human Trafficking

The United States made stopping the trafficking of women a top priority. In 2000, Congress passed the Trafficking Victims Protection Act (TVPA), which created the first comprehensive federal law to address trafficking, with a significant focus on the international dimension of the problem. The law provides a three-pronged approach: *prevention* through public awareness programs overseas and a State Department–led monitoring and sanctions program; *protection* through a new visa and services for foreign national victims; and *prosecution* through new federal crime laws and severe penalties.

As a result of the passing of the TVPA, the Office to Monitor and Combat Trafficking in Persons was established in October 2001. This enabling legislation led to the creation of a bureau within the State Department to specifically address human trafficking and exploitation on all levels and to take legal action against perpetrators. Along with the FBI, the US Immigration and Customs Enforcement (ICE) is one of the lead federal agencies charged with enforcing the TVPA. Human trafficking represents significant risks to homeland security. Would-be terrorists and criminals often can access the same routes and use the same methods as human traffickers. ICE's Human Smuggling and Trafficking Unit works to identify criminals and organizations involved in these illicit activities.

Globally, the number of countries with a statute that criminalizes most forms of trafficking in persons increased from 33 in 2003 (18 percent) to 158 in 2016 (88 percent). This rapid progress means that more victims are assisted and protected, and more traffickers are put behind bars. Nonetheless, the average number of convictions still remains low. The longer countries have had comprehensive legislation in place, the more convictions are recorded, indicating that it takes time and dedicated resources for a national criminal justice system to acquire sufficient expertise to detect, investigate, and successfully prosecute cases of trafficking in persons. Although most countries now have the appropriate legal framework for tackling trafficking crimes, the large discrepancy between the number of detected victims and convicted offenders indicates that many trafficking crimes still go unpunished.

Critical Thinking

1. If put in charge, what would you do to slow or end the international sex trade?

2. Should men who hire prostitutes be punished very severely in order to deter them from getting involved in the exploitation of these vulnerable young women?

Sources: United Nations Office on Drugs and Crime, *Global Reports on Trafficking in Persons, 2016,* https://www.unodc.org /documents/data-and-analysis/glotip/2016_Global_Report_on _Trafficking_in_Persons.pdf; Amanda Walker-Rodriguez and Rodney Hill, "Human Sex Trafficking," *FBI Law Enforcement Bulletin,* 2011, https://leb.fbi.gov/2011/march/human-sex-trafficking (URLs accessed May 2017).

---

order to procure young girls forced or sold into prostitution—a phenomenon known as *sex tourism*. In addition to sex tours, there has also been a soaring demand for pornography, strip clubs, lap dancing, escorts, and telephone sex in developing countries.[52] The outcry against human trafficking has resulted in laws and law enforcement efforts designed to stop it in its tracks. But these efforts have resulted in an ironic situation: if a 16-year-old girl is trafficked to the United States, she is considered a victim; if a 16-year-old girl who was born in the United States gets involved in the sex trade, she will be arrested for prostitution and considered a criminal.[53] The international trade in prostitution is the subject of the accompanying Policies and Issues in Criminology feature.

AP Images/Robert F. Bukaty

Prostitution can take many forms and occur in a variety of venues. Here, Alexis Wright, 30, leaves the Cumberland County Courthouse in Maine. In 2013, Wright, a Zumba fitness instructor, pleaded guilty to prostitution and tax and welfare violations; she served six months in jail and must pay back more than $57,000 in fines and restitution. The case rocked the community when authorities revealed that 68 local people were her clients, the majority of whom pleaded guilty or no contest.

Types of Prostitutes

Several different types of prostitutes operate in the United States.

STREETWALKERS Prostitutes who work the streets in plain sight of police, citizens, and customers are referred to as hustlers, hookers, or streetwalkers. Although glamorized by the Julia Roberts character in the film *Pretty Woman* (who winds up with multimillionaire Richard Gere), streetwalkers are considered the least attractive, lowest paid, most vulnerable men and women in the profession. Streetwalkers wear bright clothing, makeup, and jewelry to attract customers; they take their customers to hotels. According to legend, the term "hooker," however, is derived not from streetwalkers using their charms to "hook" clients, but from the popular name given women who followed Union General Joseph "Fighting Joe" Hooker's army and serviced the troops during the Civil War.[54] According to another legend, the term comes from the concentration of prostitutes around the shipyards and ferry terminal of the Corlear's Hook area of Manhattan in the 1820s; still others believe the origins are in North Carolina. Needless to say, the source of the term remains murky.

Research shows that there are a variety of working styles among women involved in street-based prostitution. Some are controlled by pimps who demand and receive a major share of their earnings in return for protection; in return pimps control all aspects of their lives.[55] Others are independent entrepreneurs interested in building a stable group of steady clients. Still others manipulate and exploit their customers and may engage in theft and blackmail.[56]

BAR GIRLS B-girls, as they are also called, spend their time in bars, drinking and waiting to be picked up by customers. Although alcoholism may be a problem, B-girls usually work out an arrangement with the bartender whereby they are served diluted drinks or water colored with dye or tea, for which the customer is charged an exorbitant price. In some bars, the B-girl is given a credit for each drink she gets the customer to buy. It is common to find B-girls in towns with military bases and large transient populations.[57]

BROTHEL PROSTITUTES Also called bordellos, cathouses, sporting houses, and houses of ill repute, brothels flourished in the nineteenth and early twentieth centuries. They were large establishments, usually run by madams, that housed several prostitutes. A madam is a woman who employs prostitutes, supervises their behavior, and receives a fee for her services; her cut is usually 40 to 60 percent of the prostitutes' earnings. The madam's role may include recruiting women into prostitution and socializing them in the trade.[58]

Brothels declined in importance following World War II. The closing of the last brothel in Texas is chronicled in the play and film *The Best Little Whorehouse in Texas*. Today the best-known brothels are in Nevada, where prostitution is legal outside large population centers.

CALL GIRLS The aristocrats of prostitution are call girls. They charge customers thousands of dollars per night and may net more than $200,000 per year. Some gain clients through employment in escort services; others develop independent customer lists. Many call girls come from middle-class backgrounds and serve upper-class customers. Attempting to dispel the notion that their service is simply sex for money, they concentrate on making their clients feel important and attractive. Working exclusively via telephone "dates," call girls get their clients by word of mouth or by making arrangements with bellhops, cab drivers, and so on. They either entertain clients in their own apartments or visit clients' hotels and apartments. When she retires, a call girl can sell her date book, listing client names and sexual preferences, for thousands of dollars. Despite the lucrative nature of their business, call girls run considerable risk by being alone and unprotected with strangers. They often request the business cards of their clients to make sure they are dealing with "upstanding citizens."

ESCORT SERVICES/CALL HOUSES Some escort services are fronts for prostitution rings. Both male and female sex workers can be sent out after the client calls a number published in an ad in the yellow pages. How common are adult escort services? Las Vegas has 112 yellow page listings for escort services; New York City has 179.

A relatively new phenomenon, the call house combines elements of the brothel and of call girl rings. A madam receives a call from a prospective customer, and if she finds the client acceptable, she arranges a meeting between the caller and a prostitute in her service. The madam maintains a list of prostitutes, who are on call rather than living together in a house. The call house insulates the madam from arrest because she never meets the client or receives direct payment.[59]

CIRCUIT TRAVELERS Prostitutes known as circuit travelers move around in groups of two or three to lumber, labor, and agricultural camps. They ask the foreman for permission to ply their trade, service the whole crew in an evening, and then move on. Some circuit travelers seek clients at truck stops and rest areas.

Sometimes young girls are forced to become circuit travelers by unscrupulous pimps who make them work for months as prostitutes in agricultural migrant camps. The young women are lured from developing countries such as Mexico with offers of jobs in landscaping, health care, housecleaning, and restaurants. But when they arrive in the United States, they are told that they owe their captors thousands of dollars and must work as prostitutes to pay off this debt. The young women are raped and beaten if they complain or try to escape.[60]

E-HOOKING The technological revolution has begun to alter the world of prostitution. Instead of working with a cell phone, cyberprostitutes set up personal websites or put listings on web boards, such as AdultFriendFinder, that carry personals. They may use loaded phrases such as "looking for generous older man" in their self-descriptions. When contacted, they ask to exchange emails, chat online, or make voice calls with prospective clients. They may even exchange pictures. This allows them to select whom they want to be with and avoid clients who may be threatening or dangerous.

Some cyberprostitution rings offer customers the opportunity to choose women from their Internet page and then have them flown in from around the country. In Germany, where prostitution is legal, an app called Peppr makes it easy to find a sex worker. A potential client types in his or her location and up pops a list of the nearest prostitutes, along with pictures, prices, and physical characteristics; users can arrange a session for a booking fee that averages $10.[61] Another escort app, Ohlala, allows a male user to put in a request, which includes such parameters as hours needed and desired price, then the inquiry has just 21 minutes to be accepted by a female user in the area before it disappears. If a request is accepted by a female user, the pair then have the opportunity to negotiate a bit on pricing and time before settling to meet offline; the service is being shipped overseas to such cities as New York.[62]

Becoming a Prostitute

At 38, Lt. Cmdr. Rebecca Dickinson had risen from the enlisted ranks in the Navy to its officer corps. She had an assignment to the Naval Academy in Annapolis, Maryland, where she helped teach a leadership course. But faced with money and marital problems, Dickinson also worked as a prostitute for some of the richest and most powerful men in Washington, DC. This desperate naval officer, whose career was destroyed in the scandal, was paid $130 for a 90-minute session.[63]

Why does someone turn to prostitution? Both male and female prostitutes often come from troubled homes marked by extreme conflict and hostility and from poor urban areas or rural communities. Divorce, separation, or death splits the family; most prostitutes grew up in homes without fathers.[64] Girls from the lower socioeconomic classes who get into "the life" report conflict with school authorities, poor grades, and an overly regimented school experience.[65] Young women involved in prostitution also have extensive histories of substance abuse, health problems, post-traumatic stress disorder (PTSD), social stigmatization, and isolation. Often having little family support, they turn to equally troubled peers for survival: self-medicating with drugs and alcohol and self-mutilation are the norm.[66] One survey of street-level sex workers in Phoenix, Arizona, found that women engaging in prostitution had limited educational backgrounds; most did not complete high school.[67]

Sexual abuse also plays a role in prostitution. Many prostitutes were initiated into sex by family members at ages as young as 10 to 12 years; they have long histories of sexual exploitation and abuse.[68] These early experiences with sex help teach them that their bodies have value and that sexual encounters can be used to obtain affection, power, or money.

Age may affect why girls become prostitutes. When Jennifer Cobbina and Sharon Oselin conducted 40 in-depth interviews with female street prostitutes, they discovered that younger sex workers were more likely to come from homes that were physically and sexually abusive; they turned to prostitution as an attempt to regain control of their lives. Another common theme among adolescent girls in the life is that prostitution is "normal" in the neighborhoods and environments in which they were raised. In contrast, older women are more likely to claim that supporting a drug habit and needing cash for survival were the reasons they became sex workers. Younger women tended to remain sex workers for longer periods and therefore faced the greater risk of violence, drug abuse, and other life-threatening events.[69]

DANGERS OF SEX WORK Once they get into the life, personal danger begins to escalate. Girls who may be directed toward prostitution because of childhood sexual abuse also are likely to be revictimized as adults.[70] When sociologist Jolanda Sallmann interviewed women in the Midwest with histories of prostitution, she discovered that they were hurt when people labeled and depersonalized them as "whores" or "hookers."[71] Despite their sensitivity, their lives were chaotic. The majority had suffered physical and/or sexual violence. One woman showed Sallman the scar across her neck where her pimp literally slit her throat years earlier. Another woman told how she was kidnapped and raped by a client at knifepoint while she was still a juvenile. Despite being told that she "was gonna die," she survived the incident. Considering these problems, why do women remain on the street? Even when street prostitutes try to go straight, they often return to prostitution because their limited education and lack of skills make finding employment very difficult. Without a means to support themselves and their children, they may think staying on the streets is less risky than leaving prostitution. Most self-identified as struggling with a substance use problem throughout most or all of their involvement in prostitution, typically involving crack cocaine, cocaine, and/or heroin.

Legalize Prostitution?

L05 State the arguments for and against legalizing prostitution.

Today, prostitution is considered a misdemeanor and is punishable by a fine or a short jail sentence. In practice, most law enforcement is uneven and aims at confining illegal activities to particular areas in the city.[72] Prostitution is illegal in all states except Nevada, where licensed and highly regulated brothels can operate as business enterprises in rural counties (population under 400,000; this leaves out the counties in which Las Vegas and Reno are located).

Should prostitution be legalized elsewhere? Some nations have eased control of prostitution while others have legalized it and regulate sex workers. Germany legalized sex work in 1927; there are state-run brothels. Sex workers pay taxes and are provided health insurance and a pension.[73] In most areas of the United States prostitution remains a crime, most likely because it is considered a public safety and health concern.[74]

Not surprisingly, there are strong feelings on both sides of this issue. One position is that women must become emancipated from male oppression and achieve sexual equality. The *sexual equality* view considers the prostitute a victim of male dominance. In patriarchal societies, male power is predicated on female subjugation, and prostitution is a clear example of this gender exploitation.[75] A similar view is that the fight for equality depends on controlling all attempts by men to impose their will on women. The *free choice* view is that prostitution, if freely chosen, expresses women's equality and is not a symptom of subjugation.[76] Advocates of both positions argue that the penalties for prostitution should be reduced (in other words, the activity should be decriminalized). Decriminalization would relieve already desperate women of the additional burden of severe legal punishment.

In her book *Brothel*, Alexa Albert makes a compelling case for legalization. A Harvard-trained physician who interviewed young women working at a legal brothel in Nevada, Albert found that the women remained HIV-free and felt safer working in a secure environment than alone on city streets. Despite long hours and rules that gave too much profit to the owners, the women actually took pride in their work. Besides benefiting from greater security, most were earning between $300 and $1,500 per day.[77]

Criminologist Ronald Weitzer also suggests that prostitution be legalized under strict guidelines. Weitzer believes that using law enforcement and criminal penalties to control prostitution has little effect on sex workers who will soon return to street life. After evaluating the way prostitution is dealt with around the world, Weitzer presents the argument that getting sex workers off the street by relaxing enforcement against those who work indoors is the best solution to an age-old problem. Those who operate indoors in brothels and other controlled venues are much safer and suffer far less injury from clients, pimps, and other victimizers; they also suffer less psychological hardship than those who work the streets.[78]

The argument for legalization is countered by research conducted by psychologist Melissa Farley, who surveyed brothel girls in Nevada and found that many suffered abuse and long-lasting psychological damage. Farley found that numerous brothel prostitutes are coerced into prostitution and that brothel owners are not much different from pimps who control them with an iron fist. Subject to sexual harassment, sexual exploitation, and rape, many fear for their lives. Moreover, legal prostitution does not protect women from the violence, verbal abuse, physical injury, and exposure to diseases such as HIV that occur in illegal prostitution.[79]

Similarly, Roger Matthews studied prostitution for more than two decades and found that sex workers were extremely desperate, damaged, and disorganized. Many are involved in substance abuse and experience beatings, rape, and other forms of violence on a regular basis. Prostitution is, he concludes, the world's most dangerous occupation. His solution is to treat the women forced into prostitution as victims and the men who purchase their services as the criminals. He applauds Sweden's decision to make buying sexual services a crime, thus criminalizing the "johns" rather than the women in prostitution. When governments legalize prostitution, it leads to a massive expansion of the trade, both legal and illegal.[80]

As might be expected, this is not the final word on the matter. Some experts argue that while prostitution is an inherently dangerous profession, many other professions, such as all forms of law enforcement and security, are equally dangerous but legal. The danger of prostitution is outweighed by the need for women—the most poverty-stricken class in this country—to gain a source of income that can increase their chance for independence.[81]

Pornography

The term **pornography** derives from the Greek *porne*, meaning "prostitute," and *graphein*, meaning "to write." In the heart of many major cities there are still adult stores that display and sell books, magazines, and films explicitly depicting every imaginable sex act; Miami alone has 10 adult stores. The Internet is now the main source of adult material. The purpose of this material is to provide sexual titillation and excitement for paying customers. Although material depicting nudity and sex is typically legal, protected by the First Amendment's provision limiting government control of speech, most criminal codes prohibit the production, display, and sale of obscene material.

Obscenity, derived from the Latin *caenum*, for "filth," is defined by Webster's dictionary as "deeply offensive to morality or decency, designed to incite to lust or depravity."[82]

pornography
Sexually explicit books, magazines, films, and DVDs intended to provide sexual titillation and excitement for paying customers.

obscenity
Material that violates community standards of morality or decency and has no redeeming social value.

Jason Kempin/Redux

Here's a display at the Erotic Expo at the Penn Plaza Pavilion in New York City. The adult porn industry is a multibillion-dollar business reaching hundreds of millions of consumers annually. Worldwide pornography revenue is larger than the revenues of all professional football, baseball, and basketball franchises combined. In the United States, pornography revenue exceeds the combined revenues of ABC, CBS, and NBC.

The problem of controlling pornography centers on this definition of obscenity. Police and law enforcement officials can legally seize only material that is judged obscene. "But who," critics ask, "is to judge what is obscene?" At one time, such novels as *Tropic of Cancer* by Henry Miller, *Ulysses* by James Joyce, and *Lady Chatterley's Lover* by D. H. Lawrence were prohibited because they were considered obscene; today they are considered works of great literary value. Thus, what is obscene today may be considered socially acceptable at a future time. After all, the Internet is filled with material for sale (or for free) that displays nude models in all kinds of sexually explicit poses. The uncertainty surrounding this issue is illustrated by Supreme Court Justice Potter Stewart's famous 1964 statement on how he defined obscenity: "I know it when I see it." Because of this legal and moral ambiguity, violation of obscenity laws involving adults is rarely prosecuted in the United States.

Is Pornography Harmful?

Opponents of pornography argue that it degrades both the people who are photographed and members of the public who are sometimes forced to see obscene material. Pornographers exploit their models, who often include underage children. Investigations have found that many performers and models are victims of physical and psychological coercion.[83]

One uncontested danger of pornography is "kiddie porn." Each year more than a million children are believed to be used in pornography or prostitution, many of them runaways whose plight is exploited by adults. Sexual exploitation by these rings can devastate the child victims. Exploited children are prone to such acting-out behavior as setting fires and becoming sexually focused in the use of language, dress, and mannerisms. They also may suffer physical problems ranging from headaches and loss of appetite to genital soreness, vomiting, and urinary tract infections, and psychological problems, including mood swings, withdrawal, edginess, and nervousness.[84]

Does Viewing Pornography Cause Violence?

An issue critical to the debate over pornography is whether viewing it produces sexual violence or assaultive behavior. This debate reignited when serial killer Ted Bundy claimed his murderous rampage was fueled by reading pornography.

The scientific evidence linking sexually explicit material to violence is mixed.[85] Some research has found that viewing erotic material may act as a safety valve for those whose impulses might otherwise lead them to violence; in a sense, pornography reduces violence.[86] Viewing obscene material may have the unintended side effect of satisfying erotic impulses that otherwise might result in more sexually aggressive behavior. Thus, it is not surprising to some skeptics that convicted rapists and sex offenders report less exposure to pornography than control groups of nonoffenders.[87] The lack of a clear-cut connection between viewing pornography and violence is used to bolster the argument that all printed matter, no matter how sexually explicit, is protected by the First Amendment.

However, some research does find a link between consuming pornography and subsequent violent or controlling behavior.[88] Sex researcher Michael Flood reviewed the existing literature and concluded that exposure to pornography by young people leads to sexist and unhealthy notions of sex and relationships, as well as intensification of attitudes supportive of sexual coercion while increasing their likelihood of perpetrating assault.[89]

The evidence suggests that violence and sexual aggression are not linked to erotic or pornographic films per se but that erotic films depicting violence, rape, brutality, and aggression may evoke similar feelings in viewers. A leading critic of pornography, Diana

Russell, contends that hatred of women is a principal theme in pornography and is often coupled with racism. Her research provides strong evidence linking pornography to misogyny (the hatred of women), an emotional response that often leads to rape.[90]

Pornography and the Law

The First Amendment to the US Constitution protects free speech and prohibits police agencies from limiting the public's right of free expression. However, the Supreme Court held, in the twin cases of *Roth v. United States* and *Alberts v. California*, that although the First Amendment protects all "ideas with even the slightest redeeming social importance—unorthodox ideas, controversial ideas, even ideas hateful to the prevailing climate of opinion, implicit in the history of the First Amendment is the rejection of obscenity as utterly without redeeming social importance."[91] These decisions left unclear how obscenity is defined. If a highly erotic movie tells a "moral tale," must it be judged legal even if 95 percent of its content is objectionable? A spate of movies made after the *Roth* decision claimed that they were educational or warned the viewer about sexual depravity, so they could not be said to lack redeeming social importance. Many state obscenity cases were appealed to federal courts so that judges could decide whether the films totally lacked redeeming social importance. To rectify the situation, the Supreme Court redefined its concept of obscenity in the case of *Miller v. California*:

> The basic guidelines for the trier of fact must be (a) whether the average person applying contemporary community standards would find that the work taken as a whole appeals to the prurient interest; (b) whether the work depicts or describes, in a patently offensive way, sexual conduct specifically defined by the applicable state law, and (c) whether the work, taken as a whole, lacks serious literary, artistic, political or scientific value.[92]

To convict a person of obscenity under the *Miller* doctrine, the state or local jurisdiction must specifically define obscene conduct in its statute, and the pornographer must engage in that behavior. The Court gave some examples of what is considered obscene: "patently offensive representations or descriptions of masturbation, excretory functions and lewd exhibition of the genitals."[93] Obviously, a plebiscite cannot be held to determine the community's attitude for every trial concerning the sale of pornography. Works that are considered obscene in Omaha might be considered routine in New York, but how can we be sure? There are even differences of opinion on what is considered obscene within individual communities: Surveys show that within individual communities there is little consensus even over the most extreme of pornographic materials.[94] Therefore, it does not seem possible that objective community standards actually exist and that there is a consensus on what material is outlawed and what is acceptable. To resolve this dilemma, the Supreme Court in *Pope v. Illinois* articulated a reasonableness doctrine: a work is obscene if a reasonable person applying objective (national) standards would find the material to lack any social value.[95]

These rulings are so elastic that cases involving adults are rarely if ever prosecuted and then under the most extreme circumstances—for example, sex with animals. There have been fewer than 10 federal prosecutions of adult pornography in the past decade. An Obscenity Prosecution Task Force set up by the government to vigorously enforce the law was shut down in 2011. However, while on the campaign trail President Trump vowed to renew obscenity prosecutions, and it is likely to see greater enforcement going forward.[96]

AP Images/Michael Conroy

Subway sandwich pitchman Jared Fogle, shown here, received a lengthy prison sentence after he pleaded guilty to paying for sex acts with minors and receiving child pornography. If you could, would you end obscenity enforcement efforts involving adults and put all efforts into controlling child pornography? Is there any danger to this approach?

THE LAW AND KIDDIE PORN In 2015, former Subway sandwich pitchman Jared Fogle agreed to plead guilty to allegations that he paid for sex acts with minors and was in possession of child pornography. The admission destroyed his career at the sandwich-shop chain and sent him to prison for 15 years.[97]

While few people are prosecuted for possessing, distributing, or manufacturing pornography involving adults, buying or selling kiddie porn is a totally different matter; crimes involving children are vigorously enforced. After a number of initiatives failed to meet First Amendment standards because courts ruled that they violated free speech, being over-broad or vague, Congress passed the PROTECT Act of 2003 (Prosecutorial Remedies and Other Tools to end the Exploitation of Children Today), which provides prison sentences for anyone creating and selling sexual images involving children.[98] One part of the PROTECT Act prohibits computer-generated child pornography "when such visual depiction is a computer image or computer-generated image that is, or appears virtually indistinguishable from, that of a minor engaging in sexually explicit conduct."

In *United States v. Williams*, the Supreme Court ruled that statutes prohibiting the "pandering" of child pornography (offering or requesting to transfer, sell, deliver, or trade the items) did not violate the First Amendment even if a person charged under the code did not in fact possess child pornography.[99] So it is a crime if someone offers to sell kiddie porn to another person even if they don't actually have any kiddie porn to sell or if they have virtual images they are claiming to be the real thing, as long as the purchaser *believes* they are buying kiddie porn using real children. The crime is the offer to sell and the agreement to buy, not the actual possession of the contraband.

Despite these legal changes, which make enforcement somewhat easier, the biggest challenge to those seeking to control the sale of obscene material involving children has been the shift to Internet sales. Today, the major initiative against Internet kiddie porn is the Innocent Images National Initiative (IINI) developed by the FBI, which coordinates multi-agency investigative operations worldwide. The focus is on the following:

- Online organizations, enterprises, and communities that exploit children for profit or personal gain
- Major distributors of child pornography, such as those who appear to have transmitted a large volume of child pornography via an online computer on several occasions to several other people
- Producers of child pornography
- Individuals who travel, or indicate a willingness to travel, for the purpose of engaging in sexual activity with a minor
- Possessors of child pornography

In pursuit of these offenders, FBI and other law enforcement agents go online utilizing fictitious screen names and engaging in real-time chat or email conversations with subjects in order to obtain evidence of criminal activity involving exploitation of children.[100]

Substance Abuse

L06 Discuss the causes of substance abuse.

According to the latest report by the United Nations on world drug use, an estimated 1 in 20 adults, or a quarter of a billion people between the ages of 15 and 64 years, used at least one illegal drug in the past year—roughly the equivalent of the combined populations of France, Germany, Italy, and the United Kingdom. About 29 million people are estimated to suffer from drug use disorders, and of those, 12 million are people who inject drugs, 14 percent of whom are living with HIV. There are more than 200,000 drug-related deaths each year.[101]

Drug abuse is not only a problem abroad. According to the most recent estimates, 27 million people in the United States aged 12 or older used an illegal drug in the past 30 days, which corresponds to about 1 in 10 Americans.[102] Not surprisingly, considering its extent, the cost of illegal drug abuse is staggering: the federal government estimates that the total cost of substance abuse is more than $400 billion each year; health care costs for substance abusers are close to $40 billion.[103]

Despite the scope and costs of the drug problem, some still view it as another type of victimless public order crime. There is great debate over the legalization of drugs and the control of alcohol. Some consider drug use a private matter and drug control another example of government intrusion into people's private lives. Furthermore, legalization could reduce the profit of selling illegal substances and drive suppliers out of the market. Others see these substances as dangerous, believing that the criminal activity of users makes the term "victimless" nonsensical. Still another position is that the possession and use of all drugs and alcohol should be legalized but that the sale and distribution of drugs should be heavily penalized. This would punish those profiting from drugs and would enable users to be helped without fear of criminal punishment. While this debate is unfolding, some states have legalized the use of marijuana; others are experiencing an epidemic of opioid usage. In this section we will review the history and current state of drug use and abuse.

When Did Drug Use Begin?

Chemical substances have been used to change reality and provide stimulation, relief, or relaxation for thousands of years. Mesopotamian writings indicate that opium was used 4,000 years ago—it was known as the "plant of joy."[104] The ancient Greeks knew and understood the problem of drug use. At the time of the Crusades, the Arabs were using marijuana. In the Western Hemisphere, natives of Mexico and South America chewed coca leaves and used "magic mushrooms" in their religious ceremonies.[105] Drug use was also accepted in Europe well into the twentieth century. Recently uncovered pharmacy records from 1900 to 1920 show sales of cocaine and heroin solutions to members of the British royal family; records from 1912 indicate that Winston Churchill, then a member of Parliament, was sold a cocaine solution while staying in Scotland.[106]

In the early years of the United States, opium and its derivatives were easily obtained. Opium-based drugs were used in various patent medicine cure-alls. Morphine was used extensively to relieve the pain of wounded soldiers in the Civil War. By the turn of the century, an estimated 1 million US citizens were opiate users.[107]

Alcohol and Its Prohibition

The history of alcohol and the law in the United States has also been controversial and dramatic. At the turn of the twentieth century, a drive was mustered to prohibit the sale of alcohol. This **temperance movement** was fueled by the belief that the purity of the US agrarian culture was being destroyed by the growth of cities. Urbanism was viewed as a threat to the lifestyle of the majority of the nation's population, then living on farms and in villages. The forces behind the temperance movement were such lobbying groups as the Anti-Saloon League led by Carrie Nation, the Women's Temperance Union, and the Protestant clergy of the Baptist, Methodist, and Congregationalist faiths.[108] They viewed the growing cities, filled with newly arriving Irish, Italian, and Eastern European immigrants, as centers of degradation and wickedness. Ratification of the Eighteenth Amendment in 1919, prohibiting the sale of alcoholic beverages, was viewed as a triumph of the morality of middle- and upper-class Americans over the threat posed to their culture by the "new Americans."[109]

Prohibition failed. It was enforced by the Volstead Act, which defined intoxicating beverages as those containing one-half of 1 percent or more alcohol.[110] What doomed Prohibition? One factor was the use of organized crime to supply illicit liquor. Also, the law made it illegal only to sell alcohol, not to purchase it, which reduced the deterrent effect. Finally, despite the work of Elliot Ness and his "Untouchables," law enforcement agencies were inadequate, and officials were likely to be corrupted by wealthy bootleggers.[111] In 1933, the Twenty-First Amendment to the Constitution repealed Prohibition, signaling the end of the "noble experiment."

temperance movement
The drive to prohibit the sale of alcohol in the United States, culminating in ratification of the Eighteenth Amendment in 1919.

Prohibition
The period from 1919 until 1933 when the Eighteenth Amendment to the US Constitution outlawed the sale of alcohol; also known as the "noble experiment."

Extent of Substance Abuse

Despite continuing efforts at control, the use of mood-altering substances persists in the United States. What is the extent of the substance abuse problem today? A number of national surveys attempt to chart trends in drug abuse in the general population.

MONITORING THE FUTURE One important source of information on drug use is the annual Monitoring the Future (MTF) self-report survey of drug abuse among high school students conducted by the Institute for Social Research (ISR) at the University of Michigan. This annual survey is based on the self-report responses of approximately 50,000 8th, 10th, and 12th graders and is considered the most important source of data on adolescent drug abuse. MTF survey data indicate that drug use declined from a high point late in the 1970s until 1990, when it once again began to increase, finally stabilizing around 1996 and since then there has been a decline in both lifetime and current usage. The latest survey (2016) shows a continued long-term decline in the use of many illicit substances, including marijuana, as well as alcohol, tobacco, and misuse of some prescription medications. The use of illicit drugs other than marijuana is down from recent peaks in all three grades surveyed. However, drug use is still prevalent among youth in the United States: 22 percent of high school seniors report past-month marijuana use and 6 percent report daily use. There is a higher rate of marijuana use among 12th graders in states with medical marijuana laws. In 2016, 38 percent of high school seniors in states with medical marijuana laws reported past-year marijuana use, compared to 33 percent in non–medical marijuana states.

In addition to the decline in drug abuse the MTF survey also shows significant declines in the use of alcohol and cigarettes. In 1991, when MTF first measured cigarette smoking, almost 11 percent of high school seniors smoked a half pack or more a day. Twenty-five years later, that rate has dropped to only 2 percent. There has been a similar decline in the use of alcohol, with the rate of teens reporting they have "been drunk" in the past year at the lowest ever: 37 percent of 12th graders report they have been drunk at least once, down from a peak of 53 percent in 2001. Of perhaps greater importance, the proportion of teens who report **binge drinking**—consuming five or more drinks in a row at least once in the prior two weeks—continues to significantly decline, now at only 3 percent, the lowest rate since 1991, and down from a peak of 13 percent in 1996. Binge drinking among high school seniors alone is down to 15 percent, half its peak of 31 percent in 1998.

Although nonmedical use of prescription opioids remains a serious issue in the adult population, teen use of prescription opioid pain relievers is trending downward among 12th graders, with a 45 percent drop compared to five years ago. Only 3 percent of high school seniors reported past-year misuse of Vicodin compared to nearly 10 percent a decade ago.

NATIONAL HOUSEHOLD SURVEY ON DRUG ABUSE AND HEALTH This survey, sponsored by the federal government, finds that about 10 percent of Americans used illegal drugs in the past year. Among the most recent findings:

- More than 4 million people aged 12 or older report current nonmedical use of prescription pain relievers.[112]
- Almost 2 million young adults aged 18 to 25 in the United States used cocaine in the past year (5 percent of the young adult population). This equates to about 1 out of every 20 young adults across the nation using cocaine in the past year.[113]
- About 28 million people aged 16 or older (11 percent) drove under the influence of alcohol in the past year, and 10 million (4 percent) drove under the influence of illicit drugs in the past year.[114]
- An estimated 6.4 million people reported misusing psychotherapeutic drugs in the past month, including 3.8 million people who were misusers of prescription pain relievers. Thus, the number of current misusers of pain relievers was second to marijuana among specific illicit drugs.

binge drinking
Having five or more drinks on the same occasion (that is, at the same time or within a couple of hours of one another).

FACT OR FICTION?

Fewer kids are drinking today than 20 years ago.

FACT Alcohol consumption among youths is diminishing and is actually at a 20-year low.

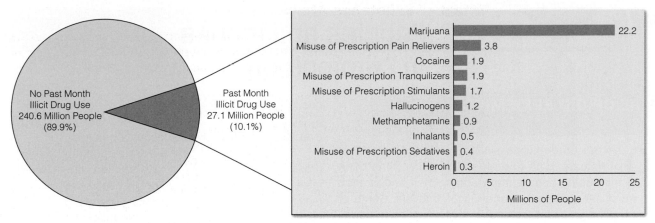

Note: Estimated numbers of people refer to people aged 12 or older in the civilian, noninstitutionalized population in the United States. The numbers do not sum to the total population of the United States because the population for NSDUH does not include people aged 11 years old or younger, people with no fixed household address (e.g., homeless or transient people not in shelters), active-duty military personnel, and residents of institutional group quarters, such as correctional facilities, nursing homes, mental institutions, and long-term care hospitals.

Note: The estimated numbers of current users of different illicit drugs are not mutually exclusive because people could have used more than one type of illicit drug in the past month.

FIGURE 13.1
Results from the National Survey on Drug Use and Health
Source: Substance Abuse and Mental Health Services Administration (SAMHSA), "Key Substance Use and Mental Health Indicators in the United States: Results from the 2015 National Survey on Drug Use and Health, 2016," https://www.samhsa.gov/data/sites/default/files/NSDUH-FFR1-2015/NSDUH -FFR1-2015/NSDUH-FFR1-2015.pdf.

Figure 13.1 shows some of the key results from the latest survey.

In sum, while these surveys show that drug usage has declined from peak years, it is still a significant social problem. The Policies and Issues in Criminology feature, The Opioid Epidemic, discusses the recent surge in opioid usage.

Causes of Substance Abuse

What causes people to abuse substances? Although there are many different views on the causes of drug use, most can be characterized as seeing the onset of an addictive career either as an environmental matter or as a personal matter.

SUBCULTURAL VIEW Those who view drug abuse as having an environmental basis concentrate on lower-class addiction. Because a disproportionate number of drug abusers are poor, the onset of drug use can be tied to such factors as racial prejudice, devalued identities, low self-esteem, poor socioeconomic status, and the high level of mistrust, negativism, and defiance found in impoverished areas.

Residing in a deteriorated inner-city area is often correlated with entry into a drug subculture. Youths living in these depressed areas, where feelings of alienation and hopelessness run high, often meet established drug users who teach them that narcotics assuage their feelings of personal inadequacy and stress.[115] The youths may join peers to learn the techniques of drug use and receive social support for their habit. Research shows that peer influence is a significant predictor of drug careers that actually grows stronger as people mature.[116] Shared feelings and a sense of intimacy lead the youths to become fully enmeshed in the drug culture.[117] Some join gangs and enter into a career of using and distributing illegal substances, while also committing property and violent crimes.[118]

PSYCHOLOGICAL VIEW Some experts have linked substance abuse to psychological deficits such as impaired cognitive functioning, personality disturbance, and emotional problems that can strike people in any economic class.[119] These produce what is called a **drug-dependent personality**. Some teens may resort to drug abuse to reduce the emotional turmoil of adolescence or to cope with troubling impulses.[120]

drug-dependent personality
A personal trait characterized by a pervasive psychological dependence on mood-altering substances.

Policies and Issues in Criminology

THE OPIOID EPIDEMIC

A heroin epidemic is sweeping the country. Use of opioids, both natural and synthetic, has been increasing substantially among men and women in most age groups and at all income levels. Some of the most significant increases have occurred in demographic groups with historically low rates of heroin use, such as higher income women. The group most at risk is young adults aged 18 to 25. Heroin use has more than doubled in the past decade among this group.

As heroin use has increased, so have heroin-related overdose deaths, which have more than quadrupled since 2010 (see Figure A). Drug-related deaths (including prescription opioids and heroin) reached an astounding 59,000 in 2016, according to preliminary data compiled by the *New York Times*. The largest increase in drug overdose deaths can be found in states along the East Coast, particularly Maryland, Florida, Pennsylvania, and Maine. Preliminary analysis indicates the rise in deaths continued in 2017. Drug overdoses are now the leading cause of death among Americans under 50.

What factors explain this rapid increase in heroin use among some groups, such as affluent young people, not just in big cities but also in rural and suburban areas? The opioid epidemic may have its roots in the explosive growth of prescription painkillers such as Vicodin, OxyContin, and Percocet, which are supplied by American pharmaceutical companies. By 2011, more than 200 million prescriptions for these drugs were issued in a single year. Potency also increased: in 2002,

one in six users took a pill more powerful than morphine; by 2012, it was one in three. Nearly half of all opioid overdose deaths involve a prescription opioid.

The threat posed by the easy availability of these prescription drugs began to have traction with state lawmakers, who cracked down on opioid abuse, creating drug-monitoring programs and prosecuting doctors who handed out unnecessary prescriptions. Pharmaceutical companies also responded by reformulating the drugs, making them less potent. Unfortunately, these reforms had unforeseen consequences: as the supply of retail painkillers dropped, users turned instead to heroin, which is both cheap and plentiful. The use of legal drugs is actually the strongest risk factor for starting heroin use and part of the progression to addiction. More than 90 percent of people who use heroin also used at least one other drug. Among new heroin users, three out of four report having abused prescription opioids prior to using heroin.

Another factor is that heroin is being imported in significantly higher quantities and high purity, at a relatively low price. To give some idea of how much heroin is entering the country, according to the Drug Enforcement Administration, the amount confiscated each year at the southwest border was approximately 1,100 pounds during 2000–2008; by 2013, this amount had more than quadrupled, to 4,841 pounds. And yet, these enforcement efforts are still not enough to stem the tide. Data released in 2017 show that the opioid epidemic is worsening, driven largely by the rise of fentanyl, a synthetic opioid painkiller 50 to 100 times more powerful than morphine. In 2016, fatal overdoses increased by 26 percent in Connecticut, 35 percent in Delaware, and 39 percent in Maine. During the first three quarters of 2016, deadly overdoses in Maryland jumped by a whopping 62 percent, prompting the state's governor to declare an official state of emergency.

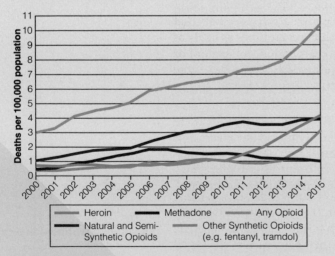

FIGURE A
Overdose Deaths Involving Opioids
Source: CDC/NCHS, National Vital Statistics System, 2016, https://wonder.cdc.gov/.

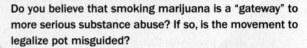

Critical Thinking

Do you believe that smoking marijuana is a "gateway" to more serious substance abuse? If so, is the movement to legalize pot misguided?

Sources: Centers for Disease Control and Prevention, "Today's Heroin Epidemic Infographics," https://www.cdc.gov/vitalsigns/heroin/infographic.html; CDC, "Heroin Overdose Data, 2017," https://www.cdc.gov/drugoverdose/data/heroin.html; "America's Opioid Epidemic Is Worsening: States Are Losing the Battle Against Deadly Drugs Like Heroin and Fentanyl," *The Economist*, March 6, 2017, http://www.economist.com/blogs/graphicdetail/2017/03/daily-chart-3; Josh Katz, "Drug Deaths in America Are Rising Faster Than Ever," *New York Times*, June 5, 2017, https://www.nytimes.com/interactive/2017/06/05/upshot/opioid-epidemic-drug-overdose-deaths-are-rising-faster-than-ever.html (URLs accessed June 2017).

Policies and Issues in Criminology

SUBSTANCE ABUSE AND PSYCHOSIS

Most estimates suggest that people diagnosed with mood or anxiety disorders are about twice as likely as the general population to also suffer from a substance use disorder. Studies exploring the link between substance use disorders and other mental illnesses have typically not included people with severe psychotic illnesses.

A study of 9,142 people diagnosed with schizophrenia, schizoaffective disorder, or bipolar disorder with psychotic features were matched with 10,195 controls according to geographic region. Mental disorder diagnoses were confirmed using the Diagnostic Interview for Psychosis and Affective Disorder (DI-PAD), and the controls were screened to verify the absence of schizophrenia or bipolar disorder in themselves or close family members. The DI-PAD was also used for all participants to determine substance use rates.

Compared to the controls, people with severe mental illness were about four times more likely to be heavy alcohol users (four or more drinks per day), 3.5 times more likely to use marijuana regularly (21 times per year), and 4.6 times more likely to use other drugs at least 10 times in their lives. The greatest increases were seen with tobacco, with patients with severe mental illness five times more likely to be daily smokers.

This is of concern because smoking is the leading cause of preventable death in the United States. The association between mental issues and substance abuse was constant when controlling for gender, age, and race.

Previous research has shown that people with schizophrenia have a shorter life expectancy than the general population, and chronic cigarette smoking has been suggested as a major contributing factor to higher morbidity and mortality from malignancy as well as cardiovascular and respiratory diseases. These new findings indicate that the rates of substance use in people with severe psychosis may be underestimated, highlighting the need to improve the understanding of the association between substance use and psychotic disorders so that both conditions can be treated effectively.

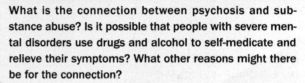

Critical Thinking

What is the connection between psychosis and substance abuse? Is it possible that people with severe mental disorders use drugs and alcohol to self-medicate and relieve their symptoms? What other reasons might there be for the connection?

Source: Sarah M. Hartz, Carlos N. Pato, Helena Medeiros, Patricia Cavazos-Rehg, Janet L. Sobell, James A. Knowles, Laura Bierut, and Michele T. Pato, "Comorbidity of Severe Psychotic Disorders with Measures of Substance Use," *JAMA Psychiatry* 71 (2014): 248–254.

Personality testing of known users suggests that a significant percentage suffer from psychotic disorders, including various levels of schizophrenia. Surveys show that youngsters with serious behavioral problems were more than seven times as likely as those with less serious problems to report that they were dependent on alcohol or illicit drugs. Youths with serious emotional problems were nearly four times more likely to report dependence on drugs than those without such issues.[121] The Policies and Issues in Criminology feature above reviews research on this topic.

What is the connection between psychological disorders and drug abuse? Drugs may help people deal with unconscious needs and impulses and relieve dependence and depression. People may turn to drug abuse as a form of self-medication to reduce the emotional turmoil of adolescence, deal with troubling impulses, or cope with traumatic life experiences such as institutional child abuse (kids who were sexually or physically abused in foster care, mental institutions, juvenile detention centers, day care centers, etc.).[122] Survivors of sexual assault and physical abuse in the home also have been known to turn to drug and alcohol abuse as a coping mechanism.[123] Depressed people may use drugs as an alternative to more radical solutions to their pain, such as suicide.[124] Kids with low self-esteem, or those who are self-conscious about their body image or who have a poor self-image, may turn to drugs to ease psychological turmoil.[125] Unfortunately, while substance abuse may relieve psychological strain in the short term, this relief is later countered by feelings of depression and anxiety in the long term.[126]

GENETIC FACTORS Substance abuse may have a genetic basis. Evidence for this has been found in research showing that biological children of alcoholics reared by non-alcoholic adoptive parents develop alcohol problems more often than the biological children of the adoptive parents.[127] In a similar vein, a number of studies comparing alcoholism among identical twins and fraternal twins have found that the degree of concordance (both siblings behaving identically) is twice as high among the identical twin groups. Nonetheless, most children of drug abusing parents do not become drug dependent themselves, which suggests that even if drug abuse is heritable, environment and socialization must play some role in the onset of abuse.[128]

SOCIAL LEARNING Social psychologists suggest that drug abuse may result from observing parental drug use. Parental drug abuse begins to have a damaging effect on children as young as 2 years old, especially when parents manifest drug-related personality problems such as depression or poor impulse control.[129] Children whose parents abuse drugs are more likely to have persistent abuse problems than the children of nonabusers.[130]

People who learn that drugs provide pleasurable sensations may be the most likely to experiment with illegal substances, and a habit may develop if the user experiences lower anxiety, fear, and tension levels.[131] Having a history of family drug and alcohol abuse has been found to be a characteristic of violent teenage sexual abusers.[132] Heroin abusers report an unhappy childhood that included harsh physical punishment and parental neglect and rejection.[133]

According to the social learning view, drug involvement begins with using tobacco and drinking alcohol at an early age, and this progresses to experimentation with marijuana and hashish and finally to cocaine and even heroin. Although most recreational users do not progress to "hard stuff," most but not all addicts begin their involvement with narcotics by first experimenting with recreational drugs. By implication, if teen smoking and drinking could be reduced, the gateway to hard drugs would be narrowed. For example, a 2003 research study found that a 50 percent reduction in the number of teens who smoke cigarettes can cut marijuana use by 16 to 28 percent.[134]

PROBLEM BEHAVIOR SYNDROME (PBS) For many people, substance abuse is just one of many problem behaviors.[135] Longitudinal studies show that drug abusers are maladjusted, alienated, and emotionally distressed and that their drug use is one among many social problems.[136] Having a deviant lifestyle begins early in life and is punctuated with criminal relationships, a family history of substance abuse, educational failure, and alienation. Kids who abuse drugs lack commitment to religious values, disdain education, spend most of their time in peer activities, engage in precocious sexual behavior, and experience school failure, family conflict, and similar social problems.[137] In adulthood, people who manifest substance abuse problems also exhibit an assortment of other social and legal problems.[138]

RATIONAL CHOICE Not all people who abuse drugs do so because of personal pathology. Some may use drugs and alcohol because they want to enjoy their effects: getting high, relaxation, improved creativity, escape from reality, and increased sexual responsiveness. Research indicates that adolescent alcohol abusers believe that getting high will make them powerful, increase their sexual performance, and facilitate their social behavior; they care little about negative future consequences.[139]

IS THERE A SINGLE "CAUSE" OF DRUG ABUSE? There are many different views of why people take drugs, and no theory has proved adequate to explain all forms of substance abuse. Recent research efforts show that drug users suffer a variety of family and socialization difficulties, have addiction-prone personalities, and are generally at risk for many other social problems.[140] One long-held assumption is that addicts progress along a continuum from using so-called gateway drugs such as alcohol and marijuana to using ever more potent substances, such as cocaine and heroin; this is known as the *gateway hypothesis*.[141] A great deal of research has attempted to find out whether there is truly a drug gateway, but results so far have been mixed. Some hard-core drug abusers have actually never smoked or used alcohol. And although many American youths have tried marijuana, few actually progress to crack or heroin abuse.[142] However, other research has found evidence that marijuana users are up to five times more likely than nonusers to escalate their drug abuse and try cocaine and heroin.[143] In sum, although most marijuana smokers do not become hard drug users, some do, and the risk of using dangerous substances may be increased by first engaging in recreational drug use.

Substance Abuse and Crime

One of the main reasons for the criminalization of particular substances is the significant association believed to exist between drug abuse and crime. Research suggests that many criminal offenders have extensive experience with alcohol and drug use and that abusers commit an enormous amount of crime. Substance abuse appears to be an important precipitating factor in a variety of criminal acts, especially income-generating crimes such as burglary.[144]

ALCOHOL AND CRIME Alcohol is a factor in 40 percent of all violent crimes; 37 percent of almost 2 million incarcerated inmates report that they were drinking at the time of their arrest.[145] Most violent crimes, including murder, rape, assault, child abuse, and spousal abuse, are committed by alcohol-involved offenders. Among violent crimes, with the exception of robberies, the offender is far more likely to have been drinking than under the influence of other drugs. Two-thirds of victims of spousal or partner abuse report that the perpetrator had been drinking.

DRUGS AND CRIME Efforts to link drug use to crime find that they are highly correlated. One source of information about the drug-crime connection comes from the ADAM II project, a federal program that monitored drug use patterns among arrestees in five US cities: Atlanta, Chicago, Denver, New York, and Sacramento.[146] Data from adult male arrestees were collected through voluntary interviews and drug tests with almost 2,000 men within 48 hours of their arrest. The sample was drawn from all adult males arrested, not just those arrested on drug charges.

What do the data show about the association between drug use and crime? Marijuana remains the drug most often detected in arrestees, ranging from 37 percent of arrestees testing positive in Atlanta to 58 percent testing positive in Chicago. In three of the five sites, over half of the adult male arrestees tested positive for marijuana. While cocaine and crack remain highly associated with arrest, they continued to show a significant decline in use everywhere. The percentage of arrestees testing positive for cocaine has declined significantly: in 2000, 50 percent of arrestees tested positive in Chicago, declining to about 19 percent today; in New York, 52 percent of arrestees tested positive for cocaine and crack in 2000, today about 25 percent. In sum, these data show that a high percentage of arrestees test positively for illicit drugs and that there are significant regional differences and trends in drug use; the drug–crime connection is strongly supported by the ADAM data.[147]

Inmate drug use is another indicator of the drug-crime connection. According to the National Center on Addiction and Substance Abuse (CASA), of more than 2 million prison and jail inmates, 85 percent were substance involved.[148] Of these about 1.5 million met the accepted psychological and medical criteria for substance abuse or addiction; about

Spencer Platt/Getty Images News/Getty Images

New York City, along with other cities, is experiencing a deadly epidemic of synthetic marijuana usage, including varieties known as K2 or "spice," which can cause extreme reactions in some users. According to New York's health department, more than 120 K2 users visited an emergency room in the city in just one week. Although the state banned ingredients used to make K2, distributors have switched to other ingredients and product names in an attempt to circumvent the law. Here, an NYPD officer speaks with men who are high on K2, along a street in East Harlem.

CONNECTIONS

Chapter 10 provides an analysis of the relationship between drugs and violence, which rests on three factors: (1) the psychopharmacological relationship, which is a direct consequence of ingesting mood-altering substances; (2) economic compulsive behavior, which occurs when drug users resort to violence to support their habit; and (3) a systemic link, which occurs when drug dealers battle for territories.

500,000 had not met the strict medical and psychological criteria but had histories of substance abuse and were under the influence of alcohol or other drugs at the time of their crime. Of these, some committed their offense to get money to buy drugs, were incarcerated for an alcohol or drug law violation, or shared some combination of these characteristics. The CASA research indicates that alcohol and other drugs were involved in:

- 78 percent of violent crimes
- 83 percent of property crimes
- 77 percent of public order, immigration, or weapons offenses and probation/parole violations

Alcohol was implicated in the incarceration of more than half of all inmates in America; illicit drugs were implicated in three-fourths of incarcerations.

What causes this linkage? Drug use interferes with maturation and socialization. Drug abusers are more likely to drop out of school, to be underemployed, to engage in precocious sex, and to become unmarried parents. Even if drug use does not turn otherwise law-abiding citizens into criminals, it certainly amplifies the extent of their criminal activities. A recent analysis of the drug–crime association found distinct evidence that the relationship between drugs and crime is complex, and drug users are not a monolithic group that behaves in a uniform and predictable manner. Among the most important findings are the following:[149]

- There are different types of drug users; many do not commit crimes.
- There are differences among criminally active drug users: (a) one group gets involved with crime before or at the same time as they get involved with drugs; (b) another group gets involved with crime only after they get involved with drugs. The onset of addiction is a turning point and causes them to initiate a criminal career.
- Drug use and criminal activity feed off each other as a deviant lifestyle, and peer affiliations reinforce each other.
- Drug addiction does not turn nonviolent criminals into violent criminals, but active addiction increases the frequency of criminal activity.
- Drug use and criminal behavior share some common roots in psychological propensity for impulsive and deviant behavior.
- Drug use impacts criminal behavior by creating the need to finance a drug habit.
- Criminal deviance increases the probability of later drug use.

In sum, research examining both the criminality of known narcotics users and the narcotics use of known criminals reveals a very strong association between drug use and crime. Even if the crime rate of drug users were actually only half that reported in the research literature, users would be responsible for a significant portion of the total criminal activity in the United States.

Drugs and the Law

The federal government first initiated legal action to curtail the use of some drugs early in the twentieth century.[150] In 1906, the Pure Food and Drug Act required manufacturers to list the amounts of habit-forming drugs on product labels but did not restrict their use. However, the act prohibited the importation and sale of opiates except for medicinal purposes. In 1914, the Harrison Narcotics Act restricted the importation, manufacture, sale, and dispensing of narcotics. It defined **narcotic** as any drug that induces sleep and relieves pain, such as heroin, morphine, and opium. The act was revised in 1922 to allow importation of opium and coca (cocaine) leaves for qualified medical practitioners. The Marijuana Tax Act of 1937 required registration and payment of a tax by all persons who imported, sold, or manufactured marijuana. Because marijuana was classified as a narcotic, those registering would also be subject to criminal penalty.

Subsequent federal laws were passed to clarify existing drug statutes and revise penalties. The Boggs Act of 1951 provided mandatory sentences for violating federal drug laws. The Durham-Humphrey Amendment of 1951 made it illegal to dispense

narcotic
A drug that induces sleep and relieves pain, such as heroin, morphine, and opium; a habit-forming drug.

barbiturates and amphetamines without a prescription. The Narcotic Control Act of 1956 increased penalties for drug offenders. In 1965, the Drug Abuse Control Act set up stringent guidelines for the legal use and sale of mood-modifying drugs, such as barbiturates, amphetamines, LSD, and any other "dangerous drugs," except narcotics prescribed by doctors and pharmacists. Illegal possession was punished as a misdemeanor and manufacture or sale as a felony. And in 1970, the Comprehensive Drug Abuse Prevention and Control Act set up unified categories of illegal drugs and attached specific penalties to their sale, manufacture, or possession. The law gave the US attorney general discretion to decide in which category to place any new drug.

Since then, various federal laws have attempted to increase penalties imposed on drug smugglers and to limit the manufacture and sale of newly developed substances. The 1984 Controlled Substances Act set new, stringent penalties for drug dealers and created five categories of narcotic and nonnarcotic substances subject to federal laws.[151] The Anti-Drug Abuse Act of 1986 again set new standards for minimum and maximum sentences for drug offenders, increased penalties for most offenses, and created a new drug penalty classification for large-scale offenses (such as trafficking in more than one kilogram of heroin), for which the penalty for a first offense was 10 years to life in prison.[152] With President George H. W. Bush's endorsement, Congress passed the Anti-Drug Abuse Act of 1988, which created a coordinated national drug policy under a "drug czar," set treatment and prevention priorities, and, clearly reflecting the government's hard-line stance against drug dealing, instituted availability of the death penalty for drug-related killings.[153] For the most part, state laws mirror federal statutes. Some apply extremely heavy penalties for selling or distributing dangerous drugs, such as prison sentences of up to 25 years.

Drug Control Strategies

Substance abuse remains a major social problem in the United States. Politicians looking for a safe campaign issue can take advantage of the public's fear of drug addiction by calling for a war on drugs. Such wars have been declared even when drug use was stable or in decline.[154] Can these efforts pay off? Can illegal drug use be eliminated or controlled?

A number of different drug control strategies have been tried, with varying degrees of success. Some aim to deter people from using drugs by stopping the flow of drugs into the country, apprehending and punishing dealers, and cracking down on street-level drug deals. Others focus on preventing drug use by educating potential users to the dangers of substance abuse (convincing them to "say no to drugs") and by organizing community groups to work with the at-risk population in their area. Still another approach is to treat known users so they can control their addictions. Some of these efforts are discussed next.

Law enforcement agents leave a clothing store after a raid in the Los Angeles fashion district. Agents raided dozens of businesses in 2014 as part of an investigation into suspected money laundering for Mexican drug cartels.

SOURCE CONTROL One approach to drug control is to deter the sale and importation of drugs through the systematic apprehension of large-volume drug dealers, coupled with the enforcement of strict drug laws that carry heavy penalties. This approach is designed to capture and punish known international drug dealers and to deter others from entering the drug trade. A major effort has been made to cut off supplies of drugs by destroying overseas crops and arresting members of drug cartels in Central and South America, Asia, and the Middle East, where many drugs are grown and manufactured. The federal government has been in the vanguard of encouraging exporting nations to step up efforts to destroy drug crops and prosecute. The United States has contributed more than a billion dollars to provide economic incentives and increased security to farmers in drug-producing regions in the Western Hemisphere.[155] However,

AP Images/Nick Ut

translating words into deeds is a formidable task. Drug lords are willing and able to fight back through intimidation, violence, and corruption. The Colombian drug cartels do not hesitate to use violence and assassination to protect their interests. Mexico has been awash in blood as cartels compete for power and control of the drug trade.

The amount of narcotics grown each year is so vast that even if three-quarters of the opium crop were destroyed, the US market would still require only 10 percent of the remainder to sustain its drug trade. The drug trade is an important source of foreign revenue for third-world nations, and destroying the drug trade undermines their economies. More than a million people in developing nations depend on the cultivating and processing of illegal substances. Adding to the problem of source control is the fact that the United States has little influence in some key drug-producing areas. War and terrorism also make source control strategies problematic. After the United States toppled Afghanistan's Taliban government, the remnants began to grow and sell poppy to support their insurgency. There has been a decline of opium production in Afghanistan mainly as a result of poor yields in the country's southern provinces. However, Afghanistan still accounted for 5,000 tons of opium in 2015 and leads the world in opium poppy cultivation.[156]

The federal government estimates that US citizens spend more than $40 billion annually on illegal drugs, and much of this money is funneled overseas. Even if the government of one nation were willing to cooperate in vigorous drug suppression efforts, suppliers in other nations, eager to cash in on the "seller's market," would be encouraged to turn more acreage over to coca or poppy production.

INTERDICTION STRATEGIES Law enforcement efforts have also been directed at intercepting drug supplies as they enter the country. Border patrols and military personnel using sophisticated hardware have been involved in massive interdiction efforts; many impressive multimillion-dollar seizures have been made. Yet the US borders are so vast and unprotected that meaningful interdiction is impossible. And even if all importation were shut down, homegrown marijuana and laboratory-made drugs, such as ecstasy, LSD, PCP, and synthetic heroin could become the drugs of choice. Even now, their easy availability and relatively low cost are increasing their popularity among the at-risk population.

LAW ENFORCEMENT STRATEGIES Local, state, and federal law enforcement agencies have been actively fighting drugs. One approach is to direct efforts at large-scale drug rings. The long-term consequence has been to decentralize drug dealing and encourage young independent dealers to become major suppliers. Ironically, it has proved easier for federal agents to infiltrate and prosecute traditional organized crime groups than to take on drug-dealing gangs. Consequently, some nontraditional groups have broken into the drug trade. Police can also target, intimidate, and arrest street-level dealers and users in an effort to make drug use so much of a hassle that consumption is cut back and the crime rate reduced. Approaches that have been tried include reverse stings, in which undercover agents pose as dealers to arrest users who approach them for a buy. Police have attacked fortified crack houses with heavy equipment to breach their defenses. They have used racketeering laws to seize the assets of known dealers. Special task forces of local and state police have conducted undercover operations and drug sweeps to discourage both dealers and users.

Although some street-level enforcement efforts have succeeded, others are considered failures. Drug sweeps have clogged courts and correctional facilities with petty

Erin Siegal/Redux

Border control is an established anti-drug policy, but one that is difficult to achieve. US Customs and Border Patrol (CBP) agents work along the US–Mexico border crossing joining Tijuana, Baja California, Mexico, to San Diego, California. Working dogs are used to track the scent of drugs and smuggled humans. Here, a woman suspected of smuggling is detained after a dog detected the scent of drugs in the vehicle she was driving. Do you believe such strategies can stem the flow of drugs, or are they doomed to failure?

offenders, while draining police resources. There are also suspicions that a displacement effect occurs; that is, stepped-up efforts to curb drug dealing in one area or city simply encourage dealers to seek friendlier territory.[157]

PUNISHMENT STRATEGIES Even if law enforcement efforts cannot produce a general deterrent effect, the courts may achieve the required result by severely punishing known drug dealers and traffickers. A number of initiatives have made the prosecution and punishment of drug offenders a top priority. State prosecutors have expanded their investigations into drug importation and distribution and assigned special prosecutors to focus on drug dealers. The fact that drugs such as crack are considered a serious problem may have convinced judges and prosecutors to expedite substance abuse cases.

However, these efforts often have their downside. Defense attorneys consider delay tactics sound legal maneuvering in drug-related cases. Courts are so backlogged that prosecutors are eager to plea bargain. The consequence of this legal maneuvering is that many people convicted on federal drug charges are granted probation or some other form of community release. Even so, prisons have become jammed with inmates, many of whom were involved in drug-related cases. Many drug offenders sent to prison do not serve their entire sentences because they are released in an effort to relieve prison overcrowding.[158]

COMMUNITY STRATEGIES Another type of drug control effort relies on the involvement of local community groups to lead the fight against drugs. Representatives of various local government agencies, churches, civic organizations, and similar institutions are being brought together to create drug prevention and awareness programs.

Citizen-sponsored programs attempt to restore a sense of community in drug-infested areas, reduce fear, and promote conventional norms and values.[159] These efforts can be classified into one of four distinct categories.[160] The first involves efforts to aid law enforcement, which may include block watches, cooperative police–community efforts, and citizen patrols. These citizen groups are nonconfrontational: they simply observe or photograph dealers, write down their license plate numbers, and then notify police.

A second tactic is to use the civil justice system to harass offenders. Landlords have been sued for owning properties that house drug dealers; neighborhood groups have scrutinized drug houses for building code violations. Information acquired from these various sources is turned over to local authorities, such as police and housing agencies, for more formal action.

A third approach is through community-based treatment efforts in which citizen volunteers participate in self-help support programs, such as Narcotics Anonymous and Cocaine Anonymous, which have more than 1,000 chapters nationally. Other programs provide youths with martial arts training, dancing, and social events as alternatives to the drug life.

A fourth type of community-level drug prevention effort is designed to enhance the quality of life, improve interpersonal relationships, and upgrade the neighborhood's physical environment. Activities might include the creation of drug-free school zones (which encourage police to keep drug dealers away from the vicinity of schools). Consciousness-raising efforts include demonstrations and marches to publicize the drug problem and build solidarity among participants.

DRUG EDUCATION AND PREVENTION STRATEGIES According to this view, substance abuse would decline if kids could be taught about the dangers of drug use. The most widely known drug education program, Drug Abuse Resistance Education (D.A.R.E.), is an elementary school course designed to give students the skills for resisting peer pressure to experiment with tobacco, drugs, and alcohol. It is unique because it employs uniformed police officers to carry the anti-drug message to the students before they enter junior high school. But even though more than 40 percent of all school districts incorporate assistance from local law enforcement agencies in their drug prevention programming, reviews of the program have not been encouraging, concluding that the program has only a marginal impact on student drug use and attitudes.[161] These negative evaluations caused D.A.R.E. to revise its curriculum. It is now aimed at older students and relies more on helping them question their assumptions about drug use than on having them listen to lectures on the subject.

DRUG-TESTING PROGRAMS Drug testing of private employees, government workers, and criminal offenders is believed to deter substance abuse. In the workplace, employees are tested to enhance on-the-job safety and productivity. In some industries, such as mining and transportation, drug testing is considered essential because abuse can pose a threat to the public.[162] Business leaders have been enlisted in the fight against drugs. Mandatory drug-testing programs in government and industry are common; more than 40 percent of the country's largest companies, including IBM and AT&T, have drug-testing programs. The federal government requires employee testing in regulated industries such as nuclear energy and defense contracting.

Criminal defendants are now routinely tested at all stages of the justice system, from arrest to parole. The goal is to reduce criminal behavior by detecting current users and curbing their abuse. Can such programs reduce criminal activity? Two evaluations of pretrial drug-testing programs found little evidence that monitoring defendants' drug use influenced their behavior.[163]

TREATMENT STRATEGIES Treatment strategies rely on helping substance abusers go straight rather than deterring their behavior through punishment. Specialized drug courts have been created whose magistrates are experts in dealing with substance abusers. There are now almost 3,000 drug courts across the nation and they handle more than 100,000 cases a year.[164]

A number of approaches are taken to treat known users, getting them clean of drugs and alcohol and thereby reducing the at-risk population (see Exhibit 13.1). One rests on the assumption that each user is an individual and successful treatment must be geared to the using patterns and personality of the individual offenders in order to build a sense of self.[165] Some programs have placed abusers in regimens of outdoor activities and wilderness training to create self-reliance and a sense of accomplishment.[166] Others focus on problem-solving skills, helping former and current addicts to deal with their real-world issues.[167] Providing supportive housing for formerly homeless drug addicts also may lead to better access to medical care, food, and job opportunities—all of which result in lower levels of addiction.[168] More intensive efforts use group therapy, relying on group leaders who have been substance abusers; through such sessions, users get the skills and support to help them reject social pressure to use drugs. These programs are based on the Alcoholics Anonymous approach, which holds that users must find within themselves the strength to stay clean and that peer support from those who understand their experiences can help them achieve a drug-free life.

There are also residential programs for the more heavily involved, and a large network of drug treatment centers has been developed. Some detoxification units use medical procedures to wean patients from the more addicting drugs to other drugs, such as methadone, that can be more easily regulated. Methadone is a drug similar to heroin, and addicts can be treated at clinics where they receive methadone under controlled conditions. However, methadone programs have been undermined because some users sell their methadone in the black market, and others supplement their dosages with illegally obtained heroin.

Other therapeutic programs attempt to deal with the psychological causes of drug use in "therapeutic communities." Hypnosis, aversion therapy (getting users to associate drugs with unpleasant sensations, such as nausea), counseling, biofeedback, and other techniques are often used. Some programs report significant success with clients who are able to complete the full course of the treatment.[169]

The long-term effects of treatment on drug abuse are still uncertain. Critics charge that a stay in a residential program can stigmatize people as addicts even if they never used hard drugs, and in treatment they may be introduced to hard-core users with whom they will associate after release. Users do not often enter these programs voluntarily and have little motivation to change. Supporters of treatment argue that

Exhibit 13.1   Effective Treatment Approaches

- *Medications.* Medications can be used to help with different aspects of the treatment process.
- *Withdrawal.* Medications offer help in suppressing withdrawal symptoms during detoxification. Patients who go through medically assisted withdrawal but do not receive any further treatment show drug abuse patterns similar to those who were never treated.
- *Treatment.* Medications can be used to help reestablish normal brain function and to prevent relapse and to diminish cravings. Medications are now available for treating opioids (heroin, morphine), tobacco (nicotine), and alcohol addiction; others are being developed for treating stimulant (cocaine, methamphetamine) and cannabis (marijuana) addiction. A significant problem: many addicts are polydrug users, requiring multiple medications.
- *Behavioral treatments.* Behavioral treatments help patients engage in the treatment process, modify their attitudes and behaviors related to drug abuse, and increase healthy life skills. These treatments can enhance the effectiveness of medications and help people stay in treatment longer. Outpatient behavioral treatment encompasses a wide variety of programs for patients who visit a clinic at regular intervals. Most of the programs involve individual or group drug counseling. Some programs also offer other forms of behavioral treatment:
  - *Cognitive-behavioral therapy* seeks to help patients recognize, avoid, and cope with the situations in which they are most likely to abuse drugs.

- *Multidimensional family therapy* was developed for adolescents with drug abuse problems as well as their families. It addresses a range of influences on their drug abuse patterns and is designed to improve overall family functioning.
- *Motivational interviewing* capitalizes on the readiness of individuals to change their behavior and enter treatment.
- *Motivational incentives* (contingency management) use positive reinforcement to encourage abstinence from drugs.
- *Residential treatment programs* can be very effective, especially for those with more severe problems.
- *Therapeutic communities* (TCs) are highly structured programs in which patients remain at a residence, typically for 6 to 12 months. TCs differ from other treatment approaches principally in their use of the community—treatment staff and those in recovery—as a key agent of change to influence patient attitudes, perceptions, and behaviors associated with drug use. Patients in TCs may include those with relatively long histories of drug addiction, involvement in serious criminal activities, and seriously impaired social functioning. TCs are now also being designed to accommodate the needs of women who are pregnant or have children. The focus of the TC is on the resocialization of the patient to a drug-free, crime-free lifestyle.

Source: National Institute on Drug Abuse, "NIDA InfoFacts: Treatment Approaches for Drug Addiction," http://www.drugabuse.gov/publications/drugfacts/treatment-approaches-drug-addiction (accessed May 2017).

many addicts are helped by intensive inpatient and outpatient treatment, and the cost saving is considerable. The biggest problem is availability: the federal government estimates that about 23 million people are in need of intense drug and alcohol treatment, but only 2.5 million are in programs.[170]

EMPLOYMENT PROGRAMS Research indicates that drug abusers who obtain and keep employment are likely to end or reduce the incidence of their substance abuse.[171] Not surprisingly, then, there have been a number of efforts to provide vocational rehabilitation for drug abusers. One approach is the supported work program, which typically involves jobsite training, ongoing assessment, and jobsite intervention. Rather than teaching work skills in a classroom, support programs rely on helping drug abusers deal with real work settings. Other programs provide training to overcome barriers to employment, including help with motivation, education, experience, the job market, job-seeking skills, and personal issues. For example, female abusers may be unaware of childcare resources that would enable them to seek employment opportunities. Another approach is to help addicts improve their interviewing skills so that once job opportunities can be identified, they are equipped to convince potential employers of their commitment and reliability.

Legalization of Drugs

"Like alcohol Prohibition in the 1920s, which was intended to banish certain substances from society, drug prohibition has not only failed its mission but has made its mission impossible. The failures of prohibition are painfully obvious: wasted money, wasted lives, and wasted opportunities. Determining what works best is less straightforward, but we have examples from all over the world and even our own states of policies that show progress and represent opportunities to improve."[172]

So claims the Drug Policy Alliance, a leading voice for reforming drug control laws and a group that believes the so-called "war on drugs" is both expensive and futile; it has cost more than $500 billion over the past 20 years. Federal and local governments now spend about $28 billion per year on drug control and treatment—money that could be spent on education and economic development.[173] The current administration budget (2017) is proposing to drastically slash spending on both control and treatment. The effect of such cuts on drug use remains to be seen.[174]

Legalization is warranted, according to drug expert Ethan Nadelmann, because the use of mood-altering substances is customary in nearly all human societies; people have always wanted—and will always find ways of obtaining—psychoactive drugs.[175] Banning drugs creates illicit networks of manufacturers and distributors, many of whom use violence as part of their standard operating procedures. Although some believe that drug use is immoral, Nadelmann questions whether it is any worse than the unrestricted use of alcohol and cigarettes, both of which are addicting and unhealthful. Far more people die each year because they abuse these legal substances than are killed in drug wars or die from abusing illegal substances.

Nadelmann also states that just as Prohibition failed to stop the flow of alcohol in the 1920s, while simultaneously increasing the power of organized crime, the policy of prohibiting drugs is similarly doomed to failure. When drugs were legal and freely available early in the twentieth century, the proportion of Americans who used drugs was not much greater than it is today. Most users led normal lives, largely because of the legal status of their drug use.

The futility of drug control efforts is illustrated by the fact that despite massive long-term efforts, the price of illegal narcotics such as crack cocaine and heroin has drifted downward as supplies have become more plentiful. In terms of weight and availability, there is still no commodity whose sale is more lucrative than illegal drugs. They cost relatively little to produce, and they provide dealers and traffickers with large profit margins. At the current average street price of $150 per gram in the United States, a metric ton of pure cocaine is worth more than $150 million; cutting it to reduce its purity can double or triple the value.[176] With that kind of profit to be made, can any strategy, whether treatment-oriented or punishment-oriented, reduce the lure of drug trafficking?

If drugs were legalized, the argument goes, price and distribution could be controlled by the government. This would reduce addicts' cash requirements, so crime rates would drop because users would no longer need the same cash flow to support their habits. Drug-related deaths would decline because government control would reduce needle sharing and the spread of AIDS. Legalization would also destroy the drug-importing cartels and gangs. Because drugs would be bought and sold openly, the government would reap a tax windfall both from taxes on the sale of drugs and from income taxes paid by drug dealers on profits that have been part of the hidden

AP Images/Brennan Linsley

While marijuana may be legally bought in Colorado by adults it is forbidden to underage minors. Here, young partygoers listen to music and smoke marijuana during the annual 4/20 marijuana festival in Denver's downtown Civic Center Park. Colorado schools are compiling data on the number of students who get busted for using marijuana, an idea aimed at gauging the impact of the drug's legalization and whether it affects usage among youth.

economy. Of course, as with alcohol, drug distribution would be regulated, keeping drugs away from adolescents, public servants such as police and airline pilots, and known felons. Those who favor legalization point to the Netherlands as a country that has legalized drugs and remains relatively free of crime.

Those who oppose drug legalization counter that this approach might indeed have the short-term effect of reducing the association between drug use and crime, but it might also have grave social consequences. Legalization might increase the nation's rate of drug usage, creating an even larger group of nonproductive, drug-dependent people who must be cared for by the rest of society. Also, while few people die from smoking marijuana, there are about 40,000 drug-related deaths each year in the United States.[177] In countries such as Thailand, where drugs are cheap and readily available, the rate of narcotics use is quite high. Historically, the availability of cheap narcotics has preceded drug use epidemics, as was the case when British and American merchants sold opium in nineteenth-century China.

If juveniles, criminals, and members of other at-risk groups were forbidden to buy drugs, who would be the customers? Noncriminal, nonabusing, middle-aged adults? And would not those prohibited from legally buying drugs create an underground market almost as vast as the current one? If the government tried to raise money by taxing legal drugs, as it now does with liquor and cigarettes, that might encourage drug smuggling to avoid tax payments; these "illegal" drugs might then fall into the hands of adolescents.

Decriminalization or legalization of controlled substances is unlikely in the near term, but further study is warranted. What effect would a national policy of legalizing personal use of marijuana, as some states have done, have on drug use rates? Would a get-tough policy help to "widen the net" of the justice system and thus (through contact with users during incarceration) actually deepen some youths' involvement in substance abuse? Can society provide alternatives to drugs that will reduce teenage drug dependency? The answers to these questions have proved elusive. The different types of drug control strategies are summarized in Concept Summary 13.1.

CHECKPOINTS

▶ Substance abuse is an ancient practice dating back more than 4,000 years.

▶ A wide variety of drugs are in use today, and alcohol is a major problem.

▶ Drug use among American youth has been in decline; despite this trend, about half of all high school seniors have tried illegal drugs at least once during their lifetime.

▶ There is no single cause of substance abuse. Some people may use drugs because they are predisposed to abuse.

▶ There is a strong link between drug abuse and crime. People who become addicts may increase their illegal activities to support their habits. Others engage in violence as part of their drug-dealing activities.

Concept Summary 13.1   Drug Control Strategies

Control Strategy	Main Focus	Problems/Issues
Source control	Destroy overseas crops and drug labs	Drug profits hard to resist; drug crops in hostile nations are off limits
Interdiction	Seal borders; arrest drug couriers	Extensive US borders hard to control
Law enforcement	Police investigation and arrest of dealers	New dealers are recruited to replace those in prison
Punishment	Deter dealers with harsh punishments	Crowded prisons promote bargain justice
Community programs	Help community members deal with drug problems on the local level	Relies on community cohesion and efficacy
Drug education	Teach kids about the harm of taking drugs	Evaluations do not show programs are effective
Drug testing	Threaten employees with drug tests to deter use	Evaluations do not show drug testing is effective; people cheat on tests
Treatment	Use of therapy to get people off drugs	Expensive, requires motivation; clients associate with other users
Employment	Provide jobs as an alternative to drugs	Requires that former addicts become steady employees
Legalization	Decriminalize or legalize drugs	Political hot potato; danger of creating more users

Thinking Like a Criminologist

Mental Illness and Crime You have been called upon by the director of the Department of Health and Human Services to give your opinion on a recent national survey that found that serious mental illness (SMI) is highly correlated with illicit drug use. This research shows that adults who used an illicit drug in the past year were three times as likely to suffer mental illness than adults who did not use an illicit drug. One possible explanation of these data is that drugs cause people to become mentally ill while another is that mentally ill people use drugs to "self-medicate." Regardless of the cause we know that (a) people who use drugs commit more crime than nonabusers and (b) that the mentally ill commit more crime than the mentally sound.

Writing Assignment

The director asks you to comment on the mental illness, substance abuse, and crime nexus. Write an essay spelling out the true association between these factors, how each may be an effect or cause, and how all three interact.

SUMMARY

LO1 **Interpret what is meant by the term *social harm*.**
According to the theory of social harm, acts become crimes when they cause injury and produce harm to others. However, some dangerous activities are not considered crimes, and some activities that do not appear harmful are criminalized.

LO2 **Discuss the activities of moral crusaders.**
Moral crusaders seek to shape the law to reflect their own way of thinking. These moral entrepreneurs go on moral crusades to take on such issues as prayer in schools, gun ownership, same-sex marriage, abortion, and the distribution of sexually explicit books. One of the most visible crusades has been efforts to control the legality of same-sex marriage, which culminated in a 2015 Supreme Court ruling striking down laws banning the practice.

LO3 **Describe the various forms of outlawed deviant sexuality.**
The outlawed sexual behaviors known as paraphilias include frotteurism (rubbing against or touching a nonconsenting person), voyeurism (obtaining sexual pleasure from spying on a stranger while he or she disrobes or engages in sexual behavior with another), exhibitionism (deriving sexual pleasure from exposing the genitals to surprise or shock a stranger), sadomasochism (deriving pleasure from receiving pain or inflicting pain on another), and pedophilia (attaining sexual pleasure through sexual activity with prepubescent children).

LO4 **Distinguish among the different types of prostitutes.**
Prostitutes who work the streets in plain sight of police, citizens, and customers are referred to as hustlers, hookers, or streetwalkers. B-girls spend their time in bars, drinking and waiting to be picked up by customers. Brothel prostitutes live in a house with a madam who employs them, supervises their behavior, and receives a fee for her services. Call girls work via telephone "dates" and get their clients by word of mouth or by making arrangements with bellhops, cab drivers, and so on. Some escort services are fronts for prostitution rings. Prostitutes known as circuit travelers move around in groups of two or three to lumber, labor, and agricultural camps. Cyberprostitutes set up personal websites or put listings on web boards that carry personal ads.

LO5 **State the arguments for and against legalizing prostitution.**
The sexual equality view considers the prostitute a victim of male dominance. The free choice view is that prostitution, if freely chosen,

expresses women's equality and is not a symptom of subjugation. Advocates of both positions argue that prostitution should be decriminalized in order to relieve already desperate women from the additional burden of severe legal punishment. However, decriminalizing prostitution does not protect women from the violence, verbal abuse, physical injury, and diseases (such as HIV, AIDS) to which they are exposed in illegal prostitution.

LO6 Discuss the causes of substance abuse.

The onset of drug use can be tied to such factors as racial prejudice, devalued identities, low self-esteem, poor socioeconomic status, and the high level of mistrust, negativism, and defiance typically found in impoverished areas. Some experts have linked substance abuse to psychological deficits such as impaired cognitive functioning, personality disturbance, and emotional problems. Substance abuse may have a genetic basis. Social psychologists suggest that drug abuse may also result from observing parental drug use. Substance abuse may be just one of many social problem behaviors. Some may use drugs and alcohol because they want to enjoy their effects: getting high, relaxation, improved creativity, escape from reality, and increased sexual responsiveness.

Key Terms

public order crime 446
victimless crime 447
social harm 449
moral entrepreneur 449

paraphilias 451
prostitution 453
pornography 461
obscenity 461

temperance
    movement 465
Prohibition 465
binge drinking 466

drug-dependent
    personality 467
narcotic 472

Critical Thinking Questions

1. Why do you think people take drugs? Do you know anyone with an addiction-prone personality, or do you believe that is a myth?

2. What might be the best strategy to reduce teenage drug use: source control, reliance on treatment, national education efforts, or community-level enforcement?

3. Under what circumstances, if any, might the legalization or decriminalization of sex-related material be beneficial to society?

4. Do you consider alcohol a drug? Should greater control be imposed on the sale of alcohol?

5. Is prostitution really a crime? Should men or women have the right to sell sexual favors if they so choose?

Notes

All URLs accessed in 2017.

1. Department of Justice, US Attorney's Office, Western District of Michigan, "Former Olympic Gymnastics Doctor Indicted on Federal Child Pornography Charges," December 19, 2016, https://www.justice.gov/usao-wdmi/pr/2016_1219_Nassar; Lindsay Kimble, "Elite Gymnast on How Dr. Larry Nassar Allegedly Preyed on Young Girls: 'I Thought He Was My Friend,'" *People*, March 20, 2017, http://people.com/sports/dominique-moceanu-us-gymnasts-on-abuse-scandal/.

2. Edwin Schur, *Crimes Without Victims* (Englewood Cliffs, NJ: Prentice Hall, 1965).

3. Raymond Hernandez, "Weiner Resigns in Chaotic Final Scene," *New York Times*, June 16, 2011, http://www.nytimes.com/2011/06/17/nyregion/anthony-d-weiner-tells-friends-he-will-resign.html.

4. Lindsey Bever, "Anthony Weiner Pleaded Guilty to 'Sexting' a Teen Girl. Then His Estranged Wife Filed for Divorce," *Washington Post*, May 19, 2017, https://www.washingtonpost.com/news/post-nation/wp/2017/05/19/anthony-weiner-disgraced-former-congressman-expected-to-plead-guilty-today-in-sexting-case-involving-minor.

5. The Bible, New International Version, Genesis 18:20.

6. Bible Hub, Ezekiel 16:49, http://biblehub.com/ezekiel/16-49.htm.

7. Wayne LaFave and Austin Scott Jr., *Criminal Law* (St. Paul, MN: West, 1986), p. 12.

8. Ibid.

9. Andrea Dworkin, quoted in "Where Do We Stand on Pornography?" *Ms.* (January–February 1994): 34.

10. Russel Falck, Jichuan Wang, and Robert Carlson, "The Epidemiology of Physical Attack and Rape Among Crack-Using Women," *Violence and Victims* 16 (2001): 79–89.

11. C. Gabrielle Salfati, Alison James, and Lynn Ferguson, "Prostitute Homicides: A Descriptive Study," *Journal of Interpersonal Violence* 23 (2008): 505–543.

12. Morris Cohen, "Moral Aspects of the Criminal Law," *Yale Law Journal* 49 (1940): 1017.

13. See Joel Feinberg, *Social Philosophy* (Englewood Cliffs, NJ: Prentice Hall, 1973), Chapters 2, 3.

14. *United States v. 12 200-ft Reels of Super 8mm Film*, 413 U.S. 123 (1973), at p. 137.

15. Robin Pogrebin and Scott Reyburn, "With $170.4 Million Sale at Auction, Modigliani Work Joins Rarefied Nine-Figure Club," *New York Times*, November 9, 2015, http://www.nytimes.com/2015/11/10/arts/with-170-4-million-sale-at-auction-modigliani-work-joins-rarefied-nine-figure-club.html.

16. John Franks, "The Evaluation of Community Standards," *Journal of Social Psychology* 139 (1999): 253–255.

17. Matthew Hussey, "Who Are the Biggest Consumers of Online Porn?" TNW News, http://thenextweb.com/market-intelligence/2015/03/24/who-are-the-biggest-consumers-of-online-porn/#gref; Sebastian Anthony, "Just How Big Are Porn Sites?" ExtremeTech, April 4, 2012, http://www.extremetech.com/computing/123929-just-how-big-are-porn-sites.

18. Irving Kristol, "Liberal Censorship and the Common Culture," *Society* 36 (September 1999): 5.

19. United Nations, World Health Organization, "Female Genital Mutilation," updated 2017, http://www.who.int/mediacentre/factsheets/fs241/en/.

20. David Kaplan, "Is It Torture or Tradition?" *Newsweek*, December 20, 1993, p. 124.

21. Howard Becker, *Outsiders* (New York: Macmillan, 1963), pp. 13–14.

22. American Library Association, "Frequently Challenged Books," http://www.ala.org/bbooks/frequentlychallengedbooks.

23. U.S. Code, Title 1 § 7. Definition of "marriage" and "spouse."

24. *Lawrence et al. v. Texas*, No. 02-102, June 26, 2003.

25. *Hillary Goodridge et al. v. Department of Public Health and Another*, SJC-08860, November 18, 2003.

26. *Obergefell v. Hodges*, 576 U.S. ___ (2015).

27. See, generally, Spencer Rathus and Jeffery Nevid, *Abnormal Psychology* (Englewood Cliffs, NJ: Prentice Hall, 1991), pp. 373–411.

28. Richard von Krafft-Ebing, *Psychopathia Sexualis: The Classic Study of Deviant Sex*, reprint ed. (New York: Arcade Publishing, 2011).

29. Curt Anderson, "Death Sentence Endorsed in Lunsford Case," *Washington Post*, March 15, 2007, http://www.washingtonpost.com/wp-dyn/content/article/2007/03/15/AR2007031500518.html.

30. Laurie Goodstein, "After Criticism, Pope Francis Confronts Priestly Sexual Abuse," *New York Times*, September 27, 2015, http://www.nytimes.com/2015/09/28/us/pope-francis-philadelphia-sexual-abuse.html.

31. Associated Press, "Ex-Baltimore Ravens Cheerleader Molly Shattuck Gets Probation for Raping a 15-Year-Old Boy," *New York Daily News*, August 21, 2015.

32. Miriam Wijkman, Catrien Bijleveld, and Jan Hendriks, "Women Don't Do Such Things! Characteristics of Female Sex Offenders and Offender Types," *Sexual Abuse: A Journal of Research and Treatment* 22 (2010): 135–156.

33. Boris Schiffer, Thomas Paul, Elke Gizewski, Michael Forsting, Norbert Leygraf, Manfred Schedlowski, and Tillmann H. C. Kruger, "Functional Brain Correlates of Heterosexual Paedophilia," *Neuroimage* 41 (2008): 80–91.

34. Ray Blanchard, Bruce K. Christensen, Scott M. Strong, James M. Cantor, Michael E. Kuban, Philip Klassen, Robert Dickey, and Thomas Blak, "Retrospective Self-Reports of Childhood Accidents Causing Unconsciousness in Phallometrically Diagnosed Pedophiles," *Archives of Sexual Behavior* 31 (2002): 111–127.

35. Michael Allan and Randolph Grace, "Psychometric Assessment of Dynamic Risk Factors for Child Molesters," *Sexual Abuse: A Journal of Research* 19 (2007): 347–367.

36. For an analysis of this issue, see Theresa Gannon and Devon Polaschek, "Cognitive Distortions in Child Molesters: A Re-examination of Key Theories

and Research," *Clinical Psychology Review* 26 (2006): 1000–1019.

37. Joel Roberts, "New Woes for Senator Caught in Sex Scandal," CBS News, July 11, 2007, http://www.cbsnews.com/news/new-woes-for-senator-caught-in-sex-scandal/.

38. Adam Nossiter, "A Senator's Moral High Ground Gets a Little Shaky," *New York Times*, July 11, 2007, http://www.nytimes.com/2007/07/11/us/11vitter.html.

39. See, generally, V. Bullogh, *Sexual Variance in Society and History* (Chicago: University of Chicago Press, 1958), pp. 143–144.

40. Spencer Rathus, *Human Sexuality* (New York: Holt, Rinehart and Winston, 1983), p. 463.

41. Michael Rutter, *Upstairs Girls: Prostitution in the American West* (Helena, MT: Far Country Press, 2012).

42. Jami Balls, "History of the Stockade and Salt Lake's Red Light District," Utah History to Go, http://historytogo.utah.gov/places/olympic_locations/stockade.html.

43. Ibid.

44. Mara Keire, "The Vice Trust: A Reinterpretation of the White Slavery Scare in the United States, 1907–1917," *Journal of Social History* 35 (2001): 5–42.

45. Nicole Bromfield, "Sex Slavery and Sex Trafficking of Women in the United States: Historical and Contemporary Parallels, Policies, and Perspectives in Social Work," *Journal of Women and Social Work* 31 (2016): 129–139.

46. Jane Addams, *A New Conscience and an Ancient Evil* (Champagne: University of Illinois Press, 2002).

47. Barbara G. Brents and Kathryn Hausbeck, "State-Sanctioned Sex: Negotiating Formal and Informal Regulatory Practices in Nevada Brothels," *Sociological Perspectives* 44 (2001): 307–335.

48. Charles McCaghy, *Deviant Behavior* (New York: Macmillan, 1976), pp. 348–349.

49. Michael Waldholz, "HTLV–I Virus Found in Blood of Prostitutes," *Wall Street Journal*, January 5, 1990, p. B2.

50. Scott Shuger, "Hookers.com: How E-commerce Is Transforming the Oldest Profession," *Slate*, http://www.slate.com/articles/briefing/articles/2000/01/hookerscom.html.

51. Nisha Lilia Diu, "Welcome to Paradise," *The Telegraph*, 2013, http://s.telegraph.co.uk/graphics/projects/welcome-to-paradise/.

52. Elizabeth Bernstein, "The Meaning of the Purchase: Desire, Demand, and the Commerce of Sex," *Ethnography* 2 (2001): 389–420.

53. Megan Annitto, "Consent, Coercion, and Compassion: Emerging Legal Responses to the Commercial Sexual Exploitation of Minors," *Yale Law and Policy Review* 30 (2011): 1–70.

54. Charles Winick and Paul Kinsie, *The Lively Commerce* (Chicago: Quadrangle, 1971), p. 58.

55. Vanessa Bouché and Stephanie Shady, "A Pimp's Game: A Rational Choice Approach to Understanding the Decisions of Sex Traffickers," *Women and Criminal Justice* 27 (2017): 91–108.

56. Celia Williamson and Lynda Baker, "Women in Street-Based Prostitution: A Typology of Their Work Styles," *Qualitative Social Work* 8 (2009): 27–44.

57. Winick and Kinsie, *The Lively Commerce*, pp. 172–173.

58. Paul Goldstein, "Occupational Mobility in the World of Prostitution: Becoming a Madam," *Deviant Behavior* 4 (1983): 267–279.

59. The Real Yellow Pages, http://www.yellowpages.com/new-york-ny/escort-service; http://www.yellowpages.com/las-vegas-nv/escort-service.

60. Mireya Navarro, "Group Forced Illegal Aliens into Prostitution, U.S. Says," *New York Times*, April 24, 1998, p. A10.

61. "More Bang for Your Buck," *The Economist*, August 9, 2014, http://www.economist.com/news/briefing/21611074-how-new-technology-shaking-up-oldest-business-more-bang-your-buck.

62. Lucas Matney, "Ohlala, an Uber for Escorts, Launches Its 'Paid Dating' Service in NYC," *TechCrunch*, February 3, 2016, https://techcrunch.com/2016/02/03/i-only-downloaded-it-as-a-joke-honey/.

63. Ginger Thompson and Philip Shenon, "Navy Officer Describes Working as a Prostitute," *New York Times*, April 12, 2008, http://www.nytimes.com/2008/04/12/us/12officer.html.

64. D. Kelly Weisberg, *Children of the Night: A Study of Adolescent Prostitution* (Lexington, MA: Lexington Books, 1985), pp. 44–55.

65. N. Jackman, Richard O'Toole, and Gilbert Geis, "The Self-Image of the Prostitute," in *Sexual Deviance*, ed. J. Gagnon and W. Simon (New York: Harper & Row, 1967), pp. 152–153.

66. Tammy Heilemann and Janaki Santhiveeran, "How Do Female Adolescents Cope and Survive the Hardships of Prostitution? A Content Analysis of Existing Literature," *Journal of Ethnic and Cultural Diversity in Social Work* 20 (2011): 57–76.

67. Lisa Kramer and Ellen Berg, "A Survival Analysis of Timing of Entry into Prostitution: The Differential Impact of Race, Educational Level, and Childhood/Adolescent Risk Factors," *Sociological Inquiry* 73 (2003): 511–529.

68. Gerald Hotaling and David Finkelhor, *The Sexual Exploitation of Missing Children* (Washington, DC: US Department of Justice, 1988).

69. Jennifer Cobbina and Sharon Oselin, "It's Not Only for the Money: An Analysis of Adolescent versus Adult Entry into Street Prostitution," *Sociological Inquiry* 81 (2011): 310–332.

70. Michael Miner, Jill Flitter, and Beatrice Robinson, "Association of Sexual Revictimization with Sexuality and Psychological Function," *Journal of Interpersonal Violence* 21 (2006): 503–524.

71. Jolanda Sallmann, "Living with Stigma: Women's Experiences of Prostitution and Substance Use," *Afillia Journal of Women and Social Work* 25 (2010): 146–159.

72. Ronald Weitzer, "The Politics of Prostitution in America," in *Sex for Sale*, ed. R. Weitzer (New York: Routledge, 2000), pp. 159–180.

73. Greggor Mattson, *The Cultural Politics of European Prostitution Reform: Governing Loose Women* (New York: Palgrave Macmillan, 2016).

74. Rebecca Hayes-Smitha and Zahra Shekarkharb, "Why Is Prostitution Criminalized? An Alternative Viewpoint on the Construction of Sex Work," *Contemporary Justice Review* 13 (2010): 43–55.

75. Andrea Dworkin, *Pornography* (New York: Dutton, 1989).

76. Annette Jolin, "On the Backs of Working Prostitutes: Feminist Theory and Prostitution Policy," *Crime and Delinquency* 40 (1994): 60–83, at 76–77.

77. Alexa Albert, *Brothel: Mustang Ranch and Its Women* (New York: Random House, 2001).

78. Ronald Weitzer, *Legalizing Prostitution: From Illicit Vice to Lawful Business* (New York: New York University Press, 2011).

79. Melissa Farley, *Prostitution and Trafficking in Nevada: Making the Connections* (San Francisco: Prostitution Research & Education, 2007).

80. Roger Matthews, *Prostitution, Politics and Policy* (London: Routledge-Cavendish, 2008).

81. Hayes-Smitha and Shekarkharb, "Why Is Prostitution Criminalized? An Alternative Viewpoint on the Construction of Sex Work," p. 54.

82. *Merriam-Webster Dictionary* (New York: Pocket Books, 1974), p. 484.

83. Attorney General's Commission, *Report on Pornography, Final Report* (Washington, DC: US Government Printing Office, 1986), pp. 837–901.

84. Michael Bourke and Andres Hernandez, "The 'Butner Study' Redux: A Report of the Incidence of Hands-on Child Victimization by Child Pornography Offenders," *Journal of Family Violence* 24 (2009): 183–191.

85. *Report of the Commission on Obscenity and Pornography* (Washington, DC: US Government Printing Office, 1970).

86. Berl Kutchinsky, "The Effect of Easy Availability of Pornography on the Incidence of Sex Crimes," *Journal of Social Issues* 29 (1973): 95–112.

87. Michael Goldstein, "Exposure to Erotic Stimuli and Sexual Deviance," *Journal of Social Issues* 29 (1973): 197–219.

88. Catherine Simmons, Peter Lehmann, and Shannon Collier-Tenison, "Linking Male Use of the Sex Industry to Controlling Behaviors in Violent Relationships: An Exploratory Analysis," *Violence Against Women* 14 (2008): 406–417.

89. Michael Flood, "The Harms of Pornography Exposure Among Children and Young People," *Child Abuse Review* 18 (2009): 384–400.

90. Diana Russell, *Dangerous Relationships: Pornography, Misogyny, and Rape* (Thousand Oaks, CA: Sage, 1998).

91. *Roth v. United States*, 354 U.S. 476; 77 S.Ct. 1304 (1957).

92. *Miller v. California*, 413 U.S. 15 (1973).

93. R. George Wright, "Defining Obscenity: The Criterion of Value," *New England Law Review* 22 (1987): 315–341.

94. Michael Fix, "A Universal Standard for Obscenity? The Importance of Context and Other Considerations," *Justice System Journal* 37 (2016): 72–88.

95. *Pope v. Illinois*, 107 S.Ct. 1918 (1987).

96. Alexandra Desanctis, "Trump Is Right to Sign Pledge Protecting Children from Pornography," August 2, 2016, http://www.nationalreview.com/corner /438610/donald-trump-signs-anti-porn-pledge.

97. Julie Jargon, "Jared Fogle Sentenced to 15 1/2 Years in Prison, Former Subway Pitchman Pleaded Guilty in Child-Sex Case," *Wall Street Journal* November 19, 2015, https://www.wsj.com/articles/jared-fogle-to -be-sentenced-thursday-1447942432.

98. Pub. L. 108-21, 117 Stat. 650, S. 151, enacted April 30, 2003.

99. *United States v. Williams*, 553 U.S. 285 (2008).

100. FBI, "Innocent Images National Initiative," http:// www2.fbi.gov/publications/innocent.htm.

101. United Nations Office on Drugs and Crime, *World Drug Report*, 2016, http://www.unodc.org/wdr2016/.

102. Substance Abuse and Mental Health Services Administration (SAMHSA), *Key Substance Use and Mental Health Indicators in the United States: Results from the 2015 National Survey on Drug Use and Health, 2016*, https://www.samhsa.gov/data/sites/default /files/NSDUH-FFR1-2015/NSDUH-FFR1-2015 /NSDUH-FFR1-2015.pdf.

103. National Institute on Drug Abuse, "Costs of Substance Abuse, 2017," https://www.drugabuse .gov/related-topics/trends-statistics.

104. James Inciardi, *The War on Drugs* (Palo Alto, CA: Mayfield, 1986), p. 2.

105. See, generally, David Pittman, "Drug Addiction and Crime," in *Handbook of Criminology*, ed. D. Glazer (Chicago: Rand McNally, 1974), pp. 209–232; Board of Directors, National Council on Crime and Delinquency, "Drug Addiction: A Medical, Not a Law Enforcement Problem," *Crime and Delinquency* 20 (1974): 4–9.

106. Associated Press, "Records Detail Royals' Turn-of-Century Drug Use," *Boston Globe*, August 29, 1993, p. 13.

107. See Edward Brecher, *Licit and Illicit Drugs* (Boston: Little, Brown, 1972).

108. James Inciardi, *Reflections on Crime* (New York: Holt, Rinehart and Winston, 1978), pp. 8–10; see also A. Greeley, William McCready, and Gary Theisen, *Ethnic Drinking Subcultures* (New York: Praeger, 1980).

109. Joseph Gusfield, *Symbolic Crusade* (Urbana: University of Illinois Press, 1963), Ch. 3.

110. McCaghy, *Deviant Behavior*, p. 280.

111. Ibid.

112. Substance Abuse and Mental Health Services Administration (SAMHSA), "Key Substance Use and Mental Health Indicators in the United States: Results from the 2015 National Survey on Drug Use and Health, 2016."

113. Arthur Hughes, Matthew R. Williams, Rachel N. Lipari, and Struther Van Horn, "State Estimates of Past Year Cocaine Use Among Young Adults: 2014 and 2015," December 20, 2016, https://www.ncbi.nlm.nih.gov/books/NBK424783/.

114. Rachel N. Lipari, Arthur Hughes, and Jonaki Bose, "Driving Under the Influence of Alcohol and Illicit Drugs," December 27, 2016, https://www.ncbi.nlm.nih.gov/books/NBK424784/.

115. C. Bowden, "Determinants of Initial Use of Opioids," *Comprehensive Psychiatry* 12 (1971): 136–140.

116. Marvin Krohn, Alan Lizotte, Terence Thornberry, Carolyn Smith, and David McDowall, "Reciprocal Causal Relationships Among Drug Use, Peers, and Beliefs: A Five-Wave Panel Model," *Journal of Drug Issues* 26 (1996): 205–228.

117. R. Cloward and L. Ohlin, *Delinquency and Opportunity: A Theory of Delinquent Gangs* (Glencoe, IL: Free Press, 1960).

118. Lening Zhang, John Welte, and William Wieczorek, "Youth Gangs, Drug Use and Delinquency," *Journal of Criminal Justice* 27 (1999): 101–109.

119. Peter Giancola, "Constructive Thinking, Antisocial Behavior, and Drug Use in Adolescent Boys With and Without a Family History of a Substance Use Disorder," *Personality and Individual Differences* 35 (2003): 1315–1331.

120. Amy Young, Carol Boyd, and Amy Hubbell, "Social Isolation and Sexual Abuse Among Women Who Smoke Crack," *Journal of Psychosocial Nursing* 39 (2001): 16–19.

121. Substance Abuse and Mental Health Services Administration, Office of Applied Studies, "The Relationship between Mental Health and Substance Abuse among Adolescents," Analytic Series: A-9, 1999.

122. Alan Carr, Barbara Dooley, Mark Fitzpatrick, Edel Flanagan, Roisin Flanagan-Howard, Kevin Tierney, Megan White, Margaret Daly, and Jonathan Egan, "Adult Adjustment of Survivors of Institutional Child Abuse in Ireland," *Child Abuse and Neglect* 34 (2010): 477–489.

123. Daniel Smith, Joanne Davis, and Adrienne Fricker-Elhai, "How Does Trauma Beget Trauma? Cognitions About Risk in Women with Abuse Histories," *Child Maltreatment* 9 (2004): 292–302.

124. Sean Kidd, "The Walls Were Closing in, and We Were Trapped," *Youth and Society* 36 (2004): 30–55.

125. David Black, Steve Sussman, Jennifer Unger, Pallay Pokhrel, and Ping Sun, "Gender Differences in Body Consciousness and Substance Use Among High-Risk Adolescents," *Substance Use and Misuse* 45 (2010): 1623–1635.

126. Sung Joon Jang, Todd Ferguson, and Jeremy R. Rhodes, "Does Alcohol or Delinquency Help Adolescents Feel Better over Time? A Study on the Influence of Heavy Drinking and Violent/Property Offending on Negative Emotions," *International Journal of Offender Therapy and Comparative Criminology*, first published online December 2014.

127. D. W. Goodwin, "Alcoholism and Genetics," *Archives of General Psychiatry* 42 (1985): 171–174.

128. For a thorough review of this issue, see John Petraitis, Brian Flay, and Todd Miller, "Reviewing Theories of Adolescent Substance Use: Organizing Pieces in the Puzzle," *Psychological Bulletin* 117 (1995): 67–86.

129. Judith Brook and Li-Jung Tseng, "Influences of Parental Drug Use, Personality, and Child Rearing on the Toddler's Anger and Negativity," *Genetic, Social and General Psychology Monographs* 122 (1996): 107–128.

130. Thomas Ashby Wills, Donato Vaccaro, Grace McNamara, and A. Elizabeth Hirky, "Escalated Substance Use: A Longitudinal Grouping Analysis from Early to Middle Adolescence," *Journal of Abnormal Psychology* 105 (1996): 166–180.

131. Denise Kandel and Mark Davies, "Friendship Networks, Intimacy, and Illicit Drug Use in Young

Adulthood: A Comparison of Two Competing Theories," *Criminology* 29 (1991): 441–471.

132. J. S. Mio, G. Nanjundappa, D. E. Verlur, and M. D. DeRios, "Drug Abuse and the Adolescent Sex Offender: A Preliminary Analysis," *Journal of Psychoactive Drugs* 18 (1986): 65–72.

133. D. Baer and J. Corrado, "Heroin Addict Relationships with Parents During Childhood and Early Adolescent Years," *Journal of Genetic Psychology* 124 (1974): 99–103.

134. The National Center on Addiction and Substance Abuse, "Reducing Teen Smoking Can Cut Marijuana Use Significantly," September 16, 2003.

135. Chie Noyori-Corbett and Sung Seek Moon, "Multifaceted Reality of Juvenile Delinquency: An Empirical Analysis of Structural Theories and Literature," *Child and Adolescent Social Work Journal* 27 (2010): 245–268.

136. John Wallace and Jerald Bachman, "Explaining Racial/Ethnic Differences in Adolescent Drug Use: The Impact of Background and Lifestyle," *Social Problems* 38 (1991): 333–357.

137. John Donovan, "Problem-Behavior Theory and the Explanation of Adolescent Marijuana Use," *Journal of Drug Issues* 26 (1996): 379–404.

138. Michael Hallstone, "Types of Crimes Committed by Repeat DUI Offenders," *Criminal Justice Studies* 27 (2014): 159–171.

139. A. Christiansen, G. T. Smith, P. V. Roehling, and M. S. Goldman, "Using Alcohol Expectancies to Predict Adolescent Drinking Behavior After One Year," *Journal of Counseling and Clinical Psychology* 57 (1989): 93–99.

140. Judith Brook, Martin Whiteman, Elinor Balka, and Beatrix Hamburg, "African-American and Puerto Rican Drug Use: Personality, Familial, and Other Environmental Risk Factors," *Genetic, Social, and General Psychology Monographs* 118 (1992): 419–438.

141. Bu Huang, Helene Raskin White, Rick Kosterman, Richard Catalano, and J. David Hawkins, "Developmental Associations Between Alcohol and Interpersonal Aggression During Adolescence," *Journal of Research in Crime and Delinquency* 38 (2001): 64–83.

142. Andrew Golub and Bruce D. Johnson, *The Rise of Marijuana as the Drug of Choice Among Youthful Adult Arrestees* (Washington, DC: National Institute of Justice, 2001).

143. Cesar Rebellon and Karen Van Gundy, "Can Social Psychological Delinquency Theory Explain the Link Between Marijuana and Other Illicit Drug Use? A Longitudinal Analysis of the Gateway Hypothesis," *Journal of Drug Issues* 36 (2006): 515–540.

144. Denise Gottfredson, Brook Kearley, and Shawn Bushway, "Substance Use, Drug Treatment,

and Crime: An Examination of Intra-Individual Variation in a Drug Court Population," *Journal of Drug Issues* 38 (2008): 601–630.

145. Data in this section come from NCADD, National Council on Alcoholism and Drug Dependence, Inc., "Alcohol, Drugs and Crime," 2017, https://www .ncadd.org/about-addiction/alcohol-drugs-and-crime.

146. Office of National Drug Control Policy, "Fact Sheet: The 2013 Arrestee Drug Abuse Monitoring Program II," May 12, 2014, https://obamawhitehouse .archives.gov/sites/default/files/ondcp/Fact_Sheets /adamfactsheet.pdf.

147. Ibid.

148. National Center on Addiction and Substance Abuse, "Behind Bars II: Substance Abuse and America's Prison Population, 2010," https://www .centeronaddiction.org/addiction-research /reports/behind-bars-ii-substance-abuse-and -america%E2%80%99s-prison-population.

149. Benjamin R. Nordstrom and Charles A. Dackis, "Drugs and Crime," *Journal of Psychiatry and Law* 39 (2011): 663–668.

150. See Kenneth Jones, Louis Shainberg, and Carter Byer, *Drugs and Alcohol* (New York: Harper & Row, 1979), pp. 137–146.

151. Controlled Substance Act, 21 U.S.C. 848 (1984).

152. Anti-Drug Abuse Act of 1986, Pub. L. No. 99-570, U.S.C. 841 (1986).

153. Anti-Drug Abuse Act of 1988, Pub. L. No. 100-690; 21 U.S.C. 1501; Subtitle A–Death Penalty, Sec. 7001, Amending the Controlled Substances Abuse Act, 21 U.S.C. 848.

154. Eric Jensen, Jurg Gerber, and Ginna Babcock, "The New War on Drugs: Grass Roots Movement or Political Construction?" *Journal of Drug Issues* 21 (1991): 651–667.

155. "The 2012 National Drug Control Strategy: Building on a Record of Reform," https://obamawhitehouse .archives.gov/sites/default/files/ondcp/list_of _actions.pdf.

156. United Nations Office on Drugs and Crime, *World Drug Report*, 2015, http://www.unodc.org/doc /wdr2016/WDR_2016_ExSum_english.pdf.

157. Mark Moore, *Drug Trafficking* (Washington, DC: National Institute of Justice, 1988).

158. Peter Rossi, Richard Berk, and Alec Campbell, "Just Punishments: Guideline Sentences and Normative Consensus," *Journal of Quantitative Criminology* 13 (1997): 267–283.

159. Robert Davis, Arthur Lurigio, and Dennis Rosenbaum, eds., *Drugs and the Community* (Springfield, IL: Charles C Thomas, 1993), pp. xii–xv.

160. Saul Weingart, "A Typology of Community Responses to Drugs," in *Drugs and the Community*, ed. Robert C. Davis, Arthur J. Lurigio, and Dennis P. Rosenbaum (Springfield, IL: C. C. Thomas, 1993), pp. 85–105.

161. Dennis Rosenbaum, Robert Flewelling, Susan Bailey, Chris Ringwalt, and Deanna Wilkinson, "Cops in the Classroom: A Longitudinal Evaluation of Drug Abuse Resistance Education (D.A.R.E.)," *Journal of Research in Crime and Delinquency* 31 (1994): 3–31. Donald R. Lynam, Rich Milich, Rick Zimmerman, Scott Novak, T. K. Logan, Catherine Martin, Carl Leukefeld, and Richard Clayton, "Project D.A.R.E.: No Effects at 10-Year Follow-Up," *Journal of Consulting and Clinical Psychology* 67 (1999): 590–593.

162. Mareanne Zawitz, Drugs, *Crime, and the Justice System* (Washington, DC: US Government Printing Office, 1992), pp. 115–122.

163. John Goldkamp and Peter Jones, "Pretrial Drug-Testing Experiments in Milwaukee and Prince George's County: The Context of Implementation," *Journal of Research in Crime and Delinquency* 29 (1992): 430–465; Chester Britt, Michael Gottfredson, and John Goldkamp, "Drug Testing and Pretrial Misconduct: An Experiment on the Specific Deterrent Effects of Drug Monitoring Defendants on Pretrial Release," *Journal of Research in Crime and Delinquency* 29 (1992): 62–78. See, generally, Peter Greenwood and Franklin Zimring, *One More Chance* (Santa Monica, CA: Rand Corporation, 1985).

164. National Drug Court Resource Center, http://www.ndcrc.org/.

165. Katherine Theall, Kirk Elifson, Claire Sterk, and Eric Stewart, "Criminality Among Female Drug Users Following an HIV Risk-Reduction Intervention," *Journal of Interpersonal Violence* 22 (2007): 85–107.

166. See, generally, Peter Greenwood and Franklin Zimring, *One More Chance* (Santa Monica, CA: Rand Corporation, 1985).

167. Daniel Rosen, Jennifer Q. Morse, and Charles F. Reynolds, "Adapting Problem-Solving Therapy for Depressed Older Adults in Methadone Maintenance Treatment," *Journal of Substance Abuse Treatment* 40 (2011): 132–141.

168. Audrey Hickert and Mary Jane Taylor, "Supportive Housing for Addicted, Incarcerated Homeless Adults," *Journal of Social Service Research* 37 (2011): 136–151.

169. George De Leon, Stanley Sacks, Graham Staines, and Karen McKendrick, "Modified Therapeutic Community for Homeless Mentally Ill Chemical Abusers: Treatment Outcomes," *American Journal of Drug and Alcohol Abuse* 26 (2000): 461–480.

170. Office of Drug Control Strategy, "The National Drug Control Strategy: A 21st Century Approach to Drug Policy," July 2014, https://csgjusticecenter.org/substance-abuse/publications/the-national-drug-control-strategy-a-21st-century-approach-to-drug-policy/.

171. The following section is based on material found in Jerome Platt, "Vocational Rehabilitation of Drug Abusers," *Psychological Bulletin* 117 (1995): 416–433.

172. Policy Statement, Drug Policy Alliance, 2015, http://www.drugpolicy.org/new-solutions-drug-policy.

173. Drug War Facts, "Economics," 2017, http://drugwarfacts.org/chapter/economics.

174. Alan Rappeport, "White House Proposes Cutting Drug Control Office Funding by 95%," *New York Times*, May 5, 2017, https://www.nytimes.com/2017/05/05/us/politics/white-house-proposes-cutting-drug-control-office-funding-by-95.html.

175. Ethan Nadelmann, "The U.S. Is Addicted to War on Drugs," *Globe and Mail*, May 20, 2003, p. 1.

176. United Nations Office on Drugs and Crime, *World Drug Report*, 2016, http://www.unodc.org/wdr2016/.

177. Karin A. Mack, "Drug-Induced Deaths, United States, 1999–2010," National Center for Injury Prevention and Control, CDC, November 22, 2013, http://www.cdc.gov/mmwr/preview/mmwrhtml/su6203a27.htm.

Crimes of the New Millennium: Cybercrime and Transnational Organized Crime

Learning Objectives

LO1 Trace the evolution of cybercrime.

LO2 Compare and contrast cybertheft, cybervandalism, and cyberwar.

LO3 Evaluate how the Internet can facilitate the sale of illegal materials.

LO4 Discuss efforts to control cybercrime.

LO5 Describe the evolution of organized crime.

LO6 List the activities of transnational organized crime.

Sounds like I haven't been forgiven by her. So I'm done being nice.. Going back to how I was before. What's the final answer??? Before I do the unthinkable. How are y'all nasty hoes doing? Been thinking [of] passing by magnolia towers to confront her boss about it. It's unethical to have a disgusting 'social worker' working there.

14

Chapter Outline

FACT OR FICTION?

▶ The next war may be conducted in cyberspace.

▶ Organized crime in the United States is still a local commodity, controlled by five Mafia families in New York City and a few other allied groups in Chicago, Los Angeles, and Miami.

On August 31, 2016, Kassandra Cruz, a 23-year-old Miami woman, was sentenced to 22 months in prison, three years of supervised release, a $100 special assessment, and $2,178.32 in restitution. Cruz had been convicted of cyberstalking, a violation of Title 18, United States Code, Section 2261(A)(2)(B). What did she do to deserve her prison sentence? Cruz was completing her criminal justice degree at Florida International University and while cruising the Net became fixated on a woman, "S.B.," whom she found on a pornography website. She tracked down the actress through her social media accounts. It turns out that when S.B. was an 18-year-old high school student she made a bad decision by appearing in an adult film, a mistake she had kept hidden from family and friends for 15 years.

In June 2015, S.B. received friend requests from Cruz on her Instagram and Facebook accounts. In an effort to gain S.B.'s friendship, Cruz created a false persona on her Instagram account, portraying herself as a US Marine named Giovanni. Under that ruse, S.B. accepted the friend request. Cruz, posing as Giovanni, "liked" and commented on pictures S.B. posted on her accounts. However, when S.B. noticed that Cruz had begun following and liking all of her friends' pages and posts, she became suspicious and blocked and "unfollowed" Cruz on her social media accounts.

Infuriated at the rejection, Cruz threatened S.B., saying she would expose her past to family, friends, and employers unless she was paid $100,000 in exchange for her silence. Cruz continually harassed S.B., sending more than 900 unwanted calls and text messages, including threats to her family. The messages continued until Cruz was arrested and taken into custody during an arranged meeting in Miami.[1] ∎

cybercrime
The use of modern technology for criminal purposes.

cybertheft
Use of computer networks for criminal profits. Illegal copyright infringement, identity theft, and Internet securities fraud are examples of cybertheft.

cybervandalism
Malicious attacks aimed at disrupting, defacing, and destroying technology.

cyberwar
Using cyberspace for acts of war, including spying and disrupting an enemy's computer network.

cyberterrorism
Internet attacks against an enemy nation's technological infrastructure.

Just a few years ago, such a complex Internet extortion scheme could not have been contemplated, let alone transacted. Innovation brings change and with it new opportunities to commit crime.

The technological revolution has provided new tools to misappropriate funds, damage property, sell illicit material, or conduct warfare, espionage, and terror. It has created **cybercrime**, a new breed of offenses that can be singular or ongoing, but typically involve the theft and/or destruction of information, resources, or funds utilizing computers, computer networks, and the Internet. In addition, the IT revolution has allowed criminal organizations that were originally local in scope and activity to extend their operations from coast to coast and across international borders, hence the term *transnational organized crime*. Integrating IT into their plans, they are able to carry out criminal schemes on a global basis.

This new array of crimes presents a compelling challenge because (a) it is rapidly evolving, with new schemes being created daily, (b) it is difficult to detect through traditional law enforcement channels, and (c) its control demands that agents of the justice system develop technical skills that match those of the perpetrators. These crimes are vast in scope and place a heavy burden on society.

While there is no entirely accurate measure of cybercrime, there is little doubt the offenses number in the millions. Take for instance what is happening in the UK. After years of decline, the crime rate in England and Wales doubled in 2015 when cybercrime began to be included in the official count. While common-law crimes declined, the overall crime rate increased because 7.5 million cybercrimes are now included in the tally.[2] England and Wales have a population of about 56 million people; the US population is closer to 320 million. If the Internet crime ratio is the same, then US citizens may now be victimized by more than 40 million cybercrime incidents each year.

Considering the explosion in Internet misconduct it is possible that the two-decade crime drop in America may in fact be a function of people switching from common-law crime to cybercrime.[3] Rather than shoplift from a department store and risk getting caught by security guards, offenders may take the safer route of engaging in online etailing fraud. Rather than walking the streets, sex workers can advertise their services online and even vet customers via Internet apps designed to weed out sketchy clients. It is not surprising, then, that cybercrime is a growth industry in which the returns are great and the risks are low. MacAfee, an Internet security company, estimates that a conservative estimate of the annual cost to the global economy from cybercrime is more than $400 billion, and losses may actually reach $575 billion. This is more than the national income of most countries and governments.[4]

In this chapter, we will first review the types of and trends in cybercrime. Then attention will be turned to transnational organized crime and how the Internet has influenced global crime organizations.

Contemporary Cybercrime

There are actually three general forms of cybercrime:

- Some cybercriminals use modern technology to accumulate goods and services. **Cybertheft** schemes range from illegally copying material under copyright protection to using technology to commit traditional theft-based offenses such as larceny and fraud.
- Other cybercriminals are motivated less by profit and more by the urge to commit **cybervandalism**, or technological destruction. They aim their malicious attacks at disrupting, defacing, and destroying online resources they find offensive.
- A third type of cybercrime is **cyberwar** or **cyberterrorism**, which consists of acts aimed at undermining the social, economic, and political system of an enemy nation. This can range from stealing secrets from foreign nations to destroying an enemy's Web-based infrastructure.

These three main types of cybercrime (outlined in Concept Summary 14.1) are discussed in detail in the following sections.

Concept Summary 14.1 Types of Cybercrime

Crime	Definition	Examples
Cybertheft	Use of cyberspace to distribute illegal goods and services or to defraud people for quick profits	Illegal copyright infringement, identity theft, Internet securities fraud, warez
Cybervandalism	Use of cyberspace for revenge, destruction, and to achieve a malicious intent	Website defacement, worms, viruses, cyberstalking, cyberbullying
Cyberwar	An effort by enemy forces to disrupt the intersection where the virtual electronic reality of computers meets the physical world	Logic bombs used to disrupt or destroy "secure" systems or networks, Internet used to communicate covertly with agents around the world

Cybertheft: Cybercrimes for Profit

The Internet can serve as a tool to facilitate illegal activity. Cybercriminals can "meet" their victims in social networking sites and forums, where they can find suitable co-offenders or get into contact with enablers.[5] Computer-based technology allows criminals to operate in a more efficient and effective manner. Cyberthieves now have the luxury of remaining anonymous, living in any part of the world, conducting their business during the day or at night, working alone or in a group, while at the same time reaching a much larger number of potential victims than ever before. No longer is the con artist or criminal entrepreneur limited to fleecing victims in a particular geographic locale; the whole world can be his or her target.

Cyberthieves target both individuals and corporations. To handle civilian complaints, the FBI created the Internet Crime Complaint Center (IC3) in 2000 to receive reports of Internet crime.[6] The IC3 now receives an average of 300,000 complaints per year from US citizens. Cyberthieves also target business enterprise (see Exhibit 14.1 for some examples). A recent (2016) global survey of industry leaders found that about one-quarter had been affected by computer-based attacks on business enterprise in the prior year; attacks are so stealthy that almost 20 percent of the CEOs were not sure if they had been attacked. Internal attacks are now outgrowing external attacks at the world's largest financial institutions. About 60 percent of US companies report being hit by computer network attacks each year. Losses can be heavy: about 50 organizations had suffered losses over $5 million; of these, nearly a third reported computer crime–related losses in excess of $100 million.

In the following sections, the most common forms of cybertheft that target both individuals and organizations are set out in some detail.

Theft from ATMs

Automatic teller machines (ATMs) attract the attention of cybercriminals looking for easy profits.[7] Rather than robbing an ATM user at gunpoint, the cybercriminal relies on stealth and technological skill to commit the crime. Take for instance the case of two brothers from Bulgaria who were charged with attempting to defraud two banks of more than $1 million by engaging in **ATM skimming**: placing an electronic device on an ATM that scoops information from a bank card's magnetic strip whenever a customer uses the machine. Skimmers can then create their own bank cards and steal from customer accounts.[8] ATM skimming now costs US banks hundreds of millions of dollars annually.

ATM skimming
Using an electronic device or camera on an ATM that copies information from a bank card's magnetic strip whenever a customer uses the machine or photographs their key strokes.

Exhibit 14.1   Examples of Cybertheft

- *Theft of information.* The unauthorized obtaining of information from a computer (hacking), including software that is copied for profit.
- *The "salami" slice.* With this type of fraud, the perpetrator carefully skims small sums from the balances of a large number of accounts in order to bypass internal controls and escape detection.
- *Software theft.* The comparative ease of making copies of computer software has led to a huge illegal market, depriving authors of very significant revenues.
- *Manipulation of accounts/banking systems.* Similar to a "salami" slice but on a much larger and usually more complex scale. Sometimes perpetrated as a "one-off kamikaze" fraud.
- *Corporate espionage.* Trade secrets are stolen by a company's competitors, which can be either

domestic or foreign. The goal is to increase the rival company's (or nation's) competitive edge in the global marketplace. Such companies as Anthem Health Care, Primera Blue Cross, Staples, and Home Depot have had their computer systems hacked and the names, Social Security numbers, birthdays, addresses, emails, employment information, and income data of current and former customers and employees stolen.

Sources: Australian Institute of Criminology, "9 Types of Cyber Crime," http://www.crime.hku.hk/cybercrime.htm; Cross Domain Solutions, "Cyber Crime," http://www.crossdomainsolutions.com/cyber-crime/; Kevin Granville, "9 Recent Cyberattacks Against Big Businesses," *New York Times*, February 5, 2015, http://www.nytimes.com/interactive/2015/02/05/technology/recent-cyberattacks.html (URLs accessed June 2017).

The devices planted on ATMs are usually undetectable because they blend right into the ATM's physical structure. Some cybercriminals attach a phony keypad on top of the real keypad which records every keystroke as customers punch in their PINs. These skimming devices are installed for short periods of time—usually just a few hours—so they're often attached to an ATM by nothing more than double-sided tape. They are then removed by the criminals, who download the stolen account information and encode it onto blank cards. The cards are used to make withdrawals from victims' accounts at other ATMs. Some cyberthieves use a realistic-looking card reader placed over the factory-installed card reader. When customers insert their ATM card into the phony reader, their account info is swiped and sent wirelessly to the criminals waiting nearby. Skimmers can also make use of a hidden camera, installed on or near an ATM, to record customers' entry of their PINs into the ATM's keypad.

Distributing Illicit or Illegal Services and Material

LO3 Evaluate how the Internet can facilitate the sale of illegal materials.

The Internet has become a prime source for the delivery of illicit or legally prohibited material. Included within this market are distribution of pornography and obscene material, including kiddie porn, and the distribution of dangerous drugs.

DISTRIBUTING OBSCENITY The IT revolution has revitalized the porn industry. The Internet is an ideal venue for selling and distributing obscene material; the computer is an ideal device for storage and viewing. It is difficult to estimate the vast number of websites featuring sexual content, including nude photos, videos, live sex acts, and webcam strip sessions among other forms of "adult entertainment."[9] Adult content is so pervasive and easily obtained that it has driven many "adult magazines" out of business; in 2015 *Playboy* announced it would no longer feature nudity in the magazine, finding it impossible to compete with what is on the Internet (a year later the magazine reneged on its pledge and brought nudity back).[10]

There is no conclusive data on the extent of Internet porn sites. Some estimates insist that about 5 percent of the top million websites, more than 40,000, are sex related and about 15 percent of all searches are for adult content.[11] That would mean that adult sites get billions of hits each year. LiveJasmin.com, a webcam site gets around 32 million visitors a month, or almost 2.5 percent of all Internet users.[12] But these data may undercount the actual number of adult sites: a search in Google on the word "porn" returned over 165 million pages, and "xxx" returned more than 370 million pages. People are often directed to these sites through "porn-napping" and "typosquatted" websites. Porn-nappers buy expired domain names of existing sites and then try to sell adult material to people who stumble on them while web surfing. Typosquat websites are those where a pornographer has deliberately registered names with typos so that people surfing the Net are directed to pornography sites if they mis-spell a word or put in the wrong keystroke—for example, typing in teltubbies.com instead of teletubbies.com.[13] There are also people who access the **darknet** to trade in kiddie porn—searches that do not show up in efforts to count visits to porn sites.

How do adult sites operate today? There are a number of different schemes in operation:[14]

- A large firm sells annual subscriptions in exchange for unlimited access to content.
- Password services charge an annual fee to deliver access to hundreds of small sites, which share the subscription revenues.
- Large firms provide free content to smaller affiliate sites. The affiliates post the free content and then try to channel visitors to the large sites, which give the smaller sites a percentage of the fees paid by those who sign up.
- Webmasters forward traffic to another porn site in return for a small per-consumer fee. In many cases, the consumer is sent to the other sites involuntarily, which is known in the industry as *mousetrapping*. Web surfers who try to close out a window after visiting an adult site are sent to another web page automatically. This can repeat dozens of times, causing users to panic and restart their computers in order to escape.
- Adult sites cater to niche audiences looking for specific kinds of adult content. While some sites cater to legal sexually related material, others cross the legal border by peddling access to obscene material or even kiddie porn.

> **darknet**
> Computer network that can only be accessed using nonstandard communications protocols and ports, with restricted access that can only be opened with specific software configurations.

PROSECUTING INTERNET PORNOGRAPHY Despite some successful prosecutions, it has been difficult to control Internet pornography and prosecutions for adult sites are extremely rate. One reason is that offenders can be scattered around the world, making identification and arrest difficult. There needs to be significant law enforcement agency cooperation to gather evidence and locate suspects. When there are prosecutions, they are aimed at kiddie porn such as the Lost Boy case, set out in the Profiles in Crime feature, which resulted in lengthy prison sentences for the principals involved.

Distributing Dangerous Drugs

The Internet has become a prime purveyor of prescription drugs, some of which can be quite dangerous when they are used to excess or fall into the hands of minors. Many websites advertising or selling controlled prescription drugs such as OxyContin, Valium, Xanax, Vicodin, Ritalin, and Adderall do not require a prescription, and few are certified by the National Association of Boards of Pharmacy as Verified Internet Pharmacy Practice Sites.[15] Relatively few require that the patient provide a prescrip-tion from his or her doctor, and of those that do, only about half require that an origi-nal prescription be provided. This allows prescriptions to be faxed, giving buyers the opportunity for multiple purchases with a single script. Other sites sell online "medi-cal consultations," where doctors see many patients a day to fill or refill prescrip-tions for controlled drugs without regard for the standards of medical practice. Some sites, such as the infamous and now shut down "Silk Road," are designed to enable its users to buy, trade, and sell illegal drugs and other unlawful goods and services anonymously and beyond the reach of law enforcement.

PROFILES IN CRIME

THE LOST BOY CASE

The Lost Boy online bulletin board was established to provide a forum for men who had a sexual interest in young boys to trade child pornography. Law enforcement authorities in the United States and abroad first became aware of the network when Norwegian and Italian authorities discovered that a North Hollywood, California, man was communicating via an Internet site with an Italian national about child pornography and how to engage in child sex tourism in Romania. Further investigation revealed that Lost Boy had 35 members; more than half were US nationals. Other members of the network were located in countries around the world, including Belgium, Brazil, Canada, France, Germany, New Zealand, and the United Kingdom.

At the time, the Lost Boy indictment was the largest-ever child exploitation enterprise investigation since the signing of the Walsh Act. Because of the sentencing enhancements, some of those prosecuted in the Lost Boy case received sentences of between 20 and 35 years in prison. One man, Jeffrey Greenwell, who produced pornographic images and videos that appeared on the Lost Boy online bulletin board, pleaded guilty to five counts of production of child pornography and was sentenced to a total of 100 years in prison. Since the Lost Boy case was prosecuted, Operation Delego, conducted by the Justice Department and the Department of Homeland Security, resulted in the indictment of 72 defendants for their participation in Dreamboard—a private, members-only, online bulletin board created to promote pedophilia.

To shield themselves from prosecution, the Lost Boy network had developed a thorough vetting process for new members to weed out law enforcement agents. Members were required to post child pornography in order to join the organization and to continue posting child pornography to remain in good standing. Lost Boy members advised one another on techniques to evade detection by law enforcement, which included using screen names to mask identities and encrypting computer data.

As the investigation unfolded, law enforcement agencies identified child molestation suspects in South America, Europe, and New Zealand. Suspects in Romania, France, Brazil, Norway, and the United Kingdom were charged and convicted, receiving long prison sentences. In the United States, offenders were prosecuted under the Adam Walsh Child Protection and Safety Act, a 2006 law with a three-tier system of categorizing sex offenders, mandated lifetime sex offender registration for tier one offenders, and increased penalties. It also allows judges to levy heavier sentences on child molesters who are engaged in cooperative, sustained criminal efforts with others, such as running the Lost Boy network. Fifteen US Lost Boy defendants have been convicted, one died in custody, and three remain at large. All told, the authorities identified 200 victims as a result of the investigation.

The Lost Boy case illustrates the difficulty of controlling Internet pornography. Getting evidence sufficient for prosecution involved the cooperation of law enforcement agencies around the world and the arrests of people in multiple countries, a very expensive and time-consuming activity. ■

Sources: Text of the Adam Walsh Child Protection and Safety Act of 2006, http://www.govtrack.us/congress/bills/109/hr4472/text; US Department of Justice, "Ohio Man Sentenced to 35 Years in Prison for His Participation in an Online Child Pornography Bulletin Board," http://www.fbi.gov/losangeles/press-releases/2012/ohio-man-sentenced-to-35-years-in-prison-for-his-participation-in-an-online-child-pornography-bulletin-board (URLs accessed June 2017).

Children are especially at risk, and more than 2 million kids are feared to be abusing an illegally obtained prescription drug. More teens have abused these drugs than many other illegal drugs, including Ecstasy, cocaine, crack, and methamphetamine. With access to a credit card, they can order opioid-based drugs (e.g., codeine, Demerol, OxyContin, Percocet, and Darvon), depressants (e.g., Xanax, Librium, and Valium), and stimulants (e.g., Adderall, Dexedrine, and Ritalin).

Denial-of-Service Attack

In 2013, David Rezendes was sentenced to serve 18 months in federal prison for intentionally damaging a protected computer. What did he do to deserve such a sentence? Rezendes was responsible for a denial-of-service attack he implemented to retaliate against the Larimer County (Colorado) government. During the attack, he saturated the county computer system with such an overwhelming amount of traffic and communications requests that Larimer County employees were unable to access email and county records; the public's ability to access county services online was also diminished. What motivated the attack? Rezendes was angry about a traffic ticket![16]

Used to harass or extort money from owners of an Internet site, a **denial-of-service attack (DoS)** involves threats or attacks designed to prevent the legitimate operation of the site. In some cases, such as the Rezendes attack, there is no monetary objective and the attack is a type of cybervandalism. In 2015, an attack against Rutgers University interrupted Internet service for students, faculty, and staff; another attack knocked out all of New York City's email accounts.[17]

denial-of-service attack (DoS)
Extorting money from an Internet service user by threatening to prevent the user from having access to the service.

While Rezendes's denial-of-service attack was motivated by anger and vengeance, other offenders are out for profit; these cybercriminals threaten to or actually flood an Internet site with millions of bogus messages or orders so that the services will be tied up and unable to perform as promised unless the site operator pays extortion. The attackers threaten to keep up the interference until real consumers become frustrated and abandon the site. Even so-called respectable businesspeople have been accused of launching denial-of-service attacks against rival business interests.[18]

Online gambling casinos—a multibillion a year industry—have proven particularly vulnerable to attack. Hundreds of attacks have been launched against online casinos located in Costa Rica, the Caribbean, and Great Britain. If the attack coincides with a big sporting event such as the Super Bowl, the casinos may give in and make payments rather than lose revenue and fray customer relations.[19] Another vulnerable target is online gaming sites. Massive attacks have disrupted service on games such as Blizzard's Battle.net, Riot Games's League of Legends, and the Origin service run by Electronic Arts.[20]

Internet Extortion/Ransomware

In 2017, computers around the nation were attacked by WannaCry, a form of ransomware, malicious software that typically installs itself when users go to a compromised website or open an infected email. Once loaded, the ransomware virus immediately locks the device, preventing its use. The screen is fixed with a pop-up message—supposedly from the FBI or another federal agency—saying that the user has violated some sort of federal law and the computer will remain locked until the victim pays a fine. There may also be a pop-up message saying that personal files have been encrypted and demanding payment to release the decryption codes. The extortionists demand anywhere from hundreds to thousands of dollars to release their hold on the computer. The victim is instructed to pay a ransom in order to get the key to unlock the computer. Unfortunately for victims, the virus is difficult to resolve and may require professional attention. Even if victims are able to unfreeze their computer, the malware may still operate in the background and gather personal information such as usernames, passwords, and credit card numbers through embedded keystroke logging programs.

The 2017 WannaCry attack infected 200,000 computers in more than 150 countries. In this case victims did not have to go to suspect websites or open a corrupted email. Instead, hackers discovered a flaw in Microsoft's Windows operating system that was first uncovered by the US National Security Agency. When computers were turned on, operators were confronted with a message that read, "Oops, your files have been encrypted!" and demanded $300 in Bitcoins to restore access. While some of the earlier ransomware scams involved having victims pay the ransom with prepaid credit cards, victims are now increasingly asked to pay with Bitcoin, a decentralized virtual currency network that attracts criminals because of the anonymity the system offers. There is evidence that the scheme netted the attackers more than $1 billion as victims—which included FedEx, Britain's National Health Service, and the Russian Interior Ministry—paid up to unlock their machines. In the aftermath of the attack, Microsoft created a new patch for its Windows software to prevent similar events.[21]

A ransomware variant called CryptoWall encrypts files on a computer's hard drive and any external or shared drives to which the computer has access. It directs the user to a personalized victim ransom page that contains the initial ransom amount (anywhere from $200 to $5,000), detailed instructions about how to purchase Bitcoins, and typically a countdown clock to notify victims how much time they have before the ransom doubles. Victims are infected with CryptoWall by clicking on links in emails that appear to be from legitimate businesses and through compromised advertisements on popular websites. Recovery can be a difficult process that may require the services of a specialist.[22]

warez
A term computer hackers and software pirates use to describe a game or application that is made available for use on the Internet in violation of its copyright protection.

Illegal copyright infringement is now a transnational crime. Here, a Chinese officer from the Shenzhen Market Supervision Administration is interviewed outside the office of Shenzhen QVOD Technology after delivering a written decision of administrative penalty to the company. China slapped the major online provider of pirated videos in the country with a 260 million yuan (US $42 million) fine. The Shenzhen Market Supervision Administration said that QVOD Technology had distributed a local movie and TV series online without the publishers' permission. The piracy amounted to 86 million yuan in illegal revenue. QVOD had not only repeatedly pirated the content but refused to stop its distribution after being caught. As a result, Chinese authorities levied a fine that was triple the amount of revenue QVOD made from the piracy. QVOD has been facing growing scrutiny from Chinese authorities. The company was found guilty of distributing pornography online and rose to notoriety after developing peer-to-peer video-sharing software called Kuaibo. The software became a popular way for bootleggers to distribute pirated movies and TV shows without paying expensive video bandwidth costs.

How common is the distribution of malware? Internet security firm Symantec discovered more than 430 million new unique pieces of malware in 2015, up 36 percent from the year before.[23]

Illegal Copyright Infringement

Groups of individuals have been working together to illegally obtain software and then "crack" or "rip" its copyright protections, before posting it on the Internet for other members of the group to use; this is called **warez**.

Frequently, these new pirated copies reach the Internet days or weeks before the legitimate product is commercially available. The government has actively pursued members of the warez community, and some have been charged and convicted under the Computer Fraud and Abuse Act (CFAA), which criminalizes accessing computer systems without authorization to obtain information,[24] and the Digital Millennium Copyright Act (DMCA), which makes it a crime to circumvent antipiracy measures built into most commercial software and also outlaws the manufacture, sale, or distribution of code-cracking devices used to illegally copy software.[25]

FILE SHARING Another form of illegal copyright infringement involves file-sharing programs that allow Internet users to download music and other copyrighted material without paying the artists and record producers their rightful royalties. Theft through the illegal reproduction and distribution of movies, software, games, and music is estimated to cost US industries more than $20 billion worldwide each year.

Although some students routinely share files and download music, criminal copyright infringement represents a serious economic threat. The United States Criminal Code provides penalties for a first-time offender of five years incarceration and a fine of $250,000.[26] Other provisions provide for the forfeiture and destruction of infringing copies and all equipment used to make the copies.[27]

On June 27, 2005, copyright protection of music and other types of entertainment distributed via the Internet was upheld by the Supreme Court in the case of *MGM Studios, Inc. v. Grokster*. The Court unanimously held that software distributors such as Grokster could be sued for inducing copyright infringement if they market file-sharing software that might induce people to illegally download copy-protected material even if that software could also be used for legitimate purposes. Justice David Souter wrote:

> We hold that one who distributes a device with the object of promoting its use to infringe copyright, as shown by the clear expression or other affirmative steps taken to foster infringement, is liable for the resulting acts of infringement by third parties.

As a result of the opinion, on November 7, 2005, Grokster announced that it would suspend its file-sharing service; it was also forced to pay $50 million to the music and recording industries.

Internet Securities Fraud

Internet security fraud schemes involve efforts to intentionally manipulate the stock market for profit. There are three major types of Internet securities fraud today:

- *Market manipulation.* Stock market manipulation occurs when an individual tries to control the price of stock by interfering with the natural forces of supply and demand. There are two principal forms of this crime: the "pump and dump" and the "cybersmear." In a pump and dump scheme, erroneous and deceptive information is posted online to get unsuspecting investors interested in a stock while those spreading the information sell previously purchased stock at an inflated price. The cybersmear is a reverse pump and dump: negative information is spread online about a stock, driving down its price and enabling people to buy it at an artificially low price before rebuttals by the company's officers reinflate the price.[28]
- *Fraudulent offerings of securities.* Some cybercriminals create websites specifically designed to fraudulently sell securities. To make the offerings look more attractive than they are, assets may be inflated, expected returns overstated, and risks understated. In these schemes, investors are promised abnormally high profits on their investments. No investment is actually made. Early investors are paid returns with the investment money received from the later investors. The system usually collapses, and the later investors do not receive dividends and lose their initial investment.
- *Illegal touting.* This crime occurs when individuals make securities recommendations and fail to disclose that they are being paid to disseminate their favorable opinions. Section 17(b) of the Securities Act of 1933 requires that paid touters disclose the nature, source, and amount of their compensation. If those who tout stocks fail to disclose their relationship with the company, information misleads investors into believing that the speaker is objective and credible rather than bought and paid for.

Identity Theft

Identity theft occurs when a person uses the Internet to steal someone's identity and/or impersonate the victim to open a new credit card account or conduct some other financial transaction. It is a type of cybercrime that has grown at surprising rates over the past few years.[29] It can also involve the misuse of personal information for other fraudulent purposes, such as obtaining government benefits or providing false information to police during a crime or traffic stop.[30]

identity theft
Using the Internet to steal someone's identity and/or impersonate the victim in order to conduct illicit transactions such as committing fraud using the victim's name and identity.

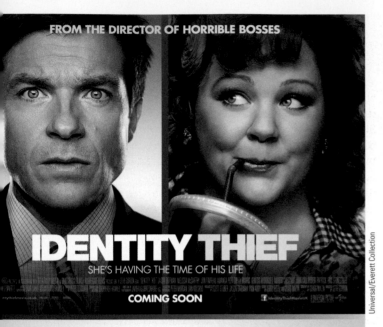

FROM THE DIRECTOR OF HORRIBLE BOSSES

IDENTITY THIEF

SHE'S HAVING THE TIME OF HIS LIFE

COMING SOON

Universal/Everett Collection

Identity theft has become so pervasive that it is now the fodder of films and books, including the hit 2013 movie *Identity Thief* with Jason Bateman and Melissa McCarthy.

phishing
Sometimes called carding or brand spoofing, phishing is a scam where the perpetrator sends out emails appearing to come from legitimate web enterprises such as eBay, Amazon, and PayPal in an effort to get the recipient to reveal personal and financial information.

spear-phishing
Targeting specific victims, sending them emails that contain accurate information about their lives obtained from social networking sites, and asking them to open an email attachment where malware harvests details such as the victims' usernames and passwords, bank account details, credit card numbers, and other personal information.

Identity theft can destroy a person's life by manipulating credit records or stealing from their bank accounts. Identity thieves use a variety of techniques to steal information. They may fill out change of address cards at the post office and obtain people's credit card bills and bank statements. They may then call the credit card issuer and, pretending to be the victim, ask for a change of address on the account. They can then charge numerous items over the Internet and have the merchandise sent to the new address. It may take months for the victim to realize the fraud because the victim is not getting bills from the credit card company.

What are the most common goals of credit card thieves? One survey found that opening new lines of credit remains the most frequently occurring use for a victim's identity, followed by using personal information to make charges on stolen credit cards and debit cards, obtaining utilities, applying for bogus personal loans and business loans, and check fraud (personal information is used to access an existing account via theft or the creation of false checks).[31]

PHISHING Some identity thieves create false emails or websites that look legitimate but are designed to gain illegal access to a victim's personal information; this is known as **phishing** (also known as *carding* and *spoofing*). At last count (2016), there were almost 290,000 unique phishing websites, a 250 percent increase in six months.[32]

There are numerous phishing scams. In one, called the account verification scam, perpetrators purchase domain names that are similar to those of legitimate companies, such as *Amazon.Accounts.net*. The real Amazon does not have *Accounts* in its domain name. These con artists then send out millions of emails asking consumers to verify their account information. By clicking the legitimate-looking address, victims are directed to a bogus website where they are informed that to fix a problem and update their account, they must submit their name, address, phone number, credit card account numbers, Social Security number, and other personal information.

In the infamous Nigerian letter scheme, victims receive a bogus email supposedly sent from an alleged representative of a foreign government asking the victim to help move money from one account to another. Some forms include requests to help a dying woman or free a political prisoner. Some claim that the victim has been the recipient of a legacy or a winning lottery ticket. Nigerian money offers now account for about 12 percent of the scam offers.[33]

Some phishing schemes involve job offers. Once the unsuspecting victims fill out the "application," answering personal questions and including their Social Security number, the phisher has them in his or her grasp. Another variation of this crime is **spear-phishing**, where cybercriminals target specific victims, sending them emails that contain accurate information about their lives, friends, and activities that was obtained from social networking sites, blogs, or other websites. Personal information makes the message seem legitimate and increases the chances the victims will open the email or go to a tainted website by clicking on a link where malware harvests details such as the victims' usernames and passwords, bank account details, credit card numbers, and other personal information. The criminals can also gain access to private networks and cause disruptions or steal intellectual property and trade secrets. One ingenious scam is referred to as *reshipping* and is discussed in Exhibit 14.2.

Once phishers have a victim's personal information, they can do three things. They can gain access to preexisting bank and credit card accounts, and buy things using those accounts. They can use the information to open brand new bank

Exhibit 14.2 Reshipping

The reshipping scheme requires individuals in the United States to receive packages at their residence and subsequently repackage the merchandise for shipment, usually abroad. Reshippers are recruited in various ways but most often through employment offers and Internet chat rooms.

Unknown subjects post help-wanted advertisements at popular Internet job search sites, and respondents quickly reply to the online advertisement. The prospective employee is required to complete an employment application, which requires him or her to divulge sensitive personal information, such as his or her date of birth and Social Security number. The "employer" then uses this information to get a credit card in the victim's name.

The applicant is informed he or she has been hired and will be responsible for forwarding, or reshipping, merchandise purchased in the United States to the company's overseas home office. The packages quickly begin to arrive and, as instructed, the employee dutifully forwards the packages to their overseas destination. The reshipper doesn't realize that the recently received merchandise was purchased with fraudulent credit cards issued in their own name—until the victim is charged for the merchandise he or she just shipped out of the country!

Source: Internet Crime Complaint Center, http://www.ic3.gov/crimeschemes.aspx#item-16 (accessed May 2017).

accounts and credit cards without the victim's knowledge. They can also implant viruses into their software that forwards the phishing email to other recipients once one person responds to the original email, thereby luring more potential victims into their net.

Phishing emails and websites have become even more of a problem now that cybercriminals can easily copy brand names, logos, and corporate personnel insignia directly into the email. The look is so authentic that victims believe the email comes from the advertised company. Most phishers send out spam emails to a large number of recipients knowing that some of those recipients will have accounts with the company they are impersonating.

COMBATING PHISHING AND IDENTITY THEFT To meet the increasing threat of phishing and identity theft, Congress passed the Identity Theft and Assumption Deterrence Act of 1998 (Identity Theft Act) to make it a federal crime when anyone:

> Knowingly transfers or uses, without lawful authority, a means of identification of another person with the intent to commit, or to aid or abet, any unlawful activity that constitutes a violation of Federal law, or that constitutes a felony under any applicable State or local law.[34]

Violations of the act are investigated by federal investigative agencies such as the US Secret Service, the FBI, and the US Postal Inspection Service. In 2004, the Identity Theft Penalty Enhancement Act was signed into law; the act increases existing penalties for the crime of identity theft, establishes aggravated identity theft as a criminal offense, and establishes mandatory penalties for aggravated identity theft. According to this law, anyone who knowingly "transfers, possesses, or uses, without lawful authority" someone else's identification will be sentenced to an extra prison term of two years with no possibility of probation. Committing identity fraud while engaged in crimes associated with terrorism—such as aircraft destruction, arson, airport violence, or kidnapping top government officials—will receive a mandatory sentence enhancement of five years.[35]

Etailing Fraud

New fraud schemes are evolving to reflect the fact that billions of dollars in goods are sold on the Internet each year. **Etailing fraud** can involve both illegally buying and selling merchandise on the Net.

etailing fraud
Illegally buying and/or selling merchandise on the Internet.

Not only do etail frauds involve selling merchandise, they can also involve buyer fraud. One scam involves purchasing top of the line electronic equipment over the Net and then purchasing a second, similar looking but cheaper model of the same brand. The cheaper item is then returned to the etailer after switching bar codes and boxes with the more expensive unit. Because etail return processing centers don't always check returned goods closely, they may send a refund for the value of the higher priced model.

In another tactic, called *shoplisting*, a person obtains a legitimate receipt from a store either by buying it from a customer or finding it in the trash and then returns to the store and, casually shopping, picks up an identical product. He then takes the product and receipt to the returns departments and attempts to return it for cash, store credit, or a gift card, which the thief then sells on the Internet at a discount for quick cash. Not surprisingly, the underground market for receipts has been growing, as stores have liberalized return policies.[36]

Cybervandalism: Cybercrime with Malicious Intent

In 2015, the online hookup site Ashley Madison was hacked; stolen information from 32 million of the site's members, such as email addresses, was posted on the Net. The hackers claimed two motivations: they objected to Ashley Madison's intent of arranging affairs between married individuals, and they objected to its requirement that users pay $19 for the privilege of deleting all their data from the site.[37] The company issued a $500,000 reward for the identity of the hackers.

Cybervandalism typically involves a cyberattack motivated by revenge and destruction, to achieve a malicious intent (such as a denial-of-service attack launched in retaliation for some slight), to hurt and embarrass someone they are angry at, or simply to hurt people because they enjoy being destructive. Cybervandals usually do not profit from their crimes other than to enjoy the havoc and harm they inflict on others; they are vandals in cyberspace.

Cybervandalism ranges from sending destructive viruses and worms to stalking or bullying people using cyberspace as a medium. Cybervandals may want to damage or deface websites or even, as Exhibit 14.3 reveals, pull a virtual fire alarm; they are motivated more by malice than greed:

- Some cybervandals target computers and networks seeking revenge for some perceived wrong.
- Some desire to exhibit their technical prowess and superiority.
- Some want to highlight the vulnerability of computer security systems.
- Some desire to spy on other people's private financial and personal information (computer voyeurism).
- Some are mean-spirited bullies who want to harm others socially rather than physically.
- Some want to destroy computer security because they believe in a philosophy of open access to all systems and programs.[38]

What forms does cybervandalism take?

In July 2015, hackers who call themselves "the Impact Team" stole user information from Ashley Madison, a website that facilitated extramarital affairs. The group threatened to release users' names and personal information if Ashley Madison was not immediately shut down. When the site stayed up, the hackers dumped 9.7 gigabytes of data to the dark web, including account details, log-ins, and credit card details. The motive? The hackers were angry at Avid Life Media, the website's owner, for their charging practices.

malware
A malicious software program.

Exhibit 14.3　Swatting

Cybervandals have developed a form of "entertainment" called "swatting": calling 911 and faking an emergency that draws a response from law enforcement—usually a SWAT team. The callers often tell tales of hostages about to be executed or bombs about to go off. The community is placed in danger as responders rush to the scene, taking them away from real emergencies. And the officers are placed in danger as unsuspecting residents may try to defend themselves. In one case, a swatter in Washington State was charged with pretending to be calling from the home of a California couple, saying he had just shot and murdered someone. A local SWAT team arrived on the scene, and the husband, who had been asleep in his home with his wife and two young children, heard something and went outside to investigate—after first stopping in the kitchen to pick up a knife. What he found was a group of SWAT assault rifles aimed directly at him. Fortunately, the situation didn't escalate, and no one was injured.

Swatters have become more sophisticated in their targets and use of technology. Consider the following Texas case. Five swatters in several states targeted people who were using online telephone party chat lines (or their family

or friends). The swatters found personal details about the victims by accessing telecommunication company information stored on protected computers. Then, by manipulating computer and phone equipment, they called 911 operators around the country. By using "spoofing technology," the swatters even made it look like the calls were actually coming from the victims! The five swatters called 911 lines in more than 60 cities nationwide, impacting more than 100 victims, causing a disruption of services for telecommunications providers and emergency responders, and resulting in up to $250,000 in losses. "Swats" that the group committed included using bomb threats at sporting events, causing the events to be delayed; claiming that hotel visitors were armed and dangerous, causing an evacuation of the entire hotel; and making threats against public parks and officials.

Sources: Liz Klimas, "'Swatting' Prank Ends Horribly for Victim—and He Has the Injury to Prove It," *The Blaze*, July 16, 2015, http://www.theblaze.com/news/2015/07/16/swatting-prank-ends-horribly-for-victim-and-he-has-the-injury-to-prove-it/; FBI, "Don't Make the Call: The New Phenomenon of 'Swatting,'" https://archives.fbi.gov/archives/news/stories/2008/february/swatting020408 (URLs accessed June 2017).

Worms, Viruses, Trojan Horses, Logic Bombs, and Spam

Some cybercriminals may not be motivated by greed or profit but by the desire for revenge or disruption. The most typical use of cyberspace for destructive intent comes in the sending or implanting of disruptive programs, called viruses, worms, Trojan horses, logic bombs, and spam.

VIRUSES AND WORMS Viruses are a type of malicious software program (also called **malware**) that disrupts or destroys existing programs and networks. The virus is then spread from one computer to another when a user sends out an infected file through email, a network, or a portable drive. **Computer worms** are similar to viruses but use computer networks or the Internet to self-replicate and send themselves to other users, generally via email, without the aid of the operator.

TROJAN HORSES Some hackers introduce a **Trojan horse** program into a computer system. The Trojan horse looks like a benign application but contains illicit codes that can damage the system operations. Sometimes hackers with a sense of irony will install a Trojan horse and claim that it is an antivirus program. When it is opened, it spreads viruses in the computer system. Though Trojan horses do not replicate themselves like viruses, they can be just as destructive.

LOGIC BOMBS A fourth type of destructive attack that can be launched on a computer system is the **logic bomb**, a program that is secretly attached to a computer system, monitors the network's work output, and waits for a particular signal such as a date to appear. Also called a *slag code*, it is a type of delayed-action virus that may be set off when a program user inserts certain input that sets it in motion. A logic bomb may cause a variety of problems ranging from displaying or printing a spurious message to deleting or corrupting data.

computer worms
Programs that attack computer networks (or the Internet) by self-replicating and sending themselves to other users, generally via email, without the aid of the operator.

Trojan horse
A computer program that looks like a benign application but contains illicit codes that can damage the system operations. Though Trojan horses do not replicate themselves like viruses, they can be just as destructive.

logic bomb
A program that is secretly attached to a computer system, monitors the network's work output, and waits for a particular signal such as a date to appear. Also called a slag code, it is a type of delayed action virus that may be set off when a program user makes certain input that sets it in motion. A logic bomb may cause a variety of problems ranging from displaying or printing a spurious message to deleting or corrupting data.

SPAM An unsolicited advertisement or promotional material, spam typically comes in the form of an unwanted email message; spammers use electronic communications to send unsolicited messages in bulk. While email is the most common form of spam, it can also be sent via instant messaging, online newsgroup, and texting, among other media.

Spam can simply be in the form of an unwanted and unwelcome advertisement. For example, it may advertise sexually explicit websites and get into the hands of minors. A more dangerous and malicious form of spam contains a Trojan horse disguised as an email attachment advertising some commodity such as free software or an electronic game. If the recipient downloads or opens the attachment, a virus may be launched that corrupts the victim's computer. The Trojan horse may also be designed to capture important data from the victim's hard drive and send it back to the hacker's email address.

Sending spam can become a crime and even lead to a prison sentence when it causes serious harm to a computer or network.

Website Defacement

Cybervandals may aim their attention at the websites of their victims. **Website defacement** is a type of cybervandalism that occurs when a computer hacker intrudes on another person's website by inserting or substituting codes that expose visitors to the site to misleading or provocative information. Defacement can range from installing humorous graffiti to sabotaging or corrupting the site. In some instances, defacement efforts are not easily apparent or noticeable—for example, when they are designed to give misinformation by substituting or replacing authorized text on a company's web page. The false information may mislead customers and frustrate their efforts to utilize the site or make it difficult for people using search engines to find the site as they surf the Net.

Almost all defacement attacks are designed to vandalize web pages rather than bring profit or gain to the intruders (though some defacers may eventually extort money from their targets). Some defacers are simply trying to impress the hacking community with their skills. Others may target a corporation when they oppose its business practices and policies (such as oil companies, tobacco companies, or defense contractors). Some defacement has political goals such as disrupting the website of a rival political party or fundraising group.

Content analysis of web page defacements indicates that about 70 percent are pranks instituted by hackers, while the rest have a political motive. Defacers are typically members of an extensive social network who are eager to demonstrate their reasons for hacking and often leave calling cards, greetings, and taunts on web pages.[39]

Website defacement is a significant and major threat to online businesses and government agencies. It can harm the credibility and reputation of the organization and demonstrate that its security measures are inadequate. As a result, clients lose trust and may be reluctant to share information such as credit card numbers and personal information. An etailer may lose business if potential clients believe the site is not secure. Financial institutions, such as web-based banks and brokerage houses, are particularly vulnerable because they rely on security and credibility to protect their clients' accounts.[40]

Cyberstalking

In 2012, a scandal rocked the nation when General David Petraeus, head of the Central Intelligence Agency, was forced to resign when word came out that he had a long-term extramarital affair with his biographer, Paula Broadwell. The affair was uncovered when Jill Kelley, a Florida socialite, asked a friend in the FBI to investigate a series of harassing emails she had received from an unknown person.[41] The FBI traced the emails to Broadwell, and found that she was also exchanging intimate messages with an email account belonging to Petraeus. The head of the CIA was brought down because his former girlfriend was cyberstalking a rival!

---

website defacement
A type of cybervandalism that occurs when a computer hacker intrudes on another person's website by inserting or substituting codes that expose visitors to the site to misleading or provocative information. Defacement can range from installing humorous graffiti to sabotaging or corrupting the site.

Cyberstalking refers to the use of the Internet, email, or other electronic communication devices to stalk another person. Traditional stalking involves repeated harassing or threatening behavior, such as following a person, appearing at a person's home or place of business, making harassing phone calls, leaving written messages or objects, or vandalizing a person's property. In the Internet age, stalkers can pursue victims through online chat rooms. Pedophiles can use the Internet to establish a relationship with the child, and later make contact for the purpose of engaging in criminal sexual activities. Internet predators are more likely to meet, develop relationships with at-risk adolescents, and beguile underage teenagers, rather than use coercion and violence.[42]

Not all cyberstalkers are sexual predators. Some send repeated threatening or harassing messages via email and use programs to send messages at regular or random intervals without being physically present at a computer terminal. A cyberstalker may trick other people into harassing or threatening a victim by impersonating the victim on Internet bulletin boards or chat rooms, posting messages that are provocative, such as "I want to have sex." The stalker then posts the victim's name, phone number, or email address hoping that other chat participants will stalk or hassle the victim without the stalker's personal involvement.

Cyberbullying

Experts define bullying among children as repeated negative acts committed by one or more children against another. These negative acts may be physical or verbal in nature—for example, hitting or kicking, teasing or taunting—or they may involve indirect actions such as manipulating friendships or purposely excluding other children from activities. Implicit in this definition is an imbalance in real or perceived power between the bully and the victim. It may come as no surprise, then, that lesbian, gay, bisexual, and transgender (LGBT) students are subject to a disproportionate amount of bullying:

- Eight in ten LGBT students have been verbally harassed at school.
- Four in ten have been physically harassed at school.
- Six in ten have felt unsafe at school.
- One in five have been the victim of a physical assault at school.[43]

Studies of bullying suggest that there are short- and long-term consequences for both the perpetrators and the victims of bullying. Students who are chronic victims of bullying experience more physical and psychological problems than their peers who are not harassed by other children, and they tend not to grow out of the role of victim. Young people mistreated by peers may not want to be in school and may thereby miss out on the benefits of school connectedness as well as educational advancement. Longitudinal studies have found that victims of bullying in early grades also reported being bullied several years later.[44] Chronically victimized students may, as adults, be at increased risk for depression, poor self-esteem, and other mental health problems, including schizophrenia.[45] While bullying is a problem that remains to be solved, it has now morphed from the physical to the virtual. With the creation of cyberspace, physical distance is no longer a barrier to the frequency and depth of harm doled out by a bully to his or her victim.[46]

Cyberbullying is defined as willful and repeated harm inflicted through the medium of electronic text. Like their real-world

AP Images/David Goldman

Cyberbullying has become common in the United States and has taken its toll on adolescent victims. Here, Alex Boston, 14, poses with her parents, Amy and Chris. In front of them is a screen shot of the phony Facebook account that was set up in Alex's name by two classmates. Alex was humiliated when they stacked the page with phony comments claiming she was sexually active, racist, and involved in drugs.

cyberstalking
Use of the Internet, email, or other electronic communications devices to stalk another person. Some cyberstalkers pursue minors through online chat rooms; others harass their victims electronically.

cyberbullying
Willful and repeated harm inflicted through the medium of electronic text.

Policies and Issues in Criminology

UPSKIRTING, DOWNBLOUSING, AND REVENGE PORN: SHOULD NONCONSENSUAL PORNOGRAPHY BE CRIMINALIZED?

In 2017, the US Marine Corps was rocked by the news that a private Facebook account had been created to post photos of naked female service members. Some of the photos of female Marines had been taken without their knowledge or consent, while others were images that had been sent to boyfriends. Though the latter photos had been taken voluntarily, they were certainly not intended to be displayed on the Internet. Marine Corps authorities later admitted during congressional hearings that they were having trouble identifying individual users, stopping the spread of spinoff websites linking to the images, and determining the proper recourse under the law to punish those responsible.

The Marine Corps photo scandal is certainly not unique. This form of digital sexual bullying has become so common that the term "revenge porn" has been coined to describe the posting of intimate and/or lewd photos or videos that were exchanged freely during a romantic relationship. When the relationship eventually falls apart, one partner decides to take revenge on the other by making the content available on private or public websites. The harm of the posting is linked to (a) embarrassment over having friends, family, and coworkers viewing the images, (b) damage to current or future romantic relationships, and (c) harm to one's reputation that can hurt employment or advancement opportunities.

Another form of this digital bullying occurs when a perpetrator who may have never met the victim posts images obtained without consent by using hidden cameras or by stealing or hacking their phones. Some involve photos taken up unsuspecting victims' skirts ("upskirting") or down their blouses ("downblousing").

The postings may be designed to attract viewers to a particular website by advertising that it now contains intimate photos of a popular celebrity such as Jennifer Lawrence. Or in some instances, the victim may be the subject of extortion or blackmail: pay up or your photos will be posted.

Surveys indicate that revenge porn has become commonplace, that 10 percent of ex-partners have threatened to post sexually explicit photos online, and about 60 percent of those threats have become a reality. These digital schemes can seriously harm the emotional and mental health of their female survivors, some of whom experience posttraumatic stress disorder (PTSD), anxiety, depression, suicidal thoughts, and other psychological effects.

Criminologist Cynthia Najdowski studied the posting of nonconsensual explicit images and found that despite the widespread threat posed by this type of harassment, criminal laws have not kept pace with technology; victims of nonconsensual pornography often have few if any avenues to seek justice.

While the federal Video Voyeurism Prevention Act of 2004 criminalized upskirting and downblousing, as of today only 37 states have followed suit. Moreover, there is currently no federal legislation prohibiting revenge porn, and most state laws still do not protect victims who recorded images themselves or consented to their recording, regardless of the fact that they did not consent to the distribution of those images. In addition, many of the states that do have laws against revenge porn require that perpetrators intended to cause distress to the victim, and proving that in court can be difficult. Najdowski's survey of existing state laws found that 33 percent of jurisdictions treat nonconsensual pornography as a misdemeanor, 23 percent as a felony, and 41 percent as either a misdemeanor or felony depending on the circumstances.

counterparts, cyberbullies are malicious aggressors who seek implicit or explicit pleasure or profit through the mistreatment of other individuals. Although power in traditional bullying might be physical (stature) or social (competency or popularity), online power may simply stem from Net proficiency. Cyberbullies are able to navigate the Net and utilize technology in a way that puts them in a position of power relative to their victim. There are two major formats that bullies can employ to harass their victims: (1) a cyberbully can use a computer and send harassing emails or instant messages, post obscene, insulting, and slanderous messages to online bulletin boards or social networking sites, or develop websites to promote and disseminate defamatory content; (2) a cyberbully can use a cell phone to send harassing text messages to the victim.[47]

Most voyeur laws criminalize photos if they are taken of women in private spaces such as a home; only 15 percent of statutes extend protection to public spaces. This restriction renders upskirting and downblousing legal in most jurisdictions. When cases are brought to court, some judges have ruled that women have no "reasonable expectation of privacy" in public places even if they have no knowledge that their image is being captured.

Existing laws contain a number of elements that make enforcement difficult. These include whether recordings were made surreptitiously, whether videographic or photographic images were recorded, what specific body parts are depicted in recordings, whether victims are identifiable from the recordings, whether the violation results in emotional and/or psychological harm to the victim. Take for instance the requirement, occurring in one-third of statutes, that recordings were made surreptitiously. High-quality recording devices are now widely available and typically included as standard equipment in mobile technology such as phones, tablets, and laptop computers. It is difficult to prove that a photo was taken stealthily when a whole crowd is around snapping photos with their cell phones.

Although half of statutes bar nonconsensual distribution of pornographic images, only 19 percent provide protection in cases in which those images were originally consensually recorded but later distributed without the victim's consent. One exception is Idaho, where the crime of video voyeurism occurs when a person disseminates "any image or images of the intimate areas of another person or persons without the consent of such other person or persons and he knows or reasonably should have known that one or both parties agreed or understood that the images should remain private."

Najdowski suggests that one way for legal and enforcement efforts against nonconsensual pornography to gain traction is to approach the problem from a

violence-against-women framework. These acts are not merely violating the right to privacy but are an assault with serious long-term effects. Identifying the deleterious effects on women's human rights, she argues, might help to increase both the visibility and perceived legitimacy of the problem. The use of violence-against-women framing might confer the benefit of attaching the issue to ongoing movements aimed at improving women's rights and status and attracting the attention of organizations that work for this cause.

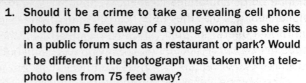

Critical Thinking

1. Should it be a crime to take a revealing cell phone photo from 5 feet away of a young woman as she sits in a public forum such as a restaurant or park? Would it be different if the photograph was taken with a telephoto lens from 75 feet away?

2. Taylor Gissell suggests that one way of reducing the risks of revenge porn is to have couples sign nondisclosure agreements before sharing intimate pictures so that there will be evidence of refusal of consent if and when one of the partners wants to pursue criminal liability if the photos are posted. Do you think this method is workable?

Sources: Cynthia J. Najdowski, "Legal Responses to Nonconsensual Pornography: Current Policy in the United States and Future Directions for Research," *Psychology, Public Policy, and Law* 23 (2017): 154–165; Barbara Starr and Zachary Cohen, "Senator Rips Top Marine Over Nude Photo Scandal," CNN, March 14, 2017, http://www.cnn.com/2017/03/14/politics/marines-nude-photo-scandal-hearing/ (accessed June 2017); Samantha Bates, "Revenge Porn and Mental Health," *Feminist Criminology* 12 (2017): 22–42; Taylor Gissell, "Felony Count 1: Indecent Disclosure," *Houston Law Review* 53 (2015): 273–301; Idaho Code, Ann. § 18-6609, Crime of Video Voyeurism; Colorado Criminal Code, § 18-7-107, Posting a Private Image for Harassment.

One form of cyberbullying receiving national attention is the nonconsensual posting of explicit photos or films, including upskirting, downblousing, and revenge porn. The Policies and Issues in Criminology feature looks at this disturbing trend.

CATFISHING Some cyberbullies want to stalk victims, and some stalkers want to bully their targets. Take the practice that has become known as *catfishing*, a term that refers to the practice of setting up a fictitious online profile, most often for the purpose of luring another into a fraudulent romantic relationship. According to the Urban Dictionary, a catfish is "someone who pretends to be someone they're not using Facebook or other social media to create false identities, particularly to pursue deceptive online romances." So, to "catfish someone" is to set up a fake social media profile with the goal of duping that person into falling for the false persona.[48]

While catfishing has been around awhile, it became a topic of public interest when 13-year-old Megan Meier began an online relationship with a boy she knew as Josh Evans. For almost a month, Megan corresponded with this boy exclusively online because he said he didn't have a phone and was homeschooled.[49] One day Megan received a message from Josh on her MySpace profile saying, "I don't know if I want to be friends with you any longer because I hear you're not nice to your friends." This was followed by bulletins being posted through MySpace calling Megan "fat" and a "slut." After seeing the messages, Megan became distraught and ran up into her room. A few minutes later, Megan's mother Tina found her daughter hanging in her bedroom closet. Though Tina rushed her to the hospital, Megan died the next day.

Six weeks after their daughter's death, the Meier family learned that the boy with whom Megan had been corresponding never existed. Josh Evans (and his on-line profile) was created by Lori Drew, a neighbor and the mother of one of Megan's friends. She created the profile as a way to spy on what Megan was saying about her daughter. Drew was charged with violations of the Computer Fraud and Abuse Act (CFAA), though her conviction was later overturned.[50]

Catfishing also created national headlines when former Notre Dame and current NFL football star Manti Te'o was the target of a catfish. Te'o developed an online relationship with someone he knew as Lennay Kekua. It is difficult to know how deep the relationship was, but he did refer to her as his "girlfriend" and mentioned repeatedly that he loved her. Te'o amassed a wide following when it was learned that his grandmother and girlfriend (Kekua) died on the same day early in the 2012 football season. While his grandmother did in fact die on that day, his girlfriend did not, and media investigations revealed that she had never existed in the first place. Kekua was a fictitious online persona created by a friend of Te'o's. In a statement to the press, Te'o maintained that he was a target: "To realize that I was the victim of what was apparently someone's sick joke and constant lies was, and is, painful and humiliating."[51]

HOW COMMON IS CYBERBULLYING? Sameer Hinduja and Justin Patchin, leading experts on cyberbullying, have conducted yearly surveys using large samples of high school youth.[52] Their most recent effort finds that on average about 28 percent of the high school and middle school students they surveyed report having been the target of some form of Internet harassment; about 16 percent of surveyed youth admitted that they had cyberbullied others at some point in their lifetimes.

Hinduja and Patchin's most important findings include:

- Adolescent girls are just as likely, if not more likely, than boys to experience cyberbullying (as a victim or offender).
- Cyberbullying is related to low self-esteem, suicidal ideation, anger, frustration, and a variety of other emotional and psychological problems.
- Cyberbullying is related to other issues in the real world, including school problems, antisocial behavior, and substance use.
- Traditional bullying is still more common than cyberbullying.
- Traditional bullying and cyberbullying are closely related: those who are bullied at school are bullied online and those who bully at school bully online.

Hinduja and Patchin's research is supported by other survey results. According to the most recent data compiled by the National Center for Education Statistics, about 21 percent of students ages 12 to 18 reported being bullied at school during the school year; girls were more likely to be bullied than boys. Students, both male and female, who self-identified as gay, lesbian, or bisexual were more likely to report that they had been bullied (34 percent of LGBTQ students compared to 19 percent of hetero-sexual students). LGBTQ students were also more likely to be electronically bullied on social media sites.[53] Less than half of all students reported bullying to adult authorities; the more frequent the bullying, the more likely it is to be reported.

Cyberspying

Spyware is a type of software that gathers personal information, including web browser histories, emails, and online purchases. Once information is gathered, it is automatically transmitted to those who installed the software either directly on the computer or when the victim opened an attachment. In some instances, the computer operator gives consent to the spying, which is legal. For example, an employee agrees to have their computer monitored by their employer to make sure they are not web surfing during business hours.

cyberspying
Illegally using the Internet to gather information that is considered private and confidential.

Parents can legally install the software on their minor child's computer if they are the owner of the machine. If their child is a legal adult, they must obtain consent. Parents (and others) can use programs such as FlexiSPY software that capture every Facebook message, email, text, and photo sent from a phone, as well as record phone calls. Such spying is legal only if the person installing the software also owns the device or was given consent by the owner.[54]

Cyberspies have a variety of motivations. Some are people involved in marital disputes who may want to seize the emails of their estranged spouse. Business rivals might hire disgruntled former employees, consultants, or outside contractors to steal information from their competitors. These commercial cyberspies target upcoming bids, customer lists, product designs, software source code, voicemail messages, and confidential email messages. Some of the commercial spying is conducted by foreign competitors who seek to appropriate trade secrets in order to gain a business advantage.

CYBERSPYING BY THE GOVERNMENT While spyware to monitor Internet messages and traffic by spouses, children, employees, and so on has become common, government agencies spying on US citizens remains quite controversial.

In Chapter 11, Edward Snowden's efforts to warn the public about the National Security Agency's domestic spying program was discussed within the context of political crime. The NSA program, code-named PRISM, is known in official government circles as the "President's Surveillance Program" and was implemented by President George W. Bush shortly after 9/11. It extracts information from the servers of nine major American Internet companies: Microsoft, Yahoo, Google, Facebook, Paltalk, AOL, Skype, YouTube, and Apple. PRISM gives the NSA access to audio, video, photographs, emails, documents, and connection logs for each of these systems. The NSA can track targeted individuals over time, while online surveillance of search terms gives them insights into their subjects' thoughts and intentions. In addition, the government receives records of calls they made—across town or across the country—to family members, coworkers, business contacts, and others.

The surveillance was undertaken without a warrant, which some legal scholars claim is in violation of the spirit of federal law and the Constitution.[55]

The Costs of Cybercrime

How common are cybercrimes, and how costly are cybercrimes to American businesses and the general public? The Internet has become a vast engine for illegal profits and criminal entrepreneurs. An accurate accounting of cybercrime will probably never be made because so many offenses go unreported, but there is little doubt that its incidence is growing rapidly.

Though thousands of breaches occur each year, most are not reported to local, state, or federal authorities. Some cybercrime goes unreported because it involves low-visibility acts—such as copying computer software in violation of copyright laws—that simply never get detected.[56] Some businesses choose not to report cybercrime because they fear revealing the weaknesses in their network security systems. However, the information that is available indicates that the profit in cybercrime is vast and continually growing.[57]

McAfee, the Internet security firm, estimates that the likely annual cost to the global economy from cybercrime is more than $400 billion and could be as much as $575 billion. These vast losses come from a number of different sources.[58] These estimates seem meager in comparison to those projected by other cybersecurity firms, such as Cybersecurity Ventures and Juniper Research, who estimate that cybercrime costs will reach $2 trillion by 2019 and $6 trillion by 2021.[59]

Losses due to phishing and identity theft are already in the billions of dollars and rising with the continuing growth of ecommerce. The Internal Revenue Service (IRS) found that during the past five years the agency paid more than $20 billion in refunds to criminals who filed false tax returns, in some cases on behalf of people who had died.[60]

McAfee believes that the cost of cybercrime will continue to increase as more business functions move online and as more companies and consumers around the world connect to the Internet.[61] Losses from the theft of intellectual property will also increase as acquiring countries make use of Net systems in manufacturing.

Combating Cybercrime

LO4 Discuss efforts to control cybercrime.

The proliferation of cybercrime and its cost to the economy have created the need for new laws and enforcement processes specifically aimed at controlling its emerging formulations. Because technology evolves so rapidly, the enforcement challenges are particularly vexing. There are numerous organizations set up to provide training and support for law enforcement agents. In addition, new federal and state laws have been aimed at particular areas of high-tech crimes.

Congress has treated computer-related crime as a distinct federal offense since the passage of the Counterfeit Access Device and Computer Fraud and Abuse Law in 1984.[62] The 1984 act protected classified US defense and foreign relations information, financial institution and consumer reporting agency files, and access to computers operated for the government. The act was supplemented in 1996 by the National Information Infrastructure Protection Act (NIIPA), which significantly broadens the scope of the law.[63]

Because cybercrime is relatively new, existing laws sometimes are inadequate to address the problem. Therefore new legislation has been drafted to protect the public from the cybercriminal. For example, before October 30, 1998, when the Identity Theft and Assumption Act of 1998 became law, there was no federal statute that made identity theft a crime. Today, federal prosecutors are making substantial use of the statute and are actively prosecuting cases of identity theft.[64]

In the wake of the 9/11 attacks, the NIIPA has been amended by sections of the USA Patriot Act (now the US Freedom Act) to make it easier to enforce laws against crimes by terrorists and other organized enemies against the nation's computer systems. Subsection 1030(a)(5)(A)(i) of the act criminalizes knowingly causing the transmission of a program, code, or command, and as a result, intentionally causing damage to a protected computer. This section applies regardless of whether the user had authorization to access the protected computer; company insiders and authorized users can be culpable for intentional damage to a protected computer. The act also prohibits intentional access without authorization that results in damage but does not require intent to damage; the attacker can merely be negligent or reckless.

In addition to these main acts, computer-related crimes can also be charged under at least 40 different federal statutes. These include the Copyright Act and Digital Millennium Copyright Act, the National Stolen Property Act, the mail and wire fraud statutes, the Electronic Communications Privacy Act, the Communications Decency Act of 1996, the Child Online Protection Act, the Child Pornography Prevention Act of 1996, and the Internet False Identification Prevention Act of 2000.[65] Movie pirates who use the Internet to sell illegally copied films led the federal government to create the Family Entertainment and Copyright Act of 2005. One part of that statute, known as the ART Act (Artists' Rights and Theft Prevention

Act of 2005), criminalizes the use of recording equipment to make copies of films while in movie theaters. The statute also makes it illegal to make a copy of a work in production and put it on the Internet so it will be accessible to members of the public when the individual making the copy knew or should have known the work was intended for commercial distribution.[66]

International Treaties

Because cybercrime is essentially global, international cooperation is required for its control. The Convention on Cybercrime, ratified by the US Senate in August 2006, is the first international treaty that addresses the definition and enforcement of cyber-crime. Now signed by 52 nations, it focuses on improving investigative techniques and increasing cooperation among nations. The convention includes a list of crimes that each signatory state must incorporate into its own law, including such cyber offenses as hacking, distribution of child pornography, and protection of intellectual property rights. It also allows law enforcement agencies new powers, including the ability to require that an Internet service provider monitor a person's online view-ing and search choices in real time. The convention also requires signatory states to cooperate whenever possible in the investigations and prosecution of cybercriminals. The vision is that a common legal framework will eliminate jurisdictional hurdles to facilitate the law enforcement of borderless cybercrimes.[67]

Carrying out this mandate may be difficult to achieve given the legal rights afforded US citizens that may not be realized by residents of other nations. First Amendment protections that restrict the definition of pornography and obscenity in this country may not apply overseas. It is not surprising that watchdog institu-tions such as the ACLU have condemned the treaty and campaigned against US participation.[68]

Cybercrime Enforcement Agencies

To enforce these laws, the federal government is now operating a number of orga-nizations to control cyberfraud. One approach is to create working groups that coor-dinate the activities of numerous agencies involved in investigating cybercrime. For example, the Interagency Telemarketing and Internet Fraud Working Group brings together representatives of numerous US attorneys' offices, the FBI, the Secret Ser-vice, the Postal Inspection Service, the Federal Trade Commission, the Securities and Exchange Commission, and other law enforcement and regulatory agencies to share information about trends and patterns in Internet fraud schemes.[69]

Specialized enforcement agencies have been created. The Internet Fraud Com-plaint Center, based in Fairmont, West Virginia, is run by the FBI and the National White Collar Crime Center. It brings together about 1,000 state and local law enforce-ment officials and regulators. Its goal is to analyze fraud-related complaints in order to find distinct patterns, develop information on particular cases, and send investiga-tive packages to law enforcement authorities in the jurisdiction that appears likely to have the greatest investigative interest in the matter. The center now receives almost 300,000 complaints each year, including auction fraud, non-delivery, and credit/debit card fraud, as well as non-fraudulent complaints such as computer intrusions, spam/unsolicited email, and child pornography; the number of annual complaints has remained relatively stable for the past five years.[70] Law enforcement has made remarkable strides in dealing with identity theft as a crime problem over the last sev-eral years.

The Secret Service maintains Electronic Crimes Task Forces (ECTFs), which focus on identifying and locating international cybercriminals connected to cyber intru-sions, bank fraud, data breaches, and other computer-related crimes. The ECTF part-ners with thousands of law enforcement agencies, the private sector, and members of academia to combat cybercrime through information sharing, coordinated investiga-tions, technical expertise, and training; there are now 4,000 private sector partners; over 2,500 international, federal, state, and local law enforcement partners; and over

350 academic partners. Since inception, the ECTFs have prevented over $13 billion in potential losses to victims and arrested approximately 10,000 individuals.[71] One of the most successful of these efforts is the New York–New Jersey Electronic Crimes Task Force (NYECTF), a partnership between the US Secret Service and a host of other public safety agencies and private corporations. The task force consists of more than 250 individual members representing federal, state, and local law enforcement, the private sector, and computer science specialists from 18 different universities. Since 1995, the task force has charged more than 1,000 individuals with electronic crime losses, exceeding $1 billion. It has trained more than 60,000 law enforcement personnel, prosecutors, and private industry representatives in cybercrime prevention. Its success has prompted similar electronic crime task forces to be set up in Boston, Miami, Charlotte, Chicago, Las Vegas, San Francisco, Los Angeles, Washington, DC, and other major cities.[72]

Cyberwar: Politically Motivated Cybercrime

No longer is warfare conducted solely by pitting one nation's military forces against another. Elements of warfare are now being conducted via the Internet. The targets are a rival nation's financial and industrial sectors rather than their army or navy. Unlike traditional military conflict, cyberwar means a small group of individuals can take on a nation-state, destroy its infrastructure, and bring it to its knees.[73]

Cyberwar enables the forces of one nation-state to penetrate another nation's computers or networks for the purposes of causing damage or disruption. Computer systems may be compromised so that vital war material is misdirected or even destroyed. Attacks are facilitated by destroying command systems and compromising air defenses. Instead of blowing up air defense radar systems and giving up the element of surprise before hitting targets, in the age of cyberwar the computers controlling the air defense are put out of action.[74]

Cyberwar can also involve attacks designed to compromise an enemy's command and control structure by hacking into missile targeting systems, rendering them ineffective during attacks. In one such attack, Israeli cyber units "blinded" Syrian antiaircraft installations guarding a secret nuclear plant that was being constructed for Syria by North Korea. While the exact methodology remains classified, Syrian computers that controlled their missile defenses were reprogrammed so that the attacking Israeli aircraft did not show up on radar screens. Israel was able to penetrate a sophisticated defense system without losing a single aircraft.[75] US cyberwar agents infiltrated the Iraqi "closed-loop" private, secure military network before the start of the second Gulf War. The agents sent email to thousands of Iraqi military officers on the Iraqi Defense Ministry email system telling them they would not be harmed if they left their tanks and weapons parked on the side of the road and went home; many did just that.

The United States and Israel are not alone in perfecting cyberwar capability. In March 2015, South Korea formally accused North Korea of cyberattacks on its nuclear reactor operating system.[76] Iran launched a major cyberattack in 2012 on Saudi Arabia's state-owned oil company, Saudi Aramco, releasing a virus named Shamoon, which replicated itself across 30,000 computers and took almost two weeks to remove. In 2017, a new variant of the Shamoon data-wiping malware was again used to

Cyberwar can be aimed at an enemy nation's infrastructure. Here, an Iranian security guard stands at the Maroun Petrochemical plant at the Imam Khomeini port, in southwestern Iran. Technicians battling a complex computer virus took the ultimate firewall measures, shutting off all Internet links to Iran's oil ministry and the terminal that carries nearly all of the country's crude exports.

AP Images/Vahid Salemi

attack high-level Saudi organizations; the Saudis believe that the Iranian government was behind the attacks.[77]

The cyberwar competition between the US and China has gotten so fierce that in 2015 the two nations reached a limited agreement not to conduct certain types of cyberattacks against each other, such as intrusions that steal corporate information and then pass it along to domestic companies. Other nations practicing cyberwar include rivals Pakistan and India; others such as Estonia and Belarus are racing to build cyber shields to counter Russia. Denmark and the Netherlands have begun programs to develop offensive computer weapons, as have Argentina and France.[78]

Cyberespionage

The 2016 presidential election was tainted by accounts of computer hacking by the Russian government, who appeared intent on shifting and shaping the outcome. This is not the only instance of Russian involvement in illegal hacking of critical computer systems in the United States. In 2017, four Russians, including two officers of the Russian Federal Security Service (FSB), were indicted for computer hacking, economic espionage, and other criminal offenses. Beginning in January 2014, the conspirators allegedly used unauthorized access to steal information from at least 500 million Yahoo accounts. They then used that stolen information to access accounts at Yahoo, Google, and other webmail providers. Of special interest to the FSB were personal accounts belonging to Russian journalists, Russian and US government officials, employees of a prominent Russian cybersecurity company, and numerous employees of other providers whose networks the conspirators sought to exploit.[79]

Intelligence agencies are now able to penetrate computer networks of an enemy nation's most sensitive military bases, defense contractors, and aerospace companies in order to steal important data or to damage their infrastructure—a practice known as **cyberespionage**. Chinese hackers are notorious for breaking into networks to gain classified information. The Chinese government has established an online warfare team to beef up the defense capabilities of the People's Liberation Army (PLA). They are thought to have used a phishing email to breach a contractor for the US Office of Personnel Management, and thus crack the agency itself, exposing the records of more than 21 million US civil service employees.[80] Though China denies involvement, its army has divisions devoted to cyberattacks. In 2016, a Chinese national, Su Bin, pleaded guilty in a California court to participating in a years-long conspiracy to hack into the computer networks of major US defense contractors, steal sensitive military and export-controlled data, and send the stolen data to China. Su would email the co-conspirators with guidance regarding what persons, companies, and technologies to target during their computer intrusions. His co-conspirators would then steal the data, using sophisticated techniques to avoid detection.[81]

The effects of a cyberattack can be devastating. A cyberattack launched on November 23, 2010, against Iran forced the shutdown of its main uranium enrichment plant at Natanz for seven days after it was targeted by the Stuxnet computer worm. Experts believe that Stuxnet was specifically designed to attack systems at the plant that control the speed at which the enrichment centrifuges spin.[82] The attack helped delay Iran's development of nuclear weapons.

Cyberterrorism

On January 21, 2016, seven Iranian nationals were indicted in the United States for their involvement in conspiracies to conduct a campaign of denial of service against the US financial sector. Each defendant was a manager or employee at either ITSec-Team or Mersad, two Iran-based companies that performed work on behalf of the Iranian government, including the Islamic Revolutionary Guard Corps. The attacks against 46 victims disabled bank websites, prevented customers from accessing their accounts online, and collectively cost the victims tens of millions of dollars. One of

cyberespionage
Efforts by Intelligence agencies to penetrate computer networks of an enemy nation in order to steal important data.

FACT OR FICTION?

The next war may be conducted in cyberspace.

FACT There have already been a number of cyberattacks on military installations in the United States and abroad.

Policies and Issues in Criminology

TERRORISM ON THE NET

In 2016, Nader Elhuzayel was sentenced to 30 years in federal prison for conspiring and attempting to provide material support to the Islamic State (IS). Elhuzayel had attempted to travel to the Middle East to join the terrorist organization. During his trial it became evident that Elhuzayel had used social media to further his plans. He discussed IS and terrorist attacks, expressed a desire to die as a martyr, and made arrangements to leave the United States to join up. In recorded conversations, Elhuzayel discussed how "it would be a blessing to fight for the cause of Allah, and to die in the battlefield," and he referred to IS as "we."

Elhuzayel used social media to communicate with IS supporters and operatives, to disseminate pro-IS information, and to assist IS supporters by distributing social media account information for those whose accounts had been suspended. Elhuzayel maintained a Facebook account with the IS flag as his profile picture. He used the account to ask Allah to grant him martyrdom and success in leaving the United States to fight for his cause and to ask Allah to "destroy your enemies and give the Islamic state victory."

Islamic State supporters such as Nader Elhuzayel routinely use the Net to recruit and raise funds. It is estimated that more than 20,000 foreign fighters have been recruited by IS to travel to Syria and join their cause. In almost every American case, social media played some part in recruitment and/or radicalization. One study of Islamic State's Twitter use found at least 46,000 Twitter accounts that supported the organization were currently in use. Twitter has suspended the accounts of Islamic State supporters in large numbers, but users create new accounts and return. Ongoing monitoring suggests there are currently a minimum of around 40,000 accounts that actively support the Islamic State, with perhaps 2,000 tweeting primarily in English.

IS recruiters use the Net to groom potential recruits. They monitor online communities trolling for receptive individuals and making themselves available to curiosity seekers. Once contact is made with a highly motivated recruit, teams keep in constant contact in order to shape their worldview and encourage direct action in support of the Islamic State. In some instances, IS agents seek out targets, while in others they respond to people who are seeking them. Agents try to insulate potential recruits against outside influences. Trips may be arranged to receive training. Online interventions are most common in countries where there are few opportunities to meet

the defendants, Hamid Firoozi, was charged with obtaining unauthorized access into the Supervisory Control and Data Acquisition (SCADA) systems of the Bowman Dam, located in Rye, New York.[83]

This Iranian intrusion could have led to a devastating terror attack against critical elements of the US infrastructure. While the Bowman Dam is relatively small, it's possible that the hackers used the intrusion as a dry run for a more disruptive invasion of a major hydroelectric generator or some other grand and indispensable element of the nation's power grid.[84]

Cyberterrorism is an element of cyberwar that involves an effort by covert forces to disrupt the intersection where the virtual electronic reality of computers meets the physical world.[85] Cyberspace is a handy battlefield for the terrorist because an attack can strike directly at a target that bombs won't affect: the economy. Because technological change plays a significant role in the development of critical infrastructures, they are particularly vulnerable to attack. And because of rapid technological change, and the interdependence of systems, it is difficult to defend against efforts to disrupt services.[86]

Cyberterrorists have many advantages. There are no borders of legal control, making it difficult for prosecutors to apply laws to some crimes. Criminals can operate from countries where cyber laws barely exist, making them almost untouchable. Cyberterrorists can also use the Internet and hacking tools to gather information on targets.[87] There is no loss of life and no need to infiltrate enemy territory. Terrorists

with the Islamic State agents in a face-to-face setting. While Americans have been recruited, there is considerably more activity in the United Kingdom, France, Belgium, and other European countries.

In addition to recruiting, IS uses the Net to instill fear and threaten reprisals. IS has issued public statements confirming the terrorist organization's determination and dedication to global terrorism. The videos IS released on the Net depicting the beheadings of American journalists James Foley and Steven Sotloff were aimed at sowing terror in the US population. The message is that IS will continue to capture American hostages in an attempt to force the US government and people into making concessions that would only strengthen IS recruiting and further its terrorist operations.

IS is not the only group using the Internet. Al-Qaeda in the Arabian Peninsula (AQAP) publishes an online English language magazine called *Inspire*, in which the group advocates simple and inexpensive lone-wolf attacks against the United States and other Western targets. The first edition of *Inspire*, released in the summer of 2010, provided specific instructions on how to build a pipe bomb. In another edition, AQAP further expanded upon these instructions to include building a pressure-cooker bomb similar to the one used in the Boston Marathon bombing.

Given the scope of the cyber threat, agencies across the federal government are making cybersecurity a top priority. The Department of Justice, including the FBI, the Department of Homeland Security, the National Security Agency, and other US intelligence community and law enforcement agencies are cooperating to combat the cyber threat. There are ongoing investigations into dangerous botnets, state-sponsored hackers, and global cyber syndicates.

Critical Thinking

Given the use of the Net by terror groups to recruit fighters and spread propaganda, would you advocate greater government control over Internet content, granting agencies a free hand to shut down websites? What problems could develop from such a policy?

Sources: Department of Justice, US Attorney's Office, Central District of California, "Orange County Man Sentenced to 30 Years in Federal Prison for Conspiring to Join ISIL and Engaging in Fraud," September 26, 2016, https://www.justice.gov/usao-cdca/pr/orange-county-man-sentenced-30-years-federal-prison-conspiring-join-isil-and-engaging; James B. Comey, Director, Federal Bureau of Investigation, Statement Before the House Homeland Security Committee, "Worldwide Threats to the Homeland," September 17, 2014, https://www.fbi.gov/news/testimony/worldwide-threats-to-the-homeland (URLs accessed June 2017).

can commit crimes from anyplace in the world, and the costs are minimal. Nor do terror organizations lack for skilled labor to mount cyberattacks. There are a growing number of highly skilled computer experts in developing countries who are available at reasonable costs. Cyberterrorism may result in a battered economy in which the government is forced to spend more on the military and cut back on social programs and education. These outcomes can weaken the terrorists' target and undermine its resolve to continue to resist.

RECRUITMENT AND FUNDRAISING Terrorist organizations are now using cyberspace in a number of different operational areas. They use the Internet to recruit new members and disseminate information. Islamist militant organizations use the Internet to broadcast anti-Western slogans and information. An organization's charter and political philosophy can be displayed on its website, which can also be used to solicit funds. The Policies and Issues in Criminology feature discusses this phenomenon further.

Terrorist groups have used the Internet to raise funds to buy arms and carry out operations.[88] One method of funding is through fraudulent charitable organizations claiming to support a particular cause such as disaster relief or food services. Charitable organizations in the United States raise more than $130 billion per year. Using bogus charities to raise money is particularly attractive to cyberterrorists because charities face far less scrutiny from the government than for-profit corporations and individuals.

LO5 Describe the evolution of organized crime.

Combating Cyberwar

There are a number of government agencies assigned with the task of countering cyberwar and cyberterror. The military has formed the United States Cyber Command (USCYBERCOM), a division that ties together the cyberwarfare arms of the various service branches. As part of the Department of Defense (DoD), USCYBERCOM coordinates the department's cyberspace operations, including:

- Plan, coordinate, integrate, synchronize, and conduct activities to lead day-to-day defense and protection of DoD information networks
- Coordinate DoD operations providing support to military missions
- Direct the operations and defense of specified DoD information networks
- Prepare to and, when directed, conduct full-spectrum military cyberspace operations

The command is charged with pulling together existing cyberspace resources, creating synergy where it does not currently exist, and synchronizing efforts to defend the information security environment.[89]

The National Security Agency/Central Security Service (NSA/CSS) encompasses both signals intelligence (SIGINT) and information assurance (IA) missions. The IA mission is to prevent foreign adversaries from gaining access to sensitive or classified national security information. The SIGINT mission is to collect, process, and disseminate intelligence information from foreign signals for intelligence and counterintelligence purposes and to support military operations.[90]

Transnational Organized Crime

The growth of the Internet has not only spurred the development of cybercrime but has also enabled and encouraged criminal syndicates that operate on a global scale, working in more than one country to plan and execute illegal business ventures. **Transnational organized crime** (also called transnational crime) involves groups or networks of individuals working in more than one state, or even across cultures and nations, to plan and execute illegal business ventures. Cross-national gangs are often large criminal organizations, some with more than 20,000 members.

According to criminologist Jay Albanese, the distinction between these new organizations that operate across borders and the traditional Mafia whose activities were bounded by neighborhood territory is actually not that great. They overlap in terms of the crimes committed, the offenders involved, and how criminal opportunities are exploited for profit. They are, he concludes, manifestations of the same

Transnational organized crime groups often prey on desperate immigrants, migrant workers, and displaced people. Here, Nigerian asylum seeker Yakubu Yahya (center), 17, is onboard the MS *Golfo Azzurro* a day after being rescued by members of Proactiva Open Arms, a Spanish nonprofit dedicated to rescuing migrant workers. Yahya went to Libya searching for his missing parents and was kidnapped by a gang in the Libyan city of Sabha while crossing the Sahara Desert. The gang members demanded $2,000, which he did not have, and he was beaten almost constantly until he managed to escape. Eventually, he found enough work in Libya to scrape together $300 to $400. That was enough to pay a smuggler to get him to the coast and then onto the smuggler's boat, from which he was rescued by the *Golfo Azzurro* team.

AP Images/Bernat Armangué

underlying conduct and the same pool of criminal offenders who exploit similar criminal opportunities.[91]

Characteristics of Transnational Organized Crime

A precise description of the characteristics of transnational organized crime is difficult to formulate, but here are some of its general traits:[92]

- Transnational organized crime is a conspiratorial activity, involving the coordination of numerous people in the planning and execution of illegal acts or in the pursuit of a legitimate objective by unlawful means (e.g., threatening a legitimate business to get a stake in it).
- An offense is transnational if:
  - It is committed in more than one state or nation.
  - It is committed in one state or nation but a substantial part of its preparation, planning, direction, or control takes place in another state or nation.
  - It is committed in one state or nation but involves an organized criminal group that engages in criminal activities in more than one state or nation.
  - It is committed in one state or nation but has substantial effects in another state or nation.[93]
- Transnational organized crime involves continuous commitment by primary members, although individuals with specialized skills may be brought in as needed.
- Transnational organized crime is usually structured along hierarchical lines—a chieftain supported by close advisers, lower subordinates, and so on.
- Transnational organized crime has economic gain as its primary goal, although power and status may also be motivating factors. Economic gain is achieved through global supply of illegal goods and services, including drugs, sex slaves, arms, and pornography.
- In addition to providing illegal material such as narcotics, contemporary global syndicates engage in business crimes such as laundering illegal money through legitimate businesses, land fraud, and computer crime.
- Transnational criminal syndicates employ predatory tactics, such as intimidation, violence, and corruption.
- Transnational organized crime groups are quick and effective in controlling and disciplining their members, associates, and victims and will not hesitate to use lethal violence against those who flaunt organizational rules.
- Transnational crime depends heavily on the instruments of the IT age: the Internet, global communications, rapid global transportation systems, universal banking systems, and global credit card and payment systems.
- Transnational organized crime groups do not include terror organizations, though there may be overlap. Some terror groups are involved in criminality to fund their political objectives, and some have morphed from politically motivated organizations to ones solely involved in for-profit criminal activity. Transnational criminal organizations may aid terror groups with transportation and communication.

Activities of Transnational Organized Crime

What are the main activities of transnational organized crime? The traditional sources of income are derived from providing illicit materials, such as narcotics, and using force to enter into and maximize profits in legitimate businesses. Income is generated from such activities as narcotics distribution, extortion, gambling, pornography, and cargo theft rings.

- Organized crime groups have become involved in trafficking in cultural property. Antiques, artifacts, and relics stolen through illegal archaeological digs are sold to gangs who then smuggle the goods out of the country and sell them either through legitimate markets such as auctions and the Internet or in underground

transnational organized crime Criminal conspiracies that cross national and international borders and involve the planning and execution of illicit ventures by groups or networks of individuals working in more than one country.

FACT OR FICTION?

Organized crime in the United States is still a local commodity, controlled by five Mafia families in New York City and a few other allied groups in Chicago, Los Angeles, and Miami.

FICTION Traditional organized crime families are in decline, being replaced by transnational crime groups originating in Europe, Asia, and Latin and South America.

L06 List the activities of transnational organized crime.

markets where collectors buy offered goods, no questions asked. Trafficking in cultural property is also becoming an important source for money laundering.

- Maritime piracy (a crime made famous in the 2013 film *Captain Phillips*, with Tom Hanks in the title role) is the specialty of Somali gangs. Pirates from this nation located on the Horn of Africa are now arming themselves with a higher grade of weaponry and basing themselves on "mother ships" from which they can send out smaller attack boats. This system allows them to hijack larger vessels over wider distances, hundreds of miles off the coast. Piracy is also linked to other forms of organized crime, since it requires sophisticated intelligence collection networks and systematic corruption of local officials. Piracy is a key source of income for many in the local communities, who receive funds from ransoms that their own governments fail to provide.

- Organized crime groups are quite active in human trafficking, the acquisition of people by improper means such as force, fraud, or deception, with the aim of exploiting them in such illegal activities as prostitution, sexual exploitation, forced labor, slavery, or similar practices. Every year, thousands of men, women, and children fall into the hands of traffickers in their own countries and abroad. Almost every country in the world is affected by trafficking, whether as a country of origin, transit, or destination for victims.

- Organized crime groups profit from smuggling migrants. Criminals are increasingly providing smuggling services to irregular migrants to evade national border controls, migration regulations, and visa requirements. Most irregular migrants resort to the assistance of profit-seeking smugglers because as border controls have improved in developed nations, migrants are deterred from attempting to illegally cross them themselves and are diverted into the hands of smugglers. Migrant smugglers are becoming more and more organized, establishing professional networks that transcend borders and regions. Nonetheless, thousands of people have lost their lives as a result of the indifferent or even deliberate actions of migrant smugglers.

- The demand for organs has outstripped supply, creating an underground market for illicitly obtained organs. Desperate recipients and donors create an avenue ready for exploitation by international organ trafficking syndicates. Traffickers exploit the desperation of donors to improve the economic situation of themselves and their families, and they exploit the desperation of recipients who may have few other options to improve or prolong their lives. Like other victims of trafficking in persons, those who fall prey to traffickers for the purpose of organ removal are vulnerable by virtue of poverty. Traffickers may enlist the services of doctors, nurses, ambulance drivers, and health care professionals who are involved in legitimate activities when they are not participating in trafficking in persons for the purpose of organ removal.[94]

Transnational Gangs

Traditional Eurocentric gangs are being replaced by transnational mega-gangs. Some, such as the Crips, Bloods, and MS-13, have expanded from local street gangs to national mega-gangs with thousands of members. The Sureños is an alliance of hundreds of individual Mexican American street gangs that originated in Southern California. Sureños gang members' main sources of income are retail-level distribution of cocaine, heroin, marijuana, and methamphetamine within prison systems and in the community as well as extortion of drug distributors on the streets. Some members have direct links to Mexican drug traffickers, brokering large drug transactions; they are also involved in other criminal activities such as assault, carjacking, home invasion, homicide, and robbery. While most members remain in Southern California cities, the gang has spread significantly and can be found throughout much of the United States.[95]

In addition to these homegrown gangs, international gangs based in Asia, Eastern Europe, North, South, and Latin America use the Internet and IT devices to facilitate their operations across nations and continents. Emerging transnational crime syndicates are primarily located in nations whose governments are too weak to present effective opposition. If they believe that the government is poised to interfere with their illegal activities, they will carry out a terror campaign, killing police and other government officials to achieve their goals. Easier international travel, expanded world trade, and financial transactions that cross national borders have enabled them to branch out of local and regional crime to target international victims and develop criminal networks within more prosperous countries and regions.[96]

Some of the most prominent transnational gang clusters are described here in some detail.

AFRICAN GANGS Africa, a continent that has experienced political turmoil, has also seen the rise of transnational gangs. African criminal enterprises in Nigeria, Ghana, and Liberia have developed quickly since the 1980s due to the globalization of the world's economies and the great advances in communications technology. Nigerian criminal enterprises, primarily engaged in drug trafficking and financial frauds, are the most significant of these groups and operate in more than 80 countries. They are infamous for their email-based financial frauds, which cost the United States alone an estimated $1 billion to $2 billion each year.

MIDDLE EASTERN GANGS Criminal groups with associations to the Middle East have been active in the US since at least the 1970s, particularly in areas with significant Middle Eastern or Southwest Asian populations. These organizations are typically loosely organized theft or financial fraud rings formed along familial or tribal lines, and include criminals from Afghanistan, Egypt, India, Iran, Iraq, Israel, Jordan, Lebanon, Morocco, Oman, Pakistan, Syria, United Arab Emirates, and Yemen. They typically use small storefronts as bases for criminal operations. Middle Eastern gangs engage in automobile theft, financial fraud, money laundering, interstate transportation of stolen property, smuggling, drug trafficking, document fraud, health care fraud, identity fraud, cigarette smuggling, trademark counterfeiting and sales of counterfeit goods, and the theft and redistribution of infant formula. These enterprises rely on extensive networks of international criminal associates and can be highly sophisticated in their criminal operations. Middle Eastern criminal organizations often engage in joint criminal ventures with one another and across ethnic lines when there is potential profit.

EASTERN EUROPEAN GANGS Eastern European gangs trace their origins to countries spanning the Baltics, the Balkans, Central/Eastern Europe, Russia, the Caucasus, and Central Asia. For example, Albanian organized crime activities in the United States include gambling, money laundering, drug trafficking, human smuggling, extortion, violent witness intimidation, robbery, attempted murder, and murder.[97]

Although ethnically based, they work with other ethnic groups when perpetrating crimes. Trading in illegal arms, narcotics, pornography, and prostitution, they operate a multibillion-dollar transnational crime cartel. Balkan organized crime groups have recently expanded into more sophisticated crimes, including real estate fraud. Take for instance Armenian Power (AP), an international organized crime group whose illegal activities allegedly range from bank fraud and identity theft to violent extortion and kidnapping. In one scheme, AP caused more than $2 million in losses when members secretly installed "skimming" devices in cash register credit card swipe machines at Southern California 99 Cents Only stores to steal customer account information and then used it to create counterfeit debit and credit cards to empty accounts. With 200 known members, AP got its start as a neighborhood gang in the 1980s but has now morphed into a transnational crime group with close ties to other gangs, including the Mexican mafia. AP's leadership also maintains ties to Armenia and Russia and deals directly with top organized crime figures in those countries, even to the point of using respected mediators from the Russian mafia to settle disputes.[98] The government began to crack down on this group and eventually indicted 90 Armenian Power leaders, members, and associates, including the head man, Mher Darbinyan, aka "Hollywood Mike" and "Capone." Darbinyan was indicted for a bank fraud scheme that used middlemen and runners to deposit and cash hundreds of thousands of dollars in fraudulent checks drawn on the accounts of elderly bank customers and businesses. He also organized and operated a complex debit card scheme that involved the installation and use of skimmers to steal thousands of customers' debit card numbers and PIN codes. He was eventually sentenced to 32 years in prison; 87 other members have been convicted. The AP case shows how today's transnational crime groups rely more on sophisticated cybercrime conspiracies than they do on the brute force of yesterday's organized criminals.[99]

Organized groups prey upon women in the poorest areas of Europe—Romania, Ukraine, Bosnia—and sell them into virtual sexual slavery. Many of these women are transported as prostitutes around the world, some finding themselves in the United States.

RUSSIAN TRANSNATIONAL CRIME GROUPS Since the collapse of the Soviet Union in 1991, criminal organizations in Russia and other former Soviet republics such as Ukraine have engaged in a variety of crimes: drugs and arms trafficking, stolen automobiles, trafficking in women and children, and money laundering.[100] No area of the world seems immune, especially not the United States. America is the land of opportunity for unloading criminal goods and laundering dirty money.

Russian organized crime is not primarily based on ethnic or family structures. Instead, it is based on economic necessity that was nurtured by the oppressive Soviet regime. A professional criminal class developed in Soviet prisons during the Stalinist period that began in 1924—the era of the gulag. These criminals adopted behaviors, rules, values, and sanctions that bound them together in what was called the thieves' world, led by the elite *vory v zakone* (thieves in law). This thieves' world, and particularly the *vory*, created and maintained the bonds and climate of trust necessary for carrying out organized crime. The following are some specific characteristics of Russian organized crime in the post-Soviet era:

- Russian criminals make extensive use of the state governmental apparatus to protect and promote their criminal activities. For example, most businesses in Russia—legal, quasi-legal, and illegal—must operate with the protection of a *krysha* (roof). The protection is often provided by police or security officials employed outside their "official" capacities for this purpose. In other cases, officials are "silent partners" in criminal enterprises that they, in turn, protect.
- As Communism collapsed, the privatization of industry resulted in the massive use of state funds for criminal gain. Valuable properties are purchased through insider deals for much less than their true value and then resold for lucrative profits.
- Criminals have been able to directly influence the state's domestic and foreign policies to promote the interests of organized crime, either by attaining public office themselves or by buying public officials.

Beyond these particular features, organized crime in Russia shares other characteristics that are common to organized crime elsewhere in the world:

- Systematic use of violence, including both the threat and use of lethal force
- Hierarchical structure
- Limited or exclusive membership
- Specialization in types of crime and a division of labor
- Military-style discipline, with strict rules and regulations for the organization as a whole
- Possession of high-tech equipment, including military weapons
- Threats, blackmail, and violence used to penetrate business management and assume control of commercial enterprises or, in some instances, to found their own enterprises with money from their criminal activities

As a result of these activities, corruption and organized crime are globalized. Russian organized crime is active in Europe, Africa, Asia, and North and South America.

Massive money laundering is now common, which allows Russian and foreign organized crime to flourish. In some cases, it is tied to terrorist funding.

The organized crime threat to Russia's national security is now becoming a global threat. Russian organized crime operates both on its own and in cooperation with foreign groups. The latter cooperation often comes in the form of joint money laundering ventures. Russian criminals have become involved in killings for hire in central and western Europe, Israel, Canada, and the United States.

In the United States, with the exception of extortion and money laundering, Russians have had little or no involvement in some of the more traditional types of organized crime, such as drug trafficking, gambling, and loan sharking. However, thousands of Russian immigrants are believed to be involved in criminal activity, primarily in Russian enclaves in New York City.[101] Russian criminal groups are extensively engaged in a broad array of frauds and scams, including health care fraud, insurance scams, stock frauds, antiquities swindles, forgery, and fuel tax evasion schemes. Russians are believed to be the main purveyors of credit card fraud in the United States. Legitimate businesses, such as the movie business and the textile industry, have become targets of criminals from the former Soviet Union, and they are often used for money laundering and extortion.

ITALIAN ORGANIZED CRIME GROUPS Italian criminal societies—aka the Mafia—are active in Italy and impact the world. There are several groups now operating in the United States: the Sicilian Mafia, the Camorra or Neapolitan Mafia, the 'Ndrangheta or Calabrian Mafia, and the Sacra Corona Unita or United Sacred Crown. These groups have approximately 25,000 members total, with 250,000 affiliates worldwide. There are more than 3,000 members and affiliates of the Italian Mafia in the United States located in the major cities in the Northeast, the Midwest, California, and the South. Their largest presence centers around New York, southern New Jersey, and Philadelphia. These groups have been involved in heroin trafficking for decades. They also engage in illegal gambling, political corruption, extortion, kidnapping, fraud, counterfeiting, infiltration of legitimate businesses, murders, bombings, and weapons trafficking. Industry experts in Italy estimate that their worldwide criminal activity is worth more than $100 billion annually.[102]

LATIN AMERICAN AND MEXICAN DRUG CARTELS Transnational crime cartels operate freely in South American nations such as Peru and Columbia. Caribbean nations such as Jamaica, the Dominican Republic, and Haiti are home to drug and gun smuggling gangs. The money from illicit trade strengthens and enlarges the gangs, enabling them to increase their involvement in intraregional and transnational dealing in order to gain more money. Furthermore, drug trafficking has contributed to a sharp increase in the availability and usage of firearms.[103]

However, while island groups flourish, it is the Mexican drug cartels that are now of greatest concern. These transnational gangs have become large-scale suppliers of narcotics, marijuana, and methamphetamines to the United States, and Mexico has become a drug-producing and transit country. In addition, an estimated 90 percent of cocaine entering the United States transits Mexico. Mexican drug gangs routinely use violence, and fighting for control of the border regions has affected US citizens. More than 60 Americans have been kidnapped, and Mexican drug cartel members have threatened to kill US journalists covering drug violence in the border region. Although Mexican drug cartels, or drug trafficking organizations, have existed for quite some time, they have become more powerful since Colombia was able to crack down on the Cali and Medellín cartels in the 1990s. Mexican drug cartels now dominate the wholesale illicit drug market in the United States. As a result, Mexican cartels are the leading wholesale launderers of drug money from the United States. Mexican and Colombian trafficking organizations annually smuggle an estimated $25 billion in drug proceeds into Mexico for laundering.

There are numerous drug cartels operating in Mexico, the main ones being Gulf, Sinaloa, Knights Templar, and Juárez. Some are dominant in local regions, while the major gangs—Gulf, Sinaloa, Los Zetas—are present throughout all of Mexico.

In recent years, new cartels have formed and others have become allies, in a constantly shifting landscape of drug activity.

ASIAN TRANSNATIONAL CRIME GROUPS Asian-based transnational crime groups are also quite active in such areas as human trafficking, narcotics, and money laundering.[104] Chinese gangs are involved in importing heroin from the neighboring Golden Triangle area and distributing it throughout the country. They are also involved in gambling and prostitution, activities that had all but disappeared under Mao Zedong's Communist regime.

The two leading organized crime problems in Cambodia are drug production/trafficking and human trafficking. Drug traffickers also use Cambodia as a transit country and traffic Cambodian women into Thailand for sexual purposes. In Taiwan, the number one organized crime problem is *heijin*, the penetration of mobsters into the legitimate business sector and the political arena. Gangs are now heavily involved in the businesses of bid-rigging, waste disposal, construction, cable television networks, telecommunications, stock trading, and entertainment. Further, starting in the mid-1980s, many criminals have successfully run for public office in order to protect themselves from police crackdowns. Taiwan's gangs are involved in gambling, prostitution, loan sharking, debt collection, extortion, and gang violence; kidnapping for ransom is also a serious concern.

Among the best-known Asian crime groups are:

- *Yakuza*. Japanese criminal group. Often involved in multinational criminal activities, including human trafficking, gambling, prostitution, and undermining licit businesses.
- *Fuk Ching*. Chinese organized criminal group in the United States. They have been involved in smuggling, street violence, and human trafficking.
- *Triads*. Underground criminal societies based in Hong Kong. They control secret markets and bus routes and are often involved in money laundering and drug trafficking.
- *Heijin*. Taiwanese gangsters who are often executives in large corporations. They are often involved in white-collar crimes, such as illegal stock trading and bribery, and sometimes run for public office.
- *Jao Pho*. Organized crime group in Thailand. They are often involved in illegal political and business activity.
- *Red Wa*. Gangsters from Thailand. They are involved in manufacturing and trafficking methamphetamine.[105]

Controlling Transnational Crime

Efforts to combat transnational organized crime are typically in the hands of federal agencies. One approach is to form international working groups to collect intelligence, share information, and plot unified strategies among member nations. The FBI belongs to several international working groups aimed at combating transnational gangs in various parts of the world. For example, to combat the influence and reach of Eurasian organized crime the FBI is involved in the following groups and activities:

- *Eurasian Organized Crime Working Group*. Established in 1994, it meets to discuss and jointly address the transnational aspects of Eurasian organized crime that impact member countries and the international community in general. The member countries are Canada, Great Britain, Germany, France, Italy, Japan, the United States, and Russia.
- *Central European Working Group*. This group is part of a project that brings together the FBI and Central European law enforcement agencies to discuss cooperative investigative matters covering the broad spectrum of Eurasian organized crime. A principal concern is the growing presence of Russian and other Eurasian organized criminals in central Europe and the United States. The initiative works on practical interaction between the participating agencies to establish lines of communication and working relationships, to develop strategies and tactics to address

transnational organized crime matters impacting the region, and to identify potential common targets.

- *Southeast European Cooperative Initiative.* This is an international organization intended to coordinate police and customs regional actions for preventing and combating transborder crime. It is headquartered in Bucharest, Romania, and has 12 fully participating member countries. The United States has been one of 14 countries with observer status since 1998. The initiative's center serves as a clearinghouse for information and intelligence sharing, allowing the quick exchange of information in a professional and trustworthy environment. The initiative also supports specialized task forces for countering transborder crime such as the trafficking of people, drugs, and cars; smuggling; financial crimes; terrorism; and other serious transborder crimes.

ANTI–ORGANIZED CRIME LAWS Congress has passed a number of laws that have made it easier for agencies to bring transnational gangs to justice. One of the first measures aimed directly at organized crime was the Interstate and Foreign Travel or Transportation in Aid of Racketeering Enterprises Act (Travel Act).[106] The Travel Act prohibits travel in interstate commerce or use of interstate facilities with the intent to promote, manage, establish, carry on, or facilitate an unlawful activity; it also prohibits the actual or attempted engagement in these activities.

In 1970, Congress passed the Organized Crime Control Act. Title IX of the act, probably its most effective measure, is the **Racketeer Influenced and Corrupt Organization (RICO) Act**.[107] RICO did not create new categories of crimes but rather new categories of offenses in racketeering activity, which it defined as involvement in two or more acts prohibited by 24 existing federal and 8 state statutes. The offenses listed in RICO include state-defined crimes (such as murder, kidnapping, gambling, arson, robbery, bribery, extortion, and narcotic violations) and federally defined crimes (such as bribery, counterfeiting, transmission of gambling information, prostitution, and mail fraud). RICO is designed to limit patterns of organized criminal activity by prohibiting involvement in acts intended to do the following:

- Derive income from racketeering or the unlawful collection of debts and use or investment of such income
- Acquire through racketeering an interest in or control over any enterprise engaged in interstate or foreign commerce
- Conduct business through a pattern of racketeering
- Conspire to use racketeering as a means of making income, collecting loans, or conducting business

An individual convicted under RICO is subject to 20 years in prison and a $25,000 fine. Additionally, the accused must forfeit to the US government any interest in a business in violation of RICO. These penalties are much more potent than simple conviction and imprisonment.

WHY IS IT SO DIFFICULT TO ERADICATE TRANSNATIONAL GANGS? While international cooperation is now common, and law enforcement agencies are willing to work together to fight transnational gangs, these criminal organizations are extremely hard to eradicate. The gangs are ready to use violence and well equipped to carry out threats. Take for instance Los Zetas, whose core followers are former members of the Mexican military's elite Special Air Mobile Force Group (*Grupo Aeromovil de Fuerzas Especiales*, or GAFES). Military trained, the Zetas are able to carry out complex operations and use sophisticated weaponry.[108] They began as enforcers for the Gulf cartel's regional domination but are now Gulf's rivals, and are considered the most powerful Mexican transnational gang. Their base is Nuevo Laredo, but the criminal organization's sphere of influence extends across Mexico and deep into Central America. Unlike most gangs, which obtain most of their income from narcotics, Los Zetas earn about half their income trafficking from arms, kidnapping, and competing for control of trafficking routes along the eastern half of the US–Mexico border. The cartel is

Racketeer Influenced and Corrupt Organizations (RICO) Act
Federal legislation that enables prosecutors to bring additional criminal or civil charges against people whose multiple criminal acts constitute a conspiracy. RICO features monetary penalties that allow the government to confiscate all profits derived from criminal activities. Originally intended to be used against organized criminals, RICO has also been used against white-collar criminals.

Transnational crime is extremely difficult to control. Here, an Afghan man harvests a poppy field in the Khogyani district of Jalalabad, east of Kabul. When foreign troops arrived in Afghanistan in 2001, one of their goals was to stem drug production. Instead, they have concentrated on fighting insurgents and have often been accused of turning a blind eye to the poppy fields. Afghanistan is now the leading provider of poppy, the basic ingredient for heroin. Controlling transnational crimes in places such as Afghanistan is all but impossible.

now considered Mexico's most brutal, and they are suspected of kidnapping and killing Central American migrants headed for the border as well as Mexican bus passengers who traveled through their territory.[109]

Even when a gang can be taken out, it is soon replaced as long as money can be made. Adding to control problems is the fact that the drug trade is an important source of foreign revenue, and destroying the drug trade undermines the economies of third-world nations. Even if the government of one nation were willing to cooperate in vigorous drug suppression efforts, suppliers in other nations, eager to cash in on the sellers' market, would be encouraged to turn more acreage over to coca or poppy production. Today, almost every Caribbean country is involved with narcotrafficking, and illicit drug shipments in the region are worth more money than the top five legitimate exports combined. Drug gangs are able to corrupt the political structure and destabilize countries. Drug addiction and violent crime are now common in Jamaica, Puerto Rico, and even small islands like St. Kitts. There are also indications that the drug syndicates may be planting a higher yield variety of coca and improving refining techniques to replace crops lost to government crackdowns.

The United States has little influence in some key drug-producing areas such as Taliban-held Afghanistan and Myanmar (formerly Burma). War and terrorism also may make gang control strategies problematic. After the United States toppled Afghanistan's Taliban government, the remnants began to grow and sell poppy to support their insurgency; Afghanistan now supplies 90 percent of the world's opium.[110] And while the Colombian guerillas may not be interested in joining or colluding with crime cartels, they finance their war against the government by aiding drug traffickers and "taxing" crops and sales. Considering these problems, it is not surprising that transnational gangs continue to flourish.

Thinking Like a Criminologist

Big Brother Is Watching You

The president's national security adviser approaches you with a problem. It seems that a tracking device has been developed that will allow people to be constantly monitored. Implanted under the skin at birth, the data surveillance device could potentially cover *everyone*, with a record of every transaction and activity they engage in entered into databases monitored by powerful search engines that would keep them under constant surveillance. The surveillance device would enable the government to keep tabs on their whereabouts as well as monitoring biological activities such as brain waves, heart rate, and so on. The benefits are immense. Once a person becomes a suspect in a crime or is believed to be part of a terrorist cell, he or she can be easily monitored from a distance without danger to any government agent. The suspect cannot hide or escape detection. Physical readings could be made to determine if the suspect is under stress, using banned substances, and so on.

The director wants you to write a paper for the NSA expressing your opinion on this device. You begin by reading what the American Civil Liberties Union has to say: "The United States is at risk of turning into a full-fledged surveillance society. The tremendous explosion in surveillance-enabling technologies, combined with the ongoing weakening in legal restraints that protect our privacy, mean that we are drifting toward a surveillance society. The good news is that it can be stopped. Unfortunately, right now the big picture is grim."

Writing Assignment:

Is the surveillance implant worthwhile considering the threats faced by America from terrorists and criminals? Or, as the ACLU suggests, would it be unethical because it violates the personal privacy and freedom of people before they have broken any law?

SUMMARY

LO1 Trace the evolution of cybercrime.

Cybercrime is a new breed of offenses that involve the theft and/or destruction of information, resources, or funds utilizing computers, computer networks, and the Internet. Cybercrime presents a challenge for the justice system because it is rapidly evolving, it is difficult to detect through traditional law enforcement channels, and its control demands that agents of the justice system develop technical skills that match those of the perpetrators. Cybercrime has grown because information technology (IT) has become part of daily life in most industrialized societies.

LO2 Compare and contrast cybertheft, cybervandalism, and cyberwar.

Some cybercrimes use modern technology to accumulate goods and services (cybertheft). Cybervandalism involves malicious attacks aimed at disrupting, defacing, and destroying technology that the attackers find offensive. Cyberwar is aimed at undermining the social, economic, and political system of an enemy nation by destroying its electronic infrastructure and disrupting its economy. A significant aspect of modern cyberwarfare is the use of the Internet by terrorists to plan operations, raise funds, and attack computer networks.

LO3 Evaluate how the Internet can facilitate the sale of illegal materials.

The Internet has become an important source for selling and distributing obscene material. While some sites cater to legal sexually related material, others cross the legal border by peddling access to obscene material or even kiddie porn. It is unlikely that any law enforcement efforts will put a dent in the Internet porn industry. It is also possible to obtain drugs via the Net without a prescription or with bogus prescriptions.

LO4 Discuss efforts to control cybercrime.

The growth of cybercrime and its cost to the economy have created the need for new laws and enforcement processes specifically aimed at controlling its new and emerging formulations. Congress has treated computer-related crime as a distinct federal offense since passage of the Counterfeit Access Device and Computer Fraud and Abuse Law in 1984. Because cybercrime is relatively new, existing laws sometimes are inadequate to address the problem. Therefore new legislation has been drafted to protect the public from this new breed of criminal. Specialized enforcement agencies have been created to crack down on cybercriminals.

LO5 Describe the evolution of organized crime.

Organized crime today is transnational. With the aid of the Internet and instant communications, groups are operating on a global scale to traffic drugs and people, to launder money, and to sell arms. Eastern European crime families are active abroad and in the United States. Russian organized crime has become a major problem for law enforcement agencies. Mexican and Latin American groups are quite active in the drug trade; Asian crime families are involved in smuggling and other illegal activities.

LO6 List the activities of transnational organized crime.

Efforts to combat transnational organized crime are typically in the hands of federal agencies. One approach is to form international working groups to collect intelligence, share information, and plot unified strategies among member nations. The FBI belongs to several international working groups aimed at combating transnational gangs in various parts of the world. While international cooperation is now common and law enforcement agencies are willing to work together to fight transnational gangs, these criminal organizations are extremely hard to eradicate. The gangs are ready to use violence and well equipped to carry out threats.

Part 3 ■ CRIME TYPOLOGIES

Key Terms

cybercrime 490
cybertheft 490
cybervandalism 490
cyberwar 490
cyberterrorism 490
ATM skimming 491
darknet 493

denial-of-service attack 495
warez 496
identity theft 497
phishing 498
spear-fishing 498
etailing fraud 499

malware 501
computer worms 501
Trojan horse 501
logic bomb 501
website defacement 502
cyberstalking 503
cyberbullying 503

cyberspying 507
cyberespionage 511
transnational organized crime 514
Racketeer Influenced and Corrupt Organization Act (RICO) 521

Critical Thinking Questions

1. Which theories of criminal behavior best explain the actions of cybercriminals, and which ones do you believe fail to explain cybercrime?
2. How would you punish a web page defacer who placed an antiwar message on a government site? Prison? Fine?
3. What guidelines would you recommend for the use of IT in law enforcement?
4. Are we creating a "Big Brother" society and is the loss of personal privacy worth the price of safety?
5. How can cyberbullies be convinced of the harmfulness of their acts? Would it be ethical to create a web page mocking them as punishment?
6. Does the media glamorize organized crime? Does it paint an inaccurate picture of noble crime lords fighting to protect their families?

Notes

All URLs accessed in 2017.

1. US Department of Justice, US Attorney's Office, Southern District of Florida, "Miami Student Sentenced for Cyberstalking on Facebook and Instagram," August 31, 2016, https://www.justice.gov/usao-sdfl/pr/miami-student-sentenced-cyberstalking-facebook-and-instagram.
2. Allan Travis, "Crime Rate in England and Wales Soars as Cybercrime Is Included for First Time," Office of Home Statistics, 2015, https://www.theguardian.com/uk-news/2015/oct/15/rate-in-england-and-wales-soars-as-cybercrime-included-for-first-time.
3. Maria Tcherni, Andrew Davies, Giza Lopes, and Alan Lizotte, "The Dark Figure of Online Property Crime: Is Cyberspace Hiding a Crime Wave?" *Justice Quarterly*, published online January 8, 2015, http://digitalcommons.newhaven.edu/criminaljustice-facpubs/43/.
4. McAfee, "Net Losses: Estimating the Global Cost of Cybercrime: Economic Impact of Cybercrime II," Center for Strategic and International Studies, June 2014, http://www.mcafee.com/us/resources/reports/rp-economic-impact-cybercrime2.pdf.
5. Rutger Leukfeldt, Edward Kleemans, and Wouter Stol, "Cybercriminal Networks, Social Ties and Online Forums: Social Ties Versus Digital Ties Within Phishing and Malware Networks," *British Journal of Criminology* 57 (2017): 704–722.
6. FBI, Internet Crime Complaint Center, *2015 Internet Crime Report*, https://pdf.ic3.gov/2015_IC3Report.pdf.
7. Brian Krebs, "Thieves Planted Malware to Hack ATMs," Krebs on Security, May 30, 2014, https://krebsonsecurity.com/2014/05/thieves-planted-malware-to-hack-atms/.
8. Steven A. Meyerowitz, "Taking a Trip to the ATM? Beware of 'Skimmers,'" Lexis/Nexis Legal Newsroom, July 15, 2011, https://www.lexisnexis.com/legalnewsroom/financial-fraud-law/b/blog/archive/2014/01/06/taking-a-trip-to-the-atm-beware-of-39-skimmers-39.aspx.

9. Andreas Philaretou, "Sexuality and the Internet," *Journal of Sex Research* 42 (2005): 180–181.

10. Mike Snider, "'Playboy' Brings Nudity Back to Magazine," *USA Today*, February 14, 2017, https://www.usatoday.com/story/money/business/2017/02/13/playboy-brings-nudity-back-magazine/97868038/.

11. Julie Ruvolo, "How Much of the Internet Is Actually for Porn?" *Forbes*, September 7, 2011.

12. Ibid.

13. Marie-Helen Maras, *Computer Forensics: Cybercriminals, Laws, and Evidence* (Sudbury, MA: Jones and Bartlett, 2011).

14. Jeordan Legon, "Sex Sells, Especially to Web Surfers: Internet Porn a Booming, Billion-Dollar Industry," CNN, December 11, 2003, http://www.cnn.com/2003/TECH/internet/12/10/porn.business/.

15. National Center on Addiction and Substance Abuse at Columbia University, "'You've Got Drugs!' IV: Prescription Drug Pushers on the Internet," 2008, http://www.casacolumbia.org/addiction-research/reports/youve-got-drugs-perscription-drug-pushers-internet-2008.

16. US Attorney's Office, District of Colorado, "Former Fort Collins Resident Sentenced for Denial of Service Attack on Larimer County Government Computers," June 6, 2013, https://www.fbi.gov/denver/press-releases/2013/former-fort-collins-resident-sentenced-for-denial-of-service-attack-on-larimer-county-government-computers.

17. Top Tech News, "Rutgers Suffers Foreign DDoS Attack," March 30, 2015, http://www.toptechnews.com/article/index.php?story_id=1320044NONV0.

18. Saul Hansell, "U.S. Tally in Online-Crime Sweep: 150 Charged," *New York Times*, August 27, 2004, p. C1.

19. Stephen Baker and Brian Grow, "Gambling Sites, This Is a Holdup," *BusinessWeek*, August 9, 2004, pp. 60–62.

20. John Callaham, "Steam and Other Online Gaming Services Hit by DDoS Attacks," January 3, 2014, http://www.neowin.net/news/steam-and-other-online-gaming-services-hit-by-ddos-attacks.

21. Russell Goldman, "What We Know and Don't Know About the International Cyberattack," *New York Times*, May 12, 2017, https://www.nytimes.com/2017/05/12/world/europe/international-cyberattack-ransomware.html.

22. FBI, "Ransomware on the Rise: FBI and Partners Working to Combat This Cyberthreat," January 2015, http://www.fbi.gov/news/stories/2015/january/ransomware-on-the-rise/ransomware-on-the-rise.

23. Symantec, Internet Security Threat Report, Volume 21, April 2016, https://www.symantec.com/content/dam/symantec/docs/reports/istr-21-2016-en.pdf.

24. The Computer Fraud and Abuse Act (CFAA), 18 U.S.C. §1030 (1998).

25. The Digital Millennium Copyright Act, Public Law 105–304 (1998).

26. Title 18, United States Code, Section 2319.

27. Title 17, United States Code, Section 506.

28. Jim Wolf, "Internet Scams Targeted in Sweep: A 10-Day Crackdown Leads to 62 Arrests and 88 Indictments," *Boston Globe*, May 22, 2001, p. A2.

29. These sections rely on APWG, "Phishing Activity Trends Report, 1st Quarter 2016," https://docs.apwg.org/reports/apwg_trends_report_q1_2016.pdf.

30. Erika Harrell, "Victims of Identity Theft, 2014," Bureau of Justice Statistics, 2015 https://www.bjs.gov/content/pub/pdf/vit14.pdf.

31. Linda Foley, Karen Barney, and Jay Foley, "Identity Theft: The Aftermath 2009," Identity Theft Resource Center (ITRC), http://www.idtheftcenter.org/images/surveys_studies/Aftermath2009.pdf.

32. APWG, "Phishing Activity Trends Report, 1st Quarter 2016."

33. Identity Theft Resource Center (ITRC), "Scams and Consumer Alerts," http://www.idtheftcenter.org/Protect-yourself/scams-alerts.html.

34. Identity Theft and Assumption Deterrence Act, as amended by Public Law 105-318, 112 Stat. 3007 (October 30, 1998).

35. Public Law 108–275 (2004).

36. Elizabeth Woyke and Dan Beucke, "Many Not-So-Happy Returns," *Business Week*, August 15, 2005, p. 10.

37. Robert Hackett, "What to Know About the Ashley Madison Hack," *Fortune*, August 26, 2015, http://fortune.com/2015/08/26/ashley-madison-hack/.

38. Anne Branscomb, "Rogue Computer Programs and Computer Rogues: Tailoring Punishment to Fit the Crime," *Rutgers Computer and Technology Law Journal* 16 (1990): 24–26.

39. Hyung-jin Woo, Yeora Kim, and Joseph Dominick, "Hackers: Militants or Merry Pranksters? A Content Analysis of Defaced Web Pages," *Media Psychology* 6 (2004): 63–82.

40. Yona Hollander, "Prevent Web Page Defacement," *Internet Security Advisor* 2 (2000): 1–4.

41. Peter Foster, "David Petraeus Scandal: Jill Kelley Issues Legal Letters," *The Telegraph*, November 28, 2012, http://www.telegraph.co.uk/news/worldnews/northamerica/usa/9709972/David-Petraeus-scandal-Jill-Kelley-issues-legal-letters.html.

42. Janis Wolak, David Finkelhor, Kimberly Mitchell, and Michele Ybarra, "Online 'Predators' and Their Victims: Myths, Realities, and Implications for Prevention and Treatment," *American Psychologist* 63 (2008): 111–128.

43. Centers for Disease Control and Prevention, "Lesbian, Gay, Bisexual and Transgender Health," http://www.cdc.gov/lgbthealth/youth.htm.

44. Jane Ireland and Rachel Monaghan, "Behaviors Indicative of Bullying Among Young and Juvenile Male Offenders: A Study of Perpetrator and Victim Characteristics," *Aggressive Behavior* 32 (2006): 172–180.

45. Dan Olweus, "A Useful Evaluation Design, and Effects of the Olweus Bullying Prevention Program," *Psychology, Crime and Law* 11 (2005): 389–402.

46. This section leans heavily on Justin Patchin and Sameer Hinduja, "Bullies Move Beyond the Schoolyard: A Preliminary Look at Cyberbullying," *Youth Violence and Juvenile Justice* 4 (2006): 148–169.

47. Sameer Hinduja and Justin Patchin, "Cyberbullying: An Exploratory Analysis of Factors Related to Offending and Victimization," *Deviant Behavior* 29 (2008): 129–156.

48. Justin Patchin, "Catfishing as a Form of Cyberbullying," Cyberbullying Research Center, http://cyberbullying.us/catfishing-as-a-form-of-cyberbullying/.

49. Fox News, "Missouri Woman Indicted in MySpace Cyber-Bullying Case that Ended in Teen's Suicide," May 15, 2008, http://www.foxnews.com/story/2008/05/15/missouri-woman-indicted-in-myspace-cyber-bullying-case-that-ended-in-teen.html.

50. Kim Zetter, "Judge Acquits Lori Drew in Cyberbullying Case, Overrules Jury," *Wired*, July 2, 2009, https://www.wired.com/2009/07/drew_court/.

51. Ned Zeman, "The Boy Who Cried Dead Girlfriend," *Vanity Fair*, April 25, 2013, http://www.vanityfair.com/culture/2013/06/manti-teo-girlfriend-nfl-draft.

52. Data in this section come from Sameer Hinduja and Justin Patchin, Cyberbullying Research Center, 2016, http://cyberbullying.org/2016-cyberbullying-data/.

53. Lauren Musu-Gillette, Anlan Zhang, Ke Wang, Jizhi Zhang, and Barbara Oudekerk, "Indicators of School Crime and Safety: 2016," National Center for Education Statistics, https://nces.ed.gov/pubs2017/2017064.pdf.

54. FlexiSPY, Inc., https://www.flexispy.com/en/employee-monitoring.htm.

55. CBS News, "NSA Surveillance Exposed," http://www.cbsnews.com/feature/nsa-surveillance-exposed/.

56. Clyde Wilson, "Software Piracy: Uncovering Mutiny on the Cyberseas," *Trial* 32 (1996): 24–31.

57. Deloitte, "2006 Global Security Survey," http://trygstad.rice.iit.edu:8000/Articles/2006GlobalSecuritySurvey-Deloitte%26Touche.pdf.

58. McAfee Corporation, "Net Losses: Estimating the Global Cost of Cybercrime: Economic Impact of Cybercrime II," Center for Strategic and International Studies, June 2014, https://www.mcafee.com/fr/resources/reports/rp-economic-impact-cybercrime2.pdf.

59. Cyber Security Ventures, "Hackerpocalypse: A Cybercrime Revelation," http://cybersecurityventures.com/hackerpocalypse-cybercrime-report-2016/.

60. Jeremy Kirk, "Identity Theft May Cost IRS $21 Billion Over Next Five Years," *PC World*, August 3, 2012, http://www.pcworld.idg.com.au/article/432584/identity_theft_may_cost_irs_21_billion_over_next_five_years/.

61. McAfee Corporation, "Net Losses: Estimating the Global Cost of Cybercrime."

62. Public Law 98-473, Title H, Chapter XXI, [sections] 2102(a), 98 Stat. 1837, 2190 (1984).

63. Public Law 104-294, Title II, [sections] 201, 110 Stat. 3488, 3491–3494 (1996).

64. Heather Jacobson and Rebecca Green, "Computer Crime," *American Criminal Law Review* 39 (2002): 273–326; Identity Theft and Assumption Act of 1998 (18 U.S.C. S 1028(a)(7)).

65. Comprehensive Crime Control Act of 1984, PL 98–473, 2101–03, 98 Stat. 1837, 2190 (1984), Adding 18 USC 1030 (1984); Counterfeit Active Device and Computer Fraud and Abuse Act, Amended by PL 99–474, 100 Stat. 1213 (1986), Codified at 18 U.S.C. 1030 (Supp. V 1987); Computer Abuse Amendments Act 18 U.S.C. Section 1030 (1994); Copyright Infringement Act 17 U.S.C. Section 506(a) 1994; Electronic Communications Privacy Act of 1986 18 U.S.C. 2510–2520 (1988 and Supp. II 1990).

66. Family Entertainment and Copyright Act of 2005, Title 18 United States Code Section 2319B.

67. Council of Europe Convention on Cybercrime, CETS No. 185, http://conventions.coe.int/Treaty/Commun/QueVoulezVous.asp?NT=185&CL=ENG.

68. ACLU Memo on the Council of Europe Convention on Cybercrime, June 16, 2004, https://www.aclu.org/technology-and-liberty/aclu-memo-council-europe-convention-cybercrime.

69. Bruce Swartz, Deputy Assistant General, Criminal Division, Justice Department, "Internet Fraud Testimony Before the House Energy and Commerce Committee," May 23, 2001.

70. IC3, "Annual Internet Crime Report 2015," https://pdf.ic3.gov/2015_IC3Report.pdf.

71. United States Secret Service, "Cyber Crime Investigations," https://www.secretservice.gov/data/investigation/USSS-Cyber-Investigations-Flyer.pdf.

72. United States Secret Service. "Electronic Crimes Task Forces," 2017, https://www.dhs.gov/sites/default/files/publications/USSS%20Electronic%20Crimes%20Task%20Force.pdf.

73. Metodi Hadji-Janev and Mitko Bogdanoski, "Swarming-Based Cyber Defense Under the Framework of Collective Security," *Security Journal* 30 (2016): 39–59.

74. Richard Stiennon, *There Will Be Cyberwar: How the Move to Network-Centric War Fighting Has Set the Stage for Cyberwar* (Birmingham, MI: IT-Harvest Press, 2015).

75. Richard A. Clarke and Rob Knake, *Cyber War: The Next Threat to National Security and What to Do About It* (New York: HarperCollins, 2012).

76. Fergus Hanson, "Norms of Cyberwar in Peacetime," Brookings Institute, November 17, 2015, http://www.brookings.edu/blogs/markaz/posts/2015/11/17-norms-of-cyberwar-peacetime-hanson.

77. Tara Seals, "Saudi Arabia Issues Shamoon 2 Alert," *Info Security*, 2017, https://www.infosecurity-magazine.com/news/saudi-arabia-issues-shamoon-2-alert/.

78. Ibid.

79. US Department of Justice, "U.S. Charges Russian FSB Officers and Their Criminal Conspirators for Hacking Yahoo and Millions of Email Accounts: FSB Officers Protected, Directed, Facilitated and Paid Criminal Hackers," March 15, 2017, https://www.justice.gov/opa/pr/us-charges-russian-fsb-officers-and-their-criminal-conspirators-hacking-yahoo-and-millions.

80. Damian Paletta, Danny Yadron, and Jennifer Valentino-Devries, "Cyberwar Ignites a New Arms Race," *Wall Street Journal*, October 11, 2015, http://www.wsj.com/articles/cyberwar-ignites-a-new-arms-race-1444611128.

81. US Department of Justice, "Chinese National Pleads Guilty to Conspiring to Hack into U.S. Defense Contractors' Systems to Steal Sensitive Military Information," March 23, 2016, https://www.justice.gov/opa/pr/chinese-national-pleads-guilty-conspiring-hack-us-defense-contractors-systems-steal-sensitive.

82. Kim Zetter, *Countdown to Zero Day: Stuxnet and the Launch of the World's First Digital Weapon* (New York: Broadway Books, 2015); William J. Broad, John Markoff, and David E. Sanger, "Israeli Test on Worm Called Crucial in Iran Nuclear Delay," *New York Times*, January 15, 2011, http://www.nytimes.com/2011/01/16/world/middleeast/16stuxnet.html.

83. US Department of Justice, "Seven Iranians Working for Islamic Revolutionary Guard Corps-Affiliated Entities Charged for Conducting Coordinated Campaign of Cyber Attacks Against U.S. Financial Sector," March 24, 2016, https://www.justice.gov/opa/pr/seven-iranians-working-islamic-revolutionary-guard-corps-affiliated-entities-charged.

84. Joseph Berger "A Dam, Small and Unsung, Is Caught Up in an Iranian Hacking Case," *New York Times*, March 25, 2016, https://www.nytimes.com/2016/03/26/nyregion/rye-brook-dam-caught-in-computer-hacking-case.html.

85. Barry C. Collin, "The Future of CyberTerrorism: Where the Physical and Virtual Worlds Converge," http://www.crime-research.org/library/Cyberter.htm.

86. Tomas Hellström, "Critical Infrastructure and Systemic Vulnerability: Towards a Planning Framework," *Safety Science* 45 (2007): 415–430.

87. Mathieu Gorge, "Cyberterrorism: Hype or Reality?" *Computer Fraud and Security* 2 (2007): 9–12.

88. John Kane and April Wall, "Identifying the Links Between White-Collar Crime and Terrorism," National White Collar Crime Center, 2004, http://www.ncjrs.gov/pdffiles1/nij/grants/209520.pdf.

89. U.S. Department of Defense, "Cyber Strategy," http://www.defense.gov/home/features/2015/0415_cyber-strategy/.

90. National Security Agency/Central Security Service, http://www.nsa.gov/.

91. Jay Albanese, "Deciphering the Linkages Between Organized Crime and Transnational Crime," *Journal of International Affairs* 66 (2012): 1–16.

92. President's Commission on Organized Crime, *Report to the President and the Attorney General, The Impact: Organized Crime Today* (Washington, DC: US Government Printing Office, 1986), pp. 7–8.

93. James O. Finckenauer and Ko-lin Chin, *Asian Transnational Organized Crime and Its Impact on the United States* (Washington, DC: National Institute of Justice, 2007), http://www.ncjrs.gov/pdffiles1/nij/214186.pdf.

94. United Nations Office on Drugs and Crime, "Emerging Crimes," https://www.unodc.org/unodc/en/organized-crime/emerging-crimes.html.

95. Ibid.

96. FBI, "African Transnational Organized Crime Groups," https://www.fbi.gov/investigate/organized-crime.

97. FBI, "Balkan Transnational Organized Crime Groups," https://www.fbi.gov/investigate/organized-crime.

98. FBI, "Operation Power Outage: Armenian Organized Crime Group Targeted," March 3, 2011, https://www.fbi.gov/news/stories/armenian-organized-crime-group-targeted.

99. FBI, "Armenian Power Leader Sentenced to 32 Years in Prison for Racketeering, Extortion, and Fraud Offenses," November 10, 2014, http://www.fbi.gov/losangeles/press-releases/2014/armenian-power-leader-sentenced-to-32-years-in-prison-for-racketeering-extortion-and-fraud-offenses.

100. Louise I. Shelley, "Crime and Corruption: Enduring Problems of Post-Soviet Development," *Demokratizatsiya* 11 (2003): 110–114; James O. Finckenauer and Yuri A. Voronin, *The Threat of Russian Organized Crime* (Washington, DC: National Institute of Justice, 2001).

101. Omar Bartos, "Growth of Russian Organized Crime Poses Serious Threat," *CJ International* 11 (1995): 8–9.

102. FBI, "Italian Transnational Organized Crime Groups," https://www.fbi.gov/investigate/organized-crime.

103. Bilyana Tsvetkova, "Gangs in the Caribbean," *Harvard International Review*, June 2009, http://hir.harvard.edu/gangs-in-the-caribbean.

104. This section leans heavily on Finckenauer and Chin, *Asian Transnational Organized Crime and Its Impact on the United States*.

105. National Institute of Justice, "Major Transnational Organized Crime Groups, 2010," http://www.nij.gov/topics/crime/organized-crime/pages/major-groups.aspx.

106. 18 U.S.C. 1952 (1976).

107. Public Law 91-452, Title IX, 84 Stat. 922 (1970) (codified at 18 U.S.C. 1961–68, 1976).

108. William Booth, "Mexican Azteca Gang Leader Arrested in Killings of 3 Tied to U.S.," *Washington Post*, March 30, 2010, http://www.washingtonpost.com/wp-dyn/content/article/2010/03/29/AR2010032903373.html.

109. Angela Kocherga, "Zeta Leader Captured in Mexico," KVUE News, July 4, 2011, http://www.kvue.com/news/zeta-leader-captured-in-mexico-/411611980.

110. White House press release, "Presidential Determination—Major Drug Transit and Drug Producing Countries for FY 2014," https://obamawhitehouse.archives.gov/the-press-office/2013/09/13/presidential-determination-major-drug-transit-and-drug-producing-countri.

Glossary

acquaintance robbery Robbery in which the victim or victims are people the robber knows.

active precipitation Aggressive or provocative behavior of victims that results in their victimization.

adolescent-limited offenders Kids who get into minor scrapes as youth but whose misbehavior ends when they enter adulthood.

age-graded theory A state dependence theory formulated by Sampson and Laub that assumes that the causal association between early delinquent offending and later adult deviant behavior involves the quality of relationships encountered at different times in human development.

aggravated assault An unlawful attack by one person upon another, accompanied by the use of a weapon, for the purpose of inflicting severe or aggravated bodily injury.

aggravated rape Rape involving multiple offenders, weapons, and victim injuries.

aging out Phrase used to express the fact that people commit less crime as they mature.

al-Qaeda (Arabic for "the base") An international fundamentalist Islamist organization comprising independent and collaborative cells, whose goal is reducing Western influence upon Islamic affairs. Also spelled al-Qa'ida.

American Dream The goal of accumulating material goods and wealth through individual competition; the process of being socialized to pursue material success and to believe it is achievable.

androgens Male sex hormones.

anomie A lack of norms or clear social standards. Because of rapidly shifting moral values, the individual has few guides to what is socially acceptable.

anomie theory The view that anomie results when socially defined goals (such as wealth and power) are universally mandated but access to legitimate means (such as education and job opportunities) is stratified by class and status.

antisocial personality Combination of traits, such as hyperactivity, impulsivity, hedonism, and inability to empathize with others, that make a person prone to deviant behavior and violence; also referred to as sociopathic or psychopathic personality.

appeal Taking a criminal case to a higher court on the grounds that the defendant was found guilty because of legal error or violation of his or her constitutional rights.

arousal theory The view that people seek to maintain a preferred level of arousal but vary in how they process sensory input. A need for high levels of environmental stimulation may lead to aggressive, violent behavior patterns.

arraignment The step in the criminal justice process in which the accused is brought before the trial judge, formal charges are read, defendants are informed of their rights, a plea is entered, bail is considered, and a trial date is set.

arrest The taking into police custody of an individual suspected of a crime.

arson The willful or malicious burning of a dwelling house, public building, motor vehicle, aircraft, personal property of another, or the like.

assault Either attempted battery or intentionally frightening the victim by word or deed (actual touching is not required).

ATM skimming Using an electronic device or camera on an ATM that copies information from a bank card's magnetic strip whenever a customer uses the machine or photographs their key strokes.

attachment theory Bowlby's theory that being able to form an emotional bond to another person is an important aspect of mental health throughout the life span.

attention deficit hyperactivity disorder (ADHD) A developmentally inappropriate lack of attention, along with impulsivity and hyperactivity.

authority conflict pathway The path to a criminal career that begins with early stubborn behavior and defiance of parents.

bail A money bond intended to ensure that the accused will return for trial.

battery Offensive touching, such as slapping, hitting, or punching a victim.

behavior modeling The process of learning behavior (notably, aggression) by observing others. Aggressive models may be parents, criminals in the neighborhood, or characters on television or in movies.

behavior theory The view that all human behavior is learned through a process of social reinforcement (rewards and punishment).

binge drinking Having five or more drinks on the same occasion (that is, at the same time or within a couple of hours of one another).

bipolar disorder An emotional disturbance in which moods alternate between periods of wild elation and deep depression.

Black Lives Matter (BLM) A movement whose aim is to reduce institutional violence and perceived systemic racism toward black people.

blue-collar crimes Traditional common-law theft crimes such as larceny, burglary, and arson.

booking Fingerprinting, photographing, and recording personal information of a suspect in police custody.

booster (heel) Professional shoplifter who steals with the intention of reselling stolen merchandise.

booster box Device with a false bottom that can be open and shut by a professional shoplifter, lined with metal or some other substance to prevent security tags from setting off alarms, placed over merchandise.

burglary The unlawful entry of a structure to commit a felony or a theft.

capable guardians Effective deterrents to crime, such as police or watchful neighbors.

capital punishment The execution of criminal offenders; the death penalty.

car cloning Using a vehicle identification number (VIN) from a legally registered car to hide the identity of a stolen vehicle for resale.

Chicago School Group of urban sociologists who studied the relationship between environmental conditions and crime.

child abuse Any physical or emotional trauma to a child for which no reasonable explanation, such as an accident or ordinary disciplinary practices, can be found.

child sexual abuse The exploitation of children through rape, incest, and molestation by parents or other adults.

chiseling Using illegal means to cheat an organization, its consumers, or both, on a regular basis.

chronic offenders (career criminals) The small group of persistent offenders who account for a majority of all criminal offenses.

classical criminology Theoretical perspective suggesting that people choose to commit crime and that crime can be controlled if potential criminals fear punishment.

cleared crimes Crimes are cleared in two ways: when at least one person is arrested, charged, and turned over to the court for prosecution; or by exceptional means, when some element beyond police control precludes the physical arrest of an offender (for example, the offender leaves the country).

Code of Hammurabi The first written criminal code, developed in Babylonia about 1750 BCE.

cognitive theory Psychological perspective that focuses on the mental processes by which people perceive and represent the world around them and solve problems.

collective efficacy Social control exerted by cohesive communities and based on mutual trust, including intervention in the supervision of children and maintenance of public order.

commitment to conformity Obedience to the rules of society and the avoidance of nonconforming behavior that may jeopardize an individual's reputation and achievement.

common law Early English law, developed by judges, which became the standardized law of the land in England and eventually formed the basis of the criminal law in the United States.

compliance strategies Methods of controlling white-collar crime that rely on the threat of economic sanctions or civil penalties to control potential violators, creating a marketplace incentive to obey the law.

computer worms Programs that attack computer networks (or the Internet) by self-replicating and sending themselves to other users, generally via email, without the aid of the operator.

concentration effect As working-class and middle-class families flee inner-city poverty-ridden areas, the most disadvantaged population is consolidated in urban ghettos.

conduct disorder (CD) A pattern of repetitive behavior in which the rights of others or social norms are violated.

conflict theory The view that human behavior is shaped by interpersonal conflict and that those who maintain social power will use it to further their own ends.

conflict view The belief that criminal behavior is defined by those in power in such a way as to protect and advance their own self-interest.

consensus view The belief that the majority of citizens in a society share common values and agree on what behaviors should be defined as criminal.

consent The victim of rape must prove that she in no way encouraged, enticed, or misled the accused rapist.

constructive possession A legal fiction that applies to situations in which persons voluntarily give up physical custody of their property but still retain legal ownership.

corporate (organizational) crime Powerful institutions or their representatives willfully violate the laws that restrain these institutions from doing social harm or require them to do social good.

covert pathway A path to a criminal career that begins with minor underhanded behavior and progresses to fire starting and theft.

crackdowns The concentration of police resources on particular problem areas, such as street-level drug dealing, to eradicate or displace criminal activity.

crime An act, deemed socially harmful or dangerous, that is specifically defined, prohibited, and punished under the criminal law.

crime discouragers People who serve as guardians of property or people.

criminal career Engaging in antisocial acts early in adolescence and continuing illegal behaviors into adulthood. A pattern of persistent offending across the life course.

criminal environmental pollution A crime involving the intentional or negligent discharge into the biosystem of a toxic waste that destroys plant or animal life.

criminal justice System made up of the agencies of social control, such as police departments, courts, and correctional institutions that handle criminal offenders.

criminal justice system The agencies of government—police, courts, and corrections—that are responsible for apprehending, adjudicating, sanctioning, and treating criminal offenders.

criminal law The written code that defines crimes and their punishments.

criminogenic knowledge structure (CKS) The view that negative life events are connected and produce a hostile view of people and relationships, preference for immediate rewards, and a cynical view of conventional norms.

criminology The scientific study of the nature, extent, cause, and control of criminal behavior.

crisis intervention Emergency counseling for crime victims.

critical criminologists Criminologists who believe that the cause of crime can be linked to economic, social, and political disparity.

critical criminology The view that crime is a product of the capitalist system.

critical feminism The study of gender from a critical perspective. It typically involves such issues as the effects of gender inequality and the unequal power of men and women in a capitalist society.

cultural deviance theory Branch of social structure theory that sees strain and social disorganization together resulting in a unique lower-class culture that conflicts with conventional social norms.

cultural transmission Process whereby values, beliefs, and traditions are handed down from one generation to the next.

culture conflict Result of exposure to opposing norms, attitudes, and definitions of right and wrong, moral and immoral.

culture of poverty A separate lower-class culture, characterized by apathy, cynicism, helplessness, and mistrust of social institutions such as schools, government agencies, and the police, that is passed from one generation to the next.

cumulative disadvantage The tendency of prior social problems to produce future ones that accumulate and undermine success.

cyberbullying Willful and repeated harm inflicted through the medium of electronic text.

cybercrime The use of modern technology for criminal purposes.

cyberespionage Efforts by intelligence agencies to penetrate computer networks of an enemy nation in order to steal important data.

cyberspying Illegally using the Internet to gather information that is considered private and confidential.

cyberstalking Use of the Internet, email, or other electronic communications devices to stalk another person. Some cyberstalkers pursue minors through online chat rooms; others harass their victims electronically.

cyberterrorism Internet attacks against an enemy nation's technological infrastructure.

cybertheft Use of computer networks for criminal profits. Illegal copyright infringement, identity theft, and Internet securities fraud are examples of cybertheft.

cybervandalism Malicious attacks aimed at disrupting, defacing, and destroying technology.

cyberwar Using cyberspace for acts of war, including spying and disrupting an enemy's computer network.

cycle of violence A hypothesis that suggests that a childhood history of physical abuse predisposes the survivor to becoming violent themselves in later years.

darknet Computer network that can only be accessed using nonstandard communications protocols and ports, with restricted access that can only be opened with specific software configurations.

date rape A rape that involves people who are in some form of courting relationship.

decriminalized Having criminal penalties reduced rather than eliminated.

defensible space The principle that crime can be prevented or displaced by modifying the physical environment to reduce the opportunity that individuals have to commit crime.

deliberation Planning a criminal act after careful thought, rather than carrying it out on impulse.

delinquent subculture A value system adopted by lower-class youths that is directly opposed to that of the larger society.

demystify To unmask the true purpose of law, justice, or other social institutions.

denial-of-service attack (DoS) Extorting money from an Internet service user by threatening to prevent the user from having access to the service.

Department of Homeland Security (DHS) An agency of the federal government charged with preventing terrorist attacks within the United States, reducing America's vulnerability to terrorism, and minimizing the damage and aiding recovery from attacks that do occur.

deterrence strategies Methods of controlling white-collar crime that rely on the punishment of individual offenders to deter other would-be violators.

developmental theories The view that criminality is a dynamic process, influenced by social experiences as well as individual characteristics.

deviance amplification Process whereby secondary deviance pushes offenders out of mainstream society and locks them into an escalating cycle of deviance, apprehension, labeling, and criminal self-identity.

deviant behavior Actions that depart from the social norm. Some are considered criminal, others merely harmless aberrations.

deviant place theory The view that victimization is primarily a function of where people live.

differential association theory The view that people commit crime when their social learning leads them to perceive more definitions favoring crime than favoring conventional behavior.

differential opportunity The view that lower-class youths, whose legitimate opportunities are limited, join gangs and pursue criminal careers as alternative means to achieve universal success goals.

differential reinforcement Behavior is reinforced by being either rewarded or punished while interacting with others; also called direct conditioning.

differential susceptibility model The belief that there is an indirect association between traits and crime.

diffusion An effect that occurs when efforts to prevent one crime unintentionally prevent another.

Director of National Intelligence (DNI) Government official charged with coordinating data from the nation's primary intelligence-gathering agencies.

discouragement An effect that occurs when crime control efforts targeting a particular locale help reduce crime in surrounding areas and populations.

displacement An effect that occurs when crime control efforts simply move, or redirect, offenders to less heavily guarded alternative targets.

diversion programs Programs of rehabilitation that remove offenders from the normal channels of the criminal justice process, thus enabling them to avoid the stigma of a criminal label.

dizygotic (DZ) twins Fraternal (nonidentical) twins.

drift Movement in and out of delinquency, shifting between conventional and deviant values.

dropout factories High schools in which the completion rate is consistently 40 percent or less.

drug-dependent personality A personal trait characterized by a pervasive psychological dependence on mood-altering substances.

early onset The view that kids who begin engaging in antisocial behaviors at a very early age are the ones most at risk for a criminal career.

economic compulsive behavior Violence committed by drug users to support their habit.

economic crime An act committed in violation of the criminal law for the purpose of monetary gain and financial benefits.

egalitarian families Families in which spouses share similar positions of power at home and in the workplace.

ego The part of the personality developed in early childhood that helps control the id and keep people's actions within the boundaries of social convention.

eldercide Murder of a senior citizen.

election fraud Illegal interference with the process of an election. Acts of fraud tend to involve affecting vote counts to bring about a desired election outcome, whether by increasing the vote share of the favored candidate, depressing the vote share of the rival candidates, or both. Varieties of election fraud include intimidation, disruption of polling places, distribution of misinformation such as the wrong election date, registration fraud, and vote buying.

embezzlement A type of larceny in which someone who is trusted with someone else's personal property fraudulently converts it to his or her own use or for the use of others.

eros The life instinct, which drives people toward self-fulfillment and enjoyment.

espionage The practice of obtaining information about a government, organization, or society that is considered secret or confidential without the permission of the holder of the information. Commonly called spying.

etailing fraud Illegally buying and/or selling merchandise on the Internet.

exploitation Forcing victims to pay for services or contracts to which they have a clear right.

expressive crimes Offenses committed not for profit or gain but to vent rage, anger, or frustration.

expressive violence Violence that is designed not for profit or gain but to vent rage, anger, or frustration.

extinction An effect that occurs when crime reduction programs produce a short-term positive effect, but benefits dissipate as criminals adjust to new conditions.

failed state A nation whose government has lost control of its own territory, is unable to provide public services and protection, and lacks the ability to interact with other states as a full member of the international community.

felony A serious offense that carries a penalty of imprisonment, usually for one year or more, and may entail loss of political rights.

felony murder A killing that accompanies a felony, such as robbery or rape.

fence A buyer and seller of stolen merchandise.

feticide Intentional or negligent killing of a human fetus.

filicide Murder of an older child.

first-degree murder Killing a person after premeditation and deliberation.

focal concerns Values, such as toughness and street smarts, that have evolved specifically to fit conditions in lower-class environments.

focused deterrence The view that police can deter crime by using every strategy possible and also by directly interacting with offenders and communicating clear consequences if they engage in criminal activity.

forcible rape Under common law, the carnal knowledge of a female forcibly and against her will. In 2012, a new broader definition of rape was implemented: "The penetration, no matter how slight, of the vagina or anus with any body part or object, or oral penetration by a sex organ of another person, without the consent of the victim."

general deterrence A crime control policy that depends on the fear of criminal penalties convincing the potential law violator that the pains associated with crime outweigh its benefits.

general strain theory (GST) The view that multiple sources of strain interact with an individual's emotional traits and responses to produce criminality.

general theory of crime (GTC) Gottfredson and Hirschi's developmental theory that links crime to impulsivity and a lack of self-control.

globalization The process of creating transnational markets, politics, and legal systems in an effort to form and sustain a global economy.

grand jury A group of citizens chosen to hear testimony in secret and to issue formal criminal accusations (indictments).

grand larceny Theft of money or property of substantial value, punished as a felony.

green-collar crimes Crimes that affect the environment.

guerilla The term means "little war" and developed out of the Spanish rebellion against French troops after Napoleon's 1808 invasion of the Iberian Peninsula. Today the term is often used interchangeably with the term *terrorist*.

harms perspective The view that all activities that cause physical, financial/economic, emotional or psychological, and cultural harm to individuals and/or the environment should be criminalized.

hate crimes (bias crimes) Violent acts directed toward a particular person or members of a group merely because the targets share a discernible racial, ethnic, religious, or gender characteristic.

hung jury A jury that is unable to agree on a decision, thus leaving the case unresolved and open for a possible retrial.

hypoglycemia A condition that occurs when glucose (sugar) in the blood falls below levels necessary for normal and efficient brain functioning.

id The primitive part of people's mental makeup, present at birth, that represents unconscious biological drives for food, sex, and other life-sustaining necessities. The id seeks instant gratification without concern for the rights of others.

identity theft Using the Internet to steal someone's identity and/or impersonate the victim in order to conduct illicit transactions such as committing fraud using the victim's name and identity.

impulsive Lacking in thought or deliberation in decision making. An impulsive person lacks close attention to details, has organizational problems, and is distracted and forgetful.

incapacitation effect The idea that keeping offenders in confinement will eliminate the risk of their committing further offenses.

income inequality The unequal distribution of household or individual income across the various participants in an economy.

indictment A written accusation returned by a grand jury charging an individual with a specified crime, based on the prosecutor's demonstration of probable cause.

individual vulnerability model Assumes there is a direct link between traits and crime; some people are vulnerable to crime from birth.

infanticide Murder of a very young child.

influence peddling Using one's institutional position to grant favors and sell information to which one's co-conspirators are not entitled.

information A filing before an impartial lower-court judge who decides whether the case should go forward (this filing is an alternative to the use of a grand jury).

information-processing theory Theory that focuses on how people process, store, encode, retrieve, and manipulate information to make decisions and solve problems.

insider trading Illegal buying of stock in a company on the basis of information provided by someone who has a fiduciary interest in the company.

institutional anomie theory The view that anomie pervades US culture because the drive for material wealth dominates and undermines social and community values.

instrumental crimes Offenses designed to improve the financial or social position of the criminal.

instrumental theory The view that criminal law and the criminal justice system are capitalist instruments for controlling the lower class.

instrumental violence Violence used in a rational, controlled, and purposeful fashion; for example, an attempt to improve the financial or social position of the criminal.

insurgent The typical goal of an insurgency is to confront the existing government for control of all or a portion of its territory, or force concessions in sharing political power. While terrorists may operate in small bands with a narrow focus, insurgents represent a popular movement and may also seek external support from other nations to bring pressure on the government.

interactionist view The belief that those with social power are able to impose their values on society as a whole, and these values then define criminal behavior.

interrogation The questioning of a suspect in police custody.

involuntary or negligent manslaughter A killing that occurs when a person's acts are negligent and without regard for the harm they may cause others.

jihad Has three meanings: (1) a true believer's internal struggle to live as a devout Muslim, (2) to build a Muslim society, (3) to defend Islam, with force if necessary, against nonbelievers.

johns Men who solicit sex workers.

larceny The unlawful taking, carrying, leading, or riding away of property from the possession or constructive possession of another.

latent trait A stable feature, characteristic, property, or condition, such as defective intelligence or impulsive personality, that makes some people crime prone over the life course.

left realism An approach that views crime as a function of relative deprivation under capitalism and that favors pragmatic, community-based crime prevention and control.

liberal feminist theory A view of crime that suggests that the social and economic role of women in society controls their crime rates.

life course persisters Delinquents who begin their offending career at a very early age and continue to offend well into adulthood.

life course theory Theory that focuses on changes in criminality over the life course brought about by shifts in experience and life events.

lifestyle theories Views on how people become crime victims because of lifestyles that increase their exposure to criminal offenders.

logic bomb A program that is secretly attached to a computer system, monitors the network's work output, and waits for a particular signal such as a date to appear. Also called a slag code, it is a type of delayed action virus that may be set off when a program user makes certain input that sets it in motion. A logic bomb may cause a variety of problems ranging from displaying or printing a spurious message to deleting or corrupting data.

malware A malicious software program.

mandatory sentences A statutory requirement that a certain penalty shall be carried out in all cases of conviction for a specified offense or series of offenses.

manslaughter Homicide without malice.

marginal deterrence Occurs when a relatively more severe penalty will produce *some* reduction in crime.

marginalization Displacement of workers, pushing them outside the economic and social mainstream.

marital exemption The formerly accepted tradition that a legally married husband could not be charged with raping his wife.

mass murder The killing of four or more victims by one or a few assailants within a single event.

merchant privilege laws Legislation that protects retailers and their employees from lawsuits if they arrest and detain a suspected shoplifter on reasonable grounds.

middle-class measuring rods The standards by which authority figures, such as teachers and employers, evaluate lower-class youngsters and often prejudge them negatively.

misdemeanor A minor crime usually punished by a short jail term and/or a fine.

monozygotic (MZ) twins Identical twins.

mood disorder A condition in which the prevailing emotional mood is distorted or inappropriate to the circumstances.

moral entrepreneurs Individuals who create moral rules that reflect the values of those in power rather than any objective, universal standards of right and wrong.

moral filtering The process of making socially and morally responsible decisions.

Mosaic Code The laws of the ancient Israelites, found in the Old Testament of the Judeo-Christian Bible.

motivated offenders People willing and able to commit crimes.

motor vehicle theft The theft of a motor vehicle.

murder The unlawful killing of a human being with malice aforethought.

murder and nonnegligent manslaughter The willful (nonnegligent) killing of one human being by another.

naive check forgers Amateurs who cash bad checks because of some financial crisis but have little identification with a criminal subculture.

narcissistic personality disorder A pattern of traits and behaviors indicating infatuation and fixation with one's self to the exclusion of all others, along with the egotistic and ruthless pursuit of one's own gratification, dominance, and ambition.

narcotic A drug that induces sleep and relieves pain, such as heroin, morphine, and opium; a habit-forming drug.

National Crime Victimization Survey (NCVS) The ongoing victimization study conducted jointly by the Justice Department and the US Census Bureau that surveys victims about their experiences with law violation.

National Incident-Based Reporting System (NIBRS) Program that requires local police agencies to provide a brief account of each incident and arrest involving 49 specific offenses, including incident, victim, and offender information.

nature theory The view that intelligence is largely determined genetically and that low intelligence is linked to criminal behavior.

negative affective states Anger, frustration, and adverse emotions produced by a variety of sources of strain.

negative reinforcement Using either negative stimuli (punishment) or loss of reward (negative punishment) to curtail unwanted behaviors.

neglect Not providing a child with the care and shelter to which he or she is entitled.

neurophysiology The study of brain activity.

neurotransmitters Chemical compounds that influence or activate brain functions.

neutralization techniques Methods of rationalizing deviant behavior, such as denying responsibility or blaming the victim.

neutralization theory The view that law violators learn to neutralize conventional values and attitudes, enabling them to drift back and forth between criminal and conventional behavior.

nolle prosequi A declaration that expresses the prosecutor's decision to drop a case from further prosecution.

nurture theory The view that intelligence is not inherited but is largely a product of environment. Low IQ scores do not cause crime but may result from the same environmental factors.

obscenity Material that violates community standards of morality or decency and has no redeeming social value.

obsessive-compulsive disorder An extreme preoccupation with certain thoughts and compulsive performance of certain behaviors.

occasional criminals Offenders who do not define themselves by a criminal role or view themselves as committed career criminals.

offender-specific crime The view that offenders evaluate their skills, motives, needs, and fears before deciding to commit the criminal act.

offense-specific crime The view that an offender reacts selectively to the characteristics of a particular criminal act.

oppositional defiant disorder (ODD) A pattern of negativistic, hostile, and defiant behavior, during which a child often loses her or his temper, often argues with adults, and often actively defies or refuses to comply with adults' requests or rules.

overt pathway Pathway to a criminal career that begins with minor aggression, leads to physical fighting, and eventually escalates to violent crime.

paraphilias Bizarre or abnormal sexual practices that may involve nonhuman objects, humiliation, or children.

parental efficacy The ability of parents to be supportive of their children and effectively control them in noncoercive ways.

Part I crimes The eight most serious offenses included in the UCR: murder and nonnegligent manslaughter, forcible rape, robbery, aggravated assault, burglary, larceny, motor vehicle theft, and arson.

Part II crimes All other crimes, aside from the eight Part I crimes, included in the UCR arrest data. Part II crimes include drug offenses, sex crimes, and vandalism, among others.

passive precipitation Personal or social characteristics of victims that make them attractive targets for criminals; such victims may unknowingly either threaten or encourage their attackers.

paternalistic families Traditional family model in which fathers assume the role of breadwinners, while mothers tend to have menial jobs or remain at home to supervise domestic matters.

patriarchy A society in which men dominate public, social, economic, and political affairs.

peacemaking An approach that considers punitive crime control strategies to be counterproductive and favors the use of humanistic conflict resolution to prevent and control crime.

penology Subarea of criminology that focuses on the correction and control of criminal offenders.

personality The reasonably stable patterns of behavior, including thoughts and emotions, that distinguish one person from another.

petit (petty) larceny Theft of a small amount of money or property, punished as a misdemeanor.

phishing Sometimes called carding or brand spoofing, phishing is a scam where the perpetrator sends out emails appearing to come from legitimate web enterprises such as eBay, Amazon, and PayPal in an effort to get the recipient to reveal personal and financial information.

plea bargain Agreement between prosecution and defense in which the accused pleads guilty in return for a reduction of charges, a more lenient sentence, or some other consideration.

political crime Illegal acts that are designed to undermine an existing government and threaten its survival. Political crimes can include both violent and nonviolent acts and range in seriousness from dissent, treason, and espionage to violent acts such as terrorism or assassination.

population All people who share a particular characteristic, such as all high school students or all police officers.

population heterogeneity The propensity to commit crime is stable; those who have it continue to commit crime over their life course.

pornography Sexually explicit books, magazines, films, and DVDs intended to provide sexual titillation and excitement for paying customers.

positivism The branch of social science that uses the scientific method of the natural sciences and suggests that human behavior is a product of social, biological, psychological, or economic forces that can be empirically measured.

posttraumatic stress disorder (PTSD) Psychological reaction to a highly stressful event; symptoms may include depression, anxiety, flashbacks, and recurring nightmares.

power–control theory The view that gender differences in crime are a function of economic power (class position, one-earner versus two-earner families) and parental control (paternalistic versus egalitarian families).

precedent A rule derived from previous judicial decisions and applied to future cases; the basis of common law.

preemptive deterrence Efforts to prevent crime through community organization and youth involvement.

preliminary hearing Alternative to a grand jury, in which an impartial lower-court judge decides whether there is probable cause sufficient for a trial.

premeditation Considering the criminal act beforehand, which suggests that it was motivated by more than a simple desire to engage in an act of violence.

premenstrual syndrome (PMS) Condition, postulated by some theorists, wherein several days before and during menstruation excessive amounts of female sex hormones stimulate antisocial, aggressive behavior.

price fixing The illegal control by agreement among producers or manufacturers of the price of a commodity to avoid price competition and deprive the consumer of reasonable prices.

primary deviance A norm violation or crime that has little or no long-term influence on the violator.

primary prevention programs Programs, such as substance abuse clinics and mental health associations, that seek to treat personal problems before they manifest themselves as crime.

probable cause A set of facts, information, circumstances, or conditions that would lead a reasonable person to believe that an offense was committed and that the accused committed that offense. It is the level of proof needed to make a legal arrest.

problem behavior syndrome (PBS) Antisocial behaviors that cluster together, including family dysfunction, substance abuse, smoking, precocious sexuality and early pregnancy, educational underachievement, suicide attempts, sensation seeking, and unemployment, as well as criminality.

professional criminals Offenders who make a significant portion of their income from crime.

Prohibition The period from 1919 until 1933 when the Eighteenth Amendment to the US Constitution outlawed the sale of alcohol; also known as the "noble experiment."

propensity theory The view that a stable unchanging feature, characteristic, property, or condition, such as defective intelligence or impulsive personality, makes some people crime prone.

prostitution The granting of nonmarital sexual access for remuneration.

psychodynamic (psychoanalytic) psychology Theory, originated by Freud, that the human personality is controlled by unconscious mental processes that develop early in childhood and involve the interaction of id, ego, and superego.

psychopharmacological relationship In such a relationship, violence is the direct consequence of ingesting mood-altering substances.

public order crimes Behaviors that are outlawed because they threaten the general well-being of society and challenge accepted moral principles.

racial profiling Police-initiated action directed at a suspect or group of suspects based solely on race.

racial threat hypothesis As the size of the black population increases, the perceived threat to the white population increases, resulting in a greater amount of social control imposed on African Americans.

Racketeer Influenced and Corrupt Organizations (RICO) Act Federal legislation that enables prosecutors to bring additional criminal or civil charges against people whose multiple criminal acts constitute a conspiracy. RICO features monetary penalties that allow the government to confiscate all profits derived from criminal activities. Originally intended to be used against organized criminals, RICO has also been used against white-collar criminals.

rape Under common law, the carnal knowledge of a female forcibly and against her will. Contemporary statues are gender neutral ("a person") and can include various acts of sexual penetration.

rational choice theory The view that crime is a function of a decision-making process in which the would-be offender weighs the potential costs and benefits of an illegal act.

reaction formation Irrational hostility evidenced by young delinquents, who adopt norms directly opposed to middle-class goals and standards that seem impossible to achieve.

recidivism Relapse into criminal behavior after apprehension, conviction, and correction for a previous crime.

recognizance Pledge by the accused to return for trial, which may be accepted in lieu of bail.

rehabilitation Treatment of criminal offenders that is aimed at preventing future criminal behavior.

Reign of Terror The origin of the term *terrorism*, the French Revolution's Reign of Terror began in 1793 and was initiated by the revolutionary government during which agents of the Committee of Public Safety and the National Convention were referred to as terrorists.

reintegrative shaming A method of correction that encourages offenders to confront their misdeeds, experience shame because of the harm they caused, and then be reincluded in society.

relational aggression Psychological and emotional abuse that involves the spreading of smears, rumors, and private information in order to harm a partner.

relative deprivation Envy, mistrust, and aggression resulting from perceptions of economic and social inequality.

reliable measure A measure that produces consistent results from one measurement to another.

replacement An effect that occurs when criminals try new offenses they had previously avoided because situational crime prevention programs neutralized their crime of choice.

resource deprivation The consequence of a lack of income and other resources, which cumulatively leads to poverty.

restitution Permitting an offender to repay the victim or do useful work in the community rather than facing the stigma of a formal trial and a court-ordered sentence.

restorative justice Using humanistic, nonpunitive strategies to right wrongs and restore social harmony.

restrictive (partial) deterrence Refers to situations in which the threat of punishment can reduce but not eliminate crime.

retributive terrorists Terror groups who refrain from tying specific acts to direct demands for change. They want to instead redirect the balance between what they believe is good and evil. They see their revolution as existing on a spiritual plane; their mission is to exact retribution against sinners.

retrospective reading The reassessment of a person's past to fit a current generalized label.

road rage Violent assault by a motorist who loses control of his or her emotions while driving.

robbery Taking or attempting to take anything of value from the care, custody, or control of a person or persons by force or threat of force or violence and/or by putting the victim in fear.

role exit behaviors In order to escape from a stifling life in male-dominated families, girls may try to break away by running away and or even attempting suicide.

Romeo and Juliet laws Apply to cases of statutory rape when both members engage in consensual sexual intercourse, but the age gap between the older alleged offender and the younger alleged victim is narrow, typically two to four years.

routine activities theory The view that victimization results from the interaction of three everyday factors: the availability of suitable targets, the absence of capable guardians, and the presence of motivated offenders.

sampling Selecting a limited number of people for study as representative of a larger group.

schemas Cognitive frameworks that help people quickly process and sort through information.

schizophrenia A severe disorder marked by hearing nonexistent voices, seeing hallucinations, and exhibiting inappropriate responses.

scientific method The use of verifiable principles and procedures for the systematic acquisition of knowledge. Typically involves formulating a problem, creating hypotheses, and collecting data, through observation and experiment, to verify the hypotheses.

secondary deviance A norm violation or crime that comes to the attention of significant others or social control agents, who apply a negative label that has long-term consequences for the violator's self-identity and social interactions.

secondary prevention programs Programs that provide treatment, such as psychological counseling, to youths and adults after they have violated the law.

second-degree murder A person's wanton disregard for the victim's life and his or her desire to inflict serious bodily harm on the victim, which results in the victim's death.

self-control A strong moral sense that renders a person incapable of hurting others or violating social norms.

self-report survey A research approach that requires subjects to reveal their own participation in delinquent or criminal acts.

sentencing circle A peacemaking technique in which offenders, victims, and other community members are brought together in an effort to formulate a sanction that addresses the needs of all.

serial killer A person who kills three or more persons in three or more separate events.

shame The feeling we get when we don't meet the standards we have set for ourselves or that significant others have set for us.

Sherman Antitrust Act Federal law that subjects to criminal or civil sanctions any person "who shall make any contract or engage in any combination or conspiracy" in restraint of interstate commerce.

shield laws Laws that protect women from being questioned about their sexual history unless such questioning directly bears on the case.

shoplifting The taking of goods from retail stores.

situational crime prevention A method of crime prevention that seeks to eliminate or reduce particular crimes in specific settings.

situational inducement Short-term influence on a person's behavior, such as financial problems or peer pressure, which increases risk taking.

snitch Amateur shoplifter who does not self-identify as a thief but who systematically steals merchandise for personal use.

social capital Positive, life-sustaining relations with individuals and institutions.

social classes Segments of the population whose members are at a relatively similar economic level and who share attitudes, values, norms, and an identifiable lifestyle.

social control theory The view that everyone has the potential to become a criminal, but most people are controlled by their bonds to society. Crime occurs when the forces that bind people to society are weakened or broken.

social disorganization theory Branch of social structure theory that focuses on the breakdown in inner-city neighborhoods of institutions such as the family, school, and employment.

social ecology school An interdisciplinary approach to the study of interdependent social and environmental problems that cause crime.

social harm The injury caused to others by willful wrongful conduct.

social learning theory The view that human behavior is modeled through observation of human social interactions, either directly from observing those who are close and from intimate contact, or indirectly through the media. Interactions that are rewarded are copied, while those that are punished are avoided.

social process theory The view that criminality is a function of people's interactions with various organizations, institutions, and processes in society.

social reaction (labeling) theory The view that people become criminals when significant members of society label them as such and they accept those labels as a personal identity.

social structure theory The view that disadvantaged economic class position is a primary cause of crime.

socialization Process of human development and enculturation. Socialization is influenced by key social processes and institutions.

socialized The process of acquiring social norms, values, behavior, and skills through interaction with significant others such as parents, peers, and teachers.

sociobiology The view that human behavior is motivated by inborn biological urges to survive and preserve the species.

sociological criminology Approach to criminology, based on the work of Émile Durkheim, that focuses on the relationship between social factors and crime.

spear-phishing Targeting specific victims, sending them emails that contain accurate information about their lives obtained from social networking sites, and asking them to open an email attachment where malware harvests details such as the victims' usernames and passwords, bank account details, credit card numbers, and other personal information.

specific deterrence The view that criminal sanctions should be so powerful that offenders will never repeat their criminal acts.

spree killers Individuals who kill multiple victims over a relatively short span of time and often follow no discernible pattern.

stalking A course of conduct that is directed at a specific person and involves repeated physical or visual proximity, nonconsensual communication, or verbal, written, or implied threats sufficient to cause fear in a reasonable person.

state dependence The propensity to commit crime is constantly changing, affected by environmental influences and changing life events.

state political crime Political crime that arises from the efforts of the state to either maintain governmental power or to uphold the race, class, and gender advantages of those who support the government. It is possible to divide state political crimes into five varieties: (1) political corruption, (2) illegal domestic surveillance, (3) human rights violations, (4) state violence such as torture, illegal imprisonment, police violence and use of deadly force, and (5) state corporate crime committed by individuals who abuse their state authority or who fail to exercise it when working with people and organizations in the private sector.

state-organized crime Acts defined by law as criminal and committed by state officials, either elected or appointed, in pursuit of their jobs as government representatives.

state-sponsored terrorism Terrorism that occurs when a repressive government regime forces its citizens into obedience, oppresses minorities, and stifles political dissent.

status frustration A form of culture conflict experienced by lower-class youths because social conditions prevent them from achieving success as defined by the larger society.

statutory crimes Crimes defined by legislative bodies in response to changing social conditions, public opinion, and custom.

statutory rape Sexual relations between an underage minor female and an adult male.

stigmatize To apply negative labeling with enduring effects on a person's self-image and social interactions.

strain The anger, frustration, and resentment experienced by people who believe they cannot achieve their goals through legitimate means.

strain theory Branch of social structure theory that sees crime as a function of the conflict between people's goals and the means available to obtain them.

stratified society Grouping according to social strata or levels. American society is considered stratified on the basis of economic class and wealth.

street efficacy A concept in which more cohesive communities with high levels of social control and social integration foster the ability for kids to use their wits to avoid violent confrontations and to feel safe in their own neighborhood. Adolescents with high levels of street efficacy are less likely to resort to violence themselves or to associate with delinquent peers.

structural theory The view that criminal law and the criminal justice system are means of defending and preserving the capitalist system.

subculture A set of values, beliefs, and traditions unique to a particular social class or group within a larger society.

subculture of violence A segment of society in which violence has become legitimized by the custom and norms of that group.

successful degradation ceremony A course of action or ritual in which someone's identity is publicly redefined and destroyed and he or she is thereafter viewed as socially unacceptable.

suitable targets Objects of crime (persons or property) that are attractive and readily available.

superego The part of the personality representing the conscience, formed in early life by internalization of the standards of parents and other models of behavior.

supranational criminology The study of war crimes, crimes against humanity, and the supranational penal system in which such crimes are prosecuted and tried.

surplus value The Marxist view that the laboring classes produce wealth that far exceeds their wages and goes to the capitalist class as profits.

systematic forgers Professionals who make a living by passing bad checks.

systemic link A link between drugs and violence that occurs when drug dealers turn violent in their competition with rival gangs.

temperance movement The drive to prohibit the sale of alcohol in the United States, culminating in ratification of the Eighteenth Amendment in 1919.

terrorism The illegal use of force against innocent people to achieve a political objective.

testosterone The principal male hormone.

thanatos The death instinct, which impels people toward self-destruction.

theft The intentional taking, keeping, or using of another's property without authorization or permission.

three-strikes policies Laws that require offenders to serve life in prison after they are convicted of a third felony.

ticking bomb scenario A scenario that some experts argue in which torture can perhaps be justified if the government discovers that a captured terrorist knows the whereabouts of a dangerous explosive device that is set to go off and kill thousands of innocent people.

torture An act that causes severe pain or suffering, whether physical or mental, that is intentionally inflicted on a person for such purposes as obtaining a confession, punishing them for a crime they may have committed, or intimidating or coercing them into a desired action.

trait theory The view that criminality is a product of abnormal biological or psychological traits.

trajectory theory The view that there are multiple independent paths to a criminal career and that there are different types and classes of offenders.

transitional neighborhood An area undergoing a shift in population and structure, usually from middle-class residential to lower-class mixed-use.

transnational organized crime Criminal conspiracies that cross national and international borders and involve the planning and execution of illicit ventures by groups or networks of individuals working in more than one country.

treason An act of disloyalty to one's nation or state.

Trojan horse A computer program that looks like a benign application but contains illicit codes that can damage the system operations. Though Trojan horses do not replicate themselves like viruses, they can be just as destructive.

turning points According to Laub and Sampson, the life events that alter the development of a criminal career.

underclass The lowest social stratum in any country, whose members lack the education and skills needed to function successfully in modern society.

Uniform Crime Report (UCR) Large database, compiled by the FBI, of crimes reported and arrests made each year throughout the United States.

USA Patriot Act (USAPA) Legislation giving US law enforcement agencies a freer hand to investigate and apprehend suspected terrorists.

valid measure A measure that actually measures what it purports to measure; a measure that is factual.

victim compensation programs Financial aid awarded to crime victims to repay them for their loss and injuries; may cover medical bills, loss of wages, loss of future earnings, and/or counseling.

victim precipitation theory The view that victims may initiate, either actively or passively, the confrontation that leads to their victimization.

victimless crimes Public order crimes that violate the moral order but have no specific victim other than society as a whole.

victim–offender reconciliation programs (VORPs) Mediated face-to-face encounters between victims and their attackers, designed to produce restitution agreements and, if possible, reconciliation.

victimologists Criminologists who focus on the victims of crime.

victimology The study of the victim's role in criminal events.

victim-precipitated homicide Refers to those killings in which the victim is a direct, positive precipitator of the incident.

victim–witness assistance programs Government programs that help crime victims and witnesses; may include compensation, court services, and/or crisis intervention.

virility mystique The belief that males must separate their sexual feelings from their need for love, respect, and affection.

voluntary or nonnegligent manslaughter A killing committed in the heat of passion or during a sudden quarrel that provoked violence.

warez A term computer hackers and software pirates use to describe a game or application that is made available for use on the Internet in violation of its copyright protection.

waterboarding Immobilizing a person on his or her back, with the head inclined downward, and pouring water over the face and into the breathing passages, producing an immediate gag reflex and an experience akin to drowning; the subject believes his or her death is imminent.

website defacement A type of cybervandalism that occurs when a computer hacker intrudes on another person's website by inserting or substituting codes that expose visitors to the site to misleading or provocative information. Defacement can range from installing humorous graffiti to sabotaging or corrupting the site.

white privilege The assumed societal privileges that benefit Caucasians and provide them with opportunities not available to non-white people under the same social, political, or economic circumstances.

white-collar crime Illegal acts that capitalize on a person's status in the marketplace. White-collar crimes may include theft, embezzlement, fraud, market manipulation, restraint of trade, and false advertising.

workplace violence Violence such as assault, rape, or murder committed at the workplace.

Name Index

Subject Index